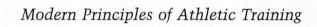

Modern Principles of Athletic Training

ANCIENT TRAINING ROOM

The palaestra, a sandcovered open court-
yard, was surrounded by small rooms
where athletes bathed, oiled, and dressed.
Right figure, a youth leaves his outer gar-
ment with an attendant; center figure, a
competitor oils his body before entering
the palaestra; left, an attendant removes a
thorn from an injured athlete.

Modern Principles of
ATHLETIC TRAINING

DANIEL D. ARNHEIM, D.P.E., A.T.,C.

Fellow, American College of Sports Medicine
Professor of Physical Education
California State University, Long Beach
Formerly at San Diego State University

Illustrated by
HELENE ARNHEIM, M.A.

SIXTH EDITION

With 1038 illustrations and
14 color photographs

TIMES MIRROR/MOSBY COLLEGE PUBLISHING

ST. LOUIS   TORONTO   SANTA CLARA   1985

To
Jennifer Lynn
and
James Daniel

Editor   Nancy K. Roberson
Developmental editor   Michelle A. Turenne
Project editor   Connie Povilat
Manuscript editors   Suzanne Seeley, Sandra L. Gilfillan
Designer   Diane M. Beasley
Production   Linda R. Stalnaker, Jeanne Genz

Cover art   *Silverdome Superbowl* by LeRoy Neiman

Part One opener photo   Bill Knight, Pro Photo Inc.
Part Two, Three, and Four opener photos   Bill Stover

SIXTH EDITION

Library of Congress Cataloging in Publication Data

Arnheim, Daniel D.
  Modern principles of athletic training.

  Rev. ed. of: Modern principles of athletic training / Carl E. Klafs. 5th ed. 1981.
  Includes bibliographies and index.
  1. Physical education and training.   2. Sports—Accidents and injuries.   3. Sports medicine.
I. Klafs, Carl E.   Modern principles of athletic training.   II. Title.
GV711.5.A76   1985   617'.1027   84-22221
ISBN 0-8016-2683-8   *58,681*

C/VH/VH 9 8 7 6 5 4   02/B/222

FOREWORD I

With the sixth edition of *Modern Principles of Athletic Training*, Dr. Arnheim has continued his tradition of presenting the latest in the field of athletic training and sports medicine. I feel he has done an excellent job of presenting the material in a very readable and interesting fashion. Though written as an introductory text, those with scientific and clinical experience will find this revised edition an excellent reference.

This edition parallels the growth in the field of athletic training and sports medicine. One can follow the advances in the field with each edition. The basics covered in the first edition have become, in this edition, specific explanations of disease and injury process. Also presented in this edition are advances in evaluation, management, and rehabilitation. New topics include computers, endorphins and enkephalins, and the effects of exercise on ligamentous structures.

Because the athletic trainer often functions as the coach for strength and conditioning, the section on physical conditioning is a welcome addition, as is a complete section on women and children in sports. A sport-specific conditioning section provides a guide for those involved in such endeavors.

The general evaluation of injuries is well presented in a systematic approach that eliminates confusion. This is also the case in the emergency procedures section. Terms are explained as the reader progresses, an important aspect for an introductory text.

The general concepts of modalities and rehabilitation are well explained in detail, including the concepts of Cyriax. The general principles of rehabilitation are well thought out and presented. The student is led step by step through the rehabilitation process.

PNF techniques, with accompanying photos, are included in the appendix. The appendix also includes the latest NATA information, as well as

v

ACSM position statements on alcohol, steroids, weight loss in wrestling, and heat stress in marathons. An expanded glossary will also be important to the student.

With the increase of knowledge in the sports medicine field, it is appropriate that Dr. Arnheim should continue this updating. He has done this with the skill of the experienced author in the field. He integrates all aspects of sports medicine, from DeLorme to isokinetics, from the art to the science of athletic training.

The strengths of *Modern Principles of Athletic Training* lie in Dr. Arnheim's ability to make it both an easily understood introductory text and to provide the latest information for the practicing clinician. The bibliographies are the most complete in the field. Without this book, the libraries of athletic trainers, physical therapists, team physicians, and others interested in sports medicine will be incomplete.

Joe H. Gieck, Ed.D., R.P.T., A.T.,C.
Head Athletic Trainer, Curriculum Director for the Master's
Program in Athletic Training, University of Virginia;
Former Chairman, Board of Directors, National Athletic Trainers Association

FOREWORD II

The scope of what has come to be known as athletic training has never been sharply defined throughout the history of sports. In the ancient Greek games it appears that physicians, known as gymnastes, were both coaches and trainers of the athletes, but others, generally described as bath attendants, also served the needs of athletes. In more recent times the coach-trainer served as masseur and diet advisor before coaching became a profession; even today the coach who works alone at any level may be responsible for providing a variety of services to athletes. Athletic training has become a profession in the United States, but not in other countries, where they sometimes have persons known as "sports physical therapists."

Since the publication of the first edition of this book in 1963, there has been a tremendous increase in knowledge and experience in the field now described as "sports medicine." This has resulted in the development of new categories of specialists who were formerly included in more general fields, such as physical education, or who have moved over from other disciplines because of their special interest in sports, such as sports psychology. A truly comprehensive text in sports medicine would have to assume the dimensions of an encyclopedia. Still, there exists a need for a text to gather together a reference source for those working with recreational and competitive athletes on a day-to-day basis. This need exists at all levels, from the formal education of such persons in an academic setting to that of the office or clinic where they may be working.

This sixth edition of *Modern Principles of Athletic Training* has been so extensively rewritten that it is virtually a new book: it encompasses as many of the developments already mentioned as possible and to express them in terms that everyone at different levels of education and experience can understand and apply. The discussion of the role of biomechanics in the prevention and occurrence of sports injuries is one example of the way in which information has been better organized and upgraded to make today's practitioners more knowledgable and effective.

The collegiate instructor in physical education, particularly in a program leading to certification in athletic training, the graduate athletic trainer, the sports team physician, the coach working at any level with athletes, and the athletes themselves may all derive great benefits from reading this book, utilizing the information it contains in practical ways and keeping it on hand as a source for reference. Techniques of play and rules undergo gradual but constant changes. The fundamentals of conditioning and the prevention of illness and injury in sports continue the same, modified only to make them more effective, and they are well described and illustrated in this book.

Allan J. Ryan, M.D.

Editor-in-Chief, *The Physician and Sports Medicine;*
Past President and Fellow, American College of Sports Medicine

PREFACE

Purpose of Text

The sixth edition of *Modern Principles of Athletic Training* continues to have as its primary purpose the presentation of the most current information possible in athletic training and sports medicine. Since the first edition over twenty years ago, this text has been at the forefront of the field of athletic training. This edition continues in this tradition, representing the major changes inherent in this ever-expanding field.

Who Is It Written For?

Modern Principles of Athletic Training is designed primarily as an introductory text to the broad field of athletic training. It can be used for a course on athletic training techniques for both coaches and athletic trainers, as well as for a course dealing with the scientific and clinical foundations of athletic training and sports medicine. Practicing athletic trainers, physical therapists, and other medical specialists should also find this text valuable.

The extent of the knowledge explosion in the field of sports medicine in general and athletic training in particular is truly mind-boggling. Since the last edition, more and more information has come forth on physical training, injury prevention, and injury management. The athletic trainer is increasingly becoming a sports therapist, and more particularly, a specialist in orthopedic therapy. Through my own intense research and observation, written reviews, feedback from instructors using the text, and comments from students, this edition was written to meet the major challenges of athletic training.

Substantive Changes

The sixth edition of *Modern Principles of Athletic Training* is more than just a revision: it is almost an entirely rewritten text. The following summarizes the major areas of additions and change.

The essential philosophy and organization of the sixth edition of *Modern Principles of Athletic Training* remains the same as in past editions. Philosophically, this text is designed to take the student from *general* to *specific* concepts. This text, as it has over the past years, still contends that preventing injuries is the most important aspect of athletic training.

Part One, Athletic Training, has been reduced from four to three chapters, to more precisely present to the reader the field of athletic training, the incidence of injury, the role of the athletic trainer, and the scope of the athletic training program. Chapter 1 provides the reader with an introduction to athletic training and sports medicine. Chapter 2 looks at who the athletic trainer is and what his or her responsibilities should be. Chapter 3 is concerned with the working of the total athletic training program.

All of the chapters in Part Two, General Principles of Sports Medicine and Athletic Training, have been considerably changed and updated. Chapter 4, Physical Conditioning and Training, presents an overview of the major physiological concepts of exercise. Chapter 5, Injury Prevention Through Physical Conditioning, presents the most up-to-date information available on how to avoid sports injuries by following proper exercise principles. Chapter 6, Nutritional Considerations and Other Intended Aids, contains information that dispels false ideas on fad diets and discusses the dangers of taking harmful substances into the body. Chapter 7, Protective Sports Equipment, covers the uses, advantages, and fitting of protective equipment. Of particular note is Chapter 8, Psychogenic Considerations, which has been completely modified to include all major aspects of the psychology of the injured and the best approaches for the coach or athletic trainer to take when caring for the injured athlete.

Part Three, Foundations of Injury Causations, Prevention, and Management, has been almost completely rewritten. Chapter 9, Body Characteristics and Mechanisms of Injury, has been extensively expanded to include more in-depth discussion on mechanisms of injuries at the tissue level. It also explores the question of why the human body is more susceptible to some injuries than to others. Chapter 10, Classifying, Recognizing, and Inspecting Sports Injuries, was previously called Injury Recognition, Evaluation, and the Healing Process. In this edition, the subject of tissue healing and pain has been removed from Chapter 10 and becomes a separate chapter. Chapter 10 defines the major categories of sports injuries and establishes the foundations for recognizing, inspecting, and evaluating these injuries. Knowledge gained here by the student will be used later in the text when specific injuries are presented. Chapter 11, Tissue Healing and Pain, elaborates how the body reacts to injury. It also provides a foundation for the use of certain therapeutic modalities and procedures. Chapter 12, Emergency Procedures in Sports, has replaced the fifth edition chapter on Crisis Procedures. The discussion is now much more thorough in the areas of immediate care of injuries, handling the seriously injured athlete, and special emergency conditions, such as heat and cold environmental stress. Chapter 13, Wound Dressing, Taping, Bandaging, Padding, and Orthotics, imparts the major fundamentals necessary for the application of these materials. Chapter 14, Therapeutic Modalities, has replaced the former chapter on physical therapy. Exercise rehabilitation is now presented in a chapter by itself. Added to Chapter 14 are basic concepts of cryokinetics, iontophoresis, phonophoresis, transcutaneous electrical nerve stimulation (TENS), Cyriax massage technique, and the principles of myofascial pain and trigger point therapy. Discussion of ultrasound diathermy techniques has also been greatly expanded. Chapter 15, Basics in Exercise Rehabilitation, presents the foundations of therapeutic exercise. Like all chapters in this section, Chapter 15 helps the reader understand principles and practices that are presented later on in the text when specific sports injuries are discussed. Chapter 16, Pharmacology in Sports, is included in Part Three so that the reader might have a more complete understanding of the majority of therapeutic approaches other than surgery used in the management of sports injuries.

In general, all of Part Four, Specific Sports Injuries and Other Problems, has been extensively revised with a new organization and many added conditions. Chapters 18 through 25 have been reorganized to include more evaluation and rehabilitation procedures and injury conditions. Chapter 18 extensively covers acute injuries, while Chapter 19, new to this edition, covers The Lower Extremity: Chronic and Overuse Injuries. Chapter 20 has been updated to include more discussion of rotary knee injuries and meniscal and patellar conditions. Chapter 21, The Thigh, Hip, and Pelvis, was formerly called The Thigh, Hip, Buttocks, and Groin. The major change was to move pelvic injuries to this chapter and to expand the number of conditions presented. Chapter 22 includes an expansion of low back conditions presented, besides an increase in the number of abdominal and thoracic injuries presented. Chapter 23 offers an expanded presentation of upper back, cervical, and cerebral conditions. Chapter 24 has been updated to include many more chronic and overuse conditions—for example, the addition of thoracic outlet conditions and impingement problems. Because of the obvious neglect of wrist and hand injuries in sports activities, this area of the text has been extensively expanded to include such conditions as carpal tunnel syndrome, Boutonnière deformity, bowler's thumb, handlebar palsy, and de Quervain's disease. Chapter 26 presents new material on the management of acute asthmatic attacks, diabetic coma, insulin shock, epileptic seizures, and the female athlete related to menstrual irregularities and reproduction.

Numerous pedagogical devices have been included in this edition:

1. Color throughout text   Color has been added throughout the text to accentuate illustrations as well as written material.

2. New color illustrations   Fourteen new full-color illustrations have been added to Chapter 17. These depict common bacterial, viral, and fungal infections, as well as common skin reactions to chemical irritants.

3. Boxed material within chapters   Important information such as special taping techniques and other skills has been boxed in to make key information easier to find and to enhance the text's flexibility and appearance.

4. Expanded anatomy   Presentation of anatomy throughout has been expanded to enable the student to more fully understand sports injuries.

5. Management plans   New to this edition are sample situations of injury management plans, which have been added to Chapters 18 through 25. The intent of this addition is to make material practical and immediately applicable to what has already been learned.

6. Injury evaluation expanded Each of the chapters discussing injuries has extensive evaluation information that is pertinent to the student, the athletic trainer, and the professional in the field.

7. Management procedures updated Injury management procedures, including therapeutic modalities and exercise rehabilitation, have been extensively revised to include the expanding requirements of athletic training.

8. More conditions added The total number of sports injuries and other health problems discussed have been extensively expanded throughout the text.

9. New photos and line drawings The line drawings have been replaced and updated, and *over 90% of the photos have been replaced.* The number of illustrations has almost doubled. These changes were made to improve the text's overall appearance, to incorporate color, to more fully highlight key points, and to generally make the book easier to use.

10. Margin information Key concepts, selected definitions, helpful training tips, salient points, and some illustrations have been placed in the margin throughout the text for emphasis and ease of reading and studying.

11. Chapter objectives Objectives have been added to each chapter to reinforce important learning goals.

12. References Each chapter provides the most complete and up-to-date references available.

13. Additional resources Pertinent and timely articles, books, and topics from the current literature have been provided to enlarge the perspective of the book's coverage.

14. Expanded glossary The number of terms has been substantially increased to help the student more successfully use the content of this text.

15. Appendixes added Four appendixes have been added to this edition. The fully illustrated Appendix I presents proprioceptive neuromuscular facilitation (PNF) patterns for the major joints. Appendix II gives National Athletic Trainers Association information, including the code of ethics, states with licensure, and approved athletic training education programs. Appendix III presents the American College of Sports Medicine position statements, including the use of alcohol in sports, the use and abuse of anabolic-androgenic steroids in sports, proper and improper weight loss programs, weight loss in wrestlers, prevention of heat injuries during distance running, and participation of the female athlete in long-distance running. Appendix IV lists units of measure, including conversions.

Ancillaries

Instructor's manual Greatly expanded, new, and practical features include:

- Brief chapter overviews
- Learning objectives
- Key terminology
- Discussion questions
- Class activities
- Appendixes include answer keys, additional resources, and transparency masters
- Perforated format, ready for immediate use

In addition, approximately 2000 examination questions are included. Each chapter contains true-false, multiple choice, and completion test questions. Worksheets including matching, short answer, listing, and essay questions can be used as self-testing tools for students or as additional sources for examination questions. The appendix includes part tests that can be used in evaluating student knowledge for each of the four parts of the text.

The instructor's manual was prepared by Marcia Anderson, M.S., A.T.,C., Director of the Athletic Training program, Bridgewater State College, Bridgewater, Massachusetts.

Transparencies New with this edition, 24 acetate transparencies are available to maximize the teaching and learning process.

Acknowledgments

No text revision of this magnitude could have been accomplished without the contributions of numerous people. First, and above all else, my deep thanks to my partner in life, my wife Helene, for her encouragement, suggestions, and countless hours of work, both drawing and typing. My thanks to my students and colleagues who, over the years, have made excellent suggestions for this revision. I want to thank Dr. Rob Carlson, chair, Department of Physical Education, San Diego State University, and the Athletic Medicine program for their cooperation in this endeavor. A special thanks goes to both Bob Moore, Ph.D., R.P.T., A.T.,C., and Carlynn Smith, A.T., C., head associate trainers of San Diego State University, as well as to Sue Laliker, A.T., C., assistant trainer, who immeasurably assisted me with suggestions and provided student trainers as photography models: Dava Reeder, A.T., C., Vicki Mosse, A.T.,C., Steve Allington, Keith Clarke, Philip Dizon, Lisa Winston, and Brad Mathers. Also, thanks to Paul Smith for his willingness to pose. Appreciation is extended to Rick McDonald, A.T.,C., R.P.T., and Mark Herschberger, A.T.,C., head and assistant athletic trainers, respectively, of the San Diego Chargers football team for allowing me to take key photos of their facilities. Also, appreciation is extended to Fred Rodriquez, Ph.D., California State University, Long Beach, for his photographic contributions.

I would be more than remiss for not thanking Times Mirror/Mosby College Publishing for their dedication and assistance in this project. A special thanks must be extended to my developmental editor, Michelle Turenne. Without her mind for details, her gentle prodding, and her encouragement, this text would have been much less than it is. Gratitude is extended to my manuscript editor, Suzanne Seeley, who made a very demanding job pleasant.

Also, the publisher's reviewers for this edition made excellent suggestions and criticisms that were carried out wherever possible. Their contributions are present in every chapter. I would like to express my sincere appreciation for their comparative and critical readings of the fifth edition, as well as for the earlier draft of this edition. They were:

Marcia Anderson, M.S., A.T.,C.   Bridgewater State College
Joel A. Bloom, Ph.D., A.T.,C.   University of Houston
Christine E. Boyd, Ph.D., A.T.,C.   University of Florida
Doris E. Flores, M.S., A.T.,C.   California State University—Sacramento

Marsha L. Grant, M.Ed., A.T.,C.	Ithaca College
Bobby Patton, D.Ed., A.T.,C.	Southwest Texas State University
William E. Prentice, Ph.D., A.T.,C., R.P.T.	The University of North Carolina—Chapel Hill
Charles J. Redmond, R.P.T., M.S.P.T., L.A.T.	Springfield College
Laura F. Rubesich, M.S., A.T.,C.	Youngstown State University
Douglas D. Sebold, Ed.D., A.T.,C.	Washington State University
Gordon Stoddard, M.S., A.T.,C.	University of Wisconsin—Madison

Finally, to Tony Succec, Ed.D., and Mike Buono, Ph.D., San Diego State University, my thanks for critically reviewing the exercise physiology aspects of Chapters 4 and 5.

Although I have spent 23 years at California State University, Long Beach, it was during a recent 2-year leave of absence to teach and coordinate the Sportsmedicine/Athletic Training curriculum at San Diego State University that the sixth edition of *Modern Principles of Athletic Training* was written.

Daniel D. Arnheim

CONTENTS

Part Two
GENERAL PRINCIPLES OF SPORTS MEDICINE

4   Physical Conditioning and Training, 78

Part Three
FOUNDATIONS OF INJURY CAUSATIONS, PREVENTION, AND MANAGEMENT

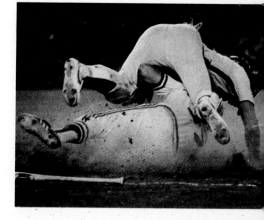

Part Four
SPECIFIC SPORTS INJURIES AND OTHER PROBLEMS

Part One | ATHLETIC TRAINING

Part One explores the origins of athletic training, the current incidence of sports injuries, and present challenges for preventing and caring for these injuries. The attributes of an athletic trainer and the athletic training program are described in detail.

Chapter 1

GENERAL CONSIDERATIONS

When you finish this chapter, you should be able to

Describe the historical foundations of athletic training

Identify epidemiological data-gathering systems

Differentiate collision, contact, and noncontact sports

Discuss reasons for the incidence of injury

Early humans were concerned solely with survival. Existence in their world demanded the utmost in survival skills, for which they needed bodies trained to make effective use of each physical ability. Since they could not afford to be incapacitated in any way, they relied on the soothsayer, medicine man, or shaman to help them maintain their physical well-being through prayer, meditation, or fasting.

The drive to compete is inherent in humans, as it is in other forms of life. Competition for status within the group, competition for a mate, competition in physical skills, or competition for survival is as necessary to humans as life itself. Their competitive nature, in time, led to competition in sports to release energy in a relatively peaceful and nonharmful way. Such competition frequently had religious overtones (still evident in many of our contemporary primitive cultures), culminating in the Panhellenic Games.

Early civilizations show little evidence of organized sports as such. It was not until the rise of Greek civilization that a strongly organized athletic picture began to evolve. Establishment of the Panhellenic Games, originally religious festivals, the most famous of which were the Olympic Games, in time produced coaches and trainers to assist athletes in achieving a peak of physical perfection.[18]

Subsequently, with the appearance of the professional athlete in Athenian society, the *gymnastes* came into existence. These men trained their pupils in the skills and techniques of the sports of their day and employed a rudimentary knowledge of anatomy, physiology, and dietetics to keep the athletes in good condition. Later, the medical *gymnastai* appeared on the scene. Their concern was conditioning the athlete and maintaining him at a high peak of physical efficiency[10,11] (Fig. 1-1). Possessing some knowledge of diet, rest, and exercise and the effect that each has on physical development and performance, they made use of hot baths, massage, anodynes, and other measures. The *paidotribai* (literally "youth or boy rubbers" who ranged in age from 7 to 20 years) and the *aleiptes* (anointers, who used various oils, powders, and massage in their ministrations) were also professional trainers, and the techniques of massage, the prescription of diet, and the general fitness of the athlete were their particular concerns.[10,18]

Professional trainers were very much a part of the scene in ancient Rome. Early in his career, Galen, who later served as court physician to Marcus Aurelius, was physician to the gladiatorial school at Pergamum. He and others of his time wrote at considerable length about the salutary effects of proper diet, rest, abstinence from strong drink and sexual indulgence, and exercise as prerequisites for physical conditioning. For certain particularly demanding events, such as boxing, wrestling, and the pankration (a combination of both), the eating of meat was stressed and a psychological approach was used in selecting athletes for certain events.

Perhaps the greatest of all the Greek trainers, Herodicus of Megara, was considered a physician as well as a trainer. He performed his duties almost 300 years before Galen, and his chief claim to fame is that he was the teacher of Hippocrates, who was to become the "father of modern medicine."[11,45] As far as can be determined, Herodicus was the first physician to recommend exercise as a method of treatment for disease. Asclepiades, in the time of Christ, used exercise and massage as a method of treatment. In

Figure 1-1

Ancient shower. The athlete removes sand, dust, and oil with a strigil (small bronze instrument at left) before showering. The strigil and oil bottle were part of the athlete's equipment.

the sixteenth century Mercuriale was the first physician known to have classified exercise is either "preventive" or "therapeutic"; Pare, another sixteenth century physician, postulated that exercise was a most necessary corollary to the rehabilitation of a fracture following treatment.

For many centuries after the fall of the Roman Empire there was a complete lack of interest in sports activities. It was not until the beginning of the Renaissance that these activities slowly gained popularity. Training as we know it came into existence during the late nineteenth century with the firm establishment of intercollegiate and interscholastic athletes in the United States. The first trainers of this era were hangers-on who "rubbed down" the athlete. Since they possessed no technical knowledge, their training techniques usually consisted of a rub, the application of some type of counterirritant, and occasionally the prescription of various home remedies and poultices. Many of those earlier trainers were persons of questionable character. As a result, it has taken a good many years for the trainer to attain the status of a bona fide member of the athletic staff.

Until the last decade, women's sports participation was governed mainly by societal patterns, which were inhibitive. Scattered references in ancient history shed scant light on women's sports. With the rise of Sparta, women were encouraged to participate in strenuous physical activities, such as running, throwing the javelin, and wrestling. The aim of Spartan society was to develop the strongest, healthiest females possible to serve as mothers of the future Spartan soldiers who would be developed to represent the epitome of physical perfection.

When the Olympic Games came into existence, women were not only forbidden to participate but were also forbidden to watch, on pain of death. In later years, the Heraea Games were instituted, to be held secretly every 4 years between the Olympiads, with participation restricted to women. As time went on, attitudes became much more liberal, and eventually women were permitted limited participation in many of the games, principally wrestling, running, and chariot racing.[18] It may well be that women's training started at this time. The Roman conquest of Greece put an end to the many games, and, as with the men, active participation by women in sports declined until it was more or less nonexistent. In the last quarter of the nineteenth century, the introduction in high schools and colleges of tennis, crew rowing, and basketball, the forerunners of the modern women's sports program, led women to current sports participation.

Athletic training evolved into a major influence in athletes' lives. Growth of the trainer's role from ancient times to the present has aptly been described thus: "The days of 'the rubber,' the know-it-all, the jack-of-all-trades and the master of all is over."[32] This change occurred rapidly after World War I and the appearance of the athletic trainer in intercollegiate athletics. During this period the major influence in developing the athletic trainer as a specialist in preventing and managing athletic injuries resulted from the work of Dr. S.E. Bilik, a physician who wrote the first major text (1917) on athletic training and care of athletic injuries.[4] Since that time more and more colleges and universities have been offering courses in athletic training, and today there are very few students majoring in physical education or physical therapy who are not offered some formal experience in athletic training and sports medicine.

Today the professional trainer is a well-qualified individual who is certified by the National Athletic Trainers Association, has an advanced academic degree, and has a thorough understanding of and special skill in the many facets of prevention and care of athletic injuries. Both men and women work in all phases of the athletic training program in a team approach with the physician and the coach.

Today the precepts of athletic training are considered a major aspect of high school athletic programs. Although budgeting for salaries, equipment, and facilities has not generally been legislated, a number of states have recently introduced or enacted such measures as the very real need becomes apparent. In the past coaches were content to confine training to management of preliminary conditioning and the use of preventive strapping. Today, with the advances of techniques and equipment, high school coaches find that they must become more familiar with the broader aspects of the athletic training program.

A big step forward was the 1950 founding of the National Athletic Trainers Association (NATA) in Kansas City, Missouri, for the express purposes of establishing professional standards and exchanging and disseminating information. In 1954 the American College of Sports Medicine was founded. The recent formation of sports medicine associations by the American Medical Association and the American Orthopaedic Society attests to the growing interest in sports training and injury prevention and management. These organizations are dedicated to the promotion of research in medical problems encountered in physical exercise and sports. They have made numerous contributions to the area of training and have increased the understanding and knowledge of coaches and trainers at professional meetings, seminars, and through the publication of technical papers and periodicals so that they can more adequately train and care for their athletes.

> Today the professional athletic trainer is well qualified in the many facets of prevention and care of athletic injuries.

SURVEILLANCE OF SPORTS INJURIES

By their very nature sports activities invite injury. The "all-out" exertion required, the numerous situations requiring body contact, and play that involves the striking and throwing of missiles establish hazards that are either directly or indirectly responsible for the many different injuries suffered by athletes.

A report on athletic injuries and deaths in secondary schools and colleges in the United States, based on the survey, mandated by section 826 of Public Law 93-380, was released by the National Center for Education Statistics, a division of the Department of Health, Education and Welfare (HEW). The report indicates that well over 4.2 million men and women participate annually in varsity sports in secondary schools, colleges, and universities throughout the United States.[6] More than 1.25 million girls and 3.5 million boys engage in interscholastic sports; over 30 million children aged 6 to 12 are involved in out-of-school programs.[26] These figures are more than double those of the early 1960s; half of the sports participants are female.

DATA COLLECTION SYSTEMS

Because of the vast number of people involved with organized and recreational sports and the number of injuries sustained from these activities, accurate data acquisition is essential. Although methods are much improved over the past, many weaknesses exist in systematic data collection and analyses of sports injuries.[5]

The state of the art of sports injury surveillance is at this time unsatisfactory.[8] Currently most local, state, and federal systems are concerned with the accident or injury only after it has happened, and they focus on injuries requiring medical assistance or that cause time loss or restricted activity.

The ideal system takes an epidemiological approach that studies the relationship of various factors that influence the frequency and distribution of sports injuries. Some of the factors that should be collected and studied are[8]:

1. The potential hazards and unique risks a sport represents
2. The need for an athlete to take injury risks
3. The exposure time in risk taking and chances to become injured
4. The personal factors of interest and motivation to participate, skill level, extent of physical maturation, and knowledge of the activity
5. The failure of sports equipment
6. The inadequacy of the sports environment, including weather, facilities, playing surface, and crowd management
7. The laxity of officials

The epidemiological approach to the study of sports injuries involves the relationship of as many facts as possible:
Hazards
Risks
Personal factors
Equipment
Environment
Officiating

TABLE 1-1

Sports accidents*

Sport	Injuries	Fatalities	Participants
Baseball	471,800	([a])	([a])
Basketball	434,200	([a])	([a])
Boating	([a])	1,208[b]	63,000,000[b]
Football[c]	443,300	9[d]	1,600,000[d]
Hang gliding	1,300	15[e]	80,000[f]
Ice skating	30,300	([a])	([a])
Parachuting	868[g]	50[g]	40,000[g]
Roller skating	205,500	([a])	50,000,000[f]
Scuba diving	1,051	([a])	2,000,000[h]
Sledding	34,400	([a])	([a])
Snowmobiling[i]	8,932	91[f]	6,500,000
Snow skiing	47,000	([a])	14,000,000[j]
Swimming	117,000	2,300[f]	100,000,000[f]
Water skiing	18,923	44[b]	15,000,000[b]

From the National Safety Council. Source: Consumer Product Safety Commission estimates for 1981 except where noted. [a]Estimate not available. [b]U.S. Coast Guard. [c]1980 data. [d]American Football Coaches Assoc. [e]U.S. Hang Gliding Assoc. [f]National Safety Council. [g]U.S. Parachuting Assoc. [h]National YMCA Center for Underwater Activities. [i]1981 fiscal year. [j]U.S. Ski Area Owners Assoc.

*Reporting methods and coverage may vary among sources and can affect comparisons between sports.

Valid, reliable sports injury data can materially help decrease injuries. If properly interpreted, the data can be used to modify rules, assist coaches and players in understanding risks, and help manufacturers evaluate their product against the overall market.[23] The public, especially parents, needs to understand the risks inherent in a particular sport, and insurance companies that insure athletes need to know risks to set reasonable costs.[23]

National Data Gathering Systems

A number of data collection systems tabulate the incidence of sports injuries. The most mentioned systems are the National Safety Council, Annual Survey of Football Injury Research, National Electronic Injury Surveillance System (NEISS), and the National Athletic Injuries Reporting System (NAIRS).

National Safety Council

The National Safety Council is a nongovernmental, nonprofit public service organization. It draws sports injuries data from a variety of sources, including educational institutions. Table 1-1 shows 1-year estimates of injuries, deaths, and participants associated with various sports.

Annual Survey of Football Injury Research

In 1931 the American Football Coaches Association (AFCA) began the first Annual Survey of Football Fatalities. In 1980 this title was changed to Annual Survey of Football Injury Research. Every year, with the exception of 1942, data have been collected about public school, college, professional, and sandlot football. Information is gathered through personal contact interviews and questionnaires.[25] The sponsoring organizations of this survey are as follows:

> American Football Coaches Association
> Durham, North Carolina
>
> National Collegiate Athletic Association
> Shawnee Mission, Kansas
>
> National Federation of State High School Associations
> Kansas City, Missouri

This survey classifies football fatalities as being *direct* or *indirect*. *Direct fatalities are those resulting directly from participation in football. Indirect fatalities are produced by systemic failure caused through the exertion of playing football or by a complication that arose from a nonfatal football injury.* (See Tables 1-1 and 1-2.)

In 1977 the AFCA and the National Collegiate Athletic Association (NCAA) instituted a national surveillance of catastrophic football injuries. Catastrophic, in this instance, refers to cervical neck injury leading to paralysis and permanent central nervous system damage (quadriplegia). Fifty-one catastrophic cervical injuries were reported from 1977 to 1982. This is a significant reduction from the period of 1971 to 1975, which averaged 35 catastrophic injuries per year.[25] Another important data collection body is the National Football Head and Neck Injury Registry, which was established by Dr. J.S. Torg at the Sports Medicine Center of the University of Pennsylvania.[41]

TABLE 1-2

Injuries associated with selected products*

Product Descriptions	Number of Cases		Estimated Number of Cases	
	Report Period	12 Mos to Date	Report Period	12 Mos to Date
Sports and recreational equipment				
Baseball, activity and related equipment	2,897	8,860	165,841	507,483
Basketball, activity and related equipment	1,413	8,219	66,239	436,384
Bicycles and accessories	5,031	10,454	256,894	553,599
Bowling, activity and related equipment	75	388	3,420	21,468
Exercise equipment	261	1,028	12,174	54,107
Fishing	372	892	25,746	62,373
Football, activity and related equipment	3,140	8,069	174,344	448,656
Golf equipment (inc, golf carts)	175	391	10,449	23,667
Guns, all types	222	841	11,905	50,717
Gymnastics and associated equipment	146	964	8,825	53,122
Hockey (field & ice) and related equipment	67	693	4,380	48,125
Ice and roller skating and skating not specified	634	3,343	33,051	198,269
Mopeds, minibikes and other such vehicles	395	891	22,460	51,841
Playground equipment	1,262	3,612	65,220	189,340
Skateboards	179	436	8,700	20,966
Snow skiing and related equipment	5	732	369	48,352
Snowmobiles (inc. apparel and protective gear)	—	147	—	12,860
Soccer, activity and related equipment	575	1,919	29,941	105,198
Swimming, swimming pools and related equipment	1,109	1,687	60,128	94,558
Tennis, badminton and squash, activity and equipment	363	1,219	20,677	71,320
Toboggans, sleds, snow discs and snow tubing	1	718	22	46,754
Track and field activities, apparel and related equip.	308	1,141	13,825	60,000
Trampolines	46	144	2,626	9,247
Volleyball, activity and related equipment	408	1,229	22,828	73,916
Water skiing, tubing and surfing and related equipment	287	451	19,275	29,405
Wrestling (organized activity) and related equip.	133	1,084	7,247	66,240

*Injuries associated with selected consumer products treated in hospital emergency departments by quarter and 12 months ended 9/30/82.
Source: National Electronic Injury Surveillance System, U.S. Consumer Product Safety Commission/Directorate for Epidemiology, National Injury Information Clearinghouse, Washington, D.C.

Estimated Number of Product-Related Injuries per 100,000 Population within the Contiguous United States which Were Treated in Hospital Emergency Rooms During the Last 12 Months Ending with This Report Period							By Sex		Estimated Mean Severity
By Age							**By Sex**		
All Ages	00-04	05-14	15-24	25-64	65+		Male	Female	12 Mos to Date
238.1	50.5	414.2	443.5	170.0	1.3		359.8	122.3	21
204.7	4.1	263.3	612.4	93.5	.9		355.9	61.0	17
259.7	277.0	913.5	245.8	64.6	14.9		366.5	157.9	35
10.1	5.7	8.3	12.7	11.7	4.6		9.2	10.9	14
25.4	22.3	38.3	53.3	14.9	1.5		37.3	14.1	36
29.3	15.1	58.0	29.1	24.1	13.5		46.4	13.0	28
210.5	7.6	469.8	594.0	32.8	1.0		410.9	20.1	20
11.1	7.4	17.5	7.6	10.6	11.3		15.9	6.6	46
23.8	4.9	37.5	45.0	17.4	3.8		42.2	6.2	95
24.9	8.5	93.3	35.8	2.3	—		16.8	32.7	21
22.6	.6	38.9	65.5	7.2	.6		37.9	8.0	22
93.0	20.3	263.9	140.7	39.7	2.3		66.4	118.1	20
24.3	6.5	49.4	53.9	10.3	2.6		39.3	10.1	48
88.8	364.3	318.1	13.0	5.8	1.9		96.2	81.8	28
9.8	5.8	35.3	13.7	1.3	—		15.5	4.4	25
22.7	.7	26.9	54.1	16.8	.6		27.1	18.4	19
6.0	.6	5.9	12.0	5.8	.5		8.7	3.4	58
49.4	1.6	121.3	112.9	14.2	.9		77.5	22.6	16
44.4	51.0	106.2	71.7	17.7	2.2		57.7	31.8	121
33.5	5.7	21.0	54.5	41.4	2.0		45.9	21.6	21
21.9	14.8	73.0	28.4	5.7	—		31.2	13.0	28
28.2	1.6	34.4	74.2	17.3	1.2		34.6	22.0	21
4.3	1.9	14.0	6.3	1.0	.5		4.9	3.8	20
34.7	.6	34.0	77.6	30.5	1.1		36.7	32.7	13
13.8	.7	6.1	36.5	12.6	—		21.4	6.5	23
31.1	6.9	55.1	96.7	5.8	—		56.9	6.4	21

National Electronic Injury Surveillance System (NEISS)

In 1972 the federal government established the Consumer Product Safety Act (CPSA), which created and granted broad authority to the Consumer Produce Safety Commission to enforce the safety standards of more than 10,000 products that may be risky to the consumer.[5] To carry out this mission, the National Electronic Injury Surveillance System (NEISS) was established. Data on injuries related to consumer products are monitored 24 hours a day from a selected sample of 5000 hospital emergency rooms nationwide. Sports injuries represent 25% of all injuries reported by NEISS.[5] It should be noted that a product may be related to an injury but not be the direct cause of that injury (Table 1-2).

Once a product is considered hazardous, the commission can seize the product or create standards to decrease the risk.[8] Also, manufacturers and distributors of sports recreational equipment must report to the commission on any product that is potentially hazardous or defective.[8] The commission can also research the reasons that a sports or recreational product is hazardous.[5]

National Athletic Injury Reporting System (NAIRS)

The National Athletic Injury Reporting System* first began functioning in 1975 as an epidemiological approach to the study of sports injuries. It was originally developed to provide an in-depth look at sports injuries and to acquire data that were complete, up to date, reliable, and valid.[30,44] A sample of 30 different sports at 200 college and high schools is taken, with certified athletic trainers collecting and reporting the data. Weekly injury reports are then submitted to NAIRS.[26] Using an epidemiological approach, NAIRS is concerned with many variables that relate to the injury. Of these, exposure time and risk are very important. For example, in football reporting, squad size, number of games played, number of practices engaged in, whether the athlete was a substitute or a starter, the athlete's height and weight, equipment used, position played, activity engaged in, and type of playing surface

---

*NAIRS, Pennsylvania State University, University Park, PA.

TABLE 1-3

Total direct football fatalities, 1976 to 1982

Year	High School	College	Total
1976	15	0	15
1977	8	1	9
1978	9	0	9
1979	3	1	4
1980	9	0	9
1981	5	2	7
1982	7	0	7
TOTAL	56	4	60

Modified from Mueller, F.O., and Blyth, C.S.: Phys. Sportsmed. **10:**135, 1982; and Mueller, F.O., and Schindler, R.D.: submitted for publication, Feb. 1983.

are some of the categories for which information is sought. Periodically reports are returned to the participating schools. Such information is useful to the athletic department in budget planning, equipment purchasing, athletic conditioning, and insurance acquisition.[30]

THE INCIDENCE OF SPORTS INJURIES

An **accident** is defined as an unplanned event capable of resulting in loss of time, property damage, injury, disablement or even death.[9] On the other hand, an **injury** may be defined as damage to the body that restricts activity and/or causes disability to such an extent that the athlete is confined to his or her bed.[9] Sports are classified by the extent to which they may produce accidents and injuries. Those sports classified as collision-type commonly have more potential for causing fatalities and severe injuries than sports catagorized as contact or noncontact.

In general an athlete runs a 50% chance of sustaining some injury. Of the 50 million estimated sports injuries per year, 50% require only minor care with no restriction of activity.[9] Ninety percent of sports injuries fall into the category of muscle contusions, minor joint sprains, and muscle strains; however, 10% of the injuries are more serious. Repeated minor injuries can lead to the complications of microtraumas and eventually to severe, chronic conditions in later life.

Collision Sports

In collision sports, athletes use their bodies to deter or punish opponents. American football, ice hockey, boxing, and rugby are the most common collision sports in the United States.

American Football

American tackle football is the nation's—if not the world's—most injurious sport. It is also one of the most popular, with approximately 3 million high school and 75,000 college participants annually. Of this number, over 300,000 high school participants, 35,000 college players, and half of all National Football League players will be injured.[43]

Football fatalities and catastrophic injuries Compared to 1970 to 1975, the period of 1976 to 1981 represented a 44% reduction in the total number of football fatalities; 42% of these were in high school and 60% in college football.[25] The incidence of direct fatalities is very low, based on 100,000-player exposure. For all football, including sandlot, professional, high school, and college, the number of fatalities was 0.88 per 100,000 and dropped to 0.53 in the 1976 to 1981 period and to zero in 1982. (Fig. 1-2). There has been a significant drop in fatalities in organized football since 1976 (Table 1-3), at which time the NCAA and the National Federation of State High School Associations (NFSHSA) made rule changes that prevented the use of the head as a primary and initial contact area of blocking and tackling.[25]

The National Operating Committee on Standards for Athletic Equipment (NOCSAE) played a role in the decline of football fatalities. NOCSAE developed helmet safety standards that were adopted and implemented in 1978 by the NCAA and in 1980 for all high school players.

accident
Occurring by chance or without intention
injury
An act that damages or hurts

Figure 1-2

Fatalities in organized football have dropped significantly since rules were adopted that prevent the head from being used as a primary and initial contact area.

TABLE 1-4

Number of fatal injuries during games compared to practices, 1976 to 1982	Games	38
	Practices	20
	Scrimmages	2
	Unknown causes	0

Modified from Mueller, F.O., and Blyth, C.S.: Phys. Sportsmed. **10**:135, 1982; and Mueller, F.O., and Schindler, R.D.: submitted for publication Feb. 1983.

TABLE 1-5

Football activity at time of fatal injury, 1976 to 1982 (%)

	1976	1982
Tackling	30	49
Tackled	16	26
Blocking	1	2
Blocked	1	2
Collision	3	5
Equipment	0	0
Unknown causes	10	16
TOTAL	61	100

Modified from Mueller, F.O., and Blyth, C.S.: Phys. Sportsmed. **10**:135, 1982; and Mueller, F.O. and Schindler, R.D.: submitted for publication Feb. 1983.

TABLE 1-6

Heatstroke fatalities, 1931 to 1982

Year	Total	Year	Total
1931-1954	0	1970	8
1955	1	1971	4
1956-1958	0	1972	7
1959	4	1973	3
1960	3	1974	0
1961	3	1975	0
1962	5	1976	1
1963	0	1977	1
1964	4	1978	4
1965	6	1979	2
1966	1	1980	1
1967	2	1981	2
1968	5	1982	2
1969	5	TOTAL	74

From Mueller, F.O., and Schindler, R.D.: submitted for publication Feb. 1983.

TABLE 1-7

Catastrophic permanent cervical cord injuries in football

Year	High School	College	Total
1977	10	2	12
1978	11	0	11
1979	7	3	10
1980	10	2	12
1981	5	1	6
TOTAL	43	8	51

Modified from Mueller, F.O., and Blyth, C.S.: Phys. Sportsmed. **10**:135, 1982; and Torg, J.S., et al.: J.A.M.A. **241**:1477, 1977.

Most direct fatalities in football occur from injury to the head, followed by neck injuries (20%) and internal injuries (9%). Most direct fatalities occurred during regularly scheduled games, and the largest number took place during October (Table 1-4).

Since 1976 tackling has claimed the majority of lives. From 1976 to 1982, 49% of the deaths occurred from tackling, and 26% from being tackled (Table 1-5).

Each year a number of football deaths are attributed to *indirect* causes. From 1931 to 1982 there were 456 such cases. In 1982 the primary cause of indirect deaths was from heart failure; the second most frequent cause was heatstroke (Table 1-6). From the 1931 beginning of the Annual Survey of Football Injury, through 1982, there were 74 deaths from heatstroke, a highly preventable condition.

Besides fatalities, there is a major concern for the catastrophic injuries sustained in football. One study listed 99 permanent spinal cord injuries and 77 deaths in high school and college football from 1971 to 1975.[42] From 1977 to 1981, 51 permanent spinal injuries were reported (Table 1-7). This represents a significant drop, which can be attributed to stricter rules on the use of the head and to better conditioning of the neck. Most catastrophic injuries occurred to backfield players during game situations when on defense and when tackling. The predominant position of the head was down, in flexion, with contact made at its top.

Although football helmets have been substantially improved since the beginning of American football, concussions continue to be a frequent injury, especially in high school. No helmet is capable of completely protecting the brain against shock. Cervical neck injuries are the result of improper techniques in blocking and tackling rather than the fault of the helmet per se, since the helmet cannot adequately protect the back of the neck.

In view of these findings several pertinent recommendations have been made, most of which are applicable to all other sports, as well as to football. In reference to football it is recommended that the athletes be drilled in the proper execution of the game fundamentals, particularly blocking and tackling, that the head and neck be particularly strengthened through the use of proper conditioning exercises, and that the use of the head as a battering ram when blocking and tackling be discouraged. The helmet should be regarded as a protective device rather than an offensive weapon. Other recommendations include the strict enforcement of game rules and health protection regulations. A mandatory complete medical examination should be given and a medical history should be taken at the beginning of the season. A physician should be in attendance at all games and, if possible, at all practice sessions. Personnel should be cognizant of the problems and the safety measures related to physical activity in hot weather, and emphasis should be placed on proper, gradual, and complete physical conditioning of the athlete.

Economic costs of catastrophic sports injuries Even though the number of catastrophic injuries from sports is relatively low, the economic cost to the athlete, to the family, and to social agencies is often staggering. Costs are direct and indirect: direct costs are those paid directly by the athlete, the athlete's family, and social agencies, whereas indirect costs are those incurred as a result of the injury.[40]

Examples of some of the direct areas of costs for a catastrophic injury are as follows:

- Initial ambulance transportation
- Initial emergency room care
- Acute care in the hospital
- Home modification (for example, wheelchair ramps, wider doorways, and bathroom modifications)
- The purchase of an electric hospital bed, electric hoist for entering and leaving the bed, and a wheelchair
- Daily assistance from an attendant
- Vocational rehabilitation
- Special drugs and medical supplies (for example, muscle relaxants, pain medication)
- Average of 15 days' yearly hospitalization for complications, such as care of decubitus ulcers (bedsores) and urinary tract infections
- Transportation (for example, special van equipped with a wheelchair lift)

Some of the possible indirect cost areas incurred are as follows:

- Reduced life span
- Reduced economic productivity
- Increased number of illnesses
- Possible legal and court costs
- Social isolation and psychological problems
- Economic dependency

Over a lifetime, a young athlete who has become a quadriplegic could require $40,000 to $50,000 or more per year in direct costs, which ultimately could amount to well over $1 million dollars. Costs for psychosocial problems are often difficult to measure in dollars unless professional assistance is obtained.

Figure 1-3

Stick and body contact injuries are prevalent in ice hockey.

G. Robert Bishop

Ice Hockey

Ice hockey is an extremely fast, physically demanding and aggressive sport. Over 2 million athletes compete in ice hockey throughout the world. As of 1979 there were approximately 268 collegiate ice hockey teams in the United States. Because of the nature of the game, injuries are prevalent (Fig. 1-3). Over an 8-year period, 1973 through 1980, there were 10 fatalities among all ages of participants. In ages 5 to 14 there were two deaths from being struck with a hockey puck or stick.[28] Of medically attended and hospital emergency room attended injuries during 1980, injuries to the head and face (35% and 44%) had the highest incidence. The areas of the arms and hands and legs and feet both sustained 18% and 21% of all injuries.

A 5-year study of a major collegiate hockey team indicated that injuries about the shoulder (34.5%), upper extremities (28.8%), and lower extremities (33.8%) were fairly equally divided into thirds. The highest percentage of injuries was sustained in game situations, with the second half of the game being the most dangerous time for both practice and actual game playing.[35] The most common injuries were incisions or lacerations (28.9%) and contusions (19.4%).

Many states have now passed legislation requiring face protection. Fifty to seventy percent of eye and face injuries result from improper stick use, and 15% to 25% from fighting or other aggressive action that is unrelated to actual play.[44] The face protection regulation has led to a dramatic decrease in facial injuries in those areas where it has been strictly enforced.

Various surveys have indicated that forwards are injured more often than defense men. Goaltenders are especially vulnerable to clavicle and neck injuries, particularly when contact with the goal itself ensues. The elbows and the insides of the knees are other vulnerable areas. Improvements in equipment design should provide better goalie protection. Figures indicate that the hockey stick is responsible for over one third of all hockey injuries, almost twice the number caused by the hockey puck. Stricter rule enforcement and perhaps an increase in the penalties for stick violations and for fighting, plus continued improvements in protective equipment, will keep injuries at a low level.[14]

Rugby Football

Rugby football is one of the safest sports. Since it is played with no protective equipment or padding and with short-cleated shoes, it does not reflect either the severity or the types of injuries usually incurred in American football. In American tackle football, in comparison, the player wears considerable protective equipment and the body and its parts become an offensive weapon. Injury rates in rugby on the international level are reported in the range from 3% to 20%. A recent study conducted in the Boston area reported an 11% injury rate.[1]

In a regional study in New England, participating colleges recorded an overall injury rate of 9.8%, with injuries to the shoulder showing the high-

Figure 1-4

A potential injury situation in rugby, a game of precision, skill, and forceful body contact.

est incidence followed by injuries to the head, the neck, and the knee successively[22] (Fig. 1-4). Generally bruises, contusions, and minor lacerations most commonly occur on the hands and face, with injuries to the knee and ankle next in frequency. Meniscal injuries are more common than ligament injuries, with occasional injuries occurring to the neck, particularly in scrum.[1] As with all sports the key to reduced injuries is proper and adequate conditioning, and as coaching techniques and facilities improve, a progressive decrease in the injury rate should be expected.

Contact Sports

Contact sports include basketball, baseball, field hockey, touch and flag football, judo, lacrosse, rodeo, soccer, softball, water polo, and wrestling. Basketball, baseball and softball, soccer football, and lacrosse are discussed as representative of contact sports.

Basketball

Figure 1-5

Basketball is increasingly becoming a contact sport. The high center of gravity of basketball players can result in heavy falls.

Basketball has the second highest rate of injury. Originally conceived as a noncontact sport, it has evolved into a body contact activity. Most of the injuries in this sport involve the wrists, elbows, and head, with sprained ankles and broken fingers at the top of the list. So-called *jumper's knee*, Achilles tendinitis, Achilles tendon rupture, and stress fractures are among the more common injuries. They result either with other players or attempts to ward off an impending collision with walls, bleachers, or other obstacles. Ankle and knee injuries occur in underbasket play or as the result of change-of-direction actions. The body build of basketball players is typically such that a high center of gravity induces relative instability, resulting in heavy falls to the floor. This is particularly obvious in rough underbasket play when a player must leap off the floor to play the ball (Fig. 1-5). In this situation even a relatively slight body contact with an opponent or a teammate anywhere below the hips could cause an upset. The acromioclavicular joint is very susceptible to injury in basketball players. Lacerations and abrasions occur more frequently in this sport than in football. Basketball has the highest incidence of injury (about double that of volleyball and field hockey, the next ranked) among women.[15] A recent analytical comparative study of high school basketball players found that the injury pattern for both genders was similar but that girls sustained more injuries, having a rate of 0.72 injuries per player as compared to 0.16 for the boys. Girls' injuries tended to become less frequent as the season progressed.[24]

Between 1973 and 1980 there were 37 deaths in basketball; six of these players were between the ages of 5 and 14, as reported by NEISS. It was also estimated by NEISS in 1980 that there were over 1.5 million injuries, resulting from organized and recreational basketball, treated in emergency rooms and by private physicians in the United States. Most of these injuries were to legs or feet and arms or hands.

Baseball and Softball

In a study of some 46 million individuals who participated in baseball and softball annually, approximately 900,000 injuries had occurred, an incidence of 1.96%.[16] Most are caused by the ball, which is not only hard but travels at an extremely high rate of speed—some professional pitchers throw at over 100 miles per hour (Fig. 1-6). Little League pitchers have been timed at 55 to 70, and a batted ball can reach a velocity of 88 to 95 miles per hour.

Injuries to the hand, wrist, and forearm predominate, with mallet finger the most common. Wrist injuries, usually incurred in sliding, and sprains and occasional fractures; spike wounds and lacerations are not uncommon, usually resulting from collisions encountered in sliding or in playing the ball.

Over the years, Little League has kept an injury register and has done a great deal of research to reduce injuries to a minimum. The result has been the elimination of steel spikes and the institution of the on-deck circle, screening the dugouts, mandating the use of face and head protectors for the batters, and installing breakaway bases, all of which have resulted in a decrease in injuries.[16] The injury frequency is less than 2%; the injuries are those considered sufficient for medical attention and are mostly minor in nature. So-called Little League elbow, the result of excessive forceful throwing, such as in pitching, during one's early formative years has come in for considerable attention and study by the medical profession. Opinion is still divided as to whether such throwing has a detrimental residual effect that will limit activity in later years. Long-term studies now under way should give some answers in the near future.

In a report on juvenile sports-related injuries, the U.S. Consumer Product Safety Commission[28] indicated that from 1973 through 1980 baseball fatalities of children between the ages of 5 and 14 were surprisingly high. During that period there were 40 deaths and 359,000 medically attended injuries. Seventeen of these deaths were from direct blows to the chest, and 21 were from being hit in the head by a bat or baseball. It can be speculated that most of these deaths were caused by individuals' not wearing protective head gear.

Soccer Football

Undoubtedly soccer football is played by more individuals than any other sport in the world. It is the most popular sport in 135 countries and sustains a television audience of over 100 million fans. In the United States the sport is enjoying an unprecedented boom; participants range in age from 6 to over 60, and there has been a marked increase in the number of spectators. Although soccer is played with a minimum of protective equipment, serious injuries are rare; however, deaths do occur.

A study reviewing 33 soccer deaths since 1938 indicated that death resulted from collision with another player or the ground, by being hit in the head with a ball, and from hitting a goalpost.[37] Death came as a result of injuries to the brain or internal organs (for example, the spleen), cardiovascular problems, or various rare medical conditions. From the 8-year period 1973 through 1980, eleven soccer deaths were reported, six of which were of children aged 5 to 14. Of these six deaths, four children died when goalposts fell on them, one from hitting his head against a goal pipe, and one from a fractured femur.[28]

Injury incidence is reported in a range of from one injury out of every 48 players to one out of every 947 players in the international professional ranks.[29]

Figure 1-6

A pitched baseball could be a lethal missile, traveling at over 100 miles per hour.

In Europe it is reported that soccer injuries compose 50% to 60% of all sports injuries and from 3.5% to 10% of all the injuries treated in hospitals.[37] A study of high school teams in the Seattle area indicated an injury rate of 30 per 100 participants and that most of the injuries occurred during games. The thigh was the area most frequently injured, and a few ankle injuries were reported, but the head injury rate was identical to that for tackle football. Eighty-one percent of those injured were able to return to full participation.

Injuries to the lower extremities seem to be most common (Fig. 1-7). Sprains to the ankle joint are most frequent, followed by ruptured ligaments, injuries to the menisci, and fractures. Contusions of the forefoot and the metatarsals often occur. Although injuries to the upper extremities are least common, when they do occur they are usually shoulder sprains with or without an accompanying rotator cuff tear. Fracture of the greater tuberosity of the humerus and separation of the acromioclavicular or the sternoclavicular joints are occasionally reported—usually the result of a fall. Many of the injuries reported, particularly those that affect the foot, the ankle, the knee, or the groin, are the result of overuse (from recurrent microtrauma).

Lacrosse and Field Hockey

Lacrosse, an original American sport, was invented by North American Indians. It is one of the fastest running sports played. It is played by both genders in more than 170 colleges and universities and in over 750 high schools and preparatory schools. Additionally there are many amateur and club lacrosse leagues.[20] Injuries in lacrosse, oddly enough, are neither as frequent nor as severe as one would expect, considering that it is a hard contact game involving the use of a stick (Fig. 1-8). The use of protective helmets, face masks, gloves, and arm protectors for the players, with the goalie having the additional protection of a chest protector, has lessened the chance of serious injury. Additionally, the use of plastic sticks with molded plastic heads further contributes to the safety of the game.[20] Sprains and

TABLE 1-8

Causes of injury in lacrosse

Cause	Number of Injuries	Percent of Total Injuries
Struck by stick	39	42.86
Collision with player	18	19.78
Struck by ball	9	9.89
Fall or trip	9	9.89
Collision with boards	5	5.49
Collision with goal	0	0.00
Other	11	12.09
TOTAL	91	100.00

From Marchant, L., Roy, E., and Warshawski, J.: Sport safety research, Fitness and Amateur Sport, Government of Canada. Used by permission.

strains, especially of the lower extremities, appear to be the most common injuries. Abrasions, lacerations, and contusions, usually the result of stick contact or collision, are not infrequent. Joint injuries usually affect the ankles or the knees, and pulled hamstring muscles occasionally occur. Field hockey injury patterns appear to be similar to those found in lacrosse.

Figure 1-7

Although frequent forceful body contact often occurs in soccer, serious injuries are relatively rare; foot and leg injuries are common.

Figure 1-8

In spite of protective equipment, stick injuries are quite common in lacrosse.
Courtesy California Lacrosse Association.

Wrestling

In high schools throughout the country, wrestling is one of the most popular sports, averaging 300,000 to 400,000 participants yearly.[34] Wrestling has a considerable number of contact-related injuries, the most common affecting the knee, shoulder, and head and neck region, injuries specifically to the menisci and the medial collateral ligament being the most common (Fig. 1-9).

One study found that 75.2 injuries were reported for 100 participants per season.[34] There are more injuries in practice than in competition, but the latter presents a higher risk situation, as does the takedown maneuver. Since 1973 there have been no deaths reported by the U.S. Consumer Product Safety Commission.[28] Not infrequently, injuries to the ear resulting in hematoma auris (cauliflower ear), elbow hyperextension injuries, lateral meniscus injuries, and costochondral or sternoclavicular separations occur as a result of the sport of wrestling.[12] In the past, severe illness and even death have occurred as a result of improper procedures followed in making weight, but fortunately a more enlightened approach in recent years seems to be reducing such incidents.

Noncontact Sports

A great number of sports are classified as noncontact, including archery, badminton, bowling, crew rowing, cross-country running, curling, fencing, golf, gymnastics, riflery, skiing, squash, swimming, diving, tennis, track and field, and volleyball. Four noncontact sports will be discussed that are representative of the vast array of physical stresses they can present: track and field, skiing, gymnastics, and tennis.

Figure 1-9

Wrestling has a potential for numerous contact-related injuries.

Track and Field

Track and field is extremely popular with men and women. Taking into consideration the high number of participants, it has very few fatalities and a relatively low injury rate. In the age range of 5 to 14, in 1980 NEISS reported that two deaths were attributed to head injuries resulting from falls; one athlete died while pole-vaulting and the other while performing a high jump. Fatalities in the past have usually indicated the presence of some organic impairment that directly or indirectly contributed to the fatality. In most cases death occurred as a consequence of a freak accident, such as the athlete's being struck with an implement or projectile.

The recent proliferation of long-distance road races held in warm weather in which runners of both genders ranging in age from 8 to 80 years has led to a significant amount of heat injury. Although the injuries may affect less than 1% of the total number of participants, 50 to 100 heat casualties are not uncommon in some of the larger events, whereas the number of subclinical injuries probably approaches 10% to 20% during marginal, adverse environmental conditions.[17] Muscle pulls, knee and ankle injuries, puncture wounds from shoe spikes, and abrasions are the most common injuries associated with this sport. Musculotendinous strains constitute about one third of the runner injuries, with approximately half of such strains affecting sprinters; stress fractures are more common in middle- and long-distance runners.

One study of high school track and field participants over a 2-year period in four high schools indicated most injuries were sustained during practice for both boys and girls, with musculotendinous injuries constituting the largest number. The thigh was the most common area of injury, with the leg and knee second (Fig. 1-10). Hamstrings constituted the major strain for both boys and girls. Shinsplints were the major problems in the lower legs.[33]

Skiing

Alpine skiing is a unique sport because of the multiple conditions to which the skier is exposed. Three factors stand out when considering the injury rate of skiing: the skier, the ski equipment, and the environment. An in-depth study conducted for nine seasons (1972 to 1981) in Vermont indicated some interesting findings.[19] Over these nine seasons the injury rate declined, but not significantly. The greatest decline of injuries was to the lower leg, primarily in ankle sprains. Twisting injuries leading to tibial fractures declined by 79%; however, boot top fractures declined only by 37%. In comparison, the grade I medial collateral ligament sprain of the knee showed decline, but more serious knee injuries remained about the same. Knee injuries represented the largest group of injuries at 20% of all injuries reported. Injuries to the upper body were not significant during this 9-year period. Injuries to the head and spine and upper body lacerations declined, while injuries to the upper extremities and trunk increased. The usual causes of reported fatalities, however, are head injuries, cardiac disease, or internal hemorrhage usually caused by laceration of the spleen, the liver, or both.

Equipment-related injuries to the lower extremities can be reduced con-

Figure 1-10

The thigh is the most common area of injury in track and field participants.

siderably by proper equipment maintenance, especially the bindings, which must be properly installed and adjusted.[19,27] They must be kept clean at all times, and they should be checked frequently as conditions change. The addition of a sole pad (friction pad) is recommended. The bindings cannot protect the leg and knee under all circumstances, but through adequate and proper conditioning, and using and maintaining good equipment at its most effective level, the skier can adjust the odds in his or her favor. Competent instruction through ski schools, strict slope discipline by ski patrols, and frequent grooming of the slopes all contribute most significantly to reducing the rate and severity of skiing accidents.[27]

Injuries of the upper extremities appear to be on the increase as a result of the forward lean prevalent in today's style of skiing, which is augmented by the forward flexion of high stiff boots.[13] Women have proportionately more lower extremity equipment-related injuries than men but do not show proportionately more of other types of injuries. Fifty percent of the injuries would be preventable if a safe, releasable ski binding were developed. Injury rates are higher in the under-25 age group, as would be expected, and tend to decrease as the skier's level of skill improves. Inexperienced skiers are especially prone to lower extremity equipment-related injuries.

Cross-country skiing, it is estimated, has well over 4 million participants in the United States each year. Because cross-country skiing is performed mostly at state and federal parks or on unattended trails, accurate injury data are difficult to obtain. With the development of touring centers, constructed tracks, and trails, some more consistent data are being made available.[7] The U.S. Consumer Product Safety Commission, via NEISS, re-

Figure 1-11

The high stiff boot and forward lean of today's alpine skier is producing a greater number of upper extremity injuries.

G. Robert Bishop

ports 0.2 medically treated injuries in 1000 skiers, and in an independent two-season study of five private cross-country touring centers, 0.72 injuries per 1000 skiers were reported.[2] From these data it might be concluded that on a well-groomed and maintained course, cross-country skiing is a relatively safe sport.

Most injuries occur while the skier is going down hill. Upper extremity injuries are the most common. The greatest number of lower limb injuries result from the rotational forces involved in controlling and maneuvering the skis. Low-cut boots with pin bindings are the major cause of injuries.[21]

Gymnastics

Gymnasts suffer from shoulder, elbow, and wrist injuries (Fig 1-12). A knee or ankle can also be injured, particularly in the tumbling phase of the floor exercise or in the execution of a dismount. Lacerations of the palm are still occasionally suffered, but the incidence is nowhere as great as it was before hand grips came into general use. Coaches or spotters not infrequently incur "spotter's elbow," medial epicondylitis, as the result of subjecting the elbow to unusually severe force in assisting a performer.

In a study of injuries of a university women's gymnastic team over a 5-year period, a number of factors were revealed.[39] Out of 70 participants there were 66 medically reportable injuries. The most prevalent injuries requiring medical attention were 17 ankle sprains out of a total of 82 injuries, representing 20%. The next highest injury incidence was tendinitis of the supraspinatus muscle (10), then nine fractures throughout the body and four elbow dislocations. During that same period there were also three torn knee menisci and a variety of hand, wrist, and leg muscle problems.

In a report of sports-related medically attended injuries in children 5 to

Figure 1-12

Gymnasts can sustain serious injuries to their shoulders, elbows, wrists, knees, and ankles.

14 years of age over an 8-year period (1973 through 1980), gymnastics ranked fourth, with 109,200 injuries. There were no fatalities during this period; however, the estimated number of head and neck injuries treated in hospital emergency rooms throughout the country was 17,865.[28]

Tennis and Other Racquet Sports

Tennis, racquetball, squash, and other racquet sports present unique injury problems to the participants. Major sports-related injuries reported to the U.S. Consumer Product Safety Commission involved injury impact with a secondary object. Although racquet sports are low in terms of fatalities, they can be hazardous. In racquet sports that are confined to a limited space, injuries are often sustained by running into a wall or being hit by a ball or racquet.[3,36] Of the estimated 75,000 reported sports-related medically attended injuries to 5- to 14-year-olds during 1980, 35% (26,488) were to the face and head and 42% (31,429) occurred to the legs and feet.

Tennis players suffer from many injuries. One of the most common is overuse microtrauma to the elbow joint. "Tennis elbow," lateral humeral epicondylitis, has been estimated to occur in 31% of all men and women players. This injury is four times as frequent as the next most prevalent injury, ankle sprains (8%).[31] On occasion the tennis player may injure a knee or shoulder and sustain bruises from falling or sliding on the court surface. As with most sports, many traumas could be prevented through a proper regimen of conditioning exercise and proper warm-up and cool down. Poor technique is believed to contribute to many tennis injury conditions.

AN OVERVIEW OF SPORTS-RELATED INJURIES

Although millions of individuals participate in organized and recreational sports, there is a relatively low incidence of fatalities or catastrophic injuries. Ninety-eight percent of individuals with injuries requiring hospital emergency room medical attention are treated and released.[28] Deaths have been attributed to chest or trunk impact by thrown objects, other players, or nonyielding objects (for example, goalposts). Deaths have occurred when players were struck in the head by sports implements (bats, golf clubs, hockey sticks) or by missiles (baseballs, soccer balls, golf balls, hockey pucks). Deaths have also resulted when an individual received a direct blow to the head from another player or the ground. On record are a number of sports deaths in which a playing structure, such as a goalpost or backstop, fell on a participant.

The highest incidence of indirect sports death stems from heatstroke. Other less common indirect causes include cardiovascular and respiratory problems or congenital conditions not previously known.

Catastrophic injuries leading to cervical injury and quadriplegia are seen mainly in American football. Although the incidence is low for the number of players involved, it could be lower if proper precautions were taken by coaches, trainers and players.

In general, in most popular organized and recreational sports activities, the legs and arms are most at risk, with the head and face next. Muscle strains, joint sprains, contusions, and abrasions are the most frequent injuries sustained by the active sports participant.

Figure 1-13

Tennis players commonly sustain serious overuse injuries to their elbows, shoulders, or wrists.

PREVENTION OF SPORTS INJURIES

Most high schools do not have access to the services of a qualified professional trainer. Consequently either the coach or a student trainer will handle this responsibility. It is the purpose of this book to provide a trainer or coach acting as a trainer with information about the adequate conditioning of athletes and the proper care of any injuries that fall within his province. The primary responsibility of the trainer is the prevention and care of injuries in athletes under his or her jurisdiction. With reasonable foresight, many accidents can be prevented. Careful and constant supervision of all playing facilities and areas with respect to maintaining safety factors at a constant level by eliminating any potential or existing hazards is mandatory. The institution of a carefully planned, specific program of conditioning the athlete *the year round* will assist greatly in reducing the number of injuries. The athlete who enters competition after insufficient preseason training or who begins preliminary training in a state of physical unfitness is an excellent prospect for injury. It is therefore mandatory that the trainer plan a conditioning program and see that the athletes follow such a program during off-season as well as in-season periods. A player who is unable to participate in competition because of injury is of no use to the team. Attention paid to the role conditioning has in preventing injuries will pay excellent dividends indeed.

Year-round conditioning is essential to sports injury prevention.

Careful attention to the selection and fitting of all gear and equipment will also minimize the probabilities of injury. Procuring the best equipment possible with the funds available should be considered a guiding rule. Additionally, the responsibility of the trainer extends to making certain that all issued equipment is worn and is worn properly. Good equipment, properly and carefully fitted, should be the guaranteed right of every athlete.

In instances in which it may be necessary for an injured athlete to enter competition before complete healing has occurred, protective strapping can protect the injury and prevent further injury. In such instances careful consideration of all factors and medical consultation as necessary should precede any decisions.

Finally, the trainer should at all times be cognizant of the physical and psychological condition of the athletes under his care, both in and out of competition. Counseling in regard to adequate rest with proper nutrition and exercise, a carefully planned program of physical conditioning, and a good emotional climate will greatly enhance the odds in favor of accident prevention and reduction.

IMPLICATIONS

In recent years the number of injuries and fatalities resulting from participation in sports activities has increased steadily. There is a general consensus among top trainers and coaches that the rate of injury can be substantially decreased by proper *preventive* measures. Appropriate and adequate conditioning and the careful fitting of athletic gear and equipment according to individual needs are prerequisites to injury prevention. The continued improvement in all types of playing surfaces, facilities, and athletic equipment is a factor in injury reduction. Public awareness has contributed much toward the growth of the training profession and in establishing a growing awareness that athletics have a built-in risk factor that can be greatly minimized if care is taken to provide proper equipment, good facilities, and properly trained personnel. In addition careful treatment and consideration of the injured athlete will assist greatly in preventing further injuries and in eliminating the dangers of permanent sequelae.

An athlete participates in sports because of personal interest in the sport and loyalty to the school. When athletes are sidelined because of injuries, they are neither deriving personal satisfaction nor benefiting their school. Hence it is the obligation of the trainer to get them back into competition as soon as it is safely possible. The high school coach and the high school trainer share a mutual obligation in this respect. They should work closely with the school officials or the team physician in making their decisions.

According to clinical records, inadequate conditioning is a contributing factor in a high percentage of athletic injuries. The most dangerous period in any sport is the first 3 to 4 weeks of the season. Often the players are somewhat overweight and generally out of good physical condition. In addition, their lack of familiarity with most fundamentals of the game results in their being awkward and therefore accident prone in situations that have injury-provoking potential. Undoubtedly the incidence of injury could be markedly reduced if the various conference and scholastic rules were modified or amended to permit a longer precompetition period devoted to physical conditioning. Such a provision would enable the trainer to prevent many of the injuries that now occur. The extension of the preseason period for the express purpose of conditioning the athlete should in no way be assumed to indicate a desire on our part to extend the competition season. Body contact, scrimmage, and other forms of all-out performance should be limited, by rules and careful regulation, to the last 2 weeks of the preseason period. By that time, assuming that from 3 to 4 weeks of carefully graded conditioning work has been carried on, athletes are ready for more strenuous effort. By developing more strength, endurance, flexibility, and speed, they are able to meet and surmount accident-provoking situations that perhaps a month earlier would have had serious implications. They are able to recuperate increasingly more rapidly and effectively from vigorous bouts of activity. Their reflexes have been sharpened, and their general kinesthetic sense is more sharply defined. The increase of flexibility and range of joint motion, coupled with the strengthening of the supporting muscles, enable them to withstand more severe strain, impact, and twisting than they could have previously.

During both the preseason period and the regular season, strict adherence to the general principles underlying training must be observed.

During the preseason period as well as during the regular season, strict adherence to the general principles underlying training must be observed. For this reason, knowing the important facts about the principles of use and disuse, intensity of use, alternation of rest and exercise, persistence, and drive is of the utmost concern to trainer and coach. Repetitive bouts of work that are progressively more concentrated induce permanent organic changes, which in turn enable the individual to perform more work and to do so more skillfully and efficiently.

Injury prevention is discussed in more depth throughout the text.

REFERENCES

1. Baake, T.: Rugby medicine: no more magic sponge, Phys. Sportsmed. **7**:138, 1979.
2. Bayle, J.J., Johnson, R.J., and Poper, M.H.: Cross-country ski injuries, a prospective study, Iowa Orthop. J. **1**:41, 1981.
3. Berson, L.B., et al.: Epidemiologic study of squash injuries, Am. J. Sports Med. **9**:103, 1981.
4. Bilik, S.E.: The trainer's bible, New York, 1956, T.J. Reed & Co.; originally published 1917.
5. Brown, V.R.: Government's role in data-gathering. In Vinger, P.F., and Hoerner, E.F. (editors): Sports injuries, Boston, 1982, John Wright, PSG, Inc.
6. Calvert, R., Jr.: Athletic injuries and deaths in secondary schools and colleges, 1975-76, Washington, D.C., National Center for Education and Statistics.
7. Clancy, W.G.: Cross-country ski injuries. In Johnson, R.J. (editor): Symposium on skiing injuries, Clinics in sports medicine, vol. 1., no. 2, Philadelphia, July 1982, W.B. Saunders Co.
8. Damron, C.F.: Injury surveillance systems for sports. In Vinger, P.F., and Hoerner, E.F.: (editors): Sports injuries, Boston, 1982, John Wright, PSG, Inc.
9. Dean, C.H., and Hoerner, E.F.: Injury rates in team sports and individual recreation. In Vinger, P.F., and Hoerner, E.F. (editors): Sports injuries, Boston, 1982, John Wright, PSG, Inc.
10. Durant, W.: The life of Greece, New York, 1939, Simon & Schuster, Inc.
11. Durant, W.: Caesar and Christ, New York, 1944, Simon & Schuster, Inc.
12. Estwanik, J.J.: The prevalence of injuries in wrestling, Med. Sci. Sports **11**:92, 1979.
13. Ettlinger, C.F., and Johnson, R.J.: The state of the art in preventing equipment-related alpine ski injuries. In Johnson, R.J. (editor): Symposium on skiing injuries, Clinics in sports medicine, vol. 1, no. 2, Philadelphia, July 1982, W.B. Saunders Co.
14. Feriencik, K.: Trends in ice hockey injuries: 1965-1977, Phys. Sportsmed. **7**:81, 1979.
15. Gillette, J.: When and where women are injured in sports, Phys. Sportsmed. **3**:61, 1975.
16. Hale, C.J.: Protective equipment for baseball, Phys. Sportsmed. **7**:59, 1979.
17. Hanson, P.G.: Heat injury in runners, Phys. Sportsmed. **6**:91, 1979.
18. Harris, H.A.: Greek athletes and athletics, London, 1964, Hutchinson & Co.
19. Johnson, R.J., and Ettlinger, C.F.: Alpine ski injuries: changes through the years. In Johnson, R.J. (editor): Symposium on skiing injuries: Clinics in sports medicine, vol. 1, no. 2, Philadelphia, July 1982, W.B. Saunders Co.
20. Kulund, D.N., Schildwachter, T.L., McCue, F.C. III, and Gieck, J.H.: Lacrosse injuries, Phys. Sportsmed. **7**:82, 1979.
21. Lyons, J.W.: Cross-country ski injuries, Phys. Sportsmed. **8**:1, 1980.
22. Micheli, L.J., and Riseborough, E.M.: The incidence of injuries in rugby football, J. Sports Med. Phys. Fitness **2**:93, 1974.
23. Milner, E.M.: Proposals for improvement. In Vinger, P.F., and Hoerner, E.F. (editors): Sports injuries, Boston, 1982, John Wright, PSG, Inc.
24. Moritz, A. III, and Grana, W.A.: High school basketball injuries, Phys. Sportsmed. **6**:92, 1978.
25. Mueller, F.O., and Blyth, C.S.: Fatalities and catastrophic injuries in football, Phys. Sportsmed. **10**:135, 1982.
26. Mueller, F.O., and Blyth, C.S.: Epidemiology of sports injuries in children. In Betts, J.M., and Eichelberger, M. (editors): Symposium on pediatric and adolescent sports medicine, Clinics in sports medicine, vol. 1, no. 3, Philadelphia, Nov. 1982, W.B. Saunders Co.
26a. Mueller, F.O., and Schindler, R.D.: Fiftieth annual survey of football injury research, 1931-1982, submitted for publication Feb. 1983.

27. O'Malley, R.D.: Trends in skiing injuries: an 18-year analysis, Phys. Sportsmed. **6**:68, 1978.

28. Overview of sports-related injuries in persons 5-14 years of age, Washington D.C., Dec. 1981, U.S. Consumer Product Safety Commission.

29. Pardon, E.T.: Lower extremities are site of most soccer injuries, Phys. Sportsmed. **5**:42, 1977.

30. Powell, J.W.: Pros and cons of data-gathering mechanisms. In Vinger, P.F., and Hoerner, E.F. (editors): Sports injuries, Boston, 1982, John Wright, PSG Publishing Co., Inc.

31. Priest, J.D., Braden, V. and Gerberich, S.G.: Elbow and tennis, Phys. Sportsmed. **8**:81, 1980.

32. Rawlinson, R.: Modern athletic training, North Palm Beach, Fla. 1980, The Athletic Institute.

33. Requa, R.K., and Garrick, J.G.: Injuries in interscholastic track and field, Phys. Sportsmed. **9**:42, 1981.

34. Requa, R.K., and Garrick, J.G.: Injuries in interscholastic wrestling, Phys. Sportsmed. **9**:44, 1981.

35. Rielly, M.F.: The nature and causes of hockey injuries: a five-year study, Ath. Train. **17**:88, 1982.

36. Rose, C.P., and Morse, J.D.: Racquetball injuries, Phys. Sportsmed. **7**:73, 1979.

37. Smodlaka, V.N.: Death on the soccer field and prevention, Phys. Sportsmed. **9**:100, 1981.

38. Smodlaka, V.N.: Rehabilitation of injured soccer players, Phys. Sportsmed. **7**:58, 1979.

39. Snook, G.A.: Injuries in women's gymnastics: five-year study, Am. J. Sportsmed. **7**:242, 1979.

40. Tolpin, H.G., and Bentkover, J.D.: The economic costs of sports injuries. In Vinger, P.F., and Hoerner, E.F. (editors): Sports injuries, Boston, 1982, John Wright, PSG, Inc.

41. Torg, J.S.: Athletic injuries to the head, neck, and face, Philadelphia, 1982, Lea & Febiger.

42. Torg, J.S., et al.: The national football head and neck injury registry, J.A.M.A. **241**:1477, 1977.

43. Underwood, J.: Football's unfolding tragedy, Reader's Digest **115**:92, 1979.

44. Vinger, P.F.: Too great a risk spurred hockey mask development, Phys. Sportsmed. **5**:70, 1977.

45. Vogt, M.: Die Olympische Spiele in Altertum, München Med. Wochenshr. **30**:1199, 1936.

ADDITIONAL SOURCES

Buckley, W.E., and Powell, J.: NAIRS: an epidemiological overview of the severity of injury in college football 1975-1980 seasons, Ath. Train. **17**:279, 1982.

Dagian, R.F., Dillman, C.J., and Milner, E.K.: Relationship between exposure time and injury in football, Am. J. Sports Med. **8**:257, 1980.

Garrick, J.G.: Epidemiologic perspective. In Torg, J.S. (editor): Symposium on ankle and foot problems in the athlete, Clinics in sports medicine, vol. 1, no. 1, Philadelphia, Mar. 1982, W.B. Saunders Co.

Garrick, J.G., and Requa, R.: Medical care and injury surveillance in the high school setting, Phys. Sportsmed. **9**:115, 1981.

Johnson, R.J. (editor): Symposium on skiing injuries, Clinics in sports medicine, vol. 1, no. 2, Philadelphia, July 1982, W.B. Saunders Co.

Marchant, L., Knopp, D., and Warshawski, J.: An analysis of head injuries in hockey and lacrosse, Fitness and Amateur Sports Branch, Department of the Secretary of State, Ottawa, Canada.

Marchant, L, Roy, L., and Washawski, J.: Sport safety research, Fitness and Amateur Sports Branch, Department of the Secretary of State, Ottawa, Canada.

Requa, R.K., and Garrick, J.G.: Injuries in interscholastic track and field, Phys. Sportsmed. **9**:42, 1981.

Shively, R.A., Grana, W.A., and Ellis, D.: High school sports injuries, Phys. Sportsmed. **9**:46, 1981.

1975 Sports participation survey, Elgin, Ill., 1975, The National Federation of State High School Associations.

Chapter 2

THE ATHLETIC TRAINER

When you finish this chapter, you should be able to

Define sports medicine and athletic training

Specify the qualifications and functions of a certified athletic trainer and where he or she carries out these functions

List a successful athletic trainer's personal qualities

Discuss the athletic trainer's relationship with other professionals

Designate the most important factors of legal liability in sports

Identify major professional organizations and publications related to athletic training

The athletic trainer is considered a paramedical specialist in sports medicine.

Athletic training and the role of the athletic trainer are unique to North America, originally emerging from the needs of American football. The athletic trainer is skilled in conditioning, injury prevention, emergency aid management, rehabilitation, education, and counseling. Today the athletic trainer is considered a paramedical specialist in sports medicine.

SPORTS MEDICINE

The term *sports medicine,* according to the American College of Sports Medicine, refers to a multidisciplinary, professional, scientific body dedicated to the generation and dissemination of knowledge concerning the motivation, responses, adaptations and health of persons engaged in exercise. Some individuals have argued that the term *medicine* refers to the art of preventing, caring for, and assisting in the care of disease and the care of the injured, and when related to sports should not encompass exercise training. In the future this separation may occur; however, to date sports medicine implies both clinical and training aspects of exercise.[5]

Specifically, the American College of Sports Medicine is concerned with[6]:

1. Basic physiology, and biochemical, biomechanical, and behavioral mechanisms associated with exercise
2. Improvement and maintenance of functional capabilities for daily living
3. Prevention and rehabilitation of chronic and degenerative diseases
4. Evaluation and conditioning of athletes
5. Prevention and treatment of injuries related to sport and exercise

In other words,

> sports medicine is the study of the physiological, biomechanical, psychosocial, and pathological phenomena associated with exercise and athletics and the clinical application of the knowledge gained from this study to the improvement and maintenance of functional capacities for physical labor, exercise, and athletics and to the prevention and treatment of disease and injuries related to exercise and athletics.[6]

ATHLETIC TRAINING

The term *athletic training* may be confusing; athletic training and the athletic trainer are traditional titles that began during the early development of the field (see Chapter 1). Training implies the act of coaching or teaching. In Europe the term *trainer* is synonymous with *coach*, whereas in the United States a trainer may also be someone who trains dogs and horses or functions in other teaching areas. A better title to describe the role of athletic trainer might ultimately be *sports therapist* or *sports medicine practitioner.*

QUALIFICATIONS OF THE CERTIFIED ATHLETIC TRAINER

The professional athletic trainer is expected to be a college graduate with extensive background in biological and health sciences as well as specifically in athletic training. A person planning to work as an athletic trainer at the high school level should also consider obtaining a teaching certificate. For full-time athletic training employment, an additional background as a licensed or registered physical therapist may be beneficial.

NATA Certification

Currently there are two ways to become certified in the National Athletic Trainers Association (NATA)*: (1) having graduated from an NATA-approved curriculum, or (2) through internship and passing the national examination. A person can become certified after successfully completing an

---

*All requirements are subject to change. Students may contact the National Athletic Trainers Association Board of Certification, 1001 E. Fourth St., P.O. Drawer 1865, Greenville, N.C. 27835-1865.

TABLE 2-1

Relative importance of each domain as assigned by 300 athletic trainers

	Percent of Items*
Prevention	18
Recognition and evaluation	24
Management/treatment and disposition	22
Rehabilitation	20
Organization and administration	9
Education and counseling	7
TOTAL	100

*Rounded.

NATA-approved athletic training education program from a college or university sponsoring an NATA-approved graduate or undergraduate program (see Appendix II-C).

Certification Through Internship

Certification by NATA may be attained under this category for schools that do not offer an approved curriculum; however, the candidate for certification must have spent a minimum of 1800 clock hours over a minimum of 2 years and not more than 5 years under the direction of an NATA-certified athletic trainer. A record of internship hours worked by the candidate must be submitted to the NATA Board of Certification annually (January 1 to December 31). Current requirements for certification can be obtained from the NATA Board of Certification. Another trend, which is highly recommended, is for athletic trainers to also obtain an emergency medical technician (EMT) certificate.

THE TRAINER'S ROLE AND FUNCTION

Athletic trainers are highly educated and well trained professionals. They are concerned with injury prevention, recognition, and evaluation, and the management, treatment, disposition, rehabilitation, organization and administration, education, and counseling of the injured.

In 1982, to determine the most appropriate content for the NATA certification examination, a role delineation study was conducted by NATA

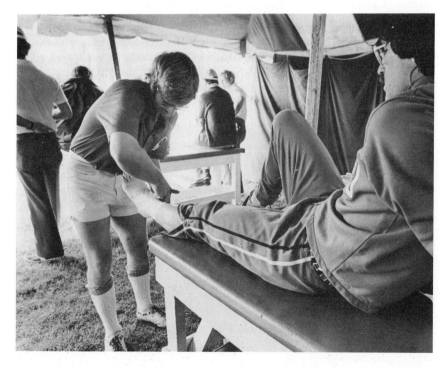

Figure 2-1

Athletic training can be a highly exciting and rewarding profession.

Courtesy Cramer Products, Inc., Gardner, Kan.

The prevention of injury is a major goal of athletic training.

and a professional examination service.[3] In this study 300 trainers, representing each geographic area of the United States, were asked to rate each major athletic training domain. Table 2-1 indicates, by percentage the average level of importance the participants assigned to each role.

Injury Prevention

The prevention of injury is a major goal of athletic training.[8] Trainers must know how to create and carry out postseason, off-season, preseason, and in-season conditioning programs to assist the athlete in gaining and maintaining maximum physical conditioning. They must be skilled in constructing and applying all types of protective devices that support body parts, including adhesive taping, orthotic devices, and braces. Trainers determine whether athletic equipment is unsafe and ensure its proper maintenance. The trainer monitors safe or unsafe environmental conditions, such as temperature and humidity. The trainer must also identify and protect preexisting physical conditions that might predispose the athlete to injury.

Injury Recognition and Evaluation

A primary aspect of athletic training is the recognition and evaluation of injuries.[8] A trainer must have a thorough knowledge of human anatomy, physiology, kinesiology, and biomechanics to properly assess the seriousness of an injury. Knowledge and application of history-taking and injury inspection are essential. Through injury site palpation and estimation of range of motion, muscle strength, and joint flexibility and through neurological, sensory, and motor tests the trainer determines the extent of injury.

Injury Management/Treatment and Disposition

The athletic trainer is skilled in administering proper emergency care and making prompt, appropriate, medical referral.[8] When an injury occurs, the trainer can skillfully apply emergency protective devices, such as spine boards, cervical collars, bandages, and dressings, and can oversee transporting the injured athlete without further tissue damage. With direction from the physician the trainer carries out a treatment regimen using a variety of therapeutic methods, supportive procedures, or other techniques to aid recovery (Fig. 2-2).

Injury Rehabilitation

Once injured, the athlete will be primarily concerned with full restoration.[8] The athletic trainer should be skilled in the use of a wide variety of means to encourage this restoration, including exercise and other therapeutic methods. The trainer must be able to establish goals and a criteria for recovery and also be able to assess when, by objective measurement, the goals have been achieved.

Program Organization and Administration

To carry out an effective athletic training program there must be detailed organization and administration of all aspects of record keeping and facility upkeep.[8] Although the athletic training budget is often one of the largest in the entire athletic program, it is limited because of the demands placed on

Figure 2-2

The athletic trainer carries out the direction of the physician in treating the athlete.

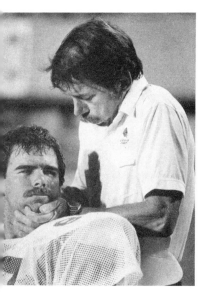

it; therefore it must be carefully managed. The purchase of supplies and equipment therefore becomes a constant concern to the athletic trainer. The trainer initiates and carries out a health care service system for each injured athlete. A final but not least important factor is that policies and procedures must be established and carried out for daily operation of the training program and support personnel.

Education and Counseling

Athletic trainers are also educators and counselors.[8] They instruct athletes about all aspects of their condition, including the nature of the condition and procedures to be followed for fastest recovery. They provide information on athletic training topics to coaches, faculty, and the community. They provide ongoing instruction to assistant trainers and paraprofessionals working in the training program. The trainer may counsel athletes on emotional problems, including sexuality, drug abuse, and personal or social problems. For serious psychosocial difficulties the trainer makes proper professional referrals.

THE TRAINER'S PERSONAL QUALITIES

A trainer's personal qualities, not the facilities and equipment, determine success. Personal qualities may be thought of as the many characteristics that identify individuals in regard to actions and reactions as members of society. Personality is a complex of the many characteristics that together give an image of the individual to those with whom he or she associates. The personal qualities of trainers are most important since they in turn work with many complicated and diverse personalities. Although no attempt has been made to establish a rank order, the qualities discussed in the following paragraphs are essential if one desires to be a good trainer.

Athletic trainer's personal qualities:
Health
Fairness
Stability
Appearance
Leadership
Compassion/empathy
Intelligence
Humor
Competence/responsibility

Health

Good mental and physical health is an absolute necessity for the trainer. The work requires abundant energy, vitality, and physical and emotional stability. Long, arduous hours of strenuous work will sap the reserve strength of a trainer who is not in the best of health. The trainer must also set an example for athletes by personally adhering to the rules of good health.

Sense of Fairness

The ethics of training demand that fairness and justice be maintained at all times. Trainers cannot allow themselves to become discriminatory in their treatment of athletes. All should be treated on an equal basis regardless of race, color, gender, creed, or athletic ability.

Maturity and Emotional Stability

The ability to get along with others and to act properly under stress and pressure is a measure of emotional stability and maturity. A trainer is subjected to much stress and emotional pressure. During the competition, trainers work in an atmosphere of constant tenseness. By expressing self-control at all times, the trainers establish a calming effect on those about them.

Trainer "Burnout"

The expression "burnout" is commonly used to describe the feelings of exhaustion and disinterest toward one's work. Clinically, it is most often associated with the helping professions; however, it is seen in athletes and other types of individuals engaged in physically or emotionally demanding endeavors. Most persons who have been associated with athletics have known athletes, coaches, or athletic trainers who just "drop out." They become dissatisfied and disinterested in what they have dedicated a major part of their lives to. Signs of burnout include excessive anger, blaming others, guilt, being tired and exhausted all day, sleep problems, high absenteeism, family problems, and self-preoccupation. Drugs or alcohol may be consumed in an attempt to cope.

As a member of a helping profession, the athletic trainer is subject to burnout. The very nature of athletic training is one of caring about and serving the athlete. When the emotional demands of work overcome the professional's resources to cope, burnout may occur. Too many athletes to care for, the expectations of coaches to return an injured athlete to action, difficulties in caring for the chronic conditions, and personality conflicts involving athletes, coaches, physicians, or administrators can leave the athletic trainer physically and emotionally drained at the end of the day. Sources of emotional drain include little reward for one's efforts, role conflicts, lack of autonomy, or a feeling of powerlessness to deal with the problems at hand.[9] Commonly, the professional trainer is in a constant state of high emotional arousal and anxiety during the working day. If burnout is not addressed early, serious mental and family problems can ensue.

> As a member of a helping profession, the athletic trainer is subject to burnout.

Good Appearance

"Your appearance as you pass by is your only message to most of the world." This maxim, old though it may be, has never lost its timeliness. Neatness and cleanliness of person and dress should be the trademark of the trainer.

Leadership

Trainers must be dynamic individuals who can lead and motivate those with whom they work, as well as those whom they serve. They must work cooperatively with many people, being able to express their opinions and views without being dogmatic. They must be able to accept, understand, and weigh the views and opinions of others and to transform the abilities of their co-workers into an organized, harmonious whole. Above all, they must be decisive. An equivocal attitude has no place in the training room or on the field where quick, knowledgeable decisions based on experience and education must be made. Procrastination could prove dangerous. The trainer who is both liked and respected has a far greater opportunity to develop those under his or her charge than the individual who is obeyed solely for strict disciplinary methods.

> Trainers who are liked and respected have a greater opportunity to develop their charges than individuals who are obeyed only for strict disciplinary methods.

Compassion and Empathy

Competence must be coupled with compassion and empathy—the ability to feel a sympathetic awareness for the suffering or distress of others with a desire to help alleviate such suffering. Empathy combined with compassion for those under his or her care are qualities that the competent trainer must possess.

Intellectual Capacity

In a broad sense intellectual capacity may be defined as the ability to deal with the many problems of life, including those encountered in one's work. It denotes one's ability to adapt to constant change, to keep up with the times. Consequently, the trainer should possess a lively intellectual curiosity both within and outside of the field, which provides stimulation to do considerable reading in professional and allied journals and books and to experiment and research in the athletic training area. More research concerning sports injuries is greatly needed, and the trainer is in an ideal position to initiate and carry through intensive and long-range programs.

Sense of Humor

Many athletes rate having a sense of humor as the most important attribute of the trainer. The ability to relax others by means of humor and wit is indeed an important asset and can release much of the tension that builds up, particularly before competition.

Competence and Responsibility

When one speaks of competence, a number of desirable characteristics are implied. A trainer inspires confidence through a quiet strength—knowing what to do, when to do it, how to do it, and then doing it properly and effectively. Self-confidence is a quality that trainers must exhibit if they expect others to have confidence in them. Versatility in a profession is yet another index of competence.

THE NATA CODE OF ETHICS

The National Athletic Trainers Association has established a codified standard of behavior. Since its inception in 1957, this code of ethics has been revised almost yearly. Its primary goal is to establish the highest possible standard of conduct for athletic training at all athletic program levels. The basic premise of this code is that the athletic trainer will act at all times with honesty, integrity, and loyalty. Members of NATA who behave in a manner that is unethical or unbecoming to the profession can be censured or placed on probation or can lose their membership.[8] (See Appendix II-A.)

EMPLOYMENT OPPORTUNITIES

Athletic trainers work in a number of different settings—in high schools, school districts, colleges or universities, for professional teams, or in sports medicine clinics.

Athletic trainers work in a number of different settings:
High schools
School districts
Colleges/universities
Professional teams
Sports medicine clinics

High Schools

It would be ideal to have certified athletic trainers serve every high school in the United States. Many of the physical problems that occur later from improperly managed sports injuries could be avoided initially if proper care from an athletic trainer had been provided. Many times a coach does all of his or her own athletic training, although in some cases, a coach is assigned additional athletic training responsibilities and is assisted by a student trainer. If a high school hires an athletic trainer, it is commonly in a faculty-trainer capacity. This individual is usually employed as a teacher of one of the school's classroom disciplines and performs training duties on a part-time or extracurricular basis. In this instance, compensation is on the same basis of released time from teaching and/or a stipend.

Another means for obtaining high school or community college athletic training coverage is when a nearby college or university provides a certified graduate student. The graduate student receives a graduate assistantship with a stipend paid by the high school or community college. In this situation both the graduate student and the school benefit.

School Districts

Some school districts have found it effective to employ a centrally placed certified athletic trainer. In this case the trainer, who may be full- or part-time, is a nonteacher who serves a number of schools. The advantage is savings; the disadvantage is that one individual cannot provide the level of service usually required by a typical school.

Colleges and Universities

At the college or university level the athletic training position varies considerably from institution to institution. With smaller institutions, the athletic trainer may be a half-time teacher in physical education and half-time trainer (Fig. 2-3). In some cases, if the trainer is a physical therapist, rather than teach, he or she may spend part of the time in the school health center and part of the time in athletic training. Increasingly at the college level, athletic training services are being offered to members of the general student body who participate in intramural and club sports. In most colleges and universities the athletic trainer is full-time, does not teach, works in the department of athletics, and is paid by the state or from student union or alumni funds.

Professional Teams

The athletic trainer for professional sports teams usually performs specific team training duties for 6 months out of the year; the other 6 months is spent in off-season conditioning and individual rehabilitation. The trainer working with a professional team is involved with only one sport and is paid according to contract, much like a player. Playoffs and championships could add substantially to the yearly income.

Sports Medicine Clinics

Because of the vast number of organized and recreational sports enthusiasts, sports medicine clinics are increasing in number throughout the country.[4] A market survey indicated that from 1961 to 1981, the number of sports participants doubled in the United States.[2] Services provided by these clinics vary considerably. Some specialize in therapy and rehabilitation; others include exercise physiology testing and biomechanics testing and analysis. Some of these programs are managed by a physician, others by a registered

Figure 2-3

Both men and women athletic trainers have work opportunities at the college or university level.

or licensed physical therapist. Commonly therapy is performed by physical therapists or physical therapy aides. In some cases, depending on state and local regulations, certified athletic trainers are employed in sports medicine clinics. Perhaps more trainers will be hired in these clinics as they acquire state licensure.

STATE LICENSURE*

A concerted effort is taking place in the United States for legislating state licensure for athletic trainers.[1] Such licensure dictates qualifications and practice requirements. It characteristically establishes the trainer's relationship with the physician, the function of athletic training, and the use of therapeutic methods. (See Appendix II-B for a list of states issuing licenses.)

PROFESSIONAL RELATIONSHIPS

It is important that the athletic trainer enjoy good relationships with many people. Rapport should be developed not only with training assistants and athletes but also with the athletic staff and medical and dental personnel. Getting to know a number of people on and off campus and engendering an understanding of athletic training will often aid in solving problems. *Establishing good public relations is a vital responsibility for all trainers.*

Athletic Staff

The athletic trainer works closely with the athletic staff. Because the trainer is vitally concerned with the safety of equipment, a cooperative relationship must be maintained with the equipment manager, who can assist by adjusting personal equipment to the needs of an injured athlete or purchasing specialized protective gear.

Since trainers work closely with coaches, they must develop an awareness and an insight into each other's problems so that they can function as effectively as possible. The trainer must develop tolerance and patience and must earn the respect of the coaches so that his or her judgment in all training matters is fully accepted. In turn the trainer must avoid questioning the abilities of the coaches in their particular fields and must restrict opinions to athletic training matters. To avoid frustration and hard feelings, the coach coaches and the trainer trains. In terms of the health and well-being of the athlete, the physician and the athletic trainer have the "last word."

To avoid frustration and hard feelings, the coach coaches and the trainer trains.

Medical Personnel

The trainer has administrative and working relationships with the school nurse, members of the school health services program, and the team physician. All these have responsibilities, direct and indirect, connected with the athletic program, and it is well for the trainer to be familiar with the place of each in the program and the relationships of each to the trainer. These relationships and responsibilities must be clearly defined.

Athletic trainer's support medical personnel:
  Nurse
  School health services
  Team physician
  Team dentist
  Team podiatrist

*NATA Licensure Committee, P.O. Drawer 1865, Greenville, N.C. 27835-1865.

The Nurse

As a rule, the nurse is not responsible for the recognition of sports injuries. Training and background, however, render the nurse quite capable in the recognition of skin disease, infections, and minor irritations. The nurse works under the direction of the physician and in liaison with the athletic trainer and the school health services.

School Health Services

Colleges and universities maintain school health services that range from a department operating with one or two nurses and a physician available on a part-time basis to an elaborate setup comprised of a full complement of nursing services with a staff of full-time medical specialists and a complete laboratory and hospital facilities. At the high school level health services are usually organized so that one or two nurses conduct the program under the direction of the school physician, who may serve a number of schools in a given area or district. This poses a problem, since it is often difficult to have qualified medical help at hand when it is needed. Local policy will determine the procedure of referral for medical care. If such policies are lacking, the trainer should see to it that an effective method is established for handling all athletes requiring medical care or opinion. The ultimate source of health care is the physician. The effectiveness of athletic health care service can be evaluated only to the extent to which it meets the following criteria:

1. Availability at every scheduled practice or contest of a person qualified and delegated to render emergency care to an injured or ill participant
2. Planned access to a physician by phone or nearby presence for prompt medical evaluation of the health care problems that warrant this attention
3. Planned access to a medical facility—including plans for communication and transportation

The Team Physician

Team physicians must have *absolute authority* in determining the health status of an athlete who wishes to participate in the athletic program.

Team physicians must have absolute authority in determining the health status of an athlete who wishes to participate in the athletic program. They are the final authority in the determination of whether or not athletes should be permitted to take part in a given sports activity and when, following injury, they should be allowed to reenter competition. The physician's judgment must be based not only on medical knowledge but also on knowledge of the psychophysiological demands of a particular sport.

Although team physicians are often orthopedic surgeons, they should serve the athlete in every respect. They must understand the entire health pattern as well as the psychological makeup of the athlete and be prepared to render medical attention to all conditions or illnesses.

When a physician is asked to serve as team physician, arrangements must be made with the employing educational institution as to specific required responsibilities. Policies must be established regarding emergency care, legal liability, facilities, personnel relationships, and duties. The physician must work cooperatively with the trainer and the coach in planning a training program for the prevention of sports injuries and for reconditioning following injury. If it is not possible for the team physician to attend all practice sessions and competitive events or games, it is sometimes possible to establish a plan of rotation involving a number of physicians. In this plan any one physician need be present at only one or two activities a year. The rotation plan has proved quite practical in situations in which the school district is unable to afford a full-time physician or has so limited a budget that it must ask for volunteer medical coverage. In some instances the attending physician is paid a per-game stipend (see Chapter 3).

The Team Dentist

The role of team dentists is somewhat analogous to that of team physicians. They serve as dental consultant for the team and should be available for first aid and emergency care. Good communication between the dentist and the trainer should ensure a good dental program (see Chapter 3).

The Team Podiatrist

Podiatry, the specialized field dealing with the study and care of the foot, has become an integral part of sports health care. Many podiatrists are trained in surgical procedures, foot biomechanics, and the fitting and construction of orthotic devices for the shoe. Like the team dentist, a podiatrist should be available on a consultancy basis for major problems.

LEGAL IMPLICATIONS IN SCHOOL SPORTS

In recent years negligence suits against teachers, coaches, trainers, school officials, and physicians because of sports injuries have increased both in frequency and in the amount of damages awarded. An increasing awareness of the many risk factors present in physical activities has had an effect on the coach and trainer in particular. A great deal more care is now taken in following coaching and training procedures that conform to the legal guidelines governing liability. Certification through the National Athletic Trainers Association and licensing by the state can go a long way toward establishing the legal parameters of the training profession and would undoubtedly reduce the vulnerability of the trainer to suits.

Athletic Training: An Auxiliary Function of Medicine

Inasmuch as athletic training is an auxiliary function of medicine in many respects, many pertinent legal factors are involved. The legal liability of the athletic trainer is not always well defined or thoroughly understood. Frequently trainers or trainer-coaches must perform training duties without benefit of medical supervision. In such situations they are well advised to confine their duties to routine bandaging and first aid procedures that can be performed in the absence of a physician. When the nature of athletic training is such that it involves the use of techniques that require either special training, medical direction, or licensing, there are some legal implications that come into play, and the athletic trainer should be aware of these before proceeding.

The legal liability of the athletic trainer is not always well defined or thoroughly understood.

Medical Diagnoses

Medical diagnoses may be made only by a licensed physician, and any final decisions regarding such diagnoses are the physician's alone. There is a fine line indeed between the recognition of an injury and its diagnosis. Debating this difference serves no useful purpose other than to further confound the distinction. In situations in which time is of the essence, as is often the case in sports injuries, the ability to evaluate quickly, accurately, and decisively is vitally important. In such situations the trainer or coach must remain within the limits of his or her ability and training and must act in full accord with professional ethics. The dispensing of pharmaceuticals by a trainer, even with the express permission of a medical doctor, is illegal in most states. Distribution of placebos, vitamins, and other similar types of ingesta may be considered questionable; the trainer should be certain that the administration of any pharmaceuticals or ingesta is well within his or her legal purview. Complete understanding of what constitutes the framework within which athletic trainers can safely operate is of paramount importance if they are to avoid pitfalls that may make them legally liable.

Liability

liability
The legal responsibility to perform an act in a reasonable, prudent manner

Liability is defined in several ways, all of which state in one way or another that it is the legal responsibility of persons in a certain situation to do a particular thing in a reasonable and prudent manner; failure to perform such action in a prudent and reasonable manner makes them legally liable for the results of said action. In most cases in which the charge has been negligence the key has been to compare the actions of a hypothetical, reasonably prudent, athletic trainer to the actions of the defendant. This is done to ascertain whether the course of action followed by the defendant was in conformity with the judgment exercised by such a reasonably prudent person. The key phase has been "reasonable care." Trainers who are licensed in athletic training or any of the other medical services such as physical therapy are in a stronger position, since not only are they trained in the use of the various techniques, but they also have a more legitimate claim to use these aids under the law than do trainers who are not licensed or who lack certification.

Variations in some phases of the interpretation of liability exist among the various states and countries. In most states in the United States the rule concept that school districts are not liable for the negligence of their agents while at the same time they act in a governmental capacity in the absence of a statute expressly imposing such liability seems to be well established. This concept has been increasingly challenged in recent years but still holds in most states. The doctrine of immunity in some states has been extended to the university but not to private schools and colleges.

Assumption of Risk

The courts generally acknowledge that hazards are present in sports through the concept of "assumption of risk." In other words, the individual either by expressed or implied agreement assumes the danger and hence relieves the other individual of legal responsibility to protect him; by so doing he agrees to take his own chances. This concept, however, is subject to many and varied interpretations in the courts. This is particularly true when a minor is involved, since he or she is not considered able to render a mature judgment about the risks inherent in the situation. Although athletes participating in a sports program are considered to assume a normal risk, this in no way exempts those in charge from exercising reasonable care and prudence in the conduct of such activities or from foreseeing and taking precautionary measures against accident-provoking circumstances.

The trainer may be held accountable for injuries or accidents resulting from the following.

Torts

Torts are legal wrongs that *legal* scholars have considerable difficulty in defining with exactitude. For our purposes a *tort* is defined as civil wrongs, other than breach of contract, for which a court will provide a remedy in the form of damages. Such wrongs may emanate from an act of "omission," wherein the individual fails to carry out a legal duty, or from an act of "commission," wherein he or she commits an act that is not legally his or hers to perform. In either instance, if injury results, the person can be held liable. In the first case trainers may fail to carry out treatment procedures after they have been instructed to do so by a physician. In the second trainers may attempt to perform minor surgery which is not within their legal province and from which serious medical complications later develop.

Medical diagnoses may be made only by a licensed physician.

Negligence

The tort concept of negligence is held by the courts when it is shown that an individual (1) does something that a reasonably prudent person would not do or (2) fails to do something that a reasonably prudent person would do under circumstances similar to those shown by the evidence. Negligence is the failure to use ordinary or reasonable care—care that persons of ordinary prudence would exercise in order to avoid injury to themselves or to others under similar circumstances. The standard as set up takes cognizance of the fact that the individual is neither the exceptionally skillful individual nor is he or she the extraordinarily cautious one, but rather a person of *reasonable* and *ordinary* prudence. Put another way, it is expected that the individual will bring a commonsense approach to the situation at hand and will exercise due care in the handling of it. A case in point might be a training situation in which the trainer, through improper or careless handling of a therapeutic agent, seriously burns an athlete. Another illustration, occurring all too often in sports, is one in which a trainer or coach moves a possibly seriously injured athlete from the field of play to permit activity to continue and does so either in an improper manner or before consulting those qualified to know the proper course of action. Should a serious or disabling injury result, the trainer or coach has made himself liable to suit.

Knowingly using dangerous or faulty equipment is another type of negligence for which the trainer can be held accountable should an accident result from such use. No equipment is 100% infallible in terms of safety. Never should a trainer or coach state or in any way indicate that a particular piece of equipment is absolutely safe or foolproof or incapable of producing injury, either directly or as an accessory to the fact. If injury in any way results from such equipment and a statement has been made indicating the absolute safety of the equipment, an implied liability could result.

It is expected that a person possessing more training in a given field or area will possess a correspondingly higher level of competence than, for example, will a student. An individual will therefore be judged in terms of his or her performance in any situation in which legal liability may be assessed. It must be recognized that liability, per se, in all of its various aspects, is not assessed at a universal level nationally but varies in interpretation from state to state and from area to area. It is therefore well to know and acquire the level of competence expected in your particular area.

Summary of Legal Implications

To safeguard both athlete and trainer the following suggestions are given:

1. Keep accurate records of all accidents and subsequent action(s).

2. Make it a point to become familiar with the health status and medical history of the athletes under your care so you will be aware of those particular problems an athlete may have that could present a need for additional care or caution on your part.

3. Establish and maintain qualified and adequate supervision of the training room, its environs, facilities, and equipment at all times.

4. Exercise extreme caution in the distribution of nonprescription medications and do not dispense prescription drugs.

5. Use only those therapeutic methods that you are qualified to and that the law states you can use.

6. Do not use or permit the presence of faulty or hazardous equipment.

7. Work cooperatively with the coach and the team physician in the selection and use of sports protective equipment and insist that the best be obtained and properly fitted.

8. Do not permit injured players to participate unless cleared by the team physician. Players suffering a head injury should not be permitted to reenter the game. In some states a player who has suffered a concussion may not continue in the sport for the balance of the season.

9. Do not under any circumstances give a local anesthetic to enable an injured player to continue participation. It is dangerous as well as unethical.

10. Develop an understanding with the coaches that an injured athlete will not be allowed to reenter competition until, in the opinion of the team physician or the trainer, he or she is mentally and physically able. Do not permit yourself to be pressured to clear an athlete until he or she is fully cleared by the physician.

11. Follow the expressed orders of the team physician at all times.

12. Use common sense.

PROFESSIONAL ORGANIZATIONS

Professional organizations have a number of purposes: (1) to upgrade the profession by devising and maintaining a set of professional standards and establishing a code of ethics with which to achieve this goal; (2) to bring together professionally competent individuals to exchange ideas and to stimulate research and critical thinking; and (3) to give individuals an opportunity to work as a group with a singleness of purpose, thereby making it possible for them to achieve objectives that, separately, they could not accomplish.

Prior to the formation of the National Athletic Trainers Association in 1950, trainers occupied a somewhat insecure place in the athletic program. Since that time, as a result of the raising of professional standards and the establishment of a code of ethics, there has indeed been considerable professional advancement. The Association accepts as members only those who are properly qualified and who are prepared to subscribe to a code of ethics and to uphold the standards of the Association. It publishes a quarterly journal, *Athletic Training: the Journal of the National Athletic Trainers Association,* and holds an annual convention at which the members have an opportunity to keep abreast of new developments and to exchange ideas through clinical programs. The organization is constantly working to improve both the quality and the status of athletic training.

Another organization that has done much to advance athletic training techniques and knowledge is the American College of Sports Medicine, organized in 1954. This organization is interested in all aspects of sports. Its membership is composed of medical doctors, doctors of philosophy, physical educators, trainers, coaches, scientists, and others interested in or associated with sports. It seeks, through study and research, to improve sports not only from the standpoint of performance but also from the standpoint of injury prevention, conditioning, and reconditioning. It holds national and regional conferences and meetings devoted to exploring the many aspects of sports medicine and publishes a quarterly magazine, *Medicine and Science in Sports.* This journal includes articles in French, Italian, German, and English and provides complete translations in English of all articles. It reports the recent developments in the field of sports medicine on a world-wide basis. Other journals to be considered are the *International Journal of Sports Medicine,* which is published in English by Thieme-Stratton, Inc., New York, and *The Journal of Sports Medicine and Physical Fitness* by Edizioni Minerva Medica S.P.A. The Orthopaedic and Sports Physical Therapy Sections of The American Physical Therapy Association publishes an excellent quarterly, *The Journal of Orthopaedic and Sports Physical Therapy.*

Other journals of considerable interest and value to the individual in athletic training are *The American Journal of Sports Medicine,* published by The Williams & Wilkins Company, which is the official publication of the American Orthopaedic Society for Sports Medicine, and *The Physician and Sportsmedicine,* published by McGraw-Hill, Inc.

The trainer should belong to at least one professional organization. An organization cannot function successfully through the support of only a few dedicated people. If professional status and advancement, better working conditions, and higher compensation are to be obtained, trainers must support their professional organizations not only as dues-paying members but also as active participants, seeking to reach a higher level of professional recognition.

The trainer should belong to at least one professional organization.

REFERENCES

1. Behnke, R.: NATA licensure annual update, Ath. Train. **17**:184, 1982.
2. Darden, E.: The athlete's guide to sports medicine, Chicago, 1981, Contemporary Books, Inc.
3. Grace, P., and Ledderman, L.: Role declineation study for the certification examination for entry-level athletic trainers, Ath. Train. **17**:264, 1982.
4. Hain, J.A.: Specialized health clinics deal with sports injuries, L.A. Times, San Diego edition, Part V, p. 1, March 24, 1983.
5. Kegerreis, S.: Sports medicine: a functional definition, J. Phys. Educ. Rec. Dance, **52**:22, 1981.
6. Lamb, D.R.: "Sports medicine"— what is it? ACSM President's report, Sports Medicine Bulletin **16**:2, 1981.
7. National Athletic Trainers Association: Code of ethics, Ath. Train. **19**:66, Spring 1984.
8. National Athletic Trainers Association: 1982 Role delineation study of the trainer, NATA Board of Certification, Greenville, N.C., 1982, The Association.
9. Vergamini, G.: Professional burnout: implications for the athletic trainer, Ath. Train. **16**:196, Fall 1981.

ADDITIONAL SOURCES

Appenzeller, H.: Athletics and the law, Charlottesville, VA, 1975, The Michie Co.

Appenzeller, H.: The right to participate, Charlottesville, VA, 1983, The Michie Co.

Appenzeller, H. and Appenzeller, T.: Sports and the courts, Charlottesville, VA, 1980, The Michie Co.

Ball, R.: The A.T.C. and the law, NATA Annual Meeting, Clinical Symposium, June 1983, Greenville, N.C., National Athletic Trainers Association. (Cassette.)

Behnke, B., et al.: Licensure mechanisms: success and failures, NATA Annual Meeting, Clinical Symposium, June 1983, Greenville, N.C., National Athletic Trainers Association. (Cassette.)

Bell, G.W. (editor): Professional preparation in athletic training, NATA, Champaign, Ill., 1982, Human Kinetics Publishing.

Delforge, G.: Athletic training: a profession? NATA Annual Meeting, Clinical Symposium, June 1983, Greenville, N.C., National Athletic Trainers Association. (Cassette.)

George, J.E.: Law and emergency care, St. Louis, 1980, The C.V. Mosby Co.

Grace, P.: NATA certification guidelines and procedures, NATA Annual Meeting, Clinical Symposium, June 1983, Greenville, N.C., National Athletic Trainers Association. (Cassette.)

Patrick, C.: Ethics and the athletic trainer, NATA Annual Meeting, Clinical Symposium, June 1983, Greenville, N.C., National Athletic Trainers Association. (Cassette.)

Weistart, J.C., and Lowell, C.H.: The law of sports, Indianapolis, 1979, The Bobbs-Merrill Co., Inc.

THE ATHLETIC TRAINING PROGRAM

When you finish this chapter, you should be able to

Describe the components of a properly maintained training room and training program

Identify appropriate personnel policies and program operations

Outfit a training program with supplies and equipment

Athletic training and sports medicine form a health care unit that requires careful organization and administration. Besides being a practitioner, the athletic trainer is an administrator who performs both managerial and supervisory duties.[2] Chapter 3 considers major policies and procedures necessary to run an athletic training program effectively.

HYGIENE AND SANITATION

Good hygiene and sanitation are essential in an athletic training program.

The practice of good hygiene and sanitation is of the utmost importance in an athletic training program. It has been shown that the greatest number of indirectly caused deaths related to sports can be ascribed to infection. The prevention of infectious conditions is a direct responsibility of the trainer, whose duty it is to see that all athletes are surrounded by as hygienic an environment as is possible and that each individual is practicing sound health habits.

Training Room

The use of the training room as a place only for the prevention and care of sports injuries must be strictly observed. Too often the training facility becomes a meeting or club room for the coaches and athletes. Unless definite rules are established and practiced, room cleanliness and sanitation become an impossible chore. Unsanitary practices or conditions must not be tolerated. The following are some important training room policies.

1. *No cleated shoes are allowed.* Dirt and debris tend to cling to cleated shoes; therefore, they should be removed before entering the training facility.

2. *Game equipment is kept outside.* Because game equipment such as balls and bats adds to the sanitation problem, it should be kept out of the training room. Coaches and athletes must be continually reminded that the training room is not a storage room for sports equipment.

3. *Shoes must be kept off treatment tables.* Besides the tendency of shoes to contaminate treatment tables, they must be removed before any care is given to the athlete.

4. *Athletes should shower before receiving treatment.* The athlete should make it a habit to shower before being treated if it is not an emergency. This procedure helps keep tables and therapeutic modalities sanitary.

5. *Roughhousing and profanity should not be allowed.* Athletes must be continually reminded that the training facility is placed for injury care and prevention. Horseplay and foul language lower the basic purpose of the athletic training room.

General cleanliness of the training room cannot be stressed enough. Through the trainer's example, the athlete may develop an appreciation for cleanliness and in turn develop wholesome personal health habits. Cleaning responsibilities in most schools are divided between the training staff and the maintenance crew. Care of permanent building structures and trash disposal are usually the responsibilities of maintenance, whereas upkeep of specialized equipment falls within the province of the training staff.

Division of routine cleaning responsibilities may be organized as follows:

1. Maintenance crew
   a. Sweep floors daily.
   b. Clean and disinfect sinks and built-in tubs daily.
   c. Mop and disinfect hydrotherapy area twice a week.
   d. Refill paper towel and drinking cup dispensers as needed.
   e. Empty wastebaskets and dispose of trash daily.
2. Training staff
   a. Clean and disinfect treatment table daily.
   b. Clean and disinfect hydrotherapy modalities daily.
   c. Clean and polish other therapeutic modalities weekly.

Gymnasium Equipment

Sanitation in sports is a continual battle in the athletic training environment. Such practices as passing a common towel to wipe off perspiration, or using common water dispensers, or failing to change dirty clothing for clean are prevalent violations of sanitation in sports. The following is a suggested health practice check list, which may be employed by the coach and trainer:

1. Facilities sanitation
   a. Are the gymnasium floors swept daily?
   b. Are drinking fountains, showers, sinks, and urinals and toilets cleaned and disinfected daily?
   c. Are lockers aired and sanitized frequently?
   d. Are mats cleaned routinely (wrestling mats and wall mats cleaned daily)?

2. Equipment and clothing issuance
   a. Are equipment and clothing fitted to the athlete to avoid skin irritations?
   b. Is swapping of equipment and clothes prevented?
   c. Is clothing laundered and changed frequently?
   d. Is wet clothing allowed to dry thoroughly before the athlete wears it again?
   e. Is individual attention given to proper shoe fit and upkeep?
   f. Is protective clothing provided during inclement weather or when the athlete is waiting on the sidelines?
   g. Are clean dry towels provided each day?

The Athletes

To promote good health among the athletes, the coach or trainer should encourage sound health habits. The following checklist may be a useful guide for coaches, trainers, and athletes:

1. Are the athletes medically cleared to participate?
2. Is each athlete insured?
3. Does the athlete promptly report injuries, illnesses, and skin disorders to the coach or trainer?
4. Are good daily living habits of resting, sleeping, and proper nutrition practiced?
5. Do they shower after practice?
6. Do they dry thoroughly and cool off before departing the gymnasium?
7. Do they avoid drinking from a common water dispenser?
8. Do they avoid use of a common towel?
9. Do they avoid exchanging gym clothes with teammates?
10. Do they practice good foot hygiene?
11. Do they avoid contact with teammates when they have a contagious disease or infection?

Location

The **training room** should be located immediately adjacent to the dressing quarters of the athletes and should have three entrances: an outside entrance from the sports field and two inside entrances, leading from the men's and women's locker rooms. This arrangement makes it unnecessary to bring injured athletes in through the building and possibly through several doors; it also permits access when the rest of the building is not in use. Entrance doorways should be at least 44 inches wide; a double door at each entrance is preferable to allow easy passage of a wheelchair or a stretcher. A ramp at the outside entrance is safer and far more functional than are stairs. If an outside entrance is present, provisions should be made to protect against drafts, particularly during cold or inclement weather.

training room
Multipurpose area where first aid, physical examination, bandaging and taping, therapy, and exercise rehabilitation are carried out.

Toilet facilities should be located adjacent to the training room and be readily accessible through a door in the training room.

The training room should be located close to the shower rooms also that showers are readily available to dirt- or mud-covered athletes coming in for treatment.

Since the training room is the place where emergency treatment is given, its light, heat, and water sources should be independent of those for the rest of the building.

The trainer's office, which is incorporated in the training quarters, should have an outside telephone line. It is advisable to have a local or campus phone as well. The installation of a field phone adjacent to the major activities area is also desirable. Strict regulations concerning use of the telephones should be established. They should be used only in connection with training business and should not be used by students. Because of the nature and character of the training room and of the equipment and supplies within, it should have an independent lock-and-key system so that it is not accessible to everyone who possesses a master key to the building. The trainer alone should possess keys for the training quarters.

FACILITIES

Essential to any sports program is the maximum use of facilities and the most effective use of equipment and supplies.

The training room (Fig. 3-1) is a special room designed to meet the many requirements of the sports training program. To accommodate the various functions of a training program, it must be designed as a multipurpose area in which first aid can be administered, physical examinations conducted, pregame and prepractice bandaging and taping done, therapy and exercise rehabilitation carried out. In addition, it must serve as a health center for athletes and as a place from which they may be supervised and treated. A place must be provided too where health records and injury histories of athletes can be kept.

Size and Construction

A training area of less than 1000 square feet is impractical. A training room 1000 to 1200 square feet in size is satisfactory for most school situations. The 1200 square foot area (40 by 30 feet) permits the handling of a sizable number of athletes at one time besides allowing ample room for the rather bulky equipment needed. A room of this size is well suited for pregame preparation. Careful planning will determine whether a larger area is needed or is desirable.

The room should have windows in at least one wall; the windows should be placed high enough above the floor to provide ample natural light and draft-free ventilation and to ensure privacy. A training room that is not properly equipped with vents can become exceedingly unpleasant smelling. To supplement natural ventilation, either an exhaust fan or, preferably, an air-conditioning system should be installed.

The walls and ceiling should be of either drywall or plaster construction and should be painted in a light pastel shade with a washable paint.

The floor should be of smooth-finished concrete, with a nonslip texture. On occasion cleats are worn in the room, and a wooden floor may in time splinter and warp. Vinyl tile, although somewhat expensive, has been used as a floor covering with considerable success. The floors should be graded to slope toward strategically placed drain outlets.

Figure 3-1

A modern training room serves to carry out numerous functions.

Illumination

The training room should be planned so that good natural illumination comes from high on one side. Work areas should be planned so that light comes from the left for right-handed trainers and from the right for left-handed trainers. Outdoor diffusers are preferable to shade for eliminating undue glare and controlling illumination.

Artificial lighting should be planned with the advice of a technical lighting engineer. The standard level of illumination recommended for training facilities is 30 foot-candles at the height of 4 feet above the floor. Ceilings and walls, acting as reflective surfaces, aid in achieving an equable distribution and balance of light.

Light fixtures may be of several types. Since an even, nonglaring light is desired, a fixture that illuminates indirectly by casting direct light on the ceiling, from which it is reflected down and outward, is an excellent type. Fluorescent lights, when used with a diffuser, also provide a good source of light. Diffusers eliminate the flickering that is otherwise often an objectionable feature.

Special Service Sections

Apart from the storage and office space, a portion of the training room should be divided into special sections, preferably by low walls or partitions. It should be noted, however, that space may not permit a separate area for each service section, and an overlapping of functions may be required.

Taping, Bandaging, and Orthotics Section

Each training room should provide a place where taping, bandaging, and applying orthotic devices can be executed. This area should have three or four taping tables adjacent to a sink and a storage cabinet.

Superficial Thermal and Mechanical Therapy Section

Superficial therapy consists of both heat and cryotherapy modalities. These modalities might include one or two infrared heat lamps, three or four tables for massage and passive mobilization, and two or three chairs or stools. This section should also facilitate cold therapy procedures such as ice massage.

Electrotherapy Area

The electrotherapy area should constitute about 20% of the total special service area and is used for treatment by ultrasound, diathermy, or other electrotherapy methods. Equipment should include at least two treatment tables, several wooden chairs, one or two dispensing tables for holding supplies, shelves, and a storage cabinet for supplies and equipment. The area should contain a sufficient number of grounded outlets, preferably in the walls and several feet above the floor. It is advisable to place rubber mats or runners on each side of the treatment tables as a precautionary measure. This area must be under supervision at all times, and the storage cabinet should be kept locked when not in use.

Hydrotherapy Area

The hydrotherapy area should constitute approximately 15% of the total special service area. The floor should slope at a good gradient toward a centrally located drain to prevent water from standing. Equipment should include two whirlpool baths, one permitting complete immersion of the body, a steam room or cabinet, several lavatories, and storage shelves. Since some of this equipment is electrically operated, considerable precaution must be observed. All electrical outlets should be placed from 4 to 5 feet above the floor and should have spring-locked covers and water spray deflectors. All cords and wires must be kept clear of the floor to eliminate any possibility of electrical shock. To prevent water from entering the other areas, a slightly raised, rounded curb should be built at the entrance to the area. When a training room is planned, ample outlets must be provided, for under no circumstances should two or more devices be operated from the same outlet. All outlets must be properly grounded.

Figure 3-2

An effective training program must have appropriate facilities that are highly organized.

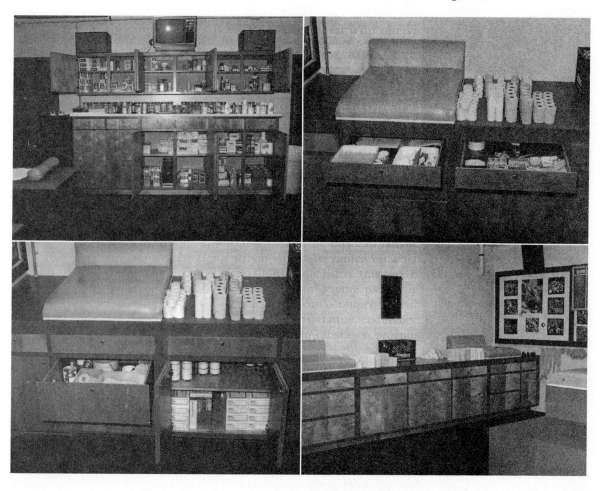

Exercise Rehabilitation Section

Ideally a training room should accommodate injury reconditioning under the strict supervision of the trainer. Selected pieces of resistance equipment should be made available. Depending on the existing space, shoulder wheels, knee exercisers, hand apparatus, and bicycle exercisers should be available to the injured athlete.

Storage Facilities

Many training quarters lack ample storage space. Often storage facilities are located a considerable distance away, which is extremely inconvenient. In addition to the storage cabinets and shelves provided in each of the three special service areas, a small storage closet should be placed in the trainer's office. All of these cabinets should be used for the storage of general supplies as well as for the small specialized equipment used in the respective areas. A large walk-in storage closet, 80 to 100 square feet in area, is a necessity for the storage of bulky equipment, medical supplies, adhesive tape, bandages, and protective devices (Fig. 3-2). A refrigerator for the storage of frozen water in styrofoam cups for ice massage, and other necessities is also an important piece of equipment. Many trainers prefer to place the refrigerator in their office, where it is readily accessible but still under close supervision. In small sports programs, a large refrigerator will probably be sufficient for all ice needs.

If at all possible, an ice-making machine should be installed in an auxiliary area to provide an ample and continuous supply of ice for treatment purposes.

The Trainer's Office

A space 10 feet by 8 feet is ample for the trainer's office. It should be located so that all areas of the training room are well under supervision without the trainer's having to leave the office. Glass partitions on two sides permit the trainer, even while seated at the desk, to observe all activities. A desk, chair, tack board for clippings and other information, telephones, and a record file are the basic equipment.

PROGRAM SCOPE AND FUNCTIONS

The athletic training program must clearly reflect its scope and major functions and the extent to which it will and can serve the athletic program, institution, and community.

The Athlete

The trainer must decide the degree to which the athlete will be served. For example, will prevention and care activities be extended to athletes for the entire year, including summer and other vacations, or only during the competitive season? Also, the trainer must decide what care will be rendered. Will it extend to all systemic illnesses or to just musculoskeletal problems?[2]

The Institution

A policy must be established as to who will be served by the athletic training program.[2] Often legal concerns and the school liability insurance dictate who is to be served. A policy should make it clear whether students other than athletes, athletes from other schools, faculty, and staff are to be cared for. If so, how are they to be referred and medically directed? Also, it must be decided whether the training program will act as a clinical setting for student trainers.

The Community

A decision must be made as to which, if any, outside group or person in the community will be served by the training staff. Again, legality and the institution's insurance program must be taken into consideration. If a policy is not delineated in this matter, outside persons may tend to abuse the services of the training facilities and staff.

PERSONNEL

The head trainer, in cooperation with the athletic director, should establish detailed policies on each personnel category related to the training program. The policies should contain work descriptions, including education and experience required, responsibilities, salary, and benefits, if any. Line of responsibilities must be spelled out in detail. For example, a student trainer usually must go through the athletic trainer on all matters. The athletic trainer goes through the athletic director on administrative matters and through the team physician on medical matters.

A student trainer must go through the athletic trainer on all matters.

The Trainer's Duties

Duties of the athletic trainer should be detailed; an example of this is as follows[2]:

1. Work cooperatively with the coaches in setting up and carrying out a program of conditioning for athletes
2. Administer first aid to injured athletes
3. Obtain ambulances
4. Apply protective or injury-preventive devices, such as taping, bandaging, or bracing
5. Advise on equipment purchases
6. Supervise fitting of protective equipment
7. Work cooperatively with and under the direction of the physician about:
   a. reconditioning procedures
   b. operation of therapeutic devices and equipment
   c. fitting of braces, guards, and other devices
   d. referrals to the physician, health services, or hospital
   e. assisting in the physical examinations and physical fitness screening
8. Direct daily training room operations including:
   a. exercise rehabilitation and therapy programs
   b. record keeping
   c. requisitioning and storage of supplies
   d. inventory and budget allocation
9. Provide training coverage of athletic events, home and away
10. Supervise and instruct assistant and student trainers

Figure 3-3

The trainer must decide the degree to which each athlete will be served.

11. Counsel and advise athletes and coaches on matters pertaining to health
12. Act as a clinical supervisor for students working toward NATA certification
13. Conduct athletic training clinics and workshops periodically

The Team Physician's Duties

The team physician's various duties and responsibilities may be summarized as follows[2]:

1. See that a complete medical history of each athlete is compiled and is readily available
2. Determine through a physical examination the athletes' health status
3. Diagnose and treat injuries and other illnesses
4. Direct and advise the athletic trainer on health matters
5. Act, when necessary, as an instructor to the trainer, assistant trainer, and student trainers on special therapeutic methods, therapeutic problems, and related procedures
6. Attend all games, athletic contests, scrimmages, and practices; if this is not feasible, arrange for attendance by other qualified medical personnel; when personal attendance is not possible, be available for emergency call
7. Decide when, on medical grounds, athletes should be disqualified from participation and when they may be permitted to reenter competition
8. Serve as an advisor to the trainer and the coach and, when necessary, as a counselor to the athlete
9. Work closely with the school administrator, school dentist, trainer, coach, and health services personnel to promote and maintain consistently high standards for the care of the athlete

The Team Dentist's Duties

There are three areas of responsibility for the team dentist:

1. Organize and carry out the preseason dental examination
2. Be available to provide emergency care when needed
3. Conduct the mouth protector program

PROGRAM OPERATIONS

It is imperative that every athletic training program develop policies and procedures that carefully delineate the everyday workings of the program. This is especially true for handling health problems and injuries.

The Health Screening Examination

The trainer and physician work closely together for the development of a program for the prevention of sports injuries and the conditioning of the athlete. Physical examinations must be given not only at the entry level but be conducted each season that the athlete participates. This program is based on the thorough examination of the athlete by the physician.

The physical examination must serve as a screening device that permits only those who are physically and psychologically fit in all respects to enter

Every athletic training program must develop policies and procedures that carefully delineate the everyday workings of the program.

athletic competition. The various cardiovascular, neurological, orthopedic, and respiratory anomalies or irregularities that may be aggravated by athletic participation or may predispose the participant to injury should be considered disqualifying conditions. Overweight and underweight athletes should be given instructions for correcting their respective weight problems.

Postural or orthopedic conditions that may prove to be a handicap or predispose the participant to injury in a particular sports activity are often revealed during an examination. In some such instances participation in another sport in which the condition will not present a serious problem is recommended. In other instances the condition may prove to be sufficiently serious to warrant a declaration of ineligibility to participate in any sports activity.

Individuals can often participate successfully in certain sports even though they may possess some organic anomaly. The physician is the judge as to the type of activity in which the athlete may participate and any limitations necessary within this activity.

The physician should rule out disease states that contraindicate participation in certain activities. Such states would include metabolic, cardiovascular, and renal disease, neurological problems, and pulmonary, musculoskeletal, and abdominal aberrations. Athletes who possess one kidney or one eye or who are obese may have to be disqualified, as should any individual who has had repeated brain concussions in one season or who has a history of head injury serious enough to have required surgery. Therapy-controlled disorders such as asthma, diabetes, and convulsive disorders must be considered individually by the physician based on circumstances before the person is permitted to participate in competitive sports.

If, in the physician's considered professional judgment, participation presents certain hazards or may prove deleterious to the health of the athlete, either at the present or in the future, the individual will be disqualified. The trainer and coach must learn to accept such decisions as best for the athlete. In most instances, although the individual is disqualified from a particular sport that contained risk factors for a medical problem, he or she can nonetheless be counseled to participate in an alternate sport that poses no particular hazard.

Obtaining a complete medical history should be the first step. Following this, a thorough physical examination, including a careful check of the cardiovascular, respiratory, musculoskeletal, and central nervous systems should be made (see Figs. 3-4 and 3-5). Care and thoroughness should prevail. Unfortunately, sometimes only a perfunctory examination, limited to cardiac auscultation and a check for inguinal hernia, is made. School administrators and the public must be made aware of the necessity for a thorough and complete physical examination of all prospective participants in school athletic programs.

Because of the hazard in all sports—especially football, track, and baseball—immunization against tetanus should be provided for each player at the time of examination. If the athlete has been immunized previous to the examination, determination should be made of whether a booster shot is required.

Examination of the Chest and Lungs

The chest and lungs should be examined by inspection, palpation, percussion, and auscultation. The general shape and size of the chest, any deformities, any growths or tumors, the distribution of hair, and the condition of the glands are noted. The pulse rate and blood pressure are checked, and the veins are examined to determine the presence of varicosities. The respiratory movements are observed and the rate and character of respiration noted. By palpation the chest wall is examined for respiratory and cardiac anomalies.

Through percussion (tapping) some abnormal chest conditions can be noted and identified and the size, shape, and position of the heart determined. By means of a stethoscope (auscultation) the examiner carefully listens to the breath sounds (respiratory murmurs) to detect any abnormal or pathological sounds. The examiner then listens to the heart, observing any modifications in sound, intensity, or rhythm. When examining the high school athlete, the physician should be alert to any heart murmurs that may be present. The murmurs may be either functional or organic. Functional murmurs often will disappear as a result of exercise. Organic murmurs are caused by some abnormality in structure resulting from either congenital malformation or disease and usually affect the valves. Exercise will cause an organic murmur to become more pronounced. In the adolescent, heart murmur may signify either incomplete closing of the valves (valvular insufficiency) or narrowing of the valves (stenosis). Organic murmurs are often a residual of rheumatic fever. Many times detectable heart murmurs found in the adolescent are idiopathic and disappear as the individual advances toward maturity.

Gallagher-Brouha step test   The Gallagher-Brouha step test or similar tests should be given to all examinees and the return of the heart rate and blood pressure to pretest levels carefully noted. Following rehabilitation, the step test may also be used for determining the athlete's fitness to return to competition. The test is easily administered. The subject steps on and off of an 18-inch platform at the rate of thirty times a minute for a total of 4 minutes. Pulse rates are then taken during recovery at 30 seconds, 1 minute, 2 minutes, and 3 minutes. The index is computed as follows:

$$\frac{\text{Duration of exercise in seconds} \times 100}{2 \times \text{Sum of any three pulse rates in recovery}}$$

An athlete scoring 65 or less is unfit for activity. The higher the index the more fit the individual may be assumed to be. Scoring tables have been devised for both high school boys and girls. If at all possible, all athletes should have an electrocardiogram. If this is not feasible, then all potential athletes who have a history of any cardiac anomaly or whose examinations have indicated possible cardiac malfunction should have one.

Examination of the Trunk

Using inspection, palpation, and percussion, the examiner notes the size and shape of the trunk, the distribution of hair, the amount of fat present, and the presence of any anomalies of the genitalia, dilated veins, growths,

Sidenotes:

With a stethoscope (auscultation) the examiner carefully listens to respiratory murmurs to detect any abnormal or pathological sounds.

The Gallagher-Brouha step test or similar tests should be given to all examinees and the return of the heart rate and blood pressure to pretest levels carefully noted.

An athlete scoring 65 or less on the Gallagher-Brouha test is unfit for activity.

and muscle spasm. The examiner further explores the tenderness, which may be indicative of strains or bruises, enteritis, or appendicitis. The physician also checks for an enlarged liver or spleen and for hernia.

Abdominal hernias are not uncommon in athletic persons, and the examiner looks carefully for their presence. The protrusion of some of the internal structures through the abdominal wall indicates a hernia, and the name of the hernia is derived from its location.

The most common hernia in men is the inguinal hernia. It occurs at the inguinal canal, located at the extreme lower border of the abdomen. The canal, which lies immediately above the inguinal (Poupart's) ligament and functions as a passageway for the spermatic cord in men, forms a weak place in the abdominal wall. Weak abdominal musculature, injury, or excessive intra-abdominal pressures, such as those resulting from lifting a heavy object, will predispose a person to hernia. An inguinal hernia may be either direct or indirect. In a direct hernia the intestine protrudes directly through the muscles and into the canal, whereas in the indirect it enters the canal at the internal abdominal ring and follows the course of the spermatic cord.

Femoral hernia, which is more prevalent among women than men, occurs at the femoral ring, an opening in the groin, approximately ½ inch (1.25 cm) in diameter or usually larger in women, located just below the inguinal ligaments. Femoral hernia is not particularly common type of hernia. Unusual growth or cysts, such as the pilonidal cyst, should be noted. The rectal area should be inspected for hemorroids.

For women athletes a gynecological examination may be advisable. Such factors as periodicity and menstrual patterns, such as flow, irregularity, and cramps, should be noted, and if possible a vaginal examination and Pap smear administered. Many physicians feel that some blood chemistry tests are important. The hemoglobin test for women and a urinalysis for diabetes for both genders are suggested. Physician availability and cost are the principal factors that limit most examinations.

> The most common hernia among men is the inguinal hernia; the femoral hernia is more prevalent in women.

Examination of the Head and Neck

Examination of the head and neck areas is confined principally to observation for the presence of oral infections, sinus infections (not unusual among athletes), and any abnormal skin, eye, ear, nose, or throat conditions. The eyes are examined and, if practicable, a hearing test is given. Current medical opinion holds that athletes who need visual correction should use soft contact lenses in the majority of sports, particularly in such sports as soccer, American football, and swimming, in preference to spectacles or hard contact lenses. Both spectacles and hard contact lenses can be easily dislodged, are less comfortable to wear, and do not afford as good protection to the eyes as do the soft lenses.

Examination of the Mouth

The preseason dental examination can be performed by the team dentist, by a group of school or dental association designated dentists, or by the family dentist. Pathological conditions of the mouth, such as broken teeth, teeth with cavities, or infections, should be screened and remedial measures undertaken.

Selection and fitting of mouth guards can also be done at this time. Athletes with pathological conditions of the mouth should not be fitted until the mouth has returned to health. Those with mouth anomalies such as cleft palate and those wearing orthodontic appliances, dentures, or bridgework will require special attention. Properly fitted mouth guards will virtually eliminate broken or chipped teeth and will do much toward preventing head or neck injuries.

Body Structure

Body structure is a definite factor in the degree of efficiency and the level of success an athlete attains. Studies have shown that certain types of body build have definite advantages over other types of certain sports.

Adolescents who are gross in body bulk are often selected to participate in activities that tax them well beyond their physical capacities. However, because their muscles and bones have not yet developed the strength and maturity necessary to adequately meet excessive stresses or above-normal physical demands, young people of this type are prone to serious injury, particularly to the skeletal system, since the epiphyseal growth centers can be seriously damaged. Orthopedists often express concern over the tendency of some coaches and physical education teachers to place such individuals in situations in which excessive weight-support demands are placed on them or in which they are subjected to severe physical contact. Athletic trainers and coaches must be careful never to overmatch an adolescent. Competition kept within the scope of the person's physical abilities will produce wholesome results, whereas overmatching or placing the individual in situations for which he or she is not physically ready can lead to trauma that may have serious permanent consequences.

Testing for Flexibility

Range of motion tests have been used by the medical profession for years. Team physicians have long recognized the relationship between injury and joint flexibility. Tight-jointed athletes seem susceptible to muscle strains, tears, tendonitis, and nerve pinch syndromes, whereas athletes who are loose-jointed are more prone to develop ligament problems, subluxations, and dislocations. Various individuals exhibit differences in the natural degree of flexibility they possess, probably because of variations in muscle and ligament lengths. There is also a varying degree of specificity of flexibility in the various joints in the body, since a specific range of motion in any one joint does not give an assessment of the range of motion in any other joint.

Range of motion tests may be made with a Leighton Flexometer or a goniometer or may consist of tests such as the sit and reach, the trunk-hip forward bend tests, and others.

Athletes who exhibit limited flexibility need to be put into a regimen of stretching to increase range of motion. The static-stretch exercises detailed in Chapter 4 can be assigned for this purpose. Those athletes who possess excessive flexibility should be put on a progressive resistance program and should limit or eliminate stretching procedures, if at all possible, until satisfactory ranges of motion are attained.

Body structure is a definite factor in the degree of efficiency and the level of success an athlete attains.

Athletes who exhibit limited flexibility need a regimen of stretching to increase range of motion.

Field or Gymnasium Procedures

The trainer's duties and responsibilities are not confined to the training room but extend to the gymnasium and the sports field as well. Most injuries occur during games or contests, and devising a proper and legal procedure for the on-the-spot handling of game or competition injuries is a joint responsibility of the team physician, the coach, the administrator, and the trainer. It may be advisable to have the county or district attorney's office check the procedures that you plan to establish to determine whether or not they comply with all medical and legal requirements. Following an approved, standard policy for taking care of athletes injured during competition or practice is sound not only from a legal standpoint but also from the standpoint of therapeutic management. Following are some suggestions that can be used as a basis for establishing standard procedures to be followed by a trainer when an accident occurs and no physician is present.

1. Make an immediate preliminary examination to ascertain the seriousness, type, and extent of the injury.
2. If the injury is recognized as being beyond the scope of your ability, send for the physician immediately.
3. Give first aid if it is indicated.
4. Should the condition of the player be such that he or she requires removal from the area, determine whether it is a condition that would warrant medical sanction before attempting movement or transportation. If the player is unconscious or is unable to move without assistance, use a stretcher. All athletic trainers should know the proper methods of transporting injured persons.
5. In some collision sports, particularly football, have an ambulance on call for all games. Sometrainers feel that the presence of an ambulance on or near the field has a negative psychological effect on the players. However, an ambulance should be available, but may be parked out of the view of both spectators and players, and the attendants should be inconspicuously seated where they can be summoned quickly if needed. If during practice an ambulance must be summoned to a school, a strict set of procedures must be adhered to, including the following:
   a. Clear, concise directions must be given as to where the injured athlete is.
   b. Someone such as a student trainer is positioned to meet and direct the ambulance onto the campus.
   c. Keys to open gates are readily available.
6. Use a standard accident report blank upon which all pertinent information may be recorded. A form of this type should contain the following:
   a. Date, time, and place of the accident
   b. Sport being played
   c. Nature and extent of the injury
   d. Brief description of how the injury occurred
   e. Emergency procedures followed and disposition of the injured athlete
   f. Names and, if possible, signatures of at least two witnesses

Devising a proper and legal procedure for on-the-spot handling of game or competition injuries is a joint responsibility of the team physician, coach, administrator, and trainer.

An accident report blank of the type described serves as a record for future reference. If the emergency procedures followed are questioned at a later date, one's memory of the details may be somewhat hazy, but a report filled out on the spot provides specific information. All reports of this nature should be filed in the trainer's office. It is well to make them out in triplicate so that one copy may be sent to the school health office, one sent to the physician, and one retained.

Training Room and Related Procedures

Trainer's assignment
procedures:
  Sports coverage
  Record keeping
  Care of supplies and
    equipment
  Maintenance of facility and
    equipment

Procedures must be established to run the training room smoothly. They should include assignment of sports coverage, record keeping, care of supplies and equipment, and maintenance of the facility and equipment.

Sports and Training Room Coverage

Ideally all sports should have professional or student trainer coverage at competitions, both home and away. However, if there are not enough trainers to go around, those sports that are most hazardous should have priority.

Depending on whether a school has a full-time training staff, a training room may operate from 9 AM to 6 PM. Mornings are commonly reserved for treatments and exercise rehabilitation, early afternoons are for treatment, exercise rehabilitation, and preparation for practice or a contest, and late afternoons and early evenings are spent in injury management.

Record Keeping

Some trainers object to record keeping, stating that they have neither the time nor the inclination to be bookkeepers. There is, however, a certain amount of paperwork that must be done, and, if properly planned, little time need be spent on it. A filing cabinet and desk are as much a part of the trainer's equipment as is a whirlpool bath. Careful records of all serious injuries should be filed and readily accessible. In schools in which there is no permanent health services program, the trainer should keep the health appraisal records of all athletes. These would include the results of the physical examination, the medical history, and other pertinent information. It is important that these records be kept up to date. In schools in which a close liaison exists between the health services and the trainer, the health records of all students, including athletes, are kept in the health services office, and such data as are thought relevant are forwarded to the trainer. Often the school health services are responsible for making out all accident reports. Pertinent information is supplied on a form by either the trainer or the coach and is sent to the health services office, where an official transcript is made in triplicate. One copy is sent to the trainer, the second is sent to the school or team physician, and the third is filed in the health services office. In addition, such records should be carefully examined and analyzed annually to determine how the total program can be made safer for the participants. Data recorded over the year should be tabulated and submitted to one or more of the national injury registries. Every program should be a participant in at at least one, preferably more, of the systematic injury reviews.

It is not feasible to keep a record of each athlete's visit to the training

Figure 3-4

Suggested medical history
form for athletes.
Courtesy D. Bailey, California State
University, Long Beach.

```
                                I
        ATHLETIC MEDICAL EXAMINATION FOR _____
                                             (Sport)

Name _____ Age_____Birthdate_____ S.S.#_____

Address _____ Phone no. _____
              (Street)          (City)         (Zip)

   Instructions:
       All questions must be answered.  Failure to disclose pertinent medical informa-
       tion may invalidate your insurance coverage  and, under NCAA rules, may cancel
       your eligibility to participate in interscholastic athletics.  Any further
       health problems must be discussed with the physician at the time of this
       examination.

   Medical history:
       Have you ever had any of the following:  If "yes" give details to the
       examining doctor.
```

		NO	YES	DETAILS (IF YES)
1.	Head injury or concussion			
2.	Bone or joint disorders, fractures (broken bones), dislocations, trick joints, arthritis, back pain			
3.	Eye or ear problems (disease or surgery)			
4.	Dizzy spells, fainting or convulsions			
5.	Tuberculosis, asthma, bronchitis			
6.	Heart trouble or rheumatic fever			
7.	High or low blood pressure			
8.	Anemia, leukemia or bleeding disorder			
9.	Diabetes, hepatitis or jaundice			
10.	Ulcers, other stomach trouble or colitis			
11.	Kidney or bladder problems			
12.	Hernia (rupture)			
13.	Mental illness or nervous breakdown			
14.	Addiction to drugs or alcohol			
15.	Surgery or advised to have surgery			
16.	Taking medication regularly			
17.	Allergies or skin problems			
18.	Other illness, injury not named above			
19.	Menstrual problems; LMP			

```
                     Signature _____

                     Date _____
```

room, but when an athlete has suffered a handicapping or serious injury and is undergoing reconditioning treatment, a progress record should be kept. Records often have the status of legal documents in that they may be used to establish certain facts should a civil suit, an insurance action, or a criminal action ensue following injury or reconditioning. It is to the trainer's advantage to keep accurate, albeit concise, records at all times.

A good trainer keeps on file an annual report of the activities in his or her area. Such a report should include the number of athletes serviced, a survey of the number and types of injuries, an analysis of the program with recommendations for improvement, a budget record, and any other information that is pertinent. Many schools require that such a report be pre-

Figure 3-5

Suggested medical examination form for athletes.

Courtesy D. Bailey, California State University, Long Beach.

II
ATHLETIC MEDICAL EXAMINATION

Name _____ S.S.# _____

Physical examination   Sport

Height_____ Weight_____ Pulse_____ B.P. _____/_____

    Vision: Right_____/_____ with/without glasses   Dip/Tet

            Left _____/_____ with/without glasses

    Hearing: Right_____ Left_____   _____
                                          (Date)

Laboratory_____ Blood: HCT_____ RPR_____ Sickledex_____
       (Date)   Urine: Sugar_____ Alb _____

Chest x-ray_____ Yes_____ no_____
          (Date)

System examination	Comments	Initials
Group 1 Eyes_____		
Ears_____		
Nose _____		
Throat_____		
Neck _____		
Group 2 Skin _____		
Heart_____		
Lungs_____ Breasts _____		
Group 3 Abdomen, groin, genitals, rectum		
Group 4 Spine, extremities		

Cleared, unrestricted_____ Not cleared_____

Cleared, restricted_____ Further evaluation_____

                  Appointment to be made_____
                                        (date)

Comments:_____

_____

_____

_____

                         Team Physician   Date

sented annually to the athletic council or to the department head. (See Figs. 3-4 through 3-9 for suggested forms.)

Insurance

Most states, although recognizing sports as a bona fide school activity, classify it as extramural and therefore do not extend to it the legal responsibilities they assume for regular class activities. In recent years there have been considerable advances in making low-cost sports injury insurance available for high school and college athletes. Such insurance usually covers the athlete against injuries incurred during practice or competition. Most of these plans are sponsored by the state athletic associations. Others are sponsored by private companies. Some of these insurance plans do not provide adequate coverage in cases in which a serious injury requires surgical intervention and a long recovery time. Of particular concern are catastrophic injuries (cervical damage) that are not adequately covered. It is essential that parents be made aware of insurance limitations.

It is not within the province of this book to detail the various forms of coverage and their advantages and disadvantages, since such information is usually included in texts dealing with the administration of school athletic programs. Nonetheless, *insurance is a responsibility of the trainer, to the extent of working closely with the school, the athletic administrator, and the coach to see that every athlete is adequately covered by a good, reliable company.* Care should be taken to be certain that the coverage is the best that can be obtained; it should provide maximum coverage for minimum cost. This responsibility entails careful study of all available plans. The trainer in charge of insurance is responsible for making injury claims and the necessary follow-up.

ATHLETIC TRAINING CARD

Name______ Age___ Sex___ Student no. (S.S. #)______

Sport______

School address______ City______ State______

Zip______ Phone______

Permanent address______ City______ State______

Zip______ Phone______

Parents' address______ City______ State______

Zip______ Phone______

Are you a junior college transfer? Yes___ No___

Give the number of seasons completed at CSULB______

Do you or your parents have private health insurance? Yes___ No___

Name of company______ Policy number______

In case of emergency notify______ Phone______ Relationship______

List major past injuries and dates______

Medic Alert______

Figure 3-6

Sports participation card.

Courtesy D. Bailey, California State University, Long Beach.

Computer Use

Increasingly computers are being used in athletic training (Fig. 3-10). Trainers who have immediate access to a computer find that a great deal of time can be saved. Its use is almost limitless in storing and retrieving important information. Some of the more popular uses are[1]:

1. Recording number of injuries for later study in regard to incidence and the conditions under which the injuries took place, level of injury, when injured (in practice or game), and so on
2. Fitness data
3. Insurance data
4. Results of therapy and rehabilitation

BUDGET CONCERNS

One of the major problems faced by athletic trainers is to obtain a budget of sufficient size to permit them to carry out a creditable job of training.

Figure 3-7

Interim health questionnaire (to be completed before resuming participation).
Courtesy D. Bailey, California State University, Long Beach.

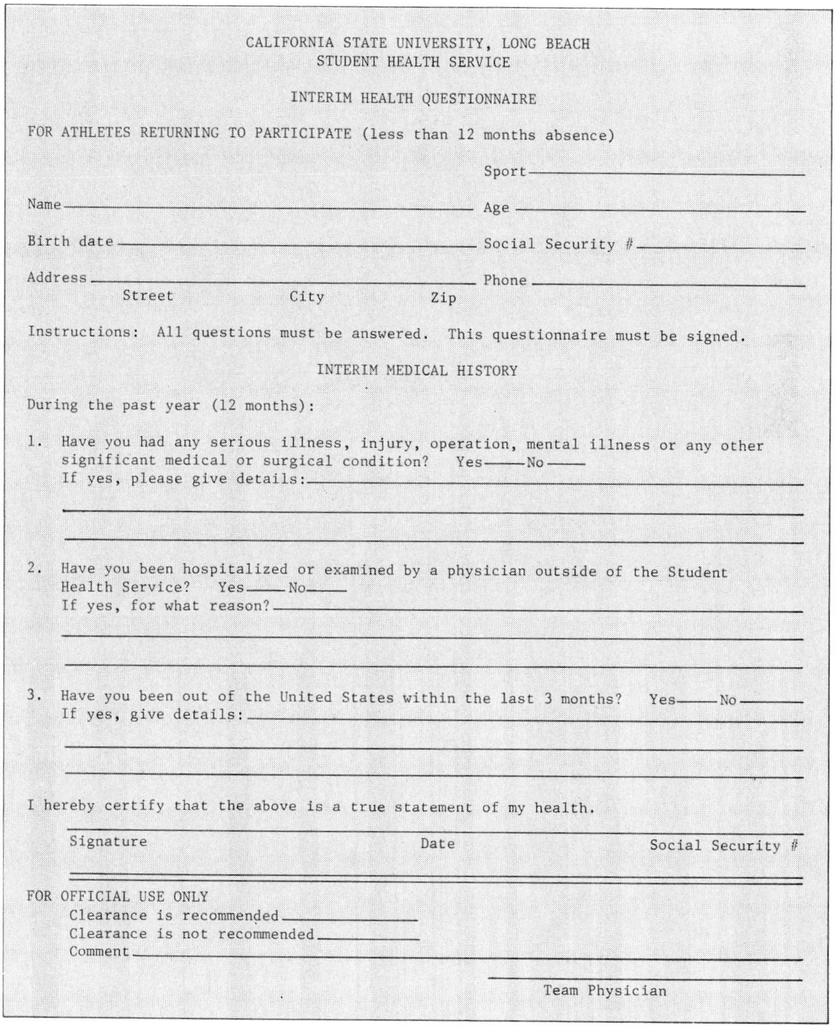

```
                    CALIFORNIA STATE UNIVERSITY, LONG BEACH
                           STUDENT HEALTH SERVICE

                         INTERIM HEALTH QUESTIONNAIRE

    FOR ATHLETES RETURNING TO PARTICIPATE (less than 12 months absence)

                                            Sport_____

        Name_____     Age _____

        Birth date_____  Social Security #_____

        Address_____   Phone _____
                   Street      City      Zip

    Instructions:  All questions must be answered.  This questionnaire must be signed.

                         INTERIM MEDICAL HISTORY

    During the past year (12 months):

    1.  Have you had any serious illness, injury, operation, mental illness or any other
        significant medical or surgical condition?  Yes_____No_____
        If yes, please give details:_____


        _____

    2.  Have you been hospitalized or examined by a physician outside of the Student
        Health Service?  Yes_____ No_____
        If yes, for what reason?_____


        _____

    3.  Have you been out of the United States within the last 3 months?  Yes_____No_____
        If yes, give details:_____


    I hereby certify that the above is a true statement of my health.

        Signature                    Date                Social Security #


    FOR OFFICIAL USE ONLY
        Clearance is recommended_____
        Clearance is not recommended_____
        Comment_____

                                        Team Physician
```

Figure 3-8

Athletic injury record form.
Courtesy D. Bailey, California State
University, Long Beach.

Name _____ Sport: _____ Age: _____ Location: _____ Date: __/__/__ Time: _____ Injury number: _____

Player I.D. _____ Recheck _____ Reinjury _____

Initial injury _____ Intercollegiate-nonintercollegiate

Incurred while participating in sport: yes ____ no ____

Preseason--Practice--Game

Description: How did it happen? _____

Initial impression: _____

Site of injury
1 Right
2 Left
3 Proximal
4 Distal
5 Anterior
6 Posterior
7 Medial
8 Lateral
9 Other _____

Site of evaluation
1 SHS
2 Athletic Trn Rm.
3 Site-Competition
4 _____

Procedures
1 Physical exam
2 X-ray
3 Splint
4 Wrap
5 Cast
6 Aspiration
7 Other _____

Disposition
1 SHS
2 Trainer
3 Hospital
4 H.D.
5 Other _____

Body part
1 Head
2 Face
3 Eye
4 Nose
5 Ear
6 Mouth
7 Neck
8 Thorax
9 Ribs
10 Sternum
11 Upper back
12 Low back
13 Shoulder
14 Rotator cuff
15 AC joint
16 Glenohumeral
17 Sternoclavicular
18 Upper arm
19 Elbow
20 Forearm
21 Wrist
22 Hand
23 Thumb
24 Finger
25 MP joint
26 PIP joint
27 Abdomen
28 Hip
29 Thigh
30 Knee
31 Patella
32 Lower leg
33 Ankle
34 Achilles tendon
35 Foot
36 Toes
37 Other

Referral
1 Arthrogram
2 Neurological
3 Int. Med.
4 Orthopedic
5 EENT
6 Dentist
7 Other

Structure
1 Skin
2 Muscle
3 Fascia
4 Bone
5 Nerve
6 Fat pad
7 Tendon
8 Ligament
9 Cartilage
10 Capsule
11 Compartment
12 Dental
13 _____

Nature of injury
1 Contusion
2 Strain
3 Sprain
4 Fracture
5 Rupture
6 Tendonitis
7 Bursitis
8 Myositis
9 Laceration
10 Concussion
11 Avulsion
12 Abrasion
13 _____

Degree
1° 2° 3°

Non-traumatic
1 Dermatological
2 Allergy
3 Influenza
4 URI
5 GU
6 Systemic infect.
7 Local infect.
8 Other

Disposition of injury
1 No part.
2 Part part.
3 Full part.

Previous injury _____

Treatment _____

Medication _____

Prescription dispensed
1 Antibiotics
2 Antiinflammatory
3 Decongestant
4 Analgesic
5 Muscle relaxant
6 Enzyme
7 _____

Injections
1 Steroids
2 Antibiotics
3 Steroids-xylo
4 _____

Most high schools fail to make any budgetary provisions for training except for the purchase of tape, ankle wraps, and a training bag that contains a minimum amount of equipment. Many fail to provide a room and any of the special facilities that are needed to establish an effective training program. Some school boards and administrators fail to recognize that the functions performed in the training quarters are an essential component of the athletic program and that even if no specialist is employed, the facilities are nonetheless necessary. Colleges and universities are not usually faced with this problem. By and large, training is recognized as an important corollary of the athletic program, and facilities and specialists are usually available. High school athletes are as much in need of training room services as are college athletes; for that reason high school coaches must strive to convince the school administrators of the need for a training program. Within the last few years there has been a pronounced trend toward wider recognition of this need. More frequently not only are schools providing well-equipped training rooms but also hiring teachers who have had preparation and experience in athletic training to serve in a dual capacity as teachers and part-time trainers.

Budget needs vary considerably. However, a reasonably good, medium-sized high school athletic training program can be operated at an annual cost of $7,000 to $12,000. The amount spent on building and equipping a training facility, of course, is entirely a matter of local option. In purchasing equipment, immediate needs as well as availability of personnel to operate specialized equipment should be kept in mind.

Budget records should be kept on file so that they are available for use in projecting the following year's budgetary needs. They present a picture of the distribution of current funds and serve to substantiate future budgetary requests.

Expenditures for individual items vary in accordance with different

Figure 3-9

Athletic injury report form.
Courtesy D. Bailey, California State University, Long Beach.

```
                  CALIFORNIA STATE UNIVERSITY, LONG BEACH
                       REPORT OF ATHLETIC INJURY


Name _____ Date _____ Sport _____ Year  1  2  3  4

History of this injury:   Time: _____ Location _____

    How did it happen?  (Student's own words): _____

_____

Previous injuries: _____

Initial impression: _____

_____

_____

Treatment: _____

Medication: _____

Disposition:  Referred (Circle)  SHS, X-ray, Hospital, Other _____

Recheck--initial injury              (Initial) _____
                                          Trainer          Team Physician
```

training philosophies. Some trainers believe in a considerable amount of strapping and therefore may expend as much as 60% of their annual budget on adhesive tape; others, holding an opposing viewpoint, may spend a rather small percentage of their allotment on tape. The trainer should keep accurate records of current funds and their distribution. Budgets must be justified, and good records aid in substantiating future requests.

Equipment and Supplies

The training personnel must be concerned with the equipment the athlete wears. It is just as important in injury prevention to be outfitted with properly fitted equipment as it is to be well conditioned and coached (see Chapter 7). Too often coaches are more concerned with the outward appearance of athletes than with the extent of protection afforded them. However, it is easy to understand why those given the responsibility for purchasing sports equipment become confused. Various claims made for a specific piece of equipment and a general lack of knowledge on what constitutes quality merchandise are but two reasons for this confusion. The best rule of thumb is always "you get what you pay for." Safety must never be sacrificed for appearance. In sports programs with limited budgets, the highest priority must be given to the best quality of protective equipment; outward appearance of the athlete must come second. In most cases coaches have the final word as to which type of equipment they want their teams to have; however, this decision should be made in consultation with the athletic trainer and equipment supervisor.

Figure 3-10

Computers are becoming an essential tool in athletic training.

Another important responsibility of the equipment supervisor and training personnel is the initial fitting of equipment to the individual athlete. Once fitted, the athlete is taught how to wear each protective device properly and to promptly report any malfunctioning or misfit. The wearing of *all* protective equipment should be mandatory in practice as well as in competition. It is desirable, particularly with young athletes, to check daily the wearing of protective or specialized equipment. Many injuries, which result in loss of sport days, can be avoided by attention to properly fitted equipment.

TABLE 3-1

Suggested basic equipment for individual programs

Item	Quantities for Number of Participants per Year		
	Up to 200	200 to 400	400 to 600
Anatomy charts (set)	1	1	1
Ankle wrap roller	1	2	2
Blankets	3	3	3
Bulletin board	1	1	1
Callus file	6	12	18
Crutches	2 pairs	4 pairs	6 pairs
Diathermy (microwave or shortwave)	1	1	1
Drinking dispenser	1	1	1
Electric clock	1	1	1
Electric muscle stimulator	1	1	1
Examining table (physician)	1	1	1
Exercise equipment (assorted)	*	*	*
Eyecup	1	2	3
Flashlight (pencil type)	1	2	3
Forceps (tweezers)	3	3	3
Hair clippers	1	2	2
Hammer	1	1	1
Ice maker	1	1	1
Massage or treatment tables	2	4	6
Medicine dropper	3	6	9
Mirror (hand)	3	5	7
Moist heat pack machine	1 small	1 small	1 large
Nail clippers	1	2	2
Neck and back board	1	2	2
Oral screw	(available for each first-aid kit)		
Oral thermometer	1	2	3
Paraffin bath	optional	optional	1
Pliers	1	2	3
Razor (safety, with blades)	1	2	3
Reconditioning equipment			
Barbells	†	†	†
Chinning bar	†	†	†
Dumbbells	†	†	†
Mats	†	†	†
Pulley weights	†	†	†
Shoe weights	†	†	†

*Assorted pieces of equipment sufficient for the given number of participants.
†Should be on hand for each participant or funds available for purchase when need arises.
‡Dry, cool storage areas should be provided to house the bulk of the training supplies.

Equipment and supplies recommendations helpful to the qualified trainer are indicated in the accompanying lists. Table 3-1 itemizes the equipment suggested as basic for individual programs, the quantities listed being applicable to situations in which the number of participants is under 200, 200 to 400, and 400 to 600, respectively.

Table 3-2 lists yearly training supplies, grouped according to areas of use in injury prevention or injury management. Table 3-3 provides a checklist for the trainer's kit suitable for use in various sports.

Item	Quantities for Number of Participants per Year		
	Up to 200	200 to 400	400 to 600
Universal or Nautilus equipment	†	†	†
Isokinetic device (Cytex, Orthotron)	†	†	†
Refrigerator	1	1	1
Resuscitator	1	1	1
Safety pins	200	400	600
Scales and weight chart	1	2	3
Scalpel	1	2	3
Scissors			
All-purpose	2	3	4
Bandage	3	5	7
Surgical	2	2	2
Screwdriver	1	1	1
Shoehorn	3	5	7
Sink and washbasin	1	1	1
Sitz bath	1	1	1
Splints (set of assorted pneumatic)	1	2	3
Sterilizer	optional	optional	1
Storage cupboards	‡	‡	‡
Stretcher (folding)	1	1	1
Surgical lamp	1	1	1
Tape adherent			
Aerosol (12-ounce spray can)	18 cans	24 cans	30 cans
Bulk	5 gallons	10 gallons	15 gallons
Tape cutters	5	8	10
Taping tables	2	3	4
Trainer's office			
Bookshelf	1	1	1
Desk	1	1	1
Filing cabinet	1	1	1
Telephone	1	1	1
Training kits	(available for each sport)		
Ultrasound	1	1	1
Waste container	2	3	4
Wheelchair	(should be available)		
Whirlpool baths	1	2	3

TABLE 3-2

Suggested yearly training supplies for individual programs

Item	Quantities for Number of Participants per Year		
	Up to 200	**200 to 400**	**400 to 600**
Adhesive tape (linen backed)—			
½-inch	3 tubes	5 tubes	7 tubes
1-inch	12 tubes	24 tubes	36 tubes
1½-inch	40 speed packs	77 speed packs	144 speed packs
2-inch	48 tubes	72 tubes	144 tubes
Ammonia ampules (box of 100)	1	1	2
Analgesic balm	*	*	*
Ankle wrap (96 inch [240 cm] for men;	20	30	40
(72 inch [180 cm] for women)	20	30	40
Antacid tablets	500	1,000	1,500
Antacid liquid (6-ounce)	2	3	4
Antiglare salve	5	10	15
Antiseptic powder (4-ounce)	1	2	3
Antiseptic soap (liquid, 6 ounce)	2	3	4
Aspirin tablets	300	600	1,200
Back braces	*	*	*
Bandages			
Band-Aids (sterile strips, box of 100)			
Assorted sizes	20 boxes	35 boxes	50 boxes
Butterfly (sterile strips)			
Medium	50	100	150
Small	50	100	150
Sterile pads (box of 100)			
2 by 2	5 boxes	10 boxes	15 boxes
3 by 3	5 boxes	10 boxes	15 boxes
Calamine lotion (4-ounce)	4	8	12
Chiropodist's felt, ⅛-inch (0.3 cm)	2 rolls	4 rolls	6 rolls
Collodion	1 pint	1 pint	2 pints
Combine (roll)	2 rolls	4 rolls	6 rolls
Cotton (sterile, 6-ounce)	2	3	4
Cotton-tipped applicators (100 box)	6	12	18
Drinking cups (paper, box of 100)	6	8	10
Elastic bandages			
3-inch (7.5 cm)	12	24	48
4-inch (10 cm)	36	72	144
6-inch (15 cm)	12	24	48
Elastic knee caps			
Large	*	*	*
Medium	*	*	*
Small	*	*	*
Elastic knee guards			
Large	*	*	*
Medium	*	*	*
Small	*	*	*
Elastic tape (3-inch [7.5 cm])	72 tubes	144 tubes	288 tubes
Elastic thigh caps			
Large	*	*	*
Medium	*	*	*
Small	*	*	*

*Should be on hand for each participant or funds available for purchase when need arises.

Item	Quantities for Number of Participants per Year		
	Up to 200	200 to 400	400 to 600
Elastic thigh guards			
Large	*	*	*
Medium	*	*	*
Small	*	*	*
Eye wash (6-ounce)	2	3	4
Felt (36 by 44 inches [90 by 110 cm])			
¼-inch (0.6 cm)	1 sheet	2 sheets	3 sheets
½-inch (1.25 cm)	1 sheet	2 sheets	3 sheets
Flexible collodion	1 pint	2 pints	2 pints
Fluromethane (4-ounce)	2	4	6
Foot antifungus powder (4-ounce)	2	3	4
Foot antifungus salve (2-ounce)	6	12	18
Fungicides			
Ointments or solutions	1 pint	6 pints	9 pints
Powders (4-ounce can)	4 cans	8 cans	12 cans
Gauze (roll)			
1-inch (2.5 cm)	25 rolls	50 rolls	100 rolls
2-inch (5 cm)	25 rolls	50 rolls	100 rolls
3-inch (7.5 cm)	25 rolls	50 rolls	100 rolls
Germicides			
Alcohol (isoproyl)	5 pints	10 pints	15 pints
Boric acid (eyewash)	1 pint	2 pints	3 pints
Merthiolate (liquid)	1 pint	2 pints	3 pints
Nitrotan (liquid)	1 pint	2 pints	3 pints
Peroxide	1 pint	2 pints	e pints
Grease (lubrication, 1-pound)	5	10	15
Gum rosin (adherent, 6-ounce)	1	1	1
Heat-treated plastic (¼-inch [0.6 cm]) (Orthoplast)	2 sheets	3 sheets	4 sheets
Heel cups (plastic)	5	10	15
Instant cold packs (dozen)	1	2	3
Internal agents			
Antacid tablets	200	300	500
Aspirin tablets	500	1000	1500
Dextrose tablets	2000	4000	6000
Knee braces (left and right)			
Large	*	*	*
Medium	*	*	*
Small	*	*	*
Liniment (6-ounce)	2	3	4
Massage lubricant	2 pints	4 pints	6 pints
Medicated ointments			
Athletic ointment	1 pound	2 pounds	3 pounds
Menthol ointment (4-ounce)	1	4	6
Zinc oxide	1 pound	2 pounds	2 pounds
Menthol spray (6-ounce)	2	3	4
Moleskin (12-inch [30 cm])	2 rolls	4 rolls	6 rolls
Neck and back board (emergency)	1	1	1
Nonadhering sterile pads, 3 by 3 (100)	2	4	6
Orthotic plastic material	*	*	*
Peroxide (6-ounce)	2	3	4
Petroleum (grease)	5 pounds	10 pounds	15 pounds

Continued.

TABLE 3-2, cont'd

Suggested yearly training supplies for individual programs

Item	Quantities for Number of Participants per Year		
	Up to 200	**200 to 400**	**400 to 600**
Powder (talcum)	1	1	1
Powdered rosin	*	*	*
Pretape material, 3 inch (7.5 cm)	1 case	2 cases	3 cases
Rubdown liniment (1-pint)	3	5	7
Shoulder harness	*	*	*
Slings (triangular bandages)	5	10	15
Splints, air	1 set	1 set	1 set
Sponge rubber (vinyls), 36 by 44 inches (90 by 110 cm)			
⅛-inch (0.3 cm)	1 sheet	2 sheets	3 sheets
¼-inch (0.6 cm)	1 sheet	2 sheets	3 sheets
½-inch (1.25 cm)	1 sheet	2 sheets	3 sheets
Stockinette (3-inch [7.5 cm] roll)	1	3	6
Sun lotion, e.g., Paba (4-ounce)	4	8	12
Tape adherent (clear)			
Bulk	1 pint	2 pints	3 pints
Spray cans (12-ounce)	10 cans	20 cans	30 cans
Tape remover	½ gallon	¾ gallon	1 gallon
Throat gargle, antiseptic (4-ounce)	4	7	12
Tongue depressors	500	1000	1500
Waterproof tape (1-inch [2.5 cm])	6 rolls	12 rolls	36 rolls

TABLE 3-3

Checklist for trainer's kit*

Item	Amount	Football-Rugby	Basketball-Volleyball-Soccer	Wrestling	Baseball	Track and Cross-country	Water Polo and Swimming	Gymnastics	Tennis
Adhesive tape									
½-inch (1.25 cm)	1 roll	X	X	X	X	X		X	X
1-inch (2.5 cm)	2 rolls	X	X	X	X	X		X	X
1½-inch (3.75 cm)	3 rolls	X	X	X	X	X		X	X
2-inch (5 cm)	1 roll	X	X	X	X	X		X	X
Alcohol (isopropyl)	4 ounces	X	X	X	X	X	X	X	X
Ammonia ampules	10	X	X	X	X	X	X	X	X
Analgesic balm	½ pound	X	X	X	X	X	X	X	X
Ankle wraps	2	X	X		X	X			X
Antacid tablets or liquid	100	X	X	X	X	X	X	X	X
Antiglare salve	4 ounces	X			X				
Antiseptic powder	4 ounces	X	X	X	X	X	X	X	X
Antiseptic soap (liquid)	4 ounces	X	X	X	X	X	X	X	X
Aspirin tablets	100	X	X	X	X	X	X	X	X
Band-Aids (assorted sizes)	2 dozen	X	X	X	X	X	X	X	X
Butterfly bandages (sterile strip)									
Medium	6 dozen	X	X	X	X	X		X	
Small	6 dozen	X	X	X	X	X		X	
Cotton (sterile)	1 ounce	X	X	X	X	X	X	X	X
Cotton-tipped applicators	2 dozen	X	X	X	X	X	X	X	X
Elastic bandages									
3-inch (7.5 cm)	2 rolls	X	X	X	X	X		X	X
4-inch (10 cm)	2 rolls	X	X	X	X	X		X	X
6-inch (15 cm)	2 rolls	X	X	X	X	X	X	X	X
Elastic tape roll (3-inch)	2 rolls	X	X	X	X	X		X	X
Eyewash	2 ounces	X	X	X	X	X	X	X	X
Felt									
¼-inch (0.6 cm)	6 by 6 sheet	X	X	X	X	X		X	X
½-inch (1.25 cm)	6 by 6 sheet	X							
Flexible collodion	2 ounces	X	X	X	X	X		X	
Foot antifungus powder	2 ounces	X	X	X	X	X	X	X	X
Forceps (tweezers)	1	X	X	X	X	X	X	X	X
Fungicide (salve)	2 ounces	X	X	X	X	X	X	X	X
Germicide (solution)	2 ounces	X	X	X	X	X	X	X	X
Grease (lubrication)		X	X	X	X	X			X
Gum rosin (adherent)	1 ounce	X	X		X	X			X
Heel cups	2				X	X		X	
Instant cold pack	2	X	X	X	X	X	X	X	X

*Extra amounts of items such as tape and protective padding are carried in other bags.

Continued.

TABLE 3-3, cont'd

Checklist for trainer's kit*

Item	Amount	Football-Rugby	Basketball-Volleyball-Soccer	Wrestling	Baseball	Track and Cross-country	Water Polo and Swimming	Gymnastics	Tennis
Liniment	2 ounces	X	X	X	X	X	X	X	X
Medicated salve	2 ounces	X	X	X	X	X	X	X	X
Mirror (hand)	1	X	X	X	X	X	X	X	X
Moleskin	6 by 6 sheet	X	X	X	X	X		X	X
Nonadhering sterile pad (3 by 3)	12	X	X	X	X	X		X	X
Oral screw	1	X	X	X	X	X	X	X	X
Oral thermometer	1	X	X	X	X	X	X	X	X
Peroxide	2 ounces	X	X	X	X	X	X	X	X
Salt tablets	50	X	X	X	X	X		X	X
Shoehorn	1	X	X	X	X	X			X
Sponge rubber									
⅛-inch (0.3 cm)	6 by 6 sheet	X	X	X	X	X		X	X
¼-inch (0.6 cm)	6 by 6 sheet	X	X	X	X	X		X	X
½-inch (1.25 cm)	6 by 6 sheet	X							
Sterile gauze pads (3 by 3)	6	X	X	X	X	X		X	X
Sun lotion	2 ounces	X	X	X	X	X	X	X	X
Surgical scissors	1	X	X	X	X	X	X	X	X
Tape adherent	6-ounce spray can	X	X	X	X	X		X	X
Tape remover	2 ounces	X	X	X	X	X	X	X	X
Tape scissors (pointed)	1	X	X	X	X	X	X	X	X
Tongue depressors	5	X	X	X	X	X	X	X	X
Triangular bandages	2	X	X	X	X	X	X	X	X
Waterproof tape (1-inch)	1 roll						X		

REFERENCES

1. Abdenour, T.E.: Computerized training room records, Ath. Train. **17**:191, 1982.
2. Gaunya, S.T.: The role of the trainer. In Vinger, P.F., and Hoerner, E.F. (editors): Sports injuries: the unthwarted epidemic, Boston, 1982, John Wright, PSG, Inc.

ADDITIONAL SOURCES

Bucher, C.A.: Administration of health and physical education programs and athletics, ed. 8, St. Louis, 1983, The C.V. Mosby Co.

Clarizo, M.: Computer use in athletic training education, Professional Preparation Conference, Newport Beach, Calif., March 1983, Greenville, N.C., National Athletic Trainers Association. (Cassette.)

Kanfush, P.: Selling athletic training in the high schools, Southwest Athletic Trainers' Association Meeting, January 1982, Greenville, N.C., National Athletic Trainers Association. (Cassette.)

Linder, C.W., et al.: Preparticipation health screening of young athletes, Am. J. Sports Med. **9**:187, 1981.

Pestolesi, R.A., and Sinclair, W.A.: Creative administration in physical education and athletics, Englewood Cliffs, N.J., 1978, Prentice-Hall, Inc.

Smilkstein, G.: Health evaluation of high school athletes, Phys. Sportsmed. **9**:73, 1981.

Part Two

GENERAL PRINCIPLES OF SPORTS MEDICINE

Part Two covers information that undergirds sports medicine and athletic training. Performance training, conditioning for injury prevention, nutrition, protective equipment, and the many psychological aspects of the athletic trainer's role are discussed.

Chapter 4

PHYSICAL CONDITIONING AND TRAINING

When you finish this chapter, you should be able to

Identify the most important elements of the physiological effects of training

Describe the most effective ways to achieve strength, flexibility, and endurance

Describe the physiological effects of stress, acclimatization, and jet lag

Explain the major physiological and morphological characteristics of the female athlete

Discuss the physiological implications of hard physical training and competition during childhood

Training is usually defined as a systematic process of repetitive, progressive exercise or work, involving also the learning process and acclimatization. The great sports medicine pioneer Dr. S.E. Bilik[2] concisely stated the primary objective of intense sports conditioning and training as follows: "To put the body with extreme and exceptional care under the influence of all the agents which promote its health and strength in order to enable it to meet extreme and exceptional demands upon it."

Through the use of systematic work increments, improved voluntary responses by the organs are attained; through constant repetition, the conscious movements become more automatic and more reflexive, requiring less concentration by the higher nerve centers and thus reducing the amount of energy expended, through the elimination of movements unnecessary of performance of the desired task. Increasing the strenuousness of exercise in the ways suggested is an application of the *overload principle,* which holds that an activity must always be upgraded to a consistently higher level through maximum or near-maximum stimulation. In this way the metabolic level and the organic responses can be increased.

Logan and Wallis[13] identified the *SAID principle,* which expressly relates to sports conditioning and training. SAID is an acronym for specific adaptation to imposed demands. The SAID principle indicates that conditioning and training are directed toward the specific demands of a given sport. "Strength, cardiovascular endurance, muscular endurance, flexibility, and neuromuscular skill may be developed by using this principle in the application of exercise."[12]

PHYSIOLOGICAL EFFECTS OF TRAINING

Proper training induces specific and identifiable physiological effects within the athlete.

Body Density

Over time, regular exercise produces density changes within the musculoskeletal system. These physical changes are of definite, recognizable types indicative of the sport for which the training has been designed. The muscles change in girth, showing increases in cross section and in density because of an increase in sarcoplasm. There is a reduction in the amount of adipose tissue in the body and an increase in the development of connective tissue within the muscle bundles, which adds to the general toughness of the muscle and enables it to better withstand the strains and stresses it must undergo.[17]

As a result of the muscle activity involved in training, additional stress is put on the bones. This results in an increase in the strength of the bones and also a rearrangement of the cancellous plates of the bones in accord with the stresses to which they have been subjected, thus decreasing the susceptibility to injury.

Ligaments also become denser through proper exercise. A process of minimal stretch and release tends to strengthen connective tissue fibers, whereas constant stretch weakens the fibers.

An immediate but temporary weight loss occurs at the onset of training as a result of water loss. This weight is immediately replaced on ingestion of food and water. However, the initial true loss of weight at the start of training is caused by a reduction in the amount of fat and is followed by a slow gain in weight, resulting from an increase in muscle bulk through development.

> Over time, regular exercise produces density changes within the musculoskeletal system.

Types of Muscle Fibers

Current opinion favors classifying muscle fibers into three basic types: the slow-twitch oxidative (SO) fiber, fast-twitch oxidative-glycolytic (FOG) fiber, and fast-twitch glycolytic (FG) fiber. Fast-twitch fibers are basically anaerobic; they do not depend on oxygen for their energy supply. In contrast, slow-twitch fibers are aerobic; they require oxygen for continued contraction. The preponderance of one fiber over another is related to inherited genetic factors that determine sports performance potential.[19] Fast-twitch fibers are responsible for speed or speed-power activities such as sprinting and weight lifting. Slow-twitch muscle fibers come into play in endurance activities such as long-distance running or cross-country skiing. The FOG fiber lies somewhere in the middle, but closer to the FG than the SO category.

The way in which an individual trains determines the type of fiber developed. Slow, low-intensity work primarily uses slow-twitch fibers. Fast-twitch fibers are suited for power and speed; slow-twitch fibers contract slowly and are fatigue resistant.[3] Athletes in ball sports exhibit a wide variety of muscle fiber types, and tend to be somewhere in the middle of the range.[3]

In physical restoration after injury or surgery, the type of activity the

> There are three basic types of muscle fibers:
> Slow-twitch oxidative (SO)
> Fast-twitch oxidative-glycolytic (FOG)
> Fast-twitch glycolytic (FG)

athlete participates in should be considered when planning the retraining program. Fast-twitch fibers increase in size with exercise and decrease in size with immobilization.[14] All work of low intensity may develop the slow-twitch fibers and fail to adequately develop strength and recruit fast-twitch fibers. The principle of specificity, which is discussed later in this chapter, must be adhered to.

Muscle Strength

Size alone is not an index of muscle strength.

Strength is defined as the capacity to exert force or as the ability to do work against resistance. The most noticeable change that takes place in the muscles as a result of regular and proper exercise is the increase in girth. However, this general rule—the girth of a muscle is proportional to the work done by it—does not always hold true. For example, the weight training of men is usually associated with marked muscular hypertrophy, whereas women who engage in heavy weight training tend to develop sizable increases in strength and have very limited hypertrophy. It has been postulated that the higher levels of testosterone (the predominant male androgen) found in the male are responsible for the muscle bulking.[26] Another important consideration is that a muscle will grow in size and strength only when a work load over and above any previous demands is placed on it. This principle of overload is one of the basic premises of strength training. Frequent repetitions, if not coincidental with increases in work load, are valueless for this purpose, although the total work load may be equal.

Size alone is not an index of the strength of a muscle, since muscles of the same size in an individual may vary considerably in strength because of the difference in the amounts of adipose or fatty tissue each contains. In essence, fat possesses an inhibiting quality with respect to muscle efficiency; it not only lacks contractile power but it also limits the speed and amount of contraction by acting as a friction brake.

Muscular strength can show an increase of three times or more without a proportional increase in muscle bulk necessarily being indicated. However, exercise must be performed against near-maximal and gradually increasing resistance. Such resistance can be obtained either by lifting, pulling, or pushing against some resistive force that requires near-maximal effort for the individual; by moving the body at an ever-increasing rate of speed that is approaching the maximum level of performance; or by a combination of the two. It is important for the trainer to know that a number of factors are involved in strength training. The speed, duration, number of repetitions, and vigor or force with which exercises are performed will determine the outcome of the program. The variable of individual difference is another factor that will affect the final result. Two athletes of the same gender following identical programs will not develop strength at the same rate, in the same manner, or to the same degree, because of varying inherent characteristics.

General consensus favors the current theory that hypertrophy, the increase in muscle cross section, is caused by a development of the existing constituent fibers when strength exercises are employed and by an increase in the toal number of capillaries called into play when exercises of endurance are employed. In other words, a gain in strength is accompanied by a significant increase in both the size of fibers and the number of capillaries in the muscle and by a resultant gain not only in power but also in speed and endurance.

Muscle Contraction and Exercise

Exercise for the development of strength is related to the type of muscle contraction.

Isometric contraction   Performance of an **isometric exercise** generates heat and energy by forcefully contracting the muscle in a **static** position, that is, with no change in the length of the muscle or in the angle of the joint at which the contraction takes place. Attempting to lift or push an object that cannot be moved places the muscles in a state of isometric, or static, contraction. Isometric exercise has been shown to be most effective when a maximal contraction is held for 6 seconds and the contraction repeated from five to ten times daily. Strength gained through an isometric program is specific to the joint angle at which the contraction takes place, so it is advisable to exercise throughout the full range of joint motion during each workout.

Isotonic contraction   Shortening or lengthening the muscle through its complete range involves an **isotonic contraction.** Isotonic exercises involve moving a resistive force, either a part of the body or some extraneous object. This type of contraction is referred to also as a *dynamic* contraction, since definite and easily discerned movement takes place. An isotonic exercise does not involve the same fibers throughout a particular movement because the load remains constant regardless of the angle of contraction or the degree of fatigue engendered; consequently, the greatest strength gain appears in those fibers used in the initial part of the movement to overcome inertia. The least gain is at the midpoint of the contraction.

The primary value of performing isotonic contraction in exercise is the increase or maintenance of joint range of motion. In addition, isotonic movements tend to promote muscular circulation and endurance. In performing an isotonic movement against resistance, the muscle should be first placed in stretch to ensure maximal innervation of muscle fibers. After full stretch, the body part is *concentrically* moved as far as possible and then *eccentrically* moved to the beginning position. A general rule for the most effective muscle training is to move the resistance as smoothly and quickly as possible and return it at a much slower rate. Slow, eccentric muscle contraction against resistance is known as **negative resistance,** enervating more muscle fibers than positive, or concentric, contraction.

Recovery from muscular fatigue is more rapid in isotonic exercises than in isometric. Isotonic exercises wherein the muscle works throughout its full range against an increasingly greater resistance are known as progressive resistance exercises (PRE) and were introduced by De Lorme and Watkins.[4] This type of exercise, and its many variations, has been shown to be superior to the isometric form for the development of strength and endurance. The De Lorme method makes use of a series of three sets of exercises with ten repetitions each. The first set is per-

isometric exercise
Contracts the muscle statically without changing its length.

isotonic exercise
Shortens and lengthens the muscle through a complete range of motion.

negative resistance
Slow eccentric muscle contraction against resistance.

formed against a resistance half of one's maximum, the second at three-quarters maximum, and the final set against full maximum. When one is able to successfully complete the full series, a weight increment (usually 5 pounds) is progressively added to the maximum. Numerous variations are employed today, but none has been significantly different in its effectiveness. A training program using three sets each workout produces greater strength improvement than a program using one or two sets. Workouts three to four times weekly, with four to eight repetitions, produces the greatest strength.

isokinetic exercise
Accommodating resistance
exercise (ARE).

Isokinetic contraction Isokinetic muscle contraction occurs through an *accommodating resistance exercise (ARE)*. It offers all the advantages of both isometric and isotonic exercises without their inherent weaknesses.[8,21] This method more nearly uses total involvement of the muscle fibers, since the resistance varies according to the angle of pull and the degree of fatigue developed throughout the exercise. The inertia of the resistance, a definite factor in the isotonic exercise, is not a factor in isokinetics, since the resistance automatically adjusts to the degree of force exerted against it, thus maintaining a constant and consistent force. Exercises can be performed throughout the entire range of the performer's speed, since most isokinetic exercise equipment has variable speed adjustments. A decided advantage of this type of exercise is that muscle soreness does not result. It is postulated that the muscle has a brief period of relaxation between repetitions, thus allowing the blood to circulate freely throughout the fibers and cleanse away the accumulated lactic acid and metabolites from the muscle cells. Isotonic exercises do not permit such relaxation, hence there is a buildup of fatigue products. Neither isokinetic nor isotonic resistance are superior to one another. The goal of training must be satisfied according to the SAID principle. Over the last few years, isokinetic resistance exercising has found a valuable place in rehabilitation, whereas free weights employing isotonic principles have become increasingly popular in sports conditioning. (See Chapter 15 for further discussion.)

TABLE 4-1

Comparison of strength exercises

	Isometric	Isotonic	Isokinetic	Variable Resistance (Nautilus)
Resistance	Accommodating at one angle	Constant	Accommodating through range of motion	Fixed ration through range of motion
Velocity (speed)	Zero	Variable	Constant	Variable
Reciprocal contraction	None	None	Yes	None
Eccentric contraction	None	Yes	None	Yes

Plyometric exercise For some years **plyometric exercises** have been in vogue in Europe. These exercises are now becoming increasingly popular in the United States. This type of exercise produces an isometric-type overload, using the myotatic, or stretch, reflex. By means of an eccentric (lengthening) contraction, the muscle is fully stretched ("on stretch") immediately preceding the concentric (shortening) contraction. The greater the stretch put on the muscle from its resting length immediately before the concentric contraction, the greater the load the muscle can lift or overcome. The rate of stretch is more critical than the magnitude of the stretch.[27]

Ways of Achieving Strength

Individuals can gain strength in numerous ways. This discussion briefly describes the more prevalent ways strength is developed; they are the nonequipment, equipment, and combined nonequipment and equipment approaches.

Nonequipment approaches Three nonequipment approaches are presently employed in sports conditioning: calisthenics, or free exercise; partner or reciprocal, resistance; and self-resistance.

Calisthenics, or free exercise, is one of the more easily available means of developing strength. Isotonic movement exercises can be graded according to intensity by using gravity as an aid, ruling gravity out, moving against gravity, or using the body or body part as a resistance against gravity. Most calisthenics require the athlete to support the body or move the total body against the force of gravity. Push-ups are a good example of a vigorous antigravity free exercise. To be considered maximally effective, the isotonic calisthenic exercise, as in all types of exercise, must be performed in an exacting manner and in full range of motion. In most cases, ten or more repetitions are performed for each exercise and repeated in sets of two or three.

Some free exercises have a holding phase instead of employing a full range of motion. Examples of these are back extensions and sit-ups. When the exercise produces maximal muscle tension, it is held between 6 and 10 seconds and then repeated one to three times.

Partner, or reciprocal, resistance exercise is an excellent approach to gaining strength and flexibility, such as in neuromuscular facilitation. It requires no equipment other than a partner who is about equal in size and strength. It is often highly motivating for both participants, and all types of exercise can be engaged using this method. When performing isokinetic resistance, the body part involved is taken into a stretched position by the partner. Resistance is accommodated through a complete range of motion. Three bouts of resistance usually are given for each exercise.

Equipment approaches Numerous devices are designed to overload the musculature and develop strength. These range from individual pieces to entire conditioning systems and are generally categorized as isotonic/isometric and isokinetic.

Isotonic/isometric equipment are almost too numerous to mention. Some of the more standard stationary apparatus, chinning bars, parallel bars, and stall bars, have numerous possibilities for increasing strength

Relaxation training is an essential aspect of any sports-conditioning program.

Another standard piece of equipment is the wall pulley weight, which progressively exercises the major joints and muscles.

Free weights are very popular and are used for developing strength through both isotonic and isometric contraction. Sports programs commonly have a variety of free weights, including dumbbells (Fig. 4-1) and barbells (Fig. 4-2). Dumbbells range from 2 to 2½ pounds to 50 to 75 pounds or more, and barbells range from 25 or 30 pounds to well over 200 pounds. Some people argue that free weights do not provide consistent muscle development through a full range of motion; however, they do help in the development of balance and coordination and exercise stabilizing and accessory muscles, which machine systems often do not provide.

Machine exercise systems, such as the *Universal Gym*, allow a variety of exercise possibilities such as sit-ups, parallel bar dips, bench presses, pull-downs, rowing exercises, knee extensions, knee curls and biceps curls, as well as arm pressing (Fig. 4-3). The Universal Gym employs graduated weights that are lifted by heavy cables as the athlete applies force against a bar.

Isokinetic machines provide an accommodating muscle resistance through a full range of motion. A maximal load is produced as the athlete dynamically performs work. The amount of resistance depends on the extent of force applied by the athlete. Machines designed for isokinetic resistance develop flexibility and coordination, as well as strength.

The *Nautilus machine* is one of the newest and most popular exercise systems. Nautilus training machines provide full range of movement and direct resistance to specific muscles or muscle groups. Both concentric and eccentric muscle contraction is maximally provided by special cams and

Figure 4-1

Dumbbell weights can
provide a variety of isotonic
resistance exercises.

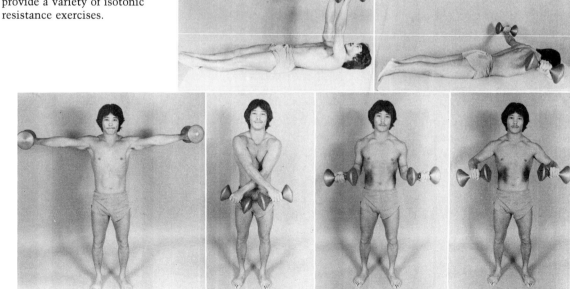

Figure 4-2

Barbell weights provide
opportunities for isotonic
resistive exercise.

Figure 4-3

The Universal Gym system
provides a variety of
resistance exercise
possibilities.

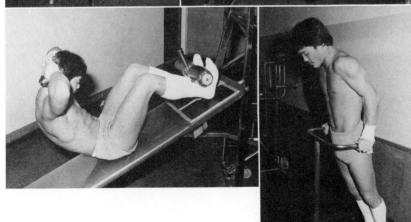

General Principles of Sports
Medicine

Figure 4-4

The Nautilus exercise system
uses variable resistance.

counterweights. In this system, negative, or eccentric, work is accentuated. Although Nautilus is not an isokinetic system, it does provide some variable resistance through a full range of motion. Each machine provides body stabilization to afford isolation of a specific muscle or muscle group (Fig. 4-4). This musculature isolation emphasizes negative, or eccentric, contraction.[20] Because the amount of resistance varies during a full range of motion, resistance is indicated by the number of plates lifted, rather than the number of pounds.

Other examples of exercise systems, such as the *Mini-Gym*, provide opportunities for specific strength development related to sports activities. Using variable resistance devices, the athlete can concentrate on specific sports requirements (Fig. 4-5).

Figure 4-4

For legend see opposite page.

Continued.

Speed Training

Speed differs from endurance in that it requires the expenditure of an enormous amount of energy in a short time and is specific to the area developed. This requires performances of extremely short duration, such as a swim sprint, dash, or rope climb, to rely almost exclusively on the oxygen within the tissues. The anaerobic activity depends on the immediate chemical release of oxidative energy by phosphocreatine and ATP, a high-energy phosphate compound, for instant use by the muscles. The amount of energy released, although high, cannot meet the tremendous requirements of prolonged intensive exercise, thus calling the fast-twitch muscles into play.

Figure 4-4, cont'd

The Nautilus exercise system uses variable resistance.

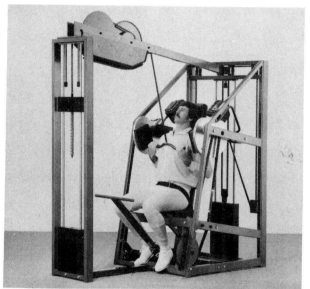

Age is a factor in attaining speed. An individual's ability in speed reaches its peak when he or she is about 20 years of age. Speed depends not only on a considerable amount of anaerobic activity, but also on the resiliency and responsiveness of the circulatory system and reaction time, flexibility, and strength. Speed ability declines rapidly after 28 years of age because it imposes a considerable task on the heart and there is a gradual increase in loss of vascular resiliency.

As previously stated, the strength gain of muscles is accompanied by a

Figure 4-4, cont'd

For legend see opposite page.

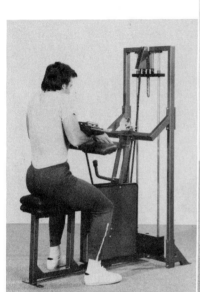

significant increase in both the size of fibers and the number of capillaries. This gain in strength results in *concomitant gains in speed* and in endurance. In training for speed one should train principally for strength by means of overload and by application of the principles employed for improving strength and power for endurance. Speed activities should be added to the program to enable the athlete to increase the ability to produce en-

Figure 4-5

For legend see opposite page.

ergy more rapidly and to accumulate a greater oxygen debt. On this basis it would be consistent to place athletes who participate in activities that require great speed into an intensive strength program, concentrating principally on the muscle groups most called on in the particular activity.

Strength training not only involves weight training or lifting, but also running and other activities to achieve the desired results, since PRE makes extremely limited demands, if any at all, on the cardiorespiratory system. Therefore, it is good practice for a sprinter to compete in cross-country in the off-season, as well as run long distances that will make heavy demands on the body during the regular competitive season. In these activities the athlete will be developing strength and endurance. A strength-endurance program of this kind must be carefully correlated with sufficient sprint activities to develop and maintain a high rate of cardiorespiratory response and efficiency.

Flexibility Training

Flexibility is defined as the range of movement of a specific joint or group of joints influenced by the associated bones and bony structures and the physiological characteristics of the muscles, tendons, ligaments, and the various other collagenous tissues surrounding the joint. Studies have indicated that an increase in the flexibility of joints tends to decrease the injuries to those joints. In most instances it is also contended that an increase in flexibility contributes to better athletic performance. Both of these considerations are important to the trainer. In general, the flexible athlete, is less injury prone and more likely to perform optimally when compared to the inflexible athlete.

Figure 4-5

Systems such as the Mini-Gym provide the athlete with opportunities to concentrate on specific sports requirements.

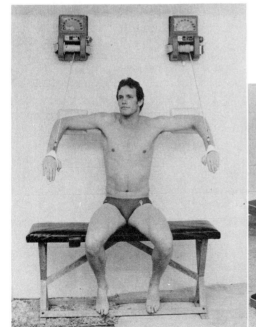

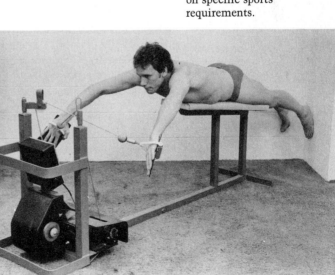

Good flexibility usually indicates that there are no adhesions or abnormalities present in or around the joints and that there are no serious muscular limitations. This allows the body to move freely and easily through the full range of joint flexion and extension without any unnecessary restrictions in the joints or the adjacent tissues.

An increase in flexibility must accompany an increase of strength, or the range of motion may be considerably affected. Exercises of flexibility can achieve their goal without decreasing strength. Conversely, exercises for the acquisition of great strength such as is sought by some weight lifters, without the use of accompanying movements designed to maintain and increase the range of joint motion, can and will result in the condition commonly called "muscle-boundedness." In this condition, because of the enormous bulk and inelasticity of the muscles, tendons, and ligaments, there is a decided inability to obtain complete flexibility and freedom of joint mobility.

An increase in flexibility is important to the athlete. With more flexibility the runner can increase stride, the hurdler can effect a more economical flight, and the swimmer can produce a better leg kick and a more efficient arm stroke. The gymnast, the wrestler, and the various other athletes all depend to a large degree on good flexibility and range of motion.

Types of Flexibility Training

There is some disagreement as to the best type of stretching procedure to use for improving flexibility. The ballistic stretch, in which the body momentum forces the muscle groups into as much extensibility as can be tolerated, has been used for many years. Evidence indicates that this type of exercise, although it will increase flexibility, may also induce muscle tears as a result of misjudging the stretch tolerance of the tissues and/or failing to control the force of the body momentum. Therefore use of the ballistic stretch should be discouraged.

The gradual (sometimes called "static") stretch, in which a position of extreme stretch on a given muscle group is assumed and held for a period of time, is thought by many to be as effective as the ballistic stretch and without the possibility of preactivity muscle strains or tears.[5] A convenient rule to use in setting up a flexibility program is to determine the comfortable range of motion for each joint, then set a goal to increase that range of motion in all directions.

Joint flexibility may be varied or affected by a number of factors: joint problems hereditary joint structural differences, elasticity of body connective tissue, reciprocal muscle coordination, and muscle viscosity. Hyperflexibility should be avoided. Such excessive flexibility contributes little to performance and can indeed increase susceptibility to joint injury. There appears to be no one single factor that either increases or decreases flexibility. Although good flexibility can be attained in a relatively short time, in most instances it is lost rather quickly unless the athlete maintains a regular regimen of stretching exercises. Several objective methods are available for measuring flexibility. The student or trainer who wishes to use such tests should refer to current books on measurement in the fields of physical education, adapted physical education, or physical therapy.

Neuromuscular Relaxation and Psychological Readiness

Relaxation is an essential aspect of any sports-conditioning program. Coordinated movement implies the ability to reciprocally contract agonist and relax antagonist muscles efficiently. This also can be called differential relaxation. Relaxation and the reduction of abnormal muscle tension allows greater lung inspiration and expiration, making the exchange of oxygen and carbon dioxide more efficient.

Establishing an attitude of readiness or "mind-set" (commonly referred to as "psyching up"), in respect to physical performance is of utmost importance to the athlete. The close relationship between emotions and muscles has long been recognized and has had considerable study. Thinking about a projected physical action affects the muscles involved. Motivational stressors that are based on *success* can induce a greater work output in the individual and serve to increase the gross mechanical and physiological efficiency, whereas motivational stressors that indicate *failure* may tend to promote an emotional reaction that would circumvent the increased gross mechanical efficiency. If the emotions are developed in intensity and then properly channeled, they can be of considerable aid to physical performance. Stress reactions are similar in both sexes. A positive attitude on the part of the athlete preparing for competition aids considerably in reducing excess tension. The champion athlete "thinks" like a champion and therefore develops a winning attitude. Relaxation also promotes better circulation, heart rate, and blood pressure. Volitional relaxation allows for neuromuscular skill learning to also take place more efficiently. An athlete who is tense and unable to relax may be more prone to a variety of musculoskeletal injuries. (See Chapter 8.)

Endurance and Stamina

The degree of ability to withstand fatigue is inherited, and the basis of the fatigue pattern is in each individual's constitution. Two factors modify an individual's capacity for improving endurance: (1) the ability to endure the pain and concomitant discomforts of fatigue while endeavoring to improve the level of work tolerance, and (2) the body's ability to effect the necessary homeostatic adjustments, which can enable an athlete to increase energy production to as much as twenty times the resting level when such a demand is made.

Endurance is the ability of the body to undergo prolonged activity or to resist stresses set up as a result of prolonged activity. Endurance involves a number of elements, each of which is partially responsible for success or failure in sustaining physical performance. Endurance primarily depends on the various aspects of cardiac efficiency, which in turn exerts influence on the performance of the other portions of the human organism.[3]

Training or conditioning builds a given economy—an efficiency in body adaptability—which is important as the body adjusts to the continued and prolonged stresses put on it in performing an activity that requires all-out or near-maximal performance over a considerable period of time. As a result of careful conditioning, the onset of fatigue is considerably delayed and the athlete is able to maintain a high rate of performance over a long period of time.

endurance
The ability of the body to undergo prolonged activity or to resist stresses set up as a result of prolonged activity.

General Principles of Sports
Medicine

As a muscle tires, it loses
some of its ability to relax.

Exercises for endurance improve muscle tonus. The improvement is primarily caused by functional involvement of more motor units as a result of work increase. Work increase improves circulation by calling into play more capillaries, thus providing the working muscles with more oxygen and fuel and facilitating removal of the metabolic by-products of exercise.

As a muscle tires, it loses some of its ability to relax. The character of a muscle is indicated not only by its ability to produce power over a protracted period of time but also by its capacity to concurrently maintain its elasticity. As the muscle works, it restores its own oxygen and fuel supplies and disposes of lactic acid and other metabolic products. As long as these two processes continue to operate at basically the same rate, the muscle can continue to work with efficiency. However, when an imbalance is reached in which the waste product accumulation rate is greater than the oxygen and fuel intake, physiological equilibrium (homeostasis) is upset and fatigue sets in. In fatigue the reaction time slows down and is accompanied by stiffening or inability of the muscle to reach a condition of relaxation. This stiffening or incomplete relaxation, coupled with a reduced ability to respond to stimulation, is one of the contributing factors to athletic injury.

Respiratory Response to Training

Training increases vital capacity (the maximal volume of air the lungs exchange in one respiratory cycle) and aids materially in establishing economy in the oxygen requirement. The conditioned athlete operates primarily on a "pay as you go" basis as a result of his increased stroke volume and reduced heartbeat. An increase in the contractile power of the respiratory muscles, particularly the diaphragm, results in deeper respiration per breath. This enables the athlete to use a greater lung capacity and, consequently, to effect increased economy in the use of oxygen. The untrained individual attempts to compensate by increasing the rate of respiration and soon reaches a state of considerable respiratory indebtedness, which severely encumbers or even halts performance.

The trained individual, through aerobic endurance training, is able to establish a steady state of oxygen consumption at higher rates of work because of greater mechanical efficiency in performing the required task. This permits more work with a lower expenditure of energy or oxygen consumption. Since less oxygen is used for a given task, a greater margin of reserve and continued high-level performance for a longer period of time, without distress, can be attained.

Endurance-type exercises will
produce significant changes
in the cardiorespiratory
system.

Endurance-type exercises will produce significant changes in the cardiorespiratory system but will have little effect on muscle strength per se. Conversely, strength (weight) training brings about gains in muscular strength but has no significant influence on the cardiorespiratory systems.

Endurance training not only significantly improves maximal oxygen consumption but is a key factor in injury prevention. The fatigued athlete not only has a diminished reaction capacity but because of muscular fatigue is less able to withstand extraneous forces so that an injury can be sustained under circumstances in which a better conditioned performer will not. Aerobic endurance training uses slow interval training. An aerobic program coupled with a good weight training program should condition the cardiorespiratory system and the neuromuscular system adequately for competition.

Anaerobic training, which enables one to sustain an oxygen debt, can be accomplished through using a fast interval program (sprints alternated with jogging or running). Anaerobic capacity is vital in all athletics, since it not only permits one to sustain a greater oxygen debt but comes into play in situations where oxygen delivery may prove to be insufficient.

Anaerobic training can be accomplished through using a fast interval program.

Cardiac and Circulatory Response to Training

Heart size will increase as the result of a training program. This is neither undesirable nor indicative of any dangerous or unusual propensity for cardiac anomalies. To the contrary, the increased heart size is caused by the thickening of the heart muscle. It results in a more powerful contraction and, accordingly, a larger volume output of blood per stroke. In other words, as a result of training or conditioning, the heart becomes considerably more efficient in its operation. Consequently, it is capable of circulating more blood with fewer contractions.

In performing a set amount of work over a period of time, the heart rate becomes slower as training progresses. Training reduces the pulse rate, sometimes by as much as ten to twenty beats per minute, during the period between pretraining and post-training measurements. The overall efficiency of the heart is high because of the slower heart rate and the more efficient use of oxygen by the coronary arteries, although the consumption of oxygen by the heart itself rises considerably with the increase in work load. One of the advantages of training is that whereas the heart rate does not show an immediate and rapid increase at the start of severe exercise, it does return to normal more rapidly than the heart of the untrained person. Hence, recuperative power becomes an important factor in proper conditioning. Precluding organic or functional anomalies, there is no evidence that strenuous or severe exercise can injure the heart of a young adult.

Training exerts considerable effect on blood pressure. Because of the increase in the systemic system, as a result of using blood from the splanchnic pool, there is more volume under higher pressure. This results in better transportation of oxygen to the tissues, when it is needed, and in more efficient removal of metabolites. As the result of prolonged effort in the untrained individual, systolic pressure falls progressively, an indication of approaching exhaustion. On the other hand, training retards this phenomenon and work can be continued for a longer time with scarcely any perceptible changes in blood pressure. During exercises of endurance, the rise in blood pressure is much greater than during exercises of speed. Many factors tend to modify the response of blood pressure to various forms of exercise. Studies have indicated that the rate, intensity, duration, and state of training of the performer will determine the blood pressure response.

Many factors modify the response of blood pressure to various forms of exercise:
  Rate
  Intensity
  Duration
  Level of training

Major Principles of Physical Training

In terms of recent research, it appears that most coaches fail to work their athletes hard enough. They are concerned with the problems of staleness and lack of motivation and with the fear of engendering some type of abnormal physiological condition; as a result, they tend to underwork their athletes. High school football players who participate in an exceedingly intensive preseason conditioning program for 6 to 8 weeks before the start of the playing season have much greater strength and stamina throughout the entire season than do players who begin an identical conditioning program only 2 or 3 weeks before the start of the season.

Intensity

The intensity at which an activity is performed is probably the most critical of the various factors that determine the amount of positive physical change to take place. Relatively few individuals ever approach their maximum in terms of work capacity during training. The various physiological and psychological changes that must necessarily be effected for greater endurance will come about only through an intensive program of work based on the overload principle of progressively increasing the loads, the number of repetitions, and the rate and intensity of these repetitions. This system applies regardless of the type of activity. There is no shortcut to attaining high standards of performance. It is a long, arduous process to which athletes must dedicate themselves without reservations if they desire to become a top-flight performer.

Specificity

Physical training for a particular sport in no way guarantees that the level of fitness reached or the degree of neuromuscular skill achieved will be adequate for other sports. Repeated practice of a skill as one attempts to perfect that skill involves a biological programming and reprogramming as the skill is constantly repeated and the movement/skill pattern is developed and eventually controlled by conditioned reflexes, thus gradually eliminating conscious control. Specificity applies to all physical activities; hence, if one wishes to improve speed, practice must be geared to speed. If endurance or strength is the objective, then practice must involve constantly raising the levels of performance in endurance or strength activities. Practice must be related to the dominant features of the specific skill itself. Specificity means relating the specific physical requirements of an activity to a practice pattern that will elicit the specific biological responses that produce that skill. To be effective, any training program involves three considerations[21]:

1. The program must be specifically planned in terms of the sport itself.
2. The program must be geared specifically to the individual using it.
3. If one wishes to increase strength at all limb speeds, isokinetic high-speed training should be used.

The use of mimetic training activities assists not only in developing the necessary neuromuscular skills but also in motivating the athlete.

Consistency

Athletes must train with as much regularity as possible. Depending on the requirements of the sport, training might be engaged in a number of times per week. Regularity of "workouts" is dispersed, and rest periods serve to apply the overload principle, producing a positive stress on the body.

Training for optimal performance requires consistency.

Overload Progression

All training must apply the SAID principle, overloading the body gradually over a long period of time. Whether for power or endurance, the work should be performed with a progressively increased load. Exercise having a specific pattern in terms of either movement, force, duration, or speed is employed to produce training results that will be peculiar to that exercise alone.

SPECIAL PHYSIOLOGICAL CONSIDERATIONS
Physiological Stress

One area that concerns the trainer is the effect of emotional factors on physical performance. Selye[24] has defined these diverse stimuli, which tend to induce psychological or physiological conditions that upset the internal environment (homeostasis) of the body, as *stressors*. Sport is a stressor; it upsets the homeostatic balance, with physical, psychic, and social stressors acting as an integrated whole to produce a response.

The various emotional states are sustained by extensive physiological adjustments comparable to the changes evoked by work and exercise. These changes are controlled to a great extent by the autonomic nervous system and include acceleration and strengthening of the heartbeat, a rise in blood pressure, a release of glucose from the liver, the secretion of a small amount of epinephrine (adrenaline) from the adrenal glands, and a relaxation of the muscles in the bronchial tubes, which permits easier breathing. These changes permit the body to function more efficiently under conditions of stress.

In addition to the physiological adaptation to the stress of exercise, there is an involvement of the higher centers of the nervous system. Continued repetitive acts become reflexive and require less concentration on their performance. This results in improved coordination, which, in turn, is reflected in more skillful and economical performance.

Acclimatization

An increasing problem in sports is acclimatization. Today athletes and sports teams are traveling farther afield in search of competition. As a result they often encounter abrupt changes in climate. In the United States it is usual for teams to leave severe wintry conditions and engage teams enjoying a subtropical climate in which playing conditions on the stadium floor approach 100° F (37.78° C). Conversely, teams from subtropical areas find themselves competing on frozen turf and encountering subfreezing temperatures. It is evident that athletes or teams competing under foreign climatic conditions will not perform as well as would be expected, unless some preliminary acclimatization takes place. This is probably more evident when the individual moves from a cold to a hot climate.

Evidence is increasing to indicate that an individual can, within a 4- to 5-day period, be completely acclimatized artificially through performing vigorous work in a hot room and that such acclimatization will suffice a minimum of 3 weeks in cold weather. This would indicate that, when competition is scheduled for a foreign hot climate, it is necessary to provide artificial acclimatization if par performance is expected. Acclimatization of

General Principles of Sports
Medicine

Cold does not affect
performance as much as heat
does.

this type results in lower rectal temperatures, more stable blood pressure for any given work load, and lower work-pulse rates.

Cold does not affect performance as much as heat does. Normally, the increase in metabolic heat is the result of activity, and the necessary heat loss is carried by radiation, convection, and sweating. The important consideration, when performing in cold environment, is to dress in such a manner as to secure heat retention during warm-up activities and rest periods and still permit heat dissipation during competition.

Training at high altitudes presents other problems of acclimatization. High altitudes often place unusual demands on the body when functioning in an atmosphere where partial oxygen pressure is significantly decreased from sea level. The ability of an athlete to use quickly and effectively the oxygen taken in is the critical factor in endurance. At an altitude of 2300 meters (7347 feet) the partial pressure of oxygen is approximately 20% less than that at sea level. Therefore, the athlete must take in not only a much greater volume of air, but must also effect a more efficient extraction and use of the oxygen in the ambient air if a sea-level performance is to be equaled in those events in which endurance is a requisite. It has been shown that in running events of 800 meters or more and in swimming events greater in distance than 200 meters a decrease in performance will occur at medium altitude. The greater the performance demand on endurance, the greater the decrement in performance. In events that are basically anaerobic, such as sprints, no significant decrements in performance are found. In fact, the decreased density of the air gives some advantages in the sprints and field events. Recovery times in all events are considerably longer than at sea level.

If activities requiring more than 1½ minutes of constant sustained effort are to be performed at an altitude of 3000 feet or more, the athlete should undergo training for a minimum of 3 to 5 weeks at an altitude comparable to that at which the competition will be held. Some changes in the techniques of performance also are needed, particularly in breathing patterns.[23] This is especially true in swimming where the strokes must be adapted to a different breathing rhythm. One advantage of altitude training has been the decided improvement of performance at sea level. Intermittent sea-level stays of as long as 11 days resulted in better performances and did not interfere with altitude acclimatization. There appears to be considerable variability between individuals in respect to acclimatization, especially in the ability to tolerate an intense performance tempo for long periods of time at high altitudes. This probably explains the failure of some top athletes to perform as well in long distance events at high altitude as they do near sea level.

Jet Lag

For some people, air travel
induces physiological stress
that results in a syndrome
called *circadian
dysrhythmia*, which reflects
desynchronization of one's
biological and biophysical
time clock.

Jet power has made it possible to travel thousands of miles in just a few hours. Athletes and athletic teams are now quickly transported from one end of the country to the other and to foreign lands. For some, such travel induces a particular physiological stress, resulting in a syndrome that is identified as a *circadian dysrhythmia* and that reflects a desynchronization of one's biological and biophysical time clock.

The term *circadian* (from the Latin *circa dies*, "about a day") implies a period of time of approximately 24 hours. The body maintains many cyclic mechanisms (circadian rhythms) that follow a pattern, for example, the daily rise and fall of body temperature or the tidal ebb and flow of the cortical steroid secretion (which produces other effects on the metabolic system that are in themselves cyclical in nature). Body mechanisms adapt at varying rates to time changes. Some, like protein metabolism, adjust immediately whereas others take time, like the rise and fall of body temperature, which takes about 8 days. Others, such as the adrenal hormones, which regulate metabolism, and other body functions, may take as long as 3 weeks. Even intellectual proficiency or the ability to think clearly is cyclical. Younger individuals adjust more rapidly to time zone changes than do older people, although the differences are not great.[10] The stress induced in jet travel occurs only when flying either east or west at high speed. Travel north or south has no effect on the body unless several time zones are crossed in an east or west progression. The changes in time zones, illumination, and environment prove somewhat disruptive to the human physiological mechanisms, particularly when one flies through five or more time zones, as occurs in some international travel. Some people are much more susceptible to the syndrome than are others, but the symptoms can be sufficiently disruptive to interfere with one's ability to perform maximally in a competitive event. The symptoms can be any one or a combination of the following: anorexia, severe headache, blurred vision, dizziness, insomnia, or extreme fatigue. For international travel a full day of recuperation should be allowed before indulging in any type of activity. It is suggested that these preventive measures be followed:

1. Depart well rested.
2. Choose daylight departures when possible.
3. Exercise moderation in eating and drinking both before and during the flight.
4. Plan no strenuous activities for the first 24 hours after arrival.

Athletes who have particular health problems such as asthma, diabetes, epilepsy, hypertension, or peptic ulcer should have medical attention if they are competing at a time of day unusual to their regular practice or competition or if traveling across time zones.[10]

Symptoms of circadian dysrhythmia can be any one or a combination of the following:
Anorexia
Severe headache
Blurred vision
Dizziness
Insomnia
Extreme fatigue

THE WOMAN ATHLETE AND PHYSICAL TRAINING

Girls and women can successfully compete in strenuous athletic activities at the highest levels of physical performance without physiological or psychological harm.

Feminine and Masculine Characteristics

Contrary to lay opinion, participation in sports does not masculinize women. Within a sex, the secretion of testosterone, progesterone, androgen, and estrogen varies considerably, accounting for significant variation in terms of muscularity and general morphology among males and females. Girls whose physiques are more masculine are stronger per unit of weight than either girls who are less masculine or boys who display considerable femininity of build.[9] Those who are of masculine type often enter sports

Many girls and women fear
that vigorous exercise will
result in bulging muscles, but
such overdevelopment is
relatively uncommon and the
result of arduous and
concentrated training over
many years.

and are usually quite successful because of mechanical advantages resulting from their masculine structure. However, such types are the exception; the majority of women participants in sports possess a feminine body build.

Many girls and women fear the development of unsightly, bulging muscles should they exercise vigorously. They point to the pronounced muscular definition of the quadriceps and the gastrocnemius seen in some women who have had intensive and prolonged ballet or dance training. Actually, such overdeveloped musculature is relatively uncommon and the result of long, arduous, and concentrated training for many years. Such excessive development is not a concomitant of sports competition. One need only observe some of the outstanding girl and women athletes to obtain complete refutation of such a premise. Indeed, physical activity develops femininity and grace. *Inherent endocrinological and morphological factors, not physical activity, are responsible for femininity and masculinity.*[21]

Running

Many girls often have difficulty in running, particularly after adolescence. The female pelvis is frequently broader and shallower, which causes the femur to articulate at a more acute angle than does that of the male, resulting in a mechanical disadvantage; the obliquity of the femur tends to induce a lateral sway of the body in running. Frequently failure to lift the knees sufficiently and compensation by casting the lower leg and foot out to the side in the forward-carry phase causes the femur to be rotated inwardly. The casting accentuates the trunk sway, which becomes quite pronounced. In conditioning and coaching, good knee elevation, directly forward, coupled with straightforward foot placement, should be stressed.

Many girls, as they run, tend to hug the upper arms and elbows tight against the body and swing the forearms out to the sides, meanwhile vigorously rotating the upper trunk and the shoulders in an attempt to offset the inward thigh rotation. In addition to showing the exaggerated trunk rotation, some girls tend to keep the clenched fists tight against the chest, meanwhile alternately thrusting the elbows forward in a vigorous manner. Stressing relaxation and a proper arm swing, linked with a strong high forward knee lift, will increase the efficiency and speed of the runner.

Jumping

One of the arguments frequently advanced against sports for women raises the point that activities such as the high jump or broad jump are harmful because they cause internal damage in the pelvic region as a result of the jarring forces encountered in landing. This, it is argued, subjects the mesenteries and other supportive tissues to tearing, with concomitant trauma to the neighboring organs. Medical findings refute this postulate. The exercise engaged in by a woman athlete in training and in conditioning, as well as in actual competition, tends to strengthen the floor of the pelvis and the surrounding tissues and brings about improved muscle tone.

Irritation or strain to the breasts can result, especially if the breasts are pendulous, unless adequate support and restraint are afforded by means of a properly designed and fitted brassiere.

Women have a lower center of gravity than do men and hence are generally more stable. Their arms and legs are proportionately shorter than men's. Both of these factors present disadvantages in jumping.

Throwing and Support Activities

The shoulder width of the female is narrower than that of the male, and the breadth of the pelvis, augmented by the adipose pads over the hips, usually causes the arm to incline inward. Most women have a pronounced hyperextension of the elbow joint, often coupled with a decided outward angling of the forearm. These skeletal differences create difficulties in throwing, circling, or rotatory movements of the arm as a whole. This is true also in activities involving the support of the body by the arms, as encountered in gymnastics. In the latter the differences provide a distinct handicap, since both elbow and shoulder joints must function at somewhat unfavorable angles for weight bearing.

Physiological Implications

Both structural and physiological differences emphasize the fact that women should not be compared with men in terms of performance. They should be judged in terms relative only to the performance standards of their own gender. Gender has a definite influence on training, principally because of physiological differences in the capacity to perform exercises.

Prepubertal and Pubertal Periods

During the prepubertal period, girls are the equal of, and often superior to, boys of the same age in activities requiring speed, strength, and endurance. The difference between men and women is not too apparent until after puberty. With the advent of puberty the gulf begins to widen, with the males continuing in a slower gradual increase in strength, speed, and endurance.

During the prepubertal period, girls are the equal of, and often superior to, boys of the same age in activities requiring speed, strength, and endurance.

Circulatory Factors

In the performance of moderate exercise there is little significant difference between young men and women in respect to standards of performance, but the significance increases as the strenuousness of the activity increases. Women are subject to the same physiological laws as are men. However, they have a smaller heart and a faster pulse rate. They indicate a greater and more rapid increase in pulse rate at the beginning of exercise and a much slower recovery after exercise. The pulse rates of trained women athletes are about ten beats per minute slower than those of nonathletes. Since the male possesses a larger heart, probably because of the fact that he has more muscle tissue, he has a larger circulation. Since heart rate is proportional to body size, a larger individual will have a slower heart rate, hence the male rate is some five to eight beats slower than that of the female, resulting in a greater cardiac output at a lower cardiac cost.

At rest the average number of red blood cells in the female is 4,500,000/mm^3 as compared to 5,000,000/mm^3 in the male. Postexercise values reflect an increase of approximately 1,000,000 for the male and a comparable rise for the female relative to the lower resting value. This rise is indicative of the compensatory adjustment to meet the demand for an increased oxygen supply. The female also has approximately 8% less hemoglobin.

At a given level of oxygen consumption women have a higher heart rate than do men. On the other hand, at a given heart rate men can transport more oxygen during submaximal and maximal work. In both sexes the maximal heart rate bears a linear relationship with an increased work load. Exhaustion, however, is reached at a lower rate of performance in women.

Blood pressure values, both diastolic and systolic, are from 5 to 10 mm Hg lower in the female. Pubertal systolic values, although reflecting some rise, are less pronounced than those of the male and will often indicate a slight decrease, which is maintained until age 18 or 19. After age 19 there is a slow but steady increase in both the male and female as age advances. After menopause most women show a systolic increase slightly higher than the comparable male.

Respiratory Function

Because of the smaller thoracic cavity, women respire more rapidly. They require less oxygen because of a lower metabolic rate and smaller body size. Trained athletes of both genders appear to use their anaerobic processes to approximately the same level. Women breathe more shallowly, that is, with the upper part of the chest, whereas men tend to breathe deeper and hence more diaphragmatically.

Vital capacity is the volume of air moved through the lungs from a maximal inspiration to a maximal expiration. It varies between the genders, since it bears a direct relationship to body size, area, and height. Although vital capacity does not predict performance by itself, it can be enhanced through training, and it determines performance capabilities. The vital capacity of the female is about 10% less than that of a male of the same size and age. The tendency to breathe with the upper part of the chest rather than from the diaphragm further limits the respiratory volume of the female. However, through training, diaphragmatic breathing can be developed.

The *oxygen pulse*, a measure used to determine how effectively the heart functions as a respiratory organ, is a relative measure involving blood volume, hemoglobin content, and body weight through which oxygen consumption is calculated in milliliters per heartbeat. There is a close relationship between the oxygen pulse rate of young women and young men who have similar heart rates while they are engaged in exercise of approximately 3600 ft-lb of work per minute. Both sexes reflect the same oxygen pulse rates at ages 12 to 15 years, but from 15 years up to ages 31 to 35 the male shows a rapid increase in values, as much as three times that of the female rate, which remains unchanged.

The *maximal aerobic power* of the female, the ability to use oxygen effectively, is also from 25% to 30% less than that of the male after age 12. Before that time both values are about the same. Both men and women peak out at age 18 years, after which there is a gradual decline. A comparison of the oxygen uptake values indicates similar levels per kilogram of body weight and it would seem that women, having a smaller body size, should have a higher value. It may well be that the smaller hemoglobin concentration restricts the full use of cardiac output for oxygen transport. Maximal oxygen uptake values (oxygen accepted by the tissues) are much higher for physically active females than for the more sedentary.

Metabolism

The metabolic rate of the female at all ages is from 6% to 10% lower than that of the male of comparable size when related to body surface area. When the basal metabolic rate is related to muscle mass, however, the gender difference disappears. This would indicate a significance to the resting heat disposition but not to muscular efficiency.

The calcium metabolic rate of the female is higher than that of the male, since ossification of her bones occurs at an earlier age. However, the bones of the male are denser and more rugged because of the slower rate of ossification and the subsequent calcium retention.

Muscular Strength

In proportion to weight and size, women's muscles are weaker than men's, possessing at maturity approximately half the strength of their male counterparts. Muscular strength is related to the size and anatomy of the body and is indicated in terms of its proportionate mass. Among males this constitutes approximately 43% and among women about 36% of the total. Differences in relative amounts of muscle tissue during puberty are the result of endocrine function, which causes the fundamental sex differences in terms of weight and development. Testosterone produces a marked increase in the weight of muscle tissue and an enlargement of the muscle fibers. Female hormones have a growth-inhibiting effect, but as with men, women's muscles develop in relation to the fundamental laws of exercise (Fig. 4-6).

Figure 4-6

As with men, women's muscles develop in relation to the fundamental laws of exercise.
Courtesy Cramer Products, Inc., Gardner, Kan.

Adiposity

Women have about 10% more adipose tissue than do men, although women long-distance runners will exhibit values well below that figure. The fat is stored at various depots around the body, as well as in a rather thick subcutaneous layer that serves as protection and insulation. Because of the subcutaneous layer, women are better able to withstand heat and cold than are men. The greater amount of adipose tissue may have some effect on the lower metabolic rate. Since fat is inert, it limits athletic performance, representing dead weight that must be carried by the athlete.

Women tend to accumulate fat on the thighs and around the hips, abdomen, and breasts, which would account generally for their greater relative weight in relation to size. The average female has about 7 pounds more of subcutaneous fat than her male counterpart, having a ratio of 22% to 25% fat to body weight as opposed to 14% for the male. Women athletes exhibit far less adiposity than nonathletes, having a range of from 10% to 15%. Among women distance runners, Wilmore has found values as low as 6%.[26] The type of athletic activity in which the sportswoman participates seems to affect her adiposity. For example, women runners are much leaner than women who compete in the weight events. Female athletes can and do approach the relative fat values attained by male athletes.[26]

Menarche

Menarche, the onset of the menses, normally occurs between the tenth and the seventeenth year, with the majority of girls usually entering it between 13 and 15 years. Menarche, like menstruation, is regular in its irregularity.

The onset of menarche may be delayed by strenuous training and competition.

There is some indication that strenuous training and competition may delay the onset of menarche. The greatest delay appears to be related to the higher caliber competition.[6,15] In itself, a delay in the first menses does not appear to pose any significant danger to the young female athlete. The late-maturing girl commonly has longer legs, narrower hips, and less adiposity and body weight for her height, all of which are more conducive to sports.[15]

Menstruation

As interest and participation in girls' and women's sports grow, the various myths that have surrounded female participation and the effects of participation on menarche, menstruation, and childbirth are gradually being dispelled. Although the effects of sustained and strenuous training and competition on the menstrual cycle and the effects of menstruation on performance still cannot be fully explained with any degree of certainty, continued and increasing research is slowly clearing away the mysteries. Some of the research in the past has been contradictory and, on occasion, open to question. Nonetheless, current research appears to be answering some of the questions, although much needs still to be done.

The menstrual cycle is considered to have four phases. These phases, based on a 28-day cycle, are as follows:

1 *The menses*—cycle days 1 to 5

2. *Postmenstrual* phase—also known as the estrogenic, proliferative, or follicular phase; cycle days 6 to 13 or 14
3. *Ovulation*—also known as the luteal or progesterone phase; cycle days 15 to 28
4. *Postovulatory* phase—also known as the premenstrual phase; cycle days 15 to 28.

The majority of women tend to show some variation in the length of their cycles, these differences occurring principally because of differences in duration of the preovulatory phase rather than the premenstrual phase.

With the onset of menarche a cyclic hormone pattern commences, which establishes the menstrual cycle. These hormonal changes result from complex feedback mechanisms and specifically controlled interactions that occur between the hypothalamus, ovaries, and pituitary gland. Two gonadotropins induce the release of the egg from the mature follicle at midcycle (ovulation). They are FSH (follicle-stimulating hormone), which stimulates the maturation of an ovarian follicle, and LH (luteinizing hormone), which stimulates the development of the corpus luteum, and endocrine structure that secretes progesterone and estrogens. The control and eventual inhibition of the production of FSH when the follicle reaches maturity is brought about by the estrogenic steroids produced by the ovaries. Progesterone, a steroid hormone produced within the corpus luteum—a small body that develops within a ruptured ovarian follicle after ovulation—eventually inhibits production of LH. Estrogen is secreted principally by the luteal cells. Before onset of a new menstrual period, FSH levels are already rising, probably to initiate maturation of new follicles to reinstitute the next cycle.

For many years medical opinion held that little or no exercise should be taken during the menstrual period. In modern medical opinion the avoidance of strenuous activity is advised for only the first 2 days. During this time, the womb is quite heavy and engorged with blood. The athlete should avoid activities involving torque or jarring forces such as jumping or twisting movements that involve the pelvis at this time. *Some athletes, however, are able to participate in heavy training or competition without experiencing any distress or involvement during their menstrual period.* The best performances usually appear during the immediate postmenstrual period and the poorest performances are observed during the immediate premenstrual period. Many world-class athletes have set records during the flow phase. As can be seen, variation is the rule, not the exception. Most authorities believe that there is little evidence that physical activities have unfavorable effects on the cycle. Variations in performance may be induced by the psychological and hormonal factors that normally accompany menstruation, as indicated by such symptoms as depression, fatigue, irritability, nervousness, and water retention. Any athlete who is healthy gynecologically and whose menstrual cycles show no unusual or unfavorable changes either during or as the result of physical stress should be permitted to participate in sports activities at all times.

Female Conditioning for Sports

The conditioning program for women in preparation for athletic participation varies little from that for the male. Since females are not usually as strong or as powerful as males, the resistance factor in activities in which strength is the prime factor may need to be reduced somewhat to fit the ability of the trainee. The same policy applies to activities of endurance.

Weight training   There has long been a belief that heavy exercise, particularly weight training, will develop unsightly and bulky muscles in women and that such exercises have a tendency to develop masculinity. The occasional slight bulking up seen in some females is probably a result of their having higher endogenous levels of testosterone (the male hormone) than are usually found in females. As women continue in a weight-training program there is an identifiable loss in adiposity as strength improves. Numerous studies have clearly indicated that strenuous muscular exercise does not result in muscle hypertrophy to the degree of that found in the male.[25]

Women should follow the same general and specific weight-training procedures advocated for men, with the exception that the amount of weight to be handled must be within their capacity to manage. The identical exercise programs, including the recommended number of repetitions, should be followed. It is suggested, however, that weight increments be in units of 2½ and 5 pounds, rather than 5 and 10 pounds, unless the individual shows herself fully capable of handling the larger increment.

Figure 4-7

Endocrine influences on the menstrual cycle.

From Klafs, C.E., and Lyon, M.J.: The female athlete: conditioning, competition, and culture, St. Louis, 1973, The C.V. Mosby Co.

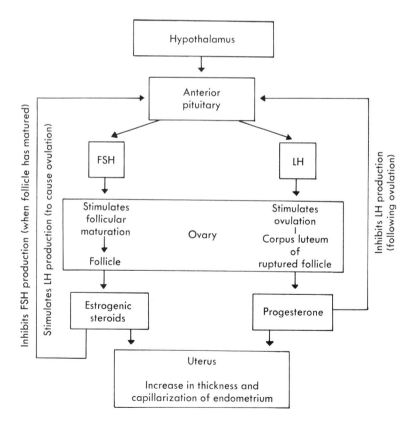

In some instances, a slight decrease in muscular strength may be noted during the days immediately preceding menstruation. Such loss is temporary. During the menstrual period it might be advisable to curtail the lifting program for a couple of days at the onset, substituting the moderate general conditioning and stretching exercises.

TRAINING AND COMPETITION IN CHILDHOOD

Parents and professionals in the area of education, psychology, and medicine have long questioned whether vigorous physical training and competition are advisable for the immature child. Increasingly, children are engaging in intense programs of training that require many hours of daily commitment and may extend over many years. Swimmers may practice 2 hours, two times a day, covering 6000 to 10,000 meters each session in the water; gymnasts may practice 3 to 5 hours per day, and runners may cover as many as 70 miles each week.[28]

The American Academy of Pediatrics has indicated that the nearly universal participation of young children of both genders in competitive sports requires realistic guidelines. It is recognized that sports have an important effect on stamina and physiology and have lifelong values as recreational activities.[1] The American Academy of Pediatrics also indicates that there is no physical reason to separate preadolescent girls and boys by gender in sports activities or recreational activities; however, separation of the genders should occur in collision-type sports when boys have acquired greater muscle mass in proportion to body weight, making participation with girls hazardous. All participants should be properly grouped by physical maturation, weight, size, and skill (Fig. 4-8). Of major importance is for the child to always be given a proper physical examination before entering organized

Participation of young children of both genders in competitive sports requires realistic guidelines.

Figure 4-8

It is particularly important to match children in sports according to physical maturity, weight, size, and skill.

From Arnheim, D.D., and Pestolesi, R.A.: St. Louis, 1978, The C.V. Mosby Co.

competitive sports. Also of importance is that coaches of children have some understanding of growth and development, injury causation, prevention of sports injuries, and the understanding and practice of correct coaching techniques.

Injury Epidemiology

There is a lack of in-depth accident statistics related to children and sports participation. Most of the current variance in data is based on personal medical opinion rather than on epidemiological study.[16] From the information available, unsupervised play is far more dangerous than organized sports for the preadolescent participant[18] (Fig. 4-9). High-participation sports such as Little League baseball and Pop Warner football report relatively few injuries in childhood.[7,22]

Children should not engage in too early specialization in any single physical activity.

Physical Immaturity

Many professionals are concerned with the young athlete who has immature skeletal structures and engages in highly competitive sports. The degree of maturation is commonly measured by skeletal ossification. The skeleton does not completely mature until early adulthood. An example of this is the femur, which reaches full ossification at about 19 years of age. The main concern of opponents of vigorous competitive youth sports programs, especially the contact or collision variety, are injuries that could cause a premature cessation of growth in a particular bone.[11] *Epiphyseal injuries* affecting growth plates, which are primarily cartilagenous in their immature state, can be injured by a number of activities. The following activities should be performed with great caution[19]:

- Falling, jumping, or landing with straight legs
- Excessive stress to the shoulder and elbow from repeated throwing motions
- Long-duration exercise involving weight bearing, such as long-distance running
- Heavy weight lifting

Many physicians also are concerned with repeated microtraumas that occur to the young athlete over a period of time. Such small traumas can compound and produce chronic and, in some cases, degenerative conditions within the immature musculoskeletal system.

The Child Athlete's Psyche

Another question that must be addressed is whether high-level sports competition is psychologically harmful to the emotionally immature. *Will a child who is placed under constant high-level competitive pressures, such as playing in all-star games, championships, or play-offs, develop emotional problems?* This is a difficult question. Some opinions indicate that no harm occurs, whereas others believe undesirable behaviors may stem from this type of stress (Fig. 4-10). Children have been known to display "burnout" from heavy training and high-pressure competition, which leads to a loss of interest in sports and exercise.[19]

Many of the psychological problems associated with sports competition can be averted by educating parents and coaches that the joy of participation is the important thing, rather than winning at all cost. This is not to say

Figure 4-9

Unsupervised play is generally more dangerous than organized sports activities.

From Arnheim, D.D., and Pestolesi, R.A.: St. Louis, 1978, The C.V. Mosby Co.

that winning is not important, but it should be viewed as a reward for successful participation.

Another major factor is that children should not engage in too early specialization in any single physical activity that requires year-round conditioning. Normal physical and emotional growth and development are enhanced by a variety of activities.

Physical Training Intensity

How hard should children engage in physical training? Will such training adversely affect a child's heart, lungs, muscles, or bones? The answers to these questions can be either positive or negative, depending on many variables. It must be remembered that exercise is an essential element for normal growth and development. Children who are deprived of proper physical activity will fail to reach their growth potential. In fact, children who engage in physical training in preparation for sports competition will commonly have wider and stronger bones than less active children.[26] However, training that is too strenuous has been known to overstress the child's body, resulting in injury.

Should a child between the ages of 9 and 12 years train with heavy resistance to increase strength? Heavy resistance, such as weight lifting, has

Figure 4-10

Constant high-level competitive psychological pressure can lead to a child's becoming disinterested in sports and exercise.

From Arnheim, D.D., and Pestolesi, R.A.: St. Louis, 1978, The C.V. Mosby Co.

been found to increase strength and the width and density of the skeletal structure.[26] Although data are inconclusive, it is speculated that growing children should not engage in heavy resistance–type training programs. A safer approach is employing a program of low weight and high repetition through a full range of motion or the use of isokinetic methods where the resistance matches the force applied by the child.[26] Of major importance is that children should avoid strength specialization. This avoidance is to prevent muscle and structural imbalances that may lead to eventual injury.

As with strength development, there is some contention as to the amount of stress that should be applied to a child's cardiovascular and respiratory system. The human body at all ages, with an absence of pathological processes, has a great capacity to adapt to cardiorespiratory stress. However, data are not available as to the effects of intense and long-term training on children. As with adults, children having low cardiorespiratory fitness respond most dramatically to such programs.[19]

REFERENCES

1. American Academy of Pediatrics: Competitive sports for children of elementary school age, Committee on Pediatric Aspects of Physical Fitness, Recreation and Sports, Pediatrics **67:**927, 1981.
2. Bilik, S.E.: The trainer's bible, ed. 9, New York, 1956, T. J. Reed & Co., Publishers.
3. Costill, D.: Endurance and strength training: an update, Proceedings of the NATA Professional Preparation Conference, Nashville, Tenn., 1978, National Athletic Trainers Association.
4. De Lorme, T.L., and Watkins, A.L.: Progressive resistance exercise, New York, 1951, Appleton-Century-Crofts.
5. deVries, H.A.: Evaluation of static stretching procedures for improvement of flexibility, Res. Q. **33:**222, 1962.
6. Erdelyi, G.J.: Effects of exercise on the menstrual cycle, Phys. Sportsmed. **4:**79, 1976.
7. Godshall, R.W.: Junior League football: risks versus benefits, J. Sport Med. **3**(4):139, 1975.
8. Johnson, J.H.: A comparison of isokinetic and isotonic training for college women, Am. Correct. Ther. J. **34:**176, Nov./Dec. 1980.
9. Klafs, C.E., and Lyon, M.J.: The female athlete: a coach's guide to conditioning and training, ed. 2, St. Louis, 1978, The C.V. Mosby Co.
10. LaDow, J.: Circadian rhythms and athletic performance, Phys. Sportsmed. **7:**87, 1979.
11. Larson, R.L.: Physical activity and the growth and development of bone and joint structures. In Rarick, G.L., editor: Physical activity: human growth and development, New York, 1973, Academic Press, Inc.
12. Logan, G.A.: Adapted physical education, Dubuque, Iowa, 1972, William C. Brown Co., Publishers.
13. Logan, G.A., and Wallis, E.L.: Recent findings in learning and performance, Paper presented at the Southern Section Meeting, California Association for Health, Physical Education, and Recreation, Pasadena, Calif., 1960.
14. MacDougall, G.C.B., et al.: Effects of strength training and immobilization on human muscle fibers, Eur. J. Applied Physiol. **43:**25, Feb. 1980.
15. Malina, R.M., et al.: Age at menarche and selected menstrual characteristics in athletes at different competitive levels and in different sports, Med. Sci. Sports **10:**218, 1978.
16. Micheli, L.J.: Sports injuries in children and adolescents. In Strauss, R.H. editor: Sports medicine and physiology, Philadelphia, 1979, W.B. Saunders Co.
17. Morehouse, L.E., and Miller, A.T.,

Jr.: Physiology of exercise, ed. 7, St. Louis, 1976, The C.V. Mosby Co.

18. National Safety Council: Accident facts, Chicago, 1982, The Council.

19. Pate, R.R.: The principles of training. In Kulund, D.N. (editor): The injured athlete, Philadelphia, 1982, J.B. Lippincott Co.

20. Peterson, J.A.: Total fitness: the Nautilus way, New York, 1978, Leisure Press.

21. Pipes, T.V., and Wilmore, J.H.: Isokinetic vs. isotonic strength training in adult men, Med. Sci. Sports **7**:262, 1975.

22. Roser, L.A., and Clauson, D.K.: Football injuries in the very young athlete, Clin. Orthop. **69**:212, 1970.

23. Ryan, A.J.: The Olympic Games at altitude. Academy of Orthopaedic Surgeons: Symposium on sports medicine, St. Louis, 1969, The C.V. Mosby Co.

24. Selye, H.: The stress of life, New York, 1956, McGraw-Hill Book Co.

25. Wilmore, J.H.: Inferiority of female athletes: myth or reality, J. Sport Med. **3**:1, 1975.

26. Wilmore, J.H.: Athletic training and physical fitness, Boston, 1977, Allyn & Bacon, Inc.

27. Wilt, F.: Plyometrics, what it is—how it works, Ath. J., 76, May 1975.

28. Zauner, C.W., and Benson, N.Y.: Physiological alterations in young swimmers during 3 years of intensive training, J. Sport Med. **21**:179, June 1981.

ADDITIONAL SOURCES

Arnheim, D.D., and Pestolesi, R.A.: Elementary physical education: a developmental approach, ed. 2, St. Louis, 1978, The C.V. Mosby Co.

Bachman, D.C., et al.: Physiology of strength, Chicago, 1900, Teach'em, Inc. (Cassette.)

O'Shea, J.P., and Wegner, J.: Power weight training and the female athlete. Phys. Sportsmed, **9**:109, June 1981.

Pappas, A.: Adolescent injuries in athletics, Eastern Athletic Trainers Association Meeting, Greenville, N.C., Jan. 1984. (Cassette.)

Rohrbaugh, J.B.: Femininity on the line, Psychol. Today **13**:30, 1979.

Sapega, A.A., and Drillings, G.: The definition and assessment of muscular power, J. Orthop. Sports. Phys. Ther. **5**:7, July/Aug. 1983.

Smith, N.J.: The young athlete—an overview. In Strauss, R.H. (editor): Sports medicine and physiology, Philadelphia, 1979, W.B. Saunders Co.

Strength: one component of a winning team, Phys. Sportsmed. **9**:116, Aug. 1981.

Thomas, C.L.: Factors to women participants in vigorous athletics. In Strauss, R.H. (editor): Sports medicine and physiology, Philadelphia, 1979, W.B. Saunders Co.

Chapter 5

INJURY PREVENTION THROUGH PHYSICAL CONDITIONING

When you finish this chapter, you should be able to

Discuss the merits of conditioning and sports injury prevention

Identify the major conditioning seasons and the types of exercise carried out in each

List the ten cardinal conditioning principles

Explain warm up, cool down, flexibility, strength, and endurance in the prevention of sports injuries

Describe the differences between muscle soreness and stiffness

Lack of physical fitness is one of the primary causes of sports injury.

Physical training for sports participation, besides preparing athletes for high-level performance, is resolutely tied into injury prevention. Coaches and trainers alike now recognize that a lack of physical fitness is one of the primary causes of sports injury. *Muscular imbalance, improper timing because of poor neuromuscular coordination, a lack of ligamentous or tendinous strength, lack of flexibility, and inadequate muscle bulk are among the major causes of injury directly attributable to insufficient or improper physical conditioning.* Inadequate nutrition and psychological problems are also factors and are discussed in detail in Chapters 6 and 8.

The amount of time spent on preseason and in-season conditioning is relative not only to the type of activity but also to the state of the athlete's physical fitness at the initiation of the conditioning program. The trainer should project the conditioning program on a timetable so that desired levels of achievement can be reached by approximately the predicted dates. In this manner a careful check can be kept on the athlete's progress. The athlete who reports for practice at the start of the season 10 pounds overweight or in a flabby condition will require a longer and more intensive schedule than a teammate who reports in a reasonably good state of fitness.

Joint range of motion must be increased to prevent tendon and ligament tears.

Team physicians and trainers report that the most serious sports injuries are those to the musculoskeletal system. These injuries can be obviated by proper and thorough physical conditioning. Muscle bulk and strength must be built up to protect the muscles and the underlying soft parts. Tendons and ligaments must be strengthened and toughened to enable them, along with the muscles, to fortify the joints that they traverse, to prevent untoward injuries, and to permit full and effective range of movement and stability. Care must be taken by the athlete to warm up properly to prevent muscle tears or strains and to raise muscle and deep body temperatures to their most effective levels. Although there is evidence to support both the positive and the negative aspects of warm-up, the preponderance favors warm-up. Coaches, athletes, and trainers generally favor adequate and proper warm-up believing that it is essential not only to prevent injury but to raise muscle and deep body temperatures to their most effective levels.[2] Flexibility and range of joint motion must be increased to prevent tendon and ligament tears, as well as to foster body mobility in all aspects. Neuromuscular skills that will effect good motor performance must be developed along with speed and endurance. The awkward, slow, or tired athlete is the one most prone to injury.

It takes time and careful preparation to bring an athlete into competition at a level of fitness that will preclude early-season injury. The most dangerous period in any sport is the first 3 or 4 weeks of the season, principally because athletes frequently are lacking in flexibility, often overweight, and many times out of good physical condition when they report for initial practice. Another factor is lack of familiarity with most of the fundamentals of a sport, resulting in awkwardness and a consequent proneness to potential injury-provoking situations.

Because many athletic trainers fear overemphasis, preseason practice schedules usually are severely limited. As a result, many athletes enter competition in a condition far from the optimal level of fitness that is reached, barring injury, at about the third week of competition. There is a considerable difference between training athletes to reach their peak for a certain performance and training them to reach a good level of fitness to reduce their injury potential. Emphasis for achieving optimal fitness should be on all-around development, whereas emphasis for peaking should be on all-around development plus gradually intensified, specialized exercise designed to secure maximal performance at the end of a particular time.

CONDITIONING SEASONS

No longer do serious athletes engage in just preseason conditioning and in-season competition. Sports conditioning is a year-round endeavor, often encompassing four training seasons: postseason, off-season, preseason, and in-

Figure 5-1

Modern sports programs often require elaborate conditioning facilities and equipment to apply sound injury prevention methods.

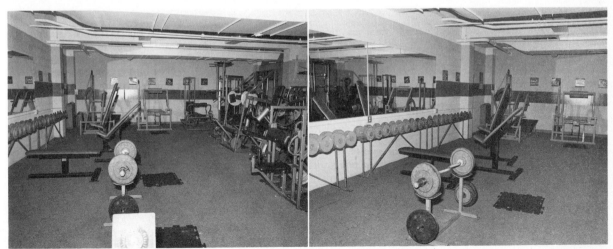

Continued.

General Principles of Sports
Medicine

Sports conditioning often falls
into four seasons: post-
season, off-season, preseason,
and in-season.

season. This plan is especially appropriate for collision-type sports, such as
football. Gaunya[8] called this approach "the quadratic training cycle." For
American tackle football, the postseason generally is from February to May;
off-season, May to July; preseason, July to September, and in-season, September to January.

Postseason

Conditioning during the postseason is commonly dedicated to physical restoration. This period is particularly appropriate when the athlete has been
injured during the in-season. This is a time when postsurgical rehabilitation
takes place and detailed medical evaluations can be obtained.[8]

Off-season

It is not essential that athletes continue an intensive conditioning program
during the off-season, although it is usually a good idea for the athletic
trainer and coach to encourage them to participate in another sport during
this period. Such an activity should make certain physical demands, em-

Figure 5-1, cont'd

For legend see p. 113.

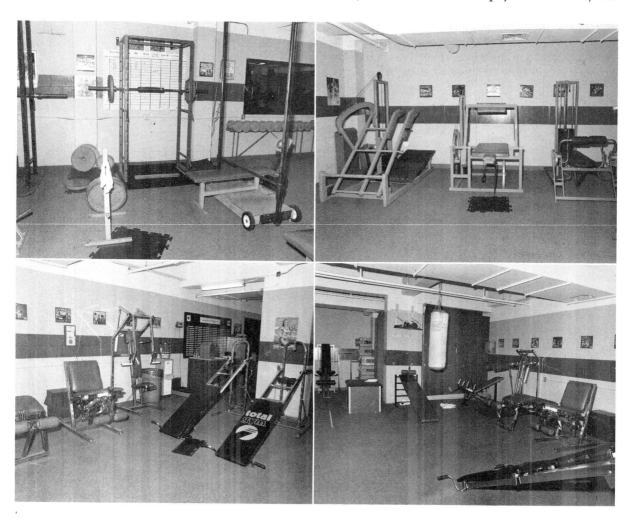

bodying strength, endurance, and flexibility by means of running and general all-around physical performance. This will assist athletes in maintaining their level of fitness. In other words, the sport must be sufficiently demanding to require a good level of fitness to participate effectively. An excellent off-season sport for the football player would be wrestling or gymnastics. Track, especially cross-country, is a conditioner. Rope skipping as a conditioning activity lends itself to all sports and makes vigorous demands on the body.

If it is not feasible for athletes to participate in an off-season sport, a *detraining program* should be planned. Such a program permits gradual decrease in the usual work load and allows the athlete to exercise less frequently and less intensively. A weekly workout of moderate to strong intensity is usually all that is required, since physical fitness is retained for a considerable length of time after an active program of competition ends. The physically vigorous athlete tends to be quite active in the off-season too and, as a rule, will stay in reasonably good condition throughout the year.[8]

It must be kept in mind, however, that caloric intake must be decreased accordingly when the exercise load is decreased, since not as much energy is then burned up. The overweight condition of many athletes when they report for preseason training is caused by their having continued a midseason appetite with an off-season activity load. Establishing regular training routines for the off-season enables the trainer to keep a close check on athletes even if they are seen only at 2- or 3-week intervals. In this way extreme overweight or poor fitness can be forestalled.

Preseason

Trainers should impress on their athletes the need for maintaining a reasonably high level of physical fitness during the off-season. If such advice is followed, the athlete will find preseason work relatively rewarding and any proneness to potential injury considerably diminished. No difficulty in reaching a state of athletic fitness suitable for competition within 6 to 8 weeks should then be experienced. During this preliminary period flexibility, endurance, and strength should be emphasized in a carefully graded developmental program. In such a program there must be wise and constant use of established physiological bases for improving physical condition and performance.

Many athletes, particularly in one-season sports, tend to reach their highest level of performance halfway through the season. As a result, they are truly efficient only half of the time. Conference and federation restrictions often hamper or prohibit effective preseason training, especially in football, and therefore compel the athlete to come into early-season competition before being physically fit for it. At the high school level 6 to 8 weeks of preseason conditioning afford the best insurance against susceptibility to injury and permit the athlete to enter competition in a good state of physical fitness, provided a carefully graded program is established and adhered to conscientiously. Recently, physicians have been adding their voices to the demands for a realistic approach to proper conditioning, and it may be that school administrators and the general public will see the need and effectiveness of permitting adequate and properly controlled preseason training.

In-season

Intensive preseason conditioning programs, which bring the athlete to the competitive season, may not be maintained by the sport itself. Unless there is strenuous conditioning throughout the season, a problem of deconditioning may occur. Athletes who do not undergo maintenance conditioning may lose their entry level of physiological fitness.[8]

THE TEN CARDINAL CONDITIONING PRINCIPLES

The following ten cardinal principles can be applied to sports conditioning to prevent injuries:

1. *Warming up.* See that proper and adequate warm-up procedures precede all activities.
2. *Gradualness.* Add small daily increments of work. REMEMBER: It takes 6 to 8 weeks to get into top-level condition.
3. *Timing.* Prevent overdoing. Relate all work to the athlete's general condition at the time. Practice periods should extend for 1 hour to 1 hour and 45 minutes, depending on the sport. REMEMBER: The tired athlete is prone to injury.
4. *Intensity.* Stress the intensity of the work rather than the quantity. Usually coaches and athletic trainers fail to work their athletes *hard* enough in terms of intensity. They make the mistake of prolonging the workout rather than increasing the tempo or the work load. As the degree of training increases, the intensity of training must also increase.
5. *Capacity level.* Expect from the athlete performance that is as close to his or her physiological limits as health and safety factors will allow. Only in working to capacity will the desired results be achieved.
6. *Strength.* Develop strength as a means of producing greater endurance and speed.
7. *Motivation.* Motivation is a prime factor in sports conditioning. Use circuit training and isometric exercises as means of further motivating the athlete.
8. *Specialization.* Exercise programs should include exercises for strength, relaxation, and flexibility. In addition, exercises geared to the demands made on the body in specific activities should be used to develop specialization.
9. *Relaxation.* Specific relaxation exercises, which aid in recovery from fatigue and tension, should be taught.
10. *Routine.* A daily routine of exercise, both in-season and off-season, should be established.

PHYSICAL ACTIVITIES DESIGNED FOR INJURY PREVENTION

Conditioning should be performed gradually, with work being added in small increments.

Three aspects of conditioning particularly apply to injury prevention: (1) warming up and cooling down, (2) increasing flexibility, and (3) strength development.

Warming Up and Cooling Down

Both the processes of properly warming up and cooling down are believed by many authorities to have major implications in the prevention of sports injuries.[15]

Warming Up

Although warm-up is still a subject of study and results are somewhat conflicting, most evidence favors its use. The use of warm-up procedures has long been traditional in sports and is still advocated by most athletic trainers, coaches, and physicians as the means of preparing the body physiologically and psychologically for physical performance, in the belief that it will not only improve performance but will lessen the possibilities of injury.[2,3,12] The term "warming up" in this discussion refers to the use of preliminary exercise procedures rather than the use of hot showers, massage, counterirritants, diathermy, or other forms of passive warm-up.

Warm-up is used as a preventive measure, although limited data exist to substantiate this. It is believed that a proper warm-up will prevent and/or reduce strains and the tearing of muscle fibers from their tendinous attachments. Most frequently the antagonist muscles are torn. Their inability to relax rapidly, plus the great contractile force of the agonist muscles added to the momentum of the moving part, subject the antagonists to a sudden severe strain that can result in a subsequent tearing of the fibers themselves, as well as their tendinous attachments.[13] Proper warm-up can reduce or prevent muscle soreness.

Physiological purposes of warming up   The main purposes of warming up are to raise both the general body and the deep muscle temperatures and to stretch collagenous tissues to permit greater flexibility. This reduces the possibility of muscle tears and ligamentous sprains and helps to prevent muscle soreness. As cellular temperature increases, it is accompanied by a corresponding increase in the speed of the metabolic processes within the cells, since such processes are temperature dependent. For each degree of internal temperature rise there is a corresponding rise in the rate of metabolism of about 13%. At higher temperatures there is a faster and more complete dissociation of oxygen from the hemoglobin and myoglobins, which improves the oxygen supply during work.[11] The transmission of nerve impulses speeds up as well. Overloading the muscle groups before power activities results in improved performance. It is thought that there is an increased level of excitation of the motor units that are called into play to handle the increased load and that these motor units are then carried over into the actual performance. The result is an increase in the athlete's physical working capacity. The following proper warm-up performance improvement ranges from 0.5 to 0.6 seconds in the 100-meter dash to as much as 4 to 6 seconds in the 800-meter run. The percentage of improvement, from 2% to 5%, is approximately the same for the various distances studied.

It takes at least 15 to 30 minutes of gradual warm-up to bring the body to a state of readiness with its attendant rise in body temperature and to adequately mobilize the body physiology in terms of making a greater number of muscle capillaries available for extreme effort and of

Proper warming up and cooling down may prevent sports injuries.

readying blood sugar and adrenaline. The time needed for satisfactory warm-up varies with the individual and tends to increase with age.

Warm-up differs in relation to the type of competition. It is advisable for athletes to warm up in activities similar to the event in which they will compete. Accordingly, a sprinter would start by jogging a bit, practice a few starts, and use some stretching techniques and general body exercises. A baseball player might first use general body exercises, swing a bat through a number of practice swings, and do preliminary throwing, alternating these activities with stretching exercises. Both overload and the use of mimetic activities appear to be important for those events in which neuromuscular coordination is paramount.

On cool days, warm-up should be increased somewhat in duration and should be performed in sweat clothing. Only when athletes are fully warmed up and ready to move directly into competition should they remove their sweat clothing. In some events, for example, field events, sweat clothing should be replaced immediately after a competitive effort. If rather long periods of time elapse between trials or events, the performer should use light warm-up procedures during the intervals.

The process of warming up Warm-up is generally considered as falling into two categories: (1) the *general*, or *unrelated*, warm-up, which consists of activities that bring about a general warming of the body without having any relationship to the skills to be performed; and (2) *specific*, or *related*, warm-up, which is mimetic, that is, similar to or the same as skills to be performed in competition (running, throwing, swinging, etc.).

Warming up involves general body warming and specific body warming to the demands of the sport.

General warm-up General warm-up procedures should consist of jogging or easy running, gradual stretching, and general exercises. These procedures should mobilize the body for action and make it supple and free. They must be of sufficient duration and intensity to raise deep tissue temperatures without developing marked fatigue. When athletes attain a state of sweating, they have raised their internal temperature to a desirable level. The nature of the warm-up varies to some degree in relation to the activity. Some procedures lend themselves well to athletic activities of all types and should be performed along with others that are specifically designed for the sport in which the athlete is to participate.

The exercises described in this discussion provide balance and depth in procedures, so that total body warm-up may be achieved. The athlete's daily workout, either for practice or for competition, should begin with running and the gradual stretches and then proceed to the calisthenic exercises.

Specific event warm-up After completing the general exercises in the warm-up, the athletes should progress to those that are specific for their events or activities. They should start at a moderate pace and then increase the tempo as they feel body temperature and cardiovascular increases taking place. The effects of warm-up may persist as long as 45 minutes. However, the closer the warm-up period is to the actual performance, the more beneficial it will be in terms of its effect on the performance. For the athlete to benefit optimally from warm-up, no more than 15 minutes should elapse between the completion of the warm-up and performing the activity itself.

The exercises on pp. 120-123, and Tables 5-1 and 5-2, pp. 124-131, for track and field sports, are to be used as specific warm-ups after the general warm-up. They serve to localize warm-up in the body areas that receive the most use during competition in a particular sport. These exercises lend themselves to a number of sports and a minimum of 30 to 50 repetitions are to be performed.

The warm-ups listed in Tables 5-1 and 5-2 are designed specifically for the sports indicated. Allow ample time for all warm-up procedures.

Cooling Down

Cooling down applies to exercise of gradually diminishing intensity that follows strenuous work and permits the return of both the circulation and various body functions to preexercise levels. From 30 seconds to 1 minute of jogging, followed by 3 to 5 minutes of walking, permits the body to effect the necessary re-adjustments.

Physiologically, an important reason for cooling down activity is that blood and muscle lactic acid levels decrease more rapidly during active recovery than with passive recovery. Also, active recovery keeps the muscle pumps going and prevents blood from pooling in the extremities.[1]

> Cooling down decreases blood and muscle lactic acid levels more rapidly.

Flexibility Training

Most authorities in sports medicine consider flexibility one of the most important objectives in conditioning athletes. Good flexibility increases the athlete's ability to avoid injury. Since it permits a greater range of movement within the joint, the ligaments and other collagenous tissues are not so easily strained or torn. It also permits greater freedom of movement in all directions. There appears to be a definite relationship between injury and joint flexibility. The "tight" or inflexible athlete performs under a considerable handicap in terms of movement, besides being much more injury prone. Tight-jointed athletes seem to be more susceptible to muscle strains and tears. Repetitive stretching of the collagenous or fascial ligamentous tissues over a long period of time permits the athlete to obtain an increased range of motion. Such stretching also provides an excellent warm-up.

Conversely, hyperflexibility must be avoided, because loose-jointed players are more prone to dislocations and subluxations.[19] Extremes of flexibility are indeed of little value and can result in weakness of the joint at certain angles. Flexibility, like strength, is quite specific to the joint and its surrounding complementary tissues. It varies in its natural degree among individuals. Flexibility and strength are independent of each other, since strength per se involves only muscle tissue, whereas stretch is concerned simply with the connective tissue.

The development of flexibility is a slow process, but persistence will pay off. The myotatic (stretch) reflex, which is invoked during a stretching maneuver, is a muscle-protective mechanism. The muscle itself actively resists stretch as the result of a reflex inhibition in the antagonistic muscle (the inverse myotatic reflex), which tends to reduce activation. The amount and rate of response of a stretch reflex are proportional to the amount and rate of stretching; hence the use of a repetitive vigorous ballistic (rebound) stretching maneuver would cause the muscle to contract with proportional

Text continued on p. 126.

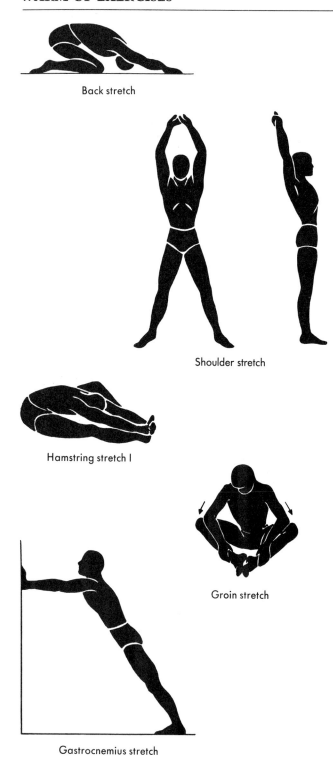

Back stretch

Shoulder stretch

Hamstring stretch I

Groin stretch

Gastrocnemius stretch

Back stretch Kneeling on both knees, feet extended, sit on the heels, with the trunk bent forward over the thighs, and arch the back as much as possible. Meanwhile retract the abdomen forcefully. Extend arms forward to full length with palms on the floor and force the head down between the arms as far as possible. Hold this position for 30 seconds; repeat 2 or 3 times. *NOTE:* This exercise also stretches the quadriceps muscle group.

Shoulder stretch Assume a small side stride stand, arms extended in front of the body and fingers interlaced. Reverse the hand position, maintaining grip (palms now face away from the body), and raise the straight arms overhead, forcing them into as much hyperextension as possible. Be sure to keep the chin firmly tucked in. Hold for 30 seconds; repeat 2 or 3 times.

Hamstring stretch I Sit on ground with one leg fully extended and the other flexed. Stretching is to one leg at a time. The trunk is flexed forward on the thigh, knee straight, and hands reaching to touch the toes. To also stretch the gastrocnemius at the knee joint, the foot should be dorsiflexed as much as possible. Hold for 30 seconds; repeat 2 to 3 times.

Groin stretch In a sitting position, place the soles of the feet together, drawing the heels as close to the buttocks as possible. With the elbows placed inside the knees, grasp the ankles and exert force outwardly with the elbows. Push the knees down toward the floor while flexing the spine forward and pulling the forehead toward the toes. Hold the terminal position for 20 to 40 seconds.

Gastrocnemius stretch Stand approximately 3 to 4 feet from a vertical surface such as a wall or upright support. Incline the straight body forward to an angle of approximately 65 degrees, supporting the body with the extended arms, the palms against the surface. *NOTE:* Stretching may be augmented by having the balls of the feet on a 2-inch elevation such as a short length of a two-by-four. Hold the position for 30 seconds; repeat 2 or 3 times.

Hamstring stretch II In a standing position, cross the right leg over the left, placing the right foot directly alongside the left. Bend the trunk slowly forward, sliding both hands down the right leg toward the ankle until a strong pull of opposition is felt. Hold this position for 6 to 10 seconds. Now try to continue sliding the hands closer to the feet until again opposition is felt. Again hold the position for 6 to 10 seconds. Repeat until no further gain in flexion can be obtained. Repeat the entire procedure to the opposite side. *NOTE:* Contracting the abdominal and quadriceps muscles during the standing procedure will augment the stretch; repeat 2 or 3 times each leg.

Running in place Run in place with vigorous arm swinging, raising the knees well above waist level for 3 to 4 minutes.

Trunk circling Starting position—straddle stand, arms free at sides. Circle the trunk 4 times to the left and then 4 times right (5 repetitions of a left and right series).

Abdominal curl Starting position—lying on back, knees bent, with feet on the floor and hands clasped across the chest. Count 1—curl upper trunk and head as close to the knees as possible. Count 2—return to starting position, (10 to 20 repetitions.) Vary the exercise by adding a trunk twist on the initial movement, touching the right elbow to the left knee and then returning to the starting position. On the next curl, touch the left elbow to the right knee and return. Alternate these movements for a total of 10 to 20 repetitions; repeat 2 or 3 times.

Arm fling Starting position—straddle stand, both arms sideward to the left, hands clenched to a loose fist. Swing relaxed arms horizontally to the left as far as they can go, meanwhile rotating the trunk in the same direction. Repeat to the right. Keep feet fixed; 10 to 20 repetitions.

Ankle suppling Starting position—feet in a small side stand. Rock up on the balls of the feet as high as possible, then back on the heels, raising the balls of the feet as much as possible. Repeat the sequence from the beginning; 8 to 10 repetitions.

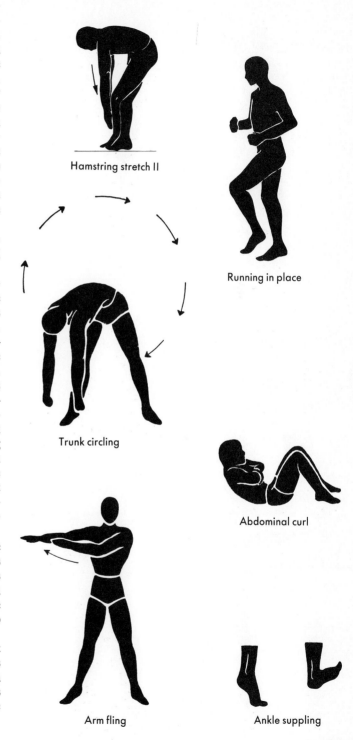

Hamstring stretch II

Running in place

Trunk circling

Abdominal curl

Arm fling

Ankle suppling

Arm circling

Half squat

High kick

Pectoral stretch

Arm circling Starting position—feet in a side stride stand, hands loosely clenched to a fist. Circle right arm backward for 8 to 10 complete arm circles, then the left arm. Circle right arm forward 8 to 10 circles; repeat with left arm. Continue alternating; 8 to 10 complete repetitions of series.

Half squat Starting position—small stride stand, hands on hips. Keeping the trunk erect and raising the heels slightly off the ground, bend both knees to a half squat position. Return to starting position. Complete 10 to 15 repetitions at a moderate tempo.

High kick Starting position—attention. Take a small step forward with the left foot, transferring the weight, and kick the extended right leg as high as possible. Step back and repeat the sequence. After 8 to 10 repetitions with the right leg, exercise the left leg.

Pectoral stretch Starting position—feet in a side stride stand and arms raised sideward to slightly above shoulder height, palms upward. Slowly and steadily pull the straight arms as far back as possible. Relax the arms momentarily and then repeat the pull; 10 to 20 repetitions.

Push-ups Starting position—front-leaning rest with back straight. Bend the arms, lowering the straight body until the chest just brushes the ground. Straighten arms and return to starting position. Execute in a moderate tempo; 6 to 10 repetitions. *CAUTION: Be sure to keep head in line with body and do not permit hips either to sag or to be carried higher than the back.*

Push-up

Ski stretch Starting position—attention. Move, either by stepping or by sliding the right foot forward into a deep-lunge position, left knee slightly flexed and hand on each side contracting the ground with the fingertips to maintain balance. Hold this position for at least 6 seconds while slowly and steadily forcing the body weight downward to increase the stretch. Shift body weight over the forward knee, meanwhile pulling the left leg forward to starting position. Repeat, moving the left leg forward. Repeat 5 to 10 times.

Anterior shoulder stretch Starting position—feet in small side stride stand, fingers hooked together in rear of buttocks. Slowly force the extended arms backward and upward as far as possible. Hold the terminal position for 6 to 10 seconds. Repeat 5 to 10 times.

Shoulder roll Starting position—attention. With a preliminary run of 5 or 6 steps, drop the right shoulder and, swinging the right arm across the body with chest high, execute a roll forward—landing on the back of the right shoulder, tucking the body by flexing the hips and knees, and rolling up on the feet to a stand. Repeat, rolling on the left shoulder; 4 to 6 repetitions to each side.

Ski stretch

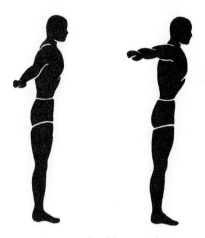

Anterior shoulder stretch

Shoulder roll

TABLE 5-1

Circuit A

Sport	Back Stretch	Shoulder Stretch	Hamstring Stretch I	Groin Stretch	Gastrocnemius Stretch	Hamstring Stretch II	Running in Place	Trunk Circling	Abdominal Curl	Arm Fling	Ankle Suppling	Arm Circling	Half Squat	High Kick	Pectoral Stretch	Push-up	Shoulder Roll	Ski Stretch	Anterior Shoulder Stretch	Warm-ups Specific to the Sport
Baseball	X	X	X	X	X	X	X	X	X	X	X	X						X	X	Warm-up throws with partner; starting easy at first, then gradually increasing force of throw; swinging weighted bat; throwing weighted ball
Basketball	X	X	X	X	X	X	X	X		X	X				X				X	Warm-up throws; one- and two-hand passing drills; dribbling warm-up drills; pregame basket shooting practice
Cross-country			X	X	X	X	X	X			X		X							Same warm-up procedures as for long distance
Cycling	X	X	X		X	X	X				X									
Diving	X	X	X		X	X	X	X	X	X	X			X				X	X	
Football (American)		X	X	X	X	X	X	X	X		X	X		X			X	X		Offensive-defensive warm-up; body contact–simulated charge and block
Gymnastics	X	X	X	X	X	X		X	X	X	X		X		X	X	X	X	X	Dip swings on parallel bars; splits; run through complete routine several times

	C1	C2	C3	C4	C5	C6	C7	C8	C9	C10	C11	C12	C13	
Ice hockey		X	X	X	X	X		X		X			X	Warm-up skating; stick handling and passing; shooting drills
Lacrosse	X	X	X	X	X	X	X	X	X	X		X	X	Running and passing drills
Rowing	X	X	X		X	X	X	X	X		X		X	
Rugby	X	X	X	X	X	X	X	X	X			X	X	Same as football
Skiing														
Cross-country	X	X		X		X		X	X			X	X	
Downhill	X	X	X	X	X	X	X	X		X		X	X	
Slalom	X	X	X	X	X	X	X	X		X		X	X	
Soccer (football)	X	X	X	X	X	X	X	X	X	X		X	X	Passing and heading drills
Swimming	X	X		X		X	X	X	X	X		X	X	Depending on event, swim 10 to 20 laps at moderate rate of speed
Tennis	X	X	X	X	X		X	X		X		X	X	After initial warm-ups, warm-up on practice board, then move on court for practice serves and volleys
Track and field*														
Volleyball	X	X	X	X	X	X	X	X	X	X		X	X	Circle-passing drills and practice serves
Water polo	X	X	X	X	X	X	X	X	X	X		X	X	Same warm-ups as for swimming; on practice days, swim 6 to 10 laps after general warm-up; ball-handling drills—deck and in water; skill drills
Wrestling	X	X		X	X	X	X	X	X	X		X	X	Sit out against token resistance

*See Table 5-2.

vigor—not at all a desirable response for either warm-ups or the attainment of flexibility.[18] It could damage the muscle fibers. It would therefore seem logical to use a sustained static-type stretch that will initiate the inverse myotatic reflex as a controlling mechanism. This inhibits the stretching muscles, which in turn facilitates further stretching. The use of static-type stretch—to the point of maximal resistance—accompanied by active con-

TABLE 5-2

Circuit A for track and field

Sport	Back Stretch	Shoulder Stretch	Hamstring Stretch I	Groin Stretch	Gastrocnemius Stretch	Hamstring Stretch II	Running in Place	Trunk Circling	Abdominal Curl	Arm Fling
Sprinters			X		X	X		X		X
High hurdlers	X		X	X	X	X		X		X
Low hurdlers	X		X	X	X	X		X		X

traction of the antagonists and then holding the position for 6 to 10 seconds before stretching them further seems to be the best way of achieving results. The amount and intensity of the movement of the various body parts through a full range of joint motion maintains an adequate degree of flexibility. To be most effective, flexibility exercises should be done several times daily performing 2 or 3 repetitions and holding all terminal positions

Ankle Suppling	Arm Circling	Half Squat	High Kick	Pectoral Stretch	Push-up	Shoulder Roll	Ski Stretch	Anterior Shoulder Stretch	Warm-ups Specific to the Sport
X		X	X				X		1. Alternate running at half speed and jogging, each for a distance of 50 yd, for a total of 400 yd. 2. Take 6 to 8 starts, running at half speed, finally working up to three-quarter speed. 3. Several sprints at half to three-quarter speed for 50 to 60 yd. 4. On competition days, do a few stretching exercises for the legs, such as the ski stretch and side straddle hop during the last 6 to 8 minutes before call. This is especially important to warm-up the hamstrings.
X		X	X				X		1. Take 6 to 8 starts, clearing first hurdle on last 2 or 3 starts. 2. Two-thirds maximal speed starts running first 2 or 3 hurdles. 3. After warm-up keep relaxed, loose, and warm through easy jogging alternated with side straddle hops and trunk circling until called to the mark.
X		X	X				X		Same as high hurdlers.

Continued.

at least 30 seconds at each exercise session. In performing flexibility exercises it is advisable to do the endurance exercises first, followed by the flexibility exercises and then the strength exercises.

The athlete who possesses good flexibility can change direction of movement easily, is able to fall properly and with less chance of injury, and

TABLE 5-2, cont'd

Circuit A for track and field

Sport	Back Stretch	Shoulder Stretch	Hamstring Stretch I	Groin Stretch	Gastrocnemius Stretch	Hamstring Stretch II	Running in Place	Trunk Circling	Abdominal Curl	Arm Fling
440 yd (400 m)			X	X	X	X	X	X		
880 yd (800 m)			X	X	X	X	X	X		
Mile run (1500 m)			X	X	X			X		

is physically more adaptable to almost any game situation. The wise athletic trainer will single out inflexible athletes and have them placed on a regimen of static stretching exercises until they achieve a satisfactory degree of flexibility. This is one way in which injury can be reduced.

The athlete who gains improved flexibility and increased range of joint

Ankle Suppling	Arm Circling	Half Squat	High Kick	Pectoral Stretch	Push-up	Shoulder Roll	Ski Stretch	Anterior Shoulder Stretch	Warm-ups Specific to the Sport
X		X							1. Alternate jogging and running at half speed, each for 100 yd, in total 400 yd. 2. Walk 2 to 3 minutes. 3. Run 200 yd at half speed. 4. Walk at least 3 minutes. 5. Take a few starts. 6. Finish with light stretching exercises.
X		X	X			X			1. Alternate running with jogging at half speed, each about 150 yd for 800 m. 2. Walk at least 3 minutes. 3. Run 300 yd at half speed. 4. Walk 3 to 5 minutes. 5. Take 6 starts. 6. Finish with light stretching exercises.
X		X							1. Alternate running with jogging at half speed, each for 200 yd—½ mile total. 2. Run ¼ mile at pace race (e.g., 4:20 mile, run 65 sec 440 yd). 3. Walk 6 to 8 minutes. 4. Jog 220 yd, walk approximately 100 yd, and finish with a fast 100-yd sprint. 5. Walk 4 to 5 minutes. 6. Take 2 or 3 starts. 7. Finish with light stretching exercises just before the race.

Continued.

movement is able to use his or her body more effectively and efficiently
and is better able to avoid a potential injury-provoking situation. In addition, when such a situation is unavoidable, the joints involved are far more
stable and can withstand a stress or torque considerably in excess of that
which can be resisted by a less flexible person. Increased flexibility further
aids in reducing impact shock such as that encountered in the contact

TABLE 5-2, cont'd

Circuit A for track and field

Sport	Back Stretch	Shoulder Stretch	Hamstring Stretch I	Groin Stretch	Gastrocnemius Stretch	Hamstring Stretch II	Running in Place	Trunk Circling	Abdominal Curl	Arm Fling
Two-mile run (3000 m)			X	X	X			X		
Long distance (5000 to 10,000 m)			X	X	X			X		
Javelin		X			X	X	X	X	X	X
Jumpers and vaulters	X	X	X	X	X	X	X	X	X	
Weight events		X	X		X	X	X	X	X	X

sports or in activities in which the body comes into forceful contact with a relatively unyielding surface (for example, the landing phase included in gymnastics, jumping, or vaulting).

Although the results of static and ballistic stretching may closely parallel each other, static stretching is preferred because it does not result in the small muscle tears and pulls that so often occur after vigorous ballistic

Ankle Suppling	Arm Circling	Half Squat	High Kick	Pectoral Stretch	Push-up	Shoulder Roll	Ski Stretch	Anterior Shoulder Stretch	Warm-ups Specific to the Sport
X		X							1. Alternately walk and jog 440 yd. 2. Walk 4 to 5 minutes. 3. Run ½ mile at intended 2-mile pace. 4. Walk 6 to 8 minutes. 5. Jog 440 yd finishing last 150 yd in a sprint. 6. Finish with light stretching exercises.
X		X							1. Upgrade specific warm-ups suggested for 2-mile run. 2. Warm-up from 2 to 3 miles—jogging, striding, and walking, terminating with short sprints. Usually jog first mile, stride second. 3. Finish with light stretching exercises.
X	X	X		X	X			X	1. Alternately jog and stride ½ mile. 2. Take 6 to 8 50-yd sprints. 3. Take warm-up throws or puts.
X	X	X		X	X			X	1. Same as for weight events. 2. Warm-up throws from easy to three-fourths maximal force. 3. Throw weighted javelin.
			X	X			X	X	1. Alternately jog and sprint ¼ to ½ mile. 2. Practice vaults or jumps.

There is a distinct difference
between weight lifting, which
is a sport, and weight
training, which is a series of
progressive resistance
exercises used to attain speed,
strength, and endurance.

stretching. When a muscle has been thoroughly warmed up through static stretching and a program of general conditioning exercises, the athlete may proceed to ballistic stretching if so desired, although it is doubtful that it will contribute any additional flexibility.

Strength Training

The inherent values of weight training are recognized by trainers, physical educators, coaches, and physicians. A cursory review of sports literature reveals various sytems of weight training. It has taken a long time, even for people in the field, to recognize that there is a distinct difference between weight lifting, which is a sport, and weight training, in which a series of progressive resistance exercises are used to attain speed, strength, and endurance.

As indicated in Chapter 4, most weight-training systems currently in use today are based on variations of the DeLorme method of progressive resistance exercises (PRE) using the overload principle.[4] If properly carried out, weight training will contribute to the general physical well-being of athletes, as well as improve their speed, "explosive power," strength, and endurance. The use of a weighted football, soccer ball, baseball, or basketball, the swinging of weighted baseball bats, and the wearing of weighted belts and other equipment—by runners, jumpers, rope climbers, and other athletes—are simply forms of weight training. Resistive devices, such as those employing friction that can be increased or decreased by means of a dial, have considerable value and are indicated when space and/or finances preclude establishing weight-lifting equipment. These devices can be used either supplemental to or in lieu of barbells and other weights.

Weight exercises are usually categorized, in terms descriptive of the type of contractions they elicit, as isotonic, isometric, or isokinetic. Each type of contraction has value.

In a weight-training program certain fundamental principles must be followed by each athlete:

1. Precede all weight training with the general warm-up.
2. Begin all isotonic contractions from a position of "on stretch," immediately moving into the concentric contraction.
3. Perform isotonic movements slowly and deliberately, at approximately one-fifth maximal speed.
4. Hold isometric movements at the terminal position for about 6 to 10 seconds, or longer if desired, holding the contractions at various angles, since strength is gained at the specific angle at which the joint is held during the contraction.
5. Apply the overload principle in all isotonic contractions. When you are able to complete the second or third series with some degree of ease, add more resistance.
6. Maintain good muscular balance by exercising both the agonist and antagonist muscles.
7. Confine heavy work to the off-season and the preseason period. A light to medium program can be maintained during the regular practice days of the competitive season, provided that it is confined to use of the weight schedule after the regular practice.
8. Work with weights every other day and no more than 4 days a week. This allows ample time for reduction of soreness and stiffness.

9. Initiate the training program first in terms of general body development and then progress to exercises tailored to the specific sport or event employing the SAID principle and geared to the type of muscle fiber involved (fast or slow twitch) in the activity.
10. After a general warm-up, begin a preliminary series of about ten repetitions using approximately half of the weight normally used. This is usually a sound procedure.
11. Observe proper breathing procedures during lifting to assist in fixing the stabilizing muscles of the trunk and therefore give a firm base from which to work. Inhale deeply just before beginning a lift and exhale somewhat forcefully on the return movement. This aids in performing the lift.

Isotonic Training Exercises

These exercises should be done about once or twice a week during the off-season, every other day during the preseason, and after regular activity periods during the competition season. Beginners are advised to start their programs during the off-season and concentrate principally on a general body-building program. They should have moved into the preseason period before concentrating on weight training that is specific in terms of their sport. The initial resistance is somewhat arbitrarily determined by ascertaining the athlete's maximal lift in each exercise to be programmed and then by setting the initial resistance from 75% to 90% of that amount. It is recommended that the exercises be performed for the suggested number of repetitions with near-maximal weight and that a 5-pound increment be added for the arms and a 10-pound increment for the legs when the ultimate series is repeated two workout periods in succession. Use three series of ten repetitions in each series for each of the exercises performed. It is difficult to prescribe a program for the various isokinetic or internal friction-type devices. Fewer repetitions are warranted; probably six repetitions in each of three sets are adequate when the work is performed in a circuit.

Isometric Training Exercises

As discussed in Chapter 4, isometric exercises produce muscular heat and energy by shortening the muscle length or changing the angle of the joint. For the best results, there should be a maximal muscle contraction for at least 6 seconds. To ensure optimal performance, the athlete should be instructed to statically contract the muscle for 10 seconds. Each exercise is repeated five to ten times.

RESISTANCE TRAINING FOR SPECIFIC ACTIVITIES

After the general program of weight training, exercises specifically designed to develop the muscle groups that are most important for successful performance in a given activity should be assigned. A thorough knowledge of kinesiology is of the utmost importance if the trainer or coach is to intelligently prescribe suitable activities. Careful analysis of an activity in terms of the types and kinds of movement employed gives clues as to which muscle groups are the most prominent in effecting the desired patterns of movement. It is then relatively simple to select routines that have been devised to properly exercise those muscles. Sports demand rotational, rather than linear, elements of the body. Exercises must be selected on the basis of their

A thorough knowledge of kinesiology is of the utmost importance for the trainer or coach to intelligently prescribe suitable activities.

Text continued on p. 140.

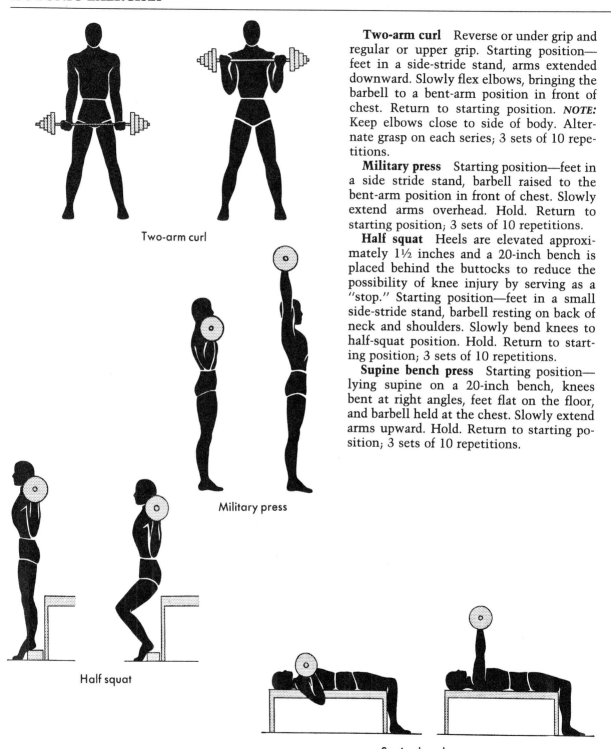

Two-arm curl

Military press

Half squat

Supine bench press

Two-arm curl Reverse or under grip and regular or upper grip. Starting position—feet in a side-stride stand, arms extended downward. Slowly flex elbows, bringing the barbell to a bent-arm position in front of chest. Return to starting position. *NOTE:* Keep elbows close to side of body. Alternate grasp on each series; 3 sets of 10 repetitions.

Military press Starting position—feet in a side stride stand, barbell raised to the bent-arm position in front of chest. Slowly extend arms overhead. Hold. Return to starting position; 3 sets of 10 repetitions.

Half squat Heels are elevated approximately 1½ inches and a 20-inch bench is placed behind the buttocks to reduce the possibility of knee injury by serving as a "stop." Starting position—feet in a small side-stride stand, barbell resting on back of neck and shoulders. Slowly bend knees to half-squat position. Hold. Return to starting position; 3 sets of 10 repetitions.

Supine bench press Starting position—lying supine on a 20-inch bench, knees bent at right angles, feet flat on the floor, and barbell held at the chest. Slowly extend arms upward. Hold. Return to starting position; 3 sets of 10 repetitions.

Rowing exercise Starting position—feet in a small side stride stand, arms extended downward with hands centered and in proximity of the bar, head resting on a folded towel placed on a table. Slowly pull the bar up to a position in front of the chest. Hold. Return to starting position; 3 sets of 10 repetitions. *NOTE:* This may also be done with the lifter assuming and maintaining an angle stand—that is, trunk flexed forward at the hips at approximately a right angle.

Side arm raises Starting position—prone or supine position on a bench, arms downward, hands grasping 10-pound dumbbells. Slowly raise arms sideward to a horizontal position. Hold. Return to starting position. *CAUTION: Avoid locking the elbow joint in a complete extension, since this exerts severe strain on the joint.* Do 3 sets of 10 repetitions, alternating the prone and supine positions daily.

Leg curl Starting position—face lying position with boot weight fixed to one foot. The leg is curled upward as far as possible and then slowly returned to its original position; 3 sets of 10 repetitions and then repeat with other leg.

Heel raise Starting position—feet in a small side-stride stand, balls of the feet on a 2-inch riser, barbell resting on the back of the neck and shoulders. Slowly rise on toes. Hold. Return to starting position. Variations may be performed by having the feet either toes out or toes in; 3 sets of 10 repetitions.

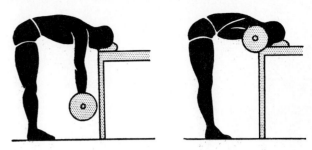

Rowing exercise

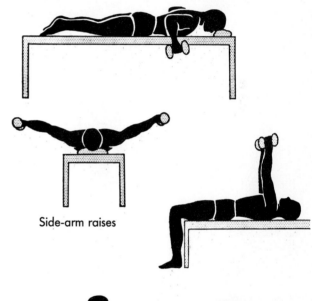

Side-arm raises

Leg curl

Heel raise

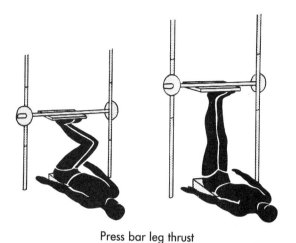

Press bar leg thrust

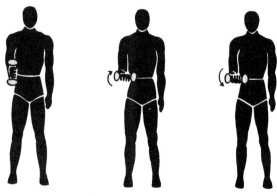

Press bar quadriceps strengthener

Supination-pronation

Press bar leg thrust Starting position—angle-lying position under the press bar, balls of the feet in contact with the bar or bar platform, legs in a half-flexed position. Slowly extend the knees, keeping the buttocks in contact with the floor. Hold. Return to starting position; 3 sets of 10 repetitions. *NOTE:* To provide for better contact, fasten to the bar an 8-inch by 12-inch board. This prevents the feet from slipping off the bar.

Press bar quadriceps strengthener Starting position—a half-crouched position under the bar, shoulders and neck in contact with the bar. (A folded towel may be used as a pad.) Slowly extend knees to an erect position. Hold. Return to starting position; 3 sets of 10 repetitions. *CAUTION: Lift with the knee extensors, not the lower back muscles.*

Abdominal curl Starting position—hook-lying, feet anchored, and dumbbell weighing 15 to 25 pounds held on the upper chest. Curl the upper trunk upward and as far forward as possible. Return slowly to the starting position. Maintain a moderate tempo and steady rhythm and avoid bouncing up from the floor; 3 sets of 10 repetitions. Number can be increased as capacity for more work increases.

Supination-pronation Start with feet in small side stride stand, elbow bent at a right angle to upper arm, and hand grasping a 20-pound dumbbell. Rotate the dumbbell alternately left and right, using the muscles of the forearm and wrist only; 3 sets of 10 repetitions.

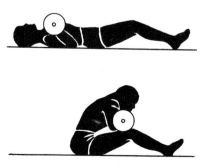

Abdominal curl

Wrist roll Begin with feet in a small side stride stand. Slowly wind up a cord to which a 25-pound weight has been attached. Reverse the action, slowly unwinding the full length of the cord; 3 sets of 5 repetitions. *NOTE:* A wrist roller is easily constructed by securing one end of a 30-inch length of sash cord to the center of a 12-inch length of broomstick or dowel of a somewhat thicker diameter and the other end to a 25-pound weight.

Boot exercise Sit on plinth or table with lower legs hanging free over the edge and clear of the floor. A 20-pound boot is strapped to the foot. Do exercises involving knee flexion and extension and inversion, eversion, flexion, and extension of the ankle. The weight should be increased in terms of ability to handle it. Each exercise should be done for 3 sets of 10 repetitions.

Crossed-arm swings Starting position—small side stride stand, a 20-pound dumbbell in each hand, arms raised directly sideward to shoulder height. Slowly swing the arms forward in a horizontal plane, continuing until each arm has progressed across the other and is carried as far as possible. Arms are extended, but elbow joints should not be locked. Return slowly toward the starting position, carrying the arms horizontally as far backward as possible; 3 sets of 10 repetitions.

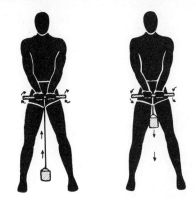

Wrist roll

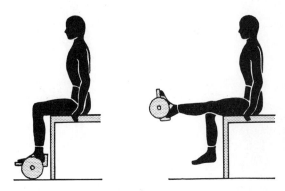

Boot exercise

Crossed-arm swing

Stationary press
bar leg thrust

Stationary press
bar leg tensor

Wall press

Shoulder-arm tensor

Stationary press bar leg thrust Starting position—angle-lying position under the press bar, balls of the feet in contact with the bar or bar platform, legs in a half-flexed position. Press bar is locked into place. Exert maximum force against the immovable bar, sustaining full pressure for 6 to 10 seconds. Following a short period of relaxation (5 to 10 seconds) repeat the procedure 2 or 3 times. *NOTE:* Hips may be elevated by a 2-inch pad.

Stationary press bar leg tensor Starting position—a half-crouched position under the bar, which is locked into place, shoulders and neck in contact with the bar. Exert maximum pressure against the bar by using the leg extensors and sustain full pressure for 6 to 10 seconds. Following a momentary relaxation, repeat the exercise 2 or 3 times.

Wall press Starting position—stand in a small stride stand in either the corner of a room or a doorway, placing the hands against the walls or the sides of the opening at about shoulder height. The elbows should be bent to about the halfway point in the normal range. Exert maximum force against the opposing surface, holding the position for at least 6 to 10 seconds. Relax pressure momentarily. Repeat 2 or 3 times.

Shoulder-arm tensor Starting position—feet in a small side stride stand. Hook the fingers of the hands together, elbows bent so that hands are above waist height. Push the hands together forcefully, at the same time tensing the arm, shoulder, neck, and abdominal muscles. Hold for 6 to 10 seconds. Relax momentarily and then repeat the tensing action but reverse the hand action by pulling against the fingers with as much force as possible. Repeat 2 or 3 times.

TABLE 5-3

Circuit B

Sport	Military Press	Two-arm Curl	Half Squat	Supine Bench Press	Rowing Exercise	Side Arm Raises	Leg Curl	Heel Raise	Press Bar Leg Thrust	Press Bar Quadriceps Strengthening	Abdominal Curl	Supination-Pronation	Wrist Roll	Boot Exercise	Crossed-Arm Swing	Stationary Press Bar Leg Thrust	Stationary Press Bar Leg Tensor	Wall Press	Shoulder-Arm Tensor
	Isotonic															Isometric			
Baseball	X	X	X		X	X	X	X	X			X	X	X		X		X	
Basketball	X	X	X		X	X	X	X	X			X	X	X		X		X	
Cycling			X				X	X	X	X				X		X	X		
Diving	X	X	X	X	X	X	X	X	X	X	X	X	X	X	X	X	X	X	X
Football (American)	X	X	X	X	X	X	X	X	X	X	X	X	X	X	X	X	X	X	X
Gymnastics	X	X	X	X	X	X	X	X	X	X	X	X	X	X	X	X	X	X	X
Ice hockey	X	X	X	X	X	X	X	X	X	X	X	X	X	X	X	X	X	X	X
Lacrosse	X	X	X	X	X	X	X	X	X	X	X	X	X	X	X	X	X	X	X
Rowing	X	X	X	X	X	X	X	X	X	X	X	X	X	X	X	X	X	X	X
Rugby	X	X	X	X	X	X	X	X	X	X	X	X	X	X	X	X	X	X	X
Skiing																			
Cross-country	X	X	X	X	X	X	X	X	X	X	X	X	X	X		X	X		
Downhill		X	X			X		X	X		X	X		X	X	X	X		
Slalom			X		X	X	X	X	X	X	X	X		X	X	X	X		
Soccer (football)		X	X	X	X		X	X	X	X		X	X	X	X	X	X		X
Swimming	X	X	X		X	X	X	X	X	X	X	X	X	X	X	X	X	X	X
Tennis	X	X	X		X	X	X	X	X	X	X	X		X	X	X	X		X
Track and field																			
Sprinters, runners, and hurdlers			X				X	X	X	X	X			X		X	X		X
Jumpers	X	X	X	X	X	X	X	X	X	X	X	X	X	X	X	X	X	X	X
Vaulters	X	X	X	X	X	X	X	X	X	X	X	X	X	X	X	X	X	X	X
Weight events	X	X	X	X	X	X	X	X	X	X	X	X	X	X	X	X	X	X	X
Javelin	X	X	X	X	X		X	X	X	X	X	X	X	X	X	X	X	X	X
Volleyball	X	X	X	X	X	X	X	X	X	X	X	X	X	X	X	X	X	X	X
Water polo	X	X	X	X	X	X	X	X	X	X	X	X	X	X	X	X	X	X	X
Wrestling	X	X	X	X	X	X	X	X	X	X	X	X	X	X	X	X	X	X	X

development construction, as well as mimetic activity. For example, arm swings similar to the crawl stroke might be employed while holding a 5-pound dumbbell in each hand. Throwing a weighted ball could be one means used in strengthening a throwing arm. Mimetic activities of this type assist in establishing the neuromuscular pattern of movement desired. Table 5-3 shows isometric and isotonic exercises for setting up a weight-training program geared to a particular sport. Additional training suggestions for each sport follow.

Baseball

A number of studies have shown that throwing speed, batting, and running speed can be improved through the use of resistance exercises. Employing a program of exercises coupled with workouts using a weighted bat and a weighted ball should result in performance improvement. Players should practice throwing, as described earlier, but should use a specially prepared ball. A baseball is weighted by opening the seam, drilling a 3/8-inch hole to the center of the ball, and pounding in a few ounces of soft-spun lead wool (such as that used for sealing pipe joints and obtainable at most plumbing supply stores). The remainder of the hole can then be filled with kapok, cotton, and some other soft material and the cover resewed. A bat in which a hole has been drilled lengthwise at the top and 4 or 5 ounces of lead inserted can be used for trunk twisting and bat swinging.

Basketball

The exercises suggested for baseball players, with the exception of those involving use of a weighted ball or bat, will also serve as specific exercises for basketball players. In addition, passing drills that use a 4-pound or 6-pound medicine ball further serve to strengthen the wrists, fingers, forearms, and shoulders. One-hand and two-hand shooting drills in which the shooter uses a medicine ball in lieu of a basketball and goes through the pattern of making a shot to a partner are also excellent for developing strength where it is needed for the sport.

To further develop the explosive power that is so vital in backboard play, players should practice rebound play while wearing a weight belt. Such belts are easily made of canvas and should be of double thickness so that several pounds of lead shot may be placed between the layers. They are secured by a small tongue and buckle. The local shoemaker can construct weight belts at a nominal charge.

Cycling

The long-distance cyclist must train as assiduously and as arduously as the marathon runner.

Cycling as a competitive sport has had popularity in Europe for many years but is just beginning to gain significant awareness in the United States. Road racing makes severe demands on the cardiovascular system, as well as on the leg muscles, and the long-distance cyclist must train as assiduously and as arduously as the marathon runner. Sprint cycling, basically a spurt activity, makes similar demands but of shorter duration. Nevertheless, sprinters must develop endurance if they are to compete successfully in elimination heats, which frequently allow little time for complete recovery from the previous sprint heat.

Many cyclists ride as much as 200 miles and more per week, especially before or early in the season. As the season progresses, interval training may be instituted and the distance rides shortened somewhat. The training programs for competitive cycling are highly specific. However, the warm-ups and weight-training exercises indicated in Tables 5-1 and 5-3 can be used to advantage to supplement the riding program.

Diving

Diving makes basically the same physical demands on the body as does gymnastics. The warm-up and weight-training exercises indicated in Tables 5-1 and 5-3 will enable the diver to gain the flexibility and strength necessary for the activity. Special attention should be given to strengthening the muscles of the legs, ankles, and feet while maintaining a high degree of suppleness. Upper body and limb strength is equally important, and the diver should select from any of the general arm and trunk strengthening exercises shown in the text.

Football (American)

Football players should follow the general weight-training program to obtain as much overall development as possible. In addition, the practice of the high kick, while using weighted shoes, is of benefit to punters and place kickers. The use of a weighted ball for passing, punting, and centering helps to develop the muscles employed in performing these skills. Such a ball can be easily constructed by stuffing an old ball with cotton waste or, preferably, sponge rubber scraps. The ball should weigh approximately 3 pounds. Passers can further develop the throwing arm by using the same arm, wrist, and shoulder exercises advocated for baseball and basketball players. Linemen can use the press bar to considerable advantage by doing additional work with the shoulder shrug and leg lift, both isotonically and isometrically.

The use of a weighted football for passing, punting, and centering helps to develop the muscles employed in performing football skills.

Gymnastics

Exercises for the arm and shoulder joint and for the leg, which have been indicated as part of the general weight-training pattern, will serve well as specific exercises for gymnasts if the concentration is increased. In addition, abdominal curls with a weight and the wrist rolls should be included. The use of a weight belt by vaulters has great value. Chinning, either with the weight belt or with weights attached to the feet, is also an excellent exercise for gymnasts.

Ice Hockey

The physical responses in ice hockey are considerable, making not only aerobic and anaerobic demands but demands on strength and power as well. Isometric and isotonic exercises, particularly the latter, should be employed to develop the wrists, forearms, shoulders, and legs. Flexibility exercises for these body areas should also be stressed, since stick handling and agility require a great deal of flexibility. The physical contact encountered in body checking, board contact, and scrimmaging calls for basically the same training program followed in conditioning for American football in addition to the specific skills involved in skating and stick handling. Cardiorespiratory training will be considered later in this chapter.

Lacrosse

This is a physically demanding sport with a great deal of running, requiring ruggedness to withstand, with little protective equipment, forceful body contact. It also requires a great deal of agility, not only in evasive tactics but also in handling, passing, throwing, and catching while the athlete is in full motion.

The player should participate in a general weight-training program as suggested in Table 5-3. In addition, optimal flexibility also must be developed. A carefully constructed weight-training and flexibility program coupled with a challenging running program to increase endurance and speed should produce a well-conditioned lacrosse player.

Rowing

This is probably the most physically demanding sport. In rowing the entire body is maximally involved—for as long as 6 minutes in some instances. The demands made on the cardiopulmonary and muscular systems are tremendous indeed, so any training program must take into account activities that will expressly stress and develop those systems. Hence emphasis must be on weight training and running. In addition, rowing itself—at tempos and time intervals over and above those usually encountered in competition—forms a considerable part of the training program. Overload, using arm and ankle weights, can be used additionally to condition the rower through any of the three aspects of the program.

Rugby

Weight training for rugby should generally follow the program for American football inasmuch as the character of play and the physical demands made on the players are more or less identical.

Skiing

Downhill and slalom skiing require a great deal of flexibility; hence a broad program of stretching and general flexibility exercises also should be performed.

Skiing makes unusually heavy demands on the hip and knee joints. Although downhill skiing does not make the intensive aerobic demands encountered in cross-country skiing, nonetheless a good weight-training program coupled with a strong running program to increase cardiorespiratory efficiency should be undertaken. Downhill and slalom, in particular, require a great deal of flexibility; hence a broad program of stretching and general flexibility exercises also should be performed. As with all other sports a year-round program of fitness should be instituted.

Exercises using a skateboard or those in which the feet are firmly fixed as in bindings and using ski poles as an exercising device all have value. Particular attention should be paid when developing an individual training program to strengthening of the knee joints, which are especially vulnerable in this sport.

Cross-country skiers, while using the weight-training procedures just listed, need to follow a program that emphasizes cardiorespiratory development.

Soccer Football

Weight training should employ those exercises which strengthen the ankle, knee, and hip joints to better withstand the starting, stopping, and changes of direction that are so vital to the game, as well as building up muscles used in kicking. In addition, the shoulder and neck musculature must be built up so as to enable the player to adequately perform "heading." Isotonic, isometric, and isokinetic exercises should be prescribed. The use of weighted shoes will be of some benefit and should assist in developing leg strength. Soccer makes tremendous aerobic demands on the player, particularly the halfbacks, since there is almost continuous running for over 70 minutes in each game. Therefore, a good cardiorespiratory aerobic program should be carried out.

Swimming

Swimmers can use both isotonic and isometric exercises to advantage. The use of mimetic exercises (arm and leg strokes) against a resistance is particularly effective. Many resistance devices can be adapted or modified for this purpose. As strength increases, resistance should be increased accordingly.

The use of mimetic exercises (arm and leg strokes) against a resistance is particularly effective.

Tennis

Tennis is basically a "spurt" sport wherein short bursts of intense activity are followed by a pause in activity. Cardiorespiratory training, as discussed later in this chapter, is of great importance. Any isometric and isotonic exercises that will strengthen the legs and the shoulder complex may be used. The wrist, forearm, and shoulder may be further strengthened through the use of a weighted racket which can be constructed by inserting lead into a hole drilled in the long axis of the handle and wrapping lead tape (obtainable at sporting goods stores) or solder around the frame.

Track and Field

Sprinters, runners, and hurdlers Emphasis for these athletes is primarily on leg development.

Weight lifters It is good practice for these athletes to work with their competitive implements weighted to values somewhat above the official weight. In particular, this group must stress the various arm and leg presses and lifts and abdominal curls.

Jumpers and vaulters The events in which these athletes engage are in some respects quite similar to phases of other events. Yet they have certain other characteristics inherently their own. Broad and high jumpers should follow the same pattern laid down for the sprinters and hurdlers but in addition should wear a weight belt some of the time while practicing.

Pole vaulting, although it has some of the characteristics of sprinting, is a gymnastic event that requires primarily great strength in the abdominal, shoulder, and back muscles. In addition to intensive work on the general weight-training program, the vaulter should follow the programs indicated for sprinters and for weight lifters. Rope climbing and pull-ups are excellent adjuncts to the weight program. Although not usually considered weight exercises, they do involve the lifting of the performer's body weight and are mimetic, in that they incorporate a basic movement in vaulting. The use of a weight belt during pull-ups and rope climbing is an excellent means of developing arm strength. Doing abdominal curls with a weight held behind the head is an excellent exercise, particularly when alternating trunk twists are added, since the oblique abdominal and rectus femoris muscles are brought into active participation. These muscles are very important in executing the pull-up and the turn.

Volleyball

Exercises that strengthen the fingers, wrists, and arms and develop the lower extremities for jumping are the prime exercise requisites for this sport. The strength-training exercise pattern should be coupled with a program of general conditioning exercises and plenty of running and jumping to develop endurance.

Water Polo

Although this sport is primarily an aquatic activity, it has many of the elements of basketball. Polo players should follow the program outlined for swimmers and in addition should work on strengthening hands, wrists, and shoulders by using the basketball exercises that involve these body parts. Dry-land passing drills, using a medicine ball, are quite effective as a means of developing good throwing ability.

Wrestling

Wrestling is an activity that requires excellent all-around development. In addition to the general weight-training exercises, a good running program coupled with circuit training not only can give variety to the training program but also can provide significant gains in strength and endurance.

SPECIAL APPROACHES TO PREVENTIVE CONDITIONING
Circuit Training

Circuit training employs both resistance training and calisthenic exercises.

Circuit training is a method of physical conditioning that employs both resistance training and calisthenic conditioning exercises. In some forms apparatus stunts have been added as a third kind of activity. The method has achieved considerable popularity in England[14] and has found favor in the United States as a means of achieving optimal fitness in a systematized, controlled fashion. The method was originally introduced by Morgan and Adamson in the late 1950s at the University of Leeds, England. It was immediately accepted by physical educators, coaches, and trainers as an excellent and self-motivating means of increasing strength, flexibility, and endurance, in an orderly fashion, within a group. The intensity and vigor of circuit training are indeed challenging and enjoyable to the performer. This system produces positive changes in motor performance. General fitness, muscular power, endurance, and speed have shown decided improvement as well.

Circuit training is based on the premise that the athlete must do the same amount of work in a shorter period of time or must do considerably more work within the limits of an assigned training period. Numerous variations of this system are in use, but all employ certain common factors:

(1) the use of PREs; (2) the use of physical conditioning and apparatus exercises, the former being performed either with or without weights; (3) a circular arrangement of the activities that permits progression from one station to another until all stations have been visited, the total comprising a "circuit"; and (4) a limiting time factor within which the circuit must be concluded.

The circuit is usually set up around the perimeter of the exercise area. When a circuit is set up, the number and types of stations desired should be selected for their value in stressing development of the body parts most commonly called into play in a particular athletic activity, as well as for their worth as activities promoting all-around body fitness. Six to twelve different stations can be set up, each with a specific exercise. The circuit should be so planned that the trainee can complete a circuit without becoming excessively fatigued.

> The circuit should be so planned that the trainee can complete a circuit without becoming excessively fatigued.

After a thorough orientation period to familiarize the trainee with the procedure and with the exercise to be done at each station, a time trial is given to ascertain the length of time required for completion of one to three laps, depending on the number of stations and the intensity and design of the various exercises. Progress is from one station to the next immediately on completion of the assignment at the first station. A "target" time, which is one third lower than the initial trial time, is then assigned. The weight exercises are usually performed at 50% to 70% of the athlete's maximal number of repetitions, and the resistance is usually arbitrarily determined by the trainer, in accordance with the athlete's capability. Two sample circuit programs that may serve as guides in developing programs to meet various requirements are shown in Figs. 5-2 and 5-3.

This system easily lends itself to handling large groups efficiently and productively. It is a practical method, entailing some preliminary planning, but beyond that it needs little coordinating. Athletes find it motivating, since it makes conditioning fun and challenging through competition against teammates and against time.

> Athletes find circuit training motivating, since it makes conditioning fun and challenging through competition against teammates and time.

Cardiorespiratory Improvement

A number of training methods are designed to enhance cardiorespiratory performance according to the requirements of a particular sport. Those which will be discussed here are continuous training, interval training, and fartlek.

Continuous Training

The continuous training approach is designed for long-endurance activities such as marathon running. Long, uninterrupted work is engaged in at a constant intensity. The steady pace in a situation of constant overload draws on the athlete's energy reserves over a long period of time. This method develops the athlete's aerobic capacity, functional stability, and energy reserves.[8]

Interval Training

All sports call for endurance. Some sports, such as soccer, football, lacrosse, hockey, and cross-country skiing, make tremendous aerobic demands on the body. Improvements in training methods have enabled athletes to significantly reduce their times in running events. Hard, intensive work is the key to the top conditioning that makes near-record and record-breaking performances possible. Resistance to the various effects of fatigue can be accomplished only through intensive, rigorous training that loads the circulorespiratory system to a level above an established threshold. In this way improvement in training, notably endurance, can occur. Below the training threshold no training effect is visible. This is the application of the *overload principle* to the cardiorespiratory system, wherein sufficient stress in the form of a specific work load and time factor is applied to develop endurance. Karvonen[9] has determined that the working pulse rate should be 60% of the heart rate reserve; therefore, the target heart rate equals the resting heart rate plus 60% of the heart rate reserve. Others have suggested 160 beats/min as a rule-of-thumb threshold. (A 10-second value of 27 beats/min may be used.)

The program of interval training must be set up to permit the athlete to achieve the greatest possible work load with the least amount of fatigue. That the body can achieve and tolerate a work load, when done intermittently, well over three times that done continuously has been well established by physiologists.

Four factors are significant in interval training: (1) a specified distance that is repeated a given number of times; (2) a recovery period during which

Figure 5-2

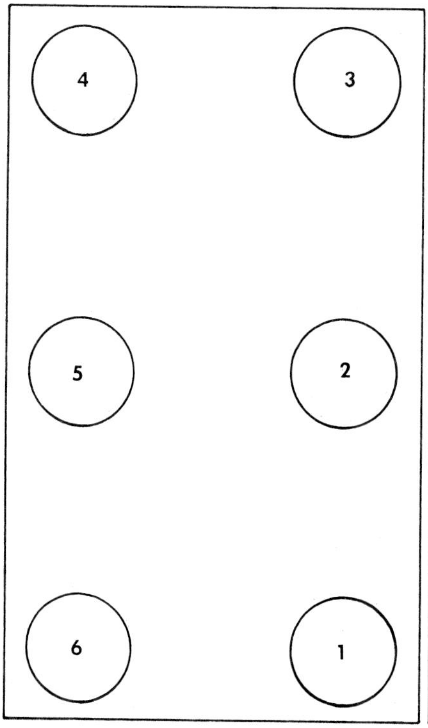

Circuit A—general conditioning. Station **1,** squat thrusts, 75% maximum number of repetitions performed in 1 minute; **2,** general flexion exercise, performed for 2 minutes; **3,** abdominal curls with weights, 75% maximum number of repetitions; **4,** two arm curls, 75% maximum number of repetitions; **5,** vertical jump (Sargent), 75% maximum number of repetitions performed in 1 minute; **6,** half squat, heels raised, exercise with weight, 75% maximum number of repetitions.

Figure 5-3

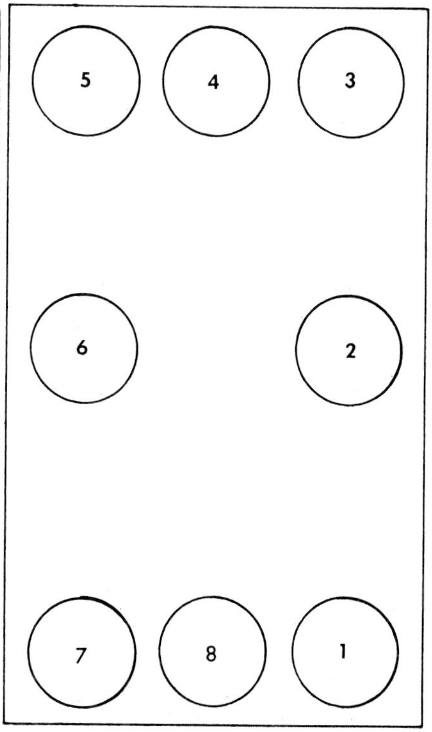

Circuit B—strength. Station **1,** rowing exercise, 70% maximum number of repetitions; **2,** chinning, 70% maximum number of repetitions; **3,** abdominal curls with weights, 75% maximum number of repetitions; **4,** two arm curls, 70% maximum number of repetitions; **5,** heel raising, toes elevated, 70% maximum number of repetitions; **6,** military press, 70% maximum number of repetitions; **7,** press bar leg thrust, 70% maximum number of repetitions; **8,** rope skipping, 1 minute, 70% maximum number of repetitions.

Figure 5-2

Figure 5-3

the athlete jogs slowly and relaxes; (3) a predetermined pace, carefully timed, at which the athlete covers the set distance; and (4) a predetermined number of repetitions in running the distance. Alternating 30-second intervals of work with rest intervals, which terminate when the pulse rate reaches 120 beats/min, appears to be the best pattern.

It is best to start the program 6 to 8 months before the opening of the competitive season. A relatively slow pace is used in the beginning and is sufficiently increased every 4 weeks to bring the runner to the desired time peak at the start of competition.

This type of conditioning program is quite flexible and permits adaptation. However, it is best not to tamper with the pace factor, since this is the key to a successful, planned performance. The number of repetitions should be increased if one wishes to intensify the workout, but the pace, recovery period, and distance should remain unchanged.

Development and improvement of the cardiorespiratory system are paramount in any training program, and probably the best method of achieving cardiorespiratory improvement is through interval training or one of its variations. It is not within the province of this text to deal with interval training to any further extent.

Fartlek

First devised in Sweden, this form of cardiorespiratory training is a type of cross-country running with pace variations, conducted over a hilly terrain. The term *fartlek*, broadly translated, means "speed play," referring to pace variations employed at the runner's whim during the period of the run. A set time period is used as the basic factor; consequently, no attention is given to pace as such in this program as in interval training. The runner starts off cross-country running at an easy pace, which is varied from time to time with short intensive sprints and with fast middle-distance runs up to ½ mile in length. Tempo and speed are entirely at the runner's discretion. The rationale for fartlek is that performance over a varied terrain and at varying paces eliminates training boredom, delays the onset of fatigue, and develops more stamina and strength than would be gained on a flat running track. Perhaps the principal objection to the sole use of this type of training is that, in all probability, the runner does not acquire pace judgment because of the variations. However, using fartlek in conjunction with interval training, as a means of developing cardiorespiratory endurance, would counter that objection. It also serves well as an off-season program to enable the athlete to remain in condition.

MUSCLE SORENESS AND STIFFNESS

Muscle soreness has long been a problem for the person engaging in physical conditioning. Two major types of muscle soreness are associated with severe exercise. The first is acute soreness occurring immediately after exercise, which is resolved when exercise has ceased. The second and more serious problem is delayed soreness, which is related mainly to early-season or unaccustomed work. Severe muscular discomfort occurs 24 to 48 hours after exercise.[7] Acute muscle soreness is considered to be related to an impedance of circulation, causing muscular ischemia. Lactic acid and potas-

The two major types of muscle soreness associated with severe exercise are acute and delayed.

sium collect in the muscle and stimulate pain receptors.

Compared to acute soreness, delayed soreness increases in intensity for 2 to 3 days and then subsides until it has completely disappeared within 7 days.[7] Four theories have been set forth as possibly causing muscle soreness: the lactic acid theory, tonic muscle spasm theory, torn tissue theory, and connective tissue theory.

Studies conducted since the beginning of this century have failed to satisfy the question of muscle soreness that occurs after exercise. Lactic acid production and accumulation may be related to acute soreness, but not to delayed soreness.[17] There is currently some question as to the spasm theory suggested by deVries[5] in 1961. Some indications do exist that delayed muscle soreness could be attributed to a disruption or tear in muscle fibers or damage to the connective tissue, particularly after eccentric contraction to the point of exhaustion.[16]

There are many ways of reducing the possibility of delayed muscle soreness. One is a gradual and complete warm-up before engaging in vigorous activity, followed by a careful cooling down. In the early part of training, careful attention should be paid to static stretching before and after activity.[5] If there is extreme soreness, the application of ice packs or ice massage to the point of numbness (about 5 to 8 minutes) followed by a static stretch will often provide relief.

Muscle stiffness is contrasted to muscle soreness because it does not produce pain. It occurs when a group of muscles have been worked hard for a long period of time. The fluids that collect in the muscles during and after exercise are absorbed into the bloodstream at a very slow rate. As a result the muscle becomes swollen, shorter, and thicker and therefore resists stretching. Light exercise, massage, and passive mobilization assist in reducing stiffness.

tonic
Muscle contraction marked by constant contraction that lasts for a period of time

clonic
Involuntary muscle contraction marked by alternate contraction and relaxation in rapid succession

Muscle Cramps

Like muscle soreness and stiffness, muscle cramps can be a problem related to hard conditioning. They are caused by the body's depletion of essential electrolytes or an interruption of synergism between opposing muscles. The most common cramp is **tonic,** where there is continuous muscle contraction. **Clonic,** or intermittent, contraction stemming from nerve irritation may rarely occur.

REFERENCES

1. Bonen, A., and Belcastro, A.N.: Comparison of self-selected recovery methods on lactic acid removal rates, Med. Sci. Sports **8:**176, 1976.
2. Burke, E.J. (editor): Toward an understanding of human performance, readings in exercise physiology for the coach and athlete, Ithaca, N.Y., 1978, Mouvement Publications.
3. DeBruyn/Provost, P.: The effects of various warming intensities and duration upon some physiological variables, Eur. J. Applied Physiol. **43:**93, 1980.
4. De Lorme, T.L., and Watkins, A.L.: Progressive resistance exercise, New York, 1951, Appleton-Century-Crofts.
5. deVries, H.A.: Electromyographic observations on the effects of static stretching upon muscular distress, Res. Q. **32:**468, 1961.
6. deVries, H.A.: Physiology of exer-

cise for physical education and athletics, ed. 3, Dubuque, Iowa, 1980, William C. Brown Co., Publishers.

7. Francis, K.T.: Delayed muscle soreness: a review, J. Orthop. Sports Phys. Ther. **5**:10, July/Aug. 1983.

8. Gaunya, S.T.: The role of the trainer. In Vinger, P.F., and Hoerner, E.F. (editors): Sports injuries, the unthwarted epidemic. Boston, 1981, John Wright, PSG Publishing Co., Inc.

9. Karvonen, M.J.: Effects of vigorous exercise on the heart. In Rosenbaum, F.F., and Belknap, E.L. (editors): Work and the heart, New York, 1959, Paul B. Hoeber, Inc.

10. Lopex, R.: Flexibility for dancers and athletes, JOHPERD **52**:29, May 1981.

11. Martin, B.J., Robinson, S., Wiegman, D.L., and Anlick, L.H.: Effect of warm-up on metabolic responses to strenuous exercise, Med. Sci. Sports **7**:146, 1975.

12. Massey, B., Johnson, W.R., and Kramer, G.F.: Effect of warm-up exercise upon muscular performance using hypnosis to control the psychological variable, Res. Q. **32**:63, 1961.

13. Morehouse, L.E., and Gross, L.: Maximum performance, New York, 1977, Simon & Schuster, Inc.

14. Morgan, R.E., and Adamson, G.T.: Circuit training, New Rochelle, N.Y., 1958, Sportshelf and Soccer Association.

15. Töttössy, M.: Warming up. In Kulund, D.N. (editor): The injured athlete, Philadelphia, 1981, J.B. Lippincott Co.

16. Tullson, P., and Armstrong, R.B.: Muscle hexose monophosphate shunt activity following exercise, Experientia **37**:1311, 1981.

17. Waltrous, B., Armstrong, R., and Schwane, J.: The role of lactic acid in delayed onset muscular exercise, Med. Sci. Sports Exerc. **13**:80, 1981.

18. Wilkerson, G.B.: Developing flexibility by overcoming the stretch reflex, Phys. Sportsmed. **9**:189, Sept. 1981.

19. Wilmore, J.H.: Athletic training and physical fitness, Boston, 1977, Allyn & Bacon, Inc.

ADDITIONAL SOURCES

Anderson, B.: Stretching, Bolinas, Calif., 1980, Shelter Publications.

Cornelius, W.L.: Two effective flexibility methods, Ath. Train. **16**:23, Spring 1981.

Kulund, D.N.: Strength and power in athletics. In Kulund, D.N. (editor): The injured athlete, Philadelphia, 1981, J.B. Lippincott Co.

Robertson, R.J.: Physiologic basis of year-round physical conditioning, Southwest Athletic Trainers Association Meeting, Jan. 1982, National Athletic Trainers Association. (Cassette.)

Sapega, A.A., and Drillings, G.: The definition and assessment of muscular power, J. Orthop. Sports Phys. Ther. **5**:7, July/Aug. 1983.

Chapter 6

NUTRITIONAL CONSIDERATIONS AND OTHER INTENDED AIDS

When you finish this chapter, you should be able to

Describe the importance of good nutrition in sports training

List essential nutrients that supply energy and promote growth and tissue repair

Identify harmful eating practices

Discuss the pros and cons of dietary supplementation

Examine problems inherent in weight control

Designate common harmful substances used in athletic performance

There is probably no field of endeavor where faddism is so prevalent as in sports participation. This chapter will present an overview of the influences of nutrition and other aids on sports participation and the health of the athlete.

NUTRITION

Exercise makes metabolic demands on the body. Although competitive activities make more demands than those made under normal circumstances, athletes are no different from other individuals in their need for proper nutrition (Fig. 6-1). The repair of damaged tissues, recuperation of fatigued muscles, and regeneration of energy necessitate a balanced and adequate diet. At the high school level the absence of a training table or other means of dietary control presents a problem for trainer and coach. This problem must be solved through developing the athlete's awareness of the elements of a good diet. To some extent this problem is encountered at the college and university level. Selecting a balanced diet and understanding the values and importance of dietary supplements and food substitutes are the responsibilities of the trainer. New developments in nutrition science and a bewildering mass of advertising claims and counterclaims make it difficult to intelligently judge products based on scientific facts. Fallacies and food fads are prevalent, especially at the high school level, and it requires constant education to establish sound dietary habits. Throughout adolescence the high school athlete must have proper nutrition if he or she is to achieve optimal growth and development. The trainer can make a very positive contribution by dispensing sound dietary advice and information at this level.

Fallacies and food fads are prevalent in sports.

Many nutritional practices are potentially harmful. From time to time various foods and drugs have been introduced to athletes for the purposes of improving performance and/or assisting in weight gain or loss. It is the trainer's and the coach's duty to know what these ingesta contain and whether or not they may be harmful to the athlete. They must also decide if taking such aids would be ethical.

Food Types

Food contains nutrients that either supply energy, regulate the various body processes, or are concerned with the growth and repair of body tissues. How much, when, and what foods are consumed depend more on social, psychological, and satiety values than on nutritional considerations.[11] The foods commonly ingested are actually chemical substances that can be broken down into simpler substances by digestive enzymes. The body then uses the energy stored in these compounds.

Food is categorized into six basic groups: carbohydrates, fats, proteins, minerals, vitamins, and water. Each is equally important in the diet. In the typical American diet from 50% to 60% of the energy is provided by carbohydrates, from 35% to 45% by fats, and from 10% to 15% by proteins.[11] However, there are variations in these percentages because of cultural, agricultural, economic, and sociological factors. There is also a trend toward using less carbohydrates and more proteins.

Carbohydrates, fats, and proteins are responsible for energy production. However, proteins are not a common source of energy but are used primarily for building and repairing tissue and are essential in the regulation of body processes.

Water, although not a food, is necessary for the various metabolic chemical reactions. It is a component in protoplasm, assists in the transportation of food and waste materials, aids in elimination of waste products, and assists in control of body temperature. Mineral salts help maintain the internal environment and are basic in formation of many tissues, particularly the bones, blood, and teeth.

Vitamins are organic substances that, although needed in very small amounts, are indispensable for normal functioning of the body.

Carbohydrates

Carbohydrates are organic compounds composed of carbon, hydrogen, and oxygen. The ratio of hydrogen to oxygen is 2:1, the same ratio found in water. Common carbohydrates are the starches and sugars found in foods such as breadstuffs, potatoes, and chocolate. During digestion the complex sugars found in foods are broken down into simple sugars that can be absorbed by the blood and tissues.

Utilizing carbohydrates The sugars are carried to the liver where they are converted either into glycogen or glucose (blood sugar). Glycogen is stored in the liver and can be readily reconverted into glucose when the demands of exercise require it. Glucose is carried by the blood to the various cells of the body. Some of the glucose may be stored as glycogen in the muscle cells, but most is utilized immediately as energy at the cellular level. This is especially true of nerve cells, since they cannot

Nutritional requirements include carbohydrates, fats, proteins, minerals, vitamins, and water.

Figure 6-1

The nutritional demands of most athletes are major, requiring an increase in the daily number of calories.

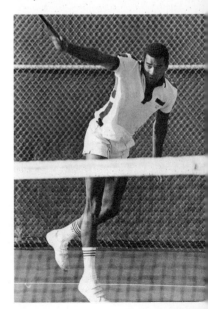

utilize any other energy-yielding nutrient. Excess glucose that is not used as energy and has not been converted into glycogen is transformed into fat and is stored as a reserve energy source. Muscles utilize the carbohydrates first during the initial stages of exercise, and they use more for strenuous work than for moderate work. Endurance is directly related to the glycogen stores in the body. Carbohydrates are usually considered to be the primary body fuels, and fats assume the role of reserve stores.

Fats

Fats and carbohydrates are composed of the same basic elements, but in fat the relative hydrogen content is higher. Fats or fatty compounds are usually referred to as *lipids* and are generally classified as *saturated, monounsaturated,* or *polyunsaturated* fats. In saturated fats each carbon atom in a molecular chain has two hydrogen atoms attached to it. Monounsaturated fats have one carbon atom in the chain that is free of hydrogen. In polyunsaturated fats two or more carbon atoms are free of hydrogen.

Fats provide more energy per gram than either carbohydrates or proteins, but body efficiency appears to be about 4.5% less with a fat diet than a carbohydrate diet. After digestion, fats are absorbed and deposited in muscle tissue and in other fat storehouses or depots around the body. These depots supply an energy reserve when needed, particularly if exercise demands are so protracted that they diminish the carbohydrate stores.

Digesting fat   Fats are not as quickly digested as are other food elements. However, they must still be considered a basic source of muscular energy, since fats are used when the carbohydrate stores are depleted. More oxygen is needed by the athlete who is on a fat diet than would be required for a carbohydrate diet. This means that greater demands will be made on the respiratory system. For this reason it would not be feasible to place a distance runner, for instance, on a high-fat diet. Slow digestion, then, is characteristic of fat. In some instances the products of fat breakdown prove to be exceedingly irritating to the linings of the stomach and the digestive tract. This can cause a considerable amount of dietary distress and in some cases may cause diarrhea.

Consuming too much fat   Americans consume too much fat. The average diet is approximately 40% fat, and most fats consumed are "hard," or saturated, fats. These fats have a higher melting point (solidification point) and are principally animal fats, dairy products, hydrogenated shortenings, chocolate, and coconut. Saturated fats tend to raise the cholesterol level of the blood. "Soft," or unsaturated, fats are classified as monounsaturated or polyunsaturated. Monounsaturated fats are generally free flowing and do not solidify even at low temperatures. Monounsaturated fats are found in fowl, olive and peanut oils, and most nuts. These fats appear to be neutral in their effect on cholesterol. Polyunsaturated fats apparently lower the cholesterol level in the blood. Polyunsaturates are found in fish, various plant oils (corn, soybean, sunflower, safflower), and special margarines.

As caloric intake is increased above normal in preparation for competition or for a heavy bout of work, there is a tendency to overemphasize the fat content of the diet. Generally, sports diets are too heavy with fatty foods, particularly dairy products and eggs. Investigations have emphasized the prominence of fatty acid as one of the causes of atherosclerosis, a common form of arteriosclerosis (hardening of the arteries). Atherosclerosis is characterized by abnormal, cholesterol-containing deposits (plaques) on the inner layers of the blood vessels. It is one of the main causes of hypertension (high blood pressure). Authorities have expressed a need for caution in prescribing an overabundance of fatty foods in the sports diet, although fats are recognized as one of the major sources of energy. Current research indicates that not more than 25% of the caloric intake should come from fats. It must be stressed that the bulk of fat intake should consist of the polyunsaturated fats.

Proteins

Proteins are nitrogenous organic compounds that break down into amino acids and are transported by the blood to the tissues. Proteins are somewhat complex substances. Basically, they are composed of a great number of carbon atoms with which atoms of hydrogen, oxygen, and nitrogen are associated. Other elements such as iron, copper, sulfur, and phosphorus are also associated with proteins, but in small amounts.

Food proteins are made up of amino acids in various and complex combinations. Twenty amino acids, usually considered the "building blocks" of proteins, are derived from digested food protein. The food proteins vary considerably in the type and number of amino acids constituting them. Amino acids are classified as either essential (indispensable) or nonessential (dispensable). Eight of the twenty amino acids are considered essential because they cannot be synthesized by the body at a rate sufficient to meet its needs for growth and maintenance. They must therefore be provided by the diet. The other twelve can be synthesized by the body to build body proteins, provided sufficient nitrogen is available. Such nitrogen (nonessential nitrogen) comes from either an excess of essential amino acids or from nonessential amino acids. Nutritional values of protein foods vary also, inasmuch as their values to the diet are determined by their amino acid pattern. Generally, animal proteins are considered more adequate than vegetable proteins, although each group has a wide range of biological values.

Utilizing protein Amino acids are absorbed from the intestine and transported via the bloodstream to the various parts of the body. Amino acid molecules are deaminized by the liver cells, with a portion forming glucose and the remainder forming urea. Those having the ability to form glucose are termed *glycogenic;* others, which bear a closer relationship to fatty acids, are classified as *ketogenic,* since they break down to acetic acid. Nitrogen is important as one of the key elements necessary for growth and repair. Amino acid that is not utilized undergoes a process of deamination during which the nitrogen is combined with carbon dioxide to form urea, which is excreted as urine within 4 hours after ingestion of this protein. This process necessitates an adequate daily intake of dietary protein to maintain a healthy growing state of the individual. In addition to their building and repairing properties, food proteins have considerable importance in maintaining the body's ability to resist infections and to effect good healing. Protein intake for the athlete should constitute 11%

to 12% of the total calories. More than this does no particular good; on the other hand, it seems to do no particular harm either, although high protein intakes may be converted to fat and stored as adipose tissue. A daily protein allowance of 0.80 g/kg of body weight should provide all of the protein needed for peak performance by an athlete.[9] Protein is not metabolized in sufficient amounts during exercise to be of any benefit.

Inorganic Requirements

Inorganic salts are essential for good health and for life itself. Through metabolization these salts perform a number of vitally important services. As stated earlier, they aid in the formation of tissues, particularly the bones and teeth, and maintain the homeostatic or internal environment of the body through stabilizing a specific ion concentration. Calcium salts help to sustain the rhythms of heartbeat and intestinal peristalsis and contribute to growth of bones and teeth, blood clotting, neuromuscular irritability, and nerve transmission. Sodium salts help to maintain the acid-base balance and osmotic pressure of the blood. Some salts trigger enzymatic reactions; others activate endocrine secretion.

Most of the inorganic requirements are present in common foods, thus obviating the need for supplemental ingesta when a properly balanced diet is followed.

Most of the necessary elements are present in the common foods, thus obviating the need for supplemental ingesta when a properly balanced diet is followed. The principal *mineral elements* are calcium, sodium, magnesium, phosphorus, potassium, chlorine, and sulfur. In addition, there are a number of important *trace elements:* cobalt, copper, fluorine, iodine, iron, manganese, molybdenum, selenium, vanadium, and zinc.

Potassium Potassium, a soluble salt found in the cells and interstices, is usually present in lean muscle meats, some leafy vegetables, and certain native waters. It is especially significant in the functioning of muscle and plays an important role in contraction. It also seems to counteract fatigue.

Calcium Calcium, although considered a common food element, is not readily absorbed from certain foods and is present only in rather minute quantities in others. Calcium phosphate is essential for the good development of teeth and bones. A small amount of magnesium, which is present in leafy vegetables, milk, and fruit, is also necessary for proper bone growth. The bulk of dietary calcium is supplied by dairy products. A very small quantity is supplied by such secondary sources as green leafy vegetables, legumes, egg yolks, nuts, and whole grains. Milk and the various milk products are particularly needed by the growing young athlete.

Sodium chloride (table salt) There is no evidence to support the common practice of increasing the salt intake of athletes, since most persons consume 10 to 12 times what is needed in a daily diet.

Sulfur and phosphorus Sulfur and phosphorus, principally obtained from protein foods, are also essential for various body needs. Sulfur assists in the formation of certain amino acids; phosphorus and calcium play an important role in the development of bones and teeth, transport of fatty acids, functioning of the buffer system, and energy metabolism.

Iron Anemia will result if there is an iron deficiency in the diet. Iron, along with cobalt and copper, regulates the body's synthesis of hemoglobin (the oxygen-carrying substance of the red blood cells). As the worn-out red blood cells are catabolized in the liver, the greater portion of the iron in the hematin, which is the iron-containing pigment, is conserved and used again. Iron is found in lean muscle meats, organ meats (particularly liver), egg yolk, seafood, green leafy vegetables, nuts, legumes, and whole wheat.

Manganese, copper, and zinc Manganese, copper, and zinc activate certain enzyme reactions and serve some functions in normal metabolism. Manganese, copper, and zinc are present in animal and plant foods. Sufficient amounts of copper for human needs are dissolved into foodstuffs and water from pasteurizing machines, copper water pipes, or copper-lined cooking vessels. Iodine, although required in small amounts, is essential to the normal functioning of the thyroid gland. An excellent source of iodine is seafood. An iodine deficiency can result in goiter. However, today's practice of iodizing table salt and the drinking water has obviated this danger, and the athlete is assured of an adequate iodine intake.

Vitamins

More misinformation has been disseminated about vitamins than about any other nutritional factor. A lack of vitamins is the underlying cause of a number of deficiency diseases. Interest in nutritional research has increased tremendously, and today probably more research in nutrition is carried on in the field of vitamins and their uses than in any other single area.

Vitamins are organic compounds, present in varying amounts in natural foods, that act as regulators or catalysts in the body processes. They assist the body in utilizing other nutrients. Although they are not chemically related, they do have certain functional similarities. More than 26 vitamins have been identified. At first it was believed that there were only a few; accordingly, they were named by the letters of the alphabet and were further identified by indicating their preventive nature against a specific disease (for example, vitamin B_1, antiberiberi). This method proved cumbersome, however, and vitamin names are currently based on their chemical nature, although the old terms are still recognized and used.

Vitamins are essential for maintaining good health. A lack of vitamins in the diet leads to deficiency conditions, which express themselves in a variety of ways. The problem of vitamin deficiency is rarely caused by the lack of a single vitamin. It is, rather, the result of a multiple vitamin deficiency. A good, varied diet that includes a balance of the "basic four" food categories will supply all vitamin requirements (Table 6-1).

Several vitamins can be made synthetically, and according to the available research, it appears that the body is unable to distinguish between the natural and the synthetic vitamins; either is utilized equally well. The body, however, cannot manufacture any of the vitamins except D, which is derived from sunshine. Thus, it must obtain its requirements from the diet. Supplementary vitamins are of considerable value during postoperative or recuperative periods after illness or injury and are often prescribed by the physician to aid in the healing process.

Although many vitamins and vitamin substances are known at the present time, there are some whose functions have been successfully demonstrated in experimental animals but whose effectiveness in humans has not been indicated with any degree of validity. Only those vitamins whose actions have been demonstrated to have specific human significance will be considered. Vitamin A, some elements in the vitamin B complex (such as thiamine, riboflavin, niacin, and B_{12}), and vitamins C and D fall into this category.

Other vitamins, such as vitamin H and P, folic acid, and inositol, have demonstrated certain actions in laboratory animals only. Since their effects have not yet been verified in humans, they will not be considered here.

Vitamins are usually identified as either fat soluble or water soluble. Fat-soluble vitamins usually persist in the diet in a reasonably intact state; they are found in butter, fortified margarines, and liver and are not usually destroyed in cooking. Vitamins A, D, E, and K are fat soluble. Little information is currently available concerning the biochemical role each of the fat-soluble vitamins plays, and there is some concern about their toxicity, since the amount of vitamin in excess of body needs is stored in the body. Vitamins A and K are present in a rather large variety of foods, whereas D and E are present in a limited number. Water-soluble vitamins grouped together as the B complex and vitamin C are often lost through cooking vitamin-containing foods in water and then disposing of the water in which they were cooked. Some vitamins are categorized as *heat labile.* These are the vitamins usually destroyed in the cooking process because of their in-

TABLE 6-1

Basic four food groups diet allowance

Food Group	Servings
Fruits and Vegetables Vitamin A, C Minerals	Four or more servings (½ cup cooked edible portion or 3 to 4 oz; 100 g raw); at least one raw portion daily
Breads and Cereals Thiamine Niacin Riboflavin Iron Protein	Four or more servings of whole grain or "enriched" cereals or breadstuffs (1 oz of cereal or 1 slice of bread or equivalent grain)
Milk and Milk Products Riboflavin Calcium Protein	Two or more servings (8 oz of milk; calcium equivalents are 1⅓ oz of hard cheese, 1⅓ cup of cottage cheese, 1½ cup of ice cream). *NOTE:* Fat and sugar contents vary from high to low with ice cream and fruit yogurt compared with milk
Meats and Meat Substitutes Protein Iron Thiamine Niacin Riboflavin	Two or more servings (2 or 3 oz of cooked lean meat, fish, or poultry; protein equivalents are two eggs, 2 oz of hard cheese, ½ cup of cottage cheese, 1 cup of cooked legumes, 4 tbsp of peanut butter, 1 oz of nuts or sunflower seeds); count cheese either in the milk group or meat group, not both

Modified from Whitney, E.N., and Hamilton, E.M.: Understanding nutrition, ed. 3, 1984, West Publishing Co.

ability to withstand heat. Vitamin C is an example of this group. Most of the vitamins, however, are *heat stable* and are not easily oxidized. Vitamins act as protein substances in the body.

Vitamin A　Vitamin A is essential for cell building, acts as a stimulus for new cell growth, and is a factor providing for skeletal growth; tooth formation; and formation of epithelial tissue composing the skin, mucous linings of the digestive, respiratory, and genitourinary tracts and sinuses. Through its action on the epithelium, it helps the body resist infections and plays a role in reproduction. It also increases longevity, delays senility, and acts as a preventive for nyctalopia (night blindness). If there is a deficiency of vitamin A in the diet, the "visual purple" (rhodopsin) that is required for red vision and the iodopsin required for cone vision are bleached out. Lack of this vitamin may also impair peripheral vision, which often results in accident proneness.

The implications of vitamin A deficiency are important to the trainer. Increased intake improves night vision and should benefit football players and other athletes who play under the lights. It may also be of benefit to players who need good peripheral vision, for example, pass catchers in football and basketball players. It is currently theorized that vitamin A is concerned with redirecting cell differentiation through its influence on RNA and DNA.

Sources　Since animals such as fish can store considerable amounts of vitamin A in their livers, this organ is one of the best sources of the substance. Cod-liver oil, which contains fat-soluble vitamin A and D, is one of the most prevalent commercial sources. A precursor of vitamin A, *carotene*, is found in plant foods such as green leafy vegetables, carrots, sweet potatoes, mangoes, artichokes, and papayas. It is converted into vitamin A in the liver. Other sources of this vitamin are liver, eggs, and dairy fat.

Vitamin B complex　The vitamin B complex group of vitamins is water soluble. Some are lost in preparation as the water is poured off and others, being heat labile, are destroyed by prolonged cooking. The various vitamins are known to be closely interrelated and involved in various enzymatic actions. Water-soluble vitamins are stored in the body in limited amounts and must therefore be included in the athlete's daily food plan.

Thiamine (vitamin B₁)　Thiamine is of the utmost importance for the proper and complete utilization of carbohydrates. Only a small amount of thiamine, enough for a few days of normal functioning, is stored in the body. Since this small reserve may readily be depleted by physiological emergencies, it is important that adequate amounts of thiamine be secured daily, preferably through normal dietary means. Thiamine is produced synthetically and thus can be made available for supplementation if indicated by a physician.

Sources　The richest dietary source of this vitamin is pork and pork products. Peas, legumes, and enriched or whole wheat bread are other good sources of thiamine. Dried brewer's yeast and wheat germ oil, both extremely high in thiamine, are not utilized regularly and so assume little importance in the average diet. In our culture there is a tendency to use refined cereals and flours; much of the thiamine is lost in the milling process unless the flour is subsequently enriched.

Riboflavin (vitamin B$_2$ or G)   Found in all living cells and a constituent of many enzymes, riboflavin also can be made synthetically. It is the link between the metabolism of carbohydrates and proteins. Its main functions are to promote growth, general health, and longevity. It is also essential to certain aspects of nerve tissue and cell respiration maintenance.

Sources   Liver is probably the richest source of riboflavin. Kidney, lean meats, chicken, peanuts, eggs, dried yeast, vegetable greens, and carrots are all excellent sources. The most common source of riboflavin is milk. Because riboflavin is easily affected by light, foods such as milk should not be stored in strong light lest they lose their riboflavin content. The body is unable to store this vitamin.

Niacin (nicotinic acid)   Niacin works quite closely with riboflavin and thiamine and enters into necessary enzyme reactions. This vitamin is quite stable in respect to heat, light, air, acids, and alkalies. As a result, it is not destroyed by ordinary cooking. Like riboflavin, it cannot be stored by the body; therefore, adequate amounts should be included in the daily diet. Niacin is an effective element in promoting and maintaining normal growth, function, and health.

Sources   Liver, dried brewer's yeast, lean muscle meats, whole wheat bread, enriched bread, milk, fresh vegetables, and fresh fruit are the principal sources of niacin.

Vitamin B$_{12}$ Vitamin B$_{12}$ comprises a group of complex compounds and is the only vitamin to contain a metal, cobalt, which is found in each of the compounds. This water-soluble vitamin is stable to heat in neutral solutions but is destroyed by heating in dilute acid or alkali.

The most essential function of vitamin B$_{12}$ is the development and production of red blood cells.

Its most essential function is in the development and production of red blood cells. Vitamin B$_{12}$ serves as an erythrocyte maturation factor and is important in respect to anemia and pernicious anemia. Not only does it act as a preventive and as a specific in treatment, but it also relieves the digestive and nervous disturbances that accompany these diseases. It is effective also in developing appetite and acting as a growth factor in children. It functions by putting weight on children who are underweight.

Since vitamin B$_{12}$ is essential in the energy metabolism of muscle, it has been postulated that injecting B$_{12}$ intramuscularly before competition would enable the athlete to perform more effectively. Studies investigating this premise indicate that vitamin B$_{12}$ supplementation is wholly unnecessary and that any advantage gained is in all probability purely psychological.

Sources   The major sources of this vitamin are liver and kidney. Milk, fish, lean beef, and pork rank as medium in terms of content.

Vitamin C   Vitamin C (ascorbic acid) is the least stable of all vitamins. It is freely soluble in water and is relatively stable in weak acids, but it is neutralized in the presence of alkalies. Because of its sensitivity to oxidation, drying or storing foods destroys or reduces their vitamin C content. Since it is extremely heat labile, cooking can easily render it ineffective. Therefore, vegetables or fruits should be eaten raw or, if cooked, should be prepared at low heat with a minimal quantity of water. Since ascorbic acid is stored in the body for extremely short periods, a daily dietary requirement is indicated.

As with other vitamins, ascorbic acid is essential to the formation of collagen, which is a bonding or cementing force between the cells. In this task vitamin C is responsible for maintaining the firmness of tissues such as the gum tissues. It further acts as a factor in maintaining the integrity or soundness of the capillaries and thus preventing the condition known as "capillary fragility," in which a hemorrhagic condition of the capillaries is induced. Vitamin C influences and plays a most important role in tooth and bone formation, development, and repair and in the healing of wounds. Vitamin C also functions in the absorption of iron from the intestinal tract. The callus that is formed in the healing of a fracture is a result of ascorbic acid action. There seems to be some relationship between vitamin C and the production of the adrenocortical hormones, especially with reference to the pituitary gland. This vitamin may also be concerned in the maintenance of normal hemoglobin levels and in the maturation of red blood cells. Recent research, although somewhat contradictory, seems to indicate that the ingestion of vitamin C tends to lessen the severity of the symptoms of the common cold.[11]

> Vitamin C influences the repair and healing of wounds.

Sources Fresh citrus fruits such as oranges, grapefruit, lemons, and limes are the best sources of ascorbic acid. Tomatoes, raw cabbage, white potatoes (cooked in their skins), and most vegetables and greens, *if eaten raw*, are also good sources.

Vitamin D Vitamin D is composed of at least 16 known substances of different forms. Of these, D_2 and D_3 are of the greatest importance, although other forms also contribute to the general good health of the individual. Vitamin D is fat soluble and is stable with reference to both heat and oxidation.

The average athlete obtaining reasonable exposure to sunlight will, in all probability, need no vitamin D supplementation.

Sources The sources of vitamin D are somewhat limited. Sunlight is an excellent source. Other good sources are irradiated milk; the liver oils of cod, tuna, halibut, and other bony fishes; eggs; and butter. Some activated margarines are also suitable sources.

Water

Water, one of the three prime necessities of life, comes from several sources to meet the body's physiological needs. Most of it is ingested in the daily diet either as fluid or as the fluid elements contained in the so-called solid foods. The remainder is a result of the oxidation of organic foodstuffs.

Water forms the bulk, about 75%, of all protoplasm, and it acts as a medium for the various enzymatic and chemical reactions. Water functions as a diluent of toxic wastes, thus preventing damage to the body and its organs from some of the toxic by-products of metabolism. This is especially true in respect to the kidneys. Water aids in the transport of body fuels, elimination of waste materials, and regulation of body temperature by dissipating excess heat from the body through perspiration (Table 6-2).

> Water functions as a diluent of toxic wastes, thus preventing damage to the body and its organs from some of the toxic by-products of metabolism.

A water balance must be maintained. Water loss usually approximates the water intake. If a salt deficit exists, the body will not retain water but will continue to eliminate it at a rate basically the same as that of the intake under normal situations. Dehydration must be prevented. Moderately severe or even severe exercise can be sustained quite comfortably over extended periods of time if the water intake is regulated to conform to the water loss. Small amounts given often are more effective in maintaining balance under severe heat and exercise conditions than are extremely large amounts given at greater intervals. Deprivation of water leads to more rapid dehydration, with subsequent impairment of performance. A daily intake of 2000 ml of water should be adequate in most instances but should be increased if sweating occurs. Some form of water should be available at all training sessions and games. It should be considered as much a part of the training/competitive regimen as any other phase. The withholding of water from athletes can neither be condoned morally nor can it be justified on physiological bases. Encourage your players to drink all the water that they want before and during competition or practice. In extremely hot weather even the thirst mechanism may fail to require adequate amounts; players should be told to drink more than their thirst tells them to. A little water sloshing about in the stomach can do no harm.

Weight loss during hot weather activity is primarily water loss. It is good practice to weigh athletes nude and dry both before and after practice to observe the amount of weight loss. Excessive loss should be noted. A loss of 2.2 pounds (1 kg) is accompanied by a loss of approximately 2 g of salt (1 level teaspoonful of salt equals about 4 g). A loss of 5 pounds requires careful observation, and a loss of 10 pounds or more during a single practice period approaches the danger level.

Electrolyte Needs

Electrolyte losses are primarily responsible for muscle cramping and intolerance to heat. Copious sweating results not only in a body water loss but in a mineral loss as well, particularly sodium, chloride, and, under extreme conditions, potassium (although generally potassium loss is negligible).

TABLE 6-2

Typical water balance in adults

Sources and Loss	Milliliters
Sources of water	
Liquid food	1100
Solid food	500-1000
Water of oxidation	300-400
TOTAL	1900-2500
Loss of water	
Urine	1000-1300
Perspiration and evaporation from skin	800-1000
Feces	100
TOTAL	1900-2500

From Guthrie, H.A.: Introductory nutrition, ed. 5, St. Louis, 1983, The C.V. Mosby Co.

These salts are electrically charged and are identified as ions or electrolytes. They are primarily concerned with the extracellular water (water outside of the cells), the significant reduction of which affects the body's control of the extracellular water. *Heavy sweating requires water replacement*, which is far more important than the replacement of electrolytes. Electrolytes can be adequately replaced after exercise by a balance diet, which can, if need be, be salted slightly more than is usual. Free access to water *(ad libitum)* before, during, and after activity should be encouraged.

Ingestion of the so-called sport or "electrolyte" beverages, of which there is a variety on the market, to replace water and electrolytes is of no special benefit; the need is more imagined than real, since the water and electrolyte losses can be met by increasing water intake and consuming food that has been slightly additionally salted. If a premixed electrolyte solution is employed, it should be diluted with water in a 2:1 ratio for faster absorption into the bloodstream. Potassium needs can be met adequately through drinking an 8-ounce glass of orange juice, whereas a glass of tomato juice or similar fluid can supplement the diet for the most essential minerals.[8]

> Replacing fluid after heavy sweating is far more important than replacing electrolytes.

Dietary Supplements

Nutritional supplementation takes the form of different liquid diet products, vitamins, proteins, mineral, iron, and anabolic steroids.[24] Anabolic steroids will be discussed later in this chapter.

Liquid Food Supplements

A number of liquid food supplements have been produced and are being used by high school, college, university, and professional teams with some indications of success. These supplements supply from 225 to 400 calories per average serving, at a cost of approximately one fifth that of the pregame meal, which usually consists of steak. Athletes who have used these supplements, usually in about 925-calorie servings, report elimination of the usual pregame symptoms of "dry mouth," abdominal cramps, leg cramps, nervous defecation, and nausea.

Under ordinary conditions it usually takes about 4 hours for a full meal to pass through the stomach and the small intestine. Pregame emotional tension often delays the emptying of the stomach, and therefore the undigested food mass remains in the stomach and upper bowel for a prolonged time, even up to or through the actual period of competition, and frequently results in nausea, vomiting, and cramps. This unabsorbed food mass is of no value to the athlete. According to team physicians who have experimented with the liquid food supplements, one of their major advantages is that they do clear both the stomach and the upper bowel before game time, thus making available the caloric energy that would otherwise still be in an unassimilated state.[13] There is merit in the use of such food supplements for pregame meals.[1]

> It takes approximately 4 hours for a full meal to pass through the stomach and small intestine.

Other Dietary Supplementation

Vitamins Since vitamin retention by the body is limited and activity requiring endurance or all-out effort mades demands on the limited

General Principles of Sports Medicine

body stores, these stores can easily become seriously depleted during a period of intense work. Deficiency diseases are not as common in the United States today as they are in other parts of the world, since most Americans eat a reasonably well-balanced diet.

Coaches and many trainers have long believed that fortifying a normal diet with relatively large dosages of vitamins would improve the athlete's performance and fitness for exercise. Vitamin requirements do not increase during exercise, nor does exercise specifically reduce the amount of vitamins C or B_{12} present. *Vitamins per se are not an energy source.* Available evidence does not justify supplementing the diet of the athlete with vitamins to improve physical performance unless a preexisting vitamin deficiency exists.[18]

Vitamin requirements do not increase during exercise.

Taking vitamins in excessive quantities (megavitamin dosage) can, in certain circumstances, have deleterious effects and lead to vitamin toxicity from storage of vitamins A, D, and E. In extreme cases it can prove fatal. At higher levels of competition the "pill freak" is rapidly becoming passé. It would seem to be more practical to attain desired vitamin levels through intelligent food selection and preparation rather than to rely on artificial supplements.

Protein Massive doses of protein supplements are being taken in the belief that extra protein will stimulate muscle protein and growth. Athletes need no more protein than the average individual; a well-balanced diet will supply adequate amounts not only of protein but also of all other nutritional needs. Protein supplementation is of no use as far as performance is concerned. Excessive protein supplementation not only leads to an increase in blood urea concentration but also may result in increased albumin excretion and nephritis. Muscle protein cannot be increased by eating high-protein foods. Only exercise can bring about an increase in muscle mass.

Iron Iron deficiency, which is much more prevalent than usually thought, can affect muscular performance. Not infrequently, teenaged boys will exhibit an iron deficiency due to an inadequate diet and the demands of a rapid growth rate. Among female athletes, iron deficiency is not at all uncommon; borderline anemia may occur as the result of not getting enough dietary iron. The loss may be further compounded, particularly in the initial phases, by a strenuous training program wherein a temporary drop in plasma and hemoglobin results in so-called sports anemia, which is due to the increased destruction of red blood cells. Should an iron deficiency be detected, iron supplementation should be introduced under medical supervision. The recommended daily dietary allowance for females from age 10 up through the reproductive years is 18 mg. Recent surveys have indicated that an average daily intake of only 11 to 12 mg, over a period of several years, results in an iron store depletion, with the hemoglobin levels falling below the anemia borderline of 12 g/ 100 ml of blood.

Emotional State at Mealtime

It is imperative that meals be eaten in an atmosphere of relaxation and in pleasant, cheerful surroundings. Negative emotions tend to upset and retard the digestive processes by shifting the blood mass away from the organs of digestion. Emotional stress over a period of time can result in chronic gastrointestinal disturbances. Pre-event stress is transitory but is often severe enough to pose problems. By establishing a near-normal situation, in terms of emotional climate, mealtimes can be pleasant and full of good fellowship and camaraderie.

Pre-event Nutrition

Too often trainers and coaches concern themselves principally with the meal immediately preceding competition and do not seem to realize that pre-event nutrition begins some time before that. Events that call for sudden bursts of all-out energy, rather than endurance or sustained effort, do not appear to be particularly affected or modified by pre-event nutrition. However, preparing for moderate or sustained effort that requires endurance includes consideration of nutrition approximately 48 hours preceding competition, since such events can be significantly affected by ingestion. The usual manifestation of precompetitive tension such as abdominal cramps, "dry mouth," acidosis, and other metabolic symptoms can be either reduced or eliminated to a considerable degree by careful attention to dietary considerations.

Pre-event nutrition should begin at least 48 hours before the competition.

It is also wise to begin to gradually decrease the training program about 48 hours before competition. This is advocated because it enables the body to replenish certain essential stores and to reduce or eliminate various metabolites that might reduce performance. As has previously been shown, the glycogen stores of the body—specifically those in the liver, which normally consist of about 1500 calories—need to be built up to a full measure if an athlete is to compete well in an endurance event. In endurance events approximately 1500 calories are consumed during the first hour of effort, and continued exertion may result in an excessive depletion of the glycogen reserves of the body, with consequent hypoglycemia (notable reduction in blood sugar) and evident fatigue.

Rest and eating a high-carbohydrate diet 2 or 3 days before competition can store additional glycogen.

The use of liquid meals—which are nutritionally sound and contain the recommended daily dietary proportions of nutrients—as the meal immediately before performance is widely used and is recommended as a means of eliminating or reducing the pregame syndrome. Fluid is much easier to digest because it eliminates the liquefaction step in the stomach, an important factor under stress conditions, since nausea and vomiting are not infrequent accompaniments to preperformance tension.

Foods to Avoid

Foods of high cellulose content such as lettuce should be avoided, since they tend to increase the need for defecation. The elimination of highly spiced and of fatty or fried foods from the diet is also desirable because of the likelihood of gastrointestinal irritation.[17]

Protein Content

It is advisable to limit protein intake during the period just preceding competition, since proteins are a source of fixed acids, which can be eliminated from the body only through urinary excretion.

Carbohydrate Content

Carbohydrate intake should be significantly increased during the precontest period. Extra helpings of breads, cereals, potatoes, and sugar should be the rule. Bread and potatoes do not deserve their reputation as fattening foods. Potatoes should be eaten plain, that is, baked or boiled without the addition of milk, cream, or butter, which are the fattening agents. Bread, preferably, should be constituted from the less-refined flours or enriched by the restoration of the vitamins and minerals lost through refining. Since carbohydrates are most readily available and most easily absorbed in terms of metabolic demands, they are the first elements utilized for muscular work. Inasmuch as the final by-products of carbohydrate metabolism—carbon dioxide and water—are eliminated from the body through the lungs and the skin, no additional acid load is accumulated in the tissues, which cannot be removed by kidney function (Table 6-3).

Carbohydrate loading The amount of glycogen stored in a muscle will determine the endurance of that muscle. In activities that continue for half an hour or more and in which the aerobic energy demand is at a

TABLE 6-3

Energy equivalents of food calories expressed in minutes of activity

Food	Calories	*Walking	Riding Bicycle†	Swimming‡	Running§	Reclining‖
			Minutes of Activity			
Apple, large	101	19	12	9	5	78
Bacon, 2 strips	96	18	12	9	5	74
Banana, small	88	17	11	8	4	68
Beans, green, 1 cup	27	5	3	2	1	21
Beer, 1 glass	114	22	14	10	6	88
Bread and butter	78	15	10	27	4	60
Cake, 2-layer, 1/12	356	68	43	32	18	274
Carbonated beverage, 1 glass	106	20	13	9	5	82
Carrot, raw	42	8	5	4	2	32
Cereal, dry, 1/2 cup with milk, sugar	200	38	24	18	10	154
Cheese, cottage, 1 tbsp	27	5	3	2	1	21
Cheese, cheddar, 1 oz	111	21	14	10	6	85
Chicken, fried, 1/2 breast	232	45	28	21	12	178
Chicken, TV dinner	542	104	66	48	28	417
Cookie, plain	15	3	2	1	1	12
Cookie, chocolate chip	51	10	6	5	3	39
Doughnut	151	29	18	13	8	116
Egg, fried	110	21	13	10	6	85
Egg, boiled	77	15	9	7	4	59
French dressing, 1 tbsp	59	11	7	5	3	45
Halibut steak, 1/4 lb	205	39	25	18	11	158
Ham, 2 slices	167	32	20	15	9	128

From Konishi, F.: J. Am. Diet. Assoc. **46**:186, 1965. Used by permission.

*Energy cost of walking for 150 lb individual = 5.2 calories per minute at 3.5 mph.

†Energy cost of riding bicycle = 8.2 calories per minute.

‡Energy cost of swimming = 11.2 calories per minute.

§Energy cost of running = 19.4 calories per minute.

‖Energy cost of reclining = 1.3 calories per minute.

constant high level, the storing or loading of glycogen seems to be of value. It has been shown that endurance can be increased but not a track athlete's speed.[2,17] The amount of stored glycogen can easily be doubled through loading by increasing the carbohydrate ingestion. Originally, athletes were instructed to deplete carbohydrate stores with heavy training and eating a low carbohydrate diet. It is now known that rest and eating a high carbohydrate diet for 2 or 3 days before competition will store sufficient glycogen.[15] Increasing pre-event ingestion of carbohydrates is of no particular use unless activity is sustained for half an hour or more, since events of short duration are not affected or modified by such "loading." Indeed, dehydration may develop. Marathon runners have shown no difference in carbohydrate stores during the first half of the race, but loading appears to have been of some advantage in the second half. Taking sweetened drinks during the latter part of the race seems to be of some help, but the explanation is open to question, since physiological evidence is moot. The apparent lift may be psychological; perhaps the fluid itself may have some bearing.

Food	Calories	Minutes of Activity				
		Walking*	Riding Bicycle†	Swimming‡	Running§	Reclining‖
Ice cream, ⅙ qt	193	37	24	17	10	148
Ice cream soda	255	49	31	23	13	196
Ice milk, ⅙ qt	144	28	18	13	7	111
Gelatin, with cream	117	23	14	10	6	90
Malted milk shake	502	97	61	45	26	386
Mayonnaise, 1 tbsp	92	18	11	8	5	71
Milk, 1 glass	166	32	20	15	9	128
Milk, skim, 1 glass	81	16	10	7	4	62
Milk shake	421	81	51	38	22	324
Orange, medium	68	13	8	6	4	52
Orange juice, 1 glass	120	23	15	11	6	92
Pancake with syrup	124	24	15	11	6	95
Peach, medium	46	9	6	4	2	35
Peas, green, ½ cup	56	11	7	5	3	54
Pie, apple, ⅙	377	73	46	34	19	290
Pie, raisin, ⅙	437	84	53	39	23	336
Pizza, cheese, ⅛	180	35	22	16	9	138
Pork chop, loin	314	60	38	28	16	242
Potato chips, 1 serving	108	21	13	10	6	83
Sandwiches						
Club	590	113	72	53	30	454
Hamburger	350	67	43	31	18	269
Roast beef with gravy	430	83	52	38	22	331
Tuna fish salad	278	53	34	25	14	214
Sherbet, ⅙ qt	177	34	22	16	9	136
Shrimp, french fried	180	35	22	16	9	138
Spaghetti, 1 serving	396	76	48	35	20	305
Steak, T-bone	235	45	29	21	12	181
Strawberry shortcake	400	77	49	36	21	308

General Principles of Sports
Medicine

It should be noted that carbohydrate loading has risks. Depositing glycogen in the muscles brings with it three times as much water as glycogen.[17] This may cause the athlete to feel heavy and stiff.

Sugar Content

All sugars tend to retard
gastric emptying; thus heavy
sugar solutions tend to
remain in the stomach for a
long time, often causing
gastric distress.

Many coaches and trainers advocate giving sugar, either in the form of lump sugar, dextrose tablets, glucose pills, or honey, as a means of improving athletic performance. Since sugar is a fuel food and therefore is active in muscle contractions, it has been reasoned that the feeding of supplementary sugar should have value. All sugars tend to notably retard gastric emptying; thus heavy sugar solutions tend to remain in the stomach for a considerable length of time, frequently causing gastric distress. Sugar feeding should be limited to weak solutions, less than 2.5 g/100 ml of water. Such drinks will help deliver sugar to the liver and aid in physical performance inasmuch as the solution leaves the stomach and enters the blood at a rapid rate. A weak drink will thus deliver approximately as much sugar to the liver as would a strong drink.

Physiologically, when an individual is fed sugar, there is a tendency for the fluid required for its digestion to be drawn into the gastrointestinal tract, thus further dehydrating the organism. A more desirable way of feeding sugar is to serve tea, lightly sweetened and with lemon, to aid in overcoming this dehydrating factor. Sugar feeding, if used, must be carried out sensibly, since indiscriminate or excessive feeding can lead to severe gastric disturbances.

Liquids

Liquids should be low in fat content and readily absorbable. Above all, they should not cause laxation; therefore fruit juices should be restricted. Items such as prune juice, which has a high laxation factor, should be eliminated from the diet. Water intake should be normal. Cocoa, whether made from milk or water, is an excellent beverage to give some variety and can be substituted for milk, juice, coffee, or tea as the occasion demands.

Coffee and tea   At the high school level, drinking tea or coffee is not the usual practice among athletes, but it becomes more prevalent at the college and university level. For many years, tea, a caffeine-containing fluid, has traditionally been a part of the pregame meal. Caffeine induces a period of stimulation of the central nervous system that is followed by a period of depression. Because the athlete is usually excited and somewhat nervous during the precontest period, the addition of caffeine to the pregame meal may not be advisable. The same statements apply to the use of coffee. Tea and coffee are also diuretics; that is, they stimulate the flow of urine and thus may cause additional discomfort during the competitive period.

However, individual tolerance or reactivity to caffeine-containing liquids varies considerably. At the college level, insistence on the complete elimination of coffee or tea from a diet in which drinking such beverages has been customary may result in a psychological effect that militates against the athlete more than would the usual intake of the mild stimulants.

Salt Intake and Electrolyte Drinks

In maintaining an adequate salt content, a daily intake of 15 to 20 g (approximately 1 tablespoon) will meet most needs. As has been previously stated, this is better obtained through the salting of foods than supplementary salt tablets. The consumption of 1 cup of bouillon and 3 glasses of liquid during the pregame meal, followed by an additional glass of water about 1½ hours after the meal, should meet the needs in terms of both salt and liquid requirements. Excessive salt intake (as with salt tablets) combined with limited water intake results in cellular dehydration.

A number of the commercial electrolyte drinks have concentrations sufficiently high in salt to cause fluid retention in the stomach and small intestine and can cause upper abdominal distress. Such drinks should be avoided, particularly before competition.

> Excessive salt intake results in cellular dehydration; therefore electrolyte drinks should be avoided.

Time of the Pre-event Meal

The number and spacing of meals and the effect of food intake has been reported by several investigators. It is generally conceded that the pre-event meal should be consumed about 3 to 4 hours before competition. Eating a meal immediately before competition is not conducive to effective performance. The acute discomfort of attempting to perform physically on a full stomach provides a psychological impediment. Also, the increase in portal circulation required for digestion is achieved by withdrawing from the systemic circulation blood that would otherwise be readily available for the maintenance of physical work.

Food Fallacies and Quackery

There is no scientific evidence that performance can generally be improved through control of the athlete's diet. Improvement in performance may be attributed to a balanced diet, if there have been previous dietary deficiencies. The main value of proper nutrition lies in preventing the deleterious effects of improper or inadequate nutrition.

> There is no scientific evidence that performance can generally be improved by controlling the athlete's diet.

Food fads are rampant among athletes. No food, vitamin, supplement, or hormone will substitute for sound nutrition and hard work. Dietary abuses are sometimes condoned by parents and coaches in the mistaken belief that they will help, whereas in reality many of them are deleterious.

Diets that have recently come into popularity such as the fruitarian, which is based on raw fruits, dried fruits, honey, and olive oil, the macrobiotic diets, and the so-called organic food diets do not, in most instances, supply all of the nutrients required by an athlete, nor does any sound scientific evidence support these diets. Reliance on such diets can be hazardous.[20] Individuals following a strictly vegetarian diet frequently suffer from a vitamin B_{12} deficiency, which could lead to pernicious anemia. Scurvy is not infrequent among the followers of the macrobiotic diet, and for the "natural" or "organic" food devotees there is always the danger of nutritional deficiencies and/or other physiological problems. "Natural" foods are no more nutritious than conventionally produced and processed foods and are purchased at greatly inflated prices.[11]

Over the years the pregame steak has been a favorite meal for athletes in the mistaken belief that the excess protein would aid performance through providing more muscle fuel and growth, thereby increasing strength. Actually, protein demand is regulated by the rate of growth, and excess protein, as has previously been stated, may be converted into fat and stored as such. Protein is not stored as protein as is fat. As a result very little protein is utilized by the body as fuel for muscular work. Protein stores are established approximately 48 hours before performance; hence the pregame steak is not only not essential, it is an expensive fad as well.

Vitamin supplementation has been touted by many trainers, coaches, and athletes as a means of improving performance. As indicated previously, such supplementation has value only when a diet is nutritionally unsound and lacking in the required values. Astrand and Rodahl state the case for vitamin supplementation in respect to water-soluble vitamins: "The ingestion of large quantities of vitamin pills is a rather expensive way of increasing the vitamin content of the urine, which serves no useful purpose in the first place."[20]

WEIGHT CONTROL

Gain or loss of weight in an athlete often poses a problem because the individual's ingrained eating habits are difficult to change. The trainer's inability to adequately supervise the athlete's meal program in terms of balance and quantity further complicates the problem. An intelligent and conscientious approach to weight control requires, on the part of both trainer and athlete, some knowledge of what is involved. Such understanding allows athletes to better discipline themselves as to the quantity and kinds of foods they should eat.

The energy requirements of individuals are not at all constant, but vary with age, sex, weight, current health status, and occupation. Body weight is determined in part by body build or somatotype. Because of these many variables, there is no shortcut or magic formula to weight control.

Overweight is simply the result of putting more energy into the body than is utilized. The principal cause is overeating coupled with inactivity. It is important that athletes develop good eating habits, restricting their use of fatty foods and modifying their carbohydrate intake. They must learn to eat less—overeating at the training table is a common fault—and to confine their intake to bulky, low-calorie foods.

TABLE 6-4

Calorie adjustment required for weight loss

To lose 1 pound a week—500 fewer calories daily

Basis of estimation

1 lb body fat	= 454 g
1 g pure fat	= 9 calories
1 g body fat	= 7.7 calories (some water in fat cells)
454 g × 9 calories/g	= 4086 calories/lb fat (pure fat)
454 g × 7.7 calories/g	= 3496 calories/lb body fat (or 3500 calories)
500 calories × 7 days	= 3500 calories = 1 lb body fat

From Williams, S.R.: Nutrition and diet therapy, ed. 5, St. Louis, 1985, The C.V. Mosby Co.

Weight Control Through Exercise

There has long been a misconception that exercise has little or no effect on caloric balance. Nothing could be further from the truth. Inactivity is probably the most important factor in weight gain. Eating habits do not readily change but activity habits do. The measured costs, in energy expenditure, of various types of physical activities give an indication of the value of exercise as a means of weight control (Table 6-4). This is exemplified by the added poundage that athletes usually acquire during the off-season. They continue their food intake at substantially the same rate but lower their activity level; therefore, the energy that is usually burned off through activity remains as adipose accretion.

Since the energy cost of exercise is proportional to body weight, overweight athletes require more energy and use more of their body reserves in performing a given activity than do persons who are not carrying excess poundage. If athletes permit themselves to become 20% or more overweight, the energy cost of their performance will increase the same amount, and they will be working at an inefficient level. A reduction in surplus weight, even when additional weight appears to be a desirable factor, generally results in a more efficiently functioning individual whose increase in usable energy will more than offset any apparent advantage dead weight would seem to give. If an increase in weight is desirable, it is better achieved through a gain in muscle bulk than through a gain in fat. Overnutrition can be a distinct hindrance to many types of performance, since the excess caloric intake causes excessive adipose tissue deposits, which

Regular exercise tends to stabilize weight once the desired level has been attained.

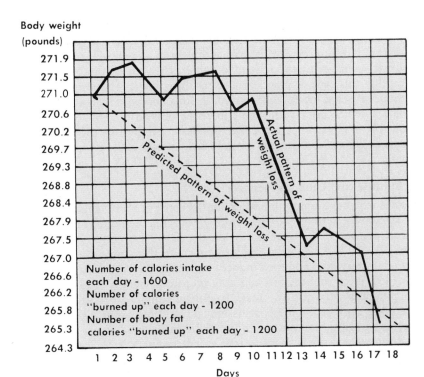

Figure 6-2

Changes in body weight of a very overweight person on a reducing diet. The progress chart of an actual patient shows how greatly body weight can fluctuate as a result of water retention even though daily calorie intake remains constant. This dieter accumulated water for 10 days while losing fat, then showed a rapid weight loss as water was eliminated.

Courtesy Pennwalt, Prescription Products Division, Pennwalt Corporation, Rochester, N.Y.

tend to restrict body movement, thus adding to the work load and reducing the effective available surface for heat loss.

Weight Reduction

To lose weight one must increase physical activity and maintain a proper diet; only in this way can caloric expenditure be increased. Regular exercise tends to stabilize the weight, once the desired level is attained. In some sports, especially wrestling and weight lifting, it is sometimes necessary for the athlete to lose a few pounds so that he may make a specific weight class. Usually, most of the loss is achieved through dehydration and/or reducing the food intake.

Intense weight reduction during a short period of time may seriously impair performance. Ordinarily, weight reduction is effected within a period of 2 to 7 days. From 2 to 4½ pounds may be lost during this time. Avoiding fat foods and limiting the fluid intake, coupled with an exercise program to induce sweating, is the method customarily used. Cross-country running in heavy clothing is preferable to the use of steam or hot baths and is far less enervating. Dehydration impairs performance; in some individuals dehydration of as little as 2% of the body weight causes a significant deterioration of work performance. If at all possible, weight reduction should be avoided. However, should trainers be faced with an athlete's need for weight reduction, they should advocate a gradual loss over as long a period of time as is feasible under the circumstances, to ensure the athlete's entering competition in a near-optimal state of fitness.[19,22]

Crash Dieting

In an attempt to lose weight the athlete may go on a "crash" diet. Diets of this nature fail to recognize the basic problem in weight reduction—that of acquiring a change in eating habits. Athletes should be discouraged from attempting this type of program. The resulting lowered vitality makes the individual susceptible to colds and infections and produces weariness and weakness, which are reflected in a lowering of both the efficiency and the magnitude of physical performance. Besides crash dieting, the athlete may become desperate and become bulimic or may eventually develop anorexia nervosa.

Bulimia and Anorexia Nervosa

Bulimia and anorexia nervosa are bizarre eating problems that possibly result from a desire to conform to an often impossible ideal.

Athletes who have an inordinate amount of concern about being overweight can develop the serious eating disorders of bulimia or anorexia nervosa. The bulimic person is most commonly female, in the age range of adolescence to middle age. She typically gorges herself with thousands of calories after a period of starvation and then induces vomiting. She is usually preoccupied with food, diets, and recipes and may prepare elaborate meals for others. Such practices can cause a stomach rupture, disrupt heart rhythm, and even cause liver damage. Stomach acids brought up from vomiting cause tooth decay and inflame the mucous lining of the mouth and throat.

Anorexia nervosa is characterized by a distorted body image and a major concern about weight gain. As with bulimia, anorexia nervosa affects mostly females. It usually begins in adolescence. It can be mild without major consequences or severe and life threatening. It has been estimated that as many as 15% to 21% of those with this disorder will die. Because these females have a distorted self-image, they believe they are overweight despite being extremely thin. They deny hunger and engage in constant exercise. Besides lack of hunger, they may use laxatives and induce vomiting.

These bizarre problems occur from a desire to conform to perhaps an impossible ideal. It has been suggested that the roots of anorexia nervosa come from fears of sexuality and separation from parents.

It is essential that a coach or athletic trainer be aware of the signs of these disturbances and make proper referral for any athlete who may be experiencing a compulsion about body weight.[4]

Weight Gain

Weight gain can be accomplished through diet enrichment and exercise regulation. At times it may be advisable to advocate dietary supplementation between meals to increase caloric intake. Some reduction in the rigor of the daily training program, with an increase in the periods of rest and relaxation, helps in adding extra ounces. Such reductions in the training program should be consistent with maintaining the status quo of performance levels.

Weight Control in Wrestling

Publicity in recent years has charged that certain coaches were requiring wrestlers to achieve excessive weight loss so that they could make a certain weight class for competition. If this is true, such practices cannot be condoned. They are not only undesirable from the standpoint of maintaining physical effectiveness but are also potentially harmful. A rapid decrease in weight, which is caused by extreme restrictions of caloric intake, is contraindicated immediately before or during periods that will require maximal physical effort. Also, weight reduction by high school athletes poses a serious problem because of the growth and maturation factors.[19,24]

Some coaches and trainers advocate "dryout" and *total fasting* in the beginning of a program of weight reduction. Usually they suggest elimination of carbohydrates and salt. Such an approach has serious implications to the athlete, since salt loss in the urine is greatly increased and this loss, coupled with the additional salt loss incurred through perspiration, greatly increases the possibility of a clinically identified sodium deficiency. When vigorous physical activity is performed, these features are not only magnified, but they may also lead to a renal shutdown. During such total fasts a decrease in heart size accompanies these hydrodynamic changes.

Total fasting as a means of weight control in wrestlers cannot be condoned.

As indicated previously in this chapter, weight control is difficult for some individuals and is easier for others. Undoubtedly, the psychological makeup of the person plays a large part in accomplishing the mental discipline for the "long haul" concept of weight reduction. *There is no easy or quick way to lose weight safely.*

It is sometimes difficult to determine whether or not a person is overweight. Some athletes who appear overweight or who tip the scales above average standards are not overweight at all; they usually possess greater musculature and larger bones. In such situations a knowledge of somatotyping would be of value to the trainer or coach.

Body fat that makes up 5% to 7% of the total body weight is ideal. One method for assessing optimal weight is by pinching the skin on the forehead at the outer upper area above the eye and then comparing its thickness to the skinfold over the abdomen and over the back of the arm (center of the triceps). All three measurements should be approximately 6 to 8 mm. Tcheng and Tipton[22] conclude that, based on their comprehensive studies of high school wrestlers,[8] a fat content of 5% of total body weight is the ideal wrestling weight.

Weight loss during training should not exceed 2 to 5 pounds a week, and the conditioning program should be started at least 5 to 6 weeks before final decisions are made as to the final weight at which the athlete is to wrestle. Once it is determined, he should not be permitted reduction to wrestle at a lower weight but should let his weight stabilize. Weight fluctuations impair physical performance.

A balanced diet, reduced somewhat in quantity, coupled with an adequate fluid and salt intake and with hard physical work is still the best way to reduce weight. The use of digitalis and other weight-loss drugs is strongly condemned (Appendixes III-C and III-D).

ERGOGENIC AIDS

For years there has been considerable interest in finding an agent that would improve athletic performance. Such an aid is classified as an *ergogenic* (literally, "work-producing") aid and is usually defined as any substance or means that improves physical performance through its effect on the body. Substances include drugs, foodstuffs, vitamins, and physical stimulants such as electricity or thermal packs. A method (means) might be hypnosis or cheering.

From time to time, there are enthusiastic claims of a wonder "aid," which subsequent, critical research fails to substantiate. In many instances, psychological effects alone are responsible for improved performance. Other substances that do have some ergogenic properties have such deleterious physiological and psychological side effects that their use cannot be tolerated under any circumstances. Aside from the medicolegal aspects of administering various substances, the use of some "aids" poses an ethical problem. Certainly an athletic trainer has no moral right to permit the use of any substance that is potentially harmful. In addition, is it sporting to "soup up" an athlete through the use of a substance that the opposition neither uses nor condones? Are the resulting performances truly indicative of athletes' potential or are they merely indicative of their reaction to an artificial stimulus? If trainers encounter potential or actual use of harmful or dangerous ergogens, they should counsel the athletes by explaining to them the agent's action on the body and its effect on physical performance. Such explanations should be done rationally rather than emotionally. Leaders in sports and in sports medicine have taken an unequivocal stand against the use of any agent that would fall into the category of dope or that would be used to enhance athletic performance through artificial means. The Amateur Athletic Union (AAU) and the International Amateur Athletic Federation (IAAF) have proscribed the use of certain substances 3 days before competition. The IAAF has established antidoping regulations and

Intended ergogens that are dangerous must be banned from use by the athlete.

forbids the use of psychomotor stimulants, sympathomimetic amines, central nervous system stimulants, narcotic analgesics, and anabolic steroids.

The International Olympic Committee has a strict drug-testing program at the Olympic Games. Urine tests are made to determine whether doping substances have been ingested. A positive urine sample is one that contains one or more of the following banned drugs[12]:

Psychomotor stimulant drugs
    Amphetamines
    Cocaine
    Diethylpropion
    Dimethylamphetamine
    Ethylamphetamine
    Fencamfamine
    Methylamphetamine
    Methylphenide
    Norpseudoephedrine
    Phendimetrazine
    Phenmetrazine
    Prolintane
    Related compounds
Narcotic analgesics
    Dextromoramide
    Dipipanone
    Heroin
    Morphine
    Methadone
    Pethidine
    Related compounds

Sympathomimetic amines
    Ephedrine
    N-Methylephedrine
    Methoxyphenamine
    Related compounds
Miscellaneous central nervous
  system stimulants
    Amiphenazole
    Bemegride
    Leptazol
    Nikethamide
    Strychnine
    Related compounds
Anabolic steroids
    Methandienone
    Nandrolone decanoate
    Nandrolone phenpropionate
    Oxymetholone
    Stanozolol
    Related compounds

It has often been argued that the use of vitamins, food supplements, and gelatin as possible ergogenic aids carries the same implications. Such measures, however, do no harm to the athlete; nor can they be considered unfair practices. Indeed, they may conceivably reduce a dietary need, although it is improbable that they contribute to the improvement of physical performance. Carbohydrate (glycogen) loading is an ergogenic process, but currently no definite stand has been taken regarding the ethics of its use.

The trainer is advised to forego the use of questionable materials and to rely on *ethically and morally sound practices*. Athletes should develop the various potentials inherent within them, rather than resort to artificial means. The more common ergogenic aids, which have been used and subjected to considerable research and testing, are discussed below to assist the trainer in developing some knowledge and awareness of their effects on human beings and human performance. Since the physiological effects of alcohol, coffee, tea, and salt have been discussed previously in this chapter, they will not be reexamined.

Amphetamines (Benzedrine, *d*-Amphetamine Sulfate)

Amphetamines are synthetic alkaloids that are extremely powerful and dangerous drugs, contrary to what uninformed individuals may say. It may be taken either in the form of tablets or by means of inhalers. Proprietary

Benzedrine functions as a
powerful stimulant to the
central nervous system.

forms are Benzedrex, Benzedrine, Dexedrine, Desyphed, Tuamine, and, in
Europe, Pervitin. Publicity regarding the use of "pep" pills or "bennies," of
which Benzedrine is the active ingredient, has made the general public quite
conscious of the dangers involved in using this drug. Such use in sports, for
the purpose of reducing fatigue, cannot be condoned.[7]

Benzedrine functions as a powerful stimulant to the central nervous
system. In most instances its effects are evidenced through increases in
blood pressure and the rate of breathing and through a general feeling of
alertness, euphoria, and peppiness. It does not seem to have any effect on
the higher mental processes. Its use also impairs sleep; for this reason it is
often used by students when preparing for examinations and by truck driv-
ers whose long and monotonous journeys frequently compel them to seek
some means of remaining awake while at the wheel.

Benzedrine may cause dizziness and a feeling of depression. It appears
to have a greater effect on individuals of a slight body build than on those
with a heavier build. Individual reaction may be highly specific. In some
instances hallucinations have led athletes to believe that they were performing far better than they actually were. They were guilty of exhibiting
extremely poor judgment in critical situations and otherwise not playing up
to their usual level of performance. In these instances amphetamines had
been taken without the knowledge of the staff.

Since Benzedrine and its derivatives constrict the mucous membranes,
their use, under medical direction, for the relief of nasal congestion is quite
safe, provided instructions are followed. Prolonged use of amphetamines
leads to extreme nervousness and may produce hallucinations and insomnia. Their continued use leads to addiction. Studies reported in the literature are somewhat contradictory in that there is some evidence that d-am-
phetamine sulfate inhibits fatigue; on the other hand, evidence supporting
the contention that improved performance results from the administration
of d-amphetamine sulfate is lacking. The fact that the drug is inherently
dangerous should mitigate against its use.[7]

Anabolic Steroids

Some athletes, particularly weight lifters, track weight athletes, and wrestlers, have been using anabolic steroids in an attempt to gain weight and
strength. Androgenic hormones are basically a product of the male testes.
Of these hormones, testosterone is the principal one and possesses the ability to function androgenically (the ability to stimulate male characteristics)
and anabolically (the ability through an improved protein assimilation to
increase muscle mass and weight, general growth, bone maturation, and
virility). When prescribed by a physician to ameliorate or improve certain
physiological conditions these drugs have value.

Within the last few years steroids have been synthetically developed
that, although related to testosterone, have a decreased androgenic effect.
Among the most commonly used are Anavar, Dianabol, Durabolin, Deca-
Durabolin, Maxibolin, Nilevar, and Winstrol. As is usual with many such
drugs, undesirable side effects, such as reversion of testicular size and function to prepubertal levels, have resulted in a manifestly decreased libido.
There is also risk of liver damage and growth of the prostate gland if ste-

roids are taken for any protracted period. There is also a strong possibility of cancer, if steroids are taken for any protracted period or in dosages greater than that which is usually medically prescribed.

If these drugs are given to the prepubertal boy, a decrease in the ultimate height, because of the cessation of long bone growth, is a most certain hazard. Acne, hirsutism, a deepening of the voice in the prepubescent boy, and in some instances development of abnormally large mammary glands are among other androgen effects. The ingestion of steroids by females can result in hirsutism and a deepening of the voice as a result of vocal cord alteration. When the dosage is halted, the hirsutism may cease but the change of the vocal cords is irreversible. As the duration and dosage increase, the possibility of producing androgen effects also increases. Since self-administered overdosage seems to be the pattern of those who use steroids, the preceding statement is most significant.

The question of whether steroids, with or without protein supplements, bring about increases in weight and strength is moot. Evidence appears somewhat contradictory. A number of studies have shown such increases.[5] Others have found no significant changes.[6] In the latter, noted increases in strength have been attributed to the effect of the strength-training program per se; increases in weight have been ascribed to water retention.

Studies such as these are conducted under carefully controlled laboratory situations in which all precautions are taken to obviate undesirable or dangerous side effects. It must be recognized that these drugs are extremely dangerous and must not be given to athletes as ergogenic aids. They are categorically condemned for this use, since *the dangers associated with their use are most insidious and can lead to effects as serious as those associated with the amphetamines* (Appendix III-B).

Blood Reinjection (Blood Doping)

Endurance, acclimatization, and altitude make increased metabolic demands on the body, which responds by increasing blood volume and red blood cells to meet the increased aerobic demands.

Recently researchers have replicated these physiological responses by removing 900 ml of blood, storing it, and reinfusing it after 6 weeks.[10] The reason for waiting at least 6 weeks before reinfusion is it takes that long for the athlete's body to reestablish a normal hemoglobin and red blood cell concentration. Using this method, endurance performance has been significantly improved.[10] From the standpoint of scientific research such experimentation has merit and is of interest. However, not only is use of such methods in competition unethical, but use by nonmedical personnel could prove to be dangerous.

Not only is the use of blood reinjection in competition unethical, but use by nonmedical personnel could prove dangerous.

Cigarette Smoking

On the basis of various investigations into the relationship between smoking and performance, the following conclusions can be drawn:

1. There is individual sensitivity to tobacco that may seriously affect performance in instances of relatively high sensitivity. Since over one third of the men studied indicated tobacco sensitivity, it may be wise to prohibit smoking by athletes.

2. As few as ten inhalations of cigarette smoke causes an average maximal decrease in airway conductance of 50%. This occurs in nonsmokers as well.

3. Smoking reduces the oxygen-carrying capacity of the blood. A smoker's blood carries from five to as much as ten times more carbon monoxide than normal, thus the red blood cells are prevented from picking up sufficient oxygen to meet the demands of the body's tissues. The carbon monoxide also tends to make arterial walls more permeable to fatty substances, a factor in atherosclerosis.

4. Smoking aggravates and accelerates the heart muscle cells through overstimulation of the sympathetic nervous system.

5. Total lung capacity and maximal breathing capacity are significantly decreased in heavy smokers; this is important to the athlete, since both changes would impair the capacity to take in oxygen and make it readily available for body use.

6. Smoking decreases pulmonary diffusing capacity.

7. After smoking, an accelerated thrombolic tendency is evidenced.

8. Smoking is a carcinogenic factor in lung cancer and is a contributing factor to heart disease.

9. Postmortem examinations indicate that smoking is implicated in the changes observed in the aorta and coronary arteries, in the development of new symptomatic coronary artery disease (angina pectoris and symptomatic myocardial infarction, for example), and in the increase in coronary heart disease mortality.

10. Freedom from coronary atherosclerosis is much more common in nonsmokers.

11. Atherosclerotic processes in smokers tend to increase with the number of cigarettes smoked daily and the smoker's age.

Only the more pertinent conclusions have been presented. The list of physiological damage continues to grow.

Certainly the amount of evidence is all on the negative side. Since smoking offers no positive contribution to either health or performance, it should be forbidden.

Marijuana

Proponents of marijuana smoking insist that marijuana is a harmless drug that induces relaxation, sharpens mental acuity and awareness, improves reflex responses, and can be used with impunity. Recent findings refute these claims. The components of marijuana smoke are similar to those of tobacco smoke and the same cellular changes are observed in the user.

Continued use leads to respiratory diseases such as asthma and bronchitis and a decrease in vital capacity from 15% to as much as 40% (certainly detrimental to physical performance). Among other deleterious effects that have been found are lowered sperm counts and testosterone levels. Evidence of interference with the functioning of the immune system and cellular metabolism has also been found. The most consistent sign is the increase in pulse rate, which averages close to 20% higher during exercise and is a definite factor in limiting performance.[3] Some decrease in leg, hand, and finger strength has been found at higher dosages. As with tobacco, marijuana must be considered carcinogenic.

Psychological effects such as a diminution of self-awareness and judgment, a slowdown of thinking, and a shorter attention span appear early in the use of the drug. Postmortem examinations of habitual users reveal not only cerebral atrophy but alterations of anatomical structures, which suggest irreversible brain damage. Marijuana also contains unique substances ("cannabinoids") that are stored, in very much the same manner as are fat cells, throughout the body and in the brain tissues for weeks and even months. These stored quantities result in a cumulative deleterious effect on the habitual user.[14,16]

A drug such as marijuana has no place in sports. Claims for its use are unsubstantiated, and the harmful effects, both immediate and long term, are too significant to permit indulgence at any time.

Cocaine

Cocaine is a recreational drug that has had increasing popularity in the sports world. In high doses it causes a sense of excitement and euphoria. On occasions it also produces hallucinations. Found in the leaves of the coca bush, when applied locally to the skin it acts as an anesthetic; however, when taken into the body through inhalation, snorting, or injection, it acts on the central nervous system.

Habitual use of cocaine will not lead to physical tolerance or dependence but will cause psychological dependence and addiction. When used recreationally the athlete feels alert, self-satisfied, and powerful. Heavy usage can produce paranoid delusions and violent behavior.

Alcohol

Alcohol is the number one abused drug in the United States.[23] Alcohol is absorbed directly into the bloodstream via the small intestine. It accumulates in the blood because alcohol absorption is faster than its oxidation. It acts as a central nervous system depressant, producing sedation and tranquility. Characteristically, alcohol consumption, at any time or in any amount, does not better mental or physical abilities and should be completely avoided by athletes (Appendix III-A).

Alcohol consumption, at any time or in any amount, does not better mental or physical abilities and should be avoided by athletes.

REFERENCES

1. Adams, M.M., et al.: Effect of a supplement on dietary intakes of female collegiate swimmers, Phys. Sportsmed. **10**:122, July 1982.

2. Astrand, P.E.: Nutrition and physical performance, World Rev. Nutr. Diet. **16**:59, 1973.

3. Avakain, E.V., et al.: Effects of smoking on cardiorespiratory responses to submaximal exercise, Med. Sci. Sports **11**:87, 1979.

4. Berkow, R. (editor): The Merck manual, ed. 14, Rahway, N.J., 1982, Merck & Co., Inc.

5. Bowers, R.W., and Reardon, J.P.: Effects of methandostenolone (Dianabol) on strength development and aerobic capacity, Med. Sci. Sports **4**:54, 1972.

6. Casner, S.W., and Early, R.G.: Anabolic steroid effects on body composition in normal young men, J. Sports Med. **11**:98, 1971.

7. Cooter, G.R.: Amphetamines and sports performance, J. Phys. Ed. Rec. **51**:63, Oct. 1980.

8. Costill, D.L.: Innovations in athletic conditioning and sports medicine: nutrition for improved performance, Berkeley, Calif., 1973, University of California Extension Media Center. (Audiotape.)

9. Food and Nutrition Board, NAS-NRC, Committee on Nutritional

Misinformation: Water deprivation and performance of athletes, Nutr. Rev. **32**:314, 1974.

10. Gledhill, N.: The ergogenic effect of blood doping, Phys. Sportsmed. **11**:87, Sept. 1983.

11. Guthrie, H.A.: Introductory nutrition, ed. 5, St. Louis, 1983, The C.V. Mosby Co.

12. Hanley, D.F.: Drug and sex testing: regulations for international competition, Symposium on Olympic sportsmedicine, Clinics in sports medicine, vol. 2, no. 1, Philadelphia, March 1983, W.B. Saunders Co.

13. Johnson, R.D.: Liquid meal called digestive aid, Med. Sci. Sports., p. 1, 1967.

14. Kolansky, H., and Moore, W.T.: Marijuana, can it hurt you? J.A.M.A. **232**:923, 1975.

14a. Konishi, F.: Food energy equivalents of various activities, J. Am. Diet Assoc. **46**:186, 1965.

15. Moore, M.: Carbohydrate loading: eating through the wall, Phys. Sportsmed. **9**:97, Oct. 1981.

16. Nahas, G.G.: The pathophysiological effect of marijuana use in man, Private Practice, p. 56, Jan. 1975.

17. Nelson, R.A.: Nutrition and physical performance, Phys. Sportsmed. **10**:55, April 1982.

18. Rasch, P.J., Klafs, C.E., and Arnheim, D.D.: Effects of vitamin C supplementation on cross-country runners, Sportzärzliche Praxis **1**:4, 1962.

19. Ryan, A.J.: A round table: weight reduction in wrestling, Phys. Sportsmed. **9**:79, Sept. 1981.

20. Smith, N.J.: Food for sports, Palo Alto, Calif., 1976, Bull Publishing Co.

21. Smith, N.J.: Nutrition and the athlete, Am. J. Sports Med. **10**:253, July/Aug. 1982.

22. Tcheng, T.K., and Tipton, C.M.: Iowa wrestling study: anthropometric measurements and the prediction of a "minimal" body weight for high school wrestlers, Med. Sci. Sports **5**:1, 1973.

23. Wells, J.: Alcohol: the number one drug of abuse in the United States, Ath. Train. **17**:172, 1982.

24. Zambraski, E.J., et al.: Iowa wrestling study: changes in urinary profiles of wrestlers prior to and after competition, Med. Sci. Sports **7**:217, 1975.

25. Ziegler, M.M.: Nutritional care of the pediatric athlete, Symposium on pediatric and adolescent sports medicine, Clinics in sports medicine, vol. 1, no. 3, Philadelphia, Nov. 1982, W.B. Saunders Co.

ADDITIONAL SOURCES

Appenzeller, O., and Atkinson, R.: Nutrition for physical performance in sports medicine, Baltimore, 1981, Urban & Schwarzenberg, Inc.

Buzzeo, R.: National scope of drug problems, NATA Annual Meeting, Clinical Symposium, June 1983, National Athletic Trainers Association. (Cassette.)

Clement, D.B.: Drug symposium—drug use survey: results and conclusions, Phys. Sportsmed. **11**:64, Sept. 1983.

Grandjean, A.: Performance nutrition, NATA Annual Meeting, Clinical Symposium, June 1983, Greenville, N.C. National Athletic Trainers Association. (Cassette.)

Olerud, J.: Nutrition and the athletic trainer, NATA Annual Meeting, Clinical Symposium, June 1982, National Athletic Trainers Association. (Cassette.)

O'Shea, J.P.: Anabolic steroids in sports: a biophysical evaluation. In Scriber, K., and Burke, E.J., editors: Relevant topics in athletic training, Ithaca, N.Y., 1978, Mouvement Publications.

Smith, G.: Drug symposium—recreational drugs in sports, Phys. Sportsmed. **11**:75, Sept. 1983.

Strauss, R.H., editor: Sports medicine, Philadelphia, 1984, W.B. Saunders Co.

Williams, M.: Ergogenic aids in sport—nutritional, pharmacological, and hematological, NATA Professional Preparation Conference, Pittsburgh, Pa., National Athletic Trainers Association. (Cassette.)

Zipes, S.J.: Recreational mood altering chemicals, NATA Annual Meeting, Clinical Symposium, June 1982, National Athletic Trainers Association. (Cassette.)

Chapter 7

PROTECTIVE SPORTS EQUIPMENT

When you finish this chapter, you should be able to

Identify important equipment for various body parts

Differentiate between good and bad features of selected equipment

Properly fit selected equipment

Protective equipment may be used to:
Disperse energy
Absorb energy
Slow down rate of energy
Deflect a blow
Transmit energy to other body areas
Protect against sharp instruments
Limit excess movement

$\mathbf{M}$odifications and improvements in sports equipment are continually being made, especially for sports in which injury is common.[7]

The proper selection and fit of sports equipment are essential in the prevention of many sports injuries. This is of course particularly true in direct contact and collision sports, such as football, hockey, and lacrosse, but it can also be true in indirect contact sports, such as basketball and soccer. Whenever protective sports equipment is selected and purchased, a major decision in the safeguarding of the athletes' health and welfare is being made.

Currently there is serious concern about the standards for protective sports equipment, particularly material durability standards—including who should set these standards, mass production of equipment, equipment testing methods, and requirements for wearing protective equipment. Some people are concerned that a piece of equipment that is protective to one athlete might in turn be a weapon against another athlete.

Standards are also needed for protective equipment maintenance, both to keep it in good repair and to determine when to throw it away. Too often old, worn-out equipment is passed down from the varsity players to the younger and often less experienced players, compounding their risk of injury. Coaches must learn to be less concerned with color, looks, and style of a piece of equipment and more concerned with its ability to prevent injury.

A major step toward the improvement of sports equipment has been through such groups as the American Society for Testing and Materials (ASTM).[1,13] Its Committee on Sports Equipment and Facilities, established in 1969, has been highly active in establishing "standardization of specifications, test methods, and recommended practices for sports equipment and facilities to minimize injury, and promotion of knowledge as it relates to protective equipment standards."[1,13] Some of the current concerns of this committee are gymnastic apparatus and the accident potential to the performer; wrestling mat protection; football headgear and body padding; hockey helmets, skates, and mesh, as well as body padding and footwear of all types with particular emphasis on fit, traction, and torque; skiing equipment of all kinds, primarily binding releases, ski boot dimensions, poles, runaway straps, and goggles, and standardization for commercial ski shops that outfit the skier; and playing surfaces and their shock-absorbing aspects. Engineering, chemistry, biomechanics, anatomy, physiology, physics, computer science, and other related disciplines are applied to solve problems inherent in safety standardization of sports equipment and facilities.

HEAD PROTECTION

Direct collision sports such as football and hockey require special protective equipment, especially for the head. Football provides more frequent opportunities for body contact than does hockey, but hockey players generally move faster and therefore create greater impact forces. Besides direct head contact, hockey has the added injury elements of swinging sticks and fast-moving pucks. Other sports using fast-moving projectiles are baseball with its pitched ball and swinging bat, and track and field with its javelin, discus, and heavy shot, which can also produce serious head injuries. In recent years most helmet research has been conducted in football and ice hockey; however, some has been on baseball headgear.[9]

Football Helmets

A major influence of football helmet standardization in the United States has been the research of Hodgson and Thomas[11] and the National Operating Committee on Standards for Athletic Equipment (NOCSAE) for football helmet certification. To be NOCSAE approved, a helmet must be able to tolerate forces applied to it at three different sites. The helmet is placed and fitted on a head-forming device raised to an appropriate height and then allowed to fall against a rubber padded steel anvil, at which time the Gadd Severity Index (GSI) is recorded. The GSI must not exceed 1500 on the second of two successive drops from a distance of 1.5 meters. Such a certification means that every football helmet worn by a player, no matter the level of the athlete's ability, ensures standardization of materials and their durability. Football helmets typically must withstand repeated blows and high mass–low velocity impacts such as running into a goalpost or hitting the ground with the head.

Testing new football helmets does not ensure that they will remain safe. A random selection of helmets from a high school football team showed that 75% of those that were 3 years old failed the NOCSAE test.[12]

There are many types of helmets in use today. Basically they fall into three categories—padded, suspension, and air and fluid. There are also helmets that are combinations of the three. In general the helmet should adhere to the following fit standards:

Football helmets must withstand repeated blows that are of high mass and low velocity.

Figure 7-1

Combination fluid and suspension football and helmet liner.

1. It should cover the base of the skull.
2. It should not come down over the eyes.
3. It should not shift when manual pressure is applied.
4. It should not recoil on impact.
5. The ear and ear cut-out should match.
6. The front edge of helmet shell should sit ¾-inch above the player's eyebrows.
7. The chin strap should be an equal distance from the center of the helmet.
8. The cheek pads should fit snugly against the sides of the face.

The suspension helmet holds the head by a series of straps within a hard plastic shell and does not come into contact with the cranium (Fig. 7-1). The suspension helmet is designed to diffuse the impact of each blow to the entire shell of the helmet rather than allowing it to be localized at a single point. In recent years research has produced a custom-fitted helmet that combines air and fluid in compartments that are adjusted to individual head shape. Air cells are first inflated over the top of the head; then the front, back, neck, and sides are inflated, respectively.

Whichever football helmet is used, it must be routinely checked for proper fit, especially in the first few days that it is worn. A check for snugness should be made by inserting a tongue depressor between the head and liner. Proper fit is determined when the tongue depressor is resisted firmly when moved back and forth.

Chin straps are also important to maintaining the proper head and helmet relationship. There are two basic types of chin straps in use today, a 2-

Figure 7-2

A, Pull down on face mask; helmet must not move. **B,** Turn helmet to position on the athlete's head. **C,** Push down on helmet; there must be no movement. **D,** Try to rock helmet back and forth; there must be no movement. **E,** Check for a snug jaw pad fit. **F,** Proper adjustment of the chin strap is necessary to ensure proper helmet fit.

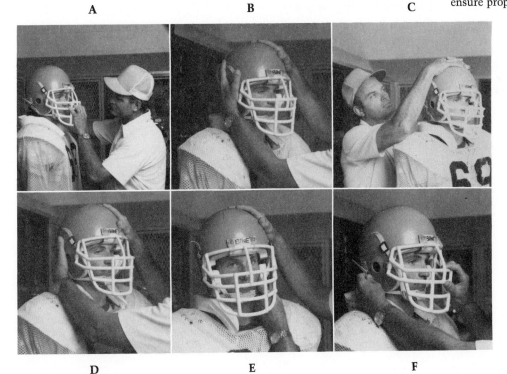

A   B   C

D   E   F

General Principles of Sports
Medicine

Even high-quality helmets are
of no avail if not properly
fitted or maintained.

Ice hockey helmets must
withstand the high-velocity
impact of a stick or puck and
the low-velocity forces of
falling or hitting a sideboard.

snap and a 4-snap strap. Many coaches prefer the 4-snap chin strap because
it tends to keep the helmet from tilting forward and backward. The chin
strap should always be locked so it cannot be released by a hard external
force to the helmet (Fig. 7-2).

Jaw pads are also essential to keep the helmet from rocking laterally.
They should fit snugly againt the player's cheek bones. Even if a helmet is
certified as to its ability to withstand the forces of the game, it is of no avail
if not properly fitted or maintained.

Ice Hockey Helmets

As with football helmets, there has been a concerted effort to upgrade and
standardize ice hockey helmets.[2] In contrast to football, blows to the head
in ice hockey are usually singular rather than multiple. An ice hockey helmet must withstand both high-velocity impacts, such as being hit with a
stick or a puck (which produces low mass and high velocity), as well as the
high mass–low velocity forces produced by running into the sideboard or
falling on the ice. In each instance, the hockey helmet, like the football
helmet, must be able to spread the impact over a large surface area through
a firm exterior shell and at the same time be able to decelerate forces that
act on the head through a proper energy-absorbing liner.[2] The standards for
hockey helmets established by the Canadian Standards Association and the
work by the American Society for Testing and Materials–F8 Hockey Committee for Standards for facial and dental protection have encouraged many
leagues to establish legislation in an attempt to reduce head and facial injuries.[10]

Baseball Batting Helmets

Like ice hockey helmets, the baseball batting helmet must withstand high-
velocity impacts. Unlike football and ice hockey, baseball has not produced
a great deal of data on batting helmets.[9] It has been suggested, however,
that football helmets do little to adequately dissipate the energy of the ball
at impact. An answer might be to add external padding or improve the helmet's suspension.[9]

FACE PROTECTION

The face may be protected by:
  Face guards
  Mouth guards
  Ear guards
  Eye protection devices

Devices that provide face protection fall into four categories: full face
guards, mouth guards, ear guards, and eye protection devices.

Face Guards

Face guards are used in a variety of sports to protect against flying or carried
objects or collision with another player. Since the adoption of face guards
and mouth guards in football, mouth injuries have been reduced over 50%
(Fig. 7-3), but the incidence of neck injuries has increased significantly. The
catcher in baseball, the goalie in hockey, and the lacrosse player all should
be adequately protected against facial injuries, particularly lacerations and
fractures (Fig. 7-4).

There is a great variety of face masks and bars available to the player,
depending on the position played and the protection needed. In football, no
face protection should have less than 2 bars. Proper mounting of the face

mask and bars is imperative for maximum safety. All mountings should be made in such a way that the bar attachments are flush with the helmet. A 3-inch space should exist between the top of the face guard and the lower edge of the helmet. No helmet should be drilled more than one time on each side. There should be a space of 1 to 1½ inches between the player's nose and the face guard. As with the helmet shell, pads, and chin strap, the face guard must be checked daily for defects.

Mouth Guards

The majority of dental traumas can be prevented if the athlete wears a correctly fitted intraoral mouth guard, as compared to an extraoral type (Fig. 7-5). In addition to protecting the teeth, it absorbs the shock of chin blows and obviates a possible cerebral concussion. The mouth protector should afford the athlete a proper and tight fit, comfort, unrestricted breathing, and unimpeded speech during competition. A loose mouthpiece will soon be ejected onto the ground or left unused in the locker room. The athlete's air passages should not be obstructed in any way by the mouthpiece. It is best when it is retained on the upper jaw and projects backward only as far as the last molar, thus permitting speech. Maximum protection is afforded

Figure 7-3

A variety of face guards used in football.

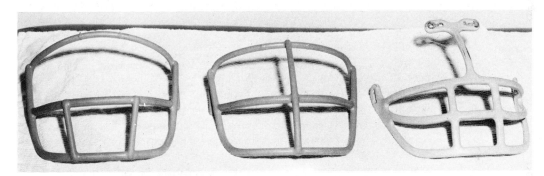

Figure 7-4

Baseball catcher's mask.

Figure 7-5

Customized mouth protector.

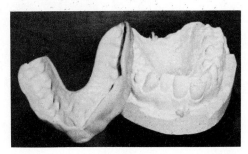

when the mouth guard is composed of a flexible, resilient material and is
formfitted to the teeth of the upper jaw.[4]

Several commercial protectors are available that can either be self-
molded or fitted by a dentist. Many high schools and colleges are now requiring that mouth guards be worn under certain circumstances. Such a
protector should be considered as much a part of standard protective equipment as is a helmet or a pad.

Ear Guards

With the exception of boxing and wrestling, most contact sports do not
make a special practice of protecting the ears. Both boxing and wrestling
can cause irritation of the ears to the point that permanent deformity may
ensue. To avoid this problem special ear guards should be routinely worn.
Recently a very effective ear protection has been developed for the water
polo player (Fig. 7-6).

Eye Protection Devices

The athlete who wears glasses must be protected during sports activities.
Of course, glasses broken during the heat of competitive battle may pose
considerable danger. The eyes of the athlete can be protected by glass
guards, case-hardened lenses, plastic lenses, or contact lenses.

*Eye protection must be worn
by all athletes who play
sports with fast-moving
projectiles.*

Spectacles

For the athlete who must wear corrective lenses, spectacles can be both a
blessing and a nuisance. They may slip on sweat, get bent when hit, fog up
from perspiration, detract from peripheral vision, or be difficult to wear
with protective headgear. Even with all these disadvantages, properly fitted
and designed spectacles can both provide adequate protection and withstand
the rigors of the sport. If the athlete has glass lenses, they must be case-
hardened to prevent them from splintering on impact. When a case-hardened lens breaks it crumbles, eliminating the sharp edges that may penetrate the eye. The cost of this process is relatively low. The only disadvan-

Figure 7-6

Ear protection. **A,** The
wrestler's ear guard. **B,** Water
polo player's ear protection.

A

B

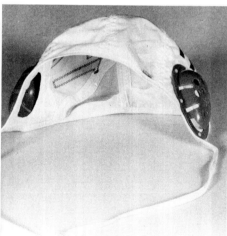

tages involved are that the weight of the glasses is heavier than average, and they may be scratched more easily than regular glasses.

Another sports advantage to glass-lens spectacles is a process by which they can become color-tinted on exposure to ultraviolet rays from the sun and then return to a clear state when removed from the sun's rays. These are known as photochromic lenses.

Plastic lenses for spectacles are becoming increasingly popular with athletes. They are much lighter in weight than glass lenses; however, they are much more prone to scratching.

Contact Lenses

In many ways the athlete who is able to wear contact lenses without discomfort can avoid many of the inconveniences of spectacles. Their greatest advantage is probably the fact that they "become a part of the eye" and move with it.

Contact lenses come in mainly two types: the corneal type, which covers just the iris of the eye, and the scleral type, which covers the entire front of the eye, including the white or scleral portion. Peripheral vision, as well as astigmatism and corneal waviness, is improved through the use of contact lenses. Unlike regular glasses, contact lenses do not normally cloud up during temperature changes. They also can be tinted to reduce glare. For example, yellow lenses can be used against ice glare and blue ones against glare from snow. One of the main difficulties with contact lenses is their high cost compared to regular glasses. Some other serious disadvantages of wearing contact lenses are the possibility of corneal irritation caused by dust getting under the lens and the possibility of a lens becoming dislodged during body contact. Besides these disadvantages, only certain individuals are able to wear contacts with comfort, and some individuals are unable to ever wear them because of certain eye idiosyncrasies. There is currently a trend for athletes to prefer the soft hydrophilic lenses to the hard type. Adjustment time to the soft lenses is shorter than for the hard, they can be more easily replaced, and they are more adaptable to the sports environment.[14]

Eye and Glass Guards

It is essential that athletes take special precautions to protect their eyes, especially in those sports that employ fast-moving projectiles and implements (Fig. 7-7). Besides the more obvious sports of ice hockey, lacrosse, and baseball, the racquet sports also cause serious eye injury. Those athletes not wearing spectacles should wear metal-rimmed frames that surround the

Figure 7-7

Eyes must be protected in sports in which projectiles are moving fast and with a force.

orbital cavity. Athletes who normally wear spectacles with plastic or case-hardened lenses are to some degree already protected against eye injury from an implement or projectile; however, greater safety is afforded by a metal-rimmed frame that surrounds and fit over the athlete's glasses. The protection the guard affords is excellent, but it does hinder vision in some planes.[5]

BODY PROTECTION

Body protection is essential in contact sports. Those areas that are most exposed to impact forces must be properly covered with some resilient material that offers protection against tissue compression injuries. Of particular concern are the hard bony protuberances of the body that have insufficient soft tissue for protection, such as the shoulders, chest, ribs, elbows, knees, and shins (Figs. 7-8 and 7-9). The protection of soft tissue body areas is also a concern (Fig. 7-10).

The problem that arises in the wearing of protective head, face, and body equipment is that while it is armor against injury to the athlete wearing it, it can also serve as a weapon against all opponents. Standards must become more stringent in determining what equipment is absolutely necessary for body protection and at the same time is not itself a source of trauma.

Recently many lightweight pads have been developed to protect the athlete against external forces. A jacket developed by Byron Donzis for the protection of a rib injury incorporates a pad composed of air-inflated, inter-

Figure 7-8

The ice hockey goalie's equipment represents the ultimate in body protection.

Figure 7-9

Standard football protective pads. This system uses open cell foam and air management to disperse a direct impact over the entire surface area of the pad, minimizing the blow to the athlete.

Courtesy Donzis Protective Equipment, Houston, Tex.

Figure 7-8

Figure 7-9

G. Robert Bishop

connected cylinders that protect against severe external forces.[3] This same principle has been used in the development of other protective pads.

Shoulder Protection

Manufacturers of shoulder pads have made great strides toward protecting the football player against direct force to the shoulder muscle complex. There are two general types of pads—flat and cantilevered. The player who uses the shoulder a great deal in blocking and tackling requires the bulkier cantilevered type as compared to the quarterback or ball receiver. Over the years the shoulder pad's front and rear panels have been extended along with the cantilever. Following are rules for fitting the shoulder pad:

1. The tip of the inside shoulder pad should come in a direct line with the lateral aspect of the shoulder and flap covering the deltoid muscle.
2. The neck opening must allow the athlete to extend the arm overhead without placing pressure on the neck but not allow sliding back and forth.
3. Straps underneath the arm must hold the pads firmly but not so they constrict soft tissue.

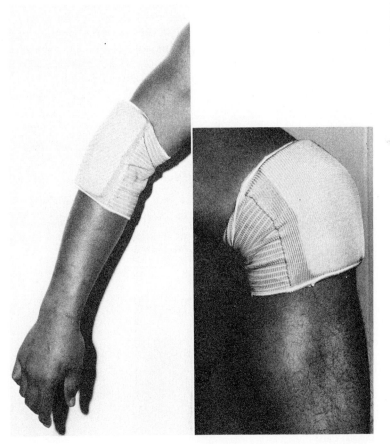

Figure 7-10

Hard, bony areas of the body such as the elbow and knee are prone to bruising.

The female athlete should
wear a protective bra that
prevents uncontrolled breast
movement when she is
running and jumping.

Breast Protection

Until recently the primary concern for female breast protection had been against external forces that may cause bruising. With the vast increase in physically active women, concern has been redirected to protecting the breasts against movement that stems from running and jumping. This is a particular problem for women with very heavy breasts. Many girls and women in the past may have avoided vigorous physical activity because of discomfort felt from uncontrolled movement of their breasts. Manufacturers are making a concerted effort to develop specialized bras for women who participate in all types of physical activity.[15]

A brassiere should hold the breasts to the chest and prevent stretching of Cooper's ligament, causing premature sagging[8] (Fig. 7-11).

KNEE, FOOT, AND ANKLE PROTECTION

Footwear can mean the difference between success, failure, or injury in competition. It is essential that the coach, athletic trainer, and equipment personnel make every effort to fit their athletes with proper shoes and socks.

Socks

Poorly fitted socks can cause abnormal stresses on the foot. For example, socks that are too short crowd the toes, especially the fourth and fifth. Socks that are too long can also cause skin irritation because of their wrinkles. Manufacturers are now providing a double-knit tubular sock without heels that considerably decreases friction within the shoe (Fig. 7-12). The tubular sock is especially good for the basketball player.

Figure 7-11

A, A sports bra must hold the breasts to the chest to avoid excessive motion. **B,** Cooper's ligament.

A courtesy Creative Support Systems, Santa Barbara, Calif.

A

Douglas Child

B

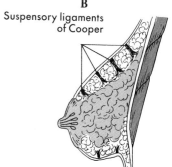

Suspensory ligaments of Cooper

Shoes

Even more damaging than poorly fitted socks are improperly fitted shoes. Chronic abnormal pressures to the foot often lead to permanent structural deformities as well as to potentially dangerous calluses and blisters (see Chapter 17). Besides these local problems occurring to the feet, improper shoeing results in mechanical disturbances affecting the body's total postural balance, which may eventually lead to pathological conditions of the muscle and joint.

Shoe Composition

The bare human foot is designed to function on uneven surfaces. Shoes were created to protect against harmful surfaces, but should never interfere with natural functioning. Sports shoes, like all shoes, are constructed of different parts, each of which is designed to provide function, protection, and durability. Each sport places unique stresses and performance demands on the foot. In general, all sport shoes, like street shoes, are made of similar parts. For example, shoes are composed of a sole, uppers, heel counter, and toe box. The sole or bottom of a shoe is divided into an outer, middle, and inner section, each of which must be sturdy, flexible, and provide a degree of cushioning, depending on the specific sport requirements. A heel counter should support and cushion the heel, while the toe box protects and provides an area so that the toes do not become crowded. The uppers must give the foot support and freedom to withstand a high degree of stress (Fig. 7-13).

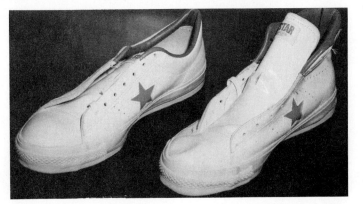

Figure 7-12

The tubular doubleknit sock can prevent friction in the shoe.

Figure 7-13

Properly fitted sports shoes can prevent foot stress.

Shoe Fitting

Fitting sports footgear is always difficult, mainly because the individual's left foot varies in size and shape from the right foot, and sports shoe manufacturers do not offer the extensive variety of shoe size possibilities that street shoe manufacturers do. To properly fit the sports shoe, the athlete should approximate the conditions under which he will perform, such as wearing his game socks, jumping up and down, or running. It is also desirable to fit the athlete's shoes at the end of the day to accommodate the gradual increase in size that occurs from the time of awakening.

Under performance conditions the new shoe should feel snug but not tight because it will stretch with wear. The length of the sports shoe should allow enough space that all toes can be fully extended without being cramped. Its width should permit full movement of the toes, flexion, extension, and some spreading. A good point to remember is that the wide part of the shoe should match the wide part of the foot. This allows the shoe to crease evenly when the athlete goes on the balls of his feet. The shoe should bend (or "break") at its widest part; when the break of the shoe and the ball joint coincide, the fit may be considered to be correct. However, if the break of the shoe is in back or in front of the metatarsophalangeal joint, the shoe and foot will be opposing one another, causing abnormal skin and structural stresses to occur. Two measurements must be considered when fitting shoes: first, the distance from the heel to the metatarsophalangeal joint, and second, the distance from the heel to the end of the longest toe. An individual's feet may be equal in length from the heels to the balls of the feet, but different between heels and toes. Shoes, therefore, should be selected for the longer of the two measurements. Other factors to consider when buying the sports shoe are the stiffness of the sole and the width of the shank or narrowest part of the sole. A shoe with a too rigid, nonyielding sole places a great deal of extra strain on the foot tendons. The shoe with too narrow a shank also places extra strain because it fails to adequately support the athlete's inner longitudinal arches. Two other shoe features to consider are inner soles to reduce friction and built-in arch supports.

The cleated or specially soled sports shoe presents some additional problems in fitting. For example, American football uses these basic shoe types: the multi–short-cleated polyurethane sole, and the five in front and

Figure 7-14

Variations in cleated shoes— the longer the cleat, the higher the incidence of injury.

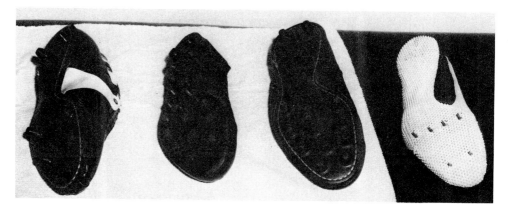

two in back cleat arrangement and the soccer-type sole, both of which have cleats no longer than 0.5 inches (Fig. 7-14). If cleated shoes are used, no matter which sport, the cleats must be positioned under the two major weight-bearing points, the first and fifth metatarsophalangeal joints.

Shoe Lacing Technique

As has been discussed, the sports shoe is major protective equipment. There are three basic lacing patterns used in sports shoes: the U-throat, the vamp pattern, and the stabilizer. The U-throat laces down to the toes and the vamp laces partway down to the toes. The stabilizer laces like the vamp pattern but has an added dimension of going around the heel counter through guides that, when tightened, secure both the uppers and the heel counter. Proper shoe lacing is also necessary to protect the foot and ankle (Fig. 7-15). Correct lacing ensures against the shoe becoming loose during activity. In the case of the high-top shoe, proper lacing can be an additional factor in preventing ankle sprains. The lacing procedure is as follows:

1. Lace the first and second shoe eyelets in an inside-out manner, making sure that the toes can move freely.
2. Lace the next 2 to 4 eyelets in an outside-in manner, making sure to pull each lace snugly but without restricting foot movement.
3. The last procedure repeats the first, by lacing the remaining eyelets in an inside-out manner. Lacing of these last eyelets should not be tight but should be left somewhat loose to allow freedom of muscle function.

HAND PROTECTION

One of the finest physical instruments, the human hand, is perhaps one of the most neglected in terms of injury, especially in sports. Special attention must be paid to protecting the integrity of all aspects of the hand when encountering high-speed missiles or receiving external forces that contuse or shear. Constant stress to the hand, as characterized by the force received by the hand of the baseball catcher, can lead to irreversible pathological damage in later life[15] (Fig. 7-16).

SPECIALIZED PROTECTIVE DEVICES

In recent years many lightweight and very strong synthetic materials have been developed. As a result, a number of very useful and specialized protec-

Figure 7-15

Shoe lacing technique.

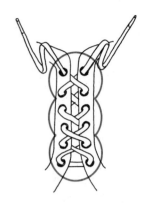

Figure 7-16

The hand is an often neglected area of the body in sports.

tive pieces of equipment are now available to the athlete and can be made
by the trainer or coach or are available commercially.

One must have a very optimistic feeling about the progress that has
been made in sports protective equipment. Researchers, physicians,
coaches, trainers, and manufacturers are working together to provide the
athlete with the safest possible equipment. Although there is continuous
need for safer protective equipment, the future is bright in this highly important area.

Ankle Supports

Most commercial ankle supports are of either *elastic* or *spat* type. The elastic type is a flexible, fibered sheath that slides over the foot and ankle,
purportedly giving mild support to a weak ankle. It has little use either as
a strong support or as a protection to the postacute or chronically weakened
ankle in sports. The spat type is usually less resilient than the elastic and
has an open front that permits it to be fitted directly over the ankle and
then snugly tied like a shoe. Some spats have vertical ribs to effect added
inversion or eversion. Though providing some assistance, no commercial
ankle support affords as much protection as does adhesive tape properly
applied directly to the skin surface. A fabricated orthoplast strip brace cut
three to four inches wide has been found to be an effective semirigid support for sprained ankles.[17]

Knee Supports and Protective Devices

Knees are next in order to ankles and feet in terms of incidence of injury in
sports. As a result of the variety and rather high frequency of knee afflictions, many protective and supportive devices have been devised. The de-

Figure 7-17

A preventive knee brace
designed to protect against a
lateral force and distribute
load away from joint. Losse
knee defender.

Courtesy Don Joy Orthopedic,
Carlsbad, Calif.

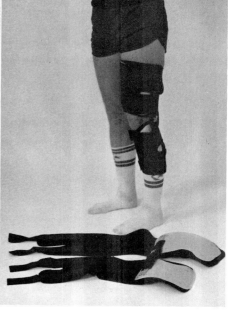

vices most frequently used in sports today are braces, elastic supports, and elastic pads.

Protective knee braces are extremely varied. Currently popular are the singular hinge-type braces that are designed to protect against a lateral force and to distribute the load away from the joint (Figs. 7-17 to 7-19). Other types of protective knee braces are the ribbed brace, consisting of a series of vertical ridged strips contained within an elastic sleeve, and the elastic sleeve, containing a rigid hinge on either side of the knee joint. Another support that is commonly used is the neoprene sleeve, which provides a great deal of pressure around the knee. Careful engineering and testing must be conducted to produce the knee brace that will protect adequately. Knee braces and rotary instability are discussed in Chapter 20.

Elastic knee pads or guards are extremely valuable in sports in which the athlete falls or receives a direct blow to the anterior aspect of the knee. An elastic sleeve containing a resilient pad helps to dissipate anterior striking force but fails to protect the knee against lateral, medial, or twisting forces.

Figure 7-18

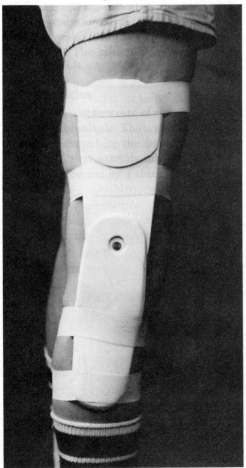

Figure 7-19

Figure 7-18

The Arco knee guard.
Courtesy Robert F. McDavid, Indiana State University.

Figure 7-19

Sleeve hinge type of knee brace.

Abdominal and Low Back Supports

Because low back strain is a national problem, there are many gimmicks on the market that claim to give relief. Such devices may be classified as abdominal and low back supports. Where freedom of activity is desired, as in sports, a rigid and nonyielding material may be handicapping. A material that permits movement and yet offers support is desirable. Such material may consist of elastic, rubberized fabric. In most cases of low back strain, supporting the abdominal viscera will alleviate considerable discomfort.

Figure 7-20

Retaining shoulder brace.

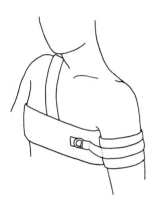

Shoulder Braces

The shoulder braces (Fig. 7-20) used in sports are essentially restraining belts for the chronically dislocated shoulder. Their purpose is to restrict the upper arm from being elevated more than 90 degrees and externally rotated, thus preventing it from being placed in a vulnerable position. Because of the ensuing limitation in range of motion of the arm, the athlete's capabilities are considerably reduced.

Other Elastic Pads and Supports

Elastic pads and supports are varied and can be suited to most body areas. Thigh, forearm, wrist, and elbow devices afford mild support and give protection from direct blows.

REFERENCES

1. American Society for Testing and Materials, Committee F-8 on Sports Equipment and Facilities: Member information packet, Philadelphia, 1978, The Society.
2. Bishop, P.J., et al.: The ice hockey helmet: how effective is it? Phys. Sportsmed. 7:96, 1979.
3. Cain, T.E., et al.: Use of the air-inflated jacket in football, Am. J. Sports Med. 9:240, 1981.
4. Castaldi, C.R.: Injuries to the teeth. In Vinger, P.F., and Hoerner, E.F. (editors): Sports injuries: the unthwarted epidemic, Boston, 1981, John Wright, PSG, Inc.
5. Eye protection for athletes, round table discussion, Phys. Sportsmed. 9:43, 1978.
6. Gardner, L.: For the problem knee, slip on a sleeve, Phys. Sportsmed. 3:111, 1975.
7. Gardenswartz, A.: Equipment for sport. In Appenzeller, O., and Atkinson, R. (editors): Sports medicine, Baltimore 1981, Urban & Schwarzenberg.
8. Gehlsen, G., and Albohm, M.: Evaluation of sports bras, Phys. Sportsmed. 8:89, 1980.
9. Goldsmith, W., and Kabo, J.M.: Performance of baseball headgear, Am. Sports Med. Vol. 10:31, 1982.
10. Hayes, D.: Reducing risks in hockey: analysis of equipment and injuries, Phys. Sportsmed. 6:67, 1978.
11. Hodgson, V.R., and Thomas, L.M.: Biomechanical study of football head impacts using a head model—condensed version; final report prepared for NOCSAE, 1973.
12. Houston, J.T.: Helmet makers seek better product, tests. In More, M. (editor): Football injury and equipment update, Phys. Sportsmed. 10:197, 1982.
13. Hulse, W.F.: Sports equipment standards. In Vinger, P.F., and Hoerner, E.F. (editors): Sports injuries: the unthwarted epidemic, Boston, 1981, John Wright, PSG, Inc.
14. Morehouse, C.A., et al.: Soft contact lenses for sports, Phys. Sportsmed. 6:106, 1978.

15. Protect catcher's hand, surgeons say, Phys. Sportsmed. **4**:14, 1976.
16. Schuster, K.: Equipment update: jogging bras hit the streets, Phys. Sportsmed. **7**:125, 1979.
17. Turner, D.J.: Use of the semi-rigid support for sprained ankles, Ath. Train. **17**:201, 1982.

ADDITIONAL SOURCES

Bahniuk, E.: Ski standards developed by the American Society for Testing Materials. In Johnson, R.J. (editor): Symposium on skiing injuries—Clinics in sports medicine, vol. 1, no. 2, Philadelphia, July 1982, W.B. Saunders Co.

Bishop, P.J., et al.: Performance of eye protectors for squash and racquetball, Phys. Sportsmed. **10**:47, 1982.

Blyth, C.S., and Hodgson, V.R.: National governing bodies. In Vinger, P.F., and Hoerner, E.F. (editors): Sports injuries: the unthwarted epidemic, Boston, 1981, John Wright, PSG, Inc.

Burns, D.: A manufacturer's perspective. In Vinger, P.F., and Hoerner, E.F. (editors): Sports injuries: the unthwarted epidemic, Boston, 1981, John Wright, PSG, Inc.

Easterbrook, M.: Eye protection for squash and racketball players, Phys. Sportsmed. **9**:78, 1982.

Goodwin, W.C., et al.: Mouth protectors in junior football players, Phys. Sportsmed. **10**:41, 1982.

Hale, C.J., and Spackman, R.R. Jr.: Protective equipment and conditioning, Audio Cassettes on Sportsmedicine, Chicago, Teach'em, Inc.

Hoerner, E.F., and Vinger, P.F.: Protective equipment: its value, capabilities and limitations (an editorial comment). In Vinger, P.F., and Hoerner, E.F. (editors): Sports injuries: the unthwarted epidemic, Boston, 1981, John Wright, PSG, Inc.

Moore, M. (editor): Football injury and equipment update, Phys. Sportsmed. **10**:197, 1982.

Morehouse, C.A.: Obsolescence in protective equipment. In Vinger, P.F., and Hoerner, E.F. (editors): Sports injuries: the unthwarted epidemic, Boston, 1981, John Wright, PSG., Inc.

Chapter 8

PSYCHOGENIC CONSIDERATIONS

When you finish this chapter, you should be able to

Discuss athletes' major personality patterns before and during competition

Identify psychological indications of abnormal stress

Describe the most important psychological elements inherent in sports injuries

Demonstrate coping skills for abnormal stress

Mens sana in corpore sano, or "a sound mind in a sound body," is the concept of mind-body relationship that we have accepted since the time of the early Greeks. In recent years we have become increasingly concerned with the effect of psychosomatic relationships and their applications to physical performance and injury management.

Sports training requires the athlete to have mental discipline. The great athlete becomes a great athlete not only because of physical endowment but also because of dedication and tenacity of purpose.

SPORTS PERFORMANCE

Psychological conditioning is as important and as much the responsibility of the trainer as physical conditioning or rehabilitation. Often an individual's psychological condition has a direct bearing on neuromuscular or physical response. Also, the trainer is a teacher and, functioning in this role, must seek to develop accepted sociological and psychological behavior in athletes. A trainer can contribute much to the emotional stability and the psychosociological maturity of those who come under his or her care.

Participation in sports occurs principally as an individual's effort to satisfy various psychogenic needs. These needs may include desires to achieve social status and prestige or the assertion of certain aggressive tendencies. Such patterns are derived from basic activity drives.

In recent years much emphasis has been placed on a need for competition—the fact that life itself is competitive and we therefore need to stimulate and encourage competition. Athletes derive satisfaction from the act of participating in a sport activity. This satisfaction sparks the competitive

Psychological conditioning is as important and as much the responsibility of the trainer as physical conditioning or rehabilitation.

drive, although the intensity of the drive tends to vary, depending on the individual and the type of activity pursued. Because of variations in human temperament, some persons become more competitive than others. It must be recognized, however, that competition and rivalry are not inherent tendencies but are learned incentives peculiar to our type of society. In many societies competition in the forms we know it is either unknown or undesirable.

THE TRAINER'S ROLE

A trainer is brought into close personal contact with the athletes and is often faced with emotional or sociological problems. Athletes by their very nature tend to develop tensions. The trainer is in an excellent position to eradicate or prevent such tensions and must have a knowledge of psychological factors and know what course of action to follow. Some situations require understanding and sympathy, others firmness. Still others require considerable restraint. The right word spoken at the right time can often resolve a situation that could otherwise develop into an unfortunate circumstance.

Injury prevention is *psychological*, as well as *physiological*. The athlete who enters a contest while angry, frustrated, or discouraged or undergoing some other disturbing emotional state is more prone to injury than is the individual who is better adjusted emotionally. The angry player, for example, wants to vent ire in some way and therefore often loses perspective of desirable and approved conduct. In the grip of emotion, skill and coordination are sacrificed, with the result that an injury that otherwise would have been avoided, can be sustained.

Studies have indicated that athletes in certain types of sport tend to manifest common characteristics. These identifiable personality characteristics may influence the choice of sport that the athlete makes. Trainers and coaches have long believed that there are "types," readily identifiable by specific personality traits, who gravitate toward specific sports. On the basis of the limited evidence available, such assumptions seem to be reasonable.

Athletes usually select an activity because they have achieved some degree of success in that activity previously, either as students in general physical education classes or as participants in recreational or sandlot competition. They have developed an interest in the activity, although their actual participation experience may be somewhat limited. Sometimes a coach or trainer, observing students in some type of physical activity, will suggest that they try out for a particular sport. To the trained eye these students have given evidence of possessing the inherent characteristics, both physical and psychological, that indicate an excellent chance for success in that activity.

Through daily contact the observant trainer soon learns to predict the responses of athletes. Generally, such responses follow a consistent pattern. It is through a knowledge and understanding of these patterns that the trainer is able to predict responses and thus be prepared to handle situations as they develop in the training room and on the field.

The training room is no place for a display of temperament on the part

The trainer is in an excellent position to eradicate or prevent tensions and must have a knowledge of psychological factors and appropriate actions.

Through daily contact the observant trainer soon learns to predict the responses of athletes.

By setting an example, the
trainer can help the athlete
maintain a fairly constant
level of behavior.

The athletic trainer must
have some counseling skills.

of the trainer, who must learn to condition and modify his or her personality so that behavior becomes a stable element in the midst of a somewhat unstable emotional climate. Students learn by precept and example. The trainer, by setting an example can aid considerably in maintaining a fairly consistent level of behavior. *The trainer must learn to respond to irritability with tranquility, to obstinacy with patience, and to anger with tolerance.* To respond with an emotion that is similar to the athlete's tends to increase tensions and may result in feelings of enmity and dislike on the part of the athlete. On occasion, however, the trainer may need to respond with such emotions to evoke a desired response from the athlete. Patience and understanding are the keys to establishing and promoting desirable relationships with students, athletes, and others. During treatment and physical restoration good communication and personal involvement with the athlete are essential.

Although athletic trainers are typically not educated as professional counselors or psychologists, they must be concerned with the feelings of the athletes they work with. No one can work closely with human beings without becoming involved with their levels of emotions and, at times, their personal problems. The athletic trainer is usually a very caring person and, as such, is placed in numerous daily situations in which close interpersonal relationships are important. The athletic trainer must have appropriate counseling skills to confront an athlete's fears, frustrations, and daily crises and to refer individuals with serious emotional problems to the proper professionals.

THE PERSONALITY PATTERN OF ATHLETES

Personality patterns are seldom found as pure types; rather, they are found in varying combinations, with one or two characteristics being somewhat outstanding in each. The different types are quite recognizable in the training room. They respond differently to treatment, and the trainer must be able to recognize and understand the dominant traits of each so that therapy and reconditioning may proceed at an optimal rate.

One type is the naturally cheerful, confident, and optimistic athlete, who is exceedingly extroverted and usually demonstrates good leadership qualities. This athlete needs constant checking, since often there is a tendency to downplay or ignore injuries and not adhere as closely to training procedures as may be desirable. Similarly, an easygoing, sometimes lackadaisical, and not easily excited athlete, who lacks drive and seldom uses full vigor in physical efforts, is a constant problem to the trainer and the coach because constant checking is required to ensure that recommended procedures are followed.

A frequent visitor to the training room may be the athlete who suffers from a host of injuries and ailments that are principally psychosomatic. As a rule this individual is somewhat introverted and hypochondriacal and can be a difficult problem unless the trainer takes a positive approach and does not become overly indulgent.

The athlete who displays tenacity, stubbornness, and irascibility often possesses strong leadership qualities. This athlete is usually fiercely competitive, quite aggressive, and a good competitor but needs careful handling by the coach and trainer to properly channel these characteristics so that they will improve rather than negate performance (Fig. 8-1).

Varsity competition at the high school and college levels tends to promote precontest emotional disturbances, in particular, an increased anxiety level.[9] Such disturbances do not appear to have deleterious effects on the health of either male or female participants. However, they can and often do have detrimental effects on the athlete's performance. These disturbances result from tensions built up within the athlete and from the emotional climate that precedes competition. The trainer is in a particularly advantageous position to aid in dispelling such tensions. Despite the bustle and demands of the training room, a word of counsel or a joke may relieve the tension, leaving the athlete relaxed and consequently better able to perform effectively.

The Pregame Syndrome

Pregame tension is a syndrome with which everyone connected with athletics is familiar. Before any event that is of significance to the performer, the symptoms manifest themselves in varying degrees. Continued exposure somewhat lessens but does not eradicate the effects; veteran athletes, public

Figure 8-1

The highly competitive athlete often has personality qualities that have to be carefully channeled to improve performances.
Courtesy Cramer Products, Inc., Gardner, Kan.

performers, politicians, and others will attest to still feeling one or more of these effects of tension.

The pregame syndrome is one of nature's ways of preparing the individual for maximal effort and is the result of adrenomedullary activity. Epinephrine is released into the system, with dramatic results. (Adrenalin is a proprietary name for epinephrine, a hormone of the adrenal medulla, which was the first hormone identified [early 1900s].) It is formed by the adrenal gland, located on the superior border of the kidney, and is released into the bloodstream in varying amounts. It is theorized that an epinephrine-like compound stimulates the adjacent dendrites and muscle cells when it is released, as a result of the nerve impulse reaching the synapse or myoneural junctions. The adrenal hormones spread throughout the body and elicit a wide range of effects. These effects increase the physical performance of an individual in an emergency. This is accomplished through the following means:

1. Speedup of circulation and respiration, which increases the delivery of fuel to the muscles and the removal of metabolites and other wastes
2. Increase in glycogenolytic action, which increases the blood sugar content and supplies more fuel to the muscles
3. Increase in the metabolism of the cerebrum, which results in an increase in alertness and in the neuromuscular responses, thus improving physical performance
4. Increase in the excitability of the neurons, which enhances motor activity and alertness

With the increase in blood pressure and heart rate and the endocrine stimulation, certain emotional symptoms appear, such as a feeling of anxiety, breathlessness, "butterflies" in the stomach, and trembling. An athlete in a state of readiness for competition will exhibit these signs in varying degrees.

Event Considerations

Numerous psychological factors are inherent in sports competition. A trainer must understand the athlete's desire to compete and behavioral problems that may be associated with competition.

The Athlete's Level of Aspiration

A champion thinks like a champion. A positive attitude toward a competitive situation aids the performer. The mind is not hindered or cluttered with doubts and countless little nagging thoughts couched in terms of failure. Rather, the champion is determined to succeed and can concentrate all conscious efforts, physical and psychological, toward achieving the goal. Players will react emotionally to the importance of a contest. If they are competing against a team that they believe will not give them much trouble, it is difficult for the coach and trainer to get them "up" psychologically for the contest. An underrated team will often play far above its usual rated level of performance simply because it aspires to win. The players are determined. Conversely, their opponents, unquestionably the better team in terms of previous performances, cannot seem to get going. Psychological readiness, or mind set, is as important to performance as is physical conditioning.

Successful players and competitors have high levels of aspiration. They constantly raise these levels and maintain hopes of success even if at times they repeatedly experience failure. On the other hand, unsuccessful players tend to lower their level of aspiration. Individuals who have a low level of aspiration and then experience failure tend to escape by removing themselves from the failure situation through various means such as rationalization or defeatism. If they are neither favorite nor underdog, they have a 50/50 chance of being successful.

The level of aspiration of either an individual or a team can be raised through pep talks, slogans, and various audiovisual materials in the training and locker rooms. Trainers can play an important role both in maintaining and in raising the level of aspiration by using their position as a means of adding to the levels of motivation and encouragement so necessary in sports.

Motivation and the Athletic Trainer

There appears to be a specific relationship between the voluntary motor system and emotion. Kinesthetic skills and performances are affected by the state of emotion existing at a given time. Motivation is facilitated when emotion is channeled as an energizing force rather than as an impediment. Such factors as cheering, excitement, and pep talks are motivational influences that assist the athlete in performing optimally, calling up reserves to sometimes exceed known ability, or staving off the onset of fatigue or exhaustion. This type of motivation is usually not within the realm of the trainer. Instead, the trainer must use other motivational incentives, such as setting achievable goals in the rehabilitative program; developing an *esprit de corps*, a pride in the team and in one's self; and establishing and maintaining good morale in the training room. The ability to communicate—to speak the athlete's language—will help establish desirable rapport that will not only be motivational during treatment but will render the injured athlete more receptive toward the rehabilitation program.

The trainer deals with motivation in terms of developing desirable attitudes and patterns of response toward training and its various procedures and instilling the athlete with a desire to participate in therapy and reconditioning with a positive attitude. To want to get well is extremely important in any therapeutic process. Thus, good motivation enables the athlete to assist the trainer and become an asset rather than a liability.

Sports Participation as a Stressor

Sports participation serves as both a physical and an emotional stressor. Stress can be a positive or negative influence. All living organisms are endowed with the ability to cope effectively with stressful situations. Pelletier[11] stated: "Without stress, there would be very little constructive activity or positive change." Negative stress can contribute to poor health, whereas positive stress produces growth and development. A healthy life must have a balance of stress; too little causes a "rusting out" and too much stress can cause "burnout."[14]

Sports participation is both a physical and an emotional stressor.

General Principles of Sports
Medicine

anxiety
A feeling of uncertainty or
apprehension

Athletes place their bodies in countless daily stress situations. Their bodies undergo numerous "fight or flight" reactions to avoid injury or other threatening situations. Inappropriate adjustment to fight or flight responses can eventually lead to emotional or physical illness.

The mind and body are inseparable in terms of stress. Daily worries, fears, and anxieties can be stress producing. **Anxiety** is one of the most common mental and emotional stress producers. It is reflected by a nondescript fear, a sense of apprehension and restlessness. Typically the anxious athlete is unable to describe the problem. The athlete feels inadequate in a certain situation but is unable to say why. Heart palpitations, shortness of breath, sweaty palms, constriction in the throat, and headache may accompany anxiety.

Pre-event Anxiety and Tension

Temporary stress reactions associated with pre-event nervous tension are dry mouth and diuresis and a desire to defecate.

Dry mouth　A dryness of the mouth (xerostomia) often accompanies the above symptoms. It results from a lack of normal secretion and is caused by stress. The use of lozenges, chewing gum, or lemons, anything that will reactivate salivary action, is indicated. This helps relieve xerostomia and aids somewhat in relieving the tension. It keeps the athlete occupied, even though to a limited extent.

Diuresis and nervous defecation　Diuresis (increased flow of urine) and nervous defecation often accompany pregame tension and may be attributed to increased hormonal and nerve action. The increase in anxiety appears to increase nerve irradiation and thus activate not only the adrenal glands but also the brain regions and visceral nerves that govern these functions, with the result that both bladder and bowel action are stimulated.

Staleness　Athletes who have been training over a long period of time or who have been involved in long periods of competition, with a resultant lack of relaxation and rest, sometimes go "stale." Staleness is evidenced by a wide variety of symptoms, among which are a deterioration in the usual standard of performance, chronic fatigue, apathy, loss of appetite, indigestion, weight loss, constipation, and inability to sleep or rest properly. Often athletes will exhibit lowered blood pressure or an increased pulse rate, both at rest and during activity, as well as increased catecholamine excretions. All these signs indicate adrenal exhaustion. The athlete becomes irritable and restless, has to force himself or herself to practice, and exhibits signs of boredom and lassitude in respect to everything connected with the activity.

When these symptoms first appear, the trainer should immediately bar the athlete from all activity, prescribing instead ample rest and relaxation. Sometimes having a chat with the individual, explaining what the problem is and how it can be met, helps to get the athlete back to normal a little faster. In severe cases of staleness it is best to refer the athlete to the team physician for evaluation and treatment. Such treatment follows the procedure for other depressed patients. The main key is the revival and stimulation of interest, motivation, and desire.

Conflict adjustment The athlete who for one reason or another is under a great deal of mental and emotional stress may react as being in conflict. The adjustments of these conflicts may be inappropriate and reflect minor or even major behavioral problems.

Ambivalence Ambivalence is typical of an individual in conflict. To want something and simultaneously reject it is characteristic of ambivalence. Some people achieve more satisfaction from one aspect and therefore encounter greater frustration in the other aspects of an activity. To express it differently, whatever they do to fulfill one motive opposes the other. Over a long period of time these people tend to develop an attitude of "Whatever I attempt to do is wrong or ends in failure." In such cases individuals tend to develop personality patterns that are revealed through various types of recognizable, overt behaviors. Thus the accident-prone athlete, the overly aggressive individual, and the complacent person all indicate outward manifestations of some hidden psychological problem. In some instances overt behavior is indicative of a specific failing or shortcoming that the individual seeks to mask by assuming a defensive posture.

Accident proneness Accident-prone athletes have more than an average share of injuries. Injuries seem to seek them out, and normally insignificant or innocuous situations assume significance when they appear on the scene. They are easily involved in situations wherein they receive some injury, although others emerge unscathed. Ogilvie and Tutko[10] categorize the accident-prone athlete into three types: (1) the bona fide injured, (2) the psychologically injured, and (3) the malingerer. The *bona fide injured* athlete may have a series of rather severe injuries as the result of hostility directed toward the self, which is manifested in reckless and daredevil performances, thus inviting injury. The *psychologically injured* individual constantly complains of injury and pain, but no medically sound evidence is recognizable. The *malingerer* intentionally lies about an injury to get out of work.

Accident-prone individuals are most likely to suffer an accident toward the end of a long or sustained period of work. Accident proneness appears to be caused by a lack of ability to coordinate properly, as the result of either fatigue or emotional imbalance. Often the discouraged or apathetic athlete is accident prone. Trainers and coaches have long observed that the competitor who is not emotionally stable stands an excellent chance of being injured.

Certain characteristics can be recognized in accident-prone athletes. Usually they are easily distracted and, as implied previously, generally exhibit emotional instability. In some instances they become extremely aggressive toward and intolerant of others, displaying an attitude of superiority. They actually enjoy some accidents because of the attention they attract. Some individuals of this type become almost permanent fixtures in the training room. Their high incidence of injury, plus the fact that they enjoy the ministrations and attention, make these individuals a real problem for the trainer and the coach alike.

Hostility and overt aggressiveness Although aggressiveness is a desirable characteristic in sports, some athletes are hostile or overaggres-

Conflict adjustment examples in an athlete include:
Ambivalence
Accident proneness
Hostility/
    overaggressiveness
Rationalization
Sarcasm/criticism
Foul language
Defeatism
Complacency
Malingering

General Principles of Sports
Medicine

Feelings of hostility are often
released through competition,
particularly in contact sports.

sive toward the opposition and team members and associates.[3] Such feelings may indicate pregame tension or they may be the result of intensive training over a long period of time. Frequently, athletes who display aggressive tendencies falling into the latter category are "drawn fine" and need to ease their rigorous schedules for a while. Often feelings of hostility are released through competition, particularly in contact sports.

The trainer can handle the overly aggressive individual in several ways. He or she can attempt to channel the tendencies into more desirable avenues through careful counseling, or if the athlete seems amenable to reason, the trainer can get the athlete to recognize the problem and to attempt to solve it through changes in behavior. The latter method is not always effective, particularly when anger or hostility is evidenced during the discussion. A person in this frame of mind soon loses the ability to listen, reason, and think coherently and often becomes more symptomatic than usual. When neither the catharsis of competition, channeling, nor reasoning produces favorable results, the individual should be remanded to proper counseling channels for assistance. This type athlete is usually difficult to recondition.

Rationalization Many times the trainer will encounter athletes who employ rationalization to a considerable degree. Such individuals advance seemingly plausible reasons for everything they do. Whenever errors, misunderstandings, or problems occur, although it is evident that the fault lies with them, they defend their position with the support of a somewhat credible explanation. The relationship to the trainer and the training program takes the form of projection, usually involving feelings of persecution. Sometimes the position is taken that the trainer is not interested in the athlete or in his or her rehabilitation and that this attitude is a result of some misunderstood action that has caused the trainer to develop a feeling of personal animosity.

Individuals who show a pattern of this type are difficult to reach. They fail to follow training or reconditioning instructions, complaining that they cannot see the use of such procedures. They are convinced the procedures are giving them no positive results or are only aggravating the particular problem. Any attempt to point out specifics usually results in more rationalization. Not only do they fail to realize shortcomings, but they also refuse to accept them when they are made apparent. They cover their failures or confusion with specious reasoning that will, in their eyes, justify their actions.

Pressuring the athlete and
consistently explaining the
objectives often have positive
results.

The difficulties in working with this type of individual are nearly insurmountable. However, pressuring the athlete and consistently explaining the objectives often bring about positive results. Extreme cases should be referred to the school psychologist.

Sarcasm and criticism Some athletes seek relief from emotional conflicts by turning to an excessive use of sarcasm or criticism. They incessantly find fault with equipment, training facilities, and gear. They are hypercritical of their wrappings and of other preventive or therapeutic actions. When queried, they take refuge in heavy sarcasm rather than attempting to critically evaluate their behavior and then take steps to eradicate their own faults. Answering such sarcasm with sarcasm tends to strengthen rather than attenuate the difficulty. Consequently, such individuals are best dealt with privately in efforts to help them recognize and overcome their shortcomings.

Foul language and profanity   The persons who persistently use foul or profane language often wish to distract attention from their failings or to compensate for feelings of insecurity. In some instances profanity may be a means of relieving inner tensions, but under no circumstances should the use of such language be tolerated. It has no place in sports. The usual, relaxed, after-practice atmosphere of the training room may reflect a feeling that the barriers are down and thus induce, in some individuals, a tendency to be careless with their language. Violators should promptly be called to task and told in no uncertain terms that such action is not and will not be tolerated.

Defeatism   Occasionally the trainer will encounter individuals who are defeatists. These individuals are quitters who give up easily, cannot see the use of continuing, and often employ rationalization in an attempt to cover shortcomings. It is difficult to ascribe a specific reason for this attitude, since it often has rather deep psychological implications. These individuals are completely unreliable in competitive situations, since it is difficult to predict just when they will give up. Because they will not persist in treatment procedures, reconditioning is difficult.

The trainer may attempt to help these individuals develop more positive attitudes through counseling, but such attempts are not usually successful. It is better for them to secure the services of someone trained in the complexities of psychological diagnosis and treatment. As a rule, the defeatists or quitters do not last long in athletic competition. They either are dropped by the coach or give up athletics voluntarily because of preconceived ideas about their inability to succeed.

Complacency   Complacent athletes are so satisfied with their own abilities and merit that they do not endeavor to improve. These individuals present a trying problem both to the trainer and to the coach because it is difficult to find adequate means of motivating such athletes. Methods that work for others are seldom effective with complacent athletes. Constant needling by the trainer or coach may occasionally effect some motivation but it is usually short lived. It is dispiriting when one recognizes that such individuals are performing well below optimum. It is difficult to get them to recognize their full potential, shake off the shackles of lethargy, and become efficiently functioning, contributing members of the team.

In the training room complacent athletes casually accept all ministrations but beyond this make little or no effort to assist with their own reconditioning. This necessitates constant checking to ensure that they are following instructions and to provoke them into action. This is time consuming and also can prove vexing. The complacent athlete who makes no effort to respond is a detriment and should be dropped from the team.

Malingering   Certain athletes seek to escape practice and other responsibilities or to gain sympathy by feigning illness or injury. Frequently, such an individual is termed "con man" by trainers and coaches,

Athletes using profanity should promptly be called to task and told that such behavior will not be tolerated.

the term being self-evident. In many instances such an action may be difficult to detect. However, a history of repeated questionable incidents warrants thorough investigation. When a case of malingering is evident, the trainer can usually handle it by direct means, that is, by letting the athlete know that the acting has been detected and that henceforth complaints had better be legitimate. Should the conduct continue, a conference between trainer and coach is indicated. A persistent malingerer is of no value to the team and should be dropped.

Pain tolerance Athletes who participate in collision and contact sports are able to tolerate more pain than ones who participate in the noncontact sports. The latter, however, are able to endure more pain than nonathletes. The contact sport athletes tend to reduce the intensity of their perception and so evince a greater pain tolerance and tend to be more extroverted than noncontact sport athletes. Noncontact-sport athletes tend to augment their perception somewhat but not to the degree that nonathletes do. Experienced trainers are well aware of the differences in pain tolerance exhibited by athletes in various sports.

PSYCHOLOGY OF SPORTS INJURIES

Every athlete is a unique person and reacts to physical injury in a personal way.

TABLE 8-1

Emotional emergency care

Type of Emotional Reaction	Outward Signs	Trainer's Reactions	
		Yes	No
Normal	Weakness, trembling Nausea, vomiting Perspiration Diarrhea Fear, anxiety Heart pounding	Calm and reassuring	Avoid pity
Overreaction	Excessive talking Argumentativeness Inappropriate joke telling Hyperactivity	Allow athlete to vent emotions	Avoid telling athlete he or she is acting abnormally
Underreactive	Depression; sitting or standing numbly Little talking if any Emotionless Confusion Failure to respond to questions	Be empathetic; encourage talking to express feelings	Avoid being abrupt; avoid pity

Modified from Hafen, B.Q.: First aid for health emergencies, ed. 2, St. Paul, Minn., 1981, West Publishing Co.

Psychological Reactions to Injury

No serious sports injuries are without their psychological reactions. Even the athlete who has learned to be "in control" will show some signs of stress.

At the time of serious injury the athlete may normally fear the experience of pain or possible disability. There may be a sense of anxiety about suddenly becoming disabled and unable to continue sport participation. There also may be a sense of guilt about being unable to help the team or "letting down" the coach. Becoming suddenly dependent and somewhat helpless can cause anxiety in the usually independent and aggressive person.[5] The athlete may regress to childlike behavior, crying or displacing anger toward the trainer who is administering first aid. Also, in the very early period of injury, and sometimes later, the athlete may deny the injury altogether.

Emotional Reactions and Emergency Care

The American Psychiatric Association has set forth major principles in the emergency care of emotional reactions to trauma.[6] Some of these principles are summarized as follows:

1. Accept everyone's right to personal feelings, since everyone comes from a unique background and has had different emotional experiences. Do not tell the injured person how he or she should feel. Show empathy, not pity.
2. Accept the injured person's limitations as real.
3. Trainers must accept their own limitations as providers of first aid.

In general, the trainer dealing with injured athletes' emotions should be empathetic and calm, making it obvious that their feelings are understood and accepted. Table 8-1 indicates the emotional reaction after trauma and what a trainer should do and not do.

The Psychology of Loss

The athlete who has sustained an injury of such an intensity as to be unable to perform for a long period will generally experience five reactions: denial or disbelief, anger, bargaining, depression, and acceptance of the situation (p. 208). These reactions are typical for anyone who has experienced a sudden serious loss.

The athletic trainer must realize that reactions to a sense of loss are normal and allow the athlete to fully experience each reaction. A common error is to try to talk the person out of being angry or depressed. Trainers must educate all of their injured charges to understand that rehabilitation and full recovery are a cooperative venture, with major responsibility resting on the athlete's shoulders.

> Psychological reactions to serious injury may include denial or disbelief, anger, bargaining, depression, or acceptance.

THE ATHLETE AND ABNORMAL PSYCHOLOGICAL STRESS

Abnormal stress can be a major problem to athletes. As with all individuals, athletes react to stress uniquely. A steady decline in performance may reflect problems coping with stress. Other signs are loss of appetite, loss of sleep, and nervous sweating. Even athletes who get a good night's sleep may feel fatigue and sluggishness during the day or even generally depressed and apathetic.

The Stress of Sports Injuries

Two psychological problem areas in the athletic training setting can benefit from coping techniques. The first area is psychological stress that is adversely affecting performance and appears to be leading to burnout or a serious physical injury. The second area of concern deals with psychological factors in the rehabilitation process.

REACTIONS TO LOSS

Denial or Disbelief

On suddenly becoming disabled and unable to perform, the athlete will commonly deny the seriousness of the condition. When indications are that the injury is serious and will not heal before the end of the season, the athlete might respond by saying, "Not so, I'll be back in 2 weeks." This irrational thinking indicates denial of the true seriousness of the injury.

Anger

Anger commonly follows disbelief. As the athlete slowly becomes aware of the seriousness of the injury a sense of anger develops. The athlete begins to ask, "Why me?" "What did I do wrong?" "Why am I being punished?" "It's not fair." Commonly, this anger becomes displaced toward other people. The trainer may be blamed for not providing a good enough tape job, or another player may be blamed for causing the situation that set up the injury.

Bargaining

As anger becomes less intense, the athlete gradually becomes aware of the real nature of the injury and, with this awareness, begins to have doubts and fears about the situation, which leads to a need to bargain. Bargaining may be reflected in prayer, "God, if you will heal this injury in 3 weeks instead of 6, I'll go to church every Sunday." Or it may be reflected by pressure being put on the trainer or physician to do their very best for a fast healing.

Depression

As the athlete becomes increasingly aware of the nature of the injury and that healing will take a specific length of time, depression can set in. Crying episodes may occur; there may be periods of insomnia, and the athlete may lose the desire for food.

Acceptance

Gradually, the athlete begins to feel less dejected and isolated and becomes resigned to the situation.

Coping with Mental and Emotional Stress

Three primary areas must be addressed in managing abnormal stress: the external environment, the mental and emotional assessment of the stressing situation, and the body's physiological response to the stressor(s).

The External Environment

If possible, it is important to identify the situations that cause the athlete to feel stressed. These situations may be actual or imagined, but nevertheless should be identified and listed. Possible problem areas may include training schedules or conditioning, relationships with a coach or peers, living conditions, or school schedules. These stressors should be listed on paper in a hierarchy from the most to the least stress producing. When feasible, these stressors should be eliminated, changed, or modified. Often when the athlete has an opportunity to carefully examine and talk over such problems, they become less stressful.

Stressors should be listed on paper in order of the most to the least stress producing.

Mental and Emotional Assessment

Situations in life do not produce stress; it is our thoughts and feelings about these situations that create the stress. An important approach to stress control is the psychoeducational approach to cognitive restructuring. Two successful methods for restructuring thoughts that lead to adverse stress are refuting irrational ideas and thought stopping.

Refuting irrational ideas   This method is designed to deal with a person's internal dialogue. Psychologist Albert Ellis[4] developed a system to change irrational ideas and beliefs. His system is called *rational emotive therapy*. The basic thesis is that actual events do not create emotions but self-talk after the event does. In other words, irrational self-talk causes anxiety, anger, and depression.

Athletes who are under severe stress should explore their self-talk. The following is an example:

Fact and events: A tennis player is losing to another player who is ranked lower. The tennis player's service and net game are badly off.

Self-talk:

"Those sure are lucky shots."

"Why do I get to play all these dinkers?"

"I should beat you badly."

"I'm a pretty bad player, today."

Emotions: Anger with self, embarrassment, depression.

Another example follows:

Fact and events: A football player who plays offensive tackle is getting beat badly by the opposing player.

Self-talk:

"That guy is really beating my tail."

"I am bigger and faster than he, I should be able to handle him easily."

"I am losing my ability. I'm no good."

Emotions: Embarrassment at looking bad, anger and frustration with
self, and fear of maybe being "pulled" from the position.

Thought stopping   Thought stopping is an excellent cognitive technique for helping the athlete overcome worries and doubts.[2,12] The anxious athlete will often repeat negative, unproductive, and unrealistic
statements during self-talk, such as "I missed that shot and will probably
miss the next one," or "I'll never play as good as I did because of this
shoulder strain."

Thought stopping is focusing
on the undesired thoughts
and stopping and emptying
the mind.

Thought stopping consists of focusing on the undesired thoughts and
stopping and emptying the mind. The command "Stop" or a loud noise
is used to interrupt the anxiety-producing thoughts.[2] After the thought
interruption, a positive statement is inserted, such as "I missed that shot,
but I'll get the next one." or "My shoulder is healed and I'll play as well,
if not better, than before." The self-statement "Stop" or a loud noise dis-
tracts the athlete from the anxiety-producing thought. Controlling negative thoughts with this technique can significantly reduce the athlete's
stress level.

Physiological Responses to Stress

When dealing with stress reduction one must keep in mind its physiological
responses. Two important aspects are reducing the athlete's muscular tension and quieting the anxious mind.

Reducing muscular tension   Relaxation is usually defined as the
elimination or diminution of tension. For our purposes, we will define it
as the constructive use of tension, or *the ability of the muscles to release
contractual tension.* Muscle tension may be induced physiologically
through exercise or psychogenically through anxiety, uncertainty, or
other mental-emotional stressors. Emotional disturbances are reflected in
muscle action, and situations that tend to increase such emotional tensions are thus indicated by increased muscular tensions. There are many
causes of tensions; generally, normal fatigue, chronic fatigue, and over-
activity are the principal ones. Before relaxation can occur, the causes for
tension must be studied. In sports we are concerned with the release of
tensions, either physical or psychogenic, within the muscles.

Emotional disturbances are
reflected in muscle action,
and situations that increase
emotional tensions are thus
indicated by increased
muscular tensions.

As muscles tire, they lose some of their ability to release contractual
tension (to relax). As a result, the elasticity of the muscle is considerably
diminished. The endurance of a muscle is characterized by its ability to
retain its elasticity. Hence, the degree of elasticity determines the degree of
muscular efficiency. A muscle carefully conditioned for endurance will assume its maximal length after a long series of repeated actions. As a muscle
fatigues, it steadily diminishes in irritability (its ability to respond to a stimulus) and elasticity because of the presence of increased metabolites. It loses
its ability to readily give up eccentric (lengthening) contraction. The capability of a muscle to recuperate after a bout of exercise is considerably enhanced by the ability of the athlete to consciously relax.

Tension is a natural concomitant of any form of competitive endeavor.
Properly channeled tension is an asset rather than a liability. Excessive ten-

sion, however, is detrimental not only to physical performance but also to the health of the athlete.

Hypertension, which may be related to extreme anxiety, sometimes occurs in athletes. Evidences of hypertension are increased tendon reflexes, increased mechanical muscle irritability or excitability, occasional mechanical nerve excitability, spasticity of certain muscle groups, and a somewhat abnormal excitability in terms of cardiac and respiratory responses. Extreme irritability, restlessness, and tremor complete the syndrome. Relaxation eliminates these symptoms of stress.

To eliminate undesirable tensions athletes should be trained to employ one of the various recognized techniques of relaxation, since reducing muscular tension decreases nervous tension and vice versa. A number of techniques for inducing relaxation have been advanced. Each has its proponents. Jacobson[7] has developed a technique that employs progressive relaxation. He recognized two types of relaxation: general and differential. General relaxation is obtained when all of the body's voluntary muscles are completely relaxed. Differential relaxation, in contrast, is the ability of agonist and antagonist muscles to reciprocally contract and relax with ease in the act of moving a body part. The Jacobson technique requires, as do other similar techniques, considerable practice before mastery is achieved. One hour, two or three times a week, is recommended. Practice can be carried out on either a group or an individual basis. Once the basic principles are acquired, the athlete can use them when convenient and, in most instances, achieve a reasonable degree of success.

Progressive muscle relaxation[7] is probably the most extensively used technique for relaxation today (pp. 211-214). It can be considered intense training in the awareness of tension and its release. Although over 200 sessions were prescribed in Jacobson's original method, a much smaller number can still be extremely effective. In the early stages of the method, the subject is instructed to actively tense major muscle groups for a few seconds and then release the muscle tension, while consciously relaxing as much as possible. Progressive relaxation may be practiced in a reclining position or while seated in a chair. Each muscle group is tensed from 5 to 7 seconds, then relaxed for 20 to 30 seconds. In most cases, one repetition of the procedure is sufficient; however, if tension remains in the area, repeated contraction and relaxation is permitted. The sequence of tensing and releasing is systematically applied to the following body areas: the dominant hand and forearm; dominant upper arm; nondominant hand and forearm; nondominant upper arm; forehead; eyes and nose; cheeks and mouth; neck and throat; chest; back; respiratory muscles; abdomen; dominant upper leg, calf, and foot; and nondominant upper leg, calf, and foot. Throughout the session, a number of expressions for relaxing may be used: "Let the tension dissolve. Let go of the tension. I am bringing my muscles to zero. Let the tension flow out of my body."

After the athlete has become highly aware of the tension in the body, the contraction is gradually decreased until little remains. At this point, the athlete focuses attention on one area and mentally wills the tension to decrease to zero, or complete relaxation. Jacobson's session normally takes longer than the time allowed in a typical session or than the individual would want to spend. A short form can be developed that, although not as satisfactory, helps the individual become better aware of the body. *The essence of Jacobson's method is recognizing muscular tension and the conscious release of that tension.* The following is an adapted form of Jacobson's progressive relaxation method:

Quieting the anxious mind Many times the athlete can reduce muscular tension at will, but is unable to quell the active mind. A good example of this often occurs at bedtime; the body may totally relax, but the mind continues to race with thoughts causing sleeplessness.

Meditation is a relaxation instrument used in virtually every culture dating back almost 3000 years. Many consider meditation to be an attitude rather than a technique or process. By increasing one's focus or attention, a greater conscious awareness is attained. It is not a pulling away from or a numbness against the realities of life. Practiced properly, meditation can reduce mental anxiety and muscular tension and create a climate for increased productivity. Meditation also affects the physiological functioning of the body in a positive way. In the sports setting, meditation is primarily important because of its potential for positively affecting various physiological aspects of the individual.

Benson[1] reported that meditation was not simply a relaxed state, but also included the individual's capacity for focused attention. In studying transcendental meditation (TM), Benson observed a relaxation response that is hypometabolic, the counterpart of the fight or flight response, and that

---

JACOBSON'S PROGRESSIVE RELAXATION

Beginning Instructions

1. Get into a position that is relaxed and comfortable.
2. Breathe in and out easily and allow yourself to relax as much as possible.
3. Make yourself aware of your total body and the tensions that your muscles might have contained within them.

Arm Relaxation

1. Clench your right fist. Increase the grip more and more until you feel the tension created in your hand and forearm.
2. Slowly let go of the grip and allow the tension to flow out slowly until there is no tension left in your hand and forearm.
3. Feel how soft and relaxed the hand and forearm are and contrast this feeling with the left hand.
4. Repeat this procedure with the left hand, gripping hard and bringing the tension into the fist and forearm.
5. Now, bend your right elbow and bring tension into the right biceps, tensing it as hard as you possibly can and observing the tightness of the muscle.
6. Relax and straighten the arm, allowing the tension to flow out.
7. Repeat the tension and relaxation technique with the left biceps.

JACOBSON'S PROGRESSIVE RELAXATION, cont'd

The Head

1. Wrinkle your forehead as hard as you can and hold that tension for 5 seconds or longer.
2. Now relax and allow the forehead and face to completely smooth out.
3. Frown and feel the tension that comes in between the eyes and eyebrows.
4. Let go to a completely blank expression. Feel the tension flow out of your face.
5. Squint your eyes tighter and tighter, feeling the tension creep into the eyes.
6. Relax and gently allow your eyes to be closed without tension.
7. Clench your jaw, bite down hard, harder. Notice the tension in your jaw.
8. Relax. When you're relaxed, allow your lips to be slightly parted and your face completely without expression, without wrinkles or tension.
9. Stick your tongue up against the roof of your mouth as hard as possible, feeling the tension in the tongue and the mouth. Hold that tension.
10. Relax, allowing the face and the mouth to be completely relaxed. Allow the tongue to be suspended lightly in the mouth. Relax.
11. Bring your lips to form an O. Purse the lips hard together forming the letter O very hard, so you feel the tension around the lips only.
12. Relax, allowing the tension to leave around the lips. Allow your lips to be slightly parted and tension completely gone from the face.

The Neck and Shoulders

1. By pressing your head back against the mat or chair you feel the tension come into the neck region. Hold that tension. Be aware of it, sense it.
2. Now slowly allow the tension to leave, decreasing the amount of pressure applied until the tension has completely gone and there is as much relaxation as possible.
3. Bring your head forward so that your chin is pressing against your chest and tension is brought into the throat and back of your neck. Hold that tension.
4. Slowly return to the beginning position and feel the tension leave the neck and relax completely.
5. Shrug your shoulders upward, raising the tips of your shoulders up as far as you can to the bottoms of the ears hunching your head between your shoulders. Feel the tension creep into the tops of the shoulders. Hold that tension.
6. Now slowly let the tension leave by returning the shoulders to their original position. Allow the tension to completely leave the neck and shoulder region. Have a sense of bringing the muscles to zero, where they're completely at ease and without strain.

Continued.

JACOBSON'S PROGRESSIVE RELAXATION, cont'd

Respiration and the Trunk

1. As the body is completely relaxed and you have a sense of heaviness, allow your tension to move to your respiration. Fill the lungs completely and hold your breath upward to 5 seconds, feeling the tension come into the chest and upper back muscles.
2. Exhale slowly, allowing the air to go out slowly as you feel the tension being released slowly.
3. Now, while your breath is coming slowly and easily, sense the contrast of the breath holding to the breath that is coming freely and gently.
4. Tighten the abdominal muscles by pressing downward on the stomach. Note the tension that comes into the abdominal region, also in the respiratory center, as well as in the back region.
5. Relax the abdominal area and feel the tension leave the trunk region.
6. Slightly arch the back against the mat or back of the chair. This should be done without hyperextending or straining. Feel the tension that creeps into and along the spine. Hold that tension.
7. Now, gradually allow the body to sink back into its original position and feel the tension leave the long muscles of the back.
8. Flatten the lower back by rolling the hips forward and feel the tension come into the lower back region. Hold that tension. Try to isolate that tension from all the other parts of your body.
9. Gradually return to the original position and feel the tension leave the body. Be aware of any of the tension that might have crept into your body regions that you have already relaxed. Allow your mind to scan your body; go back over the areas that you have released from tension and become aware of whether any tension has returned.

The Buttocks and Thighs

1. Press your buttocks muscles together, holding that area upward to 5 seconds. Try to isolate just the contraction of the buttocks region.
2. Now, slowly allow the buttocks muscles to return to their normal state, relaxing completely.
3. Contract your thighs by straightening your knees. Hold that contraction, feeling the tension, isolating the tension just to that region, focusing just on the thigh region.
4. Slowly allow the tension to leave the region, bringing the entire body to a relaxed state, especially the thighs to a tensionless state.
5. To bring the tension to the backs of the thighs, press your heels as hard as you can against the floor or mat, slightly bending the knees; bring the tension to the hamstring region and the back of the thighs. Hold this tension, study it, concentrate on it. Try to isolate the tension from other tensions that might have crept into the body.
6. Relax. Allow the tension to flow out. Return your legs to the original position, and let go of all the tensions of the body.

JACOBSON'S PROGRESSIVE RELAXATION, cont'd

The Lower Legs and Feet

1. With the legs fully extended, point your foot downward as hard as possible, bringing tension into both calves. Hold that tension. Hold it as hard as you can without cramping.
2. Slowly allow the foot to return to a neutral position and allow relaxation to occur within the calf muscle. Bring it to zero, if possible. No tension.
3. Curl the toes of the feet downward as hard as you can without pointing the foot downward, isolating the tension just in the bottoms of the feet and toes. Hold that tension. Isolate the tension, if possible, from the calves. Hold it, feel the tension on the bottoms of your feet.
4. Slowly relax and allow the tension to release from the foot as the toes straighten out.
5. Curl the toes backward toward the kneecaps and bring the foot back into dorsiflexion so you feel the tension in the tops of the toes, tops of the feet, and in the shin. Hold that tension. Be aware of it, study the tension.
6. After 5 seconds or longer, return to a neutral state where the foot is completely relaxed, and the toes have returned to their normal position. Feel the tension leave your body.

meditation affects the brain waves, as indicated on an encephalogram printout, producing calmness and relaxation. In TM it was found that after 3 to 5 minutes of meditation, the experienced meditator used 17% to 18% less oxygen and also produced less carbon dioxide. There was a slower respiratory rate and a significant fall in blood lactates, which are typically present in abnormal stress states. The heart rate and blood pressure decreased notably, brain waves that are associated with a relaxed mental state increased. Further study identified four major components that are characteristic of almost every meditation system: (1) a mental device, (2) a passive attitude, (3) a decrease in muscle tone, and (4) a quiet environment.

Meditators focus on a constant mental stimulus such as a phrase repeated silently or audibly, a sound or a single word, or perhaps they gaze steadily at some object. In the passive attitude of meditation, a "don't work at it" approach is taken. As thoughts come into the consciousness, they are quietly turned away and the individual returns to the focus of attention. For decreased muscle tone, a comfortable position is taken with the various major body areas relaxed and placed in as comfortable a position as possible. To effectively conduct a meditation session, a quiet environment is essential (p. 216). Normally, the eyes are closed unless the meditator is focusing on some external object.

Psychological Factors in the Rehabilitation Process

Rehabilitation in sports can tax the trainer's patience and ingenuity. A highly motivated athlete begrudges every moment spent out of action and can become somewhat difficult to handle if the desired ends of rehabilitation are to be attained. At the other end of the scale, the malingerer presents a problem by continuing treatment when it is no longer necessary. Between

The trainer must establish with the athlete that everything possible is being done to ensure full recovery as fast as healing will allow.

these extremes are problems of varying difficulty and complexity. To reduce problems in rehabilitation to a minimum, the trainer must establish an atmosphere of confidence and trust with the athlete. Whenever possible, the trainer establishes the fact that everything possible is being done to ensure full recovery as fast as healing will allow. The athlete must fully understand the nature of the injury, especially its prognosis. False hopes for a fast "comeback" should not be engendered when an injury is serious or full recovery is doubtful. The trainer should establish with the athlete a spirit of cooperation.

Many injured athletes lack patience. Recovery is usually a rather slow and tedious process. Patience and desire are therefore necessary adjuncts in securing a reasonable rate of recovery. Some athletes are unenthusiastic and consequently require continued motivation. Athletes must be made to realize that recovery depends on their positive attitude, as well as on the physiological healing processes and that they can aid recovery by means of conscientious and persistent effort.

Pain Control and the Healing Process

Two injury situations in the athletic training setting that can be aided by psychological means are pain and the healing process.

THE MEDITATION TECHNIQUE

Quieting the Body

The athlete sits comfortably in a position that maintains a straight back; the head is erect and the hands are placed loosely on each leg or on the arm of a chair with both feet firmly planted on the floor. To ensure a relaxed state, the meditator should mentally relax each body part, starting at the feet. If a great deal of tension is present, Jacobson's relaxation exercise might be appropriate, or several deep breaths are taken in and exhaled slowly and completely, allowing the body to settle more and more into a relaxed state after each emptying of the lungs.

The Meditative Technique

Once the athlete is in a quiet environment and fully physically relaxed, the meditative process can begin. With each exhalation the athlete emits self-talk of a short word. It is repeated over and over for 10 to 20 minutes. Such words as "peace" or "relaxed" are excellent relaxers; however, Benson[1] has suggested that the word "one" produces the same physiological responses as any other word. If extraneous thoughts come to mind, the meditator should passively disagree with the extraneous thought and return to the meditation.

After Meditating

After repeating the special word the athlete comes back to physical reality slowly and very gently. As awareness increases, physical activity should also increase. Moving too quickly or standing up suddenly might produce light-headedness or dizziness.

Dealing with pain The injured athlete can be taught relatively simple techniques to inhibit pain and discomfort. At no time should pain be completely inhibited, since pain is a protective mechanism. The athlete can reduce pain in three ways: reducing muscle tension, diverting attention away from the pain, or changing the pain sensation to another sensation.[13]

Tension reduction The pain response can be associated with general muscular tension stemming from anxiety and the pain-spasm-pain cycle of the specific injury. In both of these situations muscle tension increases the sensation of pain. Conversely, relaxation methods that reduce muscle tension can also decrease the awareness of pain. Both the Benson[1] and Jacobson[7] techniques of stress reduction can be advantageous in pain reduction.

Attention diversion A positive method for decreasing pain perception is to divert attention from the injury. This can be performed in a number of ways. The simple act of focusing on something other than the painful injury can be beneficial. An example might be to engage in mental problem solving, such as adding or subtracting a column of numbers or counting spots on the floor. Pain also can be diverted by fantasizing about pleasant events, such as sunbathing at the beach, sailing, or skiing.

Altering the pain sensation Imagination is one of the most powerful forces available to human beings. Negative imagination can be a major cause of illness, stress, and muscular tension, whereas positive imagination can produce wellness and counteract stress.

Through imagination the athlete can alter pain sensation to another sensation. For example a body part immersed in ice-cold water can change the pain to a sensation of cold dampness. The injured part might be imagined to be relaxed and comfortable instead of painful. Imagining a peaceful scene at a pleasant spot such as the beach or mountains can both relax the athlete and divert attention from the pain.

> The athlete can decrease pain sensation by reducing muscle tension, diverting attention away from the pain, or changing the pain sensation to another sensation.

Improving the Healing Process

It is important that the athlete be educated about the physiological process of healing. Once the healing process is understood, the athlete is instructed to imagine it taking place during therapy and throughout the day. If an infection is being fought, the body's phagocytes can be imagined as "Pac Men" gobbling up infectious material. When tissue is torn, clot formation and organization can be imagined, followed by tissue regeneration and healing.*

Regaining Competitive Confidence

Often an athlete returns to participation physically ready but psychologically ill prepared.[13] Although few athletes will admit it, on returning to participation they often feel anxious about the possibility of reinjury. This anxiety could lead to tension and the disruption of coordination. It is prob-

> After a disabling injury, many athletes return to participation physically ready but psychologically unprepared.

---

*Whether healing is speeded up in this manner has not been scientifically proven at this time. However, it does help the athlete psychologically to be part of the process and to take major responsibility for rehabilitation.

able under such circumstances that this athlete will sustain reinjury or injury to another body part (Fig. 8-2).

Systematic desensitization   Through a relatively simple technique called *systematic desensitization*, the trainer can help the athlete to effectively cope with anxiety-provoking feelings associated with an injury. Systematic desensitization was created by the behavior therapist Joseph Wolpe.[16] The athlete first learns to consciously relax. Wolpe's original work used Jacobson's progressive relaxation[7]; however, any method that reduces total body tension can be used. When relaxation skill has been acquired, the athlete, with the help of the trainer, develops a fear hierarchy related to returning to the sport and going "all out."

Each progressive step is imagined while in deep relaxation. If fear is felt at a specific step, the athlete stops and relaxes as much as possible. The process is repeated until no anxiety is felt at that step.[8] The athlete then goes on to the next more anxiety-producing event, and the procedure is repeated until no anxiety is felt. When the athlete is able to complete the entire list of events without anxiety, he or she is ready for competition.

Figure 8-2

Regaining competitive confidence after a serious injury is of major importance if additional injury is to be prevented.

REFERENCES

1. Benson, H.H.: The relaxation response, New York, 1975, William Morrow & Co., Inc.
2. Davis, M., McKay, M.M., and Eshelman, E.R.: The relaxation and stress reduction workbook, Richmond, Calif., 1980, New Harbinger Publications.
3. Eastwood, J.M.: The effects of viewing a film of professional hockey on aggression, Med. Sci. Sports **6:**158, 1974.
4. Ellis, A.: A new guide to rational living, North Hollywood, Calif., 1975, Wilshire Book Co.
5. Hafen, B.Q.: First aid for health emergencies, St. Paul, Minn., 1981, West Publishing Co.
6. Henderson, J.: Emergency medical guide, ed. 4, New York, 1978, McGraw-Hill Book Co.
7. Jacobson, E.: Progressive relaxation, ed. 2, Chicago, 1938, University of Chicago Press.
8. McKay, M., Davis, M., and Fanning, M.: Thoughts and feelings, Richmond, Calif., 1981, New Harbinger Publications.
9. Morgan, W.P., and Hammer, W.M.: Influence of competitive wrestling on state anxiety, Med. Sci. Sports **6:**58, 1974.
10. Ogilvie, B.C., and Tutko, T.A.: Problem athletes and how to handle them, London, 1965, Pelham Books, Ltd.
11. Pelletier, K.R.: Mind as healer, mind as slayer, New York, 1977, Dell Publishing Co., Inc.
12. Rimm, D.C., and Masters, J.C.: Behavior therapy: techniques and empirical findings, New York, 1974, Academic Press, Inc.
13. Rotella, R.J.: Psychological care of the injured athlete. In Kulund, D.: The injured athlete, Philadelphia, 1982, J.B. Lippincott Co.
14. Truck, S.: Teacher burnout and what to do about it, Navato, Calif., 1978, Academic Therapy Publications.
15. Vergamini, G.: Professional burnout: implications for the athletic trainer, Ath. Train. **18:**197, 1981.
16. Wolpe, J.: The practice of behavior therapy, ed. 2, New York, 1973, Pergamon Press, Inc.

ADDITIONAL SOURCES

Gieck, J.: Stress management for the athletic trainer, NATA Annual Meeting, Clinical Symposium, June 1983, National Athletic Trainers Association. (Cassette.)

Gieck, J., and Brown, R.S.: The burnout syndrome among athletic trainers, J. Natl. Athl. Trainers Assoc. **17:**36, Spring 1977.

Meilman, P.W.: Psychological aspects of chronic pain, J. Orthop. Sports Phys. Ther. **1:**76, Fall 1979.

Nideffer, R.M., and Sharp, R.C.: How to put anxiety behind you, Briarcliff Manor, N.Y., 1978, Stein & Day Publishers.

Ogilvie, B.C.: Walking the perilous path of the team psychologist, Phys. Sportsmed. **5:**62, 1977.

Rotella, R.: Psychological management of the injured athlete, Professional Preparation Conference, Pittsburgh, Jan. 1983, National Athletic Trainers Association. (Cassette.)

Ryan, A.J.: Moderator, round table: The emotionally disturbed athlete, **9:**67, July 1981.

Selye, H.: The stress of life, New York, 1976, McGraw-Hill Book Co.

Singer, R.N.: The learning of motor skills, New York, 1981, Macmillan Publishing Co., Inc.

Smith, R.E.: Coping with stress and burnout, NATA Clinical Symposium, Granite Falls, Wash., 1982, Marvey Productions.

Strant, W.F. (editor): Sports psychology: an analysis of athletic behavior, Ithaca, N.Y., 1978, Mouvement Publications.

Part Three | # FOUNDATIONS OF INJURY CAUSATIONS, PREVENTION, AND MANAGEMENT

P*art Three imparts the diverse information necessary in understanding the body's susceptibility to sports injury and the body's reaction to a particular injury. It also covers classification, recognition, evaluation, and management principles.*

Chapter 9

BODY CHARACTERISTICS AND MECHANISMS OF INJURY

When you finish this chapter, you should be able to

Discuss the major structural characteristics of the body that predispose it to sports injuries

Specify the characteristics of soft tissue when mechanical stresses are applied

Designate the influences of faulty posture on the athlete's susceptibility to injury

Point out the relationship of faulty mechanics in running, throwing, and jumping to sustaining microtraumas

Explain why certain exercise movements should be avoided because of their injury-producing potential

If we carefully study the mechanical structure of the human body, it is amazing that humans can move so effectively in the upright posture. Not only must constant gravitational force be overcome, but the body also must be manipulated through space by a complex system of somewhat inefficient levers, fueled by a machinery that operates at an efficiency level of about 30%. The bony levers that move the body must overcome considerable resistance in the form of inertia and muscle viscosity and must work in most instances at an extremely unfavorable angle of pull. All these factors mitigate the effectiveness of lever action to the extent that most movement is achieved at an efficiency level of less than 25%.

In addition, more than half the total body weight is located in the upper part of the body, and this weight is supported by means of rather thin, articulated bones. Thus the center of gravity, which increases stability as it is lowered, is relatively high in the erect human body.

Despite these seeming inefficiencies, the body can compensate by making modifications or adjustments that depend on the task at hand. For example, the center of gravity may be lowered by widening the stance, the segmented body parts may function either as a single unit or as a series of finely coordinated units, or an increase in muscle power may be elicited in an effort to offset certain mechanical ineptitudes. Structural changes in bones, resulting from stresses placed on them, afford broader and more secure muscle anchorage and consequently aid in the development of more power.

Although the bones of the body are not primarily designed to withstand shock, the musculature serves as a shock absorber by absorbing impact and distributing it over a relatively large area, thereby lessening the concentration of the force on a small area of bone. Bones such as the shin and skull, however, which have little or no overlying musculature and thus are more susceptible to injury, should be afforded protection, especially in sports activities in which they are particularly vulnerable to blows.

In the upright posture human legs are long and straight, and the feet are adaptable for support and propulsion. The spine has three curves in the anteroposterior plane that help maintain balance. However, along with the invaluable advantages gained through an upright posture and an increased range of movement, there are some disadvantages. The mesenteries supporting the abdominal viscera would be more effective in a quadruped position. The constant gravitational pull plus the weight of the supported organs makes humans somewhat prone to have a protruded abdomen unless the abdominal muscles maintain sufficient tonicity to withstand these forces. The head, weighing close to 14 pounds, is balanced almost precariously on top of the seven small cervical vertebrae, which are sustained by the cervical neck ligaments and neck muscles. This cervical area is particularly vulnerable to injury, especially when excessive hyperflexion or hyperextension is encountered; hence strengthening of the neck muscles as a protective measure is vital in sports. Also, because of the length and great weight of the torso and head, the lumbosacral area of the spine is subjected to considerable strain and is particularly vulnerable to injury, especially in certain activities. For example, the twisting movements of golf and tennis and the excessive supportive demands sometimes made on the lumbosacral area in weight lifting or gymnastics often lead to low back strain or injury.

When determining the mechanical reasons for sports injuries to the musculoskeletal system, many factors stand out. Hereditary, congenital, or acquired defects may predispose an athlete to a specific type of injury. Anomalies in anatomical structure or in body build (somatotype) may make an athlete prone to certain injuries.

TISSUE AND BODY STRUCTURAL CHARACTERISTICS

Understanding the body's ability to resist sports injuries requires some knowledge of tissue and structural characteristics.

Soft Tissues

Most soft tissue is composed of connective tissue, which is made up of collagen. Collagen contains protein molecules that form white fibrils which are mainly parallel to one another and are bound together into bundles to increase tensile strength. The soft tissues directly involved with vigorous activity and directly or indirectly exposed to trauma are of special concern to sports medicine. These tissues include fascia, tendons, ligaments, cartilage, and muscle. Bone, which is not considered a soft tissue, is a modification of collagen and will be discussed on p. 234.

Excessive force applied to soft tissue will cause injury. The coach or trainer should have a clear understanding of the types of forces to which athletes are subjected. The three forces particularly significant to soft tissues are compression, tension, and shear[11] (Fig. 9-1). *Compression* is a force that, with enough energy, crushes tissue. Soft tissue can withstand and absorb compressional forces; however, when the force is excessive and can no longer be absorbed, a contusion, or bruise, occurs. Tissue crushing results

Figure 9-1

Mechanical forces that can injure soft tissue.
A, Compression.
B, Tension.
C, Shear.

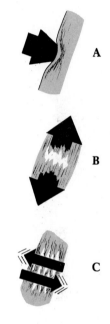

Collagen is the main organic constituent of connective tissue.

Major forces that can injure soft tissue are compression, tension, and shear.

in hemorrhage, muscle fiber disruption, and spasm. *Tension* is the force that pulls and extends tissue. *Shear* is a force that moves across the parallel organization of collagen fibers. Tendons and ligaments are designed to effectively withstand tension forces, but do not resist shear or compressional forces well. Excessive tension or shear forces can result in injuries such as sprains (ligaments) or strains (musculotendinous units) of varying degrees of severity.

Tendons

When a tendon is loaded by tension, its wavy collagen fibers straighten in the direction of the load.

The tendon contains wavy parallel collagen fibers that are organized in bundles surrounded by a gelatinous material that decreases friction.[3] Basically, a tendon attaches a muscle to a bone and concentrates a pulling force in a limited area. Tendons can produce and maintain a pull from 8700 to 18,000 pounds per square inch.[1] When a tendon is loaded by tension, the wavy collagen fibers straighten in the direction of the load; when the tension is released, the collagen returns to its original shape.[3] However, collagen fibers will break if their physiological limits have been reached. A breaking point occurs after a 6% to 8% increase in length.[3] Because a tendon is usually double the strength of the muscle it serves, tears commonly occur at the muscle belly, musculotendinous junction, or bony attachment. Clinically, however, a constant abnormal tension on tendons increases elongation by the infiltration of fibroblasts, which will cause more collagenous tissue to be produced.[1] Repeated microtraumas can evolve into chronic muscle strain that resorbs collagen fibers and eventually weakens the tendon. Collagen resorption occurs in the early period of sports conditioning and in the immobilization of a part. During resorption collagenous tissues are weakened and susceptible to injury; therefore, a gradually paced conditioning program and early mobilization in the rehabilitation process are necessary[4] (Chapter 4).

Ligaments and Capsules

Ligaments maintain anatomical integrity and structural alignment. Ligaments and capsules are similar in composition to tendons; however, they

TABLE 9-1

General strength grades in selected articulations	Articulation	Skeleton	Ligaments	Muscles
	Ankle	Strong	Moderate	Weak
	Knee	Weak	Moderate	Strong
	Hip	Strong	Strong	Strong
	Lumbosacral	Weak	Strong	Moderate
	Lumbar vertebrae	Strong	Strong	Moderate
	Thoracic vertebrae	Strong	Strong	Moderate
	Cervical vertebrae	Weak	Moderate	Strong
	Sternoclavicular	Weak	Weak	Weak
	Acromioclavicular	Weak	Moderate	Weak
	Glenohumeral	Weak	Moderate	Moderate
	Elbow	Moderate	Strong	Strong
	Wrist	Weak	Moderate	Moderate
	Phalanges (toes and fingers)	Weak	Moderate	Moderate

contain elastic fibers, and the collagen fibers, although having a wavy configuration, are irregular and have a spiral arrangement. Attaching bone to bone, ligaments are strongest in their middle and weakest at their ends.[1] When an intact ligament is traumatically stretched, the injury often produces an avulsion-type fracture or tear at the ends, rather than in the middle. Avulsion fractures are more common when bone tissue is comparatively weaker than ligamentous tissue, as is evidenced in older individuals or postmenopausal women in whom significant osteoporosis has occurred or in children in whom the epiphyseal plates are relatively wide and soft.

A major factor in ligamentous injury is the viscoelastic tissue properties of ligaments and capsules. Viscoelastic refers to an extensibility when loaded that is time dependent.[8] Constant compression or tension will cause ligaments to deteriorate, whereas intermittent compression and tension increase strength and growth, especially at the bony attachment.[1] Chronic inflammation of ligamentous, capsular, and fascial tissue causes a shrinkage of collagen fibers; therefore, repeated microtraumas over time make capsules and ligaments highly susceptible to major acute injuries.

Another unique characteristic of ligaments and capsules is that they generally heal slowly due to a poor blood supply. However, nerve innervation is plentiful and responds to injury with a high degree of pain. In comparison to ligament and capsule protection, muscles are relatively slow to respond when traumatically stimulated. For example, a muscle will begin to develop tension in just a few hundredths of a second when stimulated after injury, but will take almost a full tenth of a second to make a complete response.[2]

> Constant compression or tension will cause ligaments to deteriorate; intermittent compression and tension will increase strength and growth.

Joints

A diarthrodial (or freely moving) joint is a union of two bones. Its movement depends on inherent structures, including shape, ligamentous restraint, atmospheric pressure created by the articular surfaces, the presence of an articular disk, and the muscles acting on it.[1] All diarthrodial joints have a synovium and synovial fluid, an articular cartilage, ligaments and joint capsule, and muscles crossing the joint. They differ in strength from one another depending on their skeletal, ligamentous, and muscular arrangement. Table 9-1 indicates the relative strengths of selected articulations in terms of sports participation.

Articular Cartilage

The articular cartilage, which is classified as soft tissue, has three major mechanical functions: control of joint motion, joint stability, and force or load transmission.[6]

Motion control   The shape of the articular surface determines what motion will occur. An enarthrodial joint or a ball and socket joint, such as the hip, is considered as a universal joint, allowing movement in all planes. In contrast, a hinge joint such as the interphalangeal joint allows movement in only one plane.

Stability   In general, bones that form a joint normally closely match with one another and produce varying degrees of stability, depending on their particular shape.

Load bearing The articular cartilage assists in transmitting a joint load smoothly and uniformly. The atmospheric pressure within the joint space must be kept constant. If the bones that form a joint become out of accordance with one another because of injury or disease, an increased stress occurs that predisposes the joint to degenerative changes (e.g., osteoarthritis), which pose major challenges for the physician.

Joint Ligaments, Capsules, and Muscles

In terms of stability, ligaments and capsular structures are highly important to joints. Characteristically, joints that are shallow and relatively poor fitting must depend on their capsular structures and/or muscles for major support. The knee is an example of an articulation that lacks bony congruence and depends mainly on muscles and ligaments for its support.

Besides moving limbs, muscles also provide joint stabilization to a greater or lesser extent and absorb the forces of load transmission. Muscles help stabilize joints in the following ways: (1) muscles that cross joints assist in maintaining proper articular alignment, and (2) some muscles attach directly to the articular capsule (shunt muscles) and when stretched, also tighten the capsule. By becoming taut the shunt muscles prevent the articulations from separating and also assist in maintaining proper alignment.[1]

Major Articulations

Spine The spine, or vertebral column, consists of 26 articulated bone segments called vertebrae, which permit forward flexion, backward extension, lateral flexion, and rotation of the trunk. To achieve this con-

Figure 9-2

The spine and pelvis may be at risk in many collision and contact-type sports.

siderable variety of movement, use is made of the intervertebral disks and a number of opposing curves in the anteroposterior plane. These two features permit flexibility and resilience. In addition to permitting a wide range of movement, the spine serves as a place of support and attachment for the ribs and muscles and for the pelvis and head. It also serves as a shock absorber, as a means of distributing body weight, and as a factor in locomotion (Fig. 9-2).

The pelvic girdle consists of three fused boxes: the ilium, ischium, and pubis. The pelvis articulates with the spine at the sacroiliac joint and is, to a limited degree, an extension of the spinal column. The only observable pelvic girdle movements are those of anterior and posterior tilt.

The pelvis plays an important role in the prevention of injuries to the spine. In sports such as weight lifting, gymnastics, wrestling, and pole vaulting, in which force is conveyed to the pelvis in lifting, the abdominal muscles and the thoracic spine oppose the force, thereby reducing the stress on the lumbosacral joint by as much as 30% and that on the lower thoracic spine by as much as 50%. The ability to apply this counterforce is a sign of an experienced athlete and substantially reduces the possibilities of low back injury. Abdominal strength is essential to prevent lumbosacral injuries.

> Abdominal strength is essential to prevent lumbosacral injuries.

Shoulder complex The shoulder complex is composed of numerous joints of which the glenohumeral, acromioclavicular, and sternoclavicular can sustain sports injuries. The shoulder complex plays a critical role in many sports, and injuries to the soft tissue and to joints are common. In many sports the other parts of the body play a somewhat secondary role. Their prime function is to set the stage for the shoulder joint to assume the "star" performance role, for example, in batting, pitching, forward passing, or swinging implements of some type. It is quite possible to identify certain derangements of the shoulder joint as being peculiar to a particular sport (Fig. 9-3).

The glenohumeral joint, more commonly known as the shoulder

Figure 9-3

Wrestling severely stresses the shoulder and other major joints.

Courtesy Cramer Products, Inc., Gardner, Kan.

joint, is an enarthrodial or swivel joint, which is a rather insecure joint formed by articulation of the humerus with the glenoid fossa of the scapula. It possesses a remarkable mobility as a result of the looseness of the capsule and of the ligaments surrounding it. The joint maintains its integrity through the ligamentous structures rather than through the bony structures and is therefore susceptible to severe sprains and luxations. Subluxations and dislocations of the joint occur when the arm is forced backward well beyond its normal range in the position of throwing, forcing the proximal end of the humerus out of the shallow shoulder socket and displacing it to a position under the coracoid process of the scapula (Fig. 9-4).

Many shoulder joint injuries are caused by a descending force or impact that drives the acromion downward and away from the clavicle, which sustains its position. This is a somewhat common injury. In football it occurs when the shoulder is used as a driving force or when the shoulder forcefully contacts the ground while it is in a position of forward rotation, as may occur when the ball carrier has the ball tucked in close to the player's body and therefore is unable to properly use the carrying arm to break the player's fall. In tumbling it can occur when there is shoulder point contact with the mat. In wrestling this injury can occur when the wrestler throws the opponent and causes shoulder point contact with the mat, using his own body weight plus the opponent's weight to provide the force. Another comparatively common cause of shoulder dislocation is demonstrated when the athlete falls on either hand or the elbow, with the latter in about 90-degree flexion. This drives the head of the humerus with great force against both the glenoid fossa and the acromion, forcing them backward and exerting considerable stress on the coracoclavicular and clavicular ligaments, resulting in a sprain or a rupture. Also, a direct blow to the clavicle or a fall on the tip of the shoulder could cause a sprain or even a dislocation of the sternoclavicular joint.

Soft tissue injuries can result from the repetitive dynamic contraction of the muscle, as in pitching. The repeated microtraumas culminate in a chronic injury. A sudden all-out contraction of a muscle wherein the antagonist muscles fail to control the effort is another cause. Direct, forceful impact to the muscle, as from a blow, is still another cause of soft tissue injury.

Since the shoulder joint depends on the surrounding muscle tissue for additional support and stability, a sound exercise program that will strengthen and maintain these muscles at a high level of fitness is indicated. After an injury, the trainer should insist that the athlete maintain as much joint mobility as possible at a given time (Chapter 24).

Elbow joint   The elbow is a complex hinge joint located between the capitulum and trochlea of the humerus proximally and the head of the radius and trochlear notch of the ulna distally. The radius and ulna also articulate with each other proximally by a superior radioulnar joint and distally by an inferior radioulnar joint. The radioulnar joint allows pronation and supination of the forearm and flexion and extension. Flexion is limited either by the locking of the coronoid process on the anterior sur-

Figure 9-4

Common mechanisms of shoulder injuries.

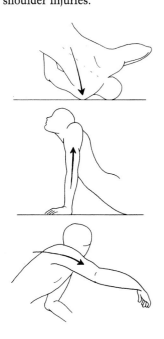

face of the humerus or, in some instances, by the bulk of the muscle masses on the forearm and upper arm. The olecranon process, a hooklike protuberance on the ulna, checks extension. The joint is enveloped by an extensive capsule, which is strengthened on all four sides by the anterior, posterior, radial, and ulnar collateral ligaments.

Forcible extension, forcible hyperextension, and impact forces are the principal causes of injury to this joint. The momentum of the forearm forcing the olecranon process against the trochlea of the humerus often results in a chipping of the bone or in a partial or complete dislocation. Muscle strains resulting from forcible hyperextension are quite common, as are capsular strains. They usually result either from a fall in which the athlete lands on an extended and locked elbow joint or when the arm and elbow are in an extended, supportive position and an impact force is directed on the posterior aspect of the arm in the vicinity of the elbow joint. Throwing, in which the arm is forcefully extended, can result in a painful traumatic elbow. In this type of injury there is irritation of the periosteum, which may become chronic as a result of the calciferous deposits that accrue (Fig. 9-5).

When the elbow or any other hinge joint is flexed at an angle of less than 90 degrees during activity, the normal stabilizing factor reverses itself and, instead of thrusting the articulating end of the excursioning bone into the joint, tends to pull it away and thus decreases the stability of the joint. It is in this position that the joint is most vulnerable to a partial or complete dislocation.

Wrist joint A diarthrodial, or freely movable, condyloid joint—formed by the articulations of the navicular, lunate, and triquetral bones with the radius—and a triangular articular disk interposed between the ulna and triquetrum constitute the wrist joint. The tendons of the extensor and flexor muscles of both the wrist and the hand reinforce the joint, and the capsular ligament that encloses the joint cavity is additionally strengthened by the dorsal and volar carpal ligaments. Basically, movements of the wrist are in two planes; therefore, the joint is often classified as biaxial. The wrist joint offers a variety of movements—among them flexion, extension, hyperextension, ulnar adduction (deviation), radial abduction (deviation), and circumduction. The freedom of action of the wrist joint plus the prehensility of the hand makes this area the most mobile of the body.

Injuries to the wrist are common. Most injuries appear to be the result of force applied when the wrist is in a hyperextended position, thus instituting a severe compression. The lunate bone is frequently injured,

229

Body Characteristics and Mechanisms of Injury

Figure 9-5

Typical mechanism of an elbow injury.

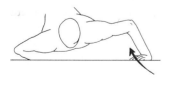

Figure 9-6

Common mechanisms of wrist injuries.

often resulting in a chipping of the bone itself. The chip may work itself loose and lodge among other carpal bones, causing pain, irritation, and limitation of normal movement.

One of the most important injuries, amounting to approximately 8% of the fractures occurring in organized sport, is fracture of the carpal navicular bone. This can occur quite easily when the athlete falls on his or her outstretched hand. Too often, such injuries are rather cursorily dismissed as simple sprains and, as a result, the fracture is neglected (Fig. 9-6).

Wrist injuries are common to many sports but achieve a considerable incidence and significance in wrestling and gymnastics. Compression injuries are fairly commonplace in the tumbling aspect of free exercise and the long horse vault. In these activities speed is added to mass to increase the resultant force thrust against the hyperextended wrist. Rotatory movements, as performed in tumbling, also create an additional hazard, since a rotational shearing action is exerted on the hyperextended wrist if the hand is improperly placed. Severe sprains or fractures are usually the result.

Hip joint   The hip joint is a diarthrodial joint formed by articulation of the head of the femur with the acetabular cavity of the pelvis. The ligamentous capsule that envelopes the joint is lined with a smooth synovial membrane and is lubricated with synovia, a viscid fluid. A cartilaginous cup or rim further deepens the cavity. The head of the femur is almost completely spherical, permitting a degree of freedom second only to that found in the shoulder joint. However, the accompanying ligaments, capsule, and adjacent muscles restrict this mobility to a considerable degree. Of interest and concern to the trainer is the Y ligament, or iliofemoral band, an extremely strong fibrous band that crosses the anterior aspect of the joint and checks extension, outward rotation, and inward rotation. As a result, hyperextension of the hip is practically nonexistent. When the thigh is flexed on the trunk, the Y ligament is slack; but when the thigh is straightened so that it falls into line with the trunk, the ligament is straightened to its full length (Fig. 9-7).

The head of the femur is the main weight-bearing point of the body and, as such, is subjected to much force. Most hip injuries occur when the athlete attempts a sudden change of direction and consequently subjects the neck of the femur to considerable torque. On occasion injuries occur because the joint is forced beyond the limits of its range of motion. In rare circumstances an impacted fracture may result when the head of the femur is driven into the acetabulum with great force.

Knee joint   The knee, a hinge joint, permits free flexion and extension and, in some instances, a slight amount of rotation of the tibia. Although formed by the articulation of only two bones, the tibia and the femur, this is not only an exceedingly complex joint but also the largest articulation in the body.

At first glance the joint appears somewhat insecure, but closer observation reveals that it is reinforced on all four sides by ligamentous support and muscle tendons. On the anterior aspect the tendon of the quadriceps fuses with the capsule, which has contained within it the patella,

Figure 9-7

Common mechanisms of hip injuries.

or kneecap, a sesamoid bone. Lateral stability is achieved through the lateral and medial collateral ligaments, anterior and posterior cruciate ligaments, articular capsule, and muscle tendons and tendinous expansions that occur on the lateral and posterior aspects of the joint. Within the joint are the semilunar menisci, which are two crescent-shaped fibrocartilaginous disks that vary in thickness from their outer rims toward the center and thus provide a concavity into which the femoral condyles fit.

The stress demands made on the knee joint in most sports are quite severe (Figs. 9-8 and 9-9). Because of the structure of the knee joint, ligamentous injuries are especially common despite the joint reinforcements. The knee is particularly vulnerable to forces delivered either laterally or medially when the joint is in a position of extension. Often the collateral ligaments, most frequently the medial collateral, are either sprained or ruptured. This injury may occur as an isolated trauma. More commonly, however, it is associated with tears of either or both cruciate ligaments and with injury to either or both of the menisci (Fig. 9-10). Such injury may involve various combinations. The menisci may be slit, severed, torn, avulsed, or broken into two or more pieces either as the result of lateral force applied when the joint is in an extended or locked position or as the result of force transmitted through the femur in a downward-angling direction, such as occurs when one lands after a jump and fails to flex the knee joint sufficiently to dissipate the shock of landing.

Figure 9-8

The demands on knee joints in football are severe.
Courtesy Cramer Products, Inc., Gardner, Kan.

Figure 9-9

Volleyball stresses the hands and knees.

Figure 9-8

Figure 9-9

Foundations of Injury

Severe twisting of the knee is often encountered, particularly in those sports for which cleated shoes are worn. The amount of torque engendered when the foot is firmly fixed and the rest of the body continues to rotate longitudinally is of considerable magnitude; consequently, the knee ligaments are subjected to tremendous stress and are frequently badly strained or torn. In those ball sports involving running and changes of direction as evasive maneuvers, cutting plays an important part and frequently provides the mechanism for injury to the knee and occasionally the ankle (Fig. 9-11). There are a number of cutting techniques employed, but the right angle pivot (sidestep cut) and the crossover step (reverse cut) are probably most frequently used and are responsible for most knee injuries in those sports. In the sidestep cut the medial ligaments of the pivot leg are subjected to severe stresses, whereas in the crossover cut

Figure 9-10

Mechanisms of knee sprains. Arrow in each case indicates direction of applied force.

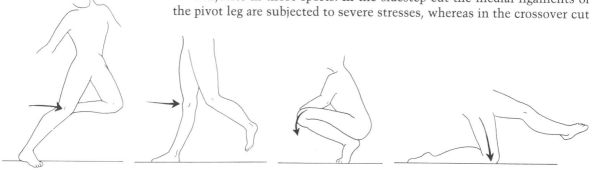

Figure 9-11

Soccer places great stress on the knees and ankles.

it is the lateral ligaments that receive the stresses. During the foot plant and the cut (change of direction) phase of either maneuver, the supporting leg is in an exceedingly vulnerable position from the standpoint of stability. The rotation of the trunk and pelvis on the supporting leg further enhances the stress and may be sufficient to cause ligament injury. Should an extraneous force be applied to the knee by, for example, a blocker or through collision with another player, an overload force occurs that the structures of the knee cannot sustain; injury to the mechanisms of the knee results.

Ankle joint The ankle joint is a freely movable hinge joint formed by the tibia and fibula articulating with the superior aspect of the talus and has the movements only of plantar flexion and dorsiflexion (extension and flexion, respectively). The tibia and fibula are strengthened by the anterior and posterior tibiofibular and talofibular, calcaneofibular, lateral talocalcaneal, deltoid, and interosseous ligaments. All these, together with the capsule that surrounds the joint, ensure its integrity. The strength of the joints is further augmented by the tendons of the long muscles of the lower leg, a number of which traverse the joint. Medial and lateral stability is increased by the extension of the tibial and fibular malleoli, which course down, respectively, the medial and lateral aspects of the talus, completely restricting lateral movement and rotation. The ankle joint has a range of motion from 75 to 80 degrees, moving from plantar flexion to dorsiflexion. The foot has about 50 to 70 degrees of movement from inversion to eversion, occurring at the subtalar and transverse tarsal articulations.

Sprains and bruises occur most often to the ankles and knees. Because of the inadequate support supplied by the muscles and ligaments, the ankle joint suffers frequent and often severe injury. Since the medial malleolus is the shorter of the two, the talus tends to rotate or slide around it so that the foot is inverted; that is, the foot is turned inward and the lateral aspect of the joint is subjected to a severe pulling or tearing action on the ligaments and surrounding tissues. If the force is unusually severe, the malleolus may break. Since body weight is transmitted through both the fibula and tibia to the talus, the joint is subjected to considerable stress. When the joint is placed in an awkward position, body weight tends to accentuate the moment of force. Approximately 85% of inversion injuries result in tearing of the lateral ligament (Fig. 9-12).

Figure 9-12

A and **B,** Common mechanisms of ankle injuries. **C,** Basketball produces a high number of serious ankle injuries.

C courtesy Cramer Products, Inc., Gardner, Kan.

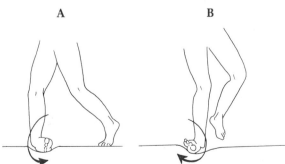

A   B   C

Long Bones

The student of sports injuries should have some understanding of the biomechanics of long bone injury. Two biomechanical factors should be considered: bone and load characteristics.[5]

Bone Characteristics

Long bones are not uniform, but have different regions along their length that respond uniquely to stress.

The skeleton varies in composition and structure, which affects its propensity for sports injury. Bones differ according to their type, the region they are in, and their makeup. The type of bone may be designed for full body support, such as the tibia, or for dexterity and fine movements, such as the radius or ulna. Long bones are not uniform, but have different regions along their length that respond uniquely to stress. The external compact bone responds to stress differently from that of the medial cortex. Also, bone makeup affects the reaction to stresses. Lamellar bone, for example, reacts differently to stress than woven bone.

Because of its viscoelastic properties, bone will bend slightly. However, bone is generally brittle and a poor shock absorber due to its mineral content. This brittleness increases under tension forces as opposed to compression forces.

Many factors of bone structure affect its strength. Anatomical strength or weakness can be affected by a bone's shape and its changes in shape or direction. A hollow cylinder is one of the strongest structures for resisting both bending and twisting as compared to a solid rod that has much less resistance to such forces.[5] This may be why bones such as the tibia are primarily cylinders. Most spiral fractures of the tibia occur at its middle and distal third, where the bone is most solid (Fig. 9-13).

Figure 9-13

Anatomical strengths or weaknesses of a long bone can be affected by its shape, changes of direction, and hollowness.

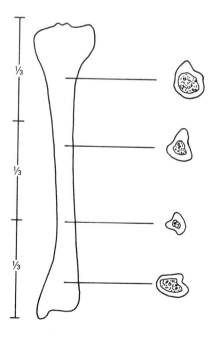

Stress forces become concentrated where a long bone suddenly changes shape and direction. Long bones that change shape gradually are less prone to injury than those which change suddenly. The clavicle, for example, is prone to fracture because it changes from round to flat at the same time it changes direction.

Load Characteristics

Long bones can be stressed or loaded to fail by *tension, compression, bending*, and *twisting* (torsion). These forces, either singularly or in combination, can cause a variety of fractures. For example, spiral fractures are caused by twisting, whereas oblique fractures are caused by the combined forces of axial compression, bending, and torsion. Transverse fractures occur by bending (Fig. 9-14).

> Long bones can be stressed by tension, compression, bending, and torsion.

Along with the type of stress, the amount of the load must be considered. The more complex the fracture, the more energy is required. Energy is used in deforming the bone and actually breaking the bony tissue, whereas some energy becomes dissipated in adjacent soft tissue.[5]

The rate of energy at which a force is applied to a long bone affects its failing point, sometimes called the *yield point*. At this point, the tissue tears or fractures. Depending on the type of bony tissue, more energy is generally required to cause fracture in a shorter period of time than over a longer period of time.[9]

Stress fractures Stress fractures have been variously called *march, fatigue* (stress), and *spontaneous* fractures; the most commonly used term is stress fracture. The exact cause is not known but there are a number of likely possibilities, such as an overload due to muscle contrac-

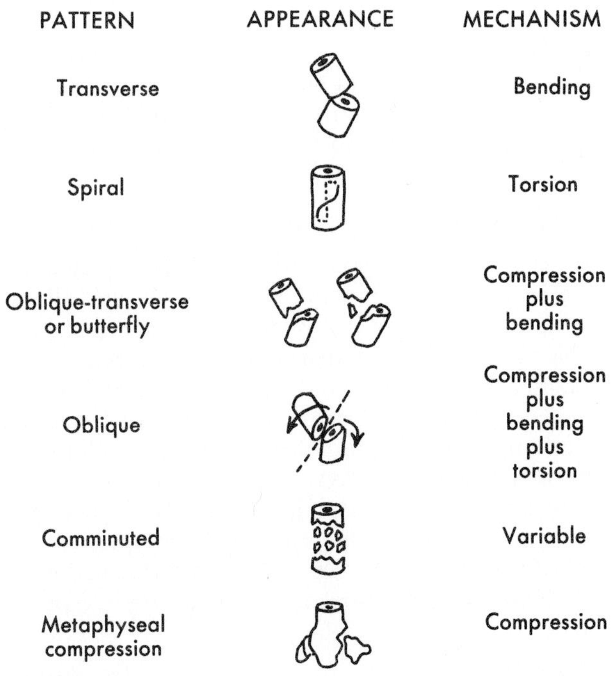

PATTERN	APPEARANCE	MECHANISM
Transverse		Bending
Spiral		Torsion
Oblique-transverse or butterfly		Compression plus bending
Oblique		Compression plus bending plus torsion
Comminuted		Variable
Metaphyseal compression		Compression

Figure 9-14

Mechanisms of bone fractures.

tion, an altered stress distribution in the bone accompanying muscle fatigue, a change in the ground reaction force, such as going from a wood surface to a grass surface, and performing a rhythmically repetitive stress leading up to a vibratory summation point. The last possibility is favored by many authorities.[10] Rhythmic muscle action performed over a period of time at a subthreshold level causes the stress-bearing capacity of the bone to be exceeded, hence a stress fracture. A bone may become vulnerable to fracture during the first few weeks of intense physical activity or training. Weight-bearing bones undergo bone resorption and become weaker before they become stronger. The sequence of events is suggested by Stanitski, McMaster, and Scranton[10] as resulting from increased muscular forces plus an increased rate of remodeling that leads to bone resorption and rarefaction, which progresses to produce increasingly more severe fractures. The four progressively more severe fractures are focal microfractures, periosteal and/or endosteal response (stress fractures), linear fractures (stress fractures), and displaced fractures.

Typical responses for stress fractures in sports are as follows:
1. Coming back into competition too soon after an injury or illness
2. Going from one event to another without proper training in the second event
3. Starting initial training too quickly
4. Changing habits or the environment, such as running surfaces, the bank of a track, or shoes

In addition to these stresses, susceptibility to fracture can be increased by a variety of postural and foot conditions. Flatfeet, a short first metatarsal bone, or a hypermobile metatarsal region can predispose an athlete to stress fractures.

Early detection of the stress fracture may be difficult. Because of their frequency in a wide range of sports, stress fractures always must be suspected in susceptible body areas that fail to respond to usual management. Until there is an obvious reaction in the bone, which may take several weeks, x-ray examination may fail to reveal any change. Although nonspecific, a bone scan can provide early indications in a given area.

POSTURAL DEVIATIONS AND INJURY POTENTIAL

Postural deviations are often a primary source of injuries.

Postural deviations are often a primary source of injuries caused by either unilateral asymmetries, bone anomalies, abnormal skeletal alignments, or poor mechanics of movement. Many sports activities are unilateral, thus leading to considerable overdevelopment of a body segment. The resulting imbalance is manifested by a postural deviation as the body seeks to reestablish itself in relation to its center of gravity. Often such deviations are a primary cause of injury. For example, a consistent pattern of injury relationship to asymmetries within the pelvis and legs (short leg syndrome) has shown these to be factors in knee injury.[7] Unfortunately, not much in the form of remedial work is usually done; as a result, an injury often becomes chronic—sometimes to the point that continued participation in a sport must be halted. When possible, the trainer should seek to ameliorate or eliminate faulty postural conditions through therapy, working under the direction of an orthopedist or other qualified medical personnel. Remedial work of this type can complement the training program and, in most instances, may assist principally in maintaining sufficient bilateral development to minimize the more obvious undesirable effects of intensive unilateral development. Development of the antagonistic muscles to offset the power and force of the agonstic muscles will reinforce and establish stability and assist in the development and maintenance of good muscular balance. A number of postural conditions offer genuine hazards to athletes by making them exceedingly prone to specific injuries. Some of the more important will be indicated in the following discussions of foot and leg anomalies, spinal anomalies, and various stress syndromes.

Foot and Leg Anomalies
Poor Mechanics of Walking and Running

Ligamentous and muscular sprains of the foot, ankle, or knee often result from poor walking or running mechanics. These injuries become chronic when faulty alignment of the foot and leg persists. When such mechanics are observed, the footgear should be checked as a first step. Improperly fitting or poorly designed shoes may cause or aggravate an undesirable condition. Therefore, considerable care must be exercised when sports gear is issued to fit the shoe to the player and not the player to the shoe.

The knee joint, by virtue of its anatomical structure, is basically an unstable joint. Thus knee injuries in both contact and noncontact sports are quite common. Pronation or toeing out, in either walking or running, exposes the medial aspect of the knee joint to such an extent that when considerable lateral force is applied (as in being tackled or in changing direction suddenly while moving at a high rate of speed) severe injury can result. Athletes who habitually walk or run in this fashion should be placed on a corrective program to obviate the habit and to reduce susceptibility to knee joint damage.

Genu Valgum (Knock-Knees)

Genu valgum is an orthopedic disorder that presents a serious hazard to the knee joints. The weight-bearing line passes to the lateral side of the center of the knee joint as a result of the inward angling of the thigh and lower leg. This causes the body weight to be borne principally on the medial aspects of the articulating surfaces, thereby subjecting the medial collateral ligament to considerable strain and rendering the joint somewhat more unstable and prone to injury (Fig. 9-15, *A*).

Genu Varum (Bowlegs)

Genu varum (Fig. 9-15, *B*) is the opposite of genu valgum. The extra stress is placed on the fibular collateral ligament. In extreme cases of either of these conditions, athletes should be directed into a noncontact activity in which they are not subjected to the conditions of stress and force encountered in contact sports.

Figure 9-15

Genu valgum (**A**), knock-knees, and genu varum (**B**), bowlegs.

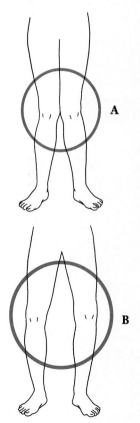

Figure 9-16

Kyphosis.

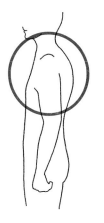

Figure 9-17

Lumbar lordosis.

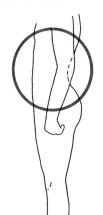

Spinal Anomalies
Kyphosis

An anteroposterior curvature of the spine wherein the convexity is directed posteriorly characterizes kyphosis, which is usually found in the cervico-thoracic region. The condition is commonly called "round back." As a rule it is accompanied by a forward-thrust head, abducted scapulae, and a flat chest. Usually, activities that make great demands on the pectoral muscles are a primary cause in fostering this condition among athletes. Kyphotic athletes who have strong and well-developed but shortened pectoral muscles (such as are found frequently among basketball players, gymnasts, weightlifters, and—as a product of football stances—among football players) are quite susceptible to anterior dislocations of the arm, particularly when the arm is forced into an abducted and extended position accompanied by outward rotation. Exercises designed to stretch the shortened pectoral muscles and to strengthen muscles in the upper back, thus obtaining a more normal shoulder alignment and reducing the possible incidence of shoulder joint injury, are advocated (Fig. 9-16).

Lumbar Lordosis

Lumbar lordosis is an abnormal anterior curvature of the lumbar spine, commonly called "hollow back" or "swayback." A tightening of the lower back extensor muscles, contraction of the lumbar fascia, and corresponding stretching of the abdominal muscles are involved. Among football linemen this condition is further aggravated by the postural demands of the offensive stance. Gymnasts, particularly female gymnasts, are also subject to lumbar lordosis as the result of the strenuous muscular and ligamentous strains imposed on the lower back. In addition, the sport demands exceptional spinal flexibility, which also can be a factor. Spondylolysis (the breaking down of a vertebra or the occurrence of a stress fracture between the anterior and posterior portions of a vertebra) or spondylolisthesis (subluxation or slipping forward of the fifth lumbar vertebra and that portion of the spine above it over the base of the sacrum) can result, the spine's response to the excessive and strenuous physical demands being made on it. Lumbosacral strain, sacroiliac strain, and coccyalgia (pain in the coccygeal area) often may be traced to a lordotic condition as the predisposing cause. During active exercise there may be an overriding of the lumbosacral facets when an excessive lordosis is present; this can and often does result in trauma. The hamstring pull, sometimes suffered by trackmen, is often associated with a lordotic condition in which a lowering of the pubic arch produces a corresponding lift of the ischial tuberosity, where the hamstrings originate. As a result, the latter are constantly in a state of stretch. Correction of the pelvic tilt by means of an exercise program designed to strengthen the abdominal muscles and stretch the lumbar extensor muscles, as well as improving the flexibility of the spine, will do much to ameliorate this condition (Fig. 9-17).

Scoliosis

Scoliosis is defined as a lateral curvature of the spine and is a condition in which there is a rotary, lateral, curving deviation of the vertebrae from the median line of the body. Many of our sports are unilateral, and others have certain phases that tend to develop or aggravate this postural-orthopedic condition. Baseball pitching and high jumping using a one-foot takeoff are examples. Scoliotic athletes may be subject to severe epiphysitis or bursitis as a result of the excessive force demands made on the joint structures of the overdeveloped segment.

When a scoliotic condition is not directly attributable to a sport or a habit, it is usually caused by another structural condition, of which the most common probably is unequal leg length. When this condition exists, a lift built into the shoe will often correct the situation and permit the athlete to function normally. As with other postural-orthopedic conditions, a prescribed exercise program designed to help the individual to increase flexibility, stretch the shortened muscles, and strengthen the stretched muscles should be administered under the direction of a trained therapist or physician (Fig. 9-18).

ABNORMAL REPETITIVE STRESS AND MICROTRAUMAS

Injuries as a result of abnormal and repetitive stress and microtraumas fall into a class with certain identifiable syndromes. Such stress injuries frequently result in either limitation or curtailment of sports performance. Most of these injuries in athletes are directly related to the dynamics of running, throwing, or jumping. The injuries may result from constant and repetitive stresses placed on bones, joints, or soft tissues; from forcing a joint into an extreme range of motion; or from prolonged strenuous activity. Some of the injuries falling into this category may be relatively minor; still, they can prove to be quite disabling. Among injuries classified as repetitive stress and microtrauma are Achilles tendinitis; splints; stress fractures, particularly of the fibula and second and fifth metatarsal bones; Osgood-Schlatter disease; runner's and jumper's knee; patellar chondromalacia; apophyseal avulsion, especially in the lower extremities of growing athletes; and intertarsal neuroma.

Dynamics of Running

Since many of the abnormal or continued stress syndromes bear a direct relationship to the act of running, the trainer should have an understanding of what is involved in this gait. Running differs from walking in that the double period of support that occurs in walking is eliminated and a period of flight during which there is no contact with the ground is achieved. Basically there are three phases to the running gait: the push-off, the flight, and the landing. In running the foot strikes the ground almost directly under the center of gravity. This is not the case in walking. The resistive force, that is, the body weight and the backward pressure of the foot as it strikes the ground ahead of the body is almost entirely eliminated in running. The supportive phase decreases, having an inverse relationship to the speed of the gait. In a sprint at a high rate of speed, the supportive phase is almost entirely propulsive. The legs alternate between a swinging phase, a brief supportive phase, and another swinging phase. Since the foot strikes the ground in advance of the body, there is a forward component of force in the

Figure 9-18

Scoliosis.

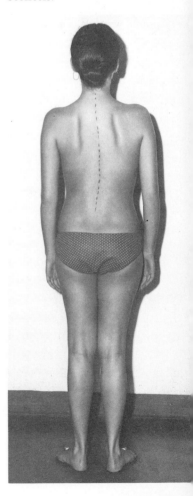

thrust of the foot against the ground, which results in a backward counter-pressure of the ground against the foot, slightly checking the forward momentum of the body. Most overuse injuries occur at the moment of impact. The counterpressure exists from the moment of foot-strike until the center of gravity has moved beyond the supporting foot. When the center of gravity has moved in front of the supporting foot, a propulsive force is engendered by the forceful thrust of the foot against the ground, resulting from the extension of the hip, knee, and ankle.

The mechanics of running are indeed similar to those of walking, differing, as previously stated, in the fact that the period of double support is eliminated and a period of flight supplants it. The force exerted consists of two components, horizontal and vertical, although the vertical component (unlike that in walking) is negligible because of the great increase in the horizontal component. Since the horizontal force is greatly increased, accompanied by a slight vertical increase, the angle between the leg and the ground during extension is smaller and the pelvis is carried lower. Therefore, the weight is brought closer to the hip. The lowering of the pelvis requires greater flexion of the knee joint of the supporting leg, thus increasing the amount of extensor force developed by the driving leg. The increased knee flexion reduces the amount of time required to carry the leg forward to a position of extension.

Since speed is considerably increased in running and the body undergoes a period of flight, the force is greatly magnified when the swinging leg and foot strike the ground. In walking the heel of the swinging foot strikes the ground; but in running the leg reaches a full extension and has initiated the beginning of a backward movement. This causes the ball of the foot, rather than the heel, to make forceful contact with the supporting surface. In slow running, contact may be made with the heel first, the runner rolling along the lateral border to the ball of the foot as the leg reaches full backward extension. In sprinting, the weight is borne principally by the toes. At the moment of impact the foot may be in either dorsiflexion or plantar flexion, depending on whether the runner is moving slowly or rapidly. Placement of the foot may be in a neutral position or it may be toed out (pronation) or toed in (inversion). The latter two placements will exert considerable stress on the medial and lateral aspects of the foot, respectively. Pronation, the weakest position of the foot, is usually associated with a decided inward rotation of the thigh, which causes additional strain on the knee and hip joints, sometimes resulting in significant trauma. Continued overuse of the foot, particularly as encountered in distance running, leads to syndromes that are relatively common in activities in which repetitive pounding of the foot occurs in the foot-strike and the takeoff thrust phases of the gait.

Dynamics of Throwing

Throwing activities account for a considerable number of acute and chronic injuries to the elbow and shoulder joints. Throwing is a unilateral action that subjects the arm to repetitive stresses of great intensity, particularly in sports activities such as pitching or javelin throwing. Should the thrower employ incorrect techniques, the joints are affected by atypical stresses that result in trauma to the joint and its surrounding tissues. Throwing is a sequential pattern of movements in which each part of the body must perform a number of carefully timed and executed acts. For example, throwing a ball or javelin employs one particular pattern of movements; hurling the discus or hammer makes use of a similar complex, but with centrifugal force substituted for linear force and the type of terminal movements employed in release being different. Putting the shot—a pushing rather than a throwing movement—has in its overall pattern a number of movements similar to those employed in throwing a ball. Discus and hammer throwing seldom result in significant injury problems. However, hammer throwers, because of improper release of the hammer, on occasion may incur shoulder girdle injuries, particularly of the rotator cuff muscles and the middle and posterior deltoid.

In the act of throwing, momentum is transferred from the thrower's body to the object that is thrown. According to physical laws, the greater and heavier the mass, the greater the momentum needed to move it. Hence, as the size and weight of the object increase, more parts of the body are used to effect the summation of forces needed to accomplish the throw. The same is true in respect to the speed of the object: the greater the speed, the more body parts that must come into play to increase the body's momentum. Timing and sequence of action are of the utmost importance. They improve with correct practice.

In throwing, the arm acts as a sling or catapult, transferring and imparting momentum from the body to the ball. There are various types of throwing, with the overhand, sidearm, and underarm styles being the most common. The act of throwing is fairly complex and requires considerable coordination and timing if success is to be achieved.

Throwing or pitching involves three distinct phases: a preparatory or cocking phase, the delivery or acceleration phase, and the follow-through or terminal phase. Specific injuries appear peculiar to each phase. In throwing, the most powerful muscle groups are brought into play initially, progressing ultimately to the least powerful but the most coordinated (i.e., the legs, trunk, shoulder girdle, arm, forearm, and finally the hand). The body's center of gravity is transported in the direction of the throw as the leg opposite the throwing arm is first elevated and then moved forward and planted on the ground, thus stopping the forward movement of the leg and permitting the body weight to be transferred from the supporting leg to the moving leg. Initially the trunk rotates backward as the throwing arm and wrist are cocked, then rotates forward, continuing its rotation beyond the planted foot as the throwing arm moves forcibly from a position of extreme external rotation, abduction, and extension through flexion to forcible and complete extension in the terminal phase of the delivery, bringing into play the powerful internal rotators and adductors. These muscles exert a tremendous force on the distal and proximal humeral epiphysis and over a period of time create cumulative microtraumas that can result in shoulder problems or the so-called pitcher's or tennis elbow and eventually traumatic arthritis in the radiohumeral joint.

In throwing, the shoulder and the elbow seem particularly vulnerable to trauma. Uncoordinated or stress movements can subject either articulation to a considerable amount of abnormal force or torque. In pitching, with considerable speed being engendered, the forearm is the crucial element. The inward or outward rotation that is used to impart additional speed and action to the ball subjects the elbow and the shoulder to appreciable torque, which may become traumatizing if the action is improperly performed over a considerable period of time. The rotator cuff muscles, long head of the biceps brachii, pronator teres, anconeus, and deltoid are the muscles that are most affected in throwing.

Lesions of the pitching arm are quite common and are not restricted to the mature college or professional player. In the adolescent, bones are immature; the epiphyses are not closed and appear to be somewhat susceptible to injury, particularly from pitching, wherein medial epicondyle epiphysis avulsion (Little League elbow) and lateral epicondylitis (pitcher's or tennis elbow) are not uncommon injuries.

The initial cocking phase may result in decreased internal and increased external humeral rotation, and tendinitis may occur in both the biceps and triceps muscles, as well as in the shoulder rotators.

The delivery or acceleration phase can cause tendinitis involving the greater pectoral and latissimus dorsi muscles. "Little League shoulder," which results in osteochondrosis of the proximal humeral epiphysis or in a fracture of the proximal portion of the humeral shaft, can also result. This phase also subjects the elbow joint to considerable torque and stress, which may cause "Little League elbow." Changes at the radiohumeral joint caused by compression forces may result in an aseptic necrosis of the radial head or osteochondritis dissecans of the capitulum of the humerus where it articulates with the radius. Bony spurs on both radius and ulna are not uncommon.

The final phase of the throw, the follow-through, has few problems other than the pronator teres syndrome, wherein pain is felt during the terminal pitching phase. This syndrome appears most frequently among adults, since the forearm pronation is more pronounced in performing a "breaking" pitch.

Careful coaching to assist athletes in developing the proper timing and sequence of movement, coupled with a training program for developing the muscles of the throwing arm, will reduce injuries to a minimum.

Dynamics of Jumping

In jumping activities the shock of takeoff and landing is transmitted to the lower limb or limbs. Improper takeoff or landing is responsible for a great many joint injuries. The force of the takeoff can cause a stress fracture to the foot or the ankle. The shock of an improper landing is frequently the cause of injury to the ankle, knee, or hip joint.

Severe torque results when the takeoff foot is either toed in or out. In either case the ligaments, particularly in the ankle or the knee joint, are subjected to an intense rotational shear force that usually results in torn ligaments, cartilages, or bone fracture. Improper landings from either the high jump or the long jump can cause lower limb injury, but the arms and neck are also vulnerable. The flop style of high jumping, wherein the bar is cleared by going over backward and the landing is on the back, can result in a cervical injury, especially to young and inexperienced jumpers.

Traumatic forces to the ankle joint frequently occur in jumping. Such twisting or shearing action can be damaging. Approximately 85% of all ankle injuries result from forced inversion, which causes tearing of the lateral ligaments. Eversion injuries usually result in the breaking off of the lateral malleolus, with some damage to the connective tissues on the medial aspect of the ankle.

Although the knee is the largest joint in the body, its shallowness renders it extremely vulnerable to injury. Medial, lateral, and twisting forces, such as encountered in most sports, subject the supportive ligamentous bands to severe strains. These injuries can occur after one violent traumatic incident, or they may result from the cumulative effects of repeated microtrauma. Such strain can result in the stretching or tearing of the supporting connective tissue, such as when the foot is firmly fixed and the body and leg go into or are in rotation. Hyperextension of the knee, wherein the knee is forced into a position beyond the normal 180-degree position, can result in severe joint trauma that may involve the synovial membrane or the deeper periosteal tissue. This commonly occurs in takeoff but can occur on landing, especially in gymnastics. Jumper's knee is an example of a condition resulting from repetitive microtrauma.

Athletes should be taught proper foot placement and the techniques of landing with the hips, knees, and ankles partially flexed and relaxed to absorb the landing shock. In some instances the addition of a body or shoulder roll as the initial landing phase is terminated may further mitigate shock.

ADDITIONAL INJURY FACTORS

In addition to the areas discussed, three injury factors should be taken into consideration: readiness, reinjury, and contraindicated movements.

Contraindicated movements
in sports include:
  Full squats
  Knee sitting
  Double leg lifts
  Straight leg sit-ups
  Hands behind the neck
    sit-ups
  Head bridge
  Back hyperextension
  Hurdler's stretch

Readiness

Muscles serve as pads to cushion and distribute any external force applied to the body. In the contact sports players should be taught to achieve a state of readiness, that is, to "set" themselves a moment before impact by partially tensing the muscles so that the body is prepared to receive the imminent force. Tensing in this fashion prevents bruising and complements the strength of the joints involved through dissipation of the force by the muscles. This decreases the amount of stress placed on the ligamentous areas. The player who is completely relaxed at the moment of player or ground contact is the one who stands an excellent chance of injury, whereas the player who is in a state of readiness can assume the impact and still be able to continue in the play situation because the muscles are ready to move into instantaneous action.

Reinjury

The problem of reinjury is a serious one in sports. Less severe injuries tend to occur and recur with increasing frequency and severity. This is usually the result of neglect or of inadequate treatment in terms of reconditioning.

Text continued on p. 246.

Full squats

Full squats

The movement employed in the full squat primarily affects the knee and ankle joints and, to a lesser extent, the hip joint. On the initial movement flexion is elicited at the hips, knees, and ankles. It is produced by the force of gravity and controlled by an eccentric or lengthening contraction of the extensor muscles of the thigh. As the athlete reaches the terminal position and is in a full squat, the anterior portion of the knee joint is thrust forward. As a result the extensors are stretched to their full length, thereby forcing the posterior aspect to support the entire weight of the body with the flexors in a state of tension. The knee joint is thus levered into what is tantamount to an open position, exerting an excessive stress on the medial, lateral, and cruciate ligaments, which may therefore become overstretched and weakened. This reduces the inherent stability of the joint. Exercises that employ the deep squat contribute to the development of chronic synovitis and may predispose the joint to arthritic changes in later life.

Exercises employing the full squat should be eliminated from the conditioning program. The inherent dangers in such exercises far outweigh the values to be gained through performing them. Orthopedists are quite concerned with this problem. Numerous clinical evaluations emphasize the need for eliminating this exercise. Substituting either the quarter or the half squat for the full squat, with the heels placed on a lift of 1 or 2 inches in height, is suggested as better exercise to develop the muscles of the knee and hip joint.

Knee sitting

Knee sitting, like full squats, should be avoided, especially in those individuals who have heavy legs. Sitting on the lower legs may adversely open the knee joint, thereby stretching ligaments and producing joint instability. This position particularly should be avoided by those athletes having a history of knee injury.

Knee sitting

Double leg lifts

The double leg raise while in a long lying position can lead to serious low back injury or strain. This is particularly true for the athlete who has heavy legs or weak lower abdominal muscles. Lifting two straightened legs together can create an adverse tension in the iliopsoas muscles, thereby pulling the lumbar spine into an abnormal curve. This may be avoided *only* if the low back can be maintained in a flattened position throughout the movement.

Double leg lift

Straight-leg sit-ups

Straight-leg sit-ups, like double leg lifts, should not be performed. These seriously strain the lower back by abnormally contracting hip flexors, primarily the iliopsoas muscles.

Straight leg sit-ups

Hands behind the neck sit-ups

Sit-ups with the hands behind the neck should be avoided. In this position, the cervical spine can be adversely stressed.

Hands behind the neck sit-ups

Head bridge

Bridging up so that the weight of the trunk is supported on the top of the head can seriously compress the cervical vertebrae. Modified bridging, however, where pressure is applied to the back of the head may be safe in selected situations.

Head bridge

Back hyperextension

Performing back hyperextensions can be dangerous. Such movements can abnormally compress the lumbar vertebrae and cause injury. A protective rule of thumb is not to arch the back more than raising the chest and head while keeping the abdomen in contact with the surface.

Back hyperextension

Hurdler's stretch

A recent addition to the list of contraindicated movements is the hurdler's stretch. The position of the back leg places abnormal stress on the medial collateral ligament of the knee and should be avoided.

Hurdler's stretch

There has always been an unfortunate tendency for many athletes to participate while hurt or before they have adequately recovered from an injury, thus exposing the condition to reinjury. This occurs in the mistaken belief that displaying fortitude in the presence of pain is traditionally not only the thing to do but also is heroic. Indeed, this is a misconception. Players who expose themselves to reinjury in this fashion do a disservice to themselves and the team.

Pain tolerance is an individual matter, since no two people respond to pain in the same way. Some possess a very high tolerance, whereas others have a very low tolerance. The athlete who possesses a high tolerance will usually continue participation when injured or before completely recovered from a previous injury, thus increasing the chances for a reinjury perhaps more severe than the initial trauma. Many sports are predicated on violent physical contact, and a participant who is not up to par is almost certain to sustain additional injury.

Before an injured athlete is permitted to reenter training or competition a number of factors must be considered: the nature of the injury, type of activity to be engaged in, inherent risks, age of the individual, and personality of the athlete.

REFERENCES

1. Cailliet, R.: Soft tissue pain and disability, Philadelphia, 1977, F.A. Davis Co.
2. Cavanagh, P.R., and Grieve, D.W.: The biomechanics of movement. In Strauss, R.H., editor: Sportsmedicine and physiology, Philadelphia, 1979, W.B. Saunders Co.
3. Ciulo, J.V., and Zarins, B.: Biomechanics of the musculotendinous unit: relation to athletic performance and injury, Symposium on Olympic sports medicine, Clinics in sports medicine, vol. 2, p. 871, Philadelphia, 1982, W.B. Saunders Co.
4. Erikson, E., and Häggmark, T.: Muscle and tendon physiology. In Mack, R.P. (editor): Symposium on the foot and leg in running sports, American Academy of Orthopaedic Surgeons, St. Louis, 1982, The C.V. Mosby Co.
5. Gozna, E.R.: Biomechanics of long bone injuries. In Gozna, E.R., and Harrington, I.J. (editors): Biomechanics of musculoskeletal injury, Baltimore, 1982, The Williams & Wilkins Co.
6. Harrington, I.J.: Biomechanics of joint injuries. In Gozna, E.R., and Harrington, I.J., editors: Biomechanics of musculoskeletal injury, Baltimore, 1982, The Williams & Wilkins Co.
7. Klein, J.: Develomental asymmetry of the weight-bearing skeleton and its implication on knee injury. In Scriber, K., and Burke, E.J. (editors): Relevant topics in athletic training, Ithaca, N.Y., 1978, Movement Publications.
8. Kotwick, J.E.: Biomechanics of the foot and ankle, Symposium on ankle and foot problems in the athlete, Clinics in sports medicine, vol. 1, p. 819, Philadelphia, 1981, W.B. Saunders Co.
9. Sammarco, G.J., Burstein, A.H., Davis, W.L., et al.: The biomechanics of torsional fractures: the effect of loading on ultimate properties, J. Biomech. 4:113, 1971.
10. Stanitski, C.L., McMaster, J.H., and Scranton, P.E.: On the nature of stress fractures, Am. J. Sports Med. 6:391, 1978.
11. Zarin, B.: Soft tissue and repair—biomechanical aspects, Int. J. Sports Med. 3(suppl. 1):9, 1982.

ADDITIONAL SOURCES

Bells, J.M., and Eichelberger, M. (editors): Symposium on pediatric and adolescent sports medicine, Clinics in sports medicine, vol. 1, Philadelphia, 1982, W.B. Saunders Co.

Butler, D.L., Grood, E.S., and Noyes, F.R.: Biomechanics of ligaments and tendons, Exerc. Sports Sci. Rev. **6:**125, 1978.

Cailliet, R.: Scoliosis: diagnosis and management, Philadelphia, 1975, F.A. Davis Co.

Carton, R.W., et al.: Elastic properties of single elastic fibers, J. Appl. Physiol. **17:**547, 1962.

Frankel, J.H., and Nordin, M.: Basic biomechanics of the skeletal system, Philadelphia, 1980, Lea & Febiger.

Gozna, E.R., and Harrington, I.J. (editors): Biomechanics of musculoskeletal injury, Baltimore, 1982, The Williams & Wilkins Co.

Mack, R.P.: Symposium on the foot and leg in running sports, American Academy of Orthopaedic Surgeons, St. Louis, 1982, The C.V. Mosby Co.

Nordin, M., and Frankel, V.H.: Biomechanics of collagenous tissues. In Frankel, V.H., and Nordin, M. (editors): Basic biomechanics of the skeletal; system, Philadelphia, 1980, Lea & Febiger.

Chapter 10

CLASSIFYING, RECOGNIZING, INSPECTING, AND EVALUATING SPORTS INJURIES

When you finish this chapter, you should be able to

Categorize and define the major exposed and unexposed sports injuries

Explain the major characteristics of musculoskeletal sports injuries

Describe the steps in on-site and off-site inspection and evaluation of sports injuries

Causative factors of sports injury[10]
Consequential (due to sports participation)
A. Primary
   1. Extrinsic (e.g., human, implemental, vehicular, environmental)
   2. Intrinsic (e.g., instantaneous, overuse)
B. Secondary (e.g., early, late)

Before injuries can be recognized, inspected, and properly evaluated they must be classified and defined. Learning to intelligently evaluate the nature and extent of sports injuries is of the utmost importance. The responsibility of evaluation to determine the extent of injury falls to the coach or trainer when a physician is not immediately available for evaluation. A decision may also have to be made as to whether continued participation would be detrimental to the athlete and whether medical referral is necessary. To reach such decisions reasonably and prudently, the responsible person must have a basic knowledge of injury characteristics. This chapter classifies and defines injuries occurring in sports and describes procedures for evaluating them.

CLASSIFYING INJURIES

Injuries in sports can be classified and discussed in a number of ways. The two most common classifications are causation and major anatomy and the forces involved.

Causative Factors

A primary injury is one that results directly from the stress imposed by a particular sport. The injury can be externally caused, such as by body contact or use of a piece of equipment. The use of some implement, such as a racquet or gymnastics equipment, can produce instantaneous trauma or overuse microtrauma from repeated stresses. Another extrinsic cause is through a vehicular accident, such as a motorcycle or racing car.[10] Environmental factors can also produce injury, such as accidents while engaged in mountaineering or water sports.

Intrinsic injuries are those occurring due to stresses created within the athlete. These can be instantaneous or chronically developed over a long period of time.

Secondary problems can arise from an injury, especially if it has not been properly treated initially or if the athlete has been allowed to return to competition too soon. An example of an early secondary problem after injury may be chronic swelling and weakness in a joint, whereas an example of later occurrence is arthritis that has developed in a joint many years after repeated sprains and improper care.

Nonconsequential causative factors refer to injuries or other problems that are not directly related to stress in a specific sport, but adversely influence it. Periodic asthma attacks are an example of a nonconsequential causative factor that can adversely affect performance.

Acute Anatomical Factors

Sport injuries also can be described according to the primary structure that has been affected and the extent of trauma. The most external anatomy is the skin and, when wounded, the injury is highly visible; on the other hand, injuries affecting muscles, tendons, ligaments, joint capsules, cartilages, and bone are usually unexposed and internal.

Exposed Skin Injuries

Exposed injuries can be classified primarily into four types of skin insults: abrasions, lacerations, puncture wounds, and incisions (Fig. 10-1). The great-

ANATOMICAL DIRECTIONS

proximal
Nearest to a point of reference

distal
Farthest from a point of reference

lateral
A position farther away from the median plane or midline

medial
Toward the median plane or midline

anterior
Situated or directed toward the front

posterior
Situated or directed toward the back

superior
Situated above

inferior
Situated below

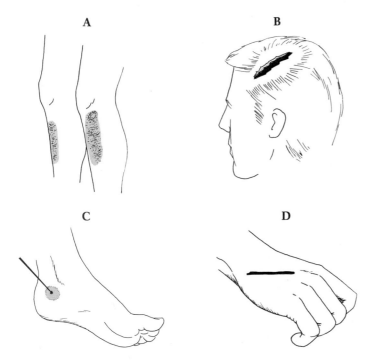

A

B

C

D

Figure 10-1

The four major skin traumatic injuries are abrasion (**A**), laceration (**B**), puncture (**C**), and incision (**D**).

Figure 10-2

A contusion can range from a superficial to a deep tissue compression *(arrow)*, injuring cells and causing relative amounts of hemorrhage.

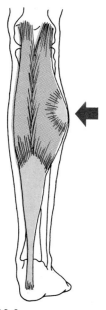

Figure 10-3

A strain can occur to any aspect of the musculo-tendinous unit. Depending on the amount of force, a strain can stretch or tear muscle fibers *(arrow)* or even avulse a tendon from a bone.

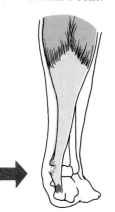

est problem these conditions present is their vulnerability to infection because of direct exposure to a contaminant (Chapter 17).

Abrasions are common conditions in which the skin is scraped against a rough surface. The epidermis and dermis are worn away, thus exposing numerous blood capillaries. This general exposure, with dirt and foreign materials scraping and penetrating the skin, increases the probability of infection unless the wound is properly debrided and cleansed.

Lacerations are also common in athletics and occur when a sharp or pointed object tears the tissues, giving a wound the appearance of a jagged-edged cavity. As with abrasions, lacerations present an environment conducive to severe infection. The same mechanism that causes a laceration also can lead to a skin avulsion. In this case a piece of skin is completely ripped from its source.

Puncture wounds can easily occur during physical activities and can be fatal. Direct penetration of tissues by a pointed object such as a track shoe spike can introduce the tetanus bacillus into the bloodstream, possibly making the athlete a victim of lockjaw. All puncture wounds and severe lacerations should be referred immediately to a physician.

Incisions are cleanly cut wounds that often appear where a blow has been delivered over a sharp bone or a bone that is poorly padded. They are not as serious as the other types of exposed wounds.

Unexposed Injuries

Unexposed or closed wounds in sports include those internal injuries which do not penetrate the epidermal skin layer. Recognizing and caring for these conditions present a definite challenge, since one's actions can mean the difference between a rapid or a prolonged period of recovery.

A bruise or contusion is received because of a sudden traumatic blow to the body. The intensity of a contusion can range from superficial to deep tissue compression and hemorrhage (Fig. 10-2).

Interrupting the continuity of the circulatory system results in a flow of blood and lymph into the surrounding tissues. A hematoma (blood tumor) is formed by the localization of the extravasated blood into a clot, which becomes encapsulated by a connective tissue membrane. The speed of healing, as with all soft tissue injuries, depends on the extent of tissue damage and internal bleeding.

Contusion or the crushing of soft tissue can penetrate to the skeletal structures, causing a bone bruise. The extent to which an athlete may be hampered by this condition depends on the location of the bruise and the force of the blow. Typical in cases of severe contusion are the following:

1. The athlete reports being struck a hard blow.
2. The blow causes pain and a transitory paralysis caused by pressure on and shock to the motor and sensory nerves.
3. Palpation often reveals a hard area, indurated because of internal hemorrhage.
4. Ecchymosis or tissue discoloration may take place.

Strains A strain, sometimes referred to as a muscle pull, is a stretch, tear, or rip in the muscle or adjacent tissue, such as the fascia or muscle tendons (Fig. 10-3). The etiology of muscle strain is often obscure because there are many possible causes. Most often a strain is produced by an abnormal muscular contraction. The cause of this abnormality has been attributed to many factors. One popular theory suggests that a fault in the reciprocal coordination of the agonist and antagonist muscles takes place. The cause of this fault or incoordination is more or less a mystery. However, among the possible explanations advanced are that it may be related to (1) a mineral imbalance caused by profuse sweating, (2) fatigue metabolites collected in the muscle itself, or (3) a strength imbalance between agonist and antagonist muscles.

A strain may range from a minute separation of connective tissue and muscle fiber to a complete tendinous avulsion or muscle rupture (graded as *first*, *second*, or *third degree*). The resulting pathology is similar to that of the contusion or sprain, with capillary or blood vessel hemorrhage. Healing takes place in a similar fashion, with the organization of a hematoma, absorption of the hematoma, and finally the formation of a cicatrix (scar) by fibroblastic repair. Detection of the injury is accomplished by understanding how the injury occurred and the administration of a muscle test to determine the specific locality. The muscles that have the highest incidence of strains are the hamstring group, gastrocnemius, quadriceps group, hip flexors, hip adductor group, spinalis group of the back, deltoid, and rotator cuff group of the shoulder. The following are signs that a strain may have occurred:

1. Snapping sound when the tissue tears
2. Muscle fatigue and spasm before the strain occurred
3. Severe weakness and loss of function
4. A sharp pain immediately on the occurrence of injury
5. Spasmodic muscle contraction of the affected part
6. Extreme point tenderness on palpation
7. An indentation or cavity where tissues have separated or a bump indicating contracted tissue occurring immediately after injury

Continued overstretching of muscle tissue can lead to chronic inflammation. Some areas of the body, such as the elbow region and Achilles tendon, are more predisposed to chronic strain.

Muscle cramps and spasms A cramp is usually a painful involuntary contraction of a skeletal muscle or muscle group. Cramps have been attributed to a lack of salt or other minerals or muscle fatigue. A reflex reaction caused by trauma of the musculoskeletal system is commonly called a spasm. The two types of cramps or spasms are the clonic type, with alternating involuntary muscular contraction and relaxation in quick succession, and the tonic type, with rigid muscle contraction that lasts over a period of time.

Sprains The sprain, one of the most common and disabling injuries seen in sports, is a traumatic joint twist that results in stretching or totally tearing stabilizing connective tissues (Fig. 10-4). When a joint is forced beyond its normal anatomical limits, microscopic and gross pathologies occur. Specifically, there is injury to ligaments, to the articular capsule and synovial membrane, and to the tendons crossing the joint. According to the extent of injury, sprains are graded in three degrees. A first degree indicates stretching of ligaments, a second degree indicates

Figure 10-4

A sprain mainly involves ligamentous and capsular tissue *(arrow)*; however, tendons also can be secondarily involved. A joint that is forced beyond its anatomical limits can stretch and tear tissue and, on occasion, avulse ligaments from their bony attachments.

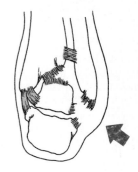

partial tearing, and a third degree describes a complete severance of ligaments. Effusion of blood and synovial fluid into the joint cavity produces joint swelling, local temperature increase, pain or point tenderness, and skin discoloration (ecchymosis). According to statistics, the joints that are most vulnerable to sprains are the ankles, knees, and shoulders. Sprains occur least often to the wrists and elbows. Since it is often difficult to distinguish between joint sprains and tendon strains, the examiner should expect the worst possible condition and manage it accordingly. Repeated joint twisting can eventually result in chronic inflammation, degeneration, and arthritis.

Dislocations Dislocations are second to fractures in terms of handicapping the athlete. The highest incidence of dislocations involves the fingers and, next, the shoulder joint (Fig. 10-5). Dislocations, which result primarily from forces causing the joint to go beyond its normal anatomical limits, are divided into two classes: *subluxations* and *luxations*. Subluxations are partial dislocations in which an incomplete separation between two articulating bones occurs. Luxations are complete dislocations, presenting a total disunion of bone apposition between the articulating surfaces.

Several important factors are important in recognizing and evaluating dislocations:

1. There is a loss of limb function. The athlete usually complains of having fallen or of having received a severe blow to a particular joint and then suddenly being unable to move that part.

2. Deformity is almost always apparent. Since such deformity can often be obscured by heavy musculature, it is important for the examiner to palpate the injured site to determine the loss of normal body contour. Comparison of the injured side with its normal counterpart often reveals distortions.

3. Swelling and point tenderness are immediately present.

At times, as with a fracture, x-ray examination is the only absolute diagnostic measure. First-time dislocations or joint separations may result in a rupture of the stabilizing ligamentous and tendinous tissues surrounding the joint and avulsion or pulling away from the bone. Trauma is often of such violence that small chips of bone are torn away with the supporting structures, or the force may separate growth epiphyses or cause a complete fracture of the neck in long bones. This indicates the importance of administering complete and thorough medical attention to first-time dislocations. It has often been said, "Once a dislocation—always a dislocation." In most cases this is true, since once a joint has been

A first-time dislocation should always be considered as a possible fracture.

Figure 10-5

A joint that is forced beyond its anatomical limits can become partially dislocated (subluxated) (**A**), or completely dislocated (luxated) (**B**).

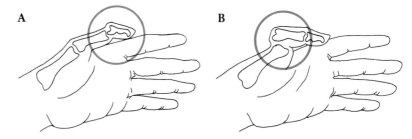

either subluxated or completely luxated the connective tissues that bind and hold it in its correct alignment are stretched to such an extent that the joint will be extremely vulnerable to subsequent dislocations. Chronic, recurring dislocations may take place without severe pain, because of the somewhat slack condition of the stabilizing tissues.

A first-time dislocation should always be considered and treated as a possible fracture. Once it has been ascertained that the injury is a dislocation, a physician should be consulted for further evaluation. However, before the patient is taken to the physician, the injury should be properly splinted and supported to prevent any further damage.

Types of fractures Fractures can be a partial or complete interruption in a bone's continuity and can occur without external exposure or can extend through the outer skin, creating a serious external wound. The fracture can be the result of a sudden traumatic event or a repetitive abnormal stress. Fractures are one of the most serious hazards of sports and should be routinely suspected in musculoskeletal injuries; pp. 254-255 illustrate the major acute fractures.

Basic acute fracture signs X-ray films can offer an accurate means of identifying an acute fracture. Whenever there is some question as to the possibility of a fracture having occurred, the athlete should be referred to a physician. An understanding of the gross fracture signs by the trainer or coach cannot be overemphasized. Trainers should familiarize themselves with them sufficiently to be able to make the following examination at the time and place of injury:

1. Determine the mechanism of the injury:
   a. In what sport was the athlete engaged?
   b. How was the athlete hit?
   c. How did the athlete fall?
   d. Did the athlete feel a sudden pain when the injury occurred?
      NOTE: Often, immediate pain subsides and numbness is present for a period of 20 to 30 minutes.
2. Inspect the area of the suspected fracture:
   a. Deformity. Compare the corresponding part to determine the deformity.
   b. Swelling. Is rapid swelling taking place?
   c. Direct tenderness. Ascertain the presence of point tenderness, especially over bony structures.
   d. Indirect tenderness. Through palpation, proximally and distally to the injury site, determine whether pain can be elicited at the probable fracture point.
   e. Bony deviations. Does palpation indicate any irregularity in the continuity of the bone?
   f. Crepitus. On examining the body part, is there a grating sound apparent at the fracture site?
   g. False joint. Is there an abnormal movement of the part, sometimes giving the appearance of an extra joint?
   h. Discoloration. Is there discoloration around the site of injury?
      NOTE: Often, discoloration does not appear until several days after the injury has occurred.

Comminuted fracture

Comminuted fractures consist of three or more fragments at the fracture site. These could be caused by a hard blow or a fall in an awkward position. From the physician's point of view, these fractures impose a difficult healing situation because of the displacement of the bone fragments. Soft tissues are often interposed between the fragments, causing incomplete healing. Such cases may need surgical intervention.

Depressed fractures occur most often in flat bones such as those found in the skull. They are caused by falling and striking the head on a hard, immovable surface or by being hit with a hard object. Such injuries also result in gross pathology of soft areas.

Greenstick fractures are incomplete breaks in bones that have not completely ossified. They occur most frequently in the convex bone surface, with the concave surface remaining intact. The name is derived from the similarity of the fracture to the break in a green twig taken from a tree.

Impacted fractures can result from a fall from a height, which causes a long bone to receive, directly on its long axis, a force of such magnitude that the osseous tissue is compressed. This telescopes one part of the bone on the other. Impacted fractures require immediate splinting by the athletic trainer and traction by the physician to ensure a normal length of the injured limb.

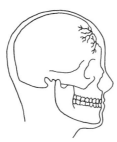

Depressed fracture

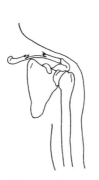

Greenstick fracture

Impacted fracture

Longitudinal fractures are those in which the bone splits along its length, often the result of jumping from a height and landing in such a way as to impact force or stress to the long axis.

Oblique fractures are similar to spiral fractures and occur when one end receives sudden torsion or twisting and the other end is fixed or stabilized.

Serrated fractures in which the two bony fragments have a sawtooth, sharp-edged fracture line are usually caused by a direct blow. Because of the sharp and jagged edges, extensive internal damage, such as the severance of vital blood vessels and nerves, often occurs.

Spiral fractures have an S-shaped separation. They are fairly common in football and skiing, in which the foot is firmly planted and then the body is suddenly rotated in an opposing direction.

Transverse fractures occur in a straight line, more or less at right angles to the bone shaft. A direct outside blow usually causes this injury.

Contrecoup fractures occur on the side opposite to the part where trauma was initiated. Fracture of the skull is at times an example of the contrecoup. An athlete may be hit on one side of the head with such force that the brain and internal structures compress against the opposite side of the skull, causing a fracture.

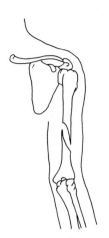

Longitudinal fracture

Oblique fracture

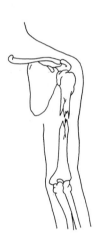

Serrated fracture

Spiral fracture

Transverse fracture

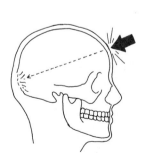

Contrecoup fracture

Stress fractures   The major signs of a stress fracture are swelling, focal tenderness, and pain. In the early stages of the fracture the athlete complains of pain when active but not at rest. Later, the pain is constant and becomes more intense at night. Percussion, by light tapping on the bone at a site other than the suspected fracture, will produce pain at the fracture site.

The most common sites of stress fracture are the tibia, fibula, metatarsal shaft, calcaneus, femur, pars interarticularis of the lumbar vertebrae, ribs, and humerus (Fig. 10-6).

The management of stress fractures varies with the individual athlete, injury site, and extent of injury. Stress fractures that occur on the compression side of bone heal more slowly and are managed more easily compared with those on the tension side. Stress fractures on the tension side can rapidly produce a complete fracture.[2]

Management usually consists of removal from sports activity, but not necessarily complete abstinence from physical activity, for 3 to 4 weeks or longer. If the stress fracture is in one of the metatarsal bones, special orthotics or shoe alterations can allow weight bearing and, in some people, full athletic participation. Stress fractures of other bones may require abstinence from participation and even casting. The major rule for the return of an athlete to full sports participation is *not to return prematurely. It is better to be held back 1 week longer than to return 1 week too early. If in doubt, hold longer.*

> Guideline for return to participation:
> Better to hold 1 week longer than to return 1 week too early.

Avulsion fractures   An avulsion fracture is a separation of a bone fragment from its cortex at an attachment of a ligament or tendon. This usually occurs as a result of a sudden, powerful twist or stretch of a body part. An example of a ligamentous episode is the sudden eversion of the foot, causing the deltoid ligament to avulse bone away from the medial malleolus. A good example of a tendinous avulsion is one that causes a patellar fracture. This occurs when an athlete falls forward while suddenly bending a knee. The stretch of the patellar tendon pulls a portion of the inferior patellar pole apart (Fig. 10-7).

Epiphyseal conditions   Three types of epiphyseal growth site injuries can be sustained by children and adolescents performing sports activities. The most prevalent age range for these injuries is from 10 to 16 years. They consist of injury to the epiphyseal growth plate, articular epiphyseal injuries, and apophyseal injuries.

> A musculoskeletal injury to a child or adolescent should always be considered as a possible epiphyseal condition.

The epiphyseal growth plate   The epiphyseal growth plate is a cartilagenous disk located near the end of each long bone. Growth of the long bones depends on these plates. Ossification in long bones begins in the diaphysis and in both epiphyses. It proceeds from the diaphysis toward each epiphysis and from each epiphysis toward the diaphysis.[1] The growth plate has layers of cartilage cells in different stages of maturity with the more immature cells at one end and mature ones at the other end. As the cartilage cells mature, immature osteoblasts replace them later to produce solid bone[7,9] (Fig. 10-8). Epiphyseal growth plates are often less resistant to deforming forces than are ligaments of nearby joints or the outer shaft of the long bones; therefore, severe twisting or a blow

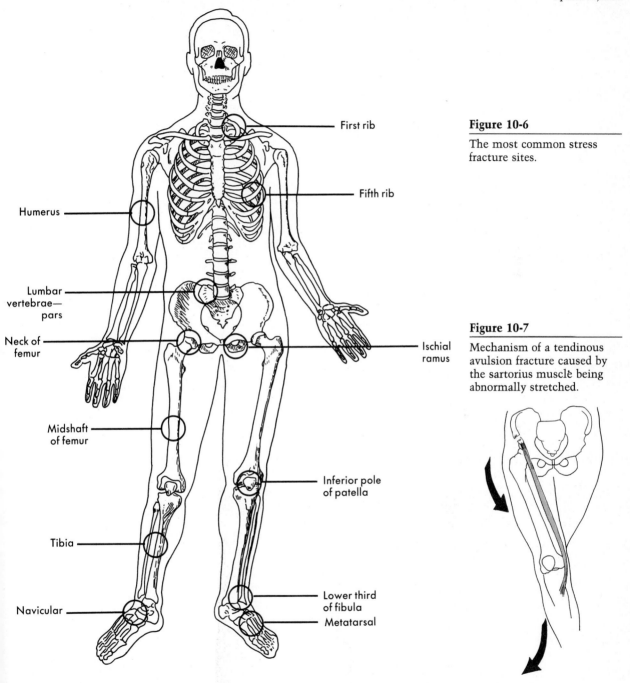

First rib

Fifth rib

Humerus

Lumbar
vertebrae—
pars

Neck of
femur

Ischial
ramus

Midshaft
of femur

Inferior pole
of patella

Tibia

Navicular

Lower third
of fibula

Metatarsal

Figure 10-6

The most common stress
fracture sites.

Figure 10-7

Mechanism of a tendinous
avulsion fracture caused by
the sartorius muscle being
abnormally stretched.

to an arm or leg can result in disruption in growth.[9] Injury could prematurely close the growth plate, causing a loss of length in the bone. Growth plate dislocation could also cause deformity of the long bone.

Epiphyseal growth plate injury is categorized into five types (Fig. 10-9); the first four types are caused by shear or avulsion forces and the fifth type is caused by crushing or compressional force. The injuries are described as follows:

Type I	Complete separation of the epiphysis in relation to the metaphysis with fracture to the bone
Type II	Separation of the growth plate and a small portion of the metaphysis
Type III	Fracture of the epiphysis
Type IV	Fracture of a portion of the epiphysis and metaphysis
Type V	No displacement of the epiphysis, but the crushing force can cause a growth deformity

Articular epiphyseal injuries The articular epiphyseal region at the end of the long bone is particularly vulnerable to injury in children and adolescents. Such conditions as chondromalacia and osteochondritis dissecans may occur as a result of microtraumas, limb malalignments, and/or circulatory impairments.

Apophyseal injuries The young, physically immature athlete is particularly prone to apophyseal injuries. The apophyses are "traction epiphyses" in contrast to the "pressure epiphyses" of the long bones. These apophyses serve as origins or insertion for muscles of growing bone that

Figure 10-8

The epiphyseal growth plate is the cartilagenous disk located near the end of each long bone.

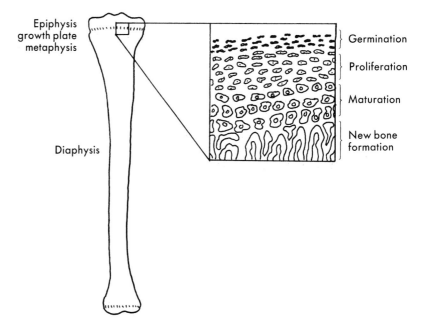

provide bone shape but not length. Common apophyseal avulsion conditions found in sports are Sever's disease and Osgood-Schlatter disease (Chapters 19 and 20).

Chronic Conditions

The chronic condition is usually of long onset and duration, but acute injuries, if not properly managed, can soon become chronic. As in acute conditions, inflammation plays an important role in chronic injuries, although it does not necessarily present the classic stages of redness, swelling, pain, heat, and loss of function. Because of the constant presence of a low-grade inflammation, there is a proliferation of fibroblasts, which develop a generalized connective tissue scarring. In sports a chronic condition may have any of several etiological factors: poor performance techniques, **sequelae** of acute injuries, or constant stress beyond physiological limits.

The use of *improper performance technique* places abnormal strain on joints and tendons, predisposing the athlete to a future chronic condition. Proper form must be stressed!

The *sequelae of acute injuries* may lead to a chronic condition if traumatic injuries are superimposed one on the other or incessant reinjury of a part occurs. The healing of an acute injury, if delayed by improper care, may result in chronic inflammation.

Stress beyond the physiological limits of the athlete (overuse syndrome)

sequela
Pathological condition occurring as a consequence of another condition or event

Figure 10-9

Types of long bone epiphyseal injuries.

Separation

Fracture—separation

Fracture—part of epiphysis

Fracture—epiphysis and
epiphyseal plate

Bony union—
premature closing

Crushing of epiphyseal plate—
may cause premature closure

may occur either grossly, as in heat exhaustion, or, more frequently, as in small, insidious micropathologies in the muscles and joints. Such conditions are frequently difficult to detect as specific single entities and as a result can cause untold loss of competitive time.

General care of chronic injuries in sports is basically the same regardless of the area condition. Of prime importance are rest, immobilization, and heat applied to the injured part. This procedure is often accompanied by an anti-inflammatory medication. Emergency care of the seriously ill and injured athlete is discussed in detail in Chapter 12.

A great number of chronic conditions are associated with sports participation. The student should be familiar with some of the unique characteristics of these conditions.

Muscle and Tendon Conditions

Commonly, chronic tendon injuries are intrinsic and involve overuse.

Tendinitis   Tendinitis has a gradual onset, diffuse tenderness because of repeated microtraumas, and degenerative changes. Obvious signs of tendinitis are swelling and pain that move with the tendon. Occasionally, tendinitis leads to deposits of minerals, primarily lime, within the tendon. This is known as calcific tendinitis.

Tenosynovitis   Tenosynovitis is inflammation of the sheath covering a tendon. In its acute state there is rapid onset, articular crepitus, and diffuse swelling. In chronic tenosynovitis the tendons become locally thickened, with pain and articular crepitus present on movement (Fig. 10-10).

Bursitis   The bursa is the fluid-filled sac found in places where friction might occur within body tissues. Bursae are predominantly located between bony prominences and muscles or tendons. Overuse of muscles or tendons at these prominences, as well as constant external compression or trauma, can result in bursitis. The signs and symptoms of bursitis

Figure 10-10

Tenosynovitis is an inflammation of the sheath covering a tendon.
A, Normal. **B,** Strained.
C, Chronic tenosynovitis.

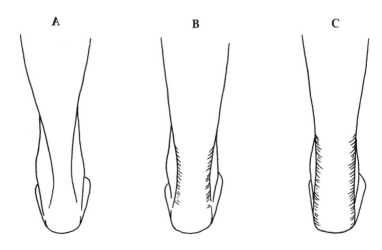

A   B   C

include swelling, pain, and some loss of function. Repeated trauma may lead to calcific deposits and degeneration of the internal lining of the bursa.[5]

Ectopic calcification   Voluntary muscles can become chronically inflamed, resulting in myositis. An **ectopic** calcification known as *myositis ossificans* can occur in a muscle that directly overlies a bone. Two common sites for this condition are the quadriceps region of the thigh and the brachial muscle of the arm. In myositis ossificans osteoid material that resembles bone rapidly accumulates. If there is no repeated injury, the growth may subside completely in 9 to 12 months, or it may mature into a calcified area, at which time surgical removal can be accomplished with little fear of recurrence.[8]

ectopic
Located in a different place than normal

Tendinitis and tenosynovitis can be the result of or lead to calcium deposits within the tendon or synovial-lined sheath. Deposits of lime produce the condition called calcific tendinitis.

Atrophy and contracture   Two complications of muscle and tendon conditions are atrophy and contracture. Muscle atrophy is the wasting away of muscle tissue. Its main cause in athletes is immobilization of a body part, inactivity, or loss of nerve stimulation. A second complication to sport injuries is *muscle contracture,* an abnormal shortening of muscle tissue where there is a great deal of resistance to passive stretch. Commonly associated with muscle injury, a contracture is associated with a joint that has developed unyielding and resisting scar tissue.

Osteochondrosis and Traumatic Arthritis

Two chronic conditions that are common in athletes are osteochondrosis and traumatic arthritis. Osteochondrosis is a category of conditions in which the etiologies are not well understood. A synonym for this condition, if it is located in a joint such as the knee, is *osteochondritis dissecans* and, if located at a tubercle or tuberosity, *apophysitis.* One suggested cause of osteochondrosis is ischemic necrosis in which circulation to the epiphysis has been disrupted. Another suggested cause is that trauma causes particles of the articular cartilage to be fractured, eventually resulting in fissures that penetrate to the subchondral bone. If trauma to a joint occurs, pieces of cartilage may be dislodged, which can cause joint locking, swelling, and pain. If the condition occurs in an apophysis, there may be an avulsion-type fracture and fragmentation of the epiphysis, along with pain, swelling, and disability.[8]

Traumatic arthritis is usually the result of microtraumas. With repeated trauma to the articular joint surfaces, the bone and synovium thicken, there is pain, muscle spasm, and articular crepitus or grating on movement. Joint insult leading to arthritis can come from repeated sprains that leave a joint with weakened ligaments. There can be malalignment of the skeleton, which stresses joints, or it can arise from an irregular joint surface that stems from repeated articular chondral injuries. Loose bodies that have been dislodged from the articular surface can also irritate and produce arthritis. Athletes with joint injuries that are improperly immobilized or who are allowed to return to activity before proper healing has occurred may eventually be afflicted with arthritis.

Athletes with improperly immobilized joint injuries or who are allowed to return to activity before proper healing has occurred may eventually be afflicted with arthritis.

Nerve Responses

A number of abnormal nerve responses can be attributed to athletic participation or injury. Some of the more common conditions are referred pain and trigger points, hypoesthesia or hyperesthesia, nerve stretch or pinch injuries, and neuritis.

Pain that is felt in a point of the body other than its actual origin is known as *referred pain*. In the muscular system a common manifestation of referred pain is the *trigger point*, which is a center of irritation that when stimulated sets off pain to distant body areas (Chapter 11).

Among the conditions affecting touch sensation, two are common to athletic injuries, hypoesthesia and hyperesthesia. *Hypoesthesia* refers to a diminished sense of feeling or numbness with associated tingling. *Hyperesthesia* refers to increased sensitivity to a stimulation. A variety of nerve injuries, such as nerve contusions and stretching, can lead to diminished or increased sensitivity, as well as pain. Direct trauma to a nerve, such as a blow, can cause such symptoms as numbness, paresthesia, and muscle weakness. Sensations associated with paresthesia are burning and prickling. A sudden *nerve stretch or pinch* can lead to a sharp burning pain that radiates down the limb together with muscle weakness. Conditions having these signs that go untreated can lead to an eventual permanent loss of function.

Like other tissues in the body, nerves can become chronically inflamed from repeated irritation. *Neuritis* can be caused by the mechanical stresses of compression, direct blows, penetrating injuries, contusion, stretching, and nerve entrapment. Symptoms of neuritis can range from minor nerve involvement to paralysis.

INJURY INSPECTION AND EVALUATION

Injury inspection and evaluation:
  Where?
    Initial on injury site
    Off injury site
  When?
    Before and during the rehabilitation process

As stated in Chapter 3, the coach or trainer is by law not allowed to diagnose injuries; however, injury inspection and evaluation are in the purview of the athletic trainer.

A logical process must be used to accurately evaluate the extent of a sport injury. One must be aware of the major signs that reveal the site, nature, and, above all, severity of the injury. Detection of these signs can be facilitated (1) *by understanding the mechanism or traumatic sequence* and (2) *by methodically inspecting the injury.* Knowledge of the mechanism of an injury is extremely important in finding which area of the body is most affected. When the injury mechanism has been determined, the examiner proceeds to the next phase, physical inspection of the affected region. At this point information is gathered by what is seen, what is heard, and what is felt. Three types of inspection and evaluation can be given to the athlete by the examiner: the initial on-injury site inspection and evaluation, the off-injury site inspection and evaluation, and the evaluation before and during rehabilitation.

Initial On-site Injury Inspection and Evaluation

In an attempt to understand the mechanism of injury, a brief history of the complaint must be taken. The athlete is asked, if possible, about the events leading up to the injury and how it occurred. The athlete is further asked what was heard or felt when the injury took place. The trainer then makes a *visual observation* of the injured site and compares it to the uninjured body part. The initial visual examination can disclose obvious deformity, swelling, and skin discoloration. Next, what was heard at the time of the injury is determined. Sounds occurring at the time of injury or during manual inspection yield pertinent information on the type and extent of pathology present. Such uncommon sounds as grating or harsh rubbing may indicate fracture. Joint sounds may be detected when either arthritis or internal derangement is present. Areas of the body that have abnormal amounts of fluid may produce sloshing sounds when gently palpated or moved. Such sounds as a snap, crack, or pop at the moment of injury often indicate a breaking of bone. Finally, the region of the injury is gently palpated. Feeling or palpating a part with trained fingers can, in conjunction with visual and audible signs, indicate the nature of the injury. As the examiner gently feels the injury and surrounding structures with the fingertips, several factors can be revealed: the extent of point tenderness, the extent of irritation (whether it is confined to soft tissue alone or extends to the bony tissue), and the determination of deformities that may not be detected by visual examination.

After a quick on-site injury inspection and evaluation the trainer makes the following decisions:

1. The seriousness of the injury
2. The type of first aid and immobilization necessary
3. Whether or not the injury warrants immediate referral to a physician for further evaluation
4. The manner of transportation from the injury site to the sidelines, training room, or hospital.

All information on the initial history, signs, and symptoms of the injury must be documented, if possible, so that they may be described in detail to the physician.

Off-site Injury Inspection and Evaluation

Once the athlete has been removed from the site of injury to a place of comfort and safety, further inspection and evaluation usually consists of six steps: (1) determination of major complaints, (2) general inspection, (3) bony palpation, (4) soft tissue palpation, (5) neurological evaluation, and (6) functional evaluation. *This same type of inspection and evaluation is given to athletes who are not in an initial or acute state of injury, but who have a recurrent or chronic complaint.*

The major complaint Without a physician immediately present, a trainer may have to acquire some general information that will be accurately passed on to the physician. Athletes should be asked to describe in their own words "their problem":

1. When did it first occur?
2. Did it come on suddenly or gradually?
3. What does the condition currently feel like?
4. If it is painful, does it burn, feel sharp or dull, ache, gnaw, throb, shoot, or feel constrictive?

Pain should further be described as to its severity, such as *mild, moderate, severe, excruciating,* or *agonizing.* The athlete should then be asked to specifically locate the area of complaint by *pointing to it with one finger only*. The trainer asks the following:

1. If the pain is generalized or local, does it radiate to another body area?
2. Is the pain constant or does it go and come?

When the complaint is chronic or recurrent, the athlete can be asked when the pain is the worst: at night, in the morning, during activity, or after activity.[3,6]

General observed inspection Along with gaining an understanding of the athlete's major complaint, the body is generally observed to determine a number of factors: *general posture, body movements,* and *asymmetrical body configurations.* How the body is habitually held can tell the trainer a lot about the athlete's condition:

1. Is the body held stiffly to protect a painful area?
2. Is the body properly aligned or does it incline in one direction or another?

A second major factor to observe is how the athlete walks or moves the limbs:

1. Is one limb obviously held rigidly in protection?
2. Are movements abnormally slow, jerky, or asynchronous?
3. Is there a limp?

The third aspect to look for is asymmetry of the body. An unnatural protrusion of a body part could mean fracture or dislocation. An abnormal limb rotation could mean severe sprain or subluxation.

Bony palpation Before the examiner undertakes bony palpation to determine a pathological condition, there must be a clear understanding of the normal anatomy of the athlete. Both the injured and noninjured sites should be palpated and compared. The sense of touch might reveal an abnormal gap at a joint, swelling on a bone, joints that are misaligned, or abnormal protruberances associated with a joint or bone.

Soft tissue palpation To perform soft tissue palpation requires a good knowledge of ligaments, capsular structures, muscles, blood vessels, and nerves. Through palpation, a normal tissue relationship can be ascertained, as well as variations from the normal. Such tissue deviations as swellings, lumps, gaps, and muscle tension can be detected. Like bony palpation, soft tissue palpation must proceed orderly and be performed on both sides of the body for comparison.

Circulatory and neurological evaluation Both circulation and neurological examination should be an important part of the evaluatory process. Visual observation can detect skin areas that are blanched from impeded blood flow or reddened from increased blood flow. Feeling the skin with the hands often can reflect varied areas of cold or warmth.

Nerve injury can result in symptoms of burning, prickliness, numbness, or loss of function. Often numbness, referred pain, or other nerve involvements will follow the segmental distribution of spinal nerves on the surface of the skin. These are called dermatomes and are the areas of skin supplied by afferent nerves (Fig. 10-11). Commonly, the physician or therapist can identify the site of spinal cord or nerve dysfunction in an area of the body that is insensitive to a pinprick.

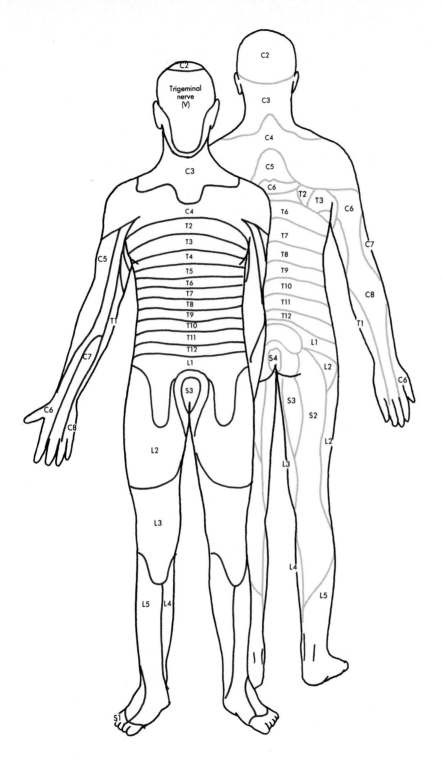

Figure 10-11

Numbness, referred pain, or
other nerve involvements
often follow the segmental
distribution of spinal nerves
on the skin's surface.

Functional evaluation To complete the inspection and evaluation, a functional examination should be given, if possible, including range of motion, grade and resistive motion, strength, and the practical use of the body part.

Passive and active range of motion The first functional evaluation should be to test both passive and active range of motion for pain and restriction. In passive movement the athlete's limb is taken through a range of motion until resistance is felt by the trainer or the athlete feels pain. Sometimes resistance is felt with or without pain. Pain may occur at any point in the range. Passive motion producing pain in a joint might mean a ligamentous or capsular condition. Conversely, active movement causing joint pain could indicate a muscular, ligamentous, or capsular condition. *NOTE: Goniometer joint measurement should be taken and recorded both passively and actively* (Chapter 15).

Active range of motion requires neuromuscular integrity and the athlete's willingness to bring the part to the point of pain. Active motion may be of normal, limited, or restricted range. Both passive and active range of motion measurements are taken, recorded, and compared to the unaffected limb.

Graded and resisted motion Whenever feasible and there is no fear of aggravating the injury, muscle strength should be tested and compared with the noninjured side.[4] Muscle grades are described as follows:

Active range of motion requires neuromuscular integrity and the athlete's willingness to bring the part to the point of pain.

Muscle Grade	Description
5 = Normal	Complete range of motion against gravity with full resistance
4 = Good	Complete range of motion against gravity with some resistance
3 = Fair	Complete range of motion against gravity alone
2 = Poor	Complete range of motion with gravity eliminated
1 = Trace	Evidence of slight contractibility with no joint motion
0 = Zero	No evidence of contractibility

Evaluation during the rehabilitation process A major value of the athletic training program is that athletes can engage in daily supervised rehabilitation. Ideally, injury evaluation is also performed daily. Range of motion, strength, and motor control can be tested before therapy. This helps make the program gradually progressive in intensity and helps to indicate when the correct amount of exercise has been carried out.

REFERENCES

1. Anthony, C.P., and Thibodeau, G.A.: Textbook of anatomy and physiology, ed. 11, St. Louis, 1983, The C.V. Mosby Co.
2. Chamay, A.: Mechanical and morphological aspects of experimental overload and fatigue in bone, J. Biomech. **3:**263, 1970.
3. Cyriax, J.: Textbook of orthopaedic medicine, ed. 8, vol. 1, Diagnosis of soft tissue lesions, Eastbourne, England, 1982, Baillière Tindall.
4. Daniels, L., and Worthingham, C.: Muscle testing techniques of manual examination, Philadelphia, 1980, W.B. Saunders Co.
5. Hafen, B.Q.: First aid for health emergencies, St. Paul, Minn., 1981, West Publishing Co.
6. Hoppenfeld, S.: Physical examination of the spine and extremities, New York, 1976, Appleton-Century-Crofts.
7. Larson, R.L.: Physical activity and the growth and development of bone and joint structures. In Rarick, G.L. (editor): Physical activity: human growth and development, New York, 1973, Academic Press.
8. Maron, B.R.: Orthopedic aspects of sports medicine. In Appenzeller, O., and Atkinson, R. (editors): Sports medicine, Baltimore, 1981, Urban & Schwarzenberg, Inc.
9. Micheli, L.J.: Sports injuries in children and adolescents. In Straus, R.H. (editor): Sports medicine and physiology, Philadelphia, 1979, W.B. Saunders Co.
10. Williams, J.G.P.: Color atlas of injury in sport, Chicago, 1980, Year Book Medical Publishers, Inc.

ADDITIONAL SOURCES

Anderson, W.A.D., and Scotti, T.M.: Synopsis of pathology, ed. 10, St. Louis, 1980, The C.V. Mosby Co.

Appenzeller, O., and Atkinson, R. (editors): Sports medicine, Baltimore, 1981, Urban & Schwarzenberg, Inc.

Muckle, D.S.: Injuries in sport, Bristol, England, 1982, John Wright & Sons, Ltd.

Prior, J.A., Silberstein, J.S., and Stang, J.M.: Physical diagnosis, ed. 6, St. Louis, 1981, The C.V. Mosby Co.

Standard Nomenclature of Athletic Injuries, Monroe, Wis., 1976, The American Medical Association.

Chapter 11

TISSUE HEALING AND PAIN

When you finish this chapter, you should be able to

Discuss the phases of both soft tissue and fracture healing

Draw a comparison between the physiological and psychological aspects of pain

A student of the human body and sports medicine has to marvel at the process of healing. A common expression, "We know more about traveling into space than how the body repairs itself," tells it all. Although highly complicated and not fully understood, the basis of inflammation and the healing process should be studied as a foundation for initiating proper injury management. This chapter presents an overview of some of the major events inherent in soft tissue and skeletal healing, pain, and the psychological response to pain.

SOFT TISSUE HEALING

Soft tissue is, in this instance, considered to be all body tissues other than bone. The healing process of soft tissue consists of three major phases: the inflammatory (reactive or substrate) phase, the repair (regeneration) phase, and the remodeling phase.

Reactive (Inflammatory) Phase

Reactive phase:
Redness
Heat
Swelling
Pain
Loss of function

Inflammation is the reaction of body tissue to an irritant or injury and is characteristic of the first 3 or 4 days after injury. The major outward signs are redness (rubor), heat (calor), swelling (tumor), pain (dolor), and, in some cases, loss of function (functio laesa). Dilation of blood vessels causes the swelling and redness by exudates. Pain may be produced by chemical substances such as histamine, serotonin and bradykinin, by pressure on nerve endings, or by anemia in the area of the injury.

Inflammation is that fundamental reaction designed to protect, localize, and rid the body of some injuring agent in preparation for healing and repair. The main causative factors are trauma, chemical agents, thermal extremes, and pathogenic organisms. The tissue irritants leading to the inflammatory process impose a number of vascular, chemical, and cellular changes.

Acute Traumatic Injury

At the time of trauma, before the usual signs of inflammation appear, a transitory **vasoconstriction,** with decreased blood flow, occurs and lasts up to 10 minutes.[14] At the moment of vasoconstriction, coagulation begins to seal broken blood vessels followed by the activation of chemical influences. Vasoconstriction is replaced by the dilation of venules, as well as arterioles and capillaries in the immediate area of the injury. **Vasodilation** brings with it a slowing of blood flow, increased blood viscosity, and stasis, which leads to swelling. With dilation also comes exudation of plasma and concentration of red blood cells (hemoconcentration). Much of the plasma **exudate** results from fluid seepage through the intact vessel lining that becomes more **permeable** and from higher pressure within the vessel. Permeability is relatively transient in mild injuries, lasting only a few minutes with restoration to a preinjury state in 15 to 30 minutes.[1] In slightly more severe situations there may be a delay in response with a late onset of permeability. In such cases, permeability may not appear for many hours and then appears with some additional irritation and a display of rapid swelling lasting for an extended period of time (Fig. 11-2).

vasoconstriction
Decrease in the diameter of a blood vessel

vasodilation
Increase in the diameter of a blood vessel

exudate
Fluid with a high protein content and cellular debris that come from blood vessels and accumulate in the area of the injury

permeable
Permitting the passage of a substance through a vessel wall

Figure 11-1

Tissue healing and the causation of pain is not clearly understood. However, what is known must be studied as a foundation for proper injury management.
Courtesy Cramer Products, Inc., Gardner, Kan.

A redistribution of leukocytes occurs within the intact vessels, caused in part by a slowing of circulation. These leukocytes move from the center of the blood flow to become concentrated and lined up and adhere to the endothelial walls. This process is known as *margination* and *pavementing* and occurs mainly in venules. The leukocytes pass through the wall of the blood vessel by ameboid action, known as *diapedesis*, and are directed to the injury site by chemotaxis (a chemical attraction to the injury)(Fig. 11-3).

Although not completely understood, it is believed that vascular dilation stems primarily from chemical mediators freed or created at the injury site, while nerve factors play a lesser role. Some of the better known chemicals are *serotonin* and *histamine*, which increase permeability, as well as *plasma kinins* (primarily *bradykinin*), which are accompanied by vasodilation and permeability. Plasma kinins are the most potent vasodilators in

Figure 11-2

The mechanism and process of acute inflammation.

From Anderson, W.A.D., and Scotti, T.M.: Synopsis of pathology, ed. 10, St. Louis, 1980, The C.V. Mosby Co.

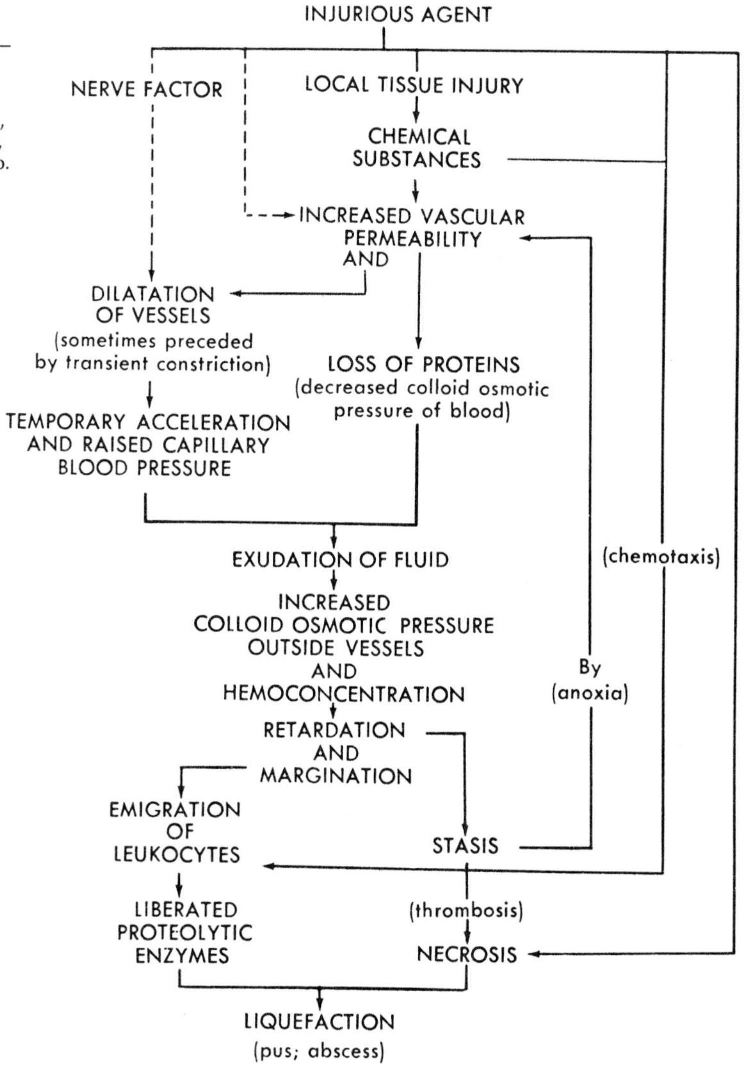

Figure 11-3

The process of margination, pavementing, and movement of leukocytes through the blood vessel wall.

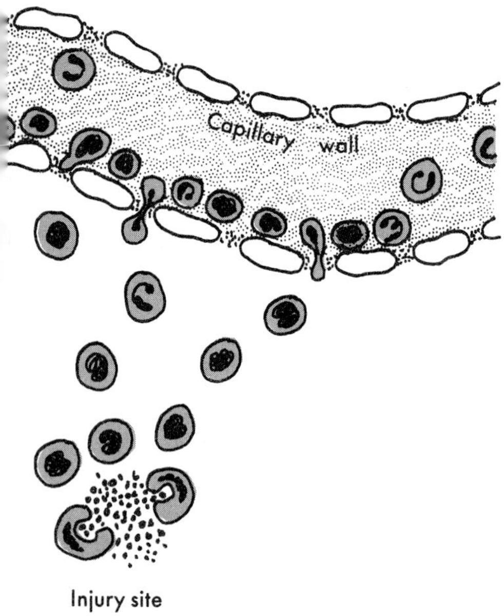

Injury site

the body thus far identified and produce the outward cardinal signs of inflammation, which include venule and capillary permeability along with pain. In the very early stage of an acute injury, histamine and other substances are explosively released, while kinins become more predominent in the later inflammatory phase. Another substance commonly associated with inflammation is *prostaglandin*, which has a histamine-like affect on injured soft tissue.[8]

Bleeding and Exudate

The extent of fluid in the injured area is highly dependent on the extent of damaged vessels and permeability of intact vessel. Blood coagulates in three stages. In the initial stage *thromboplastin* is formed, while in the second stage *prothrombin* is converted into *thrombin* under the influence of thromboplastin with calcium, and in the third stage thrombin changes from soluble *fibrinogen* into insoluble *fibrin*. The plasma exudate then coagulates into a network of fibrin and localizes the injured area.

Important to the healing process are the *cells of inflammation* found in exudate; they include different types of leukocytes, red blood cells, and giant cells. Many of these cells release key chemicals as well as stimulate **phagocytosis**. For example, mast cells found in connective tissue release histamine and serotonin, both of which produce a vasodilatory effect. Granulocytes form prostaglandins, which have vasodilator and chemotactic properties and also assist in phagocytosis. Macrophages, mainly monocytes, function to carry out phagocytosis as well as produce a chemotaxis of other macrophages.

phagocytosis
Process of ingesting microorganisms, other cells, or foreign particles, commonly by monocytes; a white blood cell

Phagocytosis

Phagocytosis is the process of ingesting material such as bacteria, dead cells, and other debris associated with disease, infection, or injury. This process is commonly accomplished by the phagocyte projecting cytoplasmic pseudopods, which engulf the object and ingest the particle through enzymes.

Repair and the Regenerative Phase

An external or internal wound is associated with tissue death. In the initial stage of injury, tissue death occurs from actual trauma. Following trauma, cellular death may continue as a result of a lack of oxygen because of a disruption of circulation. A third causative factor is when the digestive enzymes of engulfing phagocytes spill over to kill normal cells. This points up the importance of proper immediate wound care involving ice, compression, elevation, rest, and immobilization (see Chapter 12).

Cellular death continues after initial injury because of:
Lack of oxygen caused by disruption of circulation
Digestive enzymes of engulfing phagocytes spill over to kill normal cells

The term *repair* is synonymous with healing, while *regeneration* refers to the restoration of destroyed or lost tissue. Healing, which extends from the inflammatory phase to about 3 weeks, occurs in three ways: (1) by resolution, where there is little tissue damage and normal restoration; (2) by granulation tissue, occurring if resolution is delayed; and (3) by regeneration, the replacement of tissue by the same tissue.

Tissue repairs:
By resolution
By granulation tissue
By regeneration

The formation of scar tissue following trauma is a common occurrence; however, because scar tissue is less viable than normal tissue, the less scarring the better. When mature, scar tissue represents tissue that is firm, fi-

Tissue repair depends on:
  Elimination of debris
  Regeneration of endothelial
  cells
  Production of fibroblasts

brous, inelastic, and devoid of capillary circulation. The type of scar tissue known as adhesion can complicate the recovery of joint or organ disabilities. Healing by scar tissue begins with an exudate, a fluid with a large content of protein and cellular debris that collects in the area of the injury site. From the exudate, a highly vascular mass develops known as granulation tissue. Infiltrating this mass is a proliferation of immature connective tissue (fibroblasts) and endothelial cells. Dead tissue, other debris, and fibrin are removed by macrophages and granulocytes. Gradually the collagen protein substance, stemming from fibroblasts, forms a dense fibrous scar.

During this stage, two types of healing occur. *Primary healing*, healing by first intention, takes place in an injury that has even and closely opposed edges, such as a cut or incision. With this type of injury, if the edges are held in very close approximation, a minimum of granulation tissue is produced. *Secondary healing*, healing by secondary intention, results when there is a gaping lesion and large tissue loss leading to replacement by scar tissue. External wounds, such as lacerations, and internal musculoskeletal injuries commonly heal by secondary intention.

Regeneration

According to van der Meulen, "In man—unlike the salamander, which can regrow an amputated limb—the capacity for regeneration is limited to a few

Figure 11-4

Stimulated by hypoxia and action of macrophages, capillary buds begin to form in the walls of the intact vessels.

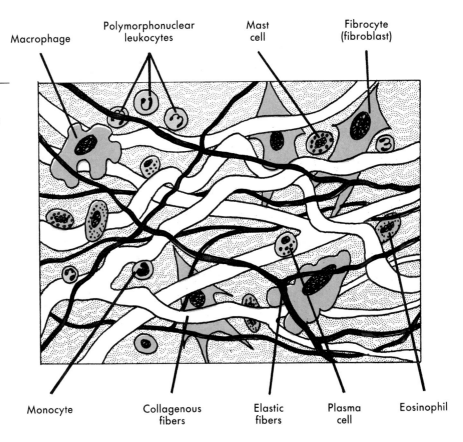

Macrophage · Polymorphonuclear leukocytes · Mast cell · Fibrocyte (fibroblast)

Monocyte · Collagenous fibers · Elastic fibers · Plasma cell · Eosinophil

cells, which comprise the endothelial cells, the fibroblasts and the epithelial cells."[14] The ability to regenerate following injury decreases with age. It is also associated with nutrition, general health of the individual, but most importantly, to the type of tissue that has been injured. The following are examples of healing capabilities within the musculoskeletal system:

> **bone** Restores easily from the endosteum or periosteum
> **cartilage** Regenerates somewhat from the perichondrium
> **connective tissue** Readily regenerates
> **peripheral nerve fibers** Can regenerate if the damaged ends are opposed
> **striated voluntary muscle tissue** Tissue that is very limited in regeneration

Repair and regeneration depend on three major factors: elimination of debris, the regeneration of endothelial cells, and the production of fibroblasts, which make up connective tissue throughout the body and form the basis of scar tissue. Typically in a traumatic event injured blood vessels become deprived of oxygen and die. Before repair and regeneration can occur, debris must first be removed by phagocytosis. Stimulated by a lack of oxygen (hypoxia) and the action of macrophages, capillary buds begin to form in the walls of the intact vessels. From these buds grow immature vessels that form connections with other vessels. As these vessels become mature, more oxygenated blood is brought to the injured area. From the perivascular cells come the fibroblasts (immature fibrocytes) that migrate to the injury and form collagen substances, often within a few days of the injury.[14] The development of collagen is stimulated by lactic acid and vitamin C and depends on the proper amount of oxygen for its development (Fig. 11-4).

Remodeling Phase

Remodeling of the traumatized area overlaps that of repair and regeneration. Normally in acute injuries the first 3 weeks are characterized by increased production of scar tissue and the strength of its fibers. Strength of scar tissue continues to increase from 3 months to 1 year following injury. Ligamentous tissue has been found to take as long as a year to become completely remodeled. To avoid a rigid, nonyielding scar, there must be a physiological balance between synthesis and lysis. If there is too early or excessive strain placed on the injury, the healing process is extended. For proper healing of muscle and tendons, there must be careful consideration as to when to mobilize the site. Early mobilization can assist in producing a more viable injury site; however, too long a period of immobilization can delay healing.

> Remodeling depends on the amount and type of scar tissue present.

Chronic Inflammation

The chronic muscle and joint problem is an ever-present concern in sports. It often results from repeated acute microtraumas and overuse. A prominent feature is the proliferation of connective tissue and tissue degeneration, which is distinct from acute inflammation. The primary cells in chronic inflammation are lymphocytes, plasma cells, and macrophages. It has been suggested that lymphocytes, although not normally phagocytic, may be used to stimulate fibroblasts to heal and form scar tissue. The role of plasma cells is not clearly understood, however. Macrophages, present in both acute and chronic inflammation, are definitely phagocytic and actively engaged in repair and healing.

Major chemicals found in chronic inflammation—although again, not fully understood—are the kinins (especially bradykinin), which produce the basic signs of inflammation, vasodilation, increased permeability, and pain. Prostaglandin, also seen in chronic conditions, does not produce pain but is a vasodilator and can be inhibited by aspirin.[3,12]

Chronic inflammation can stem from repeated acute microtraumas and overuse.

FRACTURE HEALING

Those concerned with sports must fully realize the potential seriousness of a bone fracture. Coaches often become impatient for the athlete with a fracture to return to competition and sometimes become unjust in their criticism of the physician for being conservative. *Time* is required for proper bone union to take place.

The osteoblast is the cellular component of bone and forms its matrix; the osteocyte both forms and destroys bone, while osteoclasts destroy and resorb bone. The constant ongoing remodeling of bone is caused by osteocytes, while osteoclasts are considered related mainly to pathological responses (Fig. 11-5). Osteoclasts come from the cambrium layer of the periosteum, which is the fibrous covering of the bone, and are involved in bone healing. The inner cambrium layer, in contrast to the highly vascular and dense external layer, is more cellular and less vascular. It serves as a foundation for blood vessels and provides a place for attaching muscles, tendons, and ligaments.

Figure 11-5

Bone is a complex organ in both growth and healing.

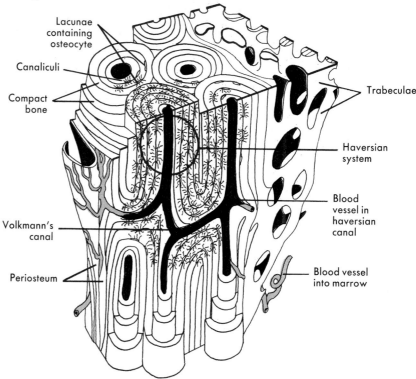

Like soft tissue injury healing, fracture healing involves a number of phases and can generally be divided into inflammatory, reparative, and remodeling phases.

Inflammatory Phase

Acute inflammation usually lasts about 4 days. When a bone fractures, there is trauma to the periosteum and surrounding soft tissue. With hemorrhaging, a hematoma accumulates in the medullary canal and surrounding soft tissue. The exposed ends of vascular channels become occluded with clotted blood accompanied by a dying back of the osteocytes, disrupting the intact blood supply. The dead bone and related soft tissue begin to elicit a typical inflammatory reaction, including vasodilation, plasma exudate, and inflammatory cells.

Reparative Phase

As with a soft tissue injury, the hematoma begins its organization in granulation tissue and gradually builds a fibrous junction between the fractured ends. At this time the environment is acid, but will slowly change to neutral or slightly alkaline. A major influx of capillary buds that carry endosteal cells from the bone's cambrium layer occurs. These cells first produce a fibrous callus, then cartilage, and finally a woven bone. It is important to note that when there is an environment of high oxygen tension, fibrous tissue will predominate, whereas when oxygen tension is low, cartilage develops. Bone will develop at the fracture site when oxygen tension and compression are in the proper amounts.

Soft and Hard Callus

The soft callus, in general, is an unorganized network of woven bone formed at the ends of the broken bone that is later absorbed and replaced by bone. At the soft callus stage, both internal and external calluses are produced that bring an influx of osteoblasts that begin to immobilize the fracture site. The internal and external calluses are formed by bone fragments that grow to bridge the fracture gap. The internal callus grows rapidly to create a rigid immobilization. Beginning in 3 to 4 weeks, and lasting 3 or 4 months, the hard callus forms. Hard callus is depicted by a gradual connecting of bone filament to the woven bone at the fractured ends. If there is less than satisfactory immobilization, a cartilagenous rather than bony union is produced.

Primary Bone Healing and Remodeling

With adequate immobilization and compression the bone ends become crossed with a new haversian system that will eventually lead to the laying down of primary bone. Remodeling occurs after the callus has been resorbed and trabecular bone is laid down along the lines of stress. It should be noted that complete remodeling may take many years. The influence of bioelectrical stimulation is the basis for development of new trabecular bone to be laid down at the point of greatest stress. This influence is predicated on the fact that bone is electropositive on its convex side and electronegative on its concave side. The convex is considered the tension side, while the con-

Fracture healing
  Inflammatory phase
    Trauma
    Hemorrhage
    Bone death
  Reparative phase
    Granulation
    Woven bone
    Soft callus
    Hard callus
  Remodeling phase
    Callus resorbed
    Trabecular bone
    Bone

cave is the compression side. Significantly, osteoclasts are drawn to a positive electrical charge and osteoblasts to a negative electrical charge. Remodeling is considered complete when a fractured bone has been restored to its former shape, or has developed a shape that can withstand imposed stresses.

Importance of Proper Fracture Care

In the treatment of fractures the bones must be immobilized completely until x-ray studies reveal that the hard callus has been formed. It is up to the physician to know the various types of fractures and the best form of immobilization for each specific fracture. During healing, fractures can keep an athlete out of participation in his or her particular sport for several weeks or months, depending on the nature, extent, and site of the fracture. During this period there are certain conditions that can seriously interfere with the healing process. Three such conditions are discussed below:

Conditions that interfere with fracture healing:
Poor blood supply
Poor immobilization
Infection

1. If there is a *poor blood supply to the fractured area* and one of the parts of the broken bone is not properly supplied by the blood, that part will die and union or healing of the fracture will not take place. This condition is known as aseptic necrosis and can often be seen in the head of the femur, the navicular bone in the wrist, the talus in the ankle, or isolated bone fragments. The condition is relatively rare among vital, healthy, young athletes, except in the navicular bone of the wrist.

2. *Poor immobilization of the fracture site* resulting from poor casting by the physician and permitting motion between the bone parts, may not only prevent proper union but may also, in the event that union does transpire, cause deformity to develop.

3. *Infection* can materially interfere with the normal healing process, particularly in the case of a compound fracture, which offers an ideal situation for development of a severe streptococcal or staphylococcal infection. The increased use of modern antibiotics has considerably reduced the prevalence of these infections coincidental with or immediately following a fracture. The closed fracture is not immune to contamination, of course, since infections within the body or a poor blood supply can render it quite susceptible. If the fracture site should become and remain infected, the infection could interfere with the proper union of the bone. The interposition of soft parts between the severed ends of the bone—such as muscle, connective tissue, or other soft tissue immediately adjacent to the fracture—can prevent proper bone union, often necessitating surgical cleansing of the area of such tissues by a surgeon.

PAIN PERCEPTION

It is important to consider pain when discussing tissue response to injury. It is often described subjectively as "burning, sharp, dull, crushing, or piercing." Chusid[7] describes a painful stimulus as causing only two sensations—sharp or dull pain. These can be further described as being fast or slow pain.

Deep structural pain is contrasted to superficial pain because of its poor localization.

The sensation of deep structural pain is contrasted to superficial pain because of its poor localization. Pain in the visceral structures is often associated with the autonomic system of sweating, blood pressure changes, and nausea. Deep visceral pain may also radiate to other body areas. If this occurs the pain becomes referred to a body structure that was developed from the same embryonic segment or dermatome as the structure in which the pain originated (dermatomal rule).[7]

A number of theories on how pain is produced and perceived by the brain have been advanced. Only in the last two decades has science demonstrated that pain is both a psychological and physiological phenomenon and is therefore unique to each individual. Sports activities demonstrate this fact clearly. Through conditioning, an athlete learns to endure the pain of rigorous activity and to block the sensations of a minor injury.

As understanding of pain increases, there is a growing distinction between chronic and acute pain. Acute pain protects the body against something harmful. On the other hand, chronic pain is a paradox that apparently serves no useful purpose. Bonica[2] indicates that acute pain is a disagreeable sensation and an emotional experience caused by tissue damage or a noxious stimulus. This noxious stimulus affects the high threshold nociceptors in skin, blood vessels, subcutaneous tissue, fascia, periosteum, viscera, and other pain-sensitive structures. Nociceptors act to convert a stimulus into impulses that travel via peripheral nerve fibers to the spinal cord and then to the brain to be perceived as pain. One concept is that nociceptors, when stimulated, transmit their impulses to the small-diameter A delta and C nerve fibers.[4]

Theories of Chronic Pain Control

Athletic training is concerned with basically healthy and physically active individuals; however, it still must address those musculoskeletal conditions that have become chronically painful. Currently there are a number of neurophysiological theories of controlling chronic pain through therapeutic means. Three of these are the "gate control" theory, control through a central biasing mechanism within the brain, and control through stimulating the endogenous, opiate-like endorphin substances produced by the pituitary gland. These theories must not be considered as discrete but as working in coordination with one another.

The Gate Theory

The gate theory, as developed by Melzack and Wall,[10] sets forth the idea that the spinal cord is organized in such a way that pain or other sensations may be experienced. An area located in the dorsal horn is thought to be able to cause an inhibition of pain impulses from ascending to the brain cortex for perception. The area, or "gate," within the dorsal horn is composed of T cells and the *substantia gelatinosa*. T cells are thought to be neurons that organize stimulus input and transmit the stimulus to the brain. The substantia gelatinosa is thought to function as a gate-control system. It determines the stimulus input sent to the T cells from peripheral nerves. If the stimulus from a noxious material exceeds a certain threshold, pain is experienced. It is thought that the smaller and slower nerve fibers carry pain impulses, whereas larger and faster nerve fibers carry other sensations. Impulses from the faster fibers arriving at the gate first inhibit pain impulses. In other words, stimulation of large, rapidly conducting fibers can selectively close the gate against the smaller pain fiber input. This concept explains why acupuncture, acupressure, cold, heat, and chemical skin irritation can provide some relief against pain. It also provides a rationale for the current success of transcutaneous electrical nerve stimulation (TENS) (see Chapter 14).

Central Biasing Mechanism

Another consideration in pain control is a central biasing mechanism located in the brainstem. Within the brainstem is the raphe magnus nucleus in which neurons respond maximally to a noxious pain stimulus.[13] It appears that by stimulating the raphe magnus nucleus a gate-type mechanism is produced. This nucleus is rich in enkephalin hormone, a morphinelike substance, and the neurotransmitter serotonin.[5]

Endogenous Opiates

In recent years specific opiate receptors have been found in the brain. Some of these opiates, such as etorphine, are 10,000 times as potent as morphine. Opiate receptors in the brain are found in the limbic system, spinoreticular tracts, thalamus, hypothalamus, and other pathways involved with pain reception. They are also found in the substantia gelatinosa and vagus nerve.[9]

Besides opioid receptors, morphinelike substances have been identified in the brain and brainstem. A general term, *endorphins*, is given to two enkephalins and beta-endorphin, which are polypeptides. Beta-endorphin is found in areas of the brain and periphery, while enkephalins have been found in the brainstem and pituitary gland. Beta-endorphin has been found to produce hypothermia and profound analgesia of the entire body.[9]

Releasing endorphin for the purpose of pain control has been attributed to low frequency, 1 to 3 cycles per second, high-voltage electrical stimulation analgesia.[13] This also indicates why electroacupuncture relieves pain at trigger point sites.

Figure 11-6

Some typical clinical presentations of referred somatic pain from organs with pathological conditions.

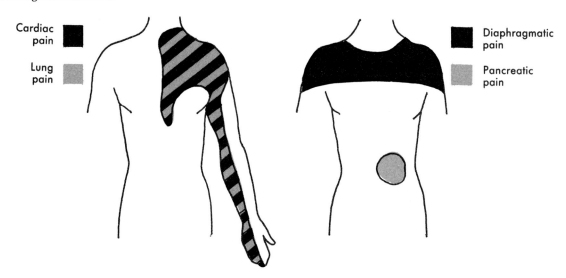

Cardiac pain

Lung pain

Diaphragmatic pain

Pancreatic pain

Referred Pain

One of the major areas of pain athletic trainers must be aware of is that produced from visceral injury. *Gray's Anatomy* states,

> Although most physiological impulses carried by visceral afferent fibers fail to reach consciousness, pathological conditions or excessive stimulation (e.g., trauma and inflammation) may bring into action those which carry pain. The central nervous system has a poorly developed power of localizing the source of such pain, and by some mechanism not clearly understood, the pain may be referred to the region supplied by the somatic afferent fibers whose central connections are the same as those of the visceral afferents.[8]

Visceral pain has a tendency to radiate and give rise to pain that becomes referred to the skin's surface.[4]

Figure 11-6, cont'd

Some typical clinical presentations of referred somatic pain from organs with pathological conditions.

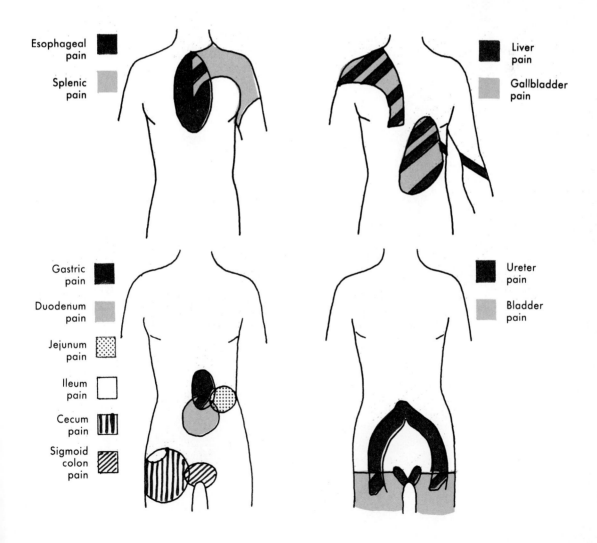

Esophageal pain
Splenic pain

Liver pain
Gallbladder pain

Gastric pain
Duodenum pain
Jejunum pain
Ileum pain
Cecum pain
Sigmoid colon pain

Ureter pain
Bladder pain

Psychological Aspects of Pain

Pain, especially chronic pain, is a subjective, psychological phenomenon. When painful injuries are treated, the total athlete must be considered, not just the pain or condition. Even in the most well adjusted person, pain will create emotional changes. Constant pain will often cause self-centeredness and an increased sense of dependency.

Athletes, like nonathletes, vary in their pain thresholds. Some can tolerate enormous pain, while others find mild pain almost unbearable. Pain appears to be worse at night because persons are alone and more aware of themselves, plus being devoid of external diversions.[11] Personality differences can also cause differences in pain toleration. For example, athletes who are anxious, dependent, and immature have less toleration for pain than those who are relaxed and emotionally in control.

Figure 11-6, cont'd

Some typical clinical presentations of referred somatic pain from organs with pathological conditions.

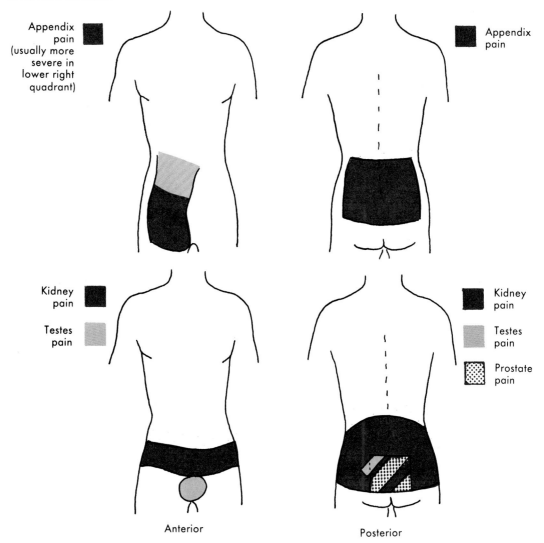

Appendix pain (usually more severe in lower right quadrant)

Appendix pain

Kidney pain

Testes pain

Kidney pain

Testes pain

Prostate pain

Anterior

Posterior

REFERENCES

1. Anderson, W.A.D., and Scotti, T.M.: Synopsis of pathology, St. Louis, 1980, The C.V. Mosby Co.
2. Bonica, J.J.: Pathophysiology in pain. In Current concepts of postoperative pain, New York, 1978, H.P. Publishing Co., Inc.
3. Bonta, I.L., and Parnham, M.J.: Prostaglandins and chronic inflammation, Biochem. Pharmacol. 27:1611, 1978.
4. Boyd, C.E.: Referred visceral pain in athletics, Ath. Train. 15:20, 1980.
5. Cailliet, R.: Soft tissue pain and disability, Philadelphia, 1977, F.A. Davis Co.
6. Casey, K.L.: Neural mechanism in pain and analgesia: an overview. In Beckman, A.L. (editor): The neural basis of behavior, New York, 1982, S.P. Medical and Scientific Books.
7. Chusid, J.G.: Correlative neuroanatomy and functional neurology, ed. 17, Los Altos, Calif., 1979, Lange Medical Publications.
8. Goss, C.M.: Gray's Anatomy of the human body, Philadelphia, 1973, Lea & Febiger.
9. Goth, A.: Medical pharmacology, ed. 10, St. Louis, 1981, The C.V. Mosby Co.
10. Melzack, R., and Wall, P.D.: Pain mechanisms: a new theory, Science 150:971, 1965.
11. Rusk, H.A.: Rehabilitation medicine, ed. 4, St. Louis, 1977, The C.V. Mosby Co.
12. Schachter, M.: Kallikreins (kininogenases)—a group of serine proteases with bioregulatory actions, Pharmacol. Rev. 31:1, 1979.
13. Stratton, S.A.: Role of endorphins in pain modulation, J. Orthop. Sports 3:200, 1982.
14. van der Meulen, J.C.H.: Present state of knowledge on processes of healing in collagen structures, J. Sports Med. (suppl. 1) 3:4, 1982.

ADDITIONAL SOURCES

Beresford, W.: The physiology of tissue injury and repair, NATA Annual Meeting and Clinical Symposium, 1980, Philadelphia, National Athletic Trainers Association. (Cassette.)

Cailliet, R.: Soft tissue pain and disability, Philadelphia, 1977, F.A. Davis Co.

Kalenak, A.: Wound healing, Thirty-fourth NATA Annual Meeting, Eastern Athletic Trainers Association, National Athletic Trainers Association. (Cassette.)

Pare, L.: Soft tissue evaluation—the Cyriax approach, Eastern Athletic Trainers Association Meeting, January, 1984, National Athletic Trainers Association. (Cassette.)

Spiker, J.C.: Implications of tissue injury repair in the rehabilitative process, NATA Annual Meeting and Clinical Symposium, 1980, Philadelphia, National Athletic Trainers Association. (Cassette.)

Zarins, B.: Soft tissue and repair—biomechanical aspects, Int. J. Sports Med. 3:9, 1982.

Chapter 12

EMERGENCY PROCEDURES IN SPORTS

When you finish this chapter, you should be able to

Assess vital signs of an injured athlete

Perform lifesaving emergency procedures

Carry out emergency procedures and first aid for musculoskeletal sports injuries

Demonstrate proper emergency procedures for environmental emergencies

Vital signs to watch for:
Pulse
Respiration
Temperature
Skin color
Pupils
State of consciousness
Movement
Abnormal nerve
  stimulation
Blood pressure

Most sports injuries do not result in life-or-death emergency situations, but when such situations do arise, prompt care is essential. Time becomes the critical factor, and assistance to the injured athlete must be based on knowledge of what to do and how to do it—how to carry out effective aid immediately. There is no room for uncertainty, indecision, or error. It is the responsibility of the individual preparing for a profession as an athletic trainer to be thoroughly conversant with the various aspects of emergency procedures. A positive approach to the situation must be used, reflecting an attitude of confidence, optimism, and reassurance to reduce the patient's anxiety.

The prime concern of emergency aid is to maintain cardiovascular function and, indirectly, central nervous system function, since failure of any or all of the systems leads to death. The key to emergency aid is the initial evaluation of the injured athlete. Time is of the essence, so this evaluation must be done rapidly and accurately so that proper aid can be rendered without delay. In some instances these first steps not only will be lifesaving but also may determine the degree and extent of residual disability. Promptness and accuracy, then, are the primary responsibilities.

RECOGNIZING VITAL SIGNS

The ability to recognize basic physiological signs of injury is essential to proper handling of critical injuries. When evaluating the seriously ill or injured athlete, the trainer or coach must be aware of nine response areas: heart rate, breathing rate, blood pressure, temperature, skin color, pupils of the eye, movement, the presence of pain, and unconsciousness.

Pulse

The pulse is the direct extension of the functioning heart. In emergency situations it is usually determined at the carotid artery at the neck or the radial artery in the wrist (Fig. 12-1). A normal pulse rate per minute for adults ranges between 60 and 80 beats and in children from 80 to 100 beats; however, it should be noted that trained athletes usually have slower pulses than the typical population.

An alteration of a pulse from the normal may indicate the presence of a pathological condition. For example, a *rapid but weak pulse* could mean shock, bleeding, diabetic coma, or heat exhaustion. A *rapid and strong pulse* may mean heatstroke or severe fright, and a *strong but slow pulse* could indicate a skull fracture or stroke, whereas *no pulse* means cardiac arrest or death.[7]

Respiration

The normal breathing rate per minute is approximately 12 breaths in adults and 20 to 25 breaths in children. Breathing may be shallow (indicating shock), irregular, or gasping (indicating cardiac involvement). Frothy blood from the mouth indicates a chest injury, such as a fractured rib, that has affected a lung. Listen for air passing in and out of the mouth or nose or both and ascertain whether the chest is rising or falling.

Temperature

Body temperature is maintained by water evaporation and heat radiation. It is normally 98.6° F (37° C). Temperature is measured with a thermometer, which is placed under the tongue, armpit, or, in case of unconsciousness, in the rectum. Changes in body temperature can be reflected in the skin. For example, a hot dry skin might indicate disease, infection, or overexposure to environmental heat. Cool, clammy skin could reflect trauma, shock, or heat exhaustion, whereas cool, dry skin is possibly the result of overexposure to cold.

A rise or fall of internal temperature may be caused by a variety of circumstances, such as the onset of a communicable disease, cold exposure, pain, fear, or nervousness. Characteristically with the lowered temperature there may be chills with chattering teeth, blue lips, goose bumps, and pale skin.

To convert Fahrenheit to centigrade (Celsius):
$$°C = (°F - 32) ÷ 1.8$$
To convert Celsius to Fahrenheit
$$°F = (1.8 × °C) + 32$$

A   **B**

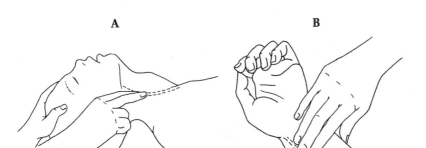

Figure 12-1

Pulse rate taken at the carotid artery (**A**) and radial artery (**B**).

Skin Color

For individuals who are lightly pigmented, the skin can be a good indicator of the state of health. In this instance, three colors are commonly identified in medical emergencies: red, white, and blue. A red skin color occurs from a lack of oxygen and may indicate heatstroke, diabetic coma, or high blood pressure. A pale, ashen, or white skin can mean insufficient circulation, shock, fright, hemorrhage, heat exhaustion, or insulin shock. Skin that is bluish in color (cyanotic), primarily noted in lips and fingernails, usually means that circulating blood is poorly oxygenated. This may indicate an airway obstruction or heart involvement.

Assessing a dark-skinned athlete is different from assessing a light-skinned athlete. These individuals normally have pink coloration of the nail beds, inside the lips, mouth, and tongue. When a dark-skinned person goes into shock, the skin around the mouth and nose will often have a grayish cast, while the tongue skin, inside the mouth, on the lips, and nail beds will have a bluish cast. Shock resulting from hemorrhage will cause the tongue and inside of the mouth to become a pale, grayish color instead of blue. Fever in these athletes can be noted by a red flush at the tips of the ears.[7]

Pupils

Some athletes normally have irregular and unequal pupils.

The pupils are extremely sensitive to situations affecting the nervous system. Although most persons have pupils of regular outline and of equal size, some individuals normally have pupils that may be irregular and unequal. This disparity requires the coach or athletic trainer to know which of their athletes deviate from the norm.

A constricted pupil may indicate that the athlete is using a central nervous system–depressant drug. If one or both pupils are dilated, the athlete may have sustained a head injury, may be experiencing shock, heatstroke, or hemorrhage, or may have ingested a stimulant drug (Fig. 12-2). The pupils' response to light should also be noted. If one or both pupils fail to accommodate to light, there may be brain injury or alcohol or drug poisoning. When examining an athlete's pupils, the athletic trainer should note the presence of contact lenses or an artificial eye.

State of Consciousness

When recognizing vital signs the examiner must always note the athlete's state of consciousness. Normally the athlete is alert, aware of the environment, and responds quickly to vocal stimulation. Head injury, heatstroke, and diabetic coma can vary an individual's level of conscious awareness (see pp. 285-287, Emergency evaluation of the unconscious athlete, including p. 286, Cerebral concussion).

Movement

The inability to move a body part can indicate a serious central nervous system injury that has involved the motor system. An inability to move one side of the body could be caused by a head injury or cerebrovascular accident (stroke). Paralysis of the upper limb may indicate a spinal injury; inability to move the lower extremities could mean an injury below the

Figure 12-2

The pupils of the eye are extremely sensitive to situations affecting the nervous system. **A,** Normal pupils. **B,** Dilated pupils. **C,** Irregular pupils.

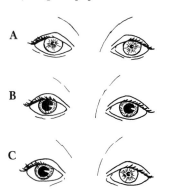

neck, and pressure on the spinal cord could lead to limited use of the limbs.[7,17]

Abnormal Nerve Stimulation

The injured athlete's pain or other reactions to adverse stimuli can provide valuable clues to the coach or trainer. Numbness or tingling in a limb with or without movement can indicate nerve or cold damage. Blocking of a main artery can produce severe pain, loss of sensation, or lack of a pulse in a limb. A complete lack of pain or awareness of serious but obvious injury may be caused by shock, hysteria, drug usage, or a spinal cord injury. Generalized or localized pain in the injured region probably means there is no injury to the spinal cord.[5]

Blood Pressure

Blood pressure, as measured by the sphygmomanometer, indicates the amount of force that is produced against the arterial walls. It is indicated at two pressure levels: systolic and diastolic. Systolic pressure occurs when the heart pumps blood, while diastolic pressure is the residual pressure present in the arteries when the heart is between beats. The normal systolic pressure for 15- to 20-year-old males ranges from 115 to 120 mm Hg. The diastolic pressure, on the other hand, usually ranges from 75 to 80 mm Hg. The normal blood pressure of females is usually 8 to 10 mm Hg lower than in males for both systolic and diastolic pressures. At the age of 15 to 20, a systolic pressure of 135 mm Hg and above may be excessive; also, 110 mm Hg and below may be considered too low. The outer ranges for diastolic pressure should not exceed 60 and 85 mm Hg, respectively. A lowered blood pressure could indicate hemorrhage, shock, heart attack, or internal organ injury.

EMERGENCY EVALUATION OF THE CONSCIOUS ATHLETE

There are two major considerations in emergency evaluation: first, control of life-threatening conditions and, second, management of non-life-threatening injuries.
1. Primary emergency evaluation
   a. Check for abnormal or arrested breathing
   b. Check for abnormal or arrested pulse
   c. Check for external bleeding
   d. Check for shock
2. Secondary emergency evaluation
   a. Check for head injury
   b. Check for spinal injury
   c. Check for dislocation and function
   d. Check for skin wounds

EMERGENCY EVALUATION OF THE UNCONSCIOUS ATHLETE

The state of unconsciousness provides one of the greatest dilemmas in sports. Whether it is advisable to move the athlete and allow the game to resume or to await the arrival of a physician is a question that too often is

TABLE 12-1

Evaluating the unconscious athlete

Functional Signs			Selected Conditions				
	Fainting	Concussion	Grand Mal Epilepsy	Brain Compression and Injury	Sunstroke	Diabetic Coma	Shock
Onset	Usually sudden	Usually sudden	Sudden	Usually gradual	Gradual or sudden	Gradual	Gradual
Mental	Complete unconsciousness	Confusion or unconsciousness	Unconsciousness	Unconsciousness gradually deepening	Delirium or unconsciousness	Drowsiness, later unconsciousness	Listlessness, later unconsciousness
Pulse	Feeble and fast	Feeble and irregular	Fast	Gradually slower	Fast and feeble	Fast and feeble	Fast and very feeble
Respiration	Quick and shallow	Shallow and irregular	Noisy, later deep and slow	Slow and noisy	Difficult	Deep and sighing	Rapid and shallow with occasional deep sigh
Skin	Pale, cold and clammy	Pale and cold	Livid, later pale	Hot and flushed	Very hot and dry	Livid, later pale	Pale, cold, and clammy
Pupils	Equal and dilated	Equal	Equal and dilated	Unequal	Equal	Equal	Equal and dilated
Paralysis	None	None	None	May be present in leg and/or arm	None	None	None
Convulsions	None	None	None	Present in some cases	Present in some cases	None	None
Breath	N/A	N/A	N/A	N/A	N/A	Acetone smell	N/A
Special features	Giddiness and sway before collapse	Signs of head injury, vomiting on recovery	Bites tongue, voids urine and feces, may injure self on falling	Signs of head injury, delayed onset of symptoms	Vomiting in some cases	In early stages, headache, restlessness, and nausea	May vomit; early stages: shivering, thirst, defective vision, and ear noises

Modified from International medical guide for ships, World Health Organization, Geneva, Switzerland.

resolved hastily and without much forethought. Unconsciousness may be defined as a state of insensibility in which there is a lack of conscious awareness. This condition can be brought about by a blow to either the head or the solar plexus, or it may result from general shock. It is often difficult to determine the exact cause of unconsciousness.

To recognize and evaluate the injury sustained by an unconscious athlete, use the following procedures:

1. Understand the sequence of the accident, either by having witnessed the event or by questioning other players and spectators.
2. After learning how the accident occurred, decide what part of the body was most affected. Often no one is fully aware of just when or how the athlete was hurt. The position or attitude in which the athlete was found may therefore present an important key as to how the injury took place. It is a normal reaction for a person to pull away from an injuring force and to grasp at the painful area.
3. Do not move the unconscious athlete from the position found until a thorough examination has been made.
4. Make the examination as follows:
   a. First, check the carotid pulse for a heartbeat and then determine whether the athlete is breathing normally. If breathing is impaired, clear airway and proceed to give mouth-to-mouth resuscitation. If a carotid pulse is not detected, closed heart massage should be initiated.
   b. Start with the head and determine first whether there is bleeding or whether there is a straw-colored fluid coming from the nose, eyes, ears, or mouth. Look for bumps, lacerations, or deformities that may indicate a possible concussion or skull fracture.
   c. Check for shock.
   d. Moving down the body, check each part for deformities and, where possible, make a bilateral comparison. Palpate for abnormal movements and uneven surfaces.

Ideally the athlete should be fully conscious before one attempts removal from the field, so that the athlete can be questioned about where the pain is and can be asked to move fingers or toes to determine possible spinal fracture or paralysis (see Table 12-1). Placing ammonia under the nose of the injured athlete will often cause arousal; however, ammonia should *not* be used on an unconscious athlete, since it tends to elicit a jerk reflex: if, for example, a cervical spine injury is present, such action could result in greater injury. Not until the trainer is completely satisfied that no serious injury is present should the athlete be moved. To avoid possible aggravation of an injury, transportation of the injured person from the playing field must be directed by the physician. When such transportation is necessary, it should always be carried out in the manner used for moving a person with a fractured spine (see pp. 299-300).

Avoid placing ammonia under the nose of an unconscious athlete.

The First Steps of CPR

Establish unresponsiveness of the athlete by tapping or gently shaking him or her and shouting, "Are you okay?" If there is no response, call out for help, position the athlete for assistance, and then proceed with the ABCs of cardiopulmonary resuscitation (CPR).[16]

The ABC Steps of CPR

The ABC mnemonic is easily remembered and indicates the sequential steps utilized for basic life support:

A Airway opened

B Breathing restored

C Circulation restored

Frequently, when A is restored, B and C will resume spontaneously, and it is then unnecessary to carry them out. In some instances, the restoration of A and B obviates the necessity for step C. If the athlete is in a position other than supine, he or she must be carefully rolled over as a unit, avoiding any twisting of the body, since CPR can be administered only with the athlete lying flat on the back with knees straight or slightly flexed (see p. 299). When performing CPR, the following prescribed sequence *must be adhered to precisely:*

Airway opened

1. *note:* A face mask may have to be cut away before CPR can be rendered (Fig. 12-3). Open the airway by using the head-tilt method. Lift neck with one hand while pushing down on victim's forehead with the other, avoiding the use of excessive force. The tongue is the most common cause of respiratory obstruction; the forward movement of the jaw raises the tongue away from the back of the throat, thus clearing the airway. *note:* In suspected head or neck injuries do not tilt the head back. Displace the jaw only, keeping the head in a fixed neutral position.

2. In an unconscious individual, since the tongue often acts as an impediment to respiration by blocking the airway, it may be necessary to use

Figure 12-3

A face mask may have to be removed before CPR can be rendered.

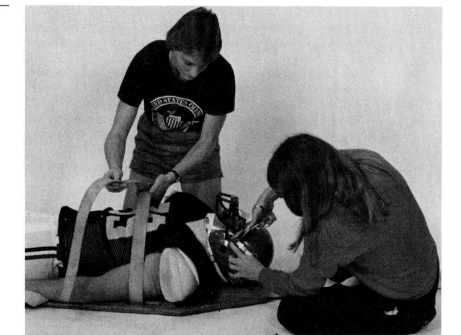

the head tilt–chin lift maneuver if the head tilt–neck lift maneuver is not effective. Lift the chin by placing the fingers of one hand under the lower jaw near the chin, lifting and bringing it forward and thus supporting the jaw and lifting the tongue. Avoid compressing the soft tissue under the jaw, since this could obstruct the airway. Avoid completely closing the mouth. The teeth should be slightly apart. Look to see if the chest rises and falls. Listen for air passing in or out of the nose or mouth. Feel on the cheek whether air is being expelled.

3. If neither of the foregoing is sufficiently effective, additional forward displacement of the jaw can be effected by grasping each side of the lower jaw at the angles, thus displacing the lower mandible forward as the head is tilted backward. In executing this maneuver, both elbows should rest on the same surface as that upon which the victim is lying. Should the lips close, they can be opened by retracting the lower lip with a thumb. In sus-

Figure 12-4

Life Support Decision Tree (unwitnessed arrest).
Reprinted with permission.
© American Heart Association.

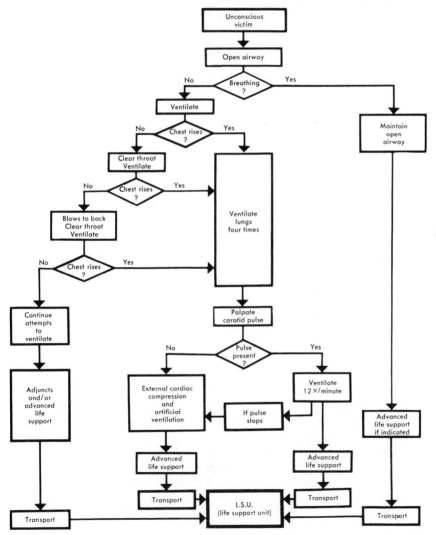

Foundations of Injury

pected neck injuries this is the maneuver that should be used, since it can be performed effectively without extending the cervical spine.

4. If necessary, clear the mouth of any foreign objects, such as vomitus, mouthpiece, dentures, or dislodged bridgework, but do not waste a great deal of time.

5. If opening the athlete's airway does not cause spontaneous breathing, proceed to step B.

BREATHING RESTORED

1. With the hand that is on the athlete's forehead, pinch the nose shut, keeping the heel of the hand in place in order to hold the head back (if there is no neck injury) (Fig. 12-5). Taking a deep breath, place your mouth over the athlete's mouth, to provide an airtight seal, and blow until you see the chest rise. Remove your mouth and listen for the air to escape through passive exhalation.

2. Should the athlete still not be breathing, give 4 quick breaths, then check the carotid artery for pulse. If pulse is present, continue rescue breathing at the rate of 12 times a minute (every 5 seconds). Recheck for continued pulse presence after each series of 12 ventilations, or after 1 minute, when a single operator is functioning.

3. If no pulse is evident, then artificial circulation must be provided through cardiac compression coupled with the rescue breathing (step C).

Figure 12-5

The procedure for conducting mouth-to-mouth resuscitation requires pinching the nose shut (A), moving the head back (if there is no neck injury) (B), and after taking a deep breath, (C), placing the mouth over the victim's mouth, thereby forming an air-tight seal and blowing until the chest rises.

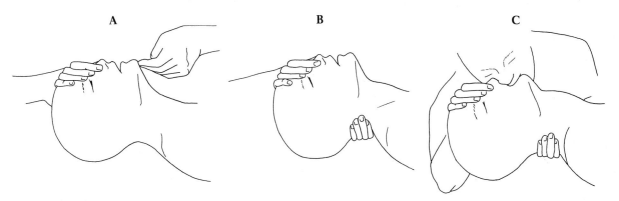

A   B   C

Figure 12-6

With the middle and index fingers of the hand closest to the waist, the lower margin of the victim's rib cage is located. The fingers are then run along the rib cage to the notch where the ribs meet the sternum. The middle finger is placed on the notch with the index finger next to it on the lower end of the sternum.

CIRCULATION RESTORED

1. Position self close to the side of the athlete's chest. With the middle and index fingers of the hand closest to the waist, locate the lower margin of the athlete's rib cage on the side next to you (Fig. 12-6).

2. Run the fingers up along the rib cage to the notch where the ribs meet the sternum.

3. Place the middle finger on the notch and the index finger next to it on the lower end of the sternum.

4. Next, the hand closest to the athlete's head is positioned on the lower half of the sternum next to the index finger of the first hand that located the notch; then the heel of that hand is placed on the long axis of the breast bone.

5. The first hand is then removed from the notch and placed on the top of the hand on the sternum so that the heels of both hands are parallel and the fingers are directed straight away from the coach or trainer (Fig. 12-7).

6. Fingers can be extended or interlaced, but they must be kept *off* of the chest.

7. Elbows are kept in a locked position with arms straight and shoulders positioned over the hands, enabling the thrust to be straight down.

8. In a normal-sized adult, enough force must be applied to depress the sternum 1½ to 2 inches (4 to 5 cm). After depression, there must be a complete release of the sternum to allow the heart to refill. The time of release should equal the time of compression. For the single operator compression must be given at the rate of 80 times per minute, maintaining a rate of 15 chest compressions to 2 quick breaths, thus alternating B and C.

9. When two rescuers are available, they are positioned at the side of

Figure 12-7

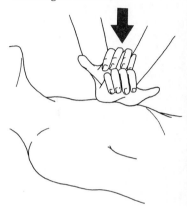

The heel of the headward hand is placed on the long axis of the lower half of the sternum next to the index finger of the first hand. The first hand is removed from the notch and placed on top of the hand on the sternum with fingers interlaced.

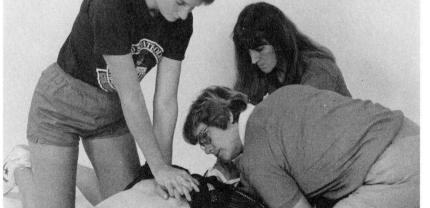

Figure 12-8

Cardiac compression, using two rescuers, interposes one breath for every five chest compressions. Third person in photo is an instructor and observer.

the athlete (Fig. 12-8). The one providing the breathing does so by interposing a breath after every 5 chest compressions, which are being administered by the other rescuer at the rate of 60 compressions per minute. The carotid pulse must be checked frequently by the ventilator during chest compression to ascertain the effectiveness of the compression. Ventilation and compression should be interrupted every 4 to 5 minutes of ventilation to determine whether spontaneous breathing and pulse have occurred. *Never interrupt CPR for more than 5 seconds.* Adequate circulation must be maintained. Any interruption in compression permits the blood flow to drop to zero.[1]

Number of Rescuers	Ratio of Compressions to Breaths	Rate of Compressions
1	15:2	80 times/min
2	5:1	60 times/min

Every trainer should be certified in CPR and should take a refresher examination at least once a year. It is wise to have all training assistants certified as well.

The Endotracheal Airway

There are a number of airways on the market; the approved Safar or S airway is very popular. It overcomes the distasteful features of direct mouth-to-mouth resuscitation and makes resuscitation easier and more effective. Use of the endotracheal airway should be reserved for the specialist in emergency aid because of the dangers inherent in the process; improper introduction of the device can injure soft tissues of the throat or push foreign objects farther down the throat.[10] The following steps should be taken in the use of the S airway[10]:

1. Remove obstructions, if any.
2. Place athlete on back.
3. Operator takes a position behind the athlete's head.

The endotracheal airway should be used *only* by the specialist in emergency aid.

Figure 12-9

The use of the endotracheal airway should be reserved for the specialist in emergency aid. **A,** With the curve of the airway away from the operator, it is inserted over the athlete's tongue. **B,** Once the airway is inserted properly, the operator blows a deep breath into the mouthpiece.

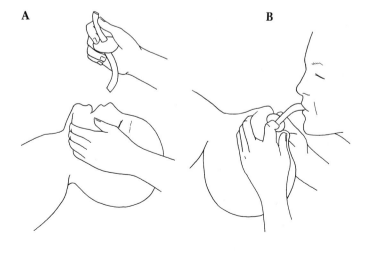

A   B

4. Athlete's head is tilted back.
5. With the curve of the airway away from the operator, it is inserted over the athlete's tongue (Fig. 12-9).
6. If insertion is impossible because of a tightly closed jaw, it must be forced open by inserting the index finger between the cheek and teeth just behind the wisdom teeth.
7. To avoid pushing the tongue into the athlete's throat, it may have to be held down by the operator's fingers.
8. The athlete's chin is then held forward while the head is tilted back.
9. The athlete's nose is pinched together with both thumbs while both the index fingers press down on the airway's lip flange to prevent leaking of air.
10. The operator then blows a deep breath into the mouthpiece.
11. Following the movement of the athlete's chest, indicating air ventilation, the operator removes the tube from the mouth, allowing the athlete to exhale air.
12. Air should be blown into the athlete deeply and fast for the first 3 or 4 breaths; then a breath is administered every 4 to 5 seconds.

Obstructed Airway Management

Death by choking on foreign objects claims close to 3000 lives every year. Choking is a possibility in many sports activities; for example, an athlete may choke on a mouth guard, a broken bit of dental work, chewing gum, or even a "chaw" of tobacco. When such emergencies arise, early recognition and prompt, knowledgeable action are necessary to avert a tragedy. An unconscious person can choke also—the tongue may fall back into the pharynx, thus blocking the upper airway. In sports, blood clots resulting from head, facial, or dental injuries may provide an impediment to normal breathing, as may vomiting. When complete airway obstruction occurs, the individual is unable to speak, cough, or breathe. If the athlete is conscious, there is a tremendous effort made to breathe, the head is forced back, and the face initially is congested and then becomes cyanotic as oxygen deprivation is incurred. If partial airway obstruction is causing the choking, some air passage can be detected, but in a complete obstruction no air movement is discernible.[15]

To relieve airway obstruction caused by foreign bodies, three maneuvers are recommended: (1) blows to the back, (2) manual thrusts (Heimlich maneuver), and (3) finger sweeps of the mouth and throat.

1. *Blows to the back* Four rapid, sharp blows are administered in succession with the heel of the hand directly over the spine between the shoulders; they can be given with the athlete standing, sitting, or lying down. The other hand should be placed on the athlete's chest for stabilization. In standing or sitting, the athlete's head should be lower than the chest as the blows are applied. If lying down, the athlete should be rolled over on the side with the face toward the trainer, chest firmly against the trainer's thigh, and the blows should be forcefully delivered in series of four and should be repeated a number of times.[1]

2. *Manual thrusts (Heimlich maneuver)* There are two methods of us-

ing the Heimlich maneuver, depending on whether the victim is in an erect position or has collapsed and is either unconscious or too heavy to lift.

Method A Stand behind the athlete. Place both arms around the waist just above the belt line, and permit the athlete's head, arms, and upper trunk to hang forward (Fig. 12-10, *A*). Grasp one fist with the other, placing the thumb side of the grasped fist immediately below the xiphoid process of the sternum, clear of the rib cage. Now sharply and forcefully pull the fists into the abdomen several times. This "hug" pushes up on the diaphragm, compressing the air in the lungs and creating forceful pressure against the blockage, thus usually causing it to be promptly expelled. Repeat the maneuver four times in each series.

Method B If the athlete is on the ground or on the floor, lay him or her on the back and straddle the hips, keeping your weight fairly centered over your knees. Place the heel of your left hand against the back of your right hand and push sharply into the abdomen just above the belt line (Fig. 12-10, *B*). Repeat as many times as needed to expel the blockage. Care must be taken in either of these methods to avoid extreme force or applying force over the rib cage because fractures of the ribs and damage to the organs can result.

A combination of these two techniques—alternating the back blows with the four manual thrusts until the object is expelled—is probably most effective.

3. *Finger sweeping* If a foreign object such as a mouth guard is lodged in the mouth or the throat and is visible, it may be possible to remove or release it with the fingers. Care must be taken that the probing does not drive the object deeper into the throat. It is usually impossible to open the mouth of a conscious victim who is in distress, so the previously described techniques should be immediately put into use. In the unconscious athlete, turn the head either to the side or face up, open the mouth by grasping the tongue and the lower jaw, holding them firmly between the thumb and

Figure 12-10

The Heimlich maneuver for an obstructed airway.
A, Standing. **B,** Reclining.

A

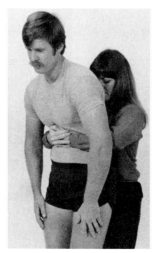

B

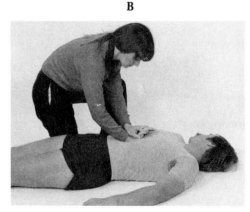

fingers and lifting—an action that pulls the tongue away from the back of the throat and from the impediment. If this is difficult to do, the crossed finger method can usually be employed effectively. The index finger of the free hand (or, if both hands are employed, an assistant can probe) should be inserted to one side of the mouth along the cheek deeply into the throat; using a hooking maneuver, free the impediment, moving it into a position from which it can be removed (Fig. 12-11).

EMERGENCY CARE OF MUSCULOSKELETAL INJURIES

Because musculoskeletal injuries are extremely common in sports, a knowledge of their immediate care is necessary. Three areas of first aid are highly important: (1) control of hemorrhage, management of early inflammation, muscle spasm, and pain; (2) splinting; and (3) handling and transportation.

Hemorrhage, Inflammation, Muscle Spasm, and Pain Management

Of major importance in musculoskeletal injuries is the initial control of hemorrhage, early inflammation, muscle spasm, and pain. The acronym for this process is ICE (ice, compression, and elevation). Added to this is the important factor of rest.

Ice, Compression, Elevation, and Rest (ICE-R)

Ice (cold application)   Cold, primarily ice in various forms, has been found to be an effective first aid agent. As a vasoconstrictor, cold applied for 5 to 10 minutes decreases the swelling that usually occurs for 4 to 6 hours following injury. It also minimizes pain and muscle spasm. Cold makes blood more viscous, lessens capillary permeability, and decreases the blood flow to the injured area.[11] Cold applied to a recent injury will lower metabolism and the tissue demands for oxygen and reduce hypoxia. This benefit extends to uninjured tissue, preventing injury-related tissue death from spreading to adjacent normal cellular structures.[11] It should be noted however, that prolonged application of cold can cause tissue damage.

For best results, ice packs (crushed ice and towel) should be applied directly to the skin. Frozen gel packs should not be used directly against the skin, because they reach much lower temperatures than ice packs. A good rule of thumb is to apply a cold pack to a recent injury for a 20-minute period and repeat every 1 to 1½ hours throughout the waking day. Depending on the severity and site of the injury, cold may be applied

ICE-R (ice, compression, elevation, and rest) are essential in the emergency care of musculoskeletal injuries.

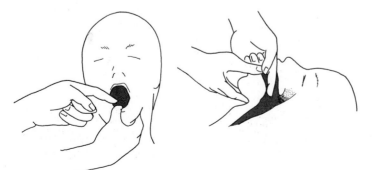

Figure 12-11

Finger sweeping of the mouth is essential in attempting to remove a foreign object from a choking victim.

Foundations of Injury

intermittently for 1 to 72 hours. For example, a mild strain will probably require one or two 20-minute periods of cold application, while a severe knee or ankle sprain might need 3 days of intermittent cold.

Compression   Immediate compression of an acute injury is considered an important adjunct to cold and elevation, and in some cases may be superior to them. Placing external pressure on an injury assists decreasing hemorrhage and hematoma formation. Fluid seepage into interstitial spaces is retarded by compression, and absorption is facilitated.

Figure 12-12

A horseshoe-shaped pad can be placed around the maleolus to reduce edema.

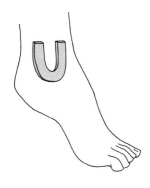

Many types of compression are available to the coach or trainer. An elastic wrap that has been soaked in water and frozen in a refrigerator can provide both compression and cold when applied to a recent injury. Pads can be cut from felt or foam rubber to fit difficult-to-compress body areas. A horseshoe-shaped pad, for example, placed around the malleolus in combination with an elastic wrap and tape, provides an excellent way to prevent or reduce ankle edema (Fig. 12-12). Although cold is applied intermittently, compression should be maintained throughout the day. At night, rather than removing the wrap completely, it should be loosened to avoid the pooling of fluids when the body processes slow down.

Elevation   Along with cold and compression, elevation reduces internal bleeding. By elevating the affected part above the level of the heart, bleeding is reduced and venous return is encouraged, further reducing swelling.

Rest   Rest is essential for musculoskeletal injuries. This can be achieved by not moving the part or can be guaranteed by the application of tape, wraps, splints, casts, and the assistance of a cane or crutches (see p. 388). Immobilization of an injury for the first 2 or 3 days after injury helps to ensure healing of the wound without complication. Too early movement will only increase hemorrhage and the extent of disability, prolonging recovery.

An ICE-R schedule

1. Evaluate the extent of injury.
2. Apply crushed ice pack on the injury.
3. Hold ice pack firmly to the injury site with an elastic wrap.
4. Elevate injured part above the level of the heart.
5. After 20 minutes, remove ice pack.
6. Replace ice pack with a compress wrap and pad.
7. Elevate injured part.
8. Reapply ice pack in 1 to 1½ hours and, depending on degree of injury, continue this rotation until injury resolution has taken place and healing has begun.
9. In a second or third degree injury, on retiring, wear a compress bandage and pad that is applied looser than during the day.
10. If possible, elevate injured part above the heart.
11. The next day the injury is again elevated.
12. With second or third degree injury, continue this same process for 2 or 3 days.

Emergency Splinting

Any suspected fracture should always be splinted before the athlete is moved.

Any suspected fracture should always be splinted before the athlete is moved. Transporting a person with a fracture without proper immobilization can result in increased tissue damage, hemorrhage, and shock. Conceivably a mishandled fracture could cause death. Therefore, a thorough knowledge of splinting techniques is important (Fig. 12-13).

The application of splints should be a simple process through the use of emergency splints. In most instances the trainer does not have to improvise a splint, since such devices are readily available in most sports settings. The use of padded boards is recommended. They are easily available, can be considered disposable, and are easy to apply. Commercially sold basswood splints are excellent, as are disposable cardboard and clear plastic commercial splints. The clear plastic splint is inflated with air around the affected part and can be used for extremity splinting, but its use requires some special training (Fig. 12-14). This provides support and moderate pressure to the part and affords a clear view of the site for x-ray examination. For fractures of the femur the half-ring type of traction splint offers the best support and immobilization (Fig. 12-15). Whatever the material used, the principles of good splinting remain the same.

Figure 12-13

Any suspected fracture should routinely be splinted.

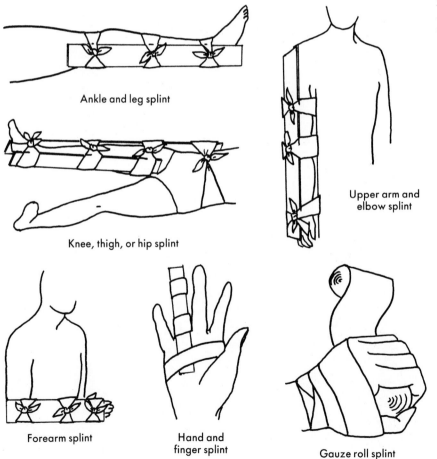

Ankle and leg splint

Knee, thigh, or hip splint

Upper arm and elbow splint

Forearm splint

Hand and finger splint

Gauze roll splint

Splinting of Lower Limb Fractures

Fractures of the ankle or leg require immobilization of the foot and knee. Any fracture involving the knee, thigh, or hip needs splinting of all the lower limb joints and one side of the trunk.

Splinting of Upper Limb Fractures

Fractures about the shoulder complex are immobilized by a sling and swathe bandages, with the upper limb bound to the body securely. Upper arm and elbow fractures must be splinted with immobilization effected in a straight arm position to lessen bone override. Lower arm and wrist fractures should be splinted in a position of forearm flexion, supported by a sling. Hand and finger dislocations and fractures should be splinted with tongue depressors or gauze rolls.

Figure 12-14

The air splint provides excellent support as well as a clear site for x-ray examination.

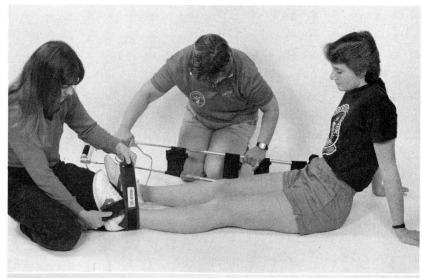

Figure 12-15

Application of a half-ring traction splint for a fracture of the femur.

Splinting of the Spine and Pelvis

Injuries involving a possible spine or pelvic fracture are best splinted and moved using a spine board (Figs. 12-16 and 12-17). When such injuries are suspected *the trainer should not, under any circumstances, move the injured athlete except under the express direction of a physician.*

Handling the Injured Athlete

Moving, lifting, and transporting the injured athlete must be executed so as to prevent further injury. Emergency aid authorities have suggested that improper handling causes more additional insult to injuries than any other emergency procedure.[7,10,15] There is no excuse for poor handling of the injured athlete.

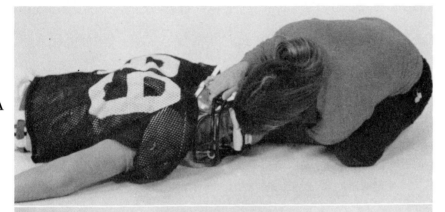

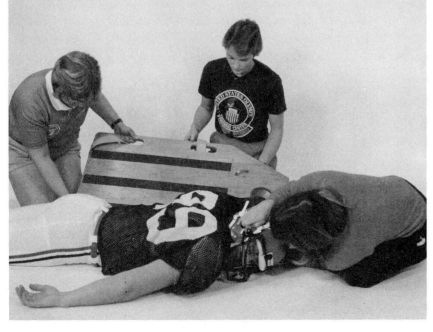

Figure 12-16

A, When moving an unconscious athlete, first establish whether the athlete is breathing and has a pulse. *An unconscious athlete must always be treated as having a serious neck injury.* If lying prone, the athlete must be turned over for CPR or to be secured to a spine board for possible cervical fracture. All of the athlete's extremities are placed in axial alignment with one trainer stabilizing the athlete's neck and head. **B,** The spine board is next placed as close to the athlete as possible.

Continued.

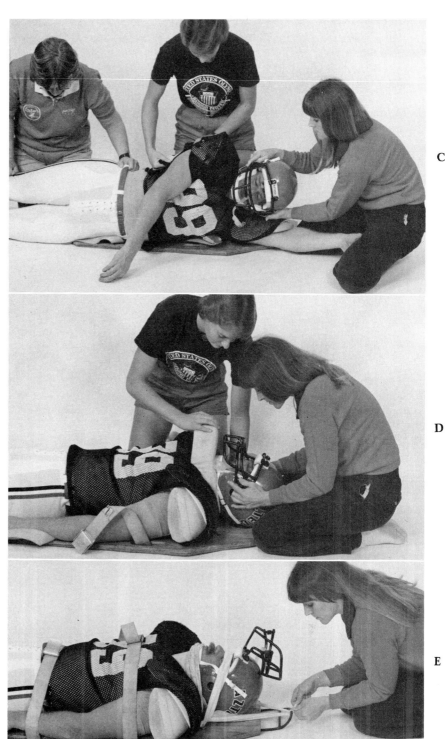

Figure 12-16, cont'd

C, Each assistant is responsible for one of the athlete's segments. When the trainer (captain) gives the command "roll," the athlete is moved as a unit onto the spine board. **D,** At all times, the captain continues to stabilize the athlete's neck. **E,** The head and neck are next stabilized onto the spine board by means of a chin strap secured to metal loops, and finally the trunk and lower limbs are secured to the spine board by straps.

Moving the Injured Athlete

It is very important that an unconscious athlete or one believed to have a spinal fracture be moved like a "log." The athlete who is unconscious and unable to describe the injury in terms of sensation and site *must be treated as having a cervical fracture.*

Suspected spinal injury   Suspected spinal injury requires extremely careful handling and is best left to ambulance attendants or paramedics who are more skilled and have the proper equipment for such transport. If such personnel are not available, moving should be done under the express direction of a medical doctor and using a spine board (see Fig. 12-16, *A-E*). One danger inherent in moving an athlete with a suspected spinal injury, and in particular a cervical injury, is the tendency of the neck and head to turn because of the victim's inability to control his or her movements. Torque so induced creates considerable possibility of spinal cord or root damage when small fractures are present. The most important principle in transporting an individual on a spine board is to keep the head and neck in alignment with the long axis of the body. In such cases it would be well to have one individual whose sole responsibility would be to ensure and maintain proper positioning of the head and neck.

Suspected severe neck injury   Once an injury to the neck has been recognized as severe, a physician and an ambulance should be summoned immediately. Primary emergency care involves maintaining normal breathing, treating for shock, and keeping the athlete quiet and in the position found until medical assistance arrives. Not until the physician has examined the athlete and given permission should transportation be

An unconscious athlete must be treated as having a cervical fracture.

Figure 12-17

An alternate method of placing the athlete on a spine board is the straddle slide method.

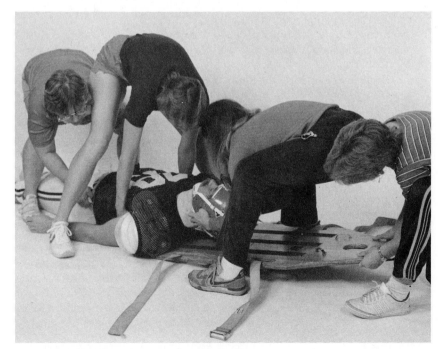

attempted. The athlete should be transported while lying on the back with the curve of the neck supported by a rolled up towel or pad or encased in a stabilization collar. Neck stabilization must be maintained throughout transportation, first to the ambulance and then to the hospital, and throughout the hospital procedure. If stabilization is not continued, additional cord damage and paralysis may ensue.

Steps in moving an unconscious athlete[4]:

1. Establish whether the athlete is breathing and has a pulse.
2. Plan to move the athlete on a spine board.
3. If the athlete is lying prone, he or she must be turned over for CPR or to be secured to the spine board. *An unconscious athlete or one with a possible cervical fracture is transported face up. An athlete with a spinal fracture other than cervical is transported face down.*
    a. Place all extremities in an axial alignment (Fig. 12-16, *A*).
    b. To roll the athlete over requires four or five persons with the "captain" of the team protecting the athlete's head and neck. The neck must be stabilized and not moved from its original position no matter how distorted it may appear.
    c. The spine board is placed close to the side of the athlete (Fig. 12-16, *B*).
    d. Each assistant is responsible for one of the athlete's body segments. One assistant is responsible for turning the trunk, another the hips, another the thighs, and the last the lower legs.
4. With the spine board close to the athlete's side, the captain gives the command to roll him or her on the board as one unit (Fig. 12-16, *C*).
5. On the board, the athlete's head and neck continue to be stabilized by the captain (Fig. 12-16, *D*).
6. If the athlete is a football player, the helmet is *not* removed; however, the face guard is removed for possible CPR.
7. The head and neck are next stabilized on the spine board by a chin strap secured to metal loops. Finally, the trunk and lower limbs are secured to the spine board by straps (Fig. 12-16, *E*).

An alternate method of moving the athlete onto a spine board, if he or she is face up, is the *straddle slide method.* Five persons are used—a "captain" stationed at the athlete's head and three or four assistants. One assistant is in charge of lifting the athlete's trunk, one the hips, and one the legs. On the command "lift" by the captain, the athlete is lifted while the fourth assistant slides a spine board under the athlete between the feet of the captain and assistants (Fig. 12-17).

Transporting the Injured Athlete

Improper transportation procedures often cause additional insult to athletic injuries.

As with moving, transporting the injured athlete must be executed so as to prevent further injury. There is no excuse for the use of poor transportation techniques in sports. Planning should take into consideration all the possible transportation methods and the necessary equipment to execute them. Capable persons, stretchers, and even an ambulance may be indicated to carry out the transportation of the injured athlete. Four modes of assisting in travel are used: ambulatory aid, manual conveyance, stretcher carrying, and vehicular transfer.

Ambulatory aid   Ambulatory aid (Fig. 12-18) is that support or assistance given to an injured athlete who is able to walk. Before the athlete is allowed to walk, there should be careful scrutiny by the trainer or coach to make sure that the injuries are minor. Whenever serious injuries are suspected, walking should be prohibited. Complete support should be given on both sides of the athlete. The athlete's arms are draped over the assistants' shoulders and their arms encircle his or her back.

Manual conveyance   Manual conveyance (Fig. 12-19) may be used to move a mildly injured individual a greater distance than could be walked with ease. As with the use of ambulatory aid, any decision to carry the athlete must be made only after a complete examination to determine the existence of potentially serious conditions. The most convenient carry is done by two assistants, with one standing behind the seated athlete and grasping the athlete around the chest, while the other, standing in front and with the back to the athlete, grasps the athlete's legs.

Stretcher carrying   Whenever a serious injury is suspected, the best and safest mode of transportation for a short distance is by stretcher. With each segment of the body supported, the athlete is gently lifted and placed on the stretcher, which is carried adequately by four assistants, two supporting the ends of the stretcher and two supporting either side (Fig. 12-20). It should be noted that any person with an injury serious enough to require the use of a stretcher must be examined by a physician before being moved.

Figure 12-18

Figure 12-19

Figure 12-18

The ambulatory aid method of transporting a mildly injured athlete.

Figure 12-19

Manual conveyance method for transporting a mildly injured athlete.

When transporting a person with a limb injury, be certain the injury is splinted properly before transport. Athletes with shoulder injuries are more comfortably moved in a semisitting position, unless other injuries preclude such positioning. If injury to the upper extremity is such that flexion of the elbow is not possible, the individual should be transported on a stretcher with the limb properly splinted and carried at the side with adequate padding placed between the arm and the body.

Vehicular transfer If an injury demands vehicular transfer, the trainer or coach should, if at all possible, use an ambulance. Only in an extreme emergency should other modes of travel be considered. Because of the liability risks involved, it is unwise for trainers or coaches to use their own cars. Most vehicles, other than ambulances, are not equipped for carrying a stretcher patient. In cases of moderate injury, when it is inadvisable for an athlete to walk home, the parents should be notified so that they may make the necessary arrangements for proper medical attention.

SPECIAL EMERGENCY CONDITIONS

Three emergency situations may face the coach or trainer that require special consideration: hemorrhage, shock, and environmental stress.

Hemorrhage

In any injury situation one must be constantly aware of the danger of hemorrhage. Hemorrhage is the escaping of blood through the walls of the blood vessels or through ruptured blood vessels. There are three basic types of

Figure 12-20

Whenever a serious injury is suspected, a stretcher is the safest method of transporting the athlete.

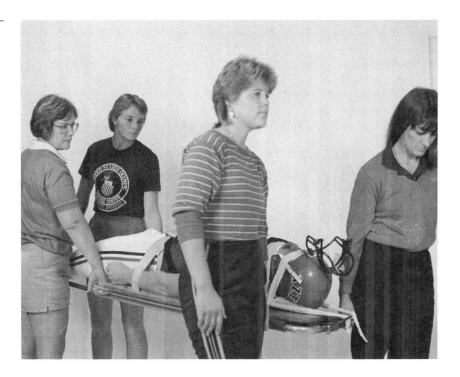

hemorrhage: arterial, venous, and capillary. It is vitally important that hemorrhaging be promptly recognized.

1. *Arterial hemorrhage* is a condition in which an artery has been damaged or severed. There is a very rapid flow of bright red blood, usually escaping in a rhythmical spurting with each heartbeat. Because of the rapidity with which the blood is lost from the body, this type of hemorrhaging is considered the most dangerous. It requires immediate attention. The trainer should promptly elevate the part and apply a compress bandage directly over the site of the hemorrhage. Direct pressure is considered the best means of control and causes the least amount of further damage to the injured area. Only when the use of direct pressure does not appear to be acting as a suitable control should a tourniquet be applied.

2. *Venous hemorrhage* is characterized by a rapid, steady effusion of dark blood from the wounded area. It is controlled by elevation of the part and application of direct pressure over the area. A tourniquet is seldom necessary to control this type of bleeding.

3. *Capillary hemorrhage* is an oozing or very gradual seeping of blood from the wounded area and is easy to control through elevation of the part and direct pressure on a sterile dressing that is placed directly over the wound.

As stated, elevation of the part and direct pressure are considered the best measures in controlling hemorrhage. When the injured area is raised above the level of the heart, there is a diminishing of the pulse pressure, resulting in a reduced amount of blood in the vessels. By applying direct pressure over the wound while the part is elevated, it is possible to keep the hemorrhage to a minimum. The pressure should be applied until the blood coagulates or until medical help has been obtained.

If direct pressure fails to control the bleeding, then a tourniquet should be used to cut off the flow of blood above the injured area. The most common error is applying the tourniquet too loosely and allowing the blood to seep out slowly. Although a loosely applied tourniquet will constrict the veins, it cannot occlude the deeper arteries; consequently, blood will still be lost. It is most important when using a tourniquet to take the pulse rate of the artery *below* the tourniquet to determine whether cessation of blood flow has taken place. A tourniquet is seldom used in athletics, and in most cases medical care can be administered in ample time. There are, of course, exceptions, such as the ones that occur in snow injuries, when the injured person must be transported for a long distance, sometimes under trying conditions with limited help. Circumstances such as these may necessitate use of a tourniquet. The time of tourniquet application should always be indicated on a card that can be secured to the person of the injured athlete so that an accurate record can be kept of when to release and reset pressure. NOTE: *It must be remembered that if a tourniquet is left on for longer than 10 minutes, or if it is too narrow, a clot may result and the loss of the limb, as a result of gangrene, may be a consequence.*

Internal hemorrhage is unexposed and therefore invisible to the eye unless hemorrhaging is manifested through the body openings or is identified through x-ray or other diagnostic techniques. Its danger lies in the difficulty of diagnosis. When internal hemorrhaging occurs either subcutaneously or intramuscularly, the athlete may be moved without danger in most instances. However, the detection of bleeding within a body cavity such as the skull or thorax is of the utmost importance, since it could mean the difference between life and death. Because the symptoms are obscure, internal hemorrhage is difficult to properly diagnose. It has been said that, as a result of this difficulty, internal injuries require hospitalization under complete and constant observation by a medical staff to determine the nature and extent of the injuries. All severe hemorrhaging will eventually result in shock and should therefore be treated on this premise. Even if there is no outward indication of shock, the athlete should be kept quiet and body heat maintained at a constant and suitable temperature. The preferred shock position is supine with all body parts level with the heart.

Shock

In any injury shock is a possibility, but when severe bleeding, fractures, or deep internal injuries are present, the development of shock is assured. Shock occurs when there is a diminished amount of fluid available to the circulatory system. As a result there are not enough oxygen-carrying blood cells available to the tissues, particularly those of the nervous system. This occurs when the vascular system loses its capacity to hold the fluid portion of the blood within its system, because of a dilation of the blood vessels within the body and a disruption of the osmotic fluid balance (Fig. 12-21). When this occurs a quantity of plasma is lost from the blood vessels to the tissue spaces of the body, leaving the solid blood particles within the vessels and thus causing stagnation and slowing up the blood flow. With this general collapse of the vascular system there is widespread death of tissues, which will eventually cause the death of the individual unless treatment is given.

Certain conditions, such as extreme fatigue, extreme exposure to heat or cold, extreme dehydration of fluids and minerals, or illness, predispose an athlete to shock.

Signs of shock:
  Blood pressure is low
  Systolic pressure is usually below 90 mm Hg
  Pulse is rapid and very weak
  Athlete may be drowsy and appear sluggish
  Respiration is shallow and extremely rapid

Figure 12-21

In shock, blood vessels dilate, causing the osmotic fluid balance to be disrupted, allowing plasma to become lost into tissue spaces.

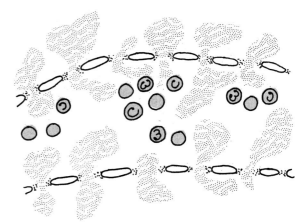
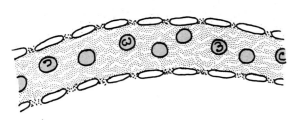

Normal capillary

Dilated capillary

In a situation in which there is a potential shock condition, there are other signs by which the trainer or coach should assess the possibility of the athlete's lapsing into a state of shock as an aftermath of the injury. The most important clue to potential shock is the recognition of a severe injury. It may happen that none of the usual signs of shock is present. To avoid shock in cases of such injury it is vitally important that immediate care be given to the athlete, as indicated below. These steps should be followed in sequence:

1. *Bleeding,* because it is one of the conditions that causes shock, should receive first consideration. If the wound is of a disturbing nature, the athlete should not be permitted to see it.
2. *Body temperature* should be kept normal, 98.6° F. (37° C), since extreme variations of temperature serve only to accentuate the condition of shock.
3. *Body position* should be arranged with the head and trunk level and with the lower limbs elevated. If the athlete is unconscious, turn the head to one side so that any fluids, such as mucus or saliva, will drain out of the mouth rather than into the throat; establish an airway; and be sure that the tongue has not been swallowed.
4. *Oxygen,* if available, can be administered to help restore starved tissues.
5. *Pain* is one of the causes of shock, and the athlete's physician will often administer sedation to enable the athlete to be more at ease.

Shock can also be compounded or initially produced by the psychological reaction of the athlete to an injury situation. Fear or the sudden realization that a serious situation has occurred can result in shock. In the case of a psychological reaction to an injury the athlete should be instructed to lie down and avoid viewing the injury. This athlete should be handled with patience and gentleness, but firmness, as well. Spectators should be kept away from the injured athlete. Reassurance is of vital concern to the injured individual. The person should be given immediate comfort through the loosening of clothing. Nothing should be given by mouth until a physician has determined that no operative procedures are indicated.

Environmental Stress

People concerned with sports are belatedly recognizing the impact of environmental stress on the performer, not only as it relates to the performance per se but in respect to the potential dangers of certain situations. One not only must be aware of the factors of temperature, humidity, and wind but also must be prepared to make appropriate recommendations to the coaching staff regarding the types of uniforms or equipment to be worn, the length and number of practice sessions, the weight loss of athletes, and any other pertinent information about the situation. In this way, the problems posed by environmental extremes can be greatly mitigated.

Hyperthermia

Concern is rising at the increase in causes of heat exhaustion and heatstroke in sports. Among football players and distance runners there have been a number of deaths in high school and college, all of which were di-

In the United States hyperthermia is the second most frequent cause of sports death.

rectly attributable to heatstroke. Findings that show uniforms and helmets to be major causative factors have led persons in sports to take a critical look at the type of equipment worn relative to temperature and humidity. Under certain conditions the uniform can be a death trap.

It is vitally important to have knowledge of temperature and humidity factors to assist the coaching staff and athletic trainer in planning practice and game uniforming and procedures. One should familiarize oneself with the use of the sling psychrometer or the instrument used in establishing the WBGT Index (wet-bulb, globe temperature index). One should be able to determine not only relative humidity but also the danger zones; then one can advise the coaching staff and athletes with a reasonable degree of authority. In addition, one should become familiar with the clinical signs and treatment of heat stress (Fig. 12-22).

Heat is eliminated from the body through conduction, convection, evaporation, and radiation. Body temperature regulation results almost entirely through cutaneous cooling from the evaporation of sweat. During exercise there is some respiratory heat loss, but the amount is relatively small. The effectiveness of sweat evaporation is strongly influenced by relative humidity and wind velocity and under the most ideal conditions does not exceed 70% to 80%.[8] When temperature exceeds 80° F (26.7° C), sweating is the only effective means that the body has of heat dissipation. However, when a high temperature is accompanied by high humidity, a condition with serious implications exists, since high humidity reduces the rate of evaporation *without* diminishing sweating. The stage is set for heat exhaustion and/or heatstroke unless certain precautionary measures have been observed. When a person's temperature reaches 106° F (41.1° C) the chances of survival are exceedingly slim.

An average runner may lose from 1.5 to 2.5 L/hr through active sweating; much greater amounts can be lost by football players in warm weather activity. Seldom is more than 50% of this fluid loss replaced, even though replacement fluids are taken ***ad libitum,*** since athletes usually find it uncomfortable to exercise vigorously with a full stomach, which could interfere with the respiratory muscles. The problem in fluid replacement is how rapidly the fluid can be eliminated from the stomach into the intestine, from which it can enter the bloodstream. Cold drinks (45° to 55° F [7.2° to 12.8° C]) tend to empty more rapidly from the stomach than do warmer

ad libitum
The amount desired

Figure 12-22

Sling psychrometer used to determine relative humidity.

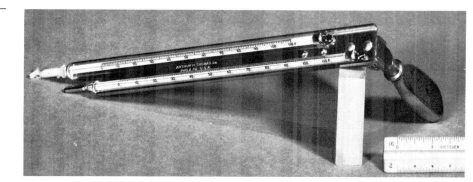

drinks and offer no particular threat to a normal heart or in inducing cramps.[3]

Sweating occurs whether or not the athlete drinks water, and if the sweat losses are not replaced by fluid intake over a period of several hours, dehydration results. Sweat is always hypotonic, that is, it contains a lower concentration of salt than does the blood, and its loss establishes a deficit of water in excess of the salt deficit. This is reflected in several physiological changes, which may manifest themselves in peripheral vascular collapse, renal decompensation, and uremia.[6]

Athletes must have unlimited access to water. Failure to permit *ad libitum* access will not only undermine their playing potentialities but also may be responsible for permitting a dangerous situation to develop that could conceivably have fatal consequences (Fig. 12-23).

Women are apparently more physiologically efficient in body temperature regulation than men; although they possess as many heat-activated sweat glands as men, they sweat less and manifest a higher heart rate when working in heat.[19] Although slight differences exist, the same precautionary measures apply to both genders.

Body build must be considered when determining individual susceptibility to heat stress. Overweight individuals may have as much as 18% greater heat production than an underweight individual, since metabolic heat is produced proportionately to surface area. It has been found that heat victims tend to be overweight. Death from heatstroke increases at a ratio of approximately 4 to 1 as body weight increases.

Prevention The following should be considered when planning a training-competitive program that is likely to take place during hot weather:

1. Gradual acclimatization This is probably the single most effective method of avoiding heat stress. Acclimatization should involve not only becoming accustomed to heat but also becoming acclimatized to exercise in hot temperatures. A good preseason conditioning program, started well before the advent of the competitive season and carefully graded as to intensity, is recommended. During the first 5 or 6 days an 80% acclimatization can be achieved on the basis of a 2-hour practice period in the morning and a 2-hour practice period in the afternoon. Each should be broken down into 20 minutes of work alternated with 20 minutes of rest in the shade.

2. Uniforms Select uniforms on the basis of temperature and humidity. Initial practices should be conducted in short-sleeved tee shirts, shorts, and socks, moving gradually into short-sleeved net jerseys, lightweight pants, and socks as acclimatization proceeds. All early season practices and games should be conducted in light-weight uniforms with short-sleeved net jerseys and socks. Long sleeves and full stockings are indicated only when the temperature is low.

3. Weight records Careful weight records of all players must be kept. Weights should be taken both before and after practice. A loss of 3% to 5% of body weight will reduce blood volumn and could be a serious health threat.[18] Remember that body build may reveal a susceptibility to heat stress.

Figure 12-23

Athletes must have unlimited access to water, especially in hot weather.

Courtesy Cramer Products, Inc., Gardner, Kan.

The prevention of hyperthermia involves:
Gradual acclimatization
Lightweight uniforms
Routine weight record keeping
Unrestricted fluid replacement
Well-balanced diet
Routine temperature/ humidity readings

4. *Fluid replacement* Intake of water should be carefully observed. (See Chapter 7.) Athletes should have unlimited access to cold water at all times.

5. *Diet* Generally, a well-balanced diet is essential. Fat intake should be somewhat minimized.

6. *Temperature/humidity readings* Dry-bulb and wet-bulb readings should be taken on the field before practice. The purchase of a sling psychrometer for this purpose is recommended (Fig. 12-22). It is relatively inexpensive and uncomplicated to use. The relative humidity should be calculated. The following suggestions regarding temperature and humidity will serve as a guide:

Temp. (°F)	Humidity	Procedure
80°-90° (26.7° C-32.2° C)	Under 70%	Watch those athletes who tend toward obesity.
80°-90° (26.7° C-32.2° C)	Over 70%	Athletes should take a 10-minute rest every hour and tee shirts should be changed when
90°-100° (32.2° C-37.8° C)	Under 70%	wet. All athletes should be under constant and careful supervision.
90°-100° (32.2° C-37.8° C) Over 100° (37.8° C)	Over 70%	Under these conditions it would be well to suspend practice. A shortened program conducted in shorts and tee shirts could be established.

Clinical indications and treatment The outline on pp. 311-312 and Tables 12-2 and 12-3 list the clinical symptoms of the various hyperthermal conditions and the indications for treatment.* Although these tables call particular attention to some of the procedures for American football, the precautions, in general, have application to all sports. Football, because of the specialized equipment worn by the players, requires special consideration. To a degree, many uniforms are heat traps and serve to compound the environmental heat problem, which is not the case with the lighter uniforms. All trainers and coaches should be aware of the temperature and the humidity and should take appropriate protective measures.

The recent popularity of distance running, especially road racing the marathon and the ultramarathon, has posed some problems in regard to potential heat stress injuries.[12,14] Accordingly, the American College of Sports Medicine has issued a position statement on the prevention of heat injuries during distance running. This statement is based on the most current research available, and the supportive statement so clearly indicates the problems encountered that it is reproduced in its entirety, with permission of the American College of Sports Medicine (see Appendix III-E).

Hypothermal Stress

Many sports played in cold weather do not require heavy protective clothing; thus weather becomes a factor in injury susceptibility.

Cold weather is a frequent adjunct to many outdoor sports in which the sport itself does not require heavy protective clothing; consequently, the weather becomes a pertinent factor in injury susceptibility. In most instances, the activity itself enables the athlete to increase the metabolic rate

---

*Courtesy Büskirk, E.R., and Grasley, W.C.: Human performance laboratory, The Athletic Institute, The Pennsylvania State University.

ENVIRONMENTAL CONDUCT OF SPORTS: PARTICULARLY FOOTBALL

I. General warning
   A. Most adverse reactions to environmental heat and humidity occur during the first few days of training.
   B. It is necessary to become thoroughly acclimatized to heat to successfully compete in hot and/or humid environments.
   C. Occurrence of a heat injury indicates poor supervision of the sports program.
II. Athletes who are most susceptible to heat injury
   A. Individuals unaccustomed to working in the heat.
   B. Overweight individuals, particularly large linemen.
   C. Eager athletes who constantly compete at capacity.
   D. Ill athletes, having an infection, fever, or gastrointestinal disturbance.
   E. Athletes who receive immunization injections and subsequently develop temperature elevations.
III. Prevention of heat injury
   A. Take complete medical history and provide physical examination. Include:
      1. History of previous heat illnesses or fainting in the heat.
      2. Inquiry about sweating and peripheral vascular defects.
   B. Evaluate general physical condition.
      1. Type and duration of training activities for previous month.
         a. Extent of work in the heat.
         b. General training activities.
   C. Measure temperature and humidity on the practice or playing fields.
      1. Make measurements before and during training or competitive sessons.
      2. Adjust activity level to environmental conditions.
         a. Decrease activity if hot or humid.
         b. Eliminate unnecessary clothing when hot or humid.
   D. Acclimatize athletes to heat gradually.
      1. Acclimatization to heat requires work in the heat.
         a. Recommended type and variety of warm weather workouts for preseason training.
         b. Provide graduated training program for first 7 to 10 days—and other abnormally hot or humid days.
      2. Provide adequate rest intervals and water replacement during the acclimatization period.
   E. Body weight loss during activity in the heat.
      1. Body water should be replaced as it is lost.
         a. Allow additional water as desired by player.
         b. Provide salt on training tables (no salt tablets should be taken).
         c. Weigh each day before and after training or competition.
            (1) Treat athlete who loses excessive weight each day.
            (2) Treat well-conditioned athlete who continues to lose weight for several days.

Continued.

F. Clothing and uniforms
1. Provide lightweight clothing that is loose fitting at the neck, waist, and sleeves. Use shorts and tee shirt at beginning of training.
2. Avoid excessive padding and taping.
3. Avoid use of long stockings, long sleeves, double jerseys, and other excess clothing.
4. Avoid use of rubberized clothing or sweatsuits.
5. Provide clean clothing daily—all items.
G. Provide rest periods to dissipate accumulated body heat.
1. Rest in cool, shaded area with some air movement.
2. Avoid hot brick walls or hot benches.
3. Loosen or remove jerseys or other garments.
4. Take water during the rest period.
IV. Trouble signs: stop activity!

Headache	Diarrhea
Nausea	Cramps
Mental slowness	Seizures
Incoherence	Rigidity
Visual disturbance	Weak, rapid pulse
Fatigue	Pallor
Weakness	Flush
Unsteadiness	Faintness
Collapse	Chill
Unconsciousness	Cyanotic appearance
Vomiting	

sufficiently to be able to function physically in a normal manner and dissipate the resulting heat and perspiration through the usual physiological mechanisms. An athlete may fail to warm up sufficiently or may become chilled because of relative inactivity for varying periods of time demanded by the particular sport either during competition or training; consequently, the athlete is exceedingly prone to injury. Low temperatures alone can pose some problems, but, when such temperatures are further accentuated by wind, the chill factor becomes critical (Fig. 12-24). For example, a runner proceeding at a pace of 10 mph directly into a wind of 5 mph creates a chill factor equivalent to a 15-mph headwind.

During strenuous physical activity in cold weather, as muscular fatigue builds up the rate of exercise begins to drop and may reach a level wherein the body heat loss to the environment exceeds the metabolic heat protection, resulting in definite impairment of neuromuscular responses and exhaustion. A relatively small drop in body core temperature can induce shivering sufficient to materially affect one's neuromuscular coordination. Shivering ceases below a body temperature of 85° to 90° F (29.4° to 32.2° C). Death is imminent if the core temperature rises to 107° F (41.6° C) or drops to between 77° and 85° F (25° and 29° C).

Low temperatures accentuated by wind can pose major problems for athletes.

TABLE 12-2

Heat disorders: treatment and prevention

Disorders	Cause	Clinical Features and Diagnosis	Treatment	Prevention
Heat cramps	Hard work in heat; sweating heavily; salt intake inadequate	Muscle twitching and cramps; spasms; usually after midday; arms, legs, abdomen; low serum sodium and chloride	Ingesting fluids and foods containing sodium chloride	Proper acclimatization; eating foods containing sodium chloride
Heat exhaustion	Prolonged sweating; inadequate replacement of body fluid losses; intestinal infection; diarrhea; predisposes to heatstroke	Excessive thirst, dry tongue and mouth; hypopyrexia; weight loss; fatigue; weakness; incoordination; mental dullness; small urine volume; elevated body temperature; high serum protein and sodium; reduced swelling	Bed rest in cool room, IV fluids if drinking is impaired, increase fluid intake to 6 to 8 L/day; sponge with cool water; keep record of body weight; keep fluid balance record; provide semiliquid food until salination is normal	Supply adequate water and other liquids Provide adequate rest and opportunity for cooling
Heatstroke	Thermoregulatory failure of sudden onset	Abrupt onset, preceded by headache, vertigo, and fatigue, absence of sweating; hot, flushed dry skin; pulse rate increases rapidly and may reach 160 to 180; respiration increases; blood pressure rises; temperature rises rapidly to 105 or 106° F (40 to 41° C); athlete feels as if he or she is burning up; diarrhea, vomiting; circulatory collapse may produce death; could lead to permanent brain damage	Heroic measures to reduce temperature must be taken immediately (e.g., full body immersion in cold water, air fan over body, massage limbs, etc.); temperature must be taken every 10 minutes and not allowed to fall below 101° F (38.5° C) to avoid converting hyperpyrexia to hypothermia; remove to hospital as soon as possible	Ensure proper acclimatization, proper hydration Educate those supervising activities conducted in the heat Adapt activities to environment Screen participants with past history of heat illness

*Modified from Berkow, R.: The Merck manual of diagnosis and therapy, ed. 14, Rahway, N.J., 1982, Merck & Co., Inc.

TABLE 12-3

Contrasting heatstroke and heat exhaustion

	Heatstroke	Heat Exhaustion
Cause	Inadequate or failure of heat loss	Excessive fluid loss
Symptoms	Headache, weakness, sudden loss of consciousness	Gradual weakness, nausea, anxiety, excess sweating, light-headedness
Signs	Hot, red, dry skin; little sweating; rapid pulse; very high temperature	Pale, grayish, clammy skin; weak, slow pulse; low blood pressure; faintness
Management	Rapid cooling by full body immersion in cold water, ice packs, fanning; immediate hospitalization	For syncope, head down, replace lost water and salt

Modified from Berkow, R.: The Merck manual of diagnosis and therapy, ed. 14, Rahway, N.J., 1982, Merck & Co., Inc.

Figure 12-24

Low temperatures can pose serious problems for the athlete, but wind chill could be a critical factor.

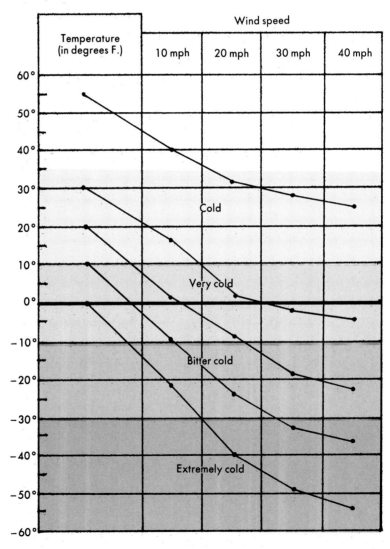

Apparel for competitors must be geared to the weather. The function of such apparel is to provide a semitropical microclimate for the body and prevent chilling. Such clothing should not restrict movement, should be as lightweight as possible, and should consist of material that will permit the free passage of sweat and body heat that would otherwise accumulate on the skin or the clothing and provide a chilling factor when activity ceases. Preliminary to exercise, during activity breaks or rest periods, and at the termination of exercise, a warm-up suit should be worn to prevent chilling. Activity in cold, wet, and windy weather poses some problem, since such weather reduces the insulative values of the clothing worn, and consequently the individual may be unable to achieve energy levels equal to the subsequent body heat losses. Runners who wish to continue outdoor work in cold weather should use lightweight insulative clothing and, if breathing cold air seems distressful, should use ski goggles and a ski face mask or should cover the mouth and nose with a free-hanging cloth. Contrary to common belief, the breathing of cold air is not harmful to pulmonary tissues.

Inadequate clothing, improper warm-up, and a high chill factor form a triad that can lead to musculoskeletal injury, chilblains, frostbite, or the minor respiratory disorders associated with lower tissue temperatures. For work or sports in temperatures below 32° F (0° C), it is advisable to add a layer of protective clothing for every 5 mph of wind.

Overexposure to cold   Severe overexposure to a cold climate is less common than hyperthermia; however, it is still a major risk of winter sports, long-distance running in cold weather, and swimming in cold water.[6]

General body cooling   A core temperature that gets below 80° F (26.7° C) leads to unconsciousness. With a rectal temperature of 86.4° F (30.2° C), the athlete displays a slurring of speech, clumsy movement, pupils that respond sluggishly, shallow respiration, and a heartbeat that may be irregular and slow.[2,6] The skin appears pale; the tissue of the lips, around the nose, and underneath the fingernails is a bluish hue (cyanosis). Muscle tonus increases, causing the neck and limbs to become stiff and rigid. Also occurring are metabolic pH changes leading to acidosis, liver necrosis, uremia, renal failure, and seizures.

Severe exposure to cold is a major medical emergency. The first concern is the maintenance of an airway. If the heart has stopped and the temperature is approximately 85° F (29° C) or less, it may be difficult to reestablish a heart rhythm. External rewarming should take place if the condition ranges from mild to moderate. Emergency rewarming at the site is to immerse the athlete's hands and forearms in water that is between 113° and 118° F (45° and 48° C). If the athlete is conscious, a hot drink may help in rewarming. Alcohol of any kind must be avoided because it vasodilates peripheral capillaries. In cases of severe cold exposure, rewarming too rapidly can cause the peripheral capillaries to become dilated, pulling blood and warmth from the core of the body. In a hospital setting, the athlete may be given warm enemas and warm intravenous solutions.

Local body cooling   Local cooling of the body can result in tissue damage ranging from superficial to deep. Exposure to a damp, freezing cold causes mild or superficial frostbite (frostnip). In contrast, exposure to dry temperatures well below freezing will more commonly produce a deep freezing type of frostbite.

Low freezing temperatures may cause ice crystals to form between or within the cells and may eventually destroy the cell. Local capillaries can be injured, blood clots may form, and blood may be shunted away from the injury site to ensure the survival of the nonaffected tissue.

PREVENTION

The primary preventive measures for local body cooling injuries are obvious but often disregarded. The athlete should wear nonconstricting, multilayered clothing, including warm gloves and socks. Because so much heat is lost via an unprotected head, warm headgear is essential in cold climates. Local cold injuries that may be seen in athletes are frostnip, superficial frostbite, deep freezing frostbite, and chilblains.

Frostnip involves ears, nose, cheeks, chin, fingers, and toes. It is commonly seen when there is a high wind, severe cold, or both. The skin initially appears very firm, with cold, painless areas that may peel or blister in 24 to 72 hours. Affected areas can be treated early by firm, sustained pressure of the hand (without rubbing), blowing hot breath on the spot, or, if the injury is to the fingertips, by placing them in the armpits.

Superficial frostbite involves only the skin and subcutaneous tissue. It appears pale, hard, cold and waxy. Palpating the injured area will reveal a sense of hardness but with yielding of the underlying deeper tissue structures. When rewarming, the superficial frostbite will at first feel numb, then will sting and burn. Later the area may produce blisters and be painful for a number of weeks.

Deep frostbite is a serious injury indicating tissues that are frozen. This is a medical emergency requiring immediate hospitalization. As with frostnip and superficial frostbite, the tissue is initially cold, hard, pale or white, and numb. Rapid rewarming is required, including hot drinks, heating pads, or hot water bottles that are 100° to 110° F (38° to 43° C). On rewarming, the tissue will become blotchy-red, swollen, and extremely painful. Later the injury may become gangrenous, causing a loss of tissue.

Chilblains result from prolonged and constant exposure to cold for many hours. In time there is skin redness, swelling, tingling, and pain in the toes and fingers. This adverse response is caused by problems of peripheral circulation and can be avoided by preventing further cold exposure.

Cold injuries in sports include:
  Frostnip
  Superficial frostbite
  Deep frostbite
  Chilblains

REFERENCES

1. American Heart Association: A manual for instructors of basic life support, Dallas, 1977, The Association.
2. Appenzeller, O., and Atkinson, R.: Temperature regulation and sports. In Appenzeller, O., and Atkinson, R. (editors): Sports medicine, Baltimore, 1981, Urban & Schwarzenberg, Inc.
3. Costill, D.L.: Fluids for athletic performance: why and what you drink during prolonged exercise. In Burke, E.J. (editor): Toward an un-

derstanding of human performance, Ithaca, N.Y., 1978, Mouvement Publications.

4. Emergency care and transportation of the sick and injured, Chicago, 1971, The Committee on Injuries, American Academy of Orthopaedic Surgeons.

5. Emergency care and transportation of the sick and injured, ed. 2, Chicago, 1977, American Academy of Orthopaedic Surgeons.

6. Gutmann, L.: Temperature-related problems in athletic and recreational activities. In Joynt, R.J. (editor): Seminars in neurology, vol. 1, no. 4, p. 242, 1981.

7. Hafen, B.Q.: First aid for health emergencies, ed. 2, St. Paul, Minn., 1981, West Publishing Co.

8. Hanson, P.G.: Heat injury to runners, Phys. Sportsmed. **7**:91, 1979.

9. Hayward, J.S.: Hyperthermia, hypothermia, and drowning. In Vinger, P.F., and Hoerner, E.F. (editors): Sports injuries: the unthwarted epidemic, Boston, 1982, John Wright, PSG, Inc.

10. Henderson, J.: Emergency medical guide, ed. 4, New York, 1978, McGraw-Hill Book Co.

11. Knight, K.L.: ICE for immediate care of injuries, Phys. Sportsmed. **10**:137, 1982.

12. Moore, M.: What are we learning from road races? Phys. Sportsmed. **10**:151, 1982.

13. Mueller, F.O., and Schindler, R.D.: Annual survey of football injury research 1981-1982, American Football Coaches Association, National Collegiate Athletic Association, and National Federation of State High School Associations.

14. O'Donnell, T.F.: Management of heat stress injuries in the athlete, Orthop. Clin. North Am. **11**:841, 1980.

15. Parcel, G.S.: First aid in emergency care, ed. 2, St. Louis, 1981, The C.V. Mosby Co.

16. Standards and guidelines for cardiopulmonary resuscitation (CPR) and emergency cardiac care (ECC), J.A.M.A. **244**:453, 1980.

17. Stephenson, H.E., Jr. (editor): Immediate care of the acutely ill and injured, ed. 2, St. Louis, 1978, The C.V. Mosby Co.

18. Stone, B.: Dehydration and its effects upon endurance activity, Ath. J. **14**:64, 1982.

19. Wells, C.L.: Sexual differences in heat stress response, Phys. Sportsmed. **5**:78, 1977.

ADDITIONAL SOURCES

Bangs, C.C.: Cold injuries. In Strauss, R.H. (editor): Sports medicine, Philadelphia, 1984, W.B. Saunders Co.

Cantu, R.C.: Sports medicine in primary care, Lexington, Mass., 1982, The Collamore Press.

Gambardella, R.: Heat and cold related injuries, Current concepts in sports medicine, Fourth Annual Symposium, Centinela Hospital, Inglewood, Calif. (Cassette.)

Heimlich, H.J.: A lifesaving maneuver to prevent food choking, J.A.M.A. **234**:398, 1975.

McArdle, W.D., Katch, F.I., and Katch, J.H.: Exercise physiology, Philadelphia, 1981, Lea & Febiger.

Nadel, E.R.: Temperature regulation. In Strauss, R.H. (editor): Sports medicine and physiology, Philadelphia, 1979, W.B. Saunders Co.

Sutton, J.R.: Heat illness. In Strauss, R.H. (editor): Sports medicine, Philadelphia, 1984, W.B. Saunders Co.

Sunderland, E.: Heat stress: physiological response to heat and exercise, NATA Annual Meeting, Clinical Symposium, June 1983, Greenville, N.C., National Athletic Trainers Association. (Cassette.)

Chapter 13

Wound Dressing, Taping, Bandaging, Padding, and Orthotics

When you finish this chapter, you should be able to

Dress wounds

Tape and bandage sports injuries

Protect sports injuries with pads and orthotics

Eight basic uses for dressings and bandages:

Protect wounds from infection

Protect wounds from further insult and contamination

Control external and internal hemorrhage

Act as a compress over exposed or unexposed injuries

Immobilize an injured part

Protect an unexposed injury

Support an injured part

Hold protective equipment in place

All wounds must be considered to be contaminated by microorganisms.

As stated in previous chapters, skill in the art of athletic training encompasses many areas. Besides the understanding of injury prevention and the ability to recognize and evaluate injuries, one must have skill in a variety of specialized training areas. Each of these skill areas requires a great deal of practice and experience before a high level of proficiency can be developed. The following skill categories are basic to the successful sports medicine program: taping, wound dressing, bandaging, padding, and orthotics.

WOUND DRESSINGS

Bandages, when properly applied, can contribute decidedly to recovery from sports injuries. Bandages carelessly or improperly applied may cause discomfort, allow wound contamination, or even hamper repair and healing. In all cases bandages must be firmly applied—neither so tight that circulation is impaired nor so loose that the dressing is allowed to slip.

Skin lesions are extremely prevalent in sports; abrasions, lacerations, and puncture wounds are almost daily occurrences. It is of the utmost importance to the well-being of the athlete that open wounds be cared for immediately. All wounds, even those that are relatively superficial, must be considered to be contaminated by microorganisms and therefore must be cleansed, medicated—when called for—and dressed. Dressing wounds requires a sterile environment to prevent infections.

Individuals who perform wound management in sports have often been criticized for not following good principles of cleanliness. It is obvious from the large number of athletes who acquire severe wound infections each year that this criticism is true. To alleviate this problem one must adhere to standard procedures in the prevention of wound contamination. (See Chapter 17 for wound management.)

Training Room Practices

The following are suggested procedures to use in the training room to cut down the possibility of wound infections.

1. Sterilize all instruments used in the care of wounds and other skin problems either by exposing them to high temperatures such as boiling water or by chemical means.
2. Never touch sterile instruments until hands are thoroughly cleansed with soap or detergent and water.
3. Place sterilized instruments such as scissors, forceps, and swabs on a clean surface.
4. Clean in and around a skin lesion thoroughly.
5. Place a nonmedicated dressing on a lesion if the athlete is to be sent for medical attention.
6. Avoid touching any parts of a sterile dressing that will come in contact with a wound.
7. Place medication on a pad rather than directly on a lesion.
8. Secure the dressing with tape or a wrap, always avoiding placing pressure directly over a lesion.

Field Practices

Although caring for wounds or other skin problems under field conditions is less than ideal, cleanliness can still be practiced. Such procedures as using sterile instruments, cleansing the hands before touching wounds, and preventing contamination of sterile pads are easily within the province of the coach or trainer.

Materials

Bandages peculiar to sports consist essentially of gauze, cotton cloth, and elastic wrapping. Plastics are also being used more frequently. Each material offers a specific contribution to the care of injuries.

Gauze   Gauze materials are used in three forms—as sterile pads for wounds, as padding in the prevention of blisters on a taped ankle, and as a roller bandage for holding dressings and compresses in place.

Cotton cloth   Cotton is used primarily for cloth ankle wraps and for triangular and cravat-type bandages. It is soft, is easily obtained, and can be washed many times without deterioration.

Elastic roller bandage   The elastic bandage is extremely popular in sports because of its extensibility, which allows it to conform to most parts of the body. Elastic wraps are "active bandages" that let the athlete move without restriction. They also act as a controlled compression bandage, in which the regulation of pressure is graded according to the athlete's specific needs. A *cohesive elastic bandage* has been developed that exerts constant, even pressure. It is lightweight and contours easily to the body part. The bandage is composed of two layers of nonwoven rayon, which are separated by strands of Spandex material. The cohesive elastic bandage is coated with a substance that makes the material adhere to itself, eliminating the need for metal clips or adhesive tape for holding it in place.

Plastics Plastics are playing an increasing role in sports medicine. Spray plastic coatings are used to protect wounds. A variety of plastic adhesive tapes are also used because they are waterproof. Many trainers use plastic food envelopes to insulate analgesic balm packs and to protect bandages and dressings from moisture. A common plastic pad used for wound dressing is the Telfa pad. Plastic materials that can be formed into a desired shape when heated are also becoming an integral part of the training room list of supplies (see p. 337).

TAPING IN SPORTS

The use of adhesive substances in care of the external lesions goes back to ancient times. The Greek civilization is credited with formulating a healing paste composed of lead oxide, olive oil, and water, which was used for a wide variety of skin conditions. This composition was only recently changed by the addition of resin and yellow beeswax and, even more recently, rubber. Since its inception, adhesive tape has developed into a vital therapeutic adjunct.[11]

Two types of tape are generally used in sports medicine—linen and elastic. Linen, the most commonly used, is only slightly yielding, if at all. Elastic tape, in comparison, is made to stretch. Where linen tape rigidly holds a dressing, bandage, or body part in place, elastic tape compresses and moves as the body moves. One possible reason for more extensive use of linen tape is its lower cost. Also, waterproof, hypoallergenic, plastic-backed tape is available for wound dressing, and moleskin with a felt backing is available for support and cushioning.[17]

Tape Usage
Injury Care

When used for sports injuries, adhesive tape offers a number of possibilities:
- Retention of wound dressings
- Stabilization of compression-type bandages that are used to control external and internal hemorrhaging
- Support of recent injuries to prevent additional insult that might result from the activities of the athlete

Injury Protection

Protecting against acute injuries is another major use of tape support. This can be achieved by limiting the motion of a body part or by securing some special device.

Linen Adhesive Tape Qualities

When purchasing linen tape, consider:
Grade of backing
Mass
Winding tension

Modern adhesive tape has great adaptability for use in sports because of its uniform adhesive mass, adhering qualities, and lightness, as well as the relative strength of the backing materials. All of these are of value in holding wound dressings in place and in supporting and protecting injured areas. It comes in a variety of sizes; 1-, 1½-, and 2-inch (2.5-, 3.75-, and 5-cm) widths are commonly used in sports medicine. The tape also comes in tubes or special packs. Some popular packs provide greater tape length on each spool. When linen tape is purchased, factors such as cost, grade of backing, quality of adhesive mass, and properties of unwinding should be considered.

Tape Grade

Linen-backed tape is most often graded according to the number of longitudinal and vertical fibers per inch of backing material. The heavier and more costly backing contains 85 or more longitudinal fibers and 65 vertical fibers per square inch. The lighter, less expensive grade has 65 or fewer longitudinal and 45 vertical fibers.

Adhesive Mass

As a result of improvements in adhesive mass, one should expect certain essentials from tape. It should adhere readily when applied and should maintain this adherence despite profuse perspiration and activity. In addition to having adequate sticking properties, the mass must contain as few skin irritants as possible and must be able to be removed easily without leaving a mass residue or pulling away the superficial skin.

Winding Tension

The winding tension that a tape roll possesses is quite important to the operator. Sports places a unique demand on the unwinding quality of tape; if tape is to be applied for protection and support, there must be even and constant unwinding tension. In most cases a proper wind needs little additional tension to provide sufficient tightness.

Using Adhesive Tape in Sports
Preparation for Taping

Special attention must be given when applying tape directly to the skin. Perspiration and dirt collected during sport activities will prevent tape from properly sticking to the skin. Whenever tape is employed, the skin surface should be cleansed with soap and water to remove all dirt and oil. Hair should be removed by shaving to prevent additional irritation when the tape is removed. If additional adherence or protection from tape irritation is needed, a preparation containing rosin and a skin-toughening preparation should be applied. Commercial benzoin or skin tougheners offer astringent action and dry readily, leaving a tacky residue to which tape will adhere firmly.

Taping directly on skin provides maximum support. However, applying tape day after day can lead to skin irritation. To overcome this problem many trainers sacrifice some support by using a protective covering to the skin. The most popular is a commercial, moderately elastic underwrap material that is extremely thin and fits snugly to the contours of the part to be taped. One commonly used underwrap material is polyester urethane foam, which is fine, porous, extremely lightweight, and resilient. Proper use of an underwrap requires the part to be shaved and sprayed with a tape adherent. It is also desirable to place a protective greased pad anterior and posterior to the ankle to prevent tape cuts and secondary infection.

Proper Taping Technique

Selection of the correct tape width for the part to be taped depends upon the area to be covered. The more acute the angles present, the narrower the tape width needed to fit the many contours. For example, the hands and feet usually require ½-inch or 1-inch (2.5- or 2.5-cm) tape, the ankles require 1½-inch (3.75-cm) tape, and the larger skin areas such as thighs and back can accommodate 2- to 3-inch (5- to 7.5-cm) tape with ease. *NOTE: Supportive tape improperly applied could aggravate an existing injury or cause the athlete to become initially injured.*

Tearing Tape

Trainers use various techniques in tearing tape (Fig. 13-1). A method should be employed that permits the operator to keep the tape roll in hand most of the time. The following is a suggested procedure: (1) Hold the tape roll in the preferred hand with the index finger hooked through the center of the tape roll and the thumb pressing its outer edge. (2) With the other hand grasp the loose end between the thumb and index finger. With both hands in place, make a quick, scissors-like move to tear the tape. When tearing is properly executed, the torn edges of the linen-backed tape appear to be relatively straight, without curves, twists, or loose threads sticking out. Learning to tear tape effectively from many different positions is essential for speed and efficiency. Many tapes other than the linen-backed type cannot be torn manually and require a knife, scissors, or razor blade cutter.

Figure 13-1

Methods of tearing linen-backed tape.

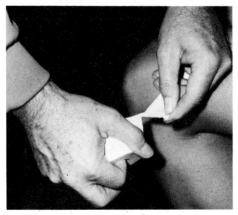

Rules for Tape Application

Included below are a few of the important rules to be observed in the use of adhesive tape. In practice the trainer will identify others.

1. If the part to be taped is a joint, *place it in the position in which it is to be stabilized* or, if the part is musculature, *make the necessary allowance for contraction and expansion.*

2. *Overlap the tape at least half the width of the tape below.* Unless tape is overlapped sufficiently, the active athlete will separate it, thus exposing the underlying skin to irritation.

3. *Avoid continuous taping.* Tape continuously wrapped around a part may cause constriction. It is suggested that one turn be made at a time and that each encirclement be torn to overlap the starting end by approximately 1 inch. This rule is particularly true of the nonyielding linen-backed tape.

4. *Keep the tape roll in hand whenever possible.* By learning to keep the tape roll in the hand, seldom laying it down, and by learning to tear the tape, an operator can develop taping speed and accuracy.

5. *Smooth and mold the tape as it is laid on the skin.* To save additional time, tape strips should be smoothed and molded to the body part as they are put in place; this is done by stroking the top with the fingers, palms, and heels of both hands.

6. *Allow tape to fit the natural contour of the skin.* Each strip of tape must be laid in place with a particular purpose in mind. Linen-backed tape is not sufficiently elastic to bend around acute angles but must be allowed "to fall as it may," fitting naturally to the body contours. Failing to allow this creates wrinkles and gaps that can result in skin irritations.

7. *Start taping with an "anchor" piece and finish by applying a "lock" strip.* Taping should commence, if possible, by sticking the tape to an anchor piece that has encircled the part. This affords a good medium for the

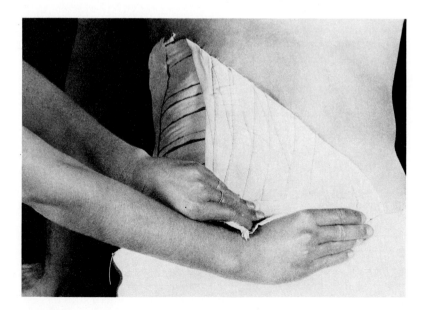

Figure 13-2

To manually remove tape from the body, pull it in a direct line with the body.

stabilization of succeeding tape strips, so that they will not be affected by the movement of the part.

8. *Where maximum support is desired, tape directly over skin surfaces.* In cases of sensitive skin, other mediums may be used as tape bases. With the use of artificial bases, one can expect some movement between the skin and the base.

Removing Adhesive Tape

Tape usually can be removed from the skin by manual methods, by the use of tape scissors or tape cutters, or by chemical solvents.

Manual removal When tape is pulled from the body, the operator must be careful not to tear or irritate the skin. Tape must not be

---

ARGUMENTS AGAINST ROUTINE ANKLE TAPING

1. Tape is applied over movable skin.[2]
2. Moisture collects under tape, increasing its looseness.[2]
3. Constant taping for activity weakens supporting muscle tendons.[2]
4. Tape support is reduced 40% after 10 minutes of vigorous activity.[14]
5. Ankle wraps loosen 34% to 77% during exercise.[14]
6. Taping often replaces the practice of thoroughly exercising the ankle joint.[2]
7. The tradition of taping is based on folklore rather than on facts.[7]
8. Taping gives the athlete false security and soon becomes a psychological crutch.[2,7]
9. Because taping does not significantly reduce ankle torque it does not decrease the athlete's potential for lower leg injury.[1,3,16]

ARGUMENTS FOR ROUTINE ANKLE TAPING

1. Wrapping or taping the ankles does not significantly hinder motor performance.[9]
2. Properly applied wraps and tapings, even though they loosen during activity, provide critical support at the limits of ankle movement.[15]
3. Because wraps and tapings do loosen in the initial period of activity, the midrange of ankle movement is allowed, thus moving adverse stress from the knee joint.[15]
4. High-risk sports, such as football, basketball, and soccer, should use ankle prophylaxis.[4]
5. Athletes having a history of recent ankle injury or chronically weak ankles should be given every possible protection against further insult.[8]
6. Statistics show that athletes who wear tape as an ankle prophylaxis have fewer injuries.[4]
7. Pressure of tape on the peroneus brevis muscle stimulates its action.[4]

wrenched in an outward direction from the skin but should be pulled in a direct line with the body (Fig. 13-2).

Use of tape scissors or cutters   The characteristic tape scissors has a blunt nose that slips underneath the tape smoothly without gouging the skin. Precautions should be taken to avoid cutting the tape too near the site of the injury, lest the scissors aggravate the condition.

Use of chemical solvents   When an adhesive mass is left on the skin after taping, a chemical agent may have to be used. Commercial cleaning solvents often contain a highly flammable agent. Extreme care must be taken to store solvents in cool places and in tightly covered metal containers. Extensive inhalation of benzene fumes has a toxic effect. Adequate ventilation should be maintained when using solvents.

Adhesive Tape and Injury Prophylaxis

Adhesive tape as a prophylaxis has routinely been applied to ankles for many years; however, recently there has been controversy as to the real benefits, if any, ankle taping provides.

The value of adhesive tape as a prophylaxis is controversial.

Tape as an Adjunct to Conditioning and Rehabilitation

Ankle taping to prevent injury should only be employed as an adjunct to proper and extensive exercise. Tape should never be applied indiscriminantly, but under highly controlled conditions.[6] The primary muscles of concern are the plantar muscles of the foot, the peroneal group, and the gastrocnemius-soleus complex. Special attention should be paid to stretching the heel cord. Heel cord tightness may be a major cause of lateral ankle sprain. When the heel cord is tight and the ankle is forced into dorsiflexion, the subtalar joint is placed into a supinated position, causing an increased stress on the ankle's lateral capsule.[10]

Ankle taping should only be used as an adjunct to proper and extensive exercise.

Athletes with normal or near normal ankles should rely more on strengthening exercises than on artificial aids. When prophylaxis is needed in a high-risk sport, wraps may be preferable to rigid taping. Ankle taping should not become routine unless an honest effort at reconditioning has failed to adequately restore function to the ankle. One must remember that an improperly applied wrap or taping can compound an injury and may even create postural imbalances that could adversely affect other parts of the body.[11]

COMMON TYPES OF BANDAGES USED IN SPORTS MEDICINE

Triangular and cravat-type bandages, usually made of cotton cloth, may be used where roller types are not applicable or available. Figure-of-eight and spica bandages are also used in sports medicine.

Triangular and Cravat Bandages

The triangular and cravat-type bandages are primarily used as first aid devices. They are valuable in emergency bandaging because of their ease and speed of application. In sports, the more diversified roller bandages are usually available and lend themselves more to the needs of the athlete. The principal use of the triangular bandage in athletic training is for arm slings.

Cervical Arm Sling

The cervical arm sling (Fig. 13-3) is designed to support the forearm, wrist, and hand. A triangular bandage is placed around the neck and under the bent arm that is to be supported.

Materials needed: One triangular bandage and one safety pin.

Position of the athlete: The athlete stands with the affected arm bent at approximately a 70-degree angle.

Position of the operator: The operator stands facing the athlete.

Procedure

1. The triangular bandage is positioned, by the operator, under the injured arm with the apex facing the elbow.
2. The end of the triangle nearest the body is carried over the shoulder of the injured arm; the other end is allowed to hang down loosely.
3. The loose end is pulled over the shoulder of the uninjured side.
4. The two ends of the bandage are tied in a square knot behind the neck. For the sake of comfort, the knot should be on either side of the neck, not directly in the middle.
5. The apex end of the triangle is brought around to the front of the elbow and fastened with a safety pin.

NOTE: In cases in which greater arm stabilization is required than that afforded by a sling, an additional bandage can be swathed about the upper arm and body (Fig. 13-5).

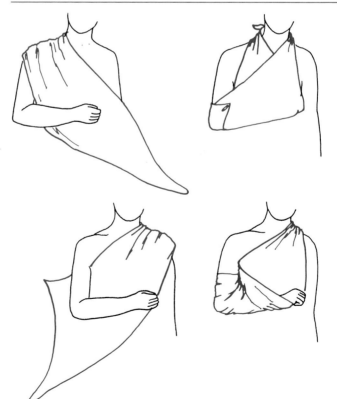

Figure 13-3

Cervical arm sling.

Figure 13-4

Shoulder arm sling.

Shoulder Arm Sling

The shoulder arm sling (Fig. 13-4) is suggested for forearm support when there is an injury to the shoulder girdle or when the cervical arm sling is irritating to the athlete.

Materials needed: One triangle bandage and one safety pin.

Position of the athlete: The athlete stands with his injured arm bent at approximately a 70-degree angle.

Position of the operator: The operator stands facing the athlete.

Procedure

1. The upper end of the shoulder sling is placed over the *uninjured* shoulder side.
2. The lower end of the triangle is brought over the forearm and drawn between the upper arm and the body, swinging around the athlete's back and then upward to meet the other end, where a square knot is tied.
3. The apex end of the triangle is brought around to the front of the elbow and fastened with a safety pin.

There are two basic kinds of slings, the cervical arm sling and the shoulder arm sling, and each has a specific purpose.

Sling and Swathe

The sling and swathe combination is designed to stablize the arm securely in cases of shoulder dislocation or fracture (Fig. 13-5).

Roller Bandages

Roller bandages are made of many materials; gauze, cotton cloth, and elastic wrapping are predominantly used in the training room. The width and length vary according to the body part to be bandaged. The sizes most frequently used are the 2-inch (5-cm) width by 6-yard (5½-m) length for hand, finger, toe, and head bandages; the 3-inch (7.5-cm) width by 10-yard (9-m) length for the extremities; and the 4-inch (10-cm) or 6-inch (15-cm) width by 10-yard length for thighs, groins, and trunk. For ease and convenience in the application of the roller bandage, the strips of material are first rolled into a cylinder. When a bandage is selected, it should be a single piece that is free from wrinkles, seams, or any other imperfections that may cause skin irritation.

Application

Application of the roller bandage must be executed in a specific manner to adequately achieve the purpose of the wrap. When a roller bandage is about to be placed on a body part, the roll should be held in the preferred hand with the loose end extending from the bottom of the roll. The back surface of the loose end is placed on the part and held in position by the other hand. The bandage cylinder is then unrolled and passed around the injured area. As the hand pulls the material from the roll, it also standardizes the bandage pressure and guides it in the proper direction. To anchor and stabilize the bandage, a number of turns, one on top of the other, are made. Circling a body part requires the operator to alternate the bandage roll from one hand to the other and back again.

Figure 13-5

Sling and swathe.

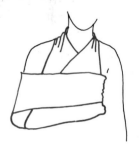

To apply a roller bandage, hold it in the preferred hand with the loose end extending from the bottom of the roll.

To acquire maximum benefits from a roller bandage, it should be applied uniformly and firmly, but not too tightly. Excessive or unequal pressure can hinder the normal blood flow within the part. The following points should be considered when using the roller bandage:

1. A body part should be wrapped in its position of maximum muscle contraction to ensure unhampered movement or circulation.
2. It is better to use a large number of turns with moderate tension than a limited number of turns applied too tightly.
3. Each turn of the bandage should be overlapped by at least one half of the overlying wrap to prevent the separation of the material while engaged in activity. Separation of the bandage turns tends to pinch and irritate the skin.
4. When limbs are wrapped, fingers and toes should be scrutinized often for signs of circulation imparment. Abnormally cold or cyanotic phalanges are signs of excessive bandage pressure.

The usual anchoring of roller bandages consists of several circular wraps directly overlying each other. Whenever possible anchoring is commenced at the smallest circumference of a limb and is then moved upward. Wrists and ankles are the usual sites for anchoring bandages of the limbs. Bandages are applied to these areas in the following manner:

1. The loose end of the roller bandage is laid obliquely on the anterior aspects of the wrist or ankle and held in this position. The roll is then carried posteriorly under and completely around the limb and back to the starting point.
2. The triangle portion of the uncovered oblique end is folded over the second turn.
3. The folded triangle is covered by a third turn, thus finishing a secure anchor.

After a roller bandage has been applied, it is held in place by a *locking technique*. The method most often used to finish a wrap is that of firmly tying or pinning the bandage or placing adhesive tape over several overlying turns.

Once a bandage has been put on and has served its purpose, removal can be performed either by unwrapping or by carefully cutting with bandage scissors. Whatever method of bandage removal is employed, extreme caution must be taken to avoid additional injury.

Circular Bandage

In training procedures the circular bandage (Fig. 13-6) is used to cover a cylindrical area and to anchor other types of bandages.

1. A turn is executed around the part at an oblique angle.
2. A small triangle of material is exposed by the oblique turn.
3. The triangle is bent over the first turn, with succeeding turns made over the turned down material locking it in place.
4. After several turns have been made, the bandage is fastened at a point away from the injury.

Figure 13-6

Circular wrist bandage.

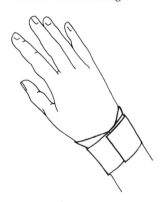

Spiral Bandage

The spiral bandage (Fig. 13-7) is widely used in sports for covering a large area of a cylindrical part.

1. The spiral bandage is anchored at the smallest circumference of the limb and is wrapped, proceeding upward in a spiral against gravity.
2. To prevent the bandage from slipping down on a moving extremity, it is suggested that two pieces of tape be folded lengthwise and placed on the bandage at either side of the limb or that tape adherent be sprayed on the part.
3. After the bandage is anchored, it is carried upward in consecutive spiral turns, each overlapping the other by at least ½ inch.
4. The bandage is terminated by locking it with circular turns, which are then firmly secured by tape.

A good example of the spiral bandage is the *recurrent finger bandage* (Fig. 13-8). The bandage is started at the base of the phalanx and carried

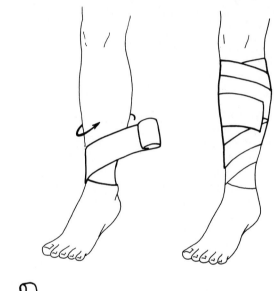

Figure 13-7

Spiral bandage.

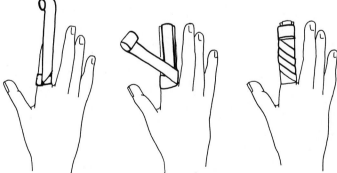

Figure 13-8

Recurrent bandage.

over the tip of the finger and then down the other side, adjacent to the starting point. The bandage is folded, and the pattern of the underlying bandage is retraced until several gauze pieces have been laid down. The recurrent finger bandage is completed and held in place by circular turns. The same recurrent overlapping technique can be used wherever there is a need to protect the padding over dressings.

Eye Bandage

For cases in which a bandage is needed to hold a dressing on an eye, the following procedure (Fig. 13-9) is suggested:
1. The bandage is started with a series of three circular turns around the head and then brought obliquely down the back of the head.
2. From behind the head the bandage is carried forward underneath the earlobe and upward, crossing respectively the cheek bone, the injured eye, and the bridge of the nose; it is then returned to the original circular turns.
3. The head is encircled by the bandage, and the procedure is repeated with each wrap overlapping at least two thirds of the underlying material over the injured eye.
4. When at least three series have been applied over the injured eye, the bandage is locked after completion of a circular turn around the head.

Jaw Bandage

Bandages properly applied can be used to hold dressings and to stabilize dislocated or fractured jaws (Fig. 13-10):
1. The bandage is started by encircling the jaw and head in front of both ears several times.
2. The bandage is locked by a number of turns around the head.
3. Each of the two sets of turns is fastened with tape strips.

Figure 13-9

Eye bandage.

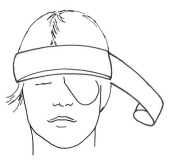
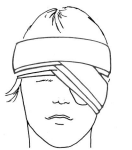

Figure 13-10

Jaw bandage.

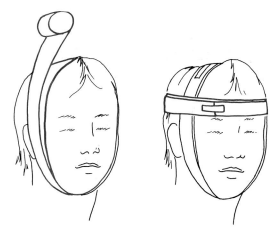

Figure-8 and Spica Bandages

Figure-8 and spica bandages are readily applicable in athletic training. They are used both for support and for holding dressings in place near highly movable joints. There is little difference between the two types. The spica has a larger loop on one end than does the figure-8.

The shoulder, elbow, hip, knee, and ankle joints are well suited for use of the figure-8 or the spica bandage.

Shoulder Spica

The shoulder spica (Fig. 13-11) is used predominantly for the retention of wound dressings or analgesic balm packs and for moderate muscular support.

1. The axilla must be well padded to prevent skin irritation and constriction of blood vessels.
2. The bandage is anchored by one turn around the affected upper arm.
3. After anchoring the bandage around the arm on the injured side, the wrap is carried around the back under the unaffected arm and across the chest to the injured shoulder.
4. The affected arm is again encircled by the bandage, continuing around the back. Every figure-8 pattern moves progressively upward with an overlap of at least one half of the previous underlying wrap.

Hand and Wrist Figure-8

A figure-8 bandage (Fig. 13-12) can be used for wrist and hand support as well as for holding dressings in place. The anchor is executed with one or two turns around the palm of the hand. The roll is then carried obliquely across the anterior or posterior portion of the hand, depending on the position of the wound, to the wrist, which it circles once; then it is returned to the primary anchor. As many figures as needed are applied.

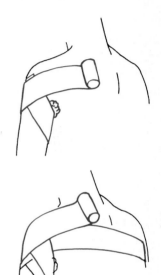

Figure 13-11

Shoulder spica.

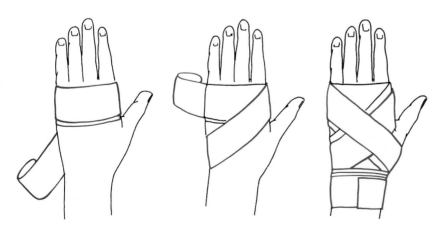

Figure 13-12

Hand and wrist figure-8.

Elbow Figure-8

The elbow figure-8 bandage (Fig. 13-13) can be used to secure a dressing in the antecubital fossa or to restrain full extension in hyperextension injuries; when it is reversed, it can be employed for conditions on the posterior aspect of the elbow.

1. Anchor the bandage by encircling the lower arm.
2. Bring the roll obliquely upward over the posterior aspect of the elbow.
3. Carry the roll obliquely upward, crossing the antecubital fossa; then pass once again completely around the upper arm and return to the beginning position by again crossing the antecubital fossa.
4. Continue the procedure as described, but for every new sequence move upward toward the elbow one half the width of the underlying wrap.

Hip Spica

The hip spica (Fig. 13-14) serves two purposes in sports. It holds analgesic packs in place and offers a mild support to injured hip adductors or flexors.

NOTE: Elastic wraps used for the hip should be double the length of the regular wrap.

1. Start the end of the roll at the upper part of the thigh and immediately encircle the upper thigh and groin, crossing the starting point.
2. When the starting end has been reached, the roll is taken completely around the waist to ensure against the wrap slipping down; it should be brought around the waist and firmly fixed above the crest of the ilium.
3. Continue by carrying the wrap around the thigh at groin level and up again around the waist; secure the end at the waist with adhesive tape.

Figure 13-13

Elbow figure-8.

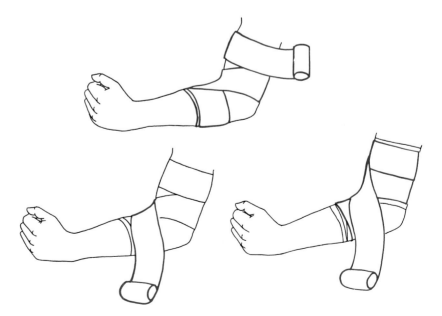

NOTE: If movement restriction of the groin is needed, a hip spica wrap should be applied in reverse to Fig. 13-14 (see Fig. 21-25).

Ankle and Foot Spica

The ankle and foot spica bandage (Fig. 13-15) is primarily used in sports for the compression of new injuries, as well as for holding analgesic balm packs or wound dressings in place.

1. An anchor is placed around the foot near the metatarsal arch.
2. The bandage is brought across the instep and around the heel and returned to the starting point.
3. The procedure is repeated several times, each succeeding revolution progressing upward on the foot and the ankle.
4. Each spica is overlapped by approximately three fourths of the preceding bandage.

Arm or Leg Figure-8

As with other figure-8 bandages, the arm or leg type (Fig. 13-16) is used for keeping dressings in position, for holding splints in place, and for giving mild or moderate muscle support.

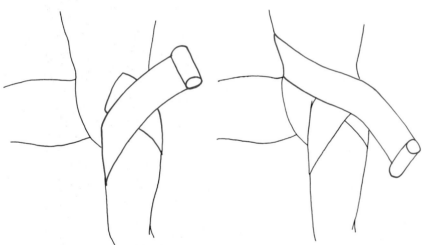

Figure 13-14

Hip spica.

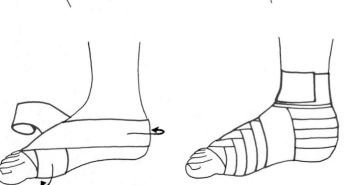

Figure 13-15

Ankle and foot spica.

1. An anchor is applied by circular turns around the wrist or ankle.
2. A spiral strip is carried diagonally upward to a point where one complete circular turn is executed.
3. The roll is then carried downward, crossing the spiral strip, to finish one figure-8.
4. The procedure is repeated until the injury site is thoroughly covered.

Demigauntlet Bandage

The demigauntlet bandage (Fig. 13-17) has considerable versatility in sports. It holds dressings on the back of the hand and it also offers support and protection to knuckles.

1. The bandage is anchored by circular turns at the wrist.
2. The roll is carried between the fourth and little fingers, encircling the little finger, and is brought once again across the back of the hand to the wrist.

Figure 13-16

Arm or leg figure-8.

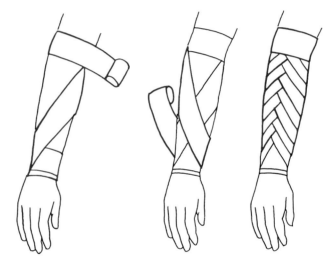

Figure 13-17

Demigauntlet bandage.

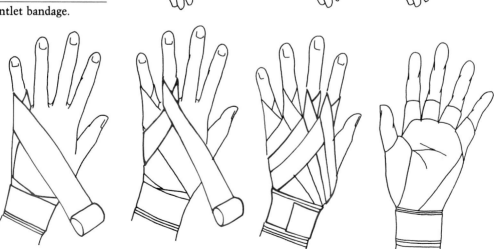

3. The wrist is again encircled by the roll, which is carried to the next fingers consecutively until all digits and thumb have been wrapped.
4. Locking is executed at the wrist.

Finger Bandage

The finger bandage (Fig. 13-18) can be used to hold dressings or tongue depressor splints in place. It is applied in a fashion similar to that used for the demigauntlet, with the exception that a spiral is carried downward to the tip of the finger and then back up to finish around the wrist.

PADS AND ORTHOSES

Besides the various bandages and protective and supportive adhesive taping used in sports medicine, there are commercial and self-constructed devices designed to aid the injured athlete. These devices may be divided generally into pads and orthoses. Pads consist of various resilient materials that cushion against injury.

In sports medicine an **orthosis** is an orthopedic device designed to support, align, prevent, or correct a deformity or to improve the function of a movable body part. Sport medicine orthotics is fast becoming an important technique requirement for all coaches and trainers.

orthosis
Orthopedic device designed to support, align, prevent, or correct a deformity or to improve function

Types of Devices
Foot Pads

Commercial foot pads are intended for use by the general public and are not usually designed to withstand the rigors of sports activities. Those commercial pads that are suited for sports are not durable enough for a limited budget. If money is no object, the ready-made commercial pad has the advantage of saving time. Commerical pads are manufactured for almost every type of common structural foot condition, ranging from corns and bunions to fallen arches. Indiscriminate use of these aids, however, may result in intensifying the pathological condition or delaying the athlete from seeing a physician for evaluation. Recently a viscoelastic polymer material, Sorbothane II, has been developed. Made into a protective foot pad, it can dis-

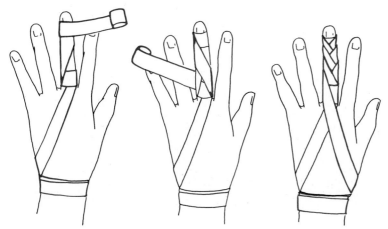

Figure 13-18

Finger bandage.

sipate over 90% of the energy that the foot produces and fully return to its orginal shape when the force is removed.[5]

Orthopedic Footwear

Devices that are built into or placed inside a shoe to permit proper functioning of the foot are defined as orthopedic footwear. The trainer or coach should never presume, without first consulting the team physician, to have an athlete wear orthopedic footwear. Postural imbalance, caused by foot conditions or by improper footwear, can affect the entire body by subjecting the body segments to atypical strains (Fig. 13-19).

Construction of Protective and Supportive Devices

Being able to construct protective and supportive devices is of considerable value in sports. The primary mediums used are sponge rubber, felt, adhesive felt or adhesive sponge rubber, gauze pads, cotton, lamb's wool, and plastic material. All these have special uses in athletic training.

Soft Materials

Sponge rubber (foam rubber) is resilient, nonabsorbent, and able to protect the body against shock. It is particularly valuable for use as a protective padding for bruised areas and it can also serve as a supportive pad. Newly formulated foam rubber is currently being used extensively as inner soles in sports shoes. Covered by a synthetic leather sheet, this new material prevents blisters and calluses by absorbing vertical, front-to-back, and rotary forces. Sponge rubber generally ranges from ⅛ to ½ inch (0.3 to 1.25 cm) in thickness.

Felt is a material composed of matted wool fibers pressed into varying thicknesses that range from ¼ to 1 inch (0.6 to 2.5 cm). Its benefit lies in its comfortable, semiresilient surface, which gives a firmer pressure than most sponge rubbers. Because felt will absorb perspiration, it clings to the skin, and it has less tendency to move about than sponge rubber. Because of its absorbent qualities it must be replaced daily.

Adhesive felt (moleskin) or *sponge rubber* is a felt or sponge rubber material containing an adhesive mass on one side, thus combining a cushioning effect with the ability to be held in specific spot by the adhesive mass. It is a versatile material that is useful on all body parts.

Gauze padding is less versatile than other pad materials. It is assembled in varying thicknesses and can be used as an absorbent or protective pad.

Common materials:
 Sponge rubber
 Felt
 Adhesive felt
 Adhesive sponge rubber
 Gauze padding
 Cotton
 Lamb's wool

Figure 13-19

Types of sports orthoses. **A,** Orthoplast with a foam rubber doughnut; **B,** Orthoplast splint; **C,** Orthoplast rib protector with a foam rubber pad; **D,** fiberglass material for splint construction; **E,** plaster of paris material for cast construction; **F,** foam rubber pad; **G,** Aloplast foam moldable material for protective pad construction.

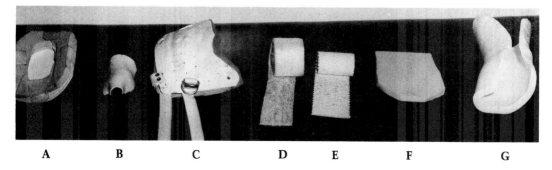

A   B   C   D   E   F   G

Cotton is probably the cheapest and most widely used material in sports. It has the ability to absorb, to hold emollients, and to offer a mild padding effect.

Lamb's wool is a material commonly used by trainers on and around the athlete's toes when circular protection is required. In contrast to cotton, lamb's wool does not pack but keeps its resiliency over a long period of time.

Protective pads can be of varying shapes and sizes, cut to fit the body contours. In addition to the flat and variously shaped compression pads, pads of two other distinct shapes, the *doughnut* and the *horseshoe*, are often used (Fig. 13-20). Each is adapted so that pressure is placed around the perimeter of an injured area, leaving the injury free from additional pressure or trauma.

Rigid Materials

A number of plastic materials are becoming widely used in sports medicine for customized orthoses. They can brace, splint, and protect a body area. They may provide casting for a fracture, support for a foot defect, or a firm nonyielding surface to protect a severe contusion.

Plastics used for these purposes differ in their chemical composition and reaction to heat. The three major categories are thermoforming and thermosetting plastics and thermoplastic foams.[13]

Thermoforming plastics are of the low temperature variety and the most popular in athletic training. When heated to between 140° and 180° F (60° and 82.2° C), depending on the material, the plastic can be accurately molded to a body part. Aquaplast (polyester sheets) and Orthoplast (synthetic rubber thermoplast) are popular types.

Thermosetting plastics require relatively higher temperatures for shaping. They are rigid and difficult to form, usually requiring a mold rather than being formed directly on the body part.[13] High-impact vinyl (polyvinyl chloride), Kydex (polyvinyl chloride acrylic) and Nyloplex (thermoplastic acrylic) are examples of the more commonly used thermoforming plastics.

Thermoplastic foams are plastics that have differences in density as a result of the addition of liquids, gas, or crystals. They are commonly used as shoe inserts and other body padding. Aloplast (polyethylene foam) and Plastazate (polyethylene foam) are two commonly used products.[13]

Figure 13-20

Protective pads can be of varying shapes and sizes and are cut to fit body contours. **A,** Doughnut shape. **B,** Horseshoe shape.

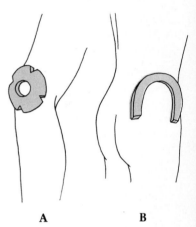

A   **B**

REFERENCES

1. Abdenour, T., Saville, W., White, R., and Abdenour, M.: The effect of ankle taping upon torque and range of motion, Ath. Train. **14:**227, 1979.
2. Freguson, A.B., Jr.: The case against ankle taping, J. Sports Med. **1:**8, 1973.
3. Fischer, R.D.: The measured effect of taping, joint range of motion, and their interaction upon the production of isometric ankle torques, Ath. Train. **17:**218, 1982.
4. Glick, J.M.: The prevention and treatment of ankle injuries, Am. J. Sports Med. **4:**4, 1976.
5. Jahn, W.T.: Visco-elastic orthotics: Sorbothane II, J. Orthop. Sports Phys. Ther. **4:**174, 1983.
6. Juvenal, J.P.: The effects of ankle taping on vertical jumping ability, Ath. Train. **7:**5, 1972.
7. Kozar, B.: Effects of ankle taping upon dynamic balance, Ath. Train. **9:**94, 1974.

8. Libera, D.: Ankle taping, wrapping and injury prevention, Ath. Train. 7:73, 1972.

9. Mayhew, J.L. and Riner, W.F., Jr.: Effects of ankle wrapping on motor performance, Ath. Train. 9:27, 1974.

10. McCluskey, G.M.: Prevention of ankle sprains, Am. J. Sports Med. 4:151, 1976.

11. Meissner, L.: Functional bandages. In Kuprian, W. (editor): Physical therapy for sports, Philadelphia, 1982, W.B. Saunders Co.

12. Metcalf, G.R., and Denegar, C.R.: A critical review of ankle taping, Ath. Train. 18:121, 1982.

13. Peppard, A., and O'Donnell, M.: A review of orthotic plastics, Ath. Train. 18:77, 1983.

14. Rarick, L.: The measurable support of the ankle joint by conventional methods of taping, J. Bone Joint Surg. 44A:1183, 1962.

15. Reid, D.C.: Ankle injuries in sports, J. Sports Med. 1:3, 1973.

16. Sammarco, J.: Beomechanics of the ankle: surface velocity and instant center of rotation in the sagittal plane, Am. J. Sports Med. 5:6, 1977.

17. Soos, T.H.: Taping the injured athlete. In Kulund, D.N. (editor): The injured athlete, Philadelphia, 1982, J.B. Lippincott Co.

ADDITIONAL SOURCES

Dixon, D.: The dixonary of athletic training, Bloomington, Ind., 1965, Bloomcraft-Central Printing, Inc.

Rivell, R.A.: Common padding and strapping used in foot injuries, NATA Annual meeting and clinical symposium, Philadelphia, 1980, Greenville, N.C., National Athletic Trainer's Association. (Cassette.)

The student trainer's manual, Cramer's of Gardner, Kan.

Walsh, W.M., and Blackburn, T.: Prevention of ankle sprains, Am. J. Sports Med. 5:6, 1977.

| # THERAPEUTIC MODALITIES

When you finish this chapter, you should be able to

Differentiate between the physiological responses to therapeutic cold and heat

Apply therapeutic cold and heat modalities

Apply electrical muscle stimulation

Describe the major principles of penetrating heat

Demonstrate therapeutic massage, manual stretching, and trigger point therapy.

Athletic trainers are becoming increasingly skillful in the use of a wide variety of therapeutic modalities. This chapter introduces those modalities that may have special implications to sports injuries.

COLD, HEAT, AND ELECTRICAL STIMULATION

It has been known for centuries that cold, heat, and electrical stimulation have therapeutic capabilities. In modern athletic training and sports medicine they are used in a variety of ways depending on their availability and the trainer's philosophy. However, all therapeutic modalities should be carried out under the direction of a physician.

Cold as Therapy

Application of cold for the first aid of trauma is a well-accepted practice (Chapter 12). When intermittently applied, it is effective from 1 to 72 hours during the initial inflammatory phase of injury (Fig. 14-1).

The major therapeutic value of cold is its ability to produce anesthesia, allowing pain-free exercise.

Although there is some confusion as to exactly how tissues respond to cold, it is becoming very popular in sports medicine as a means of follow-up injury management. The major question in the use of cold rehabilitation is whether or not it can cause significant vasodilation and increase blood flow to the extent that it becomes therapeutic. It has been speculated that the body's initial reaction to sudden cold is by shutting down the small blood vessels to conserve heat. After a period of continued cooling, the body responds by vasodilation to bring in warm blood in an effort to prevent tissue damage. This phenomenon of the body's efforts to prevent tissue damage has been called the *hunting reaction*.[14] It also has been theorized

Foundations of Injury

The extent of cooling depends on the thickness of the subcutaneous fat layer.

that when cold is removed, vasodilation will occur, causing tissue temperature to rise significantly above normal for as long as 3 hours.[16] This belief has been seriously questioned.[11] A major therapeutic value of cold, however, is to produce anesthesia and allow pain-free exercise to be performed.[11]

A great many questions remain to be answered on the effects of cold as a therapeutic modality. Some of the reasons for a lack of concrete answers are the difficulty in measuring changes and the reaction of different body areas to cold exposure.

Local application of cold increases the threshold of muscle spindles, decreasing a muscle's reaction to stretch. The muscles become relaxed, and spasm is reduced. With cold, even if exercise follows, neural activity stays lowered, and spasticity will not readily return. Once a muscle has been cooled through the subcutaneous fat layer, the fat acts as an insulator against rewarming.[12] In individuals with less than ½ inch (1.3 cm) of subcutaneous fat, significant muscle cooling occurs after 10 minutes of cold application. In persons with more than 8/10 inch (2 cm) of subcutaneous fat the muscle temperature barely drops after 10 minutes of ice application.[12] Through spasm control, the cycle of spasm-pain-spasm can be broken, permitting (1) *a greater range of motion*, (2) *an ability to stretch tight muscles*, and (3) *the ability to engage in pain-free coordinated movement*.

Another major attribute of cold therapy is its ability to act selectively on free nerve endings and on peripheral nerves to increase the pain threshold.[22] Pain is also relieved by reducing muscle spasm, swelling, and inflammation.

Other unique qualities of cold are its ability to decrease muscular fatigue, increase and maintain muscular contraction, and increase muscular strength. This is attributed to decreasing the local metabolic rate and tissue temperature.[12] The application of cold also increases collagen stiffness and strength. This reduces the tendency for tendons and ligaments to deform, but may increase joint stiffness.

Figure 14-1

Cold as therapy, intermittently applied, is effective from 1 to 72 hours during the initial inflammatory phase of injury.

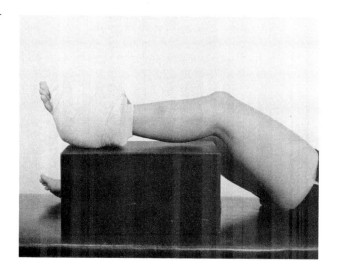

Contraindications to Cold Therapy

Although adverse reactions to therapeutic cold application are uncommon, they do happen, and are described as follows:

1. Cooling for an hour at 30.2° to 15.8° F (−1° to −9° C) produces redness and edema that lasts for 20 hours after exposure.[15] Frostbite has been known to occur in subfreezing temperatures of 26.6° to 24.8° F (−3° to −4° C).

2. Immersion at 41° F (5° C) increases limb fluid volume by 15%.

3. Exposure for 90 minutes at 57.2° to 60.8° F (14° to 16° C) can delay resolution of swelling up to 1 week.

4. Some individuals are allergic to cold, reacting with hives and joint pain and swelling.

5. **Raynaud's phenomenon** is a disease that causes vasospasm of digital arteries lasting for minutes to hours, which could lead to tissue death. The early signs of Raynaud's phenomenon are attacks of intermittent skin blanching or cyanosis of the fingers or toes, skin pallor followed by redness, and finally a return to normal color. Pain is uncommon, but numbness, tingling, or burning may occur during and shortly after an attack.

6. Paroxysmal cold hemoglobinuria is a rare disease that occurs minutes after cold exposure and may lead to renal dysfunction, secondary hypertension, and coma. Early symptoms are severe pain in the back and legs, headache, vomiting, diarrhea, and dark brown urine.

7. Extreme caution should be taken to avoid cooling a body part and allowing the athlete to participate when anesthetized.

8. Although it is relatively uncommon, application of ice can cause nerve palsy.[4] Nerve palsy occurs when cold is applied to a part that has motor nerves close to the skin surface, such as the peroneal nerve at the fibular head. Usually, the condition resolves spontaneously with no significant problem. As a general rule, ice should not be applied longer than 20 to 30 minutes at any one time.

Raynaud's phenomenon
Condition in which cold exposure causes vasospasm of digital arteries

Techniques for Application of Cold

Cold as a first aid medium has been discussed in Chapter 12. It should be applied when hemorrhaging is under control and repair has started, usually 1 to 3 days after injury, based on the nature and extent of the condition. Depending on the body site and thickness of the subcutaneous fat, the following neuromuscular response has been suggested[10]:

Cold therapy can begin 1 to 3 days after injury.

Stage	Response	Time after Initiation
1	Cold sensation	0 to 3 min
2	Burning, aching	2 to 7 min
3	Local numbness, anesthesia; pain, reflex impulses stopped; pain-spasm-pain cycle interrupted	5 to 12 min
4	Deep tissue vasodilation without increased metabolism*	12 to 15 min

Cryotherapy becomes an uncomfortable procedure during stage 2, when burning or aching occurs. This requires encouragement by the trainer or therapist, especially during the first experience. When the athlete experi-

---

*This response is questionable in my opinion.

ences the comfortable stages of 3 and 4, little further encouragement is necessary.[9]

Cryokinetics The early work of Haden[7] and Grant[6] has clearly shown the value of cold when combined with passive or active movement for the treatment of painful musculoskeletal conditions. At stage 3, cold has depressed the excitability of free nerve endings and peripheral nerve fibers with a subsequent increase in the pain threshold. With the pain-spasm-pain cycle diminished, greater pain-free motion is allowed. Although passive movement in the early stages of healing assists in developing more viable collagen tissue, voluntary active movement is preferred whenever possible. A variety of exercise techniques can be employed with cryotherapy.

Ice massage Ice massage has been used in sports to some advantage. The technique calls for massaging the affected part with an ice cylinder obtained from freezing water in a Styrofoam cup, which insulates the hand against the cold. Grasping the ice cylinder with a towel, the trainer massages the affected part in a circular manner, continuing until the part progresses from an uncomfortable chill sensation to an ache and then numbness. This will take from 5 to 10 minutes. When the part is numb, gradual stretching and mobilization are executed by the athlete or the trainer (Fig. 14-2). This technique is simple, inexpensive, and can be carried out at home.

Ice water immersion Immersion in 40° F (4° C) water is a simple means for treating a distal part. After analgesia, which occurs rapidly, the athlete is encouraged to move the part in a normal manner. A combination of cold water and the hydromassage action of a whirlpool has been found to reduce initial swelling and encourage healing.

Ice blanket or pack This is a convenient way to apply cold therapy. It may consist of plastic bags filled with crushed ice or simply toweling saturated with crushed ice. Exercise can begin after 6 to 12 minutes of chilling.[16]

Figure 14-2

Ice massage is an excellent therapeutic modality in sports medicine.

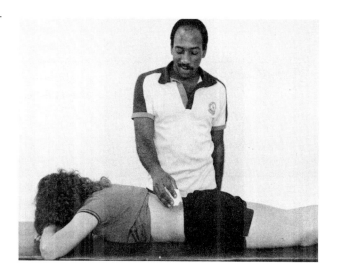

Thermotherapy

The application of heat for disease and traumatic injuries has been used for centuries. Recently, however, its use in the immediate treatment phase of a musculoskeletal injury has been replaced with cold. As with cyrotherapy, there are many unanswered questions as to how heat produces physiological responses, when it is best applied, and what types of thermotherapy are most appropriate for a given condition. The desirable therapeutic effects of heat include (1) increasing the extensibility of collagen tissues, (2) decreasing joint stiffness, (3) reducing pain, (4) relieving muscle spasm, (5) reducing inflammation, edema, and exudates, and (6) increasing blood flow.[13]

Heat affects the extensibility of collagen tissue by increasing the viscous flow of collagen fibers and subsequently relaxing the tension. From a therapeutic point of view, heating contracted connective tissue permits an increase in extensibility through stretching. Muscle fibrosis, a contracted joint capsule, and scars, can be effectively stretched while being heated or just after the heat is removed.[13] An increase in extensibility does not occur unless heat treatment is associated with stretching exercises.

> Heat has the capacity to increase the extensibility of collagen tissue.

Heat, like cold, can relieve pain but for different reasons. Whereas cold numbs the area, heat stimulates the free nerve endings and peripheral nerves by a "gating" mechanism or secretion of endorphins (Chapter 10). Muscle spasm due to **ischemia** can be relieved by heat, which increases blood flow to the area of injury. Heat is also believed to assist inflammation and swelling by a number of related factors, such as raising temperature, increasing metabolism, reducing oxygen tension, lowering the pH level, increasing capillary permeability, and releasing histamine and bradykinin, which cause vasodilation. Histamine and bradykinin are released from some cells during acute and chronic inflammation (Chapter 11). It is also produced by axon reflexes and vasomotor reflex change. Parasympathetic impulses stimulated by heat are believed to be one reason for vasodilation.[13]

> **ischemia**
> Lack of blood supply to a body part

Heat treatments can be categorized as moist, such as derived from a whirlpool or water packs, or dry, such as with an infrared lamp. Heat is provided through conduction, convection, or conversion. **Conduction** refers to direct contact with a hot medium such as a whirlpool or hot-water bath. **Convection** is indirect heat, such as the heated air obtained from a stove. **Conversion** is the production of heat by other forms of energy. An example is diathermy, which produces heat from shortwave radio frequencies. (See the discussion on penetrating heat.)

> **conduction**
> Heating by direct contact with a hot medium
>
> **convection**
> Heating indirectly through another medium such as air or liquid
>
> **conversion**
> Heating by other forms of energy

Superficial Heat

Superficial heat refers to heat that mainly affects the surface of the skin. Important contraindications and precautions regarding the use of heat from any source are as follows:

1. Never apply heat when there is a loss of sensation.
2. Never apply heat immediately after an injury.
3. Never apply heat when there is decreased arterial circulation.
4. Never apply heat directly over the eyes or genitals.
5. Never heat the abdomen during pregnancy.

Examples of superficial heat include moist hot packs, water soaks,

Figure 14-3

The commercial moist heat packs can retain heat for 20 to 30 minutes.

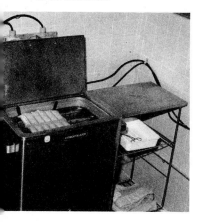

Moist heat packs afford body part relaxation and reduction of the pain-spasm-pain cycle.

whirlpool baths, contrast baths, paraffin baths, and analgesic balms and liniments.

Moist heat therapies   Heated water is one of the most widely used therapeutic modalities in sports medicine. It is readily available for use in any sports medicine program. The greatest disadvantage of hydrotherapy is the difficulty in controlling the therapeutic effects. This is primarily caused by the rapid dissipation of heat, which makes maintaining a constant tissue temperature difficult.

For the most part moist heat aids the healing process in some local conditions by causing higher superficial tissue temperatures; however, joint and muscle circulation increase little in temperature. Superficial tissue is a poor thermal conductor, and temperature rises quickly on the skin surface as compared to the underlying tissues.

Hydrotherapy is best applied to postacute conditions of sprains, strains, and contusions. It produces mild healing qualities with a general relaxation of tense, spasmed muscles.

Each hydrotherapy modality has its own technique of application. Basically, the water temperature must be kept constant, within a range of 90° to 115° F (32.2° to 46.1° C), with variances based on the texture and pigmentation of the athlete's skin. A light-complexioned individual cannot, as a rule, withstand intense moist heat. Conversely, the darker pigmented athlete is able to endure hotter temperatures.

General precautions   The contraindications to and precautions for hydrotherapy are the same as for other types of heat devices. The following considerations must be given:

1. Avoid overheating sensitive skin, the eyes, and the genitals.
2. Never apply heat to a recent injury until hemorrhage has subsided.
3. Use caution when the athlete is submerged in heated water, since light-headedness and even unconsciousness may result as blood is withdrawn from the head and centralized in other areas.

Moist heat packs   Commercial moist heat packs fall into the category of conductive heating. Silicate gel contained in a cotton pad is immersed in thermostatically controlled hot water at a temperature of 175° F (79.4° C). Each pad retains water and a constant heat level for 20 to 30 minutes. Six layers of toweling or commercial terry cloth are used between the packs and the skin. The usefulness of the moist heat pack lies in its adaptability; it can be positioned anywhere on the body.

The major value of the moist heat pack is in the general relaxation it brings and reduction of the pain-spasm-pain cycle (Fig. 14-3). There are limitations of the moist heat pack and all other superficial heating modalities: ". . . the deeper tissues, including the musculature, are usually not significantly heated because the heat transfer from the skin surface into deeper tissues is inhibited by the subcutaneous fat, which acts as a thermal insulator, and by the increased skin flow, which cools and carries away the heat externally applied."[13]

To avoid burns the athlete should not lie on the pad. It has been estimated that the greatest heating occurs within 8 minutes of application and then steadily declines.[13]

Water immersion baths Water is a reasonably good conductor of heat with little heat loss to an immersed part. The two types of immersion baths principally used in sports training are the local bath and the whirlpool hydromassage.

Heated water soak The heated water soak is an adaptable, inexpensive, and readily available method of providing hydrotherapy. Besides increasing circulation, the buoyancy of the water allows mild exercise of painful areas and produces a soothing sensation. Temperatures up to 120° F (48.89° C) can be used with complete safety for 10 to 30 minutes. The heated water soak is often used as a vehicle for selected germicides and medications used to treat infection.

Whirlpool bath A whirlpool bath is a combination therapy, giving the athlete both a massaging action and a hot water bath (Fig. 14-4). It has become one of the most popular thermotherapies used in sports medicine. Through water agitation and the heat transmitted to the injured area, local circulation can be increased, which is usually followed by a reduction in congestion, spasm, and pain. Table 14-1 describes a general treatment approach when using the whirlpool in sports.

When using the whirlpool soon after an injury the water jet should be directed toward the sides of the tank. Directing the stream of water on the injury will only aggravate the condition and perhaps cause additional bleeding.

The whirlpool bath provides both heated water and massaging action.

Figure 14-4

The whirlpool bath combines massage and water that can be at varied temperatures.

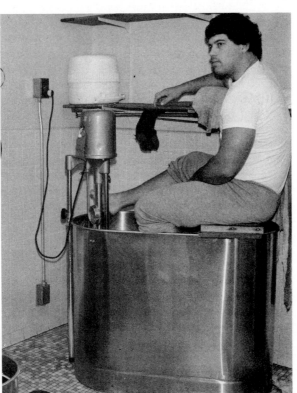

Contrast baths Contrast baths produce hyperemia in feet, ankles, hands, and wrists of individuals who have a chronic inflammatory condition. The following is a sequence of immersion time for each temperature:

The athlete is submerged for 10 minutes in water that is between 105° F and 110° F (40.6° and 43.3° C). After the initial soak, the athlete is submerged for 1 minute in water that is between 59° and 68° F (15° and 20° C) and then shifts to the hot water for 4 minutes, alternating temperatures for a period of 30 minutes.[21]

Contrast bath procedure:
2 minutes immersion in ice slush followed by 30 seconds in tepid water (93° to 98° F [33.9 to 36.7 C]).

A second method of contrast that has become popular in sports medicine uses the concept of alternatively submerging the limb in an ice slush bath for 2 minutes and then in tepid water 93° to 98° F (33.9° to 37.7° C) for 30 seconds. The baths are alternated for 15 minutes, beginning and ending with cold immersion.[1]

Paraffin bath Paraffin bath therapy is particularly effective with injuries to the more angular bony areas of the body, such as the hands, wrists, elbows, knees, ankles, and feet. Because of its high melting point and low heat conductivity, a combination of eight parts of paraffin with one part of mineral oil provides an effective means of bringing sustained heat to the affected area.

Paraffin bath therapy is particularly effective for injuries to the more angular body areas.

In the training room the paraffin mixture is usually contained in a thermostatically controlled unit at a temperature of 126° to 130° F (52° to 54° C). This constant temperature keeps the paraffin and mineral oil mixture in a molten state. Slats at the bottom of the container protect the athlete from burns and collect dirt, which settles to the bottom. This method provides an excellent means of heating the skin at higher temperatures than could ordinarily be tolerated in water.

Therapy by means of the paraffin bath can be delivered in several ways. It can be applied as a pack or a soak or by painting the molten paraffin on an affected part. Packs, soaks, or a combination are the most commonly used methods in sports medicine (Fig. 14-5).

Before therapy, the part to be treated is thoroughly cleaned and dried. Then the athlete dips the affected part into the paraffin bath and quickly

TABLE 14-1

Sample whirlpool routine

Injury Progress	Water Temperature	Duration of Treatment
Step 2 of acute injury	40° F (4.4° C) (ice cold whirlpool)	5 min
Step 3 of acute injury	60° F (15.5° C)	10 min
Step 4 of acute injury	90° F (32.2° C)	10 min
Step 5 of acute injury	100°-102° F (37.8°-38.9° C)	10-20 min
Chronic injury	102°-105° F (38.9°-40.6° C)	10-20 min
To warm part before activity	100°-102° F (37.8°-38.9° C)	5 min
Full-body immersion	90°-100° F (32.2°-37.8° C)	5-10 min

pulls it out, allowing the accumulated wax to dry and form a solid covering. The process of dipping and withdrawing is repeated 6 to 12 times until the wax coating is ¼ to ½ inch (0.62 to 1.3 cm) thick.

If the pack technique is to be employed, the accumulated wax is allowed to solidify on the last withdrawal; then it is completely wrapped in a plastic material that in turn is wrapped with a towel. The packed body part is placed in a position of rest for approximately 30 minutes or until heat is no longer generated. The covering is then removed and the paraffin is scraped back into the container.

If the soak technique is selected, the athlete is instructed to soak the wax-coated part in the hot wax container for 20 to 30 minutes without moving it, after which the part is removed from the container and the paraffin on it is allowed to solidify. The pack procedure can follow the soak or the paraffin coating can be scraped back into the container immediately after it hardens. Once the paraffin has been removed from the part, an oily residue remains that provides an excellent surface for massage.

Other superficial thermotherapies   Water percussion, heated air, and water vapor baths are other therapeutic mediums available for use in the sports program.

Water percussion can take the form of a brisk shower bath or a water stream from a hose. A shower with a temperature of between 100° and 105° F (37.7° to 40.5° C) for a period of 10 to 20 minutes can produce soothing sedation to a fatigued athlete or relieve sore muscles. A water jet from a hose nozzle played directly on a towel that covers a subacute strain or sprain can offer a deep massage effect to the injured area. The towel should be folded into four thicknesses and laid over the injured area to prevent skin irritation from the heavy water stream. The application should not exceed 10 minutes at a temperature of 110° F (43.3° C).

Saunas and *steam baths* are ancient instruments for treating ills and for causing temporary loss of body weight through profuse perspiring. Today we see these devices used by athletes who must achieve a competitive weight, such as is specified in wrestling. Often, these individuals attempt to "make" weight the day of the contest. Such intense heating of the body produces extreme fluid loss, which is fatiguing and generally harmful to the athlete.

Saunas are usually taken in cabinets or special rooms containing machines that electrically heat air. Such baths produce profuse perspiration, resulting in a high fluid loss. Saunas should be given in temperatures ranging from 130° to 160° F (54.4° to 71.1° C) and are most effective with 10- to 20-minute exposures. Heated air therapy, such as the sauna bath, is less fatiguing than vapor therapy because the slower heating of the tissue allows the skin to cool by perspiration.

Steam baths are similar to heated air baths, with the exception that highly heated water is used in its vaporized form. The temperature is maintained at 105° to 115° F (40.5° to 46.1° C) for 20 to 30 minutes in either a cabinet or a closed room. During the first 10 minutes of heating, the athlete feels physically invigorated because of the stimulation of the

Figure 14-5

Paraffin bath therapy is very effective on hands and feet.

central nervous system. If the heating continues for more than 20 minutes, a depression of the system will result. This extreme fluctuation of nervous energy causes greater physical fatigue than that which results from dry heat. Generally, both heated air baths and vapor baths aid in sedating and in producing hyperemia of muscle and articular tissue.

Analgesic balms and liniments Application of a petroleum- or oil-base rubefacient to postacute injuries is one of the most popular therapeutic agents used in sports. Analgesic balm chiefly contains methyl salicylate (oil of wintergreen), capsium (red pepper), and menthol, and it acts as a skin counterirritant (Chapter 16). Analgesic balms and liniments are not actually heat agents but give the feeling of warmth as the result of skin capillary dilation and an increase in local circulation. Because it is applied directly to the skin, it allows freedom of movement while the athlete is receiving a therapeutic increase in local circulation. Both analgesic balms and liniments can be used for massage; however, balms have the added attribute of being used for packs.

The irritation of analgesic balms and liniments is claimed by many to stimulate peripheral sensory and vasomotor nerves, creating capillary dilation and mild anesthesia at the injured site. However, the exact nature of the analgesic action of the balm is not known. The sensation of heat may be caused by the rubefacient irritation, which stimulates superficial pain fibers and increases local capillary circulation. The counterirritant effect seems to be the result of stimulation to the free nerve endings in the skin, which tends to block the pain-spasm-pain cycle.

THE ANALGESIC BALM PACK

Many and varied methods of applying analgesic balm packs have been devised. The following is the most popular procedure.

Materials needed: Analgesic balm, nonsterile cotton, a sheet of paper or plastic, and an elastic bandage.

Procedure
1. A thin layer of balm, approximately ⅛ inch (0.31 cm) thick, is spread over the injured site.
2. A layer of nonsterile cotton or cloth is placed over the balm.
3. A sheet of paper or plastic is laid over the cotton or cloth.
4. An elastic bandage from 3 to 6 inches (7.5 to 15 cm) in width (depending on the area covered) is wrapped around the back of the balm pack to hold it in place.

This method ensures an airtight medium that will generate the analgesic effect for as long as 3 hours.

Indications The use of the analgesic packs as a treatment is varied. Most posttraumatic and chronic conditions can be treated in this manner. Sprains, strains, and muscle contusions will respond adequately to the application of analgesic balm.

Precautions Blistering does not usually occur from an analgesic balm pack, if mild strength is used and if heat therapy does not precede the pack by at least 15 minutes.

Electrical Muscle Stimulation

In recent years, electrotherapy has been used as a means of controlling pain and decreasing tissue swelling and muscle spasm. In sports medicine it should be used as an adjunctive therapy with other approaches, such as cold, ultrasound, and exercise.

The human body has electrical conductivity due to positive and negative ions contained in tissue fluids. Tissue conductivity varies according to the amount of fluid it contains. For example, muscle tissue provides excellent conduction, whereas denser tissues, such as tendons and fascia, are poor conductors. An exception to this fact is that fat is a poor electrical conductor and acts as an insulator against electrical conduction.

An *electrical current* refers to a string of loose electrons that pass along a conductor, such as a nerve or wire. The intensity, or magnitude, of the current is measured in *amperes* (amp); 1 amp equals the rate of flow of 1 *coulomb* (coul) per second. A coulomb is a unit of electrical charge and is defined as the quantity of an electrical charge that can be transferred by 1 amp in 1 second.

An electrical current can alternate periodically and flow in opposite directions, or it can be direct, with the flow of electrons moving in the same direction. Medically, direct current is called *galvanic* current and can flow continuously or be interrupted.

Resistance to the passing of an electrical current along a conductor is measured in *ohms*, and the force that moves the current along is called *voltage* (V). One volt is the amount of electrical force required to send a current of 1 amp through a resistance of 1 ohm. In terms of electrotherapy, currents of 0 to 150 V are considered low-voltage currents, whereas those above 150 V are considered high voltage. The intensity of a current varies directly with the voltage and inversely with the resistance. Electrical power is measured in watts.

A frequency of an electrical current is expressed in cycles per second (cps). In electrotherapy frequencies of less than 1000 cps are low-frequency currents and 100,000 cps are considered as high-frequency currents.[23]

Low-frequency current An alternating low-frequency electrical current that has two equal strokes is known as a *sinusoidal* current. In its original form the sinusoidal, or sine, wave is a continuous, alternating current with a frequency of 60 cps. A muscle contraction can be emitted with each impulse. The current can be altered to produce a muscle contraction that slowly builds to a peak intensity and then returns to a low beginning intensity. This waveform is called *surge* and is commonly used for muscle spasm.

Galvanic and transcutaneous electrical nerve stimulation (TENS)
Two direct currents highly effective in sports medicine are galvanic stimulation and transcutaneous electrical nerve stimulation (TENS).

Galvanic stimulation Galvanic current can be of low or high frequency. The uninterrupted galvanic current does not produce muscular contraction; it is used to cause chemical reactions by breaking up nerve molecules into positively and negatively charged atoms and ions. The positively charged particles are pulled toward the negative pole and, conversely, the negatively charged particles are drawn toward the positive

Galvanic therapy increases blood flow and decreases swelling, spasm, and pain.

Figure 14-6

Electrical stimulation can serve in diagnosis of an injury site and provide a controlled muscle contraction.

pole. Because of the reaction, galvanic therapy increases blood flow and decreases swelling, spasm, and pain.[5,24] Interrupted galvanic current and other currents that cause a muscle contraction can be used for reeducation after injury. Body parts that have been immobilized for a period of time tend to lose their memory for movement. Electrical muscle stimulation can assist in regaining that memory.

Application In electrotherapy, moist electrode pads are fixed directly to the skin. The *active pad*, which brings the current to the body, can range from very small to 4 inches (10 cm) square; the *dispersal pad*, where electrons leave the body, should be as large as possible. The distance between the pads depends on the type of muscle contraction desired. The closer the pads are, the shallower and more isolated the contraction; the farther apart the pads are, the deeper and more generalized the contraction (Fig. 14-6).

In some cases a tetanizing current has been known to relieve a muscle spasm. A frequency between 30 and 40 pulses/sec will produce tetanus. The tetanizing period should be relieved by a time of relaxation. A ratio of 1 to 3 is desirable with 10 seconds of contraction followed by 30 seconds of relaxation. The treatment time should range from 15 to 30 minutes, two or three times a day.

Active exercising can be employed while the muscles are being electrically stimulated. Electrical stimulation with exercise seems to increase muscle fiber innervation. Other therapies that can be effectively combined with electrical stimulation are ice pack treatments or cold water immersion.[5] Care should be taken not to stimulate muscles immediately after an acute injury or to open wounds or incision sites.

Iontophoresis Iontophoresis is the process whereby ions in solution are carried through the intact skin by an electrical current. Using a direct current generator with positive and negative electrodes, the medication is carried into the body via the positive electrode. Medications of choice for musculoskeletal inflammatory conditions have commonly been pain relievers, such as lidocaine (Xylocaine), and anti-inflammatory agents, such as hydrocortisone.[3,8]

Transcutaneous electrical nerve stimulation In recent years, the transcutaneous electrical nerve stimulator (TENS) has become popular in sports medicine for both acute and chronic pain. It produces a direct, low-intensity current that stimulates sensory nerves to block pain transmission. Although not fully understood, it is believed that TENS works on the "gate" mechanism and endorphin concept of pain control.[5]

The electrodes of TENS are placed at trigger points, or dermatome sites adjacent to the injury or surgical incision. Because TENS does not cause muscle contraction, it can be used immediately after injury. TENS does not have to be worn continuously; ½ to 1 hour application will often relieve pain hours after it is removed. Another major value of TENS is that it allows pain-free exercise (Fig. 14-7).

Precautions and counterirritations TENS should never be used during sports participation when there is a chance of reinjury or before an injury is properly healed. It should never be used over the carotid sinus, during pregnancy or on a person who is wearing a pacemaker.

Penetrating Heat

Three major types of penetrating therapeutic heating approaches are in use today. All heat by means of conversion. They are shortwave diathermy, which uses a high electrical frequency; microwave diathermy, which heats through electromagnetic radiation; and ultrasound, which changes electrical current into sound waves.

Shortwave diathermy   The shortwave diathermy machine applies a high-frequency (over 10 megacycles), oscillating, electrical current to the deep tissues of the body. The electrical current is converted to give a homogeneous heating effect. The current is brought to the patient through two cords from the machine generator. The cords terminate in loose cables, drum electrodes, or pads, depending on the requirements of the athlete.

Shortwave diathermy has been purported to raise the internal tissue temperature as much as 9° F (5° C). With this temperature rise there is increased blood flow through the dilated vessels, which in turn accelerates the metabolic processes and phagocytosis. Maximal effects occur in about 20 minutes.

Microwave diathermy   Microwave diathermy produces 2450 megacycles/sec compared to approximately 10 megacycles in shortwave diathermy. Shortwave diathermy treats a widespread area and is generally less safe to use than microwave diathermy; microwave diathermy can be directed to a specific area. The microwave energy is generated by a magnetron tube that produces a high oscillating frequency. Microwave diathermy, in contrast to shortwave diathermy, uses electromagnetic waves for heating. These waves travel a predetermined distance from the reflector head into the athlete's body.

Ultrasound therapy   In recent years, ultrasound has been the most commonly used penetrating therapy in sports medicine. The major equipment necessary to produce therapeutic ultrasound is a generator and an ultrasound applicator. The generator produces a high-frequency alternating current that is transferred to a crystal positioned between electrodes

Major penetrating heat therapies:
   Shortwave diathermy
   Microwave diathermy
   Ultrasound diathermy

Figure 14-7

Transcutaneous electrical nerve stimulation (TENS) is a major approach to the control of pain.
Courtesy Electromedical Products, Inc., Hawthorne, Calif.

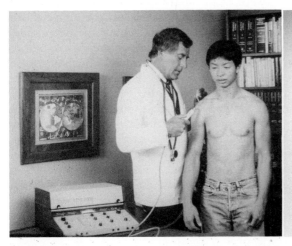
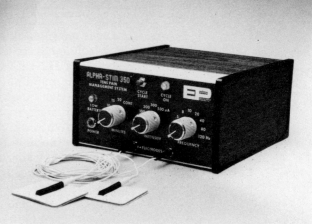

Foundations of Injury

Ultrasound can be applied
directly to the skin or
through a water medium.

in the sound applicator or transducer. Electrical current causes the crystal to vibrate, which is changed to mechanical energy.

When applied to an injured area, the mechanical energy becomes converted into heat. A micromassage action also takes place from the vibration. The greatest heating takes place in denser structures, such as bone and connective tissue. Little heating occurs in the subcutaneous fat or muscle.[13]

Localized heating results primarily at an interface of two different tissues, such as bone and ligaments or capsules. The mechanical energy causes a pressure wave to be created as it comes in contact with tissue of different viscosities. This energy then is changed into heat because of the motion of molecules within the tissue. There is a high rise of temperature at the bone and usually an increased temperature in a joint capsule and ligament. It also causes a temperature rise in scar tissue.

Indications Ultrasound therapy is of major value when combined with exercise for constricted capsular structures, ligamentous injury, muscle contractures, and tendinous injuries.[13] It can temporarily relieve pain. Ultrasound therapy has some value in calcific bursitis and tendinitis.

Operation Transducer heads that are stationary or movable are available. Stationary ultrasound employs an intermittent sound transmission to the body part. Also available are moving ultrasound machines that can be pulsed, creating a mechanical effect only, and machines that can be combined with electrical stimulation. There is some doubt as to the complete effectiveness of stationary and pulsed machines, especially if maximal therapeutic heating is a major goal.

When ultrasound is applied directly to the skin, a *coupling medium* must be used. Coupling mediums can include a variety of materials, some of which are mineral oil or water-soluble creams or gels. The purpose of a coupler is to provide an airtight contact with the skin and a slick, friction-proof surface to glide over. When a water-soluble material is used, the skin should first be washed and dried to prevent air bubbles from hampering the flow of mechanical energy into the skin.

Stroking methods Movement of the transducer can be in a circular pattern or a stroking pattern. In the circular pattern the transducer is applied in small overlapping circles. In the stroking pattern the transducer is moved back and forth, overlapping the preceding stroke by half. Both techniques are carried out slowly and deliberately. The field covered should not exceed 3 to 4 inches (7.5 to 10 cm). The pattern to use is determined mainly by the skin area to be treated. For example, the circular pattern is best for highly localized areas, such as the shoulder, whereas in larger, more diffuse injury areas, the stroking pattern is best employed. When a highly irregular surface area is to be given therapy, the underwater method should be employed.

Underwater application Underwater ultrasound is suggested for such irregular body parts as the wrist, hand, elbow, knee, ankle, and foot. The part is fully submerged in water; then the ultrasound head is submerged and positioned about 1 inch (2.5 cm) from the body part to be treated. The water medium provides an airtight coupling, allowing sound waves to travel at a constant velocity. To ensure uninterrupted therapy, air bubbles that form on the skin must be continually wiped away. The sound head is moved slowly in a circular or longitudinal pattern.

Dosage and treatment time Dosage of ultrasound varies according to the depth of the tissue treated and the state of injury, such as subacute or chronic. Basically, 0.1 to 0.8 watts/cm² is regarded as low intensity, 0.8 to 1.5 watts/cm² is medium intensity, and 1.5 to 3 watts/cm² is high intensity. The duration of treatment time ranges from 3 to 8 minutes. Treatment ranges from daily to three times per week.

Precautions and contraindications Although ultrasound is a relatively safe modality, certain precautions must be taken, and in some situations it should never be used. Great care must be taken in anesthetized areas because the sensation of pain is one of the best indicators of overdosage. In general, ultrasound must not be applied to highly fluid areas of the body, such as the eyes, ears, brain, spinal cord, or heart. Reproductive organs and a pregnant abdomen also must be avoided. Acute injuries should not be treated with ultrasound. In the past, epiphyseal growth areas were contraindicated; however, it has been determined that within therapeutic dosages, ultrasound is safe[13] (Fig. 14-8).

Ultrasonic phonophoresis Phonophoresis is a method of driving molecules through the skin by ion transfer with a direct galvanic current or by the mechanical vibration of the ultrasound.[21] Like ionophoresis, it is designed to move an entire molecule of medication into injured tissues. Some sports medicine personnel prefer this to ionophoresis, indicating that it is less hazardous to the skin and that there is greater penetra-

Figure 14-8

Ultrasound diathermy is one of the most commonly used therapies in sports medicine.

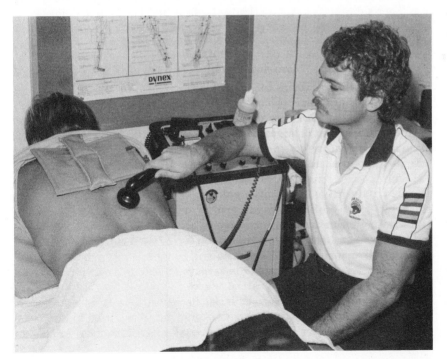

tion.[20] As with ionophoresis, phonophoresis is predominately used to introduce a hydrocortisone and an anesthetic into the tissues. This method has been successful with painful trigger points, tendinitis, and bursitis.[20]

MASSAGE

Massage is defined as a systematic manipulation of the soft tissues of the body. The movements of gliding, compressing, stretching, percussing, and vibrating are regulated to produce specific responses in the athlete.[25]

Primarily, massage is separated into five basic categories: effleurage, pétrissage, friction, tapotement, and vibration. **Effleurage** is a technique in which the body or body part is stroked with the heels and palms of the hands gliding over the body. **Pétrissage** is a technique in which soft tissue, held between the thumb and forefinger, is alternately rolled, lifted, and twisted to loosen tissue and stimulate fluid drainage. **Friction** movements are used successfully on joints and areas where there is little soft tissue and on soft tissue that is indurated or spasmed. The fingers and thumbs move in circular patterns, stretching the underlying tissue and thus increasing circulation to the part. **Tapotement** consists of cupping, hacking, and pincing movements. **Vibration** is the rapid shaking of tissue by hand or using a machine vibrator.

effleurage
Stroking

pétrissage
Kneading

friction
Heat producing

tapotement
Percussion

vibration
Rapid shaking

Therapeutic Effects of Massage

Historically, wherever sports have been seriously undertaken, massage has been used in some form. Even today it is widely used throughout the world. Manipulation of soft tissue by massage is a useful adjunct to other modalities. Sports massage causes mechanical, physiological, and psychological responses.

Mechanical Responses

Mechanical responses to massage occur as a direct result of the graded pressures and movements of the hand on the body. Such actions encourage venous and lymphatic drainage and mildly stretch superficial and scar tissue. Connective tissue can be effectively stretched by friction massage, which helps to prevent rigidity in scar formation. When enforced inactivity is imposed on the athlete, as the aftermath of an injury or when edema surrounds a joint, the stagnation of circulation may be prevented by employing certain massage techniques.

Physiological Responses

Possible physiological
responses of massage:
  Reflex responses
  Relaxation
  Stimulation
  Increased circulation

Massage can increase circulation and as a result increase metabolism to the musculature, and aid in the removal of metabolites such as lactic acid.[25] It also helps overcome venostasis and edema by increasing circulation at and around the injury site, assisting in the normal venous blood return to the heart.

The *reflex effects* of massage are processes that, in response to nerve impulses initiated through rubbing the body, are transmitted to one organ by afferent nerve fibers and then respond back to another organ by efferent fibers. Reflex responses elicit a variety of organ reactions, such as body relaxation, stimulation, and increased circulation.

Relaxation can be induced by slow, superficial stroking of the skin. It is a type of massage that is beneficial for tense, anxious athletes who may require gentle treatment.

Stimulation is attained by quick, brisk action that causes a contraction of superficial tissue. The benefits derived by the athlete are predominately psychological. He or she feels invigorated after intense manipulation of the tissue. In the early days of American sports, stimulation massage was given as a warm-up procedure, but it has gradually lost popularity because of the time involved and the recognition that it is relatively ineffectual physiologically.

Increased circulation is accomplished by mechanical and reflex stimuli. Together they cause the capillaries to dilate and be drained of fluid as a result of firm outside pressure—thus stimulating cell metabolism, eliminating toxins, and increasing lymphatic and venous circulation. In this way the healing process is aided.

Psychological Responses

The tactile system is one of the most sensitive systems in the human organism. From earliest infancy humans respond psychologically to being touched. Because massage is the act of laying on of hands, it can be an important means for creating a bond of confidence between the trainer and the athlete.

Sports Massage

Massage in sports is usually confined to a specific area and is seldom given to the full body. The time required for giving an adequate and complete body massage is excessive in athletics. It is not usually feasible to devote this much time to one athlete; 5 minutes is usually all that is required for massaging a given area.

Massage Lubricants

To enable the hands to slide easily over the body, a friction-proofing medium must be used. Rubbing the dry body can cause gross skin irritation by tearing and breaking off the hair. Many mediums can be used to advantage as lubricants, such as fine powders, oil liniments, or almost any substance having a petroleum base.

Positioning the Athlete

Proper positioning for massage is of great importance. The injured part must be made easily accessible, while the athlete is comfortable and the part to be massaged is relaxed.

Confidence

Lack of confidence by the person doing the massage is easily transmitted through inexperienced hands. Every effort should be made to think out the procedure to be used and to present a confident appearance to the athlete.

Massage Procedures
Effleurage

Effleurage, or stroking (Fig. 14-9), is divided into light and deep methods. Light stroking is designed primarily to be sedative. It is also used in the early stages of injury treatment. Deep stroking is a therapeutic compression of soft tissue, which encourages venous and lymphatic drainage. A different application of effleurage may be employed for a specific body part.

Light and deep stroking of the back   A pillow or pad is placed under the athlete's pelvis to relax the low back region. When stroking the back, the heel of the hand is pushed upward upon the back of the athlete to the heavy trapezius muscle, where the fingers encircle and lift the soft tissue (trapezial milking), and then trail down to where the stroke commenced. The stroke starts in the lower lumbar area, as close as possible to the vertebral column. The hands stroke upward, covering the entire length of the spine and over the tops of the shoulders. When the length of the spine has been covered, the fingers move out from the center about ½ inch (1.3 cm) and trail down the back to start the succeeding stroke. Progressively the hands move out to the periphery of the back until the whole area has been rubbed, then they proceed inward toward the center. To facilitate relaxation, as well as vascular drainage, the hands should maintain a definite rhythm and never lose contact with the athlete's back. Another excellent relaxation technique is to initiate a slow stroking directly over and down the full length of the spinal column.

Stroking of the lower limb   When effleurage is applied to a lower limb, the same principles as those used in back massage must be followed: begin the stroking at about the middle of the thigh, rubbing upward over the buttocks to the lower back, and then trail down to a point below the place where the stroke was initiated. Each stroke starts about ½ inch (1.3 cm) below the preceding one, until the entire limb has been massaged. A pad should be placed under the knee and the ankle. Pressure should be applied lightly in these areas.

Stroking of the shoulder and arm   Effleurage to the arm is much like that to the lower limb. Stroking begins over the scapula and then moves over the upper chest region, progressing gradually down until stroking has been performed on the entire length of the arm.

Stroking variations   There are many variations in effleurage massage; some that are of particular value to sports injuries are pressure

Figure 14-9

Effleurage.

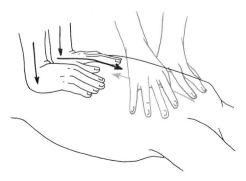

variations, the hand-over-hand method, and the cross body method.[25] *Pressure variations* range from very light to deep and vigorous stroking. Light stroking, as discussed earlier, can induce relaxation or may be used when an area is especially sensitive to the touch; on the other hand, deep massage is designed to bring about definite physiological responses. Light and deep effleurage can be used alternately when both features are desired. The *hand-over-hand* stroking method is of special benefit to those surface areas which are particularly unyielding. It is performed by an alternate stroke in which one hand strokes, followed immediately by the overlaying of the other hand, somewhat like shingles on a roof (Fig. 14-10). The *cross body* effleurage technique is an excellent massage for the low back region. The operator places a hand on each side of the athlete's spine. Both hands first stroke simultaneously away from the spine, then both hands at the same time stroke toward the spine (Fig. 14-11).

Pétrissage

Kneading, or pétrissage (Fig. 14-12), is a technique adaptable primarily to loose and heavy tissue areas such as the trapezius, the latissimus dorsi, or the triceps muscles. The procedure consists of picking up the muscle and skin tissue between the thumb and forefinger of each hand and rolling and twisting it in opposite directions. As one hand is rolling and twisting, the other begins to pick up the adjacent tissue. The kneading action wrings out the muscle, thus loosening adhesions and squeezing congestive materials into the general circulation. Picking up skin may cause an irritating pinch. Whenever possible, deep muscle tissue should be gathered and lifted.

Friction

The friction massage (Fig. 14-13) is used often around joints and other areas where tissue is thin, as well as on tissues that are especially unyielding, such as scars, adhesions, muscle spasms, and fascia. The action is initiated by bracing with the heels of the hands, then either holding the thumbs steady and moving the fingers in a circular motion or holding the fingers steady and moving the thumbs in a circular motion. Each method is adaptable to the type of area or articulation that is being massaged. The motion is started at a central point and then a circular movement is initiated, the hands moving in opposite directions away from the center point. The pur-

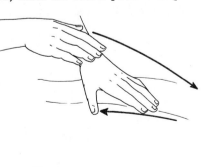

Figure 14-10

Hand-over-hand effleurage.

Figure 14-11

Cross-body effleurage.

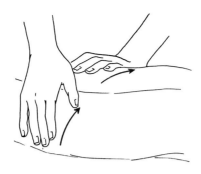

Figure 14-12

Pétrissage.

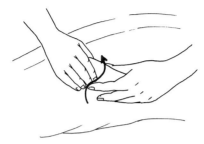

Figure 14-13

Friction massage.

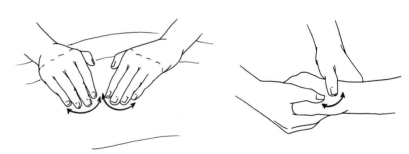

Figure 14-14

Tapotement. **A**, Cupping.
B, Hacking. **C**, Pincing.

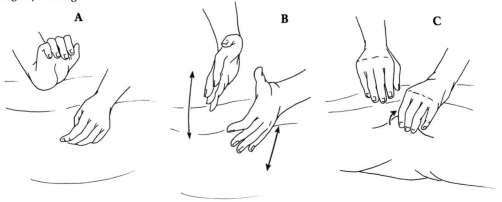

pose is to stretch the underlying tissue, develop friction in the area, and increase circulation around the joint.

Tapotement

The most popular methods of tapotement, or percussion, are the cupping, hacking, and pincerlike, or pincing, movements.

Cupping   The cupping action produces an invigorating and stimulating sensation. It is a series of percussion movements, rapidly duplicated at a constant tempo. One's hands are cupped to such an extent that the beat emits a dull and hollow sound, quite opposite to the sound of the slap of the open hand. The hands move alternately, from the wrist, with the elbow flexed and the upper arm stabilized (Fig. 14-14, A). The cupping action should be executed until the skin in the area develops a pinkish coloration.

Hacking   Hacking can be used in conjunction with cupping to bring about a varied stimulation of the sensory nerves (Fig. 14-14, B). It is similar to cupping, except the hands are rotated externally and the ulnar or little finger border of the hand is the striking surface. Only the heavy muscle areas should be treated in this manner.

Pincing   Although pincing is not in the strictest sense percussive, it is placed under tapotement because of the vigor with which it is applied. Alternating hands lift small amounts of tissue between the first finger and thumb in quick, gentle pinching movements (Fig. 14-14, C).

Vibration

Vibration is rapid movement that produces a quivering or trembling effect. It is mainly used in sports for its ability to relax and soothe. Although vibration can be done manually, the machine vibrator is usually the preferred modality.

Effective Massaging

Besides knowing the different kinds of massage, one should have an understanding of how to give the most effective massage. The following rules should be employed whenever possible:

1. Make the athlete comfortable:
   a. Place the body in the proper position on the table.
   b. Place a pad under the areas of the body that are to be massaged.
   c. Keep the training room at a constant 72° F (22.2° C) temperature.
   d. Respect the athlete's privacy by draping him or her with a blanket or towel, exposing only the body parts to be massaged.
2. Develop a confident, gentle approach when massaging:
   a. Assume a position that is easy both on you and on the athlete.
   b. Avoid using too harsh a stroke, or further insult to the injury may result.
3. To ensure proper lymphatic and venous drainage, stroke toward the heart whenever possible.
4. Know when not to use massage:
   a. Never give a massage when there may be a local or general

infection. To do so may encourage its spread or aggravate the condition.

b. Never apply massage directly over a recent injury; limit stroking to the periphery. Massaging over recent injuries may dislodge the clot organization and start bleeding.

Cyriax Massage

Cyriax massage is a method of deep transverse friction massage.

The Cyriax method of deep friction massage is being increasingly used in sports medicine. It is a specific technique for muscles, tendons, ligaments, and joint capsules. The major goal of Cyriax massage is to move transversly across a ligament or tendon to mobilize it as much as possible. This technique often precedes active exercise. According to Cyriax,[2] deep transverse friction massage restores mobility to a muscle in the same way as mobilization frees a joint.

The position of the athletic trainer's hands is very important in gaining maximal strength and control. Four positions are suggested: index finger crossed over the middle finger, middle finger crossed over the index finger, two fingers side by side, and an opposed finger and thumb (Fig. 14-15).

The massage must be directly over the site of lesion and pain. The fingers move with the skin and do not slide over it. Massage must be across the grain of the affected tissue. The thicker the structure, the more friction is given.[25] The technique is to sweep back and forth the full width of the tissue. Massage should not be given to acute injuries or over highly swollen tissues. A few minutes of this method will produce a numbness in the area, and exercise or mobilization can be instituted.

Figure 14-15

Cyriax massage is a specific technique for muscle, tendons, ligaments, and joint capsules using a variety of hand positions. **A,** Index finger crossed over the middle finger. **B,** Middle finger crossed over the index finger. **C,** Two fingers side by side. **D,** Opposed finger and thumb.

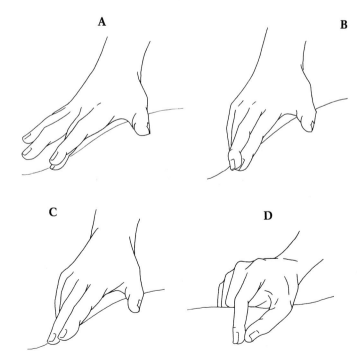

A B

C D

MANUAL STRETCHING

Any disturbance in the musculature or connective tissue surrounding a joint can restrict the amplitude of movement. Injuries in sports can cause muscle weaknesses, poor bony alignments, or abnormal tightness of the connective tissue surrounding the articulations. Abnormal muscle or fascial tightness of the trunk and lower extremities can be reflected in postural deviations. Restoration of normal joint alignment and flexibility is of the utmost importance to the athlete. The optimal range of motion must be obtained so that the athlete may perform adequately and have the postural balance and elasticity needed to withstand the majority of traumatic forces incurred in sports.

Although active motion is the most desirable, passive stretching can increase joint range of motion. Whenever feasible, it is desirable for the athlete to assist passive stretching by moving in the direction of the stretch. *Passive stretching* is the loosening of the tissue surrounding and adjacent to an articulation so that its range of motion can be increased.

Effective techniques of manipulation and stretching are invaluable as a sequel to massage and other treatment procedures for injuries. Massage and stretching procedures in sports help restore full function. Before carrying out passive stretching, there must be a complete understanding of the following: the *indications* for stretching, the correct *positioning* for most effective movement of the part, procedures for the proper *execution* of various actions, and, finally, the *precautions* to be observed. *NOTE: At no time should stretching be applied until there is absolute knowledge that no fracture is present and stretching will not aggravate a serious existing injury.*

Indications

It is well known that acute or chronic conditions may result in a limited range of motion. After the effects of an internal injury to a joint have subsided, normal movement should be encouraged whenever it is possible without deterring the healing process. Internal scar tissue and adhesions resulting from joint inactivity can often be averted through passive exercising of the part. In chronic conditions there may be a special problem, because overuse or abnormal stresses may have been the etiological factors. Hence, every precaution must be taken to maintain function without additional aggravation. This may require less passive stretching, thereby sacrificing function for adequate and complete healing.

Positioning

Poor positioning and improper isolation of the part to be treated may cause additional insult to the injury. The athlete's confidence in the ability of the trainer will be jeopardized if abnormal stresses or strains are manifested outside the injured area.

Execution

When a stretch is given, the athlete must be completely relaxed so that the connective tissue and musculature are effectively stretched. If the athlete is tense and apprehensive, a lead-up massage combined with soothing conversation may be helpful. When stretching is about to begin, the athlete should inhale deeply and then exhale slowly. When it has been decided that the athlete is at ease and thoroughly relaxed, the mobilization technique is performed directly after one of the exhalations. Exhaling helps the athlete avoid tensing a particular muscle group in anticipation of the mobilization procedure. Quick or extremely harsh moves should be avoided. Emphasis should be placed on steady, progressive movement.

Precautions

To ensure adequate and safe stretching, the following should be noted:
1. *Never attempt stretching of a suspected fracture.*
2. Always wait until internal hemorrhage has subsided before attempting stretching.
3. Increase the circulation to an area before any stretching.
4. Position the athlete to effect the best results without strain to other parts of the body.
5. Before stretching takes place, have the athlete completely relaxed to ensure the stretching of connective tissue as opposed to musculature.

Selected Techniques

The following selected stretching techniques are commonly conducted in athletic training programs by experienced trainers.

Figure 14-16

Cervical transaction stretch.

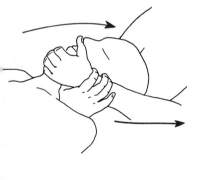

Cervical Region
Traction stretch

Indications When muscle contractures occur in the cervical region, traction may aid in securing relaxation. Traction can be given by manual stretching (Fig. 14-16) or by means of a mechanical traction device. Both have their values. When traction is needed over an extended period of time, as in a neck strain, progressive mechanical traction may be indicated by the physician. *NOTE: The traction stretch is specifically mentioned as one of the safest techniques because it does not twist the head in relation to the neck and because it is similar to the performance of the traction machine used in physical medicine.*

Positioning The athlete lies supine and completely relaxed. The operator stands at the head of the table, cupping the left hand and grasping the point of the athlete's chin. Next, the trainer's right forearm is placed under the cervical curve of the athlete's neck, and the trainer grasps his or her own left wrist. In this position the head is securely stabilized and will allow a secure, comfortable pull.

A traction device should be used only under the direction of a physician. The starting weight resistance should be no more than from 5 to 10 pounds. The athlete's tolerance increases progressively with each treatment. Application time may range from 5 to 10 minutes. It is suggested that heat in some form be applied along with the traction to produce muscle relaxation.

Execution Before traction is applied a light effleurage massage is advisable to obtain muscle relaxation. After assuming the traction position, one pulls gently until the athlete's neck is at its greatest length. At this point traction is maintained for about 2 minutes.

Precautions Traction should never be initiated by the trainer if there is any possibility of a fracture. In any severe condition of the neck a physician must be consulted before traction is applied. Massage and relaxation techniques should be applied before traction is given. Sudden movements or excessive elongation of the neck should be avoided. Before stretch is given, the operator must be sure that the athlete's chin is depressed, keeping the back of the neck as flat as possible. The force of the stretch should be felt along the entire cervical and thoracic spine.

Thoracic Region
Chest lift stretch

Indications The chest lift (Fig. 14-17) is a general thoracic stretch designed to extend the spinalis muscle group lying along the vertebral column. It may be used to advantage for mild strains and for a general loosening of the thoracic cage.

Positioning The athlete sits with legs extended and fingers interlaced behind the head. The operator stands behind the athlete and places one knee on the table. The trainer's arms are placed through the arms of the athlete, the hands are placed directly under the posterior rib cage, and the athlete is instructed to lie back on the trainer's knee.

Execution Lying with the spine directly over the operator's knee, the athlete is instructed to take a deep breath and exhale. At this time the operator pushes downward with the arms on the athlete's shoulders and pulls the athlete's rib cage upward with the hands.

Precautions Avoid stretching when possible serious rib or vertebral injuries are suspected or when there is a shoulder injury. NOTE: *Do not apply too much force to the shoulders.*

Compression stretch

Indications Upper back strains, fatigue, or muscle spasms may warrant the compression stretch (Fig. 14-18) as part of the massage procedure.

Positioning The athlete lies face down, arms to the side, and rests the forehead on the table. Padding may be placed under the chin and chest for comfort. The operator stands facing forward at the side of the table, in line with the athlete's hips. The hands are crossed over one another, placing the heels of the palms at the twelfth rib on each side of the spine, approximately over the transverse processes.

Execution The operator pushes gently downward, forward, and outward, depressing the rib cage as the athlete exhales. Each time a stretch is applied the operator should move slowly upward, initiating successive stretches, until the entire thoracic cage has been covered.

Precautions Never stretch where there may be torn cartilage or a rib or vertebral fracture. Push gently, but do not stretch hard or suddenly or trauma may be increased. The best results are obtained after circulation in the area has been increased by massage, whirlpool, or heat lamp.

Figure 14-17

Chest lift stretch.

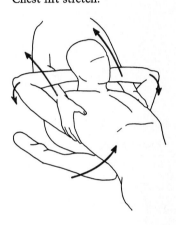

Figure 14-18

Compression stretch.

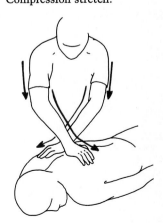

Figure 14-19

Trunk rotation stretch.

Figure 14-20

Scapular stretch.

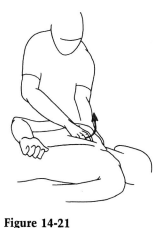

Figure 14-21

Elbow traction stretch.

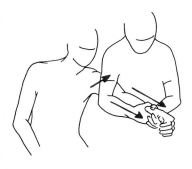

Thoracic and Lumbosacral Region
Trunk rotation stretch

Indications Limited ranges of motion on trunk rotation may be increased by use of the trunk rotation stretch.[2]

Positioning The athlete sits on a stool or chair with the hips placed against the back of the chair and the feet planted firmly on the floor (Fig. 14-19). The operator stands to one side of the chair, facing the athlete. The operator then places his or her outside leg over the knees of the athlete, stabilizing the lower limbs. Reaching around the back of the athlete's upper trunk, the athlete grasps the shoulder nearest to the back of the chair and pulls it toward him or her. Simultaneously, the operator places a free hand on the athlete's near shoulder and pushes forward, thus effecting a forced torsion of the athlete's upper trunk.

Execution The athlete exhales as the trunk is rotated, which should be executed with a slow and even pressure, beyond the point of restriction. It is desirable that the athlete have at least a 90-degree range of motion.

Precautions Make certain that the athlete's hips are maintained in a stabilized position against the back of the chair. NOTE: *Do not attempt to stretch when the athlete's lungs are expanded.*

Scapular Region
Scapular stretch

Indications The scapula pulls away from the rib cage, giving the sensation of more than normal freedom of movement at the shoulder girdle. This stretch is an excellent adjunct to the shoulder massage.

Positioning The athlete lies prone, with the arm that is to be stretched at the side in a hammer lock position; that is, the arm is bent at right angles across the back (Fig. 14-20). The operator stands facing the athlete's shoulder, places the hand closest the head underneath the point of the shoulder, and then lifts gently upward as the other hand grasps the spinal border of the scapula.

Execution With a gentle lifting of the hand and grasping the scapula, the operator pulls outward and away from the rib cage.

Precautions A pad, placed over the scapula, should be used if irritation is evident on grasping this area.

Elbow Region
Elbow traction stretch

Indications This procedure can be used to stretch out contracted capsular and tendinous tissue.

Positioning The athlete, in either a sitting or a standing position, places the affected arm underneath the operator's arm (Fig. 14-21). The operator, whose back is to the athlete, reaches over the athlete's arm and then with both hands grasps the athlete's wrist.

Execution In this position the operator gradually extends the athlete's arm forward, placing traction in the elbow joint. The elbow should never be forced into extension but should be stretched gradually. An increased range of movement can be facilitated if flexion is first initiated through several repetitions before extension is attempted.

Precautions   This traction stretch should be used only in cases of inelastic and contracted tissue, never after a recent elbow dislocation or serious strain.

Lumbosacral Region

Low back rotation stretch

Indications   Increasing the range of motion of the lower back often relieves the irritation of strain and chronic fibromyositis.

Positioning   The athlete lies in a supine position with hips turned laterally to the trunk, the upper leg flexed at a 90-degree angle. The operator stands at the middle of the table, facing the athlete, and places the hand that is on the side of the athlete's feet directly on the side of the knee, positioning the other hand on the athlete's shoulder.

Execution   In this position the operator stabilizes the athlete's shoulder and with a scissors action pushes the pelvis forward, thereby initiating a stretch (Fig. 14-22).

Precautions   Do not stretch if there is a possibility of a fracture. Do not thrust, but stretch with an even and steady movement. *Do not stretch beyond normal pain limitations.*

Low back scissors stretch

Indications   This mild stretch is to be used with an effleurage massage of the back; it helps to relax and loosen contracted tissue.

Positioning   The athlete lies prone with arms at the side. The operator stands transversely at the middle of the table, on the side opposite the one to be stretched. With the hand nearest the athlete's feet, the operator grasps the anterosuperior spine of the ilium and places the heel of the other hand on the lumbar area of the spine, directly over the transverse process (Fig. 14-23).

Execution   The operator pulls upward on the anterosuperior spine and simultaneously pushes downward on the lower thoracic and lumbar area of the spine.

Precautions   Do not stretch if there is a possibility of fracture or if the athlete complains of tenderness at the anterosuperior spine of the ilium. In the latter instance, a pad should be placed on the site before it is grasped.

MYOFASCIAL PAIN AND TRIGGER POINT THERAPY

Acute and chronic musculoskeletal pain can be due to myofascial trigger points. A **trigger point** is a specific sensitive area that has been referred to soft tissue. Such pain sites have variously been described as fibrositis, myositis, myalgia, myofacitiis, and muscular strain.[17] Trigger points are small hyperirritable areas within a muscle in which nerve impulses bombard the central nervous system and are expressed as a referred pain.[26]

There are two types of trigger points: active and latent. The active trig-

Figure 14-22

Low back rotation stretch.

Figure 14-23

Low back scissors stretch.

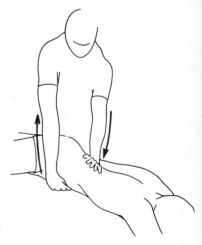

trigger points
Small hyperirritable areas within a muscle

Figure 14-24

Spraying of Fluori-Methane and passive stretching for trigger points and myofascial pain.

ger point is hyperirritable and causes an obvious complaint. The latent trigger point, on the other hand, is dormant, producing no complaint, except perhaps a loss of range of motion. The trigger point does not follow a usual area of distribution such as sclerotomes, dermatomes, or peripheral nerves. (See Fig. 10-13.) The trigger point pain area is called the *reference zone*, which could be close to the point or a considerable distance from the point.[17,18]

One method of determining an active trigger point is to reproduce the injured athlete's major pain complaint by pressing firmly on the site for 5 to 10 seconds. Another assessment technique is to elicit a "jump response" by placing the athlete's muscle under moderate tension, applying firm pressure, and briskly pulling a finger across the tight band of muscle. This procedure causes the tight band of muscle to contract and the athlete to wince or cry out.[18]

A number of techniques have been used to alleviate the active trigger point. Some of these methods include injection with a local anesthetic–like agent, ice massage, acupressure, acupuncture, ultrasound, muscle stimulation, and the spray and stretch method.[19]

The spray and stretch method for treating trigger points and myofascial pain has become a major approach (Fig. 14-24). The coolant of choice is Fluori-Methane.

Steps to the Spray and Stretch Technique

1. Position the athlete in a relaxed but well-supported position. The muscle that contains the trigger point is stretched (an exception to this is the sternocleidomastoid muscle).
2. Alert the athlete that the spray will feel cool.
3. Hold the Fluori-Methane bottle about 12 inches (30 cm) away from the skin to be sprayed.
4. Direct the spray at an acute angle in one direction toward the reference zone of pain.
5. Direct the spray to the full length of the muscle, including the reference zone of pain.
6. Begin firm stretching that is within the athlete's pain tolerance.
7. Continue spraying in parallel sweeps that are about ¼ inch (0.6 cm) apart at a speed of about 4 inches (10 cm) every second.
8. Cover the skin area one or two times.
9. Continue passive stretching while spraying (don't force the stretch; allow time for the muscle to "let go").
10. After the first session of spraying and stretching, warm the muscle with a hot pack or by vigorous massage.
11. A second session may be necessary after step 10.
12. When a stretch has been completed, have the athlete actively but gently move the part in a full range of motion.
13. Do not overload a muscle with strenuous exercise immediately after a stretch.
14. After an initial spraying and stretching session, instruct the athlete on stretch exercises that should be performed at home on a daily basis.

REFERENCES

1. Cooper, D.L., and Fair, J.: Contrast baths and pressure treatment of ankle sprains, Phys. Sportsmed. 7:143, April 1979.
2. Cyriax, J.: Treatment of manipulation and deep massage, ed. 6, New York, 1959, Paul B. Hoeber, Inc.
3. Delacerda, F.G.: Iontophoresis for treatment of shinsplints, J. Orthop. Sports Phys. Ther. 3:183, Spring 1982.
4. Driz, D., et al.: Cryotherapy and nerve palsy, Am. J. Sports Med. 9:256, July/Aug. 1981.
5. Gieck, J.H.: The athletic trainer and rehabilitation. In Kulund, D.N. (editor): The injured athlete, Philadelphia, 1982, J.B. Lippincott Co.
6. Grant, A.E.: Massage with ice (cryokinetics) in the treatment of painful conditions of the musculoskeletal system, Arch. Phys. Med. Rehab. 44:233, 1964.
7. Haden, C.A.: Cryokinetics in an early treatment program, Phys. Ther. 44:990, 1964.
8. Harris, P.R.: Iontophoresis: clinical research in musculoskeletal inflammatory conditions, J. Orthop. Sports Phys. Ther. 4:109, Fall 1982.
9. Hocutt, J.E., Jr.: Cryotherapy, Am. Fam. Physician 23:141, 1981.
10. Hocutt, J.E., Jr., et al.: Cryotherapy in ankle sprains, Am. J. Sports Med. 10:316, Sept./Oct. 1982.
11. Knight, J.L., and Londeree, B.R.: Comparison of blood flow in the ankle of uninjured subjects during therapeutic applications of heat, cold, and exercise, Med. Sci. Sports Exerc. 12:76, 1980.
12. Lehmann, J.F., and DeLateur, B.J.: Cryotherapy. In Lehmann, J.F. (editor): Therapeutic heat and cold, ed. 3, Baltimore, 1982, The Williams & Wilkins Co.
13. Lehmann, J.F., and DeLateur, B.J.: Therapeutic heat. In Lehmann J.F. (editor): Therapeutic heat and cold, ed. 3, Baltimore, 1982, The Williams & Wilkins Co.
14. Lewis, T.: Observations upon the reactions of vessels of the human skin to cold. Heart 15:177, 1930.
15. McMaster, W.C.: Cryotherapy, Phys. Sportsmed. 10:112, Nov. 1982.
16. Moore, R.J.: Uses of cold in rehabilitation of athletes: recent advances, Paper presented to the Nineteenth Annual Meeting of the American Medical Aspects of Sports, San Francisco, June 18, 1977.
17. Nielsen, A.J.: Spary and stretch for myofascial pain, Phys. Ther. 58:567, May 1978.
18. Nielsen A.J.: Case study: myofascial pain of the posterior shoulder relieved by spray and stretch, J. Orthop. Sports Phys. Ther. 3:21, Summer 1981.
19. Peppard, A., and Riegter, H.F.: Trigger point therapy for myofascial pain, Phsy. Sportsmed. 9:161, June 1981.
20. Quillin, W.S.: Ultrasonic phonophoresis, Phsy. Sportsmed. 10:211, June 1982.
21. Rusk, H.A.: Rehabilitation medicine, ed. 4, St. Louis, 1977, The C.V. Mosby Co.
22. Sherman, M.: Which treatment to recommend? Hot or cold? Am. Pharm. NS20:46, Aug. 1980.
23. Shriber, W.J.: A manual of electrotherapy, ed. 4, Philadelphia, 1975, Lea & Febiger.
24. Smith, W.: High galvanic therapy in the symptomatic management of acute tibial fracture, Ath. Train. 16:59, Spring 1981.
25. Tappan, F.M.: Massage techniques, New York, 1964, Macmillan Publishing Co., Inc.
26. Travell, J., and Rinzler, S.H.: The myofascial genesis of pain, Postgrad. Med. 11:425, 1952.

ADDITIONAL SOURCES

Chu, D.: Conventional uses of therapeutic modalities, Professional Preparation Conference, Palo Alto, Calif., Feb. 1981, National Athletic Trainers Association. (Cassette.)

Cyriax, J., and Cyriax, P.: Orthopaedic medicine, Woburn, Mass., 1983, Butterworth Publishers, Inc.

Derscheid, G.: Manual therapy: theoretical analysis for sport, NATA Annual Meeting, Clinical Symposium, June 1983, National Athletic Trainers Association. (Cassette.)

Esterson, P.: Modalities—state of the art, Mid-Atlantic Athletic Trainer's Association Meeting, May 1983, National Athletic Trainers Association. (Cassette.)

Forster, A., and Patastanga, L.: Clayton's electrotherapy: theory and practice, ed. 8, Eastbourne, England, 1981, Baillière Tindall.

Knight, J.L., et al.: A reexamination of Lewis' cold-induced vasodilatation in the finger and the ankle, Ath. Train. **15:**248, Winter 1980.

Kuprian, W.: Massage. In Kuprian, W. (editor): Physical therapy for sports, Philadelphia, 1982, W.B. Saunders Co.

Lehmann, J.F. (editor): Therapeutic heat and cold, ed. 3, Baltimore, 1982, The Williams & Wilkins Co.

Maitland, G.D.: Vertebral manipulation, ed. 4, Woburn, Mass., 1977, Butterworth Publishers, Inc.

Maitland, G.D.: Peripheral manipulation, Woburn, Mass., 1977, Butterworth Publishers, Inc.

Prentice, W.E.: The use of electroacutherapy in the treatment of inversion ankle sprains, Ath. Train. **17:**15, Spring 1982.

Shestack, R.: Handbook of physical therapy, ed. 3, New York, 1977, Springer Publishing Co., Inc.

Stillwell, G.K. (editor): Therapeutic electricity and ultraviolet radiation, Baltimore, 1983, The Williams & Wilkins Co.

Travell, J.G., and Simons, D.G.: Myofascial pain and dysfunction, Baltimore, 1983, The Williams & Wilkins Co.

Warren, C.G.: Therapeutic modalities and the athletic trainer, NATA Clinical Symposium, Granite Falls, Wash., 1982, Marvl Productions. (Cassette.)

Chapter 15

BASICS IN EXERCISE
REHABILITATION

When you finish this chapter, you should be able to

Present the major aspects of a good exercise
rehabilitation program in a sports medicine setting

Conduct exercise rehabilitation designed to increase
strength, endurance, flexibility, coordination, and
speed of movement

Establish an exercise rehabilitation plan for an
athlete's individual needs

Demonstrate a number of special exercise
rehabilitative approaches

Fit and instruct in crutch and cane usage

Although it is often neglected, exercise is one of the most important therapeutic tools available to the athletic trainer, therapist, or coach.[2] Through a carefully applied exercise program in conjunction with other therapies and directed by a physician, an athlete often can be returned safely to competition after injury. The two major categories of exercise are conditioning and rehabilitation. *Rehabilitation* is the restoration of an athlete to the level of preinjury fitness through a carefully planned and carried out program of therapeutic exercise. It is essential that the athlete return to competition with function fully restored. Too often athletes fail to regain full function and, as a result, perform at a subpar level, thereby risking permanent disability.

An injured athlete should be monitored throughout the entire convalescent and reconditioning periods by both the trainer and the physician. At no time should the immediate or future health of the athlete be endangered as a result of hasty decisions; at the same time, the dedicated athlete should be given every possible opportunity to compete, provided that such competition does not pose undue risk. The final decision in this matter must rest with the sports physician. The sports physician must decide at what point the athlete can reenter competition without the danger of reinjury, as well as when the use of supportive taping or other aids is necessary to prevent further injury.

It has been said that a good substitute is always more valuable than an injured star. There must be full cooperation between coach, trainer, and physician in helping to restore the athlete to the proper level of competitive fitness. Rehabilitation through exercise is considered one factor in the total therapy regimen.

> The physician makes the final decision as to whether an athlete returns to competition.

369

Exercise rehabilitation after a sports injury is the combined responsibility of all individuals connected with a specific sport. To devise a program that is most conducive to the good of the athlete, basic objectives that consider his or her needs must be developed. In addition to maintaining a good psychological climate, the objectives are to (1) prevent deconditioning of the total body and (2) rehabilitate the injured part without hampering the healing process.

Preventing deconditioning involves keeping the body physically fit while the injury heals. In establishing a conditioning program, emphasis should be placed on maintaining strength, flexibility, endurance, and coordination of the total body. Whenever possible, athletes should engage in activities that will aid them in their sport but will not endanger recovery from the injury. Contralateral exercises should be introduced when they can be performed without pain or stress to the injured body part. If possible, all uninvolved body parts and joints should be exercised daily so as to maintain a reasonable degree of general strength and endurance.

Restoring the injured part is so important that a rehabilitation program must be started as soon as possible. An injured part, particularly a joint or the musculature, must be prevented from developing disuse degeneration. Disuse will result in atrophy, muscle contractures, inflexibility, and delays in healing because of circulatory impairment. This is not to imply that sports injuries should be "run off or worked through." Rather, a proper balance between resting and exercising should be maintained.

As discussed in Chapter 4, a major principle that is applicable to all physical conditioning and exercise rehabilitation is the SAID principle,[1] which stands for "specific adaptations to imposed demands."[11] The SAID principle states that to be effective, exercise must be specifically adapted to the needs of the athlete.

CONSEQUENCES OF INACTIVITY

Prolonged bed rest, sitting, or immobilization of a body part can cause muscles to atrophy and joints to become rigid and unyielding.

The human body is a dynamic moving entity that requires physical activity to maintain muscle tone and joint mobility. Prolonged inactivity of the entire body or body part can produce muscle atrophy, loss of strength, and loss of joint flexibility and coordination.

Individuals suffering from severe infections are generally debilitated and may have chronic inflammations, organic involvements, or intense pain on moving a part; they may require inactivity. But if injury has been incurred by a healthy and active person, prescribing inactivity may be adding insult to insult. Lack of activity causes generalized muscle atrophy and specific degeneration surrounding the injury site. Besides muscle atrophy, the body is unable to properly rid itself of waste materials. The athlete therefore loses endurance, strength, flexibility, and coordination and may consequently experience diminished confidence and ability in the sport. To stave off problems produced by inactivity, an exercise program must be started as soon as possible after injury.

Members of the medical profession are in general agreement that prolonged bed rest and inactivity can often delay recovery.[2] This is particularly true when there is musculoskeletal involvement. Frequently, intensive exercise programs are scheduled for preoperative preparation of the athlete. Such conditioning may shorten recovery time. Postoperative exercising is also encouraged, which further decreases the period of recovery. Controlled exercise during convalescence from a soft tissue injury assists in resolution and healing by decreasing edema and the less viable scar tissue. Exercise rehabilitation should be made an integral part of the athlete's recovery program.

MUSCULAR STRENGTH AND ENDURANCE

Muscular strength allows the athlete to overcome a given resistance. It is one of the most essential factors in restoring function after injury. Muscle size and strength can be increased with use and can decrease in cases of disuse. Both isotonic and isometric muscle contractions are used to advantage in rehabilitation. All movements and exercises should be carefully controlled and initially should be guided by pain. Pain-free motion should be a goal. Every effort should be made to prevent atrophy and the loss of muscle tone when a body part or joint is immobilized. As strength is slowly regained, weight bearing may be introduced when the joint(s) is deemed capable of support. Isotonic and/or isokinetic exercises are preferable because they increase function of a part through a complete range of movement. Isometric exercises involve no movement of the joints, but develop strength primarily in the position exercised.

Immobilized parts may initially be carefully exercised through isometrics, in the beginning using a three-fourths maximal effort. Such exercise assists in preventing atrophy and reduces loss of muscular strength until movement can be executed. When at all possible a program designed to maintain cardiovascular endurance should accompany the program of musculoskeletal reconditioning. Constant evaluation of the reconditioning program must take place, with the program readjusted to meet the changing needs of the athlete. Standard muscle and flexibility tests should be used to assess the athlete's stages of recovery.

Most programs of exercise using the overload principle for restoring physical function employ the concept of "progressive resistance exercise" as set forth by DeLorme (Chapter 5).

After initial isometric exercises, as pain and swelling diminish or disappear, the athlete should begin a program of movement using either isotonic or isokinetic exercises to assist in the development of strength, endurance, and range of motion. As discussed in Chapter 4, isokinetic exercises provide one of the best means of developing strength and endurance in the rehabilitative process, since they provide uniform strength demands and resistance throughout the full range of movement at a prescribed level of resistance. Isokinetic exercise assists the training experience by increasing the muscular force at all speeds of contraction. Rehabilitation is enhanced when the injured athlete is able to perform an exercise set at a specific speed and contractive force equal to his or her sport (Figs. 15-1 and 15-2).

Muscle endurance is important to the restoration of the injured part. Muscle endurance is the ability to sustain muscle contractions at a submaximal effort over a period of time. Muscle strength and endurance are indivisible parts of a continuum. For example, exercises employing progressive resistance at near maximal effort for four to six repetitions mainly af-

Figure 15-1

A, The Orthotron is an isolated joint isokinetic exercise system. **B,** The Fitron isokinetic cycle-ergometer. **C,** Isokinetic devices have become an essential part of rehabilitation in sports medicine. Cybex II Testing System: Isokinetic Dynamometer, Dual-Channel Recorder, and speed selector. **D,** Isokinetic Dynamometer and the Upper-Body Exercise and Testing Table.

Courtesy Cybex, Bay Shore, N.Y.

A

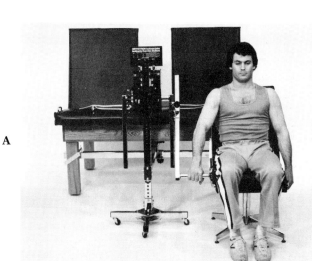

B

C

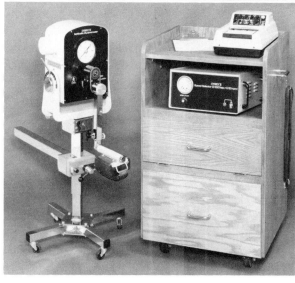

D

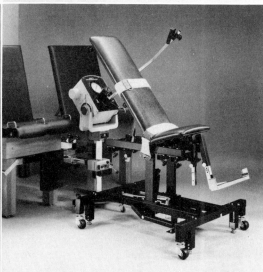

fect strength; decreasing the resistance and increasing the number of repetitions requires the ability to sustain a movement.

Remember, in developing an exercise program, if immobilization is present, begin with an isometric program, then go to the progressive resistance and isokinetic forms as recovery permits. The strength and strength ratios of the agonist and antagonist muscles should be carefully monitored so as to equate the opposition groups. Additionally, when joint functions are being restored, the ranges of motion should be carefully measured with a goniometer to assess improvement. Specificity is of the utmost importance, since it determines the muscle fiber recruitment as the patient progresses into the isotonic and/or isokinetic phases of the recovery program.

Figure 15-2

Sample Cybex chart.
Courtesy Cybex, Bayshore, N.Y.

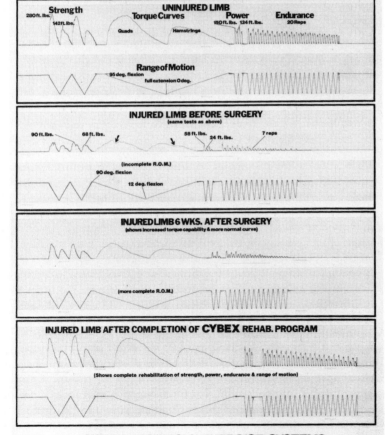

CLASSIFICATION OF ISOTONIC REHABILITATIVE EXERCISE

Reconditioning exercises can be classified into four categories: (1) passive, (2) assistive, (3) active, and (4) resistive. Each can be used to advantage in restoring the athlete to a state of competitive fitness.

Passive Exercise

Passive exercise is the movement of an affected part by another person or by a device, without effort by the athlete. This technique can be used to advantage if an injury has hampered the range of joint motion or if the apprehensive athlete must be shown that the condition has been remediated and that there is no need for fear.

Assistive Exercise

Assistive exercise is movement of an injured part by the athlete, but with the assistance of another person.

Active Exercise

Active exercise is movement that is executed by the athlete without assistance. Exercises falling into this category are those used for general conditioning and those used remedially for restoring function to an injured part.

Resistive Exercise

Resistive exercise is movement that the athlete performs against a resisting force. One type is illustrated in the progressive weight training exercises discussed in Chapter 5.

FLEXIBILITY

Flexibility must be present if a part is to be functional. A part that is immobilized in a cast or brace or is not moved regularly through a full range of movement will eventually become inflexible. Important aspects of the athletic rehabilitation regimen are the stretching and muscle release techniques. These techniques are instituted only if they will not aggravate the injury.

Static Stretching

Manual stretching using passive or proprioceptive neuromuscular facilitation (PNF) techniques (pp. 385-387 and Appendix I) and gradual or static stretching exercises are considered most effective. Static stretching should be employed as discussed in Chapter 5.

Assessing Joint Range of Motion

To ensure accuracy and reliability in the use of a goniometer, the tester must employ specific body positions and anatomical landmarks.

Goniometry, which measures joint range of motion, is an essential procedure in the early, intermediate, and late stages of injury. Full range of motion of an affected body part is a major criterion for the return of the athlete to participation.

Although a number of different types of goniometers are on the market, the most commonly used are those which measure 0 to 180 degrees in each direction. The arms of the instrument are usually 12 to 16 inches (30 to 40 cm) long, with one arm being stationary and the other fully movable.[9]

To ensure accuracy and reliability, the tester must employ specific body positions and anatomical landmarks. Figs. 15-3 to 15-19 depict proper athletic positioning and placement of the goniometer (Table 15-1).

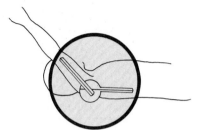

Figure 15-3

Shoulder flexion. The stationary arm is placed along the midaxillary line of the trunk in line with the greater trochanter of the femur. The moving arm is placed along the humerus and in line with the lateral condyle of the humerus.

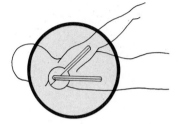

Figure 15-4

Shoulder extension using the same landmarks shown in Fig. 15-3.

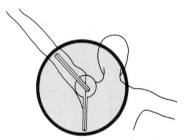

Figure 15-5

Shoulder abduction. The stationary arm is positioned parallel to floor at the side of the body posterior to the axillary line. The moving arm is placed on the posterior aspect of the arm parallel to the posterior midline of the body pointing toward the olecranon process.

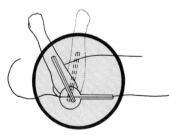

Figure 15-6

Lateral and medial shoulder rotation with the elbow flexed at 90 degrees. The stationary arm is placed parallel to the table. The center of goniometer is placed at the olecranon process, and the moving arm is placed along the dorsal midline of the forearm between the styloid process.

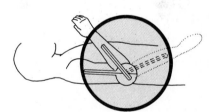

Figure 15-7

Elbow extension and flexion. The stationary arm is positioned along the lateral midline of the humerus toward the acromion process. The moving arm is positioned along the lateral midline of the radius pointing to the styloid process.

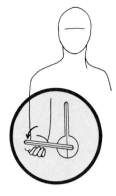

Figure 15-8

Forearm pronation. The stationary arm is placed on the back of the wrist parallel to the long axis of the humerus. The moving arm is placed along the back of the hand after movement has been performed.

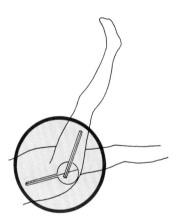

Figure 15-9

Forearm supination. The goniometer is placed on the volar (palm) side of the hand.

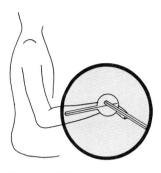

Figure 15-10

Wrist flexion and extension. The stationary arm is positioned along the lateral midline of the ulna pointing toward the medial epicondyle. The moving arm parallels the fifth metacarpal bone.

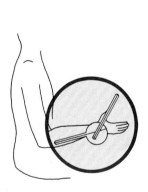

Figure 15-11

Radial flexion. The stationary arm is positioned along the midline of the back of the forearm between the ulna and radius pointing toward the lateral epicondyle of the humerus. The moving arm is positioned along the third metacarpophalangeal joint of the third digit.

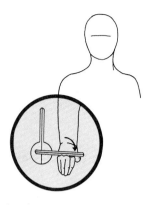

Figure 15-12

Hip flexion. The stationary arm is placed along a line from the crest of the ilium, femur, and greater trochanter. The moving arm is positioned in line with the femur and pointing toward the lateral condyle of the femur.

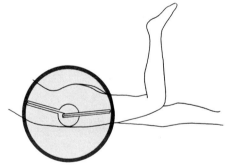

Figure 15-13

Hip extension. The goniometer is placed in the same position as in Fig. 15-2, but the athlete takes a prone position.

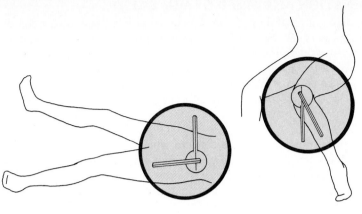

Figure 15-14

Hip abduction and adduction
with the athlete in a supine
position. The stationary arm
is positioned between the
anterior superior iliac spine.
The moving arm parallels the
anterior aspect of the femur
pointing toward the middle of
the patella.

Figure 15-15

Medial and lateral rotation in
a sitting position. The
stationary arm is positioned
along the middle of the tibia.
The center of the goniometer
is in the midpatellar region.
The moving arm is in the
same position as the
stationary arm.

Figure 15-16

Knee flexion extension in
supine position. The
stationary arm is positioned
along the lateral femur
pointing toward the lateral
condyle of the greater
trochanter. The moving arm
is placed parallel to the
lateral midline of fibula
toward the lateral malleolus.

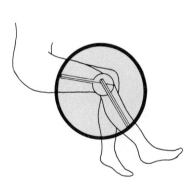

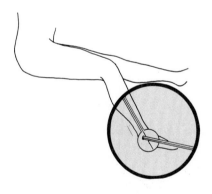

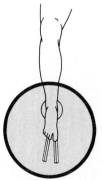

Figure 15-17

Knee extension and flexion
sitting on a table. The
stationary arm is parallel to
the lateral aspect of the
femur. The center of the
goniometer is at the lateral
condyle of the femur. The
moving arm is parallel to the
fibula.

Figure 15-18

Ankle dorsiflexion and
plantar flexion. The
stationary arm is parallel to
the lateral midline of the
fibula in line with the lateral
malleolus and head of the
fibula. The moving arm is
placed parallel to the lateral
midline of the fifth
metatarsal bone.

Figure 15-19

Foot abduction and
adduction. The stationary
arm is positioned on the
plantar aspect of the foot
from the center of the heel
and between the second and
third toes.

COORDINATION AND SPEED OF MOVEMENT

The final stages of rehabilitation are concerned with reestablishing coordination and speed of movement. Before returning to a sport ready to resume full activity, an athlete must be able to perform at the same level of proficiency and have the same potential for delaying fatigue as before he or she became hurt. An athlete who is not at full capacity or who favors an injured part will most likely become reinjured or develop associated problems.

Body Mechanics

Body mechanics must always be a concern when considering a program of physical rehabilitation. Sports afflictions often produce postural asymmetrical behavior. An arm in a sling or leg in a cast is an example of a situation that disturbs the symmetry of the body and places abnormal stress on the musculoskeletal system. The trainer should insist that the athlete maintain proper postural balance while recovering from an injury.

EXERCISE INSTRUCTION

All rehabilitative exercises should be carefully taught to the athlete. The athletic trainer or coach first demonstrates the exercise, and the athlete

TABLE 15-1

Range of joint motion

Joint	Action	Degrees of Motion
Shoulder	Flexion	180
	Extension	45
	Adduction	40
	Abduction	180
	Medial rotation	90
	Lateral rotation	90
Elbow	Flexion	145
Forearm	Pronation	80
	Supination	85
Wrist	Flexion	80
	Extension	70
	Abduction	20
	Adduction	45
Hip	Flexion	125
	Extension	10
	Abduction	45
	Adduction	40
	Medial rotation	45
	Lateral rotation	45
Knee	Flexion	140
Ankle	Flexion	45
	Extension	20
Foot	Inversion	40
	Eversion	20

Modified from Veterans Administration Standard Form 527 A, Washington, D.C., U.S. Government Printing Office.

repeats the exercise several times. It is important that the athlete fully understand the purpose of each exercise and know which muscles and body regions are primarily involved. Focusing on muscle action helps in synergy and keeps the exercise specific for a desired action. The athlete must be taught to perform at a given tempo. Isotonic exercise should be performed to four or more counts to ensure smooth movements. Two-count exercises produce jerky, arrhythmical movements.

Another major factor is to *avoid breath holding* in all strength and flexibility exercises. Breath holding creates general tension when relaxation is necessary.

> The athlete should avoid breath holding when performing strength and flexibility exercises.

The Exercise Rehabilitative Program

The proper selection and instruction in rehabilitative exercise cannot be overemphasized. All exercise forms should follow these principles:
1. Maintain a comfortable position involving the least strain possible.
2. Securely stabilize joints that are proximal to the injured part when exercising a specific body segment.
3. Perform all isotonic movements precisely and smoothly.
4. Conduct all movements within a pain-free range.

Exercise Overdosage

Engaging in exercise that is too intense or prolonged can be extremely detrimental to the progress of the athlete. The most obvious sign of overdosage is increased pain or discomfort lasting more than 3 hours. Other signs are decreased joint range of motion and strength of the injured part. In most situations, early rehabilitation involves submaximal exercise performed in short bouts that are repeated many times daily. Exercise rehabilitation in the early stages of recovery is performed two or three times a day. As recovery increases, the intensity of exercise also increases, and the exercise is performed less often during the day and, ultimately, the week.

EXERCISE PHASES

Rehabilitative exercise in sports medicine can generally be categorized into six phases. A unique phase that comes before elective surgery is the presurgical phase. After the presurgical exercise phase, five additional phases can be identified: the postsurgical or acute exercise phase (phase 1), early exercise phase (phase 2), intermediate exercise phase (phase 3), advanced exercise phase (phase 4), and the initial sports reentry phase (phase 5). Not all injured athletes experience all phases to achieve full rehabilitation. Depending on the type of injury and individual response to healing, phases may sometimes overlap.

Presurgical Exercise Phase

If surgery can be postponed, exercise may be used as a means to improve its outcome. By maintaining and, in some cases, increasing muscle tone and improving kinesthetic awareness, the athlete is prepared to continue the exercise rehabilitative program after surgery.

> Exercise performed in the presurgical phase can often assist in recovery after surgery.

Postsurgical or Acute Injury Exercise Phase (Phase 1)

Exercise is often encouraged after surgery to the musculoskeletal system. Allman states that "the optimal time for commencement of therapeutic exercise is approximately 24 hours after surgery or injury. An earlier beginning is often met by an unreceptive and confused patient. Any beginning later than 24 hours must be considered a loss of valuable time."[2] Exercise is employed to avoid muscle atrophy and to ensure return to sports participation as quickly as possible. Postsurgical exercise often repeats what was done presurgically. Commonly, the part surgically repaired is immobilized by a cast, dressing, or sling. When immobilized, muscle tensing or isometrics may be employed to maintain muscle strength. Unless contraindicated, joints that are immediately adjacent (distal and proximal) to the immobilized part should be gently exercised to maintain their strength and mobility.

When a part is immobilized after an acute injury, phase 1 allows for resolution in the healing process to occur. In many cases, muscle setting and nonflexion lifting activities such as straight leg raises may be performed while the injured part is immobilized. Muscle setting is usually performed 10 to 15 times every waking hour with each contraction held for approximately 6 seconds. Joints adjacent to the injury also may be exercised.

The postsurgical exercise phase should start 24 hours after surgery.

Early Exercise Phase (Phase 2)

The early exercise phase is a direct extension of the postsurgical, or acute injury, phase. The primary goals of this phase are to restore full muscle contraction without pain and to maintain strength in muscles surrounding the immobilized part. Muscle tensing is continued. Depending on the nature of the condition, isometric exercise against resistance may be added. Joints that are close to the injury are maintained in good condition by strengthening and mobility exercises.

Intermediate Exercise Phase (Phase 3)

When pain-free full muscle contraction has been achieved, the goals are to develop up to 50% range of motion (ROM) of the unaffected part and 50% strength. A third goal is to also restore near-normal neuromuscular coordination.

Advanced Exercise Phase (Phase 4)

The goals of phase 4 are to restore at least 90% of the athlete's range of motion and strength. Also the athlete is to undergo reconditioning for returning to his or her sport. The ideal goal in this phase is to fully restore power, flexibility, endurance, speed, and agility of the injured part, as well as the entire body.

The primary goals of the advanced phase of exercise are to fully restore power, flexibility, endurance, speed and agility to the athlete.

Initial Sports Reentry Phase (Phase 5)

Phase 5 of the exercise rehabilitation program involves returning to sports participation. In this phase, the underlying factors are gradualness and avoiding having the athlete "overdo." In some cases, this phase is a period in which muscle bulk is restored; in other instances, the athlete carefully tests the results of the exercise rehabilitation process. It is essential that the athlete not return to competition before full range of movement, strength, and coordination have been attained.

THE EXERCISE REHABILITATION PLAN

No exercise rehabilitation program can properly take place without a carefully thought out plan. It should contain at least three major elements: a clear understanding of the injury situation, an injury evaluation, and criteria for recovery and returning to a sport.

Injury Situation

Persons responsible for carrying out exercise rehabilitation must have a complete and clear understanding of the injury. This should include (1) exactly how the injury was sustained, (2) careful inspection of the injury, and (3) the medical diagnosis, consisting of the major signs, symptoms, and anatomical structures affected.

Injury Evaluation

Before an exercise program is developed, an evaluation is made. It should include range of motion, muscle strength, and functional capacity of the part. The evaluation must take into consideration factors of swelling, pain, and movements or exercises that may be contraindicated.

Exercise Plan

When there is a clear understanding of the athlete's functional capacity, exercises are selected on a progressive basis. The exercises are grouped according to phases of rehabilitation. Criteria for progressing from one phase to another are established, as are criteria for ultimate recovery.

Criteria for Full Recovery

The athlete must successfully pass a functional evaluation before obtaining a release for competition. This means having recovered full range of motion, strength, and size of the injured body part. In addition, the athlete must demonstrate full-function capabilities that are sport specific.

SPECIAL EXERCISE REHABILITATION APPROACHES
Hydrotherapeutic Exercise

A sports medicine program that has access to a swiming pool is fortunate; however, a whirlpool bath can provide some of the same benefits. Water submersion offers an excellent environment for beginning a program of exercise therapy, or it can complement all phases of rehabilitation.

Because of buoyancy and hydrostatic pressure, submersion in a pool presents a versatile exercise environment that can be easily varied according to individual needs. With the proper technique, the athlete can reduce muscle spasm, relax tense muscles, increase the range of joint motion, reestablish correct movement patterns, and, above all, increase strength, power, and muscular endurance.[4]

Using the water's buoyancy and pressure, hydrotherapeutic exercise can

The exercise rehabilitation plan must include:
  Injury situation
  Injury evaluation
  Exercise plan
  Criteria for full recovery
  Return to the sport

SAMPLE EXERCISE REHABILITATION PLAN

Injury Situation

A high school football halfback received a second degree sprain of the medial collateral ligament of the right knee joint. The athlete was given immediate care consisting of cold packs, compression, and elevation. After examination, the physician immobilized the knee to 30 degrees of flexion with a soft brace for 2 weeks. After 1 week of immobilization, the athlete was released to the trainer for exercise rehabilitation.

Injury Evaluation

Before starting exercise the trainer evaluated the following:

1. *Range of motion*—goniometry indicated that it took 15 degrees to fully lock the knee and a total of 30 degrees for flexion.

2. *Strength grade*—the quadriceps muscle was graded as fair, having only about 10% of the strength of the unaffected quadriceps muscle. The hamstring muscles on the right side also demonstrated a fair grade, having only 15% of the strength of the left side. On the other hand, the gastrocnemius muscle was graded as good, having a 5% difference between the affected and unaffected leg.

3. *Circumference measurement*—circumference measurements were taken at three sites: 3, 6, and 9 inches (7.5, 15, and 22.5 cm) above the patella. Adding all measurements and comparing them to the unaffected side yielded a 1¼ inch (3.1 cm) discrepancy.

4. *Functional capacity*—observation of the athlete indicated a decided limp with a toe walk and an inability to keep the heel flat on the floor. Even with the toe-style walking, there was an inability to bear a great deal of weight.

Management Plan

1 Management Phase

Muscle tensing was carried out from the time of immobilization. The athlete performed straight leg raises in the prone, supine, and side-lying positions and standing toe raises.

FREQUENCY: 10 to 15 times each waking hour.

2 Management Phase

Isometric exercise was added to the Phase 1 program for hamstring and quadriceps muscles (two or three contractions held for 6 seconds). Also, sandbag weights were added to the straight leg raises, starting with 5 lb and progressing to 15 lb (10 repetitions and three sets).

FREQUENCY: 2 or 3 times each day.

3	**Management Phase**	The brace was removed. The athlete performed leg swings while seated on the end of a table (10 to 20 repetitions) 3 times each day. This phase continued until 50% range of motion (ROM) and strength was achieved. The athlete walked in waist-high water daily.
4	**Management Phase**	Daily proprioceptive neuromuscular facilitation (PNF) knee patterns were initiated. The athlete began a walk/jog/run routine. Isotonic weight training was also started to restore muscle bulk. The criteria for moving to Phase 5 included 90% ROM, strength, and speed. FREQUENCY: 3 times each day.
5	**Management Phase**	The athlete practiced with the team but could not scrimmage until the criteria for recovery were satisfied. Flat footwear was worn instead of spiked shoes.

Criteria for Recovery

The ultimate goal of this reconditioning program was to return the athlete to sports participation at the same position as before injury. The criteria for recovery included the following:

1. Range of motion must be equal to the unaffected leg and must be pain free.
2. Strength of all major muscles associated with knee function must be equal to or exceed that of the unaffected leg. In rehabilitating an injured knee the lean muscle mass may be increased but adipose tissue may be decreased, thus causing the circumferential measurement to be less than that of the unaffected leg.
3. Thigh circumference of the affected leg must not be less than 90% of that of the unaffected leg.
4. The functional capabilities of the athlete must permit walking and running without a limp, running at full speed, and ten consecutive figure-8 patterns around goalposts.

be described as assistive, supportive, and resistive. As an *assistive* medium the water's upthrust can increase range of motion, strength, and control. Starting below the water level, the athlete first allows the part to be carried upward passively, keeping within pain-free limits. As the athlete gains strength, movement is actively engaged in and the buoyancy of the water becomes assistive. Progression of the movement can be initiated by increasing speed and making the water above the body part become a resistive medium (Fig. 15-20).

A second use of water buoyancy is *support.* The limb normally will float just below the water's surface. In this position the limb is parallel to the surface of the water. As with the assistive technique, increasing the speed will make the movement more difficult. Progression also can be accomplished by making the part less streamlined. In exercising the arm, the athlete can increase the difficulty by moving across the water with the flat of the hand or by using a hand paddle or webbed glove. Flippers can increase resistance to the leg.

A third use of water buoyance is *resistance.* The injured body part is moved downward against the upward thrust of the water. Maximal resistance is attained by keeping the limb at right angles to the water's surface. As with the supportive technique, the resistive technique can be made progressively more difficult by using different devices. Extra resistance is added by pushing or dragging flotation devices down into the water.

Besides specific exercising, the athlete can practice sports skills using the water's buoyancy and resistance to an advantage. For example, locomotor or throwing skills can be practiced to regain normal movement patterns.

Exercise in water provides an excellent means of rehabilitation.

Manual Resistance

Manual resistance is an excellent way to develop strength in the earlier stages of an injury or body areas in which resistive devices do not effectively work. It can be a specific approach to any body part. Manual resistance is particularly valuable when there is variable strength through a range of mo-

Manual resistance accommodates the strength capabilities of the athlete.

Figure 15-20

Use of the water's buoyance and pressure for progressive exercise. **A,** Body part floats upward passively. **B,** Using the water for buoyance. **C,** Using the water for resistance.

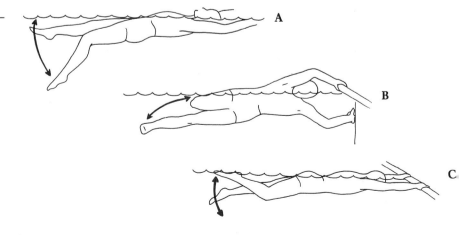

tion. Much like the isokinetic principle, the trainer applying manual resistance accommodates the strength capabilities of the body part. A special attribute of this approach is that the trainer can pay special attention to a weak range of motion. By maximizing resistance to the strong range, a carryover can be accomplished to the early part of the weak range. A variety of approaches can be applied, such as isometrics to just before the weakened range, variable speeds of movement, and exercise to both agonist and antagonist components. Exercise is performed within pain-free limits.

Proprioceptive Neuromuscular Facilitation

Proprioceptive neuromuscular facilitation (PNF) was developed by Herman Kabat, M.D., in association with Margaret Knott and Dorothy Voss, two physical therapists, for the rehabilitation of various neuromuscular problems.[7] The basis of PNF is that muscle function does not occur in a straight line but is diagonal and spiral. PNF is defined as "methods of promoting or hastening the response of the neuromuscular mechanism through stimulation of the proprioceptors."[8]

PNF employs four major neurophysiological principles: muscle and joint activity, irradiation, and Sherrington's law of successive induction and reciprocal innervation. The major muscle and joint reflexes employed are the muscle spindle, which is activated by stretch; Golgi's organ, which is activated by pressure and concerned with muscle tonus; deep pressure in receptors in joints; and the righting reflex. Irradiation or reinforcement refers to a strong voluntary muscle action against a resistance that will bring out a response in other muscle areas. Sherrington's law of successive induction indicates that flexion augments extension and extension augments flexion. Sherrington's law of reciprocal innervation refers to the voluntary or reflex contraction of a muscle that is associated with a simultaneous relaxation of its antagonist muscle because of an inhibitory response of the muscle spindle.[10]

Principles of PNF

There are six basic principles used in PNF[10]:

1. *Manual pressure*—hands are placed in the direction of the desired movement.
2. *Verbal and visual stimulation*—clear, concise instructions are given, and the movement can be seen by the athlete.
3. *Pressure and traction*—bringing the joint together causes pressure and increased stability, whereas traction pulls the joint apart and facilitates movement.
4. *Direct resistance*—isotonic and isometric. In isotonic resistance maximal resistance is given through the entire range of movement. With isometric resistance maximal tension is built up until fatigue is felt, which is followed by a gradual release.
5. *Functional patterns*—functional movements are employed using spiral and diagonal patterns, along with flexion, extension, adduction, abduction, and internal and external rotation.
6. *Proper timing*—muscles are encouraged to contract in proper sequence: distal to proximal and proximal to distal. In PNF stronger muscle components are used to facilitate weaker ones.

Techniques of PNF

There are two major categories of PNF techniques: relaxation and strengthening. Four techniques are commonly used in sports medicine. The category of relaxation includes contract-relax and hold-relax, whereas strengthening includes slow reversal and rhythmic stabilization.

Relaxation (stretching)

Contract-relax   The affected body part is passively moved until resistance is felt. The athlete is then told to isotonically contract the antagonistic muscle. The rotation is resisted as much as possible by the trainer for 10 seconds. The athlete is instructed to "relax" or "let go" up to 5 seconds. The trainer then moves the limb to a new stretch position. The exercise is repeated two or three times.

Hold-relax   The hold-relax technique is similar to contract-relax except that a maximal isometric contraction is used. The athlete moves the body part to the point of resistance and is told to "hold." The tight muscles are isometrically resisted by the trainer for 10 seconds. The athlete is then told to "let go" for up to 5 seconds, and the body part is either moved to a new range actively by the athlete or passively by the trainer. This exercise is repeated two or three times.

Strengthening techniques

Slow reversal   The athlete moves through a complete range of motion against a maximal resistance. Resistance is applied to ensure a movement pattern that is smooth and rhythmical. It is important that reversal of the movement be instituted before the previous pattern has been completed.

Rhythmic stabilization   Rhythmic stabilization uses isometric contraction of antagonistic and agonistic movement patterns that will produce a contraction of the antagonist muscle.[8] This causes a rhythmic stabilization to occur and a tremendous buildup of power.

Figure 15-21

Spiral-diagonal PNF pattern. **A,** Starting position. **B,** Finished position.

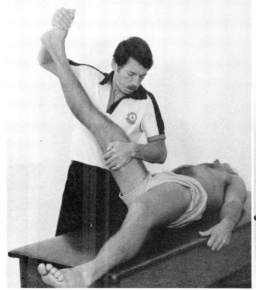 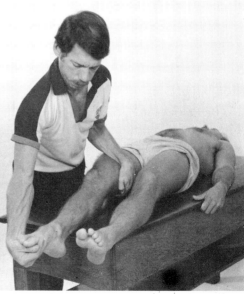

A   B

Spiral-diagonal Patterns

Spiral-diagonal patterns are used as a means of gaining relaxation or stimulating strength development through the maximal stimulation of proprioceptors. The major components of movement taking place at a joint and focal point are flexion, extension, and rotation. Movement toward and across the midline of the body takes place with adduction, and movement across and away from the midline is associated with abduction. Outward or external rotation takes place with supination and inversion, whereas inward or internal rotation is associated with pronation and eversion[8] (Fig. 15-21). Specific PNF exercises are given in Appendix I.

Cold Application Followed by Exercise

Recently the combined use of ice application and exercise has been found to benefit rehabilitation. This form of therapy is known as *cryokinetics*. Cold is applied to the injured part in the form of an ice pack for 15 minutes or by ice massage for 7 to 10 minutes (Chapter 14). In both forms, mild stretching is performed, followed by 10 to 20 repetitions of active movement of the injured part. All exercise must be pain free; if it is not, or when the analgesia wears off, activity should be stopped immediately. The major concept of this approach is that ice blocks pain impulses and reduces muscle spasm, allowing pain-free, relaxed motion.[6]

FITTING AND USING THE CRUTCH OR CANE

When an athlete has a lower limb injury, weight bearing may be contraindicated. Situations of this type call for the use of a crutch or cane. Very often, the athlete is assigned one of these aids without proper fitting or instruction in their use. An improper fit and usage can place abnormal stresses on various body parts.[5] Constant pressure of the body weight on the crutch axillary pads can cause crutch palsy. This pressure on the axillary radial nerves and blood vessels can lead to temporary or even permanent numbness in the hands. Faulty mechanics in the use of crutches or canes could produce a chronic low back and/or hip strain.

Proper fitting of a crutch or cane is essential to avoid placing abnormal stresses on the body.

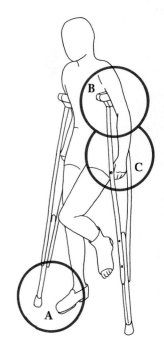

Fitting the Athlete

The adjustable, wooden crutch is well suited to the athlete. For a correct fit the athlete should wear low-heeled shoes and stand with good posture and the feet close together. The crutch length is determined first by placing the tip 6 inches (15 cm) from the outer margin of the shoe and 2 inches (5 cm) in front of the shoe. The underarm crutch brace is positioned 1 inch (2.5 cm) below the anterior fold of the axilla. Next, the hand brace is adjusted so that it is even with the athlete's hand and the elbow is flexed at an approximate 30-degree angle (Fig. 15-22).

Figure 15-22

The crutch must be properly fitted to the athlete.
A, The crutch tips are placed 6 inches (15 cm) from the outer margin of the shoe and 2 inches (5 cm) in front of the shoe. **B,** The underarm crutch brace is positioned 1 inch (2.5 cm) below the anterior fold of the axilla. **C,** The hand brace is placed even with the athlete's hand, with the elbow flexed approximately 30 degrees.

Fitting a cane to the athlete is relatively easy. Measurement is taken from the superior aspect of the greater trochanter of the femur to the floor while the athlete is wearing street shoes.

Walking with the Crutch or Cane

Many elements of crutch walking correspond with walking. The technique commonly used in sports injuries is the tripod method. In this method, the athlete swings through the crutches without making any surface contact with the injured limb or by partially bearing weight with the injured limb. The following sequence is performed:

1. The athlete stands on one foot with the affected foot completely elevated or partially bearing weight.
2. Placing the crutch tips 12 to 15 inches (30 to 37.5 cm) ahead of the feet, the athlete leans forward, straightens the elbows, pulls the upper crosspiece firmly against the side of the chest, and swings or steps between the stationary crutches (Fig. 15-23).
3. After moving through, the athlete recovers the crutches and again places the tips forward.

An alternate method is the four-point crutch gait. In this method, the athlete stands on both feet. One crutch is moved forward and the opposite foot is stepped forward. The crutch on the same side as the foot that moved forward moves just ahead of the foot. The opposite foot steps forward, followed by the crutch on the same side, and so on.

Once the athlete is able to move effectively on a level surface, negotiating stairs should be taught. As with level crutch walking, a tripod is maintained on stairs. In going upstairs, the unaffected support leg moves up one step while the body weight is supported by the hands. The full weight of the body is transferred to the support leg followed by moving the crutch tips and affected leg to the step. In going downstairs, the crutch tips and the affected leg move down one step followed by the support leg. If a handrail is available, both crutches are held by the outside hand, and a similar pattern is followed as with the crutch on each side.[3]

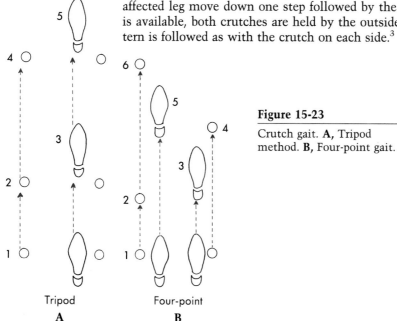

Figure 15-23

Crutch gait. **A,** Tripod method. **B,** Four-point gait.

REFERENCES

1. Allman, F.L.: Sports medicine, New York, 1974, Academic Press, Inc.
2. Allman, F.L.: Exercise in sports medicine. In Basmajian, J.V. (editor): Therapeutic exercise, ed. 3, Baltimore, 1978, The Williams & Wilkins Co.
3. Aten, D.: Crutches: essential in caring for lower extremity injuries, Phys. Sportsmed. 8:121, Nov. 1980.
4. Atkinson, G.P., and Harrison, R.A.: Implications of the Health Safety at Work Act in relation to hydrotherapy departments, Physiotherapy 76:146, Sept. 1981.
5. Flood, D.K.: Proper fitting and use of crutches, Phys. Sportsmed. 11:75, March 1983.
6. Gieck, J.H.: The athletic trainer and rehabilitation in the injured athlete, Philadelphia, 1982, J.B. Lippincott Co.
7. Kabat, H.: Proprioceptive facilitation. In Licht, S. (editor): Therapeutic exercise, Baltimore, 1965, The Williams & Wilkins Co.
8. Knott, M., and Voss, E.E.: Proprioceptive neuromuscular facilitation: patterns and techniques, ed. 2, Philadelphia, 1968, Harper & Row, Publishers, Inc.
9. Moore, M.L.: Clinical assessment of joint motion. In Basmajian, J.V. (editor): Therapeutic exercise, ed. 3, Baltimore, 1978, The Williams & Wilkins Co.
10. Surburg, P.R.: Neuromuscular facilitation techniques in sportsmedicine, Phys. Sportsmed. 9:114, Sept. 1981.
11. Wallis, E.L., and Logan, G.A.: Figure improvement and body conditioning through exercise, Englewood Cliffs, N.J., 1964, Prentice-Hall, Inc.

ADDITIONAL SOURCES

Allman, F.L., Jr.: Rehabilitation following athletic injuries. In O'Donoghue, D.H. (editor): Treatment of injuries to athletes, ed. 4, Philadelphia, 1984, W.B. Saunders Co.

Basmajian, J.V. (editor): Therapeutic exercise, ed. 3, Baltimore, 1978, The Williams & Wilkins Co.

De Lorme, T.L., and Watkins, A.L.: Progressive resistance exercises, New York, 1951, Appleton-Century-Crofts.

Friedman, M.: Assessing muscle strength isokinetically, J.A.M.A. 240:2410, Nov. 1978.

Golland, A.: Basic hydrotherapy, Physiotherapy 67:258, Sept. 1981.

Jackson, D.W., and Strizak, A.M.: Stress fractures in runners, excluding the foot. In Mack, R.P. (editor): Symposium on the foot and leg in running sports, American Academy of Orthopaedic Surgeons, St. Louis, 1982, The C.V. Mosby Co.

Moore, B.: Applied principles of therapeutic exercise, NATA Annual Meeting, Clinical Symposium, June 1983, National Athletic Trainers Association. (Cassette.)

Spiker, J.C.: Implications of tissue injury and repair in the rehabilitative process, Thirty-first NATA Annual Meeting and Clinical Symposium, June 1980, National Athletic Trainers Association. (Cassette.)

Trundle, T.: Cybex-isokinetic testing and rehabilitation, Mid-Atlantic Athletic Trainers Association Meeting, May 1983, National Athletic Trainers Association. (Cassette.)

Wilson, H.: Rehabilitation of the injured athlete. In Haycock, C.E. (editor): The athletic female, Oradell, N.J., 1980, Medical Economics Co.

| # Pharmacology In Sports

When you finish this chapter, you should be able to

Appreciate the dangers and intricacies inherent in the use of pharmaceuticals

Specify the legal ramifications related to dispensing pharmaceuticals in a sports setting

Classify pharmaceuticals that may be used by the sports participant

Describe how selective drugs work physiologically

P harmacology, an important factor in the healing arts, can be defined as the science of drugs, how they are prepared and used, and their effects on the human body. Medications of all types, both prescription and nonprescription, are commonly used by athletes.

Relatively short sports seasons make any physical incapacity a crucial factor. The anxiety created in this situation can cause athletes, trainers, coaches, and even physicians to overreact in ways that may be harmful: for example, they may advocate taking too much of a **drug** or taking it more often than indicated with the thought that "if a little bit is good, then more is better." In addition, the athlete may, unbeknownst to the team physician or trainer, be taking drugs prescribed by another physician, which could be a very dangerous practice (Fig. 16-1).

drug
Any chemical substance that affects living matter.

WHAT IS A DRUG?

The use of substances for the express purpose of treating some infirmity or disease dates back to early history. The ancient Egyptians were highly skilled in making and using medications, treating a wide range of external and internal conditions.

Many of our common drugs, such as aspirin and penicillin, originate in nature. Historically, medications were made of roots, herbs, leaves, or other natural materials when they were identified or believed to have medicinal properties. Today many medications that originally came from nature are produced synthetically.

A drug is any chemical agent that affects living matter. Used in the treatment of disease, drugs may either be applied directly to a specific tissue or organ or be administered internally to affect the body systemically. When a drug enters the bloodstream by absorption or direct injection it can affect specific tissues and organs far from the site of introduction.

DRUG VEHICLES AND THEIR ADMINISTRATION

Although trainers or coaches cannot dispense a prescription drug, they should have a basic comprehension of why, how, and by what means a drug is being delivered to the athlete's body. This section provides the reader with an elementary understanding of the vehicles in which a drug may be housed, how it may be administered, and the response it may have, both positive and negative.

A drug **vehicle** has no action on the body except to contribute to ease of administration and use by the body. A drug is housed in a certain vehicle that may be either a solid or a liquid. Some of the more common drug vehicles are listed below.

vehicle
The substance in which a drug is carried.

Liquid Preparations

1. *Aqueous solution*—sterile water containing a drug substance
2. *Elixir*—alcohol, sugar, and flavoring with a drug dissolved in solution, designed for internal consumption
3. *Liniment*—alcohol or oil containing a dissolved drug, designed for external massage
4. *Spirit*—a drug dissolved in water and alcohol or in alcohol alone
5. *Suspension*—undissolved powder in a fluid medium; must be mixed well by shaking before use
6. *Syrup*—a mixture of sugar and water containing a drug

Figure 16-1

An athlete, unbeknownst to a team physician or trainer, may be taking drugs prescribed by another physician that could lead to serious consequences.

Solid Preparations

1. *Ampule*—a closed glass receptacle containing a drug
2. *Capsule*—a gelatin receptacle containing a drug
3. *Ointment (emollient)*—a semisolid preparation of lanolin, petroleum jelly, or lard that suspends a drug
4. *Paste*—an inert powder combined with water
5. *Pill* or *tablet*—a drug powder compressed into a small oval, circle, square, or other form
6. *Plaster*—a drug in wax or resin, usually spread on a muslin cloth
7. *Poultice*—an externally applied, soft and moist paste containing a drug
8. *Powder*—a finely ground drug
9. *Suppository*—a medicated gelatin molded into a cone for placement in a body orifice, for example, the anal canal

ADMINISTRATION OF MEDICATIONS

The administration of medications in sports, as in any treatment situation, may be either internal or external and is based on the type of local or general response desired.

Internal Administration

Drugs and medications may be taken internally by means of inhalation, or they may be administered intradermally, intramuscularly, intranasally, intraspinally, intravenously, orally, rectally, or sublingually.

Inhalation is a means of bringing medication or substances to the respiratory tract. This method is most often used in sports to relieve the athlete of the discomfort of upper respiratory involvements, such as colds and coughs. The vehicle for inhalation is normally water vapor, oxygen, or highly aromatic medications.

Drugs can be internally or externally administered.

Figure 16-2

A well-outfitted trainer's kit contains carefully selected pharmaceuticals.

Courtesy Cramer Products, Inc., Gardner, Kan.

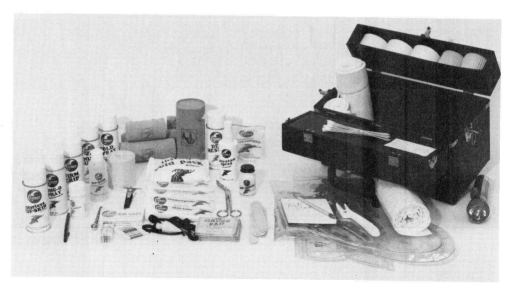

Intradermal (into the skin) or *subcutaneous* (under the cutaneous tissues) administration is usually accomplished by means of a hypodermic needle injection. Such introduction of medication is initiated when a rapid response is needed, but it does not produce as rapid a response as that following intramuscular or intravenous injection. Tests for allergic sensitivity are comonly given intradermally rather than subcutaneously.

Intramuscular injection means that the medication is given directly into the muscle tissue. The site for such an injection is usually the gluteal area or the deltoid muscle of the upper arm. The use of injections to speed the athlete's recovery is increasing in popularity. After a soft tissue injury, the physician often injects local anesthetics along with substances designed to assist in the healing process.

Intranasal application is varied according to the condition that is to be treated. The introduction of decongestants by the use of a menthol salve, a dropper, or an atomizer may relieve the discomfort of head colds and allergies. When it is difficult to control epistaxis (nosebleed), an ephedrine-saturated cotton plug may be introduced to serve as a vasoconstrictor.

Intraspinal injection may be indicated for any of the following purposes: (1) introduction of drugs to combat specific organisms that have entered the spinal cord, (2) injection of a substance such as procaine to anesthetize the lower limbs, or (3) withdrawal of spinal fluid to be studied.

Intravenous injection (into a vein) is given when an immediate reaction to the medication is desired. The drug enters the venous circulation and is spread instantly throughout the body. If large quantities of drugs are introduced into a vein, drop by drop, the process is called *intravenous infusion*.

Oral administration of medicines is the most common method of all. Forms such as tablets, capsules, powders, and liquids are easily administered orally.

Rectal administration of drugs is limited. In the past some medications have been introduced through the rectum to be absorbed by its mucous lining. Such methods have proved undesirable because of difficulties in regulating dosage. Drugs are primarily introduced into the rectum as an enema or to medicate disease conditions of the area.

Sublingual and *buccal* introductions of medicines usually consist of placing easily dissolved agents such as *troches* or *lozenges*, tablets, or pills under the tongue or in the cheek. They dissolve slowly and are absorbed by the mucous lining. This method permits slow drug administration into the bloodstream.

External Administration

Medications administered externally may include inunctions, ointments, pastes, plasters, poultices, and solutions.

Inunctions are oily or fatty substances that are rubbed into the skin and result in a local or systemic reaction. Oil-base liniments or petroleum analgesic balms used as massage lubrications are examples of inunctions.

Ointments consisting of oil, lard, petroleum jelly, or lanolin combined with drugs are applied for long-lasting topical medication.

Pastes are ointments with a nonfat base, which are spread on cloth and usually produce a cooling effect on the skin.

Plasters are thicker than ointments and are spread either on cloth or paper or directly on the skin. They usually contain an irritant and are applied as a counterirritant and used for relieving pain, increasing circulation, and decreasing inflammation.

Poultices are applied to skin areas where there is need for decongestion, absorption, stimulation, or a faster localization of suppuration. They consist mainly of a nondrug substance such as a flour paste or a mixture of water and flaxseed, which is heated and placed in a sack and then placed on the affected area. This method of heat therapy is used when other types are unavailable.

Solutions can be administered externally and are extremely varied, consisting principally of bacteriostatics. Antiseptics, disinfectants, vasoconstrictors, and liquid rubefacients are examples.

PRESCRIPTIONS

A prescription is a written order to a pharmacist by a physician. It normally contains the name or names of the drugs to be used, their quantities, special instructions to the pharmacist, and special directions to the patient. The use of extensive complicated prescriptions has been replaced with single compounds prepared by the pharmaceutical companies. Both prescription and nonprescription drugs can be obtained under their official generic, or nonproprietary, names. These are usually much less expensive than a trademark preparation developed by a single pharmaceutical company.

TABLE 16-1

A training room nonprescription medicine cabinet

Category	Ingredients	Brand (Example)
Gastrointestinal upset	Aluminum and magnesium in liquid suspension	Maalox
Constipation	Food roughage, e.g., All-Bran or agent containing psyllium	Metamucil or Mucilose
Skin wounds	Bactericide	Alcohol Betadine Achromycin Terramycin
Sunburn	Medication containing para-aminobenzoic acid	Pre-Sun or Pabanol
Insect bite or sting	Antipruritic	Alcohol, calamine lotion
Athlete's feet	Tolnaftate	Aftate
	Undecylenic acid and zinc undecylenate	Desenex
Jock itch	Drying agent	Corn starch, Zeasorb powder, talcum powder
Pain inhibition	Nerve inhibitor, counterirritants, acetylsalicylic acid	Cold producers (i.e., fluoromethane, instant cold packs), balms, and liniments Aspirin
Colds or allergy	Decongestants, Chlor-Trimeton	Sudafed, Neo-Synephrine

A typical prescription contains four parts: the superscription, inscription, subscription, and signature (Fig. 16-3).

1. The superscription (℞ or an abbreviation) means "take thou," from the Latin *recipere.*
2. Inscription refers to the ingredients indicated and their amounts.
3. Subscription provides directions to the pharmacist for dispensing (e.g., the form or vehicle for the drug).
4. Signature (Sig.) consists of the direction to the patient, such as "take one tablet three times a day."

SAFETY IN USE OF DRUGS

As stated earlier, drugs of any kind can be harmful. It is therefore essential that the trainer or coach become highly aware of the many ramifications inherent in drug safety.

Legal Concerns

The dispensing of drugs to the athlete by a member of the coaching staff or trainer, in a legal sense, is both clear and concise. At no time can a person other than a physician legally prescribe drugs for an athlete. A trainer, unless specifically allowed by state licensure, is not permitted to dispense a prescription drug. To fail to heed this fact can be a violation of the Federal Food, Drug, and Cosmetic Act and state statutes. A violation of these laws could mean legal problems for the physician, trainer, school, school district, or league. The situation is not so cut and dried for nonprescription drugs. For example, most secondary schools do not allow the trainer or coach to dispense nonprescription drugs that are to be taken internally by the athlete, including aspirin and over-the-counter cold remedies. The application of nonprescription wound medications is allowed by some secondary schools under the category of first aid. On

Unless allowed by state licensure, a trainer cannot dispense a prescription drug to an athlete.

Figure 16-3

Sample prescription.

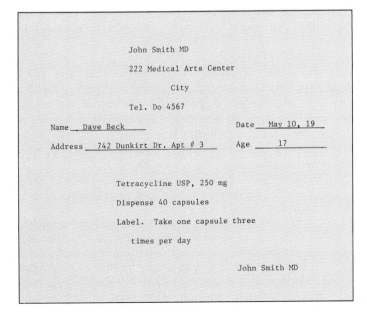

the other hand, some high school trainers in America are not allowed to apply even a wound medication in the name of first aid but can only clean the wound with soap and water; the athlete must then be sent to the school nurse for medication. The dispensing of vitamins and even dextrose may be specifically disallowed by some school districts. At the college or professional level, minors are not involved, and the dispensing of nonprescription medications may be less restrictive. A training room nonprescription medicine cabinet might contain the items listed in Table 16-1. It is assumed that athletes who are of legal age have the right to use whatever nonprescription drugs they choose; however, this right does not preclude the fact that the trainer or coach must be reasonable and prudent about the types of nonprescription drugs offered to the athlete.

Generally, dispensing nonprescription medicinals by a member of the athletic staff to any athlete depends on the philosophy of the school district and is under the direction of the team physician. As in all other areas of sports training, one is obligated to act reasonably and prudently.

What Pharmaceutical is Safe Enough?

As stated many times before, no drug can be considered to be completely safe and harmless. If a drug is truly potent enough to effect some physiological action, then it is also strong enough, under some conditions, to be dangerous. All persons react individually to any drug. A given amount of a specific medication may result in no adverse reaction in one athlete, whereas another may experience a pronounced adverse response. Both the athlete and the trainer should be fully aware of any untoward effect a drug *may* have. It is essential that the athlete be instructed clearly as to *when* to specifically take medications, with meals or not, and what not to combine with the drug, such as other drugs or specific foods. Some drugs may nullify the effect of another drug or may cause a serious antagonistic reaction. For example, calcium found in a variety of foods and even in some medications can nullify the effects of the powerful antibiotic tetracycline.[2]

Ingestion of some drugs can nullify the effects of another drug.

Responses to Drugs

Individuals react differently to the same medication, and different conditions may alter the effect of a drug on the athlete. Drugs themselves can be changed through age or improper preservation, as well as through the manner in which they are administered. Response variations also result from differences in each individual's size or age.

Following is a list of general body responses sometimes produced by drugs and medications:

1. *Addiction*—body response to certain types of drugs that produces both a physiological need and a psychological desire for the substance
2. *Antagonistic action*—result observed when medications, used together, have adverse effects or counteract one another
3. *Cumulative effect*—combination of results, effected when the body is unable to use a drug as fast as it is administered; such drug accumulation may cause unfavorable reactions
4. *Depressive action*—effect from drugs that slow down cell function

5. *Habituation*—individual's development of a psychological need for a specific medication

6. *Hypersensitivity*—allergic response to a specific drug. Such allergies may be demonstrated by a mild skin irritation, itching, a rash, or a drug that may cause a severe anaphylactic reaction, which could be fatal

7. *Idiosyncrasy*—unusual reaction to a drug; a distinctive response

8. *Irritation*—process, as well as effect, caused by substances that result in a cellular change; mild irritation may stimulate cell activity, whereas moderate or severe irritation by a drug may decrease cell activity

9. *Side effect*—the result of a medication that is given for a particular condition but affects other body areas or has effects other than those sought

10. *Potentiating*—a pharmaceutical that increases the effect of another. An example of this is codeine and aspirin. Codeine is potentiated by aspirin; therefore, less of it is required to relieve pain[10]

11. *Specific effect*—action usually produced by a drug in a select tissue or organ system

12. *Stimulation*—effect caused by drugs that speed up cell activity

13. *Synergistic effect*—result that occurs when drugs, given together, produce a greater reaction than when given alone

14. *Tolerance*—condition existing when a certain drug dosage is no longer able to give a therapeutic action and must therefore be increased

Alcohol should not be ingested with a wide variety of drugs, both prescription and nonprescription. Alcohol combined with antihistamines, sedatives, tranquilizers, and antidepressants can produce extreme drowsiness, making the performance of high-level motor tasks, such as driving an automobile, dangerous.

Alcohol and some foods, when mixed with drugs, produce adverse affects.

Other foods and chemicals also may create adverse reactions when they are mixed with pharmaceuticals. A fatty diet may decrease a drug's effectiveness. Excess acid foods, such as fruits, carbonated drinks, or vegetable juice, may cause adverse drug reactions.[10] The trainer and coach must thoroughly know the athletes they work with. The possibility of an adverse drug reaction is everpresent and requires continual education and vigilance.

The pharmacist can provide the trainer with information on the following:
  Lower cost generic drugs
  Drug effects
  Shelf age
  Dangers of drugs

Some medications are included on the list of doping substances in Chapter 6. The coach, athletic trainer, and physician must be fully aware of these substances and must prevent their use by the athlete[5] (see Table 6-5).

Buying Medicinals

One of an athletic department's best friends can be the local pharmacist. The pharmacist can assist in the selecting and purchasing of nonprescription medicines, save money by suggesting the lower priced generic drugs, and act as a general advisor on what drugs are most effective, the age of a medicine, and even the inherent dangers in a specific drug.

All pharmaceuticals must be properly labeled, indicating clearly the content, date of purchase, expiration date, and any dangers or contraindications for use. However, most pharmacists do not place the expiration date on drugs; therefore, it is up to the trainer or coach to find out this date and place it on the label. Those buying medicinals should always learn the best ways to store them, including the correct temperature and moisture and the amount of light that may be tolerated. It is generally accepted that the more complex drugs are unstable.[4]

GENERAL PHARMACEUTICAL CLASSIFICATIONS

Certain types of pharmaceuticals used in sports are briefly defined in the following list. Some of these, as well as other selected drugs, are discussed in greater detail later in the chapter.

1. *Analgesics* or *anodynes*—pain-relieving drugs.
2. *Anesthetics*—agents that produce local or general insensibility to touch, pain, or stimulation.
3. *Antacids*—substances that neutralize acidity; commonly used in the digestive tract.
4. *Anticoagulants*—agents that prevent coagulation of blood.
5. *Antidotes*—substances that prevent or counteract the action of a poison.
6. *Antipruritics*—agents that relieve itching.
7. *Antiseptics*—agents that kill bacteria or inhibit their growth and can be applied to living tissue.
8. *Antispasmodics*—agents that relieve muscle spasm.
9. *Antitussives*—agents that inhibit or prevent coughing.
10. *Astringents*—agents that cause contraction or puckering action.
11. *Bacteriostatics* and *fungistatics*—agents that retard or inhibit the growth of bacteria or fungi.
12. *Carminatives*—agents that relieve flatulence (caused by gases) in the intestinal tract.
13. *Cathartics*—agents used to evacuate substances from the bowels; active purgatives.
14. *Caustics*—burning agents, capable of destroying living tissue.
15. *Counterirritants*—agents applied locally to produce an inflammatory reaction for the relief of a deeper inflammation.
16. *Depressants*—agents that diminish body functions or nerve activity.
17. *Disinfectants*—agents that kill or inhibit the growth of microorganisms; should be applied only to nonliving materials.
18. *Diuretics*—agents that increase the secretion of urine.
19. *Emetics*—agents that cause vomiting.
20. *Hemostatics*—substances that either slow down or stop bleeding or hemorrhage.
21. *Irritants*—agents that cause irritation.
22. *Narcotics*—drugs that produce narcosis or complete insensibility.
23. *Sedatives*—agents that quiet body activity.
24. *Skeletal muscle relaxants*—drugs that depress neural activity within skeletal muscles.
25. *Stimulants*—agents that temporarily increase functional activity.
26. *Vasoconstrictors* and *vasodilators*—drugs that, respectively, constrict or dilate blood vessels.

ETHNOMEDICINE AND THE TRAINING PROGRAM

Suggestion is an extremely powerful factor in medicine generally, and in pharmacology specifically. For a pharmaceutical to be effective it is important that the athlete believe strongly that it will be beneficial; if an athlete does not believe in the medication, it is doubtful that it will be of benefit. Conversely, medications believed to be of benefit but in reality having no healing properties can have a placebo effect—the athlete strongly believes in the nonexistent ability of the drug to heal.

The trainer or coach must have some understanding of the health belief systems of the athletes with whom he or she works (Fig. 16-4).[6] An athlete may have little faith in traditional medicine or perhaps even fear typical treatment procedures. This individual may have an ethnic background that traditionally has a magical or religious conception of sickness and healing. It is necessary, therefore, to understand that typical medicinals may have little effect on these types of athletes; they require careful education and patience on the part of the physician, athletic trainer, and coach.

The trainer and/or coach must understand an athlete's belief system.

SELECTED PHARMACEUTICALS IN SPORTS

In sports the use of drugs and medicinals is widespread, as in society in general, but also is unique to the special needs of the athlete. This section is designed to discuss the most common medicinal practices in athletic

Figure 16-4

Trainers and coaches must understand the health belief system of the athletes with whom they work.

Courtesy Cramer Products, Inc., Gardner, Kan.

training to date and specific drugs that are in use. The discussion will include both prescription and nonprescription drugs, with emphasis on what should most concern the trainer or coach, and what the medications or materials are designed to accomplish.

Drugs to Combat Infection

Combating infection, especially skin infection, is of major importance in sports. Serious infection can cause countless hours of lost time and has even been the indirect cause of death.

Local Antiseptics and Disinfectants

Antiseptics are substances that can be placed on living tissue for the express purpose of either killing bacteria or inhibiting their growth. Disinfectants, on the other hand, are substances that combat microorganisms but should only be applied to nonliving objects. Other general names given to antiseptics and disinfectants are *germicides*, which are designed to destroy bacteria; *fungicides*, which kill fungi; *sporicides*, which destroy spores; and *sanitizers*, which minimize contamination by microorganisms.

Antiseptics act on disease-producing organisms by changing the protein structure of the organism, increasing its permeability, and inhibiting its metabolic processes. In essence, antiseptic agents should be selected for their ability to react selectively against the pathogen and not against the normal cells.

In sports many agents are used to combat infection. Some of the most commonly used antiseptics and disinfectants in sports are the following: phenols, dyes, mercury compounds, silver compounds, halogens, oxidizing agents, alcohols, formaldehyde, boric acid, and soap.

Alcohol is one of the most widely employed skin disinfectants. Both ethyl alcohol (70% by weight) and isopropyl alcohol (70%) are equally effective. They are inexpensive and nonirritating, killing bacteria immediately, with the exception of spores. However, they have no long-lasting germicidal action. Besides being directly combined with other agents to form tinctures, alcohol acts independently on the skin as an antiseptic and astringent. In a 70% solution it can be used for disinfecting instruments. Because of alcohol's rapid rate of evaporation, it produces a mild anesthetic action and, when used as a massage agent, gives a refreshingly cool sensation. Combined with 20% benzoin it is used in athletics as a topical skin dressing as a protective skin coating and astringent.

Benzoin is basically a resin obtained from the tree *Liquidambar orientalis*. It may also contain resorcinol, which acts medicinally as a skin dehydrant and antiseptic. Tannic acid may be present in addition to, or in place of, resorcinol; its presence initiates an astringent action on the skin, and it is advertised as a skin toughener. Alcohol also may be combined with a soft soap to make *tincture of green soap* designed for cleansing contaminated skin areas.

Acids are widely used both as antiseptics and astringents in a variety of skin preparations. Boric acid, for example, is used in powder or liquid form as a mild astringent and antiseptic. Benzoic and salicylic acids are commonly found in preparations designed to combat fungus. For example,

Classification of local antiseptics:

Alcohols—ethyl alcohol and isopropyl alcohol
Acids—acetic acid and boric acid
Surface-active agents—quaternary ammonium compounds
Phenols—hexachlorophene
Halogenated compounds—iodine and iodophors
Oxidizing agents—peroxides
Metal-containing antiseptics—mercury, silver, and zinc

one popular ointment for athlete's foot (Whitfield's) contains both benzoic and salicylic acid, whereas another popular fungicide (Desenex) contains undecylenic acid.

Surface-active agents are most commonly quaternary ammonium compounds. The most widely known and previously used is benzalkonium chloride (commonly known as Zephiran). Zephiran combined with an antirust compound is used in the disinfection of surgical instruments. More recently cetylprydinium chloride (Ceepryn) has become very popular.

Phenol was one of the earliest antiseptics and disinfectants used by the medical profession. From its inception to the present it has been used to control disease organisms, both as an antiseptic and as a disinfectant. It is available in liquids of varying concentrations and emollients. Substances that are derived from phenol and that cause less irritation are now used more extensively. Some of these derivatives are resorcinol, thymol, and the common household disinfectant Lysol. A widely used phenol derivative is hexachlorophene, often found in medical soaps and creams. Although recently there has been some question as to the safety of using hexachlorophene for total bathing, it is still considered an effective bacteriostatic skin cleanser and a treatment for staphylococcal skin infection.

Halogens are chemical substances (chlorine, iodine, fluoride, and bromine) that are used for their antiseptic and disinfectant qualities. Iodophors or halogenated compounds, a combination of iodine and a carrier, create a much less irritating preparation than tincture of iodine. A popular iodophor is povidone-iodine complex (Betadine), which is an excellent germicide commonly used as a surgical scrub by the surgeon. Betadine as an antiseptic and germicide in athletic training has proved extremely successful on skin lesions such as lacerations, abrasions, and floor burns.

Oxidizing agents as represented by hydrogen peroxide (3%) or potassium permanganate are commonly used in athletic training. Hydrogen peroxide is an antiseptic that, because of its oxidation, affects bacteria but readily decomposes in the presence of organic substances such as blood and pus. For this reason it has little effect as an antiseptic. Contact with organic material produces an effervescence, during which no great destruction of bacteria takes place. The chief value of hydrogen peroxide in the care of wounds is its ability to cleanse the infected cutaneous and mucous membranes. Application of hydrogen peroxide to wounds results in the formation of an active effervescent gas that dislodges particles of wound material and debris and, by removing degenerated tissue, eliminates the wound as a likely environment for bacterial breeding. Hydrogen peroxide also possesses a styptic action as a result of encouraging fibrin development in open wounds. Because it is nontoxic, hydrogen peroxide may be used for cleansing mucous membranes. A diluted solution (50% water and 50% hydrogen peroxide) can be used for treating inflammatory conditions of the mouth and throat.

Metal compounds are widely used as antiseptics. For example, mercury and its derivatives are considered bacteriostatic because they inhibit certain enzymatic actions of the bacteria. Some popular mercury preparations are yellow mercuric oxide for infection of the conjunctiva, thimerosal (Merthiolate), nitromersol (Metaphen), and merbromin (Mercurochrome).

Some agents containing silver have both antiseptic and astringent effects. As with mercury, silver penetrates tissue protein and disrupts the function of the microorganism by inhibiting enzymatic action. Zinc is also used in both antiseptic and astringent skin preparations. Zinc sulfate ointment is used for conjunctivitis; zinc oxide is widely used in ointments and is a main ingredient of calamine lotion.

Antifungal Agents

Many medicinal agents on the market are designed to treat fungi, which are commonly found in and around athletic facilities. The three most common fungi are *Epidermophytosis*, *Trichophyton*, and *Candida albicans*.

In recent years there has been successful development and use of antifungal antibiotics such as nystatin (Mycostatin), amphotericin B (Fungizone), and griseofulvin. Both nystatin and amphotericin B seen to be effective against deep-seated fungous infections such as those caused by the *Monilia* strain, *Candida albicans*. Griseofulvin, which is administered orally, produces an effective fungistatic action against the specific fungous species of *Microsporum*, *Trichophyton*, and *Epidermophyton*—all of which are associated with common athlete's foot. Given over a long period of time griseofulvin becomes a functioning part of the cutaneous tissues, especially the skin, hair, and nails, producing a prolonged and continuous fungistatic action. Tolnaftate (Tinactin) is a topical medication for superficial fungous infection caused by *Trichophyton* and other fungi.

Mechanical antiseptics, usually soaps that provide a cleansing and detergent action, remove pathogens from the skin.

Antibiotics

Indiscriminate antibiotic use can produce hypersensitivity and prevent immunity or resistance to infections.

Antibiotics are chemical agents that are produced by microorganisms. Their useful action is primarily a result of their interfering with the necessary metabolic processes of pathogenic microorganisms. In sports they are used by the physician as either topical dressings or systemic medications. The indiscriminate use of antibiotics can produce extreme hypersensitivity or idiosyncrasies and can prevent the acquisition of natural immunity or resistance to subsequent infections. The use of any antibiotic must be carefully controlled by the physician, who selects the drug on the basis of the most desirable type of administration and the amount of toxicity to the patient.

The antibiotics mentioned here are just a few of the many available. New types continue to be developed, mainly because, over a period of time, microorganisms often become resistant to a particular antibiotic, especially if it is indiscriminately used. Some of the more common antibiotics are penicillin, streptomycin, bacitracin, tetracycline, erythromycin, and the sulfonamides.

Penicillin is probably the most important of the antibiotics; it is useful in a variety of skin and systemic infections. In general, penicillin interferes with the metabolism of the bacteria.

Streptomycin is a potent antibiotic that inhibits protein synthesis of bacteria. It is especially beneficial in respiratory tract infections.

Bacitracin has proved to be extremely valuable in sports in the last few years. Like penicillin, it has a broad spectrum of effectiveness as an antibacterial agent. In addition, it seldom causes sensitivity reactions when used topically in a salve, an advantage over penicillin.

Tetracyclines consist of a wide group of antibiotics that have a broad antibacterial spectrum. Their application, which is usually oral, modifies the infection rather than eradicating it completely.

Erythromycin is an effective agent against staphylococci bacteria and has the same general spectrum as penicillin. It is normally employed when penicillin-resistant organisms are present.

Sulfonamides are a group of synthetic antibiotics. All sulfonamides used in treatment contain para-aminobenzenesulfonamide, which invests them with a common characteristic. Authorities indicate that sulfonamides make pathogens vulnerable to phagocytes by inhibiting certain enzymatic actions. The most commonly used drugs are sulfadiazine, sulfamerazine, sulfamethazine, and sulfisoxazole.

Drugs to Inhibit or Deaden Pain

Controlling pain in an athlete can involve innumerable drugs and procedures, depending on the beliefs of the trainer, coach, or physician. As discussed in Chapter 11, why pain is often positively affected by certain methods is not clearly understood; however, some of the possible reasons are as follows:

1. The excitatory effect of an individual impulse is depressed.
2. An individual impulse is inhibited.
3. A pattern of nervous response is disorganized.
4. The perceived impulse is decreased.
5. Anxiety created by the pain or impending pain is decreased.

Analgesics and Local Anesthetics

The inhibition of pain sensations through the skin is a major approach in sports. Analgesics give relief by causing a mild topical anesthesia in peripheral sensory nerve endings. Many chemical reactions on the skin can inhibit pain sensations through rapid evaporation, which causes a cooling action, or by counterirritating the skin. Counterirritants overcome pain responses by mildly irritating the skin, thus imposing a stronger stimuli than is imposed by the pain. This in turn causes a mild analgesic action as a result of the prevention of blood engorgement.

Cold applications also immediately act to constrict blood vessels and to numb sensory nerve endings. Applications of ice packs or submersion of a part in ice water may completely anesthetize an area. If extreme cold is used, caution must be taken that tissue damage does not result. The following are additional ingredients that can produce analgesia.

Cold applications constrict blood vessels and numb sensory nerve endings.

Alcohol evaporates rapidly when applied to the skin, causing a refreshingly cool effect that gives a temporary analgesia.

Camphor may be considered a counterirritant when applied to the skin. It has mild antiseptic and skin-irritating qualities. Acting as a rubefacient, it relieves superficial tissue areas of congestion and pressure on sensory pain receptors.

Menthol is an alcohol taken from mint oils and is principally used as a local analgesic, counterirritant, and antiseptic. Most often in sports it is used with a petroleum base for treating cold symptoms and in analgesic balms.

Spray coolants, because of their rapid evaporation, act as topical anesthetics to the skin. Several commercial coolants are presently on the market. Chloromethane is one of the most popular spray coolants used in sports today. Cooling results so quickly that superficial freezing takes place, inhibiting pain impulses for a short time. Trainers disagree as to the effectiveness of spray coolants. Some trainers use them extensively for strains, sprains, and contusions. In my opinion spray coolants are useful only when other analgesics are not available.

Methyl salicylate is synthetic wintergreen used externally in sports as an analgesic, counterirritant, and antiseptic. Together with menthol and capsicum oleoresin (red pepper), it is one of the main constituents of analgesic balms and liniments.

Local anesthetics are usually injected by the physician in and around injury sites for minor surgery procedures or to alleviate the pain of movement. Procaine hydrochloride is used extensively as a local anesthetic in sports, since its anesthesia is more concentrated than that of cocaine and does not cause blood vessel constriction.

Irritants and Counterirritants

Irritating and counterirritating substances used in sports act as rubefacients (skin reddeners) and skin stimulants. These are becoming less popular than in the past. Their application causes a local increase in blood circulation, redness, and a rise in skin temperature. Frequently mild pain can be reduced by a counterirritant, which produces a stimulus to the skin of such intensity that the athlete is no longer aware of the pain. Some examples of counterirritants include liniments, analgesic balms, and heat (hot water) and cold (ice packs).

Counterirritants reduce mild pain by stimulating the skin so intensely that the athlete is no longer aware of pain.

More specifically, liniments are liquids designed for use in massaging the body when an anodyne (pain reliever) or rubefacient is desired. These agents may contain active ingredients, such as ammonia, camphor, chloroform, methyl salicylate, or turpentine, in vehicles such as alcohol, water, oil, or soap. Vehicles such as soap and oil act as lubrication mediums for massages.

For the most part, analgesic balms contain the same ingredients as liniments, but they are carried in a petroleum base medium.

Pain can be allayed by the irritating qualities of some preparations, which to some degree overcome the pain sensations by producing a stimulus that is capable of bringing about considerable relief of a more severe pathological pain for durations that long outlast the period of stimulation. Mild pain can be allayed by a skin counterirritant, which produces a stimulus of such intensity that the athlete is no longer aware of the feeling of pain.

Anesthetics and Narcotics

Most narcotics used in medicine are derived directly from opium or are synthetic opiates. They depress pain impulses and the individual's respiratory centers. The two most often used derivatives are codeine and morphine.

Codeine resembles morphine in its action but is less potent. Its primary action is as a respiratory depressant; because of this it is found in many cough medicines.

Morphine depresses pain sensations to a greater extent than any other drug. It is also the most dangerous drug because of its ability to depress respiration and because of its habit-forming qualities. Morphine is never used in the following situations: (1) before a diagnosis has been made by the physician, (2) when the subject is unconscious, (3) when there is a head injury, or (4) when there is a decreased rate of breathing. It is never repeated within 2 hours.

Meperidine (Demerol) is often prescribed by the physician for athletes. This drug is used as a substitute for morphine in the relief of pain caused by muscular spasticity.

Hypnosis and Acupuncture

Hypnosis and acupuncture are increasingly being used, with varying success, by athletes to deal with pain. When the athlete is in an altered state of consciousness (hypnosis), the subconscious mind is available for suggestions, of which dealing with pain may be uppermost. In the altered state of consciousness the athlete is highly attentive and responsive to a suggestion that the pain can be effectively dealt with.

Acupuncture is another means by which some athletes seek relief from pain. It is often difficult for physicians trained in Western medicine and who operate under the idea that pain is elicited by specific pain receptors throughout the body to accept Eastern medicine's acupuncture. Although its mechanism of action is unclear, increasing numbers of Western physicians are beginning to use acupuncture to produce analgesia. In acupuncture analgesia methods, special stainless steel needles are inserted into the body at key sites, depending on the pain area. Sometimes the needles are rotated back and forth between the physician's fingers, or a low electrical current is applied to the needle. A possible scientific answer to the success of acupuncture as analgesia is that it modulates pain signals via the nervous system by closing the gate mechanism and blocking the pain signals to the conscious mind.

Drugs for the Central Nervous System

Drugs affect the central nervous system by either increasing or decreasing its irritability. In this section those drugs which decrease the irritability of the system will be discussed. They are classified in two groups as follows: analgesics and antipyretics, and hypnotics, sedatives, and antianxiety drugs.

Analgesics and Antipyretics

Central nervous system analgesics are those drugs designed to suppress all but the most severe pain, without the patient's losing consciousness. Their main action is on the nerves carrying the pain impulses to the brain. In most cases these drugs also act as antipyretics, inhibiting toxins from affecting the temperature control centers. They consist mainly of acetylsalicylic acid (aspirin: 5 to 15 grains), acetanilid (5 grains), acetophenetidin (5 grains), and acetaminophen. Salicylic acid (p. 411) is a remarkable compound in that it is used as an analgesic, antipyretic, and anti-inflammatory agent.

Acetaminophen (Tylenol) is an effective analgesic and antipyretic. It raises the athlete's pain threshold and decreases fever by acting on the heat-regulating center in the hypothalamus. The usual adult dosage is one or two 325 mg tablets taken every 4 to 6 hours and not to exceed 12 tablets each day. Because it does not irritate the gastrointestinal system, it is often a replacement for aspirin in noninflammatory conditions.

Propoxyphene hydrochloride (Darvon) is a mild analgesic narcotic that is slightly stronger than aspirin in its pain relief. It is not an anti-inflammatory drug. Darvon is addictive and when combined with alcohol, tranquilizers, or other sedatives or depressants it can be fatal.

Caution should always be used in dispensing analgesics for headaches and other complaints, since they may disguise symptoms of serious pathological conditions.

Hypnotics, Sedatives, and Antianxiety Drugs

Hypnotics and sedatives may be given to the athlete by the physician when the athlete either is under extreme tension, playing in an "away" game and unable to rest properly amid strange surroundings, or is abnormally apprehensive before a big contest. At such times sleep or relaxation may need to be induced with hypnotics, sedatives, or antianxiety drugs. Such drugs, in most cases, give little relief from pain. However, relaxation usually means less muscle tension, and the result is often a lessening of the pain experience.

Barbituric acid is a main ingredient in many hypnotic and sedative drugs. The most common are probably phenobarbital and pentobarbital (Nembutal). Each produces a natural sleep and inhibits nervousness. Phenobarbital quiets nervousness, and pentobarbital (Nembutal) is given orally for sleep.

Bromides give a sedative action, calming anxiety and nervousness.

Drugs to Contract Tissue

Astringents cause a contraction of cells, arrest capillary bleeding, and coagulate the albumins of local tissues. Astringents applied to mucous membranes will harden tissue cells and decrease inflammatory exudates. Applied directly to the skin, an astringent will check hemorrhage and other secretions. The most popular astringents in sports are alum, boric acid, zinc oxide, and tannic acid.

Alum is used in sports mostly in powder form and is extensively applied as a styptic in the care of mouth ulcerations and in the control of excessive foot perspiration.

Boric acid is used both as an astringent and as a mild antiseptic. As an astringent it is used in powder form; it can be dusted on capillary bleeding areas or be used on the feet to control foot odors and excessive perspiration. Toxic reaction to boric acid may occur because of its high level of absorbability.

Zinc oxide in an ointment effects a soothing and astringent action. Used in the mass (sticky portion) of the adhesive tape, it helps to prevent undue skin softening when tape is applied. As an emollient, zinc oxide ointment can be applied to denuded skin areas and can effect a mild healing action without softening the skin excessively. It also provides a good drying agent for abrasions.

Tannic acid, when administered externally, has both astringent and hemostatic qualities. It is found in many training room preparations designed to toughen skin. However, skin toughening does not really occur through the application of an astringent.

Drugs to Treat Itching

Pruritis (itching) is the result of irritation to the peripheral sensory nerves. It is a symptom, rather than a condition in itself, and leads to scratching, which in turn may cause infection. Many situations in sports can create pruritis. Perspiration combined with irritating clothing is a common cause of itching. To relieve itching, solutions and ointments containing either a mild topical anesthetic such as benzocaine or a cool, soothing agent like calamine or menthol may be applied to the skin.

Perspiration combined with irritating clothing is a common cause of itching.

Calamine is one of the oldest medications used today. It is composed of zinc oxide powder with a small amount of ferric oxide, which gives it a pinkish color. In a lotion form it is combined with glycerin, bentonite magma (a suspending agent for insoluble drugs), and a solution of calcium hydroxide (lime water). Placed on the skin, calamine lotion acts as a soothing, protective coating in cases of itching dermatitis.

Drugs to Loosen Horny Skin Layer

Because sports participation can create painful accumulations of the outermost horny layer of the skin on the hands and feet, warts, corns, and heavy calluses may require a keratolytic agent to loosen and/or encourage peeling of the top layer of skin. Resorcinol and salicylic acid are the most common drugs used for this purpose.

Protective Skin Coatings

Coatings may be applied to skin areas where protection from contamination, friction, or drying of tissues is needed. Protective coatings in sports consist mainly of substances containing storax or flexible collodion, plus adhesive tape.

Storax is a balsam derived from the trunk of *Liquidambar orientalis* or *Liquidambar styraciflua.* It occurs as a semiliquid, grayish, sticky, and opaque mass, which is used most often in a compound benzoin tincture as an adherent. Its qualities give a protective coating against tape and friction irritations.

Flexible collodion is a mixture of ethyl oxides, pyroxylin, alcohol, camphor, and castor oil. When applied to the skin, this solution evaporates rapidly, leaving a flexible cohesive film. Its use in sports is primarily for covering exposed tissue and protecting lacerated cuts from further irritation.

Adhesive tape offers a highly adaptable means for the protection of athletic affections.

Spray plastic coatings have been developed to cover external wounds, replacing the conventional cloth dressing. The danger of such coatings is that infection may be contained within the wound if it has not been properly cleansed.

Sun Screens

A number of sun screens are currently on the market. Many of these products contain para-aminobenzoic acid (PABA) which, when applied to the skin, combines with the stratum corneum to provide sun protection. Depending on the strength of the product, sunburning is prevented but tanning is allowed or both burning and tanning are prevented.[6]

Drugs to Treat Colds and Allergies

Drugs on the market designed to affect colds and allergies are almost too numerous to count. In general, they fall into three basic categories, all of which deal with the symptoms of the condition and not the causation. They are drugs dealing with nasal congestion, histamine reactions, and cough.

Nasal Decongestants and Antihistamines

Drugs that affect the nasal mucous membranes are basically vasoconstrictors, which reduce engorged tissue during upper respiratory tract involvements. They are often combined with antiseptics or antihistamines. Many decongestants that contain mild vasoconstricting agents such as phenylephrine hydrochloride (Neo-Synephrine) or naphazoline hydrochloride (Privine) are on the market. These agents, applied topically, are relatively safe. Only when used to excess do they cause undesirable side effects.

Antihistamines are often added to nasal decongestants. Histamine is a protein substance contained in animal tissues that, when released into the general circulation, causes the reactions of an allergy. Histamine causes dilation of arteries and capillaries, skin flushing, and a rise in temperature. An antihistamine is a substance that opposes histamine action. Examples are diphenhydramine hydrochloride (Benadryl) and tripelennamine hydrochloride (Pyribenzamine). Nasal vasoconstrictors or decongestants can be overused by the athlete. For example, overuse of these medications can result in a reversal of vasoconstriction, causing chronic congestion to be produced. Overuse can also cause the athlete to have elevated blood pressure, dizziness, heart palpitation, and drowsiness.

Some antihistamines have been found also to relieve the symptoms of *motion sickness* by depressing the central nervous system, particularly the nerves affecting the labyrinth of the ear. One of the most popular compounds used for motion sickness is dimenhydrinate (Dramamine).

An effective decongestant is pseudoephedrine hydrochloride (Sudafed). As a nonprescription drug it comes in tablets of 30 mg; prescription tablets for adults are 60 mg. Two tablets are recommended, four times a day. Sudafed is effective within ½ to 1 hour, by decongesting nasal passages and bronchioli.

Antitussives

Antitussives help inhibit or prevent coughing. Their action may increase the fluid content so that expectoration is made easier, or they may relieve irritated mucous membranes by soothing or healing inflamed mucosa. Antitussives are available in liquid, capsule, pill, troche, or spray form. *Ammonium chloride* is used in many cough medicines to alleviate symptoms

Overuse of nasal decongestants and antihistamines can cause elevated blood pressure, dizziness, heart palpitation, and drowsiness.

of inflamed mucous membranes. *Terpin hydrate* and *creosote* are substances that help to diminish bronchial secretions. *Codeine* is also commonly used but must be prescribed by a physician. It is a depressant and affects the reflex cough center in the brain.

Drugs to Treat Gastrointestinal Disorders

Disorders of the gastrointestinal tract include an upset stomach or formation of gas because of food incompatibilities and acute or chronic hyperacidity, which leads to inflammation of the mucous membrane of the intestinal tract. There is an ever-increasing incidence of ulcers among high school and college athletes, most of which are probably caused by the stress of anticipating sports performances. Poor eating habits may lead to involvements of the digestive tract, such as diarrhea or constipation. Drugs that elicit responses within the gastrointestinal tract are basically alkalies, carminatives, cathartics and laxatives, emetics, and hydrochloric and citric acids.

Poor eating habits may lead to digestive tract problems such as diarrhea or constipation.

Alkalies

Alkalies taken into the stomach relieve hyperacidity. The most common alkalies are sodium bicarbonate, calcium carbonate, magnesium carbonate, calcium hydroxide (lime water), and bismuth. They may be used in liquid, powder, or tablet form.

Carminatives

Carminatives are drugs that give relief from flatulence (gas). Their action on the digestive canal is to inhibit gas formation and aid in its expulsion. Peppermint and spearmint water are the most commonly used carminatives. They may be combined with alkalies to decrease the acid secretion of the stomach.

Cathartics and Laxatives

The use of cathartics in sports should always be under the direction of a physician. Constipation may be symptomatic of a serious disease condition. Indiscreet use of laxatives may render the athlete unable to have normal bowel movements. There is little need for healthy, active individuals to rely on artificial means for stool evacuation.

Cathartics are drugs that encourage bowel evacuation. They are classified into two basic types, laxatives and purgatives. *Laxatives* are mild cathartics and *purgatives* are severe ones. Bowel evacuation can be encouraged in several ways: (1) by filling the digestive tract with a bulk-type substance, such as fruits and vegetables, and thereby activating peristalsis; (2) by administering a drug to stimulate the mucous membrane, which increases its fluid secretions; or (3) by administering a substance that draws fluid from the mucous membrane. Fluid increase in the intestinal canal softens the feces, allowing it to pass more easily.

Cathartic drugs are classified according to their action on the intestinal tract. *Inorganic cathartics* include magnesium sulfate (Epsom salts), magnesia magma (milk of magnesia), sodium phosphate, and sodium sulfate. These cathartics pull fluid from the intestinal tissues, soften the feces, and increase peristalsis. Mineral oil also is used as a laxative; because of its nonabsorption, it lubricates and expands the feces for ease of evacuation. If a laxative is essential, a mild bulk-producing substance should be chosen, such as one that contains psyllium or methylcellulose.

Diarrhea is another gastrointestinal problem common to athletes. If necessary and on the advice of a physician, mild antidiarrheal agents such as kaopectate (a mixture of 20% kaolin and 1% pectin) may be given in a dose of up to 8 tablespoons for adults over 12 years of age; however, 4 tablespoons may give satisfactory relief. The trainer or coach should not indiscriminately treat an athlete's diarrhea. Diarrhea may be a symptom of a more serious problem.

Emetics

Emetics are drugs that cause reverse peristalsis, or vomiting. This is usually a first-aid measure to rid the stomach of poison. In sports it may be used to rid the stomach of disagreeable food. A glass of warm water with a tea-spoonful of powdered mustard or salt, or soapy water can cause regurgitation. A full glass of warm water and bicarbonate of soda will take the acidity from the vomitus. Probably the least time-consuming method to induce vomiting is to have the athlete tickle the back of the throat, at the gag reflex center.

Hydrochloric and Citric Acids

Hydrochloric and citric acids are seldom used in sports. Hydrochloric acid is given in a dilute form when there is a decreased amount of acid secretion in the stomach. Citric acid helps to overcome acidosis caused by an alkali reduction within the body.

Drugs to Control Bleeding

Various drugs and medicines cause selective actions on the circulatory system, including vasoconstrictors and anticoagulants.

Vasoconstrictors

In sports vasoconstrictors are most often administered externally to sites of profuse bleeding. The drug most commonly used for this purpose is epinephrine (adrenaline), which is applied directly to a hemorrhaging area. It acts immediately to constrict damaged blood vessels and has been found extremely valuable in cases of epistaxis (nosebleed) where normal procedures were inadequate.

Anticoagulants

Drugs that inhibit blood clotting may be used by the physician in cases of recent injury or in cases of blood vessel occlusion by a thrombus. The most common anticoagulants used by physicians in sports are heparin and coumarin derivatives.

Heparin is a substance that is derived from the lungs of domestic animals. It prolongs the clotting time of blood but will not dissolve a clot once it has developed. Heparin is used primarily to control extension of a thrombus that is already present.

Coumarin derivatives act by suppressing the formation of prothrombin in the liver. Given orally, they are used to slow clotting time in certain vascular disorders.

Drugs to Reduce Inflammation

Sports physicians have a wide choice of drugs at their disposal for treatment of inflammation. There is also a great variety of across-the-counter drugs that claim to deal effectively with inflammation of the musculoskeletal system. The problem of proper drug selection is tenuous, even for a physician, because of new drugs continually coming to the forefront; the situation is compounded by highly advertised over-the-counter preparations. Any drug selection, especially drugs designed to treat the inflammatory process, must be effective, must be appropriate for the highly physical athlete, and must not create any untoward adverse reactions. With these points in mind, the more generally accepted anti-inflammatory drugs will be discussed.

Salicylates (Aspirin)

A salicylate is a salt of salicylic acid, of which aspirin is the most commonly used. It is also one of the most abused drugs in use today. Salicylates have three major applications: pain, fever, and inflammation. In pain control, two 325 mg, 5-grain tablets are taken every 4 to 6 hours.

Salicylic acid (aspirin) can positively affect and control pain, fever, and inflammation.

As an anti-inflammatory agent, aspirin is effective in conditions such as tendinitis, bursitis, chondromalacia, and tenosynovitis. It is believed to inhibit the release of prostaglandins, a major factor in the inflammatory process.[3]

Adverse reactions   Aspirin has been associated with a number of adverse reactions that are primarily centered in the gastrointestinal region. These include difficulty in food digestion (dyspepsia), nausea, vomiting, and gastric bleeding. To reduce these complaints, buffered or enteric-coated aspirin should be ingested. Buffered aspirin prevents irritation because of its antacid properties, and enteric-coated aspirin dissolves in the small intestines instead of the stomach.

Other adverse reactions to aspirin, especially in high doses, are ear ringing or buzzing (tinnitus) and dizziness. In some cases, the athlete will report heart palpitations and/or tachycardia.

Dimethyl Sulfoxide

Dimethyl sulfoxide (DMSO) is one of the most controversial medicinals in sports medicine. Its unique properties have been described as a "wonder drug" by some and as "dangerous" by others. To date, the exact nature of DMSO is unknown. In 1980 it was removed from a restricted status by the FDA to the status of an investigational new drug, which means that special permisison is required to study this drug. It has been actively investigated for its use with rheumatoid arthritis, brain swelling, scleroderma, sprains, and strains. However, questions as to its effectiveness and safety remain.

Dimethyl sulfoxide (DMSO) is one of the most controversial drugs in sports medicine.

DMSO originally was a solvent used in the manufacturing of rayon and Orlon fibers, antifreeze, hydraulic fluid, paint, and varnish remover.

In terms of its medical use, DMSO is absorbed rapidly into the skin and bloodstream within 5 minutes of application.[8] Once absorbed, it permeates almost all tissue. One characteristic of DMSO is a taste and breath smell of garlic or oysters. Because of fast skin penetration it has been used as a vehicle for other drugs, such as hydrocortisone or hexachlorophene, into the body.[11] Another quality is that DMSO takes up water dramatically. It also is known to inhibit cholinesterase, which is an enzyme that catalyzes the hydrolysis of acetylcholine to choline and an anion. DMSO also breaks down collagen fibers while keeping elastic fibers intact.

In sports medicine, DMSO has been and is being used to decrease joint swelling, dispel hematomas and ecchymoses (black and blue), and generally promote the healing process. DMSO exacerbates inflammation by producing a histamine response, which promotes vasodilation. Pain is also decreased by the C nerve fibers being blocked.

The physiological mechanism of action of DMSO is still unknown. Its most appropriate therapeutic strength or dosage has not been agreed on. A 70% to 80% concentration has been suggested as a therapeutic percentage; however, when and how much to apply remain to be answered.

Reported side effects after DMSO treatment are relatively few. Some side effects are an occasional minor rash at the treatment site, generalized dermatitis, headache, nausea, and dizziness.[1] One extremely important factor is that tendons or ligaments may be weakened after prolonged DMSO treatment, thus precluding sports participation during and immediately after DMSO therapy.

Enzymes

The use of enzyme drugs has become a popular means of caring for the injured athlete. Enzymes are employed by physicians for various reasons. Some are the absorption of proteolytic enzymes and clot lysis.

Varidase (streptokinase-streptodornase) is an enzyme taken from specific strains of streptococci. This mixture of enzymes is used topically for dissolving blood clots (streptokinase) and pus (streptodornase). For an athlete it may be mixed with hydrocortisone and lidocaine (Xylocaine) in treating a swollen joint. In general, varidase is an anti-inflammatory agent designed for the relief of pain, swelling, tenderness, and redness (erythema).

Bromelain (Ananase), on the other hand, contains proteolytic enzymes produced by the pineapple plant. Taken orally it decreases edema and pain and assists in tissue repair. Other commonly used agents are salicylates, especially aspirin, indocin (Indomethacin), and corticosteroids (cortisone).

Nonsteroidal Anti-inflammatory Drugs

Indocin (Indomethacin, MSD) is a nonsteroidal drug that has anti-inflammatory, antipyretic, and analgesic properties. It is a strong inhibitor of prostaglandin synthesis and is effective for such chronic problems as rheumatoid arthritis and osteoarthritis.

Indocin can produce many adverse reactions and should be used cautiously. It can cause severe gastrointestinal tract reactions, drowsiness, headache, dizziness, depression, tinnitus, and a variety of other systemic reactions.

Ibuprofen (Motrin) is a nonsteroidal anti-inflammatory agent. Besides affecting inflammation it also acts as an antipyretic and analgesic. Tablets are available in 300 and 400 mg. It is comparable to aspirin and better tolerated by some persons. Like many other anti-inflammatory agents, ibuprofen can cause gastric irritation, dizziness, headache, nervousness, and skin itching (pruritus).

Phenylbutazone (Butazolidin) is an extremely potent nonsteroidal anti-inflammatory drug. It also is antipyretic and analgesic. Phenylbutazone is particularly useful for chronic musculoskeletal conditions such as acute arthritis, bursitis, and capsulitis. It can produce serious adverse reactions if not carefully administered by the physician. Gastric ulceration, anemia, fluid and electrolyte disturbances, liver damage, skin hemorrhaging, pruritus, kidney dysfunction, hypertension, heart inflammation, and an allergic reaction are a few of these adverse reactions.

Oxyphenbutazone (Tandearil), like butazolidin, is an extremely powerful drug. It also is a nonsteroidal agent that is anti-inflammatory, antipyretic, and pain inhibiting. The adverse reactions are similar to butazolidin.

Corticosteroids Corticosteroids, of which cortisone is the most common, are used primarily for chronic musculoskeletal and joint conditions. Cortisone is a synthetic glucocorticoid that is usually given orally or by injection. Increasingly more caution is taken in the use of corticosteroids than was practiced in the past. Prolonged use of corticosteroids can produce the following serious complications:

1. Fluid and electrolyte disturbances (e.g., water retention due to excess sodium levels)
2. Musculoskeletal and joint impairments (e.g., bone thinning and muscle and tendon weakness)
3. Dermatological problems (e.g., delayed wound healing)
4. Neurological impairments (e.g., vertigo, headache, convulsions)
5. Endocrine dysfunctions (e.g., menstrual irregularities)
6. Ophthalmic conditions (e.g., glaucoma)
7. Metabolic impairments (e.g., negative nitrogen balance, muscle wasting)

Cortisone is primarily administered by injection. Other ways are ionophoresis and phonophoresis. Studies have indicated that cortisone injected directly into tendons, ligaments, and joint spaces can lead to weakness and degeneration.[7] After cortisone treatment an athlete must not participate in sports for up to 6 weeks. Such activity will predispose the treated part to rupturing. Trigger points, tennis elbow, and plantar fasciitis have benefitted from corticosteroid treatment.[9]

Trigger points, tennis elbow and plantar fasciitis have benefitted from corticosteroid treatment.

Drugs for Muscle Dysfunctions

The two most common muscle problems in sports are the ordinary muscle cramp, stemming from physical activity, and spasms, which are associated with musculoskeletal injury. As discussed in Chapter 18, muscle cramps that commonly occur in the legs probably stem from fatigue and mineral deprivation or, perhaps, a muscle anoxia associated with some minor circulatory impairment. These cramps are often easily remediated through rest and restoration of mineral stores. However, skeletal relaxant agents designed to alleviate spasms of the musculature are widely used in both acute and chronic musculoskeletal conditions. If muscle spasms are relieved, pain can be diminished and normal function can often be resumed. In recent years skeletal relaxants have been given by physicians to athletes immediately after musculoskeletal injury.

Drugs that produce muscular relaxation are divided into "peripheral" relaxants and "central" relaxants. Peripheral relaxants act on the myoneural junction by blocking the depolarization of the motor end-plate by acetylcholine. Central relaxants inhibit specific neuromuscular reflexes. Common skeletal muscle depressants that act on the central nervous system are mephenesin, methocarbamol (Robaxin), and carisoprodol (Soma). Because centrally acting muscle relaxants also act as sedatives or tranquilizers on the higher brain centers, there is growing speculation among physicians that these drugs are less specific to muscle relaxation than was once believed.

Most of these relaxants are dispensed in tablet form and ingested orally. These drugs relieve muscle spasms that have occurred from the traumatic injuries of sprains, strains, fractures, or dislocations.

REFERENCES

1. Albrechtsen, S.J., and Harvey, J.S.: Dimethyl sulfoxide: biomechanical effects on tendons, Am. J. Sports Med. **10**:177, March 1982.
2. Biffenhagen, G., and Hawkins, W. (editors): Handbook of nonprescription drugs, Washington, D.C., American Pharmaceutical Association.
3. Caron, R.: Aspirin and athletics, Ath. Train. **16**:56, Spring 1981.
4. Graedon, J.: The people's pharmacy, New York, 1976, Avon Books.
5. Hanley, D.E.: Drug and sex testing: regulations for international competition, Symposium on Olympic sportsmedicine, Clinics in sports medicine, vol. 2, no. 1, Philadelphia, March 1983, W.B. Saunders Co.
6. Houston, B.L.: Sunscreen lotions may increase heat risks, Phys. Sportsmed. **10**:27, Sept. 1982.
7. Hughes, C.C.: Medical care: ethnomedicine. In Logan, M.H., and Hunt, E.E. (editors): Health and the human condition, North Scituate, Mass., 1978, Duxbury Press.
8. Olerud, J.: DMSO—a literature review, NATA Symposium, Granite Falls, Wash., Marvl Productions. (Cassette.)
9. Robbins, J.R.: Effects of steroids on ligaments and tendons, NATA Clinical Symposium Granite Falls, Wash., 1982, Marvl Productions. (Cassette.)
10. Wells, J.: Adverse drug interaction in sports medicine, Ath. Train. **15**:236, Winter 1980.
11. Wells, J.: An evaluation of the present indications of dimethyl sulfoxide (DMSO) in sports medicine, Ath. Train. **17**:26, Spring 1982.

ADDITIONAL SOURCES

Alford, M.: Interactions of medications with foods, NATA Annual Meeting, Clinical Symposium, June 1983, National Athletic Trainers Association. (Cassette.)
AMA drug evaluations, ed. 4, New York, 1980, John Wiley & Sons.
Berkow, R. (editor): The Merck manual, Rahway, N.J., 1983, Merck & Co., Inc.
Bowman, W.C., and Rand, M.J.: Textbook of pharmacology, ed. 2, St. Louis, 1980, The C.V. Mosby Co.
Goth, A.: Medical pharmacology: principles and concepts, ed. 11, St. Louis, 1984, The C.V. Mosby Co.
Handbook of nonprescription drugs, Washington, D.C., 1979, American Pharmaceutical Association.

Hartshorn, E.: Interactions of medications, NATA Annual Meeting, Clinical Symposium, June 1983, National Athletic Trainers Association. (Cassette.)

Hunter, L.: Pharmacology in athletics, NATA Clinical Symposium, Granite Falls, Wash., 1982, Marvel Productions. (Cassette.)

Modell, W. (editor): Drugs of choice, 1984-1985, St. Louis, 1984, The C.V. Mosby Co.

Murray, J.: Pharmacology and the athletic trainer, NATA Annual Meeting, Clinical Symposium, June 1983, National Athletic Trainers Association. (Cassette.)

Patrick, C., Kerin, T., and Lebovitz, R.: Handling prescription drugs: a panel discussion, Thirty-first NATA Annual Meeting and Clinical Symposium, Philadelphia, National Athletic Trainer's Association. (Cassette.)

Physician's desk reference, Oradell, N.J., 1983, Medical Economics Co.

Physician's desk reference for nonprescription drugs, Oradell, N.J., 1983, Medical Economics Co.

Skonieczny, P.: The use of aspirin and anti-inflammatory agents in athletics, Eastern Athletic Trainers Association Meeting, Jan. 1984, National Athletic Trainers Association. (Cassette.)

Taft, T.: Cortisones and anti-inflammatory agents—pros and cons, Mid-Adlantic Athletic Trainers Association Meeting, May 1983, National Athletic Trainers Association. (Cassette.)

Vollmer, R.R.: Physiology and pharmacology of anti-inflammatory medications in athletics, Southwest Athletic Trainers Association Meeting, Jan. 1982, National Athletic Trainers Association. (Cassette.)

Part Four

SPECIFIC SPORTS INJURIES AND OTHER PROBLEMS

T*he overall intent of this book has been to take the reader from general to specific concepts. Part Four helps the student use the knowledge acquired in preceding chapters and relate it to learning about major injuries and other conditions—their causation, prevention, evaluation, and basic management.*

Chapter 17

SKIN DISORDERS AND RELATED PROBLEMS

When you finish this chapter, you should be able to

Explain the structure and function of the skin and identify major lesions causing skin abnormalities

Contrast the pathologies of skin trauma to infection and contagion

Recognize potentially serious skin problems and make the proper physical referral

Recognize potentially serious venereal lesions

Manage common skin traumas and infections

I t is essential that athletic trainers and coaches understand conditions adversely affecting the skin and mucous membrane, especially highly contagious conditions.

THE SKIN'S STRUCTURE AND FUNCTION

The skin is the largest organ of the human body. The average adult skin varies in total weight from 6 to 7½ pounds and from ⅟₃₂ to ⅛ inch thick. It is composed of three layers—epidermis, dermis, and subcutis (Fig. 17-1).

Epidermis

The epidermis has multiple layers. It forms the outer sheath of the body and is made up of the stratum corneum, the pigment melanin, and appendages (hair, nails, sebaceous and sweat glands). It consists of two types of cells, the keratinocytes and the melanocytes. As these cells migrate outward toward the surface of the skin, the keratinocytes form the stratum corneum, which offers the greatest skin protection. The epidermis acts as a barrier against invading microorganisms, foreign particles from dirt debris, chemicals, and ultraviolet rays and also helps contain the body's water and electrolytes. Melanin, produced by melanocytes, protects the body against ultraviolet radiation.

Dermis

The dermis is a skin layer of irregular form, situated underneath the epidermis and made up of connective tissue that contains blood vessels, nerve endings, sweat glands, sebaceous glands, and hair follicles. The dermis forms a series of projections that reach into the epidermis, resulting in an interlocking arrangement and thereby preventing the epidermis from slipping off the dermis.

Hair and Sebaceous Glands

Hair grows from hair follicles contained in the skin. It extends into the dermis, where it is nourished by the blood capillaries. The sebaceous glands, which surround the hair, secrete an oily substance into the hair follicle. Persons who have overactive sebaceous glands may develop blackheads because of a plugging of the hair follicle. Small muscles called *arrectores pilorum* connect to the hair at its root and when contracted serve to constrict the hair follicles and cause a "standing on end" effect or goose pimples. Such contractions increase the emission of oil and thereby help to protect the body from cold.

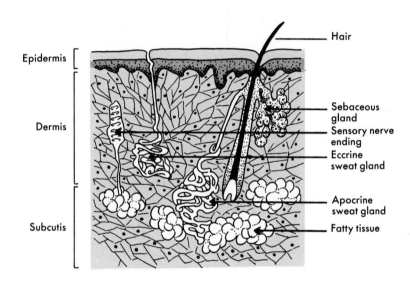

Figure 17-1

The skin is the largest organ of the human body, weighing 6 to 7½ pounds in the adult.

TABLE 17-1

Outline of the skin's structure and function

Layer	Subregion	Function
Epidermis	Stratum corneum	Prevents intrusion of microorganisms, debris, chemicals, ultraviolet radiation
		Prevents loss of water and electrolytes
		Performs heat regulation for conduction, radiation, convection
	Melanin (pigmentation)	Prevents intrusion of ultraviolet radiation
	Appendages	Contains eccrine and apocrine sweat glands, hair, nails and sebaceous glands
Dermis		Protects against physical trauma
		Contains sensory nerve endings
		Holds water and electrolytes
Subcutis		Stores fat, regulates heat

Sweat Glands

Sweat glands are necessary for cooling the surface of the body and the internal organs. There are two main types of glands: the eccrine glands, which are present at birth and are generally present throughout the skin, and the apocrine glands, which are much larger than the eccrine and mature at adolescence in conjunction with the axillary and pubic hair. Certain individuals with undersecreting sweat glands (dry skin) may be especially susceptible to various diseases. The fluid of the sweat gland contains antibacterial agents that are essential in controlling skin infections.

Nails

The nails are special horny cell structures that come from the skin (stratum germinativum) and protect the ends of the phalanges. They are embedded in skin at the base and along their sides and grow about ½ inch in 4 months.

Sensory Nerve Endings

Besides its many other functions, the dermis contains sensory nerve endings. These peripheral nerves provide the body with important protective information such as temperature changes and pain.

Subcutis

The subcutis region contains subcutaneous fat. This is the primary area for fat storage, producing internal temperature regulation and mobility of the skin over the internal body core.

Figure 17-2

Typical primary skin lesions.

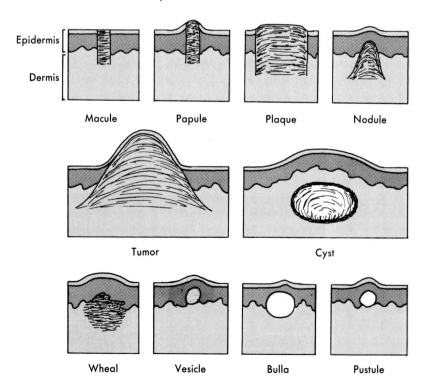

Epidermis

Dermis

Macule Papule Plaque Nodule

Tumor Cyst

Wheal Vesicle Bulla Pustule

SKIN ABNORMALITIES DEFINED

Skin that is healthy has a smooth, soft appearance. It is colored by a pigment known as melanin. An increased amount of blood in the skin capillaries may give a ruddy appearance, and an insufficient amount may give a pale effect.

The normal appearance of the skin can be altered by many factors, external and internal. Some changes may be signs of other involvements. The different intensities of paleness or redness of the skin, which is related to *redness of superficial capillaries,* may indicate a disease condition. *Excessive oiliness* or *dryness* of the skin may be hereditary, although oiliness can be indicative of a greasy diet. *Pigment variation* may result from an increase of sun exposure or from organic diseases; a yellowish discoloration, for example, is indicative of jaundice.

Skin abnormalities may be divided into primary and secondary lesions. Primary lesions include macules, papules, plaques, nodules, tumors, cysts, wheals, vesicles, bullae, and pustules (Fig. 17-2). They are summarized in Table 17-2. Secondary lesions usually develop from primary lesions

TABLE 17-2

Primary skin lesions

Type	Description	Example
Macule	A small flat circular discoloration, smaller than 1 cm in diameter	Freckle or flat nevus
Papule	A solid elevation less than 1 cm in diameter	Wart
Plaque or patch	May be a macule or papule larger than 1 cm in diameter	Vitiligo patch (patches of depigmentation)
Nodule	A solid mass less than 1 cm, deeper into the dermis than a papule	Dermatofibroma (fibrosis tumor–like)
Tumor	Solid mass larger than 1 cm	Cavernous hemangioma (tumor filled with blood vessels)
Cyst	Encapsulated, fluid filled in dermis or subcutis	Epidermoid cyst
Wheal	A papule or plaque caused by serum collection into the dermis, allergic reactions	Urticaria (hives)
Vesicle	Fluid-filled elevation less than 1 cm just below epidermis	Smallpox, chickenpox
Bulla	Like a vesicle, but larger	Second degree burn, friction blister
Pustule	Like vesicle or bullae, but contains pus	Acne

TABLE 17-3

Secondary skin lesions

Type	Description	Example
Scales	Flakes of skin	Psoriasis
Crust	Dried fluid or exudates on skin	Impetigo
Fissures	Skin cracks	Chapping
Excoriation	Superficial scrape	Abrasion
Erosion	Loss of superficial epidermis	Scratches (superficial)
Ulcer	Destruction of entire epidermis	Pressure sore
Scar	Healing of dermis	Vaccination, laceration

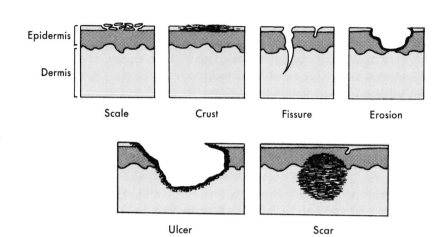

Figure 17-3

Typical secondary skin
lesions.

Figure 17-4

Common disease organisms.

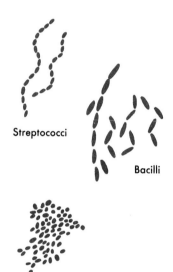

Staphylococcus
Genus of gram positive
bacteria normally present on
the skin and in the upper
respiratory tract and
prevalent in localized
infections.
Streptococcus
Genus of gram positive
bacteria found in the throat,
upper respiratory tract, and
intestinal tract.

(Fig. 17-3). Some examples are scales, crusts, fissures, erosions, ulcers, and scars (Table 17-3).

SKIN INFECTION

When the body is unable to properly defend against the microorganisms that are ever-present internally and externally, a disease or infection can occur (Fig. 17-4). The microorganisms common in infection are viruses, bacteria, fungi, protozoa, and worms. The most common infections in sports are viral, bacterial, and fungal.[20]

Viruses

Viruses are minute infectious agents lacking independent metabolism but still having the capacity to reproduce. Reproduction can only take place within a living cell. The individual chemical particle (verion) includes nucleic acid and either DNA or RNA. The virus can attach to and enter a living cell and may multiply until it kills the cell and bursts out to reinfect other cells. Instead of killing the cell, a budlike growth may occur, with harm to the cell, or the virus may remain within a cell without ever causing an infection.[20]

Bacteria

Bacteria are single-celled microorganisms that can be seen with a microscope after being stained with specific dyes. They are of three major shapes: spherical (cocci), which occur in clumps, doublets, or chains; rods (bacilli); and spirochetes, which are corkscrew shapes.

   Staphyloccocus is a genus of gram positive bacteria that appears in clumps on the skin and in the upper respiratory tract. It is the most prevalent cause of infection where pus is present. *Streptococcus* is also a gram positive strain of bacteria; however, unlike staphyloccus, they appear in long chains. Streptococcus appear in the throat and upper respiratory tract and intestinal tract. Different forms of streptococcus are associated with pneumonia, sore throat, scarlet fever, rheumatic fever, and other serious infections. The spirochete or spiral bacterium is found in a variety of infections, of which syphilis is the most common (see p. 443) (Fig. 17-4).

Fungi

Fungi such as mushrooms, yeast, and molds are organisms with a true nucleus that contains chromosomes, but fungi lack chlorophyll and rigid cell walls. In most cases they are not pathogenic; however, some, such as *Trichophyton*, will attack skin, hair, and nails. *Candida* (monilia), a yeastlike fungus that is normally part of the flora of the skin, mouth, intestinal tract, and vaginal area, can also lead to a variety of infections.

Skin Trauma

Sports participation places a great deal of mechanical stress on an individual's skin. Some of the mechanical forces that produce skin damage are compression, shearing, stretching, scraping, and avulsion.

Friction and Related Problems

The two body areas most subjected to friction are the hands and the feet, complicated by perspiration and callosity.

Excessive perspiration (hyperhidrosis) Hyperhidrosis occurs in a small segment of the population. This problem can make the handling of sports objects difficult, causing both performance and safety problems. Emotional excitement often makes the situation worse. The chemical makeup of hyperhidrotic perspiration from palms is syruplike in appearance and extremely high in sodium chloride.[10] This problem also increases the possibility of skin irritations and often makes adherence of bandages difficult, especially where adhesive tape is necessary. This condition makes callus development, blisters, and intertrigo (chafing) much more likely to occur. Treatment of excessive perspiration should include an astringent such as alcohol or an absorbent powder.

Callosity Skin, typically the epidermal skin layer, increases in thickness when constant friction or pressure is externally applied. Exces-

Excessive perspiration can be a cause of serious skin irritation.

FOOT HYGIENE FOR EXCESSIVE PERSPIRATION AND ODOR

Before Practice

1. Apply an astringent, such as 20% aluminum chloride in anhydrous ethyl alcohol (Drysol), to the skin and allow it to air dry.
2. Next, liberally apply a powder such as talcum, alum, or boric acid, to the skin, socks, and sports footwear.

After Practice

1. Following a thorough washing and drying of the feet, the same procedure is followed as before practice. An astringent is applied to the skin and an absorbent powder to street socks and shoes.
2. There should be a frequent change of footwear.
3. Sports footwear should be liberally powdered after practice to absorb moisture during storage. Ideally a different pair of shoes should be worn daily.

Excessive callus development
must be avoided.

sive callus accumulation on feet or hands is from rubbing or shearing forces over bony protuberances.

Foot calluses Foot calluses may be caused by shoes that are too narrow or too short. Calluses that develop from friction can become painful because the fatty layer loses its elasticity and cushioning effect. The excess callus moves as a gross mass, becoming highly vulnerable to tears, cracks, and ultimately infections.[16]

Athletes whose shoes are properly fitted but who still develop heavy calluses commonly have foot mechanics problems that may require special orthotics. Special cushioning devices, such as wedges, doughnuts, and arch supports, may help to distribute the weight on the feet more evenly and thus reduce skin stress.[11,16] Excessive callus accumulation can be prevented by (1) wearing two pairs of socks, a thin cotton or nylon pair next to the skin and a heavy athletic pair over the cotton pair, or a single doubleknit sock; (2) wearing shoes that are the correct size and are in good condition; and (3) routinely applying materials such as petroleum jelly to reduce friction.

Hand calluses Hand calluses can also be controlled by proper toughening procedures and direct protection through the use of a special glove as used in batting or by the application of elastic tape or moleskin. The skin of the hands can be made more resistant to callosity by the routine application of astringents such as tannic acid or by salt water soaks.

Management of excess callosity Athletes who are prone to excess calluses should be encouraged to use an emery callus file after each shower. Massaging small amounts of lanolin into devitalized calluses once or twice a week after practice may help maintain some tissue elasticity. Once excessive formation has occurred, a keratolytic ointment, such as Whitefield's ointment, may be applied. Salicylic acid, 5% to 10%, in flexible collodion, applied at night and peeled off in the morning has also been found beneficial. Before application of a keratolytic ointment, the trainer might manually decrease the calluses' thickness by carefully paring with a sharp knife, sanding, or pumicing the surface.[16] *Great care should be taken not to totally remove the callus and the protection it affords a pressure point.*

Blisters Like calluses, blisters (bullae) are often a major problem of sports participation, especially early in the season. As a result of horizontal shearing forces acting on the skin, fluid accumulates within intraepidermal slits.[13] This fluid may be clear, bloody, or purulent. Blisters are particularly associated with such sports as rowing, pole-vaulting, basketball, football, and weight events in track and field, such as the shot put and discus.

Blister prevention Soft feet and hands, coupled with shearing skin stress, can produce severe blisters. It has been found that a dusting of talcum powder or the application of petroleum jelly can protect the skin against abnormal friction. Wearing tubular socks or two pairs of socks, as for preventing calluses, is also desirable, particularly for athletes who have sensitive feet or feet that perspire excessively. If, however, a friction area ("hot spot") does arise, the athlete has several options. The athlete can cover the irritated skin with a friction-proofing material such as pe-

Figure 17-5

A direct means of preventing a blister is to "blank out" a piece of tape and fit it tightly over an irritated skin area.

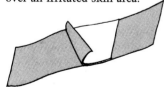

Blisters can be prevented by:
  Dusting shoes and socks
    with talcum powder
  Applying petroleum jelly
  Wearing tubular socks or
    two pairs of socks

CARING FOR A TORN BLISTER

1. Cleanse the blister and surrounding tissue with soap and water; then rinse with an antiseptic.
2. Using sterile scissors, cut the torn blister halfway around its perimeter.
3. Apply antiseptic and a mild ointment such as zinc oxide to the exposed tissue.
4. Lay the flap of skin back over the treated tissue and cover the area with a sterile dressing.
5. Within 2 or 3 days, or when the underlying tissue has hardened sufficiently, remove the dead skin. This should be done by trimming the skin on a bevel and as close as possible to the perimeter of the blister.

troleum jelly, place a "blanked-out" piece of tape (Fig. 17-5) tightly over the irritated area, or cover it with a piece of moleskin. Another method that has proved effective against blisters is the application of ice over skin areas that have developed abnormal friction.

When blisters do develop When caring for a blister, one should be aware at all times of the possibility of severe infection from contamination. Whenever a blister appears to be infected it requires medical attention. In sports, two approaches are generally used to care for blisters: the conservative and the torn blister approach. The conservative approach should be followed whenever possible. Its main premise is that a blister should not be contaminated by cutting or puncturing but should be protected from further insult by a small doughnut until the initial irritation has subsided.[11] (Fig. 17-6). If puncturing is necessary to prevent the blister from tearing, it should be done by introducing a sterilized needle underneath the epidermis, approximately ⅛ inch outside the diameter of the raised tissue. The blister should be opened wide enough that it does not become sealed. After the fluid has been dispersed a pressure pad is placed directly over the blister to prevent its refilling. When the tenderness has subsided in about 5 or 6 days, the loose skin is cut away. Conservative care of blisters is preferred for cases in which there is little danger of tearing or aggravating the blister through activity.

Corns The *hard corn (clavis durum)* is the most serious type of corn. It is caused by the pressure of improperly fitting shoes, the same mechanism that causes calluses. Hammer toes and hard corns are usually associated, with the hard corns forming on the tops of the deformed toes (Fig. 17-7, *A*). Symptoms are local pain and disability, with inflammation and thickening of soft tissue. Because of the chronic nature of this condition, it requires a physician's care.[7]

The trainer can ameliorate the situation by issuing shoes that fit properly and then having athletes with such a condition soak their feet daily in warm soapy water to soften the corn to alleviate further irritation, the corn should be protected by a small felt or sponge rubber doughnut.

Figure 17-6

The conservative approach in caring for a blister should be taken whenever possible with a protective doughnut. If the blister is torn, a flap can be formed by cutting the skin half way around its perimeter to allow treatment of the underlying tissue.

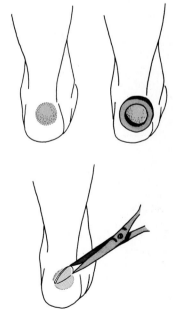

Specific Sports Injuries and
Other Problems

The *soft corn (clavis molle)* is the result of a combination of wearing narrow shoes and having excessive foot perspiration. Because of the pressure of the shoe coupled with the exudation of moisture, the corn usually forms between the fourth and fifth toes (Fig. 17-7, *B*). A circular area of thickened, white, macerated skin appears between the toes at the base of the proximal head of the phalanges. Both pain and inflammation are likely to be present.

Soft corn management   In caring for a soft corn the best procedure is to have the athlete wear properly fitting shoes, keep the skin between the toes clean and dry, decrease pressure by keeping the toes separated with cotton or lamb's wool, and apply a keratolytic agent such as 40% salicyclic acid in liquid or plasters.[11]

Ingrown toenails   It is important that the athlete's shoes be of the proper length, since continued pressure on a toenail can lead to its loss or cause it to become ingrown. The length of the sports socks is also at times a factor, since they can cause pressure on the toenails. It is important to know how to trim the nails correctly. Two things must be taken into consideration: first, the nail must be trimmed so that its margins do not penetrate the tissue on the sides (Fig. 17-8), and, second, the nail should be left sufficiently long that it is clear of the underlying tissue and still be cut short enough that it is not irritated by either shoes or socks.

Figure 17-7

A, Hard corn (clavis durum); **B,** soft corn (clavis molle).

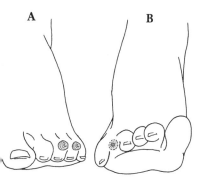

Figure 17-8

Prevention of ingrown toenails requires routine trimming so that the margins do not penetrate the skin on the side of the nail.

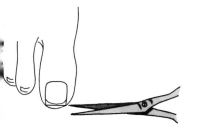

MANAGING THE INGROWN TOENAIL

1. Soak the toe in hot water (110° to 120°F.) for approximately 20 minutes, two or three times daily.
2. When the nail is soft and pliable, use forceps to insert a wisp of cotton under the edge of the nail and lift it from the soft tissue (Fig. 17-9).
3. Other methods of care include cutting a V in the center of the outer edge or shaving the toenail thin, both of which tend to pull the nail from the side.
4. Continue the chosen procedure until the nail has grown out sufficiently that it can be trimmed straight across. The correct trimming of nails is shown in Fig. 17-8.

An ingrown toenail can easily become infected. If this occurs it should be immediately referred to a physician for treatment.

Figure 17-9

Once an ingrown toenail occurs, proper management is necessary to avoid infection. **A,** A wisp of cotton being applied under the ingrown side; **B,** cutting a V in the center of the nail; **C,** shaving the top of the nail thin.

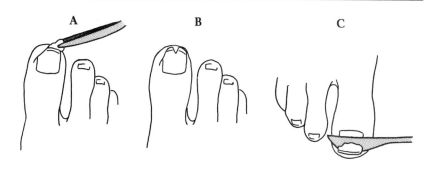

An ingrown toenail is a condition in which the leading side edge of the toenail has grown into the soft tissue nearby, usually resulting in a severe inflammation and infection. Improper clipping of toenails and use of ill-fitting shoes and socks are often etiological factors.

Intertrigo (chafing) Intertrigo or skin chafing is common in sports, particularly in athletes who are obese or heavy limbed. It results from friction and maceration (softening) of the skin in a climate of heat and moisture. Repeated skin rubbing, as in the groin and axilla, can separate the keratin from the granular layer of the epidermis. This causes oozing wounds that develop into a crusting and cracking lesion.[16]

Intertrigo or chafing is created by skin being rubbed together in a warm, moist atmosphere.

Prevention To prevent intertrigo keep the skin dry, clean, and friction free. For groin conditions the athlete should wear loose, soft, cotton underwear. A male athlete should wear his supporter over a pair of loose cotton boxer shorts. The chafed area should be cleansed once daily with mild soap and lukewarm water.

Management Treatment of a chafed area includes wet packs using a medicated solution, such as Burrows, 15 to 20 minutes three times daily.[16] This is followed by the application of a 1% hydrocortisone cream.[16]

TABLE 17-4

Care of external wounds

Type of Wound	Action of Trainer	Initial Care	Follow-up Care
Abrasion	1. Provide initial care. 2. Wound seldom requires medical attention unless infected.	1. Cleanse abraded area with soap and water; debride with brush. 2. Apply a solution of hydrogen peroxide ovaded are; continueuntil foaming has subsided. 3. Apply a petroleum-base medicated ointment to keep abraded surface moist. In sports, it is not desirable for abrasions to acquire a scab. Place a nonadhering sterile pad (Telfa pad) over the ointment.	1. Change dressing daily and look for signs of infection.
Laceration	1. Cleanse around the wound. Avoiding wiping more contaminating agents into the area. 2. Apply dry, sterile compress pad and refer to physician.	1. Complete cleansing and suturing are accomplished by a physician; injections of tetanus toxoid are given if needed.	1. Change dressing daily and look for signs of infection.
Puncture	1. Cleanse around the wound. Avoid wiping more contaminating agents into the area. 2. Apply dry, sterile compress pad and refer to physician.	1. Complete cleansing and injections of tetanus toxoid, if needed, are managed by a physician.	1. Change dressing daily and look for signs of infection.

Signs of infection:
1. Infections become
   apparent from 2 to 7
   days after injury.
2. The wound may become
   red, swollen, hot, and
   tender.
3. Lymph glands near the
   area of infection (groin,
   axilla, or neck) may
   become swollen and
   painful.
4. The athlete may have a
   mild fever and headache.

tetanus (lockjaw)
An acute, often fatal
condition characterized by
tonic muscular spasm and
hyperreflexia and lockjaw

Wounds   Traumatic skin lesions, commonly termed wounds, are extremely prevalent in sports; abrasions, lacerations, and punctures are daily occurrences. To avoid infection, any wound, no matter how slight, must be cared for immediately. In general all wounds must be cleansed with soap and water to rid them of microorganism contamination. Following cleansing, a dressing containing an antiseptic is applied. However, if the wound is to be examined by a physician, no medication should be added to the dressing (Table 17-4). Most lacerations and puncture wounds should be handled by a physician. Uninfected abrasions are not usually referred to a physician. They are managed by debridement and thorough cleansing with soap and water, followed by the application of a moist dressing, such as a medicated ointment. Using an ointment prevents accumulation of a crust and secondary infection.[18] It is advisable that abrasions heal from the inside out to avoid the formation of scabs, which serve only to cover infected areas and are easily torn off by activity.

Wound infection   All wounds are subject to infection by external contamination. The organism most often involved is the pyogenic *Staphylococcus*.

Tetanus (lockjaw) is an acute disease causing fever and convulsions. Tonic spasm of skeletal muscles is always a possibility for any nonimmunized athlete. The tetanus bacillus enters an open wound as a spore and, depending on individual susceptibility, acts on the motor end plate of the central nervous system. After initial childhood immunization by tetanus toxoid, boosters should be given every 10 years. An athlete not immunized should receive an injection of tetanus immune globulin (Hyper-Tet) immediately after injury.[9]

EMERGENCY CARE OF FACIAL LACERATIONS

The following procedure has been found beneficial in caring for lacerations during competition.

Materials needed: Antiseptic, tape adherent, flexible collodion or plastic spray, butterfly bandages, gauze, and 1-inch (2.5-cm) tape.

Position of the athlete: The athlete lies on the table, the wound upward.

Position of the operator: The operator faces toward the athlete's head, standing alongside the table on the same side as in the injury.

Procedure
1. After the injury has been washed and dried, it may have to be shaved if it is in the vicinity of the eybrow. After the shaving it is again cleansed thoroughly and an antiseptic solution is applied.
2. Tape adherent is painted around the wound, and a coating of flexible collodion is placed directly over the wound.
3. A butterfly bandage stitch or a special light and stretchable plastic tape is applied across the wound, pulling it together. Two or more bandage stitches will be needed if the laceration is over ½-inch (1.25-cm) long. Each stitch is started below the tear and pulled upward, against gravity, to ensure maximum closure.
4. A gauze bandage is placed lengthwise over the butterfly bandage stitches to give added protection.

Facial wounds Special consideration must be given to skin wounds of the head and face because of their high vascularity and nearness to the brain. The many irregular angles of the face make it susceptible to both abrasions and lacerations.

The face is generally perspiring and dirty during activity and should be cleansed thoroughly with soap and water before cleansing and debriding an abrasion. Debridement is carried out with antiseptic soap, water, and a soft brush. Once the wound has been completely cleansed, a mild antiseptic is applied, followed by a medicated ointment to keep the injury moist. A nonadhering sterile pad is placed over the wound and is taped in place. Regular daily checks should be made to ascertain whether any infection is present.

Lacerations especially common to the facial area are those occurring around the orbital socket, particularly at the brow line, and about the chin. As is done with other wounds, the facial laceration is cleansed completely and hemorrhage is controlled by the use of a cold compress or an astringent. Most lacerations about the face can be adequately protected until the game is over and can then be sutured by a physician.

Mouth lacerations Lacerations about the mouth usually occur from a blow to the mouth that forces soft tissue against the teeth. Lacerations of the mouth occur most frequently to the lips and tongue. Deep cuts will need to be sutured by a physician, but most lacerations are minor and will not keep the athelte out of activity.

For inspecting this type of injury, the athlete should rinse the mouth with water, and then the trainer should examine the teeth for possible

> Special attention should be given to facial wounds because of their close proximity to the brain.

CARE OF SCALP LACERATIONS

Materials needed: Antiseptic soap, water, antiseptic, 4-inch (10 cm) gauze pads, sterile cotton, and hair clippers.
Position of the athlete: The athlete lies on the table with the wound upward.
Position of the operator: The operator stands at the side of the table, facing the injured side of the athlete's head.
Procedure
1. The entire area of bleeding is thoroughly cleansed with antiseptic soap and water. Washing the wound to remove dirt and debris is best done in lengthwise movements
2. After the injury site is cleansed and dried, it is exposed and, if necessary, the hair is clipped away. Enough scalp should be exposed so that a bandage and tape may be applied.
3. Firm pressure or an astringent can be used to reduce bleeding if necessary.
4. Wounds that are more than ½ inch (1.25 cm) in length and ⅛ inch (0.3 cm) in depth should be referred to a physician for treatment. In less severe wounds the bleeding should be controlled and an antiseptic applied, followed by the application of a protective coating such as collodion and a sterile gauze pad. A tape adherent is then painted over the skin area to ensure that the tape sticks to the skin.

fractures. After the extent of injury has been determined, a solution of hydrogen peroxide is used as an antiseptic and is followed by an astringent-antiseptic solution. Swelling and hemorrhaging can be controlled by having the athlete suck on ice.

Scalp lacerations The care of scalp lacerations poses a special problem because of the general inaccessibility of these injuries. Bleeding is often extensive, which makes it difficult to pinpoint the site of the wound. Matted hair and dirt can also disguise the actual point of injury.

VIRAL INFECTIONS

Common viruses that attack
the skin of athletes:
  Herpes
  Verruca
  Pox virus (molluscum
      contagiosum)

As discussed earlier, viruses are ultramicroscopic organisms that do not have enzyme systems but parasitize living cells. Entering a tissue cell, the virus exists as nucleic acid. Inside, the virus may stimulate the cell chemically to produce more virus until the host cell dies and/or the virus is ejected to infect additional cells.

Of the many viral infections that can directly infect the athlete, these very common ones will be discussed: the herpesviruses, wart-causing verrucas, and molluscum contagiosum.

Herpes Simplex: Labialis and Gladiatorum

Herpes simplex is a strain of virus that is associated with skin and mucous membrane infection. Types 1 and 2 cause cutaneous lesions and are indistinguishable from one another (Color Figures C and D); however, type 1 is found, for the most part, extragenitally and type 2 genitally.[4] Both can, however, be found anywhere on the skin or mucous membrane (see Genital herpes, pp. 444-445).

Etiological Factors

Herpes simplex is highly contagious and usually transmitted directly through a lesion in the skin or mucous membrane. After the initial outbreak, it is thought to move down a sensory nerve's neurilemmal sheath to reside in a resting state in a local ganglion. Recurrent attacks can be triggered by sunlight, emotional disturbances, illness, fatigue, infection, or other situations that may stress the organism.

Symptoms and Signs

An early indication that a herpes infection is about to erupt is a tingling or hypersensitivity in the infected area 24 hours before the appearance of lesions. Local swelling occurs, followed by the appearance of vesicles. The athlete may feel generally ill with a headache and sore throat, lymph gland swelling, and pain in the area of lesions. The vesicles generally rupture in 1 to 3 days, spilling out a serous material that will form into a yellowish crust. The lesions will normally clear up in 10 to 14 days.

Of the two areas of the body affected, herpes labialis (cold sore) is usually the least symptomatic. Herpes simplex gladiatorum is the more serious, with lesions commonly on the side of the face, neck, or shoulders.

Management

Herpes simplex lesions are self-limiting. Therapy usually is directed toward reducing pain and promoting early healing.[4] Application of ice or liquid ni-

trogen during the early symptoms before the appearance of lesions effectively reduces later symptoms. Some treatment choices include drying the
lesions with dyes, germicides, and hydrogen peroxide. Anti-inflammatory
agents that contain topical hydrocortisone or other antibiotics may also be
used.

Herpes simplex infection is so highly contagious that it may run rampant through an entire team in a very short time. Wrestlers having any
signs of a herpes infection should be disqualified from body contact for at
least 120 hours (5 days).[17]

Complications

Herpes simplex, if not carefully managed, can lead to secondary infection.
A major problem is keratoconjunctivitis, an inflammation of the cornea and
conjunctiva that could lead to loss of vision and that must be considered a
medical emergency.

Verruca Virus and Warts

Numerous forms of verrucas exist, including the verruca plana (flat wart),
verruca plantaris (plantar wart), and the condyloma acuminatum (venereal
wart) (see p. 445).

The verruca virus uses the skin's epidermal layer for reproduction and
growth.[15] The verruca wart enters the skin through a lesion that had been
exposed to contaminated fields, floors, or clothing. Contamination can also
occur from exposure to other warts.[15,16]

Verruca Plana or Vulgaris

Verruca plana is associated with the common wart and is prevalent on the
hands of children (Color Figures *E* and *F*).

Symptoms and signs   This wart appears as a small, round, elevated
lesion with rough, dry surfaces. It may be painful if pressure is applied.
These warts are subject to secondary bacterial infection, particularly if
they are located on the hands or feet, where they may be constantly irritated. Vulnerable warts need to be protected until they can be treated by
a physician.

Verruca plantaris   Plantar warts are usually found on the sole of the
foot, on or adjacent to areas of abnormal weight bearing; however, they
can spread to the hands and other body parts. They most commonly result from a fallen metatarsal arch or bruises to the ball of the foot, such
as may be sustained in excessive jumping or in running on the ball of the
foot. Other names for this condition are papiloma and seed warts. Plantar
warts are seen as areas with excessive epidermal thickening and cornifi-
cation (Fig. 17-10). They produce general discomfort and point tenderness
in the areas of excessive callus formation. Commonly the athlete complains that the condition feels like having stepped on broken glass.

Symptoms and signs   A major characteristic of the plantar wart is
its punctuation of hermorrhages which looks like a cluster of small black
seeds.

Management   There are many different approaches to the treatment
of warts. In general, while the athlete is competing, a conservative approach is taken. Concern is to protect the wart against infection and keep

Figure 17-10

Plantar wart.
From Stewart, W.D., Danto, J.L.,
and Maddin, S.: Dermatology:
diagnosis and treatment of
cutaneous disorders, ed. 4, St. Louis,
1978, The C.V. Mosby Co.

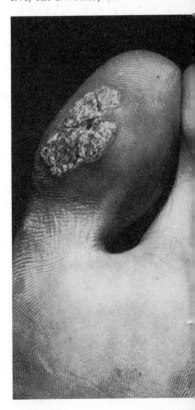

the growth of the warts under control. A common approach to controlling plantar warts is the careful paring away of accumulated callous tissue and application of a keratolytic such as the 40% salicylic acid plaster. When the competitive season is over the physician may decide to remove the wart by freezing it with liquid nitrogen or electrodesiccation. Until removal, warts should be protected by a doughnut pad.

Molluscum contagiosum (water wart) Molluscum contagiosum is a pox virus infection (Color Figure *G*). It is more contagious than warts, particularly in direct body contact activities such as wrestling.[16] It appears as a small, pinkish, slightly raised, smooth-domed papule. When this condition is identified, it must be referred immediately to a physician. Treatment often consists of cleansing throughly and employing a destructive procedure. Destructive procedures include the utilization of a powerful counterirritant such as Cantharone (cantharidin) or surgical removal of the lesion.[19]

BACTERIAL INFECTIONS

Bacteria are single-celled, plantlike microorganisms that lack chlorophyll and may destroy blood cells. Bacterial infections are common complications of skin insults. Most of them are associated with the strains of staphylococci and streptococci, particularly the *Staphylococcus aureus* strain, with the resultant production of purulent matter.

Impetigo Contagiosa

Impetigo is an acute skin infection caused by staphylococcic and mainly beta-hemolytic streptococcic organisms (Color Figure *B*). It is characterized by the eruption of small vesicles that form into pustules and, later, yellow crustations. Impetigo can be highly contagious and may spread rapidly in a gymnasium or swimming pool environment. On the suggestion of the physician the athlete may be requested to remain isolated from the team until the contagious period has passed, particularly in such sports as wrestling in which physical contact is continually made.

The treatment of impetigo requires thorough cleansing of the area and application of a medicated ointment.

Furuncles and Carbuncles

Two major skin problems affecting athletes are furuncles and carbuncles. Both, if traumatized, could lead to a serious sytemic infection.

> Athletes with bacterial infections associated with pus may pass the infection on to other athletes on direct contact.

MANAGEMENT OF IMPETIGO

1. Wash vigorously four or five times daily, using a medicated cleansing agent and hot water to remove all the crustations.
2. After cleansing, dry the area by patting gently.
3. When completely dried, an antibiotic or prescribed medicated ointment may be applied.
4. Every precaution should be taken to make sure that the athlete uses isolated gym clothing and towels to prevent the spread of the disease.

COMMON BACTERIAL INFECTIONS

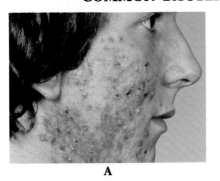

A

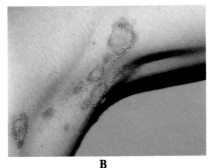

B

Figure A Acne vulgaris, a chronic inflammation of the sebaceous gland characterized by blackheads, cysts, and pustules.

Figure B Impetigo axilla; Impetigo is caused by staphylococcic and streptococcic organisms.

COMMON VIRAL INFECTIONS

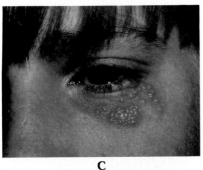

C

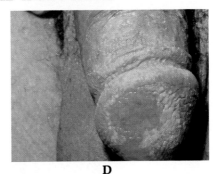

D

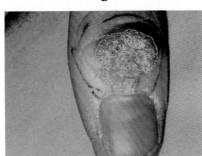

E

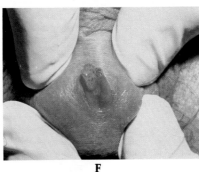

F

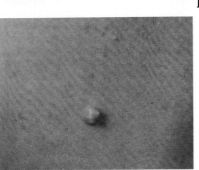

G

Figure C Herpes simplex (type 1). Herpes simplex is a virus infection associated with skin and mucous membrane infection.

Figure D Herpes simplex (type 2). Herpes simplex type 2 is associated with genital infection. After sexual contact, infection becomes apparent in about 4 to 7 days.

Figure E Verruca vulgaris (wart). Verruca vulgaris or plana is a common wart that appears on the hands.

Figure F Condyloma acuminatum (venereal warts), a venereal disease produced by a verruca virus.

Figure G Molluscum contagiosum, a pox virus skin infection producing small, slightly raised, smooth-domed papules that have a pink coloration.

COMMON FUNGAL INFECTIONS

Figure H Tinea versicolor is a yeast infection marked by multiple macular patches that appear as white or pink on black skin and on lighter colored skin as dark, white, or pink patches.

Figure I Tinea corporis, a fungal infection that appears on upper extremities and trunk.

Figure J Tinea cruris, more commonly called "jock rash," appears in the groin region.

Figure K Tinea pedis (athlete's foot), a superficial, chronic fungal infection of the skin. The fungal organisms commonly associated with this condition are *Trichophyton rubrum* and *Trichophyton mentagrophytes*.

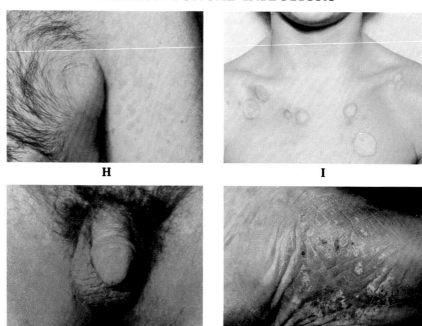

H

I

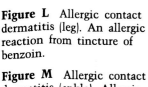

J

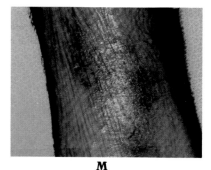

K

COMMON SKIN REACTIONS

Figure L Allergic contact dermatitis (leg). An allergic reaction from tincture of benzoin.

Figure M Allergic contact dermatitis (ankle). Allergic reaction to tape adherent.

Figure N Cold reaction. A blister reaction to a ruptured cold pack on the knee.

From Bergfeld, W.F.: Dermatologic problems in athletics. In Betts, J.M., and Eichelberger, M. (editor): Symposium on pediatric and adolescent sports medicine, Clinics in sports medicine, vol. 1, no. 3, Philadelphia, November 1982, W.B. Saunders Co.

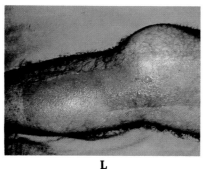

L

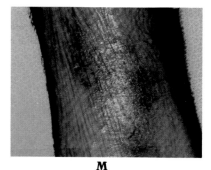

M

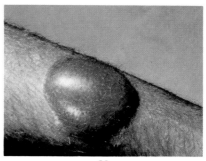

N

Furunculosis

Furuncles (boils) are common among athletes. They usually occur from irritations of hair follicles or sebaceous glands. The predominant infectious
organisms are staphylococci, which produce a pustule. The areas of the
body most affected are the back of the neck, regions about the face, and the
buttocks. The pustule becomes enlarged, reddened, and hard from internal
pressure. As pressure increases, extreme pain and tenderness develop. Most
furuncles will mature and rupture spontaneously, emitting the contained
pus. They should *not* be squeezed, since squeezing forces the infection into
adjacent tissue or extends it to other skin areas.

One should be aware that furuncles on the face can be dangerous, particularly if they drain into veins that lead to venous sinuses of the brain.
Such conditions should immediately be referred to a physician. Care of the
furuncle involves protecting it from additional irritation, referring the athlete to a physician for antibiotic treatment, and keeping the athlete from
contact with other team members while the boil is draining. The common
practice of hot dressings or special drawing salves is not beneficial to the
maturation of the boil.[11]

Carbuncles

Carbuncles are similar to furuncles in their early stages, having also developed from the staphylococci. The principal difference is that the carbuncle
is larger and deeper than a boil and usually has several openings in the skin.
It may produce fever and an elevation of white cell count. The site of greatest occurrence is the back of the neck, where it appears early as a dark red,
hard area and then in a few days emerges into a lesion that discharges yellowish red pus from a number of places.

One must be aware of the dangers inherent in carbuncles, since they
may result in the athlete's developing an internal infection or may spread
to adjacent tissue or to other athletes. The most common treatment is surgical drainage combined with penicillin medications.

Folliculitis

Folliculitis is an infection of the hair follicle. It can be caused by comedones
(blackheads) or, more commonly, by the "ingrown" hair, which grows inward and curls up to form an infected nodule. The infection occurs most
often in areas in which hair is shaved or is rubbed with clothing such as
the neck, face, buttocks, or thigh (Fig. 17-11). The injured area should be
protected from added irritation and a dressing of medicated ointment such
as systemic erythromycin or penicillin. If the infection does not respond to
this procedure, the athlete should be sent to the physician for treatment by
puncturing, curettage, and removal of the hair follicle.

Many hair follicles may become involved through the extension of infection to contiguous sebaceous glands. Such spreading causes a general
condition called *sycosis vulgaris* or "barber's itch." It frequently occurs on
the upper lip and forms a red, swollen area, exhibiting tenderness on palpation. Pus collects around the exposed hair, causing the hair to be easy to
remove. Sycosis vulgaris should always be referred to a physician for treatment.

Hidradenitis

Hidradenitis is an inflammatory condition of the apocrine glands or large sweat glands commonly found in the axilla, scrotum, labia majora, and nipples. It starts out as a keratin plug that rapidly becomes infected, growing from a relatively small papule to the size of a small tumor filled with purulent material. The contents of this lesion are highly infectious to the athlete and, when discharged, can infect other members of the team. Treatment of this problem involves avoiding the use of antiperspirants, deodorants, and shaving creams; using medicated soaps, such as those containing chlorhexidine or povidone-iodine (Betadine); and applying a prescribed antibiotic lotion.[19]

Comedones (Blackheads) and Pimples

Blackheads and pimples are common skin eruptions, which affect adolescents in particular. Both occur at the hair follicle where the oily secretion

Figure 17-11

Folliculitis.

From Stewart, W.D., Danto, J.L., and Maddin, S.: Dermatology: diagnosis and treatment of cutaneous disorders, ed. 4, St. Louis, 1978, The C.V. Mosby Co.

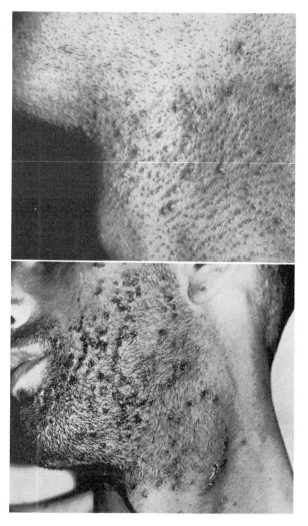

(sebum) accumulates. Sebum carries, besides its oily content, waste products that may aid in the initiation of a mild inflammatory condition, if it should stop up a hair follicle. Blackheads arise from external sebum oxidizing and forming black tips. Blackheads and pimples occur primarily where the skin is oiliest—on the face, nose, chest, and upper back. The oilier an individual's skin, the more prone it is to blackheads. Frequent and thorough cleansing of the skin, using mild soap and hot water, will remove excess oil and consequently help to prevent blackheads.

Pimples may be caused by infected blackheads, skin infections, an inadequate diet, or internal imbalances. One should caution the athlete who has pimples or blackheads that squeezing will only cause additional inflammation and infection.

Acne

A skin eruption called *acne vulgaris* (Color Figure A) occurs during adolescence. This is a chronic inflammatory disease of the sebaceous glands characterized by blackheads, cysts, and pustules. Although most adolescents experience some form of acne, only a few develop an extremely disfiguring case (Fig. 17-12). Its cause is not definitely known, but it has been suggested that sex hormone imbalance may be the major causal factor. Acne begins as an improper functioning of the sebaceous glands with the formation of blackheads and inflammation, which in turn produces pustules on the face, neck, and back in varying depths. The superficial lesions usually dry spontaneously, whereas the deeper ones may become chronic and form disfiguring scars.

The athlete with a serious case of acne vulgaris has a scarring disease and because of it may have serious emotional problems. The individual may become nervous, shy, and even antisocial, with feelings of inferiority in interpersonal relations with peer groups. The athletic trainer's major responsibility in conditions of acne is to help the athlete carry out the wishes of the physician and to give constructive guidance and counsel.

The care of acne is usually symptomatic, with the majority of cases following a similar pattern, including hormone therapy given by a physician and a routine of washing three times daily with a mild soap followed by the application of a drying agent. Other methods may be required, such as the nightly application of keratolytic lotions (sulfur zinc or sulfur resorcinol), individual drainage of crusts or blackheads by the physician, and ultraviolet treatment.

Paronychia and Onychia

Fingernails and toenails are continually subject to injury and infection in sports. A common infection is *paronychia* (Fig. 17-13), which is a purulent infection of the skin surrounding the nail. It develops from staphylococci, streptococci, and fungal organisms that accompany the contamination of open wounds or hangnails and appears as a painful, red, and swollen area. The infection may spread and cause *onychia*, an inflammation of the nail bed.

One should recognize the condition early and have the athlete soak the affected finger or toe in a hot solution of Epsom salts or boric acid three

Figure 17-12

Acne vulgaris.
From Stewart, W.D., Danto, J.L., and Maddin, S.: Dermatology: diagnosis and treatment of cutaneous disorders, ed. 4, St. Louis, 1978, The C.V. Mosby Co.

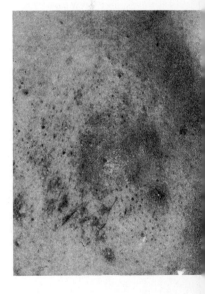

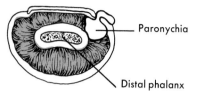

Figure 17-13

Paronychia is a common
infection of the skin
surrounding the nail.

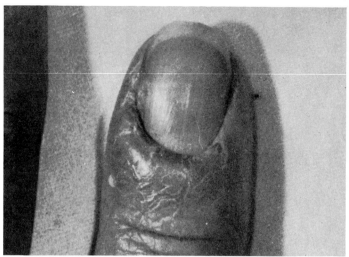

times daily. A medicated ointment, preferably penicillin or 5% ammoniated
mercury, should be applied between soakings. Every protection must be
given the infected nail while the athlete is competing. Uncontrollable paronychia may require medical intervention, consisting of pus removal by
skin incision or the removal of a portion of the infected nail.

Conjunctivitis

The conjunctiva is subject to inflammation from various causes. Colds, excessive light, dust, foreign bodies, and infections about the face may affect
the conjunctiva. Bacteria that enter the eye may cause itching, burning,
watering, and sensitivity to light. The conjunctiva appears red and swollen
with an accumulation of pus. This condition can be highly infectious,
spreading to the normal eye or to other individuals. An athlete exhibiting
signs of conjunctivitis should be sent for medical care immediately. Conjunctivitis may be an indication of a more serious disease such as iritis or
glaucoma.

Hordeolum (Sty)

A sty is an infection of the eyelash follicle or sebaceous gland at the edge
of the eyelid. The infection is usually caused by a staphylococcal organism,
which has been spread by the irritation of rubbing or by dust particles. The
condition starts as an erythema of the eye, which localizes into a painful
pustule within a few days. Treatment consists of the application of hot,
moist compresses and an ointment of 1% yellow oxide or mercury. Recurrent sties require the attention of an ophthalmologist.

Ear Conditions

The earache is a common symptom for several different ear involvements.
It often results from dermatitis of the external ear canal, from furuncles in
the external canal, from eardrum inflammation, or from infections of the
middle ear.

Infection of the external ear canal can arise from irritation caused by hardened wax (cerumen), foreign bodies, or insult caused by inserting hard objects into the ear. A general dermatitis may result or a localized infection may arise from a furuncle. The inflammation of the outer canal may infect the eardrum, causing a sharp, intermittent pain. Another and more common cause of eardrum infection is an upper respiratory infection, which irritates and closes the eustachian tube, causing increased air pressure within the middle ear. The increased middle ear pressure combines with an inflammation and tends to create sharp stabbing pain, difficulty in hearing, and ringing in the ear. Ear infections require medical attention so that antibiotics and other medical procedures may be initiated.

Swimmer's Ear

A common condition in athletes engaged in water sports is "swimmer's ear," a general term for ear infection caused by *Pseudomonas*, a type of bacillus. Contrary to current thought among swimming coaches, swimmer's ear is not usually associated with a fungal infection. Water can become trapped in the ear canal as a result of various obstructions created by cysts, bone growths, ear wax plugs, or swelling caused by allergies.[21] The athlete may complain of itching, discharge, or even a partial hearing loss. Under these circumstances the athlete should be sent immediately to a physician for treatment. Protection of the athlete with a mild ear infection can be successfully accomplished by plugging the ear with lamb's wool combined with lanolin. Prevention from ear infection can best be attained by drying the ears thoroughly with a soft towel, using ear drops containing a mild acid (3% boric acid) and alcohol solution before and after each swim, and avoiding situations that can cause ear infections, such as overexposure to cold wind or sticking foreign objects into the ear.

FUNGAL INFECTIONS

Fungi cause several of the skin diseases found among athletes because sports produce an environment, at times, that is beneficial to their cultivation. They grow best in unsanitary conditions, combined with warmth, moisture, and darkness. The fungus attacks mainly the keratin of the epidermis but may go as deep as the dermis via hair follicles.[16] Most fungal infections in sports result from the same invading fungi of which *Microsporum*, *Trichophyton*, and *Epidermophyton* are the most common genera. These organisms are given the common name of ringworm or **tinea** and are classified according to the area of the body infected. Infection takes place within superficial keratinized tissue such as hair, skin, and nails. The extremely contagious spores of these fungi may be spread by direct contact, contaminated clothing, or dirty locker rooms and showers.

tinea (ringworm)
Common name given to many different superficial fungal infections of the skin

Tinea Capitis

Tinea capitis, beginning as a small papule on the scalp and spreading peripherally, is most common among children. The lesions appear as small grayish scales resulting in scattered bald patches. The primary sources of tinea capitis infection are contaminated animals, barber clippers, hairbrushes, or combs.

Tinea Corporis

Tinea corporis (Color Figure *I*) mainly involves the upper extremities and trunk. The lesions are characterized by ring-shaped, reddish, vesicular areas that may be scaly or crusted. Excessive perspiration and friction increase susceptibility to the condition.

Tinea Unguium

Tinea unguium is a fungous infection of the toenails and fingernails. It is often seen among athletes who are involved in water sports or who have chronic athlete's foot. The nail becomes thickened, brittle, and separated from its bed (Fig. 17-14).

Tinea Cruris

Tinea cruris, more commonly called "jock rash" or "dhobie itch," appears as a bilateral and often symmetrical brownish or reddish lesion resembling the outline of a butterfly in the groin area (Color Figure *J*). The athlete complains of mild to moderate itching, resulting in scratching and the possibility of a secondary bacterial infection. A much less common condition that may be mistaken for tinea cruris is candidiasis, caused by the yeast *Candida albicans*. It is more common among individuals who are diabetic or have a tendency toward diabetes. Compared to tinea cruris, candidal infections cause severe itching and discomfort with associated infection of the scrotum.

One must be able to identify lesions of tinea cruris and handle them accordingly. Conditions of this type must be treated until cured. Infection not responding to normal management must be referred to the team physician. Most ringworm infections will respond to many of the nonprescription medications that contain such ingredients as undecylenic acid, triacetin, or propionate-caprylate compound, which are available as aerosol sprays, liquids, powders, or ointments. Powder, because of its absorbent qualities, should be the only medication vehicle used in the groin area. Medications that are irritating or tend to mask the symptoms of a groin infection must be avoided.

Atypical or complicated groin infections must have medical attention. Many prescription medications that may be applied topically or orally and show dramatic effects on skin fungus are presently on the market (Fig. 17-15).

Figure 17-14

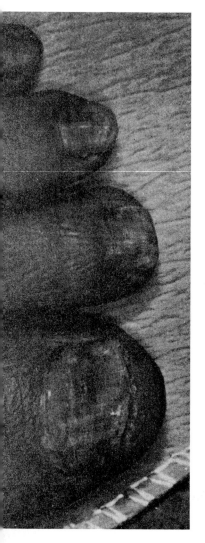

Tinea unguium.

From Stewart, W.D., Danto, J.L., and Maddin, S.: Dermatology: diagnosis and treatment of cutaneous disorders, ed. 3, St. Louis, 1974, The C.V. Mosby Co.

Figure 17-15

When managing a fungus infection, it is essential to break the chain of infection in one or more ways.

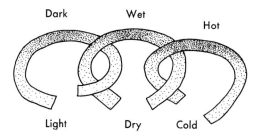

Tinea Versicolor

Tinea versicolor (Color Figure *H*) is thought to be a nonpathogenic yeast infection *(Pityrosporon obiculare)*. It is most prevalent among young adults 18 to 30 years of age. It is usually found on the athlete's chest, neck, and abdomen. On black skin it may appear as white or pink patches and on lighter skin as dark, white or pink patches. It may only be recognized in the summer because the lesions fail to tan. The usual treatment of choice is selenium sulfide (Selsum) shampoo applied at full strength for 5 minutes twice a day for five days; the scrotum should be avoided.[16]

Tinea Pedis (Athlete's Foot)

Tinea pedis, known as athlete's foot, is a condition commonly associated with the fungi *Trichophyton rubrum* and *Trichophyton mentagrophytes* (Color Figure *K*). Wherever heat, moisture, and darkness are found, athlete's foot is prevalent. However, contagion is based mainly on the athlete's individual susceptibility. There are other conditions that may also be thought to be athlete's foot, such as a dermatitis caused by allergy or eczema-type skin infection.[5]

Athlete's foot can reveal itself in many ways but appears most often as an extreme itching on the soles of the feet and between and on top of the toes. It is seen as a rash with small pimples or minute blisters that break and exude a yellowish serum (Fig. 17-16). Scratching because of itchiness may cause the tissue to become inflamed and infected, manifesting a red, white, or gray scaling of the affected area.[12]

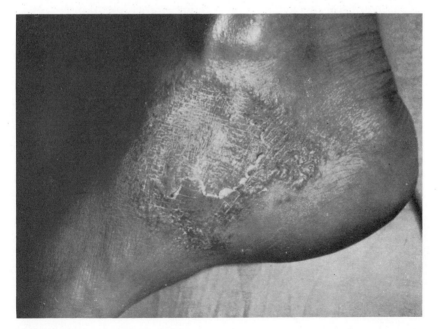

Figure 17-16

Tinea pedis.
From Stewart, W.D., Danto, J.L., and Maddin, S.: Dermatology: diagnosis and treatment of cutaneous disorders, ed. 4, St. Louis, 1978, The C.V. Mosby Co.

BASIC CARE OF ATHLETE'S FOOT

1. Keep the feet as dry as possible by frequent use of talcum powder.
2. Wear clean white socks to avoid reinfection, changing them daily.
3. Use a standard fungicide for specific medication. "Over-the-counter" medications such as Desenex and Tinactin are useful in the early stages of the infection. For stubborn cases see the team physician; a dermatologist may need to make a culture from foot scrapings to determine the best combatant to be employed.

The best cure for the problem of athlete's foot is *prevention*. To keep the condition from spreading to other athletes the following steps should be faithfully followed by individuals in the sports program:

1. All athletes should powder their feet daily.
2. One should dry the feet thoroughly after every shower, especially between and under the toes.
3. One should keep sports shoes and street shoes dry by dusting them with powder daily.
4. All athletes should wear clean sports socks and street socks daily.
5. The shower and dressing rooms should be cleaned and disinfected daily.

ALLERGIC, THERMAL, AND CHEMICAL SKIN REACTIONS

The skin can react adversely to a variety of nonpathogenic influences. Among the most common affecting athletes are allergies, temperature extremes, and chemical irritants.

Allergic Reactions

Skin reactions to allergy:
 Reddening
 Elevated patches
 Eczema

The skin displays allergic reactions in various ways (Color Figures *L-N*). An allergy is caused by an allergen, a protein toward which the body is hypersensitive. Causative factors may be food, drugs, clothing, dusts, pollens, plants, animals, heat, cold, or light, or the cause may be psychosomatic. The skin may reflect an allergy in several ways such as a reddening, elevated patches (urticaria or hives), or an eczema. Reddening and swelling of the tissue may occur either locally or generally from an increased dilation of blood capillaries. Urticaria occurs as a red or white elevation (wheal) of the skin, characterized by a burning or an itching sensation. Eczema is a skin reaction in which small vesicles are produced, accompanied by itching and a crust formation.

The athletic trainer should be able to recognize gross signs of allergic reactions and should then refer the athlete to the physician. Treatment usually includes avoidance of the sensitizing agents and use of an antipruritic agent (such as calamine lotion) and antihistamine drugs.

Allergic Contact Dermatitis

There are many substances in the sports environment to which the athlete may be allergic, causing a skin reaction. The most common plants are poison ivy, poison oak, sumac, ragweed, and primrose. Over time the athlete may become allergic to topical medications such as antibiotics, antihistamines, anesthetics, or antiseptics. Chemicals commonly found in soaps, detergents, and deodorants can create a reaction. Also, the countless chemicals used in the manufacture of shoes and clothing and other materials have been known to produce allergic contact dermatitis.[2]

Symptoms and signs The period of onset from the time of initial exposure may range from 1 day to 1 week. Skin that is continually warm will develop signs earlier. The skin reacts with redness, swelling, and the formation of vesicles that ooze fluid and form a crust. A constant itch occurs that is increased with heat and made worse with rubbing. Secondary infection is a common result of scratching.

Management The most obvious treatment approach is to determine the irritant and avoid it. This may not always be simple and may require extensive testing. In the acute phase, tap water compresses or soaks soothe and dry the vesicles. In the nonacute stage topical corticosteroids may be beneficial.

Actinic Dermatitis (Sunburn)

Sunburn is a dermatitis caused by the ultraviolet radiation from the sun and varies in intensity from a mild erythema (pink color) to a severe, second-degree burn represented by itching, swelling, and blistering. Every protection should be given to athletes who have thin, white skin. Such persons are called *heliopaths;* their skin tends to absorb a greater amount of ultraviolet radiation than more pigmented individuals. If a large area of the skin is sunburned, the athlete may display all the symptoms of severe inflammation accompanied by shock. A sunburn can cause a malfunctioning of the organs within the skin, which in turn may result in infection of such structures as hair follicles and sweat glands.

Sunburn appears 2 to 8 hours after exposure. Symptoms become most extreme in about 12 hours and dissipate in 72 to 96 hours.[3] After once receiving a severe sunburn, the skin is more susceptible to burning. The skin remains injured for months after a severe sunburn has been sustained. Prevention of sunburn should be accomplished by a gradual exposure to the rays of the sun, combined with use of a sunburn medication that will filter out most of the ultraviolet light. Individuals prone to burning should routinely wear a sunscreen such as PABA. Constant overexposure to the sun can lead to chronic skin thickening and damage.[3]

A sunburn is treated according to the degree of inflammation present. Mild burns can be aided by a soothing lotion that contains a mild anesthetic. Boric acid solution has also proved beneficial. Moderate and severe burns can be relieved by a tub bath in which a pound of cornstarch is used; a vinegar solution will also help. Severe sunburn may be treated by the physician with corticosteroids and other anti-inflammatory drugs.

Common Temperature Reactions

Miliaria (prickly heat) Prickly heat is common in sports and occurs most often during the heat of the year to those athletes who perspire profusely and who wear heavy clothing. Continued exposure to heat and moisture causes retention of perspiration by the sweat glands, resulting in itching and in burning vesicles and pustules. It occurs most often on the arms, trunk, and bending areas of the body. Care of prickly heat requires avoidance of overheating, frequent bathing with a nonirritating soap, wearing loose-fitting clothing, and the use of antipruritic lotions.

Chilblains and frostbite Chilblains is a common type of dermatitis caused by excessive exposure to cold. The tissue does not freeze but reacts with edema, reddening, possibly blistering, and a sensation of burning and itching. The parts of the body most often affected are the ears, face, hands, and feet. Treatment consists of exercise and a gradual warming of the part. Massage and application of heat are contraindicated in cases of chilblains.

Frostbite is a much more serious condition than chilblains, since an actual freezing of the superficial tissue takes place. Mild frostbite is freezing without the formation of blisters and is characterized by itching and numbness. More intensive freezing causes paresthesia, stiffness, blistering, and possibly tissue death. Authorities do not agree as to how frozen tissue should be rewarmed. Some indicate that the rewarming should be rapid, with the affected part immersed in water of 108° F until it is restored to normal temperature; others indicate gradual rewarming is best.

SEXUALLY TRANSMITTED DISEASES

Sexually transmitted diseases are discussed in this section because of their relationship to the skin and mucous membrane. It is important that athletes who appear to have a disease related to sexual activity be immediately referred for proper medical attention. The classic venereal diseases, such as gonorrhea and syphilis, are much less prevalent than in the past because effective antibiotic treatments have been developed. Diseases such as nonspecific urethritis, trichomoniasis, genital candidiasis, herpes genitalis, genital warts, molluscum contagiosum, and parasitic infestations of pediculosis pubis and scabies are more commonly seen today.

> Athletes who appear to have a disease related to sexual activity must be immediately referred for proper medical attention.

Gonorrhea

Gonorrhea, commonly called "clap," is an acute venereal disease that can infect the urethra, cervix, and rectum.

Etiological Factors

The organism of infection is the gonococcal bacteria *Neisseria gonorrhoeae*, which is usually spread by sexual intercourse.

Symptoms and Signs

In men the incubation period is from 2 to 10 days. The onset of the disease is marked by a tingling sensation in the urethra, followed in 2 or 3 hours by greenish-yellow discharge of pus and painful urination. Sixty percent of infected women are asymptomatic. For those who have symptoms, onset is between 7 and 21 days. In these cases symptoms are very mild with some vaginal discharge. Gonorrheal infection of the throat and rectum are also possible.

Management

Penicillin in high doses is usually the drug of choice. Other antibiotics may be used if the strain of bacteria is resistant to treatment.

Complications

Because of embarrassment some individuals fail to secure proper medical help and, although the initial symptoms will disappear, such an individual is not cured and can still spread the infection. Untreated gonorrhea becomes latent and will manifest itself in later years, usually causing sterility and/or arthritis. Treatment consists of large amounts of penicillin or other antibiotics. Recent experimental evidence suggests an increasing resistance of the gonococci to penicillin. Evidence of any of the symptoms should result in immediately remanding the individual to a physician for testing and treatment. *All sexual contact must be avoided* until it has been medically established that the disease is cured. Because of the latent residual effects that are the end result of several diseases in this group, including sterility and arthritis, immediate medical treatment is mandatory. Although outward signs may disappear, the disease is still insidiously present in the body. Additionally, such treatment will alleviate the discomfort that accompanies the initial stages of the disease.

Nongonococcal Urethritis (NGU)

Nongonococcal urethritis is a nonspecific infection of the genitourinary tract, which, while not as dangerous as gonorrhea, nevertheless must be medically treated. Although relatively rare among women, the incidence is quite high among men from 20 to 25 years of age. Transmission is through sexual intercourse. The symptoms are a small urethral discharge, usually in the mornings upon arising, and an itching or burning of the urethra when urinating. Usual treatment is with tetracycline group antibiotics.

Acquired Syphilis

Acquired syphilis is known as the "great imitator," since its lesions resemble those of other diseases, masking it and making detection difficult.

Etiological Factors

Syphilis is a contagious systemic disease caused by the motile spirochete *Treponema pallidum*. It enters the body through a mucous membrane or skin abrasion. In just a few hours the spirochete disseminates throughout the body.

Symptoms and Signs

Acquired syphilis is separated into three phases: primary, secondary, and tertiary. The incubation period varies from 1 to 13 weeks but most commonly 3 to 4 weeks. During the *primary phase* the site of inoculation develops a red papule that erodes into a single painless ulcer (chancre). Around the ulcer is a red areola. The lymph glands in the area become painlessly enlarged. After about 6 to 12 weeks the *secondary phase* appears. During this time there may be a mild illness including headache, loss of appetite, nausea, fever, general aching of joints, and a rash. The skin rash can imitate a variety of conditions. The rash is pinkish or pale red in light-skinned individuals and pigmented in dark-skinned individuals. The rash is found frequently on the hands and soles of the feet. The rash occurs in crops of papules, macules, or pustules. This phase, if not treated, may last a short period of time or may persist for months. Eventually the outward signs disappear and the *tertiary or late phase* may begin. In one third of the untreated cases late or tertiary syphilis occurs. In this phase the heart, spinal cord, brain, and other body organs can incur permanent damage.

Management

Penicillin in high doses is the treatment of choice for all phases of syphilis.

Trichomoniasis

Trichomoniasis affects the genitourinary of women but can also infect some men and is more correctly called *Trichomonas vaginalis.*

Etiological Factors

Trichomoniasis is associated with a protozoan organism causing vaginitis, urethritis, and cystitis.

Symptoms and Signs

The early indication of this disease in women is an abundant greenish-yellow, frothy vaginal discharge. There is complaint of irritation of the vulva and perineum and painful urination. This condition may also occur with gonorrhea.

In men, trichomoniasis is usually asymptomatic; however, some may have frothy discharge from the penis.

Management

The usual drug of choice is metronidazole, a vigorous antitrichomonal medication. As with all sexually transmitted diseases, each sexual partner who might be infected should be examined and treated.

Genital Candidiasis
Etiological Factors

Candidiasis refers to infection by fungi of the genus *Candida.* Genital candidiasis is a yeast infection usually caused by *Candida albicans.*

Symptoms and Signs

In women there is an irritation of the vulva and discharge from the vagina. The vulva may be swollen and red. In men, the glans penis may be sore and red.

Management

After identification of the *Candida albicans* organism in secretions from the vagina or penis, vigorous treatment for 2 weeks or more is carried out with a potent antifungal medication such as nystatin.

Genital Herpes
Etiological Factors

Type 2 herpes simplex virus is associated with herpes genital infection, which is now the most prevalent cause of genital ulcerations. After sexual contact signs of the disease appear in about 4 to 7 days.

Symptoms and Signs

The first signs in men are itching and soreness, but women may be asymptomatic in the vagina and cervix. It is estimated that 50% to 60% of individuals who have had one attack of herpes genitalis will have no further episodes, or if they do, the lesions are few and insignificant.[14] Like herpes labialis and gladiatorum, lesions develop that eventually become ulcerated with a red areola. Ulcerations crust and heal in about 10 days, leaving a scar.

Management

There is no cure for genital herpes. Recently systemic medications, specifically antiviral medications such as acycloguanosine (Zovirax, Acyclovir) and viderabine (Vira-A) are being used to lessen the early symptoms of the disease.[4]

Complications

Of major importance to a pregnant woman with a history of genital herpes is whether there is an active infection when she is nearing delivery. Herpes simplex can be fatal to a newborn child. There is also some relationship (although this is unclear) between a higher incidence of cervical cancer and the incidence of herpes genitalis.[16]

Condyloma Acuminata (Venereal Warts)

Another form or verruca that should be recognized and referred to a physician is condyloma acuminata or venereal warts. These warts are transmitted by sexual activity and commonly occur from poor hygiene. It appears on the glans penis, vulva, or anus.

Symptoms and Signs

This form of verruca virus produces nodules that have a cauliflower-like lesion or can be singular. In their early stage they are soft, moist, pink or red swellings that rapidly develop a stem with a flowerlike head.[1] They may be mistaken for secondary syphilis or carcinoma.

Management

Moist condylomas are often carefully treated by the physician with a solution containing 20% to 25% podophyllin. Dry warts may be treated with a freezing process such as liquid nitrogen.

PARASITIC INFESTATIONS

Certain parasites cause dermatoses or skin irritations when they suck blood, inject venom, and even lay their eggs under the skin. Athletes who come in contact with these organisms may develop various symptoms such as itching, allergic skin reactions, and secondary infections from insult or scratching. The more common parasitic infestations in sports are caused by mites, crab lice, fleas, ticks, mosquitoes, and stinging insects such as bees, wasps, hornets, and yellow jackets.[21]

Depending on the part of the country the athlete resides in, parasites such as mites, crab lice, fleas, ticks, mosquitoes and stinging insects can cause serious discomfort and infection.

TREATMENT OF SCABIES

1. The entire body should be thoroughly cleansed, with attention to skin lesions.
2. Bedding and clothing should be disinfected.
3. A coating of gamma benzene hexachloride (Kwell) should be applied on the lesions for 3 nights.
4. All individuals who have come in contact with the infected athlete should be examined by the physician.
5. Locker and game equipment must be disinfected.

Scabies (Seven-year Itch)

Scabies is a skin disease caused by the mite *Sarcoptes scabiei*, which produces extreme nocturnal itching. The parasitic itch mite is small, with the female causing the greatest irritation. The mite burrows a tunnel about ¼ to ½ inch (1.25 cm) long into the skin to deposit its eggs. These burrows appear as dark lines between the fingers, toes, body flexures, nipples, and genitalia. Excoriations, pustules, and papules caused by the resulting scratching frequently hide the true nature of the disease. The young mite matures in a few days and returns to the skin surface to repeat the cycle. The skin often develops a hypersensitivity to the mite, which produces extreme itching.

Chiggers

Several types of reddish mites known as chiggers are common to the United States, particularly the southern part. They are found in grass and on bushes and attach themselves to those who brush up against them. They puncture the skin and suck the blood, which results in a dermatitis, itching, and infection.[8]

Pediculosis (Lice)

Pediculosis is an infestation by the louse, of which three types are parasitic to man. The *Pediculus capitis* (head louse) infests the head, where its eggs (nits) attach to the base of the hair shaft. The *Phthirus pubis* (crab louse) lives in the hair of the pubic region and lays its eggs at the hair base. The *Pediculus corporis* (body louse) lives and lays its eggs in the seams of clothing. The louse is a carrier of many diseases; its bite causes an itching dermatitis, which, through subsequent scratching, provokes pustules and excoriations. Cure is quite rapid with the use of any of a number of parasiticides or lotions such as one composed of chlorophenothane 5.0 g, isopropyl alcohol 50 ml, and propylene glycol 50 ml, rubbed into the infected areas at night before retiring and again the following morning upon arising. The area should not be washed for 7 to 10 days, then the lotion is reapplied. The lice cannot survive dryness. Good hygiene is of paramount importance in all infestations. All clothing, bedding, and toilet seats must be kept clean and sterile.

Fleas

Fleas are small wingless insects that suck blood. Singly, their bites cause only minor discomfort to the recipient—unless the flea is a carrier of some contagious disease. When there are a large number of biting fleas, a great deal of discomfort can occur. After attaching themselves to some moving object, such as a dog or the leg of a human, most fleas bite in patterns of three. Fleas seem to concentrate their bites on the ankle and lower leg. Once the bite has been incurred the main concern is to prevent itching with an antipruritic lotion such as calamine. Scratching the bite should be avoided to prevent a secondary infection. Areas in which fleas abound can be sprayed with selected insecticides containing malathion or some other insecticides.

Ticks

Ticks are parasitic insects that have an affinity for the blood of many animals, including humans. They are carriers of a variety of microorganisms such as bacteria and viruses. Because ticks are commonly found on grass and bushes they can easily become attached to the athlete who brushes against them. Once attached, they burrow their head into the skin, becoming firmly fixed. To remove a tick, a heated device or alcohol is applied to its body, at which time it will withdraw its head. At no time should one attempt to pull the tick from the body; doing so may result in leaving the head of the tick still embedded in the skin.[8]

Mosquitoes

Unless it is the carrier of a disease, the mosqito, as a blood sucker, produces a bite that causes only mild discomfort and a small reddish papule. Generally mosquitoes are attracted to lights, dark clothing, and warm, moist skin.[8] Multiple bites may lead to a great deal of itching, most often relieved by the application of a topical medication such as calamine lotion.[8] In climates where mosquitoes are prevalent, repellents should be used directly on the skin.

Stinging Insects

Bees, wasps, hornets, and yellow jackets inflict a venomous sting that is temporarily painful for most individuals; however, some hypersensitive individuals may respond with an allergic reaction that may be fatal. Stings to the head, face, and neck are particularly dangerous to the athlete. Athletes having a history of allergic reactions from stings must be carefully scrutinized following a sting. The allergic athlete may respond with an increase in heart rate, fast breathing, chest tightness, dizziness, sweating, and even loss of consciousness.[21] In the uncomplicated sting cases, the stinging apparatus must be carefully removed with tweezers followed by the application of a soothing medication. Detergent soap applied directly on the sting often produces an immediate lessening in symptoms. In severe reactions to a sting the athlete must be treated for severe shock and referred immediately to a physician. For sensitive athletes who perform outdoors, it should be suggested that they avoid using scented cosmetics, soap, colognes, or aftershave lotions and colorful, floral, or dark-colored clothing.[6]

REFERENCES

1. Anderson, W.A.D., and Scotti, T.M.: Synopsis of pathology, ed. 10, St. Louis, 1980, The C.V. Mosby Co.
2. Barsky, H.E.: Allergic contact dermatitis: sensitizers, Dermatol. Allerg. **5**:37-41, 1982.
3. Bergfeld, W.F.: The skin. In Strauss, R.H. (editor): Sports medicine, Philadelphia, 1984, W.B. Saunders Co.
4. Bergfeld, W.F.: Dermatologic problems in athletes. In Symposium on pediatric and adolescent sports medicine, Clinics in sports medicine, vol. 1, no. 3, Philadelphia, Nov. 1982, W.B. Saunders Co.
5. Brodin, M.B.: Athlete's foot, Phys. Sportsmed. **7**:95, 1979.
6. de Shazo, R.E., and others: When an insect sting can mean death, Phys. Sportsmed. **4**:72, 1976.
7. Gibbs, R.C.: Calluses, corns, and warts, Am. Fam. Physician **3**:4, 1971.
8. Hemphill, W.J.: Athletic dermatology—parasitic infestation, Ath. Trainer **7**:201, 1972.
9. Henderson, J.: Emergency medical guide, ed. 4, New York, 1978, McGraw-Hill Book Co.
10. Jensen, O.: Rusters: the corrosive action of palmar sweat: sodium chloride in sweat, Acta Derm. Venereol (Stockh) **59**:135, 1979.
11. Liteplo, M.G.: Sports-related skin problems. In Vinger, P.F., and Hoerner, E.F.: Sports injuries: the unthwarted epidemic, Boston, 1982, John Wright, PSG, Inc.
12. Millikan, L.E.: Athlete's foot—scratching beneath the surface of fungal ailments, Phys. Sportsmed. **3**:51, 1975.
13. Moschella, S.L.: Physically induced blisters. In Moschella, S.L., Pillsbury, D.M., and Hurley, H.J.: Dermatology, Philadelphia, 1975, W.B. Saunders Co.
14. Murphy, K., and Corey, L.: Misinformation persists about genital herpes, Skin and Allergy News, **12**:1, 16, 1981.
15. Rees, R.B.: Warts: a clinician's view, Cutis, **28**:177, 1981.
16. Stauffer, L.W.: Abrasions, Ath. Train. **9**:138, 1974.
17. Stauffer, L.W.: Skin disorders in athletes: identification and management, Phys. Sportsmed. **11**:101, 1983.
18. Stauffer, L.W., et al.: Viral infections of athletes' skin: a round table, Phys. Sportsmed. **6**:54, 1978.
19. Stewart, W.D., Danto, J.L., and Maddin, S.: Dermatology, ed. 4, St. Louis, 1978, The C.V. Mosby Co.
20. Stossel, T.P.: Principles of infection, In Strauss, R.H. editor: Sports medicine and physiology, Philadelphia, 1979, W.B. Saunders Co.
21. Strauss, R.H.: Nontraumatic medical problems. In Strauss, R.H. (editor): Sports medicine in physiology, Philadelphia, 1979, W.B. Saunders Co.

ADDITIONAL SOURCES

Berkow, R. (editor): The Merck manual of diagnosis and therapy, ed. 14, Rahway, N.J., 1982, Merck & Co., Inc.

Bergfeld, W.F.: The skin. In Strauss, R.H. (editor): Sports medicine and physiology, Philadelphia, 1984, W.B. Saunders Co.

Knutsen, E.S.: The meaning of meditation. in The holistic health handbook, compiled by the Berkeley Holistic Health Center, Berkeley, Calif., 1978, and/or Press.

Kulund, D.N.: The injured athlete, Philadelphia, 1982, J.B. Lippincott Co.

Prior, J.A., Silberstein, J.S., and Stang, J.M.: Physical diagnosis, St. Louis, 1981, The C.V. Mosby Co.

Raab, B., Lorincz, A.L.: Genital herpes simplex: concepts and treatment, J. Am. Acad. Dermatol. **5**:249, 1981.

Rachun, A., et al., chairmen, advisory panel: Standard nomenclature of athletic injuries, Monroe, Wis., 1976, American Medical Association.

Smith, N.: Dermatology and the athletic trainer, Parts 1 and 2, NATA Clinical Symposium 1982, Granite Falls, Wash., Marvl Productions. (Cassette.)

Williams, J.G.P.: Color atlas of injury in sport, Chicago, 1980, Year Book Medical Publishers, Inc.

Chapter 18

THE FOOT, ANKLE, AND LOWER LEG: ACUTE INJURIES

When you finish this chapter, you should be able to

Identify the major anatomical components of the foot, ankle, and lower leg that are commonly injured in sports

Evaluate the foot, ankle, and lower leg following an acute injury

Report on the etiological factors, symptoms and signs, and management procedures for the major acute injuries in the foot, ankle, and lower leg

The foot, ankle, and lower leg have one of the highest incidences of sports injuries. Because of this and the complicated nature of the anatomical structures of these body parts, injuries to this area represent a major challenge to the athletic trainer and coach.

THE FOOT
Anatomy
Bony Structure

The foot is designed basically for strength, flexibility, and coordinated movement. It also transmits the stresses throughout the body that create the locomotor activities of walking and running. It is comprised of 26 bones: 14 phalangeal, 5 metatarsal, and 7 tarsal (Fig. 18-1). The tarsal bones, which form the instep or ankle portion of the foot, consists of the talus, the calcaneus (os calcis), the navicular, and the first, second, and third cuneiform bones.

Talus The talus, an irregularly shaped bone, is situated on the calcaneus over a bony projection called the sustentaculum tali in such a manner as to permit movement in only a forward and downward direction. It is stabilized by both internal and external ligaments on all four sides.

Calcaneus The calcaneus is the largest tarsal bone. It supports the talus and shapes the heel; its main functions are to convey the body weight to the ground and act as a lever attachment for the calf muscles.

Navicular, cuboid, and cuneiform bones The navicular, cuboid, and cuneiform bones, as a group, are the transverse tarsal bones, which glide upon each other in a combined movement that permits rotation, inversion, and eversion of the foot.

Because the talus fits principally into the space formed by the malleoli, little lateral movement is present unless the restrictive ligaments have been stretched. Because the uppermost articular surface of the talus is narrower posteriorly than anteriorly, dorsiflexion is limited. At a position of full dorsiflexion the anterior aspect of the medial collateral ligaments is taut,[15] while in plantar flexion internal rotation occurs because of the shape of the talus. The average range of motion is 10 degrees in dorsiflexion and 23 degrees in plantar flexion.

Metatarsals

The metatarsals are five bones that lie between and articulate with the tarsals and the phalanges, thus forming the semimovable tarsometatarsal and metatarsophalangeal joints. Although there is little movement permitted, the ligamentous arrangement gives elasticity to the foot in weight bearing. The metatarsophalangeal joints permit a hinge action to the phalanges, which is similar to the action found between the hand and fingers. The first metatarsal is the largest and strongest and functions as the main body support during walking and running.

Phalanges

The phalanges or toes are somewhat similar to the fingers in appearance but are much shorter and serve a different function. The toes are designed to give a wider base both for balance and for propelling the body forward.

The two sesamoid bones are located beneath the first metatarsophalangeal joint. Their functions are to assist in reducing pressure in weight bearing, to alleviate undue friction during movement, and to act as sliding pulleys for tendons.

Plantar Fascia

The plantar fascia is a white band of fibrous tissue originating from the medial tuberosity of the calcaneus and ending at the proximal heads of the metatarsals. Along with ligaments, the plantar fascia supports the foot against downward forces.

Figure 18-1

Bony structure of the foot.
A, Medial aspect. **B,** Lateral aspect.

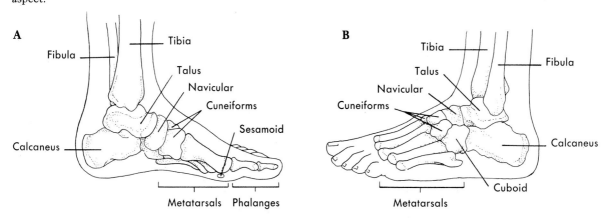

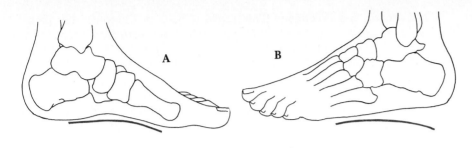

A

B

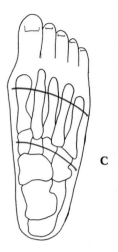

C

Arches of the Foot

The foot is structured, by means of ligamentous and bony arrangements, to form several arches. The arches assist the foot in supporting the body weight in an economical fashion, in absorbing the shock of weight bearing, and in providing a space on the plantar aspect of the foot for the blood vessels, nerves, and muscles. Their presence aids in giving the foot mobility and a small amount of prehensility. There are four arches: the medial longitudinal and lateral longitudinal, the anterior metatarsal, and the transverse (Fig. 18-2).

Figure 18-2

The arches of the foot.
A, Inner longitudinal arch.
B, Outer longitudinal arch.
C, Anterior metatarsal and transverse arches.

Medial longitudinal arch   The medial longitudinal arch originates along the medial border of the calcaneus and extends forward to the distal head of the first metatarsal. It is composed of the calcaneus, talus, navicular, first cuneiform, and first metatarsal. The main supporting ligament of the longitudinal arch is the plantar calcaneonavicular ligament, which acts as a sling by returning the arch to its normal position after it has been stretched. The tendon of the posterior tibialis muscle helps to reinforce the plantar calcaneonavicular ligament (Fig. 18-3).

Lateral longitudinal arch   The outer longitudinal arch is on the lateral aspects of the foot and follows the same pattern as that of the inner longitudinal arch. It is formed by the calcaneus, cuboid, and fifth metatarsal bones. It is much lower and less flexible than the inner longitudinal arch.

Anterior metatarsal arch   The anterior metatarsal arch is shaped by the distal heads of the metatarsals. The arch has a semiovoid appearance, stretching from the first to the fifth metatarsal.

Transverse arch   The transverse arch extends across the transverse tarsal bones, primarily the cuboid and the internal cuneiform, and forms a half dome. It gives protection to soft tissue and increases the foot's mobility.

Figure 18-3

Calcaneonavicular ligament.

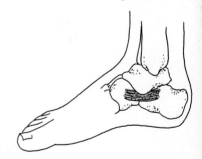

Muscles and Movement

The movements of the foot are accomplished by a complex of numerous muscles (Fig. 18-4).

Dorsiflexion and plantar flexion   Dorsiflexion and plantar flexion of the foot take place at the ankle joint. The gastrocnemius, soleus, plantaris, peroneus longus, peroneus brevis, and tibialis posterior are the plantar flexors. Dorsiflexion is accomplished by the tibialis anterior, extensor digitorum longus, extensor hallucis longus, and peroneus tertius.

Eversion and inversion   The lateral motion of the foot takes place, for the most part, at the subtalar joint, where outward movement (eversion) and inward movement (inversion) are permitted. The muscles primarily responsible for inversion and supination are the anterior tibialis and the posterior tibialis; eversion is initiated by the peroneals, primarily the longus, brevis, and tertius.

Movement of the phalanges   The movements of the phalanges are flexion, extension, abduction, and adduction. Flexion of the second, third, fourth, and fifth distal digits is executed by the flexor digitorum longus and the quadratus plantae. Flexion of the middle phalanges is performed by the flexor digitorum brevis, and flexion of the proximal phalanges is by the lumbricales and the interossei. The great toe is flexed by the flexor hallucis longus. The extension of all the middle phalanges is done by the abductor hallucis and abductor digiti quinti, the lumbricales, and the interossei. Extension of all distal phalanges is effected by the extensor digitorus longus, the extensor hallucis longus, and the extensor digitorum brevis. The adduction of the foot is carried out by the interossei plantares and the adductor hallucis; abduction is by the interossei dorsales, the abductor hallucis, and the abductor digiti quinti.

TABLE 18-1

Individual foot joints

Articulating Bones	Type	Movements
Between tarsals	Diarthrotic (gliding)	Gliding: inversion and eversion
Between metatarsals and phalanges	Diarthrotic (hinge type)	Flexion, extension, slight abduction, and adduction
Between phalanges	Diathrotic (hinge type)	Flexion and extension

Figure 18-4

The movements of the foot are accomplished by a complex of many muscles.

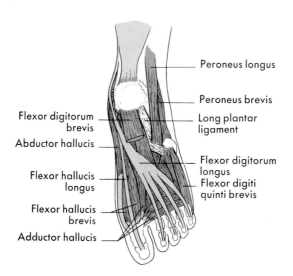

Peroneus longus

Peroneus brevis

Long plantar ligament

Flexor digitorum brevis

Abductor hallucis

Flexor hallucis longus

Flexor digitorum longus

Flexor digiti quinti brevis

Flexor hallucis brevis

Adductor hallucis

Blood and Nerve Supply

The major portion of the blood is supplied to the foot by the anterior and posterior tibial arteries. The dorsal venous arch and digital veins and dorsal digital vein stem from the short and long saphenous veins.

The tibial nerve, largest division of the sciatic nerve, supplies the muscles of the back of the leg and plantar aspect of the foot. The common peroneal nerve is a smaller division of the sciatic nerve and with its branches supplies the front of the leg and the foot (Fig. 18-5).

Evaluation

The athletic trainer is often the first to observe and assess an injury. Following initial screening, first aid is given and a decision is made as to the seriousness of the injury and whether to refer to a physician. As with all areas of the body, the acutely injured foot must be carefully evaluated.

Major Complaints

To fully understand the nature of the athlete's complaint, the following list of questions should be asked regarding an acute foot injury:
- How did the injury occur? (For example, a sudden strain, twist, or blow to the foot region.)
- What symptoms are present? (For example, pain, muscle weakness, or noises on movement such as crepitation, or any alteration in sensation such as numbness.)
- Where does it hurt?

General Observation

The athlete should be observed to determine the following:
- Whether he or she is favoring the foot, walking with a limp, or unable to bear weight
- Whether the injured part is deformed, swollen, or discolored
- Whether the foot changes color when weight bearing and non-weight bearing (changing rapidly from a darker to lighter pink when not weight bearing)
- Whether foot is well aligned and whether it maintains its shape on weight bearing

Figure 18-5

The major nerves of the foot. **A**, Dorsal aspect. **B**, Plantar aspect.

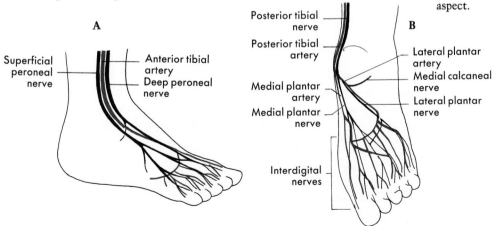

Bony Palpation

If the site of the injury is uncertain, palpate the following bony sites for point tenderness:

Medial Aspect

Medial calcaneus	First cuneiform
Medial malleolus	First metatarsal
Sustentaculum tali	First metatarsophalangeal joint
Talar head	First phalanx
Navicular tubercle	

Lateral Aspect

Lateral calcaneus	Styloid process (proximal head of the
Lateral malleolus	fifth metatarsal
Sinus tarsi	Fifth metatarsal
Peroneal tubercle	Fifth metatarsophalangeal joint
Cuboid bone	Fifth phalanx

Dorsal Aspect

Fourth, third, second metatarsals	Fourth, third, second phalanges
Fourth, third, second	Third and fourth cuneiform bones
metatarsophalangeal joints	

Plantar Aspect

Metatarsal heads	Medial calcaneal tubercle

Soft Tissue Palpation

Medial and Plantar Aspect

Tibialis posterior tendon	Plantar fascia
Deltoid ligament	Bursa head of the first metatarsal
Calcaneonavicular ligament (spring	bone
ligament)	Transverse arch
Medial longitudinal arch	

Lateral and Dorsal Aspect

Anterior talofibular ligament	Peroneal tendon
Calcaneofibular ligament	Extensor tendons of toes
Posterior talofibular ligament	Tibialis anterior tendon

Functional Evaluation

Passive, active, and resistive movement is performed in the numerous joints of the foot and adjacent ankle. Inspection is first performed while the athlete is on a table and then during weight bearing. Movement is performed in the following joints:

1. Ankle
2. Talocalcaneal
3. Mid-dorsal with heel and ankle joints stabilized
4. Metatarsophalangeal
5. Interphalangeal

The foot is then inspected while the athlete stands and walks. The posture of the foot and whether it maintains the same shape in weight bearing as in non-weight bearing is noted. (See Chapter 19 for further discussion on foot posture.)

Pulse

To ensure that there is proper blood circulation to the foot, the pulse is measured at the posterior tibial and dorsal pedis arteries.

Foot Conditions

Most people will at some time develop foot problems. This is attributed to the use of improper footwear, poor foot hygiene, or anatomical structural deviations that result from faulty postural alignments or abnormal stresses.

Many sports place exceptional demands on the feet—far beyond the normal daily requirements. The coach and athletic trainer should be well aware of potential foot problems and should be capable of identifying, ameliorating, or preventing them whenever possible. Chapter 18 is mainly concerned with those acute conditions that affect the musculoskeletal system of the foot. Skin problems of the foot and proper shoe fit were discussed in Chapter 17.

Most people will at some time in their lives develop foot problems.

Acute Conditions of the Foot

Contusions   Two common contusions of the foot are the heel and instep bruise. Each can cause the athlete a great deal of discomfort and disability.

Heel bruise   Of the many contusions and bruises that an athlete may receive, there is none more disabling than the heel bruise. Sport activities that demand a sudden stop-and-go response or sudden change from a horizontal to a vertical movement, such as basketball, jumping, or the landing action in long jumping, are particularly likely to cause heel bruises. The heel has a thick, cornified skin layer and a heavy fat pad covering, but even this thick padding cannot protect against a sudden abnormal force directed to this area.

The athlete who is prone to heel bruises should routinely wear a padded heel cup.

The major purpose of the tissue heel pad is to sustain hydraulic pressure through fat columns. Tissue compression is monitored by pressure nerve endings from the skin and plantar aponeurosis. Often the irritation is on the lateral aspect of the heel because of the heel strike in walking or running.[13]

SYMPTOMS AND SIGNS   When injury occurs the athlete complains of severe pain in the heel and is unable to withstand the stress of weight bearing.[18]

A bruise of the heel usually develops into chronic inflammation of the periosteum. Follow-up management of this condition should be started 2 to 3 days after insult, involving a variety of superficial and deep-heat therapies. If the athlete recognizes the problem in its acute stage, then the following procedures should be adhered to.

1. If possible, the athlete should not step on the heel for a period of at least 24 hours.

Specific Sports Injuries and
Other Problems

Figure 18-6

Heel protection through the
use of heel cup (**A** and **B**) and
protective heel doughnot (**C**).

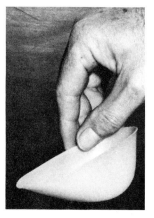

A

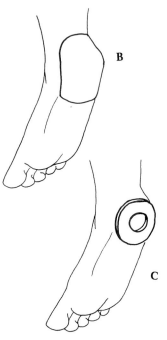

B

C

2. On the third and subsequent days warm whirlpool and ultrasound
or cold therapy can be administered.

3. If pain when walking has subsided by the third day, the athlete
may resume moderate activity—with the protecton of a heel cup, protective doughnut, or protective taping (Fig. 18-6).

NOTE: Because of the nature of the site of this condition, it may recur
throughout an entire season.

An athlete who is prone to or who needs protection from a heel
bruise should routinely wear a heel cup with a foam rubber pad as a preventive aid. By surrounding the heel with a firm heel cup, traumatic
forces are diffused.

The bruised instep The bruised instep, like the bruised heel, can cause
disability. These commonly occur by being stepped on or by being hit
with a fast-moving hard projectile, such as a baseball or hockey puck.
Immediate application of cold compresses must be performed not only to
control inflammation but, most importantly, to avoid swelling. Irritation
of the synovial sheaths covering the extensor tendon can make wearing
a shoe difficult. If the force is of great intensity there is a good chance of
fracture, requiring an x-ray.[9] Once inflammation is reduced and the athlete returns to competition a ⅛ inch (0.3 cm) pad protection should be
worn directly on the skin over the bruise and a rigid instep guard external
to the shoe.

Foot strain Insufficient conditioning of musculature, structural
imbalance, or incorrect mechanics can cause the foot to become prone to
strain. Common strains are to the metatarsal arch, the longitudinal arch,
and the plantar fascia.

Metatarsal arch strain The athlete who has acquired a fallen metatarsal arch or who has a pes cavus (high arch) is susceptible to strain. In
both cases, malalignment of the forefoot subjects the flexor tendons to
increased tension. Other conditions that produce the hypermobile and
pronated foot may predispose the athlete to a metatarsal arch strain.

Longitudinal arch strain Longitudinal arch strain is usually an
early-season injury caused by subjecting the musculature of the foot to
unaccustomed, severe exercise and forceful contact with hard playing
surfaces. In this condition there is a flattening or depressing of the longitudinal arch while the foot is in the midsupport phase, resulting in a
strain to the arch. Such a strain may appear quite suddenly, or it may
develop rather slowly throughout a considerable length of time.

SYMPTOMS AND SIGNS As a rule, pain is experienced only when running is attempted and usually appears just below the medial malleolus
and the posterior tibial tendon, accompanied by swelling and tenderness
along the medial aspects of the foot. Prolonged strain will also involve
the calcaneonavicular ligament and move progressively to the talonavicular joint, and then to the articulation of the first cuneiform with the
navicular. The flexor muscle of the great toe (flexor hallucis longus) often
develops tenderness as a result of overuse in compensating for the stress
on the arch ligaments.

MANAGEMENT The management of a longitudinal arch strain involves immediate care of ICE-R followed by appropriate therapy, reduc-

ARCH TAPING TECHNIQUE NO. 1

Arch taping with pad support. Arch taping with pad support employs the following procedures to strengthen weakened arches.

NOTE: **See Chapter 13, Arguments Against and For Routine Ankle Taping.**

Materials needed: One roll of 1½-inch (3.8 cm) tape, tape adherent, and a ⅛- or ¼-inch (0.3 to 0.6 cm) adhesive foam rubber pad cut to fit the longitudinal arch.

Position of the athlete: The athlete lies face downward on the table, with the foot that is to be taped (Fig. 18-7) extending about 6 inches (15 cm) over the edge of the table. To ensure proper position, allow the foot to hang in a relaxed position.

Position of the operator: The operator stands facing the sole of the affected foot.

Procedure

1. Place a series of strips of tape directly around the arch or, if added support is required, around an arch pad and the arch. The first strip should be put on just above the metatarsal arch.

2. Each subsequent strip should overlap the preceding piece about half the width of the tape.

   CAUTION: Avoid putting on so many strips of tape as to hamper the action of the ankle.

ARCH TAPING TECHNIQUE NO. 2

"X" taping for the longitudinal arch. When using the figure-8 method for taping the longitudinal arch, the following steps are executed.

Materials needed: One roll of 1-inch tape and tape adherent.

Position of the athlete: The athlete lies face downward on a table, with the affected foot extending approximately 6 inches (15 cm) over the edge of the table. To ensure proper position, allow the foot to hang in a relaxed natural position.

Position of the operator: The operator faces the bottom of the foot.

Procedure

1. Lightly place an anchor strip around the ball of the foot, making certain not to constrict the action of the toes.

2. Start the next strip of tape from the medial edge of the anchor, moving it upward at an acute angle, crossing the center of the longitudinal arch, encircling the heel, and descending; then, crossing the arch again, end at the lateral aspect of the anchor.

3. Lock the first "cross" and each subsequent cross individually by means of a single piece of tape placed around the ball of the foot.

Figure 18-7

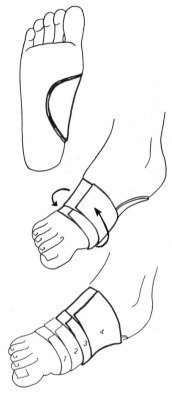

Arch taping technique no. 1, including an arch pad and circular tape strips.

Figure 18-8

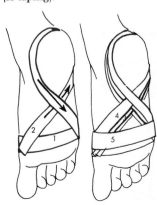

Arch taping technique no. 2 (X taping).

tion of weight bearing, and exercise rehabilitation following the procedures on p. 460. Exercise and weight bearing must be performed pain free. Employing arch taping technique no. 1 or 2 might be used to allow earlier pain-free weight bearing (Figs. 18-7 and 18-8).

Plantar fascia strain Running the length of the sole of the foot is a broad band of dense connective tissue called the plantar aponeurosis. It is attached to the undersurface of the calcaneus at the back and fans out toward the front, with fibers and their various small branches attaching to the metatarsophalangeal articulations and merging into the capsular ligaments. Other fibers, arising from well within the aponeurosis, pass between the intrinsic muscles of the foot and the long flexor tendons of the sole and attach themselves to the deep fascia below the bones. The function of the plantar aponeurosis is to assist in maintaining the stability of the foot and in securing or bracing the longitudinal arch.

ETIOLOGICAL FACTORS Strains to the fascia commonly occur during the early part of the season in sports that require running. The incidence is fairly high among tennis and basketball players and runners. The fascia is placed under strain either by extension of the toes or by depression of the longitudinal arch as the result of weight bearing. When the weight is principally on the heel, as in ordinary standing, the tension exerted on the fascia is negligible. However, when the weight is shifted to the ball of the foot (on the heads of the metatarsals), fascial tension is so increased that it equals approximately twice the body weight. In running, since the push-off phase involves both a forceful extension of the toes and a powerful thrust by the ball of the foot against a relatively unyielding surface, the degree of fascial tension is greatly increased.

Athletes who have a mild pes cavus are particularly prone to fascial strain. Modern street shoes, by nature of their design, take on the characteristics of splints and tend to restrict foot action to such an extent that the arch may become somewhat rigid because of shortening of the ligaments and other mild pathologies. The athlete, upon changing from such footgear into a flexible gymnastic slipper or soft track shoe, often experiences trauma when subjecting the foot to stresses.

Trauma may also result from running improperly, either as the result of poor techniques or because of lordosis, a condition in which the increased forward tilt of the pelvis produces an unfavorable angle of footstrike when there is considerable force exerted on the ball of the foot.

SYMPTOMS AND SIGNS The athlete complains of having a sudden pain in the arch region that is relieved by becoming non-weight bearing. There is great difficulty in walking and an inability to run. On inspection there is **point tenderness** in the plantar aponeurosis, especially in the region of the epicondyle of the calcaneus. Swelling and later ecchymosis may be associated with this problem.

MANAGEMENT Management is symptomatic. A heel doughnut may relieve some of the irritation, along with a heel lift, and a stiff shank will distribute the body weight more effectively. Also, performing a gradual stretch of the plantar muscle and the gastrocnemius-soleus complex will help to relieve tension in that region.[7,8,19] Plantar faciitis is discussed in Chapter 19.

point tenderness
Pain is produced when an injury site is palpated

TAPING FOR THE SPRAINED GREAT TOE

Figure 18-9

Taping for a sprained great
toe.

The following procedures are used for taping the great toe after a sprain (Fig. 18-9).

Materials needed: One roll of 1-inch (2.5 cm) tape and tape adherent.

Position of the athlete: The athlete assumes a sitting position.

Position of the operator: The operator faces the sole of the affected foot.

Procedure

1. The greatest support is given to the joint by a figure-8 taping. The series is started at an acute angle on the top of the foot, swinging down between the great and first toes, first encircling the great toe and then coming up, over, and across the starting point.
2. The above process is repeated, each series being started separately.
3. After the required number of figure-8 strips have been put in position, one lock piece should be placed around the ball of the foot.

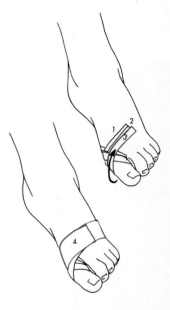

Foot sprain Two sites where foot sprain may occur are the midfoot or forefoot and the phalanges.

Midfoot or forefoot sprain Although not common, sprains of the midfoot or forefoot do occur. The most frequent mechanism is excessive dorsiflexion or plantar flexion of the toes or forefoot. Supportive ligaments are injured along with tendons.

MANAGEMENT Management usually consists of ICE-R and a limitation of weight bearing. Taping support of the forefoot will help relieve pain on weight bearing.

Midfoot and forefoot sprains are usually managed by ICE-R and limited weight bearing.

The sprained toe Sprains of the phalangeal joint of the foot are caused most often by kicking some nonyielding object. Sprains result from a considerable force applied in such a manner as the extend the joint beyond its normal range of motion ("jamming" it) or to impart a twisting motion to the toe, thereby twisting and tearing the supporting tissues. Symptoms of an acute injury appear. Management involves the following considerations:

1. The injury should be handled as an acute sprain.
2. The severity of the injury should be determined through palpation and, if there are signs of a fracture, through x-ray examination.

Fractures and dislocations Because of the foot's susceptibility to trauma in sports, fractures or dislocations can occur. Any moderate to severe contusion or twisting force must be suspected as being a fracture. X-ray examination should be routine in these situations.

Fractures and dislocations of the foot phalanges are caused by kicking an object or by stubbing a toe.

Fractures and dislocations of the foot phalanges Fractures of the phalanges (Fig. 18-10) are usually the bone-crushing type such as may be incurred in kicking an object or stubbing a toe. Generally they are accompanied by swelling and discoloration. If the fracture is of the proximal phalanx of the great toe or of the distal phalanx and also involves the interphalangeal joint, it should be referred to an orthopedist.[2] If the break

Specific Sports Injuries and
Other Problems

Figure 18-10

Fracture of the fifth phalanx.

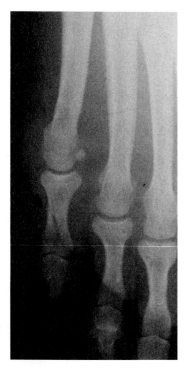

Figure 18-11

Taping for a fracture of a toe.

is in the bone shaft, an adhesive taping is applied (Fig. 18-11). However, if more than one toe is involved, a cast may be applied for a few days. As a rule 3 or 4 weeks of inactivity permits healing, although tenderness may persist for some time. A shoe with a wide toe box should be worn; in cases of great toe fracture, a stiff sole should be worn.

Dislocation of the phalanges is less common than fractures. If one occurs it is a dorsal dislocation of the middle phalanx proximal joint. The mechanism of injury is the same as for fractures. Reduction is usually performed easily without anesthesia by the physician.

Fractures of the metatarsals Fractures of the metatarsals can be caused by direct force, such as being stepped on by another player, or by abnormal stress. They are characterized by swelling and pain. The most common acute fracture is to the *base of the fifth metatarsal (Jones fracture)* (Fig. 18-12). It is normally caused by a sharp inversion and plantar flexion of the foot. It has all the appearances of a severe sprain. Treatment is usually symptomatic, with ICE-R employed to control swelling. Once swelling has subsided, a short leg walking cast is applied for 3 to 6 weeks. Ambulation is usually possible by the second week. A shoe with a large toe box should be worn. The injured toe should be taped to an adjacent toe in the same manner as for the fracture.

Fractures or dislocations of the talus A fracture or dislocation of the talus usually results from a severe ankle twist or being hit behind the leg while the foot is firmly planted on the ground (Fig. 18-13). There is extreme pain and point tenderness at the distal end of the tibia. For accurate diagnosis an x-ray is essential. If the fracture is severe, there could be a severance of the blood supply to the area—a condition that results in bone necrosis and may seriously jeopardize future sports participation by the athlete. The following procedures should be employed:

1. The foot and ankle should be immobilized and the athlete transported to a physician.

2. After the fracture has been reduced the physician will usually cast the foot in a plaster boot for about 6 weeks and then allow only limited weight bearing on the injured leg for at least another 8 weeks.

Fracture of the os calis The os calis fracture is the most common fracture of the tarsus and is usually caused by a jump or fall from a height. There is usually extreme swelling and pain. There may be a serious threat that this condition will predispose the athlete to arthritis because of injury to the articulating surface. Reduction may be delayed for as much as 24 to 48 hours or until swelling has been reduced. In the interval the following steps should be initiated:

1. Cold and a pressure bandage should be applied intermittently for 24 to 48 hours.

2. The foot should be elevated immediately after the injury and maintained in this position for at least 24 hours or until definite medical treatment has been instituted.

Exercise Rehabilitation of the Foot

In most painful conditions of the foot, weight bearing is prohibited until pain has subsided significantly. During this period and until the athlete is ready to return to full activity, a graduated program of exercise should be instituted. Exercises are divided into two stages. Each exercise should be performed three times a day with 3 to 10 repetitions of each exercise and should progress to 2 or 3 sets.

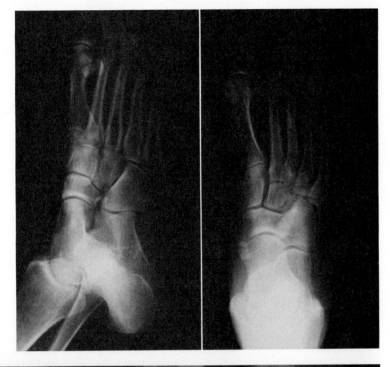

Figure 18-12

Fracture of the base of the fifth metatarsal.

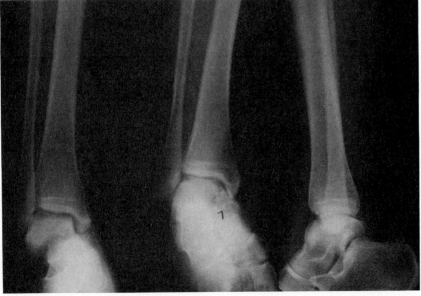

Figure 18-13

Fracture of the talar dome.

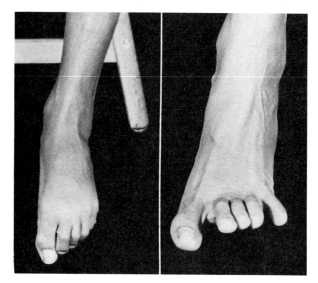

Figure 18-14

Gripping and spreading of the
toes can be an excellent
reconditioning exercise for
the injured foot.

Stage 1

In Stage 1 primary exercises are employed in the non-weight bearing or
early phase of the condition. They include "writing the alphabet," picking
up objects, ankle circumduction, and gripping and spreading.

1. *Writing the alphabet*—with the toes pointed, the athlete proceeds
   to write the complete alphabet in the air 3 times.
2. *Picking up objects*—the athlete picks up 10 small objects, such as
   marbles, with the toes and places them in a container.
3. *Ankle circumduction*—the ankle is circumducted in as extreme a
   range of motion as possible (10 circles in one direction and 10
   circles in the other).
4. *Gripping and spreading*—of particular value to toes, gripping and
   spreading is conducted up to 10 repetitions (Fig. 18-14).

Stage 2

Stage 2 exercises are added to Stage 1 when the athlete is just beginning to
bear weight. They include the "towel gather" and "scoop" exercises.

1. *Towel gathering*—a towel is extended in front of the feet. The
   heels are firmly planted on the floor, the forefoot on the end of
   the towel. The athlete then attempts to pull the towel with the
   feet without lifting the heels from the floor. As execution becomes easier, a weight can be placed at the other end of the towel
   for added resistance. Each exercise should be performed 10 times
   (Fig. 18-15).
2. *Towel scoop*—a towel is folded in half and placed sideways on the
   floor. The athlete places the heel firmly on the floor, the forefoot
   on the end of the towel. To ensure the greatest stability of the
   exercising foot, it is backed up with the other foot. Without lifting
   the heel from the floor, the athlete scoops the towel forward with
   the forefoot. As with the towel gather exercise, a weight resistance
   can be added to the end of the towel. The exercise should be repeated up to 10 times (Fig. 18-16).

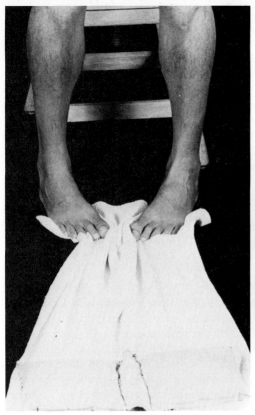

Figure 18-15

The towel gather exercise.

Figure 18-16

The towel scoop exercise.

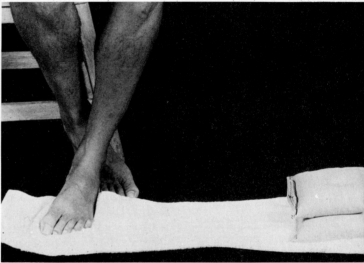

THE ANKLE

Ankle injuries, especially to the ligamentous tissue, are the most frequent injuries in sports.[1] To the athletic trainer and coach, understanding the complex nature of ankle injuries should be a major goal.

Functional Anatomy
Bony Characteristics

The ankle is a hinge joint (ginglymus), which is formed by the articulation of the tibia and fibula with the talus (Fig. 18-17). The lower ends of the tibia and fibula form a mortise into which the talus fits, thus effecting good lateral stability. The ankle is structurally quite strong because of bone and ligamentous arrangements.

The lower end of the tibia becomes enlarged as it approaches the ankle and forms a rounded subcutaneous projection, the *internal malleolus* or *medial malleolus.* The border of the internal malleolus is quite rough and provides the attachment of the supporting ligaments. The inferior aspect of the malleolus is concave and is lined with hyaline cartilage for articulating with the talus.

Figure 18-17

The ankle is a hinge type joint formed by the tibia, fibula, and talus.

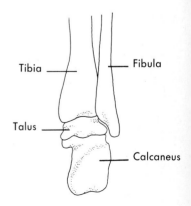

Specific Sports Injuries and
Other Problems

Because the talus is wider
anteriorly than posteriorly,
the most stable position of
the ankle is with the foot in
dorsiflexion.

The talofibular articulation is formed by the lower end of the fibula with the talus. At its lower end the fibula develops a long projection, which extends along the lateral aspect of the talus and is called the *external malleolus.* It is located posterior to, and ½ inch lower than, the internal malleolus; like that of the internal malleolus, its border is roughened for ligamentous attachment.

The talus, the second largest tarsal and the main weight bearing bone of the articulation, rests on the calcaneus and receives the articulating surfaces of the external and internal malleoli. Its almost square shape allows the ankle only two movements: dorsiflexion and plantar flexion. Because the talus is wider anteriorly than posteriorly, the most stable position of the ankle is with the foot in dorsiflexion. In this position the wider anterior aspect of the talus comes in contact with the narrower portion lying between the malleoli, gripping it tightly. By contrast, as the ankle moves into plantar flexion, the wider portion of the tibia is brought in contact with the narrower posterior aspect of the talus, a much less stable position than dorsiflexion.

Ligamentous and Capsular Support

The ligamentous support of the ankle (Fig. 18-18) additionally fortifies its great bony strength. The medial aspect has greater strength than does the lateral, since the talus is directly over the sustentaculum tali. Laterally, the major ligaments of the ankle are the anterior tibiofibular, the anterior talofibular, the lateral talocalcaneal, and the calcaneofibular. On the medial aspect, the deltoid, composed of three major segments, is the sole ligament, whereas the posterior aspect has two: the posterior talotibial and the posterior talocalcaneal.

The ankle joint is encased in a thin articular capsule, which is attached to the borders of the bone involved. It is somewhat different from most other capsules in that it is thick on the medial aspect but diminishes into a thin, gauze-like membrane at the back.

Muscular Control and Support

By far the weakest aspect of the ankle is its muscular arrangement, since the long muscle tendons that cross on all sides of the ankle afford a maximum of muscle leverage but a minimum of stabilization. The major muscles of the ankle are as follows: (1) anterior aspect—extensor hallucis longus

Figure 18-18

Major ligaments of the ankle.
A, Lateral aspect. **B,** Medial
aspect.

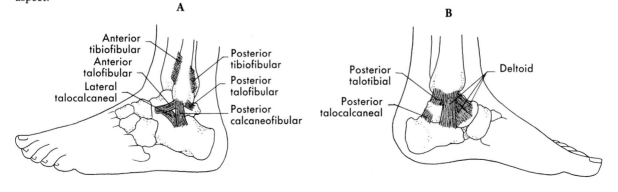

A

Anterior
tibiofibular
Anterior
talofibular
Lateral
talocalcaneal

Posterior
tibiofibular
Posterior
talofibular
Posterior
calcaneofibular

B

Posterior
talotibial

Deltoid

Posterior
talocalcaneal

and extensor digitorum longus; (2) medial aspect—posterior tibialis, flexor hallucis longus, anterior tibialis, and flexor digitorum longus; (3) lateral aspect—peroneus longus and peroneus brevis; and (4) posterior aspect—gastrocnemius and soleus. The muscles of the medial aspect aid in the support of the inner longitudinal arch.

Evaluating the Injured and Painful Ankle

The injured, or painful ankle should be carefully evaluated to determne the possibility of fracture and whether medical referral is necessary.

Most Frequent Complaints

The athlete's history may vary, depending on whether the problem is the result of sudden trauma or is of long standing.

The athlete with an acute sudden trauma to the ankle should be questioned about these factors:

1. What trauma or mechanism occurred?
2. What was the duration and intensity of pain?
3. What was heard when the injury occurred—a crack, snap, or pop?
4. How disabling was the occurrence? Could the athlete walk right away or was he or she unable to bear weight for a period of time?
5. Has a similar injury occurred before?
6. Was there immediate swelling or did the swelling occur later (or at all)?

   The athlete with a long-standing painful condition might be asked:

1. How much does it hurt?
2. Where does it hurt?
3. Under what circumstances does pain occur—when bearing weight, after activity, or on arising after a night's sleep?
4. what past ankle injuries have occurred?
5. What first aid and therapy was given for this occurrence, if any?

General Inspection

The first inspection should be observation of the athlete's walk. Is the injured individual walking in the usual manner, on the toes, or is there an inability to bear any weight? When seated, both ankles are compared for:

1. Position of the foot—a sprained ankle will usually be in a more inverted position

2. Range of ankle motion—normal range is about 20 degrees of dorsiflexion and 45 to 50 degrees of plantar flexion

Bony and Soft Tissue Palpation

Palpation in the ankle region should start with key bony sites and ligaments and progress to the musculature, especially the major tendons in the area. The purpose of palpation in this region is to detect obvious structural defects, swellings and localized tenderness (Fig. 18-19). The following anatomical areas should be palpated.

1. Medial and lateral malleolus
2. Lower interosseus membrane
3. Tarsal navicular

Figure 18-19

Local and diffused ankle swelling.

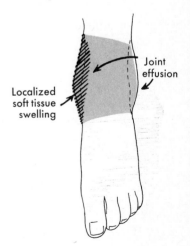

Joint effusion

Localized soft tissue swelling

4. Proximal head of the fifth metatarsal
5. Subtalar region
6. Deltoid ligament
7. Anterior talofibular ligament
8. Calcaneofibular ligament
9. Posterior talofibular ligament
10. Achilles tendon
11. Peroneal tendons
12. Posterior tibialis tendon
13. Anterior tibialis tendon
14. Region of extensor tendons
15. Other areas when indicated

If the injury might have impeded blood flow to the ankle area, a pulse should be measured at the dorsal pedal artery and the posterior tibial artery (Fig. 18-20).

Tests for Joint Stability

Where there may be ankle joint instability as a result of repeated sprains, tests should be given. The most common sprain is the inversion type, which first involves the talofibular ligament. Because this ligament prevents the talus from sliding forward, the most appropriate test is the one which elicits the anterior drawer sign (Fig. 18-21). The athlete sits on the edge of a treatment table, with legs and feet relaxed. The trainer or physician grasps the lower tibia in one hand and the calcaneus in the palm of the other hand. The tibia is then pushed backward as the calcaneus is pulled forward. A positive anterior drawer sign occurs when the foot slides forward, sometimes making a "clunking" sound as it reaches its end point.

Figure 18-20

An ankle injury may impede blood, which makes routine measurement of the pulse extremely important.

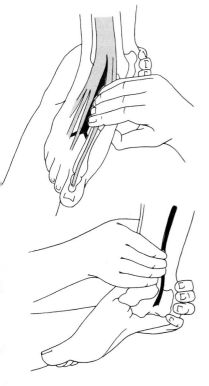

Figure 18-21

Anterior drawer test for ankle
ligament stability.

Figure 18-22

Testing lateral ankle stability.

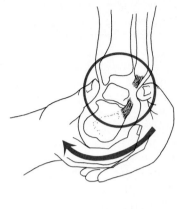

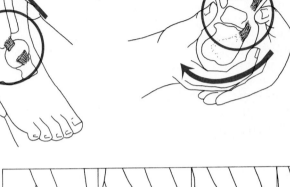

A positive drawer sign in
terms of ankle stability is
when the foot slides forward,
sometimes making a
clunking sound as it reaches
its end point.

Figure 18-23

Evaluating ankle function.

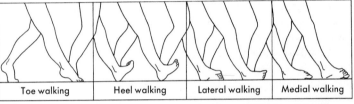

| Toe walking | Heel walking | Lateral walking | Medial walking |

Two other tests that may be used are those that test for torn anterior talofibular and calcaneofibular ligaments on the lateral side and torn side. By stabilizing the lower leg, the heel is inverted. If the talus rocks in the mortise, there is injury to both the anterior talofibular and calcaneofibular ligaments, and there is subsequent lateral ankle instability (Fig. 18-22). The deltoid ligament can be tested in the same way, except that the heel is everted. As the heel is moved into eversion, a gap is felt between the medial malleolus and calcaneus.

Functional Evaluation

Muscle function is important in evaluating the ankle injury (Fig. 18-23). *If the following movements will aggravate a recent injury, they should be avoided.* While bearing weight on both feet, the athlete:

1. Walks on toes (tests plantar flexion)
2. Walks on heels (tests dorsiflexion)
3. Walks on lateral border of feet (tests inversion)
4. Walks on medial border of feet (tests eversion)

Ankle Injury Prevention

Many ankle conditions, especially sprains, can be reduced by Achilles tendon stretching, strengthening of key muscles, proprioceptive training, proper footwear, and, in some cases, proper taping.

Preventing ankle sprains is
achieved by:
Stretching of the Achilles
    tendon
Strengthening key muscles
Proprioceptive training
Proper footwear
Taping when appropriate

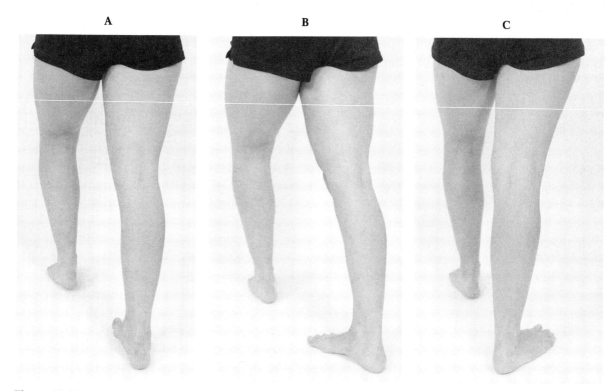

Figure 18-24

Stretching the Achilles tendon is essential for preventing ankle sprains. Stretching must be performed for all possible positions. **A,** Straight ahead. **B,** Adducted. **C,** abducted.

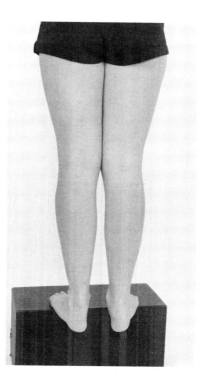
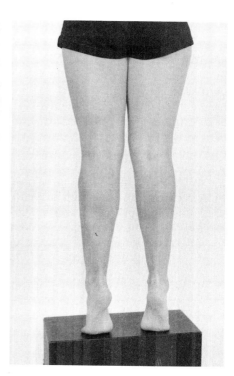

Figure 18-25

Strength training is essential for the prevention of ankle sprains.

Achilles Tendon Stretching

An ankle that can easily dorsiflex at least 15 degrees or more is essential for injury prevention. The athlete, especially one with tight Achilles tendons, should routinely stretch before and after practice (Fig. 18-24).

Strength Training

Of major importance to ankle injury prevention is to achieve both static and dynamic joint stability (Fig. 18-25). A normal range of motion must be maintained, along with strength of the peroneal, plantar flexor, dorsal flexor, and extensor muscles.[10] The peroneals, mainly the peroneus longus muscle, must be exercised to afford eversion strength and to prevent the foot's being forced into inversion.

Proprioceptive Ankle Training

Athletes who have ankle injuries or who spend most of their time on even surfaces may develop a proprioceptive deficiency.[9] Ankle ligamentous stability proprioception is also lost. The ankle and foot propioceptive sense can be enhanced by locomotion over uneven surfaces or by spending time each day on a balance board (wobble board) (Fig. 18-26).

Footwear

As discussed in Chapter 7, proper footwear can be an important factor in reducing injuries to both the foot and ankle. Shoes should not be used in activities for which they were not intended—for example, wearing running shoes designed for straight-ahead activity to play tennis, a sport demanding a great deal of lateral movement. Cleats on a shoe should not be centered in the middle of the sole but rather should be placed far enough on the border to avoid ankle sprains. High-top shoes, when worn by athletes with a history of ankle sprain, can offer greater support than low top shoes.

Preventive Ankle Wrap and Taping

As discussed in Chapter 13, there is some doubt as to whether it is beneficial to routinely tape ankles that have no history of sprain. There is some indication that tape, properly applied, can provide some prophylactic protection. It is estimated that at least $100 million is spent in the United States each year for tape for high school football.[9] Poorly applied tape will do more harm than good. Tape that constricts soft tissue or disrupts normal biomechanical function can create serious injuries. Although taping is preferred, a much cheaper cloth muslin wrap may provide some protection.

The Sprained Ankle

Because of their frequency and the disability that results, ankle sprains present a major problem for the coach, trainer, and team physician. It has been said that a sprained ankle can be worse than a fracture. Fractures are usually conservatively cared for, with immobilization and activity restriction, whereas the athlete with a sprained ankle is often rushed through management and returned to activity before complete healing has occurred. Incompletely healed, the ankle becomes chronically inflamed and unstable, eventually causing a major problem for the athlete.[6]

Figure 18-26

The wobble board is an excellent device for establishing ankle proprioception.

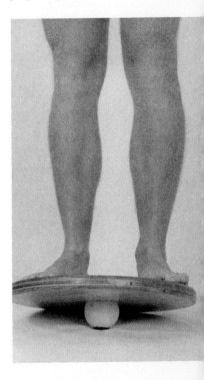

Poorly applied ankle taping can do more harm to the athlete than good.

ANKLE WRAP

Because tape is so expensive, the ankle wrap becomes an inexpensive and expedient means of protecting ankles (Fig. 18-27).

Materials needed: Each muslin wrap should be 1½ to 2 inches (3.8 to 5 cm) wide and from 72 to 96 inches (180 to 240 cm) long to ensure complete coverage and protection. The purpose of this wrap is to give mild support against lateral and medial motion of the ankle. It is applied over a sock.

Position of the athlete: The athlete sits on a table, extending the leg and positioning the foot at a 90 degree angle. To avoid any distortion, it is important that the ankle be neither overflexed nor overextended.

Position of the operator: The operator stands facing the sole of the athlete's foot.

Procedure

1. Start the wrap above the instep around the ankle; circle the ankle and move it at an acute angle to the inside of the foot.
2. From the inside of the foot move the wrap under the arch, coming up on the outside and crossing at the beginning point, where it continues around the ankle, hooking the heel.
3. Then move it up, inside, over the instep, and around the ankle, hooking the opposite side of the heel. This completes one series of the ankle wrap.
4. Complete a second series with the remaining material.

Figure 18-27

The ankle wrap.

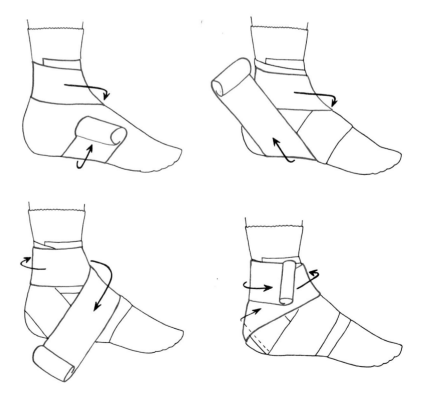

ROUTINE NONINJURY ANKLE TAPING

Ankle taping applied directly to the athlete's skin affords the greatest support; however, when applied and removed daily skin irritation will occur. To avoid this problem an underwrap material should be applied (Fig. 18-28). Before taping, follow these procedures:

1. Shave all the hair off the foot and ankle.
2. Apply a coating of a tape adherent to protect the skin and offer an adhering base.
   NOTE: It may be advisable to avoid the use of a tape adherent, especially in cases where the athlete has a history of deveoping tape blisters. In cases of skin sensitivity the ankle surface should be thoroughly cleansed of dirt and oil and an underwrap material applied; or one could elect to tape directly to the skin.
3. If underwrap is not used, apply a gauze pad coated with friction-proofing material such as grease over the instep and to the back of the heel.
4. Do not apply tape if skin is cold or hot from a therapeutic treatment.

Materials needed: One roll of 1½-inch (3.8 cm) tape and tape adherent.

Position of the athlete: The athlete sits on a table with the leg extended and the foot held at a 90 degree angle.

Position of the operator: The operator stands facing the foot that is to be taped.

Continued.

Figure 18-28

Underwrap for ankle taping.

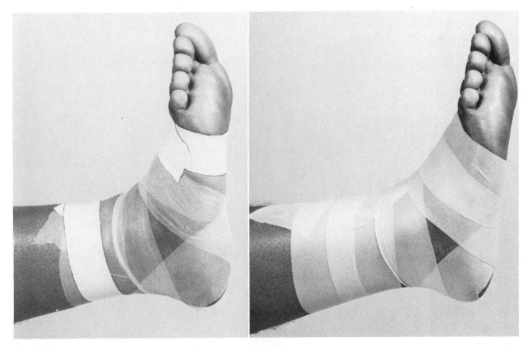

ROUTINE NONINJURY ANKLE TAPING, cont'd

Procedure
1. A single anchor is placed around the ankle about 2 or 3 inches (5 to 7.5 cm) above the malleolus (Fig. 18-29).
2. Two stirrups are applied in consecutive order, with care that each one overlaps half the width of the piece of tape it adjoins.
3. After the stirrups have been applied, 5 or 6 circular strips are put on, from the point of the anchor, moving downward until the malleolus is completely covered.
4. Next, two or three arch strips are applied.
5. The final support is given by a heel lock. Starting high on the instep, bring the tape along the ankle at a slight angle, hooking the heel, leading under the arch, then coming up on the opposite side, and finishing at the starting point. At this point the tape is torn to complete half of the heel lock. To complete the remaining half, execute the same procedure on the opposite side of the ankle (Fig. 18-30).

Figure 18-29

Routine noninjury ankle taping.

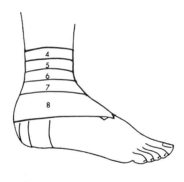

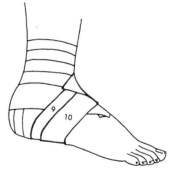

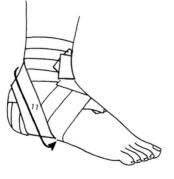

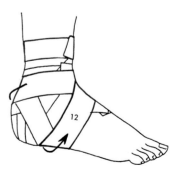

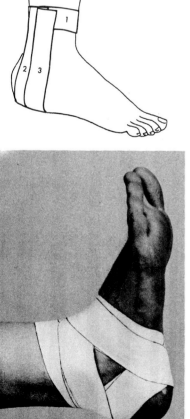

Figure 18-30

Continuous heel lock technique.

Mechanisms of Injury

Ankle sprains are generally caused by a sudden lateral or medial twist. The inversion sprain, in which the foot turns inward, is the most common type of ankle sprain. This is because there is more bony stability on the lateral side, which tends to force the foot into inversion rather than eversion. If the force is great enough, inversion of the foot continues until the medial malleolus loses its stability and creates a fulcrum to further invert the ankle.[10] The peroneal or everting muscles resist the inverting force, and when they are no longer strong enough, the lateral ligaments become stretched or torn (Fig. 18-31, *A*).

Usually a lateral ankle sprain involves either one or two torn ligaments. If it is a single ligament tear, it usually involves the *anterior talofibular ligament*, but if it is a double ligament tear with further inversion, the *calcaneal fibular ligament* also tears (Fig. 18-31, *B*). The tight heel cord forces the foot into inversion, making it more susceptible to a lateral sprain. In contrast, a foot that is pronated, hypermobile, or has a depressed medial longitudinal arch is more susceptible to an eversion type of ankle sprain (Fig. 18-32).

The eversion sprain occurs less frequently than the inversion sprain. The usual mechanism is the athlete's having suddenly stepped in a hole on the playing field, causing the foot to evert and abduct and the planted leg to rotate externally. With this mechanism the anterior tibiofibular ligament, interosseous ligament, and deltoid ligament may tear. With a tear of these ligaments, the talus is allowed to move laterally within the mortise, leading to ultimate degeneration within the joint.[3] Also, there is abnormal space between the medial malleolus and the talus (Fig. 18-33).

Figure 18-31

Mechanisms of an inversion ankle sprain.

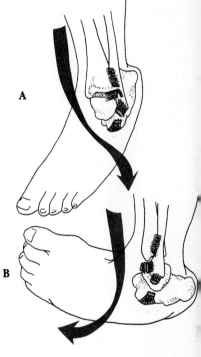

A

B

Figure 18-32

Mechanism of an eversion ankle sprain.

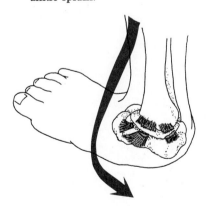

Figure 18-33

An eversion ankle sprain that creates an abnormal space between the medial malleolus and the talus.

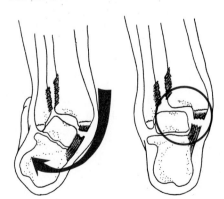

Figure 18-34

The same mechanism that
produces an ankle sprain can
also cause an avulsion
fracture.

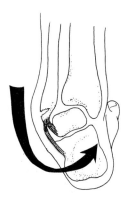

The extent of ankle swelling
is *not* an indicator of the
severity of the injury.

A sudden inversion force could be of such intensity as to produce a fracture of the lower leg. Unexpected wrenching of the lateral ligaments could cause a portion of bone to be avulsed from the malleolus (Fig. 18-34, *A* and *B*). One extreme situation is when the lateral malleolus is avulsed by the calcaneofibular bone, and the talus rocks up against the medial malleolus to produce a second fracture. This sequence of events is known as the *bimalleolar fracture*.

General First Aid Considerations

In managing a sprained ankle these first aid measures should be followed:

1. Determine the extent of the injury. The main purpose of the ankle sprain examination is to establish the injury severity and whether the ankle is stable or unstable. Swelling is *not* an indication of the severity of the injury.[17] With the athlete in a seated position, a ligament laxity test may be given by the athletic trainer or physician.[4]
2. Employ ICE-R (Fig. 18-35).
   a. Apply an elastic pressure bandage around the perimeter of the malleolus at the site of the sprain to decrease internal bleeding.
   b. After the pressure bandage has been applied, decrease the temperature of the injured area by the use of ice packs. An elastic wrap that is thoroughly soaked in ice water and applied directly to the skin will cool faster when combined with an ice pack. Ice should be applied intermittently in 20 minute periods, 5 to 6 times a day. Do not expose the tissue to prolonged cooling. If a cold medium is not available, a horseshoe pad that is cut to fit around the malleolus and is held in place by an

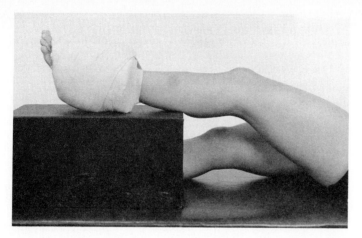

Figure 18-35

Application of ice,
compression, elevation and
rest (ICE-R) is essential first
aid for a sprained ankle.

elastic wrap will help confine the internal hemorrhage (Fig.
18-36).

c. Promptly elevate the injured limb, if at all practical, so that
fluid stasis of the internal hemorrhage does not take place.
d. The open basketweave taping technique can also be used in
conjunction with cold application.

NOTE: In most cases, if the ICE-R routine is carefully followed for 24
hours, articular and periarticular effusion can be limited.

3. If there is a possibility of fracture, splint the ankle and refer the
athlete to the physician for x-ray examination and immobilization.
4. In most cases of moderate and severe ankle sprains, continue cold
applications through the second or even the third day.
5. Begin heat therapy if hemorrhaging has stopped by the third day.

Figure 18-36

A horseshoe-shaped sponge
rubber pad provides an
excellent compress when held
in place by an elastic wrap.

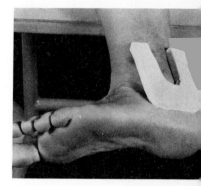

Inversion Ankle Sprains

Inversion ankle sprains are usually graded by the ligament or ligaments involved. A grade I or first degree sprain is concerned with the anterior talofibular ligament, a grade II with the calcaneofibular ligament, and a grade
III with the posterior talofibular ligament. In each instance of injury, the
foot is forcibly turned inward on the leg, as when a basketball player jumps
and comes down on the foot of another player. Inversion sprains can also
occur while an individual is walking and running on an uneven surface or
suddenly steps into a hole.

First degree inversion ankle sprains The first degree ankle sprain is
the most common type of sprain. Most result from an inversion stress
with the foot in *mild* plantar flexion, usually stretching the anterior talofibular ligament.

Symptoms and signs There is mild pain and disability with point
tenderness and localized swelling over the area of the anterior talofibular
ligament. The anterior drawer test is negative with no ecchymosis and
minimal loss of function.

OPEN BASKETWEAVE TAPING TECHNIQUE

This modification of the closed basketweave or Gibney technique is designed to give freedom of movement in dorsiflexion and plantar flexion while providing lateral and medial support and giving swelling room. Taping in this pattern (Fig. 18-37) may be used immediately after an acute sprain in conjunction with a pressure bandage and cold applications, since it allows for swelling.

Materials needed: One roll of 1½-inch (3.8 cm) tape and tape adherent.

Position of the athlete: The athlete sits on a table with the leg extended and the foot held at a 90 degree angle.

Position of the operator: The operator faces the sole of the athlete's foot.

Procedure

1. The procedures followed are the same as for the closed basketweave (see Fig. 18-38, *A-C*) with the exception of incomplete closures of the Gibney strips.
2. The gap between the Gibney ends should be locked by two pieces of tape running on either side of the instep.

   NOTE: Application of a 1½-inch (3.8 cm) elastic bandage placed over the open basketweave affords added control of swelling; however, it should be removed before retiring.

   Of the many ankle taping techniques in vogue today, those employing combinations of stirrups, basketweave pattern, and heel lock have been determined to offer the best support.

Figure 18-37

Open basketweave ankle taping is designed to allow freedom of plantar flexion and dorsiflexion and swelling room.

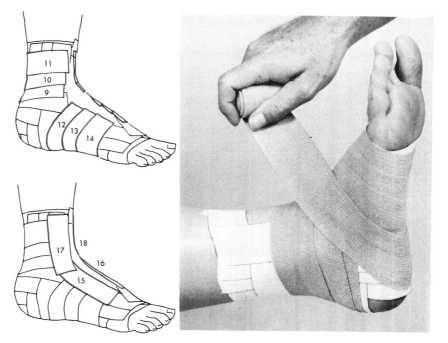

Management ICE-R is used for 20 minutes every few hours for 1 to 2 days. It may be advisable for the athlete to limit weight bearing activities for a few days. An elastic wrap might provide comfortable pressure when weight bearing begins. When the athlete's ankle is pain free and not swollen, a routine of circumduction is begun. The athlete is instructed to circle the foot first 10 times in one direction then 10 times in the other several times per day. When the athlete returns to weight bearing, application of tape may provide an extra measure of protection.

Second degree inversion ankle sprains Because it has a high incidence among sports participants and causes a great deal of disability with many days of lost time, the second degree ankle sprain is a major problem for the coach, athletic trainer, and physician.

Symptoms and signs The athlete usually complains that a tearing sensation was felt along with a pop or snap as the tissue gave way. Swelling is diffused with point tenderness at the sprain site. Some ecchymosis will occur 3 or 4 days after injury.

Pathological findings The second degree ankle sprain may completely tear the anterior talofibular ligament and stretch and tear the calcaneofibular ligament. The anterior drawer test will ilicit slight to moderate abnormal motion. Such an injury degree can produce a persistently unstable ankle that recurrently becomes sprained and later develops traumatic arthritis.

Management ICE-R therapy should be employed intermittently for 24 to 72 hours. X-ray examination should be routine for this degree of injury. The athlete should use crutches for 5 to 10 days to avoid bearing weight. A short leg walking cast may be applied for 2 or 3 days. Plantar and dorsiflexion exercises, if the athlete is pain free, may begin 48 hours after the injury occurs. Early exercise of this type helps to maintain range of motion and normal proprioception. Five to 10 minutes of ice pack application followed by 5 minutes of PNF exercise improves strength, range of motion and proprioception (see Appendix I-A). After 1 or 2 weeks of non-weight bearing, when swelling and pain have decreased, weight bearing can be resumed.

Taping in a closed basketweave technique may protect the ankle during the early stages of walking. The athlete must be instructed to avoid walking or running on uneven or sloped surfaces for 2 to 3 weeks after weight bearing has begun.

Once hemorrhage has subsided a therapy routine of superficial cold or heat should begin 3 times per day. Two or 3 weeks after the injury, circumduction exercises can be started. Gradually exercises can progress to resistive types.

Complications The second degree sprain, with its torn and stretched ligaments, tends to have a number of serious complications. Because of laxity there is a tendency to twist and sprain the ankle repeatedly. This recurrence over a period of time can lead to joint degeneration and traumatic arthritis. Once a second degree sprain has occurred, there must be a concerted effort to protect the ankle against future trauma.

Third degree inversion ankle sprains The third degree inversion ankle sprain is relatively uncommon in sports. When it does happen, it is quite disabling. Often the force causes the ankle to subluxate and then spontaneously reduce.

Symptoms and signs The athlete complains of severe pain in the region of the lateral malleolus. Swelling is diffused, with tenderness over the entire lateral area of the ankle. Where there is tearing of all three ligaments, results of the anterior and posterior drawer tests are positive.

Pathological findings This is a grade III injury that involves varying degrees of injury to the anterior talofibular, calcaneofibular, and posterior talofibular ligaments, as well as the joint capsule.

Management Normally ICE-R is employed intermittently for 2 or 3 days. It is not uncommon for the physician to apply a short leg walking cast, when the swelling has subsided, for 4 to 6 weeks. Crutches are usually given to the athlete when the cast is removed. Circumduction exercises are begun immediately after the cast is removed, followed by a progressive program of strengthening. In some cases surgery is warranted to stabilize the athlete's ankle for future sports participation.

Complications The third degree ankle sprain creates significant joint laxity and instability. Because of this laxity the ankle joint becomes prone to severe degenerative forces.

Eversion Ankle Sprains

Eversion ankle sprains have a much lower incidence than inversion sprains. Athletes who have pronated or hypermobile feet have a higher incidence of eversion sprains.

Symptoms and signs Depending on the degree of injury the athlete complains of pain, sometimes severe, that occurs over the foot and lower leg. Usually the athlete is unable to bear weight on the foot. Both abduction and adduction causes pain, but pressing directly upward against the bottom of the foot does not cause pain.

A second or third degree eversion sprain can adversely affect the medial longitudinal arch.

Complications An eversion sprain of second degree or more severity can produce significant joint instability. Because the deltoid ligament is involved with supporting the medial longitudinal arch, a sprain can cause weakness in this area. Repeated sprains could lead to pes planus (flatfoot).

Injury to the Anterior or Posterior Tibiofibular Ligaments

The possibility in both the second and third degree inversion and eversion sprain of tearing either the anterior or posterior tibiofibular ligament is always present. The anterior tibiofibular ligament can be torn in an inversion sprain, while either or both ligaments can be torn in an eversion sprain. In both mechanisms, the tearing of one or both of these ligaments can widen the ankle mortise, leaving it unstable. With the widened mortise, an eversion or inversion motion will allow the talus to move laterally and medially more than 5 degrees. This condition is known as the *talar tilt*. One method of determining a posterior tibiofibular sprain is by having the athlete bend the knee to relax the gastrocnemius muscle and passively dorsiflex the ankle. A positive test results in pain in the ankle sulcus.

A talar tilt occurs when the ankle mortise is widened.

Ankle fractures There are a number of ways that an ankle can be fractured or dislocated. A foot that is forcibly abducted on the leg can

CLOSED BASKETWEAVE (GIBNEY) TAPING TECHNIQUE

The closed basketweave technique (Fig. 18-38) offers strong tape support and is primarily used in athletic training for newly sprained or chronically weak ankles.

Materials needed: One roll of 1½-inch (3.8 cm) tape and tape adherent.

Position of the athlete: The athlete sits on a table with the leg extended and the foot at a 90 degree angle.

Position of the operator: The operator faces the sole of the athlete's foot.

Procedure

1. One anchor piece is placed around the ankle, approximately 2 or 3 inches (5 to 7.5 cm) above the malleolus, and a second anchor is placed around the arch and instep.
2. The first stirrup is then applied posteriorly to the malleolus and attached to the ankle stirrup. *NOTE:* When applying stirrups pull the foot into eversion for an inversion sprain and into a neutral position for an eversion sprain.
3. The first Gibney is started directly under the malleolus and attached to the foot anchor.
4. In an alternating series, three stirrups and three Gibneys are placed on the ankle, with each piece of tape overlapping at least one-half of the preceding strip.
5. After the basketweave series has been applied, the Gibney strips are continued on up the ankle, thus giving circular support.
6. For arch support, two or three circular strips are applied.
7. After the conventional basket weave has been completed, a heel lock should be applied to ensure maximum stability.

Figure 18-38

Closed basketweave ankle taping.

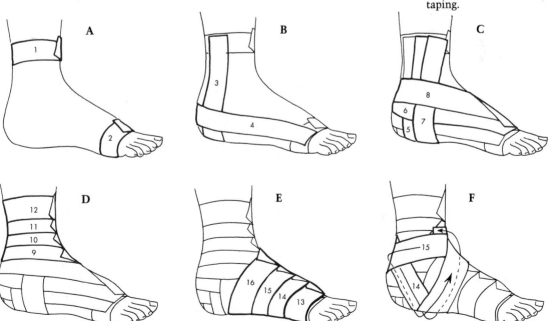

Figure 18-39

Ankle fractures or
dislocations can be a major
sports injury.

Courtesy Cramer Products, Inc.,
Gardner, Kan.

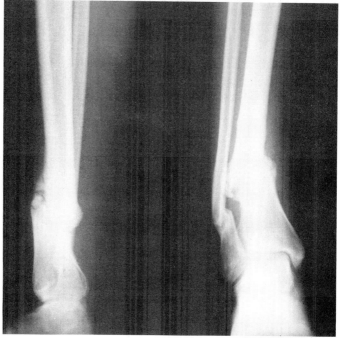

produce transverse, and on occasions even comminuted, fractures of the distal tibia and fibula. Also, forcible adduction of the foot on the leg can cause transverse fracture of the distal tibia and fibula. In contrast, a foot that is planted in combination with the leg that is forcibly rotated internally can produce a fracture to the distal fibula and posterior tibia.

There are three major situations in which ankle fractures occur: (1) when the foot is forcibly abducted or adducted, (2) when it is fixed to the ground and the lower leg is either forcibly internally or externally rotated, or (3) when the lateral or medial malleolus is forcefully avulsed (Fig. 18-39).

Avulsion fractures, in which a chip of bone is pulled off by resistance of a ligament, are common in conjunction with second or third degree eversion or inversion sprains. In most cases of fracture, swelling and pain are extreme. There may be some or no deformity; however, if fracture is suspected, splinting is essential. ICE-R is employed as soon as posible to control hemorrhage and swelling. Once swelling is reduced, casting can take place, allowing the athlete to bear weight. Immobilization will usually last for at least 6 to 8 weeks.

Achilles tendon strain Achilles tendon strains are not uncommon in sports and occur most often as a result of a lack of coordination between the agonists and the antagonists, following ankle sprains or sudden excessive dorsiflexion of the ankle.

Symptoms and signs The resulting pathology may be mild to severe. The severe injury is usually thought of as a partial or complete avulsion or rupturing of the Achilles tendon. While receiving this injury, the athlete feels acute pain and extreme weakness on plantar foot flexion.

Management The following are first aid measures to be applied:

1. As with other acute conditions, pressure is first applied with an elastic wrap together with cold application.
2. Unless the injury is minor, hemorrhage may be extensive, requiring ICE-R over an extended period of time.
3. After hemorrhaging has subsided, an elastic wrap can be lightly applied for continued pressure, and the athlete can be sent home. Management should begin the following day.

NOTE: The tendency for Achilles tendon trauma to readily develop into a chronic condition requires a conservative approach to therapy.

Management should be initiated in the following manner:

1. Follow-up therapy can usually begin on the third day and can continue on subsequent days, using hydromassage and analgesic packs until soreness has subsided.
2. Both heels, affected or unaffected, should be elevated by placing a sponge rubber pad in the heel of each street shoe. Elevation decreases the extension of the tendon and thereby relieves some of the irritation.
3. In a few days the athlete will be able to return to activity. The Achilles tendon should be restricted by a tape support and a sponge rubber heel lift placed in each athletic shoe. Heel lifts should be placed in both shoes or taped directly on the bottoms of both heels to avoid leg length asymmetry and subsequent adverse muscle and skeletal stresses.

ACHILLES TENDON TAPING

Achilles tendon taping (Fig. 18-40) is designed to prevent the Achilles tendon from overstretching.

Materials needed: One roll of 3-inch (7.5 cm) elastic tape, one roll of 1½-inch (3.8 cm) linen tape, and tape adherent.

Position of the athlete: The athlete kneels or lies face down, with the affected foot hanging relaxed over the edge of the table.

Position of the operator: The operator stands facing the plantar aspect of the athlete's foot.

Procedure

1. Two anchors are applied with 1½-inch (3.8 cm) tape, one circling the leg loosely, approximately 6 to 8 inches (15 to 20 cm) above the malleoli, and the other encircling the ball of the foot.
2. Two strips of 3-inch (7.5 cm) elastic tape are cut about 8 to 10 inches (20 to 25 cm) long. The first strip is moderately stretched from the ball of the athlete's foot along its plantar aspect up to the Achilles tendon. The second elastic strip follows the course of the first except that it is cut and split down the middle lengthwise and the cut ends are wrapped around the lower leg to form a lock. *CAUTION:* Keep the wrapped ends above the level of the strain.
3. The series is completed by placing two lock strips of elastic tape loosely around the arch and two strips around the athlete's lower leg. *NOTE:* Locking too tightly around the lower leg and foot will tend to restrict the normal action of the Achilles tendon and create more tissue irritation.

Figure 18-40

Achilles tendon taping.

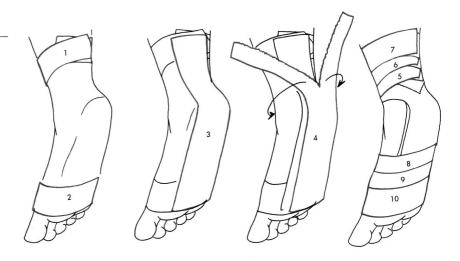

A ruptured Achilles tendon usually occurs when inflammation has been chronic.

Achilles tendon rupture A rupture of the Achilles tendon (Fig. 18-41) is a possibility in sports that require stop-and-go action. Although most common in athletes who are 30 years of age or older, rupture of the Achilles tendon can occur in athletes of any age. It usually follows a history of chronic inflammation and gradual degeneration caused by microtears. The ultimate insult normally is the result of sudden pushing-off action of the forefoot with the knee being forced into complete extension.

Symptoms and signs When the rupture occurs the athlete complains of a sudden snap or that something hit him or her in the lower leg.[5] Severe pain, point tenderness, swelling, and discoloration are usually associated with the trauma. The major problem in the Achilles tendon rupture is accurate diagnosis. Often a partial rupture is thought to be a sprained ankle. Any acute injury to the Achilles tendon should be suspected as being a rupture. Signs indicative of a rupture are obvious indentation at the tendon site and/or a positive result to a Thompson test. The Thompson test (Fig. 18-42) is performed by simply squeezing the calf muscle while the leg is extended and the foot is hanging over the edge of the table. A positive Thompson sign is one in which squeezing the calf muscle does not cause the heel to move or pull upward, or in which it moves less when compared to the uninjured leg.

Management Usual treatment of a complete Achilles tendon rupture is surgical repair. On occasion, however, the physician may decide on a conservative approach.[11] When surgical correction is necessary, the ends of the tendon are surgically fixed while the foot is positioned in plantar flexion and the knee in flexion for approximately 4 weeks. Full function following exercise rehabilitation will usually exceed 3 to 4 months.[15]

Figure 18-41

Achilles tendon rupture.

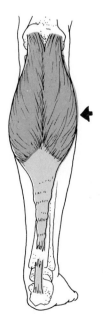

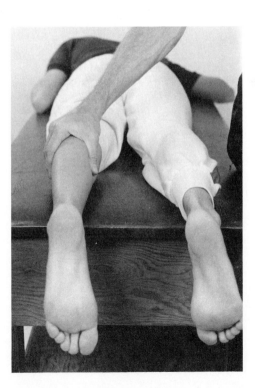

Figure 18-42

The Thompson test to determine an Achilles tendon rupture is performed by simply squeezing the calf muscle while the leg is extended. A positive result to the test is one in which the heel does not move.

MANAGEMENT PLAN FOR SECOND DEGREE ANKLE SPRAIN

Injury Situation

A male college senior-year lacrosse player stepped into a rut on the field, causing a major twist of the left ankle. At the time of injury the athlete felt a severe pain on the lateral aspect of the ankle before he fell to the ground.

Symptoms and Signs

After the injury the athlete complained of excruciating pain over the anterolateral aspect of the ankle. On palpation there was severe pain just under the lateral malleolus. A rapid, diffused swelling occurred over the lateral ankle region and an anterior drawer test showed some minor instability. X-ray examination indicated no fracture. The sprain was determined to be second degree.

Management Plan

1 Management Phase

GOALS: To control hemorrhage, swelling, pain and spasm
Estimated length of time (ELT): 2-3 days

Therapy

IMMEDIATE CARE: Ice packs (20 min) intermittently 6-8 times daily
Athlete wears elastic wrap during waking hours and elevates leg
Foot is elevated on a pillow during sleep
Crutches are used to avoid weight bearing for at least 3-4 days or until athlete can walk without a limp
Open basketweave taping is applied for hemorrhage control (2-3 days)

Exercise Rehabilitation

Toe gripping and spreading if no pain is caused (10-15 times) every waking hour starting on second day of injury
General body maintenance exercises are conducted 3 times a week as long as they do not aggravate the injury

2 Management Phase

GOALS: To decrease swelling and restore full muscle contraction without pain.
ELT: 4-7 days

Therapy

FOLLOW-UP CARE: All treatment is immediately followed by exercise
Ice pack (5-15 min) or ice massage (7 min) 2-3 times daily;
  or cold whirlpool (60° F-10 in);
  or contrast baths (20 min);
  or massage above and below injury site (5 min)

Exercise Rehabilitation

Crutch walking is continued with a toe touch if athlete is unable to walk without a limp
Grip and spread toes (10-15 times) every waking hour
PNF ankle patterns 3-4 times daily
General body maintenance exercises are conducted 3 times a week as long as they do not aggravate the injury

3 Management Phase

GOALS: To restore 50% pain-free movement and restore strength

Therapy

All treatment is immediately followed by exercise
Ice pack (5-15 min) or ice massage (7 min) 2-3 times daily;
  or whirlpool (90° to 100° F) (10 to 15 min);

	or contrast baths (20 min); or massage above and below injury site (5 min); or ultrasound (0.5 watts/cm^2) (5 min)
Exercise Rehabilitation	Avoid any exercise that produces pain or swelling Ankle circumduction (10-15 times each direction) 2-3 times daily Achilles tendon stretch from the floor (30 seconds) in each foot position (toe in, toe out, straight ahead) 3-4 times daily Toe raises (10 times—1-3 sets) 3-4 times daily Eversion exercise using a towel or rubber tube or tire resistance 3-4 times daily Shifting body weight between injured and noninjured ankle (up to 20 times and as long as pain free) 2-3 times daily Progress to toe raises (10 to 15 times) 2-3 times daily PNF ankle patterns are continued 2-3 times daily Progress to straight-ahead short step walking if it can be done without a limp General body maintenance exercises are conducted 3 times a week as long as they do not aggravate the injury

4 Management Phase

GOALS: To restore 90% ROM, power, endurance, speed, and agility
ELT: 1 week

Therapy	All treatment is immediately followed by exercise Ice pack (5 min) or ice massage (7 min) once daily; or whirlpool (100° to 120° F) (20 min); or contrast baths (20 min); or ultrasound (0.5 watts/cm^2) (5 min)
Exercise Rehabilitation	Achilles tendon stretch using slant board (30 seconds each foot position) 2-3 times daily Toe raises using slant board and resistance (10 repetitions—1-3 sets) 2-3 times daily Resistance ankle device to strengthen anterior, lateral, and medial muscles (starting with 2 lb and progressing to 10 lb) (1-3 sets) 2-3 times daily Tilt board for ankle proprioception (begin at 1 min in each direction—progress to 5 min) 3 times daily Walk-jog routine as long as symptom free; can begin to alternately walk-jog-run-walk 25 yd straight ahead, jog 25 yd straight ahead; progress to walk 25 yd in lazy S or 5 figure-8s; progress to figure-8 running as fast as possible; when athlete is able to run 10 figure-8s or Z cuts as fast as possible and able to spring up in the air on the injured leg 10 times without pain, Phase 5 can begin

5 Management Phase

The athlete is symptom free and has full ROM

Exercise Rehabilitation	With the ankle protected by a tape or splint the athlete can return to practice Strengthening and ROM exercises should be continued daily

Criteria for Full Recovery

1. The ankle is pain free on motion and no swelling is present.
2. Full ankle ROM and strength have been regained.
3. The athlete is able to run, jump, and make cutting movements as well as before injury.

THE LOWER LEG
Functional Anatomy
Bony and Interosseal Structures

The portion of the lower extremity that lies between the knee and the ankle is defined as the leg and is comprised of the tibia, the fibula, and the soft tissues that surround them.

Tibia The tibia, except for the femur, is the longest bone in the body and serves as the principal weight bearing bone of the leg. it is located on the medial or great toe side of the leg and is constructed with wide upper and lower ends to receive the condyles of the femur and the talus, respectively. The tibia is triangularly shaped in its upper two-thirds but is rounded and more constricted in the lower third of its length. The most pronounced change occurs in the lower third of the shaft and produces an anatomical weakness that establishes this area as the site of most of the fractures occurring to the leg. The shaft of the tibia has three surfaces, the posterior, the medial, and the lateral. Primarily, the posterior and lateral surfaces are covered by muscle, whereas the medial surface is subcutaneous and, as a result, quite vulnerable to outside trauma.

Fibula The fibula is long and slender and is located along the lateral aspect of the tibia, joining it in an arthrodial articulation at the upper end, just below the knee joint, and as a syndesmotic joint at the lower end. Both the upper and the lower tibiofibular joints are held in position

Figure 18-43

The four compartments of the lower leg.

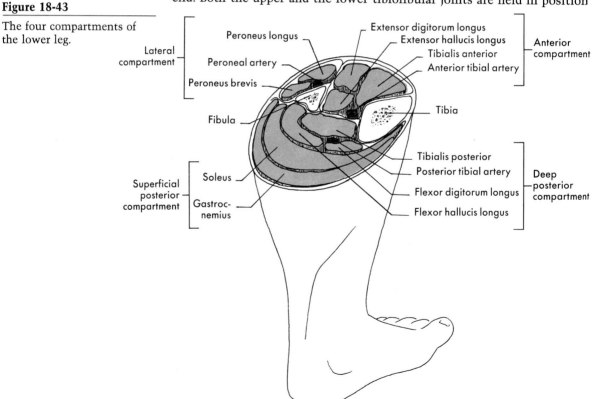

by strong anterior and posterior ligaments. The main function of the fibula is to provide for the attachment of muscles. It serves to complete the groove for the enclosure of the talus in forming the ankle joint.

Interosseous Membrane The interosseous membrane is a strong sheet of fibrous tissue that extends between the fibula and the tibia. The fibers display an oblique downward-and-outward pattern. The oblique arrangement aids in diffusing the forces or stresses placed on the leg. It completely fills the tibiofibular space, except for a small area at the superior aspect that is provided for the passage of the anterior tibial vessels.

Figure 18-44

Muscles of the lower leg. **A,** Anterior view; **B,** lateral view; **C,** posterior view superficial structures; and **D,** posterior view deep structures.

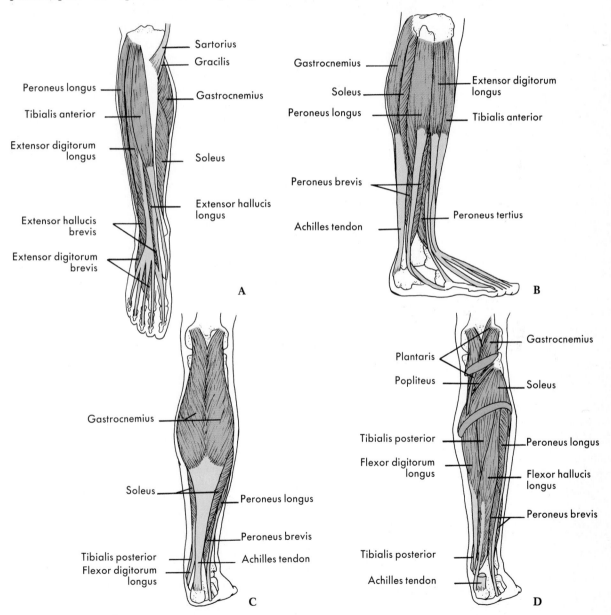

Compartments

The soft tissue of the leg is contained within four compartments bounded by heavy fascia (Fig. 18-43). The *anterior compartment* holds the major structures for ankle dorsiflexion and foot and toe extension, which are tibialis anterior, extensor hallucis longus, extensor digitorum longus, anterior tibial nerve, and the tibial artery. A *lateral compartment* houses the perneus longus, brevis, and tertius muscles and the superficial branch of the peroneal nerve. The *superficial posterior compartment* is made up of the gastrocnemius and the soleus. These muscles plantar flex the ankle and control foot inversion and toe flexion. The *deep posterior compartment* houses the tibialis posterior, flexor digitorum longus, flexor hallucis longus, and the posterior tibial artery. A major problem resulting from sports traumas can adversely affect these compartments, especially the anterior compartment. Such trauma can lead to swelling and neurological motor and sensory deficits (see further discussion later in this chapter).

Muscles

The lower leg is divided into posterior, anterior, and lateral musclar regions (Fig. 18-44). The posterior region is divided into superficial and deep muscles. The superficial muscles include the gastrocnemius, plantaris, and soleus. The deep posterior group includes the tibialis posterior, flexor digitorum longus, and flexor hallucis longus. The anterior muscles consist of the anterior tibialis, extensor digitorum longus, peroneus tertius, and extensor hallucis longus. The lateral muscles are the peroneus brevis and longus.

Blood and Nerve Supply

The major nerves of the lower leg are the tibial and common peroneal stemming from the large sciatic nerve. The major arteries often accompany the nerves and are the posterior and anterior tibial arteries (Fig. 18-45).

Figure 18-45

Blood and nerve supply of the lower leg.

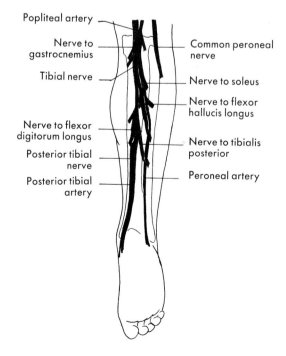

Popliteal artery

Nerve to gastrocnemius

Tibial nerve

Nerve to flexor digitorum longus

Posterior tibial nerve

Posterior tibial artery

Common peroneal nerve

Nerve to soleus

Nerve to flexor hallucis longus

Nerve to tibialis posterior

Peroneal artery

Evaluation
Major Complaints
An athlete who complains of discomfort in the lower leg region should be asked the following:
1. How long has it been hurting?
2. Where is the pain or discomfort?
3. Has the feeling changed or is it numb?
4. Is there a feeling of warmth or coldness?
5. Is there any sense of muscle weakness or difficulty in walking?
6. How did the problem occur?

General Observation
The athlete is generally observed for the following:
1. Any postural deviations such as toeing in, which may indicate internal tibial torsion, genu valgum or varum, and foot pronation should also be noted.
2. Any walking difficulty is noted, along with leg deformities or swellings.

Bony and Soft Tissue Palpation
The tibia, fibula, and the musculature are palpated for pain sites and obvious defects and swellings.

Functional Evaluation
Passive, active, and resistive movement is given to the muscles of the lower leg.

Special Tests
Where fracture may be suspected, a percussive blow can be given to the tibia or fibula below or above the suspected site. Percussion can also be applied upward on the bottom of the heel. Such blows set up a vibratory force that resonates at the fracture, causing pain.

Acute Leg Injuries
The leg is prone to a number of acute conditions, of which contusions and strains are most common. Although less common, fractures can occur in relation to direct trauma, such as being struck by a blow or through torsional forces with the foot fixed to the ground.

Leg Contusions
The shin bruise The shin, lying just under the skin, is exceedingly vulnerable and sensitive to blows or bumps. Because of the absence of muscular or adipose padding here, blows are not dissipated as they are elsewhere, and the periosteum receives the full force of any impact delivered to the shin. The periosteum surrounds bone surfaces, with the exception of the cartilaginous areas, and is composed of two fibrous layers that adhere closely to the bone, acting as a bed for blood vessels and bone-forming osteoblasts. Severe blows to the tibia often lead to a chronic inflammatory state of the cutaneous and periosteal tissue. The

shin is an extremely difficult area to heal, particularly the lower third, which has a considerably smaller blood supply than the upper portion. An inadequately cared for injury to the periosteum may develop into osteomyelitis, a serious condition that results in the destruction and deterioration of bony tissue.

In sports in which the shin is particularly vulnerable, such as football and soccer, adequate padding should be provided. All injuries in this area are potentially serious; therefore, minor shin lacerations or bruises should never be permitted to go untended.

Muscle contusions Contusions of the leg, particularly in the area of the gastrocnemius muscle, are common in sports. A bruise in this area can produce an extremely handicapping injury for the athlete. A bruising blow to the leg will cause pain, weakness, and partial loss of the use of the limb. Palpation may reveal a hard, rigid, and somewhat inflexible area because of internal hemorrhage and muscle spasm.

When this condition occurs it is advisable to stretch the muscles in the region immediately to prevent spasm and then, for approximately 1 hour, to apply a compress bandage and cold packs to control internal hemorrhaging.

If cold therapy or other superficial therapy such as massage and whirlpool do not return the athlete to normal activity within 2 to 3 days, the use of ultrasound may be warranted. An elastic wrap or tape support will serve to stabilize the part and permit the athlete to participate without aggravation of the injury.

Acute Compartment Syndrome

The acute compartment syndrome resulting from exercise is much less common than the chronic or recurrent type. It is usually caused by performing unaccustomed exercise, such as running a long distance.[14]

Symptoms and signs As an acute condition, the compartment continues to show signs of neurovascular compression after the athlete quits exercising. The following signs are characteristic of anterior compartment syndrome, by far the most common form: (1) Weakness of foot dorsiflexion or extension of the great toe, (2) decreased ability of the peroneal tendon to evert the foot, and (3) paresthesia of the web between the first and second toe or over the foot's entire dorsal region.[20]

If by chance there is an acute posterior compartment syndrome, there is (1) weakness in plantar flexion, (2) weakness of great toe and lateral toe flexion, and (3) paresthesia of the sole of the foot.

Management An acute compartment syndrome requires immediate decompression by the surgical release of the fascia covering the area.[11] The incision may be left open and leg splinted for a week.

Leg Spasms and Muscle Strains

Muscle spasms Spasms are sudden, violent, involuntary contractions of one or several muscles and may be either clonic or tonic. A *clonic* spasm is identified by intermittent contraction and relaxation, whereas the *tonic* type is identified by its constant state of muscle contraction without an intervening period of relaxation. Both of these types occur in sports. How and why muscle spasms happen to athletes is often difficult to ascertain. Fatigue, excess loss of fluid through perspiration, and inadequate reciprocal muscle coordination are some of the factors that may predispose an individual to a contracture. The leg, particularly the gastrocnemius muscle, is prone to this condition. It is usually difficult to predict the occurrence of spasm, since only the aforementioned criteria can be used as a guide.

Management When a muscle goes into spasm there is severe pain and considerable apprehension on the part of the athlete. Management in such cases includes putting the athlete at ease and relaxing the contracted site. Firmly grasping the contracted muscle, together with a mild gradual type stretching, has been found to relieve most acute spasms. Vigorously rubbing an extremity during spasm will often increase its intensity. In cases of recurrent spasm, the trainer should make certain that fatigue or abnormal mineral loss through perspiring is not a factor, since the loss of salt or other minerals can result in abnormal motor nerve impulses to skeletal muscles.

Calf strain ("tennis leg") Contrary to past beliefs, the plantaris muscle seldom ruptures; however, more commonly the medial head of the gastrocnemius becomes strained and tears near its musculotendinous attachment. Sports that require quick starts and stops, such as tennis, can cause this gastrocnemius strain. Usually the athlete makes a quick stop with the foot planted flat footed and suddenly extends the knee, placing stress on the medial head of the gastrocnemius (Fig. 18-46). In most cases

Figure 18-46

"Tennis leg" calf strain.

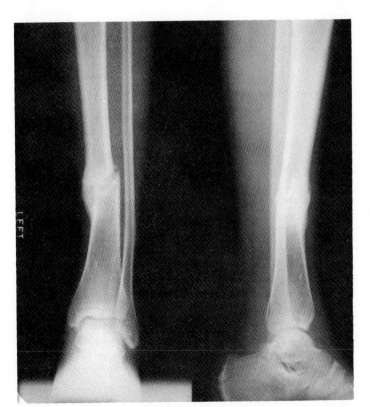

Figure 18-47

Fracture of the tibia.

it can be prevented by a regular routine of gradually stretching the calf region and exercising the antagonist and agonist muscles.[12] If the pain is sustained, immediate application of ICE-R is necessary, followed by a gentle, gradual stretch routine. Follow-up care should include a regimen of cold, heat, and mild exercise, together with walking in low-heeled shoes, accentuating a heel-toe gait.[12]

Leg fractures Fractures received during sports participation occur most often to the fingers, hands, face, and legs. Of leg fractures, the fibular fracture has the highest incidence and occurs principally to the middle third of the leg. Fractures of the tibia occur predominantly to the lower third.

Fractures of the shaft of the tibia and fibula result from either direct or indirect trauma during active participation in sports (Fig. 18-47). There is often a marked bony displacement with deformity, as a result of a strong pull of antagonistic muscles that causes an overriding of the bone ends, particularly if the athlete attempts to move or to stand on the limb following the injury. Crepitus and a temporary loss of limb function are usually present.

The pathology consists of marked soft tissue insult and extensive internal hemorrhaging. The leg appears hard and swollen. If a sharp bone edge has severed a nerve, *Volkmann's paralysis* may be present, with the characteristic dropfoot. Volkmann's paralysis is the result of great internal tension caused by hemorrhage and swelling within closed fascial compartments, inhibiting the blood supply and resulting in necrosis of muscles and in contractures. In most cases, reduction and cast immobilization are applied for 3 to 6 months, depending on the extent of the injury and any complications.

EXERCISE REHABILITATION OF THE ANKLE AND LOWER LEG

Many physicians think that a conservative approach should be taken in the treatment of sprained ankles by placing them in a cast and preventing any weight bearing for a period of at least 2 weeks. On the other hand, many sports physicians and trainers maintain that the best method is the moderately active approach, in which the athlete returns to competition much sooner than with the conservative treatment and completes the therapy through activity. The best method for returning an athlete to action should be determined by the physician.

In moderate and severe sprains the athlete should avoid weight bearing for at least 2 days and perhaps longer if there is pain and incapacitation. As the initial soreness decreases, the athlete should be encouraged to move the ankle as normally as possible—active dorsiflexion and plantar flexion should be emphasized, and inversion and eversion should be avoided. The athlete should use crutches to stand or walk. As the ankle heals, the athlete can be graduated from crutch walking to walking with a cane while the ankle is supported by tape. There must be complete healing before the athlete returns to vigorous activity. A good rule of thumb for determining when the athlete is able to return to a sport is to have the athlete stand, balancing full weight on the toes of the affected foot, and to spring up and down. If this can be done without severe discomfort, then it may be presumed that the athlete is able to resume a modified activity program with running. Maintaining tendon strength will aid the athlete when returning to the sport. The athlete's first concern should be to regain normal range of motion, after which a graded resistance exercise program can be started. All of the major muscles crossing the ankle joint must be considered in a reconditioning program. Of particular importance are the gastrocnemius and the muscles of foot inversion and eversion. The wearing of cleated shoes should be avoided until there is full injury recovery. Too often athletes are permitted to return to their sport before adequate recovery has taken place, causing the ankle joint to become chronically inflamed. Besides a daily therapy program conducted by the coach or trainer, the athlete should be encouraged to engage in a home program—for example, ICE-R treatment followed by inner tube or other resistance exercises.

In most sports injuries that affect the leg, atrophy and contracture of the leg, thigh, or hip musculature occur. In addition to these conditions, a low back imbalance may also occur and result in a shortening of the injured limb. In dealing with leg injuries, one should strive to maintain strength and complete mobility of the knee, hip, and lower back. Rehabilitation depends on the site of the injury, its nature, and its extensiveness. Mobility should be attained and encouraged through passive stretching of the plantar and dorsal areas. When pain on movement has decreased, a progressive strengthening program should be established and a daily order of exercise maintained by the athlete.

It is suggested that rehabilitation exercises be performed two to three times daily, progressing from one to three sets of 10 repetitions. The athlete must consider all the major muscles associated with the foot, ankle, and lower leg. A program of three stages might include the following:

Stage 1—early rehabilitation (all exercises must be conducted pain free).
1. *Writing the alphabet*—with toes pointed, 3 times.
2. *Picking up objects*—one at a time with the toes, such as 10 marbles, and placing them in a container.
3. *Gripping and spreading toes*—10 repetitions.
4. *Ankle circumduction*—10 circles in one direction and 10 circles in the other.
5. *Flatfooted Achilles tendon stretching*—with foot flat on the floor, the Achilles tendon is stretched first with foot straight ahead, then adducted, and finally abducted. Each stretch is maintained for 20 to 30 seconds and repeated 2 to 3 times.
6. *Toe raises*—standing flat on floor, the athlete rises onto toes as far as possible, with toes pointed straight ahead, pointed in, and finally pointed out; 10 repetitions, 2 or 3 times.
7. *Walking on toes and heels*—the athlete walks 10 spaces forward on toes and 10 paces backward on heels. Repeated 2 or 3 times.

Stage 2—intermediate rehabilitation
1. *Towel gather*—10 repetitions, 2 or 3 times.
2. *Towel scoop*—10 repetitions, 2 or 3 times.
3. *Achilles tendon stretching and toe raise*—the athlete stands with toes on a raised area such as a step with heels over the edge. The heels are raised as far as possible and then returned to stretch the Achilles tendon as much as possible. This is performed with toes pointed straight ahead, pointed in, and then pointed out; 10 repetitions, 2 or 3 times.

Too often athletes are permitted to return to their sport before adequate recovery has taken place, causing the ankle joint to become chronically inflamed.

4. *Resistance*—exercise anterior, lateral, and medial leg muscles against a resistance, such as surgical tubing or an inner tube strip. The tubing is attached around a stationary table or chair leg. The athlete then places the tubing around the foot and pulls the forefoot into dorsiflexion, eversion, then reverses position and exercises the foot in plantar flexion inversion; 10 repetitions, 3 or 4 times.

5. *Manual resistance*—manual resistance can be applied by the trainer or other person. The exercise is performed in a complete range of motion and in all four ankle movements. PNF patterns may be elected in place of straight patterns as described in Appendix I-A. Exercise is performed until fatigue or pain is felt.

6. *Proprioceptive ankle training*—the athlete spends 3 to 5 minutes daily on a balance board (wobble board) to reestablish ankle proprioception (see Fig. 18-21).

Stage 3—advanced rehabilitation

1. *Rope jumping*—5 to 10 minutes daily.

2. *Heel-toe and then on-toe running*—the athlete starts with heel-toe jogging until a mile distance can be performed easily. Jogging is then shifted to jogging 50 yards and on-toe running 50 yards, graduating to all on-toe running for 1 mile.

3. *Zigzag running*—the athlete runs a zigzag pattern graduating from slow to full speed without favoring the leg.

4. *Backward running*—a final exercise for returning full ankle and lower leg function is running backward in an on-toe manner.

REFERENCES

1. Balduini, F.C., and Tetzlaff, J.: Historical perspectives on injuries of the ligaments of the ankle, In Torg, J.S. (editor): Symposium on ankle and foot problems in the athlete, Clinics in sports medicine, vol. 1, no. 1, March 1982, Philadelphia, W.B. Saunders Co.

2. Birnbaum, J.S.: The musculoskeletal manual, New York, 1982, Academic Press, Inc.

3. Cailliet, R.: Foot and ankle pain, Philadelphia, 1968, F.A. Davis Co.

4. Cox, J.S., and Brand, R.L.: Evaluation and treatment of lateral ankle sprains, Phys. Sportsmed. **2**:6, 1977.

5. Distenfano, V.J., and Nixon, J.E.: Ruptures of the Achilles tendon, J. Sports Med **1**:4, 1973.

6. Hoerner, E.F.: Foot and ankle injuries. In Vinger, P.F., and Hoerner, E.F. (editors): Sports injuries: the unthwarted epidemic, Boston, 1982, John Wright, PSG, Inc.

7. James, S.L., et al.: Injuries to runners, Am. J. Sports Med. **6**:2, 1978.

8. Kressoff, W.B., and Ferris, W.D.: Runners injuries, Phys. Sportsmed. **7**:12, 1979.

9. Kulund, D.N.: The injured athlete, Philadelphia, 1982, J.B. Lippincott Co.

10. Mack, R.P.: Ankle injuries in athletics, In Torg, J.S. (editor): Symposium on ankle and foot problems in the athlete, Clinics in sports medicine, vol. 1, no. 1, March 1982, Philadelphia, W.B. Saunders.

11. Maron, B.R.: Orthopedic aspects of sports medicine, In Appenzeller, O., and Atkinson, R. (editors): Sports medicine, Baltimore, 1981, Urgane & Schwarzenberg.

12. Millar, A.P.: Strains of the posterior calf musculature ("tennis leg"), Am. J. Sports Med. **7**:2, 1979.

13. Miller, W.E.: The heel pad, Am. J. Sports Med **10**:19, 1982.

14. Mubarak, S., and Hargens, A.: Exertional compartment syndromes. In Mack, R.P. (editor): Symposium on the foot and leg in running sports, American Academy of Orthopaedic Surgeons, St. Louis, 1982, The C. V. Mosby Co.

15. O'Donoghue, D.H.: Treatment of injuries to atletes, ed. 4, Philadelphia, 1984, W.B. Saunders Co.

16. Reid, D.C.: Ankle injuries in sports, J. Sports Med. **1:**3, 1973.

17. Roy, S.P.: Evaluation and treatment of the stable ankle sprain, Phys. Sportsmed. **5:**8, 1977.

18. Seder, J.I.: Heel injuries incurred in running and jumping, Phys. Sportsmed. **4:**10, 1976.

19. Silva, T., et al.: Rupture of the plantar fascia in athletics, Am. J. Bone Joint Surg. **60A:**537, 1978.

20. Wallensten, R., and Eriksson, E.: Is medical lower leg pain (shinsplint) a chronic compartment syndrome? In Mack, R.P. (editor): Symposium on the foot and leg in running sports, American Academy of Orthopaedic Surgeons, St. Louis, 1982, The C.V. Mosby Co.

ADDITIONAL SOURCES

Extensor mechanism problems of the patella and ankle and foot injuries, Audiocassettes on sportsmedicine, Chicago, Teach'em, Inc.

Hayes, W.C.: Bio mechanics of the running gait, Audiocassettes on sportsmedicine, Teach'em, Inc., 160 E. Illinois, St., Chicago, Ill, 60611.

Henry, J.H.: Soft tissue injuries of the foot, Ath. Train. **16:**173, 1981.

Kuprian, W.: Physical therapy for sports, Philadelphia, 1982, W.B. Saunders Co.

Leach, R.E.: Achilles tendon ruptures. In Mack, R.P. (editor): Symposium on the foot and leg in running sports, American Academy of Orthopaedic Surgeons, St. Louis, 1982, The C.V. Mosby Co.

Leach, R.E.: Overall view of rehabilitation of the leg for running. In Mack, R.P. (editor): symposium on the foot and leg in running sports, American Academy of Orthopaedic Surgeons, St. Louis, 1982, The C.V. Mosby Co.

Mack, R.P. (editor): Symposium on the foot and leg in running sports, American Academy of Orthopaedic Surgeons, St. Louis, 1982, The C.V. Mosby Co.

Nemeth, J.A., and Thrasher, E.: Ankle sprains in athletes. In Zarins, B. (editor): Symposium on Olympic sports medicine, Clinics in sports medicine, vol. 2, no. 1, Philadelphia, March 1983, W.B. Saunders Co.

Novich, M.M., and Southmayd, W.W.: Prevention and management of injuries to the knee, leg, ankle and foot, Audiocassettes on sportsmedicine, Chicago, Teach'em, Inc.

Rachun, A., chairman, advisory panel: Standard nomenclature of athletic injuries, Monroe, Wisc., 1976, American Medical Association.

Salter, R.B.: Textbook of disorders and injuries of the musculoskeletal system, ed. 2, Baltimore, 1983, Williams & Wilkins Co.

Sammarco, G.J.: Soft tissue conditions in athletes' feet. In Torg, J.S. (editor): Symposium on ankle and foot problems in the athlete, Clinics in sports medicine, vol. 1, no. 1, Philadelphia, March 1982, W.B. Saunders Co.

Torg, J.S. (editor): Symposium on ankle and foot problems in the athlete, Clinics in sports medicine, vol 1, no. 1, Philadelphia, March 1982, W.B. Saunders Co.

Torg, J.S.: Patho-mechanics of running injuries, Audiocassettes on sportsmedicine, Chicago, Teach'em, Inc.

Waller, Jr., J.F.: Biomechanics and rehabilitation of the gastroc-soleus complex. In Mack, R.P. (editor): Symposium on the foot and leg in running sports, American Academy of Orthopaedic Surgeons, St. Louis, 1982, The C.V. Mosby Co.

Chapter 19

THE FOOT, ANKLE, AND LOWER LEG: CHRONIC AND OVERUSE INJURIES

When you finish this chapter, you should be able to

Explain the biomechanical relationships to chronic and overuse sports injuries

Relate etiological factors, symptoms and signs, and management procedures for the major chronic and overuse sports injuries of the foot, ankle, and lower leg

Develop a management plan for major chronic and overuse sports injuries

Chronic and overuse stress injuries in the foot, ankle, or leg are becoming increasingly more of a problem in athletics. Many reasons have been suggested for this situation; however, of major importance is the increase in running distance and intensity among both serious and recreational athletes (Fig. 19-1).

FOOT BIOMECHANICAL IMPLICATIONS

A study of lower extremity chronic and overuse injuries related to sports participation must include some understanding of biomechanics of the foot, especially in the act of walking and running.

> The human foot provides shock absorption for the entire body.

The human foot is designed to absorb shock for the entire body. Ankle dorsiflexion, knee and hip flexion, and eversion at the subtalar joint absorb the shock of making contact with surfaces that have no or varying resilience.[5]

Locomotion of any kind, but especially that which is imposed by sports activities, places great stress on the foot as it makes contact with a surface. If the foot is abnormally structured, pathological conditions may develop over time. A foot that functions normally will place no undue stress on itself or the other joints of the lower limb.[5] A foot with a structural malformation eventually may have overuse problems; foot malformations can lead to both soft tissue and bony deformities in the lower extremity.

The Gait Cycle

The stance phase of gait includes contact (25%), midstance (40%), and propulsion (35%). In walking from heel-strike to heel-strike, 35% of the action consists of the swing phase, and 65% consists of the stance phase. During

Figure 19-1

With the increased popularity
of distance running, chronic
and overuse injuries are on
the increase.

the initial surface contact or first 15% to 25% of the stance phase, the
lower leg is internally rotated (Fig 19-2). When in contact with a surface,
the foot is unable to rotate internally; it is the subtalar, or universal, joint
that allows for this motion. On surface contact the subtalar joint normally
pronates 6 to 8 degrees.[11] Pronation is the combined motion of calcaneal
eversion, plantar flexion, and adduction of the talus. At the same time, the
medial longitudinal arch flattens or lowers. Foot pronation is necessary for
adaption to uneven surfaces. A flatfooted athlete may have as much as 10
to 12 degrees of navicular pronation. The more the subtalar joint pronates
or everts, the more the tibia internally rotates. Tibial rotation is referred to
the knee and hip joints, which could lead to microtraumas and overuse
problems.[11] *Excessive internal rotation can be determined by the amount
of patellar rotation. The patella rotates inwardly as much in the contact
phase as it externally rotates on propulsion. More inward rotation than
external rotation leads to excessive pronation in the subtalar joint.*[15]

The more the subtalar joint
pronates or everts, the more
the tibia internally rotates.

As the foot moves to the midstance, or fully loaded, position it becomes
increasingly more stable. As the full weight of the body is supported by the
foot, the lower leg progressively moves from internal rotation to external

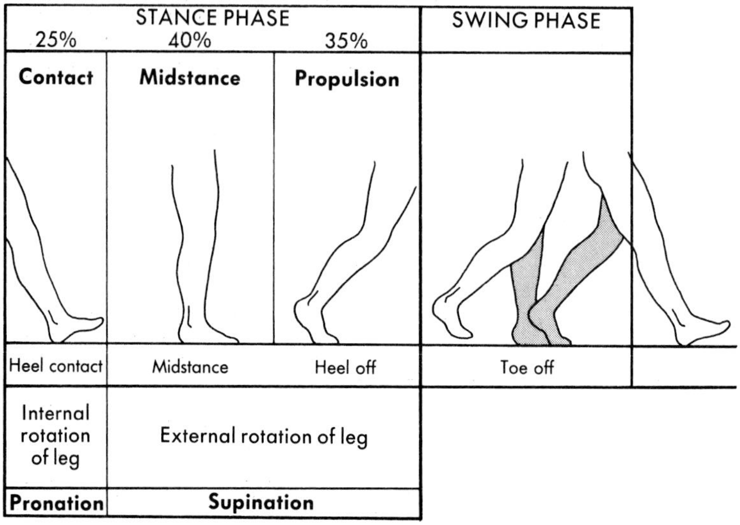

Figure 19-2

Walking gait cycle.

STANCE PHASE			SWING PHASE
25%	40%	35%	
Contact	**Midstance**	**Propulsion**	
Heel contact	Midstance	Heel off	Toe off
Internal rotation of leg	External rotation of leg		
Pronation	**Supination**		

Figure 19-3

Foot bearing weight in walking as it moves from heel-strike to toe-off.

hypermobile foot
Foot that allows too much pronation or fails at rigid stability in toe-off

rotation. As the leg externally rotates and the foot moves from a midstance position, the foot supinates. Supination begins with external rotation of the hip and raising of the medial longitudinal arch. The talus moves into dorsiflexion and the calcaneus moves into inversion as the hindfoot moves into supination. The gastrocnemius, soleus, and posterior tibial are the major muscles for foot supination[15] (Fig. 19-3). In this position the foot is normally rigid to provide a strong toe-off. Until toe-off the long peroneal muscle stabilizes the first metatarsal bone.

If an athlete has fallen arches or the stage of pronation is prolonged or the foot is inadequately stable on toe-off, injuries may occur. The converse of this is also true. A person with a cavus condition, indicated by an abnormally high arch and a rigid foot, has decreased subtalar, leg, and hip motion and subsequent shock absorption. The relative positions of the forefoot and hindfoot generate abnormal forces to the foot, which are in turn transferred to the leg (Fig. 19-4).

In running both feet are off the surface at the same time (Fig. 19-5). Sprinters are on their toes during the support phase, whereas middle-distance runners may momentarily touch their heels during the support phase. Much like walking, the jogger and long-distance runner perform a heel-foot-toe action. Whatever the type of running, a **hypermobile foot** that causes too long a pronation or fails at rigid stability in toe-off can eventually produce an injury. One indicator of how the running foot bears weight is to observe shoe wear (Fig. 19-6).

Specific Joint Segments

Parks[15] emphasizes that all of the many foot segments are interdependent of one another. If one segment is weak, it adversely affects all other segments.

The Subtalar Joint

The subtalar joint must lock completely during the toe-off phase of locomotion and unlock in the contact phase, allowing pronation to occur. The

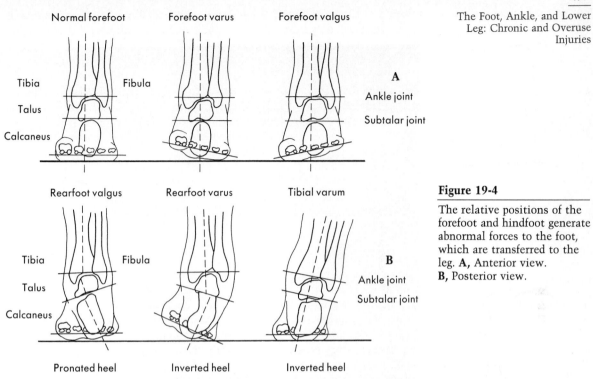

Normal forefoot   Forefoot varus   Forefoot valgus

Tibia   Fibula

Talus

Calcaneus

A

Ankle joint

Subtalar joint

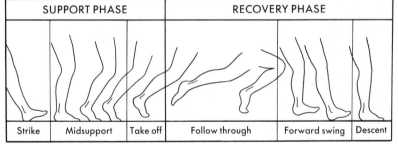

Rearfoot valgus   Rearfoot varus   Tibial varum

Tibia   Fibula

Talus

Calcaneus

B

Ankle joint

Subtalar joint

Pronated heel   Inverted heel   Inverted heel

Figure 19-4

The relative positions of the forefoot and hindfoot generate abnormal forces to the foot, which are transferred to the leg. **A,** Anterior view. **B,** Posterior view.

Figure 19-5

Running gait cycle.

SUPPORT PHASE			RECOVERY PHASE		
Strike	Midsupport	Take off	Follow through	Forward swing	Descent

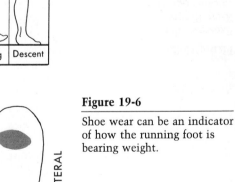

Figure 19-6

Shoe wear can be an indicator of how the running foot is bearing weight.

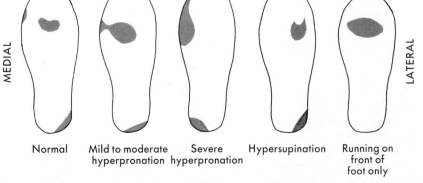

MEDIAL   LATERAL

Normal   Mild to moderate hyperpronation   Severe hyperpronation   Hypersupination   Running on front of foot only

position of the calcaneus during ambulation and stance is a good indicator of the habitual movement of the subtalar joint. At all times it should remain in a straight-line or vertical position.[15]

The Talonavicular Joint

The talonavicular joint moves independently from the hindfoot. In relation to the hindfoot it can dorsiflex and move in eversion and inversion. The talonavicular joint, like the subtalar joint, locks and unlocks. It has mobility during the first part of surface contact and should become highly stable before toe-off. Normally the talonavicular joint is positioned higher than the calcaneocuboid joint. If the subtalar joint is hypermobile, the talonavicular and calcaneocuboid joints become parallel and weakened, making them susceptible to surface forces. Another factor is that the surface stresses cause dorsiflexion of the forefoot on the hindfoot, thereby increasing hypermobility (Fig. 19-7).

The Tarsometatarsal Joint

The tarsometatarsal joint comprises the cuboid; first, second, and third cuneiform; and bases of the metatarsal bones. These bones allow for great rotational forces when engaged in weight-bearing activities. They move as a unit, depending on the funtioning of the talonavicular and subtalar joints. Also known as the Lisfranc joint, the tarsometatarsal joint is a locking device that provides foot stability. As the talonavicular joint becomes neutral or supinated, the tarsometatarsal joint becomes dorsally convex to resist the surface stress on the foot.[15] In pronation the tarsometatarsal joint loses its convexity and the bones become more parallel to one another, thus causing the forefoot to become hypermobile.[15] The primary muscle support in this region is produced by the posterior tibial muscle pulling medially and the long and short peroneal muscles pulling laterally.

The Metatarsal Region

Together with subtalar, talonavicular, and tarsometatarsal interrelationships, foot stabilization depends on the functioning of the metatarsal joints. The primary movements of the metatarsal joints are plantar flexion and dorsiflexion.

Figure 19-7

Stress sites in the
hypermobile foot.

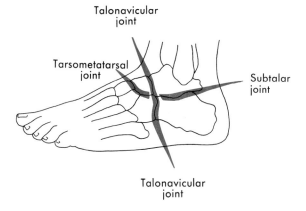

The first metatarsal bone, along with the first cuneiform (first ray) bone, moves independently from the other metatarsal bones. As a main weight bearer the first ray is concerned with body propulsion. An unstable first ray will cause forefoot pronation. Stabilization depends on the long peroneal muscle that attaches on the medial aspect of the first ray. The long peroneal muscle allows both plantar flexion of the first ray and foot abduction.[15] When there is habitual subtalar pronation, the long peroneal muscle loses its ability to effectively pull the first ray into plantar flexion and tends to adduct the foot. For mechanically effective toe-off to occur, the proximal head of the first ray must be lifted above the cuboid bone by the foot moving into a position of supination. Inadequate supination causes forefoot instability.

The fifth metatarsal bone, like the first metatarsal bone, moves independently. In plantar flexion it moves into adduction and inversion; conversely, in dorsiflexion it moves the foot into abduction and eversion. As with the other segments of the foot, stability of the fifth metatarsal bone depends on the relative position of the subtalar and talonavicular joints.[15]

FOOT CONDITIONS

Lower extremity stress injuries in sports often begin in the foot. In sports requiring extensive running, injuries can stem from biomechanical and weight transmission difficulties.

Foot Deformities and Structural Deviations
Foot Hypermobility and Rigidity

The two major foot deformities commonly seen in sports are those which are nonrigid and rigid.[5] A flexible deformed foot could eventually develop into one that is arthritic and rigid.

The degree the calcaneus is from being vertical and into the valgus, or everted, position indicates the amount of pronation. Calcaneal eversion of 5 to 10 degrees is considered mild to moderate flatfeet and 10 degrees is severe.[5]

A calcaneus that is inverted 5 degrees is associated with a high-arched foot. In the flexible, high-arched foot, pronation will occur beyond the vertical position. However, a foot that is unable to go beyond verticle reflects a moderate to severe cavus deformity.[4,5]

Arch Conditions

Painful arches are usually the result of improperly fitting shoes, overweight, excessive activity on hard surfaces, overuse, faulty posture, or fatigue—any of which may cause a pathological condition in the supporting tissue of the arch. The symptoms in these cases are divided into three stages or degrees, each characterized by specific symptoms. The first-degree stage shows itself as a slight soreness in the arch. The second-degree stage is indicated by a chronic inflammatory condition that includes soreness, redness, swelling, and a slight visible drop in the arch. In the third degree a completely fallen arch is accompanied by extreme pain, immobility, and deformity.

Fallen anterior metatarsal arch Activity on hard surfaces or prolonged stresses on the balls of the feet may cause weak or fallen anterior

Figure 19-8

Normal and fallen metatarsal arch.

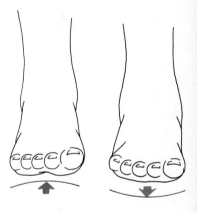

Figure 19-9

Fallen medial longitudinal arch.

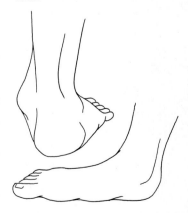

metatarsal arches (Fig. 19-8). When the supporting ligaments and muscles lose their ability to retain the metatarsal heads in a domeline shape, a falling of the arch results, thereby placing pressure on the nerves and blood vessels in the area. With this condition the athlete first notices an irritation and redness on the ball of the foot. As the condition progresses, pain, callus formation, toe cramping, and often a severe burning sensation develop. Care of fallen anterior metatarsal arch conditions should include hydrotherapy, light friction massage, exercise, and metatarsal pads.

Fallen medial longitudinal arch (flatfoot)   Various stresses weaken ligaments and muscles that support the arch, thus forcing the navicular bone downward (Fig. 19-9). The athlete may complain of tiredness and

Figure 19-10

Arch taping technique no. 3 with double X and forefoot support.

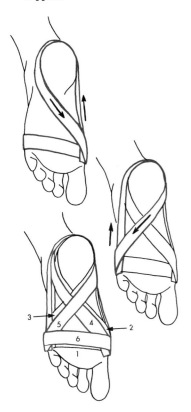

CARE FOR ARCH CONDITIONS

1. Shoes should be fitted properly.
2. Hydrotherapy, especially a whirlpool, should be given three or four times daily at a temperature of 105°F (40.6°C) until the initial inflammation has subsided.
3. Deep therapy, such as ultrasound, can be used.
4. Arch orthoses may have to be used to ameliorate irritation of the weakened ligaments. If a pathological condition of the arch can be detected in the first degree or second-degree stage, arch supports may be needed.
5. Weakened arches, if detected early, can be aided by an exercise program. If the arch is allowed to drop and the condition becomes chronic, exercising can offer little relief other than as a palliative aid.

ARCH TAPING TECHNIQUE NO. 3

The double X and forefoot support   As its name implies, this taping both supports the longitudinal arch and stabilizes the forefoot into good alignment (Fig. 19-10).

Materials needed: One roll of 1-inch (2.5 cm) tape and tape adherent.

Position of the athlete: The athlete lies face down on a table, with the foot to be taped extending approximately 6 inches (15 cm) over the edge of the table.

Position of the operator: The operator faces the bottom of the foot.

Procedure

1. Place an anchor strip around the ball of the foot.
2. Start the next strip on the side of the foot beginning at the base of the great toe. Take the tape around the heel, crossing the arch, returning to the starting point.
3. The pattern of the third strip of tape is the same as the second strip, except that it is started on the little toe side of the foot.
4. Lock each series of strips by placing tape around the ball joint. A completed procedure usually consists of a series of three strips.

tenderness in the arch and heel. Ankle sprains frequently result from weakened arches, and abnormal friction sites may develop within the shoe because of changes in weight distribution. This condition may be the result of several factors: shoes that cramp and deform the feet, weakened supportive tissues, overweight, postural anomalies that subject the arches to unaccustomed or unnatural strain, or overuse, which may be the result of repeatedly subjecting the arch to a severe pounding through participation on an unyielding surface. Commonly, the fallen medial longitudinal arch is associated with foot pronation (Fig. 19-9).

LOWDYE TECHNIQUE

The LowDye technique is an excellent method for managing the fallen medial longitudinal arch, foot pronation, arch strains, and plantar fasciitis. Moleskin is cut in 3-inch (7.5 cm) strips to the shape of the sole of the foot. It should cover the head of the metatarsal bones and the calcaneus bone (Fig. 19-11).

Materials needed: One role of 1-inch (2.5 cm), 1 roll of 2-inch (5 cm) tape and moleskin.

Position of the athlete: The athlete sits with the foot in a neutral position and the first ray in plantar flexion.

Position of the operator: The operator faces the bottom of the foot.

Procedure

1. Apply the moleskin to the sole of the foot, pulling it slightly downward before attaching it to the calcaneus.
2. Grasp the forefoot with the thumb under the distal 2 to 5 metatarsal heads, pushing slightly upward, with the tips of the second and third fingers pushing downward on the first metatarsal head. While the foot is in this position, apply two or three 1-inch (2.5 cm) tape strips laterally, starting from the distal head of the fifth metatarsal bone and ending at the distal head of the first metatarsal bone. Keep these lateral strips below the outer malleolus.
3. Secure the moleskin and lateral tape strip by circling the forefoot with four or five 2-inch (5 cm) strips. Start at the lateral dorsum of the foot, circle under the plantar aspect, and finish at the medial dorsum of the foot.

Figure 19-11

LowDye taping technique for the fallen medial longitudinal arch, foot pronation, arch strains, and plantar fasciitis.

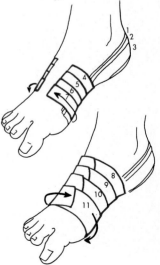

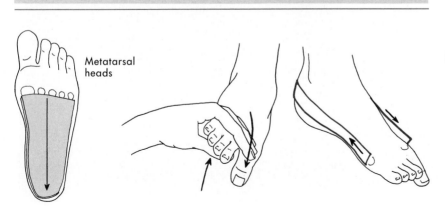

Metatarsal heads

Test for flexible and rigid flatfeet The athlete is observed as full
weight is borne on a foot and then is removed. A flexible flatfoot is one
in which the medial longitudinal arch becomes flattened on weight bearing and produces an obvious arch on removal of that weight. Conversely,
a rigid arch remains flat during both weight bearing and non-weight bearing.[6]

Care includes the use of properly fitting shoes that give sufficient
support to the arch or permit the normal anatomy of the foot to function,
exercise, arch supports, and protective taping. In addition, when there is
chronic pain, care should include daily hydrotherapy and friction massage
until the inflammation has subsided.

Pes cavus Pes cavus (Fig. 19-12), commonly called clawfoot, hollow
foot, or an abnormally high arch, is not as common as pes planus, or
flatfeet. In the rigid type of pes cavus, shock absorption is poor and can
lead to problems such as general foot pain, metatarsalgia, and clawed or
hammer toes. Pes cavus also may be asymptomatic.

The accentuated high medial longitudinal arch may be congenital or
indicate a neurological disorder. Commonly associated with this condition are clawed toes and abnormal shortening of the Achilles tendon. The
Achilles tendon is directly linked with the plantar fascia (Fig. 19-13).

Figure 19-12

Pes cavus.

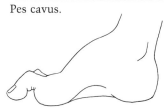

Figure 19-13

The Achilles tendon is
directly linked with the
plantar fascia. Achilles
tendon stretching releases a
tight medial longitudinal
arch.

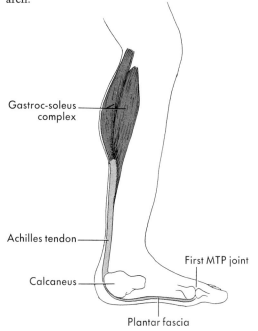

Gastroc-soleus
complex

Achilles tendon

Calcaneus

First MTP joint

Plantar fascia

Figure 19-14

Mild bunion deformity of the
left great toe.

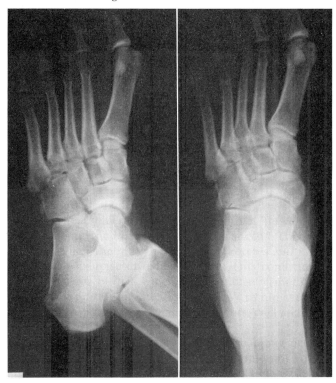

Also, because of the abnormal distribution of body weight, heavy calluses develop on the ball and heel of the foot.

Conditions of the Forefoot, Ball of the Foot, and Toe

A number of deformities and structural deviations affect the forefoot and ball of the foot. Among those seen in sports are bunions, hallux valgus, bunionettes, sesamoiditis, metatarsalgia, interdigital neuroma, and Morton's syndrome.

Bunions (hallus valgus) and bunionettes (tailor's bunions) Bunions are one of the most frequent painful deformities of the great toe (Fig. 19-14).

Etiological factors The reasons why a bunion develops are complex. Commonly it is associated with a congenital deformity of the first metatarsal head, combined with wearing shoes that are pointed, too narrow, too short, or have high heels. The bursa over the first metatarsophalangeal joint becomes inflamed and eventually thickens. The joint becomes enlarged and the great toe becomes malaligned, moving medially toward the second toe, sometimes to such an extent that it eventually overlaps it. This type of bunion is also associated with a depressed or flattened transverse arch and a pronated foot.

The bunionette, or tailor's bunion, is much less common than hallux valgus and affects the fifth metatarsophalangeal joint. In this case, the little toe angulates toward the fourth toe.

In all bunions, both the flexor and extensor tendons are malpositioned, creating more angular stress on the joint.

Symptoms and signs In the beginning of a bunion there is tenderness, swelling, and enlargement of the joint. Poor-fitting shoes increase the irritation and pain. As the inflammation continues, angulation of the toe progresses, eventually leading to instability in the forefoot.

Management Each bunion has unique characteristics. Early recognition and care can often prevent increased irritation and deformity. Following are some management procedures:

1. Wear correctly fitting shoes with a wide toe box.
2. Place a felt or sponge rubber doughnut pad or lamb's wool over the medial side of the joint.

Figure 19-15

A, Wedging of the great toe can help reduce some of the abnormal stress of a bunion. **B,** Taping for the bunion.

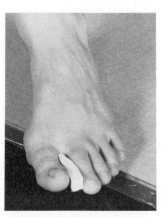

A

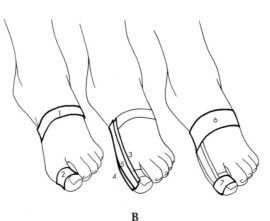

B

3. Wear a tape splint along with a resilient wedge placed between the great toe and second toe (Fig. 19-15).
4. Apply thermal therapy or cryotherapy to reduce the inflammation.
5. Engage in daily foot exercises to strengthen both the extensor and flexor muscles.

If the condition progresses, a special orthotic device may help normalize foot mechanics. Surgery might be required in the later stages of this condition.

Sesamoiditis   Pain and disability at the ball joint commonly reflect inflammation of the sesamoid bones. As the great toe passively undergoes dorsiflexion, the sesamoid bone becomes compressed upward, causing pain and discomfort.[1] This condition may be caused by roughening on the articular surface of the sesamoid bone or abnormal pressure upward. Treatment usually includes a doughnut pad around the sesamoid bone, stiff-soled shoes, and, in some cases, a series of steroid injections.

metatarsalgia
A general term to describe ball of the foot pain

Metatarsalgia   Although **metatarsalgia** is a general term to describe pain in the ball of the foot, it is more commonly associated with pain under the second and sometimes the third metatarsal head. A heavy callus often forms in the area of pain. Fig. 19-16 shows some of the more common pain sites in the foot.

Etiological factors   The most prevalant cause of this condition is the fallen metatarsal arch. Normally the head of the first and fifth metatarsal bones bear slighly more weight than the second, third, and fourth. The first metatarsal head bears two sixths of the body weight, the fifth bears slightly more than one sixth, and the second, third, and fourth bear one sixth.[2] If the foot tends toward pronation, or if the intermetatarsal ligaments are weak, allowing the foot to abnormally spread (splayed foot),

Figure 19-16

Common pain sites in the foot.

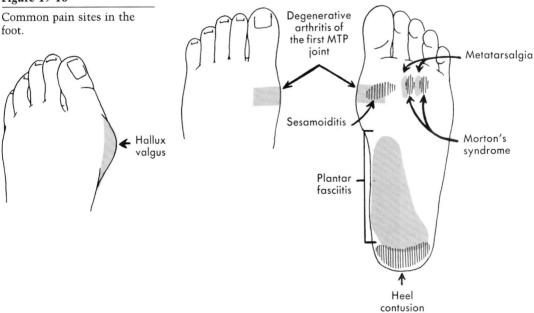

the fallen metatarsal arch is probable (Fig. 19-17). As the transverse arch becomes flattened and the heads of the second, third, and fourth metatarsal bones become depressed, pain can result. A cavus deformity can also cause metatarsalgia.

Management Management of metatarsalgia usually consists of applying a pad to elevate the depressed metatarsal heads. NOTE: *The pad is placed behind and not under the metatarsal heads* (Fig. 19-18). In severe cases a metatarsal bar may be applied (Fig. 19-19). Abnormal callus buildup should be removed by paring or filing.

A daily regimen of exercise should be practiced, concentrating on strengthening flexor and intrinsic muscles and stretching the Achilles tendon. A Thomas heel (Fig. 19-20), which elevates the medial aspect of the heel from ⅛ to ³⁄₁₆ inch (0.3 to 0.47 cm), also could prove beneficial.[2]

Figure 19-17

Normal weight bearing of the forefoot and abnormal spread (splayed foot).

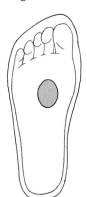

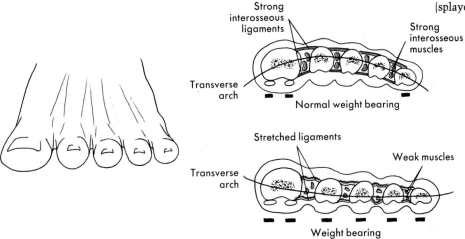

Strong interosseous ligaments

Strong interosseous muscles

Transverse arch

Normal weight bearing

Stretched ligaments

Weak muscles

Transverse arch

Weight bearing

Figure 19-18   **Figure 19-19**   **Figure 19-20**

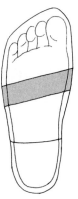   

Figure 19-18

Pad to elevate depressed metatarsal heads.

Figure 19-19

Metatarsal bar to relieve severe metatarsalgia.

Figure 19-20

The Thomas heel elevates the medial aspect of the calcaneus ⅛ to ³⁄₁₆ inch (0.3 to 0.47 cm), which can help to relieve pronation and metatarsalgia.

METATARSAL PAD SUPPORT

The purpose of the metatarsal pad is to reestablish the normal relationships of the metatarsal bones. It can be purchased commercially or constructed out of felt or sponge rubber.

Materials needed: One roll of 1-inch tape (2.5cm), a ⅛-inch (0.3 cm) adhesive felt oval cut to a 2-inch (5 cm) circumference, and tape adherent.

Position of the athlete: The athlete sits on a table or chair with the plantar surface of the affected foot turned upward.

Position of the operator: The operator stands facing the plantar aspect of the athlete's foot.

Procedure
1. The circular pad is placed just behind the metatarsal heads.
2. About two or three circular strips of tape are placed loosely around the pad and foot.

neuroma
A tumor that emanates from a nerve.

Figure 19-21

Interdigital neuroma.

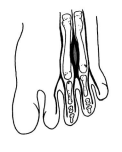

Interdigital neuroma   Interdigital nerves are those which travel between the metatarsal bones to innervate the toes. An interdigital **neuroma** emanates from and entraps the nerves. It usually involves the third plantar interdigital nerve, which innervates the third and fourth toes. Commonly, the interdigital neuroma causes a swelling of about ¾ inch (1.9 cm) long between the third and fourth distal metatarsal heads (Fig. 19-21).

Etiological factors   The interdigital nerves become entrapped between the metatarsal heads. This condition is more common among female athletes and is associated with the pronated foot and splayed toes.

Symptoms and signs   The athlete complains of severe intermittent pain in the region of the nerve impingement. The pain radiates from the distal metatarsal heads to the tips of the toes and is often relieved when no weight is borne and the shoe is removed. On palpation between the distal metatarsal heads, radiating pain may be duplicated and the tumor felt. Sometimes the skin between the metatarsal heads is numb.

Management   Conservative treatment of an interdigital neuroma includes the following:
1. Broad-toed shoe
2. Transverse arch support
3. Metatarsal bar
4. Foot orthoses
5. Injection of lidocaine and steroids

If conservative treatment is ineffective, surgical excision may provide complete relief.

Morton's syndrome   Another foot deformity causing major forefoot pain is Morton's syndrome. Metatarsalgia is produced by an abnormally short first metatarsal bone. Weight is borne mainly by the second metatarsal bone, and there is hypermobility between the first and second proximal metatarsal joints (Fig. 19-22). The treatment is the same as that for foot pronation.

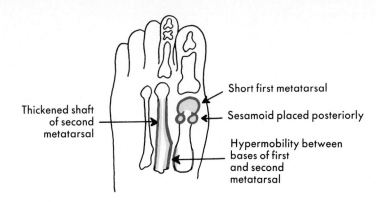

Figure 19-22

Morton's syndrome with an
abnormally short first
metatarsal bone.

Toe deformities

Hallux rigidus Hallux rigidus is a painful condition caused by fusion
or partial fusion of the first metatarsophalangeal joint. The great toe is
unable to dorsiflex, causing the athlete to toe-off on the second, third,
fourth, and fifth toes. Walking becomes awkward. Often, on complete
fusion, pain disappears.

Management usually includes a pad under the first metatarsal bone
to prevent great toe dorsiflexion. A metatarsal bar on the shoe may help
to avoid increasing the joint's irritation. Surgery may be the only means
of recovering function.[2]

Figure 19-23

Taping for hammer, or
clawed, toes.

Hammer, or clawed, toes Hammer, or clawed, toes may be congenital,
but more often the condition is caused by wearing shoes that are too
short over a long period of time, thus cramping the toes. Hammer toe
usually involves the second or third toe, whereas clawed toes involve
more than one toe. In both conditions the metatarsophalangeal and proximal interphalangeal joints become malaligned, along with overly contracted flexor tendons and overly stretched extensor tendons. A deformity
such as this eventually results in the formation of hard corns or calluses
on the exposed joints. Quite often surgery is the only cure. However,
proper shoes and protective taping (Fig. 19-23) can help prevent irritation.

Overlapping toes Overlapping of the toes (Fig. 19-24) may be congenital or may be brought about by improperly fitting footwear, particularly
shoes that are too narrow. At times the condition indicates an outward
projection of the great toe articulation or a drop in the longitudinal or
metatarsal arch. As in the case of hammer toes, surgery is the only cure,
but some therapeutic modalities, such as a whirlpool bath, can assist in
alleviating inflammation. Taping may prevent some of the contractural
tension within the sport shoe.

Figure 19-24

Overlapping toes.

Chronic and Overuse Syndromes

Because of the hard use that feet receive in many sports, they are prone
to chronic and overuse syndromes. This is especially true if weight-
transmission or biomechanical problems exist. Because distance running is
becoming increasingly popular, musculoskeletal problems of the feet are
also becoming more prevalent.

exostoses
Benign bony outgrowths that
protrude from the surface of a
bone and are usually capped
by cartilage.

Exostoses

Exostoses are benign bony outgrowths from the surface of a bone and are usually capped by cartilage. Sometimes called spurs, such outgrowths occur principally at the head of the first metatarsal bone on the dorsum of the foot (Fig. 19-25). In certain instances, what may at first appear to be an exostosis actually may be a subluxation of the joints between the metatarsal and cuneiform bones. The causes of exostoses are highly variable, including hereditary influences, faulty patterns of walking and running, excessive weight, joint impingements, and continual use of ill-fitting footwear.

Impingement exostoses   Impingement, one of the causes of exostoses, occurs when a joint is continually forced beyond the ranges of normal motion so that actual contact is effected by the bones comprising the joint. Continual contact creates inflammation and irritation. This eventually activates formation of new bone, which builds up to such a degree that the bones contact each other. Extreme dorsiflexion, such as when the foot is at the end of the support period immediately before the forward-carry, may cause exostoses to form on the anterior articular lip of the tibia and the top of the talus as a consequence of the impingement.

Symptoms and signs   Pain and tenderness are usually present and performance is impaired especially when the foot is in extreme dorsiflexion. This pain is usually apparent at the anterior aspect of the joint and may be severe enough to weaken the drive from the foot as it thrusts against the ground in the push-off, resulting in a loss of drive and speed.

Management   Some impingement spurring conditions are asymptomatic and obviously require no treatment. For cases of impingement that

Figure 19-25

Exostoses (bony overgrowths). X-ray film of a small plantar calcaneal exostotic spur.

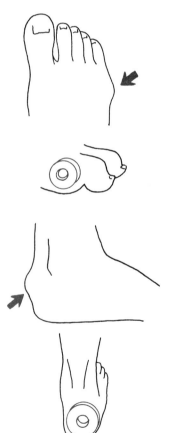

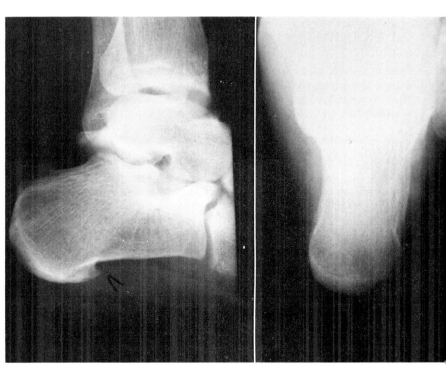

are symptomatic, surgery may be warranted to allow continued sports participation.[13]

Chronic irritation exostoses   Poorly fitting shoes or a chronic irritation may also predispose an area to exostoses, which usually appear either at the head of the fifth metatarsal bone or as a calcaneal spur. If an exostosis becomes chronically irritated or handicapping, surgery may be necessary. Sometimes protective doughnuts and custom-made pads provide relief.

Postcalcaneal Bursitis (Retrocalcaneal Bursitis)

A common bursitis of the foot is postcalcaneal bursitis located under the skin just above the attachment of the Achilles tendon (Fig. 19-26). It often occurs because of pressure and rubbing of the upper edge of a sports shoe. Irritation produces an inflamed, swollen area. At the first sign of this condition a soft resilient pad should be placed over the bursa site. If necessary, larger shoes with a softer heel contour should be worn.

Figure 19-26

Postcalcaneal bursitis.

Apophysitis of the Calcaneus (Sever's Disease)

Calcaneal **apophysitis,** or Sever's disease, is one of the many osteochondroses occurring to physically active adolescents between the ages of 8 and 13.[2] This condition can be compared to Osgood-Schlatter disease. Instead of the tibial tubercle, Sever's disease is a traction-type injury at the epiphysis of an **apophysis** (bone protusion) where the Achilles tendon attaches to the calcaneus. As with other such conditions, circulation to the epiphysis is disrupted, causing degeneration and sometimes fragmentation.

apophysitis
Inflammation of an apophysis

Symptoms and signs   Pain occurs at the posterior heel below the attachment of the Achilles tendon insertion of the child or adolescent athlete. Pain occurs during vigorous activity and does not continue at rest.

Management   This condition is usually completely resolved when the apophysis closes. Until such time, relief can be provided by restricting dorsiflexion of the foot. This can be accomplished by elevating both heels with a ¼-inch (0.6 cm) lift. Commonly, rest for several weeks will relieve the symptoms so that activity can be resumed. However, when symptoms do not resolve, a walking cast may be needed for 6 to 8 weeks.

apophysis
Bony outgrowth such as a
tubercle or tuberosity

Plantar Fasciitis (Heel Spur Syndrome)

Plantar fasciitis, or heel spur syndrome, is the most frequent hindfoot problem among distance runners.[16]

Etiological factors   Because of a narrow calcaneal attachment and broad insertions on the distal heads of the metatarsal bones, stress is centered at its narrow attachment. Stress is compounded by a tight Achilles tendon. This repeated irritation in time may cause a bone spur to form. Athletes with a cavus deformity or pronated foot are susceptible to plantar fasciitis.

Symptoms and signs   The athlete complains of anterior heel pain. On palpation the pain is usually localized on the plantar medial tuberosity of the calcaneus, radiating toward the sole of the foot. Often the pain intensifies when the athlete gets out of bed in the morning and first puts weight on the foot; however, the pain lessens after a few steps.[16] Pain also will be intensified when the toes and forefoot are forcibly dorsiflexed.

Management Management of this condition follows the same procedures as for a chronic foot strain, including longitudinal arch support or LowDye arch support. Of major importance is a vigorous regimen of Achilles tendon stretching, especially if the athlete's ankle cannot dorsiflex 10 to 15 degrees from a neutral position. Stretching should be conducted at least three times a day in the positions of straight-ahead, toe-in, and toe-out. Techniques for stretching should follow the procedures discussed on pp. 467-469. The athlete should wear a shoe that is not too stiff and has a heel that is elevated ½ to ¾ inch (1.3 to 1.9 cm) above the level of the sole.[16] An oral anti-inflammatory medication or one injection of a corticosteroid may be used.

Cuboid Syndrome

Approximately 4% of athletes with plantar foot pain have cuboid syndrome. It is associated with a pronated foot, which causes a partial displacement of the cuboid bone. The problem usually occurs in the early season after training on uneven surfaces or a sudden twist of the foot. The pain is localized on the lateral side of the foot in the region of the cuboid bone. The primary reason for pain is the stress placed on the long peroneal muscle when the foot is in pronation. In this position, the long peroneal muscle allows the cuboid bone to move medially downward.

Management of the cuboid syndrome involves manipulating the bone into a correct position, rest, and application of an arch pad and tape support or an orthotic device.

Stress Fractures of the Foot

Over 18% of all stress fractures in the body occur in the foot.[14]

Metatarsal stress fracture The most common stress fracture in the foot involves one or more metatarsal shafts. A fracture occurs most commonly to the second or third metatarsal bone (Fig. 19-27). It is seen in the runner who has suddenly changed patterns of training, such as increasing mileage, running hills, or running on a harder surface.

An athlete who has an atypical condition such as hallux valgus, flatfoot, or a short first metatarsal bone is more easily disposed toward incurring a stress fracture than is the individual whose foot is free of pathological or mechanical defects. A short first metatarsal bone is unable mechanically to make use of its strength and position to properly distribute the weight to the front part of the foot. Therefore, excessive pressure and additional weight are transferred to the second metatarsal bone, resulting in traumatic changes and, on occasion, fracture. An x-ray examination may not detect this condition, requiring a bone scan to be performed.

Management of the painful metatarsal stress fracture usually consists of 3 or 4 days of crutch walking or a short-leg walking cast for 1 to 2 weeks. Once the symptoms have significantly subsided, the athlete may resume weight bearing while walking. Shoes with firm soles should be worn. Tape support and therapy for swelling and tenderness should be given.[8]

Running should not be resumed for 3 to 4 weeks, with intensity and/

or mileage increased slowly. A more intense day should alternate with an easy day. The athlete must avoid toe running until bone tenderness is gone. Running should only be done on a soft, flat surface.

Calcaneal stress fracture   One of the bones of the foot known to develop stress fractures is the calcaneus. It is most prevalent among distance runners and is characterized by a sudden onset of constant pain in the plantar-calcaneal area. Pressure on the plantar-calcaneal tuberosity causes severe pain. The fracture fails to appear on x-ray examination for 4 to 6 weeks. Management is usually conservative for the first 2 or 3 weeks, including rest, elastic wrap compression, elevation, and active range of motion exercises of the foot and ankle.[16] After 3 weeks and when pain subsides, activity within pain limits can be resumed gradually, with the athlete wearing a cushioned shoe.[16]

Hypertrophy of the second metatarsal bone   Milers and other distance runners who have engaged in strenuous training and conditioning over a considerable span of time often suffer from hypertrophy of the second metatarsal bone. It is believed that the condition is caused by the strong thrust of the ball of the foot against the running surface during the pushing-off phase. As the foot begins its thrust, it is in a position of extreme dorsiflexion, usually with the center of gravity passing through or just forward of the ball of the foot. The extensor muscles of the foot and

Figure 19-27

Stress fractures of the third metatarsal bone.

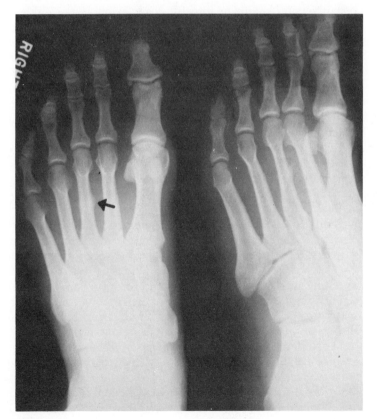

ankle bring maximal pressure to bear on the heads of the metatarsal bones. The resulting forces place great stress on this area; consequently, the second metatarsal bone, which receives a considerable share of the force, tends to enlarge or hypertrophy. This response illustrates the structure-function principle.

Chronic Ankle Tendon Condition

Achilles tendon bursitis and tendinitis   Achilles tendon bursitis and tendinitis usually occur from overstretching the Achilles tendon, resulting in constant inflammation of the Achilles bursa. This condition is chronic, developing gradually over a long period of time, and takes many days—sometimes weeks and even months—to heal properly. An excellent therapeutic approach is continued application of heat in as many forms as possible, especially by means of penetrating therapy such as ultrasound. All activity should be held to a minimum, and heel lifts should be placed in the shoes to relieve the Achilles tendon of as much tension as possible. After a workout, the tendon should be cooled down with ice packs or ice massage. Static heel cord stretching is an excellent adjunct to heat therapy.

Peroneal tendon subluxation   The long and short peroneal tendons pass through a common groove located behind the lateral malleolus. The tendon is held in place by the peroneal retinaculum. A moderate to severe inversion sprain or forceful dorsiflexion of the ankle can tear the peroneal retinaculum, allowing the peroneal tendon to tear out of its groove. A common source of this injury is when an athlete suddenly steps into a hole, forcing the foot into dorsiflexion and eversion.

Symptoms and signs   The athlete complains that in running or jumping, the tendons snap out of the groove and then back in when stress is released. Eversion against manual resistance will often replicate the subluxation. The athlete experiences recurrent pain, snapping, and ankle instability.

Management   Surgery may be warranted to repair the retinaculum; however, if not performed in the early stages, tissue atrophy may make it irreparable.[9] A more conservative approach is to stabilize the tendon into its groove by means of a horseshoe pad that surrounds the lateral malleolus and is taped into place.

Anterior tibial tendinitis   Anterior tibial tendinitis is a common condition of athletes or joggers who run downhill for an extended period of time. There is point tenderness over the anterior tibial tendon.

The athlete should be advised to rest or at least decrease the running time and distance and to avoid hills. In more serious cases ice packs, coupled with stretching before and after running, should help reduce the symptoms. A daily strengthening program also should be conducted. Oral anti-inflammatory medications may be required.

Posterior tibial tendinitis   Posterior tibial tendinitis is a common overuse condition among runners with hypermobility or pathologically pronated feet. As discussed earlier, one of the major functions of the posterior tibial muscle is to pull the first metatarsal bone into plantar flexion. When there is major foot pronation or hypermobility the posterior tibial tendon becomes overly stressed in its efforts to stabilize the first metatarsal bone.

Management consists of correcting the problem of pronation with a LowDye-type taping (p. 503) or an orthotic device. Measures such as rest or reducing the running distance should be taken to reduce the inflammation. Ice application before and after activity coupled with stretching should reduce the symptoms. A daily strengthening routine should be engaged. Anti-inflammatory medication might be decided on in more serious cases.

Peroneal tendinitis Although not particularly common, peroneal tendinitis can be a problem in athletes with pes cavus. Because in pes cavus the foot tends to be placed in constant supination, which is resisted by the peroneal tendon, a chronic inflammation can arise. Athletes who constantly bear weight on the outside of the foot also place chronic stress on the peroneal tendon.

As with all types of tendinitis in the lower extremities, the mechanics of walking and running should be observed. Where faulty mechanics occur such as running on the outside of the foot, realignment with an orthotic device or taping should be employed. In some cases a lateral heel wedge may help to reduce pain and discomfort. As with the other ankle tendons that are overused, the athlete with peroneal tendinitis should reduce activity, use ice routinely, and stretch and strengthen the tendon through eversion exercise (Fig. 19-28).

REPETITIVE AND OVERUSE LEG PROBLEMS

A number of problems of the leg can be attributed to repetitive and overuse. Three of these conditions are the medial shin stress syndrome (shinsplints), exercise-induced compartment compression syndromes, and stress fractures.

Medial Shin Stress Syndrome (Shinsplints)

Shinsplints is a general term applied to a variety of conditions that seasonally plague many athletes. It is characterized by pain and irritation in the shin region of the leg and is usually attributed to an inflammation lo-

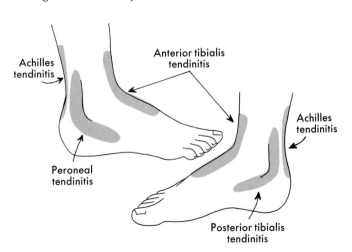

Figure 19-28

Common tendinitis of the foot and ankle region.

calized primarily in the tendon of the posterior tibial muscle or long flexor muscles of the toes. How or why inflammation is produced in this area is often a mystery. It has been believed that chronic medial shin pain was a compartment syndrome; however, recent studies have discounted this view. Speculations advanced as to the cause include faulty posture alignment, falling arches, muscle fatigue, overuse stress, body chemical imbalance, or a lack of proper reciprocal muscle coordination between the anterior and posterior aspects of the leg. All these factors, in various combinations or singly, may contribute to shinsplints.

The pathological process of this condition is regarded as a myositis or periostitis that occurs either acutely, as in preseason preparation, or chronically, developing slowly throughout the entire competitive season. One should approach this situation through deductive thinking. First, all information as to why a certain athlete may have acquired shinsplints must be gathered—examples include changing from a hard gymnasium floor activity to a soft field sport, or exhibiting general fatigue after a strenuous season. Second, one should examine the athlete for possible structural body weaknesses. From this information an empirical analysis can be made as to the probable cause of shinsplints. However, persistent shin irritation and incapacitation must be referred to the physician for thorough examination. Conditions such as stress fractures, muscle herniations, or acute anterior tibial compartment syndromes (a severe swelling within the anterior fascia chamber) may resemble the symptoms of shinsplints.

Symptoms and Signs

Jackson[7] suggests four grades of pain that can be attributed to shinsplints: grade I pain occurring after athletic activity, grade II pain occurring before and after activity but not affecting performance; grade III pain occurring before, during, and after athletic activity and affecting performance; and grade IV pain, so severe that performance is impossible.

Management

Management of shinsplints is as varied as its etiology. Constant heat in the form of whirlpools, analgesic balm packs, and ultrasound therapy give positive results and, together with supportive taping and gradual stretching, afford a good general approach to the problem.

Ice massage to the shin region and taking two aspirins have been found to be beneficial before a workout.[7] Ice massage is applied for 10 minutes or until erythema takes place. Ice application should be followed by a gradual stretch to both the anterior and posterior aspects of the leg directly after the massage. Gradual stretching should be a routine procedure before and after physical activity for all athletes who have a history of shinsplints. Exercise must also accompany any therapy program, with special considerations of the calf muscle and the plantar and dorsiflexion movements of the foot.

Exercise-Induced Compartment Compression Syndromes

As discussed in Chapter 18, the leg is made up of four compartments. Each compartment is bound by fascial sheaths or by fascial sheaths and bone (see Fig. 18-43). The anterior compartment contains the anterior tibial muscle, deep peroneal nerve, long extensor muscles of the toes, and both the ante-

TAPING FOR MEDIAL SHINSPLINTS

Proper taping can afford some relief of the symptoms of shinsplints (Fig. 19-29).

Materials needed: One roll of 1½-inch (3.75 cm) linen or elastic tape and adherent.

Position of athlete: The athlete sits on a table with the knee bent and the foot flat on the table. The purpose of this position is to fully relax the muscles of the lower leg.

Position of the operator: The operator stands facing the affected leg.

Procedure

1. The operator first applies two anchor tape strips. The first anchor strip is applied to the anterolateral aspect of the ankle and lower leg and the second to the posterolateral aspect of the midcalf.
2. Starting at the lowest end of the first anchor, run a strip of tape to the back of the lower leg, spiraling it over the shin to attach on the lower end of the second anchor strip. Apply three strips of tape in this manner, with each progressively moving upward on the leg. As each strip comes across the strip, an effort should be made to pull the muscle toward the tibia.
3. After three pieces of tape have been applied, their ends are locked by one or two cross-strips.
4. After the procedure has been completed, an elastic wrap can be applied in a spiral fashion.

Figure 19-29

Taping for shinsplints.

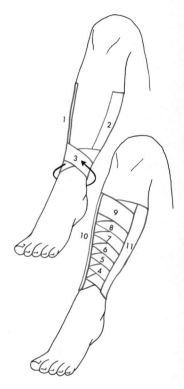

rior tibial artery and vein. The lateral compartment is made up of the superficial peroneal nerve and the long and short and peroneal muscles. Posteriorly, the leg has a deep and superficial compartment. The deep posterior compartment comprises posterior the tibial muscle and flexor muscles of the toes, as well as the peroneal artery and vein, posterior tibial artery and vein, and tibial nerve. The superficial posterior compartment is made up of the soleus muscle and gastrocnemius and plantar tendons.

The exercise-induced compartment compression syndrome is most frequently seen among runners and in sports such as soccer, which involve extensive running.[3,10] The compartments most often affected are the anterior and deep posterior, with the anterior having by far the highest incidence. On occasion, the lateral compartment may be involved.

The compartment compression syndrome occurs when the tissue fluid pressure has increased because of the confines of fascia and/or bone adversely compressing muscles, blood vessels, and nerves. With the increase in fluid pressure, muscle ischemia occurs that could lead to permanent disability.[12]

The exercise-induced compartment compression syndrome is classified as acute or chronic or recurrent. The first type is an acute syndrome and is a medical emergency, requiring immediate decompression to prevent permanent damage. The acute exercise-induced compartment compression syndrome resembles a fracture or a severe contusion.

The second type is one that is chronic or recurrent. Internal pressures rise slowly during exercise and subside after discontinuance of exercise. If

Exercise-induced
compartment compression
syndromes are most
commonly seen in runners
and soccer players.

MANAGEMENT PLAN FOR MEDIAL TIBIAL STRESS SYNDROME (SHINSPLINTS)

Injury Situation
A female college field hockey player at the end of the competition season began to feel severe discomfort in the medial aspect of the right shin.

Symptoms and Signs
The athlete complained that her shin seemed to ache all the time but became more intense after practice or a game. On palpation there was severe point tenderness about 2 inches (5 cm) in length, beginning 4½ inches (11.25 cm) from the tip of the medial malleolus. The pain was the most severe along the medial posterior edge of the tibia. Further evaluation showed the athlete to have pronated feet. X-ray examination showed no indication of stress fracture; therefore, it was considered to be medial shin stress syndrome, or shinsplints, involving the long flexor muscle of the great toe and the posterior tibial muscle.

Management Plan

1

Management Phase	GOAL: To almost completely reduce pain and point tenderness Estimated length of time (ELT): 1-2 weeks
Therapy	IMMEDIATE CARE: Ice pack (5-15 min) or ice massage (7 min) followed by stretching 3-4 times daily LowDye taping or orthosis is applied to the arch to correct pronation during weight bearing
Exercise Rehabilitation	Static stretch of Achilles tendon and anterior part of low leg hold stretch 30 sec (2-3 times); repeat set 3-4 times daily General body maintenance exercises are conducted if they do not aggravate injury, 3 times weekly

2

Management Phase	GOAL: Symptom free ELT: 1 week
Therapy	FOLLOW-UP CARE: Ice pack (5-15 min) or ice massage (7 min) and/or ultrasound (0.5-0.75 watts/cm^2 (5-10 min) 2-3 times daily Continue to wear arch taping or orthosis when bearing weight
Exercise Rehabilitation	Static stretch of lower leg followed by arch and plantar flexion exercises Towel gather (10 repetitions, 1-3 sets); progress from no resistance to 10 lb resistance, 3 times daily Towel scoop (10 repetitions, 1-3 sets); progress to 10 lb, 3 times daily Marble pickup, 3 times daily General body maintenance exercises are conducted if they do not aggravate injury, 3 times weekly

3	Management Phase	GOAL: To return to jogging ELT: 1-2 weeks
	Therapy	Cold application (5-15 min) to shin when stretching before jogging and after jogging, once daily
	Exercise Rehabilitation	Perform static stretch of lower leg before and after running, once daily Walk/jog on flat surface and avoid banked or crowned surfaces, once daily Athlete must cease activity immediately if any shin symptoms are felt
4	Management Phase	GOAL: To return to running ELT: 1 week
	Therapy	Cold application (5-15 min) before prerun stretch and again after running, once daily
	Exercise Rehabilitation	Resume training: Walk 1 mile in 15 min; then walk and jog to 8-min pace, once daily Resume running; try to run in toe-in manner
5	Management Phase	GOAL: Return to full-field hockey activity ELT: 1-2 weeks
	Therapy	Athlete practices cryokinetics before and after practice, once daily
	Exercise Rehabilitation	Athlete engages in full leg, strength, and endurance training along with reentry skill practice, once daily

Criteria for Full Recovery

1. Leg is symptom free after prolonged running.
2. The medial longitudinal arch has been strengthened along with correction of foot pronation through taping or an orthosis.

exercise is not stopped in time, an acute emergency may occur. In chronic exercise-induced compartment compression syndrome, there is a constriction of blood vessels, producing ischemia and pain, but seldom neurological involvement.

Chronic or Recurrent Compartment Compression Syndrome

The chronic or recurrent compartment compression sydrome is often confused by the coach or trainer as being shinsplints. It also may be confused with a stress fracture.

Symptoms and signs   The athlete commonly complains of an ache or sharp pain and pressure in the region of the anterior compartment on performing a particular activity. The symptoms subside or go away completely on resting. When major symptoms are present, weakness in foot and toe extension and numbness in the dorsal region may occur.[12]

Management   Often initial symptoms are aided by the application of ice and rest. However, recurrent conditions may require a surgical release of the associated fascia. Once surgery is performed, the athlete is allowed to return home and begin a light program of exercise in 10 days.

Stress Fracture of the Tibia or Fibula

Stress fractures to the tibia or fibula are a common overuse stress condition, especially among distance runners. Like many other overuse syndromes, athletes who have biomechanical foot problems are more prone to stress fractures of the lower leg. Athletes who have hypermobile pronated feet are more susceptible to fibular stress fracture, whereas those with rigid pes cavus are more prone to tibial stress fractures.[9] Runners frequently develop a stress fracture in the lower third of the leg; ballet dancers more commonly acquire one in the middle third.

The athlete with hypermobile pronated feet is more susceptible to fibular stress fracture. The athlete with rigid pes cavus is more susceptible to tibial fractures.

Symptoms and Signs

The athlete complains of pain in the leg that is more intense on activity but relieved when resting. There is usually point tenderness, but it may be difficult to discern the difference between bone pain and soft tissue pain. One technique for distinguishing bone pain from soft pain is bone percussion. The fibula or tibia is tapped firmly above the level of tenderness. Vibration travels along the bone to the fracture, which may respond with pain. Another percussive technique is to hit the heel upward from below; pain occurs at the fracture site.

Diagnosis of a stress fracture may be extremely difficult. X-ray examination may or may not detect a bone defect. A bone scan 1 to 3 hours after injection of radioactive material may reflect the stress fracture, but does not clearly distinguish between a fracture or periostitis.

Management

The following regimen may be used for a stress fracture of the leg:
1. Discontinue running or other stressful locomotor activities for at least 6 weeks.
2. When pain is severe, use crutch walking or wear a cast.
3. Weight bearing may be resumed as pain subsides.
4. Bicycling may be used before returning to running.

5. After at least 6 weeks, and a pain-free period for at least 2 weeks, running can begin again.[1]
6. Biomechanical foot correction should be made.

RELATED PROBLEMS

Although lower extremity stress injuries are usually concentrated in the foot, ankle, or leg, other body areas also can become involved. This is especially true for long-distance runners. Repetitive use and overuse of the lower extremity, particularly when there are biomechanical and subsequent weight-transmission discrepancies, can lead to problems in other regions of the body. Some of the more prevalent areas are the knee and hip.

The Knee

A common site for distance runners to have a stress problem is in the knee. In some cases there may be chronic pain and swelling in the knee joint itself. This might indicate a meniscus tear or degenerative articular cartilage changes. More commonly, it is patellar tendonitis, chondromalacia, iliotibial band tendinitis, or pes anserinus tendinitis (see Chapter 20).

The Thigh and Hip

As with the knee, the thigh and hip can sustain painful conditions that are attributed to overuse. Two conditions are on the rise in incidence because of the popularity of running. These are trochanteric bursitis and hamstring strain.

Running can place a strain on the middle gluteal muscles and the iliotibial band. When the athlete is in the stand phase, the middle gluteal muscle contracts to stabilize the pelvis. A leg-length discrepancy places additional stress on the hip that may cause the middle gluteal muscle to irritate the trochanteric bursa. The iliotibial band crossing the trochanter of the femur also can cause bursal irritation[1] (see Chapter 21).

The hamstring muscles can be adversely irritated with running. After contraction of the quadriceps muscles at heel-strike, the hamstring muscle contracts. If there is a significant difference in strength between the quadriceps muscle and the hamstring muscle or the athlete overstrides, forcing the hamstring to repeatedly contract from an extreme length, injury may occur (see Chapter 21).

Other injuries arising from the repetitive running motion are adductor groin strains or inflammation of the pubis symphysis (osteitis pubis). A foot strike that is too wide from the center line or a pelvis that abducts excessively can lead to a chronic adductor strain or osteitis pubis (see Chapter 21).

> A running foot strike that is too wide can lead to a chronic adductor strain or osteitis pubis.

Running despite constant pain is foolish. Major problems such as stress or avulsion fractures may be present. Any continuous pain over a period of time should be referred for x-ray or bone scan examination.

REFERENCES

1. Birnbaum, J.S.: The musculoskeletal manual, New York, 1982, Academic Press, Inc.
2. Cailliet, R.: Foot and ankle pain, Philadelphia, 1968, F.A. Davis Co.
3. Galstad, U.A.: Anterior tibial compartment syndrome, Ath. Train. **14:**3, 1979.
4. Halback, J.: Pronated foot disorders, Ath. Train. **16:**53, Spring 1981.

5. Hoerner, E.F.: Foot and ankle injuries. In Vinger, P.F., and Hoerner, E.F.: Sports injuries: the unthwarted epidemic, Boston, 1982, John Wright, PSG, Inc.

6. Hoppenfeld, S.: Physical examination of the spine and extremities, New York, 1976, Appleton-Century-Crofts.

7. Jackson, D.W.: Shinsplints: an update, Phys. Sportsmed. **6**:10, 1978.

8. James, S.L., et al.: Injuries to runners, Am. J. Sports Med. **6**:2, 1978.

9. Kulund, D.N.: The injured athlete, Philadelphia, 1982, J.B. Lippincott Co.

10. Leach, R.E., and Corbett, M.: Anterior tibial compartment syndrome in soccer players, Am. J. Sports Med. **7**:4, 1979.

11. Mann, R.A.: Biomechanics of running. In Mack, R.P. (editor): Symposium on the foot and leg in running sports, American Academy of Orthopaedic Surgeons, St. Louis, 1982, The C.V. Mosby Co.

12. Mubarak, S., and Hargens, A.: Exertional compartment syndromes. In Mack, R.P. (editor): Symposium on the foot and leg in running sports, American Academy of Orthopaedic Surgeons, St. Louis, 1982, The C.V. Mosby Co.

13. O'Donoghue, D.H.: Treatment of injuries to athletes, ed. 4, Philadelphia, 1984, W.B. Saunders Co.

14. Orava, S., et al.: Stress fractures caused by physical exercise, Acta Orthop. Scand. **49**:1, 1978.

15. Parks, R.M.: Biomechanics of the foot and lower extremity. In Appenzeller, O., and Atkinson, R. (editors): Sports medicine, Baltimore, 1981, Urban & Schwarzenberg, Inc.

16. Waller, J.F.: Hindfoot and midfoot problems of the runner. In Mack, R.P. (editor): Symposium on the foot and leg in running sports, American Academy of Orthopaedic Surgeons, St. Louis, 1982, The C.V. Mosby Co.

ADDITIONAL SOURCES

Allen, R.C.: Shin splints, Ath. J. **60**:59, 1979.

Andrews, J.R.: Overuse syndromes of the lower extremity, Symposium on Olympic sports medicine, Clinics in sports medicine, vol. 2, no. 1, Philadelphia, March 1983, W.B. Saunders Co.

Berman, D.L.: Etiology and management of hallus valgus in athletes, Phys. Sportsmed. **10**:103, Aug. 1982.

Bonci, C.M.: Adhesive strapping techniques, Symposium on ankle and foot problems in the athlete, Clinics in sports medicine, vol. 1, no. 1, Philadelphia, March 1982, W.B. Saunders Co.

Cavanagh, P.R.: The shoe-ground interface in running. In Mack, R.P. (editor): Symposium on the foot and leg in running sports, American Academy of Orthopaedic Surgeons, St. Louis, 1982, The C.V. Mosby Co.

Clement, D.B., et al.: A survey of overuse running injuries, Phys. Sportsmed. **9**:47, May 1981.

Deutsch, B., and Fashower, R.: Case report: anterior compartment syndrome, Athletic Training **17**:211, Fall 1982.

Drez, D., Jr.: Forefoot problems in runners. In Mack, R.P.: Symposium on the foot and leg in running sports, American Academy of Orthopaedic Surgeons, St. Louis, 1982, The C.V. Mosby Co.

Kotwick, J.E.: Biomechanics of the foot and ankle, Symposium on ankle and foot problems in the athlete, Clinics in sports medicine, vol. 1, no. 1, Philadelphia, March 1982, W.B. Saunders Co.

Newell, S.G., and Woodle, A.: Cuboid syndrome, Phys. Sportsmed. **1**:71, April 1981.

Ramig, D., et al.: The foot and its relationship to gait: a series of articles and editorial comments, J. Orthop. Sports Phys. Ther. **2**:48, Fall 1980.

Salter, R.B.: Textbook of disorders and injuries of the musculoskeletal system, ed. 2, Baltimore, 1983, The Williams & Wilkins Co.

Shields, C.L., Jr.: Achilles tendon injuries and disabling conditions, Phys. Sportsmed. **10**:77, Dec. 1982.

Torg, J.S., et al.: The recognition and management of basic "overuse syndromes," Chicago, Ill., Teach'em, Inc. (Cassette.)

Chapter 20

THE KNEE AND RELATED STRUCTURES

When you finish this chapter, you should be able to

Describe the normal structural and functional knee anatomy and relate it to major sports injuries

Evaluate the knee and related structures following injury

Establish a knee injury prevention program

Discuss etiological factors, symptoms and signs, and management procedures for the major knee joint conditions and related structures

Muscles and ligaments provide the main source of stability in the knee.

The knee is considered one of the most complex joints in the human body. Because so many sports place extreme stress on the knee, it is also one of the most traumatized joints. The knee, commonly considered a hinge joint (ginglymus), performs two principal actions, flexion and extension. Medial and lateral rotations of the tibia are possible but only to a limited degree. Since the knee is extremely weak in terms of its bony arrangement, compensation is provided through the firm support of ligaments and muscles (Fig. 20-1). The knee is designed primarily for stability in weight bearing and mobility in locomotion; however, it is especially unstable laterally and medially (Fig. 20-2).

ANATOMY
Structural Relationships
The distal end of the femur expands and forms the convex *lateral* and *medial condyles,* which are designed to articulate with the tibia and the patella. The articular surface of the medial condyle is longer from front to back than is the surface of the lateral condyle. Anteriorly, the two condyles form a hollowed-out area to receive the patella. The upper end of the tibia, designed to receive the condyles of the femur, consists of two *tuberosities,* which are divided posteriorly by a groove called the popliteal notch. Superiorly, the tuberosities have two shallow concavities that articulate with their respective femoral condyles. Separating these concavities or articular facets is a roughened area where the cruciate ligaments attach and from which a process commonly known as the tibial spine arises. The *patella* is the largest sesamoid bone in the body and lies within the tendon of the quadriceps muscles. Its function is to give anterior protection to the knee joint and increased leverage to the knee on extension. All the articular sur-

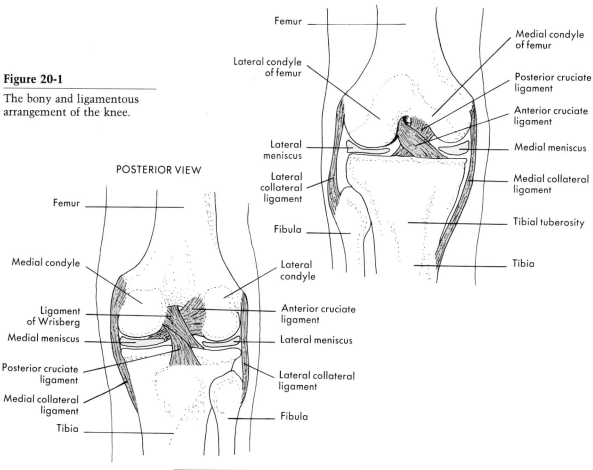

ANTERIOR VIEW

Femur

Lateral condyle
of femur

Lateral
meniscus

Lateral
collateral
ligament

Fibula

Medial condyle
of femur

Posterior cruciate
ligament

Anterior cruciate
ligament

Medial meniscus

Medial collateral
ligament

Tibial tuberosity

Tibia

POSTERIOR VIEW

Femur

Medial condyle

Ligament
of Wrisberg

Medial meniscus

Posterior cruciate
ligament

Medial collateral
ligament

Tibia

Lateral
condyle

Anterior cruciate
ligament

Lateral meniscus

Lateral collateral
ligament

Fibula

Figure 20-1

The bony and ligamentous
arrangement of the knee.

Figure 20-2

The knee is a highly
complicated joint that is
often traumatized in
competitive sports.

faces of the femur, tibia, and patella are covered by *hyaline cartilage,* a smooth and pearly substance that serves mainly to reduce friction.

Articulations

The knee joint consists of several articulations: those between the two femoral condyles and menisci, between the tibia and menisci, and between the patella and femur. The condyles of the femur move in a shallow depression, formed by the tibia and additionally deepened by two semilunar cartilages (menisci).

Menisci

The *menisci* (Fig. 20-3) are two oval-shaped (semilunar) fibrocartilages that deepen the articular facets of the tibia and cushion any stresses placed on the knee joint. They are located medially and laterally on the tibial tuberosity.

Medial meniscus   The medial meniscus is a C-shaped fibrocartilage, the circumference of which is attached firmly to the medial articular facet of the tibia and to the joint capsule by the coronary ligament. Posteriorly, it is also attached to fibers of the semimembranous muscle.

Lateral meniscus   The *lateral meniscus* forms an almost complete O and is attached to the lateral articular facet on the superior aspect of the tibia. The consistency of the menisci is much like that of the intervertebral disks. They are held much less rigidly, however, being loose except at the outer edges, which are by the anterior and posterior horns. The lateral meniscus also attaches loosely to the lateral articular capsule and to the popliteal tendon. The *Wrisberg ligament* is the part of the lateral meniscus that projects upward, close to the attachment of the posterior or cruciate ligament. The *transverse ligament* joins the anterior portions of the lateral and medial menisci.

Meniscal blood supply   Blood is supplied to each meniscus by the medial genicular artery. Although the menisci are, for the most part, **avascular,** the outer third does receive direct circulation. The inner two thirds of the menisci receive nourishment from being bathed by synovial fluid (Figs. 20-3 and 20-8).

Generally the meniscus has a poor blood supply.

avascular
Devoid of blood circulation

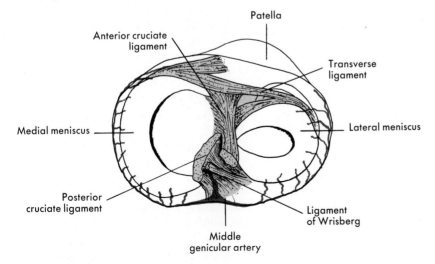

Figure 20-3

Menisci of the knee.

Stabilizing Ligaments

The major ligaments of the knee, primarily the cruciate, capsular, and collateral, are secondary to the musculature in providing joint stability.

The cruciate ligaments The *cruciate ligaments* account for a considerable amount of knee stability. They are two ligamentous bands that cross one another within the joint cavity of the knee. The *anterior cruciate ligament* attaches below and in front of the tibia; then, passing backward, it attaches laterally to the inner surface of the lateral condyle. The *posterior cruciate ligament*, the stronger of the two and primary stabilizer of the knee, crosses from the back of the tibia in an upward, forward, and medial direction and attaches to the anterior portion of the lateral surface of the medial condyle of the femur.

The anterior cruciate ligament The anterior cruciate ligament comprises three twisted sections: the anteromedial, intermediate, and posterolateral sections. In general, the anterior cruciate ligament prevents the femur from moving posteriorly during weight bearing. It also stabilizes against the tibia to prevent abnormal internal and external rotation.

When the knee is fully extended, the anteromedial section of the cruciate ligament is tight. In flexion the anteromedial fibers loosen and the posterolateral fibers tighten.[29]

The posterior cruciate ligament Some portion of the posterior cruciate ligament is taut throughout the full range of motion. It acts as a drag during the gliding phase of motion and resists internal rotation of the tibia. In general, the posterior cruciate ligament prevents hyperextension of the knee and femur, sliding forward during weight bearing.

Capsular and collateral ligaments Additional stabilization is provided the knee by the capsular and collateral ligaments. Besides stability, they also direct movement in a correct path. Although they move in synchrony, they are divided into the medial and lateral complexes.

Medial collateral ligament The superficial position of the medial (tibial) collateral ligament is separate from the deeper capsular ligament at the joint line. It attaches above on the medial epicondyle of the femur and below on the tibia, just beneath the attachment of the pes anserinus. The posterior aspect of the ligament blends into the deep posterior capsular ligament and semimembranous muscle. Fibers of the semimembranous muscle go through the capsule and attach to the posterior aspect of the medial meniscus, pulling it backward during knee flexion. Some of its fibers are taut through flexion and extension. Its major purpose is to prevent the knee from valgus and external rotating forces.

Deep medial capsular ligaments The deep medial capsular ligament is divided into three parts: the anterior, medial, and posterior capsular ligaments. The *anterior capsular ligament* connects with the extension mechanism and the medial meniscus via the coronary ligament. It relaxes during knee extension and tightens during knee flexion. The primary purposes of the *medial capsular ligaments* are to attach the medial meniscus to the femur and to allow the tibia to move on the meniscus inferiorly. The *posterior capsular ligament* is sometimes called the posterior oblique ligament and attaches to the posterior medial aspect of the meniscus and intersperses with the semimembranous muscle.

Lateral collateral ligament and related structures   The lateral (fibular) collateral ligament is a round, fibrous cord shaped like a pencil. It is attached to the lateral epicondyle of the femur and to the head of the fibula. The lateral collateral ligament is taut during knee extension but relaxed in flexion.

Another stabilizing ligament of importance is the *arcuate ligament.* It is formed by a thickening of the lateral articular capsule. Its posterior aspect attaches to the fascia of the popliteal muscle and the posterior horn of the lateral meniscus.

Other structures that stabilize the knee laterally are the iliotibial band, popliteal muscle, and biceps muscle of the thigh. The iliotibial band, stemming from the tensor muscle of the fascia lata, attaches to the lateral epicondyle of the femur and lateral tibial tubercle. It becomes tense both on extension and flexion. The popliteal muscle stabilizes the knee during flexion and, when contracting, protects the lateral meniscus by pulling it posteriorly.

The biceps muscle of the thigh also stabilizes the knee laterally by inserting into the fibular head, iliotibial band, and capsule.

Synovial Membrane and Bursae

The synovial membrane lines all of the articular surfaces and is internal to the cruciate ligaments. It is a highly vascularized, tubelike tissue, that extends upward along the anterior aspect of the femur and forms the suprapatellar bursa (Fig. 20-4).

Bursae are those protective synovia-filled sacs located in tissue sites that otherwise would become irritated because of friction (Fig. 20-5). The knee has at least eleven bursae situated at points where friction is highly probable:

1. Suprapatellar   4. Prepatellar
2. Popliteal   5. Superficial infrapatellar
3. Medial gastrocnemius 6. Infrapatellar

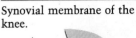

Figure 20-4

Synovial membrane of the knee.

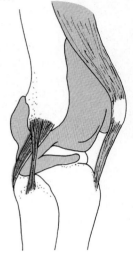

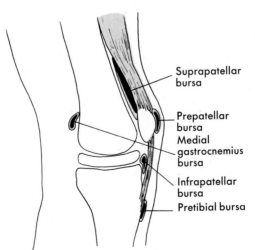

Figure 20-5

Common bursae of the knee.

Suprapatellar
bursa

Prepatellar
bursa
Medial
gastrocnemius
bursa

Infrapatellar
bursa

Pretibial bursa

7. Between the semimembranous and gastrocnemius muscles
8. Between the semimembranous muscle and tibial condyle
9. Between the lateral collateral ligament and biceps muscle of the thigh
10. Between the medial collateral ligament and biceps muscle of the thigh
11. Between the medial collateral ligament and pes anserinus

Patella

The patella is the largest sesamoid bone in the human body. It is located in the tendon of the quadriceps femoris muscle and is divided into three medial facets and a lateral facet that articulate with the femur (Fig. 20-6). The lateral aspect of the patella is wider than the medial aspect. The patella articulates between the concavity provided by the femoral condyles. Tracting within this groove depends on the pull of the quadriceps muscle, infrapatellar ligament, depth of the femoral condyles, and shape of the patella.

Knee Musculature

For the knee to function properly, a number of muscles must work together in a highly complex fashion. The following is a list of knee actions and the muscles that initiate them (Fig. 20-7):

1. Knee flexion is executed by the biceps muscle of the thigh, semitendinous, semimembranous, gracilis, sartorius, gastrocnemius, popliteal and plantar muscles.
2. Knee extension is executed by the quadriceps muscle of the thigh, consisting of three vasti—the vastus medialis, vastus lateralis, and vastus intermedius—and by the rectus femoris.
3. Outward rotation of the tibia is controlled by the biceps muscle of the thigh—the anterior cruciate ligament and the quadriceps also control external rotation.

Figure 20-6

Patella.

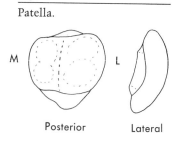

M   L

Posterior   Lateral

Major actions of the knee:
Flexion
Extension
Gliding
Rotation

Figure 20-7

Musculature of the knee.

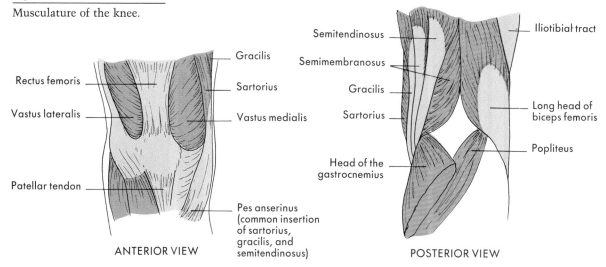

Rectus femoris

Vastus lateralis

Patellar tendon

Gracilis

Sartorius

Vastus medialis

Pes anserinus
(common insertion
of sartorius,
gracilis, and
semitendinosus)

ANTERIOR VIEW

Semitendinosus

Semimembranosus

Gracilis

Sartorius

Head of the
gastrocnemius

Iliotibial tract

Long head of
biceps femoris

Popliteus

POSTERIOR VIEW

4. Inward rotation is accomplished by the popliteal, semitendinous, semimembranous, sartorius, and gracilis muscles. Rotation of the tibia is limited and can occur only when the knee is in a flexed position.

Blood and Nerve Supply

The main blood supply of the knee consists of the popliteal artery, which stems from the femoral artery. From the popliteal artery, five branches supply the knee: the medial and lateral superior genicular, middle genicular, and medial and lateral inferior genicular arteries. The primary nerves supplying the knee are the tibial and common peroneal nerves (Fig. 20-8).

Functional Anatomy

The primary actions of the knee are flexion, extension, gliding, and rotation. Secondary movements consist of a slight internal (medial) and external (lateral) rotation of the tibia. The movements of flexion and extension take place above the menisci, whereas rotation is performed below the menisci. Rotation is caused mainly by the greater length of the medial condyle of the femur, which rolls forward more than does the lateral condyle.

The capsular ligaments are taut during full extension and to some extent relaxed during flexion. This is particularly true of the lateral collateral ligament; however, portions of the medial collateral ligament relax as flexion occurs. Relaxation of the more superficial collateral ligaments allows rotation to occur. In contrast, the deeper capsular ligament tightens to prevent excessive rotation of the tibia.

During extension there is external rotation of the tibia during the last 15 degrees of which the anterior cruciate ligament unwinds. In full extension the anterior cruciate ligament is taut and loosens during flexion. As the femur glides on the tibia, the posterior cruciate ligament becomes taut and prevents further gliding. In general, the anterior cruciate ligament stops excessive external rotation, stabilizes the knee in full extension, and prevents hyperextension. The posterior cruciate ligament prevents internal ro-

Figure 20-8

Knee blood and nerve supply.

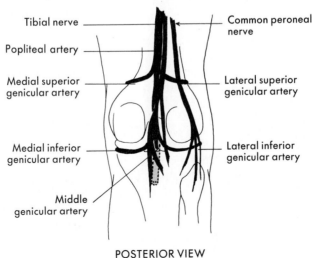

Tibial nerve

Common peroneal nerve

Popliteal artery

Medial superior genicular artery

Lateral superior genicular artery

Medial inferior genicular artery

Lateral inferior genicular artery

Middle genicular artery

POSTERIOR VIEW

tation, guides the knee in flexion, and acts as a drag during the initial glide phase of flexion.

In complete flexion, approximately 140 degrees, the range of knee movement is limited by the extremely shortened position of the hamstring muscles, the extensibility of the quadriceps muscles, and the bulk of the hamstring muscles. In this position the femoral condyles rest on their corresponding menisci at a point that permits a small degree of inward rotation.

EVALUATING THE KNEE JOINT

It is the responsibility of the team physician to diagnose the severity and exact nature of a knee injury. Although the physician is charged with the final evaluation, the coach or athletic trainer is usually the first person to observe the injury; therefore he or she is charged with initial evaluation and immediate care. The most important aspect of understanding what pathological process has taken place is to become familiar with the traumatic sequence and mechanisms of injury, either through having seen the injury occur or through learning its history(Fig. 20-9). Often the team physician is not present when the injury occurs, and the athletic trainer must relate the pertinent information.

Major Complaints

To determine the history and major complaints involved in a knee injury, the following questions should be asked:

Current Injury

1. What were you doing when the knee was hurt?
2. What position was your body in?
3. Did the knee collapse?
4. Did you hear a noise or feel any sensation at the time of injury, such as a pop or crunch? (A pop could indicate an anterior cruciate tear, a crunch could be a sign of a torn meniscus, and a tearing sensation might indicate a capsular tear.)
5. Could you move the knee immediately after the injury? If not, was it locked in a bent or extended position? (This position could mean a meniscus tear.) After being locked, how did it become unlocked?
6. Did swelling occur? If yes, was it immediate or did it occur later? (Immediate swelling could indicate a cruciate or tibial fracture, whereas later swelling could indicate a capsule, synovium, or meniscus tear.)
7. Where was the pain? Was it local, all over, or did it move from one side of the knee to the other?
8. Have you hurt the knee before?

When first studying the injury, the athletic trainer or coach should observe whether the athlete is able to support body weight flatfootedly on the injured leg or whether it is necessary to stand and walk on the toes. Toe walking is an indication that the athlete is holding the knee in a splinted position to avoid pain or that the knee is being held in a flexed position by a wedge of dislocated meniscus. In first-time acute knee sprains, fluid and

Figure 20-9

It is extremely important to understand the sequence and mechanism of the knee injury before the pathological process can be understood.
Courtesy Cramer Products, Inc., Gardner, Kan.

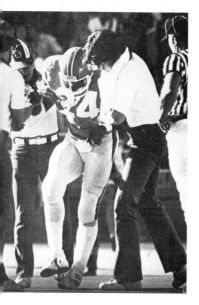

blood effusion is not usually apparent until after a 24-hour period. Swelling and ecchymosis will occur unless such effusion has been arrested by the use of compression and cold packs.

Recurrent or Chronic Injury

1. What is your major complaint?
2. When did you first notice the condition?
3. Is there recurrent swelling?
4. Does the knee ever lock or catch? (If yes, it may be a torn meniscus or a loose body in the knee joint.)
5. Is there severe pain? Is it constant or does it come and go?
6. Do you feel any grinding or grating sensations? (If yes, it could indicate chondromalacia or traumatic arthritis.)
7. Does your knee ever feel like it is going to give way or has it actually done so? (If yes and often, it may be a capsule, cruciate, or meniscus tear; loose body; or subluxating patella.)
8. What does it feel like to go up and down stairs? (Pain may indicate a patellar irritation or meniscus tear.)
9. What past treatment, if any, have you received for this condition?

Observation

A visual examination should be done after the major complaints have been determined. The athlete should be observed in a number of situations: walking, half-squatting, and going up and down stairs. The leg also should be observed for alignment and symmetry or asymmetry.

If possible, the athlete with an injured knee should be observed in the following actions:
Walking
Half-squatting
Going up and down stairs

Walking

1. Does the athlete walk with a limp or is it a free and easy walk? Is the athlete able to fully extend the knee during heel-strike?
2. Can the athlete fully bear weight on the affected leg?
3. Is the athlete able to perform a half-squat to extension?
4. Can the athlete go up and down stairs with ease? (If stairs are unavailable, stepping up on a box or stool will suffice.)

Leg Alignment

The athlete should be observed for leg alignment. Anteriorly, the athlete is evaluated for genu valgus, genu varum, and the position of the patella. Next, the athlete is observed from the side to ascertain conditions such as the hyperflexed or hyperextended knee.

Deviations in normal leg alignment may or may not be a factor in knee injury, but should always be considered as a possible cause. As with any other body segment, leg alignment differs from person to person; however, obvious discrepancies could predispose the athlete to an acute or chronic injury.

Anteriorly, with the knees extended as much as possible, the following points should be noted:

1. Are the kneecaps level with each other?
2. Are the kneecaps facing forward?
3. Can the athlete touch the medial femoral condyles and medial malleoli?

Looking at the athlete's knees from the side:

1. Are the knees fully extended with only slight hyperextension?
2. Are both knees equally extended?

Leg alignment deviations that may predispose to injury Four major leg deviations could adversely affect the knee and patellofemoral joints: patellar malalignment, genu valgum (knock-knees), genu varum (bow-legs), and genu recurvatum (hyperextended knees).

Patellar malalignment Kneecaps that are rotated inward or outward from the center may be due to a complex set of circumstances. For example, a combination of genu recurvatum, genu varum, and internal rotation, or anteversion, of the hip and internal rotation of the tibia could cause the kneecap to face inward. Internal rotation of the hip also may be associated with knock-knees, along with external rotation of the tibia, or tibial torsion. Athletes who toe-out when they walk may have an externally rotated hip, or retroversion. The normal angulation of the femoral neck after 8 years of age is 15 degrees; an increase of this angle is considered anteversion and a decrease is considered retroversion. If this seems to be a factor in a kneecap, malalignment or tibial torsion angles should be measured.

Measuring for tibial torsion Tibial torsion is determined by having the athlete kneel on a stool with the foot relaxed. An imaginary line is drawn along the center of the thigh and lower leg, bisecting the middle of the heel and the bottom of the foot. Another line starts at the center of the middle toe and crosses the center of the heel. The angle formed by the two lines is measured (Fig. 20-10); an angle measuring more or less than 15 degrees is a sign of tibial torsion.

Femoral anteversion or retroversion can be determined by the number of degrees the thigh rotates in each direction. As a rule, external and internal rotation added together equals close to 100 degrees. If internal rotation exceeds 70 degrees, there may be anteversion of the hip.[4]

Hyperextension of the knee may result in internal rotation of the femur and external rotation of the tibia. The primary muscle that allows rotation in the lower leg is the posterior popliteal muscle, which normally rotates the lower leg inward on the femur. If there is posterior muscle weakness resulting in chronic knee hyperextension, the lower leg may be allowed to rotate outward on the femur. Internal rotation at the hip is due to weak external rotator muscles or from foot pronation.

Genu valgum The cause of genu valgum, or knock-knees, can be multiple. Normally, toddlers and very young children display knock-knees. When the legs have strengthened and the feet have become positioned more in line with the pelvis, the condition is usually corrected; however, obesity may prevent proper leg alignment from taking place. Commonly associated with knock-knees are pronated feet. Genu valgum places chronic tension on the ligamentous structures of the medial part of the knee, abnormal compression of the lateral aspect of the knee surface, and abnormal tightness of the iliotibial band. One or both legs may be affected, along with a weakening of the hip's external rotator muscles.

Genu varum The two types of genu varum, or bowlegs, are structural and functional. The structural type, which is seldom seen in sports, re-

A Q angle greater than 20 degrees could predispose the athlete to patellar femoral chondromalacia.

Figure 20-10

Measuring for tibial torsion.

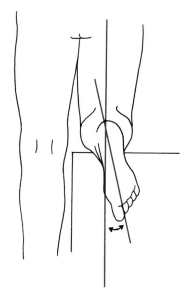

flects a deviation of the femur and tibia. The more common functional, or postural, type usually is associated with knees that are hyperextended and femurs that are internally rotated. Quite often when genu recurvatum is corrected, so is genu varum.

Genu recurvatum Genu recurvatum, or hyperextended knees, commonly occurs as a compensation for lordosis, or swayback. There is notable weakness and stretching of the hamstring muscles. Chronic hyperextension can produce undue anterior pressure on the knee joint and posterior ligaments and tendons.

Knee Symmetry or Asymmetry

The athletic trainer must establish whether both of the athlete's knees look the same:

1. Do the knees appear symmetrical?
2. Is one knee obviously swollen?
3. Is muscle atrophy apparent?

Leg-Length Discrepancy

Discrepancies in leg length can cause lateral tipping of the pelvis with some minor spinal curvature. In the nonactive person such discrepancies may not cause symptoms; however, in the physically active person a short leg could lead to problems of the entire lower limb, including the knee joint[21,34] (p. 593).

Bony Palpation

The bony structures of the knee are palpated for pain and deformities that might indicate a fracture or dislocation. The athlete sits on the edge of the training table or a bench. With the athlete's knee extended to 90 degrees, the trainer palpates the following bony structures:

Medial Aspect

1. Medial tibial plateau
2. Tibial tubercle
3. Medial femoral condyle
4. Adductor tubercle

Lateral Aspect

1. Lateral tibial plateau
2. Lateral tubercle
3. Lateral femoral condyle
4. Lateral epicondyle
5. Head of the fibula

Patella

1. Superior aspect
2. Around periphery with the knee relaxed
3. Around periphery with the knee in full extension

Capsular and Ligamentous Tissue Palpation

After palpation of the bony structures, the supportive structures should be palpated for pain and defects (Fig. 20-11). The palpation sequence is the anterior capsule, lateral collateral ligament, and medial collateral ligament and capsular structures. Capsular tissue should be palpated at the joint line where most tears occur.

Soft Tissue Palpation

Soft tissue about the knee should be palpated for symmetry of definition, defects of continuity indicating rupture or tears, and specific pain sites. Systematically the quadriceps muscle; patellar tendon; sartorius, gracilis, semitendinous, and semimembranous muscles; biceps tendon of the thigh; iliotibial band; popliteal fossa; popliteal muscle; and head of the gastrocnemius muscle should be felt for pain and defects.

Swelling Palpation

hemarthrosis
Blood in a joint cavity

Of major importance to knee inspection and evaluation is palpating for joint effusion (Fig. 20-12). Swelling due to synovia or blood in the joint, or **hemarthrosis,** must be determined. Blood in the knee joint feels heavy and moves like jelly, whereas synovial effusion feels light and, when pushed, runs easily back and forth.

Tests for Knee Ligament Stability

Both acute and chronic injury to the knee can produce ligamentous instability. It is advisable that the injured knee be evaluated, as to its stability, as soon after injury as possible. However, tests of this type should be performed only by well-trained professionals. The injured and uninjured knees are tested and contrasted to determine any differences in their stability.

Figure 20-11

Typical pain sites about the knee.

Figure 20-12

Typical swelling sites about the knee.

Valgus and Varus Stress Tests

Valgus and varus stress tests are intended to reveal laxity of the medial and lateral stabilizing complexes, especially the collateral ligaments (Fig. 20-13, *A*). The athlete lies supine with the leg extended. To test the medial side the examiner holds the ankle firmly with one hand, while placing the other over the head of the fibula. The examiner then places a force inward in an

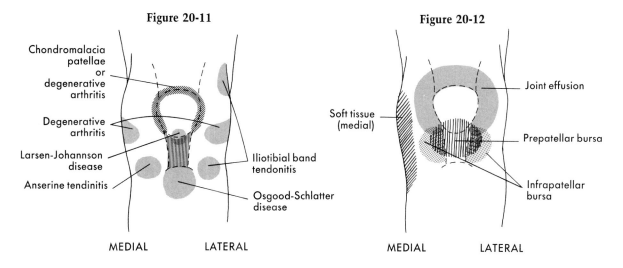

Figure 20-11

Chondromalacia
patellae
or
degenerative
arthritis

Degenerative
arthritis

Larsen-Johannson
disease

Anserine tendinitis

Iliotibial band
tendonitis

Osgood-Schlatter
disease

MEDIAL   LATERAL

Figure 20-12

Soft tissue
(medial)

Joint effusion

Prepatellar bursa

Infrapatellar
bursa

MEDIAL   LATERAL

attempt to open the side of the knee. Valgus stress is applied with the knee fully extended or at 0 degrees and at 30 degrees of flexion. The examiner reverses hand positions and tests the lateral side with a varus force on the fully extended knee and then with 30 degrees of flexion (Fig. 20-13, *B*).

Cruciate Ligament Tests

A number of tests are currently being used to establish the integrity of the cruciate ligaments. They can generally be listed as the drawer test at 90 degrees of flexion, Lachman drawer test, and pivot-shift test.

Drawer test at 90 degrees of flexion   The athlete lies on the training table with the injured leg flexed, while the operator, facing the anterior aspect of the athlete's leg, encircles the upper portion of the leg, immediately below the knee joint, with both hands. The fingers of the tester are positioned in the popliteal space of the affected leg, with the thumbs on the medial and lateral joint lines (Fig. 20-14, *A*). The tibia sliding forward from under the femur is considered a positive anterior drawer sign; conversely, the tibia sliding backward is a positive posterior drawer sign.[16] If a positive anterior drawer sign occurs, the test should be repeated with the athlete's leg rotated internally 20 degrees and externally 15 degrees (Fig. 20-14, *B* and *C*). Sliding of the tibia forward when the leg is externally rotated is an indication that the posteromedial aspect of the joint capsule, the anterior cruciate ligament, or possibly the medial collateral ligament could be torn. Movement when the leg is internally rotated indicates that the anterior cruciate ligament and posterolateral capsule may be torn.[32]

Figure 20-13

Valgus and varus knee stress tests. **A,** Valgus. **B,** Varus.

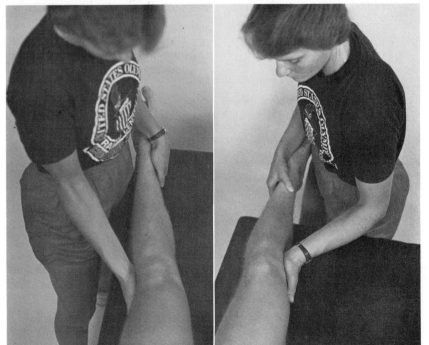

A

B

Specific Sports Injuries and
Other Problems

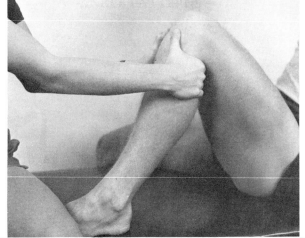

A

Figure 20-14

Drawer test for cruciate
laxity. **A,** Knee at 90 degrees
with the foot pointing
straight. **B,** Knee at 90
degrees, with the leg
internally rotated. **C,** Knee at
90 degrees, with the leg
externally rotated.

B

C

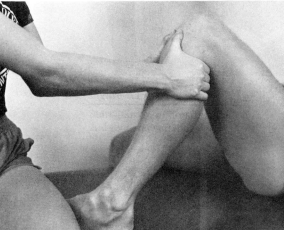

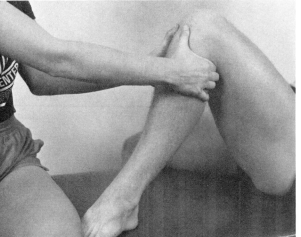

The posterior cruciate ligament is tested in the same way as the anterior cruciate ligament, but with the tibia moving posteriorly. A normal anterior shear is 5 mm. Cailliet[8] indicates that shears of ½ inch, ½ to ¾ inch, and ¾ inch or more (1.3 cm, 1.3 to 1.9 cm, and 1.9 or more) correspond to 1, 2, and 3 degrees, respectively.

Lachman drawer test In recent years the Lachman drawer test has become preferred by many over the drawer test at 90 degrees of flexion (Fig. 20-15). This is especially true for examinations immediately after injury.[11,18] One reason for using it immediately after an injury is that it does not force the knee into the painful 90-degree position, but tests it at a more comfortable 15 degrees. Another reason for its increased popularity is that it reduces the contraction of the hamstring muscles. The contraction causes a secondary knee stabilizing force that tends to mask the real extent of injury.[35] The Lachman drawer test is administered by positioning the knee in approximately 15 degrees of flexion, with the leg externally rotated. One hand of the examiner stabilizes the leg by grasp-

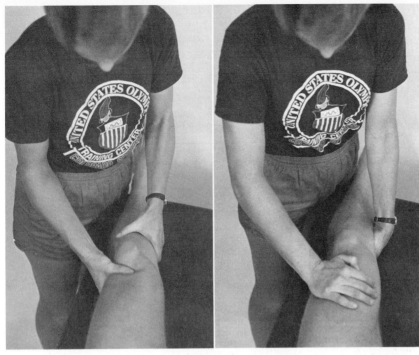

A   B

Figure 20-15

A, Lachman drawer test for
cruciate laxity. **B,** Alternate
method.

Figure 20-16

Pivot-shift test for
anterolateral rotary
instability.

ing the distal end of the thigh, and the other hand graps the proximal
aspect of the tibia, attempting to move it anteriorly.

Pivot-shift test   The pivot-shift test is designed to determine anterolateral rotary instability (Fig. 20-16). It is most often used in chronic conditions and is a sensitive test when the anterior cruciate ligament has
been torn. The athlete lies supine; one hand of the examiner is pressed
against the head of the fibula, and the other hand grasps the athlete's
ankle. To start, the lower leg is internally rotated and the knee is fully
extended. The thigh is then flexed 30 degrees at the hip while the knee
is also flexed and a valgus force is applied by the examiner's upper hand.
If there is anterior cruciate instability, a palpable shift will be felt or a
pop will be heard in the early stages of flexion.[12]

Meniscal Tests

Determining a torn meniscus often can be difficult. The three most common tests used are the McMurray test and the Apley compression and distraction tests.

The McMurray meniscal test   The McMurray test (Fig. 20-17) is
used to determine the presence of loose bodies within the knee. The ath
lete is positioned face up on the table, with the injured leg fully flexed.
The examiner places one hand on the foot and one hand over the top of
the knee, fingers touching the medial joint line. The ankle hand scribes
a small circle and pulls the leg into extension. As this occurs the hand
on the knee feels for a "clicking" response. Medial meniscus tears can be

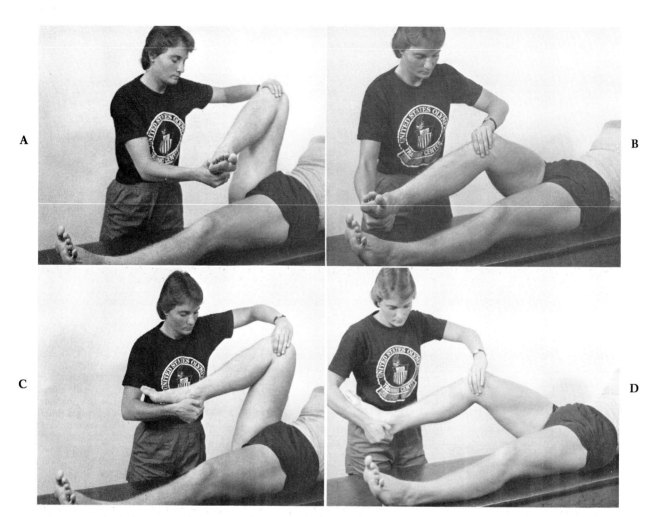

Figure 20-17

The McMurray meniscal test. **A** and **B,** Internal rotation of the lower leg into knee extension. **C** and **D,** External rotation of the lower leg into knee extension.

detected when the lower leg is externally rotated whereas internal rotation allows detection of lateral tears.

The Apley compression test The Apley compression test (Fig. 20-18) is performed with the athlete lying face down and the affected leg flexed to 90 degrees. While stabilizing the thigh, a hard downward pressure is applied to the leg. The leg is then rotated back and forth. If pain results, a meniscal injury has occurred. A medial meniscus tear is noted by external rotation, and a lateral meniscus tear is noted by internal rotation of the lower leg.

The Apley distraction test In the same position as for the Apley compression test, the examiner applies traction to the leg while moving it back and forth (Fig. 20-19). This maneuver distinguishes collateral ligament tears from capsule and meniscus tears. If the capsule or ligaments are affected, pain will occur; if the meniscus is torn, no pain will occur from the traction and rotation.[16]

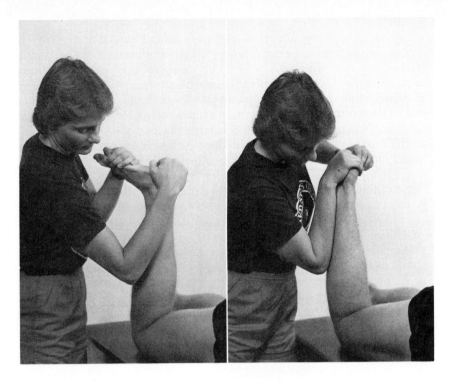

Figure 20-18

The Apley compression test.

Figure 20-19

The Apley distraction test.

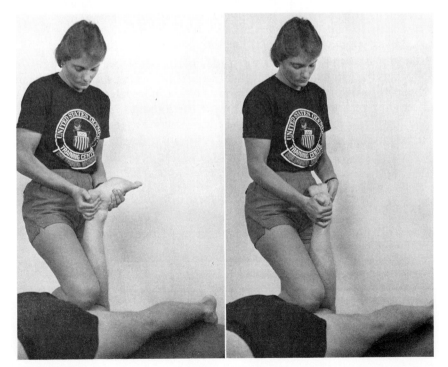

Because the musculature of
the knee atrophies so readily
after an injury, girth
measurements must be
routinely taken.

Figure 20-20

The five sites for girth
measurement.

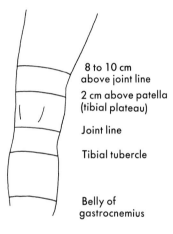

8 to 10 cm
above joint line

2 cm above patella
(tibial plateau)

Joint line

Tibial tubercle

Belly of
gastrocnemius

Figure 20-21

Testing quadriceps (**A**) and
hamstring (**B**) strength.

Girth Measurement

A knee injury is almost always accompanied by an eventual decrease in the
girth of the thigh musculature. The muscles most affected by disuse are the
quadriceps group, which are "antigravity muscles" and assist humans in
maintaining an erect, straight-leg position. They are in constant use in effecting movement. Atrophy results when a lower limb is favored and is not
used to its potential. Measurement of the circumference of both thighs can
often detect former leg injuries or determine the extent of exercise rehabilitation. Five sites have been suggested for girth measurement.[33] These sites
are the joint line, 8 to 10 cm above the tibial plateau, the level of the tibial
tubercle, the belly of the gastrocnemius muscle measured in centimeters
from the tibial tubercle, and 2 cm above the superior border of the patella
recorded in centimeters above the tibial tubercle (Fig. 20-20).

Functional Examination

It is important that the athlete's knee also be tested for function. The athlete should be observed walking and, if possible, running, turning, performing figure-8s, backing up, and stopping. If the athlete can do a deep knee
bend or duck walk without discomfort, it is doubtful that there is a meniscal tear. The resistive strength of the hamstring and quadriceps muscles
should be compared to the knee known to be uninjured (Fig. 20-21).

Patellar Examinations

Any knee evaluation should include inspection of the patella. Numerous
evaluation procedures are associated with the patella and its surroundings.
The following evaluation procedures can provide valuable information on
possible reasons for knee discomfort and problems in functioning.

Observation of the Patellar Position, Shape, and Alignment

The first aspect of examining the patella is one of observation. In terms of
position, the patella may ride higher than usual, causing a tendency toward
abnormal articulation. An indication of this condition is the patella that
faces upward (patella alta) or downward (patella infra) rather than straight
ahead when the athlete sits with the legs hanging over the end of a table

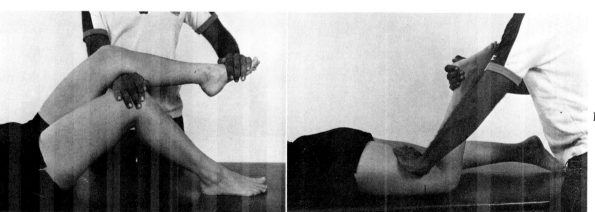

A   B

and the knees are flexed at a 45-degree angle. Observation can also tell the shape and size of the patella. Some patellas are smaller or larger than usual and some display an abnormal shape, especially at the inferior pole. The symptomatic patella also should be observed for alignment with the non-symptomatic patella. As discussed earlier, leg alignment problems such as hip anteversion, genu valgum, tibial torsion, and foot pronation can cause the patella to rotate inward, causing a tracting problem within the femoral groove.

The Q Angle

The Q angle is created when lines are drawn from the middle of the patella to the anterosuperior spine of the ilium and from the tubercle of the tibia through the center of the patella (Fig. 20-22). It should be measured with the knee fully extended and flexed at 30 degrees. The normal angle is 10 degrees for males and 15 degrees for females. Q angles that exceed 20 degrees are considered excessive and could lead to a pathological condition in the patella.

Palpation of the Patella

With the quadriceps muscle fully relaxed, the patella is palpated around its periphery and under its sides for pain sites (Fig. 20-23).

Patellar Compression, Patellar Grinding, and Apprehension Tests

With a rolled towel placed underneath the knee or held to create approximately 20 degrees of flexion, the patella is pressed downward into the femoral groove; it is then moved forward and backward (Fig. 20-24). If the athlete feels pain or a grinding sound is heard, a pathological condition is probably present. With knee still flexed, the patella is forced forward and held in this position as the athlete extends the knee (Fig. 20-25). A positive test sign is when pain and grinding are experienced by the athlete. Another

Figure 20-22

Measuring the Q angle of the knee.

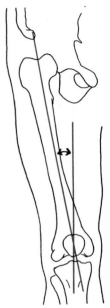

Figure 20-23

Palpating the periphery of the patella while the quadriceps muscle is fully relaxed.

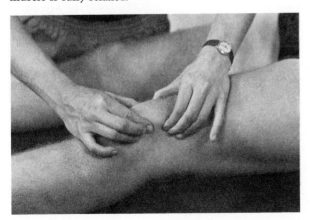

Figure 20-24

Patellar compression test. The patella is pressed downward in the femoral groove and moved forward and backward to elicit pain or crepitus.

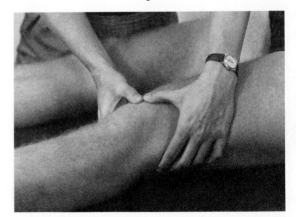

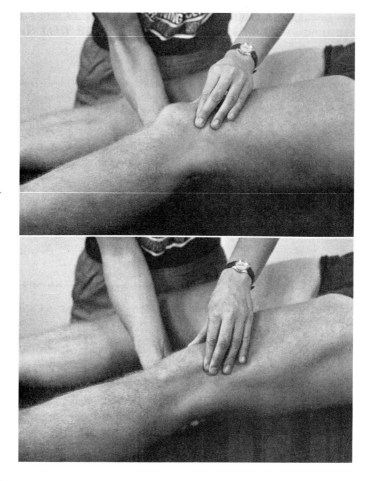

Figure 20-25

Patellar grind test. While the
knee is flexed, the patella is
forced forward, followed by
the athlete actively extending
the knee. The test is positive
if the athlete feels pain or
grinding.

Figure 20-26

Patellar apprehension test for
the easily subluxated or
dislocated patella.

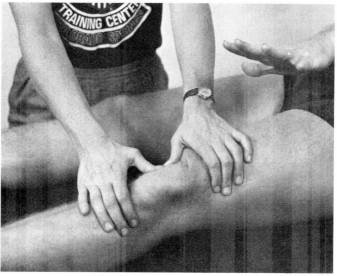

test that indicates whether the patella can easily be subluxated or dislocated (Fig. 20-26) is known as the patellar apprehension test. With the knee and patella in a relaxed position, the examiner pushes the patella laterally. The athlete will express sudden apprehension at the point where the patella begins to dislocate.[16]

PREVENTION OF KNEE INJURIES

Knee injuries, especially in football, can be prevented by increasing muscle strength, using protective bracing, and wearing proper shoes.

Muscle Strength

It is highly important that the muscles surrounding the knee be as strong as possible. The hamstrings muscles should have 60% to 70% of the strength of the quadriceps muscles. The gastrocnemius muscle also should have maximal strength. Although maximizing muscle strength may prevent some injuries, it fails to prevent rotary-type injuries.

Protective Bracing

There is an increasing trend toward football players wearing protective knee braces to avoid injury. Devices such as the Losse knee brace and the McDavid brace (Chapter 7) provide medial and lateral protection, but not rotary injury protection. The Lenox Hill (Fig. 20-27) and Pro-Am braces (Fig. 20-28) are examples of braces that help stabilize the knee with rotary problems.

Shoe Type

Over recent years, collision-type sports such as football have been using soccer-style shoes. The change from a few long conical cleats to a large number of cleats that are short (no longer than ½ inch [1.3 cm]) and broad has significantly cut down on knee injuries in football.[28] The higher number and shorter cleats are better because the foot does not become fixed to the surface and the shoe still allows for controlled running and cutting.

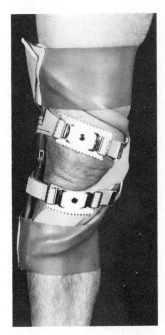

Figure 20-27

The Lenox Hill derotation knee brace.

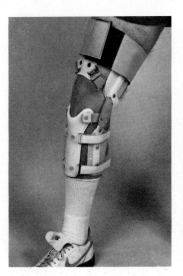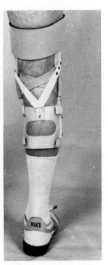

Figure 20-28

The Pro-Am knee brace.
Courtesy Pro-Fit Orthotics, Linnfield, Mass.

Specific Sports Injuries and
Other Problems

MECHANISMS OF ACUTE KNEE INJURIES

Although it is the largest joint in the body, the knee is extremely vulnerable to traumatic injuries. This shallow joint is especially defenseless against medial, lateral, compressional, and rotational forces and, because of a lack of muscle or fat padding, is also prone to contusional forces.

Ligamentous Injuries

The major ligaments of the knee can be torn in isolation or in combination. Depending on the application of forces, injury can occur from a direct straight-line or single-plane force or from a rotary force.

Single-Plane Injuries

Usually, single-plane knee injuries occur when the athlete's foot is fixed. The traumatic force may be direct, such as being hit in the knee by another player, or indirect, through a sudden valgus, varus, anterior, or posterior movement by the athlete. In sustaining direct or indirect ligamentous injury, the knee may be in a position of extension or flexion.

Injuries to the medial collateral ligament The medial collateral and capsular ligaments can be torn by a direct blow to the lateral aspect of the athlete whose foot is firmly planted. They also can be indirectly torn by a valgus force with the tibia in external rotation (Fig. 20-29). This same mechanism can occur to skiers who catch the inside of their skis in the snow.[17] The indirect valgus force with the tibia in external rotation could also tear the anterior or posterior cruciate ligaments and the medial meniscus.

Injuries to the lateral collateral ligament Sprain of the lateral collateral ligament of the knee is much less prevalent than sprain of the medial collateral ligament. The force to tear this ligament is one of varus, often with the tibia internally rotated (Figs. 20-30 and 20-31). Because of

Figure 20-29

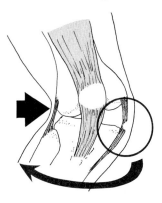

A valgus force with the tibia in external rotation injures the medial collateral and capsular ligaments, medial meniscus, and sometimes the anterior cruciate ligaments.

Figure 20-30

Competitive skiing places extreme medial, lateral, and rotary stresses on the knee.

G. Robert Bishop

the usually inaccessible medial aspect, a direct blow is rare. In skiing, the lateral collateral ligament can be injured when the skier fails to hold a snowplow and the tips cross, throwing the body weight to the outside edge of the ski.[17] If the force or blow is severe enough, both cruciate ligaments, the attachments of the iliotibial band, and the biceps muscle may be torn. This same mechanism could also disrupt the lateral and even the medial meniscus.

Injuries to the anterior cruciate ligament   Although the anterior cruciate ligament is most vulnerable to injury when the tibia is externally rotated and the knee is in a valgus position, single-plane forces can also produce injury. Hyperextension or an anterior force with the foot planted can tear this ligament (Fig. 20-32). Also, the same mechanism that sprains the medial collateral ligament, if severe enough, can tear the anterior cruciate ligament.

Injuries to the posterior cruciate ligament   The posterior cruciate ligament is vulnerable to injury after the anterior cruciate ligament has been torn and the knee has been forced into hyperextension. (Fig. 20-32). The posterior cruciate ligament is most at risk when the knee is flexed to 90 degrees. Falling with full weight on the anterior aspect of the bent knee or receiving a hard blow to the front of the bent knee can tear the posterior cruciate ligament (Fig. 20-33).

Rotary Ligament Injuries

A major mechanism of knee ligamentous injury is that of rotation with the foot fixed (Fig. 20-34). In internal rotation and external rotation of the tibia, the anterior cruciate ligament becomes taut. An athlete who is running fast and suddenly decelerates and makes a sharp "cutting" motion could produce an isolated tear of the anterior cruciate ligament. The same mechanism could be true of the skier when the ski catches in the snow and the body twists medially or laterally. The two most common rotary injuries leading to knee instability are the anteromedial and anterolateral types. Anteromedial rotary motion can tear the medial collateral ligament or both the medial and anterior cruciate ligaments. In anterolateral instability, the anterior cruciate ligament is also involved, along with a tear or laxity of the posterolateral capsule.

Figure 20-31

A varus force with the tibia internally rotated injures the lateral collateral ligament, and in some cases both the cruciate ligaments and attachments of the iliotibial band and biceps muscle of the thigh may be torn.

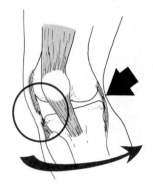

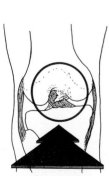
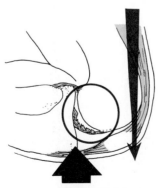

Figure 20-32

Figure 20-33

Figure 20-34

Figure 20-32

An anterior force with the foot planted can tear the anterior cruciate ligament.

Figure 20-33

A fall or being hit on the anterior aspect of the bent knee can tear the posterior cruciate ligament.

Figure 20-34

A major mechanism causing an anterior cruciate tear is when a running athlete suddenly decelerates and makes a sharp "cutting" motion.

Meniscal Tears

The medial meniscus has a higher rate of injury than the lateral meniscus. The most common mechanism is weight bearing combined with a rotary force while extending or flexing the knee. A "cutting" motion while running can distort the medial meniscus. Stretching of the anterior and posterior horns of the meniscus can produce a bowstring, or longitudinal-type, tear (Fig. 20-35, *A*). Another way a longitudinal tear occurs is by forcefully extending the knee from a flexed position while the femur is internally rotated. During extension the medial meniscus is suddenly pulled back, causing the tear (Fig. 20-35, *B*). In contrast, the lateral meniscus can sustain an oblique tear by a forceful knee extension with the femur externally rotated.[8]

KNEE JOINT INJURIES
Acute Conditions
Joint Contusions

Etiological factors   A blow struck against the muscles crossing the knee joint can result in a handicapping condition. One of the muscles frequently involved is the vastus medialis of the quadriceps group, which is primarily involved in locking the knee in a position of full extension.

Symptoms and signs   Bruises of the vastus medialis produce all the appearances of a knee sprain, including severe pain, loss of movement, and signs of acute inflammation. Such bruising is often manifested by swelling and discoloration caused by the tearing of muscle tissue and blood vessels. If adequate first aid is given immediately, the knee will usually return to functional use 24 to 48 hours after the trauma.

Bruising of the capsular tissue that surrounds the knee joint is often associated with muscle contusions and deep bone bruises. A traumatic force delivered to capsular tissue may cause capillary bleeding, irritate the synovial membrane, and result in profuse fluid effusion into the joint cavity and surrounding spaces, thereby producing intra-articular swelling. Effusion often takes place slowly and almost imperceptibly. It is advisable to prevent the athlete from engaging in further activity for at least 24 hours after receipt of a capsular bruise. Activity causes an increase in

Because the knee joint and patella are poorly padded, they are prone to bruising.

Figure 20-35

Common mechanisms of injury to the meniscus.

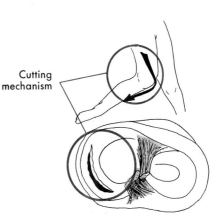

circulation and may cause extensive swelling and hematoma at the knee joint. Scar tissue develops wherever internal bleeding with clot organization is present. If this condition is repeated time after time, chronic synovitis or an arthritic sequela may develop.

Management of knee contusions   Care of a bruised knee depends on many factors. However, management principally depends on the location and severity of the contusion. The following procedures are suggested:

1. Apply compression bandages and cold until resolution has taken place.
2. Prescribe inactivity and rest for 24 hours.
3. If swelling occurs, continue cold application for 72 hours. If swelling and pain are intense, refer the athlete to the physician.
4. Once the acute stage has ended and the swelling has diminished to little or none, cold application with active range of motion exercises should be conducted within a pain-free range. If a gradual use of heat is elected, great caution should be taken to avoid swelling.
5. Allow the athlete to return to normal activity, with protective padding, when pain and the initial irritation have subsided.
6. If swelling is not resolved within a week, a chronic condition of either synovitis or bursitis may exist, indicating the need for rest and medical attention.

Bursitis

Bursitis in the knee can be acute, chronic, or recurrent. Although any one of the numerous knee bursae can become inflamed, anteriorly the prepatellar, deep infrapatellar, and pretibial bursae have the highest incidence of irritation in sports (Fig. 20-5).

Etiological factors   The prepatellar bursa often becomes inflamed from continued kneeling, and the deep infrapatellar becomes irritated from overuse of the patellar tendon.

Symptoms and signs   Swelling in the knee posteriorly indicates an irritation of one of the bursae in this region. Swelling in the popliteal fossa could be a sign of *Baker's cyst* (Fig. 20-36), which indicates distension of the gastrocnemius-semimembranous bursae.[16] Baker's cyst is commonly painless, causing no discomfort or disability. Some inflamed bursae may be painful and disabling because of the swelling and should be treated accordingly.

Management   Management usually follows a pattern of eliminating the cause, prescribing rest, and reducing inflammation. Contrast baths may help to reduce swelling. When the bursitis is chronic or recurrent and the synovium has thickened, aspiration and a steroid injection may be warranted.

Collateral Ligament and Capsular Injuries

Ligament and capsular sprains are the most frequently reported injury among the knee injuries that occur in sports.

Etiological factors   Most knee sprains affect the medial collateral ligament as a result either of a direct blow from the lateral side, in a medial

The knee has many bursae—the infrapatellar and pretibial bursae are most often irritated.

Figure 20-36

Baker's cyst in the popliteal fossa.

direction, or of a severe outward twist. Greater injury results from medial sprains than from lateral sprains because of their more direct relation to the articular capsule and the medial meniscus. Medial and lateral sprains appear in varying degrees, depending on knee position, previous injuries, the strength of muscles crossing the joint, the force and angle of the trauma, fixation of the foot, and conditions of the playing surface.

The position of the knee is important in establishing its vulnerability in traumatic sprains. Any position of the knee, from full extension to full flexion, can result in injury if there is sufficient force. Full extension tightens both lateral and medial ligaments. However, flexion affords a loss of stability to the lateral ligament but maintains stability in various portions of the broad medial ligament.[10] Medial collateral ligament sprains occur most often from a violently adducted and internally rotated knee. The most prevalent mechanism of a lateral collateral ligament or capsular sprain is one where the foot is everted and the knee is forced laterally into a varus position.

Speculation among medical authorities is that torn menisci seldom happen as the result of an initial trauma; most occur after the collateral ligaments have been stretched by repeated injury. Many mild to moderate sprains leave the knee unstable and thus vulnerable to additional internal derangements. The strength of the muscles crossing the knee joint is important in assisting the ligaments to support the articulation. These muscles should be conditioned to the highest possible degree for sports in which knee injuries are common. With the added support and protection of muscular strength, a state of readiness may be developed through proper training.

The force and angle of the trauma usually determine the extent of injury that takes place. Even after having witnessed the occurrence of a knee injury, it is difficult to predict the amount of tissue damage. The most revealing time for testing joint stability is immediately after injury, before effusion masks the extent of derangement.

Acute medial knee sprains Medial injuries of the knee can involve the medial collateral and/or capsular ligaments.

First degree medial collateral ligament sprain A first degree medial collateral ligament injury of the knee has the following characteristics (Fig. 20-37):

1. A few ligamentous fibers are torn and stretched.
2. The joint is stable in valgus stress tests.
3. There is little or no joint effusion.
4. There may be some joint stiffness and point tenderness just below the medial joint line.
5. Even with minor stiffness, there is almost full passive and active range of motion.

Management

Immediate care consists of ICE-R for at least 24 hours. After immediate care, the following procedures should be undertaken:

1. Crutches are prescribed if the athlete is unable to walk without a limp.
2. Follow-up care may involve cryokinetics, including 5 minutes of ice

Figure 20-37

First degree medial collateral ligament sprain.

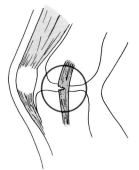

pack treatment preceding exercise or a combination of cold and compression and/or ultrasound.

3. Proper exercise is essential, starting with Phase 1 of the knee joint rehabilitation procedures on p. 566.

Isometrics and straight-leg exercises are important until the knee can be moved without pain. The athlete then graduates to stationary bicycle riding or a high-speed isokinetic program. Proprioceptive neuromuscular function can also be an excellent means for rehabilitation (Appendix I-B).

The athlete is allowed to return to full participation when the knee has regained normal strength, power, flexibility, endurance, and coordination. Usually 1 to 3 weeks is necessary for recovery. On returning to activity, the athlete may require tape support for a short period.

Second degree medial collateral ligament sprain   Second degree medial collateral ligament knee sprain indicates both miscroscopic and gross disruption of ligamentous fibers (Fig. 20-38). The only structures involved are the medial collateral ligament and the medial capsular ligament. It is characterized by the following:

1. A complete tear of the deep capsular ligament and partial tear of the superficial layer of the medial collateral ligament or a partial tear of both areas.[26]

2. There is no gross instability, but minimal or slight laxity is indicated in full extension, but at 30 degrees of flexion, and when the valgus stress test is performed, as much as 5 to 15 degrees.

3. Swelling is slight or absent unless the meniscus or anterior cruciate ligament has been torn. An acutely torn or pinched synovial membrane, subluxated or dislocated patella, or an osteochondral fracture can produce extensive swelling and hemarthrosis.

4. Moderate to severe joint tightness with an inability to fully, actively extend the knee. The athlete is unable to place the heel flat on the ground.

5. Definite loss of passive range of motion.

6. Pain in the medial joint line, with general weakness and instability.

Management

1. ICE-R for 48 to 72 hours.

2. Crutches are used with a three-point gait until the acute phase of injury is over and the athlete can walk without a limp.

3. Depending on the severity and possible complications, a full-leg cast or postoperative knee immobilizing splint may be applied by the physician (Fig. 20-39).

4. Cryokinetics or other therapeutic modalities are employed three or four times daily.

5. Isometric exercise along with exercise to all the adjacent joints is performed three or four times daily.

6. Depending on the extent of injury and swelling, the immobilizing splint is removed, and gentle range of movement may be performed. (See pp. 550-551 for a sample exercise rehabilitation program.)

7. Taping may be appropriate to provide some support and confidence to the athlete.

Figure 20-38

Second degree medial collateral ligament sprain.

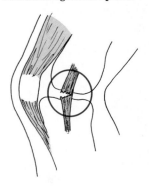

Figure 20-39

Knee immobilizer after a ligamentous injury.

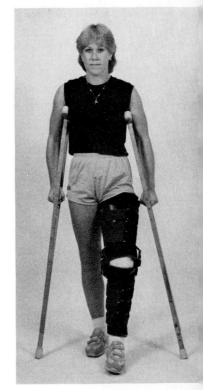

MANAGEMENT PLAN FOR MEDIAL COLLATERAL LIGAMENT SPRAIN OF THE KNEE

Injury Situation

A female college soccer player injured her right knee in a game. The injury occurred in an attempt to recover the ball when she tripped on an opponent's foot, forcing her knee into a sudden valgus position. As the knee was forced inward, the athlete felt a sharp pain and a sense that the knee "gave way."

Symptoms and Signs

On inspection, the athlete complained of severe pain in the knee region. She was unable to bear full weight on the leg or to walk other than on the toe of the foot. Palpation by the athletic trainer revealed pain along the medial joint line. Varus and valgus stress tests were performed and found negative at full extension (0 degrees), but revealed some minor excursion at 30 degrees of flexion in the valgus test. All other knee tests proved negative. X-ray examination for fracture was negative. The injury was considered by the physician to be between a grade II and III medial collateral ligament sprain.

Management Plan

Because the knee was basically stable in all tests, surgery was ruled out, and a conservative therapy program was considered to be the best approach.

---

1 **Management Phase**

GOALS: To control hemorrhage, swelling, and pain
Estimated length of time (ELT): 3 days

Therapy

IMMEDIATE CARE: Apply ice pack (20 min) intermittently, 6-8 times daily
Soft splint: an elastic wrap is worn
Leg is elevated whenever possible during day and night

Exercise Rehabilitation

Avoid weight bearing by crutch walking until athlete can walk without limp, 3-4 days
Isometric exercise (within pain-free limits; 10-15 times) to quadriceps and hamstring muscles (each contraction held 6 sec); may be done in conjunction with TENS, every waking hour
Straight leg raises in all hip positions are added to isometrics 3-4 days after injury (each exercise is performed 10-15 times), every waking hour
General body maintenance exercises are conducted as long as they do not aggravate injury, 3 times a week

2	**Management Phase**	GOALS: To restore 50% range of motion (ROM), full muscle contraction ELT: 4-7 days
	Therapy	FOLLOW-UP CARE (all cold therapy is followed by exercise): Ice pack (5-15 min) or ice massage (7 min) or cold whirlpool (60° F [15.5° C] for 10 min), 3-4 times daily
	Exercise Rehabilitation	Crutch walking is continued until athlete can walk without limp Isometrics and straight leg raises are continued, 3-4 times daily Active range of motion exercises are begun within pain-free limits using active movements and/or PNF hip and knee patterns, 3-4 times daily TENS is continued General body maintenance exercises are conducted as long as they do not aggravate injury, 3 times a week
3	**Management Phase**	GOALS: To restore 75% ROM, 50% full strength ELT: 10-14 days
	Therapy	Ice pack (5-15 min) or ice massage (10 min) followed by exercise
	Exercise Rehabilitation	Avoid any exercise that causes pain or swelling Isokinetic exercise starting at high speeds, once daily Isotonic exercise employing progressive resistance exercise using DAPRE concept (see pp. 570-571) or PNF knee patterns or jogging in waist-high pool (20 min), once daily General body maintenance exercises are conducted as long as they do not aggravate injury, 3 times a week
4	**Management Phase**	GOALS: To restore 90% ROM, power, speed, and endurance and coordination ELT: 14 days
	Therapy	If symptom free, no therapy is required Continue program of DAPRE, 3-4 times a week Begin jogging on flat surfaces and progress from walk-run to running (3 miles) Begin figure-8 runs with obstacles 10 feet (3 m) apart, then decrease to 5 feet (1.5 m) apart at full speed
5	**Management Phase**	GOAL: To restore full muscle bulk and playing skill Work on maximal resistance, 3-4 times a week Begin practice while protected with tape and brace, once daily
Criteria for Full Recovery		1. The knee is symptom free. 2. The knee has full range of motion and strength equal to or exceeding the unaffected knee. 3. The athlete has full function and is able to jump and run a figure-8 at full speed.

Figure 20-40

Third degree medial collateral
ligament sprain.

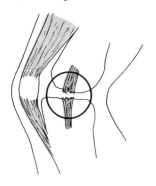

Third degree medial collateral ligament sprain Third degree medial
collateral ligament sprain means a complete tear of the supporting ligaments. The following are major symptoms and signs (Fig. 20-40):

1. Complete loss of medial stability
2. Minimal to moderate swelling
3. Medial pain and point tenderness
4. Loss of range of motion because of effusion and hamstring spasm
5. The valgus stress test reveals some joint opening at full extension
   and significant opening at 30 degrees of flexion.

An anterior cruciate ligament tear or medial meniscus disruption
may be present and should be tested for.

Immediate and follow-up care ICE-R for 20 minutes every 2 hours
during the waking day should be performed for at least 72 hours. In many
cases, such an injury is surgically repaired as soon as possible after the
acute inflammatory phase of 3 or 4 days after injury.

Acute lateral knee sprains Lateral knee sprains are due to a varus
stress to the articular capsule and/or lateral collateral ligament. The most
common situation for injury is when the tibia is internally rotated, and
the knee is suddenly forced into adduction. If the force is great enough,
bony fragments can be avulsed from the femur or tibia. An avulsion can
also occur by the combined pull of the lateral collateral ligament and
biceps muscle on the head of the fibula.[26]

A lateral knee sprain can be
caused by a varus force when
the tibia is internally rotated.

The major symptoms and signs include the following:

1. Pain and point tenderness along the joint line.

2. Depending on the degree of injury, there is usually some joint instability with joint opening on the varus stress test at 30 degrees of knee
flexion.

3. Swelling is usually minimal because of bleeding into joint spaces.

4. The greater the ligamentous injury, the less pain is felt on a varus
stress test.

An injury can also occur to the peroneal nerve, causing temporary or
permanent palsy. The common peroneal nerve originates from the sciatic
nerve. It lies behind the head of the fibula and winds laterally around the

Figure 20-41

Taping for knee collateral
ligament injuries.

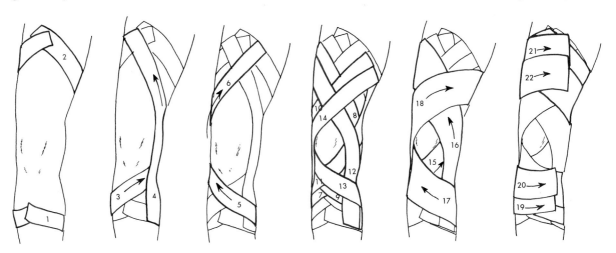

TAPING FOR COLLATERAL LIGAMENT KNEE INJURIES

As with ankle instabilities the athlete with an unstable knee should never use tape and bracing as a replacement for proper exercise rehabilitation. If properly applied, taping can help protect the knee and become an aid in the rehabilitation process[13] (Fig. 20-41).

Materials needed: One roll of 2-inch (5 cm) linen tape, a roll of 3-inch (7.5 cm) elastic tape, a 1-inch (2.5 cm) heel lift, and skin adherent.

Position of the athlete: The athlete stands on a 3-foot (90 cm) table with the injured knee held in a moderately relaxed position by means of a 1-inch (2.5 cm) heel lift. The hair is completely removed from a point 6 inches (15 cm) above to 6 inches (15 cm) below the kneecap.

Position of the operator: The operator stands facing the anterior aspect of the athlete's knee.

Procedure

1. A circular, 2-inch (5 cm) linen tape anchor strip is placed lightly around the thigh and leg at the hairline.
2. The first linen tape strip is carried from the lateral side of the leg anchor, running obliquely across the tibial tubercle and crossing slightly behind the medial femoral condyle.
3. The second linen strip begins at the medial aspect of the leg anchor and is carried upward across the medial femoral condyle, ending on the anterior portion of the thigh anchor.
4. The third linen strip is taken from the medial aspect of the leg anchor, placed obliquely across the tibial tubercle crossing slightly behind the lateral femoral condyle, and ends on the lateral aspect of the thigh anchor.
5. The fourth strip is started from the lateral leg anchor, carried upward across the lateral femoral condyle, and ends on the anterior portion of the thigh anchor. *This first series forms a self-locking X on each side of the knee joint.*
6. The second series is applied in the same sequence as the first but is applied forward, overlapping at least two thirds of the first series' tape width.
7. The third and last series of the linen tape is applied forward, overlapping two thirds of the width of the second series. As this last series is laid in place, tuck ¼ inch (0.6 cm) of the tape edge nearest the kneecap in for approximately 3 inches (7.5 cm) on either side of the knee bend to prevent the tape from tearing during activity.
8. Four elastic tape strips are cut, each about 9 inches (22.5 cm) long. Stretched to their utmost, the elastic strips are placed directly over the linen tape series, forming an X on both sides of the knee. *Elastic tape provides a flexible reinforcement to the rigid linen tape. It also helps to prevent tearing during activity and loosening caused by perspiration.*
9. Elastic tape is applied as locks for the basket weave. Two or three strips of tape are cut to encircle the thigh and the leg. Some individuals find it advantageous to complete a knee taping by wrapping loosely with an elastic wrap, thus prividing an added precaution against the tape becoming loose from perspiration.

neck of the fibula, where it branches into deep and superficial peroneal nerves (Fig. 20-8). Tears or entrapment of this nerve can produce varying weaknesses and paralysis of the lateral aspect of the lower leg. Injury of peroneal nerve requires immediate medical attention.

Management of the lateral collateral ligament injury should follow similar procedures as the medial collateral ligament injuries.

Internal knee joint conditions As discussed earlier, the knee can sustain acute and chronic injuries from a variety of mechanisms. The most common internal knee joint conditions are injury to the cruciate ligament and meniscus. Other joint conditions to consider are knee plica, loose bodies, osteochondral fractures, osteochondritis dissecans, and traumatic arthritis.

Acute anterior cruciate ligament tear Until recently, the medial collateral ligament tear was considered much more prevalent than the complete anterior cruciate ligament tear. Today the anterior cruciate is considered the most commonly disrupted ligament in the knee.[18]

The anterior cruciate ligament tear is extremely difficult to diagnose. The earlier the determination, the better, because swelling will often mask the full extent of injury. Besides swelling, this injury is associated with joint instability, and a positive drawer sign may be present. Ligament stress tests should be employed as soon as possible.[11]

Symptoms and signs The athlete often experiences a "pop," followed by immediate disability. The athlete complains that the knee feels like it is "coming apart." Although the tear may be isolated, it could be associated with a meniscus or medial collateral ligament tear. The anterior cruciate ligament can be injured in a number of ways, including internal rotation of the thigh with the knee flexed while the foot is planted and forced hyperextension. Forced hyperflexion could conceivably injure both the anterior and posterior cruciate ligaments.

Management

IMMEDIATE CARE Even with proper first aid and immediate ICE-R, swelling begins within 1 to 2 hours and becomes a notable hemarthrosis within 4 to 6 hours.[3] The athlete typically cannot walk without help.

If a clinical evaluation is inconclusive, an arthroscopic examination may be warranted to make a proper diagnosis.

FOLLOW-UP CARE Anterior cruciate ligament injury could lead to serious knee instability; an intact anterior cruciate ligament is necessary for a knee to function in high-performance situations. Controversy exists among physicians as to how to best treat an acute anterior cruciate ligament rupture and when surgery is warranted. It is well accepted that an unsatisfactorily treated anterior cruciate ligament rupture will eventually lead to major joint degeneration.[27] Therefore, a decision for or against surgery must be based on the athlete's age, the type of stress applied to the knee, and the amount of instability present, as well as the techniques available to the surgeon.[3] A simple surgical repair of the ligament may not establish the desired joint stability. Surgery may involve joint reconstruction with transplantation of some external structure such as the pes anserinus, semitendinous muscle, tensor fascia lata, or patellar tendon to replace the lost anterior cruciate support. This type of surgery involves a significant hospital stay, 8 weeks or longer in casts and braces, and 6 months to 1 year of rehabilitation.[3]

The routine use of braces such as the Lenox-Hill derotation brace, along with rotary and hyperextension taping, can provide some protection during activity.

ROTARY INJURY KNEE TAPING

The rotary taping method is designed to provide the knee with support when it is unstable from injury to the medial collateral and anterior cruciate ligaments (Fig. 20-42).

Materials needed: One roll of 3-inch (7.5 cm) elastic tape, skin adherent, 4-inch (10 cm) gauze pad, and scissors.

Position of the athlete: The athlete sits on a table with the affected knee flexed 15 degrees.

Position of the operator: The operator stands facing the side of the athlete's flexed knee.

Procedure

1. A 10-inch (25 cm) piece of elastic tape is cut with both the ends snipped. The gauze pad is placed in the center of the 10-inch (25 cm) piece of elastic tape.
2. The gauze with the elastic tape backing is placed in the popliteal fossa of the athlete's knee. Both ends of the tape are stretched to the fullest extent and are torn. The divided ends are placed firmly around the patella and interlocked.
3. Starting at a midpoint on the gastrocnemius muscle, a 3-inch (7.5 cm) elastic tape strip is spiraled to the front of the leg, then behind, crossing the popliteal fossa, and around the thigh, finishing anteriorly.
4. Procedure 3 is repeated on the opposite side.
5. Three or four spiral strips may be applied for added strength.
6. Once in place, the spiral strips are locked by the application of two circular strips around the thigh and two around the calf. *NOTE:* More rigidity can be achieved by tracing the spiral pattern with linen tape.

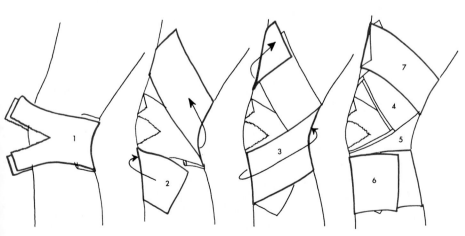

Figure 20-42

Rotary injury knee taping.

CRUCIATE LIGAMENT AND HYPEREXTENSION TAPING

Cruciate ligament and hyperextension taping (Fig. 20-43) is designed to prevent the knee from hyperextending and also may be used for strained hamstring muscles or slackened cruciate ligaments.

Materials needed: One roll of 2½ (5.5 cm) tape or 2-inch (5 cm) elastic tape, cotton or a 4-inch (10 cm) gauze pad, tape adherent, underwrap, and a 2-inch (5 cm) heel lift.

Position of the athlete: The athlete's leg should be completely shaved above midthigh and below midcalf. The athlete stands on a 3-foot (90 cm) table with the injured knee flexed by means of a 2-inch (5 cm) heel lift.

Position of the operator: The operator stands facing the back of the athlete's knee.

Procedure

1. Place two anchor strips at the hairlines, two around the thigh, and two around the leg. These should be applied loosely to allow for muscle expansion during exercise.
2. A gauze pad is placed at the popliteal space to protect the popliteal nerves and blood vessels from constriction by the tape.
3. Start the supporting tape strips by forming an X over the popliteal space.
4. Cross the tape again with two more strips and one up the middle of the leg.
5. Complete the technique by applying four or five locking strips around the thigh and calf.
6. Apply an additional series of strips if the athlete is heavily muscled.
7. Lock the supporting strips in place by applying two or three overlapping circles around the thigh and leg.

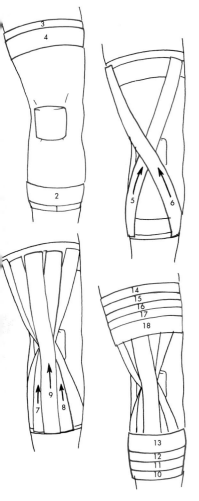

Figure 20-43

Cruciate ligament and hyperextension taping.

Meniscal lesions The medial meniscus has a much higher incidence of injury than the lateral meniscus. The higher number of medial meniscus tears is basically a result of the coronary ligament attaching the meniscus peripherally to the tibia and also to the capsular ligament. The lateral meniscus does not attach to the capsular ligament and is more mobile during knee movement. Because of the attachment to the medial structures, the medial meniscus is prone to disruption from valgus and torsional forces.

Etiological factors A blow from the lateral side directed inward forces the knee into adduction, which often tears and stretches the medial collateral ligament; meanwhile its fibers twist the medial meniscus outward. Repeated mild sprains reduce the strength of the knee to a state favorable for a cartilage tear through lessening its normal ligamentous stability. A large number of medial meniscus lesions are the outcome of a sudden, strong internal rotation of the femur with a partially flexed knee while the foot is firmly planted. As a result of the force of this action, the cartilage is pulled out of its normal bed and pinched between the femoral condyles.

Meniscus tears can be longitudinal, oblique, or transverse (Fig. 20-35). Tears close to the periphery of a meniscus because of its proximity to the coronary ligament and blood circulation may heal over time if stress in the area is kept to a minimum.[2] Tears that occur within the cartilage fail to heal due to lack of adequate blood supply.[26]

Acute symptoms and signs An absolute diagnosis of cartilage injury is difficult. For determining the possibility of such an injury, a complete history should be obtained, which consists of information about past knee injury and an understanding of how the present injury occurred. Diagnosis of menisci injuries should be made immediately after the injury has developed and before muscle spasm and swelling obscure the normal shape of the knee.

A meniscal tear may or may not result in the following:
1. Severe pain and loss of motion
2. A locked knee with inability to fully flex or extend
3. Pain in the area of the tear

Management of the acute meniscal tear If the knee is not locked but shows indications of a tear, the physician might obtain an arthrogram, which is an x-ray film of a joint that has been injected with radiopaque material. An arthrogram should rule out a fracture. An arthroscopic examination may also be given, whereby the physician can physically look inside the knee for deviations.

The knee that is locked by a displaced cartilage may require unlocking under anesthesia so that a detailed examination can be conducted. If discomfort, disability, and locking of the knee continue, surgery may be required. For the nonlocking acute meniscus tear, immediate care should follow a second or third degree sprain management pattern. The knee is managed by splinting, crutch walking, muscle setting, and isometric exercise followed by gradual ROM and progressive resistance exercises.

Chronic symptoms and signs Once a knee cartilage has been fractured, its ruptured edges harden and may eventually atrophy. On occasion, portions of the meniscus may become detached and wedge themselves between the articulating surfaces of the tibia and femur, thus imposing a locking, "catching," or "giving way" of the joint. Chronic meniscus lesions may also display recurrent swelling and obvious muscle atrophy about the knee. The athlete may complain of an inability to perform a full squat or to change direction quickly when running without pain, a sense of the knee collapsing, or a "popping" sensation. Such symptoms and signs usually warrant surgical intervention. NOTE: *Symptomatic meniscus tears can eventually lead to serious articular degeneration with major impairment and disability.*

Knee plica The fetus has three synovial knee cavities whose internal walls, at 4 months, are gradually absorbed to form one chamber; however, in 20% of all individuals, the knee fails to fully absorb these cavities. In adult life these septa form synovial folds known as plicae.

Etiological factors The most common synovial fold is the infrapatellar plica, which originates from the infrapatellar fat pad and extends superiorly in a fanlike manner. The second most common synovial fold is the suprapatellar, located in the suprapatellar pouch. The least common, but most subject to injury, is the mediopatellar plica, which is bandlike and begins on the medial wall of the knee joint and extends downward to insert into the synovial tissue that covers the infrapatellar

Simple surgical repair of the torn anterior cruciate ligament may not establish proper stability.

fat pad.[23] Because most synovial plicae are pliable, most are asymptomatic; however, the mediopatellar plica may be thick, nonyielding, and fibrotic, causing a number of symptoms. The mediopatellar plica is associated with chondromalacia of the medial femoral condyle and patella.[5]

Symptoms and signs The athlete may or may not have a history of knee injury. If symptoms are preceded by trauma, it is usually one of a blunt force, such as falling on the knee, or of twisting with the foot planted. A major complaint is recurrent episodes of painful pseudolocking of the knee when sitting for a period of time. As the knee passes 15 to 20 degrees of flexion, a snap may be felt or heard. Such characteristics of locking and snapping could be misinterpreted as a torn miniscus. The athlete complains of pain on ascending or descending stairs or on squatting. Unlike meniscus injuries, there is little or no swelling and no ligamentous laxity.

Management A knee plica that becomes inflamed due to trauma is usually treated conservatively with rest, anti-inflammatory agents, and local heat. If the condition recurs, causing a chondromalacia of the femoral condyle or patella, the plica will require surgical excision.[14]

Osteochondral knee fractures Occasionally the same mechanisms that produce collateral ligament, cruciate ligament, or meniscus tears can shear off a piece of bone attached to the anterior cartilage or cartilage alone. Twisting, sudden cutting, or being struck directly in the knee are typical causes of this condition. The athlete commonly hears a snap and feels the knee give way. Swelling is immediate and extensive because of hemarthrosis, and there is considerable pain. The diagnosis is usually confirmed by arthroscopic examination. Surgery is performed to replace the fragment as soon as possible to avoid joint degeneration and arthritis.

Osteochondritis dissecans Osteochondritis dissecans is a painful condition involving partial or complete separation of a piece of articular cartilage and subchondral bone. Both teenagers and adults can have this condition. The vast majority of fragments, over 85%, occur on the medial femoral condyle near the posterior cruciate ligament attachment.

Etiological factors The exact cause of osteochondritis dissecans is unknown. It usually has a very slow onset. A disruption of blood circulation has been suggested as a possible reason for this condition. Other possible factors are as follows[8]:

1. Repeated trauma to the medial condyle by the tibial tuberosity
2. Endocrine imbalance
3. Heredity

Symptoms and signs The athlete with osteochondritis dissecans complains of a knee that aches, has recurrent swelling and, on occasion, may catch or lock. There may be atrophy of the quadriceps muscle and point tenderness.

Management For children usually rest and immobilization using a cylinder cast are prescribed. This affords proper resolution of the injured cartilage and normal ossification of the underlying bone. As with many other osteochondroses, resolution may take as long as 1 year. For the teenager and adult surgery may be warranted, such as multiple drilling in the area to stimulate healing, pinning loose fragments, or bone grafting.

Knee plicae that have become thick and hard are often mistaken for meniscus injuries.

A knee that locks and unlocks during activity may indicate a fractured meniscus.

Loose bodies within the knee ("joint mice") Because of repeated trauma to the knee in sports activities loose bodies can develop within the joint cavity. Loose bodies can stem from osteochondritis dissecans, fragments from the menisci, pieces of torn synovial tissue, or a torn cruciate ligament. The loose body may move around in the joint space and become lodged to cause locking, popping, and giving way. When the loose body becomes wedged between articulating surfaces, irritation can occur. If not surgically removed, the loose body can create conditions that lead to joint degeneration.

Injury to the infrapatellar fat pad The two most important fat pads of the knee are the infrapatellar fat pad and the suprapatellar fat pad. The infrapatellar fat pad lies between the synovial membrane on the anterior aspect of the joint and the patellar ligament, and the suprapatellar fat pad lies between the anterior surface and the suprapatellar bursa. Of the two pads, the infrapatellar is more often injured in sports, principally as a result of its large size and particular vulnerability during activity.

Etiological factors The fat pad may become wedged between the knee articulations, irritated by chronic kneeling pressures, or traumatized by direct blows.

Symptoms and signs Repeated injury to the fat pad produces a capillary hemorrhaging and swelling of the fatty tissue; if the irritation continues, scarring and calcification may develop. The athlete may complain of pain below the patellar ligament, especially on knee extension, and the knee may display weakness, mild swelling, and stiffness on movement.

Management Care of acute fat pad injuries involves rest from irritating activities until inflammation has subsided, heel elevation of ½ to 1 inch (1.3 to 1.5 cm) and the therapeutic use of heat. Heel elevation prevents added irritation on full extension; it may also be necessary to prevent full extension from taking place by applying hyperextension taping. Therapy should include heat applied throughout the day in the form of moist heat packs, whirlpool, or analgesic balm packs. Massage around the inflamed area may assist lymphatic drainage. However, avoid massaging directly over the joint itself. Quadriceps atrophy may be prevented by assigning a daily program of quadriceps "setting" or isometric exercises.

PATELLAR AND RELATED CONDITIONS

The position and function of the patella and surrounding structures expose it to a variety of traumas and diseases related to sports activities.

Patellar Fracture

Fractures of the patella can be caused by either direct or indirect trauma.

Etiological factors Most fractures are the result of indirect violence in which a severe pull of the patellar tendon occurs against the femur when the knee is semiflexed. This position subjects the patella to maximal stress from the quadriceps tendon and the patellar ligament. Forcible muscle contraction may then fracture the patella at its lower half. Direct injury most often produces fragmentation with little displacement. Falls, jumping, or running may result in a fracture of the patella.

Specific Sports Injuries and
Other Problems

Symptoms and signs The fracture causes hemorrhage and joint effusion, resulting in a generalized swelling. Indirect fracture causes capsular tearing, separation of bone fragments, and possible tearing of the quadriceps tendon. Direct fracture involves little bone separation.

Management Diagnosis is accomplished by use of the history, palpation of separated fragments, and an x-ray confirmation. As soon as the examiner suspects a patellar fracture, a cold wrap should be applied, followed by an elastic compression wrap and splinting. The athletic trainer should then refer the athlete to the team physician. The athlete will normally be immobilized for 2 to 3 months.

Acute Patellar Subluxation or Dislocation

When an athlete plants his or her foot, decelerates, and simultaneously cuts in an opposite direction from the weight-bearing foot, the thigh rotates internally while the lower leg rotates externally, causing a forced knee valgus. The quadriceps muscle attempts to pull in a straight line and as a result pulls the patella laterally—a force that may dislocate the patella. As a rule, displacement takes place outwardly with the patella resting on the lateral condyle (Fig. 20-44).

With this mechanism the patella is forced to slide laterally into a partial or full dislocation. Some athletes are more predisposed to this condition than others because of the following anatomical structures[15]:

1. A wide pelvis with anteverted hips
2. Genu valgum, increasing the Q angle
3. Shallow femoral grooves
4. Flat lateral femoral condyles
5. High riding and flat patellas

Knees that "give way" or "catch" can have a number of possible pathological conditions:
 Subluxating patella
 Meniscus tear
 Anterior cruciate ligament
  tear
 Hemarthrosis

Figure 20-44

Fracture and dislocation of the patella.

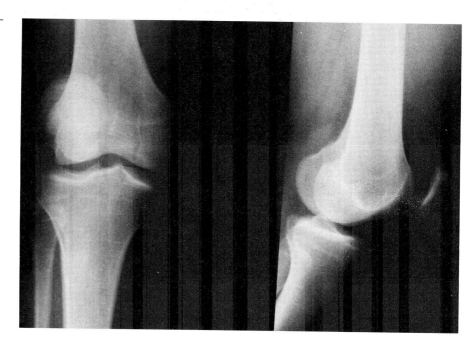

6. Vastus medialis and ligamentous laxity with genu recurvatum and externally rotated tibias
7. Pronated feet
8. Externally pointing patellas

Symptoms and Signs of the Subluxated Patella

An athlete who has a subluxated patella will complain that the knee catches or gives way. The knee may be swollen and painful. Pain is due to swelling, but also because the medial capsular tissue has been stretched and torn. Because of the hemarthrosis, the knee is restricted in flexion and extension.

The Dislocated Patella

An acute patellar dislocation is often associated with sudden twisting of the body while the foot or feet are planted.

Symptoms and signs The athlete experiences a complete loss of knee function, pain, and swelling, with the patella resting in an abnormal position. The physician immediately reduces the dislocation by applying mild pressure on the patella with the knee extended as much as possible. If a period of time has elapsed before reduction, a general anesthesia may have to be used. After aspiration of the joint hematoma, ice is applied and the joint is splinted. A first-time patellar dislocation is always associated with a chondral or osteochondral fracture. X-ray evaluation is performed before and after reduction.[26]

Management To reduce a dislocation, the hip is flexed and the patella is gently moved medially as the knee is slowly extended. After reduction the knee is immobilized in extension for 4 weeks or longer, and the athlete is instructed to use crutches when walking. During immobilization, isometric exercises are performed at the knee joint. After immobilization the athlete should wear a horseshoe-shaped felt pad that is held in place around the patella by an elastic wrap or is sewn into an elastic sleeve that is worn while running or performing in sports (Fig. 20-45). Commercial braces are also available.

Muscle rehabilitation should be concerned with all the musculature of the knee, thigh, and hip. Knee exercise should be confined to straight leg raises.[15]

If surgery is performed, it is usually to release constrictive ligaments or to reconstruct the patellofemoral joint. It is important to strengthen and balance the strength of all musculature associated with the knee joint. Postural malalignments must be corrected as much as possible. Shoe orthoses may be employed to reduce foot pronation, tibial torsion, and subsequently to reduce stress to the patellofemoral joint.

Patellofemoral Arthralgia

The patella, in relation to the femoral groove, can be subject to direct trauma or disease, leading to chronic pain and disability. Of major importance among athletes are those conditions which stem from abnormal patellar tracting within the femoral goove; of which the two most common are chondromalacia and degenerative arthritis.

Figure 20-45

Special pads for the dislocating patella.

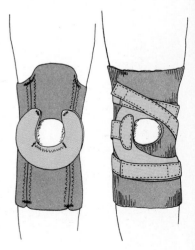

Chondromalacia

Occurring most often among teenagers and young adults, chondromalacia is a gradual degenerative process (Fig. 20-46). Cailliet[8] describes chondromalacia as undergoing three stages:

Stage 1   Swelling and softening of the articular cartilage
Stage 2   Fissuring of the softened articular cartilage
Stage 3   Deformation of the surface of the articular cartilage due to fragmentation

Etiological factors   The exact cause of chondromalacia is unknown. As indicated earlier, abnormal patellar tracting could be a major etiological factor; however, individuals with normal tracting have acquired chondromalacia and some individuals with abnormal tracting are free of it.[8] Abnormal patellofemoral tracting can be produced by the following:

1. Genu valgum
2. External tibial torsion
3. Foot pronation
4. Femoral anteversion
5. A quadriceps Q angle greater than 15 to 20 degrees
6. Patella alta
7. A shallow femoral groove
8. A shallow articular angle of the patella
9. An abnormal articular contour of the patella
10. Laxity of the quadriceps tendon

Symptoms and signs   The athlete may experience pain in the anterior aspect of the knee while walking, running, ascending and descending stairs, or squatting. There may be recurrent swelling around the kneecap and a grating sensation on flexing and extending the knee.

The patella displays crepitation with the patellar grind test. On palpation there may be pain on the inferior border of the patella or when the patella is compressed within the femoral groove while the knee is passively flexed and extended. The athlete is found to have one or more lower limb alignment deviations.

Degenerative Arthritis

Degenerative arthritis, in contrast to chondromalacia, occurs on the medial facet of the patella, which makes contact with the femur when the athlete performs a full squat.[8,23] Degeneration first occurs in the deeper portions of the articular cartilage, followed by a blistering and fissuring that stems from the subchondral bone and appears on the surface of the patella.[8]

Management   In some cases, patellofemoral arthralgia is initially treated conservatively as follows:

1. Avoidance of irritating activities such as stair climbing and squatting
2. Isometric exercises that are pain free to strengthen the quadriceps and hamstring muscles[9,25]
3. Oral anti-inflammatory agents, small doses of aspirin[26]
4. Wearing of a chrondromalacia brace (Fig. 20-47)
5. Wearing of an orthotic device to correct pronation and reduce tibial torsion

Figure 20-46

Chondromalacia with chipping away of the articular surface.

If conservative measures fail to help, surgery may be the only alternative. Some of the following surgical measures may be indicated[8,26]:

1. Realignment procedures, such as lateral release of the retinaculum, moving the insertion of the vastus medialis muscle forward
2. Shaving and smoothing the irregular surfaces of the patella and/or femoral condyle
3. In cases of degenerative arthritis the blister may be removed by drilling
4. Elevating the tibial tubercle
5. As a last resort the patella may be completely removed

Other Extensor Mechanism Problems

Many other extensor mechanism problems can occur in the physically active individual. They can occur in the immature knee or through jumping and running.

The Immature Extensor Mechanism

Two conditions common to the immature adolescent knee are Osgood-Schlatter disease and Larsen-Johansson disease.

Osgood-Schlatter disease Osgood-Schlatter disease is an apophysitis under the general classification of osteochondritis. To call this condition a disease is misleading because it is a number of conditions related to the epiphyseal growth center of the tibial tubercle. The tibial tubercle is an apophysis for the attachment of the patellar tendon.

Etiological factors The most commonly accepted cause is repeated avulsion of the patellar tendon at the epiphysis of the tibial tubercle. Complete avulsion of the patellar tendon is a major complication of Osgood-Schlatter disease.

Symptoms and signs Repeated irritation causes swelling, hemorrhage, and gradual degeneration of the epiphysis due to impaired circulation. The athlete complains of severe pain on kneeling, jumping, and running. There is point tenderness over the anterior proximal tibial tubercle (Fig. 20-48).

Conditions that may be mistaken for one another:
Osgood-Schlatter disease
Larsen-Johansson disease
Jumper's or kicker's knee

Figure 20-47   **Figure 20-48**

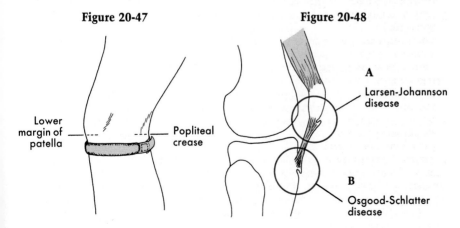

Lower margin of patella — Popliteal crease

A
Larsen-Johannson disease

B
Osgood-Schlatter disease

Figure 20-47

The chondromalacia brace.

Figure 20-48

Two conditions of the immature extensor mechanism.
A, Osgood-Schlatter disease.
B, Larsen-Johansson disease.

Management Management is usually conservative and includes the following:

1. Decreasing stressful activities until the epiphyseal union occurs, within 6 months to 1 year.
2. Severe cases may require a cylindrical cast.
3. Ice application to the knee before and after activities.
4. Isometric strengthening of quadriceps and hamstring muscles.
5. Surgery is performed only in the most severe cases.

Larsen-Johansson disease Larsen-Johansson disease is similar to Osgood-Schlatter disease, but it occurs at the inferior pole of the patella (Fig. 20-48). As with Osgood-Schlatter disease, the cause is believed to be excessive repeated strain by the patellar tendon. Swelling, pain, and point tenderness characterize Larsen-Johansson disease. Later, degeneration can be noted on x-ray examination.

Jumper's and Kicker's Knee Problems

Jumping, as well as kicking or running, may place extreme tension on the knee extensor muscle complex. As a result of either one or more commonly repetitive injuries, tendinitis occurs in the patellar or quadriceps tendon.[6,24,31] On rare occasions, a patellar tendon may completely fail and rupture.

Patellar or quadriceps tendinitis Sudden or repetitive forceful extension of the knee may begin an inflammatory process that will eventually lead to tendon degeneration.

Symptoms and signs Patellar or quadriceps tendinitis can be described in three stages of pain[6]:

Stage 1 Pain after sports activity
Stage 2 Pain during and after activity (the athlete is able to perform at the appropriate level)
Stage 3 Pain during activity and prolonged after activity (athletic performance is hampered) may progress to constant pain and complete rupture

Management Any pain in the extensor mechanism must preclude sudden explosive movement such as that characterized by heavy plyometric-type exercising. Athletes with first or second stage tendinitis should carefully warm the tendons for 5 to 10 minutes in a whirlpool at 100° to 102° F (37.7° to 38.8° C) before performing an activity. Moist heat packs can be used instead of the whirlpool. After warming, a gradual static stretch should be applied as the tendons return to normal preexercise temperature. A gradual exercise warmup should follow. The athlete should cease all activity at once if there is pain during exercise. An ice massage or pack should follow exercise. Third stage jumper's knee should be rested until it is symptom free.

Patellar or quadriceps tendon rupture An inflammatory condition of the knee extensor mechanism over a period of time can cause degeneration and weakness at the tendon attachment. Seldom does a rupture occur in the middle of the tendon, but usually it is torn from its attachment. The quadriceps tendon ruptures from the superior pole of the patella, whereas the patellar tendon ruptures from the inferior pole of the patella. Proper conservative care of jumper's knee is essential to avoid such a major injury. For athletes who use anti-inflammatory drugs, such as steroids, intense exercise involving the knee must be avoided.[23] Steroids injected directly into these tendons are known to weaken collagen fibers and mask pain.[20,23]

Runner's and Cyclist's Knee

Runner's knee is a general expression for many repetitive and overuse conditions. Many runner's knee problems can be attributed to malalignment and structural asymmetries of the foot and lower leg, including leg-length discrepancy. Common are patellar tendinitis and patellofemoral problems that may lead to chondromalacia. Two conditions that are becoming increasingly prevalent among joggers, distance runners, and cyclists are iliotibial band tendinitis and pes anserinus tendinitis or bursitis.

Iliotibial band tendinitis　Iliotibial band tendinitis commonly occurs in runners and cyclists having genu varum. Irritation develops at the band's insertion and, where friction is created, over the lateral femoral condyle. Conducting Ober's test (p. 593) will cause pain at the point of irritation.

iliotibial band tendinitis
Runner's knee

Pes anserinus tendinitis or bursitis　The pes anserinus is where the sartorius, gracilis, and semitendinous muscles join to the tibia (Fig. 20-7). Associated with this condition is pes anserinus bursitis. In contrast to iliotibial band tendinitis, inflammation results from excessive genu valgum and weakness of the vastus medialis muscle. This condition is commonly produced by running on a slope with one leg higher than the other.

pes anserinus tendinitis
Cyclist's knee

Management　Management of runner's or cyclist's knee involves correction of foot and leg alignment problems. Therapy includes cold packs or ice massage before and after activity, proper warmup and stretching, and avoiding activities that aggravate the problem, such as running on inclines.

The Collapsing Knee

Knee collapse can stem from a variety of reasons. The most common causes of frequent knee collapse include a weak quadriceps muscle; chronic instability of the medial collateral ligament, anterior cruciate ligament, or posterior capsule; a torn meniscus; loose bodies within the knee; and a subluxating patella. Chondromalacia and a torn meniscus have also been known to cause the knee to give way.

KNEE JOINT REHABILITATION

The knee rehabilitation program has as its primary goal to restore the athlete's muscle strength, power, endurance, flexibility, and agility. In general, knee rehabilitation falls into six major phases[1]:

Preoperative phase
Phase 1　Postoperative or postinjury period
Phase 2　Early intermediate rehabilitation
Phase 3　Late intermediate rehabilitation
Phase 4　Advanced rehabilitation
Phase 5　Return to competition

Preoperative Phase

If there is to be elective knee surgery, it is essential that muscles surrounding the joint be as strong as possible. A well-conditioned knee will undergo surgery with less negative effects than one that is deconditioned. In addition to the knee joint, all adjacent joints should be conditioned as much as possible. Any exercise decided on must not aggravate the condition (Table 20-1) by forcing the knee through a full range of motion (Fig. 20-49).

Phase 1

Rehabilitative exercise during the immediate postoperative or postinjury phase depends on the nature of surgery or type of injury sustained. Usually both are initiated 24 hours after an operation or an acute injury.[1] This phase ideally should be a continuation of the presurgical phase to maintain normal function and to prevent muscle atrophy but without knee flexion and extension.

Progression from one phase to another depends on the extent of soft tissue healing, pain, joint mobilization, and residual joint instability.

Exercise rehabilitation of the postsurgical anterior instability may take as long as 1 year. The immediate postoperative period continues with the preoperative isometric exercises. Contractile muscle ability is emphasized during this period.[19] To augment the exercise, electrical stimulation or biofeedback training may be performed.[19] In knee rehabilitation after knee reconstruction, 4 to 6 weeks of immobilization may be needed while early healing takes place. This ensures that the sutures or attachments are maintained in a secure position. All joints adjacent to the knee are exercised maximally. During this phase only active motion is encouraged, along with crutch walking using a three-point gait.[30] In anterior instability surgical cases, from 6 to 8 weeks of knee motion is progressively allowed through the use of a cast brace that allows 30 to 60 degrees of flexion. Each week 5

TABLE 20-1

Sample 3-week preoperative phase for uncomplicated injury

Exercise	First Week*	Second Week	Third Week
Quadriceps setting (6 sec maximal contraction, 2 sec rest for 5 min each waking hour)	+	+	+
Straight leg raises against maximal resistance (hold 6 sec in up position followed by 2 sec rest)(in cases of anterior instability, the knee is bent between 20 and 30 degrees)			
Into hip extension	+	+	−
Into hip abduction	+	+	−
Into hip adduction	+	+	−
Into hip flexion	+	+	−
Wall pulley (maximal resistance 10-15 repetitions three times a day)			
Into hip extension		+	+
Into hip flexion		+	+
Into hip abduction		+	+
Into hip adduction		+	+
Isokinetic knee flexion (of special importance to anterior instability repair)		+	+
PNF patterns for ankle, knee, and hip		+	+

* +, Performed; −, optional.

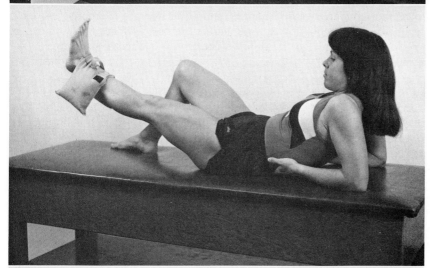

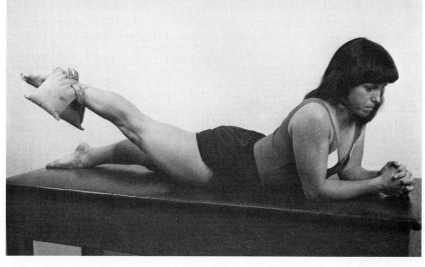

Figure 20-49

Knee exercises performed in
the presurgical period and
stage 1. **A,** Muscle setting.
B, Straight leg raise with hip
flexion. **C,** Straight leg raise
with hip extension.

A

B

C

degrees of extension and 10 degrees of flexion are added until 90 degrees of
flexion and − 15 degrees of extension have been achieved.[30] On leaving the
hospital the athlete is encouraged to engage in general conditioning activities to maintain the level of fitness.

Phase 2

Phase 2 is considered the early intermediate period of rehabilitation. It usually begins at the end of immobilization and when swelling is controlled,
pain is minimal, and the athlete can flex the knee 90 degrees and extend it
to − 15 degrees. For the knee that has been surgically corrected for anterior
instability, this phase may not commence for 10 to 12 weeks after surgery.
Less complicated knee problems may begin this phase 3 to 4 weeks after
injury. A major goal of Phase 2 is to restore biomechanical efficiency and
achieve full mobilization and pain-free extension and flexion. Both the
quadriceps and hamstring muscle groups must be strengthened; however,
in anterior cruciate ligament repair, hamstring strength is emphasized over
the quadriceps. Employing isotonic hamstring exercise does not produce an
anterior drawer force on the tibia, as does isotonic quadriceps exercise (Table 20-2) (Fig. 20-50).

Phase 3

Phase 3 is considered as the later intermediate stage of rehabilitation. The
criteria for beginning Phase 3 are no swelling or inflammation and minimal
to no pain with almost full range of motion. The athlete is able to walk
without a limp. For the athlete who has undergone reconstruction of anterior instability, this phase may not be reached for 6 months or longer. This
phase involves more intense exercising. Isokinetic or PNF exercises, isotonic or isometric resistance, and cycling exercises are those of choice (Table 20-3) (Fig. 20-51).

Phase 4

To enter Phase 4 of knee joint rehabilitation the athlete must have full
range of motion, no symptoms, functional stability, and no more than a
10% deficit in strength, power, and endurance compared to the uninvolved
leg. Phase 4 represents the functional stage of the rehabilitation program

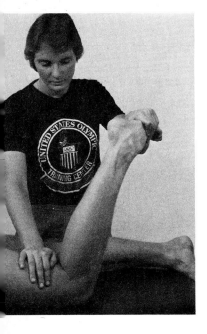

Figure 20-50

It is essential that hamstring
muscle strength be increased
in cases of knee injury and
surgery.

TABLE 20-2

Phase 2 knee joint rehabilitation

Exercise	Repetitions or Duration	Times a Day
Straight leg raises from all positions, maximal resistance (sandbags)	15-20	3
Straight leg pulling exercise in all positions, maximal resistance	15-20	3
Toe raises	15-20	3
PNF exercises (emphasize hamstring muscles for anterior cruciate ligament repair)	15-20	2-3
Stationary cycling; first both legs, then affected leg only	10-20 min	1-2
Modified isokinetic exercise (begin with low speed and progress gradually)	5-15	2-3

Figure 20-51

When an athlete is able to
almost fully extend an
injured knee against some
resistance, he or she is ready
for stage 4 rehabilitation.

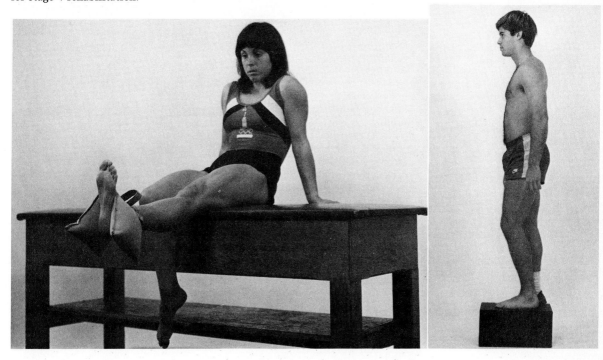

TABLE 20-3

Phase 3 knee joint rehabilitation

Exercise	Repetitions or Duration	Times a Day
Isokinetic	Starting at 120 degrees/sec and progressing to 300 degrees/sec	1-2
PNF exercises		1
Stationary bicycling	3-5 miles as fast as possible (varied resistance)	1
Pes anserinus isometric exercise	6 sec contact	2-3
Isotonic exercise, maximal resistance		
Leg extension	15-20 repetitions	1
Leg flexion	15-20 repetitions	1
Leg press	15-20 repetitions	1
Balance activities		
On one leg	2-3 min	3
On 2-inch (5 cm) board (eyes open)	2-3 min	3
On wobble board (eyes closed)	2-3 min	3
Active static stretching of quadriceps and hamstring muscles	30 sec each repeated 3 times	2-3
Jogging (jog-run for uncomplicated knee)	1-3 miles	1

TABLE 20-4

Phase 4 knee joint rehabilitation

Exercise	Repetitions or Duration	Times a Day or Week
Isokinetic	300 degrees/sec, 5 min	1 a day
Isotonic, maximal resistance		
Leg extension	15-20 repetitions, 3 sets of 10	3 times a week
Leg curls		
Leg presses		
Half knee squats		
Toe raises		
Rope jumping	10-20 min	1 time a day
Stationary bicycling	10-20 min	1 time a day
Running	20 min	
Progress from slow running to fast and straight jog or straight run	2-3 miles	1 time a day
Progress to running circles in each direction, large figure-of-eights, weaving in and out of obstacles, and cutting maneuvers	1-2 miles	2 times

TABLE 20-5

DAPRE technique

Set	Weight	Repetitions
1	Half working weight	10
2	Three fourths working weight	6
3	Full working weight	Maximum*
4	Adjusted working weight	Maximum†

From Knight, K.L.: Am. J. Sports Med. 7:336, 1979.
*The number of repetitions performed during the third set is used to determine the working weight for fourth set according to the guidelines in Table 20-6.
†The number of repetitions performed during the fourth set is used to determine the working weight for the next session.

TABLE 20-6

General guidelines for adjustment of working weight

| Repetitions in Each Set | Adjusted Working Weight | |
	Fourth Set*	Next Session†
0-2	Decrease 5-10 lb	Decrease 5-10 lb
3-4	Decrease 0-5 lb	Keep same
5-6	Keep same	Increase 5-10 lb
7-10	Increase 5-10 lb	Increase 5-15 lb
11-	Increase 10-15 lb	Increase 10-20 lb

From Knight, K.L.: Am. J. Sports Med. 7:336, 1979.
*Repetitions performed during the third set are used to determine the adjusted working weight for the fourth set. (See Table 20-5.)
†Repetitions performed during the fourth set are used to determine the working weight for the next session (usually the next day). (See Table 20-5.)

(Fig. 20-52). For the surgical knee, especially anterior instability reconstruction, this phase may not arrive until the tenth or twelfth month (Table 20-4).

Phase 5

Phase 5 is the athlete's reinstatement to competition. Exercise is no longer directed toward therapy, but toward competitive conditioning. The knee now is symptom free and equal in every respect to the uninjured knee in terms of strength, power, and size.

Modification of the DeLorme Method

An excellent modification to the DeLorme method of progressive-resistance exercise (PRE) has been developed: it is called *daily adjustable progressive-resistive exercise* (DAPRE).[22] In this method daily strength increases are noted. In this method the athlete exercises at near optimal level. In the third and fourth sets as many full repetitions are performed as possible, with the number being executed determining the weight to be added for the fourth set and for the first set in the next exercise session (Tables 20-5 and 20-6).

Criteria for Recovery and Returning to Sports

The criteria for recovery after a knee injury are sport specific. Every sport has certain requirements such as jumping, running, or cutting from one side to the other. These are feats that can be tested. As indicated earlier, full range of motion, equal or almost equal circumference to the unaffected side, and full strength, power, endurance, and proprioception are also of major importance.

Maintenance

Once a serious knee injury has occurred, the knee tends to decondition quickly. It is important for the athlete to engage in a daily maintenance

DAPRE

Daily adjustable progressive resistive exercise; a modification of the DeLorme method of exercise rehabilitation

Figure 20-52

In stage 4 exercise rehabilitation the athlete has gained almost full strength, power, and flexibility.

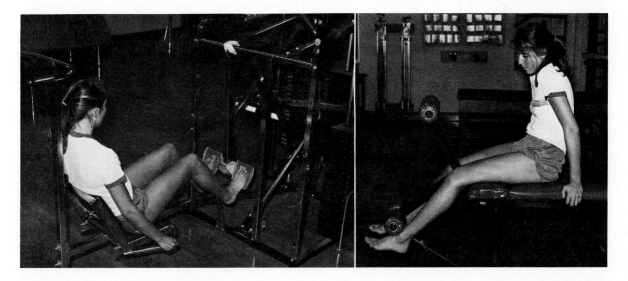

program. Immediately after practice the athlete should use either an isokinetic machine or exercise isotonically with weight resistance. Fifty percent of maximal resistance should keep the knee strong.

A collapse after a sudden change of direction may indicate ligamentous instability or a kneecap that has moved out of its articular groove. Catching and collapse can occur in a knee that has a disrupted meniscus, a patella that has an irregular articular surface, or a piece of articular cartilage that has broken loose in osteochondritis dissecans. If these recur, bracing or surgery may be the treatment of choice.

Patellofemoral Joint Rehabilitation

Patellofemoral joint exercise rehabilitation should be performed conservatively.

Injuries to the patellofemoral joint should be rehabilitated conservatively. All exercises should be pain free. Primarily, exercise rehabilitation consists of muscle setting and isometrics[8] (Table 20-7).

TABLE 20-7

Patellofemoral joint rehabilitation

Exercise*	Repetitions or Duration	Times a Day
While lying on back, with knee in full extension, contract quadriceps muscle isometrically pulling patella toward abdomen; when pain free progress to next exercise	Hold for 6 sec, rest 2 sec; repeat 2-3 times a session	1-2 times every waking hour
With 4-inch (10 cm) thick pad underneath popliteal fossa, extend knee fully	With 2-10 lb weight on ankle, hold extended position for 6 sec; repeat 2-3 times	1-2 times every waking hour
With 4-inch (10 cm) thick pad underneath popliteal fossa, and knee fully extended, slowly, eccentrically lower knee to table	With 2-10 lb weight on ankle, repeat 2-3 times	1-2 times every waking hour
In front-lying position with pillow under abdomen, slowly curl knee to approximately 30-degree angle	With 2-10 lb weight on ankle, hold terminal position for 6 sec; repeat 2-3 times	1-2 times every waking hour
In front-lying position with pillow under abdomen, slowly lower leg eccentrically from 30-degree angle of flexion	With 2-10 lb weight on ankle, repeat leg exercise 2-3 times	1-2 times every waking hour

*All exercises must be within pain-free limitations.

REFERENCES

1. Allman, F.L.: Exercise in sports medicine. In Basmajian, J.V. (editor): Therapeutic exercise, ed. 3, Baltimore, 1978, The Williams & Wilkins Co.
2. Arnoczky, S.P., and Warren, R.F.: Microvasculature of the human meniscus, Am. J. Sports Med. **10**:90, March/April 1982.
3. Berfeld, J.A.: Injury to the anterior cruciate ligament, Phys. Sportsmed. **10**:47, Nov. 1982.
4. Birnbaum, J.S.: The musculoskeletal manual, New York, 1982, Academic Press, Inc.
5. Blackburn, T.A., Jr., Eiland, W.G., and Bandy, W.D.: An introduction to the plica, J. Orthop. Sports Phys. Ther. **3**:171, Spring 1982.
6. Blazina, M.E., et al.: Jumper's knee, Orthop. Clin. North Am. **4**:665, 1973.
7. Bowers, K.D., Jr.: Patella tendon avulsion as complication of Os-

good-Schlatter's disease, Am. J. Sports Med. **9**:356, Nov./Dec. 1981.

8. Cailliet, R.: Knee pain and disability, ed. 2, Philadelphia, 1983, F.A. Davis Co.

9. Dehaven, K.E., et al.: Chondromalacia patella in athletics, Am. J. Sports Med. **1**:5, 1979.

10. Derscheid, F.L., and Garrick, J.G.: Medial collateral ligament injuries in football, Am. J. Sports Med. **9**:365, Nov./Dec. 1981.

11. DiStefano, V.J.: The enigmatic anterior cruciate ligament Ath. Train. **16**:244, 1981.

12. Galway, R.D., Beaupré, A., and MacIntosh, D.L.: Pivot-shift: a clinical sign of symptomatic anterior cruciate insufficiency, J. Bone Joint Surg. **54B**:763, 1972.

13. Handling, K.A.: Taping procedure for an unstable knee, Athletic Training **16**:248, Winter 1981.

14. Hardacker, W.T., Jr., Whipple, T.L., and Bassett, F.H.: Diagnosis and treatment of the plica syndrome of the knee, J. Bone Joint Surg. **62A**:221, 1980.

15. Henry, J.H., and Crosland, J.W.: Conservative treatment of patellofemoral subluxation, Am. J. Sports Med. **7**:1, 1979.

16. Hoppenfeld, S.: Physical examination of the spine and extremities, New York, 1976, Appleton-Century-Crofts.

17. Howe, J., and Johnson, R.J.: Knee injuries in skiing, Symposium on skiing injuries, Clinics in sports medicine, vol. 1, no. 2, Philadelphia, July 1982, W.B. Saunders Co.

18. Johnson, R.J.: The anterior cruciate: a dilemma in sports medicine, Int. J. Sports Med. **2**:71, May 1982.

19. Jones, A.L.: Rehabilitation for anterior instability of the knee: preliminary report, J. Orthop. Sports Phys. Ther. **3**:121, Winter 1982.

20. Kennedy, J.C., and Willis, R.B.: The effects of local steroid injections on tendons: a biomechanical and microscopic correlative study, Am. J. Sports Med, **4**:11, 1976.

21. Klein, K.K.: Developmental asymmetries of the weight bearing skeleton and its implications on knee stress and knee injury, Ath. Train. **17**:207, 1982.

22. Knight, K.L.: Knee rehabilitation by daily adjustable progressive resistive exercise technique, Am. J. Sports Med. **7**:336, 1979.

23. Kulund, D.N.: The injured athlete, Philadelphia, 1982, J.B. Lippincott Co.

24. Larson, R.L.: Problems of the extensor mechanism, Ath. Train. **13**:4, 1978.

25. Levine, J.: Chondromalacia patellae, Phys. Sportsmen. **7**:8, 1979.

26. Maron, B.R.: Orthopedic aspects of sports medicine. In Appenzeller, O., and Atkinson, R. (editors): Sports medicine, Baltimore, 1981, Urban & Schwarzenberg, Inc.

27. McDaniel, J.W., and Dameron, T.B.: Untreated ruptures of the anterior cruciate ligament: a follow-up study, J. Bone Joint Surg. **62A**:696, 1980.

28. Mueller, F.O., and Blyth, C.S.: North Carolina High School football injury: equipment and prevention, J. Sport Med. **2**:1, 1974.

29. Norwood, L.A., Jr., and Cross, M.J.: Anterior cruciate ligament: functional anatomy of its bundles in rotary instabilities, Am. J. Sports Med. **7**:23, 1979.

30. Noyes, R., Grood, E., and Butler, D.L.: Knee rehabilitation after anterior cruciate ligament reconstruction and repair, Am. J. Sports Med. **9**:140, May 1981.

31. Roels, J., et al.: Patellar tendinitis (jumper's knee), Am. J. Sports Med. **6**:6, 1978.

32. Slocum, D.B., and Larson, R.I.: Rotary instability of the knee and its pathogenesis and clinical test to demonstrate its presence, J. Bone Joint Surg. **50**:211, 1968.

33. Southmayd, W., and Hoerner E.F.: Injuries to the lower extremities. In Vinger, P.F., and Hoerner, E.F. (editors): Sports injuries: the unthwarted epidemic, Boston, 1982, John Wright, PSG, Inc.

34. Subotnick, S.I.: Limb length dis-

crepancies of the lower extremity
(short leg syndrome), J. Orthop.
Sports Phys. Ther. **3:**11, Summer
1981.

ADDITIONAL SOURCES

Allman, F.: Rehabilitation following
knee injury, Southwest Athletic
Trainers Association Meeting, Jan.
1982, National Athletic Trainers Association. (Cassette.)

Arnold, J.A., et al.: Natural history of
anterior cruciate tears, Am. J. Sports
Med. **7:**6, 1979.

Black, S.: Postknee arthroscopy rehabilitation, Eastern Athletic Trainers Association Meeting, Jan. 1984. National Athletic Trainers Association.
(Cassette.)

Examination of the knee and contusions and strains of the lower extremities, Chicago, Teach'em, Inc.
(Cassette.)

Cyriax, J.: Textbook of orthopaedic
medicine, vol. I, Diagnosis of soft tissue lesions, ed. 8, Eastbourne, 1982,
Bailliére Tindall.

Fulkerson, J.P.: Awareness of the retinaculum in evaluating patellofemoral pain, Am. J. Sports Med.
10:147, 1982.

Klien, K.K., and Allman, F.L., Jr.: The
knee in sports, Austin, Tex., 1969,
The Pemberton Press.

35. Torsten, J., et al.: Clinical diagnosis of ruptures of the anterior cruciate ligament, Am. J. Sports Med.
10:100, 1982.

Pope, M.H.: The biomechanics of tibial
shaft and knee injuries, Symposium
on skiing injuries, Clinics in sports
medicine, vol. 1, no. 2, Philadelphia,
1982, W.B. Saunders Co.

Ray, R.L.: Alterations and long-term
implications in knee function following trauma, Southwest Athletic
Trainers Association Meeting, Jan.
1982, National Athletic Trainers Association. (Cassette.)

Sperryn, P.N.: Sport and medicine,
Woburn, Mass., 1983, Butterworths
Publishers, Inc.

Sprains and internal derangements of
the knee and other injuries to lower
extremities, Chicago, Teach'em, Inc.
(Cassette.)

Waskowitz, W.: Knee arthroscopy in
perspective, Eastern Athletic Trainers Association Meeting, National
Athletic Trainers Association. (Cassette.)

Wild, J., et al.: Patella pain and quadriceps rehabilitation—an EMG study,
Am. J. Sports Med. **10:**12, Jan./Feb.
1982.

Chapter 21

THE THIGH, HIP, AND PELVIS

When you finish this chapter, you should be able to

Discuss the major anatomical features of the thigh, hip, and pelvis as they relate to sports injuries

Recognize and evaluate the major sports injuries to the thigh, hip, and pelvis

Establish a management plan for a sports injury to the thigh, hip, and pelvis

Although the thigh, hip, and pelvis have relatively lower incidences of injury than the knee and lower limb, they still receive considerable trauma from a variety of sports activities. Of major concern are thigh strains and contusions and chronic and overuse stresses affecting the thigh and hip.

THE THIGH REGION
Anatomy

The thigh is generally considered that part of the leg between the hip and the knee. Several important anatomical units must be considered in terms of their relationship to sports injuries: the shaft of the femur, musculature, nerves and blood vessels, and the fascia that envelops the thigh.

The Femur

The femur (Fig. 21-1) is the longest and strongest bone in the body and is designed to permit maximum mobility and support during locomotion. The cylindrical shaft is bowed forward and outward to accommodate the stresses placed on it during the bending of the hip and knee and in weight bearing.

Thigh Musculature

The muscles of the thigh may be divided into four classes according to the type of action for which they are responsible: flexors, extensors, abductors, and adductors.

Quadriceps femoris Normally the strongest of the thigh muscles, the quadriceps femoris muscle group (Fig. 21-2) consists of four muscles: rectus femoris, vastus medialis and lateralis, and vastus intermedius.

Specific Sports Injuries and
Other Problems

Rectus femoris The rectus femoris muscle is attached superiorly to the anterior inferior iliac spine and the ilium above the acetabulum and inferiorly to the patella and patellar ligament which in turn attaches to the tibial tuberosity.

Vasti muscles The vastus medialis and lateralis originate from the lateral and medial linea aspera of the femur, while the vastus intermedius muscle originates mainly from the anterior and lateral portion of the femur. Inferiorly, the three vasti muscles are attached to the rectus femoris muscle and to the lateral and proximal aspects of the patella.

Function The function of the quadriceps femoris muscle group is extension of the lower leg or the thigh on the lower leg. The rectus femoris muscle, with its pelvic attachment of the quadriceps muscles, is the only flexor of the thigh at the hip joint. This muscle group is innervated by the femoral nerve.

Hamstring muscles Located posteriorly, the hamstring muscle group (Fig. 21-3) consists of three muscles: the biceps femoris, semimembranosus, and semitendinosus muscles.

Biceps femoris The biceps femoris, as its name implies, has two heads. Its long head originates with the semitendinosus at the medial aspect of the ischial tuberosity. Its short head is attached to the linea aspera below the gluteus maximus attachment on the femur and medial to the attachment of the vastus lateralis. Both muscle heads attach with a common tendon to the head of the fibula. Both muscle heads are supplied by branches of the sciatic nerve.

Semitendinosus The semitendinosus originates at the medial aspect of the ischial tuberosity along with the biceps femoris. Together with the semimembranosus, the semitendinosus muscle attaches to the medial aspect of the proximal tibia. This attachment is just behind those of the sartorius and gracilis muscles, which all together form the pes anserinus tendon. The tibial branch of the sciatic nerve supplies this muscle.

Figure 21-1

Femur (os femoris).

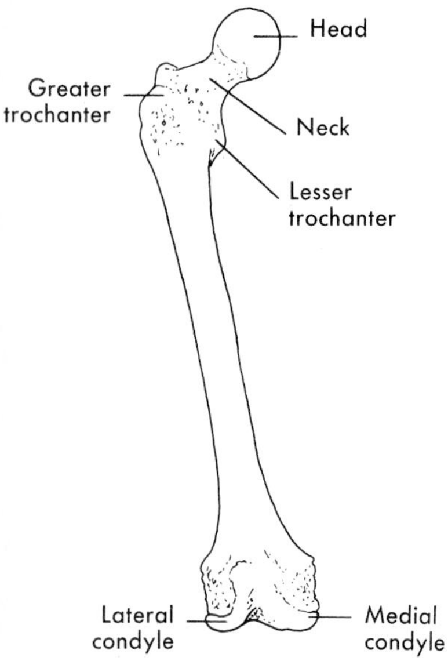

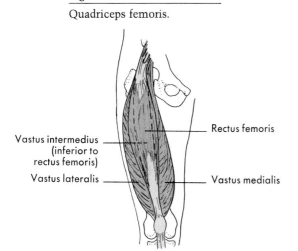

Figure 21-2

Quadriceps femoris.

Vastus intermedius (inferior to rectus femoris)

Vastus lateralis

Rectus femoris

Vastus medialis

Figure 21-3

Hamstring muscles.

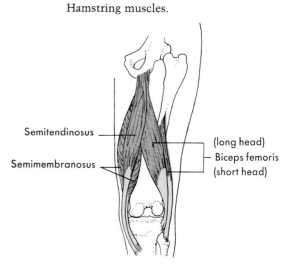

Semitendinosus

Semimembranosus

(long head)

Biceps femoris (short head)

Semimembranosus The semimembranosus originates from the lateral aspect of the upper half of the ischeal tuberosity. Moving downward, it attaches into the medial femoral condyle. It also attaches to the medial side of the tibia, the popliteus muscle fascia, and the posterior capsule of the knee joint. The tibial branch of the sciatic nerve supplies this muscle.

The hamstring muscles are biarticular; acting as extensors at the hip and flexors at the knee joint. Assisting the hamstrings in knee flexion are the sartorius, gracilis, popliteus, and gastrocnemius muscles. At the hip, hamstrings work in cooperation with the gluteus maximus to extend the hip. Lateral rotation of the leg at the knee is conducted by the biceps femoris, while medial rotation is caused by both the semitendinosus and semimembranosus muscles.

Sartorius, gracilis, adductor longus, brevis, and magnus Five muscles serve to make up the medial bulk of the thigh. They are the sartorius, gracilis, adductor longus, brevis, and magnus. All act as adductors and lateral rotators of the thigh at the hip joint (Fig. 21-4).

Sartorius The sartorius muscle attaches above to the anterior superior iliac spine and inferiorly to the proximal medial aspect of the tibia. It serves as a flexor of the thigh at the hip and as a flexor of the leg at the knee, as well as a lateral rotator of the thigh at the hip. A branch of the femoral nerve innervates this muscle.

Gracilis The gracilis is attached superiorly to the body of the inferior ramus of the pubis and inferiorly to the medial aspect of the proximal tibia. It is a relatively narrow-appearing muscle that adducts the thigh at the hip and flexes and medially rotates the leg at the knee joint. The anterior branch of the obturator nerve serves this muscle.

Adductor longus and adductor brevis Both the adductor longus and adductor brevis originate at the body and the inferior ramus of the pubis. They attach inferiorly on the linea aspera of the femur. Both muscles adduct the thigh at the hip and are served by the anterior branch of the obturator nerve.

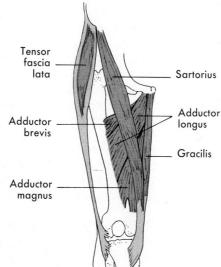

Figure 21-4

Hip adductors.

Adductor magnus The adductor magnus is the largest of the adductor muscles that adduct the thigh at the hip. It also originates from the ischial tuberosity and attaches to the linea aspera of the femur. Its upper part is supplied by the posterior branch of the obturator nerve and the lower aspect by a branch of the sciatic nerve.

Tensor fascia lata The tensor fascia lata muscle is located on the upper anterior aspect of the lateral thigh. It is attached superiorly to the iliac crest just behind the anterior superior iliac spine and is inserted inferiorly into the iliotibial tract. Its primary action is flexion and medial rotation of the thigh. It is innervated by the superior gluteal nerve.

Fascia of the thigh The deep fascia lata, which surrounds and invests the muscles of the thigh, is thick anteriorly, laterally, and posteriorly, but becomes much thinner where it covers the adductor muscles. Laterally, it provides an attachment for the tensor fascia lata muscle and the major part of the gluteus maximus muscle.

Thigh Injuries

Injuries to the thigh muscles are among the most common in sports. Contusions and strains appear most often, with the former having the higher incidence.

Quadriceps Contusions

The quadriceps group is continually exposed to traumatic blows in a variety of vigorous sports. Contusions of the quadriceps display all the classic symptoms of most muscle bruises. They usually develop as the result of a severe impact to the relaxed thigh, compressing the muscle against the hard surface of the femur. At the instant of trauma, pain, a transitory loss of function, and immediate capillary effusion usually occur. The extent of the force and the degree of thigh relaxation determine the depth of the injury and the amount of structural and functional disruption that take place.

Symptoms and signs Early detection and avoidance of profuse internal hemorrhage are vital, both in effecting a fast recovery by the athlete and in the prevention of widespread scarring. Detection of the "charleyhorse" is based on a history of injury, palpation, and a muscle function test. The athlete usually describes having been hit by a sharp blow to the thigh, which produced an intense pain and weakness. Palpation may reveal a circumscribed swollen area that is painful to the touch. A function test is given to the quadriceps muscle. Injury to the quadriceps produces varying degrees of weakness and a decreased range of motion.

First Degree Contusions

The first degree quadriceps contusion causes little pain or swelling and mild point tenderness at the site of trauma. There is little restriction of range of motion, with the athlete able to flex the knee 90 degrees or more.[2]

Second Degree Contusions

The moderate quadriceps contusion causes pain, swelling, and limited range of knee flexion. Range of knee motion is restricted to less than 90 degrees. An obvious limp is present.

Third Degree Contusions

The severe quadriceps contusion represents a major disability. A blow may have been so intense as to split the fascia lata, allowing the muscle to protrude through (muscle herniation) (Fig. 21-5). Pain is severe, and swelling may lead to hematoma. There is severely restricted movement of the knee.

Management   Compression by pressure bandage and the application of a cold medium can help control superficial hemorrhage, but it is doubtful whether pressure and cold will affect a deep contusion (Fig. 21-6). This condition is managed in three stages:

Stage 1—minimizing hemorrhaging through the ICE-R procedure, combined with performing isometric exercises for the quadriceps muscle. Crutches may be warranted in second or third degree contusions. Gentle passive stretching is done while a cold pack is applied.

Stage 2—employing hydromassage, deep thermal therapy, or cryotherapy and stretching to regain normal range of movement.

Stage 3—increasing to full function by a graduated program of resistive exercise and sports participation.[7]

Generally the rehabilitation of a thigh contusion should be handled conservatively. Cold packs combined with gentle stretching may be a preferred treatment. If heat therapy is employed, it should not be initiated until the acute phase of the injury has clearly passed. An elastic bandage should be worn to provide constant pressure and mild support to the quadriceps area. Manual massage and hydromassage are best delayed until resolution of the injury has begun. Exercise should be graduated from mild stretching

Figure 21-5

Quadriceps contusion.

Figure 21-6

Immediate care of the thigh contusion; applying cold pack with a pressure bandage along with a mild stretch may provide some relief.

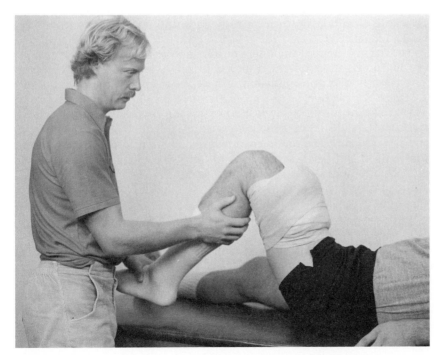

of the quadriceps area in the early stages of the injury to swimming, if possible, and then to jogging and running. Exercise should not be conducted if it produces pain.

Medical care of a thigh contusion may include surgical repair of a herniated muscle or aspiration of a hematoma. Some physicians administer enzymes either orally or through injection for the dissolution of the hematoma.[11]

Once an athlete has sustained a second or third degree thigh contusion, great care must be taken to avoid sustaining another one. The athlete should routinely wear a protective pad held in place by an elastic wrap while engaged in sports activity.

Myositis Ossificans Traumatica

Myositis ossificans
traumatica can occur from:
  A single severe blow
  Many blows to a muscle
    area
  Improper care of a
    contusion

A severe blow or repeated blows to the thigh, usually the quadriceps muscle, can lead to ectopic bone production. It commonly follows bleeding into the quadriceps muscle and a hematoma.[12] The contusion to the muscle causes a disruption of muscle fibers, capillaries, fibrous connective tissue, and periosteum of the femur. Acute inflammation follows resolution of hemorrhage. The irritated tissue may then produce tissue formations resembling cartilage or bone. In 2 to 4 weeks, particles of bone may be noted under x-ray examination. If the injury is a muscle belly, complete absorption or a decrease in size of the formation may occur.[12] This is less likely, however, if calcification is at a muscle origin or insertion. In terms of bone attachment, some formations are completely free of the femur, while one is stalklike and another is broadly attached[6] (Fig. 21-7).

Improper care of a thigh contusion can lead to *myositis ossificans traumatica*, bony deposits or ossification in muscle. The following can initially cause the condition or, once present, aggravate it, causing it to become more pronounced:

1. Attempting to "run off" a quadriceps contusion
2. Too vigorous treatment of a contusion—for example, massage directly over the contusion, ultrasound therapy, or superficial heat to the thigh

Management Once myositis ossificans traumatica is apparent, treatment should be extremely conservative. If the condition is painful and restricts motion, the formation may be surgically removed after 1 year with much less likelihood of its return. Too early removal of the formation may cause it to return. Recurrent myositis ossificans may indicate a blood clotting problem such as hemophilia, which is a very rare condition.[10]

Thigh Strains

The two major areas for thigh strains are the quadriceps and hamstring groups. (Adductor muscle strain will be discussed under hip and pelvic conditions.)

Quadriceps muscle strain Quadriceps tendon strain was discussed under jumper's problems in Chapter 20. However, on occasion, the rectus femoris muscle will become strained by a sudden stretch, such as falling on a bent knee or sudden contraction, as in jumping in volleyball or kick-

Figure 21-7

Myositis ossificans.

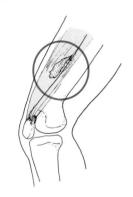

ing in soccer. Usually it is associated with a muscle that is weakened or one that is overly constricted.

A tear in the region of the rectus femoris muscle may cause partial or complete disruption of muscle fibers. The incomplete tear may be located centrally within the muscle or more peripheral to the muscle.

Symptoms and signs A peripheral quadriceps femorus tear causes fewer symptoms than the deeper tear. In general, there is less point tenderness and development of a hematoma.[15] A more centrally located partial muscle tear causes the athlete more pain and discomfort than the peripheral tear. With the deep tear there is a great deal of pain, point tenderness, spasm and loss of function but with little discoloration from internal bleeding. In contrast, complete muscle tear of the rectus femoris muscle may leave the athlete with little disability and discomfort but with some deformity of the anterior thigh.

Management Immediate care involves employing ICE and proper rest. The extent of the tear should be ascertained as soon as possible before swelling, if any, masks the degree of injury. Crutches may be warranted for the first, second, and third days. After the acute inflammatory phase has progressed to resolution and healing has begun, a regimen of isometric muscle contraction, within pain-free limits, can be initiated along with cryotherapy. Other therapy approaches such as cold whirlpool

Figure 21-8

Quadriceps tape support.

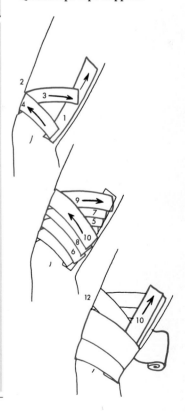

QUADRICEPS TAPE SUPPORT

The taping of the quadriceps muscle group (Fig. 21-8) is designed to give support against the pull of gravity. In cases of moderate or severe contusions or strains, taping may afford protection or mild support and give confidence to the athlete. Various techniques fitted to the individual needs of the athletes can be used.

Materials needed: One roll of 2- or 1½-inch (5 or 3.75 cm) tape, skin toughener, and a 6-inch (15 cm) elastic bandage.

Position of the athlete: The athlete stands on the massage table with leg extended.

Position of the operator: The operator stands facing the anterior aspect of the athlete's injured thigh.

Procedure

1. Two anchor strips, each approximately 9 inches (22.5 cm) long, are placed respectively on the lateral and medial aspects of the thigh and are positioned half the distance between the anterior and posterior aspects.
2. Strips of tape are applied to the thigh, crossing one another to form an X. The crisscrosses are begun 2 or 3 inches (5 or 7.5 cm) above the kneecap and carried upward, overlapping one another. It is important that each tape strip be started from the anchor piece and carried upward and diagonally over the quadriceps, thus lifting against gravity. This procedure is continued until the quadriceps is completely covered.
3. After the diagonal series has been applied, a "lock strip" is placed longitudinally over the medial and lateral borders of the series.
4. To ensure a more effective stability of the quadriceps taping, it is suggested that the entire thigh be encircled by either a 3-inch (7.5 cm) elastic tape or a 6-inch (15 cm) elastic bandage.

Specific Sports Injuries and
Other Problems

In order of incidence of sports
injury to the thigh,
quadriceps contusions rank
first, and hamstring strains
rank second.

and ultrasound may also be employed. Gentle stretching should not be begun until the thigh is pain free.

Hamstring strains   Hamstring strains rank second in incidence of sports injuries to the thigh; of all the muscles of the thigh that are subject to strain, the hamstring group ranks the highest.

Mechanism of injury   The exact cause of hamstring strain is not known. It is speculated that a quick change of the hamstring muscle from one of knee stabilization to that of extending the hip when running could be a major cause of strain. What leads to this muscle failure and deficiency in the complementary action of opposing muscles is not clearly understood. Some possible reasons are muscle fatigue, faulty posture, leg length discrepancy, tight hamstrings, improper form, or imbalance of strength between hamstring muscle groups.

NOTE: In most athletes the hamstring muscle group should be 60% to 70% of that of the quadriceps group.

It has been theorized that because the short head of the biceps femoris may contract at the same time as the quadriceps muscle as a result of an idiosyncracy of nerve innervation, it is subject to the highest incidence of hamstring strain.[1]

Symptoms and signs   Hamstring strain can involve the muscle belly or bony attachment. The extent of injury can vary from the pulling apart of a few muscle fibers to a complete rupture or an avulsion fracture (Fig. 21-9).

Capillary hemorrhage, pain, and immediate loss of function vary according to the degree of trauma. Discoloration may occur a day or two after injury.

First degree hamstring strain usually is evidenced by muscle soreness on movement, accompanied by point tenderness. These strains are often difficult to detect when they first occur. Not until the athlete has cooled down after activity do irritation and stiffness become apparent. The sore-

Figure 21-9

Hamstring tear.

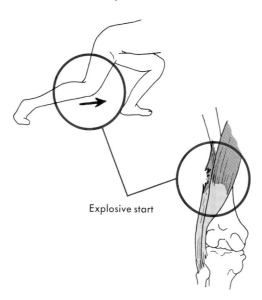

Explosive start

ness of the mild hamstring strain in most instances can be attributed to muscle spasm rather than to the tearing of tissue.

A second degree strain of a hamstring muscle represents partial tearing of muscle fibers, identified by a sudden snap or tear of the muscle accompanied by severe pain and a loss of function on knee flexion.

Third degree hamstring strains constitute the rupturing of tendinous and/or muscular tissue, involving major hemorrhage and disability.

Management Initially an ice pack, with crushed ice, and compression by an elastic wrap should be employed. Activity should be cut down until soreness has been completely alleviated. Ballistic stretching and explosive sprinting must be avoided.

In first degree hamstring strain, as with the other degrees, before the athlete is allowed to resume full sports participation, complete function of the injured part must be restored.

Second and third degree strains should be treated very conservatively. For second degree strains, ICE-R should be used for 24 to 48 hours, and for third degree strains, from 48 to 72 hours. After the early inflammatory phase of injury has stabilized, a treatment regimen of isometric exercise, cryotherapy, and ultrasound may be of benefit. In later stages of healing, gentle stretching within pain limits, jogging, stationary cycling, and isokinetic exercise at high speeds may be beneficial. Following elimination of soreness, the athlete may begin isotonic knee curls. Full recovery may take from 1 month to a full season.

Strains are always a problem to the athlete, because they tend to re-

Figure 21-10

Hamstring taping.

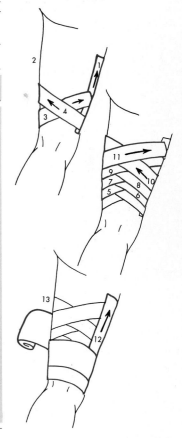

HAMSTRING TAPING

It is extremely difficult to completely relieve the injured hamstring muscles by any wrapping or taping technique, but some stabilization can be afforded by each. The hamstring taping technique (Fig. 21-10) is designed to stabilize the moderately to severely contused or torn hamstring muscles, enabling the athlete to continue to compete.

Materials needed: One roll of 2- or 1½-inch (5 or 3.75 cm) tape, skin toughener, and a roll of 3-inch (7.5 cm) elastic tape or a 6-inch (15 cm) elastic wrap.

Position of the athlete: The athlete lies face downward or may stand on the table, with the affected limb flexed at about a 15-degree angle at the knee, so the hamstring muscle is relaxed and shortened.

Position of the operator: The operator stands at the side of the table, facing the athlete's injured thigh.

Procedure

1. This taping is applied in a way similar to the quadriceps technique. An anchor strip is placed on either side of the thigh, and then strips of approximately 9 inches (22.5 cm) in length are crisscrossed diagonally upward on the posterior aspect of the thigh, forming an X.
2. After the hamstring area is covered with a series of crisscrosses, a longitudinal lock is applied on either side of the thigh.
3. Three-inch (7.5 cm) elastic tape or a 6-inch (15 cm) elastic wrap may be placed around the thigh to aid in holding the crisscross taping in place.

Femoral stress fractures are
becoming more prevalent
because of the increased
popularity of repetitive,
sustained activities, such as
distance running.

Figure 21-11

Old healed fracture of the
femur.

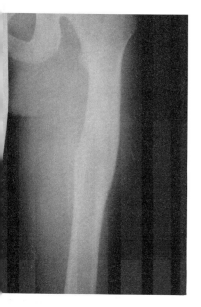

cur as a result of their sometimes healing with inelastic, fibrous scar tissue. The higher the incidence of strains at a particular muscle site, the greater the amount of scar tissue and the greater the likelihood of further injury. The fear of "another pulled muscle" becomes to some individuals almost a neurotic obsession, which is often more handicapping than the injury itself.

Femoral Fractures
Acute Fractures

In sports, fractures of the femur occur most often in the shaft rather than at the bone ends and are almost always caused by a great force, such as falling from a height or being hit directly by another participant. A fracture of the shaft most often takes place in the middle third of the bone because of the anatomical curve at this point, as well as the fact that the majority of direct blows are sustained in this area (Fig. 21-11). Shock generally accompanies a fracture of the femur, as a result of the extreme amount of pathology and pain associated with this injury. Bone displacement is usually present as a result of the great strength of the quadriceps, which causes an overriding of the bone fragments. Direct violence produces extensive soft tissue injury with lacerations of the vastus intermedius, hemorrhaging, and muscle spasms.

A fractured femur is recognized by the classic signs of (1) deformity, with the thigh rotated outward; (2) a shortened thigh, caused by bone displacement; (3) loss of function; (4) pain and point tenderness; and (5) swelling of the soft tissues.

To prevent danger to the athlete's life and to ensure adequate reconditioning, immediate immobilization and referral to a physician must be made.

Femoral stress fractures   Although relatively uncommon, stress fractures of the femur are seen more often than in the past. The possible reason for this is the popularity of jogging and the increased mileage that serious runners engage in. Stress fractures should always be considered as a possibility when there is persistent pain.[3,13] The most common site is in the area of the femoral neck. For incomplete fractures rest and limited weight bearing constitute the usual treatment of choice. Complete stress fractures may have to be surgically pinned.

THE HIP AND PELVIC REGION
Anatomy
Structural Relationships

The pelvis is a bony ring formed by the two innominate bones, the sacrum, and the coccyx (Fig. 21-12). The innominate bones are each made up of an ilium, ischium, and pubis. The functions of the pelvis are to support the spine and trunk and to transfer their weight to the lower limbs. In addition to providing skeletal support, the pelvis serves as a place of attachment for the trunk and thigh muscles and a protection for the pelvic viscera. The basin formed by the pelvis is separated into a false and a true pelvis. The false pelvis is composed of the wings of the ilium, and the true pelvis is made up of the coccyx, the ischium, and the pubis.

The *innominate bones* are composed of three bones that ossify and fuse early in life. They include the ilium, which is positioned superiorly and posteriorly; the pubis, which forms the anterior part; and the ischium, which is located inferiorly. Lodged between the innominate bones is the wedge-shaped *sacrum* composed of five fused vertebrae. The sacrum is joined to other parts of the pelvis by strong ligaments, forming the sacroiliac joints. A small backward-forward movement is present at the sacroiliac junction. The *coccyx* is composed of four or five small, fused vertebral bodies that articulate with the sacrum.

The hip joint is formed by articulation of the femur with the innominate, or hip, bone. The spherical head of the femur fits into a deep socket, the acetabulum, which is padded at its center by a mass of fatty tissue. Surrounding its rim is a fibrocartilage known as the glenoid labrum. A loose sleeve of articular tissue is attached to the circumference of the acetabulum above and to the neck of the femur below. The capsule is lined by an extensive synovial membrane, and the iliofemoral, pubocapsular, and ischiocapsular ligaments give it strong reinforcement. Hyaline cartilage completely covers the head of the femur, with the exception of the fovea capitis, a small area in the center to which the ligamentum teres is attached. The ligamentum teres gives little support to the hip joint, having as its main function the carrying of nutrient vessels to the head of the femur. Because of its bony, ligamentous, and muscular arrangements, this joint is considered by many to be the strongest articulation in the body.

Acetabulum The acetabulum, a deep socket in the innominate bone, receives the articulating head of the femur. It forms an incomplete bony ring that is interrupted by a notch on the lower aspect of the socket. The ring is completed by the transverse ligament that crosses the notch. The socket faces forward, downward, and laterally.

Femoral head The femoral head is a sphere fitting into the acetabulum in a medial, upward, and slightly forward direction.

Synovial membrane The synovial membrane is a vascular tissue en-

Figure 21-12

Pelvis.

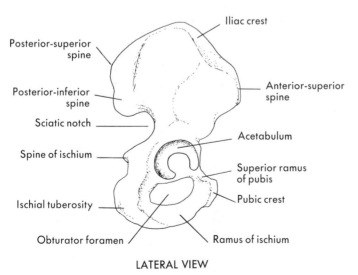

Iliac crest

Posterior-superior spine

Posterior-inferior spine

Sciatic notch

Spine of ischium

Ischial tuberosity

Obturator foramen

Anterior-superior spine

Acetabulum

Superior ramus of pubis

Pubic crest

Ramus of ischium

LATERAL VIEW

closing the hip joint in a tubular sleeve, with the upper portion surrounding the acetabulum. The lower portion is fastened to the circumference of the neck of the femur. Except the ligamentum teres, which lies outside the synovial cavity, the membrane lines the acetabular socket.

Articular capsule   The articular capsule is a fibrous, sleevelike structure covering the synovial membrane, its upper end attaching to the glenoid labrum and its lower end to the neck of the femur. The fibers surrounding the femoral neck consist of circular fibers that serve as a tight collar. This area is called the *zona orbicularis* and acts in holding the femoral head in the acetabulum.

Ligaments   Many strong ligaments—the iliofemoral, the pubofemoral, and the ischiofemoral—reinforce the hip joint (Fig. 21-13).

The *iliofemoral ligament* (Y ligament of Bigelow) is the strongest ligament of the body. It prevents hyperextension, controls external rotation and adduction of the thigh, and limits the pelvis in any backward rolling of the femur head during weight bearing. It reinforces the anterior aspect of the capsule and is attached to the anterior iliac spine and the intertrochanteric line on the anterior aspect of the femur.

The *pubofemoral ligament* prevents excessive abduction of the thigh and is positioned anteriorly and inferior to the pelvis and femur.

The *ischiofemoral ligament* prevents excessive internal rotation and adduction of the thigh and is located posteriorly and superior to the articular capsule.

Bursae   The hip joint has been described as having many bursae. Clinically, the most important of these are the iliopsoas bursa and the deep trochanteric bursa. The iliopsoas bursa is located between the articular capsule and the iliopsoas muscle on the anterior aspect of the joint. The deep trochanteric bursa lies between the greater trochanter and the deep fibers of the gluteus maximus muscle.

Musculature

The hip joint is capable of flexion, extension, adduction, abduction, circumduction, and rotation. The thigh muscles discussed earlier serve to produce major hip movements; however, the following are also muscles that move the hip.

The gluteal region   The gluteus maximus muscle forms the buttocks in the hip region. Lateral to and underneath the gluteus maximus is the

Figure 21-13

Ligaments of the hip.

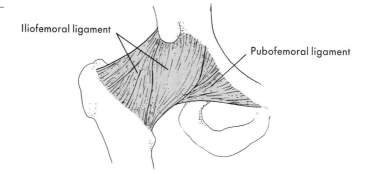

gluteus medius and minimus (Fig. 21-14, *A*). Underneath these larger muscles are much smaller muscles; the piriformis, the obturator internus, and the genilli (Fig. 21-14, *B* and *C*).

Gluteus maximus   This muscle is attached above to the posterior aspect of the iliac crest, the sacrum and the coccyx, as well as to the fascia in the area. Inferiorly, the gluteus maximus attaches to the iliotibial tract and into the fluteal tuberosity of the femur between the linea aspera and greater trochanter. It acts as a lateral rotator of the thigh at the hip joint, as well as allows the body to rise from a sitting to a standing position and, through the attachment to the iliotibial tract, helps to extend the flexed knee. The inferior gluteal nerve supplies this muscle.

Gluteus medius   The gluteus medius is located lateral to the hip. It is attached superiorly to the lateral aspect of the ilium and inferiorly to the lateral aspect of the trochanter. The gluteus maximus covers this muscle posteriorly and anteriorly by the tensor fascia lata. It acts primarily as a thigh abductor at the hip, with some flexion and medial rotation occurring from its anterior aspect, as well as extension and lateral rotation occurring from its posterior aspect. It is innervated by the superior gluteal nerve.

Gluteus minimus   This muscle originates above the lateral aspect of the ilium and attaches inferiorly to the anterior aspect of the greater trochanter of the femur. Its main action is to cause a medial rotation at the hip joint, while its secondary action is abduction of the thigh at the hip joint. It is innervated by the superior gluteal nerve.

Piriformis   The piriformis is a small intrinsic muscle that extends from the anterior aspect of the middle sacrum to the upper aspect of the border of the greater trochanter. It extends from the pelvis through the sciatic notch. As a lateral rotator of the thigh at the hip, it is supplied by the first and second sacral nerves.

Figure 21-14

Gluteal muscles.

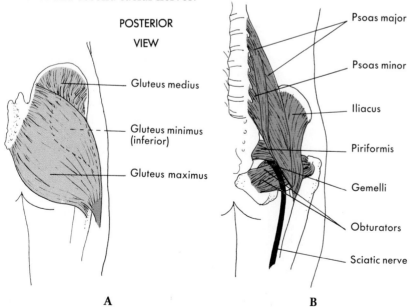

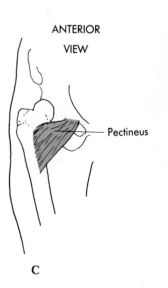

POSTERIOR VIEW

Gluteus medius

Gluteus minimus (inferior)

Gluteus maximus

Psoas major

Psoas minor

Iliacus

Piriformis

Gemelli

Obturators

Sciatic nerve

ANTERIOR VIEW

Pectineus

A   B   C

Obturator internus and gemelli The obturator internus is attached to the obturator foramen. It leaves the pelvis through the lesser sciatic foramen and attaches to the upper aspect of the greater trochanter. Two related muscles, the superior and inferior gemelli, originate at the ischium below the lesser sciatic foramen and attach to the greater trochanter. Both the obturator internus and gemelli are lateral rotators of the thigh at the hip joint. The sacral nerve supplies these muscles.

Psoas major and iliacus The psoas major and iliacus, in coordination with one another, act as flexors of the thigh at the hip joint. The psoas major originates from the lateral aspect of the lumbar spine and attaches to the lesser trochanter of the femur. Its primary action is flexion of the thigh at the hip; however, it also flexes the lumbar spine on the pelvis. It is assisted in flexion by the iliacus, pectineus, and the sartorius muscles. It is innervated by the second and third lumbar nerves. The iliacus muscle originates at the greater iliac fossa and then attaches to the lateral side of the psoas tendon and the lesser trochanter. This muscle is supplied by the femoral nerve.

Pectineus The pectineus muscle is both a flexor and adductor of the thigh at the hip joint. It is attached superiorly to the superior ramus of the pubis and interiorly to the femur below the lesser trochanter. It is innervated by a branch of the femoral nerve.

Obturator externus The obturator externus originates at the outer margins of the obturator foramen and obturator membrane. From this origin it passes below the hip joint and winds posteriorly around the neck of the femur to finally attach to the fossa of the trochanter. It acts as a lateral rotator of the thigh at the hip. It is supplied by a branch of the obturator nerve.

Blood and Nerve Supply
Arteries

The aorta opposite the fourth lumbar vertebra divides to become the two common iliac arteries (Fig. 21-15). They in turn pass downward to divide, opposite the sacroiliac joint, into the internal and external iliac arteries. Most of the branches of the internal iliac artery supply blood to the pelvic viscera. The external iliac artery, on the other hand, is the primary artery to the lower limb. It becomes the femoral artery as it passes behind the inguinal ligament, then moves in front of the thigh, to the medial side, and passes in back of the thigh two thirds of the way down. It then becomes the popliteal artery, which then goes behind the knee between the femoral condyles. For the most part, the femoral artery and its branches supply the muscles of the thigh.

Nerve Supply

The lumbar plexus is created by the intertwining of the fibers stemming from the first four lumbar nerves. The femoral nerve, a major nerve emerging from this plexus, later divides into many branches to supply the thigh and lower leg. Nerve fibers from the fourth and fifth lumbar nerves and the first, second, and third sacral nerves form the sacral plexus with the pelvic cavity anterior to the piriformus muscle. Along with other nerves, the tibial

Figure 21-15

Blood and nerve supply of the hip region.

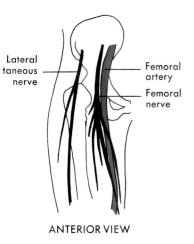

Lateral
taneous
nerve

Femoral
artery

Femoral
nerve

ANTERIOR VIEW

and common peroneal nerve emerge from the sacral plexus and form the large sciatic nerve in the thigh (see Fig. 21-15).

Evaluating the Hip and External Pelvis

The hip and pelvis form the body's major power source for movement. The body's center of gravity is located just in front of the upper part of the sacrum. Injuries to the hip or pelvis cause the athlete major disability in either the lower limb or trunk or both.

Because of the close proximity of the hip and pelvis to the low back region, many evaluative procedures overlap.

Major Complaints

The athlete should be questioned about the site and type of pain, the extent of disability, and when the injury first occurred.

Observation

The athlete should be observed for postural asymmetry, standing on one leg, and ambulation.

The athlete with an external pelvic pain must be observed for postural asymmetry.

Postural asymmetry

1. From the front view, do the hips look even? A laterally tilted hip could mean a leg length discrepancy and/or abnormal muscle contraction on one side of the hip or low back region.
2. From the side view, is the pelvis abnormally tilted anteriorly or posteriorly? This may indicate lordosis or flat back, respectively.
3. In lower limb alignment, is there indication of genu valgum, genu varum, foot pronation, or genu recurvatum? The patella should also be noted for relative position and alignment.
4. The posterior superior iliac spines, represented by the skin depressions above the buttocks, should be horizontal to one another. Uneven depressions could indicate that the pelvis is laterally tilted.

Standing on one leg Standing on one leg may produce pain in the hip, abnormal movement of the symphysis pubis, or a fall of the pelvis on the opposite side as a result of abductor weakness.

Ambulation The athlete should be observed during walking and sitting. Pain in the hip and pelvic region will normally be reflected in movement distortions.

Bony Palpation

The following bony sites should be palpated for pain and continuity:

Anteriorly
1. Anterior superior iliac spine
2. Iliac crest
3. Greater trochanter
4. Pubic tubercles

Posteriorly
1. Posterior superior iliac spines
2. Ischial tuberosity
3. Sacroiliac joint

Soft Tissue Palpation

The soft tissue sites of major concern are those lying in the groin region, the femoral triangle, sciatic nerve, and major muscles.

Groin palpation Groin pain could result from swollen lymph glands, indicating an infection, or from an adductor muscle strain. The

Figure 21-16

Manual muscle tests of the
hip. **A**, Abduction.
B, Adduction. **C**, Flexion
(iliopsoas muscle).
D, Extension. **E**, Internal
rotation. **F**, External rotation.
G, Rectus femoris at the hip.

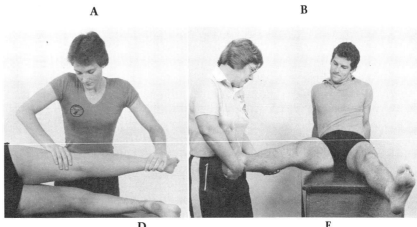

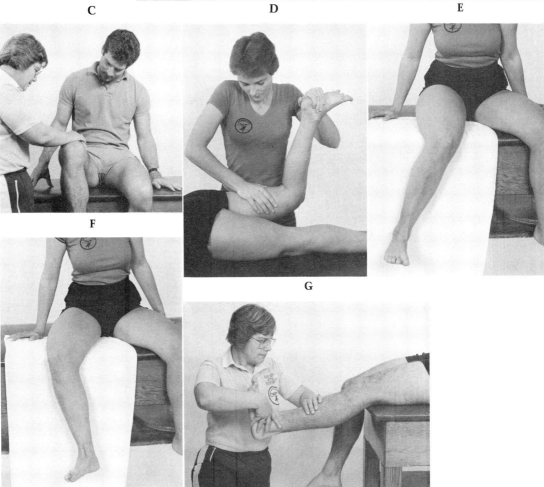

adductors may have point tenderness at any point along their length. Resisted motion may make pain worse.

Muscle palpation The following muscles should be palpated for pain, swelling, or fiber disruption:

Iliopsoas

Sartorius

Rectus femoris at the hip joint

Gracilis

Pectineus

Adductor longus and brevis

Adductor magnus

Gluteus medius

Gluteus maximus

Hamstring muscles at their origin

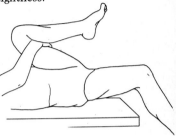

Figure 21-17

Kendall test for hip flexor tightness.

Functional Evaluation

The athlete is led through all possible hip movements, both passive and active, to evaluate range of motion and active and resistive strength. These movements are as follows:

Hip abduction

Hip adduction

Hip flexion

Hip extension

Hip internal and external rotation

Figure 21-18

Demonstrating (**A**) extensible and (**B**) tight hip flexors.

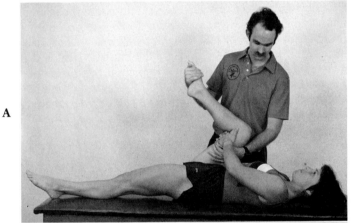

Tests for hip flexion tightness Contractures of the hip flexors are major causes of lordosis and susceptibility to groin pain and discomfort. Two tests can be used—the Kendall test and the Thomas test.

Kendall test The athlete lies supine on a table with one knee flexed on the chest and the back completely flat (Fig. 21-17). The other knee is flexed over the table's end. Normal extensibility of the hip flexors allows the thigh to touch the table, with the knee flexed approximately 70 degrees. Tight hip flexors are revealed by inability of the thigh to lie flat on the table. If only the rectus femoris muscle is tight, the thigh will touch the table but the knee will extend more than 70 degrees (Fig. 21-18).

Thomas test The Thomas test indicates whether hip contractures are present (Fig. 21-19). The athlete lies supine on a table, arms across the chest, legs together and fully extended. The athletic trainer places one hand under the athlete's lumbar curve; one thigh is brought to the chest, flattening the spine. In this position the extended thigh should be flat on the table. If not, there is a hip contracture. On fully extending the leg again, the curve in the low back returns.

Femoral Anteversion and Retroversion

The athlete with a painful hip problem may also have a deformity in the relationship between the neck of the femur and the shaft of the femur. The normal angle of the femoral neck is 15 degrees anterior to the long axis of the shaft of the femur and femoral condyles.[5] Athletes who walk in a toe-in manner may be reflecting a hip deformity in which the femoral neck is directed anteriorly (femoral anteversion). In contrast, athletes who walk in a pronounced toe-out manner may be displaying a condition where the femoral neck is directed posteriorly (femoral retroversion) (Fig. 21-20). Characteristic of femoral anteversion is internal hip rotation in excess of 35 de-

Figure 21-19

Thomas test for hip contractures.

Figure 21-20

A, Anteversion of the femoral neck. When the knee is directed anteriorly, the femoral neck is directed *anteriorly* to some degree. **B,** Retroversion of the femoral neck. When the knee is directed anteriorly, the femoral neck is directed *posteriorly* to some degree.

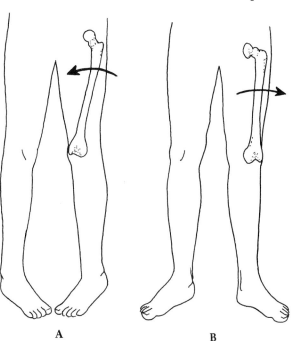

A   B

grees, and, in the case of femoral retroversion, an excess of the normal 45 degrees of external rotation.

Test for pathological conditions of the hip and sacroiliac joint The Patrick test detects pathological conditions of the hip and sacroiliac joint (Fig. 21-21). The athlete lies supine on the table and places the foot of the painful side of the knee of the extended nonaffected leg. Pressure is then applied on the bent knee downward. Pain may be felt in the hip or sacroiliac joint.

Testing the Tensor Fascia Lata and Iliotibial Band

Three tests that can be used to discern iliotibial band tightness and inflammation of the bursa overlying the lateral femoral epicondyle or direct irritation of the iliotibial band and periosteum are the Renne, Nobel, and Ober[14] (Fig. 21-22).

Renne's test While standing, the athlete supports full weight on the affected leg with the knee bent at 30 to 40 degrees. A positive response of fascia lata tightness occurs when pain is felt at the lateral femoral condyle.[14]

Nobel's test The athlete's knee is flexed to 90 degrees, and pressure is applied to the lateral femoral epicondyle while the knee is gradually extended. A positive response occurs when severe pain is felt at the lateral femoral epicondyle with the knee at 30 degrees of flexion.[14]

Ober's test The athlete lies on the unaffected side. With the knee flexed at 90 degrees, the affected thigh is abducted as far as possible. With the pelvis stabilized, the abducted thigh is then relaxed and allowed to drop into adduction. A contracted tensor fascia lata or iliotibial band will keep the thigh in an abducted position, not allowing it to fall into adduction.[5,14]

Leg Length Discrepancy

In individuals who are not physically active, leg length discrepancies of over 1 inch may produce symptoms[15]; however, a shortening of as little as 3 mm (1/8 inch) may cause symptoms in highly active athletes. Such discrepancies can cause cumulative stresses to the lower limbs, hip, and pelvis or low back.

Measuring leg length discrepancy There are two types of leg length discrepancy—true or anatomical shortening and apparent or functional shortening. X-ray examination is the most valid means of measurement. It is difficult to be completely accurate because of mobility of the soft tissue over bony landmarks.

Anatomical discrepancy In an anatomical discrepancy, shortening may be equal throughout the lower limb or localized within the femur or lower leg. The athlete lies supine and fully extended on the table. Measurement is taken between the medial malleoli and the anterior superior iliac spine of each leg (Fig. 21-23, *B*).

Functional discrepancy Functional leg shortening can occur as the result of lateral pelvic tilt (obliquely) or from a flexion or adduction deformity (Fig. 21-23, *C*). Measurement is taken from the umbilicus to the medial malleoli of each ankle.

Figure 21-21

Test for a pathological condition of the hip and sacroiliac joint.

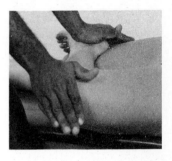

Figure 21-22

Testing for iliotibial band tightness.

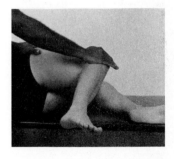

Leg length discrepancy in an athlete can lead to stress-related physical injuries.

Figure 21-23

A, Measuring for leg length
discrepancy. **B,** Anatomical
discrepancy. **C,** Functional
discrepancy.

A

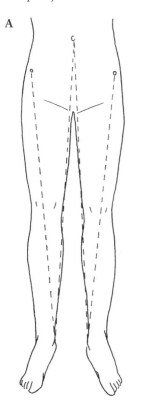

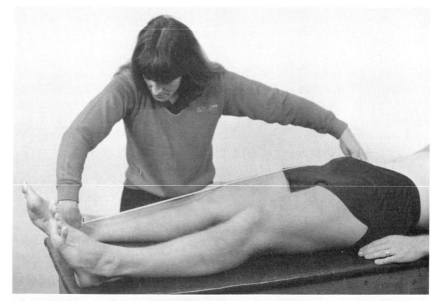

B

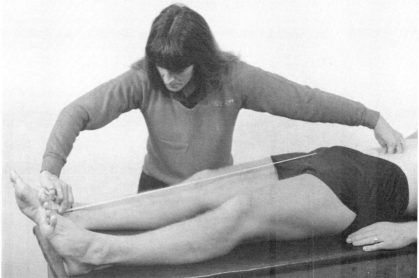

C

Groin Strain

The groin is that depression which lies between the thigh and the abdominal region. The musculature of this area includes the iliopsoas, the rectus femoris, and the adductor group (the gracilis, pectineus, adductor brevis, adductor longus, and adductor magnus). Any one of these muscles can be torn in sports activity and elicit what is commonly considered a groin strain (Fig. 21-24). Any overextension of the groin musculature may result in a strain. Running, jumping, or twisting with external rotation can produce such injuries. Contrary to some opinions, the adductor group is more often torn than is the iliopsoas.

The groin strain presents one of the most difficult injuries to care for in sports. The strain can appear as a sudden twinge or feeling of tearing during an active movement, or it may not be noticed until after termination of activity. As is characteristic of most tears, the groin strain also produces pain, weakness, and internal hemorrhage. If it is detected immediately after

GROIN SUPPORT WRAP (HIP SPICA)

The following procedure is used to support the groin strain.

Materials needed: One roll of extra long 6-inch (15 cm) elastic bandage, a roll of 1½-inch (3.8 cm) adhesive tape, and nonsterile cotton.

Position of the athlete: The athlete stands on a table with weight placed on the uninjured leg. The affected limb is relaxed and internally rotated. This procedure is different from that described earlier in which the wrap was used for pressure only.

Position of the operator: The operator stands facing the anterior aspect of the injured limb.

Procedure (see Fig. 21-25, p. 598)

1. A piece of nonsterile cotton is placed over the injured site.
2. The end of the elastic bandage is started at the upper part of the inner aspect of the thigh and is carried posteriorly around the thigh. Then it is brought across the lower abdomen and over the crest of the ilium on the opposite side of the body.
3. The wrap is continued around the back, repeating the same pattern and securing the wrap end with a 1½-inch (3.8 cm) adhesive tape.

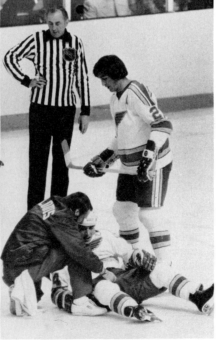

Figure 21-24

Many sports that require a severe stretch of the hip region can cause a groin strain (*see arrow*).

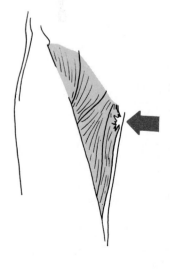

MANAGEMENT PLAN FOR GROIN STRAIN

Injury Situation

A woman varsity basketball player had a history of tightness in her groin. During a game she made a sudden rotation of the trunk while also stretching to the right side. There was a sudden sharp pain and a sense of "giving way" in the left side of the groin that caused the athlete to immediately stop play and limp to the sidelines.

Symptoms and Signs

As the athlete described it to the trainer, there was severe pain when rotating her trunk to the right and flexing her left hip. Inspection revealed that:

1. There was major point tenderness in the groin, especially in the region of the adductor magnus muscle.
2. There was no pain on passive movement of the hip, but severe pain did occur on both active and resistive motion.
3. When the groin and hip were tested for injury, the hip joint, illiopsoas, and rectus femoris muscles were ruled out as having been injured; however, when the athlete adducted the hip from a stretch position, it caused her extreme discomfort.

Management Plan

Based on the trainer's inspection, with findings confirmed by the physician, it was determined that the athlete had sustained a second degree strain of the groin, particularly to the adductor magnus muscle.

1 Management Phase	GOALS: To control hemorrhage, pain, and spasms Estimated length of time (ELT): 2-3 days	
Therapy	IMMEDIATE CARE: ICE-R (20 min) intermittently, 6 to 8 times daily The athlete wears a 6-inch elastic hip spica	
Exercise Rehabilitation	No exercise—as complete rest as possible	
2 Management Phase	GOALS: To reduce pain, spasm, and restore full ability to contract without stretching the muscle ELT: 4 to 6 days	
Therapy	FOLLOW-UP CARE: Ice massage (1 min) 3 to 4 times daily Bipolar muscle stimulation above and below pain site (7 min)	

	Exercise Rehabilitation	PNF for hip rehabilitation 3 to 4 times daily (beginning about 6 days following injury) OPTIONAL: "Jogging" in chest-level water (10 to 20 min) 1 or 2 times daily; must be done within pain-free limits General body maintenance exercises are conducted 3 times a week as long as they do not aggravate the injury
3	Management Phase	GOALS: To reduce inflammation and return strength and flexibility
	Therapy	Muscle stimulation using the surge current at 7 or 8, depending on athlete's tolerance, together with ultrasound, set at 1 watt/cm^2 (7 min) once daily and cold therapy in the form of ice massage or ice packs (7 min) followed by exercise, 2 to 3 times daily
	Exercise Rehabilitation	PNF hip patterns 2 to 3 times daily following cold application progressing to progressive-resistive exercise using pulley, isokinetic, or free weight (10 reps, 3 sets) once daily OPTIONAL: Flutter kick swimming once daily General body maintenance exercises are conducted 3 times a week as long as they do not aggravate the injury.
4	Management Phase	GOALS: To restore full power, endurance, speed, and extensibility
	Therapy	If symptom free, precede exercise with ice massage (7 min) or ice pack (5 to 15 min)
	Exercise Rehabilitation	Added to Phase 3 program, jogging on flat course slowly progressing to a 3-mile run once daily and then progressing to figure-8s starting with obstacles 10 feet apart and gradually shortening distance to 5 feet—full speed
5	Management Phase	GOAL: To return to sports competition
	Exercise Rehabilitation	Athlete gradually returns to precompetition exercise and a gradual return to competition while wearing a figure-8 elastic hip spica bandage for protection.

Criteria for Returning to Competitive Basketball

1. As measured by an isokinetic dynamometer, the athlete's injured hip should have strength equal to that of the uninjured hip.
2. Hip has full range of motion.
3. The athlete is able to run figure-8s around obstacles set 5 feet apart at full speed.

Figure 21-25

Groin support wraps.

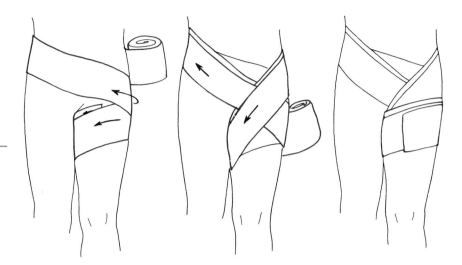

it occurs, the strain should be treated by intermittent ice, pressure, and rest for 48 to 72 hours.

Both passive, active, and resistive muscle tests should be given to ascertain the exact muscle or muscles that are involved.

Difficulty is frequently encountered when attempting to care for a groin strain. In these cases rest has been found to be the best treatment. Daily whirlpool therapy or cryotherapy are palliative; ultrasound offers a more definite approach. Exercise should be delayed until the groin is pain free. Exercise rehabilitation should emphasize gradual stretching and restoring the normal range of motion. Until normal flexibility and strength are developed, a protective spica bandage should be applied (Fig. 21-25).

Trochanteric Bursitis

An increased Q angle and/or leg length discrepancy can lead to trochanteric bursitis in women runners.

Trochanteric bursitis is a relatively common condition of the greater trochanter of the femur. Although commonly called bursitis, it also could be an inflammation at the site the gluteus medius inserts or the iliotibial band as it passes over the trochanter. It is most common among women runners who have an increased Q angle and/or a leg length discrepancy. Management should include the stopping of running on inclined surfaces and correcting faulty running form and leg length discrepancy. Cold packs or ice massage together with gentle stretching and rest with anti-inflammatory medication may be helpful.

Conditions of the Hip Joint

The hip joint, the strongest and best protected joint in the human body, is seldom seriously injured during sports activities.

Sprains of the Hip Joint

The hip joint is substantially supported by the ligamentous tissues and muscles that surround it, so any unusual movement that exceeds the normal range of motion may result in tearing of tissue. Such an injury may occur as the result of a violent twist, either produced through an impact

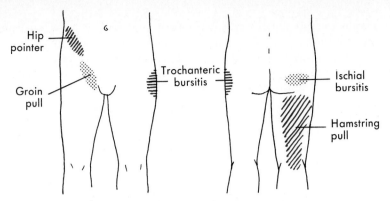

Figure 21-26

Tenderness sites in the region of the hip and pelvis.

force delivered by another participant or by forceful contact with another object, or sustained in a situation in which the foot is firmly planted and the trunk forced in an opposing direction. A hip sprain displays all the signs of a major acute injury but is best revealed through the athlete's *inability to circumduct* the thigh.

Dislocated Hip Joint

Dislocation of the hip joint rarely occurs in sports, and then usually only as the end result of traumatic force directed along the long axis of the femur. Such dislocations are produced when the knee is bent. The most common displacement is one posterior to the acetabulum and with the femoral shaft adducted and flexed.

The luxation presents a picture of a flexed, adducted, and internally rotated thigh. Palpation will reveal that the head of the femur has moved to a position posterior to the acetabulum. A hip dislocation causes serious pathology by tearing capsular and ligamentous tissue. A fracture is often associated with this injury, accompanied by possible damage to the sciatic nerve.

Management Medical attention must be secured immediately after displacement, or muscle contractures may complicate the reduction. Immobilization usually consists of 2 weeks of bed rest and the use of a crutch for walking for a month or longer.

Complications Complication of the posterior hip dislocation is likely, with the possibilities of a palsy of the sciatic nerve and/or later the development of osteoarthritis. Also, hip dislocation could lead to disruption of the blood supply to the head of the femur, which eventually leads to the degenerative condition known as avascular necrosis.

Immature Hip Joint Problems

The coach or athletic trainer working with a child or adolescent should understand two major problems stemming from the immature hip joint. They are Legg-Perthe's avascular necrosis (coxa plana) and the slipped capital femoral epiphysis.

Legg-Perthes Disease (Coxa Plana)

Legg-Perthes disease is avascular necrosis of the femoral head (Fig. 21-27). It occurs in children ages 3 to 12 and in boys more often than in girls. The

Figure 21-27

Legg-Perthes disease (coxa plana). Arrow indicates avascular necrosis of the femoral head.

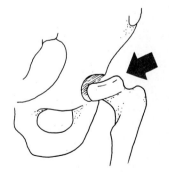

reason for this condition is not clearly understood. It is listed under the broad heading of osteochondroses. Because of a disruption of circulation at the head of the femur, articular cartilage becomes necrotic and flattens.

Symptoms and signs   The young athlete commonly complains of pain in the groin that sometimes is referred to the abdomen or knee. Limping is also typical. The condition can have a rapid onset, but more often it comes on slowly over a number of months.[8] Examination may show limited hip movement and pain.

Management   Care of this condition could mean complete bed rest to alleviate synovitis. A special brace to avoid direct weight bearing on the hip may have to be worn. If treated in time, the head of the femur will revascularize and reossify.

Complications   If the condition is not treated early enough, the head of the femur will become ill shaped, creating problems of osteoarthritis in later life.

A young athlete complaining of pain in the groin, abdomen, or knee and walking with a limp may display signs of Legg-Perthes disease or a slipped capital femoral epiphysis.

Slipped Capital Femoral Epiphysis

The problem of a slipped capital femoral epiphysis (Fig. 21-28) is found mostly in boys between the ages of 10 and 17 who are characteristically very tall and thin or are obese. Although idiopathic, it may be related to the effects of a growth hormone. One quarter of those seen are in both hips.

Symptoms and signs   As with Legg-Perthes disease, the athlete has a pain in the groin that comes on suddenly as a result of trauma or over weeks or months as a result of prolonged stress. In the early stages of this condition signs may be minimal; however, in its most advanced stage there is hip and knee pain on passive and active motion, limitations of abduction, flexion, medial rotation, and a limp. X-ray examination may show femoral head slippage posteriorly and inferiorly.

Management   In minor slippage rest and non-weight bearing may prevent further slipping. Major displacement usually requires corrective surgery.

Complications   If the slippage goes undetected or if surgery fails to properly restore normal hip mechanics, severe hip problems may occur in later life.

Figure 21-28

Slipped capital femoral epiphysis (*see arrow*).

The Snapping Hip Phenomenon

The snapping hip phenomenon is common to dancers, gymnasts, and hurdlers, who employ similar use of their hips.

Etiological factors   The problem stems from habitual movements that predispose muscles about the hip to become imbalanced.[9] This condition commonly occurs when the individual laterally rotates and flexes the hip joint as part of the exercise or dance routine. This condition is related to a structurally narrow bi-iliac width, greater range of motion of hip abduction, less range of motion in lateral rotation. With hip stability becoming lessened, the hip joint capsule and ligaments and adductor muscles become less stable.[9]

Symptoms and signs   The athlete complains that snapping occurs, especially when balancing on one leg. Such a problem should not go unattended, especially if pain and inflammation are associated with the snapping.

Management Management should focus on cryotherapy and ultrasound to stretch tight musculature and strengthen weak musculature in the hip region.

Pelvic Conditions

Athletes who perform activities involving violent jumping, running, and collisions can sustain serious acute and overuse injuries to the pelvic region (Fig. 21-29).

Contusion (hip pointer) Iliac crest contusion, commonly known as a hip pointer, occurs most often in contact sports (Fig. 21-30).

Etiological factors The hip pointer results from a blow to the inadequately protected iliac crest. The hip pointer is considered one of the most handicapping injuries in sports and one that is difficult to manage. A direct force to the unprotected iliac crest causes a severe pinching action to the soft tissue of that region.

Symptoms and signs Such an injury produces immediate pain, spasms, and transitory paralysis of the soft structures. As a result, the athlete is unable to rotate the trunk or to flex his thigh without pain.

Figure 21-29

Sports that include violent extension of the body can produce serious pelvic injuries.

Figure 21-30

Hip pointer.

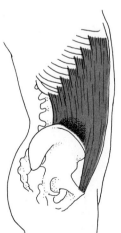

Figure 21-31

Iliac tape support.

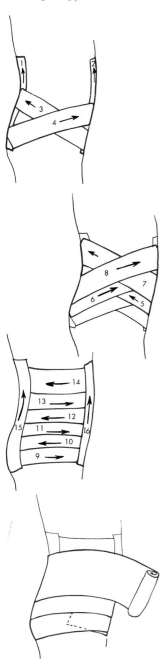

ILIAC TAPE SUPPORT

Iliac crest adhesive taping (Fig. 21-31) is designed to support, protect, and immobilize the soft tissue surrounding the iliac crest.

Materials needed: One roll of 2-inch (5 cm) adhesive tape, 6-inch (15 cm) bandage, skin toughener, and tape adherent.

Position of the athlete: The athlete stands on the floor, bending slightly laterally toward the injured side.

Position of the operator: the operator faces the injured side of the athlete.

Procedure

1. Two anchor strips, each approximately 9 inches (22.5 cm) long, are applied. One is placed longitudinally, just lateral to the sacrum and lumbar spine, and the other is placed lateral to the umbilicus.
2. Commencing 2 to 3 inches (5 to 7.5 cm) below the crest of the ilium, tape crisscrosses are placed from one anchor to the other, lifting the tissue against the pull of gravity. The crisscrosses are carried upward to a point just below the floating rib.
3. Lock strips are placed over approximately the same positions as the anchor strips.
4. If additional support is desired, horizontal strips should be laid on alternately in posteroanterior and anteroposterior directions.
5. Finally, a 6-inch (15 cm) elastic bandage is applied to additionally secure the tape in place and to prevent perspiration from loosening the taping.

Management Cold and pressure should be applied immediately after injury and should be maintained intermittently for at least 48 hours. In severe cases bed rest for 1 to 2 days will speed recovery. It should be noted that the mechanisms of the hip pointer are the same as those for an iliac crest fracture or epiphyseal separation.

Referral to a physician must be made and an x-ray examination given. A variety of treatment procedures can be employed for this injury. Ice massage and ultrasound have been found beneficial. Initially the injury may be injected with a steroid. Later, oral anti-inflammatory agents may be used. Recovery time usually ranges from 1 to 3 weeks. When the athlete resumes normal activity, a protective pad must be worn to prevent reinjury.

Osteitis Pubis

Since the popularity of distance running has increased, a condition known as osteitis pubis has become more prevalent. It is also caused by the sports of soccer, football, and wrestling. As the result of repetitive stress on the pubic symphysis and adjacent bony structures by the pull of muscles in the area, a chronic inflammatory condition is created (Fig. 21-32). The athlete has pain in the groin region and area of the symphysis pubis. There is point tenderness on the pubic tubercle and pain when such movements as running, sit-ups, and squats are performed.[4]

Management Follow-up care usually consists of rest and an oral anti-inflammatory agent with a gradual return to activity.

Fractures of the Pelvis

The pelvis is an extremely strong structure and fractures from sports activities are rare. Those that occur are usually the result of direct trauma. A pelvic fracture should be suspected if an athlete has received a crushing type of trauma. Severe pain, loss of function, and shock are commonly associated with this injury. To further substantiate the possibility of a pelvic girdle fracture, one should gently examine the injury in the following manner:

1. Both hands are placed on the anterior superior spines of the ilium and are pressed downward and outward. If there is a fracture of the pelvic ring, pain will be elicited with little pressure.
2. Pressure is again gently applied by forcing the iliac spines inward and outward. In cases of pelvic ring fracture, pain will be produced on compression and spreading.
3. The possibility of acetabular and femoral head fractures also should be remembered. The distance between the anterior superior spine and the internal malleolus of both legs should be determined by a careful examination.
4. After measurement is taken, upward pressure should be applied to the femur against the acetabulum. A fracture at this point will produce pain on pressure.

If a pelvic fracture is suspected, the athlete should be immediately treated for shock and sent to a physician. The seriousness of a pelvic fracture depends mainly on the extent of shock and the possibility of internal organ injury.

Apophysitis and avulsion fractures The pelvis has a number of apophyses where major muscles make their attachments. An apophysis or traction epiphysis are bony outgrowths and are contrasted to pressure epiphyses, which are the growth plates for long bones. The three most common sites are the iscial tuberosity and the hamstring attachment, the anterior inferior iliac spine and the rectus femoris muscle attachment, and finally the anterior superior iliac spine where the sartorius muscle makes its attachment (Fig. 21-33). Pain at these sites could mean an apophysitis. Severe pain and disability may be an indication of an avulsion fracture. X-ray examination should be routine for the possibility of avulsion or stress fracture in the area. Apophysitis demands rest, limited

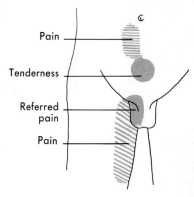

Figure 21-32

Osteitis pubis and other pain sites in the region of the pelvis.

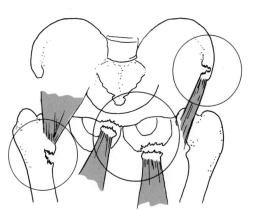

Figure 21-33

Avulsion fractures to pelvic apophyses.

Figure 21-34

Some basic exercises for hip
rehabilitation. **A,** Hip flexion.
B, Hip abduction.
C, Abduction against
resistance.

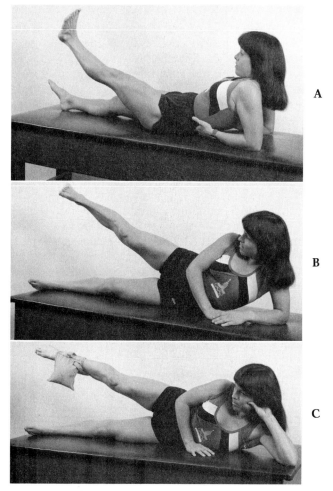

activity, and graduated exercise rehabilitation. Complete avulsion fractures require surgical repair.

Thigh Rehabilitative Exercise

In general, exercise rehabilitation of the thigh is primarily concerned with
the quadriceps and hamstring muscles. Hip adductors and abductor muscles
are discussed in the hip exercise rehabilitation section. (Because of the relationship of thigh rehabilitation to the knee region, the reader is reminded
to see Chapter 20.) Normally the progression for strength is first muscle
setting and isometric exercise until the muscle can be fully contracted, followed by active isotonic contraction and then by isotonic progressive-resis-
tant exercise or isokinetic exercise. PNF that employs both knee and hip
patterns (see Appendices I-B and I-C) is also an excellent means of thigh
rehabilitation. Flexibility exercises include gentle passive stretching followed by gradual static stretching. PNF relaxation methods and/or more
vigorous manual stretching may also be employed. As with strengthening,
flexibility exercises are performed within pain-free limits.

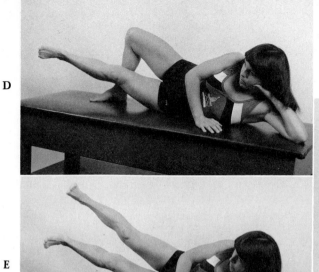

D

E

F

Hip Rehabilitative Exercise

When considering the reconditioning of the hip and groin region, one must consider its major movements: internal rotation, external rotation, adduction, abduction, extension, flexion, and the combined movement of internal and external circumduction. Because of the wide variety of possible movements, it is essential that exercise be conducted as soon as possible after injury, without aggravating the condition. When exercise is begun it should be practiced within a pain-free range of movement. A program should be organized to start with free movement leading up to resistive exercises. A general goal is to perform each exercise up to 10 to 15 repetitions, progressing from one set to three sets two or three times daily (Fig. 21-34).

Figure 21-34, cont'd

D, Hip adduction.
E, Combining abduction and adduction. **F,** Stretching the iliopsoas.

REFERENCES

1. Burkett, L.N.: Investigation into hamstrings: the case of the hybrid muscle, Am. J. Sports Med. **3:**5, 1975.
2. Cooper, D.L., and Fair, J.: Trainer's corner, treating the charley horse, Phys. Sportsmed. **7:**157, 1979.
3. Dimitris-Stilianos, K.: Stress fractures of femoral neck in young athletes—report of 7 cases, J. Bone Joint Surg. **63B:**33, 1981.
4. Hanson, P.G., et al.: Osteitis pubis

in sports activities, Phys. Sportsmed. **6**(10), 1978.
5. Hoppenfeld, S.: Physical examination of the spine and extremities, New York, 1976, Appleton-Century-Crofts.
6. Jackson, D.W.: Managing myositis ossificans in the young athlete, Phys. Sportsmed. **3**(10):56-61, 1975.
7. Jackson, D.W., and Feagin, J.A.: Quadriceps contusions in young athletes: relation of severity of in-

jury to treatment and prognosis, J. Bone Joint Surg. **55A:**95, 1973.

8. Jacobs, B.: Legg-Calvé-Perthe's disease, the "obscure affection," Contemp. Surg. **10:**62, 1977.

9. Jacobs, M., and Young R.: Snapping hip phenomenon among dancers, Am. Corrective Therapy J. **32**(3):92, 1978.

10. Jokl, P., and Federico, J.: Myositis ossificans traumatica with hemophilia (factor XI deficiency) in a football player, J.A.M.A. **237:**2215, 1977.

11. Kalenak, A., and others: Treating thigh contusions with ice, Phys. Sportsmed. 3:65-67, 1975.

12. Lipscomb, A.B.: Treatment of myositis ossificans traumatica in athletics, Am. J. Sports Med. **4:**61, 1976.

13. Lomardo, S.J., and Benson, D.W.: Stress fractures of the femur in runners, Am. J. Sports Med. **10:** 219, 1982.

14. Nobel, H.B., Hajek, M.R., and Porter, M.: Diagnosis and treatment of iliotibial band tightness in runners, Phys. Sportsmed. **19:**67, 1982.

15. Sperryn, P.N.: Sport and medicine, Boston, 1983, Butterworth (Publishers), Inc.

ADDITIONAL SOURCES

Berkow, R. (editor): The Merck manual, ed. 14, Rahway, N.J., 1982, Merck & Co., Inc.

Carmichael, S.W., et al.: Myositis ossificans: report of an unused case, J. Orthop. Sports Phys. Therapy **2:**184, 1981.

Cooper, D.L., and Fair, J.: Trainer's corner: hamstring strains, Phys. Sportsmed. **6:**104, 1978.

Prior, J.A., et al.: Physical diagnosis, ed. 6, St. Louis, 1981, The C.V. Mosby Co.

| # THE ABDOMEN, THORAX, AND LOW BACK

When you finish this chapter, you should be able to

Explain the anatomical ramifications of sports injuries of the abdomen, thorax, and low back

Recognize major sports injuries of the abdomen

Recognize, evaluate, and manage sports injuries of thorax

Recognize, evaluate, and manage low back conditions

This chapter deals with major sports injuries to the trunk region—specifically, the abdomen, thorax, and low back. Although lower in incidence of injuries than the lower limbs, injury in the trunk region could be life threatening or could cause major long-term disability (Fig. 22-1).

THE ABDOMEN
Anatomy

The abdominal cavity lies between the diaphragm and the pelvis and is bounded by the margin of the lower ribs, the abdominal muscles, and the vertebral column. Lying within this cavity are the abdominal viscera, which include the stomach and the lower intestinal tract, the urinary system, the liver, the kidneys, and the spleen.

The abdominal muscles are the rectus abdominis, the external oblique, the internal oblique, and the transverse abdominis (Fig. 22-2). They are invested with both superficial and deep fasciae.

A heavy fascial sheath encloses the rectus abdominis, holding it in its position but in no way restricting its motion. The inguinal ring, which serves as a passageway for the spermatic cord, is formed by the abdominal fascia.

Musculature

Rectus abdominis The rectus abdominis muscle, a trunk flexor, is attached to the rib cage above and to the pubis below. It is divided into three segments by means of transverse tendinous inscriptions; longitudi-

Specific Sports Injuries and
Other Problems

nally it is divided by the linea alba. It functions in trunk flexion, rotation, and lateral flexion and in compression of the abdominal cavity.

External oblique   The external oblique muscle is a broad, thin muscle that arises from slips attached to the borders of the lower eight ribs, runs obliquely forward and downward, and inserts on the anterior two thirds of the crest of the ilium, the pubic crest, and the fascia of the rectus abdominis and the linea alba at their lower front. Its principal functions are trunk flexion, rotation, lateral flexion, and compression.

Internal oblique   The internal oblique muscle forms the anterior and lateral aspects of the abdominal wall. Its fibers arise from the iliac crest, the upper half of the inguinal ligament, and the lumbar fascia. They run principally in an obliquely upward direction to the cartilages of the tenth, eleventh, and twelfth ribs on each side. The main functions of the internal oblique are trunk flexion, lateral flexion, and rotation.

Figure 22-1

Collision sports can produce serious trunk injuries.

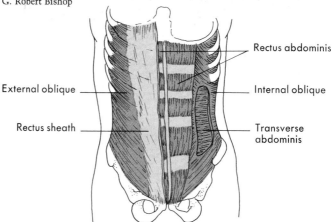

G. Robert Bishop

Figure 22-2

The abdominal musculature.

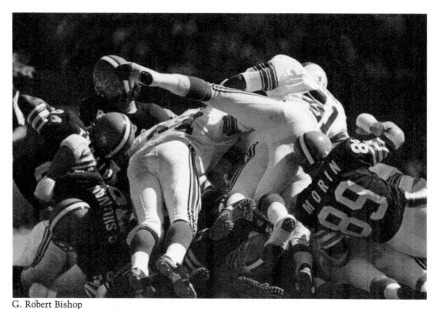

Transverse abdominis The transverse abdominis is the deepest of the abdominal muscles. Its fibers run transversely across the abdominal cavity, arising from the outer third of the inguinal ligament, the iliac crest, the lumbar fascia of the back, and the lower six ribs. It inserts into the linea alba and the front half of the iliac crest. The main functions of the transverse abdominis are to hold the abdominal contents in place and to aid in forced expiration. All the abdominal muscles work together in performing defecation, micturition, and forced expiration.

Abdominal Viscera

The abdominal viscera are composed of both hollow and solid organs. The hollow organs include vessels, tubes, and receptacles, such as the stomach, intestines, gallbladder, and urinary bladder. The solid organs are the kidneys, spleen, liver, suprarenals, and pancreas (Fig. 22-3). In those internal injuries of the abdomen that occur in sports, the solid organs are most often affected. If a hollow organ is distended by its contents, it may have the same injury potential as a solid organ. Therefore, it is desirable for athletes to have finished eating at least 3 hours before a sports contest so they can participate with stomach and bladder empty. Special anatomical considerations should be given to the kidney and spleen because of their relatively high incidence of injury in sports.

Figure 22-3

Abdominal viscera and the genitalia.

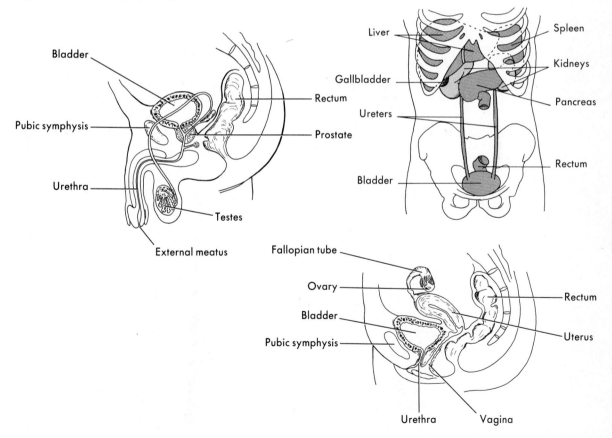

Kidneys The kidneys are situated on each side of the spine, approximately in the center of the back. They are bean-shaped, about 4½ inches (11.25 cm) long, 2 inches (5 cm) wide, and 1 inch (2.5 cm) thick. The right kidney is usually slightly lower than the left because of the pressure of the liver. The uppermost surfaces of the kidneys are connected to the diaphragm by strong, ligamentous fibers. As breathing occurs, the kidneys move up and down as much as ½ inch (1.25 cm). The inferior aspect is positioned 1 to 2 inches (2.5 to 5 cm) above the iliac crest. Resting anterior to the left kidney are the stomach, spleen, pancreas, and small and large intestines. Organs that are situated anterior to the right kidney are the liver and the intestines. The peritoneum (the membrane that lines the abdominal cavity) does not invest the kidneys. Rather, the kidneys are surrounded by a fibrous capsule and by a layer of fat that in turn is encased in another fatty layer that connects it to the niche in which it lies.

Spleen The spleen is the largest lymphatic organ in the body. It weighs about 6 ounces and is approximately 5 inches (12.5 cm) long. It lies under the diaphragm on the left side and behind the ninth, tenth, and eleventh ribs. It is surrounded by a fibrous capsule that is firmly invested by the peritoneum. Its main functions are to serve as:

1. A reservoir of red blood cells
2. A regulator of the number of red blood cells in the general circulation
3. A destroyer of ineffective red cells
4. A producer of antibodies for immunological function[13]
5. In addition, the spleen produces lymphocytes

Abdominal Injuries

The abdominal area is particularly vulnerable to injury in all contact sports. A blow may produce superficial or even deep internal injuries, depending on its location and intensity.[23] Strong abdominal muscles give good protection when they are tensed, but when relaxed they are easily damaged. It is very important to properly protect the trunk region against the traumatic forces of collision sports. Good conditioning is essential, as is proper protective equipment and application of safety rules. Any suspected internal injury must be referred immediately to a physician.[21]

Injuries to the Abdominal Wall

Contusions Compressive forces that injure the abdominal wall are not common in sports. When they do happen, more often they are in collision sports, such as football or ice hockey; however, any sports implements or high-velocity projectiles can injure. Hockey goalies and baseball catchers would be very vulnerable to injury without their protective torso pads. Contusion may occur superficially to the abdominal skin or subcutaneous tissue or much deeper to the musculature. The extent and type of injury will vary, depending on whether the force is blunt or penetrating.[21]

A contusion of the rectus abdominis can be very disabling. A severe blow may cause a hematoma that develops under the fascial tissue surrounding the rectus abdominis muscle. The pressure that results from hemorrhage causes pain and tightness in the region of the injury. A cold pack and a compression elastic wrap should be applied immediately after injury. Signs of possible internal injury must also be looked for in this type of injury.

Abdominal muscle strains A sudden twisting of the trunk or reaching overhead can tear an abdominal muscle. Potentially these types of injuries can be very incapacitating, with severe pain and hematoma formation. Initially ice and an elastic wrap compress should be employed. Treatment should be conservative, with exercise staying within pain-free limits.

Hernia The term *hernia* refers to the protrusion of abdominal viscera through a portion of the abdominal wall. Hernias may be congenital or acquired. A congenital hernial sac is developed before birth and an acquired hernia after birth. Structurally a hernia has a mouth, a neck, and a body. The mouth, or hernial ring, is the opening from the abdominal cavity into the hernial protusion; the neck is the portion of the sac that joins the hernial ring and the body. The body is the sac that protrudes outside the abdominal cavity and contains portions of the abdominal organs.

The acquired hernia occurs when a natural weakness is further aggravated by either a strain or a direct blow. Athletes may develop this condition as the result of violent activity. An acquired hernia may be recognized by the following:

1. Previous history of a blow or strain to the groin area that has produced pain and prolonged discomfort
2. Superficial protrusion in the groin area that is increased by coughing
3. Reported feeling of weakness and pulling sensation in the groin area

The danger of a hernia in an athlete is the possibility that it may become irritated by falls or blows. Besides the aggravations caused by trauma, a condition may arise, commonly known as a strangulated hernia, in which the inguinal ring constricts the protruding sac and occludes normal blood circulation. If the strangulated hernia is not surgically repaired immediately, gangrene and death may ensue.

Hernias resulting from sports most often occur in the groin area; inguinal hernias, which occur in men (over 75%), and femoral hernias, most often occurring in women, are the most prevalent types. Externally the inguinal and femoral hernias appear similar because of the groin protrusion, but a considerable difference is indicated internally. The inguinal hernia results from an abnormal enlargement of the opening of the inguinal canal through which the vessels and nerves of the male reproductive system pass. In contrast to this, the femoral hernia arises in the canal that transports the vessels and nerves that go to the thigh and lower limb.

Under normal circumstances the inguinal and femoral canals are protected against abnormal opening by muscle control. When intra-abdominal tension is produced in these areas, muscles produce contraction around these canal openings. If the muscles fail to react or if they prove inadequate in their shutter action, abdominal contents may be pushed through the opening. Repeated protrusions serve to stretch and increase the size of the opening. Most physicians think that any athlete who has a hernia should be prohibited from engaging in hard physical activity until surgical repair has been made.

The treatment preferred by most physicians is surgery. Mechanical devices such as trusses, which prevent hernial protrusion, are for the most part unsuitable in sports because of the friction and irritation they produce. Exercise has been thought by many to be beneficial to a mild hernia, but such is not the case. Exercise will not affect the stretched inguinal or femoral canals positively.

Intra-abdominal Conditions

Stitch in the side A "stitch in the side" is the name given an idiopathic condition that occurs in some athletes. It is best described as a cramplike pain that develops on either the left or right costal angle during hard physical activity. Sports that involve running apparently produce this condition.

The cause is obscure, although several hypotheses have been advanced. Among these are the following:
1. Constipation
2. Intestinal gas
3. Overeating
4. Diaphragmatic spasm as a result of poor conditioning
5. Lack of visceral support because of weak abdominal muscles
6. Distended spleen
7. Faulty breathing techniques leading to a lack of oxygen in the diaphragm
8. Ischemia of either the diaphragm or the intercostals

Immediate care of a stitch in the side demands relaxation of the spasm, for which two methods have proved beneficial. First, the athlete is instructed to stretch the arm on the affected side as high as possible. If this is inadequate, flexing the trunk forward on the thighs may prove of some benefit.

Athletes with recurrent abdominal spasms may need special study. The identification of poor eating habits, poor elimination habits, or an inadequate training program may explain the athlete's particular problem. It should be noted that a stitch in the side, although not considered serious, may require further evaluation by a physician if abdominal pains persist.

Blow to the solar plexus A blow to the sympathetic celiac plexus (solar plexus) produces a transitory paralysis of the diaphragm ("wind knocked out").

Symptoms and signs Paralysis of the diaphragm stops respiration and leads to anoxia. When the athlete is unable to inhale, hysteria because of fear may result; it is necessary to allay such fears and instill confidence in the athlete.

Management In dealing with an athlete who has had the wind knocked out, the athletic trainer should adhere to the following procedures:
1. Help the athlete overcome apprehension by talking in a confident manner.

2. Loosen the athlete's belt and the clothing around the abdomen; have the athlete bend the knees.

3. Encourage the athlete to relax by initiating short inspirations and long expirations.

There should always be some concern that a blow hard enough to knock the wind out could also cause internal organ injury.

Ruptured spleen Every year there are reports of athletes who suddenly die—hours, days, or even weeks after a severe blow received in a sports event. These deaths are often attributed to delayed hemorrhage of the spleen, the organ most often injured by blunt trauma.[9]

Etiological factors Injuries to the spleen usually result from a fall or a direct blow to the left upper quadrant of the abdomen.

Infectious mononucleosis predisposes the spleen to blunt trauma and may enlarge and weaken the spleen. Splenomegaly is present in 50% of the cases affected. An athlete with mononucleosis must not engage in any jarring activities.

Symptoms and signs The gross indications of a ruptured spleen must be recognized so that an immediate medical referral can be made. Indications include a history of a severe blow to the abdomen and possibly signs of shock, abdominal rigidity, nausea, and vomiting. There may be a reflex pain occurring about 30 minutes after injury, called Kehr's sign, which radiates to the left shoulder and one third of the way down the left arm (see Chapter 11).

Complications The great danger in a ruptured spleen lies in its ability to splint itself and then produce a delayed hemorrhage. Splinting of the spleen is formed by a loose hematoma formation and the constriction of the supporting and surrounding structures. Any slight strain may disrupt the splinting effect and allow the spleen to hemorrhage profusely into the abdominal cavity, causing the athlete to die of internal bleeding days or weeks after the injury.[24] A ruptured spleen must be surgically removed.

Liver contusion Compared to other organ injuries from blunt trauma, injuries to the liver rank second.[20] In sports activities, however, liver injury is relatively infrequent. A hard blow to the right side of the rib cage can tear or seriously contuse the liver, especially if it has been enlarged as a result of some disease, such as hepatitis. Such an injury can cause hemorrhage and shock, requiring immediate surgical intervention. Liver injury commonly produces a referred pain that is just below the right scapula, right shoulder, and substernal area and, on occasion, the anterior left side of the chest (see Chapter 11).

Hollow viscus organ injuries When compared to hollow organs, the solid organs are more often injured in sports; however, on rare occasions a severe blunt blow to the abdomen may cause rupture or laceration of the duodenum or other structures of the small intestine.

Injuries to the Genitourinary System

Kidney contusion The kidneys are seemingly well protected within the abdominal cavity. However, on occasion, contusions and even ruptures of these organs occur. The kidney may be susceptible to injury be-

An athlete with mononucleosis must not engage in any jarring activities

Athletes who complain of external pain in shoulders, trunk, or pelvis following a severe blow to the abdomen or back may be describing a referred pain from an injury to an internal organ.

Solid internal organs are more at jeopardy from an injury than are hollow organs.

cause of its normal distention by blood. A severe outside force, usually one applied to the back of the athlete, will cause abnormal extension of an engorged kidney, which results in injury. The degree of renal injury depends on the extent of the distention and the angle and force of the blow. An athlete who has received a contusion of the kidney may display signs of shock, nausea, vomiting, rigidity of the back muscles, and hematuria (blood in the urine). As with other internal organs, kidney injury may cause referred pain to the outside of the body. Pain may be felt high in the costovertebral angle posteriorly and may radiate forward around the trunk into the lower abdominal region (see Chapter 11). Any athlete who reports having received a severe blow to the abdomen or back region should be instructed to urinate 2 or 3 times and to look for the appearance of blood in the urine. If there is any sign of hematuria, immediate referral to a physician must be made.

Medical care of the contused kidney usually consists of a 24-hour hospital observation with a gradual increase of fluid intake. If the hemorrhage fails to stop, surgery may be indicated. Controllable contusions usually require 2 weeks of bed rest and close surveillance after activity is resumed. In questionable cases complete withdrawal from one active playing season may be required.

Injuries of the ureters, bladder, and urethra On rare occasions a blunt force to the lower abdominal region may avulse a ureter or contuse or rupture the urinary bladder. Injury to the urinary bladder only arises if it is distended by urine.

After a severe blow to the pelvic region, the athlete may display the following recognizable signs:

1. Pain and discomfort in the lower abdomen, with the desire but inability to urinate
2. Abdominal rigidity
3. Nausea, vomiting, and signs of shock
4. Blood dripping from the urethra
5. Passing a great quantity of bloody urine, which indicates possible rupture of the kidney

In any contusion to the abdominal region, the possibility of internal damage must be considered, and after such trauma the athlete should be instructed to check periodically for blood in the urine. To lessen the possibility of rupture, the athlete must always empty the bladder before practice or game time. The bladder can also be irritated by intra-abdominal pressures in long-distance running. In this situation repeated impacts to the bladder's base are produced by the jarring of the abdominal contents, resulting in hemorrhage and blood in the urine.[5] Bladder injury commonly causes referred pain to the lower trunk, including the upper thigh anteriorly and suprapubically (see Chapter 11).

Injury to the urethra is more common in men, because the male's urethra is longer and more exposed than the female's. Injury may produce severe perineal pain and swelling.[26]

Scrotal contusion As the result of its considerable sensitivity and particular vulnerability, the scrotum may sustain a contusion that causes a very painful, nauseating, and disabling condition. As is characteristic of any contusion or bruise, there is hemorrhage, fluid effusion, and muscle spasm, the degree of which depends on the intensity of the impact to the tissue. Immediately following a scrotal contusion, the athlete must be put at ease and testicular spasms must be reduced.

The following technique is used to relieve testicular spasm: The athlete is placed on his back and instructed to flex his thighs to his chest. This position will aid in reducing discomfort and relax the muscle spasm. After the pain has diminished, the athlete is helped from the playing area and a cold pack is applied to the scrotum (Fig. 22-4).

Spermatic cord torsion   Traumatic torsion of the spermatic cord occurs by the testicle's revolving in the scrotum following a direct blow to the area. Cord torsion produces acute testicular pain, nausea, vomiting, and inflammation in the area. In this case, the athlete must receive immediate medical attention to prevent irreparable complications. Twisting of the spermatic cord may present the appearance of a cluster of swollen veins and may cause a dull pain combined with a heavy, dragging feeling in the scrotum. This condition may eventually lead to atrophy of the testicle. A physician should be consulted when this condition is suspected.

Traumatic hydrocele of the tunica vaginalis   Traumatic hydrocele of the tunica vaginalis is an excess of fluid accumulation caused by a severe blow to the testicular region. After trauma the athlete complains of pain, swelling in the lower abdomen, and nausea. Cold packs should be applied to the scrotum, and referral to the physician should be made.

Gynecological injuries   In general the female reproductive organs have a low incidence of injury in sports; however, women water skiers do injure their valvas when water is forced into the vagina and fallopian tubes, later causing infection. On occasion the external genital organs (vulva) of the female may become contused, resulting in hematoma.

Figure 22-4

Reducing testicular spasm.

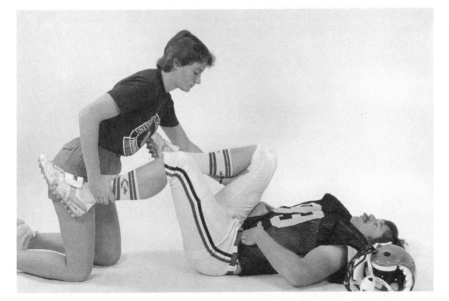

Paramore's experiment graphically shows how well the uterus is supported on a fluid bed and cushioned against landing and torque shock. A jar is partially filled with cool water in which a fresh, raw, intact egg is introduced. This is followed by filling the jar to its brim and tightly applying a lid. The jar is then shaken vigorously and bumped in any fashion, to the point of breaking the glass. Regardless of force used, the egg yolk will remain intact, demonstrating the type of protection with which the uterus is endowed.

Other Reasons for Abdominal Pain

Pain at McBurney's point may be indicating the athlete is having an appendicitis attack.

A number of other abdominal pain sites can be disabling to the athlete. The athletic trainer should be able to discern the potentially more serious pain sites and refer the athlete accordingly. Indigestion or dyspepsia commonly causes pain just below the sternum. Appendicitis, typically when the appendix is in a normal position, creates pain at McBurney's point, which is one third the distance between the anteriosuperior iliac spine and the umbilicus. Fig. 22-5 shows some of the pain sites in the abdomen.

THE THORAX
Anatomy

The thorax is that portion of the body commonly known as the chest, which lies between the base of the neck and the diaphragm. It is contained within the thoracic vertebrae and the twelve pairs of ribs that give it conformation (Fig. 22-6). Its main functions are to protect the vital organs of respiration and circulation and to assist the lungs in inspiration and expiration during the breathing process. The ribs are flat bones that are attached to the thoracic vertebrae in the back and to the sternum in the front. The upper seven ribs are called sternal or true ribs, and each rib joins the sternum by a separate costal cartilage. The eighth, ninth, and tenth ribs (false ribs) have cartilages that join each other and the seventh rib before uniting with the sternum. The eleventh and twelfth ribs (floating ribs) remain unattached to the sternum but do have muscle attachments. The individual rib articulation produces a slight gliding action.

Figure 22-5

Common sites of abdominal pain.

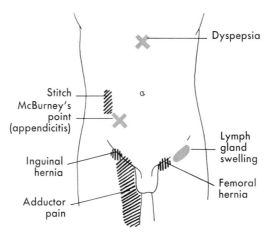

Thoracic Injuries

The chest is vulnerable to a variety of soft tissue injuries, depending on the nature of the sport.

Breast Problems

It has been suggested that many women athletes can have breast problems in connection with their sports participation.[27] Violent up and down and lateral movements of the breasts, such as are encountered in running and jumping, can bruise and strain the breast, especially in large-breasted women. Constant uncontrolled movement of the breast over a period of time can stretch Cooper's ligament, which supports the breast at the chest wall, leading to premature ptosis of the breasts.[12]

Wearing a well-designed bra that has minimal elasticity and allows little vertical or horizontal breast movement is most desirable (see Fig. 7-11). Breast injuries usually occur during physical contact with either an opponent or equipment. In sports such as fencing or field hockey, women athletes must be protected by wearing plastic cup-type brassieres.

Rib Contusions

A blow to the rib cage can contuse intercostal muscles or, if severe enough, produce a fracture. Because the intercostal muscles are essential for the breathing mechanism, when they are bruised, both expiration and inspiration become very painful. Characteristically the pain is sharp on breathing and there is point tenderness. X-ray examination should be routine in such an injury. ICE-R and anti-inflammatory agents are commonly employed. As with most rib injuries, contusions to the thorax are self-limiting, responding best to rest and cessation of sports activities.

Rib Fractures

Rib fractures (Fig. 22-7) are not uncommon in sports and have their highest incidence in contact sports, particularly in wrestling and football.

Figure 22-6

The thorax.

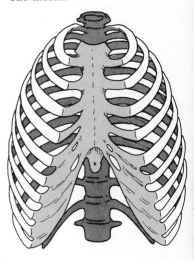

Figure 22-7

A rib fracture.

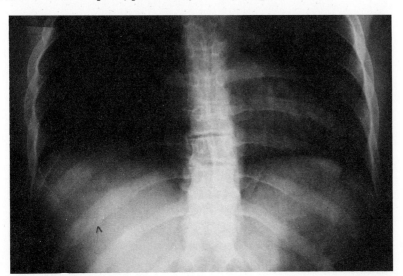

A rib fracture is usually
indicated by a severe, sharp
pain on breathing.

Etiological factors   Fractures can be caused by either direct or indirect traumas and can, infrequently, be the result of violent muscular contractions. A direct injury is the type caused by a kick or a well-placed block, with the fracture developing at the site of force application. An indirect fracture is produced as a result of a general compression of the rib cage, such as may occur in football or wrestling.

The structural and functional disruption sustained in rib fracture varies according to the type of injury that has been received. The direct fracture causes the most serious damage, since the external force fractures and displaces the ribs inwardly. Such a mechanism may completely displace the bone and cause an overriding of fragments. The jagged edges of the fragments may cut, tear, or perforate the tissue of the pleurae, causing hemothorax, or they may collapse one lung (pneumothorax). Contrary to the pattern with direct violence, the indirect type usually causes the rib to spring and fracture outward, which produces an oblique or transverse fissure.

Symptoms and signs   The rib fracture is usually quite easily detected. The history informs the athletic trainer of the type and degree of force to which the rib cage has been subjected. After trauma, the athlete complains of having a severe pain on inspiration and has point tenderness. A fracture of the rib will be readily evidenced by a severe sharp pain and possibly crepitus on palpation.

Management   The athlete should be referred to the team physician for x-ray examination if there is any indication of fracture.

An uncomplicated rib fracture is often difficult to identify on x-ray film. Therefore the physician plans the treatment according to the symptoms presented. The rib fracture is usually managed with support and rest. Simple transverse or oblique fractures heal within 3 to 4 weeks. A rib brace can offer the athlete some rib cage stabilization and comfort (Fig. 22-8).

Figure 22-8

A commercial rib brace can
provide moderate support to
the thorax.

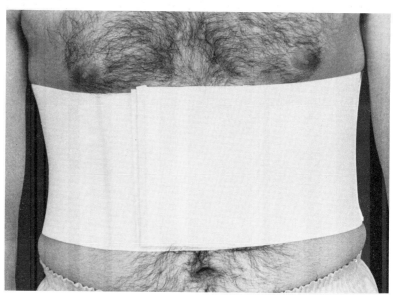

Sternal Fracture

Fracture of the sternum occurs infrequently in sports. It can develop from a direct blow to the sternum, from a violent compression force applied posteriorly, or from hyperflexion of the trunk. The most frequently affected area of the sternum is the manubrium. This fracture results in sharp chest pain that occurs particularly on inhalation and is localized over the sternum, and as the result of this injury the athlete assumes a position in which the head and shoulders are dropped forward.

Palpation indicates mild swelling and, possibly, displaced fragments. An x-ray film must be taken to determine the extent of displacement.

The treatment may require bed rest for 2 to 3 weeks with immobilization by adhesive taping or the use of a sand weight over the fracture site. After activity is resumed a posterior figure-8 bandage is applied to maintain the shoulders in an erect position.

Costochondral Separation and Dislocation

In sports activities the costochondral separation or dislocation has a higher incidence than fractures. This injury can occur from a direct blow to the anterolateral aspect of the thorax or indirectly from a sudden twist or a fall on a ball, compressing the rib cage. The costochondral injury displays many signs similar to the rib fracture, with the exception that pain is localized in the junction of the rib cartilage and rib (Fig. 22-9).

Symptoms and signs   The athlete complains of sharp pain on sudden movement of the trunk, with difficulty in breathing deeply. There is point tenderness with swelling. In some cases there is a rib deformity and a complaint that the rib makes a crepitus noise as it moves in and out of place.

Management   As with a rib fracture, the costochondral separation is managed by rest and immobilization by tape or a rib brace. Healing takes anywhere from 1 to 2 months, precluding any sports activities until the athlete is symptom free.

Muscle Conditions of the Thorax

The muscles of the thorax are the intercostals and the erector spinae, latissimus dorsi, trapezius, serratus anterior, serratus posterior, and pectoralis major—all of which are subject to contusions and strains in sports. The intercostals are especially assailable. Traumatic injuries occur most often from direct blows or sudden torsions of the athlete's trunk. Their care requires immediate pressure and applications of cold for approximately 1 hour; after hemorrhaging has been controlled, immobilization should be employed.

Internal Complications

Internal complications in the thorax resulting from sports trauma are rare. They pertain principally to injuries of the lung, pleurae, and/or intercostal arteries. Because of the seriousness of internal injuries, the athletic trainer should be able to recognize their basic signs. The most serious of the conditions are (1) pneumothorax, (2) hemothorax, (3) hemorrhaging into the lungs, (4) traumatic asphyxia, and (5) heart contusion.

Figure 22-9

Costochondral separation.

Pneumothorax   Pneumothorax is a condition in which the pleural cavity becomes filled with air that has entered through an opening in the chest. As the negatively pressured pleural cavity fills with air, the lung on that side collapses. The loss of one lung may produce pain, difficulty in breathing, and anoxia.

Hemothorax   Hemothorax is the presence of blood within the pleural cavity. It results from the tearing or puncturing of the lung or pleural tissue involving the blood vessels in the area. As with pneumothorax, pain, difficulty in breathing, and cyanosis develop.

A violent blow or compression of the chest without an accompanying rib fracture may cause a *lung hemorrhage.* This condition results in severe pain on breathing, dyspnea (difficult breathing), the coughing up of frothy blood, and signs of shock. If these signs are observed, the athlete should be treated for shock and immediately referred to a physician.

Traumatic asphyxia   Traumatic asphyxia occurs as the result of a violent blow to or a compression of the rib cage, causing a cessation of breathing. Signs include a purple discoloration of the upper trunk and head, with the conjunctivae of the eyes displaying a bright red color. A condition of this type demands immediate mouth-to-mouth resuscitation and medical attention.

Heart contusion   A heart contusion may occur when the heart is compressed between the sternum and the spine by a strong outside force, such as being hit by a pitched ball or bouncing a barbell off the chest in a bench press. This injury produces severe shock and heart pain. Death may ensue if medical attention is not administered immediately.

THE LOW BACK
Anatomy of the Vertebral Column

The low back must be considered in the context of the entire spine. The lumbar, sacral, and coccygeal portions of the spine will be discussed in this chapter, and the thoracic and cervical spine will be discussed in Chapter 23.

Bony Structure

The spine or vertebral column is composed of 33 individual bones called vertebrae. Twenty-four are classified as movable, or true, and nine classified as immovable, or false. The false vertebrae, which are fixed by fusion, form the sacrum and the coccyx. The design of the spine allows a high degree of flexibility forward and laterally and limited mobility backward. Rotation about a central axis in the areas of the neck and the lower back is also permitted.

The movable vertebrae are separated into three different divisions, according to location and function. The first division comprises the seven cervical vertebrae; the second, the twelve thoracic vertebrae; and the third, the five lumbar vertebrae. As the spinal segments progress downward from the cervical region, they grow increasingly larger to accommodate the upright posture of the body as well as to contribute in weight bearing. Physiological curves also are present in the spinal column for adjusting to the upright stresses. These curves are, respectively, the cervical, thoracic, lumbar, and sacrococcygeal curves. The cervical and lumbar curves are convex anteriorly, whereas the thoracic and sacrococcygeal curves are convex posteriorly. The shape of the vertebrae is irregular, but they possess certain characteristics that are common to all. Each vertebra consists of a neural arch through which the spinal cord passes and several projecting processes that serve as attachments for muscles and ligaments. Each neural arch has two laminae and two pedicles. The latter are bony processes that project backward from the body of the vertebrae and connect with the laminae. The laminae are flat bony processes occurring on either side of the neural arch, which project backward and inward from the pedicles. With the exception of the first and second cervical vertebrae, each vertebra has a spinous and transverse process for muscle and ligament attachment and all have an articular process.

Intervertebral Articulations

Intervertebral articulations take place between vertebral bodies and vertebral arches. Articulation between the bodies is of the symphysis type. There is an intervertebral disk made up of two components, the *annulus fibrosus* and the *nucleus pulposus.* The annulus fibrosus forms the periphery of the intervertebral disk and is composed of strong, fibrous tissue, with its fibers running in several different directions for strength. In the center is the semifluid nucleus pulposus compressed under pressure. The disks act as important shock absorbers for the spine. Besides motion at articulations between the bodies of the vertebrae, movement takes place at four articular processes that derive from the pedicles and laminae. The direction of movement of each vertebra is somewhat dependent on the direction in which the articular facets face.

Major Ligamentous Structures

The major ligaments that join the various vertebral parts are the anterior longitudinal, the posterior longitudinal, and the supraspinous (Fig. 22-10). The anterior longitudinal ligament is a wide, strong band that extends the full length of the anterior surface of the vertebral bodies. The posterior longitudinal ligament is contained within the vertebral canal and extends the full length of the posterior aspect of the bodies of the vertebrae. The *ligamenta flava* connect one lamina to another. The interspinous, supraspinous, and intertransverse ligaments stabilize the transverse and spinous process, extending between adjacent vertebrae.

Figure 22-10

Major ligaments of the lumbar spine.

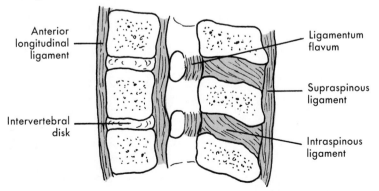

Anterior longitudinal ligament

Intervertebral disk

Ligamentum flavum

Supraspinous ligament

Intraspinous ligament

Movements of the Vertebral Column

The movements of the vertebral column are flexion and extension, right and left lateral flexion, and rotation to the left and right. The degree of movement differs in the various regions of the vertebral column. The cervical and lumbar regions allow extension and flexion. Although the thoracic vertebrae have minimal movement, their combined movement between the first and twelfth thoracic vertebrae can account for 20 to 30 degrees of flexion and extension. Flexion and extension are most extensive at the fifth lumbar and the first sacral vertebrae and atlantooccipital joints.

Flexion of the trunk primarily involves the lengthening of the deep and superficial back muscles and the contraction of the rectus abdominus. The psoas muscles also flex the lumbar spine. Trunk rotation is conducted by the oblique abdominal muscles, obliquus externus abdominis and obliquus internus abdominis. Lateral flexion is produced by the longitudinal muscles on the opposite side and the same side of the lumbar spine and by the intercostal muscles of the opposite side of the lumbar spine.

The Lumbar Vertebrae

The lumbar spine is usually composed of five vertebrae (Fig. 22-11). They are the major support of the low back and are the strongest and most massive of the vertebrae. Movement occurs in all of the lumbar vertebrae; however, there is much less flexion than extension. Seventy-five percent of flexion occurs at the lumbosacral junction (L5 S1), whereas 15% to 70% occurs between L4 and L5; the rest of the lumbar vertebrae execute 5% to 10% of flexion.[6] The major muscle of extension is the erector spinae or sacrospinalis, which is separated into the iliocostal, longissimus, and spinalis bands.

The Sacrum and Coccyx
The Sacrum

The sacrum is formed in the adult by the fusion of five vertebrae and, as part of the two hip bones, makes up the pelvis (Fig. 22-12). The roots of the lumbar and sacral nerves, which form the lower portion of the cauda equina, pass through four foramina lateral to the five fused vertebrae.

The sacrum joins with the ilium to form the sacroiliac joint, which has a synovium and is lubricated by synovial fluid. In both sitting and standing

Figure 22-11

The lumbar vertebrae.

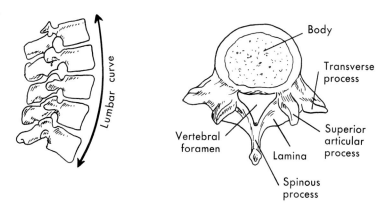

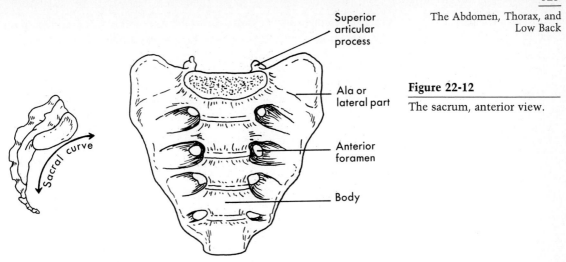

Superior
articular
process

Ala or
lateral part

Anterior
foramen

Body

Sacral curve

Figure 22-12

The sacrum, anterior view.

TABLE 22-1

Spinal nerves of the lumbar, sacral, and coccygeal regions

Spinal Nerves	Plexus Formed from Anterior Rami	Spinal Nerve Branches from Plexuses	Parts Supplied
Lumbar 1 2 3 4 5 Sacral 1 2 3 4 5 Coccygeal 1	Lumbosacral plexus	Iliohypogastric Ilioinguinal } Sometimes fused	Sensory to anterior abdominal wall
		Genitofemoral	Sensory to anterior abdominal wall and external genitalia; motor to muscles of abdominal wall
		Lateral cutaneous of thigh Femoral	Sensory to skin of external genitalia and inguinal region
			Sensory to outer side of thigh
		Obturator Tibial (medial popliteal)	Motor to quadriceps, sartorius, and iliacus muscles; sensory to front of thigh and medial side of lower leg (saphenous nerve)
		Common peroneal (lateral popliteal)	Motor to adductor muscles of thigh
		Nerves to hamstring muscles Gluteal nerves, superior and inferior	Motor to muscles of calf of leg; sensory to skin of calf of leg and sole of foot
		Posterior cutaneous nerve	Motor to evertors and dorsiflexors of foot; sensory to lateral surface of leg and dorsal surface of foot
		Pudendal nerve	Motor to muscles of back of thigh
			Motor to buttock muscles and tensor fasciae latae
			Sensory to skin of buttocks, posterior surface of thigh, and leg
			Motor to peroneal muscles; sensory to skin of perineum

From Anthony, C.P., and Thibodeau, G.: Textbook of anatomy and physiology, ed. 11, St. Louis, 1983, The C.V. Mosby Co.

the body's weight is transmitted through these joints. A complex of numerous ligaments serve to make these joints very stable.

The Coccyx

In the child the coccyx has four or five separate vertebrae, of which the lower three fuse in adulthood. The gluteus maximus muscle attaches to the coccyx posteriorly and to the levator ani anteriorly.

Spinal Nerves and Peripheral Branches

Table 22-1 indicates the major spinal nerves and their peripheral branches in the lumbar region.

Evaluation of the Low Back

The athletic trainer should have a general knowledge of low back pain evaluation techniques. Differentiating superficial muscular conditions from deeper, more potentially disabling conditions is important in determining when or when not to refer the individual to a physician. Evaluation techniques are also essential in determining the progress of rehabilitation (Fig. 22-13).

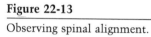

Figure 22-13

Observing spinal alignment.

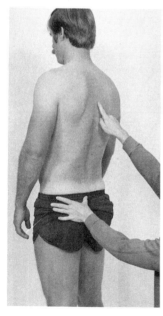

Major Complaints

To determine the basis for the back pain, the following questions should be answered by the athlete:
1. Where does it hurt, and how long does the pain last?
2. What events precipitated the pain? Was there sudden, direct trauma, such as being hit in the back, or was there a strain from a twist or lifting a heavy object? Did the pain come on slowly?
3. Does the pain radiate into the legs?
4. Is there a feeling of weakness, numbness, or tingling (paresthesia) in the legs or feet?
5. Which activities make the pain worse and what things, if any, relieve the pain?
6. Has there been back pain before? What was done for it?

General Observation

The athlete should be observed with the entire body as exposed as possible. Observation should include kinetic activities such as walking and sitting, as well as static postural evaluation.

Kinetic observation The athlete should be observed while walking, sitting, and rising from a chair. The following points should be noted:
1. Ease or lack of ease of movement
2. Whether the athlete favors one side of the body or body part more than the other
3. Movements that are painful or cannot be accomplished
4. Musculature that appears asymmetrically contracted
5. Observation of moving postural alignment from all positions, including feet, legs, pelvis, back, shoulders, and neck

Static Postural Observation

It is important next to observe the athlete's total static posture, with special attention paid to the low back, pelvis, and hips. When observing static posture, the athletic trainer must accept the fact that postural alignment varies considerably among individuals; therefore, only obvious asymmetries should be considered. The athlete should be observed from all views—front, side, and back. The entire body is looked at for vertical and horizontal alignment. To ensure accuracy of observation, a plumb line or posture screen may be of use (Fig. 22-14). A trained observer with a good background in postural observation devices may not require any special devices. Fig. 22-15, *A-C*, shows typical vertical alignment landmarks and more common postural deviations. Horizontal landmarks and deviations are indicated in Fig. 22-16, *A* and *B*.

An important factor in low back pain is scoliosis, a lateral rotary curvature of the spine. The athlete with low back pain should be routinely evaluated for the possibility of scoliosis.[3] The following general postural signs should be looked for:

1. Head is tilted to one side.
2. Shoulder is lower on one side.
3. One shoulder carried forward.

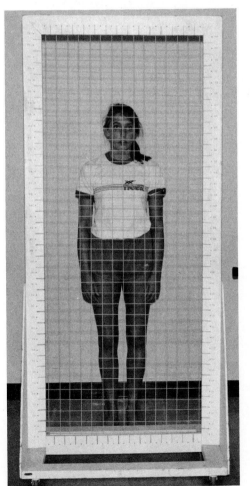

Figure 22-14

Using a grid can produce more accurate results in posture screening.

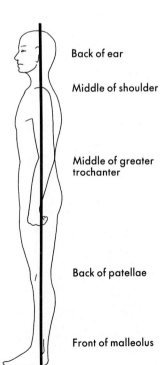

Back of ear

Middle of shoulder

Middle of greater trochanter

Back of patellae

Front of malleolus

Figure 22-15

Typical vertical alignment landmarks.

Specific Sports Injuries and
Other Problems

Figure 22-16

Typical horizontal alignment
landmarks. (Colored line
indicates vertical landmarks.)

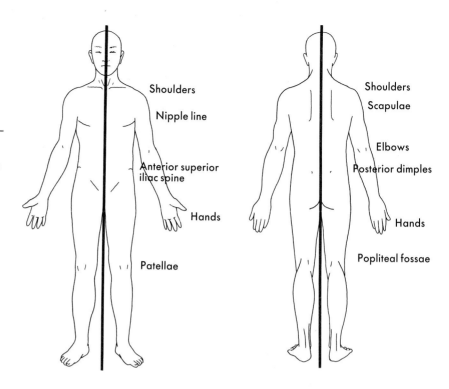

Shoulders

Nipple line

Anterior superior
iliac spine

Hands

Patellae

Shoulders

Scapulae

Elbows

Posterior dimples

Hands

Popliteal fossae

Figure 22-17

Marking spinous processes
can often reveal lateral rotary
curvatures.

Figure 22-18

Bending forward may or may
not straighten the scoliotic
spine.

Figure 22-17

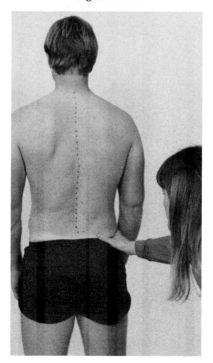

Figure 22-18

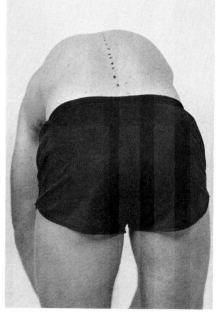

4. One scapula is lower and more prominent than the other.
5. Trunk is habitually bent to one side.
6. Space between the body and arm is greater on one side.
7. One hip is more prominent than the other.
8. Hips are tilted to one side (hip obliquity).
9. Ribs are more pronounced on one side.
10. One arm hangs longer than the other.
11. One arm hangs farther forward than the other.
12. One patella is lower than the other.
13. Marking spinous process reveals a curvature (Fig. 22-17).
14. Bending forward, the marked spine may straighten (functional) or remain twisted (structural). In this position, one side of the spine may be more prominent than the other (Fig. 22-18). *NOTE:* The athlete should be observed for asymmetries while standing and sitting.

Postural changes resulting from chronic low back pain Postural malalignment can produce low back pain, and chronic low back pain may result in spasm and postural asymmetries. Loss of the normal lordotic curve can be caused by a postural problem or muscle spasm. A lateral curvature of the low back region may be a structural deformity of function resulting from muscle spasm.

Both static and dynamic postural evaluations must be made in cases of low back injuries.

More Detailed Inspection of the Low Back

Following general observation, a more detailed inspection should be given while the athlete stands, lies supine, lies prone, and lies on the side.

Standing

1. The athlete is asked to point to the exact site of the pain.
2. The athlete's pelvis is palpated for unevenness (Fig. 22-19, *A-C*).
3. Pain sites noted by the athlete are palpated for point tenderness.
4. Skeletal and musculature sites other than those noted by the athlete are also palpated to determine trigger points that may be referring pain.
5. The athlete is asked to actively flex forward, extend, flex laterally to the left and right, and rotate the trunk in each direction. Restricted motion, painful movements, and asymmetries are noted (Fig. 22-20, *A-D*).

Figure 22-19

A, Testing hip level by comparing the level of the anterior superior iliac spine. **B,** Comparing hip level by palpating the crests of the ilium. **C,** Comparing hip level by palpating the posterior iliac spine.

| A | B | C |

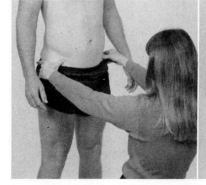 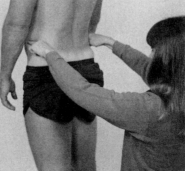 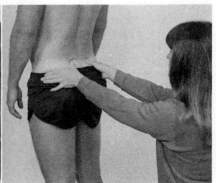

Figure 22-20

Looking for asymmetries and
muscle spasms as the athlete
goes into (**A**) forward flexion,
(**B**) back extension, (**C**) lateral
flexion, and (**D**) trunk
rotation.

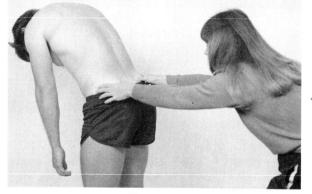

A

B   C   D

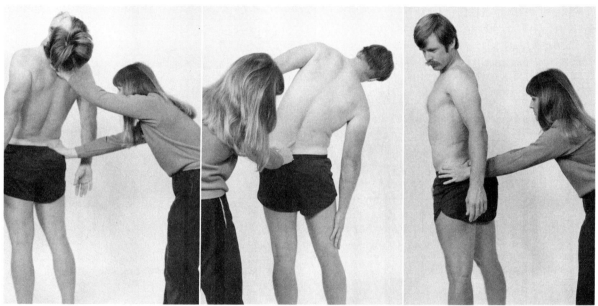

Figure 22-21

Testing the sacroiliac for a
pathological condition by
compression of the ilium.

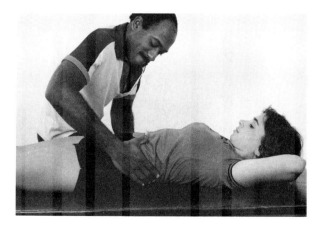

6. The sacroiliac joint can be tested for pain while the athlete is standing by firmly palpating its posterior aspects or by percussing it with the fist.

Supine

1. The athlete is measured for leg length discrepancy (see Chapter 21, p. 593).
2. The sacroiliac joint is tested again by compression inward on each side of the hip or downward and outward on each anterosuperior spine of the ilium (Fig. 22-21).
3. The Patrick test (see p. 593) for hip problems can also determine pathological conditions of the sacroiliac.

Tests for nerve root irritation   Straight leg raising (Lasèque's sign) and its variations have been found to place a stretching movement on the dura mater.[8] It tests the fourth and fifth lumbar roots and the first, second, and third sacral nerve roots, which become the sciatic nerve, the largest nerve in the body.

Straight leg raising (affected side)   With the athlete lying flat on the table, the leg on the affected side is lifted by the heel as far as possible. If the test is positive the athlete feels pain radiating down the leg as well as in the low back region (Fig. 22-22). To confirm that pain stems from a nerve root involvement and not hamstring tightness, the leg is lowered to a point at which pain ceases. In this position the foot is then dorsiflexed and the neck flexed. If pain returns, it is a verification of a pathological condition of the nerve root.

Straight leg raising (unaffected side)   The examiner raises the athlete's unaffected leg. If pain occurs in the low back on the affected side as well as radiating along the sciatic nerve, this provides additional proof of nerve root inflammation.

The bowstring test   The bowstring test is another way to determine sciatic nerve irritation. The leg on the affected side is lifted until pain is felt. The knee is then flexed until the pain is relieved, at which time pressure is applied to the popliteal fossa. The test result is positive if pain is felt on palpation along the sciatic nerve (Fig. 22-23).

A number of tests for low back injuries are designed to stretch the dura mater and subsequently test possible impingement on spinal nerves.

Figure 22-22

Straight leg raising test to stretch the spinal cord or sciatic nerve.

Figure 22-23

Bowstring test for nerve root involvement of the lumbar spine.

Figure 22-22

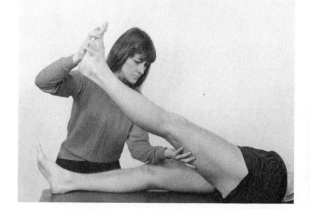

Figure 22-23

Figure 22-24

Sacroiliac compression test.
The downward pressure of
the hands on the pelvis, if
possible, will elicit pain in
the S1 joint.

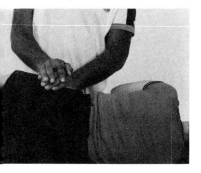

Side lying The athlete lies on the pain-free side.

1. Sacroiliac compression test: The examiner places pressure downward on the lateral pelvis in line with the sacroiliac joint. If the athlete complains of pain in the sacroiliac joint, a pathological condition may be present (Fig. 22-24).
2. When evaluating low back problems, the hip should also be evaluated (see Chapter 21).

Prone lying

1. Reverse straight leg raise: The athlete lies face down while the examiner lifts the affected leg.
2. If pain occurs in the low back, an L4 root compression may be present.

Functional Evaluation

Of major importance to the examination and evaluation of the low back is the testing of muscle strength in the lower extremities, sensory loss, and reflex inhibition.

Muscle strength To help ascertain the nerve root involvement, strength of major lower limb muscles should be determined (Table 22-2).

Sensation When there is a nerve root involvement, sensation can be partially or completely disrupted. Table 22-3 indicates general disruption or loss of sensation as a result of the low back nerve root involvement (Fig. 22-25).

Reflexes Two reflexes are routinely measured—knee (patellar) and the Achilles tendon. A diminished or absent patellar reflex is an indication of an L4, L5, or S1 nerve root problem. In contrast, the Achilles tendon reflex can determine the presence or absence of an L3, L4, or L5 nerve root problem.

TABLE 22-2

Muscle weakness and
nerve involvement

Muscles	Nerve Involvement			
Iliopsoas	T12	L1	L3	
Quadriceps	L2	L3	L4	Femoral nerve
Hip adductor group	L2	L3	L4	Obturator nerve
Extensor hallucis longus	L5	Deep peroneal nerve		
Anterior tibialis				
Gluteus medius				
Extensor digitorum longus and brevis				
Gastrocnemius, hamstring, gluteus maximus, peroneus longus and brevis	S1			

TABLE 22-3

Sensation

Region	Nerve Involvement		
Anterior thigh	L1	L2	L3
Knee	L4		
Inner lower leg and dorsum of foot	L5		
Heel, lateral malleolus, and plantar aspect of foot	S1		

Along with the evaluation procedures mentioned in this chapter, further inspection would include a thorough testing of the pelvic and thigh regions (see Chapter 21).

Mechanisms of Low Back Pain in the Athlete

Back afflictions, particularly those of the lower back, are second only to foot problems in order of incidence to humans throughout their lives. In sports, back problems are relatively common and are most often the result of congenital, mechanical, or traumatic factors. Congenital back disorders are conditions that are present at birth. Many authorities think that the human back is still undergoing structural changes as a result of upright position and therefore that humans are prone to slight spinal defects at birth, which later in life may cause improper body mechanics.

Congenital Anomalies

Anomalies of bony development are the underlying cause of many back problems in sports. Such conditions would have remained undiscovered had it not been for a blow or sudden twist that created an abnormal stress in the area of the anomaly. The most common of these anomalies are excessive length of the transverse process of the fifth lumbar vertebra, incomplete closure of the neural arch (spina bifida occulta), nonconformities of the spinous processes, atypical lumbosacral angles or articular facets, and incomplete closures of the vertebral laminae. All these anomalies may produce mechanical weaknesses that make the back prone to injury when it is subjected to excessive postural strains.

An example of a congenital defect that may develop into a more serious condition when aggravated by a blow or a sudden twist in sports is the condition of spondylolisthesis. Spondylolisthesis is a forward subluxation of the body of a vertebra, usually the fifth lumbar.

Mechanical Defects of the Spine

Mechanical back defects are caused mainly by faulty posture, obesity, or faulty body mechanics—all of which may affect the athlete's performance in sports. Traumatic forces produced in sports, either directly or indirectly, can result in contusions, sprains, and/or fractures. Sometimes even minor injuries can develop into chronic and recurrent conditions, which may have serious implications for the athlete. To aid fully in understanding a back complaint, a logical investigation should be made into the history and the site of any injury, the type of pain produced, and the extent of impairment of normal function.

Maintaining proper segmental alignment of the body during standing, sitting, lying, running, jumping, and throwing is of utmost importance for keeping the body in good condition. Habitual violations of the principles of good body mechanics occur in many sports and produce anatomical deficiencies that subject the body to constant abnormal muscular and ligamentous strain. In all cases of postural deformity the trainer should determine the cause and attempt to rectify the condition through proper strength and mobilization exercises.

Figure 22-25

Nerve root irritation in the low back region and alteration of lower limb sensation.

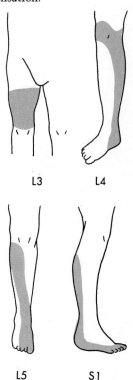

L3   L4

L5   S1

Back Trauma

That the athletic trainer possesses skill in recognizing and evaluating the extent of a sports injury to the back is of vital importance. Every football season there are stories of an athlete who has become paralyzed because of the mishandling of a fractured spine. Such conditions would not occur if field officials, coaches, and athletic trainers would use discretion, exercise good judgment, and be able to identify certain gross indications of serious spine involvement.

Preventing Initial Low Back Injuries in Sports

All conditioning programs in sports should include work for the prevention of back injuries. Prevention involves:
1. Correction, amelioration, or compensation of functional postural deviations
2. Maintenance or increase of trunk and general body flexibility
3. Increase of trunk and general body strength

One should be aware of any postural anomalies that the athletes possess; with this knowledge, one should establish individual corrective programs. Basic conditioning should include an emphasis on trunk flexibility. Every effort should be made to produce maximum range of motion in rotation and both lateral and forward flexion. Strength should be developed to the ultimate, with stress placed on developing the spinal extensors (erector spinae) and on developing abdominal strength to ensure proper postural alignment.

Conditions Causing Low Back Pain
Soft Tissue Injuries

Soft tissue injuries of the back most often occur to the lower back. Those that occur in sports are produced by acute twists, direct blows, or chronic strains resulting from faulty posture or from the use of poor body mechanics in the sport. Tearing or stretching of the supporting ligamentous tissue with secondary involvement of the musculature occurs. Repeated strains or sprains cause the stabilizing tissues to lose their supporting power, thus producing tissue laxity in the lower back area.

Back contusions Back contusions rank second to strains and sprains in incidence. Because of its large surface area the back is quite liable to bruises in sports; football produces the greatest number of these injuries. A history indicating a violent blow to the back could indicate an extremely serious condition. Contusion of the back must be distinguished from a vertebral fracture; in some instances this is possible only by means of an x-ray examination. The bruise causes local pain, muscle spasm, and point tenderness. A swollen area may be visible also. Cold and pressure should be applied immediately for about 24 hours or longer, followed by rest and a gradual introduction of various forms of superficial heat. If the bruise handicaps the movement of the athlete, deep therapy in the form of ultrasound or microwave diathermy may hasten recovery. Ice massage combined with gradual stretching has been found to benefit soft tissue injuries in the region of the lower back. The time of incapacitation usually ranges from 2 days to 2 weeks.

Considerations in preventing low back injuries:
Postural deviations must be corrected or compensated for. A balance of strength and flexibility in the trunk and pelvis must be maintained.

Lower back strain and sprain The mechanism of the typical lower back strain or sprain in sports activities usually occurs in two ways.[7] The first happens from a sudden, abrupt, violent extension contraction on an overloaded, unprepared, or underdeveloped spine, primarily in combination with trunk rotation. The second is the chronic strain commonly associated with faulty posture, usually excessive lumbar lordosis; however, conditions such as flat lower back or scoliosis can also predispose one to strain or sprain.[7]

Evaluation of the acute injury Evaluation must be performed immediately after injury. The possibility of fracture must first be ruled out. Discomfort in the low back may be diffused or localized in one area. There is no radiating pain farther than the buttocks or thigh, or neurological involvement causing muscle weakness, sensation impairment, or reflex impairments.

Immediate and follow-up care In the acute phase of this injury, it is essential that cold packs and/or ice massage be used intermittently throughout the day to decrease muscle spasm. Injuries of moderate to severe intensity may require complete bed rest to help break the pain-muscle spasm cycle. The physician may prescribe oral analgesic medication.

Cryotherapy, ultrasound, and an abdominal support is often beneficial following the acute phase. A graduated program begins slowly in the subacute stage, following the suggested regimen on p. 639. Exercise must not cause pain.

The recurrent and chronic low back pain condition Once an athlete has a moderate to severe episode of acute back strain or sprain there is high probability that it will occur again. With each subsequent episode the stage is set for the common problem of "chronic low back pain." Recurrent or chronic low back pain can have many possible causes. Many episodes of strain or sprain can produce malalignment of the vertebral facets or eventually produce discogenic disease causing nerve root compression and pain. Gradually this problem could lead to muscular weakness, impairments in sensation, and reflex responses. The older the athlete, the more prone he or she is to lower back injury. Incidence of this injury at the high school level is relatively low but becomes progressively greater at college and professional levels. In most cases, because of postural anomalies and numerous small injuries, a so-called acute back condition is the culmination of a progressive degeneration of long duration that is aggravated or accentuated by a blow or sudden twist. The injury is produced as the result of an existing anatomical vulnerability. The trunk and vertebral column press downward on the sacrum, while the lower limbs and pelvis force upward; thus an abnormal strain can be exerted when the athlete's trunk is twisted in one direction, while the hamstring muscles pull downward on the pelvis on the opposite side. Such stress, if applied to an inelastic, structurally deformed, or muscularly weak lower back, will produce pathology.

Sciatica Sciatica is an inflammatory condition of the sciatic nerve that can accompany recurrent or chronic low back pain. It produces pain that follows the nerve pathway, posterior and medial to the thigh.

Figure 22-26

An abdominal brace must both support the abdomen and flatten the lumbar curve.

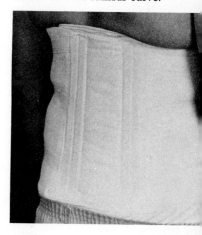

MANAGEMENT PLAN FOR LUMBOSACRAL STRAIN

Injury Situation

A high school shot-putter came into the training room complaining of a very sore back. He indicated that he woke up with the problem and was not sure how it occurred. Perhaps he had hurt it by doing dead lifts the day before, or by throwing the shot wrong.

Symptoms and Signs

The athlete complained of a constant dull ache and an inability to flex, extend, or rotate the trunk without increasing the pain. Inspection of the injury indicated:

1. The athlete had a pronounced lumbar lordosis.
2. There was an obvious muscle contraction of the right erector spinae.
3. There was severe point tenderness in the right lumbar region.
4. The right pelvis was elevated.
5. Passive movement did not cause pain; however, active and resistive movements produced severe pain.
6. Range of movement in all directions was restricted.
7. All tests for nerve root, hip joint, and sacroiliac joint were negative.
8. Leg length was measured and the athlete was found to have a functional shortening but no apparent structural shortening.
9. Both the left and right hamstring muscle groups and iliopsoas muscles were found to be abnormally tight.
10. X-ray examination showed no pathological conditions of the lumbar vertebrae.

Based on the examination, it was concluded that the athlete had sustained between a first and second degree strain of the lumbar muscles, primarily the right erector spinae region

Management Plan

1 Management Phase	GOALS: To relieve muscle spasm and pain. Estimated length of time (ELT): 2 or 3 days
Therapy	IMMEDIATE CARE: Ice pack (20 min) followed by exercise and then by TENS (15-20 min), 3 to 4 times daily
Exercise Rehabilitation	Following cold application, gentle passive stretch of low back region and hamstring and iliopsoas muscles—all within pain tolerance levels, 3 to 4 times daily

2	**Management Phase**	GOALS: To increase low back, hamstring, and iliopsoas ROM to at least begin postural correction ELT: fourth to seventh day of injury
	Therapy	FOLLOW-UP CARE: Ice massage followed by exercise 2 to 3 times daily If still painful, TENS therapy should be employed
	Exercise Rehabilitation	Repeat Phase 1 exercise and begin PNF to hip and low back regions, 2 to 3 times daily; or static low back, hamstring, and iliopsoas stretching (2 to 3 reps) and lower-abdominal strengthening 2 to 3 times daily Practice realigning pelvis General body maintenance exercises are conducted as long as they do not aggravate the injury 3 times a week
3	**Management Phase**	GOALS: 50% normal extensibility of the low back hamstring and iliopsoas muscles; appropriate abdominal strength ELT: eighth to twelfth day of injury
	Therapy	Ice massage or whirlpool once daily Ultrasound 1 to 1.5 watts/cm^2 once daily
	Exercise Rehabilitation	Repeat Phase 2 exercises once daily to continue reeducation of pelvis and lumbar alignment Add resistance training for abdominal strength General body maintenance exercises are conducted 3 times a week as long as they do not aggravate the injury
4	**Management Phase**	GOALS: To restore 90% of ROM, strength, and proper back alignment
	Exercise Rehabilitation	Return to weight training and shot-putting program 3 times a week Athlete is instructed on proper back alignment when shot-putting Athlete is to avoid dead lifting and to wear a lifting belt while weight training
5	**Management Phase**	GOALS: To return to full competition
	Exercise Rehabilitation	Return to normal training 3 times a week Gradual reentry into competition Using an abdominal support belt is advisable during practice and competition
	Criteria for Returning to Shot-putting	The athlete's back must be: 1. Pain and spasm free 2. Near normal in hamstring, low back, and iliopsoas extensibility 3. Making good progress toward correcting lumbar lordosis 4. Able to perform the shot-put with the spine and pelvis in good alignment

Individuals with lumbar disk
disease should avoid
performing forward-bending
activities.

Figure 22-27

Intervertebral disk syndrome.

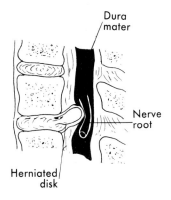

Figure 22-28

Spondylolysis.

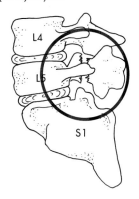

The term *sciatica* has incorrectly been used as a general term to describe all lower back pain, without reference to exact causes. It is commonly associated with peripheral nerve root compression from intervertebral disk protrusion or structural irregularities within the intervertebral foramen. This nerve is particularly vulnerable to torsion or direct blows that tend to impose abnormal stretching and pressure on it as it emerges from the spine, thus effecting a traumatic condition. The sciatic nerve is also subject to trauma at the point at which it crosses over the ischial spine. Such a contusion can cause muscular spasm, placing direct pressure on the nerve.

Lumbar disk disease (intervertebral disk syndrome) The lumbar disk is subject to constant abnormal stresses stemming from faulty body mechanics, trauma, or both, over a period of time can cause degeneration, tears and cracks in the annulus fibrosus. Various pressures within the intervertebral disks have been established.[22] When using intervertebral pressure in the standing position as a constant, it was found that pressure was *decreased* by 75% in the supine position and by 25% in the side lying position. Pressure was *increased* by 33% percent while sitting; by 33% while standing when slightly bent forward; by 45% while sitting when slightly bent forward; 52% while standing when bent far forward; and 63% while sitting when bent well forward.[22]

The area most often injured is the lumbar spine, particularly the disk lying between the fourth and fifth lumbar vertebrae. In sports, the mechanism of a disk injury is the same as for the lumbosacral sprain—a sudden twist that places abnormal strain on the lumbar region. Besides injuring soft tissues, such a strain may herniate an already degenerated disk by increasing the size of crack and allowing the nucleus pulposus to spill out (Fig. 22-27) This protusion of the nucleus pulposus may place pressure on the cord of spinal nerves, thus causing radiating pains similar to those of sciatica.[25]

The movement that produces a herniation or bulging of the nucleus pulposus may be excessive and pain may be minimal or even absent. However, even without severe pain the athlete may complain of numbness along the nerve root and muscle weakness in the lower extremity.

Examination commonly reveals point tenderness and restricted movement. Straight leg and nerve root tests prove positive. Tendon reflexes are partially or completely blocked and dermatome sensation becomes decreased relative to the affected nerve root. Muscle weaknesses also become apparent. These symptoms and signs require an immediate referral to an othopedic surgeon or neurologist.

Immediate and follow-up care Treatment of disk disease usually includes[4,6]:

1. Strict bed rest for 1 to 2 weeks
2. Progressive ambulation
3. Anti-inflammatory agent and on occasion muscle relaxants
4. Analgesics and cryotherapy to break the pain–muscle spasm cycle (heat may be of value for its ability to relax muscles)
5. Tranquilizers to decrease the anxiety of the athlete forced to stay in bed

A condition that leads to a progressive bladder or bowel malfunction or severe paresis is considered a medical emergency. When symptom free, the athlete begins a daily program of exercise rehabilitation and postural education.

Spondylolysis   Spondylolysis refers to a breaking down of the vertebrae and, more commonly, a defect in the pars intermedia of the articular processes of the vertebrae (Fig. 22-28). It is attributed to a congenital predisposition and/or repeated stress to this area. It may produce no symptoms unless a disk herniation occurs or there is sudden trauma as hyperextension. Sports movements that characteristically hyperextend the spine, such as the back arch in gymnastics, lifting weights, blocking in football, serving in tennis, spiking in volleyball, and the butterfly stroke in swimming, are most likely to cause this condition.[11,15-17] Commonly spondylolysis begins unilaterally and then extends to the other side of the vertebrae (Fig. 22-29).

Management usually involves restricted activity and complete bed rest; bracing may also be required.

Rehabilitation exercise usually involves resolution of hyperlordosis.

Spondylolisthesis   The condition of spondylolisthesis is a forward slippage of a vertebra on the one below; it is commonly accompanied by spondyloylsis and has the highest incidence with L5 on S1 (Fig. 22-30). The athlete with this condition will usually have a lumbar hyperlordosis postural impairment. A direct blow or sudden twist or chronic low back strain may cause the defective vertebra to displace itself forward on the

Spondylolysis can lead to the condition of spondylolisthesis.

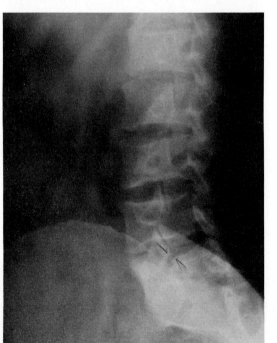

Figure 22-29

Spondylolysis of the fifth lumbar vertebrae.

Figure 22-30

Spondylolisthesis.

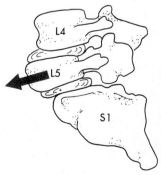

sacrum. When this happens, the athlete complains of localized pain or a pain that radiates into both buttocks, stiffness in the lower back, and increased irritation after physical activity.[19] The athlete with serious spondylolisthesis displays a short torso, heart-shaped buttocks, low rib cage, high iliac crest, and vertical sacrum; tight hamstring muscles and restricted hip extension may also be present.[17] For the most part, these symptoms are the same for the majority of lower back problems; therefore, an x-ray film should be made to enable the physician to diagnose accurately. Discovery of a defective vertebra may be grounds for medical exclusion from collision and contact-type sports.[11]

Conservative management of acute problems usually consists of bed rest and flexion of the lumbar spine.[6] Casting to reduce hyperlordosis may also be employed. A slippage of 50% or more may cause a medical emergency, requiring surgical fusion of the spine.

Sacroiliac joint   The sacroiliac is the junction formed by the ilium and the sacrum, and it is fortified by ligamentous tissue that allows little motion to take place. When the pelvis is abnormally rotated downward anteriorly, the majority of the weight of the upper trunk is carried back of the pelvis, producing stress at the sacroiliac joint.[10] This abnormal postural alignment can cause pain and disability.

Lumbar vertebral fracture and dislocation   Fractures of the vertebral column, in terms of bone injury, are not serious in themselves; but they pose dangers when related to spinal cord damage. Imprudent movement of a person with a fractured spine can cause irreparable damage to the spinal cord. All sports injuries involving the back should be considered fractures until proved differently by the physician. Lifting and moving the athlete should be executed in such a manner as to preclude twisting, and each body segment (neck, trunk, hips, and lower limbs) should be firmly supported. Vertebral fractures of the greatest concern in sports are compression fractures and fractures of the transverse and spinous processes.

The *compression fracture* may occur as a result of violent hyperflexion or jackknifing of the trunk. Falling from a height and landing on the feet or buttocks may also produce a compression fracture. The vertebrae that are most often compressed are those in the dorsolumbar curves. The vertebrae usually are crushed anteriorly by the traumatic force of the body above the site of injury. The crushed body may spread out fragments and protrude into the spinal canal, compressing and possibly even cutting the cord.

Recognition of the compression fracture is difficult without an x-ray examination. A basic evaluation may be made with a knowledge of the history and point tenderness over the affected vertebrae.

Fractures of the transverse and spinous processes result most often from kicks or other direct blows to the back. Since these processes are surrounded by large muscles, fracture produces extensive soft tissue injury. As fractures, these present little danger and will usually permit the athlete considerable activity within the range of pain tolerance. Most care and treatment will be oriented toward therapy of the soft tissue pathology.

Coccyx Injuries

Coccygeal injuries in sports are prevalent and occur primarily from such direct blows as those that are received in forcibly sitting down, falling, or being kicked by an opponent. Most injuries to the coccyx are the result of contusions.

Persistent coccyalgia should be referred to a physician for x-ray and rectal examination. Pain in the coccygeal region is often prolonged and at times chronic. Such conditions are identified by the term *coccygodynia* and occur as a result of an irritation to the coccygeal plexus.

Treatment consists of analgesics and a ring seat to relieve the pressure on the coccyx while sitting. Palliative measures such as sitz baths or whirlpool in warm water might serve to alleviate some of the pain. It should be noted that pain with a fractured coccyx may last for many months. Once a coccygeal injury has healed, the athlete should be protected against reinjury by appropriately applied padding.

Rehabilitation of Low Back Pain

The following treatment procedures are employed to a greater or lesser degree, depending on the type and extent of the pathological condition:

1. Limitation of activity
2. Anti-inflammatory and muscle relaxant medications
3. Cold and/or heat application and ultrasound
4. Passive exercise
5. Active progressive exercise
6. Relaxation training
7. Transcutaneous electrical nerve stimulation (TENS) application
8. Education for proper back usage

Limitation of Activity

Limiting physical activity is essential in the acute episodes of low back pain. It can also be a positive influence in chronic pain. The least strain on the back is in the fully recumbant position. In the case of a chronic or a subacute lower back condition, a *firm mattress will afford better rest and relaxation of the lower back.* Placing a ¾ inch plywood board over the entire area of the bed underneath the athlete's mattress prevents the mattress from sagging in the wrong places and gives a firm, stable surface for the injured back. The athlete lies supine with hips flexed by elevating the legs with pillows. It is also interesting to note that sleeping on a water bed will often relieve the symptoms of a low back problem if the athlete lies on the back. However, in some cases, the firm mattress or water bed may create more pain and discomfort. The value of a water bed is that it supports the body curves equally, decreasing abnormal pressures to any one body area.

Medications

Analgesics and oral anti-inflammatory agents are commonly given to inhibit pain. If a highly active athlete becomes severely depressed over suddenly being severely physically restricted, an antidepressant may be given. On occasion muscle relaxants are also given.

Cold or Heat Application

Local ice application reduces the pain–muscle spasm cycle. Superficial heat can also provide relaxation and reduction of spasm. Ultrasound and mild muscle stimulation can be used to relieve spasm and discomfort.

Passive Exercise

If the condition is muscular and discogenic disease has been ruled out, a mild passive stretch can help to reduce muscle spasm. Passive stretching of the hamstrings and iliopsoas muscle may allow a more coordinated lumbar pelvic rhythm to take place without pain and discomfort. Lumbar vertebral mobilization techniques may also be of some benefit if performed gently (see Chapter 14).

Active Progressive Exercise

Active exercise is a major aspect of low back rehabilitation. Once the pain and spasm have subsided, active exercise should begin. The major goals of exercise are to establish normal flexibility and strength and to develop good postural habits in all aspects of daily activities.

Exercise should not be engaged in too vigorously before pain has diminished significantly. The first exercise phase should include pelvic tilt, alternate knees to chest, and double knee to chest. *NOTE: All exercises within each phase should start with 3 repetitions and be increased each day by 1, until 10 repetitions can be performed (if a position is held, it should be done for a count of 6).*

Stage 1—low back exercises

Pelvic tilt   The athlete lies supine in a "hook-lying" position with feet flat on the mat or floor. The abdomen is contracted and the back flattened firmly against the surface.

After 10 repetitions of this exercise, the athlete, while keeping the lumbar spine as flat as possible, raises the pelvis 3 to 4 inches and holds this position for 6 seconds (Fig. 22-31).

Figure 22-31

Pelvic tilt and raise.

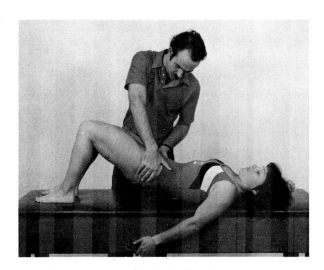

Alternate knee to chest While the athlete is lying supine, one knee is brought slowly towards the chest. Both hands grasp the posterior thigh and gently pull it slowly to an end point for a count of 6. The leg is returned slowly to its starting point and the other leg is exercised in the same way.

Double knee to chest While in a hook-lying position the athlete grasps under both bent knees and pulls them slowly and gently as far as possible toward the chest and holds the end point (Fig. 22-32).

Stage 2—low back exercises

When the low back is relatively pain free, the athlete can move to Phase 2 exercises, which include overhead low back stretch, hip flexor stretch, hamstring stretch, single leg raise, abdominal curl-up, and lateral flexion stretch.

Overhead low back stretch The athlete lies on the back and brings both legs overhead. Depending on the athlete's muscle restriction, it may be impossible to touch toes to the mat or to touch both toes and knees. Great care must be taken not to place too much pressure on the neck, especially if there is a history of injury (Fig. 22-33).

Hip flexor stretch The hip flexor stretch releases tension associated with the lumbar curve. Placing one leg upon the seat of a chair or bench with the support leg fully extended, the athlete settles the body weight downward, stretching the iliopsoas muscle on the side of the extended leg (Fig. 22-34).

Single leg raise The single leg raise stretches the low back and hamstrings and strengthens hip flexors and abdominal muscles. The athlete takes a supine position with one knee bent and the other straight. Keeping the back flat, the straight leg is raised as far as possible and returned slowly. The athlete completes up to 10 repetitions and then changes legs. This exercise can be made progressively more difficult by gradually extending the bent knee over a period of time until it is extended like the exercising leg.

Figure 22-32

Double knee to chest.

Figure 22-33

Overhead low back stretch.

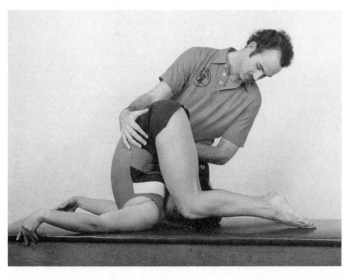

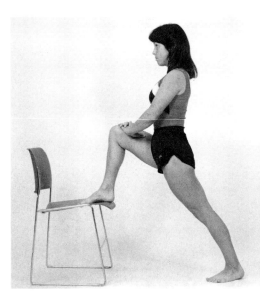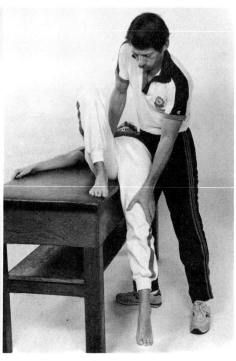

Figure 22-34

Hip flexor stretches.

Abdominal curl-up The athlete takes a hook-lying position, squeezes the buttocks together, contracts abdominal muscles, flexes the neck and places the chin on the chest, rolls shoulders forward and slowly slides hands up the thighs to an end point (Fig. 22-35, *A-C*). This exercise progresses from hands sliding up the thighs to arms crossing the chest, to finally hands laced behind the neck.

Lateral trunk flexion The athlete stands with feet apart and slightly bends the knee on the side of the direction of the stretch. The trunk is then laterally flexed without backward extension or forward flexion. All movements are gently but progressively increased.[6]

Hamstring stretching for low back pain Hamstring stretching for low back pain should not be conducted with both legs extended.[6] To protect the back against further irritation, one leg is stretched at a time. The leg not being stretched is placed in a hooked position to alleviate strain on the back. The stretch should be gradually increased, not ballistically stretched (Fig. 22-36).

Wall back flattener The wall back flattener exercise is designed to educate the athlete about the proper pelvic position, to stretch low back muscles, and to strengthen the lower abdominal muscles. The athlete stands about 8 to 12 inches from a wall facing outward, knees slightly bent, with the pelvis and low back pressed flat against the wall. The athlete then bends forward, rounding the back as much as possible, and then slowly returns to a fully upright position, attempting to touch each vertebrae to the wall.

Manual resistance, using the principles of PNF, has been found extremely valuable for the rehabilitation of low back pain. With the slow

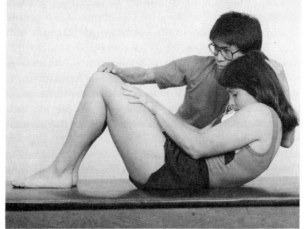

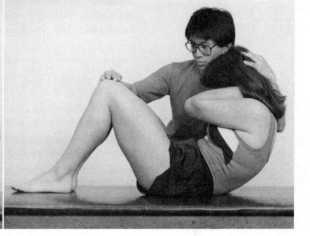

A

B

C

Figure 22-35

Abdominal curl-up.

reversal technique the athlete can strengthen and educate muscles essential for proper pelvic lumbar rhythm (see Appendix I-D).

Relaxation and Low Back Pain

An important aspect of treating athletes with low back pain is through progressive relaxation. With constant pain comes anxiety and increased muscular tension that compounds the low back problem. By systematically contracting and completely "letting go" of the body's major muscles, the athlete learns to recognize abnormal tension and to consciously relax them. The most popular method of progressive relaxation is the Jacobson[18] method, which can be found in modified form in a number of different texts.[1,2]

Transcutaneous Electrical Nerve Stimulation (TENS)

Application of a TENS device has been found beneficial in a high percentage of cases of low back pain.[6] However, not every machine is equally effective in all cases of low back pain. There must be experimentation as to type of machine, wave form, and sites of application[6] (see Chapter 13).

Figure 22-36

Hamstring stretching for low back strain.

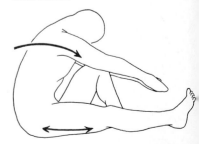

Educating for the Proper Care of the Back
Bed rest
1. Do not stay in one position too long.
2. The bed should be flat and firm.
3. Do not sleep on the abdomen.
4. Do not sleep on the back with legs fully extended.
5. If sleeping on the back, a pillow should be placed under the knees.
6. Ideally, sleep on the side.
7. Arms should never be extended overhead.

Sitting
1. Do not sit for long periods.
2. Avoid sitting forward on a chair with back arched.
3. Sit on a firm, straight-backed chair.
4. The low back should be slightly rounded or positioned firmly against the back of the chair.
5. The feet should be flat on the floor with knees above the level of the hips (if unable to adequately raise the hips, the feet should be placed on a stool).
6. Avoid sitting with legs straight and raised on a stool.

Driving
1. Move seat so that knees are higher than the hips (pedals must be reached without stretching).
2. Avoid leaning forward.
3. Wear seat and shoulder harnesses.

Standing
1. If standing in one spot for a long period of time:
   a. Shift position from one foot to another.
   b. Place one foot on a stool.
2. Stand tall, flatten low back, and relax knees.
3. Avoid arching back.

Lifting and carrying
1. To pick up an object:
   a. Bend at knees and not the waist.
   b. Do not twist to pick up an object—face it squarely.
   c. Tuck in buttocks and tighten abdomen.
2. To carry an object:
   a. Hold object close to body.
   b. Hold object at waist level.
   c. Do not carry object on one side of the body—if it must be carried unbalanced, change from one side to the other.

REFERENCES

1. Arnheim, D.D., and Sinclair, W.A.: Physical education for special populations, Englewood Cliffs, N.J., 1985, Prentice-Hall.
2. Auxter, D., and Pyfer, J.: Principles and methods of adapted physical education, St. Louis, 1985, Times Mirror/Mosby College Publishing.
3. Becker, T.: Scoliosis in the adolescent athlete, Sports Medicine Guide 2(4):1, Nov. 1983.
4. Birnbaum, J.S.: The musculoskeletal manual, New York, 1982, Academic Press.
5. Blacklock, N.J.: Bladder trauma in the long-distance runner, Am. J. Sports Med. 7:239, 1979.
6. Cailliet, R.: Low back pain, ed. 3, Philadelphia, 1981, F.A. Davis Co.
7. Cantu, R.C.: Low back injuries. In Vinger, P.F., and Hoerner, E.F. (editors): Sports injuries: the unth-

warted epidemic, Boston, 1982, John Wright, PSG, Inc.

8. Cyriax, J.: Textbook of orthopaedic medicine, vol. 1, Diagnosis of soft tissue lesions, ed. 8, London, 1982, Bailliere Tindall.

9. Davis, J.J., Cohn, I., and Nance, F.C.: Diagnosis and management of blunt abdominal trauma, Ann. Surg. 183:672, 1976.

10. Dontigny, R.L.: Dysfunction of the sacroiliac joint and its treatment, J. Orthop. Sports Phys. Ther. 1:23, 1979.

11. Ferguson, R.J., et al.: Low back pain in college football linemen, Am. J. Sports Med. 2:63, 1974.

12. Gehlsen, G., and Albohm, M.: Evaluation of sports bras, Phys. Sportsmed. 8:89, 1980.

13. Hahn, D.B.: The ruptured spleen: implications for the athletic trainer, Ath. Train. 13:190, 1978.

14. Hoppenfeld, S.: Physical examination of the spine and extremities, New York, 1976, Appleton-Century-Crofts.

15. Jackson, D.W.: Low back pain in young athletes: evaluation of stress reaction and discogenic problems, Am. J. Sports Med. 7:361, 1979.

16. Jackson, D.W., et al.: Spondylolysis in the female gymnast, Clin. Orthop. 117:68, 1976.

17. Jackson, D.W., and Wiltse, L.L.: Low back pain in young athletes, Phys. Sportsmed 2:53, 1974.

18. Jacobson E.: Progressive relaxation ed. 2, Chicago, 1938, University of Chicago Press.

19. Leach, R.E.: Disc disease, spondylolysis and spondylolisthesis, Ath. Train. 12:13, 1977.

20. Madding, G.F., and Kennedy, P.A.: Trauma to the liver, Philadelphia, 1971, W.B. Saunders Co.

21. Moncure, A.C., and Wilkins, E.W.: Injuries involving the abdomen, viscera, and genitourinary system. In Vinger, P.F., and Hoerner, E.F. (editors): Sports injuries: the unthwarted epidemic, Boston, 1982, John Wright, PSG, Inc.

22. Nachemson, A., and Elfström, G.: Intravital dynamic pressure measurements in lumbar discs, Scand. J. Rehab. Med. (Suppl. 1), 1969.

23. O'Donoghue, D.H.: Treatment of injuries in athletes, Philadelphia, 1984, W.B. Saunders Co.

24. Rutkow, I.M.: Rupture of the spleen in infectious mononucleosis, Arch. Surg. 113:718, 1978.

25. Ryan, A.J.: What causes low back pain? Phys. Sportsmed. 2:36, 1974.

26. Schiller, W.R.: General surgery and sports medicine. In Appenzeller, O., and Atkinson, R. (editors): Sports medicine, Baltimore, 1981, Urban & Schwarzenberg.

27. Schuster, K.: Equipment update: jogging bras hit the streets, Phys. Sportsmed. 7:125, 1979.

ADDITIONAL SOURCES

Anderson, W.A.D., and Scotti, T.M.: Synopsis of pathology, ed. 10, St. Louis, 1980, The C.V. Mosby Co.

Collins, H.R.: Low back injuries in athletics, National Athletic Trainers Symposium, 1982, Granite Falls, Neb., Marvl Productions. (Cassette).

Eichelberger, M.R.: Torso injuries in athletes, Phys. Sportsmed. 9:87, 1981.

Go, M.: Low back evaluation, National Athletic Trainers Association Annual Meeting, Clinical Symposium, June 1983, The Association. (Cassette.)

Mendell, J.R.: The nervous system. In Strauss, R.H. (editor): Sports medicine, Philadelphia, 1984, W.B. Saunders Co.

Prior, J.A., Silberstein, J.S., and Stang, J.M.: Physical diagnosis, ed. 6, St. Louis, 1981, The C.V. Mosby Co.

Rutledge, B.J.: Injuries to the cranium and central nervous system during athletics. In O'Donoghue, D.H.: Treatment of injuries to athletes, ed. 4, Philadelphia, 1984, W.B. Saunders Co.

Ryan, A.J.: Prevention and management of injuries to lower back, groin, hip and thigh, Audiocassettes on Sportsmedicine, Teach'em, Inc.

Urban, L.M.: The straight-leg-raising test: a review, J. Orthop. Sports Phys. Ther. 2:117, 1981.

Wooden, M.J.: Preseason screening of the lumbar spine, J. Orthop. Sports Phys. Ther. 3:6, 1981.

Chapter 23

THE UPPER SPINE, HEAD AND FACE

When you finish this chapter, you should be able to

Describe the anatomy of the upper spine, head, and face and relate it to sports injuries

Recognize and evaluate major sports injuries of the upper spine, head, and face

Perform proper immediate and follow-up management of injuries of the upper spine, head, and face

Sports injuries to the upper spine, head or face could have major consequences for the athlete. A serious facial injury could lead to disfigurement or loss of sight or might even be life threatening. Injury to the head could result in major cerebral involvement, whereas an upper spinal injury could result in paralysis.

THORACIC SPINE
Anatomy

The thoracic spine consists of 12 vertebrae. The first through the tenth thoracic vertebrae articulate with ribs by means of articular facets. Attached to all thoracic spinous processes are the trapezius muscle, the rhomboid muscle to the upper spinous processes, and the latissimus dorsi to the lower spinous processes. Deeper muscles of the back also attach to spinous and transverse processes (Fig. 23-1).

Evaluating the Thoracic Spine
Major Complaints

Pain in the upper back can be caused by a variety of conditions: pain could be referred from some visceral disorder, it could be of muscular origin, or it could be caused by a nerve root irritation. Having the athlete respond to the following questions should provide important information:

1. What kind of pain do you feel? Describe it.
2. What is the duration, location, and intensity of the pain? (For example, is it constant? intermittent?)

3. What makes the pain more or less intense?
4. Did the pain come on gradually or suddenly?
5. Do you feel numbness or tingling anywhere?
6. Have you been treated for this problem before? If so, was the result satisfactory?

General observation   The athlete is examined posteriorly and laterally for the following:

1. Kyphosis (abnormal convexity of the curvature of the thoracic spine)
2. Flat back (decreased curvature of the thoracic spine)
3. Scoliosis (lateral rotary deviation of the spine)

A collapsed vertebra will often produce a thoracic back protrusion, while a flat low back or kyphosis of the upper lumbar and lower thoracic spine may indicate Scheuermann's disease (adolescent osteochondrosis).[7] Viewed laterally, a decrease of the normal lumbar curve with an extensive kyphosis of the thoracic spine could indicate ankylosing spondylitis.[7]

In evaluating the thoracic spine, all postural deviations must be noted.

Young athletes who complain of thoracic spine pain may in fact have:
  Spondylolysis
  Spondylolisthesis
  Scoliosis
  Scheuermann's disease

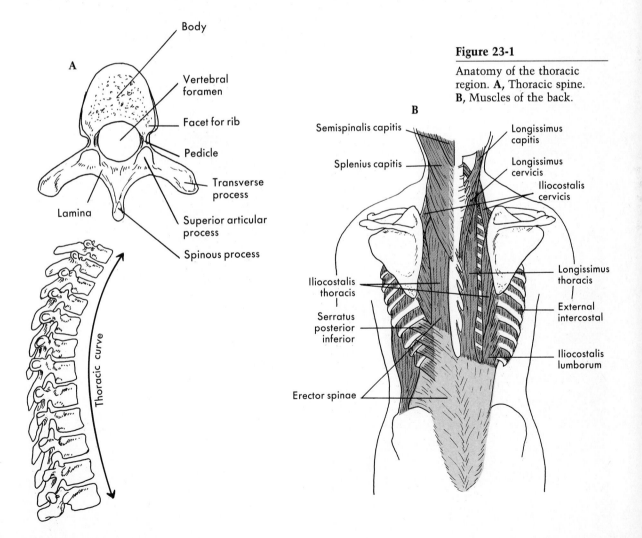

Figure 23-1

Anatomy of the thoracic region. **A,** Thoracic spine. **B,** Muscles of the back.

A

Body
Vertebral foramen
Facet for rib
Pedicle
Transverse process
Superior articular process
Spinous process
Lamina

Thoracic curve

B

Semispinalis capitis
Splenius capitis
Iliocostalis thoracis
Serratus posterior inferior
Erector spinae

Longissimus capitis
Longissimus cervicis
Iliocostalis cervicis
Longissimus thoracis
External intercostal
Iliocostalis lumborum

Bony and Soft Tissue Palpation

Starting at the twelfth thoracic vertebra, all thoracic and cervical vertebrae are palpated for pain and possible defects. Also palpated are the spinous and transverse processes, adjacent ribs in the thoracic region, and the intercostal and posterior back and shoulder muscles.

Active resistive and passive movement

Active movement   The athlete is first asked to flex, extend, laterally flex, and rotate the neck. Pain accompanying the movement in the upper back region could be referred from a lesion of the cervical disk. Additionally, pain in the scapular area could stem from an irritation of the long thoracic or suprascapular nerves, requiring evaluation of the shoulder complex (see Chapter 24). The athlete should also be asked to flex forward and laterally and to extend and rotate the trunk. Pain felt on movement may indicate nerve root irritation to the lower thoracic region.

After active movement, the same motions are resisted. Pain accom-

Figure 23-2

Many sports place a great deal of stress on the upper spine.

panying resisted movements can reveal muscle strains in the thorax and abdominal region.

Following active movement, the athlete is passively moved while seated in a chair with hips and legs stabilized. The athlete's trunk is passively rotated first one direction and then the other. Pain accompanying this passive movement may be indicate a pathological condition of the joint.

Thoracic Spine Injuries
Back Conditions in the Young Athlete

Because young athletes are much less likely to sustain back strains and nerve root irritation, back pain could indicate a vertebral growth disturbance. Three such conditions that could have serious disabling consequences are spondylolisthesis (see Chapter 22), scoliosis, and Scheuermann's disease.

Scoliosis Scoliosis was discussed in Chapter 9 in relation to injury mechanism and in Chapter 22 in relation to low back pain. Any time a young athlete complains of back pain, scoliosis should be considered. Because a lateral-rotary condition of the spine can be progressively quite disabling if not promptly treated, referral to a physician must be made at once by the trainer.

Scheuermann's disease (osteochondrosis of the spine) Scheuermann's disease is a degeneration of vertebral epiphyseal endplates. This degeneration allows the disk nucleus pulposus to prolapse into a vertebral body. Characteristically there is an accentuation of the kyphotic curve and backache in the young athlete. Adolescents engaging in such sports as gymnastics and swimming—the butterfly stroke particularly—are prone to this condition.[23]

Etiological factors Scheuermann's disease is idiopathic, but the occurrence of multiple minor injuries to the vertebral epiphyses seems to be an etiological factor. These injuries apparently disrupt circulation to the epiphyseal endplate, causing avascular necrosis.

Symptoms and signs In the initial stages, the young athlete will have kyphosis of the thoracic spine and lumbar lordosis without back pain. In later stages, there is point tenderness over the spinous processes and the young athlete may complain of backache at the end of a very physically active day. Hamstring muscles are characteristically very tight.

Management The major goal of management is to prevent progressive kyphosis. In the early stages of the disease, extension exercises and postural education are beneficial. Bracing, rest, and anti-inflammatory medication may also be helpful. The athlete may stay active, but avoid aggravating movements.

CERVICAL SPINE
Anatomy

Because of the vulnerability of the cervical spine to sports injuries, athletic trainers should be familiar with its anatomy and mechanism and with means of evaluating injuries. The cervical spine consists of seven vertebrae, with the first two differing from the other true vertebrae (Fig. 23-3). These first two are called the atlas and axis, respectively, and they function together to support the head on the spinal column and to permit cervical rotation. The *atlas*, named for its function of supporting the head, displays no body or spinous processes and is composed of lateral masses that are connected to the anterior and posterior arches. The upper surfaces articulate with the occipital condyles of the skull and allow flexion and extension but little lateral movement. The arches of the atlas form a bony ring sufficiently large to accommodate the odontoid process and the medulla of the spinal cord. The *axis* or epistropheus is the second cervical vertebra and is designed to allow the skull and atlas to rotate on it. Its primary difference from a typical vertebra is the presence of a tooth-like projection from the vertebral body that fits into the ring of the atlas. This is called the odontoid process. The great mobility of the cervical spine is attributed to the flattened, oblique facing of its articular facets and to the horizontal positioning of the spinous processes.

The *spinal cord* is that portion of the central nervous system that is contained within the vertebral canal of the spinal column. It emerges from the foramen magnum of the cranium, to the filum terminale in the vicinity of the first or second lumbar vertebra. The lumbar roots and the sacral nerves form a horse-like tail called the cauda equina.

Thirty-one pairs of *spinal nerves* extend from the sides of the spinal cord: eight cervical, twelve thoracic, five lumbar, five sacral, and one coccygeal (Fig. 23-4). Each of these nerves has an anterior root (motor root) and a posterior one (sensory root). The two roots in each case join together and form a single spinal nerve, which passes downward and outward through the intervertebral foramen. As the spinal nerves are conducted through the intervertebral foramen they pass near the articular processes of the vertebrae. Any abnormal movement of these processes, as in a dislocation or a fracture, may expose the spinal nerves to injury. Injuries that occur below the third lumbar vertebra usually result in nerve root damage but do not cause spinal cord damage.

Cervical Spine Injuries

The very mobile neck carrying the relatively heavy head can incur a wide range of sports injuries.

Because the neck is so mobile, it is extremely vulnerable to a wide range of sports injuries. Although relatively uncommon, severe sports injury to the neck can produce a catastrophic impairment of the spinal cord.

Figure 23-3

Cervical spine, atlas, and axis.

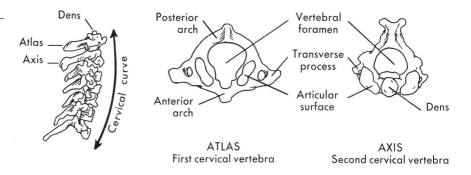

Evaluation of Neck Injuries

Evaluation of the neck injury can be divided into on-site emergency evaluation and off-site (sidelines or training room) evaluation.

On-site emergency evaluation Unconscious athletes should be treated as if they have a cervical fracture (see Chapter 12, Evaluation of the conscious and unconscious athlete). Every sports program should have an emergency system for caring for the severely injured athlete, especially when a neck injury is suspected.

An athlete who has sustained a neck injury, where fracture has been ruled out, should be carefully evaluated. Any one or more of the following signs should preclude the athlete from further sports participation:

1. Neck pain on passive, active, or resistive movement
2. Tingling or burning sensation in the neck, shoulder, or arm
3. Neck motion that causes paresthesia or hypoesthesia
4. Muscle weakness in the upper or lower limbs

Off-site evaluation Even when an athlete comes into the training room from an evaluation of neck discomfort, fracture should always be considered as a possibility until it is ruled out. If there is doubt about a fracture, immediate referral to a physician for x-ray examination should be made.

Major complaints

The following factors should be considered:

1. How did the pain begin? (For example, a sudden twist, a hit to the head or neck)
2. Does the athlete have faulty posture?
3. Does the athlete complain of radiating pain or tingling or prickling sensations?
4. Is there numbness in the arm or hand?
5. Is there a crackling or creaking sensation on movement?
6. What precipitates pain? (For example, tension stress, sitting for long periods, sudden head movements)
7. What activities relieve the neck pain?
8. Does the athlete have a history of neck problems or injuries? If so, what actions were taken? (For example, x-ray films, physical therapy, traction, manipulation)

General observation

The athlete is observed for the following:

1. Postural alignment
2. How the head is carried
3. Favoring the neck by holding it in a restricted position

Bony Palpation

The following areas are palpated:

1. Transverse processes
2. Spinous processes
3. Mastoid processes
4. Occiput processes

Soft Tissue Palpation

Muscles in the region of the neck are palpated from their origin to their insertion. Trigger points and tonus asymmetries are also noted for the following:

Figure 23-4

Relation of cord and spinal nerves to the vertebral column.

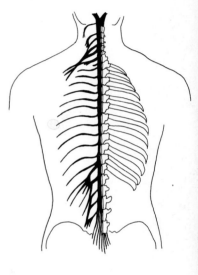

TABLE 23-1

Resistive motion to determine muscle weakness related to neck injury

Resistive motion	Major Muscles Involved	Nerves
Neck flexion	Sternocleidomastoidius	Cranial 11 Cervical 2 and 3
Neck extension	Upper trapezius	Cranial 11 Cervical 3 and 4 Dorsal, primary divisions of the cervical nerves
Neck lateral flexion	Splenius capitis Scalenus anticus, medius, and posticus	Cervical 4-8 Anterior, primary divisions of the lower nerves
Neck lateral rotation	Sternocleidomastoidius	Cranial 11 Cervical 2 and 3
Shoulder shrug (scapular elevation)	Upper trapezius Levator scapulae	Cranial 11 Cervical 3 and 4
Shoulder flexing	Anterior deltoidius Coracobrachialis	Cervical 5 and 6 Cervical 6 and 7
Shoulder extension	Deltoidius Teres major Latissimus dorsi	Cervical 5 and 6 Cervical 5 and 6 Cervical 6-8
Shoulder abduction	Middle deltoidius Supraspinatus	Cervical 5 and 6 Cervical 5
Shoulder lateral rotation	Subscapularis Pectoralis major Latissimus dorsi Teres major	Cervical 5 and 6 Cervical 5-8 Thoracic 1 Cervical 6-8 Cervical 5 and 6
Elbow flexion	Biceps brachii Brachialis Brachioradialis	Cervical 5 and 6 Cervical 5 and 6 Cervical 5 and 6
Elbow extension	Triceps brachii	Cervical 7 and 8
Forearm supination	Biceps brachii Supinator	Cervical 5 and 6 Cervical 6
Forearm pronation	Pronator teres Pronator quadratus	Cervical 6 and 7 Cervical 8 Thoracic 1
Wrist flexion	Flexor carpi radialis Flexor carpi ulnaris	Cervical 6 and 7 Cervical 8 Thoracic 1
Wrist extension	Extensor carpi radialis Extensor carpi radialis brevis Extensor carpi ulnaris	Cervical 6 and 7 Cervical 6 and 7 Cervical 6-8
Finger flexion	Flexor digitorum superficialis	Cervical 7 and 8 Thoracic 1
Finger extension	Extensor digitorum Extensor indicis Extendor digiti minimi	Cervical 6-8 Cervical 6-8 Cervical 6-8

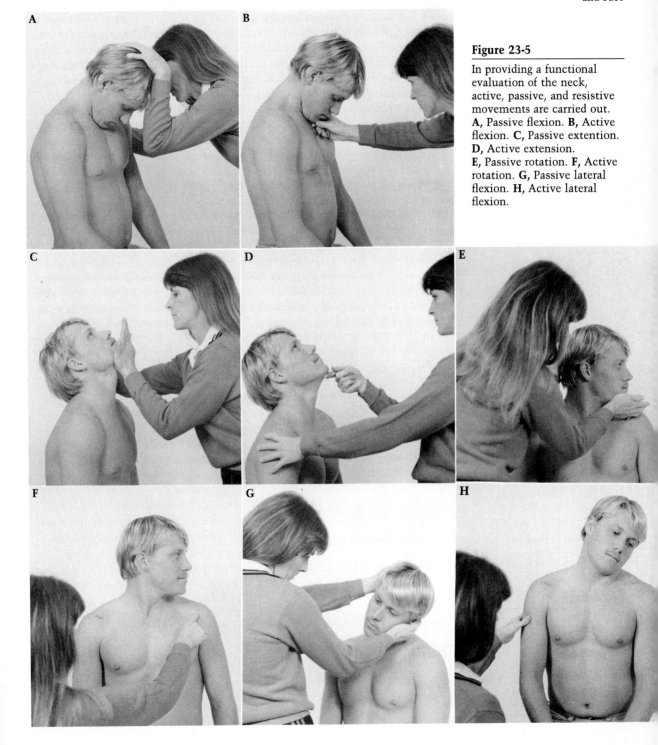

Figure 23-5

In providing a functional
evaluation of the neck,
active, passive, and resistive
movements are carried out.
A, Passive flexion. **B,** Active
flexion. **C,** Passive extention.
D, Active extension.
E, Passive rotation. **F,** Active
rotation. **G,** Passive lateral
flexion. **H,** Active lateral
flexion.

1. Sternocleidomastoid
2. Upper trapezius
3. Throat areas (cartilages, etc.)

Functional evaluation Both active and passive movements are observed for range of motion including flexion, extension, rotation, and lateral flexion. (Fig. 23-5). Strength of the major neck muscles is next determined followed by the shoulders and arms (Table 23-1).

Distraction and compression tests Two tests for nerve root inflammation in the neck region are the distraction test and the compression test. By placing traction on the cervical spine pain can be relieved in cases of a narrowing of nerve foramens (Fig. 23-6). Conversely, a compression to the top of the head downward may narrow the neural foramina and may produce localized or referred pain.[14]

Sensation Nerve root irritation within the neck can alter skin sensations, depending on the peripheral nerves involved. As a result the athlete may complain of a "pins and needles" sensation corresponding to selected dermatome regions (Fig. 23-7).

Mechanisms of Neck Injuries

The neck can be seriously injured by the following traumatic events (see Fig. 23-8):

1. A compressional force to the top of the head
2. A flexion force
3. A hyperextension force
4. A flexion rotation force
5. A hyperextension rotation force
6. A lateral flexion force

The neck is also prone to subtle injuries stemming from stress, tension, and postural malalignments.

Sports and Neck Injuries A number of sports can place the cervical spine at risk. Among those activities in the highest risk category are diving, tackle football, and wrestling. Diving into shallow water causes many catastrophic neck injuries. The diver usually dives into water that is less than 5 feet deep, failing to keep the arms extended in front of the face; the head strikes the bottom, producing a cervical fracture at the C5 level.

Figure 23-6

A, Distraction and
B, compression tests for
determining nerve root
irritation.

A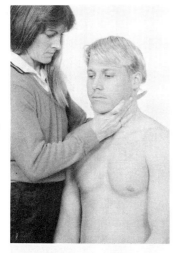

B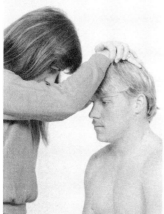

Figure 23-7

Alternations of skin sensation
reflected in dermatomes
resulting from nerve root
irritation.

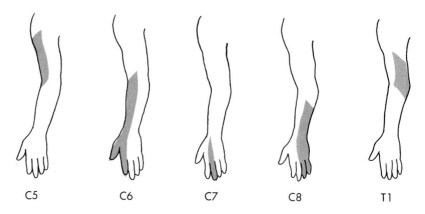

C5 C6 C7 C8 T1

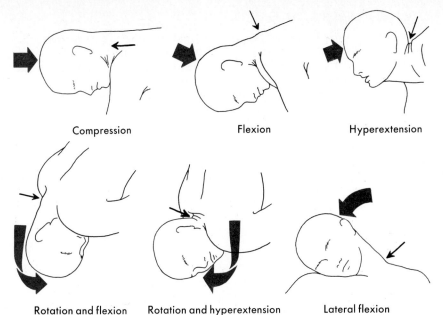

Compression   Flexion   Hyperextension

Rotation and flexion   Rotation and hyperextension   Lateral flexion

Figure 23-8

Mechanisms of neck injuries.

Football helmets do not protect players against neck injury. In the illegal "spearing" situation, the athlete uses the helmet as a weapon by striking the opponent with its top. If the athlete's neck is flexed at the time of contact, energy of the forward-moving body mass cannot be fully absorbed, and fracture or dislocation or both can occur. Many of the same forces can be applied in wrestling. In the instance of such trauma, paraplegia, quadriplegia, or death can result.

Prevention of Neck Injuries

Prevention of neck injuries depends on the flexibility of the neck, its muscle strength, the state of readiness of the athlete, a knowledge of proper technique, and the use of proper protective equipment.[15] A normal range of neck movement is necessary. Therefore, neck flexibility exercises coupled with neck-strengthening exercises should be performed by the athlete daily.

During participation the athlete should constantly be in a "state of readiness" and, when making contact with an opponent, should "bull" the neck. This is accomplished by elevating both shoulders and isometrically contracting the muscles surrounding the neck.

Strength   Athletes with long, weak necks are especially at risk. Tackle football players and wrestlers must have highly stable necks. Specific strengthening exercises are essential for the development of this stability; a variety of different exercises can be employed that incorporate isotonic, isometric or isokinetic contractions. One of the best methods is manual resistance by the athlete or by a partner who selectively uses isometric and isokinetic resistance exercises.

Manual resistance should *not* be performed just before an individual engages in a collision-type sport, such as football or ice hockey, to avoid the danger of participating in these activities with fatigued neck muscles.

Long-necked football players or wrestlers are at risk and need to establish neck stability through strengthening exercises.

Figure 23-9

Manual resistance can
provide an excellent means
for helping to prevent neck
injuries. **A,** Extension. **B,**
Flexion. **C,** Lateral flexion.
D, Rotation.

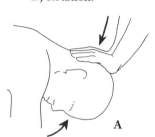

Manual Neck Resistance

1. Extension, flexion, lateral flexion, and rotation are performed.
2. Each exercise is repeated 4 to 6 times in sets of 3.
3. The resisting partner accommodates to the varied strength of the mover, through a full range of motion.
4. Weaker spots in the range of motion can be strengthened with isometric resistance that is held for 6 seconds (Fig. 23-9).

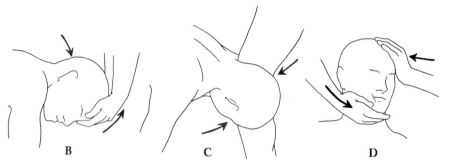

Flexibility In addition to strong muscles, the athlete's neck should have a full range of motion. Ideally the athlete should be able to place the chin on the chest and to extend the head back until the face is parallel with the ceiling. There should be at least 40 to 45 degrees of lateral flexion and enough rotation to allow the chin to reach a level even with the tip of the shoulder. Flexibility is increased by stretching exercises and strength exercises that are in full range of motion. Where flexibility is restricted, manual static stretching can be beneficial.

Protective neck devices The protective neck roll and restrictive neck strap are used to reduce the severity of football neck injuries. The neck roll or collar can be custom-made with stockinette placed over sponge rubber, a towel, or other resilient material, or can be of the commercial inflatable type. It should encircle the entire neck (Fig. 23-10).

Restrictive neck straps are being used by some football teams on a trial basis. A 1½-inch (3.75 cm) wide semielastic strap is fixed to the back of the helmet and shoulder pad to restrict excessive flexion.

Figure 23-10

A collar for neck protection
in football.

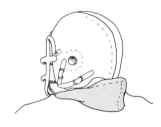

Neck Injuries

Acute torticollis (wryneck) Acute torticollis is a very common condition, more frequently called wryneck or "stiff neck." The athlete usually complains of pain on one side of the neck on awakening. This problem typically follows exposure to a cold draft of air or holding the head in an unusual position over a period of time.

On inspection, there is palpable point tenderness and muscle spasm. Head movement is restricted to the side opposite the irritation. X-ray examination will rule out a more serious injury. Management usually involves the wearing of a cervical collar for several days to relieve muscle stress and daily therapy with superficial heat (Fig. 23-11).

Acute strains of the neck and upper back In a strain of the neck or upper back the athlete has usually turned the head suddenly or has forced flexion or extension. Muscles involved are typically the upper trapezius or sternocleidomastoid. Localized pain, point tenderness, and restricted motion are present. Care usually includes use of ICE-R immediately after the strain occurs and the wearing of a soft cervical collar. Follow-up management may include cryotherapy or superficial heat and analgesic medications as prescribed by the physician.

Cervical sprain (whiplash) A cervical sprain can occur from the same mechanism as the strain but usually results from a more violent motion. More commonly the head snaps suddenly such as when the athlete is tackled or blocked while unprepared (Fig. 23-12).

The sprain displays all the signs of the strained neck but to a much greater degree. Besides injury to the musculature, the sprained neck also produces tears in the major supporting tissue of the nuchal ligament and the interspinous and the supraspinous ligaments. Along with a sprain of the neck, an intervertebral disk may be ruptured.

Symptoms and signs Pain in not experienced initially but appears the day after the trauma. Pain stems from tissue tear and a protective muscle spasm that restricts motion.

Management As soon as possible the athlere should have an x-ray examination to rule out the possibility of fracture, dislocation, or disk injury. Neurological examination is performed by the physician to ascertain spinal cord or nerve root injury. A soft cervical collar is applied to reduce muscle spasm. ICE-R is employed for 48 to 72 hours while the injury is in the acute stage of healing. In severe injury the physician may prescribe 2 to 3 days of bed rest, along with analgesics and anti-inflammation agents. Therapy might include cryotherapy or heat and massage. Mechanical traction may also be prescribed to relieve pain and muscle spasm.

Contusions to the throat and neck Blows to the neck are not frequent in sports, but occasionally an athlete may receive a kick or blow to the throat. One type of trauma is known as "clotheslining," in which the athlete strikes or is struck in the throat region. Such a force could conceivably injure the carotid artery, causing a clot to form that occludes the blood flow to the brain. This same clot could become dislodged and migrate to the brain.[18] In either case, serious brain damage may result. Immediately after throat trauma the athlete could experience severe pain and spasmodic coughing, speak with a hoarse voice, and complain of difficulty in swallowing.

Fracture of throat cartilages is rare, but it is possible and may be indicated by an inability to breathe and expectoration of frothy blood. Cyanosis may be present. Throat contusions are extremely uncomfortable and are often frightening to the athlete.

If the more severe signs appear, a physician should be called. In most situations cold may be applied intermittently to control superficial hemorrhage and swelling, and, after a 24-hour rest period, moist hot packs may be applied. For the most severe neck contusions, stabilization with a well-padded collar is beneficial.

Cervical fractures The cervical vertebrae can be fractured in a number of ways. A compression fracture is created by a sudden forced flexion

Figure 23-11

Wearing a soft cervical collar helps reduce pain and spasm in an injured neck.

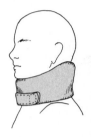

Figure 23-12

Whiplash.

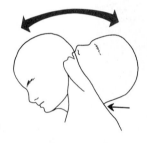

A throat contusion could ultimately lead to brain damage.

MANAGEMENT PLAN FOR WHIPLASH SPRAIN OF THE NECK

Injury Situation

A male ice hockey player, while at practice, was checked hard against the boards. Not being properly set for the force, his head was snapped vigorously backward into extension and forward into flexion. In this process the athlete experienced a sudden sharp pain and a tearing sensation at the base of the posterior neck region.

Symptoms and Signs

Initially the athlete complained to the trainer that immediately after the injury there was a dull ache, stiffness, and weakness in the neck region. He also complained of headache, dizziness, and nausea about 1 hour after the injury.

Palpation revealed severe muscle spasm and point tenderness of the erector spinae muscles and the lateral aspect of the neck and upper shoulder. Gentle passive movement produced some pain. A soft neck collar was applied for immobilization. X-ray examination ruled out fracture, dislocation, or spinal cord injury. On further evaluation there was pain on both gentle active and resistive movement. The condition was considered to be a second degree neck sprain with muscle involvement produced by a whiplash mechanism.

Management Plan

The nature of a neck sprain dictates that management should follow a conservative course. A soft cervical collar was to be worn 24 hours a day for the first 2 weeks or until the athlete was symptom free. This could be followed by wearing the brace just during the waking hours for 1 or 2 additional weeks.

1	Management Phase	GOALS: To control initial hemorrhage, swelling, spasm and pain Estimated length of time (ELT): 2-3 days
	Therapy	IMMEDIATE CARE: Apply ice pack (20 min) intermittently 6-8 times daily In some cases, transcutaneous electrical nerve stimulation (TENS) has been used successfully to reduce spasm and pain in the early stages of injury
	Exercise Rehabilitation	Wear soft cervical collar and avoid movement of the neck for 2 weeks Athlete is taught to hold head in good alignment in relation to shoulder and spine; this should be practiced every waking hour

2	Management Phase	GOALS: To restore 50% active neck motion within pain free limits ELT: 7 days
	Therapy	FOLLOW-UP CARE: Ice pack (5-15 min) or ice massage (7 min) 3-4 times; precedes active motion
	Exercise Rehabilitation	Active stretching 2-3 times daily, including neck flexion with depressed shoulders lateral neck flexion and right and left head rotation; each position held 5-10 sec and repeated 5 times or within pain free limits
3	Management Phase	GOALS: To restore 90% neck range of motion and 50% strength ELT: 4-7 days
	Therapy	Ice pack (5-15 min) or ice massage (7 min) preceding exercise 2 to 3 times daily
	Exercise Rehabilitation	Gentle passive static stretching to the within pain free limits (2 or 3 times each direction) once daily; each stretch held for 20-30 seconds Manual isotonic resistive exercise to the neck performed once daily by the athlete or trainer (5 repetitions)
4	Management Phase	GOALS: To restore full range of motion and full strength ELT: 4-7 days
	Therapy	Ice pack (5-15 min) or ice massage (7 min) once daily preceding exercise
	Exercise Rehabilitation	Continue manual resistive exercise once daily; add resistance devices such as weighted helmet and/or Nautilus neck strengthener (3 sets of 10 repetitions) using DAPRE concept, 3 times a week
5	Management Phase	GOALS: To return to ice hockey competition and full neck muscle bulk
	Exercise Rehabilitation	Work on maximum neck resistance 3-4 times daily Begin practice once daily with a neck roll protective brace during first few weeks of return

Criteria for Full Recovery

The neck of the athlete:
1. Is completely symptom free
2. Has full range of motion
3. Has full strength and bulk

of the neck, such as striking the head when diving into shallow water. If the head is also rotated when making contact, a dislocation may occur along with the fracture. Fractures can also occur in a sudden forced hyperextension of the neck (Fig. 23-13).

Symptoms and signs The athlete may have one or more of the following signs of cervical fracture:

1. Cervical pain and pain in chest and extremities
2. Numbness in trunk and/or limbs
3. Weakness or paralysis in limbs and/or trunk
4. A loss of bladder and/or bowel control
5. Neck point tenderness and restricted movement
6. Cervical muscle spasm

Management

NOTE: An unconscious athlete should be treated as if a serious neck injury is present until this is ruled out by the physician. Extreme caution must be used in moving the athlete. The athlete trainer must always be thinking of the possibility of the athlete's sustaining a catastrophic spinal injury from improper handling and transportation (see Chapter 12 for Emergency care of spinal injuries).

Cervical dislocations Cervical dislocations are not common but occur much more frequently in sports than do fractures. They usually result from violent flexion and rotation of the head. Most injuries of this type happen in pool diving accidents. The mechanism is analogous to the situation that occurs in football when blocks and tackles are poorly executed. The cervical vertebrae are more easily dislocated than are the vertebrae in other spinal regions, principally because of their nearness to the horizontally facing articular facets. The superior articular facet moves be-

Figure 23-13

Fracture of the third cervical vertebra from playing football.

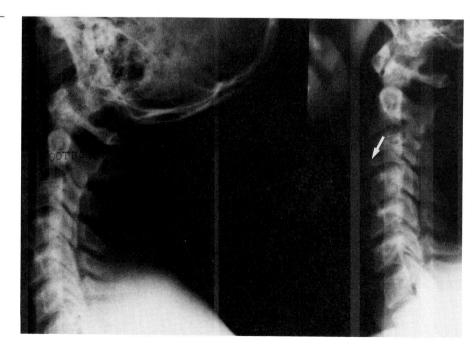

yond its normal range of motion and either completely passes the inferior facet (luxation) or catches on its edge (subluxation). The latter is far more common and, as in the case of the complete luxation, most often affects the fourth, fifth, or sixth vertebra.

For the most part, a cervical dislocation produces many of the same signs as a fracture. Both can result in considerable pain, numbness, and muscle weakness or paralysis. The most easily discernible difference is the position of the neck in a dislocation: a unilateral dislocation causes the neck to be tilted toward the dislocated side with extreme muscle tightness on the elongated side and a relaxed muscle state on the tilted side.

Cervical cord and peripheral nerve injuries Neck and back injuries should always be treated with caution, since they may cause paralysis. Because the spinal cord is well protected by a connective tissue sheath, fat, and fluid cushioning, vertebral dislocations and fractures seldom result in paralysis.

The spinal cord and nerve roots may be injured in five basic ways: *laceration by bony fragments, hemorrhage* (hematomyelia), *contusion, shock* and *stretching*. These may be combined into a single trauma or may act as separate conditions.

Laceration Laceration of the cord is usually produced by the combined dislocation and fracture of a cervical vertebra. The jagged edges of the fragmented vertebral body cut and tear nerve roots or the spinal cord and cause varying degrees of paralysis below the point of injury.

Hemorrhage Hemorrhage develops from all vertebral fractures and from most dislocations, as well as from sprains and strains. It seldom causes harmful effects in the musculature, extradurally or even within the arachnoid space, where it dissipates faster than it can accumulate. However, hemorrhage within the cord itself causes irreparable damage.

Contusion Contusion in the cord or nerve roots can arise from any force applied to the neck violently but without causing a cervical dislocation or fracture. Such an injury may result from a sudden displacement of a vertebra that compresses the cord and then returns to its normal position. This compression causes an edematous swelling within the cord, resulting in various degrees of temporary and/or permanent damage.

Spinal cord shock Occasionally a situation arises in which an athlete, after receiving a severe twist or snap of the neck, presents all the signs of a spinal cord injury. The athlete is unable to move certain parts of the body and complains of a numbness and a tingling sensation in his or her arms. After a short while all these signs leave; the athlete is then able to move his limbs quite freely and has no other symptoms other than a sore neck. This condition is considered a spinal cord shock and is caused by a mild compression of the spinal cord. In such cases athletes should be cared for in the same manner employed in any severe neck injury.

Cervical nerve stretch syndrome ("burner") Stretching (cervical nerve stretch syndrome) or cervical nerve pinch is a condition that has received more recognition in recent years. Other terms for this condition are cervical radiculitis, "hot shots," "pinched nerve," or "burner." The mechanism of injury is one in which an athlete receives a violent lateral

A unilateral cervical dislocation can cause the neck to be tilted toward the dislocated side, with tight muscles on the elongated side and relaxed muscles on the tilted side.

Figure 23-14

Active neck stretching is important in increasing neck mobility following injury.
A, Forward flexion.
B, Extension. **C,** Lateral flexion. **D,** Rotation.

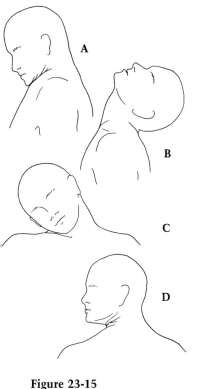

Figure 23-15

Stretching the lateral neck flexors by the Billig method.

wrench of the neck from a head or shoulder block. The player complains of a burning sensation and pain extending from the neck down the arm to the base of the thumb with some numbness and loss of function of the arm and hand which lasts 10 to 20 seconds. It is speculated than an over-riding of the articular facet has caused the electric-shock—like sensation. However, it also may be an indication of a slipped cervical disk or a congenital vertebral defect. Repeated nerve stretch may result in neuritis, muscular atrophy, and permanent damage. This condition requires immediate medical evaluation. After cervical nerve stretch, medical clearance is required before the athlete can return to sports activity. In some cases functional damage is such that the athlete must not participate in certain sports. Conditions for returning to the sport include above-average neck strength, wearing of protective neckwear, and using the head and neck in a sports activity. A similar condition can be produced by a nerve compression.

Neck Rehabilitation

The neck should be pain free before exercise rehabilitation begins. The first consideration should be restoration of the neck's normal range of motion. If the athlete had a prior restricted range of motion, increasing it to a more normal range is desirable. A second goal is to strengthen the neck as much as possible.

Increasing Neck Mobility

All mobility exercises should be performed pain free. Stretching exercises include passive and active movement.

Passive and active stretching The athlete sits in a straight-backed chair while the athletic trainer applies a gentle passive stretch. Extension, flexion, lateral flexion, and rotation in each direction is sustained for a count of 6 and repeated 3 times. Passive stretching should be conducted daily.

The athlete is also instructed to actively stretch the neck 2 or 3 times daily. Each exercise is performed for 5 to 10 repetitions with each end point held for a count of 6. All exercises are performed without force. Fig. 23-14, *A-D,* shows forward flexion, extension, lateral flexion, and rotation.

Stretching can progress gradually to a more vigorous procedure, such as the Billig procedure. In this exercise the athlete sits on a chair with one hand firmly grasping the seat of the chair and the other hand, over the top of the head, placed on the ear on the side of the support hand. Keeping that hand in place, the athlete gently pulls the opposite side of the neck. Stretch should be held for 6 seconds (Fig. 23-15). A rotary stretch in each direction can also be applied in the same manner by the athlete.

Manual neck-strengthening exercises When the athlete has gained near-normal range of motion, a strength program should be instituted. All exercises should be conducted pain free. In the beginning each exercise is performed with the head in an upright position facing straight forward. Exercises are performed isometrically with each resistance held for a

count of 6, starting with 5 repetitions and progressing to 10 repetitions
(Fig. 23-16).

1. Flexion — Press forehead against palm of hand.
2. Extension — lace fingers behind head and press head back against
   hands.
3. Lateral flexion — place palm on side of head and press head into
   the palm.
4. Rotation — put one palm on side of forehead and the other at the
   back of the head. Push with each hand, attempting to rotate head.
   Change hands and reverse direction.

Strengthening progresses to isotonic exercises through a full range of motion using manual resistance, special equipment such as a towel, or
weighted devices (Fig. 23-17). Each exercise is performed for 10 repetitions
and 2 to 3 sets.

Figure 23-16

Manual neck strengthening.

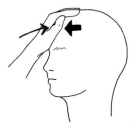
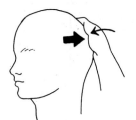
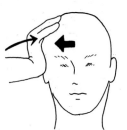

| Flexion | Extension | Lateral flexion | Rotation |

A

Figure 23-17

Neck strengthening through
the use of resistive devices.
A, Towel. **B**, Weight.
C, Nautilus.

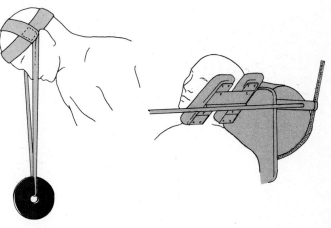

B

C

THE HEAD
Anatomy

The *brain* or encephalon is the part of the central nervous system that is contained within the bony cavity of the cranium and is divided into four sections: the cerebrum, the cerebellum, the pons, and the medulla oblongata.

Investing the spinal cord and the brain are the *meninges*, which are three membranes that give protection to the brain and spinal cord. Outermost is the dura mater, consisting of a dense, fibrous, and inelastic sheath that encloses the brain and cord. In some places it is attached directly to the vertebral canal, but for the most part a layer of fat that contains the vital arteries and veins separates this membrane from the bony wall and forms the epidural space. The arachnoid, an extremely delicate sheath, lines the dura mater and is attached directly to the spinal cord by many silklike tissue strands. The space between the arachnoid and the pia mater, the membrane that helps contain the spinal fluid, is called the subarachnoid space. The subarachnoid cavity projects upward and, running the full length of the spinal cord, connects with the ventricles of the brain. The pia mater is a thin, delicate, and highly vascularized membrane that adheres closely to the spinal cord and to the brain—the large extension of the cord that is housed within the skull (Fig. 23-18).

Cerebrospinal fluid is contained between the arachnid and the pia mater membrane and completely surrounds and suspends the brain. Its main function is to act as a cushion, helping to diminish the transmission of shocking forces.

Evaluation of Cerebral Injuries

Cases of serious head injury almost always represent a life-threatening situation that requires that the athlete be admitted to a hospital within a crucial 30-minute period.

On-site Evaluation

One must be adept at recognizing and interpreting the signs that an unconscious athlete presents. Priority first aid for any head injury must always deal with any life-threatening condition such as impaired airway or hem-

Figure 23-18

The meninges covering the brain.

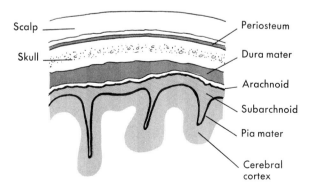

orrhage.[15,19] When an athlete is unconscious, a neck injury is also assumed. Without moving the athlete, evaluation includes:

1. Looking for the possibility of airway obstruction. If breathing is obstructed:
   a. Remove face mask by cutting it away from the helmet, but leave helmet in place
   b. Stabilize head and neck
   c. Bring jaw forward to clear air passage (do not hyperextend neck)
   d. Take pulse: if absent, CPR is given; if present, oxygen may be given
   e. **NOTE:** *Ammonia fumes should not be used for reviving an injured person.* The athlete who is dazed or unconscious, after smelling the pungent ammonia fumes may jerk the head and exacerbate a spinal fracture.
2. A quick observation of the following physical signs of concussion and/or skull fracture:
   a. Face color may be red or pale
   b. Skin may be cool or moist
   c. Pulse, if present, may be strong and slow or rapid and weak
   d. Breathing, if present, may be deep or shallow
   e. Pupils may be dilated and/or unequal
   f. Head may show swelling or deformity over area of injury
3. The athlete is removed carefully from the playing site on a spine board as per Chapter 12 instructions

> If neck injuries are suspected in the unconscious athlete, the jaw is brought forward, but the neck is not hyperextended to clear the airway.

Further Evaluation of the Athlete with a Cerebral Injury

Athletes with grade III or IV concussions having district clinical signs should automatically be sent to the hospital for medical care (for further discussion, see p. 668). In grade I and II concussions it is often difficult for the athletic trainer to determine exactly how serious the problem is. Also, grade I and II conditions can slowly—or even quickly—deteriorate to a higher grade. This makes certain evaluative procedures inperative even in so-called very minor cases (Table 23-2).

Questioning the athlete When the athlete regains consciousness, testing for mental orientation and memory should be done. Questions might include:

- What is your name?
- How old are you?
- Where are you?
- What game are you playing?
- What period is it?
- What is the score?
- What is your assignment on the 23 trap play?

Testing eye signs Because of the direct connection between the eye and the brain, pupillary discrepancies provide important information. The athlete should be observed and tested for:

1. Dilated and/or irregular pupils. A check on pupil sizes may be particularly difficult at night and under artificial lights. To ensure accuracy, the athlete's pupil size should be compared with that of an official or

> Checking eye signs can yield crucial information about possible brain injury.

another player present. It should be remembered, however, that some individuals normally have pupils that differ in size.

2. Blurred vision determined by a difficulty or inability to read a game program or the score board.

3. Inability for the pupils to rapidly accommodate to light variance. Eye accommodation should be tested by covering one eye with a hand. The covered eye normally will dilate, while the uncovered pupil will remain the same. When the hand is removed, the previously covered pupil normally will accommodate readily to the light. A slow accommodating pupil may be an indicator of cerebral injury.

4. Ability of eyes to track smoothly. The athlete is asked to hold the head in a neutral position, eyes looking straight ahead. The athlete is then asked to follow the top of a pen or pencil, first up as far as possible, then down as far as possible. The eyes are observed for smooth movement and any signs of pain. Next, the tip of the pen or pencil is slowly moved from left to right to determine whether the eyes follow the tip smoothly across the midline of the face or whether they make involuntary movements. A constant involunary back and forth, up and down, or rotary movement of the eyeball is call *nystagmus*, indicating possible cerebral involvement.

Testing balance   If the athlete can stand, the degree of unsteadiness must be noted. A cerebral concussion of grade II or more can produce balance difficulties (positive Romberg's sign). To test Romberg's sign the athlete is told to stand tall with the feet together, arms at sides, eyes closed. A positive sign is one in which the athlete begins to sway, cannot keep eyes closed, or obviously loses balance. Having the athlete attempt to stand on one foot is also a good indicator of balance.

Finger-to-nose test   The athlete stands tall with eyes closed and arms out to the side. The athlete is then asked to touch the index finger of one hand to the nose and then to touch the index finger of the other

Table 23-2

Cerebral concussion

	First Degree Grade I	Grade II	Second Degree Grade III	Third Degree Grade IV
Disorientation	+	+	+ +	+ + +
Dizziness		+	+ +	+ + +
Amnesia		+	+ +	+ + +
Headache			+ / + +	+ + +
Loss of consciousness			+ / + +	+ + +
Problems in concentrating		+	+ +	+ + +
Tinnitus		+	+ +	+ + +
Balance problems		+	+ +	+ + +
Automatism			+ / + +	+ + +
Pupillary discrepancies			+ / + +	+ + +

+ Mild
+ + Moderate
+ + + Severe

hand to the nose. Inability to perform this task with one or both fingers is an indication of physical disorientation and precludes reentry to the game.

Babinski test A major test indicating injury to the brain from trauma is the Babinski. A pointed object is stroked across the plantar aspect of the sole of the foot, from the calcaneus along the lateral aspect of the sole of the forefoot. A positive Babinski's sign is extension of the great toe and, on occasion, a spreading of the other toes. A normal reaction is one in which the toes curl downward.

Monitoring the Grade I and II Head Concussion

An athlete with any degree of concussion should be sent immediately to the sports physician for treatment and observation. Brain injury may not be apparent until hours after the trauma occurs. The athlete may have to be observed closely throughout the night and be awakened about every 1 to 2 hours to check the level of consciousness and orientation.

Cerebral Injuries

Despite its considerable protection, the brain is subject to traumatic injury, and a great many of the head injuries incurred in sports have serious consequences. For this reason it is necessary to give special consideration to this part of the body. A constant supply of oxygen and blood to the brain is vital and critical to its survival. Although the incidence of serious head injuries from football has decreased in past years when compared to catastrophic neck injuries, their occurrence is of major concern. Every coach and athletic trainer must be able to recognize the signs of serious head injury and to act appropriately.

Most traumas of the head result from direct or indirect blows and may be classified as concussion injuries. Literally, "concussion" means an agitation or a *shaking from being hit,* and "cerebral concussion" refers to the *agitation of the brain* by either a direct or an indirect blow. Surgeons define concussion as *a clinical syndrome characterized by immediate and transient impairment of neural function, such as alteration of consciousness, disturbance of vision, equilibrium, and so on, caused by mechanical forces.*[16] The indirect concussion most often comes either from a violent fall, in which sitting down transmits a jarring effect through the vertebral column to the brain, or from a blow to the chin. In most cases of cerebral concussion there is a short period of unconsciousness, having mild to severe results.

Most authorities agree that unconsciousness comes from a brain anoxia that is caused by constriction of the blood vessels. Depending on the force of the blow and the tolerance of the athlete to withstand such a blow, varying degrees of cerebral hemorrhage, edema, and tissue laceration may occur that in turn will cause tissue changes. Because of the fluid suspension of the brain, a blow to the head can effect an injury to the brain either at the point of contact or on the opposite side. After the head is struck, the brain continues to move in the fluid and may be contused against the opposite side. This causes a *contrecoup type of injury.* An athlete who is knocked unconscious by a blow to the head may be presumed to have received some degree of concussion. Most often the blow simply stuns the athlete, who recovers quite rapidly.

In determining the extent of head injury one must be aware of basic gross signs by which concussions may be evaluated. Concussions are described as being mild, moderate, or severe and graded from I through IV.

Grade I Concussion

Grade I concussions are minimal in intensity and represent the most common type in sports. In general the athlete becomes dazed and disoriented but does not become amnesic or have other signs associated with a more serious condition.

Grade II Concussion

A grade II cerebral concussion is also considered to be of mild intensity. There is no loss of consciousness but there may be a slight temporary memory loss at the moment of impact or 5 to 10 minutes later, some minor mental confusion, unsteadiness, a ringing in the ears (tinnitus), and perhaps minor dizziness. A dull headache may also follow.[18] This is what is commonly called being "dinged" or having one's "bells rung." These athletes may also develop a postconcussion syndrome, characterized by difficulty in concentrating, recurring headaches, and irritability.

Grade III Concussion

Considered moderate in intensity, the grade III concussion can pose a serious medical problem. There is a loss of consciousness (up to 4 minutes); moderate tinnitus; retrograde amnesia, which constitutes a condition in which the athlete is unable to remember recent events; mental confusion; balance disturbance; and headache. Automatism—automatic behavior before consciousness or full awareness has been achieved—may occur.[5]

Grade IV Concussion

The grade IV cerebral concussion is obviously the most severe of the so-called knocked-out states. It implies many serious consequences: a prolonged period of unconsciousness (over 5 minutes); mental confusion for an extended period with retrograde amnesia (lasting over 5 minutes); and other symptoms such as tinnitus, dizziness, balance difficulties, automatic behavior, and convulsions.

Intracranial Hemorrhage

Figure 23-19

Intracranial hemorrhage.

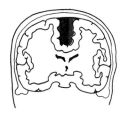

A blow to the head can cause intracranial bleeding. It may arise from rupture of a blood vessel aneurysm or tearing of a sinus separating the two brain hemispheres (Fig. 23-19). Venous bleeding may be slow and insidious, whereas arterial hemorrhage may be evident in a hew hours. In the beginning the athlete may be quite lucid, with few or none of the symptoms of serious head injury, and then gradually display severe head pains, dizziness, nausea, inequality or pupil size, or sleepiness.[1] Later stages of cerebral hemorrhage are characterized by deteriorating consciousness, neck rigidity, depression of pulse and respiration, and convulsions. Of course, this becomes a life-and-death situation necessitating urgent neurosurgical care.

Skull fracture Any time an athlete sustains a severe blow to the unprotected head, a skull fracture should be suspected. Skull fractures can be difficult to ascertain. Swelling of the scalp may mask a skull depression or deformity.[21] Until the more obvious signs caused by intracranial bleeding are present, the skull fracture, even on x-ray examination, can be missed.

Epidural, subdural, and intracerebral hemorrhage There are three major types of intracranial hemorrhage: epidural, subdural, and intracerebral.

Epidural bleeding A blow to the head can cause a tear in one of the arteries in the dural membrane that covers the brain (Fig. 23-20). It can result from a skull fracture or sudden shift of the brain. Because of arterial blood pressure, blood accumulation and the creation of a hematoma is extremely fast.[18] Often in only 10 to 20 minutes the athlete goes from appearing to be all right to having major signs of serious head injury. The pressure of the hematoma must be surgically relieved as soon as possible to avoid the possibility of death or permanent disability.

Subdural bleeding In subdural bleeding, veins are torn that bridge the dura mater to the brain.[17,21] A common mechanism of injury is one of contrecoup, in which the skull decelerates suddenly and the brain keeps moving, tearing blood vessels (Fig. 23-21). Because of lower pressure, veins are the primary type of blood vessel injured. Hemorrhage is slow. Signs of brain injury may not appear for many hours after injury. Thus athletes who have sustained a hard blow to the head must be carefully observed for a 24-hour period for signs of pressure buildup within the skull.

Intracerebral bleeding Intracerebral hemorrhage is bleeding within the brain itself. Most commonly it results from a compressive force to the brain[18] (Fig. 23-22). Deterioration of neurological function occurs rapidly, requiring immediate hospitalization.

Returning to Competition Following Cerebral Injury

There is always the question of whether an athlete who has been "knocked out" several times should continue in the sport. The team physician must be the final authority on whether an athlete continues to participate in a collision sport following head injury. Each athlete must be evaluated individually. One serious concussion may warrant exclusion from the sport; on the other hand, a number of minor episodes may not. In making this decision, the physician must make sure that the athlete is:

1. Normal neurologically
2. Normal in all vasomotor functions
3. Free of headaches
4. Free of seizure and has a normal electroencephalogram
5. Free of lightheadedness on suddenly changing body positions[18]

Secondary Conditions Associated with Cerebral Injury

Besides initial injury to the brain, many secondary conditions can also arise following head trauma. Some of the prevalent ones are cerebral hyperemia (primarily in children), cerebral edema, postinjury epilepsy and seizures, and migraine headaches.

The three major types of intracranial hemorrhage are:
  Epidural
  Subdural
  Intracerebral

Figure 23-20

Epidural bleeding.

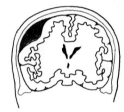

Figure 23-21

Subdural bleeding.

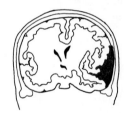

Figure 23-22

Intracerebral bleeding.

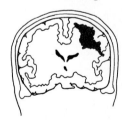

Following a cerebral injury, an athlete must be free of symptoms and signs before returning to competition.

Secondary brain injury
conditions include:
  Cerebral hyperemia
  Cerebral edema
  Cerebral seizure
  Migraine headache

Cerebral hyperemia A condition common to children with head injuries is cerebral hyperemia resulting from cerebral blood vessel dilation and a rise in intracranial blood pressure.[1,3] As a result children develop headache, vomiting, and lethargy. It can occur within a few minutes of injury and subside in 12 hours.[1]

Cerebral edema Cerebral edema is a localized swelling at the injury site. Within a 12-hour period the athlete may begin to develop edema, which causes headache and, on occasion, seizures.[1,5,18] This may last as long as 2 weeks and is not related to the intensity of trauma.

Seizures Seizures can occur immediately after head trauma, indicating the possibility of brain injury. They have a higher incidence when the brain has been actually contused or there is intracranial bleeding. A small number of individuals who have sustained a severe cerebral injury will in time develop epilepsy.[1]

For athletes having a grand mal epileptic seizure, the following measures should be taken:

1. Maintain airway
2. Make sure athlete is safe from injury
3. Avoid sticking fingers into the athlete's mouth in an effort to withdraw the tongue
4. Turn athlete's head to the side so that saliva and blood can drain out of the mouth

The seizure will normally last only a couple of minutes. The athlete with epilepsy is discussed more fully in Chapter 26.

Migraine headaches Migraine is a disorder characterized by recurrent attacks of severe headache with sudden onset, with or without visual or gastrointestinal problems. The athlete who has a history of repeated minor blows to the head such as those that may occur in soccer or who has sustained a major cerebral injury may, over a period of time, develop migraine headaches.[2,11] The exact cause in unknown, but it is believed by many to be a vascular disorder. Flashes of light, blindness in half the field of vision (hemianopia), and paresthesia are thought to be caused by vasoconstriction of intercerebral vessels. Headache is believed to be caused by dilation of scalp arteries. The athlere complains of a severe headache that is diffused throughout the head and often accompanied by nausea and vomiting. There is evidence of a familial predisposition for those athletes who experience migraine headaches following head injury.

THE FACE
Anatomy

The facial skin covers primarily subcutaneous bone with very little protective muscle, fascia, or fat. The supraorbital ridges house the frontal sinuses. In general the facial skeleton is composed of dense bony buttresses combined with thin sheets of bone.[24] The middle third of the face consists of the maxillary bone, which supports the nose and nasal passages.[24] The lower aspect of the face consists of the lower jaw or mandible. Besides supporting teeth, the mandible also supports the larynx, trachea, upper airway, and upper digestive tract [24] (Fig. 23-23).

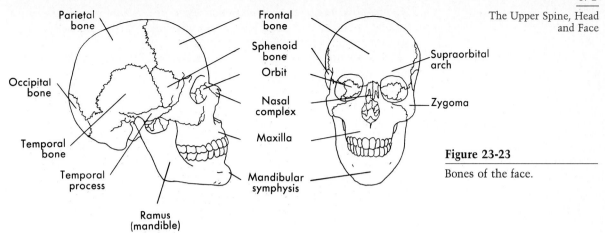

Figure 23-23

Bones of the face.

Figure 23-24

Mandibular fracture.

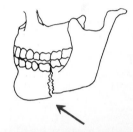

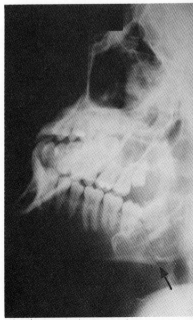

Facial Injuries

Serious injuries to the face have been reduced significantly from the past by requiring proper protection in high-risk sports. The most prevalent cause of facial injury is a direct blow that injures soft and bony tissue. Very common are skin abrasions, lacerations, and contusions; less common are fractures. Lacerations and abrasions are discussed in Chapter 17.

Injuries of the Mandible (Jaw)

Jaw fracture Fractures of the lower jaw (Fig. 23-24) occur most often in collision sports. They are second in incidence of all facial fractures. Because it has relatively little padding and sharp contours, the lower jaw is prone to injury from a direct blow. The most frequently fractured area is near the jaw's frontal angle.

Symptoms and signs The main indications of a fractured mandible are deformity, loss of normal occlusion of the teeth, pain on biting down, bleeding around teeth, and lower lip anesthesia.[12]

Management Management usually includes cold packs to the side of the face, immobilization by a four-tailed bandage, and immediate referral to a physician.

Jaw dislocations A dislocation of the jaw, or *mandibular luxation,* involves the temporomandibular joint, which is formed by the condyle of the mandible and the mandibular fossa of the temporal bone (Fig. 23-25). This area has all the features of a hinge and gliding articulation. Because of its wide range of movement and the inequity of size between the mandibular condyle and the temporal fossa, the jaw is somewhat prone to dislocation. The mechanism of injury in dislocations is usually initiated by a side blow to the open mouth of the athlete, thus forcing the mandibular condyle forward out of the temporal fossa. This injury may occur as either a luxation (complete dislocation) or a subluxation (partial dislocation).

Symptoms and signs The major signs of the dislocated jaw are a locked-open position, with jaw movement being almost impossible, and/or an overriding malocclusion of the teeth.

Management In cases of first-time jaw dislocation the initial treatment includes immediately applying a cold compress to control hemorrhage, splinting the jaw by the use of a four-tailed bandage, and referring

---

REDUCING A RECURRENT DISLOCATION OF THE JAW

The following method is used to reduce a recurrent jaw dislocation.

Materials needed: Sterile gauze pads to protect the thumbs of the operator.

Position of the athlete: The athlete sits on a chair or stool.

Position of the operator: The operator faces the athlete. Both thumbs are padded with sterile gauze.

Procedure

1. The operator grasps the jaw of the athlete and inserts both thumbs, hooking them over the back molars.
2. A gentle pressure is applied downward on the molars and then, depending on the position of the jaw, forward or backward. As the condyles slip back into their fossa, a click may be heard.

Figure 23-25

A dislocation of the jaw (right temporomandibular joint).

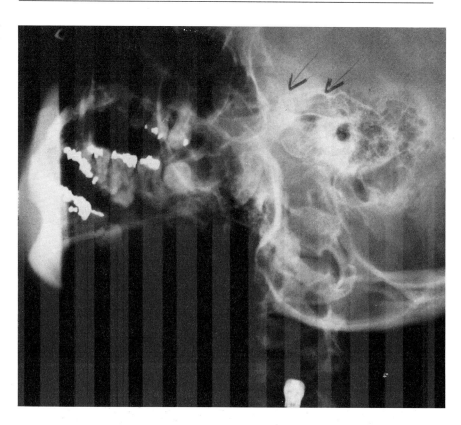

the athlete to a physician for reduction. Without a physician it is not advisable to attempt the reduction of a jaw dislocation unless it is of a chronically recurrent type.

Zygoma (cheekbone) fracture A zygoma fracture represents the third most common facial fracture.[24] Because of its nearness to the eye orbit, visual problems may also occur.

Symptoms and signs An obvious deformity occurs in the cheek region or a bony discrepancy on palpation. There is usually a nosebleed (epistaxis), and the athlete commonly complains of seeing double (diplopia).

Management Care by the athletic trainer usually involves cold application for the control of edema and immediate referral to a physician.

Maxilla fracture A severe blow to the upper jaw such as would be incurred by being struck by a hockey puck or stick can fracture the maxilla. This ranks fourth in incidence of facial fracture.

Symptoms and signs After being struck a severe blow to the upper jaw, the athlete complains of pain on chewing, malocclusion, nosebleed, double vision and numbness in the lip and cheek region.

Management Because bleeding is usually profuse, airway passages must be maintained. A brain injury may also be associated with this condition as with all injuries to the face and must be evaluated and managed accordingly. The athlete must be referred immediately for medical attention.

Dental Injuries

The tooth is a composite of mineral salts of which calcium and phosphorus are most abundant. That portion protruding from the gum, called the crown, is covered by the hardest substance within the body, the enamel. The portion that extends into the alveolar bone of the mouth is called the root and is covered by a thin, bony substance known as cementum. Under-

Epistaxis
Nosebleed

Diplopia
Seeing double

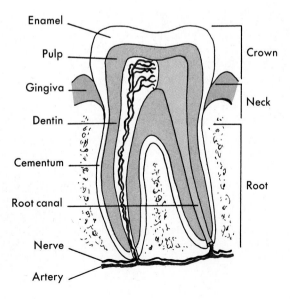

Figure 23-26

Normal tooth anatomy.

Enamel

Pulp

Gingiva

Dentin

Cementum

Root canal

Nerve

Artery

Crown

Neck

Root

neath the enamel and cementum lies the bulk of the tooth, a hard material known as dentin. Within the dentin is a central canal and chamber containing the pulp, a substance composed of nerves, lymphatics, and blood vessels that supply the entire tooth (Fig. 23-26).

With the use of face guards and properly fitting mouth guards most dental injuries can be prevented (see Chapter 7). Any blow to the upper or lower jaw can potentially injure the teeth.[22] Injuries to the tooth below the gum line may repair themselves because of the abundant blood supply. However, fractures of the tooth below the gum line may not heal if there is an injury to the tooth pulp. Even though not obvious, a tooth could sustain a mild blow that disrupts its blood and nerve supply.[4]

The Fractured Tooth

Fracture of the crown of the tooth is an enamel fracture and can usually be repaired by smoothing, capping, or even removal of the entire tooth. In contrast, fractures that involve the dentin exposing the pulp may predispose the tooth to infection and tooth death.[13]

Teeth in which the enamel or dentin is chipped fail to rejuvenate because they lack a direct blood supply. They can be capped for the sake of appearance. A tooth that is fractured or loosened may be extremely painful because of the damaged or exposed nerve. In such cases a small amount of calcium hydroxide (Dycol) applied to the exposed nerve area will inhibit the pain until the athlete is seen by a dentist.[6]

A fractured tooth is usually very sensitive to air and requires the athlete to keep the mouth closed. If there is no bleeding of the gums the athlete can continue to play and see the dentist after the game.[4]

Partially or Completely Dislocated Tooth

A tooth that has been completely dislocated intact should be rinsed off with water and replaced in the socket.

A tooth that has been knocked crooked should be manually realigned to a normal position as soon as possible. One that has been totally knocked out should be cleaned off with water and replaced in the tooth socket, if possible. If repositioning the dislocated tooth is difficult, the athlete should keep it under the tongue until the dentist can replace it.[4] If this is inconvenient, a dislodged tooth can also be kept in a glass of water. If a completely dislodged tooth is out of the mouth for more than 30 minutes the chances of saving it are very tenuous; therefore, the athlete should immediately be sent to a dentist for splinting.

Nasal Injuries
Nasal Fractures and Chondral Separation

Figure 23-27

Nasal fracture.

A fracture of the nose is one of the most common fractures of the face. It appears frequently as a separation of the frontal processes of the maxilla, a separation of the lateral cartilages, or a combination (Fig. 23-27).

Symptoms and signs   The force of the blow to the nose may either come from the side or be a straight frontal force. A lateral force causes greater deformity than a "straight-on" blow. In nasal fractures hemorrhage is profuse because of laceration of the mucous lining. Swelling is immediate. Deformity is usually present if the nose has received a lateral

NOSE SPLINTING

The following procedure is used for nose splinting.

Materials needed: Two pieces of gauze, each 2 inches (5 cm) long and rolled to the size of a pencil; 3 strips of 1½-inch (3.75 cm) tape, cut about 4 inches (10 cm) long; and clear tape adherent.

Position of the athlete: The athlete lies supine on the training table.

Position of the operator: The operator stands facing the athlete's head.

Procedure

1. The rolled pieces of gauze are placed on either side of the athlete's nose.
2. Gently but firmly, 4-inch (10 cm) lengths of tape are laid over the gauze rolls.

Figure 23-28

Splinting the fractured nose.

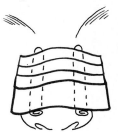

blow. Gentle palpation may reveal abnormal mobility and emit a grating sound (crepitus).

Management One should control the bleeding and then refer the athlete to a physician for x-ray examination and reduction of the fracture. Simple and uncomplicated fractures of the nose will not hinder or be unsafe for the athlete, and he or she will be able to return to competition within a few days, adequate protection can be provided by splinting (Fig. 23-28).

Nosebleed (Epistaxis)

Nosebleeds in sports are usually the result of direct blows that cause varying degrees of contusion to the septum.

Symptoms and signs Hemorrhages arise most often from the highly vascular anterior aspect of the nasal septum. In most situations the nosebleed presents only a minor problem and stops spontaneously after a short period of time. However, there are persistent types that require medical attention and, probably, cauterization.

Management The care of the acute nosebleed is as follows:

1. The athlete lies on the same side as the bleeding septum, his or her head comfortably elevated. (In this position the blood will be confined to one nostril.)

2. A cold compress is placed over the nose.

3. The athlete applies finger pressure to the affected nostril for 5 minutes.

If the above method fails to stop the bleeding within 5 minutes, more extnsive measures should be taken. With an applicator, paint the hemorrhage point with an astringent or a styptic such as tannic acid or epinephrine hydrochloride solution. The application of a gauze or cotton pledget will provide corking action and encourage blood clotting. If a pledget is used, the ends should protrude from the nostrils at least ½ inch to facilitate removal. After bleeding has ceased the athlete may resume activity, but should be reminded not to blow the nose under any circumstances for at least 2 hours after the initial insult.

Foreign Body in the Nose

During participation the athlete may have insects or debris become lodged in one of his or her nostrils; if the object is large enough, the mucous lining of the nose reacts by becoming inflamed and swollen. In most cases the foreign body will become dislodged if the nose is gently blown while the unaffected side in pinched shut. Probing and blowing the nose violently will only cause additional irritation. The removal of difficult objects may be aided by placing a few drops of olive or mineral oil into the nostril to soothe and prevent swelling of the mucosa. If oil is unavailable, the application of a nasal vasoconstrictor will help to shrink the mucous membranes.

Ear Injuries

The ear (Fig. 23-29) is responsible for the sense of hearing and equilibrium. It is composed of three parts: the external ear; the middle ear (tympanic membrane) lying just inside the skull; and the internal ear (labyrinth), which is formed, in part, by the temporal bone of the skull. The middle ear and internal ear are structured to carry auditory impulses to the brain. Aiding the organs of hearing and equalizing pressures between the middle and the internal ear is the eustachian tube, a canal that joins the nose and the middle ear.

Sports injuries to the ear occur most often to the external portion. The external ear is separated into the auricle (pinna) and the external auditory canal (meatus). The auricle, which is shaped like a shell, collects and directs waves of sound into the auditory canal. It is made up of flexible yellow cartilage, muscles, and fat padding, and is covered by a closely adhering, thin layer of skin. Most of the blood vessels and nerves of the auricle turn around its borders, with just a few penetrating the cartilage proper.

Hematoma Auris (Cauliflower Ear)

Contusions, wrenching, or extreme friction of the ear can lead to hematoma auris, commonly known as a "cauliflower ear" (Fig. 23-30).

Etiological factors This condition usually occurs from repeated injury to the ear and is seen most frequently in boxers and wrestlers. How-

Figure 23-29

Ear anatomy. **A,** Normal external ear. **B,** Inner ear.

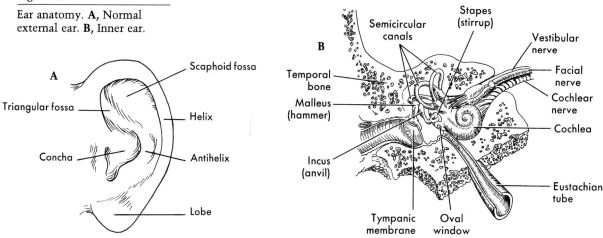

ever, recently it has been held to a minimum because of the protective
measures that have been initiated.

Symptoms and signs Trauma may tear the overlying tissue away
from the cartilaginous plate, resulting in hemorrhage and fluid accumulation. A hematoma usually forms before the limited circulation can absorb the fluid. If the hematoma goes unattended, a sequence of coagulation, organization, and fibrosis results in a keloid that appears elevated,
rounded, white, nodular, and firm, resembling a cauliflower. Quite often
it forms in the region of the helix fossa or concha; once developed, the
keloid can be removed only by surgery. To prevent this disfiguring condition from arising, some friction-proofing agent such as petroleum jelly
should be applied to the ears of athletes susceptible to this condition. They
should also routinely wear ear guards in practice and in competition.

Figure 23-30

The cauliflower ear.

Management If an ear becomes "hot" because of excessive rubbing
or twisting, the immediate application of a cold pack to the affected spot
will alleviate hemorrhage. Once swelling is present in the ear, special
care should be taken to prevent the fluid from solidifying; a cold pack
should be placed immediately over the ear and held tightly by an elastic
bandage for at least 20 minutes. If the swelling is still present at the end
of this time, aspiration by a physician is needed, usually followed by a
rigid compress such as the silicone cast.

Foreign Body in the Ear

The ears offer an opening as do the nose and eyes, in which objects can
become caught. Usually these objects are pieces of debris or flying insects.
They can be dislodged by having the athlete tilt the head to one side. If
removal is difficult, syringing the ear with a solution of lukewarm water
may remove the object. Care should be exercised to avoid striking the eardrum with the direct stream of water.

Pressure Injury (Otitic Barotrauma)

Pressure injury to the ear, or otitic barotrauma, occurs to athletes who are
involved in such pursuits as diving, scuba diving, parachuting, and sports
flying. Usually any change of ear pressure is equalized by swallowing,
yawning, or chewing, which helps the eustachian tube to equalize the external air pressure with that on the eardrum.

With otitic barotrauma the eustachian tube does not allow for air pressure equalization. Lack of pressure equalization may be attributed to nasal
congestion from a cold, allergy, or other infection. Increased pressure can
cause middle ear hemorrhaging and even a bursting of the tympanic membrane (eardrum). It is wise for an athlete with nasal congestion to avoid
pressure changes. Referral should be made to an otolaryngologist.

Eye Injuries

The eye has many anatomical protective devices. It is firmly retained
within an oval socket formed by the bones of the head. A cushion of soft
fatty tissue surrounds it, and a thin skin flap (the eyelid), which functions
by reflex action, covers the eye for protection. Foreign particles are prevented from entering the eye by the lashes and eyebrows, which act as a

filtering system. A soft mucous lining that covers the inner conjunctiva carries and spreads tears, which are secreted by many accessory lacrimal glands. A larger lubricating organ is located above the eye and secrets heavy quantities of fluid through the lacrimal duct to help wash away foreign particles. The eye proper is well protected by the sclera, a tough white outer layer possessing a transparent center portion called the cornea (Fig. 23-31).

Eye Protection

The eye can be injured in a number of different ways. Shattered eyeglass or goggle lenses can lacerate; ski pole tips can penetrate; fingers, raquetballs, and larger projectiles can seriously compress and injure the eye. High injury sports such as ice hockey, football, and lacrosse require full-face and helmet protection while low energy sports such as racquetball and tennis require eye guards that rest on the face.[8,22] Protective devices must provide protection from front and lateral blows.[9,10]

On-site Evaluation

It is essential that any eye injury be evaluated immediately. The first concern is to understand the mechanism of injury and if there is a related condition to the head, face, or neck. Evaluation steps are as follows[20]:

1. Inspect the external occular structures for swelling and discoloration, penetrating objects, deformities, and movement of the lid.
2. Palpate the orbital rim for point tenderness or bony deformity.
3. Inspect the globe of the eye for lacerations, foreign bodies, hyphema, or deformities.
4. Inspect the conjunctiva and sclera for foreign bodies, hemorrhage, or deformities.
5. Determine pupillary response, as for a possible cerebral injury, including pupil dilation and accommodation by covering the eye and then exposing it to light.
6. Determine visual acuity by asking the athlete to report what is seen when looking at some object with the unaffected eye covered. There may be a blurring of vision, diplopia, or floating black specks or flashes of light, indicating serious eye involvement.[20]

Figure 23-31

Eye anatomy.

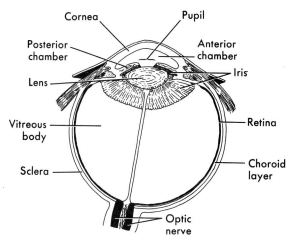

Initial Management of Eye Injuries

Proper care of eye injuries is essential. The athletic trainer must use extreme caution in handling eye injuries. If there appears to be a retinal detachment, perforation of the globe, foreign object embedded in the cornea, blood in the anterior chamber, decreased vision, loss of the visual field, poor pupillary adaptation, double vision, laceration, or impaired lid function, the athlete should be immediately referred to a hospital or an ophthalmologist.[20,22] Ideally, the athlete with a serious eye injury should be transported to the hospital by ambulance in a recumbent position. Both eyes must be covered during transport. At no time should pressure be applied to the eye. In cases of surrounding soft tissue injury, a cold compress can be applied for 30 to 60 minutes to control hemorrhage.[20]

Extreme care must be taken with any eye injury:
Transport the athlete in a recumbent position
Cover both eyes but put no pressure on the eye

Orbital Hematoma (Black Eye)

Although well protected, the eye may be bruised during sports activity. The severity of eye injuries varies from a mild bruise to an extremely serious condition affecting vision to the fracturing of the orbital cavity. Fortunately, most of the eye injuries sustained in sports are mild. A blow to the eye may initially injure the surrounding tissue and produce capillary bleeding into the tissue spaces. If the hemorrhage goes unchecked, the result may be a classic "black eye." The signs of a more serious contusion may be displayed in a subconjunctival hemorrhage or in faulty vision.

Care of an eye contusion requires cold application of at least half an hour, plus a 24-hour rest period when the athlete has distorted vision. Under no circumstances should an athlete blow the nose following an acute eye injury. By doing so hemorrhaging might be increased.

Foreign Body in the Eye

Foreign bodies in the eye are a frequent occurrence in sports and are potentially dangerous. A foreign object produces considerable pain and disability. No attempt should be made to rub the body out or to remove it with the fingers. Have the athlete close the eye until the initial pain has subsided

---

REMOVING A FOREIGN BODY FROM THE EYE

Materials needed: One applicator stick, sterile cotton-tipped applicator, eyecup, and eyewash (solution of boric acid).

Position of the athlete: The athlete lies supine on a table.

Position of the operator: The operator should stand facing the athlete, on the side of the affected eye.

Procedure

1. Gently pull the eyelid down and lay an applicator stick crosswise at its base.
2. Have the athlete look down; then grasp the lashes and turn the lid back over the stick.
3. Holding the lid and the stick in place with one hand, use the sterile cotton swab to lift out the foreign body.

---

and then attempt to determine if the object is in the vicinity of the upper or lower lid. Foreign bodies in the lower lid are relatively easy to remove by depressing the tissue and then wiping it with a sterile cotton applicator. Foreign bodies in the area of the upper lid are usually much more difficult to localize. Two methods may be used; the first technique, being quite simple, is performed as follows: Gently pull the upper eyelid over the lower lid, as the subject looks downward. This causes tears to be produced, which may flush the object down on to the lower lid. If this method is unsuccessful, the second technique should be used. (Fig. 23-32).

After the foreign prticle is removed, the affected eye should be washed with a boric acid eye solution or with a commercial eye-wash. Quite often after debridement there is a residual soreness, which may be alleviated by the application of petroleum jelly or some other mild ointment. If there is extreme difficulty in removing the foreign body or if it has become embedded in the eye itself, the eye should be closed and "patched" with a gauze pad, which is held in place by strips of tape. The athlete is referred to a physician as soon as possible.

Corneal Abrasions

An athlete who gets a foreign object in the eye will usually try to rub it away. In doing so, the cornea can become abraded. The athlete will complain of severe pain and watering of the eye, photophobia, and a spasm of the orbicular muscle of the eyelid. The eye is patched and the athlete is sent to a physician. Corneal abrasion is diagnosed by application of a fluorescein strip to the abraded area, staining it a bright green.[22]

Hyphema

A blunt blow to the anterior aspect of the eye can produce a hyphema, which is a collection of blood within the anterior chamber. The blood settles inferiorly or may fill the entire chamber. Vision is partially or completely blocked. The athlete trainer must be aware that a hyphema is a major eye injury that can lead to serious problems of the lens, choroid, or retina.[22]

Rupture of the Globe

A blow to the eye by an object smaller than the eye orbit produces extreme pressure that can rupture the globe. A golf ball or rachquetball fits this category; however larger objects such as a tennis ball or a fist will often fracture the bony orbit before the eye is overly compressed.[22] Even if it does

Figure 23-32

Removing foreign body from the eye.

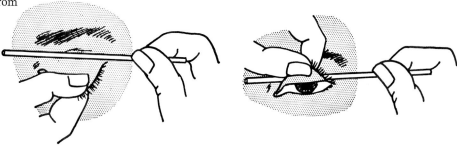

not cause rupture, such a force can cause internal injury that may ultimately lead to blindness.

Blowout Fracture

A blow to the face that strikes the eye and orbital ridge can cause what is commonly called a *blowout fracture* of the orbit. Because of the sudden increase in internal pressure of the eye, the very thin bone located in the inferior aspect of the orbit can fracture. Hemorrhage occurs around the inferior margins of the eye. The athlete commonly complains of double vision and pain on moving the eye. With such symptoms and signs, immediate referral to a physician is necessary.

Retinal Detachment

A blow to the athlete's eye can partially or completely separate the retina from its underlying retinal pigment epithelium. Retinal detachment is more common among athletes who have myopia (nearsightedness). Detachment is painless; however, early signs include seeing specks floating before the eye, flashes of light, or blurred vision. As the detachment progresses, the athlete complains of a "curtain" falling over the field of vision. Any symptoms of detachment must be immediately referred to an ophthalmologist.

REFERENCES

1. Albright, L.: Head and neck injuries. In Smith, N.J. (editor): Sports medicine: health care for young athletes, Evanston, Ill., 1983, American Academy of Pediatrics.
2. Bennett, D.R., et al.: Migraine precipitated by head trauma in athletes, Am. J. Sports Med. **8:**202, 1980
3. Bruce, D.A., et al.: Diffuse cerebral swelling following head injuries in children: the syndrome of "malignant brain edema," J. Neurosurg. **54:**170, 1981.
4. Castaldi, C.R.: Injuries to the teeth. In Vinger, P.F., and Hoerner, E.F. (editors): Sports injuries: the unthwarted epidemic, Boston, 1982, John Wright, PSG, Inc.
5. Cooper, D.L.: This sporting life, Emerg. Med. **11:**287, 1979
6. Cooper, D.L., and Fair, J.: On-the-field emergency dental care, Phys. Sportsmed. **4:**82, 1976
7. Cyriax, J.: Textbook of orthopaedic medicine, vol. 1, Diagnosis of soft tissue lesions, ed. 8, London, 1982, Baillière Tindall.
8. Diamond, G.R. et al.: Ophthalmologic injuries. In Betts, J.M., and Eichelberger, M. (editors): Symposium on pediatric and adolescent sports medicine, Clinics in sports medicine, vol. 1, no. 3, Philadelphia, Nov. 1982, W.B. Saunders Co.
9. Esterbrook, M.: Eye injuries in racket sports: a continuing problem, Phys. Sportsmed. **9:**91, 1981.
10. Esterbrook, M.: Eye protection for squash and racquetball players, Phys. Sportsmed. **9:**79, 1981.
11. Garfinkel, D.: Headache in athletes, Phys. Sportsmed. **11:**67, 1983.
12. Halling, A.H.: The importance of clinical signs and symptoms in the evaluation of facial fractures, Ath. Train. **17:**102, 1982.
13. Hildebrandt, J.R.: Dental and maxillofacial injuries. In Betts, J.M., and Eichelberger, M. (editors): Symposium on pediatric and adolescent sports medicine, Clinics in sports medicine, vol. 1, no. 3, Philadelphia, 1982, W.B. Saunders Co.
14. Hoppenfeld, S.: Physical examination of the spine and extremities, New York, 1976, Appleton-Century-Crofts.
15. Mueller, F.O., and Blyth, C.S.: Catastrophic head and neck injuries, Phys. Sportsmed. **7:**74, 1979.

16. Ommaya, A.K.: Surgical management of head injuries in athletics, Phys. Sportsmed. **4**:29,1976.

17. Rimel, R.W., et al.: Epidural hematoma in lacrosse, Phys. Sportsmed. **11**:140, 1983.

18. Rockett, F.Y.: Injuries involving the head and neck: clinical anatomic aspects. In Vinger, P.F., and Hoerner, E.F. (editors): Sports injuries: the unthwarted epidemic, Boston, 1982, John Wright, PSG, Inc.

19. Ryan, A.J.: On-field head injuries in athletics, Sportsmedicine **4**:63, 1976

20. Sandusky, J.C.: Field evaluation of eye injuries, Ath. Train. **16**:254, 1981.

21. Torg, J.S.: Life-threatening conditions. In Straus, R.H. (editor): Sports medicine and physiology, Philadelphia, 1979, W.B. Saunders Co.

22. Vinger, P.F.: Eye injuries. In Vinger, P.F., and Hoerner, E.F. (editors): Sports injuries: the unthwarted epidemic, Boston, 1982, John Wright, PSG, Inc.

23. Wilson, F.D. and Lindseth, R.E.: Adolescent "swimmer's back," Am. J. Sports Med. **10**:174, 1982.

24. Wilson, K.S.: Injuries to the face, ear-nose-throat and airway. In Vinger, P.F., and Hoerner, E.F. (editors): Sports injuries, Boston, 1982, John Wright, PSG, Inc.

ADDITIONAL SOURCES

Atkinson, T., et al.: The evaluation of facial, head, neck and temporomandibular joint, J. Orthop. Sports Phys. Therapy **3**:193, 1982.

Bachman, D.C. (editor): Head-neck injuries and helmetry, 1981, Riddell Inc.

Bruce, D.A., et al.: Brain and cervical spine injuries occurring during organized sports activities in children and adolescents. In Betts, J.M., and Eichelberger, M. (editors): Symposium on pediatric and adolescent sports medicine, Clinics in sports medicine, vol. 1, no. 3, Philadelphia, Nov. 1982, W.B. Saunders Co.

Cailliet, R.: Neck and arm pain, ed. 2, Philadelphia, 1981, F.A. Davis Co.

Godwin, W.C.: Mouth protectors in junior football players, Phys. Sportsmed. **10**:41, 1982.

Handler, S.D., and Wetmore, R.: Otolaryngologic injuries. In Betts, J.M., and Eichelberger, M. (editors): Symposium on pediatric adolescent sports medicine, Clinics in sportsmedicine, vol. 1., no. 3, Philadelphia, Nov. 1982, W.B. Saunders Co.

Harris, J.B.: Neurological injuries in winter sports, Phys. Sportsmed. **11**: 111, 1983.

Heintz, W.: The status of sports dentistry, Phys. Sportsmed. **10**:19, 1982.

Hodgson, J.R.: Injuries involving the head and neck: experimental and biomechanical aspects. In Vinger, P.F., and Hoerner, E.F. (editors): Sports injuries: the unthwarted epidemic, Boston, 1982, John Wright, PSG, Inc.

Maroon, J.C.: Catastrophic neck injuries from football in western Pennsylvania, Phys. Sportsmed. **9**:83, 1981.

Maroon, J.C.: Pathophysiology and mechanisms of cervical spine fractures, Southwest Athletic Trainers Association Meeting, January 1982, Greenville, N.C., National Athletic Trainers Association. (Cassette.)

Maroon, J.C., and Haycock, C.E.: Prevention and management of head, neck, forearm, wrist and hand injuries, Chicago, Audio Cassettes on Sportsmedicine, Teach'em, Inc. (Cassette.)

Onstad, M.: Ocular, facial and oral trauma, NATA Annual Meeting and Clinical Symposium, June 1983, Greenville, N.C., National Athletic Trainers Association.

Smith, S.D.: Sports dentistry: protection and performance from mouth guards and bites splints, Ath. Train., **16**:100, 1981.

Torg, J.S. (editor): Athletic injuries to the head, neck and face, Philadelphia, 1982, Lea & Febiger.

Warmath B.: Cranial cervical trauma: clinical evaluation by the athletic trainer, NATA Annual Meeting, Clinical Symposium, June 1983, Greenville, N.C., National Athletic Trainers Association. (Cassette.)

Chapter 24

THE SHOULDER COMPLEX

When you finish this chapter, you should be able to

Identify the major structural and functional anatomical features and relate them to sports injuries of the shoulder complex

Recognize and evaluate major sports injuries of the shoulder complex

Carry out proper immediate and follow-up injury management

The shoulder complex, as the name implies, is an extremely complicated region of the body. Sports using the shoulder in repetitive activities, such as throwing, blocking, tackling, or rolling over as in tumbling, may produce a serious injury.

ANATOMY
Bony Structure

The bones that make up the shoulder complex and shoulder joint are the clavicle, scapula, and humerus (Fig. 24-1).

Clavicle

The clavicle is a slender bone approximately 6 inches (15 cm) long and shaped like a crank or the letter S. It supports the anterior portion of the shoulder, keeping it free from the thoracic cage. It extends from the sternum to the tip of the shoulder where it joins the acromion process of the scapula. The shape of the medial two thirds of the clavicle is primarily circular, whereas its lateral third takes on a flattened appearance. Also, the medial two thirds bend convexly forward, and the lateral third is concave. The point at which the clavicle changes shape and contour presents a structural weakness, and the largest number of fractures to the bone occur at this point. Lying superficially with no muscle or fat protection makes the clavicle subject to direct blows.

Scapula

The scapula is a flat, triangularly shaped bone that serves mainly as an articulating surface for the head of the humerus. It is located on the dorsal aspect of the thorax and has two prominent projections, the spine and the coracoid process. The spine divides the posterior aspect unequally. The superior dorsal aspect is a deep depression called the supraspinous fossa, and the area below, a more shallow depression, is called the infraspinous fossa. A hooklike projection called the coracoid process arises anteriorly from the scapula. It curves upward, forward, and outward in front of the glenoid fossa, which is the articulating cavity for the reception of the humeral head. The glenoid cavity is situated laterally on the scapula below the acromion.

Humerus

The head of the humerus is spherical with a shallow, constricted neck; it faces upward, inward, and backward, articulating with the scapula's shallow glenoid fossa. Circumscribing the humeral head is a slight groove called the anatomical neck, which is the attachment for the articular capsule of the glenohumeral joint. The greater and lesser tuberosities are located adjacent and immediately inferior to the head. The lesser tuberosity is positioned anteriorly and medially, with the greater tuberosity placed somewhat higher and laterally. Lying between the two tuberosities is a deep groove called the bicipital groove, which retains the long tendon of the biceps brachii muscle.

Articulations

In all, there are four major articulations associated with the shoulder complex: the sternoclavicular joint, acromioclavicular joint, coracoclavicular joint, and glenohumeral joint (Fig. 24-2).

Sternoclavicular Joint

The clavicle articulates with the manubrium of the sternum to form the sternoclavicular joint, the only direct connection between the upper extremity and the trunk. The sternal articulating surface is larger than the sternum, causing the clavicle to rise much higher than the sternum. A fibrocartilaginous disk is interposed between the two articulating surfaces. It functions as a shock absorber against the medial forces and also helps to prevent any displacement upward. The articular disk is placed so that the clavicle moves on the disk, and the disk, in turn, moves separately on the sternum. The clavicle is permitted to move up and down, forward and backward, in combination, and in rotation.

The sternoclavicular joint is extremely weak because of its bony arrangement, but it is held securely by strong ligaments that tend to pull the sternal end of the clavicle downward and toward the sternum, in effect an-

Figure 24-1

Bones of the shoulder complex.

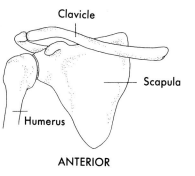

Clavicle

Scapula

Humerus

ANTERIOR

Figure 24-2

Shoulder complex articulations.

   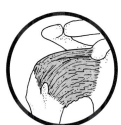

Sternoclavicular   Acromioclavicular   Coracoclavicular   Glenohumeral

choring it. The main ligaments are the anterior sternoclavicular, which prevents an upward displacement of the clavicle; the posterior sternoclavicular, which also prevents an upward displacement of the clavicle; the interclavicular, which prevents lateral displacement of the clavicle; and the costoclavicular, which prevents lateral and upward displacement of the clavicle.

Some muscular support is given to the sternoclavicular joint by the subclavius, sternocleidomastoid, and sternohyoid muscles.

Acromioclavicular Joint

The acromioclavicular joint is a gliding articulation of the lateral end of the clavicle with the acromion process. This is a rather weak junction. A thin, fibrous sleeve surrounds the joint; additional reinforcement is given by the superior and inferior acromioclavicular ligaments and by coracoclavicular ligaments.

Coracoclavicular Joint

The coracoclavicular joint is an amphiarthrodial, syndesmotic joint that permits only slight movement. It serves an important function in suspending the scapula and the clavicle and also in giving additional strength to the acromioclavicular joint. The coracoid process and the clavicle are joined by the coracoclavicular ligament, which is divided into the conoid part and the trapezoid part. The coracoclavicular ligament, because of the rotation of the clavicle on its long axis, develops some slack, which permits movement of the scapula at the acromioclavicular joint to take place.

Glenohumeral Joint (Shoulder Joint)

The glenohumeral joint (shoulder joint) is an enarthrodial, or ball-and-socket, joint in which the round head of the humerus articulates with the shallow glenoid cavity of the scapula. The cavity is deepened slightly by a fibrocartilage rim called the glenoid labrum. Surrounding the articulation is a loose, articular capsule. This capsule is strongly reinforced by the superior, middle, and inferior glenohumeral ligaments and by the tough coracohumeral ligament, which attaches to the coracoid process and to the greater tuberosity of the humerus. The long tendon of the biceps brachii passes across the head of the humerus and then through the bicipital groove. In the anatomical position the long head of the biceps moves in close relationship with the humerus. The transverse ligament retains the long biceps tendon within the bicipital groove by passing over it from the lesser and the greater tuberosities converting the bicipital groove into a canal.

Bursa

Several bursae are located around the shoulder joint, the most important of which is the subacromial (subdeltoid) bursa (Fig. 24-3), located between the acromial arch and the capsule and is reinforced by the supraspinous tendon. It is easily subjected to traumatization by the deltoid muscle, which, as it contracts, may force the deeply seated bursa against the acromial shelf.

Musculature

The muscles that cross the shoulder joint assist in establishing stability to compensate for the weak bony and ligamentous arrangement. They may be

Figure 24-3

Synovial capsule and bursae of the shoulder.

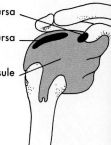

Subacromial bursa

Subcoracoid bursa

Synovial capsule

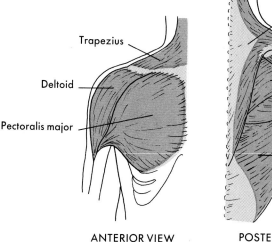

ANTERIOR VIEW   POSTERIOR VIEW

Figure 24-4

Musculature of the shoulder.

separated into two groups, one comprised of the more superficial muscles
and the other made up of the deeper muscles (Fig. 24-4). The superficial
muscles arise from the thorax and shoulder complex and attach to the humeral shaft. They consist of the deltoid, greater pectoral, latissimus dorsi,
and teres major. The deeper muscles originate from the scapula and attach
to the humeral head. They consist of the supraspinous, infraspinous, subscapular, and teres minor and major muscles. These muscles constitute the
short rotator muscles, commonly called the *rotator cuff*, whose tendons
adhere to the articular capsule and serve as reinforcing structures.

Blood and Nerve Supply

The subclavian artery, which lies distal to the sternoclavicular joint, arches
upward and outward, passes the anterior scalene muscle, and then moves
downward laterally in back of the clavicle and in front of the first ribs. The
subclavian artery continues on to become the axillary artery at the outer
border of the first rib and, in the region of the teres major muscle in the
upper arm, it becomes the brachial artery (Fig. 24-5).

The five anterior nerve rami, emanating from the fifth cervical through
the first thoracic vertebrae, subdivide, and supply fibers to the skeleton and
skin of the upper extremities. The subdivisions of the anterior rami create
the complex nerve network called the *brachial plexus*. Stemming from this
plexus are the much smaller nerves that serve the shoulders, arms, and
hands. Trauma to the shoulder complex in athletes can place the brachial
plexus in jeopardy of serious injury (Fig. 24-5).

MOVEMENTS OF THE SHOULDER COMPLEX

Injuries to the shoulder joint usually result from its structural vulnerability,
coupled with its extensive freedom of movement, and a relatively poor correlation between the articular surfaces and the great strength of some of the
surrounding musculature.

Figure 24-5

Brachial plexus and
subclavian artery.

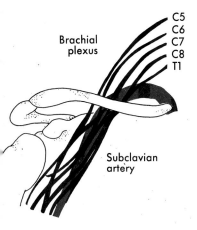

To have a more comprehensive knowledge of the shoulder and its vulnerability to injury in sports, its complex movements must be understood. To assist in the understanding, consider the following analysis of the scapulohumeral rhythm, with the arm moving from the anatomical position through abduction to the vertical position.

Ratio: Arm to Scapular Movement

All the various components of the shoulder complex must move together rhythmically to perform a specific movement. The ratio of arm movement to scapular movement is considered to be approximately 2:1; in other words, 10 degrees of arm movement are comparable to 5 degrees of scapular movement. Although this ratio holds true for a complete 0 to 180 degrees of scapulohumeral movement, it is variable between individuals. In some persons the scapula will rotate downward before it rotates upward, whereas in other individuals it will remain stabilized for the first 30 degrees. This preparatory period is called *scapular setting*.

Scapulohumeral Rhythm

Throughout the complete 0 to 180 degrees of scapulohumeral movement, 120 degrees are attributed to the arm and 60 degrees are considered as being accomplished within the shoulder complex. In the first 90 degrees of movement the arm moves approximately 50 degrees and the shoulder complex moves 40 degrees, primarily within the sternoclavicular joint. As the arm moves upward it rotates externally to allow the greater trochanter of the humerus to move out of the way of the acromion process; after 135 degrees of movement have taken place, or in the last stages of the vertical lift, approximately 20 degrees of motion take place within the acromioclavicular joint to complete the scapulohumeral rhythm. It also should be noted that the clavicle moves on its long axis posteriorly, in addition to elevating 40 degrees in the sternoclavicular joint and 20 degrees in the acromioclavicular joint. This posterior rotation slackens the coracoclavicular ligament, thus allowing the scapula to move in the acromioclavicular joint.

Faulty scapulohumeral rhythm is one cause of chronic shoulder injuries.

Muscles of the Scapulohumeral Rhythm

The muscles moving the arm in the scapulohumeral rhythm of arm abduction are (1) the prime moving muscles of arm abduction: the deltoid, supraspinous and long head of the biceps when the arm is externally rotated; and (2) the guiding muscles (adductor group): the teres major, latissimus dorsi, greater pectoral, biceps brachii, and triceps muscles. It is important that the head of the humerus be stabilized and maintained in relationship with the glenoid fossa. This requires depression to the head of the humerus by the infraspinous, teres minor, and subscapular muscles to counteract the upward force of the deltoid muscle. If the depressor muscles were not present, the head of the humerus would be jammed up against the acromion process and would traumatize the soft tissue lying principally between the subacromial bursa and the tendon of the supraspinous muscle. This depressor action is called a *force couple*.

The muscles moving the shoulder complex in scapulohumeral rhythm of arm abduction are (1) the prime moving muscles of upward rotation: the upper and lower trapezius and the serratus anterior (considered most important) muscles; and (2) the guiding muscles: the greater and lesser rhomboid, levator scapulae, lesser pectoral, and subscapular muscles. The deltoid muscle tends to pull downward on the shoulder complex when the arm is at the side, and the upper trapezius stabilizes the shoulder complex in the first 30 degrees of arm abduction.

EVALUATION OF THE SHOULDER COMPLEX

Pain in the shoulder region may be referred from injury to an internal organ such as the spleen.

The athlete who complains of pain in the shoulder region may be reflecting conditions other than in that area. Pain could be referred from a neck nerve root irritation or from an intrathoracic problem emanating from the heart, lungs, gallbladder, or other internal organs.

The shoulder complex is one of the most difficult regions of the body to evaluate. One reason for this difficulty is that the biomechanical demands placed on these structures during overhand accelerations and decelerations are, as yet, not clearly understood.[4,25]

Major Complaints

It is essential that the evaluator understand the athlete's major complaints and possible mechanism of the injury. It is also necessary to know whether the condition was produced by a sudden trauma or was of slow onset. If the injury was of sudden onset, it must be determined whether the precipitating cause was from external and direct trauma or from some resistive force.[25] The following questions in regard to the athlete's complaints can help the evaluator determine the nature of the injury:

1. If the onset was gradual, what appeared to be the cause?
2. What is the duration and intensity of the pain? Where is the pain located?
3. Is there crepitus on movement, numbness, or distortion in temperature, such as a cold or warm feeling?
4. Is there a feeling of weakness or a sense of fatigue?
5. What movement or body positions seem to aggravate or relieve the pain?
6. If therapy has been given before, what offered pain relief, if anything, such as cold, heat, massage, or analgesic medication?

General Observations

The athlete should be generally observed while walking and standing. Observation during walking can reveal asymmetry of arm swing or a leaning toward the painful shoulder.

The athlete is next observed from the front, side, and back while in a standing position. The evaluator looks for any postural asymmetries, bony or joint deformities, or muscle contractions and laxities.

Front View Observation

1. Are both shoulder tips even with one another or is one depressed (indicating acromioclavicular sprain or dislocation)?
2. Is one shoulder pulled upward from a contracted muscle?
3. Is the lateral end of the clavicle prominent (indicating acromioclavicular sprain or dislocation)?

4. Is one lateral acromion process more prominent than the other (indicating a possible glenohumeral dislocation)?
5. Does the clavicular shaft appear deformed (indicating possible fracture)?
6. Is there a loss of the normal lateral deltoid muscle contour (indicating glenohumeral dislocation)?
7. Is there an indentation in the upper biceps region (indicating rupture of bicipital tendon)?

Side View Observation

1. Is there thoracic kyphosis or shoulders slumped forward (indicating weakness of the erector muscles of the spine and tightness in the pectoral region)?
2. Is there forward or backward hang of the arm (indicating possible scoliosis)?

Back View Observation

1. Is there asymmetry, such as a low shoulder, uneven scapulae, or winging of one scapula winged and not the other (indicating scoliosis)?
2. Is the scapula protracted because of constricted pectoral muscles?
3. Is there a distracted or winged scapula on one or both sides? (A winged scapula on both sides could indicate a general weakness of the serratus anterior muscles; if only one side is winged, the long thoracic nerve may be injured.)

Bony Palpation

With the evaluator standing behind the athlete, the shoulder is palpated anteriorly, laterally, and posteriorly. Both shoulders are palpated at the same time for pain sites and deformities.[12]

Anterior palpation
1. Sternoclavicular articulation
2. Clavicular shaft
3. Acromioclavicular articulation
4. Coracoid process
5. All aspects of the acromion process
6. Greater tuberosity of the humerus
7. Bicipital groove

Lateral palpation
1. Underneath the acromion process
2. Greater tuberosity of the humerus

Posterior palpation
1. Scapular spine
2. Vertebral border of the scapula
3. Lateral border of the scapula

Soft Tissue Palpation

Palpation of the soft tissue of the shoulder detects pain sites, abnormal swelling or lumps, overly contracted muscle tissue, and trigger points. Trigger points are commonly found in the following muscles: levator scapulae, lesser rhomboid, supraspinous, infraspinous, scalene, deltoid, subscapular,

Specific Sports Injuries and
Other Problems

teres major, trapezius, serratus anterior, and greater and lesser pectoral muscles.[26] As with bony palpation, the shoulder is palpated anteriorly, laterally, and posteriorly.

Anterior palpation	Lateral palpation
1. Anterior deltoid muscle	1. Glenohumeral capsule
2. Rotator cuff	2. Lateral deltoid muscle
3. Subdeltoid bursa	3. Upper trapezius muscle
4. Greater pectoral muscle	**Posterior palpation**
5. Sternocleidomastoid muscle	1. Rhomboid muscles
6. Biceps muscle and tendon	2. Latissimus dorsi muscle
	3. Serratus anterior muscle

Temperature

Injury to the shoulder complex can adversely affect skin sensation and temperature in the arm and leg.

Skin temperature is subjectively assessed comparing the back of the athlete's hands. A cold temperature can be an indication of blood vessel constriction, whereas an overly warm temperature may indicate an inflammatory condition.[25]

Circulatory and Neurological Evaluation
Arterial Pulses

It is essential that athletes with shoulder complaints be evaluated for impaired circulation. In cases of shoulder complaints pulse rates are routinely obtained over the axillary, brachial, and radial arteries (Fig. 24-6). The axillary artery is found in the axilla against the shaft of the humerus.[12] The brachial artery is a continuation of the axillary artery and follows the medial border of the biceps brachii muscle toward the elbow. The radial pulse is found at the anterior medial aspect of the wrist. Taking the radial pulse provides an indication of the total circulation of the shoulder and arm.[25]

Sensation Testing

When there is injury to the shoulder complex, a routine test of cutaneous sensation should be made. Dermatome levels are tested for pain and light pressure (Fig. 24-7).

Figure 24-6

Arterial pulses related to the shoulder.

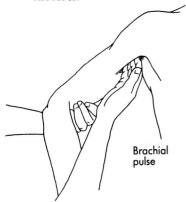

Brachial pulse

Figure 24-7

Shoulder dermatomes.

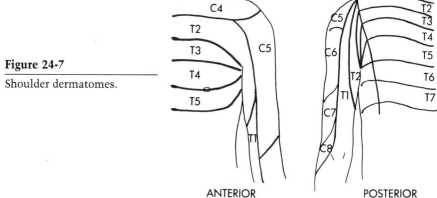

ANTERIOR   POSTERIOR

Functional Evaluation
Range of Motion

The shoulder's range of motion is noted in all directions and compared to the nonsymptomatic limb. All motions should be performed both passively and then actively (Chapter 15).

Of major importance is noting whether the scapula and humerus are moving in a coordinated manner. This is tested with the athlete abducting the arm through a full range of motion. The evaluator stands behind the athlete and notes when the arm first abducts 90 degrees without scapular motion. Second, the humerus and scapula move together with a 2:1 ratio to full abduction. If the athlete's shoulder joint fails to follow this coordinated action, a fixation of the joint (frozen joint) may be present (Fig. 24-8).

Muscle Strength

All major muscles associated with the shoulder complex should be tested for strength and pain (Table 24-1).

Special Evaluation Procedures

A number of evaluation procedures can be used to determine the possibility of selected problems.

Serratus Anterior Weakness

The athlete performs a push-up movement against a wall. Winging of the scapula indicates weakness of the serratus anterior muscle. Winging of only one scapula could indicate an injury to the long thoracic nerve.

Evaluation of Acromioclavicular Joint Stability

The acromioclavicular joint is first palpated to ascertain separation of the acromion process and distal head of the clavicle (Fig. 24-9, *A*). Next, pressure is applied inward from the anterior and posterior aspects of the shoulder. An unstable acromioclavicular joint will show some excursion and pain (Fig. 24-9, *B*). Finally, the evaluator grasps the athlete's wrist and pulls downward on the arm to detect whether the acromion process can be depressed (Fig. 24-9, *C*).

Figure 24-8

Scapulohumeral rhythm.

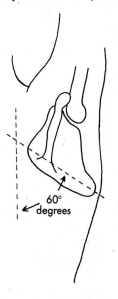

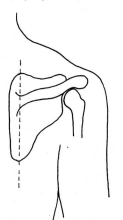 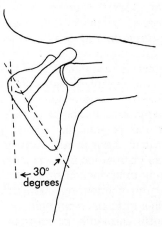

A   B   C

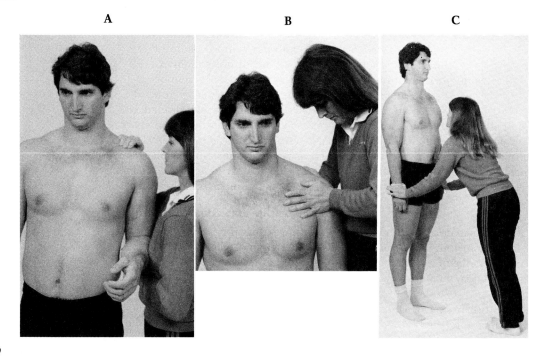

Figure 24-9

Evaluating the
acromioclavicular joint.
A, Palpating the
acromioclavicular joint.
B, Inward pressure on the
shoulder to test excursion.
C, Pulling down on the arm
to depress the acromion
process.

TABLE 24-1

Resistive motion to determine muscle weakness related to shoulder injury

Resistive Motion	Major Muscles Involved	Nerves
Scapular	Serratus anterior	Cervical 6-8
Abduction	Trapezius (superior)	Accessory cranial
Elevation	Levator scapulae	Cervical 3 and 4
	Trapezius (inferior)	Accessory cranial
Depression	Trapezius (middle)	Accessory cranial
Adduction	Rhomboid	Cervical 5
Glenohumeral		
Flexion	Deltoid (anterior)	Cervical 5 and 6
Extension	Coracobrachial	Cervical 6 and 7
	Latissimus dorsi	Cervical 6-8
	Teres major	Cervical 5 and 6
	Deltoid (posterior)	Cervical 5 and 6
Abduction	Deltoid (middle)	Cervical 5 and 6
	Supraspinous	Cervical 5
Horizontal abduction	Deltoid (posterior)	Cervical 5 and 6
Horizontal adduction	Greater pectoral	Cervical 5-8
		Thoracic 1
Lateral rotation	Infraspinous	Cervical 5 and 6
	Teres minor	Cervical 5
Medial rotation	Teres major	Cervical 5 and 6

Supraspinous Muscle Function

Drop arm test   The drop arm test is designed to determine tears of the rotator cuff, primarily of the supraspinous muscle. The athlete abducts the arm as far as possible and then slowly lowers it to 90 degrees. From this position the athlete with a torn supraspinous muscle will be unable to lower the arm further with control (Fig. 24-10). If the athlete can hold the arm in a 90-degree position, a light tap on the wrist will cause the arm to fall.

Centinela supraspinous muscle test   Another test for supraspinous muscle strength and pain was developed at the Centinela Hospital Medical Center Biomechanics Laboratory in Inglewood, California (Fig. 24-11).[29] The athlete brings both arms into 90 degrees of forward flexion and 30 degrees of horizontal abduction. In this position the arms are internally rotated as far as possible, thumbs pointing downward. A downward pressure is then applied by the evaluator. Weakness and pain can be detected, as well as comparative strength between the two arms.

The rotator cuff muscle that is most commonly injured is the supraspinous muscle.

A   B

 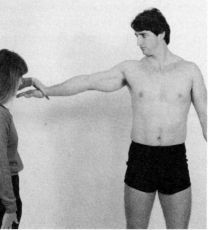

Figure 24-10

Drop arm test for supraspinous muscle stability. **A,** Lower the arm to 90 degrees. **B,** The trainer lightly taps the wrist. The test is positive if the athlete is unable to hold the 90-degree position.

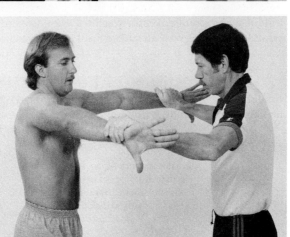

Figure 24-11

Centinela supraspinous test.

Bicipital Tendinitis and Subluxation Test

The bicipital tendinitis and subluxation test indicates function of the long head of the biceps tendon. Keeping the elbow at 90 degrees, the athlete attempts to externally rotate the humerus against the resistance of the evaluator as it is also being pulled downward.[12] The test is positive if pain is felt in the region of the bicipital groove. If there is instability, the tendon will snap out of its groove (Fig. 24-12).

Glenohumeral Instability

A number of procedures can be employed to determine glenohumeral instability.

Pressure displacement With the athlete's shoulder flexed and the arm supported in a completely relaxed position, an anteriorly unstable joint can be manually subluxated forward (Fig. 24-13).

Apprehension test With the arm abducted 90 degrees, the shoulder is slowly and gently externally rotated as far as the athlete will allow. The athlete with a history of anterior glenohumeral dislocation will show great apprehension that is reflected by a facial grimace before an end point can be reached. At no time should the evaluator force this movement[25,29] (Fig. 24-14).

Posterior instability also can be determined through an apprehension maneuver. A posterior force is applied to the glenohumeral joint while the arm is internally rotated and moved into various degrees of flexion.[25]

Anterior and Posterior Capsular Pain

The anterior and posterior capsule of the shoulder can be examined by pulling the arm into hyperextension and horizontal adduction (Fig. 24-15).

Figure 24-12

The bicipital tendinitis and subluxation test.

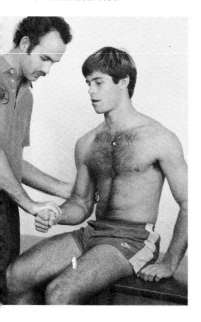

Figure 24-13

Pressure displacement test.

Figure 24-14

Shoulder apprehension test.

Figure 24-13

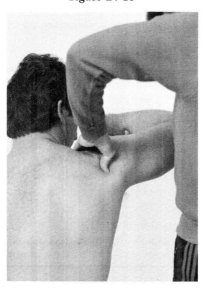

Figure 24-14

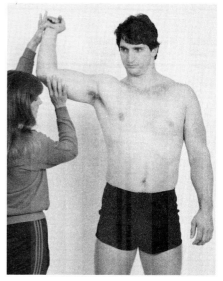

A   B

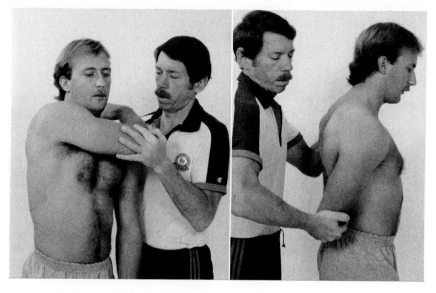

Figure 24-15

Horizontal adduction (**A**) and hyperextension (**B**) for anterior and posterior capsular stability and/or pain.

Impingement Syndrome Tests

One reliable impingement syndrome test consists of a forced flexion of the arm so that the head of the humerus is forced under the acromion process (Fig. 24-16). A positive sign is indicated if the athlete feels pain and reacts with a grimace.[10]

In another test the arm is flexed to 90 degrees and then vigorously rotated internally. This forces the greater tuberosity beneath the coracoacromial arch.

Special Tests for Neurovascular Syndromes of the Neck and Shoulders
Thoracic outlet compression syndrome tests

Anterior scalene syndrome test   The purpose of this test is to indicate whether the subclavian artery is being compressed as it enters into the outlet canal that lies between the heads of the anterior and middle scalene muscles. Compression can also occur between the cervical rib and the anterior scalene muscle.[6] This maneuver is performed with the athlete seated on a stool and both hands resting on the thighs. The athlete's radial pulse is taken, first with the arm relaxed and then extended, while at the same time elevating the chin, turning the face toward the extended hand, and holding the breath (Fig. 24-17). A positive test is one in which the pulse is depressed or stopped completely in the testing position.

Costoclavicular syndrome test   This test indicates whether the subclavian artery is being compressed between the first rib and the clavicle. The radial pulse is taken while the athlete stands in a stiff, military posture. The shoulders are in posterior abduction, the arms are extended, and the neck is hyperextended.[6] A positive test is one where the pulse is obliterated partially or totally (Fig. 24-18).

Figure 24-16

Impingement syndrome test.

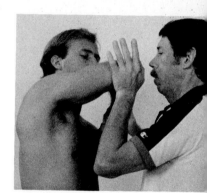

Figure 24-17

Anterior scalene syndrome test.

Hyperabduction syndrome test In hyperabduction syndrome the subclavian and axillary vessels and brachial plexus are compressed as they move behind the pectoral muscle and beneath the coracoid process (Fig. 24-19). To test for this syndrome, the athlete's radial pulse is taken while both hands are raised and the arms are fully extended overhead.

Mechanism of Injury

Chapter 9 discussed how the shoulder becomes injured in sports participation. Incorrectly performing the overhand throw, falling on the outstretched arm or shoulder tip, and forcing the shoulder into external or internal rotation while the arm is abducted are the most common mechanisms of shoulder injury.

Figure 24-18

Costoclavicular syndrome test.

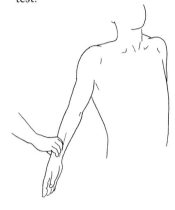

PREVENTING SHOULDER INJURIES

Proper physical conditioning is of major importance in preventing many shoulder injuries. As with all preventive conditioning, a program should be directed to general body development and development of specific body areas for a given sport.[18] If a sport places extreme, sustained demands on the arms and shoulders, or if the shoulder is at risk for sudden traumatic injury, extensive conditioning must be employed. Maximal strength of both intrinsic and extrinsic muscles must be gained, along with a full range of motion in all directions.

Proper warm-up must be performed gradually before explosive arm movements are attempted. This includes gaining a general increase in body temperature followed by sport-specific stretching of selected muscles[9] (Chapter 15).

All athletes in collision and contact sports should be instructed and drilled on how to fall properly. They must be taught to avoid trying to catch themselves with an outstretched arm. Performing a shoulder roll is a safer way to absorb the shock of the fall. Specialized protective equipment, such as shoulder pads, must be properly fitted to avoid some shoulder injuries in tackle football.

To avoid overuse shoulder injuries, it is essential that athletes be correctly taught in the appropriate techniques of throwing, spiking, overhead smashing, overhand serving, proper crawl and butterfly swimming strokes, and tackling and blocking.

Figure 24-19

Hyperabduction syndrome test.

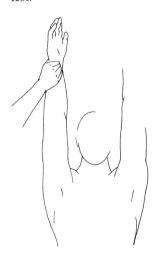

SHOULDER COMPLEX INJURIES
Overuse Syndromes of the Shoulder Complex

Overuse syndromes of the shoulder complex occur mainly in athletes who use repetitive throwing-type motions in activities such as baseball pitching, tennis serving and overhead smashing, and swimming the crawl or butterfly (Fig. 24-20). Quarterbacking and volleyball spiking also can cause microtraumas, which can lead to an overuse syndrome. In general, these sport actions have three phases in common: cocking, acceleration, and follow-through and deceleration phase.[20]

Cocking phase The cocking phase can cause anterior shoulder pain as a result of strain of the greater pectoral muscle insertion and origin of the anterior deltoid, long head of the biceps, or internal rotator muscles.

Acceleration phase Friction injuries causing an impingement syndrome or bursitis in the region of the scapula and fatigue injuries can result in the following:

1. Tendinitis of the greater pectoral major muscle insertion
2. Tendinitis of the coracobrachial muscle and short head of the biceps where it joins the coracoid process
3. Synovitis of the sternoclavicular or acromioclavicular joint
4. "Little League shoulder" or osteochondrosis of the proximal humeral epiphysis
5. Spontaneous throwing fractures of the proximal humerus stemming from a stress fracture

Follow-through and deceleration phase In this phase an eccentric load from throwing may cause pain over the posterior rotator cuff and capsule ("posterior capsule syndrome").

Contusions and Strains

Injuries to the soft tissue in the area of the shoulder complex are common in sports.

Contusions

Blows about the shoulder that produce injury are most prevalent in collision and contact sports. The muscles with the highest incidence are the upper trapezius and deltoid muscles. Characteristically, bruises of this area result in pain and restricted arm movement. The subcutaneous areas of the shoulder complex are subject to bruising in contact sports.

Contusion to the distal end of the clavicle ("shoulder pointer") The most vulnerable part of the clavicle is the enlarged lateral end (acromial end), which forms a projection just before it joins the acromion process. Contusions of this type are often called *shoulder pointers,* and they may cause the athlete severe discomfort. Contusion to the lateral end of the clavicle causes a bone bruise and subsequent irritation to the periosteum. On initial inspection this injury may be mistaken for a first-degree acromioclavicular separation. Management requires proper immediate first aid and follow-up therapy. In most cases these conditions are self-limiting; when the athlete is able to freely move the shoulder, he or she may return to sports activities.

Strains and Impingements

Strains about the shoulder complex are common in those sports which use the arms to overcome a resistance or propel an object. Strains to the musculature of the shoulder joint frequently affect the deltoid superficially and affect the tendons of the rotator cuff internally.

Rotator cuff strains The principal rotator cuff tendon injured is that of the supraspinous muscle. The mechanism of shoulder strains occurs mainly as the result of a violent pull to the arm, an abnormal rotation, or a fall on the outstretched arm, tearing or even rupturing tendinous tissue.[13] The throwing mechanism can produce a variety of abnormal stresses to the soft tissues of the shoulder, for example, impingement, overstretching, torsion, subluxation, and entrapment of nerves and blood

Figure 24-20

The tennis serve can be a major cause of overuse syndromes of the shoulder.

MANAGEMENT PLAN FOR ROTATOR CUFF TEAR

Injury Situation During a match, a male wrestler had his left arm severely forced into external rotation while it was partially abducted. At the time of trauma, the athlete felt a sudden sharp pain and a "giving way" of the shoulder.

Symptoms and Signs As the athlete left the mat, his injured arm was dangling limply. He complained to the trainer that there was moderate to severe pain and weakness in the shoulder region. On inspection, there was point tenderness over the greater tuberosity of the humerus. Tests for supraspinous muscle injury were positive. Passive movement, however, did not produce pain, but active minimal resistance movement caused extreme pain. It was determined that the wrestler had sustained a second degree rotator cuff tear.

Management Plan The physician and athletic trainer decided on a nonsurgical, active exercise rehabilitation approach that included a short period of sling support and immobilization until the shoulder complex was pain free (approximately 1 week).

1

Management Phase	GOALS: To control hemorrhage and full static contraction of shoulder Estimated length of time (ELT): 2-3 days
Therapy	IMMEDIATE CARE: ICE-R (20 min) or intermittently, 6-8 times daily
Exercise Rehabilitation	Ball squeeze (10-15 repetitions), each waking hour Muscle setting while in sling; each contraction held 6 sec (10-15 repetitions), each waking hour General body maintenance exercises are conducted 3 times a week as long as they do not aggravate injury

2

Management Phase	GOALS: To be free of pain and swelling and be able to fully contract shoulder muscles ELT: 1-2 weeks
Therapy	FOLLOW-UP CARE: Ice pack applied (5-15 min) before exercise, 3-4 times daily

	Exercise Rehabilitation	While supine, athlete abducts and externally rotates arm and squeezes ball; each maximal squeeze is held for 6 sec (3-4 times) as arm moves slowly into adduction and internal rotation within pain-free limits, each waking hour Codman's pendulum exercise (3 sets of 10) within pain-free limits, each waking hour Finger wall or ladder climb (3-4 times, 10-15 repetitions) within pain-free limits, each waking hour General body maintenance exercises are conducted 3 times a week as long as they do not aggravate injury
3	**Management Phase**	GOALS: 50% of normal pain-free range of motion (ROM), with 50% of normal strength and coordination ELT: 1-2 weeks
	Therapy	Ice pack (5 min) precedes pain-free exercise, 2-3 times daily
	Exercise Rehabilitation	Isolated movement against gravity with resistance as tolerated; each exercise progresses to 3 sets of 10, 2-3 times daily Isotonic and/or isokinetic exercise can be employed; all shoulder movements are exercised Proprioceptive neuromuscular facilitation (PNF) and pool exercising also should be considered General body maintenance exercises are conducted as long as they do not aggravate injury, 3 times a week
4	**Management Phase**	GOALS: To restore at least 90% ROM, power, endurance, speed, and coordination ELT: 1-3 weeks
	Exercise Rehabilitation	Progressive resistance exercise using DeLorme specifications or DAPRE concept, 3 times a week, using equipment such as free weights, Universal gym, and Nautilus equipment
5	**Management Phase**	GOALS: To restore usual shoulder muscle bulk for full sports participation
	Exercise Rehabilitation	Heavy overload program using Olympic weight equipment, 3-4 times a week

Criteria for Full Recovery

1. The shoulder is symptom free in all movements.
2. The shoulder has full range of motion.
3. The shoulder has full strength and coordination.

vessels. Besides throwing, swimming in freestyle and butterfly events also places great stress on the shoulder rotating mechanisms and can lead to an acute or chronic injury. A tear or complete rupture of one of the *rotator cuff tendons* (the subscapular, supraspinous, infraspinous, or teres minor) produces an extremely disabling condition in which pain, loss of function (particularly with the arm in abduction or external rotation), swelling, and point tenderness are symptoms. In a strain, passive movements seldom yield pain.

Rotator cuff impingement syndrome   The continual use of the arm or arms above the horizontal plane in an athletic endeavor has been known to lead to an impingement syndrome (Fig. 24-21).

Impingement commonly happens to the supraspinous muscle at the anterior edge of the acromion and coracoacromial ligament.[9] It is seen most often in athletes under 25 years old, in the weekend athlete 25 to 40 years old, and in workers 40 years or older.[3] (See p. 695 for impingement syndrome test.)

The major reason for impingement is the reduction of space for the supraspinous muscle to pass underneath the anterior acromion and coracoacromial ligament. This space reduction may be attributed to muscle hypertrophy and inflammation due to microtraumas or contraction of the biceps tendon, forcing the humeral head forward.[3,9]

The rotator cuff injury impingement syndrome has been described in four stages.[14,15,19]

Stage I   A beginning injury to the supraspinous muscle and/or long head of the biceps tendon will produce the following symptoms and signs:

1. Aching after activity
2. Supraspinous muscle symptoms
   a. Point tenderness over the greater tuberosity of the humerus
   b. Pain on abduction that becomes worse at 90 degrees
   c. Positive impingement sign
3. Biceps tendon symptoms
   a. Point tenderness over the biceps tendon
   b. Pain at the biceps tendon on straight-arm full flexion
   c. Positive sign on resisted supination–external rotation test
4. No palpable muscle defect

Figure 24-21

The butterfly stroke can be a major cause of the rotator cuff impingement syndrome.
Courtesy Cramer Products, Inc., Gardner, Kan.

5. Inflammation with edema
6. Temporary thickening of the rotator cuff and subacromial bursa
7. Muscles in the region of the shoulder joint may be atrophied and constricted

Stage II An impingement syndrome involving the supraspinous muscle and at times also the long head of the biceps tendon and subacromial bursa will have the following symptoms and signs:

1. Aching during activity that becomes worse at night
2. Some restriction of arm movement
3. No obvious muscle defect
4. Some muscle fiber separation
5. Permanent thickening of the rotator cuff and acromial bursa with scar tissue

Stage III In this stage the athlete has the following symptoms and signs:

1. A long history of shoulder problems
2. Shoulder pain during activity that increases at night
3. A muscle defect of 1 cm or less
4. A possible partial muscle tear
5. Permanent thickening of the rotator cuff and acromial bursa with scar tissue

Stage IV Stage IV of the rotator cuff impingement syndrome includes:

1. A long history of shoulder problems
2. An obvious infraspinous and supraspinous wasting
3. Point tenderness over the greater tuberosity of the humerus, the anterior acromion, and acromioclavicular joint
4. A great deal of pain when abducting the arm to 90 degrees
5. A muscle defect greater than 1 cm
6. Permanent thickening of the rotator cuff and acromial bursa with scar tissue
7. Limited active and full passive range of motion
8. Weakness in abduction and external rotation
9. Possible degeneration of the clavicle
10. A positive impingement sign

Management of shoulder impingement injuries Stages III and IV are usually treated by surgery. Stages I and II may be treated conservatively with cold or heat modalities or by a combination of electrostimulation and therapeutic exercise.[9]

Conservative treatment For stage I and initially in stage II shoulder impingement injuries, a conservative approach to treatment is taken. If this approach is unsatisfactory in a stage II condition, surgery may be warranted.

Early prevention and proper training Proper training methods to prevent shoulder injuries must be undertaken for sports that involve throwing. Gradual warm-up should emphasize slow stretching and maximizing the extensibility of all major shoulder muscles. Strengthening shoulder muscles should be general at first and then emphasize the external and internal rotator muscles for good glenohumeral joint control.

Athletes displaying early symptoms of shoulder impingement must modify their arm movements. A swimmer may have to decrease the distance or change to a different stroke. Those athletes who throw or who perform throwinglike motions may have to decrease their force or develop a different technique.

Cold application   Athletes experiencing shoulder pain and inflammation might benefit from cold application after workouts. This could be in the form of ice massage or an ice chip pack.

Heat   Heat of any form should be avoided after workouts. However, heat may be beneficial before workouts or at other times. Ultrasound is valuable in many cases of impingement syndrome. Between 0.8 and 1.2 watts/cm^2, 5 minutes daily, for 10 days is suggested.[10]

Transcutaneous electrical nerve stimulation   In many cases TENS is effective in relieving pain from shoulder impingement.

Anti-inflammatory medication   The physician may prescribe an oral anti-inflammatory drug for a short period of time.

Rest   A change of activity or complete rest may be warranted. Because a stage I condition is reversible, it is essential to avoid the movement causing the irritation until the shoulder is symptom free.

Sprains

Sternoclavicular Sprain

Sprains can occur in the three major joints of the shoulder complex:
    Sternoclavicular joint
    Acromioclavicular joint
    Glenohumeral joint

A sternoclavicular sprain (Fig. 24-22) is a relatively uncommon occurrence in sports, but occasionally one may result from one of the various traumas affecting the shoulder complex.

Etiological factors   The mechanism of the injury can be initiated by an indirect force transmitted through the humerus of the shoulder joint by direct violence such as a blow that strikes the poorly padded clavicle or by twisting or torsion of a posteriorly extended arm. Depending on the direction of force, the medial end of the clavicle can be displaced upward and forward, either posteriorly or anteriorly. Generally the clavicle is displaced upward and forward, slightly anteriorly.

Symptoms and signs   Trauma resulting in a sprain to the sternoclavicular joint can be described in three degrees. The *first degree* is characterized by little pain and disability with some point tenderness but with no joint deformity. A *second degree* sprain displays subluxation of the sternoclavicular joint with visible deformity, pain, swelling, point tenderness, and an inability to abduct the shoulder in full range or to bring the arm across the chest, indicating disruption of stabilizing ligaments.

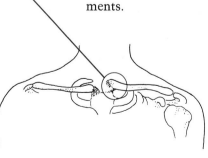

Figure 24-22

Sternoclavicular sprain and dislocation.

STERNOCLAVICULAR IMMOBILIZATION

Materials needed: A felt pad of ¼-inch (0.63 cm) thickness, cut to a circumference of 4 inches (10 cm), 3-inch (7.5 cm) roll of elastic tape, two gauze pads, and tape adherent

Position of the athlete: Reduction of the most common sternoclavicular dislocation is performed by traction with the athlete's arm abducted. Traction and abduction are maintained by an assistant while the immobilization taping is applied.

Position of the operator: The operator stands on the affected side of the athlete.

Procedure

1. An anchor strip is applied around the chest at the level of the tenth rib while the chest is expanded.
2. A felt pad is laid over the sternoclavicular joint and gauze pads are applied over the athlete's nipples.
3. Depending on the direction of displacement, tape pressure is applied over the felt pad. With the most common dislocation (that which is upward, forward, and anterior) taping is started from the back and is moved forward over the shoulder. The first pressure strip is taken from the anchor tape on the unaffected side and crosses over the injured site to finish on the front anchor strip
4. A second strip is taken from the anchor strip on the affected side and crossed over the unaffected side to finish on the front anchor strip
5. As many series of strips are applied as are needed to give complete immobilization. All series are locked in place by a tape strip placed over the ends.

Figure 24-23

Sternoclavicular immobilization.

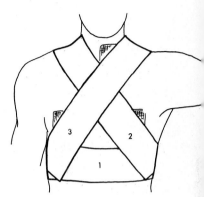

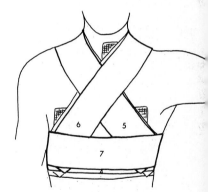

The *third degree*, which is the most severe, presents a picture of complete dislocation with gross displacement of the clavicle at its sternal junction, swelling, and disability, indicating complete rupture of the sternoclavicular and costoclavicular ligaments. If the clavicle is displaced posteriorly, pressure may be placed on the blood vessels, esophagus, or trachea, causing a life or death situation.

Management Care of this condition is based on returning the displaced clavicle to its original position, which is done by a physician, and immobilizing it at that point so that healing may take place. A deformity, primarily caused by formation of scar tissue at that point, is usually apparent after healing is completed. There is no loss of function. Immobilization (Fig. 24-23) is usually maintained for 3 to 5 weeks, followed by graded reconditioning exercises. There is a high incidence of recurrence of sternoclavicular sprains.

Acromioclavicular Sprain

The acromioclavicular joint is extremely vulnerable to sprains among active sports participants, especially in collision sports. A program of prevention

Figure 24-24

Mechanism of an
acromioclavicular sprain.

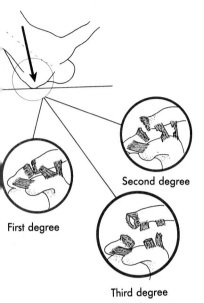

First degree

Second degree

Third degree

Figure 24-25

Comparison of a normal
shoulder (**A**) with a separated
shoulder (**B**).

should entail proper fitting of protective equipment, conditioning to provide a balance of strength and flexibility to the entire shoulder complex, and teaching proper techniques of falling and the use of the arm in sports.

Mechanism   The mechanism of an acromioclavicular sprain is most often induced by a direct blow to the tip of the shoulder, pushing the acromion process downward, or by an upward force exerted against the long axis of the humerus (Fig. 24-24). The position of the arm during indirect injury is one of adduction and partial flexion. Depending on the extent of ligamentous involvement, the acromioclavicular sprain is graded as first, second, or third degree.

Symptoms and signs   The *first degree* acromioclavicular sprain reflects point tenderness and discomfort on movement at the junction between the acromion process and the outer end of the clavicle. There is no deformity, indicating only a mild stretching of the acromioclavicular ligaments.

A *second degree* sprain indicates rupture of the supporting superior and inferior acromioclavicular ligaments. There is a definite displacement and prominence of the lateral end of the clavicle when compared to the unaffected side (Fig. 24-25). In this moderate sprain there is point tenderness on palpation of the injury site, and the athlete is unable to fully abduct through a full range of motion or to bring the arm completely across the chest.[7,22] *NOTE:* The second degree sprain may require surgery to restore stability.[2]

Although occurring infrequently, the *third degree* injury is considered a dislocation, involving rupture of the acromioclavicular and coracoclavicular ligaments. The mechanics of a completely separated shoulder consist most often of a direct blow that forces the acromion process downward, backward, and inward while the clavicle is pushed down against the rib cage. In such an injury there is gross deformity and prominence of the outer clavicular head, severe pain, loss of movement, and instability of the shoulder complex.[2,28]

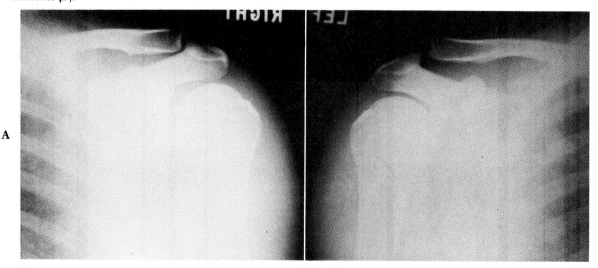

A   B

Management Immediate care of the acromioclavicular sprain involves three basic procedures: (1) cold and pressure to control local hemorrhage, (2) stabilization of the joint by a sling and swathe bandage, and (3) referral to a physician for definitive diagnosis and treatment. Complete severance of the coracoclavicular ligament demands corrective surgery. Most second-degree sprains require 4 to 6 weeks for fibrous healing to take place, and an extended period is needed for the restoration of general shoulder strength and mobility. A regimen of superficial moist heat will aid in resolving soreness. Movement in the pain-free range will be restored after the use of ice packs.[7]

Rehabilitative exercise is concerned with reconditioning the shoulder complex to the state it was before the injury. Full strength, flexibility, endurance, and function must be redeveloped. (See p. 719 for rehabilitation exercises.) Protective taping may help support the first-degree injury.

Glenohumeral Joint Sprain

Sprains of the shoulder joint involve injury to the articular capsule. The pathological process of the sprain is comparable to that of an internal strain and often affects the rotator cuff muscles.

Figure 24-26

Protective acromioclavicular taping.

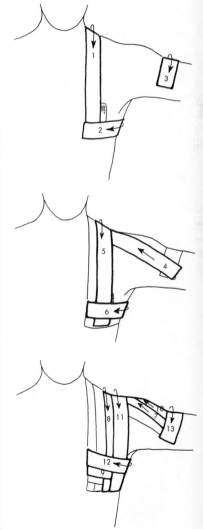

PROTECTIVE ACROMIOCLAVICULAR TAPING

Protective acromioclavicular taping (Fig. 24-26) is designed to stabilize the acromioclavicular articulation in proper alignment and still allow normal movement of the shoulder complex.

Materials needed: One ¼-inch (0.63 cm) thick felt pad, roll of 2-inch (5 cm) adhesive tape, tape adherent, 2-inch (5 cm) gauze pad, and 3-inch (7.5 cm) elastic bandage.

Position of the athlete: The athlete sits in a chair with the affected arm resting in a position of abduction.

Position of the operator: The operator stands facing the athlete's abducted arm.

Procedure

1. Three anchor strips are applied: the first in a three-quarter circle just below the deltoid muscle; the second, just below the nipple, encircling half the chest; and the third, over the trapezius muscle near the neck and then attaching to the second anchor in front and back.
2. The first and second strips of tape are applied from the front and back of the first anchor, crossing each other at the acromioclavicular articulation and attaching to the third anchor strip.
3. The third support strip is placed over the ends of the first and second pieces, following the line of the third anchor strip.
4. A fourth support strip is laid over the second anchor strip.
5. This basketweave pattern is continued until the entire shoulder complex is covered. It is followed by the application of a shoulder spica with an elastic bandage.

Mechanism   The cause of this injury is the same as that which produces dislocations and strains. Anterior capsular sprains occur when the arm is forced into abduction, such as making an arm tackle in football. Sprains can also occur from external rotation of the arm. A direct blow to the shoulder could also result in a sprain. The posterior capsule can be sprained by a forceful movement of the humerus posteriorly when the arm is flexed.

Symptoms and signs   The athlete complains of pain on arm movement, especially when the sprain mechanism is reproduced. There may be decreased range of motion and pain on palpation.

Management   Care after acute trauma to the shoulder joint requires the use of a cold pack for 24 to 48 hours, elastic or adhesive compression, rest, and immobilization by means of a sling. After hemorrhage has subsided, a program of cryotherapy or ultrasound and massage may be added, and mild passive and active exercise is advocated for regaining a full range of motion. Once the shoulder can execute a full range of movement without signs of pain, a resistance exercise program should be initiated. Any traumatic injury to the shoulder joint can lead to a subacute and chronic condition of either synovitis or bursitis, which in the absence of shoulder movement will allow muscle contractures, adhesions, and atrophy to develop, resulting in an ankylosed shoulder joint.

Subluxations and Dislocations

Dislocation of the humeral head is second only to finger dislocations in order of incidence in sports. The extreme range of all of its possible movements makes the shoulder joint highly susceptible to dislocation. The most common kind of displacement is that occurring anteriorly (Fig. 24-27). Of those dislocations caused by direct trauma, 85% to 90% recur.[11]

Anterior Glenohumeral Dislocation

Mechanism   The anterior glenohumeral dislocation or subcoracoid dislocation is often caused when an arm is abducted and externally rotated (Fig. 24-28). An arm tackle or an abnormal force to an arm that is executing a throw can produce a sequence of events resulting in a severe shoulder strain or dislocation. Less often a fall or inward rotation and abduction of an arm may result in serious shoulder joint injury.

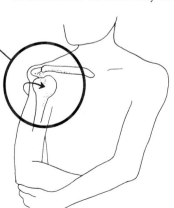

Figure 24-27

Anterior shoulder subluxation and dislocation.

Symptoms and signs The athlete with an anterior dislocation displays a flattened deltoid contour. Palpation of the axilla will reveal prominence of the humeral head. The athlete carries the affected arm in slight abduction and external rotation and is unable to touch the opposite shoulder with the hand of the affected arm. There is often severe pain and disability.

Pathological process In an anterior glenohumeral dislocation, the head of the humerus is forced out of its articular capsule in a forward direction past the glenoid labrum and then upward to rest under the coracoid process. The scope of the pathological process is quite extensive, with torn capsular and ligamentous tissue, possibly tendinous avulsion of the rotator cuff muscles, and profuse hemorrhage. Additional complications may arise if the head of the humerus comes into contact with and injures the brachial nerves and vessels. The bicipital tendon also may be pulled from its canal as the result of a rupture of its transverse ligament.

Management The athlete with an anterior dislocation displays a flattened or indented deltoid contour. Palpation of the axilla will reveal a prominence of the humeral head. The athlete carries the affected arm in slight abduction and is unable to touch the opposite shoulder with the hand of the affected arm.

Management of the shoulder dislocation requires immediate reduction by a physician, control of the hemorrhage by cold packs, immobilization, and the start of muscle reconditioning as soon as possible. The question often arises as to whether a first-time dislocation should be reduced or should receive medical attention. *Physicians generally agree that a first-time dislocation may be associated with a fracture, and, therefore, it is beyond the scope of a coach's or trainer's duties.* Recurrent dislocations do not present the same complications or attendant dangers as the acute type; however, risk is always involved. Reducing the anterior dislocation usually can be accomplished by applying traction on the abducted and flexed arm.[17]

After the dislocation has been reduced, immobilization and muscle rehabilitation are carried out. Immobilization takes place for about 3 weeks after reduction, with the arm maintained in a relaxed position of adduction and internal rotation.[17] While immobilized, the athlete is instructed to perform isometric exercises for strengthening the internal and external rotator muscles. After immobilization, the strengthening program progresses from isometrics to resisting rubber tubing and then to dumbbells and other resistance devices. (See pp. 715-718 for rehabilitation of rotator cuff injuries.) A major criterion for the athlete's return to sports competition is that there must be internal and external rotation strength equal to 20% of the athlete's body weight.[17]

Posterior Glenohumeral Dislocation

The posterior glenohumeral dislocation accounts for only 1% to 4.3% of all shoulder dislocations.[21]

Mechanism The mechanism of injury is usually a forced adduction and internal rotation of the shoulder or a fall on an extended and internally rotated arm.

Figure 24-28

Subcoracoid dislocation of the humerus at the glenohumeral joint.

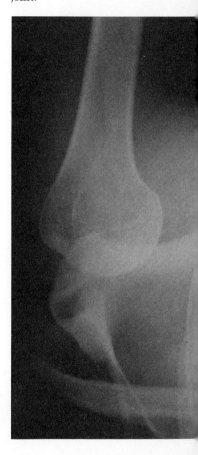

After exercise rehabilitation of an anterior shoulder dislocation, the athlete should have an internal and external rotation strength of at least 20% of body weight.

Symptoms and signs Posterior glenohumeral dislocation produces severe pain and disability. The arm is often fixed in adduction and internal rotation. The deltoid muscle is flattened, the acromion and coracoid are prominent, and the head of the humerus also may be seen posteriorly.

Management The athlete must be promptly referred to an orthopedic physician for x-ray examination and reduction. Reduction may have to be performed under anesthesia. The procedure usually involves traction on the arm with the elbow bent, followed by adduction of the arm with posterior pressure being applied to the humeral head anteriorly. While in traction the arm is slowly externally rotated and then internally rotated.[5,21]

The shoulder is immobilized in a position of external rotation and slight abduction for 3 to 6 weeks. After immobilization, an active program of range of motion and strengthening exercises are begun (p. 719).

The Unstable Shoulder: Recurrent Subluxation and Dislocation

Recurrent subluxation Subluxation of the shoulder usually begins with one traumatic event that places an abnormal stress on the joint or by repeated less forceful movements that stress the joint capsule. Pitching, tennis serving, and crawl swimming may produce anterior capsular complaints, whereas swimming the backstroke or backhand stroking in tennis can cause problems with the posterior capsule. As the articular capsule becomes increasingly lax, more mobility of the glenohumeral head is allowed, eventually damaging the glenoid lip. With this damage and stretching of supportive ligamentous and tendinous structures, subluxation and dislocation can occur.[27]

When subluxation occurs, the athlete may complain that the shoulder felt like it came out of its socket, followed by sudden pain along the arm and numbness in the fingers.[24,27] The pain and numbness may last for several minutes, followed by extreme weakness of the entire arm. Tests for apprehension will be positive, and there is often point tenderness of the humeral head and positive signs of injury to the rotator cuff.[27]

In conservative management, the shoulder is immobilized with a sling and swathe for 5 to 6 weeks. After immobilization and a decrease in inflammation, an exercise program is instituted emphasizing the rotator cuff, rhomboid, latissimus dorsi, and serratus anterior muscles.[27] A gradual program of strength and flexibility development is carried out over a 4- to 6-week period, followed by a slow return to sports activity over a period of 6 weeks.[27]

If a conservative approach is unsuccessful, surgery is usually performed. After surgery, a strength and development program is instituted.[8]

Shoulder protection Every protection should be given to the athlete who may be prone to recurrent dislocations. Restraint by means of adhesive taping and a harness appliance should be used during any sports activity. Repeated dislocations continue to stretch the supporting structures and damage the articulating hyaline cartilage, which may eventually result in an arthritic condition.

Recurrent shoulder subluxation and dislocation reduction With the permission of the team physician, the trainer can assist the athlete in

TAPING FOR SHOULDER SUPPORT AND RESTRAINT

This taping is designed to support the soft tissues of the shoulder complex and to restrain the arm from abducting more than 90 degrees (Fig. 24-29).

Materials needed: One roll of 2-inch (5 cm) tape, 2-inch (5 cm) gauze pad, cotton pad, tape adherent, and 3-inch (7.5 cm) elastic bandage

Position of the athlete: The athlete stands with the affected arm flexed at the elbow and the shoulder internally rotated.

Position of the operator: The operator stands facing the affected arm.

Procedure

1. The first phase is designed to support the capsule of the shoulder joint. After a cotton pad has been placed in the axilla, a series of three loops around the shoulder joint is applied. The first loop is started at the top of the athlete's scapula, is pulled forward across the acromion process, around the front of the shoulder, back underneath the axilla, over the back of the shoulder, crossing the acromion process again, and then is terminated at the clavicle. Each of the subsequent strips is begun down the shoulder half the width of the preceding strip.
2. Strips of tape are next run upward from a point just below the insertion of the deltoid muscle and crossed over the acromion process, completely covering the outer surface of the shoulder joint.
3. Before the final application of a basketweave shoulder taping, a gauze pad is placed over the nipple area. A strip of tape is laid over the shoulder near the neck and is carried to the nipple line in front and to the scapular line in back.
4. A second strip is taken from the end of the first strip, passes around the middle of the upper arm, and ends at the back end of the first strip.
5. The above alternation is continued with an overlapping of each preceding strip by at least half its width until the shoulder has been completely capped.
6. A shoulder spica is applied to keep the taping in place.

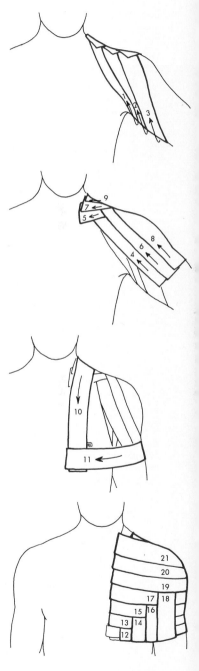

Figure 24-29

Taping for shoulder support and restraint.

reducing a recurrent shoulder subluxation or dislocation. The safest method is by the *weight on the wrist technique.* In this method the athlete lies between two tables, with the head resting on one table and the body on the other. The affected arm extends between the two tables with a 5- to 10-pound weight tied to the wrist. As the muscles of the shoulder relax, a spontaneous reduction occurs.

Shoulder Synovitis and Bursitis

The shoulder joint is subject to subacute chronic inflammatory conditions resulting from trauma or from overuse in an abnormal fashion. An injury of this type may develop from a direct blow, a fall on the outstretched hand, or the stress incurred in throwing an object. Inflammation can occur in the shoulder, extensively affecting the soft tissues surrounding it or specifically affecting various bursae (Fig. 24-30). The bursa that is most often injured is

Figure 24-30

Sports such as pole vaulting
place extreme stress on the
arm and shoulder complex;
such overuse can lead to joint
bursitis or inflammation of
the synovium.

the subacromial bursa, which lies underneath the deltoid muscle and the articular capsule and extends under the acromion process. The apparent pathological process in these conditions is fibrous buildup and fluid accumulation developing from a constant inflammatory state.

Recognition of these conditions follows the same course as in other shoulder affections.

Symptoms and Signs

The athlete is unable to move the shoulder, especially in abduction; rotation and muscle atrophy also may ensue because of disuse.

Management

Management of low-grade inflammatory conditions must be initiated somewhat empirically. In some instances both the superficial heat from moist pads or infrared rays and the deep heat of diathermy or ultrasound are beneficial. In other instances heat may be aggravating, so cold applications by cold pack may be more useful. Whatever the mode of treatment, the athlete must maintain a consistent program of exercise, with the emphasis placed on regaining a full range of motion, so that muscle contractures and adhesions do not immobilize the joint.

The *"frozen shoulder"* is a condition more characteristic of an older person, but occasionally it does occur in the athlete. It results from a chronically irritated shoulder joint that has had improper care. Constant, generalized inflammation causes degeneration of the soft tissues in the vicinity of the shoulder joint, resulting in an extreme limitation of movement. The main care of the frozen shoulder is a combination of deep heat therapy and mobilization exercise.

Figure 24-31

Clavicular fracture.
A, Associated brachial blood
vessels and nerves. **B,** X-ray
film of a comminuted
clavicular fracture.

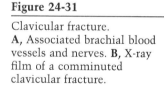

A

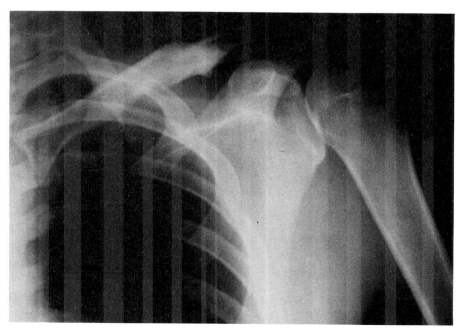

B

Fractures of the Shoulder Complex

Fractures in the shoulder complex can be caused by a direct blow on the bone or indirectly by a fall on either an outstretched arm or the point of the shoulder.

Clavicular Fractures

Clavicular fractures (Fig. 24-31) are one of the most frequent fractures in sports. Over 80% occur in the middle third of the clavicle, which lacks ligamentous support.[16]

Etiological factors   Clavicular fractures are caused by either a direct blow or a transmitted force resulting from a fall on the outstretched arm. In junior and senior high school athletes these fractures are usually the greenstick type.

Symptoms and signs   The athlete with a fractured clavicle usually supports the arm on the injured side and tilts his or her head toward that side, with the chin turned to the opposite side. On inspection the injured clavicle appears a little lower than the unaffected side. Palpation may also reveal swelling and mild deformity.

Management   The clavicular fracture is cared for immediately by applying a sling and swathe bandage and by treating the athlete for shock, if necessary. The athlete is then referred to a physician, who in most instances will perform an x-ray examination of the area and then apply a shoulder figure-of-eight wrapping that will stabilize the shoulder in an upward and backward position.

Scapular Fractures

Fracture of the scapula is an infrequent injury in sports (Fig. 24-32). Although the scapula appears extremely vulnerable to trauma, it is well protected by a heavy outer bony border and a cushion of muscle above and below. Those fractures which do occur happen as a result of force applied to the hand, elbow, or shoulder joint. The fracture usually occurs when the humerus carries a force to the scapula, as the serratus anterior muscle violently pulls the scapula forward at the same time. Such a fracture may cause the athlete to have pain on shoulder movement, swelling, and point tenderness. When this injury is suspected, the athlete should be given a supporting sling and sent directly to the sports physician.

Thoracic Outlet Problems

A number of neurovascular problems can occur in the neck and shoulder that involve compression of the brachial plexus and subclavian artery.

Etiological Factors

Four possible causes have been identified[6]:

1. Compression over a cervical rib
2. Spasm of the anterior scalene muscle
3. Compression of the brachial plexus, subclavian artery, and subclavian vein in the narrowed space between the first rib and clavicle
4. Compression of the smaller pectoral muscle over the subclavian and axillary vessels and brachial plexus as they pass beneath the coracoid process or between the clavicle and first rib

Over 80% of all fractures to the clavicle occur in the middle third.

Figure 24-32

Fractures of the scapula are infrequent in sports.

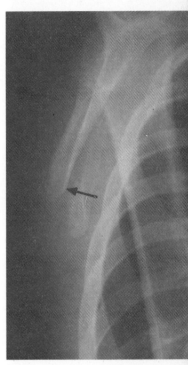

A number of neurovascular problems can occur within the thoracic outlet of the shoulder.

Symptoms and Signs

Abnormal pressure on the subclavian artery, subclavian vein, and brachial plexus produces a variety of symptoms:

1. Paresthesia and pain
2. Sensation of cold
3. Impaired circulation that could lead to gangrene of the fingers
4. Muscle weakness
5. Muscle atrophy

Three tests can be given to determine vascular compression: the anterior scalene test, costoclavicular test, and hyperabduction test (pp. 695-696).

Management

A conservative approach should be taken in early and mild cases of thoracic outlet syndromes. The following measures may prove helpful:

1. Sling support and tension reduction
2. Anti-inflammatory medication
3. Exercises to strengthen the trapezius, serratus anterior, and erector muscle of the spine
4. Postural correction, especially in cases of drooped shoulders

UPPER ARM CONDITIONS

The upper arm can sustain varied stress and trauma, depending on the nature of the sport. Crushing blows may be directed to the area by collision and contact sports; severe strain can be imposed by the throwing sports and sports that afford muscle resistance, such as gymnastics.

Contusions

Contusions of the upper arm are frequent in contact sports. Although any muscle of the upper arm is subject to bruising, the area most often affected is the lateral aspect, primarily the brachial muscle and portions of the triceps and biceps muscles.

Symptoms and Signs

Bruises to the upper arm area can be particularly handicapping, especially if the radial nerve is contused through forceful contact with the humerus, producing transitory paralysis and consequent inability to use the extensor muscles of the forearm.

Management

Cold and pressure should be applied from 1 to 24 hours after injury, followed by cryotherapy or superficial heat therapy and massage. In most cases this condition responds rapidly to treatment, usually within a few days. If swelling and irritation last more than 2 or 3 weeks, *myositis ossificans* may have been stimulated, and massage must be stopped and protection afforded the athlete during sports participation.

Strains

Acute and chronic strains are common in the arm. The muscles most commonly affected are the biceps, triceps, and pectoral muscles.[23] Management of acute problems should follow usual procedures in immediate management. Two conditions that are unique to the arm area are bicipital tenosynovitis and biceps brachii rupture.

Bicipital Tenosynovitis

Tenosynovitis of the long head of the biceps muscle is common among athletes who execute a throwing movement as part of their event.

Etiological factors   It is more prevalent among pitchers, tennis players, and javelin throwers, for whom the repeated forced internal rotations of the upper arm may produce a chronic inflammatory condition in the vicinity of the synovial sheath of the long head of the biceps muscle. A complete rupture of the transverse ligament, which holds the biceps in its groove, may take place, or a constant inflammation may result in degenerative scarring or a subluxated tendon.

Symptoms and signs   The athlete may complain of an ache in the anterior and medial areas of the shoulder; deep palpation reveals point tenderness in the region of the bicipital tendon.

Management   Such conditions are best cared for by a period of complete rest for 1 to 2 weeks, with daily applications of cryotherapy or ultrasound. After the initial aching has gone, a gradual program of reconditioning is begun.

Biceps Brachii Ruptures

Ruptures of the biceps brachii (Fig. 24-33) occur mainly in gymnasts who are engaged in power moves. The rupture commonly takes place near the origin of the muscle. The athlete usually hears a resounding snap and feels a sudden, intense pain at the point of injury. A protruding bulge may appear near the middle of the biceps. When asked to flex the elbow joint of the injured arm, the gymnast displays a definite weakness. Treatment should include immediately applying a cold pack to control hemorrhage, placing the arm in a sling, and referring the athlete to the physician. Surgical repair is usually indicated.

Fractures

Fractures of the humeral shaft (Fig. 24-34) happen occasionally in sports, usually as the result of a direct blow or a fall on the arm. The type of fracture is usually comminuted or transverse, and a deformity is often produced because the bone fragments override each other as a result of strong muscular pull.

The pathological process is characteristic of most uncomplicated fractures, except that there may be a tendency for the radial nerve, which encircles the humeral shaft, to be severed by jagged bone edges, resulting in radial nerve paralysis and causing wrist drop and inability to perform forearm supination.

Recognition of this injury requires immediate application of a splint, treatment for shock, and referral to a physician. The athlete will be out of competition for approximately 3 to 4 months.

Fracture of the Upper Humerus

Fractures of the upper humerus (Fig. 24-35) pose considerable danger to nerves and vessels of that area.

Figure 24-33

Biceps brachii rupture.

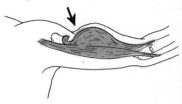

Figure 24-34

Humeral shaft fracture.

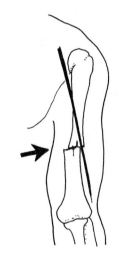

Figure 24-35

Fracture of the upper humerus.

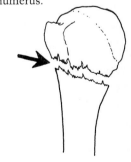

Etiological factors Such fractures can result from a direct blow, a dislocation, or the impact received in falling onto the outstretched arm. Various parts of the end of the humerus may be involved, such as the anatomical neck, tuberosities, or surgical neck. Such a fracture may be mistaken for a shoulder dislocation. The greatest number of fractures take place at the surgical neck.

Symptoms and signs It may be difficult to recognize a fracture of the upper humerus by visual inspection alone; therefore, x-ray examination gives the only positive proof. Some of the more prevalent signs that may be present are pain, inability to move the arm, swelling, point tenderness, and discoloration of the superficial tissue. Because of the proximity of the axillary blood vessels and the brachial plexus, a fracture to the upper end of the humerus may result in severe hemorrhaging or paralysis.

Management A suspected fracture of this type warrants immediate support with a sling and swathe bandage and referral to a physician. Incapacitation may range from 2 to 6 months.

Epiphyseal Fracture

Figure 24-36

Epiphyseal fracture.

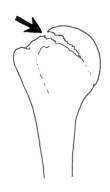

Epiphyseal fracture of the head of the humerus (Fig. 24-36) is much more common in the young athlete than is a bone fracture. An epiphyseal injury in the shoulder region occurs most frequently in individuals 10 years of age and younger.[16] It is caused by a direct blow or by an indirect force traveling along the length of the axis of the humerus. This condition causes shortening of the arm, disability, swelling, point tenderness, and pain. There also may be a false joint. This type of injury should be suspected when the above signs appear in young athletes. Initial treatment should include splinting and immediate referral to a physician. Healing is initiated rapidly; immobilization is necessary for only about 3 weeks. The main danger of an injury such as this lies in the possibility of damage to the epiphyseal growth centers of the humerus.

REHABILITATION OF THE SHOULDER COMPLEX

The shoulder complex and especially the glenohumeral joint have a tendency to become highly restricted in motion after an injury and/or immobilization. In some cases, serious injury and immobilization lead to contractures and a tendency to develop fibrosis of the articular capsule. To prevent these problems, pain-free mobility is started as soon as possible without aggravating the injury.

Shoulder rehabilitation is highly complicated and depends on the nature of the injury and whether surgery has been performed. In general, rehabilitation progresses through early, intermediate, and advanced exercise stages.[1] Types of exercise can vary from isometrics, isotonics, isokinetics, stretching, and manual resistance using the principles of PNF (Appendix I-E). Often, all six are used in rehabilitation. Rotator cuff and impingement injuries, glenohumeral dislocations and subluxations, and acromioclavicular injuries will be discussed to provide the student with an example of shoulder rehabilitation.

Rotator Cuff Injury Rehabilitation
Early Rehabilitation

At this stage, the rotator cuff is in a state of constriction after an injury or surgery. The primary goals are to establish pain-free active movement and minimal strength. TENS may be effective in reducing minor pain while exercising.

Ball squeeze   The athlete squeezes a tennis ball while performing pain-free shoulder movements in a sequence from abduction to flexion to external rotation and then moving to adduction, extension, and internal rotation (see Fig. 25-62). This exercise is performed twice daily, ten times in each direction.

Codman's pendular exercise   While bent over with the arm fully extended and the shoulder relaxed, the athlete moves the shoulder first in small circles in each direction and then in straight-line movements of flexion-extension and adduction-abduction. The distance of the swing is gradually increased. Exercises are performed twice daily with ten movements in each direction (Fig. 24-37).

Bar hang   The athlete grasps a horizontal bar overhead while supporting the body weight and standing on a chair. Gradually, the athlete allows the shoulder to take some of the body weight until it can take the entire weight without pain. The bar hang is performed one to three times for a count of five to ten daily. *NOTE:* The bar hang, even in the last stages of rotator cuff rehabilitation, may cause impingement.

Finger wall climb   Standing an arm's distance away from a wall, the athlete finger-walks up until there is pain. The first walking occurs facing the wall and then while the athlete stands sideways to the wall. This is performed two or three times, twice daily (Fig. 24-38).

Intermediate Rehabilitation

The athlete begins the intermediate phase of rehabilitation when the shoulder is pain free on muscle contraction. The goals of this stage are to increase range of motion and strength to almost preinjury status.

Codman's pendular exercise with resistance   Light dumbbell resistance is added to Codman's pendular exercise. As the weight is increased, the athlete stands upright, directing the dumbbell upward and outward and then upward and inward (Fig. 24-39). The exercises are performed twice daily, ten times in each direction.[1]

Shoulder wheel   The shoulder wheel provides an excellent means of gaining both shoulder flexibility and strength. The athlete stands sideways to the wheel and performs ten repetitions in each direction (Fig. 24-40). The exercises are repeated two or three times and performed three or four times a week.

Dumbbell stretches   The athlete lies supine on a table or bench. Holding a 2- to 5-pound dumbbell in the hand with the elbow bent 90 degrees and the shoulder abducted 90 degrees, the athlete externally rotates as far as possible (Fig. 24-41). Each stretch is maintained for 20 to 30 seconds and repeated two or three times.

The next exercise takes place with the athlete supine and the arm externally rotated and elevated 135 degrees in the frontal plane. The el-

Figure 24-37

Codman's pendular exercise.

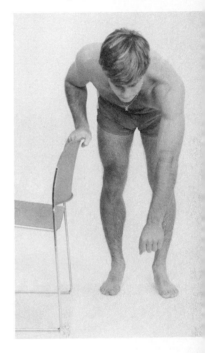

Figure 24-38

Finger wall climb.

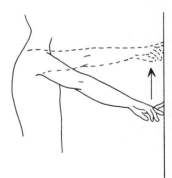

bow is extended. While holding the dumbbell, the arm is extended as far
as possible overhead.[18]

Self-stretching To stretch the posterior capsule, the athlete moves
the arm to 90 degrees of flexion and with the opposite hand pulls the
elbow into horizontal adduction.[18] The exercise is performed twice daily,
two or three times, holding each stretch for 20 to 30 seconds.

The inferior capsule is next stretched by placing the arm overhead as
far as possible with the elbow flexed. The other hand grasps the opposite
elbow to initiate the stretch[18] (Fig. 24-42).

Dumbbell exercises Strengthening the supraspinous muscle entails
having the athlete sit with the arms abducted 90 degrees and horizontally
flexed 30 degrees and internally rotated. The athlete then lifts and lowers
a dumbbell in each hand. The exercise is performed ten times and repeated two or three times, three or four times a week.

Figure 24-39

Codman's pendular exercise
with resistance.

Figure 24-40

Reconditioning with the
shoulder wheel.

Figure 24-41

Dumbbell stretches.

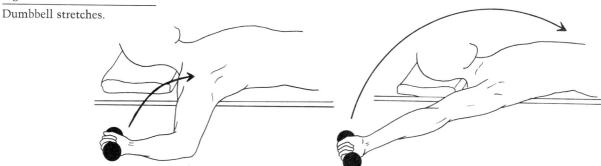

To exercise the infraspinous and teres minor muscles, the athlete lies on the side, with the arm close to the body, and the elbow bent 90 degrees. From a position of internal rotation, the athlete externally rotates the arm as far as possible (Fig. 24-43). This exercise is repeated ten times, twice for three sets, three or four times a week.

To exercise the subscapular muscle, the athlete lies supine, with the arm close to the side, and the elbow flexed 90 degrees. From a position of full external rotation, the dumbbell is internally rotated as far as possible. The exercise is performed ten times for two or three sets, three or four times a week.

Bench presses   The athlete progresses slowly from supporting a barbell or Universal weight in a bench-press position in a "locked-out" position (Fig. 24-44). Gradually, the athlete begins to bend the elbows until a press can be performed from a full range of motion. Ten presses are performed for two or three sets, three times a week.

Upright rowing   A barbell is grasped in its center with both hands raised to a position underneath the athlete's chin (Fig. 24-45). The exercise is performed ten times for two or three sets, three times a week.

Isokinetic exercises   Isokinetic exercises also can be beneficial at this stage of rehabilitation. The athlete engages in shoulder flexion, abduction, adduction, internal and external rotation, elbow extension and flexion, and horizontal adduction and abduction (Fig. 24-46).

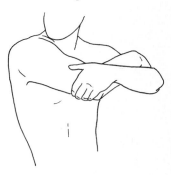

Figure 24-42

Self-stretching.

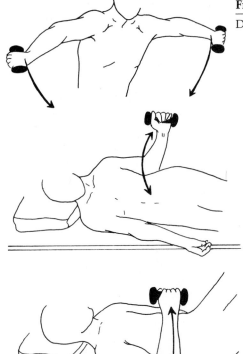

Figure 24-43

Dumbbell exercises.

Figure 24-44

Bench presses.

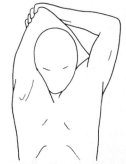

Figure 24-45

Upright rowing.

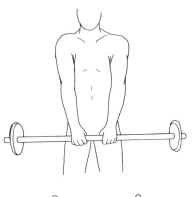

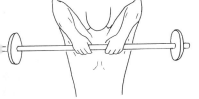

Advanced Rehabilitation

Once the athlete has progressed to the advanced stage, there is full range of motion and near-normal strength. The purpose of advanced rehabilitation is to restore the athlete to competitive fitness. One program to develop extra strength along with flexibility might include the following[1]:

1. Dumbbell alternate presses or barbell presses behind the neck
2. Dumbbell bench presses, incline dumbbell presses, flyers, or parallel bar dips
3. Bent-arm pullovers with a barbell
4. High pulls with a snatch grip
5. Straight-arm barbell pullovers with a weight of 30 pounds (grip progressively wider, with the weight remaining the same)

Exercise rehabilitation after rotatory cuff surgery   Exercise rehabilitation is begun the day after surgery.[14] The following is one rehabilitation approach for a pitcher recovering from rotator cuff surgery[14]:

1. Passive shoulder abduction and external rotation are carried out in the first month.
2. Active assistive exercise takes place during the second month.
3. Active range of motion, stretching, and more difficult exercises are carried out from the third month on.
4. When full range of movement is acquired, usually by the end of the third month, throwing a ball for 30 feet is permitted.
5. Over the fourth and fifth months, throwing distances are increased slowly.
6. In the sixth month, three-fourths speed throwing is allowed.
7. The seventh to twelfth months are spent in regaining general physical strength and endurance.
8. By the twelfth month, competitive pitching is allowed.

Figure 24-46

Shoulder exercises using the Cybex isokinetic system.

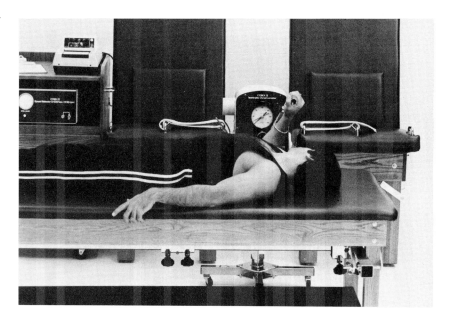

Glenohumeral Dislocation and Subluxation Rehabilitation

Exercise must be cautiously performed.[1] For athletes who have not had surgery, exercise should be performed as follows:

1. In cases of anterior dislocation, avoid positions of abduction and external rotation and emphasize adduction, forward flexion, and internal rotation.
2. In cases of posterior dislocation, avoid positions of abduction and internal rotation.
3. Avoid wide barbell grips or dumbbell positions.
4. Exercises performed on a bench should be executed only in the top third of the movement.
5. Pressing exercises should be performed in the lower half of the range.
6. For the anterior glenohumeral dislocation, special emphasis should be paid to strengthening the subscapular and teres major muscles for internal rotation (Fig. 24-47).
7. Exercise programming, in general, follows that for rotator cuff rehabilitation.

Acromioclavicular Injury Rehabilitation
Early Rehabilitation

Early rehabilitation begins after the acute stage of injury or after a surgical intervention and stays within pain-free limits. Because of tightness and/or weakness, the trapezius, pectoral, deltoid, latissimus dorsi, and arm muscles receive major emphasis.[1]

Shoulder range of motion Shoulder range of motion is gently increased by first free movements that include flexion, abduction, and internal and external rotation. Each movement is repeated five to ten times, twice daily. When these movements can be performed pain free, the athlete progresses to a towel-stretch sequence, including raising the arms overhead and stretching behind the back (Fig. 24-48).

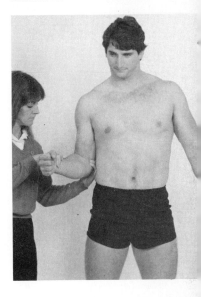

Figure 24-47

Strengthening the subscapular muscle for internal rotation.

Figure 24-48

Improving shoulder range of motion through towel exercising.

Figure 24-49

Dumbbell shoulder shrugs.

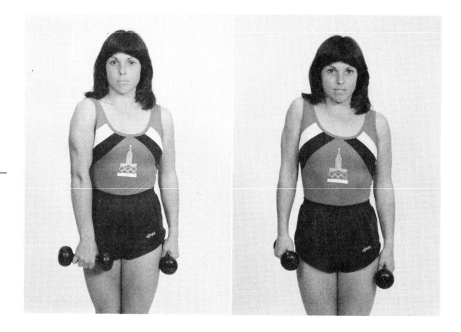

Figure 24-50

Shoulder shrugs with heavier
resistance.

Light-resistance shrugs The athlete exercises the upper trapezius muscle by performing shrugs against a light dumbbell resistance. *NOTE:* The weight should not be allowed to hang loosely, which strains the acromioclavicular joint. Light-resistance shrugs are performed five to ten times, twice daily (Fig. 24-49). This exercise should take the shoulder from an anterior position to elevation (shrugs) and then to a posterior position.

Upright rowing with light resistance For strengthening the anterior deltoid muscle, the athlete performs upright rowing against a light resistance. Each exercise is performed for five to ten repetitions, twice daily.

Resistance exercises for arm biceps and triceps muscles Elbow curls and extensions are performed with dumbbell resistance. The weight of the dumbbell should not be so much as to pull the shoulder downward. Each exercise is repeated five to ten times, twice daily.

Codman's pendular exercises As in Figs. 24-37 and 24-39, the athlete performs free exercise of Codman's pendular movement with limited weight. Movements are performed in a limited, pain-free range. This exercise is performed twice daily, and each movement is repeated five to ten times.

Intermediate Rehabilitation

When the shoulder is pain free and has almost full range of motion, intermediate rehabilitation can begin. Exercise can now be performed with more resistance and vigor.

Shrugs with heavier resistance Shoulder shrugs are performed against heavier resistance, such as that provided by the Universal apparatus (Fig. 24-50). The emphasis is on the strength development of the

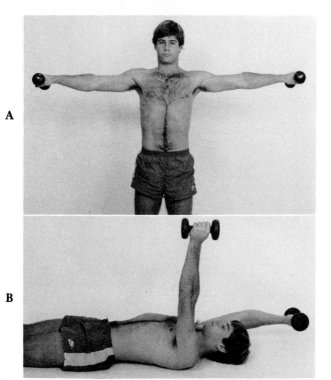

Figure 24-51

Variations in dumbbell
exercise. **A,** Adduction.
B, Flexion. **C,** Extension.
D, Presses. **E,** Chest crosses.

Specific Sports Injuries and
Other Problems

Figure 24-52

Overhead press.

Figure 24-53

Push-ups.

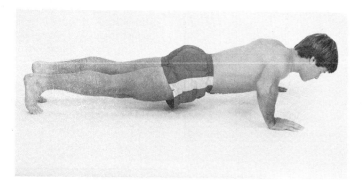

Figure 24-54

Variations in pulley exercises.
A, Cross-chest pulley
exercise. **B,** High shoulder
flexion. **C,** Horizontal
abduction.

A	B	C

  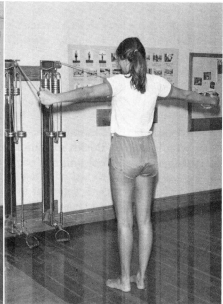

upper trapezius muscle. This exercise is performed in two or three sets of ten repetitions, three or four times a week.

Dumbbell exercises A variety of exercises with progressively heavier dumbbells are performed as indicated in Fig. 24-51. These exercises are performed in two or three sets of ten repetitions, three or four times a week.

Overhead presses Pressing a resistance overhead is valuable for strengthening the anterior deltoid muscle. Using a barbell or the Universal apparatus, the athlete presses as much weight as possible. This exercise is performed in two or three sets for ten repetitions, three or four times a week (Fig. 24-52).

Push-ups Push-ups are an excellent way to strengthen the shoulder complex, especially the anterior aspect of the shoulder and chest. Push-ups are performed in two or three sets for ten repetitions, three or four times a week (Fig. 24-53).

Pulley exercises Pulley exercises provide excellent intermediate rehabilitation for an acromioclavicular injury. Some of the possible exercises available are depicted in Fig. 24-54. Each exercise should be conducted for two or three sets with ten repetitions in each set, three or four times a week.

Dips and pull-ups Parallel bar dips and horizontal bar pull-ups are also excellent intermediate exercises for shoulder rehabilitation. As with the other exercises, they should be performed in two or three sets of ten repetitions, three or four times a week.

PNF for Shoulder Rehabilitation

PNF provides an excellent means of shoulder rehabilitation after an athletic injury. The principles of slow reversal described in Chapter 13 can help the injured shoulder develop strength and coordination (Appendix I-E).

REFERENCES

1. Allman, F.L.: Exercise in sports medicine. In Basmagian, J.V. (editor): Therapeutic exercise, ed. 3, Baltimore, 1978, The Wiliams & Wilkins Co.

2. Bowers, K.D.: Treatment of acromioclavicular sprains in athletes, Phys. Sportsmed. **11**:79, Jan. 1983.

3. Brunet, M.E., Haddad, R.J., and Porche, E.B.: Rotator cuff impingement syndromes in sports, Phys. Sportsmed. **10**:86, Dec. 1982.

4. Clancy, W.G.: Shoulder problems in overhead-overuse sports-introduction, Am. J. Sports Med. **7**:138, 1979.

5. Connolly, J.F. (editor): De Palma's the management of fractures and dislocations, vol. 1, ed. 3, Philadelphia, 1981, W.B. Saunders Co.

6. Fields, W.S.: Neurovascular syndromes of the neck and shoulders. In Joynt, R.J. (editor): Seminars in neurology, vol. 1, no. 4, New York, 1981, Thieme-Stratton, Inc.

7. Gieck, J.: Injuries to the acromioclavicular joint—mechanisms, diagnosis, and treatment, Ath. Train. **14**(1):22, 1979.

8. Hastings, D.E., and Coughlin, L.P.: Recurrent subluxation of the glenohumeral joint, Am. J. Sports Med. **9**:352, 1981.

9. Hawkins, R.J., and Hobeika, P.E.: Impingement syndrome in the athletic shoulder, Symposium on injuries to the shoulder in the athlete, Clinics in sports medicine, vol. 2, no. 2, Philadelphia, July 1983, W.B. Saunders Co.

10. Hawkins, R.J., and Kennedy, J.C.: Impingement syndromes in athletes, Am. J. Sports Med. **8**:151, 1980.

11. Henry, J.H., and Genung, J.A.: Natural history of glenohumeral dislocation—revisited, Am. J. Sports Med. **10**(3):135, 1982.

12. Hoppenfeld, S.: Physical examination of the spine and extremities, New York, 1976, Appleton-Century-Crofts.

13. Jobe, F.W.: Thrower problems, Am. J. Sports Med. **7**(2):139, 1979.

14. Jobe, F.W.: Serious rotator cuff injuries, Symposium on injuries to the shoulder in the athlete, Clinics in sports medicine, vol. 2, no. 2, Philadelphia, July 1983, W.B. Saunders Co.

15. Jobe, F.W., and Moynes, D.: Delineation of diagnostic criteria and a rehabilitation program for the rotator cuff injuries, Am. J. Sports Med. **10**:336, 1982.

16. Larsen, R.R.: Fractures about the shoulder, Am. J. Sports Med. **2**(1):48, 1974.

17. Matsen, F.A., and Zuckerman, J.D.: Anterior glenohumeral instability, Symposium on injuries to the shoulder in the athlete, Clinics in sports medicine, vol. 2, no. 2, Philadelphia, July 1983, W.B. Saunders Co.

18. Moynes, D.R.: Prevention of injury to the shoulder through exercises and therapy, Symposium on injuries to the shoulder in the athlete, Clinics in sports medicine, vol. 2, no. 2, Philadelphia, July 1983, W.B. Saunders Co.

19. Neer, C.S., and Walsh, R.P.: The shoulder in sports, Orthop. Clin. North Am. **8**:583, 1977.

20. Richardson, A.B.: Overuse syndrome in baseball, tennis, gymnastics and swimming, Symposium on injuries to the shoulder in the athlete: Clinics in sports medicine, vol. 2, no. 2, Philadelphia, July 1983, W.B. Saunders Co.

21. Samilson, R.L., and Prieto, V.: Posterior dislocation of the shoulder in athletes, Symposium on injuries to the shoulder in the athlete, Clinics in sports medicine, vol. 2, no. 2, Philadelphia, July 1983, W.B. Saunders Co.

22. Smith, M.J., and Stewart, M.J.: Acute acromioclavicular separations, Am. J. Sports Med. **7**(1):62, 1979.

23. Stoddard, G.: The physical rehabilitation of selected shoulder injuries, Athletic Training **7**:343, 1979.

24. Strauss, M.B., et al.: The shrugged-off shoulder: a comparison of patients with recurrent shoulder subluxations and dislocations, Phys. Sportsmed. **11**:85, March 1983.

25. Tank, R., and Halbach, J.: Physical therapy evaluation of the shoulder complex in athletes, J. Orothop. Sports Phys. Ther. **3**:108, Winter 1982.

26. Travell, J.G., and Simons, D.G.: Myofascial pain and dysfunction, Baltimore, 1983, The Williams & Wilkins Co.

27. Warren, R.F.: Subluxation of the shoulder in athletes, Symposium on injuries to the shoulder in the athlete, Clinics in sports medicine, vol. 2, no. 2, Philadelphia, July 1983, W.B. Saunders Co.

28. Wickiewicz, T.L.: Acromioclavicular and sternoclavicular injuries, Symposium on injuries to the shoulder in the athlete, Clinics in sports medicine, vol. 2, no. 2, Philadelphia, July 1983, W.B. Saunders Co.

29. Yocum, L.A.: Assessment of the shoulder, Symposium on injuries to the shoulder in the athlete, Clinics in sports medicine, vol. 2, no. 2, Philadelphia, July 1983, W.B. Saunders Co.

ADDITIONAL SOURCES

Birnbaum, J.S.: The musculoskeletal manual, New York, 1982, Academic Press, Inc.

Cailliet, R.: Neck and arm pain, ed. 2, Philadelphia, 1981, F.A. Davis Co.

Cantu, R.C.: Sports medicine in primary care, Lexington, Mass., 1982, The Collamore Press.

Cowen, M.H., and Torg, J.S.: Prevention and management of injuries to shoulder and elbow, Chicago, Teach'em, Inc. (Cassette.)

Davies, G.J., Gould, J.A., and Larson, R.L.: Functional examination of the shoulder girdle, Phys. Sportsmed. 9:82, June 1981.

Delacerda, F.G.: A comparative study of three months of treatment for shoulder girdle myofascial syndrome, J. Orthop. Sports Phys. Ther. 4:51, Summer 1982.

Gael, F.: Injuries of the hand. In O'Donoghue, D.H.: Treatment of injuries to athletes, ed. 4, Philadelphia, 1984, W.B. Saunders Co.

Huss, C.D., and Puhl, J.J.: Myositis ossificans of the upper arm, Am. J. Sports Med. 8(6):419, 1980.

Jobe, F.W. (editor): Symposium on injuries to the shoulder in the athlete, Clinics in sports medicine, vol. 2, no. 2, Philadelphia, July 1983, W.B. Saunders Co.

The management and prevention of injuries to shoulders and upper extremities, Chicago, Teach'em, Inc. (Cassette.)

McCue, F.: Throwing injuries of the shoulder complex, Mid-Atlantic Athletic Trainers Association Meeting, May 1983, National Athletic Trainers Association. (Cassette.)

O'Donoghue, D.H.: Treatment of injuries to athletes, Philadelphia, 1983, W.B. Saunders Co.

Penny, J.N., et al.: Shoulder impingement syndrome in athletes and their surgical management, Am. J. Sports. Med. 9(1):11, 1981.

Chapter 25

THE ELBOW, FOREARM, WRIST, AND HAND

When you finish this chapter, you should be able to

Describe the structural and functional anatomy and relate it to elbow, forearm, wrist, and hand sports injuries

Recognize and evaluate the major sports injuries to the elbow, forearm, wrist, and hand

Perform proper immediate and follow-up management of upper limb injuries

The upper limb including the elbow forearm, wrist, and hand is second to the lower limb in the number of sports injuries. Due to how it is used and its relative exposure, the upper limb is prone to acute and over use syndromes.

THE ELBOW JOINT
Anatomy
Structural Relationships

The elbow joint is composed of three bones: the humerus, the radius, and the ulna (Fig. 25-1). The lower end of the humerus forms two articulating condyles. The lateral condyle is the capitulum and the medial condyle is called the trochlea. The rounded capitulum articulates with the concave head of the radius. The trochlea, which is spool shaped, fits into an articulating groove, the semilunar notch, which is provided by the ulna between the olecranon and coronoid processes. Above each condyle is a projection called the epicondyle. The structural design of the elbow joint permits flexion and extension by the articulation of the trochlea with the semilunar notch of the ulna. Forearm pronation and supination are made possible because the head of the radius rests against the capitulum freely without any bone limitations.

The capsule of the elbow, both anteriorly and posteriorly, is relatively thin and covered by the brachial muscle in front and the triceps brachii behind. The capsule is reinforced by the ulnar and radial collateral ligaments. The ulnar collateral ligament is composed of a strong anterior band with weaker transverse and middle sheets. The radial collateral ligament does not attach to the radius, which is free to rotate. The radius rotates in the radial notch of the ulna and is stabilized by a strong annular ligament. The annular ligament is attached to the anterior and posterior margins of the radial notch and encircles the head and neck of the radius.

Synovium and Bursa

A common synovial membrane invests the elbow and the superior radioulnar articulations, lubricating the deeper structures of the two joints; a sleevelike capsule surrounds the entire elbow joint. The most important bursae in the area of the elbow are the bicipital and olecranon bursae. The bicipital bursa lies in the anterior aspect of the bicipital tuberosity and

Figure 25-2

Synovium and bursa of the elbow.

Figure 25-1

Bones and ligaments of the elbow.

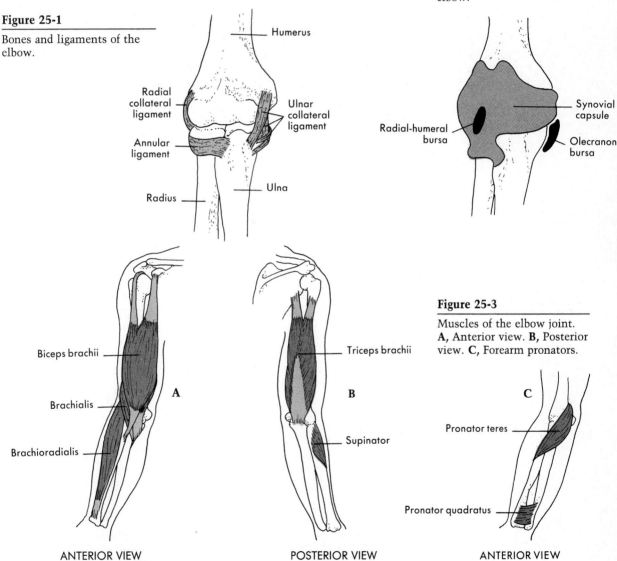

Humerus

Radial collateral ligament

Ulnar collateral ligament

Annular ligament

Radius

Ulna

Synovial capsule

Radial-humeral bursa

Olecranon bursa

Figure 25-3

Muscles of the elbow joint. **A,** Anterior view. **B,** Posterior view. **C,** Forearm pronators.

Biceps brachii

Brachialis

Brachioradialis

A

Triceps brachii

Supinator

B

C

Pronator teres

Pronator quadratus

ANTERIOR VIEW

POSTERIOR VIEW

ANTERIOR VIEW

Specific Sports Injuries and
Other Problems

cushions the tendon when the forearm is pronated. The olecranon bursa lies between the olecranon process and the skin, forming a liquid cushion (Fig. 25-2).

Muscles

The muscles of the elbow consist of the biceps brachii, and the brachial and brachioradial muscles, all of which in some way act in flexion. Extension is controlled by the triceps brachii (Fig. 25-3).

The biceps brachii and supinator muscles allow supination of the forearm, whereas the pronator teres and pronator quadratus act as pronators.

Blood and Nerve Supply

Superficial and close to the skin in front of the elbow lie the veins that return the blood of the forearm to the heart. Deep within the antecubital fossa lie the brachial and medial arteries that supply the area with oxygenated blood (Fig. 25-4).

Nerves stemming from the fifth to eighth cervical vertebrae and first thoracic vertebra control the elbow muscles. In the cubital fossa these nerves become the musculocutaneous, radial, and median nerves (Table 25-1).

Evaluation of the Elbow
Complaints

As with all sports injuries, the evaluator must first understand the possible mechanism of injury. The following questions will aid in evaluation of the elbow:

1. Is the pain or discomfort due to a direct trauma such as falling on an outstretched arm or landing on the tip of a bent elbow?
2. Can the problem be attributed to a sudden overextension of the elbow or to repeated overuse of a throwing-type motion?

The location and duration should be ascertained. As with shoulder pain, elbow pain or discomfort could be from internal organ dysfunction or referred from a nerve root irritation or nerve impingement.

1. Are there movements or positions of the arm that increase or decrease the pain?
2. Has a previous elbow injury been diagnosed or treated?
3. Is there a feeling of locking or crepitation on movement?

Figure 25-4

Arteries and nerves supplying the elbow joint, wrist, and hand.

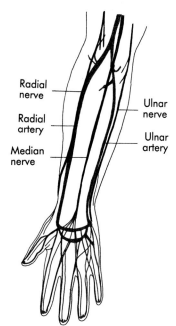

Radial
nerve

Radial
artery

Median
nerve

Ulnar
nerve

Ulnar
artery

TABLE 25-1

Resistive motion to determine muscle weakness related to elbow injury

Resistive Motion	Major Muscles Involved	Nerves
Elbow flexion	Biceps brachii	Musculocutaneous (cervical 5 and 6)
	Brachial	Musculocutaneous (cervical 5 and 6)
	Brachioradial	Radial (cervical 5 and 6)
Elbow extension	Triceps brachii	Radial (cervical 7 and 8)
Forearm supination	Biceps brachii	Musculocutaneous (cervical 5 and 6)
	Supinator	Radial (cervical 6)
Forearm pronation	Pronator teres	Median (cervical 6 and 7)
	Pronator quadratus	Median (cervical 8, thoracic 1)

General Observation

The athlete's elbow should be observed for obvious deformities and swellings. If permissible, the carrying angle, flexion, and extensibility of the elbow should be observed. If the carrying angle is abnormally increased, a cubitus valgus is present; if it is abnormally decreased, a cubitus varus is present (Fig. 25-5). Too great or too little of an angle may be indication of a bony or epiphyseal fracture. The athlete is next observed for the extent of elbow flexion and extension. Both elbows are compared (Fig. 25-6). A de-

Figure 25-5

Testing for elbow carrying angle and the extent of cubitus valgus and varus.

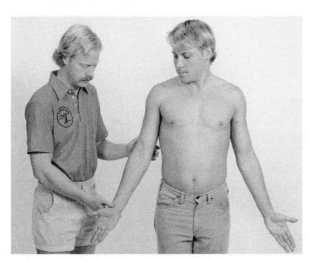

Figure 25-6

Testing for elbow flexion and extension.

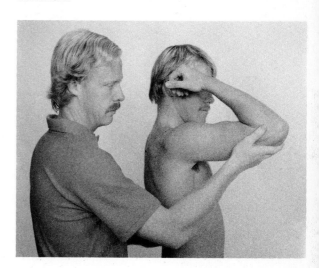

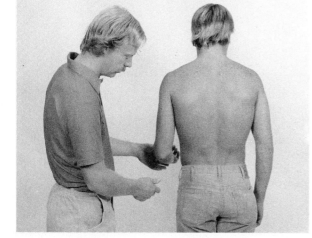

Figure 25-7

Testing for cubitus recurvatus (elbow hyperextension).

Figure 25-8

Determining whether the lateral and medial epicondyles, along with the olecranon process, form an isosceles triangle.

Specific Sports Injuries and
Other Problems

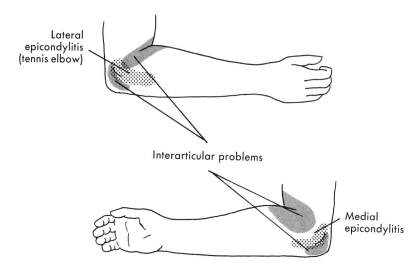

Figure 25-9

Typical pain sites in the
elbow region.

crease in normal flexion or an inability to fully extend or extending beyond
a normal extension (cubitus recurvatus) could be precipitating reasons for
joint problems (Fig. 25-7). Next, the elbow is bent to a 45-degree angle and
observed from the rear to determine whether or not the two epicondyles
and olecranon process form an isosceles triangle (Fig. 25-8).

Bony Palpation

Pain sites and deformities are determined by careful bony palpation of the
epicondyles, olecranon process, distal aspect of the humerus, and proximal
aspect of the ulna (Fig. 25-9). The radial head also must be palpated with
the athlete's arm abducted and the elbow bent. The radial head is located
approximately 1 inch (2.5 cm) distal to the lateral epicondyle. The athlete
supinates and pronates the forearm while pressure is applied to the radial
head. Pain on pressure may indicate a sprain of the annular ligament, a
fracture, or a chronic articular condition of the radial head.[10]

Soft Tissue Palpation

Soft tissue includes the following:
1. Distal aspect of the wrist flexor muscles
2. Pronator teres
3. Distal aspect of the wrist extensor muscles
4. Medial and lateral collateral ligaments
5. Brachioradial muscle
6. Biceps tendon
7. Cubital fossa and its contents, including the brachial artery, pulses,
   and median nerve

Circulatory and Neurological Evaluation

With an elbow injury, a pulse routinely should be taken of the brachial
artery located in the cubital fossa and the radial artery at the wrist.
   Alteration of skin sensation also should be noted, which could indicate
nerve root compression or irritation in the cervical or shoulder region or in

Figure 25-10

Functional evaluation
includes passive resistance
flexion and extension for
joint restrictions and pain.

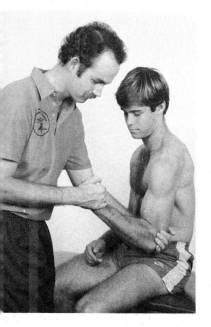

the elbow itself. Additional nerve evaluation is made through testing active and resistive motion (Table 25-1).

Functional Evaluation

The joint and muscles are evaluated for pain sites and weakness by passive, active, and resistive motions consisting of elbow flexion and extension (Fig. 25-10) and forearm pronation and supination (Fig. 25-11). Range of motion is particularly noted in passive and active pronation and supination (Fig. 25-12).

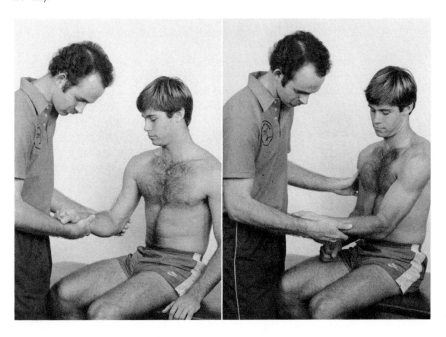

Figure 25-11

Elbow evaluation includes passive, active, and resistive forearm pronation and supination.

Figure 25-12

The range of motion of the forearm pronation and supination is routinely observed in elbow conditions.

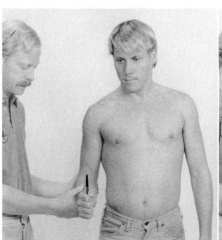
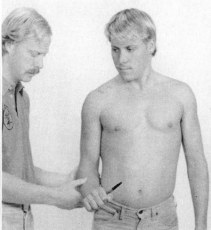
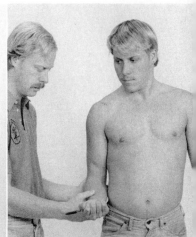

Specific Sports Injuries and
Other Problems

Figure 25-13

Testing for capsular pain
following a hyperextension of
the elbow. **A,** Wrist flexion.
B, Wrist extension.

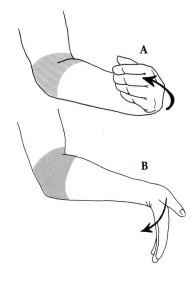

Tests for Ligamentous and Capsular Injury

A test for capsular pain after hyperextension of the elbow is as follows:

1. Flex the elbow in a 45-degree position.
2. Flex the wrist as far as possible.
3. Extend the wrist as far as possible (Fig. 25-13).

If joint pain is severe on this test, a moderate to severe sprain or fracture should be suspected.

The next test is for lateral and medial collateral ligament stability in the elbow. The following procedures should be conducted:

1. Grasp the athlete's wrist and extend the arm in an anatomical position.
2. The other hand of the evaluator is placed either over the lateral or medial epicondyle.
3. With the hand over the epicondyle acting as a fulcrum, the hand holding the athlete's wrist attempts to move the forearm.
4. In applying the stress, the evaluator notices whether there is an excursion or gapping of the lateral or medial collateral ligament (Fig. 25-14).

Symptoms and signs   The athlete complains of severe pain on the medial aspect of the elbow that becomes relieved by flexing the elbow. There is point tenderness on the medial epicondyle, distal aspect of the ulna, or lateral collateral ligament.

Tennis Elbow Test

Resistance is applied to the athlete's extended hand with the elbow flexed 45 degrees. A positive test will be moderate to severe pain at the lateral epicondyle (Fig. 25-15).

Figure 25-14

Collateral ligament test of
the elbow.

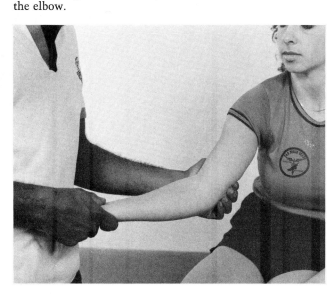

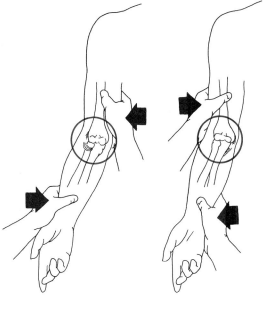

Mechanism of Elbow Injuries

As discussed in Chapter 9, elbow injuries can occur from a variety of mechanisms. The most common causes of injury are the overuse throwing mechanism and falling on the outstretched hand.

Injuries to the Elbow Region

The elbow is subject to injury in sports because of its broad range of motion, weak lateral bone arrangement, and relative exposure to soft tissue damage in the vicinity of the joint.

Contusions, Strains, and Sprains

Contusions Because of its lack of padding and its general vulnerability, the elbow often becomes contused in contact sports. Bone bruises arise from a deep penetration or a succession of blows to the sharp projections of the elbow. A contusion of the elbow may swell rapidly after an irritation of the olecranon bursa or the synovial membrane and should be treated immediately with cold and pressure for at least 24 hours. If injury is severe, the athlete should be referred to a physician for x-ray examination to determine if a fracture exists.

Olecranon bursitis The olecranon bursa (Fig. 25-16), lying between the end of the olecranon process and the skin, is the most frequently injured bursa in the elbow. Its superficial location makes it prone to acute or chronic injury, particularly as the result of direct blows. The inflamed bursa produces pain, marked swelling, and point tenderness. Occasionally, swelling will appear almost spontaneously and without the usual pain and heat. If the condition is acute, a cold compress should be applied for at least 1 hour. Chronic olecranon bursitis requires a program of superficial therapy. In some cases, aspiration will hasten healing. Although seldom serious, olecranon bursitis can be annoying and should be well protected by padding while the athlete is engaged in competition.

Strains The acute mechanisms of muscle strain associated with the elbow joint are usually excessive resistive motion, such as a fall on the outstretched hand with the elbow in extension that forces the joint into hyperextension. Repeated microtears causing chronic injury will be discussed under epicondylitis.

The biceps, brachial, and triceps muscles should be tested by active and resistive movement. The muscles of pronation and supination are also tested.

Symptoms and signs On active or resistive movement, the athlete complains of pain. There is usually point tenderness in the muscle, tendon, or lower part of the muscle belly.

Management Immediate care includes ICE-R and sling support for the more severe cases. Follow-up management may include cryotherapy, ultrasound, and rehabilitative exercises. Conditions that cause moderate to severe loss of elbow function should routinely be referred for x-ray examination. It is important to rule out the possibility of an avulsion or epiphyseal fracture.

Elbow sprains Sprains to the elbow are usually caused by hyperextension or valgus forces.

The two most common mechanisms of elbow injury:
  Throwing
  Falling on the outstretched hand

Figure 25-15

Tennis elbow test.

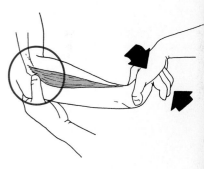

Figure 25-16

Olecranon bursitis.

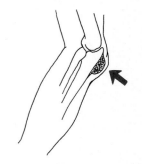

ELBOW EXTENSION RESTRICTION TAPING

The procedure for taping the elbow to prevent hyperextension is as follows:

Materials needed: One roll of 1½-inch (3.8 cm) tape, tape adherent, and 2-inch (5 cm) elastic bandage.

Position of the athlete: The athlete stands with the affected elbow flexed at 90 degrees.

Position of the operator: The operator stands facing the side of the athlete's affected arm.

Procedure

1. Apply two anchor strips loosely around the arm, approximately 2 inches (25 cm) to each side of the curve of the elbow (antecubital fossa).
2. Construct a checkrein by cutting a 10-inch (25 cm) and a 4-inch (10 cm) strip of tape and laying the 4-inch (10 cm) strip against the center of the 10-inch (25 cm) strip, blanking out that portion. Next place the checkrein so that it spans the two anchor strips, with the blanked-out side facing downward.
3. Place five additional 10-inch (25 cm) strips of tape over the basic checkrein.
4. Finish the procedure by securing the checkrein with three lock strips on each end. A figure-of-eight elastic wrap applied over the taping will prevent the tape from slipping because of perspiration.

Figure 25-17

Elbow extension restriction taping.

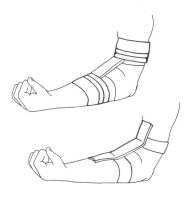

Management Immediate care for elbow sprains consists of cold and a pressure bandage for at least 24 hours with sling support fixed at 45 degrees of flexion. After hemorrhage has been controlled, superficial heat treatments in the form of the whirlpool may be started and combined with massage above and below the injury. Like fractures and dislocations, strains also may result in abnormal bone proliferation if the area is massaged directly and too vigorously or exercised too soon. The main concern should be to gently aid the elbow in regaining a full range of motion and then, when the time is right, to commence active exercises until full mobility and strength have returned. Taping can help and should restrain the elbow from further injury, or it may be used while the athlete is participating in sports (Fig. 25-17).

Epicondylitis Epicondylitis is a chronic condition that may affect athletes who execute repeated forearm pronation and supination movements such as are performed in tennis, pitching, golf, javelin throwing, and fencing. The elbow is particularly predisposed to mechanical trauma in the activities of throwing and striking.[1,12,16]

Epicondylitis is variously identified as "pitcher's elbow," "tennis elbow," "javelin thrower's arm," or "golfer's elbow." It is caused by the continuous forceful extension of the forearm accompanied by a severe twisting motion, such as when a pitcher throws a curve or screwball or when a tennis player applies English in returning a ball.

Pitcher's elbow   Baseball players who have begun curve ball pitching at too early an age appear especially vulnerable. The constant, repetitive, and violent torsion and extension to which the elbow joint is subjected over a period of time, as in pitching a baseball game, results in the pronator teres muscle being torn from its origin on the lower aspect of the inner condyloid ridge of the humerus. Stress can also sprain and even rupture the medial collateral ligament. Inadequate warm-up before throwing is another cause of this condition.

Tennis elbow   In tennis, improper techniques, poor conditioning, and a racket that is inappropriate for the level of play can cause severe stress in the elbow.[9] Usually this syndrome appears to be the result of continuous abuse, but on occasion it may result from a single incident.

Javelin thrower's elbow   Javelin throwers, like baseball pitchers, can place a great deal of stress on the elbow. The medial collateral ligament can be sprained or ruptured; forceful extension of the elbow can fracture the olecranon process (Fig. 25-18).

Golfer's elbow   The golfer's elbow, for example, on a right-handed player, involves microtears of the common flexor tendon of the medial condyle of the right elbow much like tennis elbow, but on the opposite arm and epicondyle.[5]

Symptoms and signs of epicondylitis   Regardless of the sport or exact location of the injury, the symptoms and signs are similar. Pain around the lateral aspect of the epicondyle of the humerus is produced

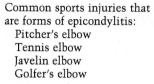

Common sports injuries that are forms of epicondylitis:
  Pitcher's elbow
  Tennis elbow
  Javelin elbow
  Golfer's elbow

Figure 25-18

Javelin throwing places a great strain on the elbow joint.

Elbow osteochondritis is
similar to that in the knee,
but less common.

on pronation and supination. The pain may be centered at the epicondyle
or it may radiate down the arm. There is usually point tenderness and in
some cases mild swelling. Passive movement of the arm in pronation and
supination seldom elicits pain, although active movement does.

Management of epicondylitis   Conservative management of moderate to severe epicondylitis usually includes a sling, rest, cryotherapy,
and/or heat through the application of ultrasound. Analgesic and/or anti-
inflammatory agents may be prescribed. A curvilinear brace applied just
below the bend of the elbow is highly beneficial in reducing stress to the
elbow. A conical brace provides counterforce, disseminating stress over a
wide area and relieving the concentration of forces directly on the bony
muscle attachments (Fig. 25-19). *NOTE:* In cases in which epicondylitis is
related to tennis, there must be a concern for proper grip size and string
tension.

Elbow Osteochondritis Dissecans

Although osteochondritis dissecans is more common in knees, it also occurs in elbows. Its cause is unknown; however, impairment of the blood
supply to the anterior surfaces leads to fragmentation and separation of a
portion of the articular cartilage and bone, creating a loose body within the
joint.

Symptoms and signs   The adolescent athlete usually complains of
sudden pain and locking of the elbow joint. Range of motion returns
slowly over a few days. Swelling, pain, and crepitation may also occur.

Management   If there are repeated episodes of locking, surgical removal of the loose bodies may be warranted. If they are not removed,
traumatic arthritis can occur.

Ulnar Nerve Injuries

Because of the exposed position of the medial humeral condyle, the ulnar
nerve is subject to a variety of problems. The athlete with a pronounced
cubitus valgus may develop a friction problem. The ulnar nerve can also
become recurrently dislocated due to a structural deformity. The ulnar
nerve can become impinged by the arcuate ligament in flexion-type activities. Repeated direct pressure is another source of elbow joint irritation.

Symptoms and signs   Rather than being painful, ulnar nerve injuries
usually respond by a paresthesia to the fourth and fifth fingers.[5] The athlete complains of burning and tingling in the fourth and fifth fingers.

Management   The management of ulnar nerve injuries is conservative; aggravation of the nerve, such as placing direct pressure on it, is
avoided. When stress on the nerve cannot be avoided, surgery may be
performed to transpose it anteriorly to the elbow.

Dislocation of the Elbow

Dislocation of the elbow (Fig. 25-20) has a high incidence in sports activity
and is caused most often either by a fall on the outstretched hand with the
elbow in a position of hyperextension or by a severe twist while it is in a
flexed position. The bones of the ulna and radius may be displaced backward, forward, or laterally. By far the most common dislocation is one in
which both the ulna and the radius are forced backward. The appearance of

Figure 25-19

Curvelinear brace for tennis
elbow.

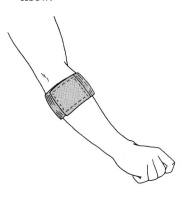

Athletes with a pronounced
elbow valgus are prone to
injuring the ulnar nerve.

the foward-displaced ulna or radius appears deformed. The olecranon process extends posteriorly, well beyond its normal alignment with the humerus. This dislocation may be distinguished from the supracondylar fracture by observing that the lateral and medial epicondyles are normally aligned with the shaft of the humerus.

Symptoms and signs Elbow dislocations involve rupturing and tearing of most of the stabilizing ligamentous tissue, accompanied by profuse hemorrhage and swelling. There is severe pain and disability. The complications of such traumas include injury to the median and radial nerves, as well as to the major blood vessels and arteries, and—in almost every instance—myositis ossificans.

Management The primary responsibility is to immediately apply cold and pressure, then a sling, and to refer the athlete to a physician for reduction. Reducing an elbow dislocation should never be attempted by anyone other than a physician. It must be performed as soon as possible to prevent prolonged derangement of soft tissue. In most cases the physician will administer an anesthetic before reduction to relax spasmed muscles. After reduction, the physician will often immobilize the elbow in a position of flexion and apply a sling suspension, which should be used for approximately 3 weeks. While the arm is maintained in flexion, the athlete should execute hand gripping and shoulder exercises. When initial healing has taken place, heat and gentle, passive exercise may be applied to help regain a full range of motion. Above all, massage and joint movements that are too strenuous should be avoided before complete healing has occurred because of the high probability of encouraging myositis ossificans. Both range of movement and a strength program should be initiated by the athlete, but forced stretching must be avoided.

Fractures of the Elbow

An elbow fracture can occur in almost any sports event and is usually caused by a fall on the outstretched hand or the flexed elbow or by a direct

Figure 25-20

Elbow dislocation.

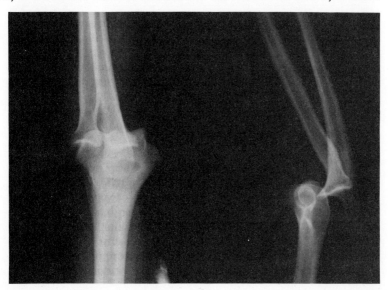

MANAGEMENT PLAN FOR POSTERIOR ELBOW DISLOCATION

Injury Situation	A female athlete fell from the uneven bars, landing on her outstretched left hand. The elbow was forced into hyperextension, dislocating the radial head posteriorly.
Symptoms and Signs	The athlete complained of extreme pain in the elbow region and numbness in the forearm and hand. From the side view the forearm appeared shortened. An obvious deformity was that the radial head stuck out beyond the posterior aspect of the elbow.
Management Plan	The athlete was referred immediately to a physician who performed an x-ray examination of the elbow to rule out fracture. After the x-ray examination, the elbow was reduced by the physician and placed in a cast and sling at 60 degrees for 6 weeks.

1 **Management Phase**

GOAL DURING IMMOBILIZATION PHASE: To maintain wrist and hand strength and shoulder range of motion while elbow is immobilized
Estimated length of time (ELT): 6 weeks

Exercise Rehabilitation

Ball squeeze (10-15 repetitions), each waking hour
Shoulder circles in all directions (10-15 repetitions), each waking hour. General body maintenance exercises are conducted 3 times a week as long as they do not aggravate injury

2 **Management Phase**

GOAL AFTER CAST IS REMOVED: To increase isometric strength and begin active range of motion
ELT: 2-3 weeks

Therapy

Ice packs (5-15 min) preceding exercise, 3-4 times daily

Exercise Rehabilitation

Continue exercises performed during immobilization phase, 3-4 times daily
Isometric exercise (2 or 3 times), every waking hour
Pain-free active flexion and extension and forearm pronation and supination (10-15 repetitions), every waking hour; *avoid forcing movement*
Proprioceptive neuromuscular facilitation (PNF) also can be beneficial
General body maintenance exercises are conducted 3 times a week as long as they do not aggravate injury

3 **Management Phase**

GOALS: 50% full range of motion, 50% strength and coordination
ELT: 4-6 weeks

Therapy

Ice packs (5-15 min) preceding exercise, 2-3 times daily

Exercise Rehabilitation

Isokinetic or isotonic exercise against dumbbell resistance, once daily, using DAPRE concept
PNF is also beneficial, emphasizing elbow flexion and extension and forearm supination and pronation.
General body maintenance exercises are conducted 3 times a week, as long as they do not aggravate injury.

4	Management Phase	GOALS: To restore 90% of elbow range of motion and strength, including power, endurance, and coordination ELT: 4-6 weeks
	Therapy	Ice packs (5-15 min) preceding exercise
	Exercise Rehabilitation	Continue Phase 3 exercises and add isotonic machine resistance or free-weight barbell exercises; bar dips and chin-ups (10 repetitions), 3-4 times a week, can be added to routine
5	Management Phase	GOAL: To reenter competition ELT: 4-6 weeks
	Exercise Rehabilitation	Continue Phase 4 exercises 3-4 times a week Return to daily gymnastic practice within pain-free limits If elbow becomes symptomatic in any way, such as pain, swelling, or decreased range of motion, athlete is to return to Phase 3 or 4 exercise program

Criteria for Returning to Gymnastics Competition

The athlete must be able to do the following:

1. Extend and flex the elbow to at least 95% of the uninjured elbow
2. Pronate and supinate the forearm to at least 95% of the uninjured arm
3. Perform an elbow curl 10 times, for 3 sets, against a resistance equal to or greater than that which can be handled by the uninjured elbow (This could be measured by an isokinetic testing device)
4. Perform an elbow extension 10 times, for 3 sets, against a resistance equal to or greater than that which can be handled by the uninjured elbow (This also can be measured by an isokinetic testing device)
5. Pronate and supinate the forearm against a resistance equal to or greater than that which can be handled by the uninjured forearm
6. Perform 10 full bar dips
7. Perform 10 chin-ups
8. Perform a full routine on the uneven bars without causing discomfort

Specific Sports Injuries and
Other Problems

blow to the elbow (Fig. 25-21). Children and young athletes have a much higher rate of this injury than do adults. A fracture can take place in any one or more of the bones that compose the elbow. A fall on the outstretched hand quite often fractures the humerus above the condyles, the condyles proper, or the area between the condyles. The ulna and/or radius also may be the recipients of trauma, and direct force delivered to the olecranon process of the ulna or a force transmitted to the head of the radius may cause a fracture. An elbow fracture may or may not result in visible deformity. There usually will be hemorrhage, swelling, and muscle spasm in the injured area.

Volkmann's Contracture

Volkman's contracture is a major complication of a serious elbow injury.

It is essential that athletes sustaining a serious elbow injury have their brachial or radial pulse monitored periodically. It is most often associated with a humeral supracondylar fracture. A possible complication of the humeral fracture is Volkmann's contracture or paralysis, which is caused by muscle spasm, swelling, or bone pressure on the brachial artery that inhibits blood circulation to the forearm, wrist, and hand.

Such a contracture can become permanent. The first indication of this problem is pain in the forearm that becomes greater when the fingers are passively extended. This is followed by cessation of the brachial and radial pulses.

Figure 25-21

Fracture in region of the elbow. **A,** Fracture of the head of the radius and also shaft of ulna. **B,** Impacted fracture of the head of the radius.

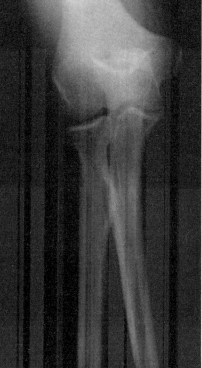

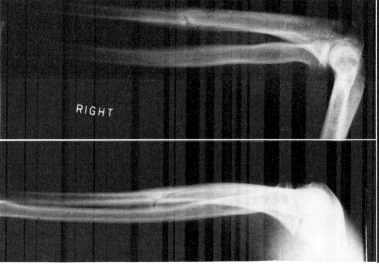

RIGHT

A

B

Rehabilitation of the Elbow

While the elbow is immobilized after an acute injury, the athlete should perform general body exercises, as well as exercises specific to the shoulder and wrist joint. In some cases isometric exercise is appropriate while the elbow is immobilized. Maintaining the strength of these articulations will speed the recovery of the elbow. After the elbow has healed and free movement is permitted by the physician, the first consideration should be restoration of the normal range of movement. Lengthening the contracted tendons and supporting tissue around the elbow requires daily mild active exercises. *NOTE:* Passive stretching may be detrimental to the athlete regaining full ROM. Forced stretching must be avoided at all times. PNF and isokinetic exercises are valuable in the early and intermediate active stage of rehabilitation. When the full range of motion has been regained (Fig. 25-22), a graded, progressive, resistive exercise program should be initiated, including flexion, extension, pronation, and supination (Fig. 25-23). Protective taping must be continued until full strength and flexibility have been restored. Long-standing chronic conditions of the elbow usually cause gradual debilitation of the surrounding soft tissue. Elbows with conditions of this type should be restored to the maximal state of conditioning without encouraging postinjury aggravation.

THE FOREARM
Anatomy
Structural Relationships

The bones of the forearm are the ulna and the radius (Fig. 25-24). The ulna, which may be thought of as a direct extension of the humerus, is long, straight, and larger at its upper end than at its lower end. The radius, considered an extension of the hand, is thicker at its lower end than at its upper end. The forearm has three articulations: the superior, middle, and distal radioulnar joints. The superior radioulnar articulation is a pivot joint, moving in a ring that is formed by the ulna and the annular ligament. The middle radioulnar joint, which is the junction between the shafts of the ulna and the radius, is held together by the oblique cord and the interosseous membrane. The oblique cord is a small band of ligamentous fibers that are attached to the lateral side of the ulna and pass downward and laterally to the radius. The interosseous membrane is a thin sheet of fibrous tissue that runs downward from the radius of the ulna and transmits forces directly through the hand from the radius to the ulna. The middle radioulnar joint provides a surface for muscle attachments; also, at the upper end, as at the lower end, there is an opening for blood vessels. The distal radioulnar joint is a pivot joint formed by the articulation of the head of the ulna with a small notch on the radius. It is held securely by the anterior and posterior radioulnar ligaments. The inferior ends of the radius and ulna are bound by an articular, triangular disk that allows a radial movement of 180 degrees into supination and pronation.

Muscles

The forearm muscles consist of flexors and pronators that are positioned anteriorly and of extensors and supinators that lie posteriorly. The flexors

Figure 25-22

Restoring full range of movement is essential in elbow rehabilitation.

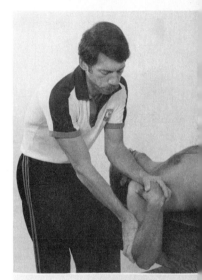

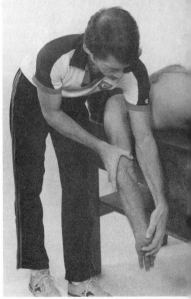

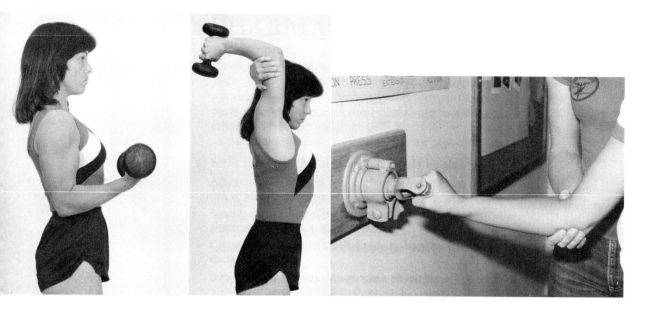

Figure 25-23

A very gradual program of progressive resistance exercise is important to elbow rehabilitation.

Figure 25-24

Bones of the forearm.

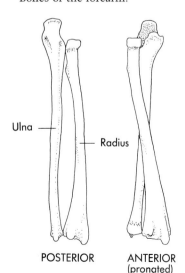

POSTERIOR   ANTERIOR (pronated)

of the wrist and fingers are separated into superficial muscles and deep muscles (Fig. 25-25). The deep flexors arise from the ulna, radius, and interosseous tissue anteriorly, whereas the superficial flexors come from the internal humeral condyle. The extensors of the wrist and fingers originate on the posterior aspect and the external condyle of the humerus.

Blood and Nerve Supply

The major blood supply stems from the brachial artery, which divides into the radial and ulnar artery in the forearm.

Except for the flexor carpi ulnaris and half of the flexor digitorum profundus, most of the flexor muscles of the forearm are supplied by the median nerve. The majority of the extensor muscles are controlled by the radial nerve.

Evaluating Forearm Injuries

Sports injuries of the forearm are easily detectable because of the amount of exposure of both the ulna and the radius. Recognition of an injury is accomplished mainly through observation of the range of motion present and visible deviations and through the use of palpation. The forearm is first tested as to the amount of pronation and supination possible, 150 degrees being considered average. Next it is tested for wrist flexion and extension, with 150 degrees again considered normal. Injury may be reflected in the visible indications of deformity or paralysis. Palpation can reveal a false joint, bone fragments, or a lack of continuity between bones.

Injuries to the Forearm

Lying between the elbow joint and the wrist and hand, the forearm is indirectly influenced by injuries to these areas; however, direct injuries can also occur.

Contusions

The forearm is constantly exposed to bruising in contact sports such as football. The ulnar side receives the majority of blows in arm blocks and, consequently, the greater amount of bruising. Bruises to this area may be classified as acute or chronic. The acute contusion can result in a fracture; but this happens only rarely.

Symptoms and signs   Most often a muscle or bone develops varying degrees of pain, swelling, and hematoma. The chronic contusion develops from repeated blows to the forearm with attendant multiple irritations. Heavy fibrosis may take the place of the hematoma, and a bony callus has been known to arise out of this condition.

Management   Care of the contused forearm requires proper attention in the acute stages by application of ICE-R for at least 1 hour, followed the next day by cryotherapy or superficial heat. Protection of the forearm is important for athletes who are prone to this condition. The best protection consists of a full-length sponge rubber pad for the forearm early in the season.

Strains

Forearm strain can occur in a variety of sports; most such injuries come from a severe static contraction. Repeated static contraction can lead to forearm splints.

Forearm splints   Forearm splints, like shinsplints, are difficult to manage. They occur most often in gymnasts, particularly to those who perform on the side horse.

Symptoms and signs   The main symptom is a dull ache between the extensor muscles, crossing the back of the forearm. There also may be

Forearm splints, like shin splints, commonly occur early and late in the sports season.

Figure 25-25

Muscles of the forearm. **A,** Anterior view. **B,** Posterior view.

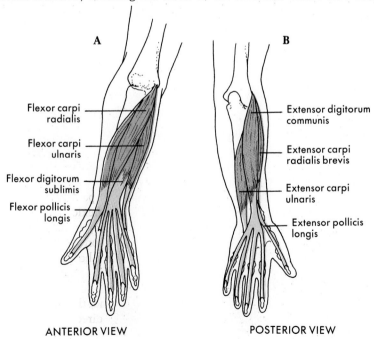

Flexor carpi radialis

Flexor carpi ulnaris

Flexor digitorum sublimis

Flexor pollicis longis

Extensor digitorum communis

Extensor carpi radialis brevis

Extensor carpi ulnaris

Extensor pollicis longis

A

B

ANTERIOR VIEW

POSTERIOR VIEW

weakness and extreme pain on muscle contraction. Palpation reveals an irritation of the interosseous membrane and surrounding tissue. The cause of this condition is uncertain; like shinsplints, forearm splints usually appear either early or late in the season, which indicates poor conditioning or fatigue, respectively. The pathological process is believed to result from the constant static muscle contractions of the forearm, for example, those required to stabilize the side horse participant. Continued isometric contraction causes minute tissue tears in the area of the interosseous membrane.

Management Care of forearm splints is symptomatic. If the problem occurs in the early season, the athlete should concentrate on increasing the strength of the forearm through resistance exercises, but if it arises late in the season, emphasis should be placed on rest, cryotherapy, or heat and use of a supportive wrap during activity.

Fractures

Fractures of the forearm (Fig. 25-26) are particularly common among active children and youths and occur as the result of a blow or a fall on the outstretched hand. Fractures to the ulna or the radius singly are much rarer than simultaneous fractures to both. The break usually presents all the features of a long bone fracture: pain, swelling, deformity, and a false joint. If there is a break in the upper third, the pronator teres muscle has a tendency to pull the forearm into an abduction deformity, whereas fractures of the lower portion of the arm are often in a neutral position. The older the athlete, the greater the danger is of extensive damage to soft tissue and the greater the possibility of paralysis from Volkmann's contractures.

To prevent complications from arising, a cold pack must be applied immediately to the fracture site, the arm splinted and put in a sling, and the athlete referred to a physician. The athlete will usually be incapacitated for about 8 weeks.

Figure 25-26

A fracture of the radius and ulna.

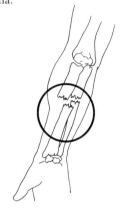

Figure 25-27

Colles fracture. **A,** Common appearance of the forearm in Colles fracture. **B,** Fracture of the distal radius and ulna styloid process.

A

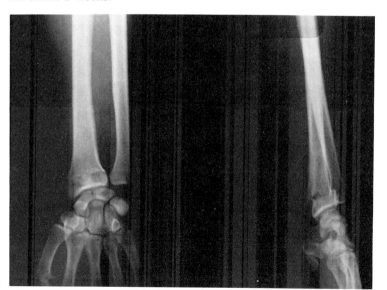

B

Colles' fracture Colles' fractures (Fig. 25-27) are among the most common types and involve the lower end of the radius and/or ulna. The mechanism of injury is usually a fall on the outstretched hand, forcing the radius and ulna backward and upward (hyperextension).

Symptoms and signs In most cases there is a forward displacement of the radius that causes a visible deformity to the wrist. Sometimes no deformity is present, and the injury may be passed off as a bad sprain—to the detriment of the athlete. Bleeding is quite profuse in this area with the extravasated fluids causing extensive swelling in the wrist and, if unchecked, in the fingers and forearm. Ligamentous tissue is usually unharmed, but tendons may be torn and avulsed, and there may possibly be median nerve damage.

Management The main responsibility is to apply a cold compress, splint the wrist, put the limb in a sling, and then refer the athlete to a physician for x-ray examination and immobilization. Severe sprains should always be treated as possible fractures. Lacking complications, the Colles' fracture will keep an athlete out of sports for 1 to 2 months. It should be noted that what appears to be a Colles' fracture in children and youths is often a lower epiphyseal separation. *NOTE:* Forearm exercise rehabilitation is discussed on p. 475.

THE WRIST AND HAND
Anatomy
Structural Relationships

The wrist, or carpus, is formed by the union of the distal aspect of the radius and the articular disk of the ulna with three of the four proximal (of the eight diversely shaped) carpal bones. Appearing in order from the radial to the ulnar side in the first or proximal row are the navicular, lunate, triangular (triquetral), and pisiform bones; the distal row consists of the

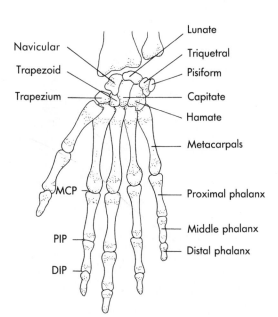

Figure 25-28

Bones of the wrist and hand.

Navicular
Trapezoid
Trapezium
MCP
PIP
DIP

Lunate
Triquetral
Pisiform
Capitate
Hamate
Metacarpals
Proximal phalanx
Middle phalanx
Distal phalanx

greater multangular (trapezium), lesser multangular (trapezoid), capitate, and hamate bones (Fig. 25-28).

The concave surfaces of the lower ends of the radius and ulna articulate with the curved surfaces of the first row of carpal bones, with the exception of the pisiform, which articulates with the articular disk interposed between the head of the ulna and the triquetral bone. This radiocarpal joint is a condyloid joint and permits flexion, extension, abduction, and circumduction. Its major strength is drawn from the great number of tendons that cross it rather than from its bone structure or ligamentous arrangement. The articular capsule is a continuous cover formed by the merging of the radial and the ulnar collateral, volar radiocarpal, and dorsal radiocarpal ligaments.

The carpal bones   The carpal bones articulate with one another in arthrodial or gliding joints and combine their movements with those of the radiocarpal joint and the carpometacarpal articulations. They are stabilized by anterior, posterior, and connecting interosseous ligaments.

The metacarpal bones and phalanges   The metacarpal bones are five bones that join the carpal bones above and the phalanges below, forming metacarpophalangeal articulations of a condyloid type and permitting flexion, extension, abduction, adduction, and circumduction. As is true for the carpal bones each joint has an articular capsule that is reinforced by collateral and accessory volar ligaments.

The interphalangeal articulations are of the hinge type, permitting only flexion and extension. Their ligamentous and capsular support is basically the same as that of the metacarpophalangeal (**MCP**) joints.

The thumb varies slightly at its carpometacarpal joint and is classified as a saddle joint that allows rotation on its long axis in addition to the other metacarpophalangeal movements.

Ligaments

There are numerous wrist and hand ligaments; however, only those concerned with sports injuries will be emphasized.

Ligaments of the wrist   The wrist is composed of many ligaments that bind the carpal bones to one another, to the ulna and radius, and to the proximal metacarpal bones. Of major interest in wrist injuries are the collateral ulnar ligament, extending from the tip of the styloid process of

Figure 25-29

Ligaments of the wrist.

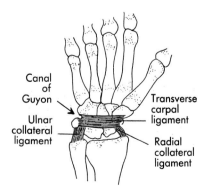

Canal
of
Guyon

Ulnar
collateral
ligament

Transverse
carpal
ligament

Radial
collateral
ligament

Figure 25-30

Ligaments of the phalanges.

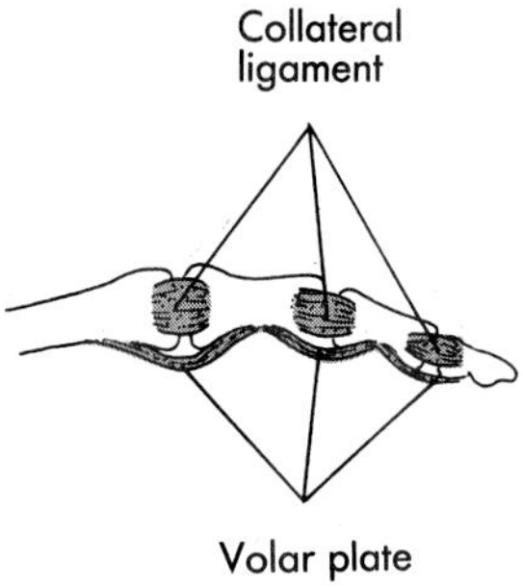

Collateral
ligament

Volar plate

Figure 25-31

Tendons of the phalanges.

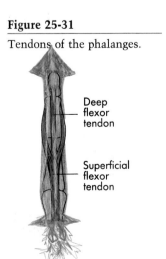

Deep
flexor
tendon

Superficial
flexor
tendon

the ulna to the pisiform bone, and the triquetral bone and collateral radial ligament that extends from the styloid process of the radius to the navicular bone (scaphoid). Crossing the volar aspect of the carpal bones is the transverse carpal ligament. This ligament serves as the roof of the carpal tunnel, in which the median nerve is often compressed (Fig. 25-29).

Ligaments of the phalanges The proximal interphalangeal (**PIP**) joints have the same design as the metacarpophalangeal joints. They comprise the collateral ligaments, palmar fibrocartilages, and a loose dorsal capsule or synovial membrane protected by an extensor expansion (Fig. 25-30).

Musculature

The wrist and hand are a complex of extrinsic and intrinsic muscles. See Table 25-2 for a discussion of the major muscles in the hand and wrist.

Blood and Nerve Supply

The arteries that supply the wrist and hand are the radial and ulnar arteries. They create two arterial arches; the superficial palmar arch is the largest and most distal to the hand, and the second is the deep palmar arch (Fig. 25-31).

The three major nerves of the hand are the ulnar, radial, and median nerves. The ulnar nerve comes to the hand by passing between the pisiform bone and the hook of the hamate bone. The radial nerve enters the wrist from the back of the forearm between the superficial and deep extensor muscles where it terminates in the back of the carpus. The median nerve enters the palm of the hand via the carpal tunnel (Table 25-2).

The sensory pattern of peripheral nerves can be seen in Fig. 25-32. The radial nerve may or may not follow this pattern.[4]

Evaluation of the Wrist and Hand
Complaints

As with other conditions, the evaluator asks about the location and type of pain:

1. What increases or decreases the pain?
2. Has there been a history of trauma or overuse?
3. What therapy or medications, if any, have been given?

Observations

As the athlete is observed, arm and hand asymmetries are noted:

1. Are there any postural deviations?
2. Does the athlete hold the part in a stiff or protected manner?
3. Is the wrist or hand swollen?

Hand usage such as writing or unbuttoning a shirt is noted. The general attitude of the hand is observed (Fig. 25-33). When the athlete is asked to open and close the hand, the evaluator notes whether this can be performed fully and rhythmically. Another general functional activity is to have the athlete touch the tip of the thumb to each fingertip several times. The last factor to be observed is the color of the fingernails. Nails that are very pale instead of pink may indicate a problem in blood circulation.

MCP
Metacarpophalangeal joint

PIP
Proximal interphalangeal joint

DIP
Distal interphalangeal joint

Circulation impairment must be noted as soon as possible in any wrist and hand injury.

Figure 25-32

Sensory patterns of peripheral nerves in the hand.

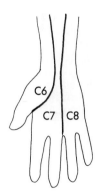

Bony Palpation

Wrist region   The bones of the wrist region are felt for pain and defects. The following anatomical sites are palpated:
With the wrist in ulnar flexion
1. Radial styloid process
2. Navicular bone (scaphoid) through the anatomical snuffbox
3. Trapezium
4. First metacarpal bone

TABLE 25-2

Resistive motion to determine muscle weakness related to wrist and hand injury

Resistive Motion	Major Muscles Involved	Nerves
Wrist flexion	Flexor carpi radialis	Median, cervical 6 and 7
	Flexor carpi ulnaris	Ulnar, cervical 8, thoracic 1
Wrist extension	Extensor carpi radialis longus	Radial, cervical 6 and 7
	Extensor carpi radialis brevis	Radial, cervical 6 and 7
	Extensor carpi ulnaris	Radial, cervical 6-8
Flexion of MCP joints of fingers	Lumbrical	Median, ulnar, cervical 6-8
	Interossei dorsalis	Ulnar, cervical 8, thoracic 1
	Interossei palmares	Ulnar, cervical 8, thoracic 1
Flexion of PIP and DIP joints of fingers	Flexor digitorum superficialis	Median, cervical 7 and 8, thoracic 1
Extension of MCP joints of fingers	Extensor digitorum	Radial, cervical 6-8
	Extensor indicis	
	Extensor digiti minimi	Radial, cervical 6-8
Finger abduction	Interossei dorsalis	Ulnar
	Abductor digiti	Cervical 8, thoracic 1
Finger adduction	Interossei palmares	Ulnar, cervical 8, thoracic 1
Thumb flexion	Flexor pollicis brevis	
	Lateral portion	Median, cervical 6 and 7
	Medial portion	Ulnar, cervical 8, thoracic 1
	Flexor pollicis longus	Cervical 8, thoracic 1
Thumb extension	Extensor pollicis brevis	Radial, cervical 6 and 7
	Extensor pollicis longus	Radial, cervical 6-8
Thumb abduction	Abductor pollicis longus	Radial, cervical 6 and 7
	Abductor pollicis brevis	Median, cervical 6 and 7
Thumb adduction	Adductor pollicis	Ulnar, cervical 8, thoracic 1
Thumb opposition	Opponens pollicis	Median, cervical 6 and 7
Fifth-finger opposition	Opponens digiti minimi	Ulnar, cervical 6 and 7

With the wrist straight
1. Distal head of the radius
2. Lunate bone
3. Capitate bone
4. Ulnar styloid
5. Triquetral bone
6. Pisiform bone
7. Hook of the hamate bone

Hand region
1. First metacarpal bone
2. MCP joint
3. Each phalanx, starting with the PIP joint, progressing to the distal interphalangeal (**DIP**) joint

At rest

Figure 25-33

General normal attitudes of the hand.

Normal fist   Clenched fist

Soft Tissue Palpation

Wrist region   Each tendon is palpated as it crosses the wrist region. Of major importance is the palpation of the six dorsal wrist tunnels, the carpal tunnel, and the tunnel of Guyon on the volar aspect. Pain at the site of the first tunnel may indicate stenosing tenosynovitis or de Quervain's disease. Point tenderness is an indication for administering the de Quervain's test.

Hand region   The soft tissue of the hand is palpated as follows:
1. Thenar and hypothenar region
2. Palmar aponeurosis
3. Flexor muscles

Dorsal aspect
1. Extension tendons
2. Phalanges

Special Tests for the Hand and Wrist

Test for de Quervain's disease   The athlete makes a fist with the thumb tucked inside. The wrist is then deviated into ulnar flexion. Sharp pain is good evidence of stenosing tenosynovitis.[10] Pain over the carpal tunnel could mean a carpal tunnel syndrome affecting the median nerve. On occasion the flexor tendons also become trapped, making finger flexion difficult. Any symptoms of carpal tunnel syndrome are an indication for testing using the tapping sign and wrist press test.

The tapping sign for carpal tunnel syndrome   The tapping sign for carpel tunnel syndrome is performed by tapping over the transverse carpal ligament. It is a positive test if pain or paresthesia is elicited (Fig. 25-34).

Wrist press   Another common test for carpal tunnel syndrome is the wrist press test. The athlete is instructed to flex both wrists as far as possible and press them together. This position is held for approximately 1 minute.[10] If this test is positive, pain will be produced in the region of the carpal tunnel (Fig. 25-35).

Figure 25-34

Tapping over the transverse carpal ligament to test for carpal tunnel syndrome.

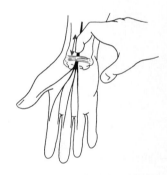

Figure 25-35

Wrist press for carpal tunnel syndrome.

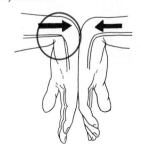

Circulatory and Neurological Evaluation

The hands should be inspected as to whether circulation is being impeded. The hands should be felt for their temperature. A cold hand or portion of a hand is a sign of decreased circulation. Pinching the fingernails can also help to indicate circulatory problems. Pinching will blanch the nail, and on release there should be rapid return of a pink color. Another objective test is Allen's test.

Testing the radial and ulnar arteries of the hand Allen's test is used to determine the function of the radial and ulnar arteries supplying the hand.[10] The athlete is instructed to squeeze the hand tightly into a fist and then open it fully three or four times. While the athlete is holding the last fist, the evaluator places firm pressure over each artery. The athlete is then instructed to open the hand. The palm should now be blanched. One of the arteries is then released and, if normal, the hand will instantly become red. The same process is repeated with the other artery (Fig. 25-36).

The hand is next evaluated for sensation alterations, especially in cases of suspected tunnel impingements. Nerve involvements will be further evaluated when active and resistive movements are initiated.

Functional Evaluation

Range of motion is noted in all movements of the wrist and fingers. Active and resistive movements are then compared to the uninjured wrist and hand. The following sequence should be conducted:

Wrist: Flexion, extension, radial and ulnar deviation
MCP: Flexion, extension
PIP and DIP joints: Flexion, extension
Finger: Abduction, adduction
MCP, PIP, and DIP joints of the thumb: Flexion and extension
Thumb: Abduction, adduction, opposition
Fifth finger: Opposition

Figure 24-36

Testing the radial and ulnar
arteries of the hand.

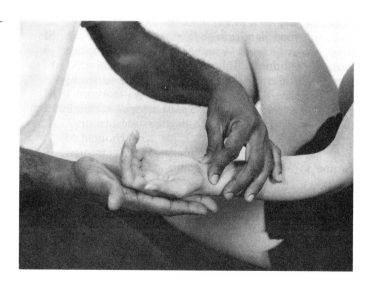

Passive, active, and resistive movements are performed in the wrist and hand. Table 25-2 indicates the extent of strength of the major wrist and hand muscles.

Injuries to the Wrist

Injuries to the wrist usually occur from a fall on the outstretched hand or repeated flexion, extension, or rotary movements[6] (Fig 25-37).

Figure 25-37

Wrist injuries commonly occur from falls on the outstretched hand or from repeated flexion, extension, lateral, or rotary movements.

A, courtesy St. Louis Baseball Cardinals.

G. Robert Bishop

Strains and Sprains

It is often very difficult to distinguish between injury to the muscle tendons crossing the wrist joint or the supporting structure of the carpal region. Therefore, emphasis will be placed on the condition of wrist sprain, whereas strain will be considered in the discussion of the hand.

A sprain is by far the most common wrist injury and in most cases is the most poorly managed injury in sports. It can arise from any abnormal, forced movement of the wrist. Falling on the hyperextended wrist is the most common cause, but violent flexion or torsion will also tear supporting tissue. Since the main support of the wrist is derived from posterior and anterior ligaments that carry the major nutrient vessels to the carpal bones and stabilize the joint, repeated sprains may disrupt the blood supply and consequently the nutrition to the carpal bones.

Symptoms and signs   The sprained wrist may be differentiated from the carpal navicular fracture by recognition of the generalized swelling, tenderness, inability to flex the wrist, and absence of appreciable pain or irritation over the navicular bone. All athletes having severe sprains should be referred to a physician for x-ray examination to determine possible fractures.

Management   Mild and moderate sprains should be given cold therapy and compression for at least 24 to 48 hours, after which cryotherapy is carried out or there is a gradual increase in heat therapy. It is desirable to have the athlete start hand-strengthening exercises almost immediately after the injury has occurred.

Nerve Compression in the Wrist Region

Because of the narrow spaces that some nerves must travel via the wrist to the hand, compression neuropathy or entrapment can occur. The two most common entrapments are of the median nerve, which travels through the carpal tunnel, and the ulnar nerve compressed in the tunnel of Guyon between the pisiform bone and the hook of the hamate bone.

Such compression causes a sharp or burning pain that is associated with an increase or decrease of skin sensitivity or paresthesia.[4] When chronic entrapment may cause irreversible nerve damage, unsuccessful conservative treatment can lead to surgical decompression. Conservative treatment of the athlete usually includes rest and anti-inflammatory medication. Varying degrees of muscle weakness can also follow.

Dislocations   Dislocations of the wrist are relatively infrequent in sports activity. Most occur from a forceful hyperextension of the hand. Of those dislocations which do happen, the bones that could be involved are the distal ends of the radius and ulna (Fig. 25-38) and a carpal bone, the lunate being the most commonly affected.

Dislocation of the lunate bone   Dislocation of the lunate (Fig. 25-39) is considered the most common dislocation of a carpal bone.

Etiological factors   Dislocation occurs as a result of a fall on the outstretched hand, forcing open the space between the distal and proximal carpal bones. When the stretching force is released, the lunate bone is dislocated anteriorly (palmar side).

Symptoms and signs   The primary signs of this condition are pain, swelling, and difficulty in executing wrist and finger flexion. There also

Figure 25-38

Dislocation of the lunate carpal bone.

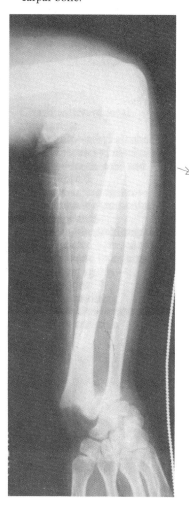

may be numbness or even paralysis of the flexor muscles, because of lunate pressure on the median nerve.

Management This condition should be treated as acute and the athlete sent to a physician for reduction of the dislocation. If it is not recognized early enough, bone deterioration may occur, requiring surgical removal.[14] The usual time of disability and subsequent recovery totals from 1 to 2 months.

Fractures

Fractures of the wrist commonly occur to the distal ends of the radius and ulna and to the carpal bones; the carpal navicular bone is most commonly affected, the hamate bone is affected less often.

Navicular fracture The navicular bone is the most frequently fractured of the carpal bones.

Etiological factors The injury is usually caused by a force on the out-stretched hand, which compresses the navicular bone between the radius and the second row of carpal bones (Fig. 25-40). This condition is often mistaken for a severe sprain, and as a result the required complete immobilization is not carried out. Without proper splinting, the navicular fracture often fails to heal because of an inadequate supply of blood, thus degeneration and necrosis occur. This condition is often called *"aseptic necrosis"* of the navicular bone. It is necessary to try, in every way possible, to distinguish between a wrist sprain and a fracture of the navicular bone because a fracture necessitates immediate referral to a physician.

Symptoms and signs The signs of a recent navicular fracture include swelling in the area of the carpal bones, severe point tenderness of the navicular bone in the anatomical snuffbox (Fig. 25-41), and navicular pain that is elicited by upward pressure exerted on the long axis of the thumb and by radial flexion.

Management With these signs present, cold should be applied, the

Figure 25-39

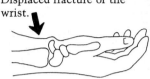

Displaced fracture of the wrist.

Figure 25-40

Carpal navicular fracture.

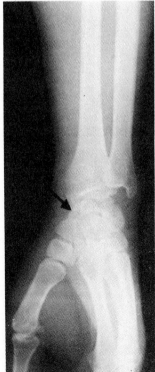

WRIST TAPING TECHNIQUE NO. 1

The wrist taping (Fig. 25-42) is designed for mild wrist strains or sprains.

Materials needed: One roll of 1-inch (2.5 cm) tape and tape adherent.

Position of the athlete: The athlete stands with the affected hand flexed toward the injured side and the fingers moderately spread to increase the breadth of the wrist for the protection of nerves and blood vessels.

Position of the operator: The operator stands facing the athlete's affected wrist.

Procedure

1. A strip of 1-inch (2.5 cm) tape, starting at the base of the wrist, is brought from the palmar side upward and around both sides of the wrist.
2. In the same pattern, with each strip overlapping the preceding one by at least half its width, three additional strips are laid in place.

Specific Sports Injuries and
Other Problems

Figure 25-41

Anatomical "snuff box"
formed by extensor tendons
of the thumb.

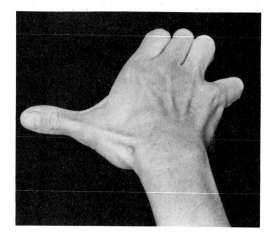

Figure 25-42

Wrist taping technique no. 1.

Figure 25-43

Wrist taping technique no. 2.

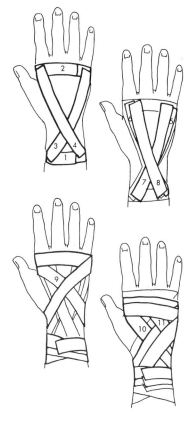

area splinted, and the athlete referred to a physician for x-ray study and casting. In most cases, cast immobilization lasts for about 8 weeks and is followed by strengthening exercises coupled with protective taping.

Hamate fracture A fracture of the hamate bone can occur from a fall, but more commonly occurs from being struck by an implement such as the handle of a tennis racket, a baseball bat, or a golf club.[14] Wrist pain and weakness are experienced. Pull of the muscular attachments can cause nonunion; therefore, casting is usually the treatment of choice.

Wrist taping Taping support should be maintained until the athlete has regained full strength and mobility.

WRIST TAPING TECHNIQUE NO. 2

This wrist taping (Fig. 25-43) is designed to stabilize and protect a badly injured wrist. The materials and positioning are the same as in technique 1.
Procedure

1. One anchor strip is applied around the wrist approximately 3 inches (7.5 cm) from the hand; another anchor strip encircles the spread hand.
2. With the wrist flexed toward the side of the injury, a strip of tape is taken from the anchor strip near the little finger and carried obliquely across the wrist joint to the wrist anchor strip. Another strip is taken from the anchor strip on the index finger side and carried across the wrist joint to the wrist anchor. This forms a crisscross over the wrist joint. A series of four or five crisscrosses may be applied, depending on the extent of splinting needed.
3. Over the crisscross taping, two or three series of figure-8 tapings are applied. Start by encircling the wrist once, carry a strip over the back of the hand obliquely, encircling the hand twice, and then carry another strip obliquely upward across the back of the hand to where the figure-8 started. This procedure should be repeated to ensure a strong, stabilizing taping.

Wrist ganglion of the tendon sheath

The wrist ganglion (Fig. 25-44) is often seen in sports. It is considered by many to be a herniation of the joint capsule or of the synovial sheath of a tendon; other authorities believe it to be a cystic structure. It usually appears slowly, after a wrist strain, and contains a clear, mucinous fluid. The ganglion most often appears on the back of the wrist but can appear at any tendinous point in the wrist or hand. As it increases in size, it may be accompanied by a mild pressure discomfort. An old method of treatment was to first break down the swelling by means of digital pressure and then apply a felt pressure pad for a period of time to encourage healing. A newer approach is the use of a combination of aspiration and chemical cauterization, with subsequent application of a pressure pad. Neither of these methods prevents the ganglion from recurring. Surgical removal is the best of the various methods of treatment.

Figure 25-44

Wrist ganglion.

Injuries to the Hand

Injuries to the hand occur frequently in sports, yet the injured hand is probably the most poorly managed of all body areas.

Contusions and Pressure Injuries of the Hand and Phalanges

The hand and phalanges, having irregular bony structure combined with little protective fat and muscle padding, are prone to bruising in sports. This condition is easily identified from the history of trauma and the pain and swelling of soft tissues. Cold and compression should be applied immediately until hemorrhage has ceased followed by gradual warming of the part in whirlpool or immersion baths. Although soreness is still present, protection should be given by a sponge rubber pad (Fig. 25-45).

A particularly common contusion of the finger is bruising of the distal phalanx, which results in a *subungual hematoma* (contusion of the fingernail). This is an extremely painful condition because of the accumulation of blood underneath the fingernail. The athlete should place the finger in ice water until the hemorrhage ceases and the pressure of blood should then be released (Fig. 25-46).

BRUISED HAND TAPING

The following method is used to tape a bruised hand:

Materials needed: One roll of 1-inch (2.5 cm) adhesive tape, role of ½-inch (1.3 cm) tape, ¼-inch (0.63 cm) thick sponge rubber pad, and tape adherent.

Position of the athlete: The fingers are spread moderately.

Position of the operator: The operator faces the athlete's hand.

Procedure

1. The protective pad is laid over the bruise and held in place by three strips of ½-inch (1.3 cm) tape laced through the webbing of the fingers.
2. A basic figure-of-eight, made of 1-inch (2.5 cm) tape, is applied.

Figure 25-45

Bruised hand taping.

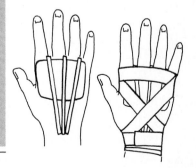

RELEASING BLOOD FROM BENEATH THE FINGERNAIL

The following are two common methods for releasing the pressure of the subungual hematoma.

Materials needed: Scalpel, small-guage drill or paper clip, and antiseptic.

Position of athlete: The athlete sits with the injured hand, palm downward, on the table.

Position of the operator: The operator sits facing the athlete's affected finger and stabilizes it with one hand.

Technique 1

1. The injured finger should first be coated with an antiseptic solution.
2. A sharp scalpel point, small-gauge drill, or paper clip, is used to penetrate the injured nail by a rotary action. If the hematoma extends out as far as the end of the nail, it may be best to release the blood by slipping the scalpel tip under the end of the nail.

Technique 2

1. A paper clip is heated to a red-hot temperature.
2. The red-hot paper clip or small-gauge drill is laid on the surface of the nail with moderate pressure. This results in melting a hole through the nail to the site of the bleeding.

Figure 25-46

Releasing blood from beneath the fingernail, technique no. 1.

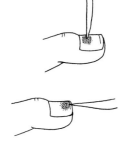

Bowler's thumb A perineural fibrosis of the subcutaneous ulnar digital nerve of the thumb can occur from the pressure of a bowling ball thumbhole. With the development of fibrotic tissue around the ulnar nerve, the athlete senses pain, tingling on pressure to the irritated area, and numbness.[11]

Early management includes a decrease in the amount of bowling and padding of the thumbhole. If the condition continues, however, surgery may be warranted.

Handlebar palsy Handlebar palsy or ulnar neuropathy in bicyclists comes from an abnormal amount of pressure on the hands. The bicyclist experiences numbness, weakness, and a loss of coordination of the ulnar side of the fourth and fifth fingers. It can occur in one or both hands.[3] To avoid this condition the bicyclist should wear gloves and have padded handlebars. It is also essential that the bicycle be of the proper size and handlebar height to avoid excessive body weight being forced forward onto the hands. Hand positions should be changed frequently on long trips. With prolonged symptoms the rider should avoid bicycling and be referred to a physician for treatment.

Tendon Conditions

Tenosynovitis The tendons of the wrist and hand can sustain irritation from repeated movement that results in tenosynovitis. An inflammation of the tendon sheath results in swelling, crepitation, and painful movement. Most commonly affected are the extensor tendons of the

Two important forms of tenosynovitis:
  de Quervain's disease
  Trigger finger or thumb

wrist: the extensor carpi ulnaris, extensor pollicis longus, extensor pollicis brevis, and abductor pollicis longus.

de Quervain's disease de Quervain's disease is a stenosing tenosynovitis. The first tunnel of the wrist becomes contracted and narrowed due to inflammation of the synovial lining. The tendons that go through the first tunnel are the extensor pollicis brevis and abductor pollicis longus, which move through the same synovial sheath. Because the tendons move through a groove of the radiostyloid process, constant wrist movement can be a source of irritation.

Symptoms and signs Athletes who use a great deal of wrist motion in their sport are prone to de Quervain's disease. The symptoms are aching, which may radiate into the hand or forearm.[4] Movements of the wrist tend to increase the pain, and there is a positive de Quervain's test. There is point tenderness and weakness in thumb extension and abduction, and there may be a painful snapping and catching of the tendons on movement.

Management Management of de Quervain's disease involves immobilization, rest, cryotherapy, and anti-inflammatory medication. Ultrasound and ice massage also have been found to be beneficial.

Trigger finger or thumb The trigger finger or thumb is another example of stenosing tenosynovitis. It most commonly occurs in a flexor tendon that runs through a common sheath with other tendons. A thickening of the sheath or tendon can occur, thus constricting the sliding tendon. A nodule in the synovium of the sheath adds to the difficulty of gliding.

Symptoms and signs The athlete complains that when the finger or thumb is flexed, there is a resistance to reextension, producing a snapping that is both palpable and audible. On palpation, tenderness is produced and a lump can be felt at the base of the flexor tendon sheath.

Management Treatment initially is the same for de Quervain's disease; however, if it is unsuccessful, steroid injections may produce relief. If steroid injections do not provide relief, splinting the tendon sheath is the last option.

Mallet finger The mallet finger is common in sports, particularly in baseball and basketball. It is caused by a blow from a thrown ball that strikes the tip of the finger and avulses the extensor tendon from its insertion along with a piece of bone.

Symptoms and signs The athlete is unable to extend the finger, carrying it at about a 30-degree angle. There is also point tenderness at the site of the injury and the avulsed bone often can be palpated (Fig. 25-47).

Management Pain, swelling, and discoloration from internal hemorrhage are present. The distal phalanx should immediately be splinted in a position of extension, cold applied to the area, and the athlete referred to a physician. Most physicians will splint the mallet finger into extension and the proximal phalanx into flexion for 4 to 6 weeks (Fig. 25-48).

Boutonnière deformity The boutonnière, or buttonhole, deformity is caused by a rupture of the extensor tendon of the middle phalanx. Trauma occurs to the top of the middle finger, which forces the PIP joint into excessive flexion.

Three finger injuries that could lead to deformity if not cared for properly:
 Mallet finger
 Boutonniere deformity
 Volar plate injury

Figure 25-47

Mallet finger.

Figure 25-48

Splinting of the mallet finger.

Figure 25-49

Boutonniere deformity.

Symptoms and signs The athlete complains of severe pain and inability to extend the PIP joint. There is swelling, point tenderness, and an obvious deformity (Fig. 25-49).

Management Management of the boutonnière deformity includes cold application followed by splinting of the PIP joint in extension. *NOTE:* If this condition is inadequately splinted, the classic boutonnière deformity will develop. Splinting is continued for 5 to 8 weeks. While splinted, the athlete is encouraged to flex the distal phalanx[4] (Table 25-3).

Sprains, Dislocations, and Fractures

The phalanges, particularly the thumb (Fig. 25-50), are prone to sprains caused by a blow delivered to the tip or by violent twisting. The mechanism of injury is similar to that of fractures and dislocations. The sprain, however, mainly affects the capsular, ligamentous, and tendinous tissues. Recognition is accomplished primarily through the history and the sprain symptoms: pain, marked swelling, and hematoma.

Sprains of the Metacarpophalangeal Joint

Fingers A sprain of the MCP joint often consists of a disruption of the extensor tendon and an inability of the athlete to fully extend the joint. There may be an obvious slipping of the extensor tendon[2] (Table 25-3).

Gamekeeper's thumb A sprain of the ulnar collateral ligament of the MCP joint of the thumb is common among athletes, especially skiers and tackle football players. The mechanism of injury is usually by a forceful abduction of the proximal phalanx, which is occasionally combined with hyperextension.[7]

Since the stability of pinching can be severely deterred, proper imme-

Figure 25-50

Sprained thumb.

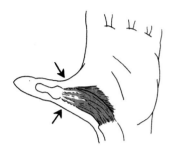

TABLE 25-3

Conservative treatment and splinting of finger injuries

Injury	Constant Splinting	Begin Motion	Additional Splinting During Competition	Joint Position
Mallet finger	6-8 wk	6-8 wk	6-8 wk	Slight DIP hyperextension
Collateral ligament sprains	3 wk	2 wk	4-6 wk	30-degree flexion
PIP and DIP dislocations	3 wk	3 wk	3 wk	30-degree flexion
Phalangeal fractures	4-6 wk	4-6 wk	3 wk	N/A
PIP and DIP fractures	9-11 wk	3 wk	3 wk	30-degree flexion
Pseudoboutonnière volar plate injuries	5 wk	3 wk	3 wk	20- to 30-degree flexion
Boutonnière deformity	6-8 wk	6-8 wk	6-8 wk	PIP in extension; DIP and MCP not included
MCP fractures	3 wk	3 wk	4-6 wk	30-degree flexion
Flexor digitorum profundus repair	5 wk	3 wk	3 wk	Depends on repair

From Gieck, J.H., and McCue, F.C., III: Ath. Train. **17**:215, Fall 1982.

SPRAINED THUMB TAPING

Sprained thumb taping (Fig. 25-51) is designed to give both protection for the muscle and joint and support to the thumb.

Materials needed: One role of 1-inch (2.5 cm) tape and tape adherent.

Position of the athlete: The athlete should hold the injured thumb in a relaxed neutral position.

Position of the operator: The operator stands in front of the athlete's injured thumb.

Procedure

1. An anchor strip is placed loosely around the wrist and another around the distal end of the thumb.
2. From the anchor at the tip of the thumb to the anchor around the wrist, four splint strips are applied in a series on the side of greater injury (dorsal or palmar side) and are held in place by one lock strip around the wrist and one encircling the tip of the thumb.
3. A series of three thumb spicas is now added. The first spica is started on the radial side at the base of the thumb and is carried under the thumb, completely encircling it, and then crossing the starting point. The strip should continue around the wrist and finish at the starting point. Each of the following spica strips should overlap the preceding strip by at least ⅔ inch (1.7 cm) and move downward on the thumb. The thumb spica with tape provides an excellent means of protection during recovery from an injury (Fig. 25-52).

Figure 25-51

Sprained thumb taping.

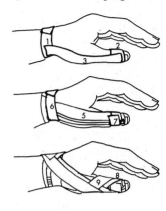

Figure 25-52

Thumb spica.

diate and follow-up care must be carried out. If there is instability in the joints, the athlete should be immediately referred to an orthopedist. If the joint is stable, x-ray examination should routinely be performed to rule out fracture. Splinting of the thumb should be applied for protection over a 3-week period or until it is pain free. The splint is applied with the thumb in a neutral position extending from the end of the thumb to above the wrist.[13] After splinting a thumb spica taping should be worn during sports participation.

Sprains of the interphalangeal joints of the fingers Interphalangeal finger sprains can include the PIP joint or the DIP joint. Injury can range from minor to complete tears of the collateral ligament, a volar plate tear, or a central extensor slip tear (Table 25-3).

Collateral ligament sprain A collateral ligament sprain of the interphalangeal joint is very common in sports such as basketball, volleyball, and football. A common mechanism is an axial force producing the "jammed finger."

Symptoms and signs There is severe point tenderness at the joint site, especially in the region of the collateral ligaments. There may be a lateral or medial instability when the joint is in 150 degrees of flexion. Collateral ligament injuries may be evaluated by the application of a valgus and varus joint stress test.

Management Management includes ice packs for the acute stage, x-ray examinations, and splinting. Splinting of the PIP joint is usually at 30 to 40 degrees of flexion for 10 days. If the sprain is to the DIP joint, splinting a few days in full extension assists in the healing process. If the sprains are minor, taping the injured finger to a noninjured one will provide protective support. Later, a protective checkrein can be applied for either thumb or finger protection.

Volar plate injury The volar plate of the PIP joint is most commonly injured in sports from a severe hyperextension force. A distal tear

Figure 25-53

Finger and thumb checkreins.

FINGER AND THUMB CHECKREINS

The finger or thumb that has been sprained may require the additional protection afforded by a restraining checkrein (Fig. 25-53).

Materials needed: One role of 1-inch (2.5 cm) tape.

Position of the athlete: The athlete spreads the injured fingers widely but within a range free of pain.

Position of the operator: The operator faces the athlete's injured finger.

Procedure

1. A strip of 1-inch (2.5 cm) tape, after encircling the middle phalanx of the injured finger, is brought over to the adjacent finger and encircles it also. The tape left between the two fingers, which are spread apart, is called the checkrein.
2. Additional strength is given by means of a lock strip that encircles the center of the checkrein.

Figure 25-54

Being hit on the tip of a finger can produce enough force to dislocate it.

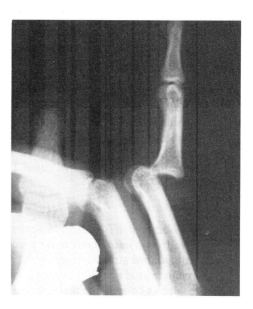

may cause a "swan-neck deformity," whereas injury to the proximal part of the plate may cause a "pseudoboutonnière deformity."[15] A major indication of a tear is that the PIP joint can be passively hyperextended in comparison to other PIP joints.

Management usually consists of splinting in 20 to 30 degrees of flexion for 5 weeks, followed by 3 weeks of active motion. A 30-degree extension block splint might be used after flexion splinting.[8]

Dislocations of the phalanges   Dislocations of the phalanges (Fig. 25-54) have a high rate of occurrence in sports and are caused mainly by being hit on the tip of the finger by a ball (Fig. 25-55). The force of injury is usually directed upward from the palmar side, displacing either the first or second joint dorsally. The resultant problem is primarily a tearing of the supporting capsular tissue, accompanied by hemorrhaging. However, there may be a rupture of the flexor or extensor tendon and chip fractures in and around the dislocated joint. It is advisable to splint the dislocation as it is and refer all first-time dislocations to the team physician for reduction.

To ensure the most complete healing of the dislocated PIP and DIP joints, splinting should be maintained for about 3 weeks in 30 degrees of

Figure 25-55

Volleyball produces a high percentage of finger injuries.

Figure 25-56

A thumb dislocation, if not properly managed, can seriously affect hand functioning.

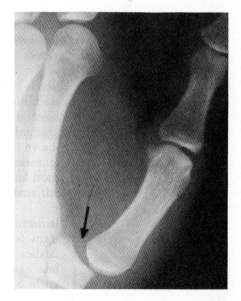

Specific Sports Injuries and
Other Problems

flexion because an inadequate immobilization could cause an unstable joint and/or excessive scar tissue and, possibly, a permanent deformity.

Special consideration must be given to dislocations of the thumb and any MCP finger joints (Fig. 25-56). A properly functioning thumb is necessary for hand dexterity; consequently, any traumatic injury to the thumb should be considered serious. Thumb dislocations occur frequently at the second joint, resulting from a sharp blow to the distal end, with the trauma forcing the thumb into hyperextension and dislocating the second joint downward. Any dislocation of the MCP finger joints can lead to complications and require the immediate care of an orthopedist.[2]

Fractures of the metacarpal bones and phalanges   The same mechanism that produces strains, sprains, and dislocations can cause fractures of the metacarpal bones and phalanges. Other mechanisms are of crushing injuries.

Fractures of the metacarpal bones   Fractures of the metacarpal bones (Fig. 25-57) are common in contact sports. They arise from striking an object with the fist or from having the hand stepped on. There is often pain, deformity, swelling, and abnormal mobility. In some cases no deformity occurs, and by palpation one is unable to distinguish between a severe contusion and a fracture. In this situation, digital pressure should be placed on the knuckles and the long axes of the metacarpal bones. Pressure will often reveal pain at the fracture site. After the fracture is located, the hand should be splinted over a gauze roll splint, cold and pressure applied, and the athlete referred to a physician. Uncomplicated metacarpal fractures take approximately 1 month for complete healing.

Fractures of the phalanges   Fractures of the phalanges are among the most common fractures in sports and can occur as the result of a variety of mechanisms: the fingers being stepped on, hit by a ball, or twisted. More concern should be given to fractures of the middle and proximal phalanges because of possible involvement with the extensor or flexor tendons. Transverse, oblique, or spiral fractures should be referred to an orthopedist. Avulsion fractures are usually treated like a corresponding sprain[2] (Table 25-4). A deformity in an anterior direction usually occurs in proximal fractures. The finger must be splinted in flexion around a gauze roll or a curved splint to avoid full extension of the digit, which must be avoided at all times. Flexion splinting reduces the deformity by relaxing the flexor tendons. Fracture of the distal phalanx is less compli-

Figure 25-57

Fractures of the metacarpals.

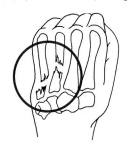

TABLE 25-4

Avulsion fractures

Avulsion Fracture	Corresponding Sprain
Corner of base of middle phalanx	Collateral ligament
Volar base of middle phalanx	Volar plate injury
Dorsal base of middle phalanx	Central extensor slip tear
Volar base of distal phalanx	Flexor profundus tear
Dorsal base of distal phalanx	Mallet finger

From Birnbaum, J.S.: The musculoskeletal manual, New York, 1982, Academic Press, Inc.

cated than fracture of the middle or proximal phalanges, but it constitutes a painful injury that sometimes becomes complicated by a subungual hematoma (Fig. 25-58). The major concerns are to control bleeding, apply a splint properly, and then refer the athlete to a physician.

Rehabilitation of the Forearm, Wrist, and Hand

Reconditioning of the hand, wrist, and forearm must commence as early as possible. Immobilization of the forearm or wrist requires that the muscles be exercised almost immediately after an injury occurs if atrophy and contractures are to be prevented. The athlete is not ready for competition until full strength and mobility of the injured joint have been regained. Grip strength is an excellent way to determine the state of reconditioning of the hand, wrist, and forearm. The hand dynamometer may be used to ascertain strength increments during the process of rehabilitation. Full range of movement and strength must be considered for all the major articulations and muscles.

Once ligament or tendon injuries have healed to the point that movement will not disrupt, active mobilization is carried out.[17,18] Exercise is graduated to increase grip and pinch strength. Some of the following exercises can be employed with success. *NOTE:* All exercises should be performed in a pain-free range of motion. Such exercises should be performed in sets of ten, working toward an ultimate program of three sets of ten, two, or three times daily.

Figure 25-58

A fracture of the proximal phalanx is usually more serious than a fracture of the distal end.

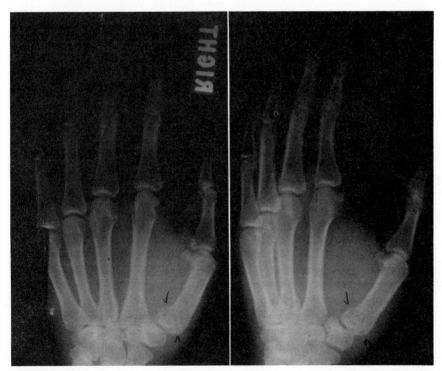

Specific Sports Injuries and
Other Problems

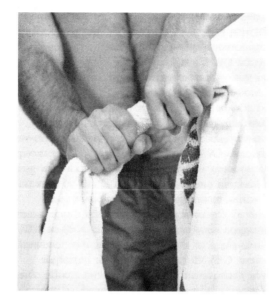

FIG. 1.3

The towel twist exercise.

FIG. 1.5

Wrist roll.

FIG. 1.4

Wrist circles and finger spread
and grip.

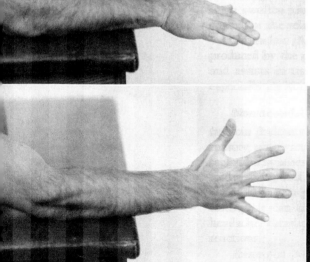

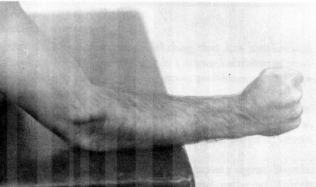

Suggested Forearm and Wrist Exercises

Proper forearm reconditioning is extremely important for injuries to the wrist and hand, as well as the forearm. An excellent beginning exercise is the towel twist, in which the athlete twists the towel in each direction as if wringing out water (Fig. 25-59). A wrist roll exercise (Fig. 25-60) against a resistance is also an excellent forearm, wrist, and hand strength developer. More specific strength development can be employed by the use of a resistance device such as a dumbbell. By stabilizing the bent elbow, the athlete can perform wrist flexion and extension and also forearm pronation and supination.

Wrist strength depends on forearm strength and freedom of movement in the wrist joint. Circumduction exercise helps to maintain joint integrity. Circling must be performed in each direction (Fig. 25-61).

Suggested Hand and Wrist Exercises

Two exercises that are highly beneficial are gripping and spreading. Resistance exercises also can be used successfully for restoring grip strength (Fig. 25-62).

Figure 25-62

Restoring grip strength.

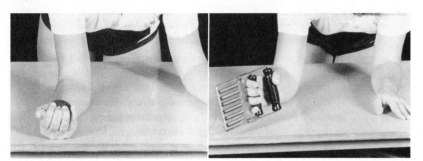

REFERENCES

1. Berhang, A.M., et al.: Tennis elbow: a biomechanical approach, J. Sports Med. **2**(5):235, 1974.
2. Birnbaum, J.S.: The musculoskeletal manual, New York, Academic Press, Inc.
3. Burke, E.R.: Ulnar neuropathy in bicyclists, Phys. Sportsmed. **9**:53, April 1981.
4. Cailliet, R.: Hand pain and impairment, ed. 3, Philadelphia, 1982, F.A. Davis Co.
5. Cyriax, J.: Textbook of orthopaedic medicine, vol. 1, Diagnosis of soft tissue lesions, ed. 8, Eastbourne, England, 1982, Baillière Tindall.
6. Dobyns, J.H., et al.: Sports stress syndrome of the hand and wrist, Am. J. Sports Med. **6**(5):236, 1978.
7. Gerber, C., et al.: Skier's thumb: surgical treatment of recent injuries to the ulnar collateral ligament of the thumb's metacarpophalangeal joint, Am. J. Sports Med. **9**:171, May/June 1981.
8. Gieck, J.H., and McCue, F.C., III: Splinting of finger injuries—a tip from the field, Athletic Training **17**:215, Fall 1982.
9. Gruchow, H.W., and Pelletier, D.: An epidemiologic study of tennis elbow, Am. J. Sports Med. **7**(4):234, 1979.
10. Hoppenfeld, S.: Physical examination of the spine and extremities, New York, 1976, Appleton-Century-Crofts.
11. Kisner, W.H.: Thumb neuroma: a hazard of ten pin bowling, Br. J. Plast. Surg. **29**:225, 1976.
12. Lipscomb, A.B.: Baseball pitching

injuries, J. Sports Med. 3(1):25,
1975.

13. Maroon, B.R.: Orthopedic aspects
of sports medicine. In Appenzeller, O., and Atkinson, R. (editors): Sports medicine, Baltimore,
1981, Urban & Schwarzenberg, Inc.

14. McCue, F.C., III, et al.: Hand
and wrist injuries in the athlete,
Am. J. Sports Med. 7(5):275, 1979.

15. McCue, F.C., III: The elbow, wrist,
and hand. In Kulund, D.N.: The
injured athlete, Philadelphia, 1982,
J.B. Lippincott Co.

16. Nirschl, R.P.: The etiology and
treatment of tennis elbow, J.

Sports Med. 2(6):308, 1974.

17. Wilson, R.L., and Carter, M.S.:
Joint injuries in the hand: pres-
ervation of proximal interphalan-
geal joint function. In Hunter,
J.M., et al. (editors): Rehabilita-
tion of the hand, ed. 2, St.
Louis, 1984, The C.V. Mosby
Co.

18. Wilson, R.L., and Carter, M.S.:
Management of hand fractures.
In Hunter, J.M., et al. (editors):
Rehabilitation of the hand, ed.
2, St. Louis, 1984, The C.V.
Mosby Co.

ADDITIONAL SOURCES

Carr, D., et al.: Upper extremity injuries in skiing, Am. J. Sports Med.
9(6):378, 1981.

Flatt, A.E.: The care of minor injuries,
ed. 4, St. Louis, 1979, The C.V.
Mosby Co.

Hunter, J.M., et al. (editors): Rehabilitation of the hand, ed. 2, St. Louis,
1984, The C.V. Mosby Co.

Pappas, A.M.: Injuries of the upper extremities. In Vinger, P.R., and Hoerner, E.F. (editors): Sports injuries:
the unthwarted epidemic, Littleton,
Mass., 1981, John Wright, PSG, Inc.
Mass., 1981, John Wright, PSG, Inc.

Priest, J.D., and Weise, D.J.: Elbow injury in women's gymnastics, Am. J.
Sports Med. 9(5):288, 1981.

Chapter 26

COMMON ILLNESS AND OTHER HEALTH CONDITIONS

When you finish this chapter, you should be able to

Recognize symptoms and signs of common respiratory and gastrointestinal tract problems

Differentiate diabetic coma from insulin shock and provide appropriate emergency care for both

Recognize common contagious viral diseases

Respond appropriately to an athlete having an epileptic seizure

Recognize the signs of hypertension

Describe major menstrual irregularities and the many aspects of female reproduction in relation to sports participation

Respiratory tract infections can be highly communicable to sports teams.

As with individuals who do not engage in sports, athletes acquire a number of illnesses and adverse health conditions. Chapter 26 discusses some of the more pertinent conditions as they relate to sports performance.

THE RESPIRATORY TRACT

The respiratory tract is an organ system through which various communicable diseases can be transmitted. It is commonly the port of entry for acute infectious diseases that are spread from person to person or by direct contact. Some of the more prevalent conditions affecting athletes are the common cold, sinusitis, sore throat, asthma, hay fever, air pollution, and the "childhood" diseases of measles, chickenpox, and mumps.

The Common Cold (Coryza)

Upper respiratory tract infections, especially colds and associated conditions, are common in the sports program and can play havoc with entire teams. The common cold is attributed to a filterable virus, which produces an infection of the upper respiratory tract within a susceptible individual.

Symptoms and Signs

The susceptible person is believed to be one who has, singly or in combination, any of the following characteristics:
1. Physical debilitation for overwork or lack of sleep
2. Chronic inflammation from a local infection

767

3. Inflammation of the nasal mucosa from an allergy
4. Inflammation of the nasal mucosa from breathing foreign substances such as dust
5. Sensitivity to stress

The onset of coryza is usually rapid, with symptoms varying in each individual. The typical effects are a general feeling of malaise with an accompanying headache, sneezing, and nasal discharge. Some individuals may register a fever of 100° to 102° F (38° to 39° C) and have chills. Various aches and pains may also accompany the symptoms. The nasal discharge starts as a watery secretion, gradually becoming thick and discolored from the inflammation. A cold may be centered in a specific area or may extend throughout the upper respiratory tract. Sinusitis and pharyngitis often result from the common cold. Many disorders begin with the same symptoms that a cold presents.

Management

Management of the cold is usually symptomatic, with emphasis placed on isolation, bed rest, and light eating. Palliative medications include aspirin for relieving general discomfort, rhinitis tablets for drying the secreting mucosa, and nasal drops or an inhaler containing ephedrine to relieve nasal congestion. If a cough is present, various syrups may be given to afford relief. Caution should be taken in disguising basic cold symptoms so that the athlete may return to activity sooner. Activity before complete recovery will only delay full recuperation and may possibly cause chronic associated conditions.

Prevention

The prevention of colds is much more important than is caring for them after they have become established. The methods of cold prevention that have proved most beneficial are (1) eating regular, well-balanced meals, (2) avoiding extreme fatigue, (3) avoiding undue temperature changes without adjustments of clothing to meet such changes, (4) maintaining cleanliness at all times, and (5)attempting to eliminate undue emotional stress.

Sinusitis

There are numerous sinuses in the facial bony structure. These sinuses are hollow cavities lined with a mucous membrane, and each sinus is connected by a canal to the nasal passages. There are two basic groups of facial sinuses: (1) an anterior group made up of the maxillary, frontal, and ethmoidal sinuses and (3) a posterior group consisting of the sphenoidal and ethnoidal sinses.

Etiology

Inflammation of the sinuses may be acute, subacute, or chronic and can occur from any condition that hampers normal sinus ventilation and drainage. Sinusitis may occur after a cold, an allergy, measles, or other diseases that involve the upper respiratory tract. It is usually associated with streptococcal, pneumococcal, and staphylococcal organisms.

Symptoms and Signs

Sinusitis can develop gradually or suddenly and is associated with headache, nasal and postnasal discharge, and a general feeling of malaise. There also may be accompanying fever and sore throat.

Management

Because the infected sinuses lie close to the brain, sinusitis can be extremely dangerous. Cases of sinusitis should be managed by a physician, who uses various methods to help evacuate and heal the inflamed sinuses. The most common treatment procedure consists of inhalation of steam and the use of vasoconstricting nose drops combined with symptomatic therapy such as rest, a light diet, and aspirin.

The athlete should be instructed as to the proper way to apply nose drops (Fig. 26-1) and the safe way to blow the nose. The nose should be blown with the mouth open and pressure applied to one nostril at a time to avoid additional sinus irritation or the spread of the infection.

Sore Throat (Pharyngitis)

The sore throat, or pharyngitis, is usually of viral origin or due to streptococcal, pneumococcal of straphylococcal organisms.[2] A sore throat usually is associated with a common cold or sinusitis, as the result of the postnasal drip. It may also be an indication of a more serious condition.

Symptoms and Signs

Frequently it starts as a dryness in the throat, progressing to soreness, with pain and swelling. It is sometimes accompanied by a headache, a fever of 101° to 102° F (38° to 39° C), chills, coughing, and a general feeling of fatigue. On examination, the throat may appear dark red and swollen, and mucous membranes may be coated.

Management

In most cases bed rest is considered the best treatment, combined with the use of symptomatic medications such as aspirin and a hot saltwater gargle. Antibiotics and a silver nitrate throat swab may be used by a physician if other measures are inadequate.

A   **B**

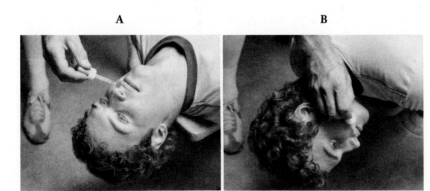

Figure 26-1

Proper application of nose drops. **A,** Head tilted back. **B,** Head down.

Asthma

As one of the most common respiratory diseases, bronchial asthma can be produced from a number of stressors, such as a viral respiratory tract infection, emotional upset, changes in barometric pressure or temperature, exercise, inhalation of a noxious odor, or exposure to a specific allergen.[2]

Symptoms and Signs

Bronchial asthma is characterized by a spasm of the bronchial smooth muscles, edema, and inflammation of the mucous lining. In addition to narrowing of the airway, copious amounts of mucus are produced. Difficulty in breathing may cause the athlete to hyperventilate, resulting in dizziness. The attach may begin with coughing, wheezing, shortness of breath, and a sense of fatigue.

The Asthmatic Athlete and Physical Activity

An asthmatic attack has been known to be stimulated by exercise in some individuals and may be provoked in others only on rare occasions during

---

MANAGEMENT OF THE ACUTE ASTHMATIC ATTACK

Athletes who have a history of asthma usually know how to care for themselves when attack occurs. However, the trainer must be aware of what to look for and what to do if called on.

Early Symptoms and Signs

Anxious appearance
Sweating and paleness
Flared nostrils
Breathing with pursed lips
Fast breathing
Vomiting
Hunched over body posture
Physical fatigue unrelated to activity
Indentation in the notch below the Adam's apple
Rib spaces sink in as the athlete inhales
Coughing for no apparent reason
Excess throat clearing
Irregular, labored breathing or wheezing

Actions to Take

Attempt to relax and reassure the athlete.
If medication has been cleared by the team physician, have the athlete use it.
Encourage the athlete to drink water.
Have the athlete perform controlled breathing along with relaxation exercises.
If an environmental factor triggering the attack is known, remove it or the athlete from the area.
If these procedures do not help, immediate medical attention may be necessary.

moderate exercise.[17] The exact cause of exercise-induced asthma (EIA) is not clear. Metabolic acidosis, postexertional hypocapnia, stimulation of tracheal irritant receptors, adrenergic abnormalities such as a defective catecholamine metabolism, and psychological factors have been suggested as possible causes.[13,17]

Management

A number of studies have been carried out to determine the most desirable exercise and training methods for EIA. Long continuous running compared to intermittent running causes the most severe bronchospasm.[18] Swimming was found to be the least bronchospasm producing, which may be due to the moist, warm air environment.[3] It is generally agreed that a regular exercise program can benefit asthmatics and nonasthmatics. Fewer symptoms occur with short intense work followed by rest compared to sustained exercise.[17] There should be gradual warm-up and cool-down. The duration of exercise should build up slowly to 30 to 40 minutes, four or five times a week. Exercise intensity and loading also should be graduated slowly. An example would be 10 to 30 seconds of work, followed by 30 to 90 seconds of rest. Aerosol asthmatic agents are taken before exercise. Asthmatic athletes who receive medication for their condition should make sure that what they take is legal for competition[17] (Chapter 6).

The athlete undergoing a sudden asthmatic attack should:

- Be relaxed and reassured
- Use a previously specified medication
- Drink water
- Perform controlled breathing
- Be removed from what might be triggering the attack

Hay Fever (Pollinosis)

Hay fever is an acute seasonal allergic condition that occurs from airborne pollens.

Symptoms and Signs

In the early stages, the athlete's eyes, throat, mouth, and nose begin to itch. This is followed by watering of the eyes, sneezing, and a clear, watery, nasal discharge. The athlete may complain of a sinus-type headache, emotional irritability, difficulty in sleeping, red and swollen eyes and nasal mucous membranes, and a wheezing cough.[2] Relief is usually fast after the oral ingestion of an antihistamine.

Air Pollution

Air pollution can adversely affect the performance and health of the athlete. Exposure to airborne chemicals and contaminants not only adversely affects cardiovascular function but can cause emphysema, chronic bronchitis, and lung cancer.[11] Athletes who must train where there may be air pollution should do so in the early morning or in the evening when contaminants are at their lowest.

THE GASTROINTESTINAL TRACT

Like any other individual, the athlete may develop various complaints of the digestive system. The athlete may display various disorders of the gastrointestinal tract as a result of poor eating habits or the stress engendered from competition. The responsibility in such cases is to be able to recognize the more severe conditions so that early referrals to a physician can be made. The following discussion of the digestive system disorders that are common in sports provides information on how to (1) give proper counsel to the athlete on the prevention of mouth and intestinal disorders, (2) recommend a proper diet, and (3) recognize deviations from the normal in these areas.

Mouth Disorders

Many different conditions involving the mouth appear during the course of a regular training program. Of these, the most commonly observed is dental caries (tooth decay), which is indicated by a local decalcification of the tooth. Tooth decay is the result of an increase in mouth acids, usually from food fermentation. Any disorder within the oral environment that raises its acid content without adequate neutralization may result in tooth decay. Proper oral hygiene is necessary and should include the following: (1) eating wholesome foods and (2) brushing the teeth properly, immediately after meals.

The greatest single cause of tooth loss is gum disease, the symptoms of which usually display the following pattern: (1) gingivitis, (2) periodontitis, and (3) pyorrhea. Gingivitis is an inflammation of the gum tissue surrounding the teeth and can arise from irritation brought about by tartar (calculus) or bacterial infection. If not cared for properly, gingivitis can extend to the periodontal tissue and eventually to the alveolar bone that supports the teeth, resulting in eventual loss of the teeth.

Infections associated with dental caries and gum disease can completely debilitate an athlete. Therefore, an immediate referral to a dentist is important.

Indigestion

Some athletes have certain food idiosyncrasies that cause them considerable distress after eating. Others develop reactions when eating before competition. The term given to digestive upset is indigestion (dyspepsia).

Etiological Factors

Indigestion can be caused by any number of conditions. The most common in sports are emotional stress, esophageal and stomach spasms, and/or inflammation of the mucous lining of the esophagus and stomach.

Symptoms and Signs

These conditions cause an increased secretion of hydrochloric acid (sour stomach), nausea, and flatulence (gas).

Management

Care of acute dyspepsia involves the elimination of irritating foods from the diet, development of regular eating habits, and avoidance of anxieties that may lead to gastric distress.

Constant irritation of the stomach may lead to chronic and more serious disorders such as gastritis, an inflammation of the stomach wall, or ulcerations of the gastrointestinal mucosa. Athletes who appear nervous and high-strung and suffer from dyspepsia should be examined by the sports physician.

Diarrhea

Diarrhea is the abnormal looseness or passage of a fluid, unformed stool and is categorized as acute and chronic, according to the type present.

Symptoms and Signs

It is characterized by abdominal cramps, nausea, and possibly vomiting, coupled with frequent elimination of stools, ranging from 3 to 20 a day. The infected person often has a loss of appetite and a light brown or gray, foul-smelling stool. Extreme weakness caused by the fluid dehydration is usually present.

Management

The cause of diarrhea is often difficult to establish. It is conceivable that any irritant may cause the loose stool. This can include an infestation of parasitic organisms or an emotional upset. Management of diarrhea requires a knowledge of its cause. Less severe cases can be cared for by (1) omitting foods that cause irritation, (2) drinking boiled milk, (3) eating bland food until symptoms have ceased, and (4) using pectins two or three times daily for the absorption of excess fluid.

Constipation

Some athletes are subject to constipation, the failure of the bowels to evacuate feces.

Etiological Factors

There are numerous causes of constipation, the most common of which are (1) lack of abdominal muscle tone, (2) insufficient moisture of the feces, causing it to be hard and dry, (3) lack of a sufficient proportion of roughage and bulk in the diet to stimulate peristalsis, (4) poor bowel habits, (5) nervousness and anxiety, and (6) overuse of laxatives and enemas.

Management

The best means of overcoming constipation is to regulate eating patterns to include foods that will encourage normal defecation. Cereals, fruits, vegetables, and fats stimulate bowel movement, whereas sugars and carbohydrates tend to inhibit it. Some persons become constipated as the result of psychological factors. In such cases, it may be helpful to try to determine the causes of stress and, if need be, to refer the athlete to a physician or school psychologist for counseling. Above all, laxatives or enemas should be avoided unless their use has been prescribed by a physician.

Hemorrhoids (Piles)

Hemorrhoids are varicosities of the hemorrhoidal venous plexus of the anus. There are both internal and external anal veins.

Etiological Factors

Chronic constipation or straining at the stool may tend to stretch the anal veins, resulting in either a protrusion (prolapse) and bleeding of the internal or external veins or a thrombus of the external veins.

Symptoms and Signs

Most often hemorrhoids are painful nodular swellings near the sphincter of the anus. There may be slight bleeding and itching. The majority of hemorrhoids are self-limiting and spontaneously heal within 2 to 3 weeks.

Management

The management of hemorrhoids is mostly palliative and serves to eliminate discomfort until healing takes place. The following measures can be suggested:

1. Use of proper bowel habits
2. Ingestion of 1 tablespoon of mineral oil daily to assist in lubricating dry stool
3. Application of an astringent suppository (tannic acid)
4. Application of a local anesthetic to control pain and itching (dibucaine)

If palliative measures are unsuccessful, surgery may be required.

Appendicitis

Appendicitis is discussed because of the importance of its early detection and the possibility of mistaking it for a common gastric complaint.

Etiological Factors

Inflammation of the vermiform appendix can be chronic or acute; it is caused by a bacterial infection. In its early stages the appendix becomes red and swollen; in later stages it may become gangrenous, rupturing into the bowels or peritoneal cavity and causing peritonitis.

Symptoms and Stages

The athlete may complain of a mild to severe cramp in the lower abdomen, associated with nausea, vomiting, and a low-grade fever ranging from 99° to 100° F (37° to 38° C). Later, the cramps may localize into a pain in the right side, and palpation may reveal tenderness at a point midway between the anterior superior spine of the ilium and the umbilicus (McBurney's point).

Management

If appendicitis is suspected, the athlete must be referred immediately to a physician for diagnostic tests. Surgery is the usual treatment.

Food Poisoning (Gastroenteritis)

Food poisoning, which may range from mild to severe, results from infectious organisms (bacteria of the salmonella group, certain staphylococci, streptococci, or dysentery bacilli) that enter the body in either food or drink.

Etiological Factors

Contaminated foods result, especially during warm weather, when improper food refrigeration permits the organisms to multiply rapidly. Contamination can also occur if the food is handled by an infected food handler.

Symptoms and Signs

Infection results in nausea, vomiting, cramps, diarrhea, and anorexia. The symptoms of staphylococcal infections usually subside in 3 to 6 hours. Salmonella infection symptoms may last from 24 to 48 hours or more.

Management

Management requires rapid replacement of lost fluids and electrolytes, which in severe cases may need to be replaced intravenously. Bed rest is desirable in all but mild cases; as long as the nausea and vomiting continue, nothing should be given by mouth. If tolerated, light fluids or foods such as clear strained broth, bouillon with a small amount of added salt, soft-cooked eggs, or bland cereals may be given.

DIABETES MELLITUS

Diabetes mellitus is a complex hereditary or developmental disease of carbohydrate metabolism. Decreased effectiveness of or insufficient insulin is responsible for most cases. Until recently diabetics were usually discouraged or forbidden competitive sports participation. Today an ever-increasing number of diabetics are active sports participants, functioning effectively in almost all sports. Since the key to the control of diabetes is the control of blood sugar, the insulin-dependent athlete must constantly juggle food intake, insulin, and exercise to maintain the blood sugar in its proper range if he or she is to perform to maximum.[1] Diet, exercise, and insulin are the major factors in the everyday life-style of the diabetic athlete, who must of necessity develop an ordered and specific living pattern to cope with the demands of daily existence and strenuous physical activity.

Diabetic athletes engaging in vigorous physical activity should eat before exercising, and, if the exercise is protracted, should have hourly glucose supplementation. As a rule, the insulin dosage is not changed but food intake is increased.[19] The response of diabetics varies among individuals and depends on many variables. Although there are some hazards, with proper medical evaluation and planning by a consultant in metabolic diseases, diabetics can feel free to engage in most physical activities.

Management of the Diabetic Coma and Insulin Shock

It is important that trainers who work with athletes who have diabetes mellitus are aware of the major symptoms of diabetic coma and insulin shock and the proper actions to take when either one occurs.

Diabetic Coma

If not treated adequately through proper diet and/or intake of insulin the diabetic athlete can develop acidosis. A loss of sodium, potassium, and ketone bodies through excessive urination, produces a problem of ketoacidosis that can lead to coma.

Symptoms and signs
Labored breathing or gasping for air
Fruity smelling breath caused by acetone
Nausea and vomiting

Specific Sports Injuries and
Other Problems

TABLE 26-1

Some infectious diseases*

Disease	Sites Involved	Mode of Transmission	Incubation Period	Chief Symptoms	Duration	Period of Contagion	Treatment	Prophylaxis
Measles (rubeola)	Skin, respiratory tract, and conjunctivae	Contact or droplet	7-14 days	Appearance—like common cold with fever, coryza, cough, conjunctivitis, photophobia, and spots in throat followed by skin rash	4-7 days after symptoms appear	Just before coldlike symptoms through about 1 week after rash appears	Bed rest and use of smoked glasses; symptomatic	Vaccine available
German measles (rubella)	Skin, respiratory tract, and conjunctivae	Contact or droplet	14-21 days	Cold symptoms, skin rash, and swollen lymph nodes behind ear	1-2 days	2-4 days before rash through 5 days afterward	Symptomatic	Vaccine available; gamma globulin given in postexposure situations
Chickenpox (varicella)	Trunk; then face, neck, and limbs	Contact or droplet	14-21 days	Mild cold symptoms followed by appearance of vesicles	1-2 weeks	1 day before onset through 6 days afterward	Symptomatic	None; avoid exposure

Disease	Part of body affected	How spread	Incubation period	Symptoms	Duration			
Mumps (epidemic parotiditis)	Salivary glands	Prolonged contact or droplet	18-21 days	Headache, drowsiness, fever, abdominal pain, pain on chewing and swallowing, swelling of neck under jaw	10 days	1 week	Symptomatic	Temporary immunization by virus vaccine
Influenza (grippe)	Respiratory tract	Droplet	1-2 days	Aching of low back, generalized aching, chills, headache, fever, and bronchitis	2-3 days	Symptomatic	Moderate temporary protection by polyvalent influenza virus	
Cold (coryza)	Respiratory tract	Droplet	12 hours to 4 days	Mild fever, headache, chills, and nasal discharge	1-2 weeks	Symptomatic	Possible help from vitamins and/or cold vaccine; avoid exposure	
Infectious mononucleosis†	Trunk	Contact	7-14 days	Sore throat, fever, skin rash, general aching, and swelling of lymph glands	3-4 weeks	Symptomatic	None; avoid extreme fatigue	

*Except as indicated, the common cause of each disease included in this table is a virus.

†Common cause, undetermined; probably a virus.

Thirst

Dry mucous lining of the mouth and flushed skin

Mental confusion or unconsciousness followed by coma

Management Because of the life-threatening nature of diabetic coma, early detection of ketoacidosis is essential. The injection of insulin into the athlete will normally prevent coma.

Insulin Shock

Unlike diabetic coma, insulin shock occurs when too much insulin is taken into the body and hypoglycemia or shock results. It is characterized by the following:

Physical weakness

Moist and pale skin

Drooping

Normal or shallow respirations

Management The diabetic athlete who engages in intense exercise and metabolizes large amounts of glycogen could inadvertently take too much insulin and thus have a severe reaction. To avoid this problem the athlete must adhere to a carefully planned diet that includes a snack before exercise. The snack should contain a combination of a complex carbohydrate and protein such as cheese and crackers. Activities that last for more than 30 to 40 minutes should be accompanied by snacks of simple carbohydrates. Some diabetics carry with them a lump of sugar or have candy or orange juice readily available in the event an insulin reaction seems imminent.

COMMON CONTAGIOUS VIRAL DISEASES

It is not within the purview of this text to describe in detail all the various infectious diseases to which athletes may be prone. However, on occasion an athlete may exhibit recognizable symptoms of such a disease; one should know the symptoms and be able to identify them (Table 26-1). A player or other athlete indicating such symptoms should be remanded to a physician without delay.

epilepsy
Recurrent paroxysmal disorder characterized by sudden attacks of altered consciousness, motor activity, sensory phenomena, or inappropriate behavior

CONVULSIVE DISORDERS (EPILEPSY)

Epilepsy is not a disease but a symptom that can be manifested by a large number of underlying disorders. **Epilepsy** is defined as "a recurrent paroxysmal disorder of cerebral function characterized by sudden, brief attack of

TABLE 26-2

Age and blood pressure limits

Age	Upper Blood Pressure Limits at Rest*
< 10	130/75 mm Hg
10-15	140/85 mm Hg
15-20	145/90 mm Hg
> 20	150/95 mm Hg

*If the upper limits of blood pressure are exceeded after three abnormal measurements have been taken, the athlete may have hypertension.

altered consciousness, motor activity, sensory phenomena, or inappropriate behavior."[2] For some types of epilepsy there is a genetic predisposition and a low threshold to having seizures. In others, altered brain metabolism or a history of injury may be the cause. A seizure can range from extremely brief episodes (petit mal seizure) to major episodes (grand mal seizures) unconsciousness and tonic-clonic muscle contractions.

Each person with epilepsy must be considered individually as to whether or he or she should engage in competitive sports. It is generally agreed that if an individual has daily or even weekly major seizures, collision sports should be prohibited.[14,20] This prohibition is not because hitting the head will trigger a seizure, but that unconsciousness during participation could result in a serious injury. If the seizures are properly controlled by medication or only occur during sleep, little, if any, sports restriction should be imposed, except for scuba diving, swimming alone, or participation at a great height.

For individuals who have major daily or weekly seizures, collision-type sports may be prohibited.

Management of the Epileptic Seizure

Often the epileptic athlete will experience an aura, which is a sign of an impending seizure. In such instances the athlete can take measures to provide protection, such as sitting or lying down. When a seizure occurs without warning, the following steps should be taken by the trainer:

Be emotionally composed.

If possible, cushion the athlete's fall.

Keep the athlete from injury-producing objects.

Loosen restricting clothing.

Prevent the athlete from biting the mouth by placing a soft cloth between the teeth.

Allow the athlete to awaken normally after the seizure.

HYPERTENSION

Hypertension, or high blood pressure, that goes uncontrolled for a long time can lead to disease of the cardiovascular system (Table 26-2).

Athletes who are believed to have mild to moderate hypertension should not participate in competitive sports until a thorough physical examination has been given, including a maximal exercise stress test.[16] The hypertensive athlete should avoid isometric exercises and heavy isotonic resistance such as in weight lifting.

Hypertension may be an excluding factor from sports participation.

THE FEMALE ATHLETE: MENSTRUAL IRREGULARITIES AND REPRODUCTION

Since women in the United States participate more in sports and are training harder than ever before in history, the question arises as to what impact these factors have on menstruation and reproduction.

Menstrual Irregularities

As reported earlier, menarche may be delayed in highly physically active women[8] (Chapter 4). Amenorrhea (absence of menses) and oligomenorrhea (diminished flow) have been common in professional female ballet dancers, gymnasts, and long-distance runners.[4,5,15] Runners who decrease training, such as when they have an injury, often report a return of regular menses.[6] Weight gain, together with less intense exercise, also are reported to reverse amenorrhea and oligomenorrhea.[5] Although these irregularities may be a normal aspect of thinness and hard physical training, it is advisable that a physician be consulted. To date, there is no indication that these conditions will adversely affect reproduction.[20] Almost any type of menstrual disorder can be caused by overly stressful and demanding sports activity—amenorrhea, dysmenorrhea, menorrhagia (excessive menstruation), oligomenorrhea, polymenorrhea (abnormal frequent menstruation), irregular periods, or any combination of these.[7]

Dysmenorrhea

Girls who have moderate to severe dysmenorrhea require examination by a physician.

Dysmenorrhea (painful menstruation) appears to be less prevalent among more active women; however, it is inconclusive whether specific sports participation can alleviate or produce dysmenorrhea. For girls with moderate to severe dysmenorrhea, gynecological consultation is warranted to rule out a serious pathological condition.[20]

Dysmenorrhea is caused by ischemia (a lack of normal blood flow to the pelvic organs) or by a possible hormonal imbalance. This syndrome, which is identified by cramps, nausea, lower abdominal pain, headache, and on occasion emotional lability, is the most common disorder. Mild to vigorous exercises that help ameliorate dysmenorrhea are usually prescribed by physicians. Physicians generally advise a continuance of the usual sports participation during the menstrual period, provided the performance level of the individual does not drop below her customary level of ability. Among athletes, swimmers have the highest incidence of dysmenorrhea; it, along with menorrhagia, are found most often, quite probably as the result of strenuous sports participation during the menses. Generally, oligomenorrhea, amenorrhea, and irregular or scanty flow appear more common to those sports which require strenuous exertion over a long period of time, for example, long-distance running, rowing, cross-country skiing, basketball, tennis, or field hockey. Since great variation exists among female athletes in respect to the menstrual pattern, its effect on physical performance, and the effect of physical activity on the menstrual pattern, each individual must learn to make adjustments to her cycle that will permit her to function effectively and efficiently with a minimum of discomfort or restriction.[12] The use of pills, devices, etc., to alter or stop the menstrual cycle is unadvisable. Evidence to date indicates that top performances are possible in all phases of the cycle.

Contraceptives

Female athletes have been known to take extra oral contraceptive pills to delay menstruation during competition. This practice is not recommended because the pills should be taken no more than 21 days, followed by a 7-day break.[20] Side effects range from nausea, vomiting, fluid retention, and amenorrhea to the extreme effects of hypertension, double vision, and thrombophlebitis.[10] Any use of oral contraceptives related to physical performance should be under the express direction and control of a physician.

In general, athletes who wear intrauterine devices are free of problems.

However, intrauterine devices are not recommended for nulliparous (never borne a viable child) adolescents because of the associated risk of pelvic inflammatory disease.[20] On occasion the athlete may complain of a lower abdominal cramp while being active. In such cases referral to a physician should be made.

Reproduction

For years it was widely stated that stressful physical exertion would strain or permanently damage the female reproductive organs. Experience and research, however, have indicated that this was but another myth. Clinical data compiled by a number of medical researchers add up to one conclusion: sports participation does not affect childbearing or childbirth in an adverse way but, on the contrary, serves this biological function in a positive way. Pregnancy may well be considered a training period for the maternal organism inasmuch as the increases in blood volume and metabolism make rather intensive demands on the physiological systems. Strenuous to moderate physical activity continuing to the latter months of pregnancy should be viewed as preparatory.

> In general, childbirth is not adversely affected by a history of hard physical exercise.

During pregnancy women athletes exhibit high levels of muscle tonicity. It has been determined that women who suffer from a chronic disability after childbirth usually have a record of little or no physical exercise in the decade immediately preceding pregnancy.[9] Generally, competition may be engaged in well into the third month of pregnancy, unless bleeding or cramps are present, and can frequently be continued until the seventh month, if no handicapping or physiological complications arise. Such activity makes pregnancy, childbirth, and postparturition less stressful. Many women athletes do not continue beyond the third month because of a drop in their performance that can result from a number of reasons, some related to their pregnancy, others perhaps psychological. It is during the first 3 months of pregnancy that the dangers of disturbing the pregnancy are greatest. After that period there is less danger to the mother and fetus, since the pregnancy is stabilized.

Another statement commonly expressed is that women athletes have pelvises which are narrower than normal and that, consequently, they experience various disorders in pregnancy and childbirth. The skeletal measurements of women athletes indicate no departure from normal dimensions. It is a matter of record that they are less subject to uterine disorders that nonathletes. Fertility and gestation among women athletes are within normal ranges. Athletes have a significantly shortened duration of labor and have fewer disorders and complications during the process of giving birth than do nonathletes. After childbirth many athletes have recorded better performances; it has been postulated that pregnancy and childbirth activate latent endocrinological forces that manifest themselves in an improved physical efficiency. Female athletes have stated that they feel stronger and perform better after having children.

Many athletes compete during pregnancy with no ill effects. Most physicians, although advocating moderate activity during this period, believe that especially vigorous performance, particularly in activities in which there may be severe body contact or heavy jarring or falls should be avoided.

REFERENCES

1. Berg, K.: The insulin-dependent runner, Phys. Sportsmed. 7:71, 1979.
2. Berkow, R. (editor): The Merck Manual, ed. 10, Rahway, N.J., 1983, Merck & Co., Inc.
3. Bundgaord, A., et al.: Exercise induced asthma after swimming and bicycle exercise, Eur. J. Respir. Dis. 63:245, May 1982.
4. Caldwell, F.: Menstrual irregularity in athletes: the unanswered question, Phys. Sportsmed. 10:142, May 1982.
5. Cohen, J.L., et al.: Exercise, body weight, and amenorrhea in professional ballet dance, Phys. Sportsmed. 10:79, April 1982.
6. Dale, E., et al.: Menstural dysfunction in distance runners, Obstet. Gynecol. 54:47, 1979.
7. Erdelyi, G.J.: Effects of exercise on the menstrual cycle, Phys. Sportsmed. 4:79, 1976.
8. Frisch, R.E., et al.: Delayed menarche and amenorrhea in ballet dancers, N. Engl. J. Med. 303:17, 1980.
9. Gendel, E.: Psychological factors and menstrual extraction, Phys. Sportsmed. 4:72, 1976.
10. Giulian, K.A.: Gynecology for the athletic trainer, Proceedings of the NATA Professional Preparation Conference, Nashville, Tenn., 1978, National Athletic Trainers Association.
11. Hage, P.: Air pollution: adverse effects on athletic performance, Phys. Sportsmed. 10:126, March 1982.
12. Klafs, C.E., and Lyon, M.J.: The female athlete: a coach's guide to conditioning and training, ed. 2, St. Louis, 1978, The C.V. Mosby Co.
13. Kolski, G.B.: The athlete with asthma and allergies, Symposium on pediatric and adolescent sports medicine, Clinics in sports medicine, vol. 1, no. 1, Philadelphia, Nov. 1982, W.B. Saunders Co.
14. Livingston, S., and Berman, W.: Participation of the epileptic child in contact sports, J. Sports Med. 2:170, 1974.
15. Malina, R.M., et al.: Age at menarche and selected menstrual characteristics in athletes at different competitive levels and in different sports, Med. Sci. Sports 10:218, 1978.
16. Martin, R.P.: The heart in athletics. In Kulund, D.N.: The injured athlete, Philadelphia, 1982, J.B. Lippincott, Co.
17. Morton, A.R.: Physical activity and the asthmatic, Phys. Sportsmed. 9:51, March 1981.
18. Morton, A.R., et al.: Continuous and intermittent running in the provocation of asthma, Ann. Allergy 48:123, Feb. 1982.
19. Ryan, A.J.: Diabetes and exercise, a round table, Phys. Sportsmed. 7:48, 1979.
20. Smith, N.J. (editor): Sports participation for children and adolescents with chronic health problems. In Sports medicine: health care for young athletes, Evanston, Ill., 1983, American Academy of Pediatrics.

ADDITIONAL SOURCES

Arnheim, D.D., and Sinclair, W.A.: Physical education for special populations, Englewood Cliffs, N.J., 1985, Prentice-Hall, Inc.

Cantu, R.C.: Diabetes and exercise, New York, 1982, Elsevier-Dutton Publishing Co., Inc.

Dameshek, H.L.: Participation for the athlete with acute or chronic systemic disease, Southwest Athletic Trainers Association Meeting, Jan. 1982, National Athletic Trainers Association. (Cassette.)

Hanson, P.: Illness among athletes: an overview. In Strauss, R.H. (editor): Sports medicine, Philadelphia, 1984, W.B. Saunders Co.

Kennell, J.H.: Sports participation for the child with a chronic health problem. In Strauss, R.H. (editor): Sports medicine, Philadelphia, 1984, W.B. Saunders Co.

Morris, A.F.: Sports medicine: prevention of athletic injuries, Dubuque, Iowa, 1984, Wm. C. Brown Co., Publishers.

Smith, N.J.: Children and parents: growth, development, and sports. In Strauss, R.H. (editor): Sports medicine, Philadelphia, 1984, W.B. Saunders Co.

Thomas, C.L.: Factors important to women participants in vigorous athletics. In Strauss, R.H. (editor): Sports medicine and physiology, Philadelphia, 1979, W.B. Saunders Co.

GLOSSARY

accident Unexpected mishap occurring by chance.

acidosis Increased or excessive acidity in the body.

Adrenalin Proprietary name for epinephrine, $C_9H_{13}NO_3$.

aerobic Requiring the presence of oxygen.

alkali reserve Total of alkaline salts in the blood available for buffering acids other than carbonic acid and acting to keep up the normal blood alkalinity.

ambient Environmental; as temperature or air that invests one's immediate environment.

ambivalence Coexistence of conflicting and opposite feelings, for example, love and hate.

amine Any of a class of organic compounds containing nitrogen.

amino acids Basic structural units from which proteins are built; a group of organic compounds.

aminolytic Capable of splitting up amines.

amylase Any starch-digesting enzyme that converts starch into sugar.

anaerobic Nonoxidative; not requiring free oxygen; opposite of aerobic.

analgesic Agent that relieves pain without causing a complete loss of sensation.

anaphylaxis Increased susceptibility or sensitiveness to a foreign protein or toxin as the result of previous exposure to it.

andric rating Maleness.

androgen Any substance that aids the development and controls the appearance of male characteristics.

androgyny Hermaphroditism.

ankylosis Abnormal immobility of a joint.

anodyne Medicine that removes or ameliorates pain.

anorexia Lack or loss of appetite; aversion to food.

anoxia Oxygen deficiency; inadequate supply of oxygen to the tissues.

antiphlogistic Pertaining to the checking or diminishing of inflamation and fever.

antipyretic An agent that relieves or reduces fever.

apophysis A bony outgrowth from a bone such as a process, tubercle, or tuberosity.

arthogram Radiopaque material injected into a joint to facilitate the taking of an x-ray.

aspect necrosis Death of tissue without infection.

aspirate To remove fluids, usually by suction.

ATP Adenosine triphosphate; a high-energy phosphate compound stored in muscles; a source of quick energy.

atrophy Wasting away of tissue or of an organ; diminution of the size of a body part.

avascular Devoid of blood circulation.

avulsion Forcible tearing away of a part or a structure.

bacteriostatic Halting the growth of bacteria.

B.M.R. Basal metabolic rate.

bromhidrosis Secretion of foul-smelling perspiration.

buccal Pertaining to the cheek or mouth.

buffer Compound that minimizes the change that occurs in pH (the degree of alkalinity or acidity) of a fluid, for example, the blood, when alkalis or acids are added.

calorie (large) The amount of heat required to raise 1 kg of water 1° C; used to express the fuel or energy value of food or the heat output of the organism; the amount of heat required to heat 1 pound of water to 4° F.

cancellous Latticelike or meshlike structure in bone.

carcinogenic Producing or causing cancer.

cardiac cycle Total sequence of cardiac movement, including the valve actions and the pressure and volume changes, during one complete period of relaxation and contraction.

cardiac output Volume of blood pumped by both ventricles in a 1-minute period.

cardiac reserve Ability of the heart to increase its rate and/or its stroke volume, thus increasing its output of blood.

cardiant Any medicine stimulating the heart.

catalyst Substance that accelerates a chemical reaction.

chemotaxis Response to influence of chemical stimulation.

chondromalacia Abnormal softening of cartilage.

cicatrix Scar or mark, formed by fibrous connective tissue; left by a wound or sore.

circadian rhythm Biological time clock by which the body functions.

circumduction Movement in which the part describes a cone with the apex at the joint.

collagen Main organic constituent of connective tissue.

colloid Liquid or gelatinous substance that retains particles of another substance in a state of suspension.

core temperature Internal or deep body temperature monitored by cells in the hypothalamus, as opposed to shell or peripheral temperature, which is registered by that layer of insulation provided by the skin, subcutaneous tissues, and the superficial portions of the muscle masses.

corticoid A hormone of the adrenal cortex.

crepitus Grating sound produced by the contact of the fractured ends of bones.

cubital fossa Triangular area on the anterior aspect of the forearm directly opposite the elbow joint (the bend of the elbow).

curettement (curettage) Surgical scraping.

cyanosis Bluish discoloration or lividness of the skin, caused by deficient oxygenation of the blood.

cystitis Inflammation of the urinary bladder.

dermatomes Area of skin supplied with afferent nerve fibers by a single posterior spinal root.

diapedesis Passage of blood cells through the walls of the blood vessels; term sometimes used to refer to the oozing of blood.

distal Remote; farther from any point of reference.

diuretic Agent or medicinal substance that increases or stimulates the flow or urine.

dyspepsia Impairment of the function of digestion.

dyspnea Labored or difficult breathing.

ecchymosis Extravasation of blood; tissue discoloration caused by the extravasation of blood.

edema Swelling as a result of the collection of fluid in the connective tissue.

emesis Vomiting.

endorphin Any of a group of endogenous polypeptide substances in the brain that bind to opiate receptors in various areas of the brain and thereby raise the pain threshold.

enthesitis Group of conditions characterized by inflammation, fibrosis, and calcification around tendons, ligaments, and muscle insertions.

enzyme Complex organic sybstance, originating from living cells, which acts as a catalyst in certian chemical changes; digestive enzyme.

eosinophil White blood cell easily stained by eosin, a red coloring matter.

epiphysis Portion of a bone that in early life is formed independently and later is joined to complete the whole bone through further ossification.

erythema redness of the skin.

estrogen Any substance that influences estrus or produces changes in female sexual characteristics.

etiology Science dealing with causes of disease.

eversion Turning outward.

excoriation Removal of a piece or strip of skin.

extravasation Escape of a fluid from its proper vessels into the surrounding tissues.

exudate Fluid with a high content of protein and cellular debris which has escaped from blood vessels and has been deposited in tissues or on tissue surfaces, usually a result of inflammation.

fibroblast Any cell component from which fibers are developed.

fibrosis Development of excessive fibrous connective tissue; fibroid degeneration.

force couple Depressor action by the subscapularis, infraspinatus, and teres minor to stabilize the head of the humerus and to counteract the upward force exerted by the deltoid during abduction of the arm.

FSH The follicle stimulating hormone in the female; stimulates follicle growth and maturation and estrogen secretion.

glucocorticoid Corticoid that raises the concentration of liver glycogen and blood sugar.

glucose Simle sugar; blood sugar; dextrose.

glycogenesis Formation of glycogen from lactic acid or simple sugar.

glycogenolytic Splitting of glycogen.

glycolysis Transformation of glycogen to lactic acid during muscle contraction.

glycosuria Abnormally high proportion of sugar in the urine.

gonadotropins Follicle-stimulating hormone (FSH) and luteinizing hormone (LH).

gynic rating Femaleness.

hemarthrosis Blood in a joint cavity.

hematolytic Pertaining to the degeneration and disintegration of the blood.

hematoma Localized collection of extravasated blood, usually clotted, in an organ, space, or tissue.

hematopoiesis Process of formation and development of blood cells.

hematuria Passing of blood in the urine.

hemianopia Defective vision or blindness in half of the visual field.

hemoglobin Iron-containing protein that is the coloring matter of the red blood cells.

hertz (Hz) Number of sound waves per second.

histamine A chemical substance stemming from damaged tissue.

histology Science dealing with the minute structure, composition, and function of tissues.

homeostasis Maintenance of a steady state in the body's internal environment.

hook-lying position Basic starting position in exercise in which the subject, lying supine and keeping the feet flat on the floor, flexes the knees and brings the heels as close to the buttocks as possible.

hyperemia Increase of blood in any part of the body.

hyperextension Extension of a joint beyond straight alignment.

hyperglycemia Excess of glucose in the blood.

hyperhidrosis Excessive sweating; excessive foot perspiration.

hyperkeratosis Increased callus development.

hyperpnea Hyperventilation; increased minute volume of breathing; exaggerated deep breathing.

hypertension High blood pressure; abnormally high tension.

hypertrophy Enlargement of a part, caused by an increase in the size of its cells.

hyperventilation Abnormal breathing that is deep and prolonged; hyperpnea.

hyponatremia Deficiency of sodium (salt) in the blood.

hypoxia Reduction of oxygen supply to a tissue.

idiopathic Caused by an unknown factor; self-originated.

indurated tissue Area of hardened tissue.

injury A harm, hurt, wound, or maim; usually inflicted by an external force.

intertrigo Chafing of the skin.

iontophoresis Introduction of ions of soluble salts into the body by means of electric current.

ipsilateral Situated on the same side.

irritability Ability of a muscle to respond to a stimulus.

ischemia Lack of blood supply to a part.

keloid Fibrous tumor.

ketogenic Forming ketones, acids produced during fat metabolism.

kinesthesia; kinesthesis Sensation or feeling of movement; the awareness one has of the spatial relationships of his body and its parts.

lactic acid A by-product of muscle contraction, producing fatigue and pain in the muscle; it evolves through glycolysis.

LH Luteining hormone, which causes the postovulatory follicle to transform into a corpus luteum through vascularization, follicular cell hypertrophy, and lipid accumulation.

lipid Fat or ester.

maceration Softening of the skin by soaking.

malocclusion Improper relationship of opposing teeth.

margination Accumulation of leukocytes on blood vessel walls at the site of injury in early stages of inflammation.

menarche Onset of the menstrual function.

mesentery Fold of peritoneum that supports the intestine from the posterior abdominal wall.

microtrauma Microscopic lesion or injury.

micturition Urination.

mimetic Imitative.

mnemonic Assisting or aiding memory..

morphology Science of form and structure.

muscle viscosity Internal resistance factor of the muscle.

myoglobinuria Myoglobin secreted in the urine.

myopia Nearsightedness.

necrosin Chemical substance that stems from inflamed tissue, bringing about changes in normal tissue.

necrosis Death of a tissue or organ, especially bone.

neuroma Tumor consisting mostly of nerve cells and nerve fibers.

nociceptor A receptor of pain.

nystagmus Constant and involuntary rolling movement of the eyeball.

orthopedic surgeon One who corrects deformities of the musculoskeletal system.

orthosis Appliance or apparatus used to support, align, prevent, or correct deformities or to improve fuction of movable parts of the body.

orthotics The field of knowledge relating to orthoses and their use.

oscillometer An instrument that measures any kind of oscillation, for example, the arterial volumetric changes that accompany the heart beat.

osteochondritis Inflammation of bone and cartilage.

osteochondritis dissecans Splitting of pieces of cartilage into the affected joint.

otolaryngologist Physician who specializes in diseases of the ear, nose, and throat.

parenteral Not given through the alimentary canal.

paresis Slight or incomplete paralysis.

paresthesia Abnormal or morbid sensation such as itching or prickling.

patent Open, unobstructed; permitting flow.

pathogenic Disease-producing.

pathology Science of the structural and functional manifestations of disease.

phagocytosis Destruction of injurious cells or particles by the phagocytes (white blood cells).

phonophoresis Introdction of ions of soluble salt into the body by means of ultrasound.

phosphocreatine Organic phosphate base, which functions as an important source of muscular energy.

placebo Medicine given merely to please the patient; in research, an innocuous pill or capsule given a subject to aid in eliminating psychological or other variables.

plasma kinins Any endogenous peptides that increase vascular permeability.

pledget small tuft of absorbent cotton.

podiatrist Practioner who specializes in the study and care of the foot.

post-parturition The period following childbirth.

prognosis Prediction as to probable result of a disease or injury.

proprioceptor One of several receptors, each of which responds to stimuli elicited from within the body itself; for example, the muscle spindles that invoke the myotatic or stretch reflex.

prosthesis Replacement of an absent body part with an artificial part; the artificial part.

proteolytic That which brings about the digestion of proteins.

proximal Nearest to the point of reference.

pruritus Itching.

psychogenic Of psychic origin; that which originates in the mind.

psychosomatic Showing effects of mind-body relationship; a physical disorder caused or influenced by the mind, that is, by the emotions.

purulent Consisting of or containg pus.

pyrogenic Inducing fever.

residual That which remains; often used to describe a permanent condition resulting from injury or disease, for example, a limp or a paralysis.

rhabdomyolysis Disintegration of striated muscle fibers.

Romberg's sign (or symptom) Experiencing difficulty when standing with the eyes closed.

rotation Turning about an axis in an angular motion.

rotor cuff Tendinous attachments of the subscapularis, supraspinatus, infraspinatus, and teres minor, on the head of the humerus.

SAID principle Specific *a*daptation to *i*mposed *d*emands.

sequela Pathological condition that occurs as a consequence of another condition or event.

seratonin A hormone and neurotransmitter.

spermatogenesis Formation of spermatozoa, male sex cell formed within the testes.

splanchnic Pertaining to the internal organs, the viscera.

sporicide Any agent that destorys a spore.

stasis Blocking or stoppage of circulation.

steroid A large group of compounds that contain no fatty acids in their molecules (cholesterol, adrenocortical hormones, sex hormones).

sterol Any one of a group of alcohols that are of vegetable or animal origin and have characteristics similar to fats.

stressor Anything that affects the body's physiological or psychological condition, upsetting the homeostatic balance.

subacute Relatively acute; a stage between acute and chronic.

syndrome Group of typical symptoms or conditions that characterize a deficiency or a disease.

telemetry Making physiological measurements of a subject from a distance by means of radio signals.

testosterone A male sex hormone.

topical Pertaining to a certain area of the body.

torque Anything that cases torsion, the turning moment of force.

torsion Act or state of being twisted.

trauma (Plural form, traumas or traumata) Wound or injury.

vascularization Process of becoming vascular; that is, having a great many blood vessels.

venostasis Pooling of blood in a vein.

viscosity Resitance to flow.

vital capacity Volume of air that can be forcefully expired after a maximal inspiration.

volar Referring to the palm or the sole.

PROPRIOCEPTIVE NEUROMUSCULAR FACILITATION (PNF) PATTERNS

Proprioceptive neuromuscular facilitation patterns should not be begun at the site of a sprain injury until resolution is well under way.

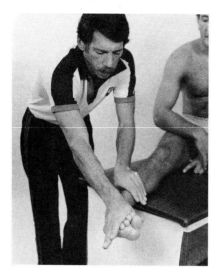

Figure A1

Start—ankle in dorsiflexion
and foot in eversion.

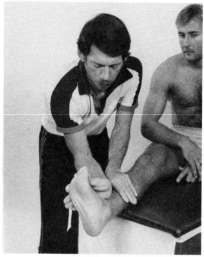

Figure A2

Finish.

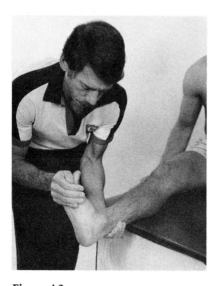

Figure A3

Start—ankle in plantar
flexion and foot in inversion.

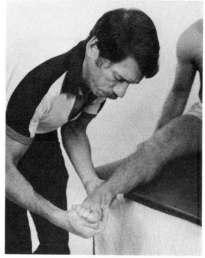

Figure A4

Finish.

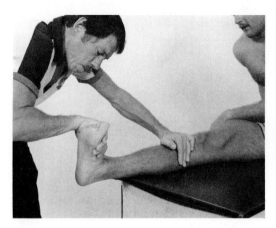

Figure A5

Start—ankle in dorsiflexion
and foot in inversion.

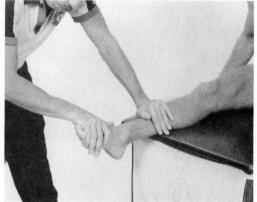

Figure A6

Finish.

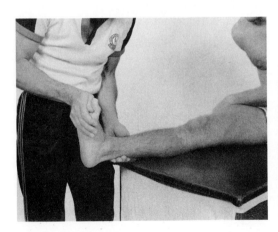

Figure A7

Start—ankle in plantar
flexion and foot in eversion.

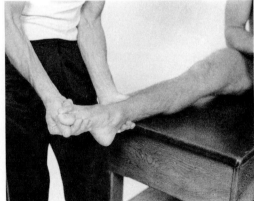

Figure A8

Finish.

B KNEE PATTERNS

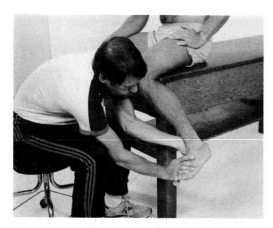

Figure B1

Start—knee extension with tibial external rotation, ankle dorsiflexion, and foot inversion with toes in tibial extension.

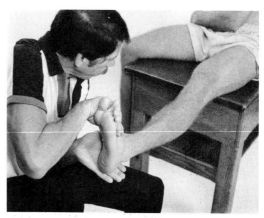

Figure B2

Finish.

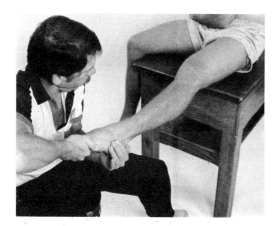

Figure B3

Start—knee flexion with tibial internal rotation, ankle plantar flexion, and foot eversion with toes in fibular flexion.

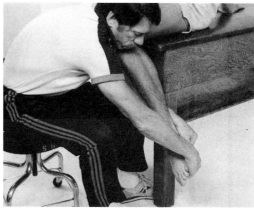

Figure B4

Finish.

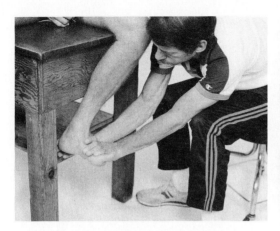

Figure B5

Start—knee extension with tibial internal rotation, ankle dorsiflexion, and foot eversion with toes in fibular extension.

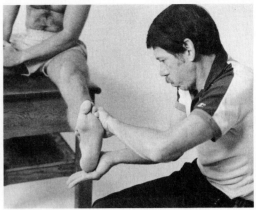

Figure B6

Finish.

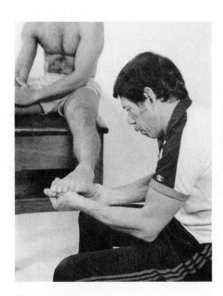

Figure B7

Start—knee flexion with tibial external rotation, ankle plantar flexion, and foot inversion with toes in tibial flexion.

Figure B8

Finish.

C HIP PATTERNS

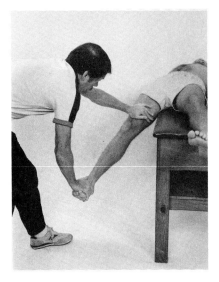

Figure C1

Start—hip flexion, adduction, and external rotation. The knee is extended, ankle dorsiflexed, foot inverted, and toes tibial extended.

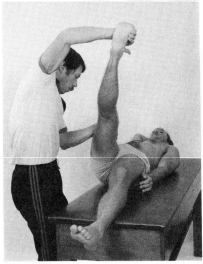

Figure C2

Finish.

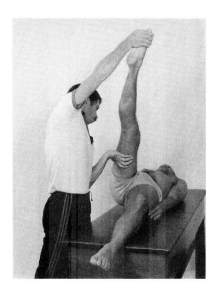

Figure C3

Start—hip moving in extension, abduction, and internal rotation. The knee is extended, ankle is plantar flexed, foot everted, and toes flexed toward the fibula.

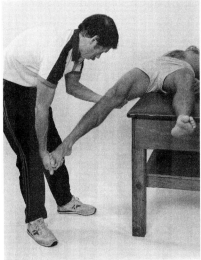

Figure C4

Finish.

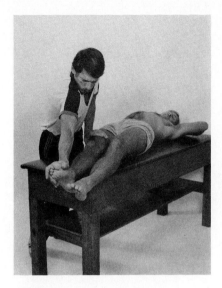

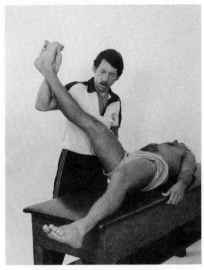

Figure C5

Start—hip flexed, abducted, and internally rotated. The ankle is dorsiflexed, foot everted, and toes in fibular extension.

Figure C6

Finish.

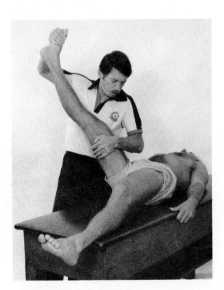

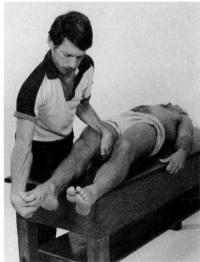

Figure C7

Start—hip in extension, adducted, externally rotated with knee extended. The ankle is plantar flexed, foot everted, and toes flexed tibially.

Figure C8

Finish.

D BILATERAL HIP PATTERNS FOR ABDOMINAL AND LOW BACK REHABILITATION

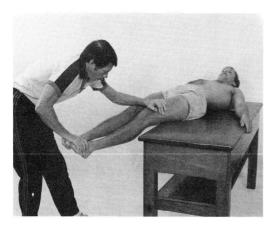

Figure D1

Start—bilateral asymmetrical hip flexion with knee flexion for trunk flexors to left. *Athlete's right leg:* hip flexion, adduction, external rotation, and knee flexion. Ankle dorsiflexed, foot in-verted, and toes in tibial extension. *Athlete's left leg:* hip flexion, abduction, internal rotation, and knee flexion. Ankle is dorsiflexed, foot everted, and toes in fibular extension.

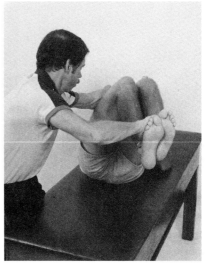

Figure D2

Finish.

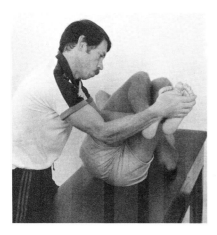

Figure D3

Start—bilateral asymmetrical hip extension with knee extended for back extensors to the right. *Athlete's right leg* moves into hip extension, abduction, internal rotation, and knee extension. Ankle is plantar flexed, foot everted, and toes in fibular flexion. *Athlete's left leg* moves in hip extension, adduction, external rotation, and knee extension. Ankle is plantar flexed, foot inverted, and toes in tibial flexion.

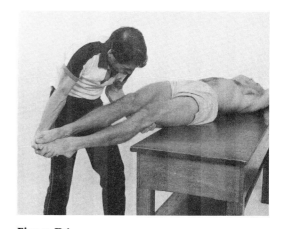

Figure D4

Finish.

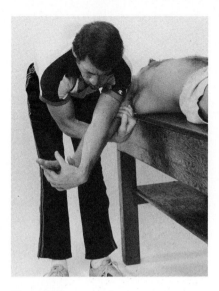

Figure E1

Start—shoulder flexion, adduction, external rotation. Forearm is supinated with wrist and fingers in radial flexion.

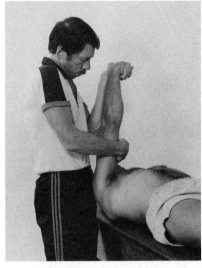

Figure E2

Continue motion.

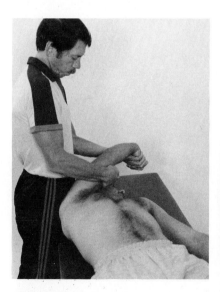

Figure E3

Finish.

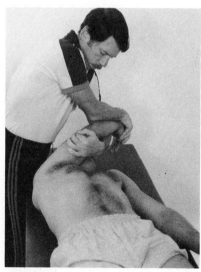

Figure E4

Start—shoulder extension, abduction, internal rotation. Forearm moves into pronation, wrist and fingers in ulnar extension.

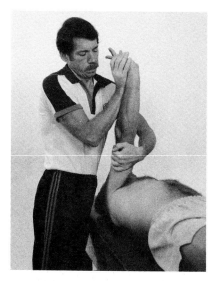

Figure E5

Continue motion.

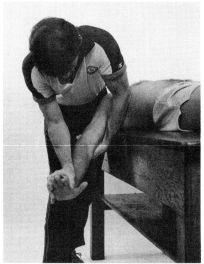

Figure E6

Finish.

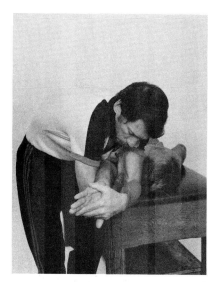

Figure E7

Start—shoulder extension,
adduction, and internal
rotation. Forearm is pronated
with wrist and fingers in
ulnar flexion.

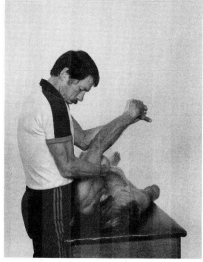

Figure E8

Continue motion.

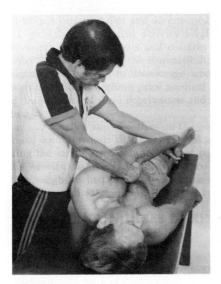

Figure E9

Finish.

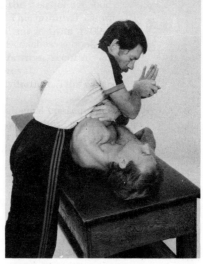

Figure E10

Start—shoulder extension, adduction and external rotation. Forearm is supinated with wrist and fingers in radial flexion.

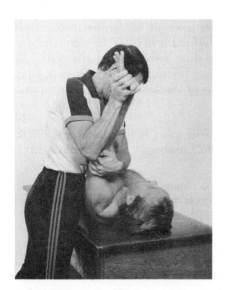

Figure E11

Continue motion.

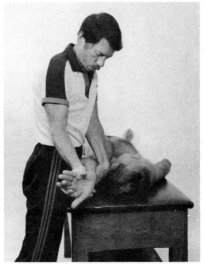

Figure E12

Finish.

NATIONAL ATHLETIC TRAINERS' ASSOCIATION INFORMATION

A   NATIONAL ATHLETIC TRAINERS' ASSOCIATION CODE OF ETHICS

Preamble

One outstanding characteristic of a profession is that its members are dedicated to rendering service to humanity. Also, they are committed to the improvement of standards of performance. In becoming a member of the athletic training profession, the individual assumes obligations and responsibilities to conduct himself/herself in accordance with its ideals and standards. These are set forth in the Constitution and By-Laws and are emphasized in the CODE OF ETHICS. Any athletic trainer who does not feel that he/she can or does not deem it necessary to comply with the principles set forth in the CODE should have no place in this profession.

The members of the athletic training profession must adhere to the highest standards of conduct in carrying out their significant roles in athletic programs at all levels. It is for this reason that the Board of Directors of the National Athletic Trainers' Association has continually revised the CODE which has been in effect since June, 1957.*

In approving the Code, the Board of Directors recognizes and believes that unless the standards and principles that are set forth in this document are accepted in good faith and followed sincerely, it will not be effective in continuing to improve the contributions of the profession and its members to athletics and sports medicine.

Ethics is generally considered as conduct in keeping with moral duty and making the right actions relative to ideal principles. Let it be understood that all members of the National Athletic Trainers' Association will understand and apply the principles set forth in this CODE and make every effort to do the right thing at the right time to the best of their ability and judgment.

Purpose

The purpose of this CODE is to clarify the ethical and approved professional practices as distinguished from those that might prove harmful or detrimental and to instill into the members of the Association the value and importance of the athletic trainers' role.

Objectives

The stated objectives of the National Athletic Trainers' Association in its Constitution are:

1. The advancement, encouragement and improvement of the athletic training profession in all its phases and to promote a better working relation-

---

*1971, 1973, 1974, 1976, 1977, 1978, 1979, 1980, 1982, 1983; Rev. 830926.

ship among those persons interested in the problems of training.
2. To develop further the ability of each of its members.
3. To better serve the common interest of its members by providing a means for free exchange of ideas within the profession.
4. To enable the members to become better acquainted personally through casual good fellowship.

Article I—Basic Principles

The essential basic principles of this CODE are Honesty, Integrity and Loyalty. Athletic trainers who reflect these characterstics will be a credit to the Association, the institution they represent and to themselves.

When a person becomes a member of this Association he/she assumes certain obligations and responsibilities. A trainer whose conduct is not in accordance with the principles set forth in the following sections shall be considered in violation of the CODE.

Section 1–Athletics in General

An athletic trainer shall show no discrimination in his/her efforts while performing his/her duties.

Section 2–Drugs

The membership of the National Athletic Trainers' Association does not condone the unauthorized and/or nontherapeutic use of drugs. The Association recognizes that the best and safest program is comprised of good conditioning and athletic training principles.

Section 3–Testimonials and Endorsements

In any endorsement in which the trainer's name and/or reference to the athletic training profession is included, the wording and illustration, including any implications of the endorsement shall be such that no discredit to the training profession may be construed. (Any endorsement that is not in keeping with the highest principles and standards of the athletic training profession shall be considered unethical.) The NATA name, logo, trademark and/or insignia may not be used in any testimonials and/or endorsement service products, programs, publications and facilities by individual members or groups of members of the Association.

Section 4–Sportsmanship

Members of this Association shall not condone, engage in or defend unsportsman-like practices.

Section 5–Fellow Trainers

Any trainer who by his/her conduct or comments, publicly discredits or lowers the dignity of members of the profession is guilty of breach of ethics.

Section 6–Membership

It is unethical for a member to sponsor a candidate for membership in the National Athletic Trainers' Association who does not know the candidate and his/her qualifications.

Section 7–Misrepresentation

It is unethical for a member to misrepresent his/her membership status and/or classification.

Article II–Educational Preparation and Certification

Any certified member of this Association must be considered an educator if he/she is involved with the professional preparation of students pursuing

National Athletic Trainers' Association Certification through any of the approved certification routes.

Section 1–Educational Standards

The athletic trainer-educator must adhere to the educational standards and criteria set forth by this Association.

Section 2–Selection of Students

The athletic trainer-educator is responsible for the selection of students for admission into a professional preparation program and must ensure that policies are non-discriminatory with respect to race, color, sex, or national origin.

Section 3–Publication and Representation

Publication and representation of the professional preparation program by the athletic trainer-educator must accurately reflect the program offered.

Section 4–Evaluation of Students

Evaluation of student achievement by the athletic trainer-educator must be done in a prudent manner.

Section 5–Recommendation for Certification

It is unethical for a member to knowingly recommend a candidate for the national certification examination who has not fulfilled all eligibility requirements as specified by the Board of Certification.

Section 6–Confidentiality of National Certification Examination

It is unethical for any member to reproduce in written form or reveal in any other manner, any part of the written or oral-practical examination for the purpose of aiding certification candidates in passing the examination.

Article III—Enforcement

Section 1–Reporting of Unethical Conduct

Any member of the Association who becomes aware of conduct that he/she considers unethical and that he/she believes warrants investigation, shall report the incident(s) in writing to the President and the Executive Director of the Association, who will in turn initiate investigation through the Ethics Committee. He/she shall include in the communication all pertinent data.

Section 2–Investigation and Action

In accordance with the By-Laws of the Association, the Ethics Committee investigates reported incidents of unethical conduct and if, in the judgment of a majority of the committee members, it finds that the accused person has violated the National Athletic Trainers' Association CODE OF ETHICS, it communicates its decision to the accused and to the Board of Directors in writing and recommends to the Board one of the following disciplinary actions:

1. *Letter of Censure*
   Copies to immediate supervisor and District Director.
2. *Period of Probation*
   During the period of probation the member shall not be eligible for any of the following: (This shall be determined by the Board of Directors.)
   a) Hold an office at any level in the Association.
   b) Represent NATA in the capacity of liaison with another organization.
3. *Initiate Procedure for Cancellation of Membership*

Section 3—Action by the Board of Directors

This decision of the Board of Directors in CODE OF ETHICS is final, except that if the decision is to initiate cancellation of membership. This shall be done as prescribed in Article VI, Sections 1 and 2 of the Constitution.

B STATES WITH LICENSURE OF ATHLETIC TRAINERS

Georgia	North Dakota
Kentucky	Oklahoma
Massachusetts	Rhode Island
Missouri	Texas
New Mexico	South Carolina

C NATIONAL ATHLETIC TRAINERS' ASSOCIATION APPROVED ATHLETIC TRAINING EDUCATION PROGRAMS

Programs listed here are approved by the National Athletic Trainers' Association. For detailed information, write to the program director whose name is given in parentheses in the listing. Two basic plans of education for athletic training are listed according to the following key:

1 Undergraduate Athletic Training Education Programs
2 Graduate Athletic Training Education Programs

ARIZONA
UNIVERSITY OF ARIZONA (2)
  Department of Physical Education
  Tucson, Arizona 85721
ARIZONA STATE UNIVERSITY (1)
  Department of Health, Physical Education & Recreation
  Tempe, Arizona 85281

CALIFORNIA
CALIFORNIA STATE UNIVERSITY, FULLERTON (1)
  Department of Health, Physical Education & Recreation
  Fullerton, California 92634
CALIFORNIA STATE UNIVERSITY, LONG BEACH (1)
  Department of Physical Education
  Long Beach, California 90840
CALIFORNIA STATE UNIVERSITY, NORTHRIDGE (1)
  Department of Physical Education & Athletics
  Northridge, California 91324
CALIFORNIA STATE UNIVERSITY, SACRAMENTO (1)
  Department of Athletics and Sport
  Sacramento, California 95819

DELAWARE
UNIVERSITY OF DELAWARE (1)
  Department of Physical Education & Athletics
  Newark, Delaware 19711

IDAHO
BOISE STATE UNIVERSITY (1)
  Department of Physical Education
  Boise, Idaho 83725

ILLINOIS
EASTERN ILLINOIS UNIVERSITY (1)
  School of Health, Physical Education & Recreation
  Charleston, Illinois 61920

ILLINOIS STATE UNIVERSITY (2)
Department of Health, Physical Education and Dance
Normal, Illinois 61761
SOUTHERN ILLINOIS UNIVERSITY (1)
127 Davies Gym
Carbondale, Illinois 62901
UNIVERSITY OF ILLINOIS (1)
Department of Physical Education
Urbana, Illinois 61801
WESTERN ILLINOIS UNIVERSITY (1)
College of Health, Physical Education & Recreation
Macomb, Illinois 61455

INDIANA
BALL STATE UNIVERSITY (1)
Department of Men's Physical Education
Muncie, Indiana 47306
INDIANA UNIVERSITY (1,2)
School of Health, Physical Education & Recreation
Bloomington, Indiana 47401
INDIANA STATE UNIVERSITY (1,2)
School of Health, Physical Education & Recreation
Terre Haute, Indiana 47809
PURDUE UNIVERSITY (1)
Department of Physical Education, Health, and Recreation Studies
West Lafayette, Indiana 47907

IOWA
UNIVERSITY OF IOWA (1)
Department of Physical Education for Men
Iowa City, Iowa 52242

KENTUCKY
EASTERN KENTUCKY UNIVERSITY (1)
College of Health, Physical Education, Recreation and Athletics
Richmond, Kentucky 40475

LOUISIANA
LOUISIANA STATE UNIVERSITY (1)
Department of Health, Physical Education and Recreation
Baton Rouge, Louisiana 70803

MASSACHUSETTS
BRIDGEWATER STATE COLLEGE (1)
Department of Physical Education
Bridgewater, Massachusetts 02324
NORTHEASTERN UNIVERSITY (1)
Department of Physical Education
Boston, Massachusetts 02115
SPRINGFIELD COLLEGE (1)
Division of Health, Physical Education & Recreation
Springfield, Massachusetts 01109

MICHIGAN
CENTRAL MICHIGAN UNIVERSITY (1)
Physical Education Department
Mount Pleasant, Michigan 48859

GRAND VALLEY STATE COLLEGE (1)
  Department of Physical Education & Recreation
  Allendale, Michigan 49401
WESTERN MICHIGAN UNIVERSITY (2)
  Department of Health, Physical Education & Recreation
  Kalamazoo, Michigan 49009

MINNESOTA
MANKATO STATE UNIVERSITY (1)
  Physical Education Department
  Mankato, Minnesota 56001

MISSISSIPPI
UNIVERSITY OF SOUTHERN MISSISSIPPI (1)
  Department of Athletic Administration & Coaching
  Hattiesburg, Mississippi 39401

MISSOURI
SOUTHWEST MISSOURI STATE UNIVERSITY (1)
  Hammons Student Center
  901 S. National
  Springfield, Missouri 65802

MONTANA
UNIVERSITY OF MONTANA (1)
  Department of Health and Physical Education
  Missoula, Montana 59801

NEBRASKA
UNIVERSITY OF NEBRASKA (1)
  University Health Center
  Lincoln, Nebraska 68588

NEVADA
UNIVERSITY OF NEVADA-LAS VEGAS (1)
  Department of Physical Education
  Las Vegas, Nevada 89119

NEW JERSEY
KEAN COLLEGE OF NEW JERSEY (1)
  Department of Physical Education
  Union, New Jersey 07083
WILLIAM PATTERSON COLLEGE OF NEW JERSEY (1)
  Department of Movement Sciences and Leisure Studies
  Wayne, New Jersey 07470

NEW MEXICO
UNIVERSITY OF NEW MEXICO (1)
  Department of Health, Physical Education & Recreation
  Albuquerque, New Mexico 87131

NEW YORK
CANISIUS COLLEGE (1)
  Department of Physical Education
  Buffalo, New York 14208
STATE UNIVERSITY COLLEGE AT CORTLAND (1)
  Division of Health, Physical Education & Recreation
  Cortland, New York 13045

ITHACA COLLEGE (1)
  Department of Health, Physical Education & Recreation
  Ithaca, New York 14850

NORTH CAROLINA
APPALACHIAN STATE UNIVERSITY (1)
  Department of Health, Physical Education & Recreation
  Boone, North Carolina 28608
EAST CAROLINA UNIVERSITY (1)
  Department of Health, Physical Education, Recreation & Safety
  Greenville, North Carolina 27834
MARS HILL COLLEGE (1)
  Physical Education Department
  Mars Hill, North Carolina 27854
UNIVERSITY OF NORTH CAROLINA (2)
  Department of Physical Education
  Chapel Hill, North Carolina 27514

NORTH DAKOTA
NORTH DAKOTA STATE UNIVERSITY (1)
  Department of Health, Physical Education, Recreation and Athletics
  Fargo, North Dakota 58102
UNIVERSITY OF NORTH DAKOTA (1)
  Department of Health, Physical Education & Recreation
  Grand Forks, North Dakota 58201

OHIO
BOWLING GREEN STATE UNIVERSITY (1)
  School of Health and Physical Education and Recreation
  Bowling Green, Ohio 43403
MIAMI UNIVERSITY OF OHIO (1)
  Withrow Court, Room 6
  Oxford, Ohio 45056
OHIO UNIVERSITY (1)
  School of Health, Physical Education & Recreation
  Athens, Ohio 45701
TOLEDO UNIVERSITY (1)
  Department of Physical Education
  Toledo, Ohio 43606

OREGON
OREGON STATE UNIVERSITY (1)
  Physical Education Department
  Corvallis, Oregon 97331
UNIVERSITY OF OREGON (2)
  Department of Physical Education
  Eugene, Oregon 97403

PENNSYLVANIA
EAST STROUDSBURG STATE COLLEGE (1)
  Koehler Fieldhouse
  East Stroudsburg, Pennsylvania 18301
LOCK HAVEN STATE COLLEGE (1)
  School of Health, Physical Education & Recreation
  Lock Haven, Pennsylvania 17745

THE PENNSYLVANIA STATE UNIVERSITY (1)
  College of Health, Physical Education & Recreation
  University Park, Pennsylvania 16802
UNIVERSITY OF PITTSBURGH (1)
  Health, Physical Education & Recreation
  Pittsburgh, Pennsylvania 15261
SLIPPERY ROCK STATE COLLEGE (1)
  Health Sciences Department
  Slippery Rock, Pennsylvania 16057
WEST CHESTER STATE COLLEGE (1)
  Physical Education Department
  School of Health Sciences
  West Chester, Pennsylvania 19380

SOUTH DAKOTA
SOUTH DAKOTA STATE UNIVERSITY (1)
  Department of Health, Physical Education & Recreation
  Brookings, South Dakota 57007

TEXAS
LAMAR UNIVERSITY (1)
  Department of Intercollegiate Athletics
  P.O. Box 10066, Lamar Station
  Beaumont, Texas 77710
SOUTHWEST TEXAS STATE UNIVERSITY (1)
  Department of Health & Physical Education
  San Marcos, Texas 78666
STEPHEN F. AUSTIN STATE UNIVERSITY (1)
  Department of Health and Physical Education
  Nacogdoches, Texas 79562
TEXAS CHRISTIAN UNIVERSITY (1)
  Department of Athletics
  Fort Worth, Texas 76129

UTAH
BRIGHAM YOUNG UNIVERSITY (1)
  Department of Physical Education
  Provo, Utah 84602

VERMONT
UNIVERSITY OF VERMONT (1)
  Intercollegiate Athletics and Physical Education Department
  Burlington, Vermont 05405

VIRGINIA
JAMES MADISON UNIVERSITY (1)
  Department of Intercollegiate Athletics
  Harrisonburg, Virginia 22807
OLD DOMINION UNIVERSITY (2)
  Department of Intercollegiate Athletics
  Norfolk, Virginia 23508
UNIVERSITY OF VIRGINIA (2)
  Athletic Department
  Charlottesville, Virginia 22903

WASHINGTON

WASHINGTON STATE UNIVERSITY (1)
Department of Physical Education for Men & Women
Pullman, Washington 99163

WEST VIRGINIA

WEST VIRGINIA UNIVERSITY (1)
Department of Professional Physical Education
Morgantown, West Virginia 26505

WISCONSIN

UNIVERSITY OF WISCONSIN-LACROSSE (1)
150 Mitchell Hall
LaCrosse, Wisconsin 54601

AMERICAN COLLEGE OF SPORTS MEDICINE POSITION STATEMENTS

A   THE USE OF ALCOHOL IN SPORTS

Based upon a comprehensive analysis of the available research relative to the effects of alcohol upon human physical performance, it is the position of the American College of Sports Medicine that:

1. The acute ingestion of alcohol can exert a deleterious effect upon a wide variety of psychomotor skills such as reaction time, hand-eye coordination, accuracy, balance, and complex coordination.
2. Acute ingestion of alcohol will not substantially influence metabolic or physiological functions essential to physical performance such as energy metabolism, maximal oxygen consumption (Vo_2max), heart rate, stroke volume, cardiac output, muscle blood flow, arteriovenous oxygen difference, or respiratory dynamics. Alcohol consumption may impair body temperature regulation during prolonged exercise in a cold environment.
3. Acute alcohol ingestion will not improve and may decrease strength, power, local muscular endurance, speed, and cardiovascular endurance.
4. Alcohol is the most abused drug in the United States and is a major contributing factor to accidents and their consequences. Also, it has been documented widely that prolonged excessive alcohol consumption can elicit pathological changes in the liver, heart, brain, and muscle, which can lead to disability and death.
5. Serious and continuing efforts should be made to educate athletes, coaches, health and physical educators, physicians, trainers, the sports media, and the general public regarding the effects of acute alcohol ingestion upon human physical performance and on the potential acute and chronic problems of excessive alcohol consumption.

Research Background for the Position Statement

This position statement is concerned primarily with the effects of acute alcohol ingestion upon physical performance and is based upon a comprehensive review of the pertinent international literature. When interpreting these results, several precautions should be kept in mind. First, there are varying reactions to alcohol ingestion, not only among individuals, but also within an individual depending upon the circumstances. Second, it is virtually impossible to conduct double-blind placebo research with alcohol because subjects can always tell when alcohol has been consumed. Nevertheless, the results cited below provide us with some valid general conclusions relative to the effects of alcohol on physical performance. In most of the

---

From American College of Sports Medicine: Position statement on the use of alcohol in sports, 1982.

research studies, a small dose consisted of 1.5-2.0 ounces (45-60 ml) of alcohol, equivalent to a blood alcohol level (BAL) of 0.04-0.05 in the average-size male. A moderate dose was equivalent to 3-4 ounces (90-120 ml), or a BAL of about 0.10. Few studies employed a large dose, with a BAL of 0.15.

1. Athletes may consume alcohol to improve psychological function, but it is psychomotor performance that deteriorates most. A consistent finding is the impairment of information processing. In sports involving rapid reactions to changing stimuli, performance will be affected most adversely. Research has shown that small to moderate amounts of alcohol will impair reaction time* hand-eye coordination[8,9,14,40] accuracy,[36,39] balance,[3] and complex coordination or gross motor skills.[4,8,22,36,41] Thus, while Coopersmith[10] suggests that alcohol may improve self-confidence, the available research reveals a deterioration in psychomotor performance.

2. Many studies have been conducted relative to the effects of acute alcohol ingestion upon metabolic and physiological functions important to physical performance. Alcohol ingestion exerts no beneficial influence relative to energy sources for exercise. Muscle glycogen at rest was significantly lower after alcohol compared to control.[30] However, in exercise at 50% maximal oxygen uptake (Vo_2max), total glycogen depleted in the leg muscles was not affected by alcohol.[30] Moreover, Juhlin-Dannfelt et al.[29] have shown that although alcohol does not impair lipolysis or free fatty acid (FFA) utilization during exercise, it may decrease splanchnic glucose output, decrease the potential contribution from liver gluconeogenesis, elicit a greater decline in blood glucose levels leading to hypoglycemia, and decrease the leg muscle uptake of glucose during the latter stages of a 3-k run. Other studies[17,19] have supported the theory concerning the hypoglycemic effect of alcohol during both moderate and prolonged exhaustive exercise in a cold environment. These studies also noted a significant loss of body heat and a resultant drop in body temperature and suggested alcohol may impair temperature regulation. These changes may impair endurance capacity.

In one study,[5] alcohol has been shown to increase oxygen uptake significantly during submaximal work and simultaneously to decrease mechanical efficiency, but this finding has not been confirmed by others.[6,15,33,44] Alcohol appears to have no effect on maximal or near-maximal Vo_2.[5-7,44]

The effects of alcohol on cardiovascular-respiratory parameters associated with oxygen uptake are variable at submaximal exercise intensities and are negligible at maximal levels. Alcohol has been shown by some investigators to increase submaximal exercise heart rate[5,20,23] and cardiac output,[5] but these heart rate findings have not been confirmed by others.[6,15,33,36,44] Alcohol had no effect on stroke volume,[5] pulmonary ventilation,[5,15] or muscle blood flow[16,30] at submaximal levels of exercise, but did decrease peripheral vascular resistance.[5] During maximal exercise, alcohol ingestion elicited no significant effect upon heart rate,[5-7] stroke volume and cardiac output, arteriovenous oxygen difference, mean arterial pressure and peripheral vascular resistance, or peak lactate,[5] but did significantly reduce tidal volume resulting in a lowered pulmonary ventilation.[5]

In summary, alcohol appears to have little or no beneficial effect on the metabolic and physiological responses to exercise. Further, in those studies reporting significant effects, the change appears to be detrimental to performance.

---

*References 8, 25, 26, 34-36, 42.

3. The effects of alcohol on tests of fitness components are variable. It has been shown that alcohol ingestion may decrease dynamic muscular strength,[24] isometric grip strength,[36] dynamometer strength,[37] power[20] and ergographic muscular output.[28] Other studies[13,20,24,27,43] reported no effect of alcohol upon muscular strength. Local muscular endurance was also unaffected by alcohol ingestion.[43] Small doses of alcohol exerted no effect upon bicycle ergometer exercise tasks simulating a 100-m dash or a 1500-m run, but larger doses had a deleterious effect.[2] Other research has shown that alcohol has no significant effect upon physical performance capacity,[15,16] exercise time at maximal levels,[5] or exercise time to exhaustion.[7]

   Thus, alcohol ingestion will not improve muscular work capacity and may lead to decreased performance levels.

4. Alcohol is the most abused drug in the United States.[11] There are an estimated 10 million adult problem drinkers and an additional 3.3 million in the 14-17 age range. Alcohol is significantly involved in all types of accidents—motor vehicle, home, industrial, and recreational. Most significantly, half of all traffic fatalities and one-third of all traffic injuries are alcohol related. Although alcohol abuse is associated with pathological conditions such as generalized skeletal myopathy, cardiomyopathy, pharyngeal and esophageal cancer, and brain damage, its most prominent effect is liver damage.[11,31,32]

5. Because alcohol has not been shown to help improve physical performance capacity, but may lead to decreased ability in certain events, it is important for all those associated with the conduct of sports to educate athletes against its use in conjunction with athletic contests. Moreover, the other dangers inherent in alcohol abuse mandate that concomitantly we educate our youth to make intelligent choices regarding alcohol consumption. Anstie's rule, or limit,[1] may be used as a reasonable guideline to moderate, safe drinking for adults.[12] In essence, no more than 0.5 ounces of pure alcohol per 23 kg body weight should be consumed in any one day. This would be the equivalent of three bottles of 4.5% beer, three 4-ounce glasses of 14% wine, or three ounces of 50% whiskey for a 68-kg person.

REFERENCES

1. Anstie, F.E.: On the uses of wine in health and disease, London, 1877, Macmillan.

2. Asmussen, E., and Boje, O.: The effects of alcohol and some drugs on the capacity for work, Acta Physiol. Scand. 15:109-118, 1948.

3. Begbie, G.: The effects of alcohol and of varying amounts of visual information on a balancing test, Ergonomics 9:325-333, 1966.

4. Belgrave, B., et al.: The effect of cannabidiol, alone and in combination with ethanol, on human performance, Psychopharmacology 64:243-246, 1979.

5. Blomqvist, G., Saltin, B., and Mitchell, J.: Acute effects of ethanol ingestion on the response to submaximal and maximal exercise in man, Circulation 42:463-470, 1970.

6. Bobo, W.: Effects of alcohol upon maximum oxygen uptake, lung ventilation, and heart rate, Res. Q. 43:1-6, 1972.

7. Bond, V.: Effect of alcohol on cardiorespiratory function. In Abstracts: research papers of 1979 AAHPER convention, Washington, D.C., AAHPER, 1979, p. 24.

8. Carpenter, J.: Effects of alcohol on some psychological processes, Q. J. Stud. Alcohol 23:274-314, 1962.

9. Collins, W., Schroeder, D., Gilson, R., and Guedry, F.: Effects of alcohol ingestion on tracking performance during angular acceleration, J. Appl. Psycol. 55:559-563, 1971.

10. Coopersmith, S.: The effects of alcohol on reaction to affective stimuli, Q. J. Stud. Alcohol 25:459-475, 1964.

11. Department of Health, Education, and Welfare: Third special report to the U.S. Congress on alcohol and health, NIAAA Information and Feature Service, DHEW Publication No. (ADM) 78-151, November 30, 1978, pp. 1-4.

12. Dorland's Illustrated Medical Dictionary, ed. 24, Philadelphia, 1974, p. 1370, W.B. Saunders Co.

13. Enzer, N., Simonson E., and Ballard, G.: The effect of small doses of alcohol on the central nervous system, Am. J. Clin. Pathol. **14**: 333-341, 1944.

14. Forney, R., Hughes, F., and Greatbatch, W.: Measurement of attentive motor performance after alcohol, Percept. Mot. Skills **19**:151-154, 1964.

15. Garlind, T., et al.: Effect of ethanol on circulatory, metabolic, and neurohumoral function during muscular work in man, Acta Pharmacol. Toxicol. **17**:106-114, 1960.

16. Graf, K., and Strom, G.: Effect of ethanol ingestion on arm blood flow in healthy young men at rest and during work, Acta Pharmacol. Toxicol. **17**:115-120, 1960.

17. Graham, T.: Thermal and glycemic responses during mild exercise in $+5$ to $-15°$ C environments following alcohol ingestion, Aviat. Space Environ. Med. **52**:517-522, 1981.

18. Graham, T., and Dalton, J.: Effect of alcohol on man's response to mild physical activity in a cold environment, Aviat. Space Environ. Med. **51**:793-796, 1980.

19. Haight, J., and Keatinge, W.: Failure of thermoregulation in the cold during hypoglycemia induced by exercise and ethanol, J. Physiol. (Lond.) **229**:87-97, 1973.

20. Hebbelinck, M.: The effects of a moderate dose of alcohol on a series of functions of physical performance in man, Arch. Int. Pharmacol. **120**:402-405, 1959.

21. Hebbellinck, M.: The effect of a moderate dose of ethyl alcohol on human respiratory gas exchange during rest and muscular exercise, Arch. Int. Pharmacol. **126**:214-218, 1960.

22. Hebbelinck, M.: Spierarbeid en Ethylalkohol, Brussels, Arsica Uitgaven, N.V., 1961, pp. 81-84.

23. Hebbelinck, M.: The effects of a small dose of ethyl alcohol on certain basic components of human physical performance: the effect on cardiac rate during musclar work, Arch. Int. Pharmacol. **140**:61-67, 1962.

24. Hebbelinck, M.: The effects of a small dose of ethyl alcohol on certain basic components of human physical performance, Arch. Int. Pharmacol. **143**:247-257, 1963.

25. Huntley, M. Effects of alcohol, uncertainty and novelty upon response selection, Psychopharmacologia **39**:259-266, 1974.

26. Huntley, M.: Influences of alcohol and S-R uncertainty upon spatial localization time, Psychopharmacologia **27**:131-140, 1972.

27. Ikai, M., and Steinhaus, A.: Some factors modifying the expression of human strength, J. Appl. Physiol. **16**:157-161, 1961.

28. Jellinek, E.: Effect of small amounts of alcohol on psychological functions. In Yale University Center for Alcohol Studies: Alcohol, Science and Society, New Haven, Ct., Yale University, 1954, pp. 83-94.

29. Juhlin-Dannfelt, A., et al.: Influence of ethanol on splanchnic and skeletal muscle substrate turnover during prolonged exercise in man, Am. J. Physiol. **233**:E195-E202, 1977.

30. Juhlin-Dannfelt, A., et al.: Influence of ethanol on non-esterified fatty acid and carbohydrate metabolism during exercise in man, Clin. Soc. Mol. Med. **53**:205-214, 1977.

31. Lieber, C.S.: Liver injury and adaptation in alcoholism, N. Engl. J. Med. **288**:356-362, 1973.

32. Lieber, C.S.: The metabolism of alcohol, Sci. Am. **234**:25-33, 1976.

33. Mazess, R., Picon-Reategui, E., and Thomas, R.: Effects of alcohol and altitude on man during rest and work, Aerospace Med. **39**:403-406, 1968.

34. Moskowitz, H., and Burns, M.: Effect of alcohol on the psychological

refractory period, Q. J. Stud. Alcohol **32:**782-790, 1971.

35. Moskowitz, H., and Roth, S.: Effect of alcohol on response latency in object naming, Q. J. Stud. Alcohol **32:**969-975, 1971.

36. Nelson, D.: Effects of ethyl alcohol on the performance of selected gross motor tests, Res. Q. **30:**312-320, 1959.

37. Pihkanen, T.: Neurological and physiological studies on distilled and brewed beverages, Ann. Med. Exp. Biol. Fenn. **35:**(Suppl.) 9, 1-152, 1957.

38. Riff, D., Jain, A., and Doyle, J.: Acute hemodynamic effects of ethanol on normal human volunteers, Am. Heart J. **78:**592-597, 1969.

39. Rundell, O., and Williams, H.: Alcohol and speed-accuracy tradeoff, Hum. Factors **21:**433-443, 1979.

40. Sidell, F., and Pless, J.: Ethyl alcohol blood levels and performance decrements after oral administration to man, Psychopharmacologia **19:**246-261, 1971.

41. Tang, P., and Rosenstein, R.: Influence of alcohol and Dramamine, alone and in combination, on psychomotor performance, Aerospace Med. **39:**818-821, 1967.

42. Tharp, V., Rundell, O., Lester, B., and Williams, H.: Alcohol and information processing, Psychopharmacologia **40:**33-52, 1974.

43. Williams, M.H.: Effect of selected doses of alcohol on fatigue parameters of the forearm flexor muscles, Res. Q. **40:**832-840, 1969.

44. Williams, M.H.: Effect of small and moderate doses of alcohol on exercise heart rate and oxygen consumption, Res. Q. **43:**94-104, 1972.

B THE USE OF ANABOLIC-ANDROGENIC STEROIDS IN SPORTS

Based on a comprehensive literature survey and a careful analysis of the claims concerning the ergogenic effects and the adverse effects of anabolic-androgenic steroids, it is the position of the American College of Sports Medicine that:

1. Anabolic-androgenic steroids in the presence of an adequate diet can contribute to increases in body weight, often in the lean mass compartment.
2. The gains in muscular strength achieved through high-intensity exercise and proper diet can be increased by the use of anabolic-androgenic steroids in some individuals.
3. Anabolic-androgenic steroids do not increase aerobic power or capacity for muscular exercise.
4. Anabolic-androgenic steroids have been associated with adverse effects on the liver, cardiovascular system, reproductive system, and psychological status in therapeutic trials and in limited research on athletes. Until further research is completed, the potential hazards of the use of the anabolic-androgenic steroids in athletes must include those found in therapeutic trials.
5. The use of anabolic-androgenic steroids by athletes is contrary to the rules and ethical principles of athletic competition as set forth by many of the sports governing bodies. The American College of Sports Medicine supports these ethical principles and deplores the use of anabolic-androgenic steroids by athletes.

This document is a revision of the 1977 position stand of the American College of Sports Medicine concerning anabolic-androgenic steroids.[4]

Background

In 1935 the long-suspected positive effect of androgens on protein anabolism was documented.[56] Subsequently, this effect was confirmed,[53,77] and the development of 19-nortestosterone heralded the synthesis of steroids that have greater anabolic properties than natural testosterone but less of its virilizing effect.[39] The use of androgenic steroids by athletes began in the early 1950s[106] and has increased through the years,* despite warnings about potential adverse reactions[4,83,106,112] and the banning of these substances by sports governing bodies.

Anabolic-Androgenic Steroids, Body Composition and Athletic Performance

Body composition Animal studies investigating the effect of anabolic-androgenic steroids on body composition have shown increases in lean body mass, nitrogen retention, and muscle growth in castrated males[37,57,58] and normal females.[26,37,71] The effects of anabolic-androgenic steroids on the body weights of normal, untrained, male animals,[37,40,71,105,114] treadmill-trained[43,97] or isometrically-trained rats,[82] or strength-trained monkeys[80] have been minimal to absent; however, the effects of steroids on animals undergoing heavy resistance training have not been adequately studied. Human males who are deficient in natural androgens by castration or other causes have shown significant increases in nitrogen retention and muscular development with anabolic-androgenic steroid therapy.[23,58,103] Human males and females involved in experimental[38] and therapeutic trials of anabolic steroids[15,16,93] have shown increases in body weight.

The majority of the strength-training studies in which body weight was reported showed greater increases in weight under steroid treatment than under placebo.† Other training studies have reported no significant changes in body weight.‡ The weight gained was determined to be lean body mass in three studies that made this determination with hydrostatic weighing techniques.[41,42,107] Four other studies found no significant differences in lean body mass between steroid and placebo treatments,[17,21,27,34] but in two of those the mean differences favored the steroid treatment.[21,27] The extent to which increased water retention accounts for steroid-induced changes in body composition is controversial[17,42] and has yet to be resolved.

In summary, anabolic-androgenic steroids can contribute to an increase in body weight in the lean mass compartment of the body. The amount of weight gained in the training studies has been small but statistically significant.

Muscular strength Strength is an important factor in many athletic events. The literature concerning the efficacy of anabolic steroids for promoting strength development is controversial. Many factors contribute to the development of strength, including heredity, intensity of training, diet, and the status of the psyche.[112] It is very difficult to control all of

---

*References 60, 62, 83, 98, 104, 106.
†References 17, 41, 42, 50, 61, 74, 94, 96, 107.
‡References 21, 27, 31, 34, 100, 108.

these factors in an experimental design. The additional variable of dosage is included when drug research is undertaken. Some athletes claim that doses greater than therapeutic are necessary for strength gains[106] even though positive results have been reported using therapeutic (low-dose) regimens.[50,74,94,107] Double-blind studies using anabolic-androgenic steroids are also difficult to conduct because of the physical and/or psychological effects of the drug that, for example, allowed 100% of the participants in one "double-blind" study to correctly identify the steroid phase of the experiment.[32] The placebo effect has been shown to be a factor in studies of anabolic-androgenic steroids as in all drug studies.[6]

In animal studies, the combination of anabolic-androgenic steroids and overload training has not produced larger gains in force production than training alone.[80,97] However, steroid-induced gains in strength have been reported in experienced[42,74,94,107] and inexperienced weight trainers[50,51,96] with[50,51,74,94] and without dietary control of supplemental protein.[42,96] In contrast, no positive effect of steroids on gains in strength over those produced by training alone were reported in other studies involving experienced[21,34,54] and inexperienced weight trainers* with[21,34,61,100] and without dietary control or supplemental protein.† The studies that reported no changes in strength with anabolic-androgenic steroids have been criticized[112] for the use of inexperienced weight trainers, lack of dietary control, low-intensity training,[17,27,31,61] and nonspecific testing of strength.[21] The studies that have shown strength gains with the use of anabolic-androgenic steroids have been criticized[83] for inadequate numbers of subjects,[74,94,107] improper statistical designs, inadequate execution, and the unsatisfactory reporting of experimental results.

There have been no studies of the effects of the massive doses of steroids used by athletes over periods of several years. Similarly, there have been no studies of the use of anabolic-androgenic steroids and training in women or children. Theoretically, anabolic and androgenic effects would be greater in women and children because they have naturally lower levels of androgens than men.

Three proposed mechanisms for the actions of the anabolic-androgenic steroids for increases in muscle strength are:

1. Increase in protein synthesis in the muscle as a direct action of the anabolic-androgenic steroid.[81,82,92]
2. Blocking of the catabolic effect of glucocorticoids after exercise by increasing the amount of anabolic-androgenic hormone available.[1,92,112]
3. Steroid-induced enhancement of aggressive behavior that promotes a greater quantity and quality of weight training.[14]

In spite of the controversial and sometimes contradictory results of the studies in this area, it can be concluded that the use of anabolic-androgenic steroids, especially by experienced weight trainers, can often increase strength gains beyond those seen with training and diet alone. This positive effect on strength is usually small and obviously is not exhibited by all

---

*References 17, 27, 31, 41, 54, 61, 100, 108.
†References 17, 27, 31, 41, 54, 108.

individuals. The explanation for this variability in steroid effects is unclear. When small increments in strength occur, they can be important in athletic competition.

Aerobic capacity　The effect of anabolic-androgenic steroids on aerobic capacity has also been questioned. The potential of these drugs to increase total blood volume and hemoglobin[88] might suggest a positive effect of steroids on aerobic capacity. However, only three studies indicated positive effects,[3,51,54] and there has been no substantiation of these results in subsequent studies.[27,41,50,52] Thus, the majority of evidence shows no positive effect of anabolic-androgenic steroids on aerobic capacity over aerobic training alone.

Adverse Effects

Anabolic-androgenic steroids have been associated with many undesirable or adverse effects in laboratory studies and therapeutic trials. The effects of major concern are those on the liver, cardiovascular, and reproductive systems, and on the psychological status of individuals who are using the anabolic-androgenic steroids.

Adverse effects on the liver　Impaired excretory function of the liver, resulting in jaundice, has been associated with anabolic-androgenic steroids in a number of therapeutic trials.[76,84,90] The possible cause-and-effect nature of this association is strengthened by the observation of jaundice remission after discontinuance of the drug.[76,84] In studies of athletes using anabolic-androgenic steroids (65 athletes tested),[89,98,104] no evidence of cholestasis has been found.

Structural changes in the liver following anabolic steroid treatment have been found in animals[95,101] and in humans.[73,86] Conclusions concerning the clinical significance of these changes on a short- or long-term basis have not been drawn. Investigations in athletes for these changes have not been performed, but there is no reason to believe that the athlete using anabolic-androgenic steroids is immune from these effects of the drugs.

The most serious liver complications associated with anabolic-androgenic steroids are peliosis hepatis (blood-filled cysts in the liver of unknown etiology) and liver tumors. Cases of peliosis hepatis have been reported in individuals treated with anabolic-androgenic steroids for various conditions.* Rupture of the cysts or liver failure resulting from the condition was fatal in some individuals.[9,70,102] In other case reports the condition was an incidental finding at autopsy.[8,10,66] The possible cause-and-effect nature of the association between peliosis hepatis and the use of anabolic-androgenic steroids is strengthened by the observation of improvement in the condition after discontinuance of drug therapy in some cases.[7,35] There are no reported cases of this condition in athletes using anabolic-androgenic steroids, but investigations specific for this disorder have not been performed in athletes.

Liver tumors have been associated with the use of anabolic-androgenic steroids in individuals receiving these drugs as a part of their treatment

---

*References 7-10, 13, 35, 65, 66, 70, 88, 102.

regimen.* These tumors are generally benign, but there have been malignant lesions associated with individuals using these drugs.[28,99,115] The possible cause-and-effect nature of this association between the use of the drug and tumor development is strengthened by a report of tumor regression after cessation of drug treatment.[49] The 17-alpha-alkylated compounds are the specific family of anabolic steroids indicated in the development of liver tumors.[46,49] There is one reported case of a 26-year-old male body builder who died of liver cancer after having abused a variety of anabolic steroids for at least four years.[75] The testing necessary for discovery of these tumors is not commonly performed, and it is possible that other tumors associated with steroid use by athletes have gone undetected.

Blood tests of liver function have been reported to be unchanged with steroid use in some training studies[31,41,54,94] and abnormal in other training studies[32,51] and in tests performed on athletes known to be using anabolic-androgenic steroids.[54,89,104] However, the lesions of peliosis hepatis and liver tumors do not always result in blood test abnormalities,† and some authors state that liver radioisotope scans, ultrasound, or computed tomography scans are needed for diagnosis.[28,29,113]

In summary, liver function tests have been shown to be adversely affected by anabolic-androgenic steroids, especially the 17-alpha-alkylated compounds. The short- and long-term consequences of these changes, though potentially hazardous, have yet to be reported in athletes using these drugs.

Adverse effects on the cardiovascular system The steroid-induced changes that may affect the development of cardiovascular disease include hyperinsulinism and altered glucose tolerance,[111] decreased high-density lipoprotein cholesterol levels,[72,98] and elevated blood pressure.[68] These effects are variable for different individuals in various clinical situations. Triglycerides are lowered by anabolic-androgenic steroids in certain individuals[24,72] and are increased in others.[18,78] Histological examinations of myofibrils and mitochondria from cardiac tissue obtained from laboratory animals have shown that administration of anabolic steroids leads to pathological alterations in these structures.[5,11,12] The cardiovascular effects of the anabolic-androgenic steroids, though potentially hazardous, need further research before any conclusions can be made.

Adverse effects on the male reproductive system The effects of the anabolic-androgenic steroids on the male reproductive system are oligospermia (small number of sperm) and azoospermia (lack of sperm in the semen), decreased testicular size, abnormal appearance of testicular biopsy material, and reductions in testosterone and gonadotropic hormones. These effects have been shown in training studies,[19,41,100] studies of normal volunteers,[38] theapeutic trials,[44] and studies of athletes who were using anabolic-androgenic steroids.[55,79,104] In view of the changes shown in the pituitary-gonadal axis, the dysfunction accounting for these abnormalities is believed to be steroid-induced suppression of gonadotrophin production.[19,36,38,79] The changes in these hormones are ordinarily

---

*References 28, 29, 49, 67, 69, 99, 115.
†References 8, 28, 29, 49, 67, 115.

reversible after cessation of drug treatment, but the long-term effects of altering the hypothalamic-pituitary-gonadal axis remain unknown. However, there is a report of residual abnormalities in testicular morphology of healthy men 6 months after discontinuing steroid use.[38] It has been reported that the metabolism of androgens to estrogenic compounds may lead to gynecomastia in males.[23,58,98,112]

Adverse effects on the female reproductive system The effects of androgenic steroids on the female reproductive system include reduction in circulating levels of luteinizing hormone, follicle-stimulating hormone, estrogens, and progesterone; inhibition of folliculogenesis and ovulation; and menstrual cycle changes including prolongation of the follicular phase, shortening of the luteal phase, and amenorrhea.[20,63,91]

Adverse effects on psychological status In both sexes, psychological effects of anabolic-androgenic steroids include increases or decreases in libido, mood swings, and aggressive behavior,[38,98] which is related to plasma testosterone levels.[25,85] Administration of steroids causes changes in the electroencephalogram similar to those seen with psycho-stimulant drugs.[47,48] The possible ramifications of uncontrollably aggressive and possible hostile behavior should be considered prior to the use of anabolic-androgenic steroids.

Other adverse effects Other side effects associated with the anabolic-androgenic steroids include: ataxia[2]; premature epiphysial closure in youths[23,58,64,109,110]; virilization in youths and women, including hirsutism,[45] clitoromegaly,[63,112] and irreversible deepening of the voice[22,33]; acne; temporal hair recession; and alopecia.[45] These adverse reactions can occur with the use of anabolic-androgenic steroids and are believed to be dependent on the type of steroid, dosage and duration of drug use.[58] There is no method for predicting which individuals are more likely to develop these adverse effects, some of which are potentially hazardous.

The Ethical Issue

Equitable competition and fair play are the foundation of athletic competition. If competition is to remain on this foundation, rules are necessary. The International Olympic Committee (IOC) has defined "doping" as "the administration of or the use by a competing athlete of any substance foreign to the body or of any physiological substance taken in abnormal quantity or taken by an abnormal route of entry into the body, with the sole intention of increasing in an artificial and unfair manner his performance in competition." Accordingly, the medically unjustified use of anabolic steroids with the intention of gaining an athletic advantage is clearly unethical. Anabolic-androgenic steroids are listed as banned substances by the IOC in accordance with the rules against doping. The American College of Sports Medicine supports the position that the eradication of anabolic-androgenic steroid use by athletes is in the best interest of sport and endorses the development of effective procedures for drug detection and of policies that exclude from competition those athletes who refuse to abide by the rules.

The "win at all cost" attitude that has pervaded society places the athlete in a precarious situation. Testimonial evidence suggests that some athletes would risk serious harm and even death if they could obtain a drug that would ensure their winning an Olympic gold medal. However, the use of anabolic-androgenic steroids by athletes is contrary to the ethical principles of athletic competition and is deplored.

REFERENCES

1. Aakvaag, A., Bentdol O., Quigstod, K., Walstod, P., et al.: Testosterone and testosterone binding globulin (TeBg) in young men during prolonged stress, Int. J. Androl. 1:22-31, 1978.

2. Agrawal, B.L.: Ataxia caused by fluoxymesterone therapy in breast cancer, Arch. Intern. Med. 141:953-959, 1981.

3. Albrecht, H., and Albrecht, E.: Ergometric, rheographic, reflexographic and electrographic tests at altitude and effects of drugs on human physical performance, Fed. Proc. 28:1262-1267, 1969.

4. American College of Sports Medicine: Position statement on the use and abuse of anabolic-androgenic steroids in sports, Med. Sci. Sports 9(4):xi-xiii, 1977.

5. Appell, H.-J., Heller-Umpfenbach, B., Feraudi, M., and Weicker, H.: Ultrastructural and morphometric investigations on the effects of training and administration of anabolic steroids on the myocardium of guinea pigs, Int. J. Sports Med. 4:268-274, 1983.

6. Ariel, G. and Saville, W.: Anabolic steroids: the physiological effects of placebos, Med. Sci. Sports 4:124-126, 1972.

7. Arnold, G.L., and Kaplan, M.M.: Peliosis hepatis due to oxymetholone—a clinically benign disorder, Am. J. Gastroenterol. 71:213-216, 1979.

8. Asano, A., Wakasa, H., Kaise, S., Nichimaki, T., et al.: Peliosis hepatis. Report on two autopsy cases with a review of literature, Acta Pathol. Jpn. 32:861-877, 1982.

9. Bagheri, S., and Boyer, J.: Peliosis hepatis associated with androgenic-anabolic steroid therapy—a severe form of hepatic injury, Ann. Intern. Med. 81:610-618, 1974.

10. Bank, J.I., Lykkebo, D., and Hagerstrand, I.: Peliosis hepatis in a child, Acta Ped. Scand. 67:105-107, 1978.

11. Behrendt, H.: Effect of anabolic steroid on rat heart muscle cells. I. Intermediate filaments, Cell Tissue Res. 180:305-315, 1977.

12. Behrendt, H., and Boffin, H.: Myocardial cell lesions caused by anabolic hormone, Cell Tissue Res. 181:423-426, 1977.

13. Benjamin, D.C., and Shunk, B.: A fatal case of peliosis of the liver and spleen, Am. J. Dis. Child. 132:207-208, 1978.

14. Brooks, R.V.: Anabolic steroids and athletes, Phys. Sportsmed. 8(3):161-163, 1980.

15. Buchwald, D., Argyres, S., Easterling, R.E., et al.: Effects of Nandrolone Decanoate on the anemia of chronic hemodialysis patients, Nephron 18:232-238, 1977.

16. Carter, C.H.: The anabolic steroid, Stanozolol, its evaluation in debilitated children, Clin. Pediatr. 4:671-680, 1965.

17. Casner, S.W., Early, R.G., and Carlson, B.R.: Anabolic steroid effects on body composition in normal young men. J. Sports Med. Phys. Fitness 11:98-103, 1971.

18. Choi, E.S.K., Chung, T., Morrison, R.S., Myers, C., et al.: Hypertriglyceridemia in hemodialysis patients during oral dromostanolone therapy for anemia, Am. J. Clin. Nutr. 27:901-904, 1974.

19. Clerico, A., Ferdeghini, M., Palombo, C., et al.: Effects of anabolic treatment of the serum levels of gonadotropins, testosterone, prolactin, thyroid hormones and myoglobin of male athletes under physical training, J. Nuclear Med. Allied Sci. 25:79-88, 1981.

20. Cox, D.W., Heinrichs, W.L., Paulsen, C.A., et al.: Perturbations of the human menstrual cycle by oxymetholone, Am. J. Obstet. Gynecol. 121:121-126, 1975.

21. Crist, D.M., Stackpole, P.J., and Peake, G.T.: Effects of androgenic-anabolic steroids on neuromuscular power and body composition, J. Appl. Physiol. 54:366-370, 1983.

22. Damste, P.H.: Voice change in adult women caused by virilizing agents, J. Speech Hear. Disord. 32:126-132, 1967.

23. Dorfman, R.I., and Shipley, R.A.: Androgens: biochemistry, physiology and clinical significance, New York: J. Wiley & Sons, 1956.

24. Doyle, A.E., Pinkus, N.B., and Green, J.: The use of oxandrolone in hyperlipidaemia, Med. J. Australia 1:127-129, 1974.

25. Ehrenkranz, J., Bliss, E., and Sheard, M.H.: Plasma testosterone correlation

with aggressive behavior and social dominance in man, Psychosom. Med. **36**:469-475, 1974.

26. Exner, G.U., Staudte, H.W., and Pette, D.: Isometric training of rats—effects upon fast and slow muscle and modification by an anabolic hormone (Nandrolone Decanoate) I. Female rats, Pflügers Arch. **345**:1-14, 1973.

27. Fahey, T.D., and Brown, C.H.: The effects of an anabolic steroid on the strength, body composition and endurance of college males when accompanied by a weight training program, Med. Sci. Sports **5**:272-276, 1973.

28. Falk, H., Thomas, L., Popper, H., and Ishak, H.G.: Hepatic angiosarcoma associated with androgenic-anabolic steroids, Lancet **2**:1120-1123, 1979.

29. Farrell, G.C., Joshua, D.E., Uren, R.F., et al.: Androgen-induced hepatoma, Lancet **1**:430, 1975.

30. Forsyth, B.T.: The effect of testosterone propianate at various protein calorie intakes in malnutrition after trauma, J. Lab. Clin. Med. **43**:732-740, 1954.

31. Fowler, W.M., Jr., Gardner, G.W., and Egstrom, G.H.: Effect of an anabolic steroid on physical performance in young men, J. App. Physiol. **20**:1038-1040, 1965.

32. Freed, D.L., Banks, A.J., Longson, D., and Burley, D.M.: Anabolic steroids in athletics: crossover double-blind trial on weightlifters, Br. Med. J. **2**:471-473, 1975.

33. Gelder, L.V.: Psychosomatic aspects of endocrine disorders of the voice, J. Commun. Disord. **7**:257-262, 1974.

34. Golding, L.A., Freydinger, J.E., and Fishel, S.S.: The effect of an androgenic-anabolic steroid and a protein supplement on size, strength, weight and body composition in athletes, Phys. Sportsmed. **2**(6):39-45, 1974.

35. Groos, G., Arnold, O.H., and Brittinger, G.: Peliosis hepatis after long-term administration of oxymetholone, Lancet **1**:874, 1974.

36. Harkness, R.A., Kilshaw, B.H., and Hobson, B.M.: Effects of large doses of anabolic steroids, Br. J. Sports Med. **9**:70-73, 1975.

37. Heitzman, R.J.: The effectiveness of anabolic agents in increasing rate of growth in farm animals; report on experiments in cattle. In Anabolic agents in animal production, Lu, F.C., and Rendell, J., (editors), Stuttgart, George Thieme Publishers, 1976, pp. 89-98.

38. Heller, C.G., Moore, D.J., Paulsen, C.A., Nelson, W.O., et al.: Effects of progesterone and synthetic progestins on the reproductive physiology of normal men, Fed. Proc. **18**:1057-1065, 1959.

39. Hershberger, J.G., Shipley, E.G., and Meyer, R.K.: Myotrophic activity of 19-nortestosterone and other steroids determined by modified levator ani muscle method, Proc. Soc. Exper. Biol. Med. **83**:175-180, 1953.

40. Hervey, G.R., and Hutchinson, I.: The effects of testosterone on body weight and composition in the rat, J. Endocrinol. **57**:xxiv-xxv, 1973.

41. Hervey, G.R., Hutchinson, I., Knibbs, A.V., et al.: Anabolic effects of methandienone in men undergoing athletic training, Lancet **2**:699-702, 1976.

42. Hervey, G.R., Knibbs, A.V., Burkinshaw, L., et al.: Effects of methandienone on the performance and body composition of men undergoing athletic training, Clin. Sci. **60**:457-461, 1981.

43. Hickson, R.C., Heusner, W.W., Van Huss, W.D., et al.: Effects of Diabanol and high-intensity sprint training on body composition of rats, Med. Sci Sports **8**:191-195, 1976.

44. Homa, P. and H. Aldercreutz. Effect of an anabolic steroid (metandienon) on plasma LH, FSH, and testosterone and on the response to intravenous administration of LRH, Acta Endocrinol. **83**:856-864, 1976.

45. Houssay, A.B.: Effects of anabolic-androgenic steroids on the skin including hair and sebaceous glands. In Anabolic-androgenic steroids, C.D. Kochakian (editor), New York, Springer-Verlag, 1976, pp. 155-190.

46. Ishak, K.G.: Hepatic lesions caused by anabolic and contraceptive steroids, Sem. Liver Dis. **1**:116-128, 1981.

47. Itil, T.M.: Neurophysiological effects of hormones in humans: computer EEG profiles of sex and hypothalamic hormones. In Hormones, behavior and psychotherapy, E.J. Sacher (editor), New York, Raven Press, 1976, pp. 31-40.

48. Itil, T.M., Cora, R., Akpinar, S., Herrmann, W.M., and Patterson, C.J.: Psychotropic action of sex hormones: computerized EEG in establishing the immediate CNS effects of steroid hormones, Curr. Ther. Res. **16**:1147-1170, 1974.

49. Johnson, F.L., et al.: Association of androgenic-anabolic steroid therapy with development of hepatocellular carcinoma, Lancet **2**:1273, 1972.

50. Johnson, L.C., Fisher, G., Silvester, L.J., and Hofheins, C.C.: Anabolic steroid:

effects of strength, body weight, oxygen uptake and spermatogenesis upon mature males, Med. Sci. Sports **4**:43-45, 1972.

51. Johnson, L.C., and O'Shea, J.P.: Anabolic steroid: effects on strength development, Science **164**:957-959, 1969.

52. Johnson, L.C., et al.: Effect of anabolic steroid treatment on endurance, Med. Sci. Sports **7**:287-289, 1975.

53. Kenyon, A.T., Knowlton, K., and Sandiford, I.: The anabolic effects of the androgens and somatic growth in man, Ann. Intern. Med. **20**:632-654, 1944.

54. Keul, J., Deus, H., and Kinderman, W.: Anabole hormone: Schadigung, Leistungsfahigkeit und Stoffwechses, Med. Klin. **71**:497-503, 1976.

55. Kilshaw, B.H., Harkness, R.A., Hobson, B.M., and Smith, A.W.M.: The effects of large doses of the anabolic steroid, methandrostenolone, on an athlete, Clin. Endocrinol. **4**:537-541, 1975.

56. Kochakian, C.D., and Murlin, J.R.: The effect of male hormones on the protein and energy metabolism of castrate dogs, J. Nutr. **10**:437-458, 1935.

57. Kochakian, C.D., and Endahl, B.R.: Changes in body weight of normal and castrated rats by different doses of testosterone propionate, Proc. Soc. Exper. Biol. Med. **100**:520-522, 1959.

58. Kruskemper, H.L.: Anabolic Steroids, New York, Academic Press, 1968, pp. 128-133, 162-164, 182.

59. Landau, R.L.: The metabolic effects of anabolic steroids in man, In Anabolic-androgenic steroids, C.D. Kochakian (editor), New York, Springer-Verlag, 1976, pp. 45-72.

60. Ljungqvist, A.: The use of anabolic steroids in top Swedish athletes, Br. J. Sports Med. **9**:82, 1975.

61. Loughton, S.J., and Ruhling, R.O.: Human strength and endurance responses to anabolic steroid and training, J. Sports Med. **17**:285-296, 1977.

62. MacDougall, J.D., Sale, D.G., Elder, G.C.B., and Sutton, J.R.: Muscle ultrastructural characteristics of elite powerlifters and bodybuilders, Eur. J. Applied Physiol. **48**:117-126, 1982.

63. Maher, J.M., Squires, E.L., Voss, J.L., and Shideler, R.K.: Effect of anabolic steroids on reproductive function of young mares, J. Am. Vet. Med. Assoc. **183**:519-524, 1983.

64. Mason, A.S.: Male precocity: the clinician's view. In The Endocrine Function of the Human Testis, V.H.T. James, Serra, M., and Martini, L. (editors), New York, Academic Press, 1974, pp. 131-143.

65. McDonald, E.C., and Speicher, C.E.: Peliosis hepatis associated with administration of oxymetholone, JAMA **240**:243-244, 1978.

66. McGiven, A.R.: Peliosis hepatis: case report and review of pathogenesis, J. Pathol. **101**:283-285, 1970.

67. Meadows, A.T., Naiman, J.L., and Valdes-Dapena, M.: Hepatoma associated with androgen therapy for aplastic anemia, J. Pediatr. **85**:109-110, 1974.

68. Messerli, F.H., and Frohlich, E.D.: High blood pressure: a side effect of drugs, poisons, and food, Arch. Intern Med. **139**:682-687, 1979.

69. Mulvihill, J.J., et al.: P.B.T. Haughton. Hepatic adenoma in Fanconi anemia treated   with oxymetholone. J. Pediatr. **87**:122-124, 1975.

70. Nadell, J. and Kosek, J.: Peliosis hepatis, Arch. Pathol. Lab. Med. **101**:405-410, 1977.

71. Nesheim, M.C.: Some observations on the effectiveness of anabolic agents in increasing the growth rate of poultry. In Anabolic agents in animal production, F.C. Lu and J. Rendel (editors), Stuttgart, Georg Thieme Publishers, 1976, pp. 110-114.

72. Olsson, A.G., Oro, L., and Rossner, S.: Effects of oxandrolone on plasma lipoproteins and the intravenous fat tolerance in man, Atherosclerosis **19**:337-346, 1974.

73. Orlandi, F., Jezequel, A., and Melliti, A.: The action of some anabolic steroids on the structure and the function of human liver cell, Tijdschr. Gastro-Enterol. **7**:109-113, 1964.

74. O'Shea, J.P.: The effects of an anabolic steroid on dynamic strength levels of weightlifters, Nutr. Rep. Int. **4**:363-370, 1971.

75. Overly, W.L., Dankoff, J.A., Wang, B.K., and Singh, U.D.: Androgens and hepatocellular carcinoma in an athlete, Ann. Intern. Med. **100**:158-159, 1984.

76. Palva, I.P., and Wasastjerna, C.: Treatment of aplastic anaemia with methonolone, Acta Haematol. **47**:13-20, 1972.

77. Papanicolaou, G.N., and Falk, G.A.: General muscular hypertrophy induced by androgenic hormone, Science **87**:238-239, 1938.

78. Reeves, R.D., Morris, M.D., and Barbour, G.L.: Hyperlipidemia due to oxymetholone therapy, JAMA **236**:464-472, 1976.

79. Remes, K., et al.: Effect of short-term treatment with an anabolic steroid (methandienone) and dehydroepian-

drosterone sulphate on plasma hormones, red cell volume and 2,3-diphosphoglycerate in athletes, Scand. J. Clin. Lab. Invest. **37**:577-586, 1977.

80. Richardson, J.H.: A comparison of two drugs on strength increase in monkeys, J. Sports Med. Phys. Fitness **17**:251-254, 1977.

81. Rogozkin, V.A.: The role of low molecular weight compounds in the regulation of skeletal muscle genome activity during exercise, Med. Sci. Sports **8**:1-4, 1976.

82. Rogozkin, V.A.: Anabolic steroid metabolism in skeletal muscle, J. Steroid Biochem. **11**:923-926, 1979.

83. Ryan, A.J.: Anabolic steroids are fool's gold, Fed. Proc. **40**:2682-2688, 1981.

84. Sacks, P., Gale, D., Bothwell, T.H., and Stevens, K.: Oxymetholone therapy in aplastic and other refractory anaemias, S. Afr. Med. J. **46**:1607-1615, 1972.

85. Scarmella, T.J., and Brown, W.A.: Serum testosterone and aggressiveness in hockey players, Psychosom. Med. **40**:262-265, 1978.

86. Schaffner, F., Popper, H., and Perez, V.: Changes in bile canaliculi produced by norethandrolone: electron microscopic study of human and rat liver, J. Lab. Clin. Med. **56**:623-628, 1960.

87. Shahidi, N.T.: Androgens and erythropoeisis, N. Engl. J. Med. **289**:72-80, 1973.

88. Shapiro, P., et al.: Multiple hepatic tumors and peliosis hepatitis in Fanconi's anemia treated with androgens, Am. J. Dis. Child. **131**:1104-1106, 1977.

89. Shephard, R.J., Killinger, D., and Fried, T.: Responses to sustained use of anabolic steroid, Br. J. Sports Med. **11**:170-173, 1977.

90. Skarberg, K.O., et al.: Oxymetholone treatment in hypoproliferative anaemia, Acta Haematol. **49**:321-330, 1973.

91. Smith, K.D., Rodriguez-Rigau, L.J., Tcholakian, R.K., and Steinberg, E.: The relation between plasma testosterone levels and the lengths of phases of the menstrual cycle, Fertil. Steril. **32**:403-407, 1979.

92. Snochowski, M., Dahlberg, E., Eriksson, E., and Gustafsson, J.A.: Androgen and glucocorticoid receptors in human skeletal muscle cytosol, J. Steroid Biochem. **14**:765-771, 1981.

93. Spiers, A.S.D., et al.: Beneficial effects of an anabolic steroid during cytotoxic chemotherapy for metastatic cancer, J. Med. **12**:433-445, 1981.

94. Stamford, B.A., and Moffatt, R.: Anabolic steroid: effectiveness as an ergogenic aid to experienced weight train-

ers, J. Sports Med. Phys. Fitness **14**:191-197, 1974.

95. Stang-Voss, C., and Appel, H-J.: Structural alterations of liver parenchyma induced by anabolic steroids, Int. J. Sports Med. **2**:101-105, 1981.

96. Steinbach, M.: Uber den Einfluss Anaboler wirkstoffe auf Korpergewicht, Muskelkraft und Muskeltraining, Sportarzi Sportmed. **11**:485-492, 1968.

97. Stone, M.H., Rush, M.E., and Lipner, H.: Responses to intensive training and methandrostenelone administration. II. Hormonal, organ weights, muscle weights and body composition, Pflugers Arch. **375**:147-151, 1978.

98. Strauss, R.H., Wright, H.E., Finerman, G.A.M., and Catlin, D.H.: Side effects of anabolic steroids in weight-trained men. Phys. Sportsmed. **11**(12):87-96, 1983.

99. Stromeyer, F.W., Smith, D.H., and Ishak, K.G.: Anabolic steroid therapy and intrahepatic cholangiocarcinoma, Cancer **43**:440-443, 1979.

100. Stromme, S.B., Meen, H.D., and Aakvaag, A.: Effects of an androgenic-anabolic steroid on strength development and plasma testosterone levels in normal males, Med. Sci. Sports **6**:203-208, 1974.

101. Taylor, W., Snowball, S., Dickson, C.M., and Lesna, M.: Alterations of liver architecture in mice treated with anabolic androgens and diethylnitrosamine, NATO Adv. Study Inst. Series, Series A **52**:279-288, 1982.

102. Taxy, J.B.: Peliosis: a morphologic curiosity becomes an iatrogenic problem, Hum. Pathol. **9**:331-340, 1978.

103. Tepperman, J.: Metabolic and endocrine physiology, Chicago, 1973, Yearbook Medical Publishers, p. 70.

104. Thomson, D.P., Pearson, D.R., and Costill, D.L.: Use of anabolic steroids by national level athletes (abstract), Med. Sci. Sports Exerc. **13**:111, 1981.

105. Vander Wal, P.: General aspects of the effectiveness of anabolic agents in increasing protein production in farm animals, in particular in bull calves. In Lu, F.C., and Rendel, J. (editors): Anabolic agents in animal production, Stuttgart, 1976, Georg Thieme Publishers, pp. 60-78.

106. Wade, N.: Anabolic steroids: doctors denounce them, but athletes aren't listening, Science **176**:1399-1403, 1972.

107. Ward, P.: The effect of an anabolic steroid on strength and lean body mass, Med. Sci. Sports **5**:277-282, 1973.

108. Weiss, V., and Muller, H.: Aur Frage der Beeinflussung des Kraft-trainings

durch Anabole Hormone, Schweiz. Z. Sportsmed. **16**:79-89, 1968.

109. Whitelaw, M.J., Foster, T.N., and Graham, W.H.: Methandrostenolone (Dianabol): a controlled study of its anabolic and androgenic effect in children, Pediatric. Pharm. Ther. **68**:291-296, 1966.

110. Wilson, J.D., and Griffin, J.E.: The use and misuse of androgens, Metabolism **29**:1278-1295, 1980.

111. Woodard, T.L., Burghen, G.A., Kitabchi, A.E., and Wilimas, J.A.: Glucose intolerance and insulin resistance in aplastic anemia treated with oxymetholone, J. Clin. Endocrinol. Metab. **53**:905-908, 1981.

112. Wright, J.E.: Anabolic steroids and athletes, Exerc. Sport Sci. Rev. **8**:149-202, 1980.

113. Yamagishi, M., Hiraoka, A., and Uchino, H.: Silent hepatic lesions detected with computed tomography in aplastic anemia patients administered androgens for a long period, Acta Haematol. Jpn. **45**:703-710, 1982.

114. Young, M., Crookshank, H.R., and Ponder, L.: Effects of an anabolic steroid on selected parameters in male albino rats, Res. Q. **48**:653-656, 1977.

115. Zevin, D., Turani, H., Cohen, A., and Levi, J.: Androgen-associated hepatoma in a hemodialysis patient, Nephron **29**:274-276, 1981.

C PROPER AND IMPROPER WEIGHT LOSS PROGRAMS

Millions of individuals are involved in weight reduction programs. With the number of undesirable weight loss programs available and a general misconception by many about weight loss, the need for guidelines for proper weight loss programs is apparent.

Based on the existing evidence concerning the effects of weight loss on health status, physiologic processes, and body coposition parameters, the American College of Sports Medicine makes the following statements and recommendations for weight loss programs.

For the purposes of this position statement, body weight will be represented by two components, fat and fat-free (water, electrolytes, minerals, glycogen stores, muscular tissue, bone, etc.):

1. Prolonged fasting and diet programs that severely restrict caloric intake are scientifically undesirable and can be medically dangerous.
2. Fasting and diet programs that severely restrict caloric intake result in the loss of large amounts of water, electrolytes, minerals, glycogen stores, and other fat-free tissue (including proteins within fat-free tissues), with minimal amounts of fat loss.
3. Mild calorie restriction (500 to 1000 kcal less than the usual daily intake) results in a smaller loss of water, electrolytes, minerals, and other fat-free tissue, and is less likely to cause malnutrition.
4. Dynamic exercise of large muscles helps to maintain fat-free tissue, including muscle mass and bond density, and results in losses of body weight. Weight loss resulting from an increase in energy expenditure is primarily in the form of fat weight.
5. A nutritionally sound diet resulting in mild calorie restriction coupled with an endurance exercise program along with behavioral modification of existing eating habits is recommended for weight reduction. The rate of sustained weight loss should not exceed 1 kg (2 lb) per week.
6. To maintain proper weight control and optimal body fat levels, a lifetime commitment to proper eating habits and regular physical activity is required.

From American College of Sports Medicine: Position statement on proper and improper weight loss programs, 1983.

Research Background for the Position Statement

Each year millions of individuals undertake weight loss programs for a variety of reasons. It is well known that obesity is associated with a number of health-related problems.[3,4,57] These problems include impairment of cardiac function due to an increase in the work of the heart[2] and to left ventricular dysfunction[1,40]; hypertension[6,22,80]; diabetes[83,97]; renal disease[95]; gall bladder disease[55,72]; respiratory dysfunction[19]; joint diseases and gout[90]; endometrial cancer[15]; abnormal plasma lipid and lipoprotein concentrations[56,74]; problems in the administration of anesthetics during surgery[93]; and impairment of physical working capacity.[49] As a result, weight reduction is frequently advised by physicians for medical reasons. In addition, there are a vast number of individuals who are on weight reduction programs for aesthetic reasons.

It is estimated that 60 to 70 million American adults and at least 10 million American teenagers are overfat.[49] Because millions of Americans have adopted unsupervised weight loss programs, it is the opinion of the American College of Sports Medicine that guidelines are needed for safe and effective weight loss programs. This position statement deals with desirable and undesirable weight loss programs. Desirable weight loss programs are defined as those that are nutritionally sound and result in maximal losses in fat weight and minimal losses of fat-free tissue. Undesirable weight loss programs are defined as those that are not nutritionally sound, that result in large losses of fat-free tissue, that pose potential serious medical complications, and that cannot be followed for long-term weight maintenance.

Therefore, a desirable weight loss program is one that:

1. Provides a caloric intake not lower than 1200 kcal $\cdot$ d^{-1} for normal adults in order to get a proper blend of foods to meet nutritional requirements. (Note: this requirement may change for children, older individuals, athletes, etc.)
2. Includes food acceptable to the dieter from the viewpoints of sociocultural background, usual habits, taste, cost, and ease in acquisition and preparation.
3. Provides a negative caloric balance (not to exceed 500-1000 kcal $\cdot$ d^{-1} lower than recommended), resulting in gradual weight loss without metabolic derangements. Maximal weight loss should be 1 kg $\cdot$ wk^{-1}.
4. Includes the use of behavior modification techniques to identify and eliminate dieting habits that contribute to improper nutrition.
5. Includes an endurance exercise program of at least 3 d/wk, 20-30 min in duration, at a minimum intensity of 60% of maximum heart rate (refer to ACSM Position statement on the recommended quantity and quality of exercise for developing and maintaining fitness in healthy adults, Med. Sci. Sports **10**:vii, 1978).
6. Provides that the new eating and physical activity habits can be continued for life in order to maintain the achieved lower body weight.

1. Since the early work of Keys et al.[50] and Bloom,[16] which indicated that marked reduction in caloric intake or fasting (starvation or semistarvation) rapidly reduced body weight, numerous fasting, modified fasting, and fad diet and weight loss programs have emerged. While these programs promise and generally cause rapid weight loss, they are associated with significant medical risks.

The medical risks associated with these types of diet and weight loss programs are numerous. Blood glucose concentrations have been shown to be markedly reduced in obese subjects who undergo fasting.[18,32,74,84] Further, in obese non-diabetic subjects, fasting may result in impairment of glucose tolerance.[10,52] Ketonuria begins within a few hours after fasting or low-carbohydrate diets are begun[53] and hyperuricemia is common among subjects who fast to reduce body weight.[18] Fasting also results in high serum uric acid levels with decreased urinary output.[59] Fasting and low-calorie diets also result in urinary nitrogen loss and a significant decrease in fat-free tissue[7,11,17,42,101] (see section 2). In comparison to ingestion of a normal diet, fasting substantially elevates urinary excretion of potassium.[*] This, coupled with the aforementioned nitrogen loss, suggests that the potassium loss is due to a loss of lean tissue.[78] Other electrolytes, including sodium,[32,53] calcium,[30,84] magnesium,[30,84] and phosphate[84] have been shown to be elevated in urine during prolonged fasting. Reductions in blood volume and body fluids are also common with fasting and fad diets.[18] This can be associated with weakness and fainting.[32] Congestive heart failure and sudden death have been reported in subjects who fasted[48,79,80] or markedly restricted their caloric intake.[79] Myocardial atrophy appears to contribute to sudden death.[79] Sudden death may also occur during refeeding.[25,79] Untreated fasting has also been reported to reduce serum iron binding capacity, resulting in anemia.[47,73,89] Liver glycogen levels are depleted with fasting[38,60,63] and liver function[†] and gastrointestinal tract abnormalities[‡] are associated with fasting. While fasting and calorically restricted diets have been shown to lower serum cholesterol levels,[88,96] a large portion of the cholesterol reduction is a result of lowered HDL-cholesterol levels.[88,96] Other risks associated with fasting and low-calorie diets include lactic acidosis,[12,26] alopecia,[73] hypoalaninemia,[34] edema,[23,78] anuria,[101] hypotension,[18,32,78] elevated serum bilirubin,[8,9] nausea and vomiting,[53] alterations in thyroxine metabolism,[71,91] impaired serum triglyceride removal and production,[86] and death.[25,37,48,61,80]

2. The major objective of any weight reduction program is to lose body fat while maintaining fat-free tissue. The vast majority of research reveals that starvation and low-calorie diets result in large losses of water, electrolytes, and other fat-free tissue. One of the best controlled experiments was conducted from 1944 to 1946 at the Laboratory of Physiological Hygiene at the University of Minnesota.[50] In this study subjects had their base-line caloric intake cut by 45% and body weight and body composition changes were followed for 24 wk. During the first 12 wk of semistarvation, body weight declined by 25.4 lb (11.5 kg) with only an 11.6-lb (5.3 kg) decline in body fat. During the second 12-wk period, body weight declined an additional 9.1 lb (4.1 kg) with only a 6.1-lb (2.8 kg) decrease in body fat. These data clearly demonstrate that fat-free tissue significantly contributes to weight loss from semistarvation. Similar results have been reported by sev-

---

*References 10, 32, 37, 52, 53, 78.
†References 29, 31, 37, 75, 76, 92.
‡References 13, 32, 53, 65, 85, 91.

eral other investigators. Buskirk et al.[20] reported that the 13.5-kg weight loss in six subjects on a low-calorie mixed diet averaged 76% fat and 24% fat-free tissue. Similarly, Passmore et al.[64] reported results of 78% of weight loss (5.3 kg) as fat and 22% as fat-free tissue in seven women who consumed a 400-kcal · d^{-1} diet for 45 d. Yang and Van Itallie[101] followed weight loss and body composition changes for the first 5 d of a weight loss program involving subjects consuming either an 800-kcal mixed diet, an 800-kcal ketogenic diet, or undergoing starvation. Subjects on the mixed diet lost 1.3 kg of weight (59% fat loss, 3.4% protein loss, 37.6% water loss), subjects on the ketogenic diet lost 2.3 kg of weight (33.2% fat, 3.8% protein, 63.0% water), and subjects on starvation regimens lost 3.8 kg of weight (32.3% fat, 6.5% protein, 61.2% water). Grande[41] and Grande et al.[43] reported similar findings with a 1000-kcal carbohydrate diet. It was further reported that water restriction combined with 1000-kcal · d^{-1} of carbohydrate resulted in greater water loss and less fat loss.

Recently, there has been renewed speculation about the efficacy of the very-low-calorie diet (VLCD). Krotkiewski et al.[51] studied the effects on body weight and body coposition after 3 wk on the so-called Cambridge diet. Two groups of obese middle-aged women were studied. One group had a VLCD only, while the second group had a VLCD combined with a 55-min/d, 3-d/wk exercise program. The VLCD-only group lost 6.2 kg in 3 wk, of which only 2.6 kg was fat loss, while the VLCD-plus-exercise group lost 6.8 kg in 3 wk with only a 1.9-kg body fat loss. Thus it can be seen that VLCD results in undesirable losses of body fat, and the addition of the normally protective effect of chronic exercise to VLCD does not reduce the catabolism of fat-free tissue. Further, with VLCD, a large reduction (29%) in HDL-cholesterol is seen.[94]

3. Even mild calorie restriction (reduction of 500 to 1000 kcal · d^{-1} from base-line caloric intake), when used alone as a tool for weight loss, results in the loss of moderate amounts of water and other fat-free tissue. In a study by Goldman et al.,[39] 15 female subjects consumed a low-calorie mixed diet for 7-8 wk. Weight loss during this period averaged 6.43 kg (0.85 kg · wk^{-1}), 88.6% of which was fat. The remaining 11.4% represented water and other fat-free tissue. Zuti and Golding[102] examined the effect of 500 kcal · d^{-1} calorie restriction on body composition changes in adult females. Over a 16-wk period the women lost approximately 5.2 kg; however, 1.1 kg of the weight loss (21%) was due to a loss of water and other fat-free tissue. More recently, Weltman et al.[96] examined the effects of 500 kcal · d^{-1} calorie restriction (from base-line levels) on body composition changes in sedentary middle-aged males. Over a 10-wk period subjects lost 5.95 kg, 4.03 kg (68%) of which was fat loss and 1.92 kg (32%) was loss of water and other fat-free tissue. Further, with calorie restriction only, these subjects exhibited a decrease in HDL-cholesterol. In the same study, the two other groups who exercised and/or dieted and exercised were able to maintain their HDL-cholesterol levels. Similar results for females have been presented by Thompson et al.[88] It should be noted that the decrease seen in HDL-cholesterol with weight loss may be an acute effect. There are data that indicate that stable weight loss has a beneficial effect on HDL-cholesterol.[21,24,46,88]

Further, an additional problem associated with calorie restriction alone for effective weight loss is the fact that it is associated with a reduction in basal metabolic rate.[5] Apparently exercise combined with calorie restriction can counter this response.[14]

4. There are several studies that indicate that exercise helps maintain fat-free tissue while promoting fat loss. Total body weight and fat weight are generally reduced with endurance training programs[70] while fat-free weight remains constant[36,54,69,70,98] or increases slightly.[62,96,102] Programs conducted at least 3 d/wk,[66-69,98] of at least 20-min duration[58,69,98] and of sufficient intensity and duration to expend at least 300 kcal per exercise session have been suggested as a threshold level for total body weight and fat weight reduction.[27,44,69,70] increasing caloric expenditure above 300 kcal per exercise session and increasing the frequency of exercise sessions will enhance fat weight loss while sparing fat-free tissue.[54,102] Leon et al.[54] had six obese male subjects walk vigorously for 90 min, 5 d/wk for 16 wk. Work output progressed weekly to an energy expenditure of 1000 to 1200 kcal/session. At the end of 16 wk, subjects averaged 5.7 kg of weight loss with a 5.9-kg loss of fat weight and a 0.2-kg gain in fat-free tissue. Similarly, Zuti and Golding[102] followed the progress of adult women who expended 500 kcal/exercise session 5 d/wk for 16 wk of exercise. At the end of 16 wk the women lost 5.8 kg of fat and gained 0.9 kg of fat-free tissue.

5. Review of the literature cited above strongly indicates that optimal body composition changes occur with a combination of calorie restriction (while on a well-balanced diet) plus exercise. This combination promotes loss of fat weight while sparing fat-free tissue. Data of Zuti and Golding[102] and Weltman et al.[96] support this contention. Calorie restriction of 500 kcal · d^{-1} combined with 3 to 5 d of exercise requiring 300 to 500 kcal per exercise session results in favorable changes in body composition.[96,102] Therefore, the optimal rate of weight loss should be between 0.45 to 1 kg (1 to 2 lb) per wk. This seems especially relevant in light of the data which indicates that rapid weight loss due to low caloric intake can be associated with sudden death.[79] In order to institute a desirable pattern of calorie restriction plus exercise, behavior modification techniques should be incorporated to identify and eliminate habits contributing to obesity and/or overfatness.*

6. The problem with losing weight is that, although many individuals succeed in doing so, they invariably put the weight on again.[45] The goal of an effective weight loss regimen is not merely to lose weight. Weight control requires a lifelong commitment, an understanding of our eating habits and a willingness to change them. Frequent exercise is necessary, and accomplishment must be reinforced to sustain motivation. Crash dieting and other promised weight loss cures are ineffective.[45]

REFERENCES

1. Alexander, J.K., and Pettigrove, J.R.: Obesity and congestive heart failure, Geriatrics **22:**101-108, 1967.
2. Alexander, J.K., and Peterson, K.L.: Cardiovascular effects of weight reduction, Circulation **45:**310-318, 1972.
3. Angel, A.: Pathophysiologic changes in obesity, Can. Med. Assoc. J. **119:**1401-1406, 1978.

---

*References 28, 33, 35, 81, 87, 99, 100.

4. Angel, A., and Roncari, D.A.K.: Medical complications of obesity., Can. Med. Assoc. J. **119**:1408-1411, 1978.

5. Appelbaum, M., Bostsarron, J., and Lacatis, D.: Effect of caloric restriction and excessive caloric intake on energy expenditure, Am. J. Clin. Nutr. **24**:1405-1409, 1971.

6. Bachman, L., Freschuss, V., Hallberg, D., and Melcher, A.: Cardiovascular function in extreme obesity, Acta Med. Scand. **193**:437-446, 1972.

7. Ball, M.F., Canary, J.J., and Kyle, L.H.: Comparative effects of caloric restrictions and total starvation on body composition in obesity, Ann. Intern. Med. **67**:60-67, 1967.

8. Barrett, P.V.D.: Hyperbilirubinemia of fasting, J.A.M.A. **217**:1349-1353, 1971.

9. Barrett, P.V.D.: The effect of diet and fasting on the serum bilirubin concentration in the rat, Gastroenterology **60**:572-576, 1971.

10. Beck, P., et al.: Studies of insulin and growth hormone secretion in human obesity, J. Lab. Clin. Med. **64**:654-667, 1964.

11. Benoit, F.L., Martin, R.L., and Watten, R.H.: Changes in body composition during weight reduction in obesity, Ann. Intern. Med. **63**:604-612, 1965.

12. Berger, H.: Fatal lactic acidosis during "crash" reducing diet, N.Y. State J. Med. **67**:2258-2263, 1967.

13. Bilich, C., et al.: Absorptive capacity of the jejunum of obese and lean subjects: effect of fasting, Arch. Intern. Med. **130**:377-387, 1972.

14. Bjorntorp, P., Sjostrom, L., and Sullivan, L.: The role of physical exercise in the management of obesity. In The treatment of obesity, J.F. Munro (editor), Lancaster, England, MTP Press, 1979.

15. Blitzer, P.H., Blitzer, E.C., and Rimm, A.A.: Association between teenage obesity and cancer in 56,111 women, Prev. Med. **5**:20-31, 1976.

16. Bloom, W.L.: Fasting as an introduction to the treatment of obesity, Metabolism **8**:214-220, 1959.

17. Bolinger, R.E., et al.: Metabolic balances of obese subjects during fasting, Arch. Intern. Med. **118**:3-8, 1966.

18. Bray, G.A., Davidson, M.B., and Drenick, E.J.: Obesity: a serious symptom, Ann. Intern. Med. **77**:779-805, 1972.

19. Burwell, C.S., Robin, E.D., Whaley, R.D., and Bickelmann, A.G.: Extreme obesity associated with alveolar hypoventilation—a Pickwickian syndrome, Am. J. Med. **21**:811-818, 1956.

20. Buskirk, E.R., Thompson, R.H., Lutwak, L., and Whedon, G.D.: Energy balance of obese patients during weight reduction: influence of diet restriction and exercise, Ann. NY Acad. Sci. **110**:918-940, 1963.

21. Caggiula, A.W., et al.: The multiple risk factors intervention trial: IV intervention on blood lipids Prev. Med. **10**:443-475, 1981.

22. Chaing, B.M., Perlman, L.V., and Epstein, F.H.: Overweight and hypertension: a review, Circulation **39**:403-421, 1969.

23. Collison, D.R.: Total fasting for up to 249 days, Lancet **1**:112, 1967.

24. Contaldo, F., et al.: Plasma high density lipoprotein in severe obesity after stable weight loss, Atherosclerosis **37**:163-167, 1980.

25. Cruickshank, E.K.: Protein malnutrition. In Proceedings of a conference in Jamaica (1953), J.C. Waterlow (editor), Cambridge University Press, 1955, p. 107.

26. Cubberley, P.T., Polster, S.A., and Shulman, C.L.: Lactic acidosis and death after the treatment of obesity of fasting, N. Engl. J. Med. **272**:628-633, 1965.

27. Cureton, T.K.: The physiological effects of exercise programs upon adults, Springfield, IL, 1969, Charles C Thomas, Publisher.

28. Dahlkoetter, J., Callahan, E.J., and Linton, J.: Obesity and the unbalanced energy equation: exercise versus eating habit change, J. Consult. Clin. Psychol. **47**:898-905, 1979.

29. Drenick, E.J.: The relation of BSP retention during prolonged fasts to changes in plasma volume, Metabolism **17**:522-527, 1968.

30. Drenick, E.J., Hunt, I.F., and Swendseid, M.E.: Magnesium depletion during prolonged fasting in obese males, J. Clin. Endoctrinol. Metab. **29**:1341-1348, 1969.

31. Drenick, E.J., Simmons, F., and Murphy, J.F.: Effect on hepatic morphology of treatment of obesity by fasting, reducing diets and small-bowel bypass, N. Engl. J. Med. **282**:829-834, 1970.

32. Drenick, E.J., Swendseid, M.E., Blahd, W.H., and Tuttle, S.G.: Prolonged starvation as treatment for severe obesity, J.A.M.A. **187**:100-105, 1964.

33. Epstein, L.H., and Wing, R.R.: Aerobic exercise and weight, Addict. Behav. **5**:371-388, 1980.

34. Felig, P., Owen, O.E., Wahren, J., and Cahill, G.F., Jr.: Amino acid metabolism during prolonged starvation, J. Clin. Invest. **48**:584-594, 1969.

35. Ferguson, J.: Learning to eat: behavior modification for weight control, Palo Alto, Calif., Bull Publishing, 1975.

36. Franklin, B., et al.: Effects of physical conditioning on cardiorespiratory function, body composition and serum lipids in relatively normal-weight and obese middle-aged women, Int. J. Obesity **3**:97-109, 1979.

37. Garnett, E.S., et al.: Gross fragmentation of cardiac myofibrils after therapeutic starvation for obesity, Lancet **1**:914, 1969.

38. Garrow, J.S.: Energy balance and obesity in man, New York, American Elsevier, 1974.

39. Goldman, R.F., Bullen, B., and Seltzer, C.: Changes in specific gravity and body fat in overweight female adolescents as a result of weight reduction, Ann. NY Acad. Sci. **110**:913-917, 1963.

40. Gordon, T., and Kannel, W.B.: The effects of overweight on cardiovascular disease, Geriatrics **28**:80-88, 1973.

41. Grande, F.: Nutrition and energy balance in body composition studies. In Techniques for measuring body composition, J. Brozek and A. Henschel (editors): Washington, D.C., National Academy of Sciences—National Research Council, 1961. (Reprinted by the Office of Technical Services, U.S. Department of Commerce, Washington, D.C., as U.S. Government Research Report AD286, 1963, 560.)

D WEIGHT LOSS IN WRESTLERS

Despite repeated admonitions by medical, educational and athletic groups,[2,8,17,22,33] most wrestlers have been inculcated by instruction or accepted tradition to lose weight in order to be certified for a class that is lower than their preseason weight.[34] Studies[34,40] of weight losses in high school and college wrestlers indicate that from 3-20% of the preseason body weight is lost before certification or competition occurs. Of this weight loss, most of the decrease occurs in the final days or day before the official weigh-in[34,40] with the youngest and/or lightest members of the team losing the highest percentage of their body weight.[34] Under existing rules and practices, it is not uncommon for an individual to repeat this weight losing process many times during the season because successful wrestlers complete in 15-30 matches/ year.[13]

Contrary to existing beliefs, most wrestlers are not "fat" before the season starts.[35] In fact, the fat content of high school and college wrestlers

From American College of Sports Medicine. 1976. Position stand on weight loss in wrestlers.

weighing less than 190 pounds has been shown to range from 1.6 to 15.1 percent of their body weight with the majority possessing less than 8%.[14,28,31] It is well known and documented that wrestlers lose body weight by a combination of food restriction, fluid deprivation and sweating induced by thermal or exercise procedures.[20,22,34,40] Of these methods, dehydration through sweating appears to be the method most frequently chosen.

Careful studies on the nature of the weight being lost show that water, fats and proteins are lost when food restriction and fluid deprivation procedures are followed.[10] Moreover, the proportionality between these constituents will change with continued restriction and deprivation. For example, if food restriction is held constant when the volume of fluid being consumed is decreased, more water will be lost from the tissues of the body than before the fluid restriction occurred. The problem becomes more acute when thermal or exercise dehydration occurs because electrolyte losses will accompany the water losses.[16] Even when 1-5 hours are allowed for purposes of rehydration after the weigh-in, this time interval is insufficient for fluid and electrolyte homeostasis to be completely reestablished.[11,37,39,40]

Since the "making of weight" occurs by combinations of food restriction, fluid deprivation and dehydration, responsible officials should realize that the single or combined effects of these practices are generally associated with (1) a reduction in muscular strength[4,15,30]; (2) a decrease in work performance times[24,26,27,30]; (3) lower plasma and blood volumes[6,7,24,27]; (4) a reduction in cardiac functioning during sub-maximal work conditions which are associated with higher heart rates,[1,19,23,24,27] smaller stroke volumes,[27] and reduced cardiac outputs[27]; (5) a lower oxygen consumption, especially with food restriction[15,30]; (6) an impairment of thermoregulatory processes[3,9,24]; (7) a decrease in renal blood flow[21,25] and in the volume of fluid being filtered by the kidney[21]; (8) a depletion of liver glycogen stores[12]; and (9) an increase in the amount of electrolytes being lost from the body.[6,7,16]

Since it is possible for these changes to impede normal growth and development, there is little physiological or medical justification for the use of the weight reduction methods currently followed by many wrestlers. These sentiments have been expressed in part within Rule 1, Section 3, Article 1 of the *Official Wrestling Rule Book*[18] published by the National Federation of State High School Associations which states, "The Rules Committee recommends that individual state high school associations develop and utilize an effective weight control program which will discourage severe weight reduction and/or wide variations in weight, because this may be harmful to the competitor. . . ." However, until the National Federation of State High School Associations defines the meaning of the terms "severe" and "wide variations," this rule will be ineffective in reducing the abuses associated with the "making of weight."

Therefore, it is the position of the American College of Sports Medicine that the potential health hazards created by the procedures used to "make weight" by wrestlers can be eliminated if state and national organizations will:

1. Assess the body composition of each wrestler several weeks in advance of the competitive season.[5,14,28,31,38] Individuals with a fat content less than

five percent of their certified body weight should receive medical clearance before being allowed to compete.

2. Emphasize the fact that the daily caloric requirements of wrestlers should be obtained from a balanced diet and determined on the basis of age, body surface area, growth and physical activity levels.[29] The minimal caloric needs of wrestlers in high schools and colleges will range from 1200 to 2400 KCal/day[32]; therefore, it is the responsibility of coaches, school officials, physicians and parents to discourage wrestlers from securing less than their minimal needs without prior medical approval.

3. Discourage the practice of fluid deprivation and dehydration. This can be accomplished by:
   a. Educating the coaches and wrestlers on the physiological consequences and medical complications that can occur as a result of these practices.
   b. Prohibiting the single or combined use of rubber suits, steam rooms, hot boxes, saunas, laxatives, and diuretics to "make weight."
   c. Scheduling weigh-ins just prior to competition.
   d. Scheduling more official weigh-ins between team matches.

E PREVENTION OF HEAT INJURIES DURING DISTANCE RUNNING

The purpose of this position statement is:

(a) To alert local, national and international sponsors of distance running events of the health hazards of heat injury during distance running, and

(b) To inform said sponsors of injury preventive actions that may reduce the frequency of this type of injury.

The recommendations address only the manner in which distance running sports activities may be conducted to further reduce incidence of heat injury among normal athletes conditioned to participate in distance running. The recommendations are advisory only.

Recommendations concerning the ingested quantity and content of fluid are merely a partial preventive to heat injury. The physiology of each individual athlete varies; strict compliance with these recommendations and the current rules governing distance running may not reduce the incidence of heat injuries among those so inclined to such injury.

Research Findings

Based on research findings and current rules governing distance running competition, it is the position of the American College of Sports Medicine that:

1. Distance races (> 16 km or 10 miles) should *not* be conducted when the wet bulb temperature—globe temperature (adapted from Minard, D. Prevention of heat casualties in Marine Corps recruits. *Milit. Med.* **126**:261, 1961. WB-GT = 0.7 [WBT] + 0.2 [GT] + 0.1 [DBT] exceeds 28° C (82.4° F).[1,2]

2. During periods of the year, when the daylight dry bulb temperature often exceeds 27° C (80° F), distance races should be conducted before 9:00 A.M. or after 4:00 P.M.[2,7,8,9]

From American College of Sports Medicine. 1975. Position statement on prevention of heat injuries during distance running.

3. It is the responsibility of the race sponsors to provide fluids which contain small amounts of sugar (less than 2.5 g glucose per 100 ml of water) and electrolytes (less than 10 mEq sodium and 5 mEq potassium per liter of solution).[5,6]

4. Runners should be encouraged to frequently ingest fluids during competition and to consume 400-500 ml (13-17 oz.) of fluid 10-15 minutes before competition.[5,6,9]

5. Rules prohibiting the administration of fluids during the first 10 kilometers (6.2 miles) of a marathon race should be amended to permit fluid ingestion at frequent intervals along the race course. In light of the high sweat rates and body temperatures during distance running in the heat, race sponsors should provide "water stations" at 3-4 kilometer (2-2.5 mile) intervals for all races of 16 kilometers (10 miles) or more.[4,8,9]

6. Runners should be instructed in how to recognize the early warning symptoms that precede heat injury. Recognition of symptoms, cessation of running, and proper treatment can prevent heat injury. Early warning symptoms include the following: piloerection on chest and upper arms, chilling, throbbing pressure in the head, unsteadiness, nausea, and dry skin.[2,9]

7. Race sponsors should make prior arrangements with medical personnel for the care of cases of heat injury. Responsible and informed personnel should supervise each "feeding station." Organizational personnel should reserve the right to stop runners who exhibit clear signs of heat stroke or heat exhaustion.

It is the position of the American College of Sports Medicine that policies established by local, national, and international sponsors of distance running events should adhere to these guidelines. Failure to adhere to these guidelines may jeopardize the health of competitors through heat injury.

The requirements of distance running place great demands on both circulation and body temperature regulation.[4,8,9] Numerous studies have reported rectal temperatures in excess of 40.6° C (105° F) after races of 6 to 26.2 miles (9.6 to 41.9 kilometers).[4,8,9] Attempting to counterbalance such overheating, runners incur large sweat losses of 0.8 to 1.1 liters/m²/hr.[4,8,9] The resulting body water deficit may total 6-10% of the athlete's body weight. Dehydration of these proportions severely limits subsequent sweating, places dangerous demands on circulation, reduces exercise capacity and exposes the runner to the health hazards associated with hyperthemia (heat stroke, heat exhaustion and muscle cramps).[2,3,9]

Under moderate thermal conditions, e.g., 65-70° F (18.5-21.3° C), no cloud cover, relative humidity 49-55%, the risk of overheating is still a serious threat to highly motivated distance runners. Nevertheless, distance races are frequently conducted under more severe conditions than these. The air temperature at the 1967 U.S. Pan American Marathon Trial, for example, was 92-95° F (33.6-35.3° C). Many highly conditioned athletes failed to finish the race and several of the competitors demonstrated overt symptoms of heat stroke (no sweating, shivering and lack of orientation).

The above consequences are compounded by the current popularity of distance running among middle-aged and aging men and women who may possess significantly less heat tolerance than their younger counterparts. In recent years, races of 10 to 26.2 miles (16 to 41.9 kilometers) have attracted several thousand runners. Since it is likely that distance running enthusiasts will continue to sponsor races under adverse heat conditions, specific steps should be taken to minimize the health threats which accompany such endurance events.

Fluid ingestion during prolonged running (two hours) has been shown to effectively reduce rectal temperature and minimize dehydration.[4] Although most competitors consume fluids during races that exceed 1-1.5 hours, current international distance running rules prohibit the administration of fluids until the runner has completed 10 miles (16 kilometers). Under such limitations, the competitor is certain to accumulate a large body water deficit (- 3%) before any fluids would be ingested. To make the problem more complex, most runners are unable to judge the volume of fluids they consume during competition.[4] At the 1968 U.S. Olympic Marathon Trial, it was observed that there were body weight losses of 6.1 kg, with an average total fluid ingestion of only 0.14 to 0.35 liters.[4] It seems obvious that the rules and habits which prohibit fluid administration during distance running preclude any benefits which might be gained from this practice.

Runners who attempt to consume large volumes of sugar solution during competition complain of gastric discomfort (fullness) and an inability to consume fluids after the first few feedings.[4,5,6] Generally speaking, most runners drink solutions containing 5-20 grams of sugar per 100 milliliters of water. Although saline is rapidly emptied from the stomach (25 ml/min), the addition of even small amounts of sugar can drastically impair the rate of gastric emptying.[5] During exercise in the heat, carbohydrate supplementation is of secondary importance and the sugar content of the oral feedings should be minimized.

REFERENCES

1. Adolph, E.I.: Physiology of man in the desert, New York: Interscience, 1947.
2. Burskirk, E.R., and Grasley, W.C.: Heat injury and conduct of athletes. Ch. 16 in Science and medicine of exercise and sport, 2nd edition, W.R. Johnson and E.R. Buskirk (editors), New York, Harper and Row, 1974.
3. Buskirk, E.R., Iampietro, P.F., and Bass, D.E.: Work performance after dehydration: effects of physical conditioning and heat acclimatization, J. Appl. Physiol. **12**:189-194, 1958.
4. Costill, D.L., Kammer, W.F., and Fisher, A.: Fluid ingestion during distance running, Arch. Environ. Health **21**:520-525, 1970.
5. Costill, D.L., and Saltin, B.: Factors limiting gastric emptying during rest and exercise, J. Appl. Physiol. **37(5)**:679-683, 1974.
6. Fordtran, J.A., and Saltin, B.: Gastric emptying and intestinal absorption during prolonged severe exercise, J. Appl. Physiol. **23**:331-335, 1967.
7. Myhre, L.G.: Shifts in blood volume during and following acute environmental and work stresses in man, doctoral dissertation, Indiana University: Bloomington, Indiana, 1967.
8. Pugh, L.G.C., Corbett, J.I., and Johnson, R.H.: Rectal temperatures, weight losses and sweating rates in marathon running, J. Appl. Physiol. **23**:347-353, 1957.
9. Wyndham, C.H., and Strydom, N.B.: The danger of an inadequate water intake during marathon running, S. Afr. Med. J. **43**:893-896, 1969.

F THE PARTICIPATION OF THE FEMALE ATHLETE IN LONG-DISTANCE RUNNING

In the Olympic Games and other international contests, female athletes run distances ranging from 100 meters to 3,000 meters, whereas male athletes run distances ranging from 100 meters through 10,000 meters as well as the marathon (42.2 km). The limitation on distance for women's running events has been defended at times on the grounds that long-distance running may be harmful to the health of girls and women.

Opinion Statement

It is the opinion of the American College of Sports Medicine that females should not be denied the opportunity to compete in long-distance running. There exists no conclusive scientific or medical evidence that long-distance running is contraindicated for the healthy, trained female athlete. The American College of Sports Medicine recommends that females be allowed to compete at the national and international level in the same distances in which their male counterparts compete.

Supportive Information

Studies[10,20,32,41,54] have shown that females respond in much the same manner as males to systematic exercise training. Cardiorespiratory function is improved as indicated by significant increases in maximal oxygen uptake.[4,6,13,16,30] At maximal exercise, stroke volume and cardiac output are increased after training.[30] At standardized submaximal exercise intensities after training, cardiac output remains unchanged, heart rate decreases, and stroke volume increases.[6,30,31] Also, resting heart rate decreases after training.[30] As is the case for males, relative body fat content is reduced consequent to systematic endurance training.[33,35,51]

Long-distance running imposes a significant thermal stress on the participant. Some differences do exist between males and females with regard to thermoregulation during prolonged exercise. However, the differences in thermal stress response are more quantitative than qualitative in nature.[36,38,47] For example, women experience lower evaporative heat losses than do men exposed to the same thermal stress[29,40,53] and usually have higher skin temperatures and deep body temperatures upon onset of sweating.[3,18,45] This may actually be an advantage in reducing body water loss so long as thermal equilibrium can be maintained. In view of current findings,* it appears that the earlier studies which indicated that women were less tolerant to exercise in the heat than men[36,53] were misleading because they failed to consider the women's relatively low level of cardiorespiratory fitness and heat acclimatization. Apparently, cardiorespiratory fitness as measured by maximum oxygen uptake is a most important functional capacity as regards a person's ability to respond adequately to thermal stress.[9,11,15,47] In fact, there has been considerable interest in the seeming cross-adaptation of a life style characterized by physical activity involving

---

From American College of Sports Medicine. 1979. Opinion statement on the participation of the female athlete in long-distance running.
*References 10, 11, 15, 40, 48-50

regular and prolonged periods of exercise hyperthermia and response to high environmental temperatures.[1,37,39] Women trained in long-distance running have been reported to be more tolerant of heat stress than non-athletic women matched for age and body surface area.[15] Thus, it appears that trained female long-distance runners have the capacity to deal with the thermal stress of prolonged exercise as well as the moderate-to-high environmental temperatures and relative humidities that often accompany these events.

The participation of males and females in road races of various distances has increased tremendously during the last decade. This type of competition attracts the entire spectrum of runners with respect to ability—from the elite to the novice. A common feature of virtually all of these races is that a small number of participants develop medical problems (primarily heat injuries) which frequently require hospitalization. One of the first documentations of the medical problems associated with mass participation in this form of athletic competition was by Sutton and co-workers.[46] Twenty-nine of 2,005 entrants in the 1971 Sydney City-to-Surf race collapsed; seven required hospitalization. All of the entrants who collapsed were males, although 4% of the race entrants were females. By 1978 the number of entrants increased approximately 10 fold with females accounting for approximately 30% of the entrants. In the 1978 race only nine entrants were treated for heat injury and again all were males.[43] In a 1978 Canadian road race, in which 1,250 people participated, 15 entrants developed heat injuries—three females and 12 males, representing 1.3% and 1.2% of the total number of female and male entrants, respectively.[27] Thus, females seem to tolerate the physiological stress of road race competition at least as well as males.

Because long-distance running competition sometimes occurs at moderate altitudes, the female's response to an environment where the partial pressure of oxygen is reduced (hypoxia) should be considered. Buskirk[5] noted that, although there is little information about the physiological responses of women to altitude, the proportional reduction in performance at Mexico City during the Pan American and Olympic Games was the same for males and females. Drinkwater et al.[13] found that women mountaineers exposed to hypoxia demonstrated a similar decrement in maximal oxygen uptake as that predicted for men. Hannon et al.[23,24] have found that females tolerate the effects of altitude better than males because there appears to be both a lower frequency and shorter duration of mountain sickness in women. Furthermore, at altitude women experience less alteration in such variables as resting heart rate, body weight, blood volume, electrocardiograms, and blood chemistries than men.[23,24] Although one study has reported that women and men experience approximately the same respiratory changes with altitude exposure,[44] another[22] reports that women hyperventilate more than men, thereby increasing the partial pressure of arterial oxygen and decreasing the partial pressure of arterial carbon dioxide. Thus, females tolerate the stress of altitude at least as well as men.

Long-distance running is occasionally associated with various overuse syndromes such as stress fracture, chondromalacia, shinsplints, and tendinitis. Pollock et al.[42] have shown that the incidence of these injuries for males engaged in a program of jogging was as high as 54% and was related to the frequency, duration, and intensity of the exercise training. Franklin et al.[19] recently reported the injury incidence of 42 sedentary females exposed to a 12-week jogging program. The injury rate for the females appeared to be comparable to that found for males in other studies although, as the investigators indicated, a decisive interpretation of presently available information may be premature because of the limited orthopedic injury data available for women. It has been suggested that the anatomical differences between men's and women's pelvic width and joint laxity may lead to a higher incidence of injuries for women who run.[26] There are no data available, however, to support this suggestion. Whether or not the higher intensity training programs of competitive male and female long-distance runners result in a difference in injury rate between the sexes is not known at this time. It is believed, however, that the incidence of injury due to running is related more to distances run in training, the running surfaces encountered, biomechanics of back, leg and foot, and to foot apparel.[28]

Of particular concern to female competitors and to the American College of Sports Medicine is evidence which indicates that approximately one-third of the competitive female long-distance runners between the ages of 12 and 45 experience amenorrhea or oligomenorrhea for at least brief periods.[7,8] This phenomenon appears more frequently in those women with late onset of menarche, who have not experienced pregnancy, or who have taken contraceptive hormones. This same phenomenon also occurs in some competing gymnasts, swimmers, and professional ballerinas as well as sedentary individuals who have experienced some instances of undue stress or severe psychological trauma.[25] Apparently, amenorrhea and oligomenorrhea may be caused by many factors characterized by loss of body weight.[7,21,25] Running long distances may lead to decreased serum levels of pituitary gonadotrophic hormones in some women and may directly or indirectly lead to amenorrhea or oligomenorrhea. The role of running and the pathogenesis of these menstrual irregularities remains unknown.[7,8]

The long-term effects of these types of menstrual irregularities for young girls that have undergone strenuous exercise training are unknown at this time. Eriksson and coworkers[17] have reported, however, that a group of 28 young girl swimmers, who underwent strenuous swim training for 2.5 years, were normal in all respects (e.g., childbearing) 10 years after discontinuing training.

UNITS OF MEASURE

TEMPERATURE

To convert a Fahrenheit temperature to Celsius (centigrade):

$$°C = (°F - 32) ÷ 1.8$$

To convert a Celsius temperature to Fahrenheit:

$$°F = (1.8 × °C) + 32$$

On the Fahrenheit scale, the freezing point of water is 32° F and the boiling point is 212° F. On the Celsius scale, the freezing point of water is 0° C and the boiling point is 100° C.

DISTANCE

Equivalent Metric Unit	Equivalent English Unit
1 centimeter (cm)	0.3937 inch
2.54 centimeters	1 inch
1 meter (m)	3.28 feet; 1.09 yards
0.304 meters	1 foot
1 kilometer (km)	0.62 mile
1.61 kilometers	1 mile

POWER AND ENERGY

$$\text{Power} = \text{Work divided by time; measured in horsepower (HP), watts, etc.}$$
$$1 \text{ HP} = 746 \text{ watts}$$
$$\text{Energy} = \text{Application of a force through a distance}$$
$$1 \text{ kilocalorie (kcal)} = \text{Amount of energy required to heat } 1 \text{ kilogram (kg) of water } 1° \text{ Celsius}$$

INDEX